The BABY NAME COUNTDOWN

The BABY NAME COUNTDOWN

The Definitive Baby Name Book

5th Edition

by Janet Schwegel

MARLOWE & COMPANY

NEW YORK

Published by
Marlowe & Company
An Imprint of Avalon Publishing Group, Incorporated
245 West 17th Street, 11th Floor
New York, NY 10011

AVALON
publishing group incorporated

THE BABY NAME COUNTDOWN: *The Definitive Baby Name Book*
Copyright © 1988, 1990, 1996, 1997, 2001 by Janet Schwegel

Library of Congress Cataloging-in-Publication Data

Schwegel, Janet, 1959–
    The baby name countdown : popularity and meanings of today's names / Janet Schwegel. -- 2nd ed.
        p. cm.
    ISBN 1-56924-735-8 (paper)
    1. Names, Personal – Canada. 2. Names, Personal – United States.
I. Title.
CS2377.S285   1997   97-25248
929.4'03--dc21   CIP

ISBN-10: 1-56924-590-8
ISBN-13: 978-1-56924-590-3

9 8 7 6
Printed in the United States of America
Distributed by Publishers Group West

Dedication

To Bryan and Allison, who continue to give my work meaning (if not origin and popularity).

⧈ Contents ⧈

▣ Introduction ▣

In some ways, names don't change. The name Ashley, for example, comes from an English word meaning "from the ash tree meadow." The meaning and origin of Ashley is unchanging.

In other ways, names change dramatically over time. In the 1950s the name Ashley was rare for a girl. A generation later, it was one of the most popular names given to baby girls. Many of the Ashleys' parents no doubt thought they were giving their girl an unusual name, because when they were children, they didn't know any girls named Ashley. A few years after their babies were born, though, kindergarten classes sprouted Ashleys.

To help you choose the perfect name for your baby, *The Baby Name Countdown* gives you all the information you need: meanings, origins, and popularity. This edition of *The Baby Name Countdown* contains over 120,000 first names, with an indication of how often each name was used in North America. As well, *The Baby Name Countdown* contains meanings and origins of popular names. (Meanings and origins are generally unavailable for unusual names.) All the names in this book are first names actually given to babies born in North America in recent years.

Most children born in North America, now and a century ago, have a popular name. But you may not realize that most children receive one of the top 200 names.

In the first decade of the twentieth century (1900 to 1909):

- 20% of girls and 27% of boys received one of the top ten names,

- 63% of girls and 66% of boys received one of the top 100 names, and

- 76% of girls and boys received one of the top 200 names.

In the last decade of the twentieth century (1990 to 1999):

- 11% of girls and 15% of boys received one of the top ten names,

- 43% of girls and 58% of boys received one of the top 100 names, and

- 54% of girls and 69% of boys received one of the top 200 names.

Names in the top 200 of the baby name ranks have a popularity rating of .07 or higher. Popularity ratings represent frequency of use per thousand children born. In other words, at least seven out of every 100,000 children received each of the top 200 names. A popularity rating of .07 is the cutoff for appearing in the list of "Popular Names with popularity ratings, origins and meanings" in Section II of this book. Names with popularity ratings of less than .07 appear in the list of "Popular and Unusual Names with popularity ratings" in Section III.

Over the last 50 years, more and more parents have given their children unusual names. For example, Michael has been the number one name for boys for the last five decades. In the 1950s, 1960s, and 1970s, it had a popularity rating of 40 (out of 1000). In the 1980s, although it was still the number one name for boys, the popularity rating for Michael decreased to 34. In the 1990s, the popularity rating for Michael was 23. Although Michael continued to be the most popular name for boys, it became less popular over time.

Similarly, over the last decade, the popularity of the top 200 names declined from 76% to 62%. The table below charts the percentage of babies given one of the top 200 names in the United States over the last century. It shows a slow increase from 76% of babies getting a popular name in the first decade, up to 80% in the 1940s. Then the percentages decrease until only 62% of babies in the 1990s have a "popular" name.

Percentage of babies receiving a top 200 (popular) name in each decade of the 20th century:

	1900s	1910s	1920s	1930s	1940s	1950s	1960s	1970s	1980s	1990s
Percentage:	76%	76%	77%	78%	80%	80%	76%	70%	68%	62%

Another surprising feature of baby naming in North America is that there are many more names for girls than for boys. This book contains approximately 73,700 different names for girls and 49,200 different names for boys — almost 25% more names for girls than for boys. Perhaps this difference reflects the wide range of roles women have in our society, from exotic dancers to supreme court judges. Perhaps it reflects a desire for boys just to be traditional members of society. Or it may reflect a belief that while a girl can have a frivolous name, a boy's name is a serious matter.

The main force in the popularity of a name seems to be fashion. Our idea of what is a good name for a baby changes over time, just as clothing styles change over time, for little discernible reason. Names for children are also strongly influenced by popular culture: television and movie characters, musicians, celebrities, sports figures, and heroes. For example, the name Shania was "unusual" in the mid-1980s — one in 100,000 girls or fewer were named Shania. Ten years later, in the mid-1990s, the name Shania had a popularity rating of .46 — one in every 2,000 girls was named Shania. This dramatic change in popularity

may be attributable to the celebrity of Shania Twain, a country music singer.

Similarly, the popularity ratings of most of the names of the characters in the 1990s sitcom *Friends* rose with the rise in popularity of the television show:

Monica — 1.4 in the mid-1980s, 2.2 in the mid-1990s;
Rachel — 5.7 in the mid-1980s, 7.6 in the mid-1990s;
Phoebe — .05 in the mid-1980s, .14 in the mid-1990s;
Ross — .55 in the mid-1980s, .44 in the mid-1990s;
Chandler— .04 in the mid-1980s, .59 in the mid-1990s;
Joey — .25 in the mid-1980s, .43 in the mid-1990s.

The Baby Name Countdown is divided into three main sections: the top 100 lists, the popular names section with meanings and origins, and all the names collected — over 120,000. This edition starts with a chart of the top 100 names of the last century, showing the change in rank of each name over the ten decades from 1900 to 1999. It's fascinating reading, not just for prospective parents. Several lists follow, including the 100 most popular names in 2000, in 1999, and in 1998; the 100 most popular first names for babies born in the mid-1990s in all of North America and in particular regions of North America; and the 100 most popular first names in the mid-1980s in North America, from an earlier edition of *The Baby Name Countdown*. The second section is a listing of currently popular names along with their meanings and origins, as well as popularity ratings. The third section contains a list of all the names collected from states and provinces in North America and includes an indication of the popularity of each name.

Popularity rating numbers indicate how many babies per thousand born were given that first name. For example, a popularity rating of 1.0 indicates that one of every thousand babies born was given that first name. (Although it doesn't sound like much, a name with a frequency of one per thousand is a quite popular name.) Similarly, a popularity rating of .10 indicates that one of every ten-thousand babies was given that name, and a popularity rating of .01 indicates that one of every hundred-thousand babies was given that first name. Names in section three "Popular and Unusual Names" which do not have a popularity rating indicated are rare names with a rating of one in a million or less.

The simplest way to understand the popularity ratings is to view them as a relative ranking: the higher the number, the more popular the name. So, for instance, you can use the popularity ratings to choose the most (or least) popular spelling of a name. But the ratings are not simply rankings; they can be multiplied or added: a name with a rating of 2.0 is twice as popular as one with a rating of 1.0. And you could add up the ratings for all the variant spellings of the name Christopher to find out whether it is actually more popular than Michael. The ratings give popularity per thousand boys or girls, but by moving the decimal places in the population and the popularity rating to the right or left, you can quickly calculate other statistical frequencies.

For example, my own name, Janet, had a popularity of:

.50 per 1,000 in the 1990s

which is equivalent to:

.05 per 100

5.7 per 10,000

57   per 100,000

and   570 per 1,000,000 (million).

You can go further with the data in *The Baby Name Countdown* and estimate roughly how many children in any geographical location will receive a certain name. Start with this fact: the birth rate in the United States and Canada is approximately 15 per thousand, meaning that for every thousand people in the population, 15 children are born in a year.

To calculate the approximate number of children that will be born in any geographical location, multiply that location's population by .015 (15 divided by 1000):

(1) $b = g \times .015$

where b is the number of births, and g is the population of some geographical location.

Once you know the number of children born in a year in a community, you can estimate how many will be named a certain name using formula (2):

(2) $n = b \times p/1000$

where n is the number of children who will receive a particular name, and p is the popularity rating of that name.

For example, the city I live in has a population of about 800,000. To estimate how many children will be named Janet this year in this city, first I calculate the approximate number of children that will be born here:

(1) $b = g \times .015$

$b = 800,000 \times .015$

$b = 12,000$

The popularity rating for the name Janet is .50. So to estimate how many children will be named Janet, I use the second formula:

(2) $n = b \times p/1000$

$n = 12,000 \times .50/1000$

$n = 6$

Based on current trends, roughly six children born in this city this year will be named Janet.

You could also estimate the frequency of use of a name among a population, using the following formula:

(3) $n = s \times p/1000$

where s is the number of children in the sample.

For example, if I'm curious how many children might have the name Michael in a kindergarten class of 30 children in four or five years, I can plug values into formula (3) thus:

$s = 30$ [the number of children in the class]

$p = 23.2$ [the popularity rating for Michael in the 1990s]

$n = s \times p/1000$

$n = 30 \times 23.2/1000$

$n = .696$

In other words, I estimate that there will be a boy named Michael in most kindergarten classes in the next few years.

The point of these examples is that you can play with the popularity ratings to estimate statistical likelihood of a certain number of children having a particular name in a particular place. The term statistical is used to remind you that any calculations based on the data do not give you actual frequencies of use of names, but estimated — or statistical — probabilities based on all of the data collected being summed together. Further, due to rounding and regional variations, these estimated probabilities are rough approximations.

Fortunately for prospective parents searching for the perfect name for their baby, *The Baby Name Countdown* contains all the information needed to make the choice. As prospective parents, it isn't enough to know what a name means, or where it came from — we need to know how popular that name is. Whether you want to ensure your child is in synch with the times by giving him or her a popular name, or you want to give your child something unique — a name of his or her own, you'll find what you need among the tens of thousands of names in *The Baby Name Countdown*.

The BABY NAME COUNTDOWN

Section I —

The Top 100 Names

Names are listed in order of popularity. The popularity rating to the left of each name
indicates how frequently the name is used per thousand children born during the
time period. For example, a popularity rating of 1.23 means that approximately one of every
thousand girls or boys born was given that name. The data for the twentieth century
and for the years 2000, 1999, and 1998 comes from the United States.
Other data is from the regions indicated.

The 100 most popular names of the twentieth century

Girls

Names are listed in order of overall popularity in the twentieth century. For each decade the rank of the name (out of 1000) is provided. Rank 1 to 10 are "black," 11 to 100 are "bold," and over 500 are 50% gray.

Overall pop.	Name	1900s	1910s	1920s	1930s	1940s	1950s	1960s	1970s	1980s	1990s
31.9	Mary	1	1	1	1	1	1	2	15	34	41
10.3	Margaret	3	4	5	8	14	23	54	101	95	107
10.1	Elizabeth	6	8	10	17	23	20	17	11	9	8
10.1	Dorothy	7	3	2	6	20	60	124	218	354	565
10.0	Helen	2	2	3	10	32	74	138	241	324	317
9.7	Patricia	287	170	30	5	4	3	6	32	61	126
9.5	Barbara	143	85	18	3	3	6	22	73	153	296
8.2	Linda	327	338	324	95	2	2	7	63	133	224
7.7	Jennifer					210	105	19	1	2	14
7.6	Ruth	5	5	6	14	33	69	109	188	228	306
7.6	Betty	92	44	4	2	11	35	104	244	434	779
6.4	Anna	4	7	12	33	72	103	101	86	53	40
6.3	Susan	156	185	219	121	10	4	4	28	96	240
6.2	Nancy	125	100	66	9	7	9	26	74	116	153
5.7	Sarah	46	52	59	62	75	109	91	18	5	4
5.3	Karen	929			141	15	8	3	24	80	128
5.2	Frances	16	9	11	19	35	88	151	211	261	355
5.2	Virginia	51	12	7	15	28	62	116	160	186	274

Overall pop.	Name	1900s	1910s	1920s	1930s	1940s	1950s	1960s	1970s	1980s	1990s
5.1	Jessica	913	953			539	448	234	10	1	2
5.1	Lisa					464	38	1	6	31	113
5.1	Carol	340	243	116	11	5	16	38	128	280	417
5.0	Sandra		942	606	50	6	12	11	39	94	168
5.0	Shirley	239	143	17	4	13	32	102	243	398	601
4.9	Donna	392	278	113	22	16	10	8	67	217	461
4.8	Marie	8	10	15	32	51	89	119	153	163	294
4.8	Laura	50	61	75	99	89	39	15	19	23	45
4.8	Mildred	9	6	9	35	94	168	289	526	996	
4.8	Alice	10	13	14	23	42	87	149	236	319	382
4.6	Catherine	19	21	28	43	46	34	58	72	63	86
4.5	Maria	59	69	61	38	39	36	32	26	41	42
4.3	Kathleen	128	104	81	72	18	15	33	68	71	124
4.2	Martha	31	25	24	26	30	46	93	163	209	289
4.2	Kimberly					683	92	5	5	18	35
4.2	Evelyn	34	11	13	31	61	98	142	209	224	205
4.1	Rose	14	15	23	37	58	65	126	234	252	309
4.1	Michelle					304	96	9	4	12	31
4.1	Sharon			763	87	9	14	24	65	168	301
4.0	Amanda	205	269	387	534	477	400	206	17	3	7
3.9	Melissa	824	973		917	513	160	34	3	7	27
3.9	Rebecca	161	169	176	169	68	29	40	13	22	24
3.9	Doris	72	36	8	13	45	102	183	414	683	973
3.9	Deborah	674	774	773	413	66	5	12	61	175	360
3.8	Stephanie	473	335	475	511	200	122	45	9	6	11
3.7	Cynthia	407	406	357	198	48	11	10	31	64	103
3.7	Amy	196	244	284	356	331	136	35	2	16	61
3.7	Katherine	53	49	63	102	73	68	78	53	32	26
3.6	Ashley							662	142	4	1
3.6	Angela	212	195	247	246	175	106	21	7	27	73
3.5	Jean	97	50	16	18	36	61	110	239	439	934
3.5	Carolyn	223	174	127	30	12	25	56	114	162	222
3.5	Janet	234	153	114	25	21	21	49	127	199	283

Overall						Rank					
pop.	Name	1900s	1910s	1920s	1930s	1940s	1950s	1960s	1970s	1980s	1990s
3.4	Joan	360	206	60	7	25	47	112	350	543	866
3.4	Christine	137	124	124	129	55	30	27	22	48	101
3.4	Ann	63	45	50	34	38	45	60	102	180	325
3.4	Florence	11	14	22	59	135	272	420	661		
3.3	Joyce	390	237	65	12	19	31	87	221	424	609
3.3	Lillian	13	16	26	61	127	194	258	371	404	312
3.3	Irene	21	17	19	46	100	143	220	312	350	422
3.3	Brenda				301	27	18	20	54	114	123
3.1	Pamela			863	478	41	13	13	49	118	305
3.1	Louise	24	18	25	42	84	146	273	614	973	
3.1	Gladys	15	20	31	60	123	198	302	515	613	780
3.0	Emily	98	105	142	173	188	229	257	64	24	3
2.9	Edna	17	19	34	53	118	196	318	493	797	
2.9	Diane		726	459	113	22	17	39	125	242	485
2.9	Heather					585	381	127	8	10	38
2.9	Grace	18	26	42	86	139	210	248	366	226	96
2.8	Judith	448	383	293	40	8	33	97	255	395	481
2.8	Gloria	452	291	36	29	26	40	98	190	244	273
2.8	Rachel	142	155	159	166	179	191	147	33	15	15
2.8	Annie	28	34	33	41	83	155	291	405	307	348
2.8	Debra					323	7	23	94	288	713
2.8	Nicole					1006	881	186	12	8	17
2.8	Kathryn	76	63	89	111	71	59	88	93	50	70
2.8	Ruby	42	24	27	48	104	179	294	362	380	264
2.8	Julia	45	40	62	97	105	128	113	129	88	59
2.8	Ethel	12	22	41	81	144	239	471	890		
2.7	Lois	86	51	21	24	49	119	236	601		
2.7	Julie	530	517	483	311	140	44	18	20	51	125
2.6	Theresa	94	96	76	74	90	41	43	82	135	256
2.6	Josephine	33	23	32	66	121	199	300	428	440	426
2.5	Edith	25	29	38	80	126	206	301	489	588	551
2.5	Marilyn		539	88	16	29	56	139	263	359	462
2.5	Christina	278	323	349	400	256	181	75	16	19	36

Overall						Rank					
pop.	Name	1900s	1910s	1920s	1930s	1940s	1950s	1960s	1970s	1980s	1990s
2.5	Jane	134	70	57	47	40	54	96	264	334	365
2.5	Janice	501	328	187	45	24	24	67	177	318	517
2.5	Emma	29	39	58	84	124	207	323	420	270	71
2.5	Beverly	834	340	98	21	31	37	85	224	406	655
2.4	Kelly						209	31	14	29	55
2.4	Cheryl				624	44	19	28	80	196	671
2.4	Hazel	20	27	44	92	154	302	569	834		854
2.4	Phyllis	189	107	43	27	37	77	152	511		
2.4	Thelma	38	28	35	67	143	237	391	711		
2.4	Esther	30	35	49	93	137	190	270	322	293	297
2.3	Teresa	195	228	200	208	134	28	25	48	124	228
2.3	Anne	79	57	83	90	86	83	81	123	130	206
2.3	Marjorie	89	41	20	44	99	173	274	431	596	
2.3	Clara	23	37	52	79	136	223	363	535	542	433
2.3	Sara	129	116	126	133	131	166	161	50	30	44
2.3	Judy		675	464	110	17	27	79	268	444	781

Boys

Names are listed in order of overall popularity in the twentieth century. For each decade the rank of the name (out of 1000) is provided.

Overall						Rank					
pop.	Name	1900s	1910s	1920s	1930s	1940s	1950s	1960s	1970s	1980s	1990s
36.8	John	1	1	2	3	3	4	3	6	9	14
34.2	James	3	3	3	2	1	2	4	5	7	13
32.2	Robert	7	4	1	1	2	3	5	7	8	20
29.0	William	2	2	4	4	4	6	7	9	15	19
21.8	Michael	39	43	49	35	9	1	1	1	1	1
19.2	David	29	30	22	11	6	5	2	4	5	11
17.4	Joseph	5	5	7	10	13	13	12	12	10	10
17.4	Charles	6	7	5	6	7	10	17	23	34	43
16.3	Richard	25	17	8	5	5	7	8	16	27	41
14.3	Thomas	12	11	11	9	8	8	9	21	25	27
12.7	George	4	6	6	8	15	25	33	49	72	105
10.0	Edward	9	8	9	12	18	23	29	40	57	80

Overall pop.	Name	Rank 1900s	1910s	1920s	1930s	1940s	1950s	1960s	1970s	1980s	1990s
9.9	Donald	51	20	10	7	12	14	25	44	67	125
9.5	Paul	17	14	13	14	17	17	19	27	40	64
9.1	Daniel	56	55	44	40	22	19	18	11	6	7
9.1	Christopher	333	349	385	367	155	49	20	2	2	2
8.1	Frank	8	9	12	16	21	34	44	65	91	152
8.0	Kenneth	47	27	20	15	16	16	21	31	47	61
7.0	Anthony	43	35	42	46	44	30	22	22	20	18
6.7	Mark	194	215	226	199	57	9	6	18	33	49
6.7	Matthew	168	159	180	225	205	100	36	10	3	3
6.3	Ronald	252	172	98	13	10	15	24	45	70	135
6.3	Steven	382	313	302	257	31	11	11	19	24	34
6.0	Raymond	22	15	16	17	23	37	46	66	77	109
5.9	Andrew	40	46	57	71	86	67	38	28	13	6
5.8	Walter	11	10	15	22	27	52	80	107	158	245
5.7	Brian				324	113	35	16	8	16	36
5.3	Henry	10	12	18	25	35	58	97	118	133	143
5.3	Harold	15	13	14	19	28	64	102	160	251	411
5.3	Kevin			830	444	185	27	14	13	23	25
5.2	Timothy	284	378	378	249	65	22	13	20	26	38
4.9	Jeffrey				619	89	24	10	15	30	55
4.8	Jason	717	707	667	679	563	420	87	3	11	45
4.8	Gary	747	677	525	47	14	12	26	48	80	170
4.7	Arthur	14	16	19	28	36	56	99	126	178	243
4.7	Stephen	95	89	120	109	24	20	28	32	36	48
4.6	Joshua	487	557	639	732	644	548	346	25	4	4
4.6	Larry	401	327	209	33	11	18	35	57	94	200
4.5	Albert	16	18	21	32	48	76	103	123	147	211
4.2	Carl	20	24	26	29	39	48	60	94	116	204
4.2	Harry	13	19	23	36	52	89	142	203	290	388
4.2	Eric	254	427	487	317	159	74	27	14	21	29
4.2	Jack	41	29	17	18	37	57	106	161	176	113
4.1	Jose	80	95	65	52	47	47	43	35	37	32
3.9	Scott	406	412	454	441	177	36	15	17	39	75

Overall							Rank				
pop.	Name	1900s	1910s	1920s	1930s	1940s	1950s	1960s	1970s	1980s	1990s
3.8	Samuel	31	41	46	60	61	71	83	61	52	35
3.7	Ralph	23	21	24	30	45	62	109	186	272	448
3.7	Jerry	180	169	108	23	19	31	41	63	114	192
3.6	Willie	28	28	27	31	34	54	98	121	164	263
3.6	Nicholas	132	112	130	162	141	144	147	51	19	8
3.6	Peter	46	48	59	59	42	39	42	55	63	87
3.6	Gregory	497	502	375	319	66	26	23	29	46	70
3.5	Louis	21	22	30	43	55	80	108	143	161	217
3.5	Lawrence	34	37	38	37	29	41	67	101	150	227
3.5	Patrick	114	156	142	107	58	40	32	37	38	44
3.5	Ryan						622	242	26	14	15
3.5	Roy	24	32	32	39	43	63	95	120	180	299
3.4	Dennis	227	204	181	74	20	21	40	62	97	173
3.4	Joe	38	38	33	27	38	60	64	110	179	234
3.3	Fred	19	25	34	34	53	99	138	242	391	619
3.2	Jonathan	631	708	583	459	216	141	82	33	17	21
3.2	Clarence	18	23	29	45	80	112	172	222	278	489
3.2	Justin	662	666	618	682	590	514	320	39	12	17
3.1	Eugene	49	40	25	24	51	83	118	162	226	390
3.1	Howard	30	26	28	38	54	85	124	196	323	561
3.1	Douglas	200	154	112	72	30	28	30	52	76	151
3.1	Gerald	120	83	45	21	26	46	62	104	175	269
3.1	Benjamin	64	73	88	124	130	126	131	42	31	30
2.8	Ernest	26	33	37	51	67	92	129	171	222	382
2.8	Brandon						726	379	54	18	12
2.8	Earl	27	31	31	44	72	111	163	210	288	486
2.8	Jacob	96	126	173	234	283	329	344	83	35	5
2.7	Roger	209	135	92	42	25	38	51	93	163	257
2.6	Francis	37	34	35	50	71	102	157	218	260	353
2.5	Russell	53	49	54	68	70	65	56	80	113	213
2.5	Billy	770	329	48	20	41	69	74	84	140	255
2.5	Stanley	52	36	41	58	63	70	120	182	248	394
2.4	Leonard	48	44	39	53	64	90	122	170	233	373

Overall						Rank					
pop.	Name	1900s	1910s	1920s	1930s	1940s	1950s	1960s	1970s	1980s	1990s
2.4	Adam	178	200	280	376	444	407	144	38	22	39
2.4	Aaron	193	208	218	274	279	232	132	36	32	31
2.3	Jesse	68	77	89	110	115	127	139	69	49	50
2.3	Keith	422	254	151	128	105	42	34	46	66	124
2.3	Alfred	33	42	40	61	92	120	164	224	296	434
2.3	Juan	111	115	96	85	95	98	91	59	59	51
2.3	Wayne	150	108	74	49	33	43	63	111	186	330
2.3	Herbert	32	39	36	55	98	139	207	284	421	623
2.2	Philip	77	78	75	69	60	66	85	88	86	161
2.2	Terry	650	611	501	150	32	29	37	71	125	233
2.2	Alexander	101	99	141	188	199	212	204	102	48	24
2.2	Bruce	236	182	137	87	40	32	48	133	177	318
2.1	Victor	79	67	79	97	91	91	89	92	88	83
2.1	Norman	76	51	43	41	69	113	143	235	346	525
2.0	Jeremy					981	740	368	24	28	47
2.0	Martin	66	79	84	94	93	78	70	108	127	142
2.0	Frederick	62	56	62	70	74	88	115	137	201	315
2.0	Kyle	718	780	772	669	650	318	176	90	29	22
2.0	Edwin	55	53	56	77	100	105	125	148	162	164
1.9	Bobby			135	26	49	77	79	98	134	249
1.9	Melvin	85	61	50	54	73	97	133	192	241	350
1.9	Nathan	140	138	229	269	292	244	189	50	41	40

🔤 The 100 most popular names in 2000

Girls									
14.0	Hannah	4.5	Haley	2.9	Sierra	1.9	Bailey	11.5	Andrew
13.5	Emily	4.4	Katherine	2.8	Caroline	1.9	Christina	11.3	William
10.3	Madison	4.3	Amanda	2.8	Kaylee	1.9	Courtney	11.2	Joshua
10.0	Elizabeth	4.3	Megan	2.8	Kimberly	1.9	Molly	10.8	Daniel
9.3	Alexis	4.3	Rachel	2.8	Vanessa	1.8	Angel	10.6	Tyler
8.8	Sarah	4.1	Chloe	2.7	Allison	1.8	Brittney	10.3	Ryan
8.3	Taylor	4.1	Jasmine	2.7	Faith	1.8	Claire	10.2	Anthony
8.1	Lauren	3.9	Natalie	2.7	Gabrielle	1.8	Leslie	9.7	Alexander
8.0	Jessica	3.9	Stephanie	2.6	Erin	1.8	Margaret	9.7	Zachary
7.7	Ashley	3.8	Amber	2.6	Michelle	1.8	Mariah	9.2	David
7.5	Samantha	3.8	Julia	2.5	Cheyenne	1.8	Miranda	9.1	James
7.1	Brianna	3.6	Savannah	2.5	Jenna	1.8	Sabrina	9.0	John
6.6	Kayla	3.5	Kaitlyn	2.4	Makayla	1.7	Autumn	8.9	Christian
6.4	Olivia	3.5	Mackenzie	2.4	Mary	1.7	Erica	8.9	Justin
6.2	Abigail	3.5	Sophia	2.4	Paige	1.7	Lindsey	8.5	Benjamin
6.2	Anna	3.3	Hailey	2.3	Kelsey	1.7	Marissa	8.0	Austin
6.1	Alyssa	3.2	Brooke	2.3	Diana	1.7	Zoe	7.7	Brandon
5.9	Emma	3.1	Danielle	2.3	Jordan	1.7	Jade	7.7	Samuel
5.6	Jennifer	3.1	Katelyn	2.3	Melanie	1.7	Jocelyn	7.5	Nathan
5.6	Nicole	3.1	Maria	2.2	Alexandria	1.7	Kathryn	7.4	Dylan
5.4	Grace	3.0	Andrea	2.2	Briana	**Boys**		7.4	Noah
5.1	Alexandra	3.0	Brittany	2.2	Kylie	17.7	Michael	7.2	Jose
5.0	Sydney	3.0	Isabella	2.2	Trinity	16.0	Jacob	7.0	Ethan
4.9	Destiny	3.0	Rebecca	2.1	Audrey	15.4	Matthew	6.9	Jonathan
4.7	Victoria	3.0	Sara	2.1	Katie	11.9	Joseph	6.9	Robert
4.6	Morgan	3.0	Madeline	2.0	Jada	11.8	Christopher	6.8	Hunter
		3.0	Melissa	2.0	Mia	11.8	Nicholas	6.8	Cameron

5.7	Kevin	4.1	Steven	3.3	Isaac	2.7	Trevor	2.3	Gavin
5.5	Kyle	4.0	Cody	3.3	Richard	2.6	Jackson	2.3	Paul
5.2	Aaron	3.8	Isaiah	3.2	Chase	2.6	Maxwell	2.2	Jesus
5.2	Logan	3.8	Sean	3.2	Patrick	2.6	Nathaniel	2.1	Antonio
5.2	Thomas	3.8	Connor	3.1	Cole	2.6	Spencer	2.1	Colin
4.9	Gabriel	3.7	Juan	3.1	Jesse	2.5	Timothy	2.1	Dominic
4.8	Caleb	3.7	Mason	3.0	Angel	2.5	Victor	2.1	Xavier
4.8	Jason	3.6	Adam	3.0	Blake	2.3	Carson	2.0	Kenneth
4.8	Jordan	3.6	Evan	3.0	Carlos	2.3	Dalton	2.0	Marcus
4.6	Devin	3.6	Luis	2.9	Bryan	2.3	Elijah	2.0	Raymond
4.6	Jack	3.5	Mark	2.9	Garrett	2.3	Ian	1.9	Jeffrey
4.3	Eric	3.5	Seth	2.8	Dakota	2.3	Shane		
4.2	Brian	3.4	Luke	2.7	Alex	2.3	Stephen		
4.2	Jared	3.3	Charles	2.7	Lucas	2.3	Bryce		

🔠 The 100 most popular names in 1999

Girls		5.0	Nicole	3.1	Gabrielle	2.3	Kaylee	1.8	Katie
13.5	Emily	4.9	Sydney	3.1	Brooke	2.3	Madeline	1.8	Caitlin
11.0	Hannah	4.9	Morgan	2.9	Jordan	2.3	Caroline	1.8	Isabel
9.7	Alexis	4.7	Jasmine	2.9	Sierra	2.2	Kelsey	1.8	Miranda
9.6	Samantha	4.7	Grace	2.9	Sara	2.2	Marissa	1.7	Lindsey
9.6	Sarah	4.6	Anna	2.8	Kimberly	2.2	Breanna	1.7	Kelly
9.2	Ashley	4.6	Destiny	2.8	Sophia	2.2	Kiara	1.7	Catherine
9.2	Madison	4.4	Julia	2.8	Mackenzie	2.2	Christina	1.7	Cassidy
8.6	Taylor	4.2	Alexandra	2.7	Andrea	2.1	Faith	1.7	Leslie
8.3	Jessica	4.2	Haley	2.7	Michelle	2.1	Autumn	*Boys*	
7.7	Elizabeth	4.1	Natalie	2.7	Hailey	2.0	Laura	17.1	Jacob
7.1	Alyssa	4.1	Kaitlyn	2.7	Vanessa	2.0	Tiffany	16.5	Michael
7.1	Lauren	4.0	Katherine	2.7	Katelyn	2.0	Jacqueline	14.7	Matthew
6.7	Kayla	4.0	Stephanie	2.7	Erin	1.9	Briana	13.4	Joshua
6.3	Brianna	4.0	Brittany	2.6	Isabella	1.9	Alexandria	12.6	Christopher
6.2	Megan	3.8	Rebecca	2.6	Shelby	1.9	Cheyenne	12.4	Nicholas
6.0	Victoria	3.7	Maria	2.6	Jenna	1.9	Mikayla	11.5	Andrew
6.0	Emma	3.6	Allison	2.5	Chloe	1.9	Cassandra	11.2	Joseph
5.9	Abigail	3.5	Amber	2.5	Melissa	1.9	Claire	11.0	Daniel
5.9	Rachel	3.5	Savannah	2.5	Bailey	1.9	Alexa	11.0	Tyler
5.7	Olivia	3.4	Danielle	2.4	Makayla	1.9	Sabrina	10.5	Brandon
5.4	Jennifer	3.3	Courtney	2.4	Paige	1.8	Angela	10.2	Ryan
5.0	Amanda	3.2	Mary	2.3	Mariah	1.8	Kathryn	10.1	Austin

10.0	William	6.2	Thomas	3.6	Charles	2.8	Jesus	2.2	Miguel
9.9	John	6.1	Nathan	3.6	Isaiah	2.7	Mark	2.1	Victor
9.9	David	6.0	Cameron	3.6	Jack	2.7	Ian	2.1	Lucas
9.7	Zachary	5.6	Hunter	3.6	Carlos	2.7	Mason	2.0	Spencer
9.5	Anthony	5.6	Ethan	3.5	Jared	2.6	Cole	2.0	Bryce
9.0	James	4.8	Aaron	3.5	Sean	2.5	Adrian	1.9	Paul
8.9	Justin	4.6	Eric	3.4	Alex	2.5	Chase	1.9	Brendan
8.6	Alexander	4.5	Jason	3.3	Evan	2.5	Jeremy	1.9	Jake
8.4	Jonathan	4.5	Caleb	3.2	Elijah	2.5	Dakota	1.9	Tristan
7.8	Dylan	4.4	Logan	3.2	Richard	2.5	Garrett	1.9	Jeffrey
7.3	Christian	4.3	Brian	3.1	Patrick	2.5	Antonio	1.9	Marcus
7.2	Noah	4.1	Luis	3.1	Nathaniel	2.4	Jackson		
7.1	Robert	4.0	Adam	3.1	Isaac	2.4	Jesse		
6.8	Samuel	4.0	Juan	3.0	Seth	2.3	Blake		
6.7	Kyle	3.8	Steven	3.0	Trevor	2.2	Dalton		
6.6	Benjamin	3.8	Cody	3.0	Angel	2.2	Tanner		
6.5	Jose	3.8	Gabriel	3.0	Luke	2.2	Stephen		
6.3	Jordan	3.7	Connor	2.9	Devin	2.2	Alejandro		
6.3	Kevin	3.7	Timothy	2.8	Bryan	2.2	Kenneth		

The 100 most popular names in 1998

Girls		6.1	Brianna	4.1	Allison	3.0	Kimberly	2.4	Tiffany
13.4	Emily	5.7	Amanda	4.1	Amber	3.0	Vanessa	2.3	Hailey
10.9	Hannah	5.7	Abigail	4.1	Kaitlyn	3.0	Sierra	2.3	Christina
10.2	Samantha	5.4	Jennifer	4.0	Haley	2.9	Kelsey	2.3	Laura
10.2	Ashley	5.4	Emma	4.0	Destiny	2.9	Michelle	2.2	Makayla
10.2	Sarah	5.4	Olivia	3.9	Courtney	2.8	Erin	2.2	Caroline
10.0	Alexis	5.3	Morgan	3.8	Danielle	2.8	Grace	2.2	Sophia
9.6	Taylor	5.3	Nicole	3.7	Natalie	2.7	Melissa	2.2	Cheyenne
9.4	Jessica	5.1	Brittany	3.7	Jordan	2.7	Katelyn	2.2	Caitlin
9.1	Madison	4.8	Jasmine	3.6	Maria	2.7	Bailey	2.2	Breanna
7.7	Elizabeth	4.5	Stephanie	3.3	Brooke	2.7	Andrea	2.1	Briana
7.0	Alyssa	4.5	Alexandra	3.3	Savannah	2.6	Mariah	2.1	Miranda
6.9	Megan	4.4	Sydney	3.2	Mary	2.6	Paige	2.1	Alexandria
6.8	Kayla	4.3	Rebecca	3.2	Gabrielle	2.5	Jenna	2.0	Autumn
6.7	Lauren	4.3	Julia	3.1	Sara	2.5	Mackenzie	2.0	Diana
6.3	Rachel	4.3	Anna	3.1	Madeline	2.4	Marissa	2.0	Mikayla
6.2	Victoria	4.2	Katherine	3.0	Shelby	2.4	Sabrina	2.0	Cassandra

1.9	Kaylee	11.8	Brandon	6.5	Noah	3.5	Alex	2.5	Stephen
1.9	Kelly	11.7	Tyler	6.4	Benjamin	3.4	Richard	2.4	Antonio
1.9	Chloe	11.6	Andrew	6.2	Thomas	3.4	Patrick	2.4	Garrett
1.9	Isabella	11.6	Austin	5.6	Nathan	3.2	Trevor	2.3	Tanner
1.9	Katie	11.3	Daniel	5.5	Hunter	3.1	Nathaniel	2.3	Blake
1.9	Kathryn	11.3	Joseph	5.5	Cameron	3.1	Isaiah	2.3	Kenneth
1.9	Erica	10.2	William	5.2	Aaron	3.1	Jack	2.3	Spencer
1.9	Alexa	10.2	Zachary	5.1	Ethan	3.1	Carlos	2.3	Mason
1.9	Claire	10.2	John	4.9	Eric	3.0	Devin	2.3	Miguel
1.8	Chelsea	10.1	David	4.6	Jason	3.0	Evan	2.2	Dalton
1.8	Lindsey	9.9	Ryan	4.5	Brian	2.9	Bryan	2.2	Seth
1.8	Amy	9.6	Anthony	4.4	Caleb	2.8	Mark	2.1	Paul
1.8	Monica	9.5	James	4.3	Cody	2.8	Isaac	2.1	Victor
1.8	Jacqueline	8.7	Justin	4.2	Logan	2.8	Jeremy	2.1	Tristan
1.8	Alicia	8.7	Jonathan	4.2	Luis	2.7	Chase	2.1	Jeffrey
1.7	Michaela	8.7	Alexander	4.1	Adam	2.7	Angel	2.0	Alejandro
Boys		7.6	Kyle	4.1	Steven	2.7	Elijah	2.0	Bryce
18.1	Michael	7.5	Robert	4.0	Connor	2.7	Ian	2.0	Lucas
17.6	Jacob	7.2	Christian	3.8	Timothy	2.7	Adrian	1.9	Brendan
15.2	Matthew	7.1	Dylan	3.8	Charles	2.6	Jesse	1.9	Travis
13.9	Joshua	7.1	Jordan	3.8	Sean	2.6	Dakota	1.9	Marcus
13.3	Christopher	6.8	Samuel	3.8	Juan	2.6	Luke	1.9	Jake
12.8	Nicholas	6.7	Jose	3.7	Jared	2.6	Jesus		
		6.5	Kevin	3.6	Gabriel	2.6	Cole		

The 100 most popular names in North America in the mid-1990s

Girls

16.6	Jessica	4.8	Morgan	2.8	Brooke	2.0	Briana
13.6	Ashley	4.7	Melissa	2.7	Marissa	2.0	Angela
11.8	Emily	4.5	Kelsey	2.6	Emma	2.0	Destiny
11.7	Sarah	4.4	Katherine	2.6	Kristen	1.9	Kathryn
10.6	Samantha	4.4	Michelle	2.5	Paige	1.9	Breanna
10.1	Taylor	4.0	Madison	2.5	Cassandra	1.8	Madeline
8.4	Brittany	3.9	Anna	2.5	Miranda	1.8	Cynthia
8.3	Amanda	3.8	Haley	2.5	Erica	1.8	Caroline
7.9	Megan	3.8	Kimberly	2.5	Gabrielle	1.7	Jamie
7.8	Kayla	3.5	Kaitlyn	2.5	Katelyn	1.7	Mackenzie
7.7	Elizabeth	3.5	Chelsea	2.5	Amy	1.7	Diana
7.6	Hannah	3.5	Allison	2.5	Julia	1.7	Erika
7.6	Rachel	3.4	Shelby	2.4	Sierra	1.6	Cheyenne
7.5	Nicole	3.4	Vanessa	2.4	Jacqueline	1.6	Brittney
7.4	Stephanie	3.4	Christina	2.4	Catherine	1.6	Kaitlin
6.8	Jennifer	3.4	Mary	2.4	Kelly	1.5	Gabriela
6.5	Lauren	3.3	Tiffany	2.3	Shannon	1.5	Hailey
5.9	Courtney	3.3	Sara	2.2	Crystal		
5.8	Alexandra	3.3	Olivia	2.2	Savannah		**Boys**
5.8	Alexis	3.3	Laura	2.2	Katie	19.5	Michael
5.8	Victoria	3.2	Maria	2.1	Mariah	15.6	Matthew
5.7	Jasmine	3.1	Andrea	2.1	Alexandria	15.5	Christopher
5.6	Danielle	3.1	Erin	2.1	Lindsey	14.7	Joshua
5.3	Amber	3.1	Abigail	2.0	Jenna	14.2	Jacob
5.2	Rebecca	3.1	Natalie	2.0	Caitlin	13.9	Tyler
4.9	Alyssa	3.0	Sydney	2.0	Alicia	13.7	Brandon
4.8	Brianna	3.0	Heather	2.0	Sabrina	13.0	Daniel
		2.9	Jordan	2.0	Monica	12.8	Nicholas

12.3	Andrew
11.6	Austin
11.4	David
11.2	Ryan
10.9	Joseph
10.8	Zachary
10.5	James
9.9	Alexander
9.8	John
9.8	Justin
9.7	William
9.3	Anthony
8.7	Jonathan
8.7	Robert
8.7	Kyle
8.2	Kevin
7.6	Cody
7.3	Jordan
6.7	Samuel
6.1	Thomas
6.1	Aaron
6.1	Benjamin
6.0	Eric
5.8	Dylan
5.6	Christian
5.3	Steven
5.3	Jose
5.2	Adam

4.8	Nathan	3.3	Connor	2.7	Mitchell	2.2	Kenneth	1.9	Tanner
4.8	Brian	3.1	Mark	2.6	Dustin	2.2	Corey	1.9	Victor
4.3	Timothy	3.1	Juan	2.6	Dakota	2.1	Nathaniel	1.9	Ethan
4.3	Jason	3.0	Trevor	2.5	Jared	2.1	Marcus	1.9	Antonio
4.2	Jesse	2.9	Taylor	2.5	Bryan	2.1	Blake	1.8	Dalton
4.1	Patrick	2.9	Stephen	2.4	Hunter	2.1	Garrett	1.8	Adrian
4.0	Sean	2.8	Travis	2.4	Carlos	2.1	Lucas	1.8	Brett
3.9	Richard	2.8	Luis	2.4	Paul	2.0	Gregory	1.8	Alejandro
3.8	Jeremy	2.7	Evan	2.4	Derek	2.0	Spencer	1.8	Cole
3.7	Charles	2.7	Jeffrey	2.4	Ian	2.0	Vincent	1.8	Edward
3.6	Cameron	2.7	Caleb	2.3	Bradley	2.0	Miguel	1.8	Shane
3.5	Alex	2.7	Devin	2.3	Scott	1.9	Luke		
3.4	Gabriel	2.7	Logan	2.2	Jesus	1.9	Peter		

The 100 most popular names by region in the mid-1990s

Northeastern United States

Girls									
		7.6	Katherine	4.1	Jacqueline	3.2	Amy	2.3	Julie
18.0	Emily	7.6	Danielle	4.1	Kimberly	3.2	Tiffany	2.3	Lindsay
16.5	Samantha	6.7	Brianna	4.1	Haley	3.1	Lindsey	2.3	Christine
16.2	Sarah	6.6	Kelsey	4.0	Christina	3.0	Jasmine	2.2	Alison
16.1	Jessica	6.5	Alyssa	4.0	Mary	3.0	Erica	2.2	Alexa
15.6	Ashley	6.1	Abigail	4.0	Katelyn	2.9	Alicia	2.2	Sabrina
13.6	Nicole	6.0	Erin	4.0	Kelly	2.8	Shelby	2.1	Grace
13.1	Amanda	5.9	Julia	3.9	Marissa	2.8	Jillian	2.1	Colleen
10.5	Elizabeth	5.7	Shannon	3.9	Catherine	2.7	Casey	2.1	Madison
10.4	Taylor	5.7	Olivia	3.9	Cassandra	2.7	Katie	2.1	Maria
10.2	Kayla	5.3	Melissa	3.9	Caroline	2.7	Miranda	2.1	Kristina
9.6	Rachel	5.3	Allison	3.8	Laura	2.6	Briana	2.0	Madeline
9.0	Megan	5.1	Emma	3.7	Kristen	2.6	Jordan	2.0	Rachael
8.8	Jennifer	4.8	Michelle	3.6	Kathryn	2.6	Margaret		
8.7	Brittany	4.7	Alexis	3.6	Jenna	2.6	Mariah	**Boys**	
8.6	Hannah	4.7	Morgan	3.6	Chelsea	2.5	Andrea	29.8	Michael
8.5	Rebecca	4.6	Meghan	3.5	Heather	2.5	Angela	25.5	Matthew
8.5	Stephanie	4.5	Molly	3.4	Michaela	2.5	Leah	22.6	Nicholas
8.4	Victoria	4.4	Amber	3.3	Paige	2.5	Vanessa	22.1	Christopher
8.3	Alexandra	4.4	Anna	3.3	Brooke	2.4	Natalie	18.1	Joseph
8.2	Lauren	4.3	Sara	3.3	Gabrielle	2.4	Alexandria	17.9	Ryan
8.0	Courtney	4.1	Kaitlyn	3.2	Caitlin	2.3	Kathleen	17.9	Tyler

17.8	Andrew	9.1	Patrick	5.1	Brendan	3.0	Nathaniel	2.1	George
17.7	John	9.0	Brian	5.0	Austin	3.0	Shane	2.1	Gabriel
16.9	Daniel	8.6	Samuel	4.9	Evan	3.0	Shawn	2.1	Seth
15.4	Zachary	8.5	Timothy	4.7	Jeffrey	3.0	Trevor	2.0	Brett
15.3	Joshua	8.5	Adam	4.7	Peter	2.9	Devin	2.0	Jack
14.7	James	8.2	Dylan	4.6	Derek	2.8	Colin	1.9	Cory
13.8	Alexander	8.1	Cody	4.6	Alex	2.8	Bryan	1.8	Isaac
13.4	Jacob	8.0	Sean	4.5	Christian	2.7	Ethan	1.8	Marcus
13.0	Kyle	7.8	Eric	4.5	Paul	2.6	Mitchell	1.8	Keith
12.7	David	6.7	Nathan	4.3	Jeremy	2.6	Travis	1.7	Bradley
12.4	Robert	6.2	Steven	4.2	Ian	2.6	Jose	1.7	Devon
11.4	Thomas	6.1	Connor	4.2	Charles	2.5	Luis	1.7	Erik
11.4	Brandon	6.0	Aaron	4.1	Corey	2.3	Kenneth	1.7	Hunter
11.3	Kevin	6.0	Cameron	3.8	Jared	2.3	Lucas	1.7	Logan
11.3	William	5.7	Jordan	3.6	Jesse	2.3	Luke	1.7	Carlos
10.8	Benjamin	5.4	Richard	3.6	Scott	2.2	Taylor	1.6	Henry
10.7	Anthony	5.4	Stephen	3.4	Gregory	2.2	Caleb	1.6	Troy
10.3	Jonathan	5.2	Jason	3.2	Edward	2.2	Alec		
9.9	Justin	5.2	Mark	3.1	Jake	2.2	Conor		

⬛ Southeastern United States

Girls		7.6	Jasmine	4.4	Kelsey	3.0	Laura	2.3	Catherine
15.6	Ashley	7.6	Amanda	4.2	Allison	3.0	Lindsey	2.2	Whitney
14.3	Jessica	7.2	Morgan	4.1	Shelby	2.9	Melissa	2.2	Julia
12.4	Taylor	5.7	Brianna	4.1	Jordan	2.9	Sierra	2.1	Breanna
12.2	Emily	5.6	Haley	4.0	Heather	2.8	Michelle	2.1	Paige
12.2	Brittany	5.6	Mary	4.0	Sydney	2.8	Gabrielle	2.1	Kaitlin
11.9	Sarah	5.3	Stephanie	3.9	Savannah	2.8	Natalie	2.1	Maria
10.3	Kayla	5.2	Madison	3.9	Olivia	2.8	Miranda	2.1	Marissa
10.1	Hannah	5.2	Jennifer	3.7	Christina	2.8	Caroline	2.0	Amy
9.4	Samantha	4.9	Danielle	3.7	Kristen	2.7	Katie	2.0	Brittney
8.4	Alexis	4.8	Anna	3.6	Brooke	2.7	Erica	2.0	Crystal
8.3	Megan	4.7	Katherine	3.6	Kimberly	2.6	Briana	1.9	Cheyenne
8.2	Amber	4.7	Tiffany	3.5	Alyssa	2.6	Caitlin	1.9	Jamie
8.1	Courtney	4.7	Rebecca	3.4	Destiny	2.5	Kelly	1.8	Emma
8.1	Rachel	4.5	Alexandra	3.2	Erin	2.5	Alexandria	1.8	Brandi
7.9	Elizabeth	4.5	Kaitlyn	3.2	Katelyn	2.4	Andrea	1.8	Jenna
7.7	Lauren	4.5	Nicole	3.2	Abigail	2.3	Shannon	1.8	Angela
7.7	Victoria	4.4	Chelsea	3.1	Sara	2.3	Kathryn	1.7	Bethany

1.7	Casey	12.8	Nicholas	5.6	Samuel	3.2	Taylor	2.1	Seth
1.7	Autumn	12.8	John	5.6	Timothy	3.1	Kenneth	2.1	Shawn
1.7	Cassidy	12.4	Justin	5.2	Eric	2.9	Alex	2.0	Gabriel
1.7	Bailey	11.8	Zachary	5.0	Steven	2.9	Mark	2.0	Wesley
1.7	Mariah	11.2	Joseph	5.0	Hunter	2.8	Evan	1.9	Luke
1.7	Madeline	11.1	Andrew	4.6	Brian	2.8	Trevor	1.9	Mason
1.7	Margaret	10.8	David	4.5	Adam	2.8	Marcus	1.8	Edward
1.6	Summer	10.7	Daniel	4.4	Richard	2.7	Jeffrey	1.8	Spencer
1.6	Mackenzie	10.5	Robert	4.4	Patrick	2.7	Bradley	1.8	Dillon
1.6	Alicia	9.4	Ryan	4.3	Dustin	2.7	Dalton	1.8	Derek
1.6	Jacqueline	9.2	Jonathan	4.2	Cameron	2.7	Jared	1.8	Darius
		9.1	Cody	4.0	Jeremy	2.6	Connor	1.7	Mitchell
Boys		8.5	Alexander	4.0	Caleb	2.6	Bryan	1.7	Elijah
19.4	Michael	8.3	Anthony	3.9	Stephen	2.5	Blake	1.7	George
17.7	Christopher	7.4	Jordan	3.9	Logan	2.5	Gregory	1.7	Juan
17.4	Joshua	7.0	Thomas	3.8	Jason	2.4	Garrett	1.6	Carlos
15.9	Brandon	6.8	Kyle	3.8	Nathan	2.4	Nathaniel	1.6	Lucas
15.5	Matthew	6.8	Aaron	3.6	Sean	2.3	Ethan	1.6	Tanner
15.4	Austin	6.7	Kevin	3.6	Dakota	2.3	Ian	1.6	Scott
15.0	William	6.3	Christian	3.6	Devin	2.3	Paul	1.6	Phillip
14.6	James	6.3	Dylan	3.5	Corey	2.2	Jose	1.6	Cory
14.5	Tyler	5.7	Benjamin	3.5	Jesse	2.2	Antonio		
14.4	Jacob	5.6	Charles	3.4	Travis	2.1	Chase		

🅰️🅱️ Midwestern United States

Girls		9.0	Nicole	5.9	Jasmine	4.2	Michelle	3.4	Marissa
15.7	Jessica	8.5	Lauren	5.9	Rebecca	4.2	Erin	3.3	Erica
15.5	Ashley	8.5	Kayla	5.6	Alexandra	4.1	Chelsea	3.3	Katelyn
15.0	Emily	7.6	Alexis	5.5	Allison	3.9	Jordan	3.3	Miranda
13.7	Samantha	7.2	Courtney	5.4	Victoria	3.9	Mary	3.2	Heather
12.8	Taylor	7.1	Danielle	5.2	Katherine	3.9	Melissa	3.2	Kelly
12.3	Sarah	6.7	Stephanie	5.2	Abigail	3.8	Olivia	3.1	Natalie
10.8	Megan	6.5	Alyssa	5.2	Kaitlyn	3.8	Sara	3.1	Emma
9.7	Amanda	6.5	Kelsey	5.2	Shelby	3.7	Brooke	3.1	Laura
9.6	Rachel	6.4	Jennifer	4.9	Anna	3.7	Sydney	3.0	Katie
9.4	Brittany	6.3	Morgan	4.9	Haley	3.6	Andrea	2.9	Mariah
9.3	Hannah	6.3	Brianna	4.6	Paige	3.6	Tiffany	2.9	Kimberly
9.3	Elizabeth	6.1	Amber	4.5	Madison	3.5	Christina	2.9	Alexandria

2.8	Shannon	2.0	Vanessa	10.5	David	4.1	Dakota	2.7	Brett
2.8	Jenna	2.0	Meghan	10.3	Anthony	4.0	Mitchell	2.7	Taylor
2.8	Gabrielle	1.9	Kaylee	10.0	Cody	3.9	Jason	2.6	Corey
2.7	Madeline	1.8	Claire	9.7	Justin	3.9	Connor	2.6	Ethan
2.7	Sierra	1.8	Kylie	9.3	Robert	3.8	Mark	2.6	Marcus
2.7	Lindsey	1.8	Whitney	8.2	William	3.7	Devin	2.5	Garrett
2.7	Briana	1.8	Catherine	8.1	Jordan	3.7	Travis	2.4	Seth
2.7	Kristen	1.8	Brittney	7.7	Kevin	3.7	Logan	2.3	Tanner
2.6	Maria			7.6	Thomas	3.7	Jesse	2.3	Antonio
2.6	Kathryn	***Boys***		7.6	Aaron	3.6	Cameron	2.3	Hunter
2.6	Amy	21.7	Michael	7.4	Benjamin	3.5	Richard	2.3	Gregory
2.5	Cassandra	20.7	Jacob	7.3	Jonathan	3.5	Blake	2.2	Cole
2.5	Angela	18.1	Tyler	7.1	Eric	3.4	Evan	2.2	Peter
2.5	Caitlin	17.3	Matthew	7.0	Samuel	3.4	Derek	2.2	Alec
2.5	Breanna	16.9	Nicholas	6.9	Dylan	3.3	Jared	2.1	Brendan
2.4	Mackenzie	15.2	Zachary	6.8	Adam	3.2	Bradley	2.1	Spencer
2.3	Julia	14.9	Joshua	6.6	Nathan	3.2	Stephen	2.1	Grant
2.3	Molly	14.5	Austin	5.8	Steven	3.1	Dalton	2.1	Devon
2.3	Jacqueline	14.5	Brandon	5.6	Brian	3.0	Jose	2.1	Chase
2.3	Crystal	14.2	Christopher	5.4	Timothy	3.0	Luke	2.1	Shane
2.2	Jamie	14.2	Andrew	5.0	Christian	3.0	Scott	2.1	Juan
2.2	Alicia	13.5	Joseph	4.9	Patrick	2.9	Lucas	2.0	Bryan
2.2	Margaret	13.4	Ryan	4.5	Trevor	2.9	Dustin	2.0	Colton
2.2	Michaela	13.0	Daniel	4.4	Sean	2.9	Jeffrey	1.9	Gabriel
2.2	Cheyenne	12.1	Alexander	4.3	Alex	2.8	Ian	1.9	Erik
2.1	Destiny	11.6	Kyle	4.3	Charles	2.8	Nathaniel	1.8	Edward
2.1	Bailey	11.1	John	4.2	Jeremy	2.8	Paul		
2.0	Grace	10.8	James	4.2	Caleb	2.7	Kenneth		

🎲 Northwestern United States

Girls									
16.4	Jessica	9.3	Amanda	6.2	Courtney	5.3	Jennifer	4.7	Haley
13.9	Emily	8.9	Megan	5.8	Stephanie	5.2	Kelsey	4.6	Amber
13.8	Ashley	8.7	Rachel	5.7	Alexis	5.1	Brianna	4.4	Shelby
12.0	Samantha	8.0	Kayla	5.6	Alyssa	4.9	Victoria	4.1	Sara
11.9	Sarah	7.7	Elizabeth	5.5	Anna	4.8	Danielle	4.1	Jordan
10.3	Taylor	7.3	Nicole	5.4	Alexandra	4.8	Sierra	4.0	Maria
10.2	Hannah	6.5	Madison	5.3	Rebecca	4.8	Morgan	4.0	Emma
		6.3	Brittany	5.3	Lauren	4.8	Katherine	4.0	Mariah

4.0	Abigail	2.6	Mckenzie	16.8	Michael	5.0	Eric	3.1	Chase
3.8	Olivia	2.6	Julia	15.4	Joshua	4.8	Connor	3.1	Derek
3.8	Miranda	2.6	Alexandria	13.6	Andrew	4.8	Jose	3.1	Charles
3.7	Kaitlyn	2.6	Breanna	13.4	Matthew	4.7	Timothy	2.9	Cole
3.6	Jasmine	2.5	Kathryn	13.0	Brandon	4.7	Caleb	2.8	Lucas
3.6	Allison	2.5	Kylie	12.8	Christopher	4.7	Steven	2.8	Isaac
3.6	Mackenzie	2.5	Bailey	12.8	Nicholas	4.7	Cameron	2.8	Wyatt
3.5	Christina	2.4	Gabrielle	12.6	Daniel	4.7	Sean	2.8	Levi
3.5	Madeline	2.4	Kaylee	12.5	Zachary	4.7	Adam	2.7	Ethan
3.5	Michelle	2.3	Grace	12.3	Ryan	4.7	Tanner	2.7	Bradley
3.5	Savannah	2.3	Jamie	12.0	Alexander	4.6	Dakota	2.7	Jeffrey
3.5	Heather	2.2	Molly	11.4	Kyle	4.4	Brian	2.7	Juan
3.5	Melissa	2.1	Kendra	11.0	David	4.3	Jason	2.7	Riley
3.4	Chelsea	2.1	Vanessa	10.9	Joseph	4.3	Trevor	2.6	Scott
3.3	Katie	2.1	Caitlin	10.7	Cody	3.9	Logan	2.5	Mark
3.3	Hailey	2.1	Natasha	9.7	James	3.8	Richard	2.5	Stephen
3.3	Marissa	2.1	Angela	9.2	Jordan	3.7	Travis	2.5	Dalton
3.3	Sydney	2.1	Brittney	9.2	Justin	3.6	Ian	2.5	Casey
3.1	Andrea	2.1	Monica	9.0	John	3.5	Devin	2.4	Kenneth
3.0	Erin	2.0	Mikayla	8.0	Benjamin	3.5	Gabriel	2.4	Shane
3.0	Mary	2.0	Michaela	8.0	Anthony	3.5	Garrett	2.4	Seth
2.9	Brooke	1.9	Cassidy	7.8	William	3.5	Jared	2.3	Bryce
2.9	Katelyn	1.9	Shannon	7.6	Samuel	3.5	Patrick	2.3	Erik
2.9	Natalie	1.8	Erica	7.6	Robert	3.5	Alex	2.3	Marcus
2.8	Paige	1.8	Kristen	6.8	Jonathan	3.5	Spencer	2.2	Jake
2.8	Lindsey	1.8	Alexa	6.7	Aaron	3.3	Jeremy	2.2	Paul
2.8	Tiffany	1.8	Kelly	6.6	Dylan	3.3	Blake	2.2	Peter
2.8	Amy	1.8	Makayla	6.6	Nathan	3.3	Colton	2.2	Luke
2.8	Cassandra			6.4	Thomas	3.2	Mitchell	2.2	Mason
2.7	Cheyenne		*Boys*	6.1	Kevin	3.2	Hunter	2.2	Bryan
2.7	Kimberly	19.8	Jacob	5.7	Christian	3.2	Dustin	2.1	Hayden
2.7	Laura	17.4	Austin	5.5	Jesse	3.2	Evan		
2.7	Alicia	17.3	Tyler	5.2	Taylor	3.2	Nathaniel		

🔠 Southwestern United States

Girls		11.7	Ashley	9.7	Jennifer	8.6	Sarah	8.3	Emily
18.4	Jessica	9.9	Stephanie	9.2	Samantha	8.4	Elizabeth	8.1	Amanda

7.6	Nicole	2.9	Karina	2.0	Kaitlyn	5.9	Aaron
6.8	Vanessa	2.8	Angelica	2.0	Emma	5.9	Carlos
6.7	Taylor	2.8	Karen	2.0	Cindy	5.3	Jordan
6.5	Kimberly	2.8	Cassandra	2.0	Shannon	5.2	Cody
6.5	Jasmine	2.7	Erica	1.9	Jasmin	5.0	Samuel
6.4	Maria	2.7	Veronica	1.9	Jazmin	5.0	Richard
6.4	Melissa	2.7	Nancy	1.9	Katelyn	5.0	Alejandro
6.2	Michelle	2.7	Ana			4.9	Miguel
6.1	Megan	2.6	Haley	**Boys**		4.8	Jason
5.9	Rachel	2.6	Adriana	17.2	Michael	4.8	Eduardo
5.7	Lauren	2.6	Anna	16.7	Daniel	4.8	Thomas
5.6	Alexis	2.6	Amy	14.4	Jose	4.8	Jesse
5.5	Danielle	2.6	Daisy	14.2	Christopher	4.8	Benjamin
5.4	Alexandra	2.6	Allison	13.5	David	4.7	Angel
5.3	Alyssa	2.5	Abigail	13.0	Andrew	4.5	Nathan
5.2	Hannah	2.5	Mariah	12.9	Joshua	4.5	Gabriel
5.1	Brittany	2.5	Olivia	12.8	Anthony	4.3	Victor
5.1	Victoria	2.5	Sierra	12.5	Matthew	4.3	Jorge
5.0	Kayla	2.4	Chelsea	11.4	Brandon	4.3	Adam
4.7	Andrea	2.4	Julia	11.1	Jacob	4.1	Dylan
4.6	Brianna	2.4	Jocelyn	10.9	Jonathan	4.0	Sean
4.5	Rebecca	2.4	Yesenia	10.6	Kevin	3.9	Oscar
4.3	Diana	2.4	Heather	10.6	Joseph	3.9	Bryan
4.3	Katherine	2.4	Erika	10.2	Ryan	3.8	Francisco
4.3	Natalie	2.4	Shelby	10.1	Nicholas	3.7	Adrian
4.2	Jacqueline	2.3	Alicia	9.6	Tyler	3.7	Ricardo
3.9	Monica	2.3	Kelly	9.1	Alexander	3.7	Timothy
3.9	Christina	2.3	Angela	8.7	Christian	3.5	Cristian
3.8	Amber	2.3	Miranda	8.3	Austin	3.4	Alex
3.8	Laura	2.3	Breanna	8.2	Robert	3.3	Edgar
3.8	Gabriela	2.3	Briana	8.2	Juan	3.2	Cameron
3.7	Brenda	2.3	Guadalupe	8.0	James	3.2	Mark
3.7	Alejandra	2.2	Sabrina	8.0	John	3.2	Jeremy
3.6	Crystal	2.2	Jordan	7.9	Justin	3.1	Manuel
3.6	Marissa	2.2	Leslie	7.4	Zachary	3.1	Patrick
3.5	Cynthia	2.2	Alexandria	7.2	Luis	3.0	Erik
3.5	Courtney	2.2	Erin	7.1	Kyle	2.9	Antonio
3.4	Madison	2.1	Brooke	6.9	Eric	2.9	Jeffrey
3.3	Sara	2.1	Mary	6.5	William	2.8	Connor
3.2	Tiffany	2.1	Bianca	6.5	Jesus	2.8	Omar
2.9	Kelsey	2.1	Sydney	6.0	Steven	2.7	Taylor
2.9	Morgan	2.0	Savannah	6.0	Brian	2.7	Sergio

2.7	Trevor
2.6	Mario
2.6	Javier
2.6	Charles
2.6	Cesar
2.5	Martin
2.5	Edward
2.5	Paul
2.5	Andres
2.5	Ivan
2.4	Fernando
2.4	Hector
2.4	Ian
2.4	Stephen
2.3	Isaac
2.3	Garrett
2.3	Marcus
2.3	Roberto
2.3	Travis
2.2	Kenneth
2.2	Ruben
2.2	Vincent
2.1	Evan
2.1	Spencer
2.1	Jared

Non-continental United States

Girls

9.8	Jessica	3.2	Tiffany	2.1	Brandi
9.1	Ashley	3.1	Brianna	2.1	Shelby
8.9	Taylor	3.1	Tiana	2.0	Alexandria
7.9	Rachel	3.0	Alexis	2.0	Brenda
7.0	Kayla	3.0	Kimberly	2.0	Briana
6.4	Mary	3.0	Abigail	2.0	Cassandra
6.4	Nicole	3.0	Angelica	2.0	Christiana
5.9	Maria	3.0	Crystal	2.0	Dana
5.3	Courtney	3.0	Jasmin	2.0	Hanna
5.3	Amanda	3.0	Tiara	2.0	Janelle
5.3	Amber	2.9	Elizabeth	2.0	Kamarin
5.1	Sarah	2.8	Mariah	2.0	Karen
5.0	Samantha	2.8	Rebecca	2.0	Paige
4.7	Lauren	2.8	Sierra	2.0	Rita
4.5	Emily	2.7	Kristen	2.0	Sharon
4.4	Jacqueline	2.7	Marissa	2.0	Stephanie
4.4	Alyssa	2.7	Melissa	2.0	Tasi
4.3	Kiana	2.6	Sara	2.0	Teresa
4.2	Megan	2.6	Brittney	2.0	Veronica
4.1	Jasmine	2.6	Christina	1.5	Agnes
4.1	Michelle	2.6	Sydney	1.5	Alexandra
4.0	Brittany	2.5	Alicia	1.5	Alisha
3.9	Camarin	2.5	Camille	1.5	Amy
3.9	Christine	2.5	Charlene	1.5	April
3.8	Jennifer	2.5	Jade	1.5	Celine
3.8	Kylie	2.5	Jenny		
3.7	Chelsea	2.5	Kathleen		
3.7	Victoria	2.5	Kelly		
3.6	Hannah	2.5	Lisa		
3.5	Andrea	2.5	Marie		
3.5	Catherine	2.5	Naomi		
3.5	Kristina	2.5	Natasha		
3.5	Shannon	2.5	Rachelle		
3.5	Gabrielle	2.5	Sabrina		
3.5	Malia	2.4	Cheyenne		
3.4	Kelsey	2.3	Anna		
3.3	Danielle	2.1	Chloe		
		2.1	Angela		

Boys

14.9	Joshua	8.5	Austin	3.7	Keith
14.5	Michael	8.4	David	3.6	Eric
11.6	Brandon	8.4	Kevin	3.6	Samuel
11.1	Matthew	8.4	Nicholas	3.3	Elijah
10.7	Justin	7.9	Jose	3.3	Richard
10.5	Christopher	7.7	Christian	3.2	Dennis
10.3	Tyler	7.6	Jordan	3.2	Edward
9.7	Joseph	7.4	Kyle	3.2	Nicolas
9.0	Ryan	7.4	Kenneth	3.2	Paul
8.8	John	7.4	James	3.2	Tommy
8.7	Jacob	7.0	Peter	3.2	Jared
		6.9	Aaron	3.1	Brian
		6.8	Daniel	3.1	Jesse
		6.4	Andrew	3.1	Noah
		6.4	Zachary	3.0	Taylor
		6.4	Cody	2.9	Charles
		6.1	Jonathan	2.8	Benjamin
		5.9	Dylan	2.8	Chase
		5.8	Anthony	2.8	Devin
		5.7	William	2.8	Shane
		5.5	Robert	2.8	Cameron
		5.4	Alexander	2.8	Corey
		5.1	Jason	2.8	Cory
		5.1	Darren	2.8	Donovan
		4.7	Isaiah	2.8	George
		4.7	Sean	2.8	Timothy
		4.7	Thomas	2.7	Ian
		4.6	Shawn	2.7	Isaac
		4.6	Vincent	2.7	Kainoa
		4.5	Nathan	2.6	Patrick
		4.5	Micah	2.6	Bryson
		4.2	Lance	2.6	Travis
		4.0	Mark	2.4	Adam
		3.9	Keanu	2.4	Gabriel
		3.7	Jeremy	2.3	Albert
		3.7	Dominic	2.3	Angelo
		3.7	Jay	2.3	Bryan
		3.7	Jeffrey	2.3	Don

2.3	Evan	2.3	Juan	2.3	Raymond	2.2	Logan	2.1	Steven
2.3	Jake	2.3	Lawrence	2.3	Bradley	2.2	Mason		
2.3	Joel	2.3	Nathaniel	2.3	Keoni	2.1	Kekoa		

Western Canada

Girls

17.5	Jessica	4.6	Amber	2.6	Caitlin	1.8	Claire
13.1	Sarah	4.4	Natasha	2.6	Alexis	1.8	Jacqueline
11.3	Taylor	4.3	Jenna	2.5	Mikayla		
11.2	Ashley	4.2	Kaitlyn	2.5	Katelyn		
10.9	Nicole	4.2	Morgan	2.5	Lindsay		
10.5	Emily	4.1	Lauren	2.5	Bailey		
10.4	Samantha	4.0	Laura	2.5	Breanna		
8.7	Megan	4.0	Cassandra	2.4	Jamie		
8.6	Amanda	3.9	Elizabeth	2.4	Kennedy		
7.7	Brittany	3.8	Brooke	2.4	Tiffany		
7.7	Courtney	3.8	Kimberly	2.3	Jordan		
7.5	Jennifer	3.8	Julia	2.3	Alicia		
7.5	Kayla	3.6	Brianna	2.3	Marissa		
7.0	Rachel	3.5	Olivia	2.2	Hayley		
6.9	Rebecca	3.5	Mackenzie	2.2	Brittney		
6.7	Madison	3.4	Katherine	2.1	Carly		
6.6	Stephanie	3.4	Sara	2.1	Michaela		
6.6	Alexandra	3.4	Shania	2.1	Crystal		
6.5	Danielle	3.3	Miranda	2.1	Allison		
6.3	Kelsey	3.3	Jasmine	2.1	Christine		
5.9	Melissa	3.3	Cassidy	2.1	Meghan		
5.8	Sydney	3.2	Kristen	2.0	Kaitlin		
5.8	Michelle	3.2	Anna	2.0	Katrina		
5.6	Hannah	3.1	Heather	1.9	Shannon		
5.5	Chelsea	3.1	Haley	1.9	Kirsten		
5.3	Amy	3.1	Christina	1.9	Leah		
5.3	Alyssa	2.9	Vanessa	1.9	Chloe		
5.0	Emma	2.8	Natalie	1.9	Sierra		
5.0	Paige	2.8	Lisa	1.9	Tara		
4.8	Erin	2.8	Hailey	1.9	Mariah		
4.8	Shelby	2.7	Angela	1.8	Destiny		
4.6	Victoria	2.7	Andrea	1.8	Catherine		
		2.7	Kendra	1.8	Cheyenne		

Boys

18.3	Matthew	6.2	Mitchell
15.2	Brandon	6.2	Aaron
14.6	Michael	6.2	Robert
14.4	Tyler	6.2	Connor
13.9	Ryan	6.1	Jason
13.8	Joshua	6.0	Benjamin
13.7	Jordan	5.8	Joseph
12.1	Nicholas	5.7	Brett
11.9	Kyle	5.7	Thomas
11.8	Daniel	5.5	John
11.4	Christopher	5.4	Riley
11.3	Justin	5.2	Taylor
11.1	Austin	5.2	Logan
10.8	Alexander	4.9	Steven
10.1	Andrew	4.7	Samuel
9.3	Dylan	4.7	Jeremy
8.6	James	4.6	Evan
8.4	Cody	4.5	Scott
8.0	Zachary	4.5	Liam
7.7	Jacob	4.4	Sean
7.7	Jesse	4.3	Anthony
7.3	Adam	4.2	Cameron
6.9	David	4.2	Travis
6.8	Nathan	4.2	Spencer
6.5	Kevin	4.1	Dustin
6.5	Cole	4.1	Colton
6.4	Eric	4.1	Mark
6.3	Jonathan	4.0	Lucas
6.2	William	4.0	Bradley
		3.9	Tanner
		3.8	Jared
		3.8	Trevor
		3.8	Tyson

3.7	Brendan	3.0	Tristan	2.7	Luke	2.4	Stephen	2.1	Alex
3.6	Joel	3.0	Devon	2.7	Colin	2.4	Braden	2.1	Jake
3.4	Patrick	3.0	Jeffrey	2.6	Curtis	2.4	Shawn	2.0	Clayton
3.4	Derek	2.9	Brayden	2.5	Ethan	2.4	Chase	2.0	Garrett
3.4	Wyatt	2.9	Brian	2.5	Mathew	2.4	Aidan	2.0	Caleb
3.2	Christian	2.8	Peter	2.5	Paul	2.3	Devin	2.0	Chad
3.1	Dakota	2.8	Levi	2.5	Bryce	2.3	Shane		
3.1	Richard	2.8	Timothy	2.4	Mackenzie	2.2	Ian		

Eastern Canada

Girls									
21.0	Jessica	5.2	Danielle	3.1	Andrea	2.3	Hannah	11.6	Kevin
15.9	Sarah	5.1	Gabrielle	3.0	Marie	2.3	Frederique	11.3	Nicholas
12.9	Stephanie	4.9	Valerie	3.0	Shannon	2.2	Erika	10.9	Joshua
12.3	Alexandra	4.9	Emilie	3.0	Myriam	2.2	Lisa	10.8	Tyler
11.0	Samantha	4.7	Amelie	2.9	Sophie	2.2	Tiffany	10.7	Gabriel
10.7	Emily	4.4	Lauren	2.9	Erin	2.2	Meghan	10.7	Andrew
9.7	Melissa	4.4	Sara	2.7	Jenna	2.1	Sydney	10.6	Jonathan
9.3	Nicole	4.4	Elizabeth	2.7	Joanie	2.1	Kimberly	10.6	William
8.7	Ashley	4.2	Laurence	2.6	Jasmine	2.0	Allison	10.5	Alexander
8.3	Catherine	4.1	Emma	2.6	Kim	2.0	Carly	9.6	Justin
8.0	Amanda	3.9	Roxanne	2.6	Cynthia	2.0	Shelby	9.3	Maxime
7.6	Rebecca	3.9	Katherine	2.6	Kristen	2.0	Erica	9.1	Jordan
7.5	Jennifer	3.8	Christina	2.6	Amy	2.0	Paige	8.8	Jacob
7.1	Rachel	3.7	Noemie	2.5	Madison	1.9	Jacqueline	8.6	Kyle
6.8	Audrey	3.7	Julia	2.5	Isabelle	1.9	Ariane	8.1	Anthony
6.7	Taylor	3.7	Olivia	2.5	Mackenzie	1.9	Patricia	7.6	Mathieu
6.5	Sabrina	3.6	Alyssa	2.4	Christine	1.9	Kathleen	7.6	James
6.5	Victoria	3.5	Melanie	2.4	Claudia			7.5	Vincent
6.3	Megan	3.5	Caroline	2.4	Justine	*Boys*		7.3	Nicolas
6.0	Brittany	3.5	Natasha	2.4	Amber	20.5	Michael	7.2	Eric
5.9	Vanessa	3.4	Courtney	2.4	Kelly	16.1	Matthew	7.1	Adam
5.8	Michelle	3.4	Jade	2.4	Laurie	14.9	Samuel	7.0	Joseph
5.6	Cassandra	3.4	Chloe	2.4	Bianca	13.7	Alexandre	6.9	Dylan
5.6	Kayla	3.3	Julie	2.4	Heather	13.1	Brandon	6.6	Francis
5.5	Camille	3.3	Kelsey	2.4	Alicia	13.1	David	6.5	Patrick
5.3	Laura	3.3	Kaitlyn	2.4	Genevieve	12.2	Christopher	6.2	Benjamin
5.2	Maude	3.2	Chelsea	2.3	Veronique	12.1	Ryan	6.1	Alex
		3.2	Natalie	2.3	Lindsay	12.1	Daniel	6.1	Robert

6.1	Simon	4.3	Nathan	3.2	Jeffrey	2.5	Derek	2.2	Jimmy
6.0	Jeremy	4.2	Connor	3.2	Mark	2.5	Taylor	2.1	Jake
5.9	Jesse	4.2	Felix	3.2	Scott	2.5	Colin	2.1	Alexis
5.9	Steven	4.2	Sebastien	3.1	Frederic	2.5	Brian	2.1	Brett
5.9	Jason	4.0	Charles	2.9	Etienne	2.4	Gregory	2.0	Cedric
5.7	Olivier	4.0	Zachary	2.9	Peter	2.4	Spencer	2.0	Ian
5.7	Thomas	4.0	Antoine	2.8	Christian	2.4	Cole	2.0	Luke
5.4	Philippe	3.7	Lucas	2.8	Paul	2.3	Shawn	2.0	Travis
5.4	John	3.6	Austin	2.8	Stephen	2.2	Jeremie	2.0	Martin
4.9	Mitchell	3.5	Cameron	2.7	Richard	2.2	Timothy	1.9	Trevor
4.8	Cody	3.3	Bradley	2.7	Evan	2.2	Dominic	1.9	Shane
4.7	Aaron	3.2	Raphael	2.7	Joel	2.2	Tommy		
4.4	Guillaume	3.2	Sean	2.5	Julien	2.2	Keven		

The 100 most popular names in North America in the late-1980s

Girls		5.7	Tiffany	2.8	Allison	1.4	Kristina	1.1	Dana
27.7	Jessica	5.6	Samantha	2.7	Alicia	1.4	Brandy	1.1	Katrina
26.5	Ashley	5.1	Emily	2.6	Jenna	1.4	Brandi	1.0	Karen
21.6	Amanda	5.0	Rebecca	2.5	Kathryn	1.4	Alexandra	1.0	Bethany
19.8	Jennifer	4.7	Vanessa	2.5	Christine	1.4	Caitlin	1.0	Brooke
15.7	Sarah	4.4	Erin	2.3	Victoria	1.4	Monica	1.0	Stacy
12.4	Stephanie	4.2	Sara	2.3	April	1.4	Chelsea	1.0	Jasmine
11.8	Nicole	4.2	Kelly	2.2	Holly	1.3	Patricia	1.0	Valerie
10.9	Brittany	3.9	Jamie	2.2	Anna	1.3	Mallory	1.0	Jillian
10.3	Heather	3.8	Whitney	2.2	Kristin	1.2	Leah		
10.2	Melissa	3.8	Katherine	2.2	Tara	1.2	Krista	**Boys**	
9.6	Megan	3.8	Courtney	2.2	Natalie	1.2	Hannah	32.4	Michael
9.2	Elizabeth	3.7	Angela	2.2	Kayla	1.2	Marie	28.9	Christopher
8.8	Amber	3.6	Andrea	2.1	Julie	1.2	Leslie	24.1	Matthew
8.1	Lauren	3.5	Mary	2.0	Natasha	1.2	Candice	19.7	David
8.0	Danielle	3.4	Lisa	1.9	Brittney	1.2	Stacey	19.4	Daniel
7.7	Michelle	3.4	Lindsay	1.8	Cassandra	1.2	Candace	18.9	Joshua
7.4	Christina	3.4	Lindsey	1.6	Krystal	1.2	Casey	17.9	Andrew
6.8	Crystal	3.4	Erica	1.6	Kathleen	1.2	Julia	17.2	James
6.2	Laura	3.3	Shannon	1.6	Meghan	1.1	Alison	16.1	Robert
5.9	Kimberly	3.2	Katie	1.6	Catherine	1.1	Kendra	15.0	Ryan
5.7	Rachel	3.1	Maria	1.5	Jacqueline	1.1	Margaret	14.4	John
5.7	Amy	3.0	Kristen	1.5	Melanie	1.1	Felicia	14.1	Joseph

12.1	Brandon	5.4	Mark	3.6	Jordan	1.7	Donald	1.3	Jeffery
11.9	Jason	5.3	Richard	3.4	Travis	1.7	Keith	1.2	Nathaniel
11.3	Justin	5.2	Benjamin	3.4	Jesse	1.7	Marcus	1.2	Wesley
11.3	Jonathan	5.0	Stephen	3.1	Shawn	1.6	Ian	1.2	Derrick
11.0	Nicholas	4.5	Charles	3.0	Kenneth	1.6	Phillip	1.2	Brent
10.4	Anthony	4.5	Dustin	2.9	Bryan	1.5	Trevor	1.2	Raymond
9.8	William	4.5	Patrick	2.9	Cody	1.5	Ronald	1.0	Mitchell
9.7	Eric	4.4	Jacob	2.9	Derek	1.5	Craig	1.0	Terry
9.6	Steven	4.4	Aaron	2.6	Corey	1.5	George	1.0	Blake
8.3	Adam	4.3	Scott	2.6	Samuel	1.4	Joel	1.0	Luke
8.3	Kyle	4.3	Sean	2.5	Chad	1.4	Gary	1.0	Colin
7.7	Kevin	4.2	Zachary	2.2	Shane	1.3	Evan	0.9	Austin
7.3	Brian	4.1	Nathan	2.1	Jared	1.3	Curtis	0.9	Seth
6.5	Thomas	4.0	Alexander	2.1	Peter	1.3	Douglas	0.9	Mathew
6.4	Jeremy	4.0	Jose	2.1	Cory	1.3	Alex	0.9	Larry
6.4	Timothy	3.7	Bradley	1.9	Brett	1.3	Philip	0.9	Randy
5.6	Tyler	3.7	Paul	1.9	Jonathon	1.3	Antonio		
5.5	Jeffrey	3.7	Gregory	1.8	Edward	1.3	Casey		

Section II —

Popular Names

with popularity ratings, origins, and meanings

This section contains the current top 200 most popular names for girls and boys.
To make the list, each name had to have a popularity rating of .07 or better, which means
that at least 7 out of every 100,000 children received that name.

Popular Girls Names

Rating · Name · Origin and meaning

-A-

Rating	Name	Origin and meaning
1.8	**A**	initial used as a first name
0.6	**Aaliyah**	Arabic sublime, exalted; Hebrew ascend
0.1	**Abagail**	Hebrew father of joy
0.2	**Abbey**	Hebrew father of joy
0.2	**Abbie**	Hebrew father of joy
0.1	**Abbigail**	Hebrew father of joy
0.6	**Abby**	Hebrew father of joy
3.2	**Abigail**	Hebrew father of joy
0.1	**Addison**	last name used as a first name, son of Adam
0.1	**Adela**	German noble, kind
0.2	**Adilene**	German noble, kind
0.1	**Adrian**	Latin dark one; rich
1.3	**Adriana**	Latin dark one; rich
0.4	**Adrianna**	Latin dark one; rich
0.1	**Adrianne**	Latin dark one; rich
0.4	**Adrienne**	Latin dark one; rich
0.1	**Aganetha**	origin unknown
0.1	**Aileen**	Irish form of Helen; Gaelic light bearer
0.1	**Aime**	French from Latin beloved
0.5	**Aimee**	French from Latin beloved
0.1	**Ainsley**	Scottish from one's own meadow
0.2	**Aisha**	African life
0.1	**Aja**	Hindu goat (Capricorn in the Zodiac)
0.3	**Alaina**	Irish fair, beautiful
0.5	**Alana**	Irish fair, beautiful
0.3	**Alanna**	Irish fair, beautiful
0.1	**Alannah**	Irish fair, beautiful
0.2	**Alayna**	Irish fair, beautiful
0.1	**Aleah**	Arabic high, exalted; Persian God's being
0.1	**Alecia**	German noble; Greek truthful
0.1	**Aleisha**	German noble; Greek truthful
1.5	**Alejandra**	Greek defender of mankind
0.1	**Alena**	Greek a torch, light
0.2	**Alesha**	German noble; Greek truthful
0.2	**Alessandra**	Greek defender of mankind
0.2	**Alessia**	German noble; Greek truthful
0.2	**Alex**	Greek defender of mankind
1.5	**Alexa**	Greek defender of mankind
6.1	**Alexandra**	Greek defender of mankind
0.1	**Alexandre**	Greek defender of mankind
0.2	**Alexandrea**	Greek defender of mankind
2.4	**Alexandria**	Greek defender of mankind
0.1	**Alexandrine**	variant of Alexandra Greek defender of mankind
0.1	**Alexane**	Alex + Anne

0.2	**Alexanne**	Alex + Anne
0.2	**Alexe**	Greek defender of mankind
0.1	**Alexi**	variant of Alexandra Greek defender of mankind
0.5	**Alexia**	Greek defender of mankind
0.1	**Alexie**	Greek defender of mankind
6.0	**Alexis**	Greek defender of mankind
0.5	**Alexus**	Greek defender of mankind
0.1	**Ali**	contemporary American form of Alice or Alison
0.1	**Alia**	Arabic high, exalted; Persian God's being
0.4	**Alice**	German noble; Greek truthful
2.2	**Alicia**	German noble; Greek truthful
0.3	**Alina**	Polish and Russian bright, beautiful
0.3	**Alisa**	German noble; Greek truthful
0.7	**Alisha**	German noble; Greek truthful
1.1	**Alison**	German noble; Greek truthful
0.5	**Alissa**	German noble; Greek truthful
0.1	**Alivia**	Latin olives
0.1	**Alix**	Greek defender of mankind
0.4	**Aliyah**	Hebrew to ascend, to go up
0.3	**Allie**	Greek defender of mankind; German noble Greek truth
3.5	**Allison**	German noble; Greek truthful
0.6	**Allyson**	German noble; Greek truthful
0.1	**Allyssa**	German noble; Greek truthful
0.4	**Alma**	Arabic learned; Italian soul
0.2	**Alondra**	origin unknown
0.2	**Alycia**	German noble; Greek truthful
0.1	**Alysa**	German noble; Greek truthful
0.1	**Alyse**	German noble; Greek truthful
0.3	**Alysha**	German noble; Greek truthful
0.1	**Alysia**	German noble; Greek truthful
0.3	**Alyson**	German noble; Greek truthful
5.1	**Alyssa**	Greek logical one
0.1	**Alyssia**	German noble; Greek truthful
0.1	**Amairani**	origin unknown
0.1	**Amal**	Hebrew work, toil
0.1	**Amalia**	German industrious one
7.3	**Amanada**	origin unknown
8.6	**Amanda**	Latin worthy of love
0.2	**Amandeep**	Punjabi light of peace
0.1	**Amara**	Latin imperishable
0.1	**Ambar**	French amber
5.3	**Amber**	French amber
0.1	**Amber-Lynn**	Amber + Lynn
0.7	**Amelia**	Latin work
1.8	**Amelie**	Latin work
0.1	**Amely**	Latin work
0.1	**America**	German chief or king; place name used as a first name
0.1	**Amie**	Latin beloved
0.1	**Amilie**	Latin work
0.1	**Amina**	Arabic security
0.2	**Amrit**	Sanskrit nectar
2.6	**Amy**	Latin beloved
1.3	**Ana**	Greek resurrection
0.1	**Anabel**	Anna + Belle
0.2	**Anabelle**	Anna + Belle
0.2	**Anahi**	origin unknown
0.2	**Anais**	Hebrew one of grace, gracious (Anna)
0.1	**Anakaren**	Anna + Karen
0.4	**Anastasia**	Greek resurrection
3.5	**Andrea**	Greek valiant, strong, courageous; Latin womanly
0.2	**Andreane**	Andree + Ann
1.9	**Andreanne**	Andree + Ann

0.1	**Andree**	Greek valiant, strong, courageous; Latin womanly
0.4	**Andree Ann**	Andree + Ann
1.2	**Andree Anne**	Andree + Ann
0.1	**Andria**	Greek valiant, strong, courageous; Latin womanly
0.8	**Angel**	Latin angelic
2.1	**Angela**	Latin angelic
1.7	**Angelica**	Latin angelic
0.5	**Angelina**	Latin angelic
0.3	**Angelique**	Latin angelic
0.2	**Angelle**	Latin angelic
0.2	**Angie**	Latin angelic
0.1	**Anik**	variant of Anna, Hebrew gracious
0.1	**Anika**	Hebrew gracious
0.1	**Anisa**	Spanish variant of Anna, Hebrew gracious
0.1	**Anisha**	Hebrew gracious
0.3	**Anissa**	Spanish variant of Anna, Hebrew gracious
0.3	**Anita**	Hebrew gracious
0.1	**Anjelica**	Latin angelic
0.3	**Ann**	Hebrew gracious
0.2	**Ann Sophie**	Ann + Sophie
3.9	**Anna**	Italian, German, Russian forms of Hebrew one of grace, gracious
0.2	**Annabelle**	Anna + Belle
0.1	**Annalise**	Anna + Lise
0.7	**Anne**	Hebrew gracious
0.2	**Anne Catherine**	Anne + Catherine
0.6	**Anne Julie**	Anne + Julie
0.3	**Anne Marie**	Anne + Marie
2.0	**Anne Sophie**	Anne + Sophie
0.1	**Anne-Marie**	Anna + Mary
0.2	**Annette**	Hebrew gracious
0.1	**Annick**	variant of Anna, Hebrew gracious
0.6	**Annie**	Hebrew gracious
0.4	**Annie Claude**	Annie + Claude
0.4	**Annie Pier**	Annie + Pierre
0.1	**Annika**	Hebrew gracious
0.3	**Anouk**	origin unknown
0.1	**Ansleigh**	last name used as a first name, place name in England
0.2	**Ansley**	last name used as a first name, place name in England
0.2	**Antoinette**	Latin priceless
0.2	**Antonia**	Latin priceless
1.1	**April**	Latin open
0.4	**Araceli**	Latin altar of heaven
0.1	**Aracely**	Latin altar of heaven
0.1	**Areli**	Latin gold
0.1	**Arely**	Latin gold
1.0	**Ariana**	Greek most holy
0.4	**Ariane**	Greek most holy
0.6	**Arianna**	Greek most holy
0.1	**Arianne**	Greek most holy
1.0	**Ariel**	Hebrew likeness of God
0.3	**Arielle**	Hebrew likeness of God
0.2	**Arlene**	Irish pledge
0.1	**Asha**	Hindi hope; Arabic sunset; living, prosperous; wife of Muhammed
0.1	**Ashanti**	a west African ethnic group
0.1	**Ashely**	English from the ash tree meadow
0.8	**Ashlee**	English from the ash tree meadow
0.6	**Ashleigh**	English from the ash tree meadow
13.4	**Ashley**	English from the ash tree meadow
0.1	**Ashli**	English from the ash tree meadow
0.2	**Ashlie**	English from the ash tree meadow
0.2	**Ashly**	English from the ash tree meadow
0.6	**Ashlyn**	English from the ash tree pool
0.2	**Ashlynn**	English from the ash tree pool

0.4	**Ashton**	English from the ash tree farm
0.1	**Ashtyn**	English from the ash tree farm
0.6	**Asia**	Greek resurrection
0.1	**Aspen**	English aspen
0.1	**Astrid**	Norse strength of God
0.2	**Athena**	Greek wisdom
0.1	**Aubree**	French blond ruler; elf ruler
0.5	**Aubrey**	French blond ruler; elf ruler
0.1	**Aubrie**	French blond ruler; elf ruler
0.1	**Aude**	Old French old, rich
0.1	**Audra**	English noble strength
0.3	**Audreanne**	Audrey + Anne
1.6	**Audrey**	English noble strength
1.4	**Audrey Ann**	Audrey + Ann
1.9	**Audrey Anne**	Audrey + Anne
0.2	**Audrey Maude**	Audrey + Maude
0.4	**Aurelie**	Latin gold
0.2	**Aurora**	Latin daybreak
0.1	**Austin**	Latin queenly one
1.2	**Autumn**	Latin autumn
0.1	**Ava**	Latin birdlike
0.3	**Avery**	French blond ruler; elf ruler
0.2	**Avneet**	origin unknown
0.1	**Axelle**	French feminine form of Axel: Hebrew father of peace; Old German small oak tree
0.1	**Ayan**	origin unknown
0.1	**Ayana**	Hindi innocent being; Swahili beautiful flower
0.1	**Ayanna**	Hindi innocent being; Swahili beautiful flower
0.1	**Ayla**	Hebrew oak tree
0.1	**Azucena**	Arabic lily

-B-

0.9	**B**	initial used as a first name
0.1	**Bailee**	English fortification; English/French public official, person in charge
1.4	**Bailey**	English fortification; English/French public official, person in charge
0.4	**Barbara**	Latin stranger
0.2	**Baylee**	English fortification; English/French public official, person in charge
0.2	**Beatrice**	Latin she who makes others happy
0.3	**Beatriz**	Latin she who makes others happy
0.1	**Belen**	Spanish Bethlehem
0.1	**Belinda**	Spanish beautiful
0.3	**Benedicte**	Latin blessed
0.3	**Berenice**	Greek bringer of victory
0.1	**Bernadette**	French brave warrior
0.1	**Bernice**	Greek bringer of victory
0.1	**Bertha**	German brilliant, glorious one
0.2	**Beth**	Hebrew house of God; short form of names containing beth
1.1	**Bethany**	Greek and Latin house of figs
0.1	**Betsy**	Hebrew God's oath (Elizabeth)
0.1	**Betty**	Hebrew God's oath (Elizabeth)
0.1	**Beverley**	English from the beaver meadow
0.2	**Beverly**	English from the beaver meadow
1.6	**Bianca**	Italian white
0.1	**Billie**	English strong willed
0.2	**Blair**	Scottish dweller on the plain
0.1	**Blake**	English white
0.4	**Blanca**	Italian white
0.1	**Bobbi**	English shining with fame; Latin stranger
0.2	**Bobbie**	English shining with fame; Latin stranger
0.3	**Bonnie**	Latin, French, Scottish good; pretty

1.1	**Brandi**	Dutch brandy
0.1	**Brandie**	Dutch brandy
0.6	**Brandy**	Dutch brandy
0.1	**Brea**	Latin from the boundary line (Sabrina); Latin from England
0.3	**Breana**	Irish strong
0.1	**Breann**	Irish strong
2.1	**Breanna**	Irish strong
0.4	**Breanne**	Irish strong
0.1	**Bree**	Latin from the boundary line (Sabrina); Latin from England
0.1	**Breeanna**	Irish strong
1.7	**Brenda**	English firebrand
0.5	**Brenna**	Irish raven
0.1	**Breonna**	newly-created African-American name
0.1	**Brett**	English a Briton
0.4	**Bria**	Latin from the boundary line (Sabrina); Latin from England
2.2	**Briana**	Irish strong
0.1	**Brianda**	origin unknown
4.8	**Brianna**	Irish strong
0.5	**Brianne**	Irish strong
0.8	**Bridget**	Irish strong
0.1	**Bridgett**	Irish strong
0.2	**Bridgette**	Irish strong
0.1	**Brieanna**	Irish strong
0.1	**Brielle**	origin unknown, possibly an invented name
0.2	**Brigitte**	Irish strong
0.1	**Brionna**	newly-created African-American name
0.1	**Britany**	Latin from England
0.5	**Britney**	Latin from England
0.1	**Brittaney**	Latin from England
0.3	**Brittani**	Latin from England
0.1	**Brittanie**	Latin from England
8.1	**Brittany**	Latin from England
0.1	**Brittnee**	Latin from England
1.8	**Brittney**	Latin from England

0.2	**Brittni**	Latin from England
0.1	**Bronwyn**	Welsh white breast
0.2	**Brook**	English brook
2.9	**Brooke**	English brook
0.4	**Brooklyn**	place name used as a first name: New York borough
0.1	**Brooklynn**	place name used as a first name: New York borough
0.1	**Bryana**	Irish strong
0.3	**Bryanna**	Irish strong
0.1	**Bryce**	English son of Rice; Welsh form of Price, son of the ardent one
0.1	**Brylee**	origin unknown
0.1	**Brynn**	Latin from the boundary line (Sabrina)

-C-

0.4	**C**	initial used as a first name
2.1	**Caitlin**	Greek pure (Katherine)
1.0	**Caitlyn**	Greek pure (Katherine)
0.1	**Caleigh**	Greek beautiful
0.4	**Callie**	Greek beautiful
0.2	**Cameron**	Scottish crooked nose
0.1	**Camila**	Latin young attendant
0.1	**Camilla**	Latin young attendant
1.1	**Camille**	Latin young attendant
0.5	**Candace**	Greek glittering white, incandescent
0.4	**Candice**	Greek glittering white, incandescent
0.1	**Candy**	Greek glittering white, incandescent
0.4	**Cara**	Irish friend
0.4	**Carina**	Latin keel
0.4	**Carissa**	Latin charity
0.4	**Carla**	French little and womanly
0.2	**Carlee**	French little and womanly
0.1	**Carleigh**	French little and womanly
0.3	**Carley**	French little and womanly
0.2	**Carli**	French little and womanly
0.2	**Carlie**	French little and womanly

1.3	**Carly**	French little and womanly
0.6	**Carmen**	Latin a song
0.2	**Carol**	Latin strong and womanly; French song of joy
1.2	**Carol Ann**	Carol + Ann
0.7	**Carol Anne**	Carol + Anne
3.2	**Carolane**	Carol + Anne
0.2	**Carolanne**	Carol + Anne
0.3	**Carole Ann**	Carol + Anne
0.7	**Carole Anne**	Carol + Anne
0.7	**Carolina**	French little and womanly
1.8	**Caroline**	French little and womanly
0.6	**Carolyn**	French little and womanly
0.4	**Carrie**	French little and womanly; Latin strong and womanly; French song of joy
0.1	**Carson**	Old Norse son of Carr
0.3	**Casandra**	Greek not believed
1.1	**Casey**	Irish brave
2.8	**Cassandra**	Greek not believed
0.1	**Cassandre**	Greek not believed
1.4	**Cassidy**	Irish clever, quick one
0.4	**Cassie**	Greek not believed
0.2	**Catalina**	Spanish form of Greek pure (Katherine)
2.6	**Catherine**	Greek pure
0.1	**Cathy**	Greek pure (Katherine)
0.1	**Catrina**	Greek pure (Katherine)
0.2	**Cayla**	form of Katherine: Greek pure, unsullied
0.4	**Cecelia**	Latin blind
0.3	**Cecilia**	Latin blind
0.1	**Ceilidh**	Irish country dance
0.1	**Celena**	Latin heavenly (Celeste)
0.6	**Celeste**	Latin heavenly
0.2	**Celia**	Latin blind
0.4	**Celina**	Latin heavenly (Celeste)
0.2	**Celine**	Latin heavenly (Celeste)
0.3	**Chandler**	Old English candlemaker
0.3	**Chanel**	English channel
0.1	**Chanelle**	English channel
0.3	**Chantal**	French a song
0.4	**Chantel**	French a song

0.3	**Chantelle**	French a song
0.1	**Charissa**	Latin charity, loving; Greek grace
0.2	**Charity**	Latin and Greek charity, loving
0.3	**Charlene**	French little and womanly (Carolyn)
0.1	**Charlie**	French little and womanly (Carolyn)
0.7	**Charlotte**	French little and womanly (Carolyn)
0.1	**Charmaine**	French little and womanly (Carolyn)
0.2	**Chasity**	Latin pure
3.6	**Chelsea**	English a port
0.7	**Chelsey**	English a port
0.2	**Chelsi**	English a port
0.3	**Chelsie**	English a port
0.1	**Cherish**	French beloved; Latin charity, loving
0.2	**Cheryl**	French beloved
0.3	**Cheyanne**	American Indian tribal name
1.6	**Cheyenne**	American Indian tribal name
0.1	**China**	place name used as a first name: country in Asia
1.4	**Chloe**	Greek blooming green bird
0.3	**Christa**	Greek a Christian, anointed one (Christina)
0.1	**Christen**	Greek a Christian, anointed one (Christina)
0.3	**Christian**	Greek a Christian, anointed one (Christina)
0.2	**Christiana**	Greek a Christian, anointed one (Christina)
0.2	**Christie**	Greek a Christian, anointed one (Christina)
0.2	**Christin**	Greek a Christian, anointed one (Christina)
3.7	**Christina**	Greek a Christian, anointed one
1.6	**Christine**	Greek a Christian, anointed one

0.3	**Christy**	Greek a Christian, anointed one (Christina)
0.1	**Chrystal**	Greek brilliant glass
0.7	**Ciara**	Irish black
0.3	**Ciera**	Irish black
0.7	**Cierra**	Irish black
1.1	**Cindy**	Greek moon
0.1	**Cinthia**	Greek moon
1.2	**Claire**	Latin clear, bright
0.3	**Clara**	Latin clear, bright
0.2	**Clare**	Latin clear, bright
0.2	**Clarisa**	Greek most brilliant
0.5	**Clarissa**	Greek most brilliant
1.1	**Claudia**	Latin lame
0.2	**Claudie**	Latin lame
0.1	**Claudine**	Latin lame
0.1	**Clemence**	Latin mild, merciful
0.2	**Cloe**	Greek blooming green bird
0.1	**Codi**	Anglo Saxon a cushion
0.1	**Colette**	Latin and French successful in battle
0.7	**Colleen**	Irish girl
0.3	**Connie**	Latin constant, firm
0.1	**Constance**	Latin constant, firm
0.1	**Consuelo**	Latin consolation
0.2	**Cora**	Greek maiden
0.1	**Coral**	Latin coral from the sea
0.1	**Coralie**	Latin coral from the sea
0.1	**Corey**	Irish from the hollow
0.1	**Cori**	Irish from the hollow
0.2	**Corina**	Greek maiden
0.3	**Corinne**	Greek maiden
0.1	**Corrina**	Greek maiden
0.3	**Cortney**	French from the king's court
0.1	**Courteney**	French from the king's court
5.8	**Courtney**	French from the king's court
0.3	**Cristal**	Greek brilliant glass
0.7	**Cristina**	Greek a Christian, anointed one (Christina)
2.5	**Crystal**	Greek brilliant glass
0.1	**Cydney**	French from the city of St. Denis
2.0	**Cynthia**	Greek moon

0.1	**Cyntia**	Greek moon

-D-

0.2	**D**	initial used as a first name
0.1	**Daija**	origin unknown
0.1	**Daisha**	origin unknown
1.1	**Daisy**	Old English eye of the day
0.5	**Dakota**	American Indian tribal name
0.4	**Dalia**	Mexican flower named after Swedish botanist Dahl
0.3	**Dallas**	English valley
0.1	**Damaris**	Greek heifer; of a gentle, trusting nature
0.8	**Dana**	Latin bright, pure as day; from Denmark
0.1	**Danae**	Latin bright, pure as day; from Denmark
0.2	**Danica**	Slavic morning star
0.7	**Daniela**	Hebrew God is my judge
0.3	**Daniella**	Hebrew God is my judge
5.8	**Danielle**	Hebrew God is my judge
0.2	**Danika**	Slavic morning star
0.1	**Danyelle**	Hebrew God is my judge (Danielle)
0.3	**Daphne**	Greek laurel tree
2.7	**Daphnee**	Greek laurel tree
0.1	**Dara**	Hebrew compassionate
0.2	**Darby**	English place name Derby, a village with a deer park
0.1	**Darcy**	Irish dark man; Norman place name Arcy
0.4	**Darian**	Persian wealthy; Anglo-Saxon dear
0.1	**Darien**	Persian wealthy; Anglo-Saxon dear
0.2	**Darlene**	French little darling; Old English dear beloved
0.1	**Dasia**	Hebrew the law of the Lord
0.2	**Dawn**	English dawn
0.3	**Dayana**	variant of Diana: Latin divine
0.2	**Dayna**	Latin bright, pure as day; from Denmark

0.1	**De'ja**	French already, before
0.1	**Deana**	Latin divine
0.9	**Deanna**	Latin divine
0.1	**Debbie**	Hebrew a bee
0.3	**Deborah**	Hebrew a bee
0.1	**Debra**	Hebrew a bee
0.1	**Deidra**	Irish sorrow; wanderer
0.3	**Deja**	French already, before
0.4	**Delaney**	last name used as a first name
0.1	**Delia**	Greek visible
0.1	**Delilah**	Hebrew brooding
0.1	**Delphine**	Latin dolphin
0.1	**Demetria**	Greek goddess of grain (fertility symbol)
0.2	**Demi**	possibly Greek variant of Demeter earth goddess
0.8	**Denise**	Greek from Dionysius, god of wine and drama
0.2	**Denisha**	origin unknown, possibly an invented name
0.2	**Denisse**	Greek from Dionysius, god of wine and drama
0.2	**Desirae**	French to crave
1.1	**Desiree**	French to crave
0.1	**Desiree'**	French to crave
0.3	**Desireé**	French to crave
0.3	**Destinee**	French destiny
0.2	**Destiney**	French destiny
0.2	**Destini**	French destiny
0.1	**Destinie**	French destiny
2.1	**Destiny**	French destiny
0.1	**Devan**	Irish poet; English from Devon
0.4	**Devin**	Irish poet; English from Devon
0.4	**Devon**	Irish poet; English from Devon
0.1	**Devyn**	Irish poet; English from Devon
0.8	**Diamond**	Latin precious stone
2.0	**Diana**	Latin divine
0.3	**Diane**	Latin divine

0.1	**Dianna**	Latin divine
0.1	**Dianne**	Latin divine
0.1	**Dina**	Hebrew judgement
0.1	**Dolores**	Spanish sorrows
1.1	**Dominique**	French belonging to the Lord
0.1	**Dominque**	French belonging to the Lord
0.1	**Domonique**	French belonging to the Lord
0.1	**Donisha**	newly-created African-American name
0.3	**Donna**	Latin lady, madam
0.1	**Doriane**	Greek ancient people of Doris region
0.1	**Doris**	Greek from the sea
0.1	**Dorothee**	Greek gift of God
0.2	**Dorothy**	Greek gift of God
0.1	**Drew**	Greek manly, valiant, courageous, strong (Andrew)
0.3	**Dulce**	Latin agreeable
0.1	**Dylan**	Welsh the sea

-E-

0.2	**E**	initial used as a first name
0.1	**Eboni**	Greek a hard, dark wood
0.4	**Ebony**	Greek a hard, dark wood
0.2	**Eden**	Hebrew delight
0.3	**Edith**	Old English rich gift
0.2	**Eileen**	Greek a torch, light
0.1	**Elaina**	Greek a torch, light
0.3	**Elaine**	Greek a torch, light
0.1	**Elana**	Greek a torch, light
0.2	**Eleanor**	Greek a torch, light
0.5	**Elena**	Greek a torch, light
0.1	**Eleni**	Greek a torch, light
0.1	**Eliana**	Hebrew God has answered me
0.1	**Eliane**	Hebrew God has answered me
0.1	**Elide**	Greek region in Peloponnesus
0.3	**Elisa**	Hebrew God's oath (Elizabeth)

0.5	**Elisabeth**	Hebrew God's oath (Elizabeth)
0.5	**Elise**	Hebrew God's oath (Elizabeth)
0.1	**Elisha**	Hebrew God's oath (Elizabeth)
0.1	**Elissa**	Hebrew God's oath (Elizabeth)
0.2	**Eliza**	Hebrew God's oath (Elizabeth)
7.7	**Elizabeth**	Hebrew God's oath
0.2	**Ella**	Old English beautiful fairy maiden
0.1	**Elle**	origin unknown
0.6	**Ellen**	Greek a torch, light
0.2	**Ellie**	English: short form of English names beginning with El-
0.3	**Elodie**	Greek shore, plain, marsh
0.1	**Eloise**	Greek hale, complete
0.1	**Elsa**	German noble one
0.1	**Elsie**	Danish form of Elsa: noble one
0.1	**Elvia**	Latin variety of yellow
0.2	**Elyse**	Hebrew God's oath
0.1	**Elyssa**	Hebrew God's oath
0.1	**Emely**	German industrious
0.1	**Emerald**	Old French the green gem
0.4	**Emie**	short form of Emily: German industrious
0.3	**Emilee**	German industrious
0.1	**Emilia**	German industrious
0.8	**Emilie**	German industrious
11.6	**Emily**	German industrious
2.8	**Emma**	Greek grandmother
0.3	**Emmanuelle**	Hebrew God is with us
0.2	**Emy**	short form of Emily: German industrious
2.6	**Erica**	German honorable ruler
0.3	**Ericka**	German honorable ruler
1.9	**Erika**	German honorable ruler
3.2	**Erin**	Irish peace
0.1	**Eryn**	Irish peace
0.5	**Esmeralda**	Spanish emerald

0.1	**Esperanza**	Latin hope
0.2	**Essence**	origin unknown
0.1	**Estefani**	Spanish variant of Stephen: Greek crown
0.1	**Estefania**	Spanish variant of Stephen: Greek crown
0.1	**Estefany**	Spanish variant of Stephen: Greek crown
0.1	**Estelle**	Latin Star
0.5	**Esther**	Persian a star
0.1	**Estrella**	Latin Star
0.2	**Eugenie**	Greek well-born
0.2	**Eunice**	Greek happy in victory
0.4	**Eva**	Latin life
0.1	**Evan**	Welsh form of John, young warrior
0.1	**Evangelina**	Greek bearer of good tidings
0.2	**Eve**	Latin life
0.1	**Evelin**	Celtic pleasant
0.8	**Evelyn**	Celtic pleasant
0.2	**Evelyne**	Celtic pleasant

-F-

0.2	**Fabiola**	Latin belonging to the Roman emperor Fabius
0.7	**Faith**	English fidelity
0.1	**Fallon**	Irish grandchild of the ruler
0.1	**Fannie**	French free (Francis)
0.2	**Fanny**	French free (Francis)
0.3	**Fatima**	Arabic a daughter of Muhammed
0.1	**Faviola**	Latin belonging to the Roman emperor Fabius
0.8	**Felicia**	Latin happy
0.1	**Felisha**	Latin happy
0.1	**Fernanda**	German to make peace, to be bold
0.2	**Fiona**	Celtic white
0.6	**Flavie**	Latin yellow or blond
0.1	**Flor**	Latin blooming
0.3	**Florence**	Latin blooming

0.3	**Frances**	French free
0.3	**Francesca**	French free
0.1	**Francis**	French free
0.1	**Francisca**	French free
0.1	**Frankie**	French free (Francis)
0.1	**Frederike**	German peace, king, ruler
2.1	**Frederique**	German peace, king, ruler

-G-

0.1	**Gabriel**	Hebrew God is my strength
1.8	**Gabriela**	Hebrew God is my strength
0.9	**Gabriella**	Hebrew God is my strength
2.7	**Gabrielle**	Hebrew God is my strength
0.2	**Gagandeep**	Sikh light of the sky
0.1	**Geena**	Latin queen
0.5	**Genesis**	Latin birth, origin, descent
0.1	**Geneva**	French juniper tree
0.5	**Genevieve**	Celtic white wave
0.2	**Georgia**	Latin farmer
0.1	**Georgina**	Latin farmer
0.1	**Geraldine**	Old German and French mighty with the spear
0.3	**Gianna**	Italian form of Jane: Hebrew gracious, merciful
0.2	**Gillian**	Latin young; Greek soft-haired, youthful
0.7	**Gina**	Latin queen
0.1	**Giovanna**	Italian form of Jean: Hebrew gracious, merciful
0.2	**Giselle**	German pledge; hostage
0.2	**Gladys**	Latin lame; small sword
0.5	**Gloria**	Latin glory
1.6	**Grace**	Latin grace, agreeable, pleasantness
0.2	**Graciela**	Spanish variant of Grace: Latin grace, agreeable, pleasantness
0.1	**Grecia**	origin unknown
0.1	**Gretchen**	German form of Margaret: Greek a pearl
0.2	**Griselda**	Teutonic stone, heroine, patience, gray eyes

1.2	**Guadalupe**	Spanish reference to St. Mary of Guadalupe; Arabic valley of wolf
0.2	**Gurleen**	Sikh one who is absorbed in the guru
0.1	**Gurneet**	origin unknown
0.1	**Gurpreet**	Punjabi attached to guru, religious
0.1	**Gwendolyn**	Welsh white

-H-

0.4	**H**	initial used as a first name
0.2	**Hailee**	Scottish hero
1.6	**Hailey**	Scottish hero
0.1	**Haily**	Scottish hero
0.1	**Halee**	Scottish hero
0.2	**Haleigh**	Scottish hero
3.8	**Haley**	Scottish hero
0.1	**Hali**	Scottish hero
0.2	**Halie**	Scottish hero
0.1	**Halle**	Scottish hero
0.2	**Hallie**	Scottish hero
0.1	**Hana**	Hebrew gracious
0.6	**Hanna**	Hebrew gracious
7.3	**Hannah**	Hebrew gracious
0.1	**Harjot**	Sikh God's light
0.1	**Harleen**	Sikh one absorbed in the Lord's love
0.4	**Harley**	Old English hare meadow
0.1	**Harlie**	Old English hare meadow
0.1	**Harmony**	Latin complete peace
0.1	**Harneet**	origin unknown
0.1	**Harpreet**	Punjabi loves God, devoted to God
0.1	**Haven**	origin unknown
0.3	**Haylee**	Scottish hero
1.3	**Hayley**	Scottish hero
0.1	**Haylie**	Scottish hero
0.1	**Hazel**	Old English hazel tree or nut
3.0	**Heather**	English a heath, a plant
0.2	**Heaven**	the word used as a name
0.6	**Heidi**	German noble, kind

0.1	**Heidy**	German noble, kind
0.5	**Helen**	Greek a torch, light
0.2	**Helena**	Greek a torch, light
0.1	**Helene**	Greek a torch, light
0.3	**Heloise**	Germanic hale, complete
0.2	**Hilary**	Latin cheerful
0.1	**Hilda**	Teutonic he who is outstanding in combat
0.2	**Hillary**	Latin cheerful
0.1	**Hollie**	English holly
1.4	**Holly**	English holly
0.6	**Hope**	English trust, faith, hope
0.4	**Hunter**	Old English a huntsman

-I-

0.1	**Idil**	Latin idyll, poem dealing with rural life, hence pleasing or simple
0.1	**Iesha**	Arabic woman
0.1	**Ileana**	Greek brilliant, resplendent
0.2	**Iliana**	Greek brilliant, resplendent
0.1	**Ilse**	German from Hebrew God's oath; Teutonic noble cheer
0.1	**Iman**	Arabic faith, belief
0.4	**Imani**	origin unknown
0.3	**India**	the name of the country as a first name
0.2	**Ingrid**	Old Norse a hero's daughter
0.4	**Irene**	Greek peace
0.3	**Iris**	Greek rainbow
0.1	**Irma**	German force
0.7	**Isabel**	Spanish consecrated to God
0.8	**Isabella**	Spanish consecrated to God
0.5	**Isabelle**	Spanish consecrated to God
0.1	**Isamar**	origin unknown
0.1	**Isela**	Teutonic hostage
0.1	**Isis**	Egyptian earth or throne, goddess of nature
0.4	**Itzel**	Basque variant of Amparo: Spanish protection

0.1	**Ivana**	Russian feminine form of John: Hebrew Jehovah has been gracious
0.2	**Ivette**	French archer (Yvonne)
0.1	**Ivey**	English ivy
0.2	**Ivonne**	French archer
0.3	**Ivy**	English ivy

-J-

0.9	**J**	initial used as a name
0.1	**Jacey**	invented name, possibly from initials J and C
0.2	**Jacinthe**	Spanish hyacinth flower
0.1	**Jackeline**	Hebrew to supplant
0.1	**Jackie**	Hebrew to supplant
0.2	**Jacklyn**	Hebrew to supplant
0.6	**Jaclyn**	Hebrew to supplant
2.7	**Jacqueline**	Hebrew to supplant
0.5	**Jacquelyn**	Hebrew to supplant
0.1	**Jacynthe**	Spanish hyacinth flower
0.4	**Jada**	Spanish jade, a precious stone
1.3	**Jade**	Spanish jade, a precious stone
0.1	**Jaden**	origin unknown
0.1	**Jadyn**	origin unknown
0.3	**Jaime**	Hebrew supplanter
0.1	**Jaimee**	Hebrew supplanter
0.1	**Jaimie**	Hebrew supplanter
0.1	**Jalisa**	newly-created African-American name
0.1	**Jameka**	newly-created African-American name
0.1	**Jamesha**	newly-created African-American name
0.1	**Jami**	Hebrew supplanter
1.9	**Jamie**	Hebrew supplanter
0.1	**Jamie-Lynn**	Jamie + Lynn
0.1	**Jamila**	Arabic beautiful
0.1	**Jana**	Hebrew gracious, merciful
0.2	**Janae**	Hebrew gracious, merciful
0.1	**Janay**	Hebrew gracious, merciful

0.4	**Jane**	Hebrew gracious, merciful	7.3	**Jennifer**	Welsh white, fair
0.1	**Janel**	Hebrew gracious, merciful	0.7	**Jenny**	Welsh white, fair
0.1	**Janell**	Hebrew gracious, merciful	0.1	**Jerica**	origin unknown, possibly an invented name
0.5	**Janelle**	Hebrew gracious, merciful			
0.2	**Janessa**	Hebrew gracious, merciful	0.1	**Jerrica**	origin unknown, possibly an invented name
0.7	**Janet**	Hebrew gracious, merciful			
0.1	**Janeth**	origin unknown	0.1	**Jesenia**	origin unknown
0.2	**Janette**	Hebrew gracious, merciful	0.1	**Jesica**	Hebrew God's grace
0.2	**Janice**	Hebrew gracious, merciful	0.2	**Jesse**	Hebrew God's grace
0.1	**Janick**	newly-created African-American name	0.1	**Jessenia**	Arabic flower (Yesenia)
			0.1	**Jessi**	Hebrew God's grace
0.2	**Janie**	Hebrew gracious, merciful	16.8	**Jessica**	Hebrew God's grace
0.2	**Janine**	Hebrew gracious, merciful	0.8	**Jessie**	Hebrew God's grace
0.1	**Janna**	Hebrew gracious, merciful	0.2	**Jessika**	Hebrew God's grace
0.2	**Jaqueline**	Hebrew to supplant	0.1	**Jessy**	Hebrew God's grace
0.1	**Jasleen**	Sikh one who sings praises to the Lord	0.2	**Jill**	Latin young; Greek soft-haired, youthful
0.1	**Jasmeet**	origin unknown	0.8	**Jillian**	Latin young; Greek soft-haired, youthful
1.1	**Jasmin**	Persian jasmine			
5.9	**Jasmine**	Persian jasmine	0.2	**Joana**	Hebrew gracious, merciful
0.1	**Jasmyn**	Persian jasmine	1.0	**Joanie**	Hebrew gracious, merciful
0.1	**Jasmyne**	Persian jasmine	0.9	**Joanna**	Hebrew gracious, merciful
0.2	**Jaspreet**	Punjabi virtuous, loves virtue	0.2	**Joanne**	Hebrew gracious, merciful
0.1	**Jayde**	Spanish jade, a precious stone	0.3	**Joannie**	Hebrew gracious, merciful
			0.3	**Joanny**	Hebrew gracious, merciful
0.1	**Jayden**	origin unknown	0.1	**Joany**	Hebrew gracious, merciful
0.1	**Jayla**	origin unknown	1.4	**Jocelyn**	German supplanted, substituted
0.2	**Jayme**	Hebrew supplanter			
0.9	**Jazmin**	Persian jasmine	0.1	**Jocelyne**	German supplanted, substituted
0.8	**Jazmine**	Persian jasmine			
0.1	**Jazmyn**	Persian jasmine	0.2	**Jodi**	Hebrew praise
0.1	**Jazmyne**	Persian jasmine	0.1	**Jodie**	Hebrew praise
0.1	**Jazzmin**	Persian jasmine	0.2	**Joelle**	Hebrew the Lord is winning
0.1	**Jazzmine**	Persian jasmine	0.1	**Johana**	Hebrew gracious, merciful
0.1	**Jean**	Hebrew gracious, merciful	0.6	**Johanie**	Hebrew gracious, merciful
0.3	**Jeanette**	Hebrew gracious, merciful	0.3	**Johanna**	Hebrew gracious, merciful
0.1	**Jeanne**	Hebrew gracious, merciful	0.2	**Johannie**	Hebrew gracious, merciful
0.1	**Jeannette**	Hebrew gracious, merciful	0.1	**Joi**	Latin joy
0.1	**Jena**	Arabic small bird	0.1	**Jolene**	English he will increase
0.1	**Jenifer**	Welsh white, fair	0.2	**Jolyane**	origin unknown
0.1	**Jeniffer**	Welsh white, fair	2.8	**Jordan**	Hebrew descending
2.2	**Jenna**	Arabic small bird	0.6	**Jordyn**	Hebrew descending
0.2	**Jennie**	Welsh white, fair	0.2	**Josee**	Hebrew he shall increase

0.1	**Josefina**	Hebrew he shall increase	0.4	**Kailey**	Arabic beloved
0.1	**Joseline**	German supplanted, substituted	0.1	**Kailyn**	Arabic beloved
0.2	**Joselyn**	German supplanted, substituted	1.6	**Kaitlin**	Greek pure, unsullied (Katherine)
0.4	**Josephine**	Hebrew he shall increase	3.4	**Kaitlyn**	Greek pure, unsullied (Katherine)
0.8	**Josiane**	Josie + Anne	0.4	**Kaitlynn**	Greek pure, unsullied (Katherine)
0.3	**Josianne**	Josie + Anne	0.2	**Kala**	Hindi black; time
0.3	**Josie**	Hebrew he shall increase	0.1	**Kalee**	Sanskrit energy
0.1	**Joslyn**	German supplanted, substituted	0.2	**Kaleigh**	Sanskrit energy
0.3	**Joy**	Latin joy	0.3	**Kaley**	Sanskrit energy
0.2	**Joyce**	Latin joyous	0.3	**Kali**	Sanskrit energy
0.2	**Juana**	Spanish form of Joan: Hebrew gracious, merciful	0.1	**Kalie**	Sanskrit energy
			0.1	**Kalli**	Sanskrit energy
0.2	**Juanita**	Spanish form of Joan: Hebrew gracious, merciful	0.1	**Kallie**	Sanskrit energy
			0.1	**Kalyn**	Arabic beloved
0.3	**Judith**	Hebrew of Judah	0.1	**Kami**	Shintoism divine power or aura
0.1	**Judy**	Hebrew of Judah			
2.7	**Julia**	Greek soft-haired, youthful	0.1	**Kandace**	Greek glittering white, incandescent
0.4	**Juliana**	Greek soft-haired, youthful			
0.3	**Julianna**	Greek soft-haired, youthful	0.1	**Kanesha**	newly-created African-American name
0.2	**Julianne**	Greek soft-haired, youthful			
1.5	**Julie**	Greek soft-haired, youthful	0.1	**Kanisha**	newly-created African-American name
0.3	**Julie Anne**	Julie + Anne			
0.1	**Juliet**	Greek soft-haired, youthful	1.0	**Kara**	Danish form of Katherine: Greek pure, unsullied
0.1	**Juliette**	Greek soft-haired, youthful			
0.1	**Julissa**	Latin Jupiter, God the Father	0.1	**Karel**	variant of Carol: Latin strong and womanly; French song of joy
0.4	**Justice**	Latin just, honest			
0.2	**Justina**	Latin just, honest			
0.9	**Justine**	Latin just, honest	0.3	**Karelle**	variant of Carol: Latin strong and womanly; French song of joy

-K-

			1.4	**Karen**	Danish form of Katherine: Greek pure, unsullied
1.3	**K**	initial used as a first name			
0.1	**Kacey**	Irish brave	0.2	**Kari**	Danish form of Katherine: Greek pure, unsullied
0.1	**Kaci**	Irish brave			
0.2	**Kacie**	Irish brave	0.3	**Kariane**	Kari + Anne
0.2	**Kadijah**	Arabic trustworthy	0.1	**Karianne**	Kari + Anne
0.1	**Kaela**	Arabic beloved	1.4	**Karina**	Latin a keel
0.1	**Kaelyn**	Arabic beloved	0.4	**Karine**	Danish form of Katherine: Greek pure, unsullied
0.3	**Kaila**	Arabic beloved			
0.2	**Kailee**	Arabic beloved			

0.4	**Karissa**	origin unknown, possibly an invented name
0.7	**Karla**	French little and womanly
0.2	**Karlee**	French little and womanly
0.1	**Karleigh**	French little and womanly
0.2	**Karley**	French little and womanly
0.2	**Karli**	French little and womanly
0.2	**Karlie**	French little and womanly
0.2	**Karly**	French little and womanly
0.4	**Karol Ann**	Carol + Ann
0.7	**Karolane**	Carol + Anne
0.4	**Karolann**	Carol + Ann
0.2	**Karolanne**	Carol + Anne
0.1	**Karolina**	Carol + Anne
0.2	**Kasandra**	Greek not believed
0.5	**Kasey**	Irish brave
1.0	**Kassandra**	Greek not believed
0.3	**Kassidy**	Greek not believed
0.1	**Kassie**	Greek not believed
0.3	**Katarina**	Greek pure, unsullied
0.1	**Katarzyna**	origin unknown
0.4	**Kate**	Greek pure, unsullied
0.2	**Katelin**	Greek pure, unsullied
2.6	**Katelyn**	Greek pure, unsullied
0.5	**Katelynn**	Greek pure, unsullied
0.2	**Katerina**	Greek pure, unsullied
0.1	**Katerine**	Greek pure, unsullied
0.3	**Katharine**	Greek pure, unsullied
4.5	**Katherine**	Greek pure, unsullied
0.1	**Katheryn**	Greek pure, unsullied
1.3	**Kathleen**	Greek pure, unsullied
0.1	**Kathrine**	Greek pure, unsullied
2.1	**Kathryn**	Greek pure, unsullied
0.3	**Kathy**	Greek pure, unsullied
0.1	**Katia**	Greek pure, unsullied
2.2	**Katie**	Greek pure, unsullied
0.1	**Katlin**	Greek pure, unsullied
0.5	**Katlyn**	Greek pure, unsullied
0.1	**Katlynn**	Greek pure, unsullied
1.1	**Katrina**	Greek pure, unsullied
0.1	**Katrine**	Greek pure, unsullied
0.2	**Katy**	Greek pure, unsullied
0.1	**Kaycee**	Irish brave
7.6	**Kayla**	Hebrew a crown, a laurel
0.1	**Kaylah**	Hebrew a crown, a laurel
0.1	**Kaylan**	origin unknown
1.1	**Kaylee**	Hebrew a crown, a laurel
0.1	**Kayleen**	Hebrew a crown, a laurel
0.3	**Kayleigh**	Hebrew a crown, a laurel
0.1	**Kayley**	Hebrew a crown, a laurel
0.1	**Kayli**	Hebrew a crown, a laurel
0.2	**Kaylie**	Hebrew a crown, a laurel
0.2	**Kaylin**	Hebrew a crown, a laurel
0.1	**Kaylon**	Hebrew a crown, a laurel
0.2	**Kaylyn**	Hebrew a crown, a laurel
0.1	**Kaylynn**	Hebrew a crown, a laurel
0.1	**Kaytlin**	Greek pure, unsullied
0.1	**Keana**	newly-created African-American name
0.1	**Keanna**	newly-created African-American name
0.1	**Keara**	Irish dark, black
0.1	**Keely**	Gaelic beautiful one
0.1	**Keira**	Irish dark, black
0.2	**Keisha**	African favorite; variation of Lakeisha
0.2	**Kelley**	Irish warrior
0.5	**Kelli**	Irish warrior
0.4	**Kellie**	Irish warrior
2.5	**Kelly**	Irish warrior
0.3	**Kelly Ann**	Kelly + Ann
0.2	**Kelsea**	Scottish from the ship island
4.4	**Kelsey**	Scottish from the ship island
0.2	**Kelsi**	Scottish from the ship island
0.5	**Kelsie**	Scottish from the ship island
0.1	**Kelsy**	Scottish from the ship island
0.1	**Kendal**	Celtic ruler of the valley
0.8	**Kendall**	Celtic ruler of the valley
1.3	**Kendra**	English knowledgeable
0.2	**Kenia**	origin unknown
0.1	**Kenna**	Old English knowledge
0.5	**Kennedy**	last name used as a first name: head of the house
0.3	**Kenya**	Hebrew horn (of an animal); Russian short form of Innokenti

0.1	**Kenyatta**	origin unknown
0.1	**Kenzie**	Scottish the fair one
0.1	**Keosha**	origin unknown
0.2	**Keri**	Irish dark-haired
0.1	**Kerri**	Irish dark-haired
0.2	**Kerry**	Irish dark-haired
0.1	**Keyana**	newly-created African-American name
0.1	**Keyanna**	newly-created African-American name
0.1	**Keyonna**	newly-created African-American name
0.6	**Khadijah**	Arabic trustworthy
0.1	**Kia**	African season's beginning
0.6	**Kiana**	variant of Anna: one of grace, gracious
0.2	**Kianna**	variant of Anna: one of grace, gracious
0.7	**Kiara**	origin unknown; possibly a variant of Kiera
0.3	**Kiera**	Irish dark, black
0.4	**Kierra**	Irish dark, black
0.2	**Kiersten**	Greek a Christian, anointed one (Christina)
0.2	**Kiley**	Irish handsome; Western Australian Aboriginal curled, stick or boomerang
0.4	**Kim**	English chief, ruler
0.1	**Kimberlee**	English chief, ruler
0.2	**Kimberley**	English chief, ruler
4.2	**Kimberly**	English chief, ruler
0.1	**Kindra**	English knowledgeable
0.1	**Kinsey**	Old English offspring, relative
0.4	**Kira**	Persian sun
0.1	**Kirandeep**	origin unknown
0.8	**Kirsten**	Greek a Christian, anointed one
0.1	**Kirstin**	Greek a Christian, anointed one
0.2	**Kori**	Irish from the hollow
0.1	**Kortney**	French from the king's court
0.3	**Kourtney**	French from the king's court

0.8	**Krista**	Greek a Christian, anointed one
0.1	**Kristal**	Greek brilliant glass
2.6	**Kristen**	Greek a Christian, anointed one (Christina)
0.2	**Kristi**	Greek a Christian, anointed one (Christina)
0.1	**Kristian**	Greek a Christian, anointed one (Christina)
0.1	**Kristie**	Greek a Christian, anointed one (Christina)
1.2	**Kristin**	Greek a Christian, anointed one (Christina)
1.3	**Kristina**	Greek a Christian, anointed one (Christina)
0.3	**Kristine**	Greek a Christian, anointed one (Christina)
0.3	**Kristy**	Greek a Christian, anointed one (Christina)
0.1	**Kristyn**	Greek a Christian, anointed one (Christina)
0.1	**Krysta**	Greek a Christian, anointed one (Christina)
0.9	**Krystal**	Greek brilliant glass
0.1	**Krystel**	Greek brilliant glass
0.2	**Krystelle**	Greek brilliant glass
0.1	**Krysten**	Greek a Christian, anointed one (Christina)
0.1	**Krystina**	Greek a Christian, anointed one (Christina)
0.4	**Kyla**	Irish handsome
0.4	**Kylee**	Irish handsome
0.1	**Kyleigh**	Irish handsome
1.3	**Kylie**	Irish handsome; Western Australian Aboriginal curled, stick or boomerang
0.1	**Kym**	English chief, ruler
0.4	**Kyra**	Greek lord or god

-L-

0.6	**L**	initial used as a first name
0.1	**La**	a popular prefix

0.6	**Lacey**	Latin cheerful		0.2	**Leonie**	Latin lion
0.1	**Laci**	Latin cheerful		0.1	**Lesley**	English meadowlands
0.1	**Lacie**	Latin cheerful		1.2	**Leslie**	English meadowlands
0.2	**Lacy**	Latin cheerful		0.1	**Lesly**	English meadowlands
0.1	**Lakeisha**	fashionable prefix La +		0.4	**Leticia**	Latin gladness
		Aisha or Aiesha		0.1	**Lexi**	short form of Alexandra:
0.1	**Laken**	origin unknown				Greek defender of mankind
0.1	**Lana**	Latin woolly		0.1	**Lexie**	short form of Alexandra:
0.2	**Lara**	Latin shining; famous				Greek defender of mankind
0.4	**Larissa**	Latin cheerful		0.2	**Lexus**	origin unknown
0.1	**Lashay**	newly-created African-		0.1	**Lia**	Hebrew to be weary
		American name		0.1	**Liana**	English from the meadow
0.1	**Latasha**	La + tasha (possibly from		0.1	**Libby**	variant of Elizabeth: Hebrew
		Natasha)				God's oath
0.1	**Latisha**	La + tisha (possibly from		0.2	**Lidia**	Greek from Lydia
		Natasha);		0.1	**Lila**	Hindi free, playful will of God
0.1	**Latoya**	Greek a powerful		0.1	**Lilia**	Latin lily
		mythological deity		0.1	**Lilian**	Latin lily
0.1	**Latrice**	La + element from Patrice:		0.6	**Liliana**	Latin lily
		Latin of noble descent		0.4	**Lillian**	Latin lily
3.5	**Laura**	Latin laurel		0.4	**Lily**	Latin lily
0.3	**Laurel**	Latin laurel		0.1	**Lina**	Latin temptress
6.7	**Lauren**	Latin laurel		0.7	**Linda**	Spanish pretty
4.2	**Laurence**	Latin laurel		1.5	**Lindsay**	English the camp near the
0.3	**Lauriane**	Laurie + Anne				stream
1.4	**Laurianne**	Laurie + Anne		2.2	**Lindsey**	English the camp near the
0.4	**Laurie**	Latin laurel				stream
0.2	**Laurie Ann**	Laurie + Ann		0.1	**Linnea**	Old Norse lime tree
0.7	**Laurie Anne**	Laurie + Anne		0.1	**Linsey**	English the camp near the
0.4	**Laury**	Latin laurel				stream
0.1	**Lauryn**	Latin laurel		1.4	**Lisa**	Hebrew God's oath
0.1	**Layla**	Arabic dark as night				(Elizabeth)
0.2	**Lea**	Hebrew to be weary		0.1	**Lisa Marie**	Lisa + Marie
1.4	**Leah**	Hebrew to be weary		0.1	**Lisbeth**	Hebrew God's oath
0.1	**Leandra**	Latin like a lioness				(Elizabeth)
0.1	**Leann**	English from the meadow		0.2	**Lisette**	Hebrew God's oath
0.2	**Leanna**	English from the meadow				(Elizabeth)
0.2	**Leanne**	English from the meadow		0.1	**Lissette**	Hebrew God's oath
0.1	**Leigh**	English from the meadow				(Elizabeth)
0.1	**Leigha**	Hebrew to be weary		0.1	**Liza**	Hebrew God's oath
0.1	**Leila**	Arabic dark as night				(Elizabeth)
0.2	**Leilani**	Hawaiian heavenly child		0.4	**Lizbeth**	Hebrew God's oath
0.2	**Lena**	Latin temptress				(Elizabeth)

0.1	**Lizet**	Hebrew God's oath (Elizabeth)
0.2	**Lizeth**	Hebrew God's oath (Elizabeth)
0.3	**Lizette**	Hebrew God's oath (Elizabeth)
0.4	**Logan**	Middle English a felled tree
0.1	**London**	place name used as a first name
0.1	**Lora**	Latin laurel
0.2	**Loren**	Latin laurel
0.5	**Lorena**	Latin laurel
0.2	**Lori**	Latin laurel
0.1	**Lorraine**	Latin sorrowful
0.1	**Louise**	German famous warrior
0.2	**Lourdes**	French place name
0.3	**Lucero**	Latin light
0.3	**Lucia**	Latin light
0.3	**Lucy**	Latin light
0.1	**Luisa**	German famous warrior
0.1	**Lupita**	short form of Guadalupe; Arabic valley of the wolf
0.2	**Luz**	Latin light
0.8	**Lydia**	Greek from Lydia
0.1	**Lyndsay**	English the camp near the stream
0.2	**Lyndsey**	English the camp near the stream
0.1	**Lynette**	Celtic graceful
0.2	**Lynn**	English waterfall
0.1	**Lynsey**	English the camp near the stream
0.2	**Lyric**	origin unknown
0.1	**Lysa**	Hebrew God's oath (Elizabeth)
0.4	**Lysandre**	origin unknown
0.3	**Lysanne**	origin unknown

-M-

0.4	**M**	initial used as a first name
0.1	**M.**	initial used as a first name
0.3	**Ma Kayla**	origin unknown

0.1	**Macey**	African-American name
0.1	**Macie**	African-American name
1.9	**Mackenzie**	Irish son of the wise leader
0.3	**Macy**	African-American name
0.1	**Madalyn**	Greek a high tower
0.2	**Maddison**	son of Maude; English good
0.1	**Madelaine**	Greek a high tower
0.6	**Madeleine**	Greek a high tower
1.9	**Madeline**	Greek a high tower
0.3	**Madelyn**	Greek a high tower
0.1	**Madisen**	son of Maude; English good
4.0	**Madison**	son of Maude; English good
0.1	**Madyson**	son of Maude; English good
0.2	**Maegan**	Greek a pearl (Margaret)
0.2	**Magali**	Hebrew from Magdala, place of high tower
0.3	**Magalie**	Hebrew from Magdala, place of high tower
0.1	**Magaly**	Hebrew from Magdala, place of high tower
0.2	**Magdalena**	Greek tower
0.6	**Maggie**	Greek a pearl (Margaret)
0.3	**Maggy**	Greek a pearl (Margaret)
0.1	**Mai**	Swedish from Greek pearl; Navajo Indian coyote
0.1	**Maia**	Old English kinswoman; Middle English maiden
0.2	**Maika**	variant of Michael: Hebrew who is like God
0.2	**Maira**	Welsh variant of Mary: Hebrew sea of sorrow; Spanish from Latin marvelous
0.1	**Makala**	possibly a variant of Makala: Hawaiian myrtle
0.8	**Makayla**	possibly a variant of Makala: Hawaiian myrtle
0.3	**Makell**	origin unknown
0.2	**Makenna**	origin unknown
0.3	**Makenzie**	Irish son of the wise leader
0.2	**Malia**	Hawaiian form of Mary: Hebrew sea of sorrow
0.8	**Mallory**	French armour mailed

0.1	**Mandeep**	Punjabi mind full of light, enlightened being	0.5	**Marie Joelle**	Marie + Joelle
0.2	**Mandy**	form of Amanda: Latin worthy of love	0.3	**Marie Josee**	Marie + Josee
0.1	**Manjot**	origin unknown	0.3	**Marie Kim**	Marie + Kim
0.1	**Manpreet**	Punjabi mind full of love	0.9	**Marie Laurence**	Marie + Laurence
0.2	**Mara**	Hebrew bitter	1.1	**Marie Lou**	Marie + Lou
0.3	**Maranda**	Latin strange, wonderful	0.8	**Marie Michele**	Marie + Michele
0.1	**Marcela**	Latin brave, warlike	0.6	**Marie Michelle**	Marie + Michelle
0.1	**Marcella**	Latin brave, warlike	0.3	**Marie Pascale**	Marie + Pascale
0.1	**Maren**	origin unknown	0.6	**Marie Philippe**	Marie + Philippe
1.4	**Margaret**	Greek a pearl	8.1	**Marie Pier**	Marie + Piere
0.4	**Margarit**	Greek a pearl	0.5	**Marie Pierre**	Marie + Pierre
0.4	**Margarita**	Greek a pearl	1.7	**Marie Soleil**	Marie + Soleil
0.1	**Marguerite**	Greek a pearl	0.1	**Marie-Claude**	Marie + Claude
0.1	**Mari**	Hebrew sea of sorrow	0.1	**Marie-Eve**	Mary + Eve
3.6	**Maria**	Latin, French, Italian, Spanish, Swedish of Mary: Hebrew sea of sorrow	0.3	**Marie-Pier**	Mary + Pierre
			0.1	**Mariel**	German form of Mary: Hebrew sea of sorrow
0.1	**Mariaguadalupe**	Maria + Guadalupe	0.3	**Mariela**	German form of Mary: Hebrew sea of sorrow
2.2	**Mariah**	Hebrew sea of sorrow	0.2	**Marieve**	Mary + Eve
0.2	**Mariam**	form of Mary + Ann	0.1	**Marika**	Slavic form of Mary: Hebrew sea of sorrow
0.1	**Marian**	form of Mary + Ann			
0.4	**Mariana**	form of Mary + Ann	0.4	**Marilou**	Marie + Lou
0.2	**Mariane**	form of Mary + Ann	0.1	**Marily**	Mary + Lee
0.1	**Marianna**	form of Mary + Ann	0.3	**Marilyn**	Hebrew descendants of Mary
0.3	**Marianne**	form of Mary + Ann			
0.4	**Maribel**	Hebrew beautiful but bitter	0.2	**Marilyne**	Hebrew descendants of Mary
0.2	**Maricela**	Latin Mars, the Roman god of war	0.8	**Marina**	Latin the sea
			0.1	**Marion**	French form of Mary: Hebrew sea of sorrow
0.1	**Maricruz**	Marie + Cruz	1.0	**Marisa**	Latin the sea
0.7	**Marie**	Latin, French, Italian, Spanish, Swedish forms of Mary: Hebrew sea of sorrow	0.2	**Marisela**	Spanish Maris sea and Marcella brave martial or a hammer
0.6	**Marie Andree**	Marie + Andree	0.5	**Marisol**	origin unknown
0.8	**Marie Anne**	Marie + Anne	2.9	**Marissa**	Latin the sea
1.1	**Marie Christine**	Marie + Christine	0.5	**Maritza**	Arabic blessed
0.3	**Marie Claire**	Marie + Claire	0.4	**Marjolaine**	French flower name
1.1	**Marie Claude**	Marie + Claude	0.1	**Marjorie**	Scottish form of Mary: Hebrew sea of sorrow
8.3	**Marie Eve**	Marie + Eve			
0.6	**Marie France**	Marie + France	0.1	**Marla**	Greek a high tower
1.0	**Marie Helene**	Marie + Helene	0.1	**Marlee**	Greek a high tower
0.5	**Marie Jeanne**	Marie + Jeanne			

0.2	**Marlen**	origin unknown
0.1	**Marlena**	Greek a high tower
0.4	**Marlene**	Greek a high tower
0.1	**Marley**	Greek a high tower
0.1	**Marlyn**	origin unknown
0.1	**Marquita**	Spanish form of Marcia: Latin brave, warlike
0.1	**Marta**	Aramaic a lady; sorrowful
0.5	**Martha**	Aramaic a lady; sorrowful
0.1	**Martina**	Aramaic a lady; sorrowful
0.1	**Martine**	Aramaic a lady; sorrowful
3.3	**Mary**	Hebrew sea of sorrow
0.1	**Mary Kate**	Mary + Kate
0.1	**Maryam**	form of Mary + Ann
0.1	**Maryann**	Mary + Ann
0.1	**Marykate**	Mary + Kate
0.1	**Marylou**	Mary + Lou
0.1	**Maryse**	French form of Mary: Hebrew sea of sorrow
0.3	**Mathilde**	Greek battle maid
0.1	**Mattie**	Aramaic a lady; sorrowful (Martha)
1.9	**Maude**	Teutonic heroine
0.1	**Maura**	Latin dark
0.1	**Maureen**	French dark-skinned
0.2	**Maxime**	Latin son of Maximus
0.1	**Maxine**	Latin greatest
0.6	**Maya**	Latin great
0.8	**Mayra**	origin unknown
0.1	**Mc**	part of a surname used as a first name
0.6	**Mc Kenna**	surname used as first name
0.2	**Mc Kenzie**	Irish son of the wise leader
0.2	**Mckayla**	origin unknown
0.6	**Mckaylee**	origin unknown
0.3	**Mckell**	origin unknown
0.4	**Mckenna**	surname used as first name
0.8	**Mckenzie**	surname used as first name
0.8	**Meagan**	Greek a pearl (Margaret)
0.4	**Meaghan**	Greek a pearl (Margaret)
7.9	**Megan**	Greek a pearl (Margaret)
1.3	**Megane**	Greek a pearl (Margaret)
0.1	**Meggie**	Greek a pearl (Margaret)
0.4	**Meggy**	Greek a pearl (Margaret)
1.6	**Meghan**	Greek a pearl (Margaret)
1.6	**Melanie**	Greek black, dark appearance
0.3	**Melina**	Greek a song
0.3	**Melinda**	Latin brave, martial
0.1	**Melisa**	Greek a bee, honey
5.2	**Melissa**	Greek a bee, honey
0.1	**Melodie**	Greek a melody
0.4	**Melody**	Greek a melody
0.2	**Melyna**	Greek a song
0.1	**Meranda**	Latin strange, wonderful
0.7	**Mercedes**	Latin reward, payment
0.5	**Meredith**	Welsh protector of the sea
0.1	**Merissa**	Latin the sea (Marisa)
0.4	**Mia**	Italian mine, my
0.3	**Micaela**	Hebrew who is like God
0.1	**Micah**	Hebrew who is like God
1.4	**Michaela**	Hebrew who is like God
0.1	**Michaella**	Hebrew who is like God
0.3	**Michele**	Hebrew who is like God
4.8	**Michelle**	Hebrew who is like God
0.5	**Mikaela**	Hebrew who is like God
0.1	**Mikala**	Hebrew who is like God
1.0	**Mikayla**	Hebrew who is like God
0.1	**Mina**	Old German love
0.2	**Mindy**	Latin brave, martial; Old German love
0.1	**Miracle**	origin unknown
2.6	**Miranda**	Latin strange, wonderful
0.1	**Mireille**	Latin wonderful
0.2	**Mireya**	Hebrew God has spoken
0.5	**Miriam**	Hebrew sea of sorrow
0.2	**Misty**	English obscure, covered with mist
0.2	**Mollie**	Irish see Mary
1.5	**Molly**	Irish see Mary
2.2	**Monica**	Greek solitary Latin advisor
0.2	**Monika**	Greek solitary Latin advisor
1.0	**Monique**	Greek solitary Latin advisor
0.1	**Monserrat**	Latin saw-like mountain
0.2	**Montana**	Spanish mountain; place name used as a first name

4.6	**Morgan**	Welsh edge of the sea
0.2	**Moriah**	French dark-skinned (Maureen)
0.1	**Mya**	Danish and Swedish short form of Maria
0.1	**Myesha**	newly-created African-American name
0.4	**Mylene**	Greek black, dark
0.1	**Myra**	Hebrew sea of sorrow (Miriam)
0.1	**Myranda**	Latin strange, wonderful
0.5	**Myriam**	Hebrew sea of sorrow (Miriam)

-N-

0.1	**N**	initial used as a first name
0.4	**Nadia**	French, Slavic hope
0.2	**Nadine**	French, Slavic hope
0.1	**Nakia**	Arabic pure
0.1	**Nallely**	origin unknown
1.3	**Nancy**	Hebrew gracious
0.7	**Naomi**	Hebrew beautiful, pleasant
0.3	**Naomie**	Hebrew beautiful, pleasant
0.1	**Naomy**	Hebrew beautiful, pleasant
0.2	**Natacha**	Latin to be born
0.1	**Natali**	Latin to be born
0.4	**Natalia**	Latin to be born
3.4	**Natalie**	Latin to be born
0.3	**Nataly**	Latin to be born
1.5	**Natasha**	Latin to be born
0.3	**Nathalie**	Latin to be born
0.1	**Nathaly**	Latin to be born
0.1	**Natori**	origin unknown
0.1	**Navdeep**	Sikh the ever new light, the new lamp
0.1	**Navjot**	Sikh the new light, always bright
0.1	**Navneet**	Sikh one who is ever new
0.2	**Nayeli**	origin unknown
0.1	**Nelly**	nickname for Helen: Greek a torch, light
0.1	**Ngoc**	Vietnamese jade
0.2	**Nia**	Welsh figure in Irish legend

0.6	**Nichole**	Greek victory of the people
0.1	**Nicola**	Greek victory of the people
8.0	**Nicole**	Greek victory of the people
0.4	**Nicolette**	Greek victory of the people
0.1	**Nicolle**	Greek victory of the people
0.1	**Niki**	Greek victory of the people
0.1	**Nikita**	Greek victory of the people
0.4	**Nikki**	Greek victory of the people
0.1	**Nikole**	Greek victory of the people
0.5	**Nina**	Spanish girl
0.1	**Noel**	Latin Christmas
0.3	**Noelle**	Latin Christmas
0.3	**Noemi**	origin unknown
3.2	**Noemie**	origin unknown
0.1	**Noemy**	origin unknown
0.2	**Nohely**	Latin Christmas
0.3	**Nora**	short form of Eleanor: Greek a torch, light
0.3	**Norma**	Latin rule, pattern
0.5	**Not**	origin unknown

-O-

0.1	**Octavia**	Latin eighth
0.2	**Olga**	Old Norse holy
3.4	**Olivia**	Latin olive

-P-

0.2	**P**	initial used as a first name
2.7	**Paige**	English child, young
0.1	**Paloma**	Latin wild dove
0.5	**Pamela**	Greek all-honey
0.6	**Paola**	Latin small
0.3	**Paris**	French place name
0.1	**Parveen**	Muslim the Pleiades; Sikh capable, skilful, efficient
0.3	**Pascale**	Latin born during Passover, Easter season
0.1	**Patience**	French endurance
0.1	**Patrice**	Latin of noble descent
1.3	**Patricia**	Latin of noble descent
0.3	**Paula**	Latin small

0.3	**Paulina**	Latin small
0.1	**Pauline**	Latin small
0.3	**Payton**	last name used as a first name, from a town in England
0.1	**Penelope**	Greek type of duck or goose noted for red stripes
0.3	**Perla**	Latin bone
0.2	**Peyton**	last name used as a first name, from a town in England
0.1	**Phoebe**	Greek the shining
0.2	**Pier Ann**	Pierre + Anne
0.1	**Pooja**	origin unknown
0.1	**Porsha**	Latin an offering
0.4	**Precious**	word used as a name
0.1	**Presley**	last name used as a first name: shrubs, brushwood, meadow
0.1	**Princess**	word used as a name
0.8	**Priscilla**	Latin from ancient times
0.1	**Priya**	Hindi beloved, very sweet natured
0.1	**Puneet**	Sikh one who is very pure and holy

-Q-

0.1	**Quanisha**	newly-created African-American name
0.1	**Quinn**	Old English queen

-R-

0.4	**R**	initial used as a first name
1.3	**Rachael**	Hebrew a female sheep
0.1	**Racheal**	Hebrew a female sheep
7.6	**Rachel**	Hebrew a female sheep
0.4	**Rachelle**	Hebrew a female sheep
0.1	**Raegan**	Celtic, Old French, royal
0.1	**Rafaelle**	Spanish form of Raphael: Hebrew God has healed
0.1	**Raina**	Old German mighty
0.1	**Raman**	origin unknown

0.2	**Ramandeep**	Sikh absorbed in the light of the Lord's love
0.3	**Randi**	English shield-wolf
1.2	**Raphaelle**	Spanish form of Raphael: Hebrew God has healed
0.6	**Raquel**	Hebrew a female sheep
0.9	**Raven**	English like a raven
0.1	**Ravneet**	origin unknown
0.1	**Raylene**	origin unknown
0.1	**Rayna**	Yiddish pure, clean
0.2	**Reagan**	Celtic, Old French, royal
0.1	**Reanna**	Rachel + Ann
0.1	**Reba**	Hebrew to tie, to bind
0.2	**Rebeca**	Hebrew to tie, to bind
5.4	**Rebecca**	Hebrew to tie, to bind
1.0	**Rebekah**	Hebrew to tie, to bind
0.2	**Regan**	Latin queen (Regina)
0.3	**Regina**	Latin queen
0.1	**Regine**	Latin queen
0.1	**Reina**	Latin queen (Regina)
0.1	**Renae**	French to be born again
0.6	**Renee**	French to be born again
0.2	**Reyna**	Greek peace
0.1	**Rhianna**	Welsh maiden
0.2	**Rhiannon**	Welsh a mythological witch, nymph, goddess
0.1	**Rhonda**	Welsh grand
0.1	**Richelle**	German powerful ruler
0.1	**Ricki**	Latin true image (Veronica)
0.2	**Rikki**	Latin true image (Veronica)
0.5	**Riley**	Irish valiant
0.2	**Rita**	Sanskrit brave, honest
0.4	**Robin**	English shining with fame
0.4	**Robyn**	English shining with fame
0.3	**Rochelle**	French from the large stone
0.4	**Rocio**	Latin covered with dew
0.7	**Rosa**	Latin rose
0.2	**Rosalie**	Rose + Lee
0.1	**Rosalinda**	Spanish fair rose
0.1	**Rosanne**	Rose + Anne
0.1	**Rosario**	Latin rose garden
0.4	**Rose**	Latin rose
0.4	**Rose Marie**	Rose + Marie

0.1	**Roseline**	Spanish fair rose	
0.1	**Rosemarie**	Rose + Marie	
0.2	**Rosemary**	Rose + Mary	
0.1	**Rosie**	Latin rose	
0.1	**Rosio**	origin unknown	
0.1	**Rowan**	last name used as a first name: Irish little red one	
0.2	**Roxana**	Persian dawn, light	
0.2	**Roxane**	Persian dawn, light	
0.1	**Roxanna**	Persian dawn, light	
0.6	**Roxanne**	Persian dawn, light	
0.1	**Rubi**	French ruby	
0.6	**Ruby**	French ruby	
0.1	**Rupinder**	Sanskrit of the greatest beauty	
0.4	**Ruth**	Hebrew friendship	
0.2	**Ryan**	Irish little king	
0.1	**Ryann**	Irish little king	
0.2	**Rylee**	German, Dutch a small stream; Irish valiant	

-S-

0.9	**S**	initial used as a first name
0.1	**Sabina**	Latin from the Sabine, a tribe in ancient Italy
2.2	**Sabrina**	Latin from the boundary line
0.1	**Sabryna**	Latin from the boundary line
0.1	**Sade**	Hebrew princess, noble
0.5	**Sadie**	Hebrew princess, noble
0.1	**Sagal**	origin unknown
0.1	**Sage**	Latin wise
0.1	**Salena**	Latin saline, salty
0.2	**Salina**	Latin saline, salty
0.2	**Sally**	Hebrew princess, noble (Sarah)
10.9	**Samantha**	Aramaic the listener
0.1	**Samara**	Hebrew ruled by God
0.1	**Samaria**	newly-created African-American name
0.4	**Samuelle**	Hebrew God has heard
0.1	**Sandeep**	Punjabi enlightened being

1.1	**Sandra**	Greek defender of mankind (Alexandra)
2.8	**Sandrine**	variant of Alexandra: Greek defender of mankind
0.4	**Sandy**	Greek defender of mankind (Alexandra)
0.1	**Santana**	Spanish saint
3.5	**Sara**	Hebrew princess, noble
0.3	**Sara Eve**	Sara + Eve
0.1	**Sara Jane**	Sara + Jane
0.3	**Sara Maude**	Sara + Maude
11.4	**Sarah**	Hebrew princess, noble
0.1	**Sarah Ann**	Sarah Ann
0.5	**Sarah Eve**	Sarah + Eve
0.2	**Sarah Jane**	Sarah + Jane
0.3	**Sarah Jeanne**	Sarah + Jeanne
0.9	**Sarah Maude**	Sarah + Maude
0.2	**Sarai**	Hebrew quarrelsome
0.1	**Sarina**	form of Sarah: Hebrew princess, noble
0.3	**Sasha**	Russian form of Alexandra: Greek defender of mankind
0.2	**Savanah**	Spanish barren
0.5	**Savanna**	Spanish barren
2.3	**Savannah**	Spanish barren
0.1	**Scarlett**	English bright red color
0.6	**Selena**	Greek moon
0.1	**Selene**	Greek moon
0.4	**Selina**	Greek moon
0.4	**Serena**	Latin peaceful
0.1	**Serina**	Latin peaceful
0.1	**Shae**	Hebrew asked for
0.1	**Shae-Lynn**	origin unknown
0.2	**Shaina**	Hebrew beautiful
0.1	**Shakeria**	newly-created African-American name
0.2	**Shakira**	newly-created African-American name
0.1	**Shameka**	newly-created African-American name
0.2	**Shana**	Hebrew God is gracious
0.1	**Shanaya**	origin unknown
0.1	**Shanelle**	English channel

0.5	**Shania**	origin unknown
0.3	**Shanice**	newly-created African-American name
0.1	**Shanika**	newly-created African-American name
0.2	**Shaniqua**	newly-created African-American name
0.2	**Shanna**	Hebrew God is gracious
2.5	**Shannon**	Irish small; wise
0.1	**Shanny**	origin unknown
0.1	**Shante**	French a song
0.2	**Shantel**	French a song (Chantel)
0.1	**Shantell**	French a song (Chantel)
0.1	**Shantelle**	French a song (Chantel)
0.2	**Shanteria**	origin unknown
0.1	**Shany**	Swahili marvellous
0.4	**Sharon**	Hebrew a plain
0.2	**Shauna**	Hebrew God is gracious
0.1	**Shaunya**	Hebrew God is gracious
0.4	**Shawna**	Hebrew God is gracious
0.1	**Shay**	Hebrew asked for
0.4	**Shayla**	Irish from the fairy fort
0.2	**Shaylee**	origin unknown, possibly an invented name
0.1	**Shaylene**	origin unknown
0.3	**Shayna**	Hebrew beautiful
0.2	**Shea**	Hebrew asked for
0.1	**Sheena**	Irish form of Jane: Hebrew gracious, merciful
0.2	**Sheila**	Irish form of Cecilia: Latin blind
0.2	**Shelbi**	English from the ledge estate
0.1	**Shelbie**	English from the ledge estate
3.4	**Shelby**	English from the ledge estate
0.1	**Shelley**	English from the meadow on the ledge
0.1	**Shelly**	English from the meadow on the ledge
0.1	**Sheridan**	last name used as first name, English descendant of Siridean
0.1	**Sherry**	French beloved
0.2	**Shirley**	English from the bright meadow
0.1	**Shyann**	American Indian tribal name
0.2	**Shyanne**	American Indian tribal name
0.1	**Shyla**	Irish form of Cecilia: Latin blind (Sheila)
0.4	**Sidney**	French from the city of St. Denis
0.1	**Sienna**	origin unknown
2.4	**Sierra**	place name; Irish black
0.3	**Silvia**	Latin forest
0.3	**Simone**	Hebrew one who hears
0.1	**Simran**	Sikh one who is absorbed in God
0.1	**Siobhan**	Irish form of Joan: Hebrew gracious, merciful
0.2	**Skye**	Arabic water giver; Scottish surname
0.3	**Skylar**	Dutch a shelter
0.2	**Skyler**	Dutch a shelter
0.3	**Sofia**	Greek wisdom
0.1	**Sommer**	English summer; summoner; Arabic black
0.5	**Sonia**	Slavic and Russian form of Sophia: Greek wisdom
0.1	**Sonja**	Slavic and Russian form of Sophia: Greek wisdom
0.2	**Sonya**	Slavic and Russian form of Sophia: Greek wisdom
0.9	**Sophia**	Greek wisdom
0.6	**Sophie**	Greek wisdom
0.5	**Stacey**	Irish form of Anastasia: Greek resurrection
0.1	**Staci**	Irish form of Anastasia: Greek resurrection
0.1	**Stacie**	Irish form of Anastasia: Greek resurrection
0.4	**Stacy**	Irish form of Anastasia: Greek resurrection
0.1	**Stefani**	Greek crown
0.3	**Stefanie**	Greek crown
0.1	**Stella**	Latin star
8.1	**Stephanie**	Greek crown

0.3	**Stephany**	Greek crown
0.2	**Stevie**	Greek crown
0.1	**Stormie**	Old English impetuous by nature
0.1	**Stormy**	Old English impetuous by nature
0.1	**Sukhdeep**	Sikh the lamp of peace and bliss
0.2	**Sumaya**	origin unknown
1.0	**Summer**	English summer
0.5	**Susan**	Hebrew a rose, a lily
0.4	**Susana**	Hebrew a rose, a lily
0.1	**Susanna**	Hebrew a rose, a lily
0.1	**Suzanna**	Hebrew a rose, a lily
0.2	**Suzanne**	Hebrew a rose, a lily
0.1	**Sydnee**	French from the city of St. Denis
3.0	**Sydney**	French from the city of St. Denis
0.1	**Sydni**	French from the city of St. Denis
0.1	**Sydnie**	French from the city of St. Denis
0.3	**Sylvia**	Latin forest
0.3	**Sylvianne**	Sylvia + Anne
0.1	**Symone**	Hebrew one who hears

-T-

0.2	**T**	initial used as a first name
0.1	**T'keyah**	newly-created African-American name
0.2	**Tabatha**	Greek, Aramaic a gazelle
0.6	**Tabitha**	Greek, Aramaic a gazelle
0.3	**Talia**	Hebrew dew Greek blooming
0.6	**Tamara**	Hebrew palm tree
0.1	**Tamera**	Hebrew palm tree
0.1	**Tamika**	origin unknown
0.2	**Tammy**	Hebrew perfection
0.1	**Tanesha**	Hausa Monday
0.5	**Tania**	Slavic fairy queen

0.1	**Tanis**	form of Tanya: Slavic fairy queen
0.3	**Tanisha**	Hausa Monday
0.5	**Tanya**	Slavic fairy queen
1.0	**Tara**	Arabic a measurement Aramaic to throw, carry
0.4	**Taryn**	Arabic a measurement; Aramaic to throw, carry
0.3	**Tasha**	form of Natasha: Latin to be born
0.6	**Tatiana**	Slavic fairy queen
0.1	**Tatianna**	Slavic fairy queen
0.1	**Tatum**	Anglo Saxon cheerful
0.2	**Tatyana**	Slavic fairy queen
0.1	**Tayla**	origin unknown
0.4	**Tayler**	origin unknown
9.9	**Taylor**	English tailor
0.1	**Teagan**	origin unknown
0.1	**Tegan**	Welsh beautiful and fair
0.1	**Tenisha**	Hausa Monday
0.6	**Teresa**	Greek to reap
0.1	**Teri**	Greek to reap
0.1	**Terra**	Arabic a measurement Aramaic to throw, carry
0.1	**Terri**	Greek to reap
0.6	**Tersea**	Greek to reap
0.3	**Tess**	Greek to reap
0.6	**Tessa**	Greek to reap
0.2	**Thalia**	Greek bloom, muse of comedy
0.5	**Theresa**	Greek to reap
0.2	**Thi**	Vietnamese poem
0.5	**Tia**	Greek princess
0.5	**Tiana**	Greek princess
0.3	**Tianna**	Greek princess
0.5	**Tiara**	Latin crown
0.1	**Tiarra**	Latin crown
0.1	**Tichina**	newly-created African-American name
0.1	**Tiera**	Latin crown
0.4	**Tierra**	Latin crown
0.3	**Tiffani**	Latin trinity
0.1	**Tiffanie**	Latin trinity

3.4	**Tiffany**	Latin trinity
0.4	**Tina**	short form of names ending in tina
0.4	**Toni**	form of Antoinette: Latin priceless
0.1	**Tonya**	Slavic fairy queen
0.9	**Tori**	Japanese bird
0.1	**Tory**	Japanese bird
0.1	**Tracey**	Latin brave
0.1	**Traci**	Latin brave
0.3	**Tracy**	Latin brave
0.1	**Tricia**	form of Patricia: Latin of noble descent
0.1	**Trina**	nickname for Katherine: Greek pure, unsullied
0.2	**Trinity**	Latin three in one
0.2	**Trisha**	form of Patricia: Latin of noble descent
0.1	**Trista**	Latin melancholy
0.2	**Tristan**	Latin melancholy
0.1	**Tristen**	Latin melancholy
0.5	**Trycia**	form of Patricia: Latin of noble descent
0.1	**Tyeisha**	origin unknown
0.2	**Tyesha**	origin unknown
0.5	**Tyler**	occupational surname
0.2	**Tyra**	origin unknown

-U-

0.1	**Unique**	origin unknown

-V-

0.2	**V**	initial used as a first name
0.1	**Valentina**	Latin strong and healthy
0.5	**Valeria**	Latin to be strong
1.4	**Valerie**	Latin to be strong
0.2	**Vanesa**	Greek butterfly
3.9	**Vanessa**	Greek butterfly
0.1	**Vasiliki**	origin unknown
1.6	**Veronica**	Latin true image
0.7	**Veronique**	Latin true image

0.1	**Vianey**	origin unknown
0.3	**Vicky**	Latin victorious
6.1	**Victoria**	Latin victorious
0.1	**Violet**	Old French little purple flower
0.4	**Virginia**	Latin pure, virgin
3.7	**Virginie**	Latin pure, virgin
0.2	**Viridiana**	Italian belonging to the third order of St. Francis — known for penitence and miracles
0.6	**Vivian**	Latin alive
0.4	**Viviana**	Latin alive
0.1	**Viviane**	Latin alive

-W-

0.7	**Wendy**	form of Gwendolyn: Welsh white
0.1	**Whitley**	origin unknown
1.4	**Whitney**	English from the white island

-X-

0.1	**Xiomara**	Teutonic glory of forest
0.1	**Xochitl**	Aztec where flowers abound

-Y-

0.3	**Yadira**	newly-created African-American name
0.1	**Yajaira**	origin unknown
0.1	**Yanira**	origin unknown
0.2	**Yaritza**	newly-created African-American name
0.1	**Yasmeen**	Persian jasmine
0.3	**Yasmin**	Persian jasmine
0.2	**Yasmine**	Persian jasmine
0.2	**Yazmin**	Persian jasmine
1.3	**Yesenia**	Arabic flower
0.1	**Yesica**	origin unknown

0.3	**Yessenia**	newly-created African-American name
0.1	**Yessica**	origin unknown
0.1	**Yoana**	newly-created African-American name
0.3	**Yolanda**	Greek violet flower
0.1	**Yoselin**	origin unknown
0.4	**Yvette**	French archer (Yvonne)
0.3	**Yvonne**	French archer

-Z-

0.1	**Zaira**	Arabic flower
0.1	**Zana**	English modern coinage, a short form of Suzanna
0.1	**Zeinab**	origin unknown
0.1	**Zhane**	origin unknown
0.9	**Zoe**	Greek life
0.1	**Zoey**	Greek life

🅰🅱 Popular Boys Names

Rating · Name · Origin and meaning

-A-

Rating	Name	Origin and meaning
0.1	**A**	initial used as a first name
6.2	**Aaron**	Hebrew to sing, to shine, to teach or a mountain, enlightened; Arabic a messenger
0.1	**Abdirahman**	Arabic God the merciful
0.1	**Abdullahi**	Arabic servant of God
0.3	**Abel**	Hebrew breath, evanescence
0.6	**Abraham**	Hebrew father of the multitude
0.1	**Abram**	Hebrew exalted father
5.5	**Adam**	Hebrew earth, man of the red earth; Phoenician man, mankind
0.2	**Adan**	Irish warmth of the home
0.2	**Addison**	Old English son of Adam
0.2	**Adolfo**	Spanish variant of Germanic Adolf, noble wolf or noble hero
2.1	**Adrian**	Greek rich; Latin black, dark
0.1	**Adrien**	French Adrian
0.2	**Agustin**	Latin majestic, dignified
0.2	**Ahmad**	Arabic the most praised
0.2	**Ahmed**	Arabic most highly praised
0.5	**Aidan**	Irish warmth of the home
0.1	**Aiden**	Irish warmth of the home
0.1	**Akeem**	Hebrew God will establish
0.1	**Alain**	Celtic harmony, peace
1.1	**Alan**	Celtic harmony, peace
0.7	**Albert**	French noble, bright
0.8	**Alberto**	French noble, bright
0.1	**Aldo**	Italian rich
1.5	**Alec**	Greek helper of mankind, protector of man
2.2	**Alejandro**	Greek helper of mankind, protector of man
0.1	**Aleksandar**	Greek helper of mankind, protector of man
0.1	**Alessandro**	Greek helper of mankind, protector of man
3.8	**Alex**	Greek helper of mankind, protector of man
10.3	**Alexander**	Greek helper of mankind, protector of man
1.7	**Alexandre**	Greek helper of mankind, protector of man
0.1	**Alexandro**	Greek helper of mankind, protector of man
0.9	**Alexis**	Greek helper of mankind, protector of man
0.3	**Alfonso**	Italian and Spanish form of Old German noble and eager

0.2	**Alfred**	Old English elfin counsellor
0.7	**Alfredo**	Old English elfin counsellor
0.4	**Ali**	Arabic greatest
0.3	**Allan**	Celtic harmony, peace
0.7	**Allen**	Celtic harmony, peace
0.1	**Alonso**	Spanish form of Old German noble and eager
0.2	**Alonzo**	Spanish form of Old German noble and eager
0.1	**Alton**	English from the old town
0.3	**Alvaro**	Latin fair
0.3	**Alvin**	German beloved by all
0.1	**Amandeep**	Punjabi light or lamp of peace
0.1	**Amir**	Arabic prince; Punjabi wealthy; king's minister
0.2	**Amrit**	Indian nectar
0.1	**Anderson**	origin unknown
1.0	**Andre**	Greek manly, valiant, courageous, strong
0.2	**Andre'**	Greek manly, valiant, courageous, strong
0.1	**Andreas**	Greek manly, valiant, courageous, strong
1.2	**Andres**	Greek manly, valiant, courageous, strong
12.5	**Andrew**	Greek manly, valiant, courageous, strong
0.7	**Andy**	Greek manly, valiant, courageous, strong
0.1	**Anfernee**	African-American original
2.1	**Angel**	Italian messenger
0.3	**Angelo**	Greek angel, a messenger or a saintly person
0.1	**Angus**	Gaelic very strong
0.1	**Anmol**	origin unknown
10.0	**Anthony**	Greek flourishing; Latin worthy of praise
0.1	**Antione**	origin unknown
0.6	**Antoine**	Greek flourishing; Latin worthy of praise
0.2	**Anton**	Greek flourishing; Latin worthy of praise
2.1	**Antonio**	Greek flourishing; Latin worthy of praise
0.1	**Antony**	Greek flourishing; Latin worthy of praise
0.1	**Antwan**	Arabic form of Anthony: flourishing; worthy of praise
0.1	**Ari**	Hebrew lion of God
0.1	**Aric**	Old English ruler
0.2	**Ariel**	Hebrew lion of God
0.1	**Arjun**	Indian one of the Pandavas
0.8	**Armando**	Old German army man
0.1	**Armani**	origin unknown
0.3	**Arnaud**	French form of Arnold, strong as an eagle, eagle ruler
0.1	**Arnold**	German strong as an eagle, eagle ruler
0.1	**Arnulfo**	Spanish variant of Germanic, wolf eagle
0.1	**Aron**	Hebrew to sing, to shine, to teach or a mountain, enlightened; Arabic a messenger
0.1	**Arron**	Hebrew to sing, to shine, to teach or a mountain, enlightened; Arabic a messenger
0.1	**Arshdeep**	origin unknown
0.6	**Arthur**	Gaelic a rock, noble, lofty, hill
0.7	**Arturo**	Spanish and Italian form of Gaelic a rock, noble, lofty, hill
0.1	**Asa**	Biblical one of the early kings of Judah; Hebrew doctor, healer
0.4	**Ashton**	Old English one who lives at the ash-tree farm
0.1	**Aubrey**	Old French ruler of the elves
0.1	**August**	Latin exalted and sacred
0.2	**Austen**	Latin exalted and sacred

11.0	**Austin**	Latin majestic, dignity; form of August
0.1	**Auston**	Latin majestic, dignity; form of August
0.1	**Austyn**	Latin majestic, dignity; form of August
0.5	**Avery**	Old English leader of the elves
0.1	**Axel**	Hebrew father of peace

-B-

0.9	**B**	initial used as a first name
0.2	**B.**	initial used as a first name
0.3	**Bailey**	English fortification; English/French public official, person in charge
0.1	**Balraj**	Hindi strongest
0.1	**Barry**	Welsh form of Harry, son of Harry; Irish spear-like, pointed
0.7	**Bastien**	Greek venerable
0.3	**Beau**	English handsome
0.2	**Ben**	Hebrew son of my right hand
0.1	**Benito**	Latin blessed
6.1	**Benjamin**	Hebrew son of my right hand
0.1	**Bennett**	Latin little blessed one
0.1	**Benny**	Hebrew son of my right hand
0.7	**Benoit**	English yellow-flowered plant of the rose family
0.2	**Bernard**	Greek brave bear
0.1	**Bernardo**	Spanish variant of German Bernald governing, ordering
0.1	**Bilal**	Arabic chosen
0.5	**Billy**	English resolute protector
0.2	**Blaine**	Irish thin, lean
0.1	**Blair**	Celtic a place
2.3	**Blake**	English white
0.1	**Bo**	Gaelic soft, marshy ground
0.5	**Bobby**	German bright fame
0.2	**Brad**	English from the broad river crossing

0.5	**Braden**	English a broad lea, a meadow
0.1	**Bradford**	Old English dweller on the broad meadow
2.4	**Bradley**	English a broad lea, a meadow; English from the broad river crossing
0.1	**Bradly**	English a broad lea, a meadow; English from the broad river crossing
0.8	**Brady**	English broad island
0.1	**Braedan**	English a broad lea, a meadow
0.2	**Braeden**	English a broad lea, a meadow
0.1	**Braedon**	English a broad lea, a meadow
0.1	**Braiden**	English a broad lea, a meadow
0.1	**Brandan**	Irish a raven; English a sword
0.5	**Branden**	Irish a raven; English a sword
13.6	**Brandon**	Irish a raven; English a sword
0.1	**Brandyn**	Irish a raven; English a sword
0.1	**Brantley**	English proud
0.1	**Braulio**	Spanish variant of German sword
0.3	**Braxton**	Anglo Saxon Brock's town
0.1	**Brayan**	Celtic strong; Irish strength, virtue
0.4	**Brayden**	English a broad lea, a meadow
0.2	**Braydon**	English a broad lea, a meadow
1.6	**Brendan**	Irish a raven; English a sword
0.4	**Brenden**	Irish a raven; English a sword
0.3	**Brendon**	Irish a raven; English a sword

0.5	**Brennan**	Irish a raven; English a sword
0.1	**Brennen**	Irish a raven; English a sword
0.8	**Brent**	Irish a raven; English a sword
0.1	**Brenton**	Irish a raven; English a sword
0.1	**Breon**	origin unknown
0.2	**Bret**	Celtic a Breton, a native of Brittany
1.9	**Brett**	Celtic a Breton, a native of Brittany
5.1	**Brian**	Celtic strong; Irish strength, virtue
0.2	**Brice**	Welsh form of Price, son of the ardent one; English son of Rice
0.2	**Bridger**	English lives at the bridge
0.5	**Brock**	Gaelic a badger
0.1	**Brodie**	Irish ditch
0.3	**Brody**	Irish ditch
0.1	**Bronson**	Old English son of the dark-skinned one
0.1	**Brooks**	Old English from the brook
0.4	**Bruce**	English from the brushwood thicket
0.1	**Bruno**	Old English with a dark complexion
2.7	**Bryan**	Celtic strong; Irish strength, virtue
0.8	**Bryant**	Celtic strong; Irish strength, virtue
1.2	**Bryce**	English son of Rice; Welsh form of Price, son of the ardent one
0.1	**Bryden**	origin unknown
0.1	**Brydon**	origin unknown
0.3	**Bryson**	Welsh son of Bryce
0.1	**Bryton**	newly-created African-American name
0.3	**Byron**	Old French from the cottage

-C-

0.2	**C**	initial used as a first name
0.2	**C.**	initial used as a first name
0.2	**Cade**	Irish spirit of battle
0.1	**Caden**	origin unknown
2.7	**Caleb**	Hebrew a dog, faithful, bold one
0.1	**Callum**	Scottish Gaelic form of Latin dove
0.1	**Calum**	Scottish Gaelic form of Latin dove
0.9	**Calvin**	Latin bald
0.1	**Camden**	Old English dweller in the winding valley
3.8	**Cameron**	Celtic bent nose
0.2	**Camille**	Latin child of free and noble birth
0.1	**Camron**	Celtic bent nose
0.7	**Carl**	English manly, strong; German farmer
0.1	**Carlo**	English manly, strong; German farmer
2.8	**Carlos**	English manly, strong; German farmer
0.2	**Carlton**	Old English from the town of the farmer
0.5	**Carson**	English son of the family on the marsh
0.4	**Carter**	Old English cart driver
1.2	**Casey**	Celtic valorous; Irish brave
0.1	**Cecil**	Latin blind
0.5	**Cedric**	Old English chieftain
0.2	**Cedrick**	Old English chieftain
0.1	**Cedrik**	Old English chieftain
1.1	**Cesar**	Latin long-haired
1.3	**Chad**	Celtic battle or warrior; English warlike
0.1	**Chadwick**	Celtic battle or warrior; English warlike
0.6	**Chance**	Old English secretary to the throne
0.6	**Chandler**	Old English candlemaker

3.7	**Charles**	English manly, strong; German farmer
0.4	**Charles Alexander**	Charles + Alexander
1.2	**Charles Antoine**	Charles + Antoine
0.5	**Charles Eric**	Charles + Eric
0.6	**Charles Etien**	Charles + Etien
0.4	**Charles Olivier**	Charles + Olivier
0.2	**Charlie**	English manly, strong; German farmer
1.7	**Chase**	English the hunt, hunter
0.1	**Chauncey**	Middle English chancellor church official
0.2	**Chaz**	English manly, strong; German farmer
0.1	**Chi**	origin unknown
0.2	**Chris**	Greek Christ-bearer
6.0	**Christian**	Greek Christ-bearer
0.6	**Christophe**	Greek Christ-bearer
15.3	**Christopher**	Greek Christ-bearer
0.1	**Chun**	Chinese spring
0.2	**Clarence**	Latin famous
0.2	**Clark**	French scholar
0.1	**Claude**	Latin lame
0.1	**Claudio**	Latin lame
0.3	**Clay**	English a town built upon clay land
1.1	**Clayton**	English a town built upon clay land
0.2	**Clifford**	English a crossing near the cliff
0.1	**Clifton**	English from the town near the cliffs
0.2	**Clint**	English a town on a hill, from the headland form
0.3	**Clinton**	English a town on a hill, from the headland form
0.1	**Codey**	English a cushion
0.1	**Codie**	English a cushion
7.5	**Cody**	English a cushion
0.7	**Colby**	Old English from the black farm
1.9	**Cole**	English cola miner; Latin a man who farms cabbage
0.2	**Coleman**	English cola miner; Latin a man who farms cabbage
1.5	**Colin**	Irish child; Celtic a cub, whelp; short form of Nicholas: victory
1.0	**Collin**	Irish child; Celtic a cub, whelp; short form of Nicholas: victory
0.1	**Colt**	Old English from the dark town
0.2	**Colten**	Old English from the dark town
0.1	**Colter**	Old English from the dark town
1.5	**Colton**	Old English from the dark town
0.7	**Conner**	Irish wise aid
3.5	**Connor**	Irish wise aid
0.5	**Conor**	Irish wise aid
0.2	**Conrad**	German bold, wise, counsellor
0.3	**Cooper**	Old English barrel maker
0.3	**Corbin**	Latin the raven
0.1	**Cordell**	Old French ropemaker
2.1	**Corey**	Latin a helmet, from the hollow
0.1	**Cornelius**	Latin horn
0.3	**Cortez**	Spanish place name or surname used as a first name
1.4	**Cory**	Latin a helmet, from the hollow
0.1	**Coty**	English a cushion
0.1	**Courtney**	Old English dweller in the court
0.7	**Craig**	Celtic from the crag or rugged rocky mass
1.6	**Cristian**	Greek Christ-bearer
0.1	**Cristobal**	Greek Christ-bearer
0.1	**Cristopher**	Greek Christ-bearer
0.1	**Cruz**	Latin crux — a symbol of Christ
0.1	**Cullen**	Gaelic handsome

| 1.1 | **Curtis** | Latin an enclosure, court; English courteous |
| 0.1 | **Cyrus** | Persian sun |

-D-

0.3	**D**	initial used as a first name
0.1	**D Andre**	newly-created African-American name
0.1	**D'andre**	newly-created African-American name
0.1	**Da'quan**	newly-created African-American name
2.6	**Dakota**	American Indian tribal name
0.1	**Dakotah**	American Indian tribal name
0.3	**Dale**	English a hollow, a small valley
0.7	**Dallas**	Old English from the waterfall
0.1	**Dallen**	Anglo Saxon from the dale
0.2	**Dallin**	Anglo Saxon from the dale
0.2	**Dallyn**	Anglo Saxon from the dale
1.9	**Dalton**	Old English dweller in the town in the valley
0.1	**Damarcus**	origin unknown
0.7	**Damian**	Greek divine power or fate
0.4	**Damien**	Greek divine power or fate
0.2	**Damion**	Greek divine power or fate
0.4	**Damon**	Greek tamer
0.1	**Dan**	Hebrew God is my judge
0.1	**Dana**	Scottish from Denmark
0.3	**Dane**	Norse inhabitant of Denmark
0.4	**Danick**	origin unknown
13.6	**Daniel**	Hebrew God is my judge
0.1	**Danik**	origin unknown
0.3	**Dannick**	origin unknown
0.8	**Danny**	Hebrew God is my judge
0.3	**Dante**	Latin enduring
0.1	**Dante'**	Italian to endure
0.1	**Dantrell**	newly-created African-American name
0.2	**Dany**	Hebrew God is my judge

0.2	**Daquan**	newly-created African-American name
0.1	**Darcy**	Irish dark; English of the Arsy (Oise River)
0.3	**Darian**	Anglo-Saxon dear, darling; Persian wealthy, king
0.2	**Darien**	Anglo-Saxon dear, darling; Persian wealthy, king
0.1	**Darin**	English a small, rocky hill
0.1	**Dario**	Anglo-Saxon dear, darling; Persian wealthy, king
0.2	**Darion**	Anglo-Saxon dear, darling; Persian wealthy, king
0.9	**Darius**	Greek wealthy
0.2	**Darnell**	Old English from the hidden niche
0.3	**Darrell**	English beloved; English a grove of oak trees
0.7	**Darren**	English a small, rocky hill
0.1	**Darrien**	Anglo-Saxon dear, darling; Persian wealthy, king
0.1	**Darrin**	English a small, rocky hill
0.1	**Darrion**	Anglo-Saxon dear, darling; Persian wealthy, king
0.2	**Darrius**	Greek wealthy
0.3	**Darryl**	English beloved; English a grove of oak trees
0.2	**Daryl**	English beloved; English a grove of oak trees
0.1	**Dashawn**	origin unknown
0.2	**Dave**	Hebrew beloved
11.8	**David**	Hebrew beloved
0.1	**David Alexander**	David + Alexander
0.1	**Davin**	Scandinavian brilliance of the Finns
0.1	**Davion**	origin unknown
0.3	**Davis**	Old Scottish son of the beloved
0.2	**Davon**	Scandinavian brilliance of the Finns
0.1	**Davonte**	origin unknown
0.1	**Dawson**	son of David

0.1	**Dayton**	Middle English day town; bright cheerful town
0.1	**De**	origin unknown
0.1	**De'andre**	prefix De + Andre
0.4	**Dean**	English head, leader; English from the valley
0.4	**Deandre**	prefix De + Andre
0.1	**Deandre'**	prefix De + Andre
0.1	**Deangelo**	prefix De + Angelo
0.1	**Dedrick**	newly-created African-American name
0.2	**Deion**	Greek god of wine
0.1	**Demarco**	prefix De + Marco
0.2	**Demarcus**	prefix De + Marcus
0.5	**Demetrius**	Greek belonging to Demeter, the Greek god of fertility
0.1	**Demond**	newly-created African-American name
0.1	**Denis**	English from Latin and Greek, wild, frenzied
0.9	**Dennis**	English from Latin and Greek, wild, frenzied
0.1	**Denver**	Old English from the edge of the valley
0.3	**Denzel**	English from a Cornish place name
0.2	**Deon**	Greek god of wine
0.1	**Deondre**	newly-created African-American name
0.2	**Deonte**	newly-created African-American name
0.1	**Deonte'**	newly-created African-American name
0.1	**Dequan**	newly-created African-American name
2.5	**Derek**	English from German Hrodrich, famous ruler
0.2	**Derick**	English from German Hrodrich, famous ruler
1.0	**Derrick**	English from German Hrodrich, famous ruler
0.3	**Deshawn**	prefix De + Shawn
0.3	**Desmond**	Old English kindly protector

0.1	**Destin**	origin unknown
0.3	**Devan**	Irish poet; English place name
0.3	**Devante**	newly-created African-American name
0.2	**Devante'**	newly-created African-American name
0.2	**Deven**	Irish poet; English place name
2.7	**Devin**	Irish poet; English place name
1.6	**Devon**	Irish poet; English place name
0.1	**Devonta**	newly-created African-American name
0.4	**Devonte**	newly-created African-American name
0.2	**Devonte'**	newly-created African-American name
0.1	**Devyn**	Irish poet; English place name
0.1	**Dewayne**	prefix De + Wayne
0.2	**Dexter**	Latin dexterous
0.1	**Dickson**	English Dick's son
0.1	**Didier**	French longing
0.7	**Diego**	Spanish form of James: held by the heel, supplanter
0.1	**Dillan**	Irish faithful
0.1	**Dillion**	Irish faithful
1.5	**Dillon**	Irish faithful
0.1	**Dimitri**	Greek belonging to Demeter, the Greek god of fertility
0.2	**Dion**	Greek god of wine
0.1	**Domenic**	Latin belonging to or pertaining to God
1.4	**Dominic**	Latin belonging to or pertaining to God
0.4	**Dominick**	Latin belonging to or pertaining to God
0.5	**Dominique**	Latin belonging to or pertaining to God
0.1	**Don**	Irish brown stranger, world ruler

1.1	**Donald**	Irish brown stranger, world ruler
0.1	**Donavan**	Irish dark warrior
0.1	**Donnell**	Celtic brave black man
0.1	**Donnie**	Irish brown stranger, world ruler
0.5	**Donovan**	Irish dark warrior
0.1	**Dontavious**	origin unknown
0.1	**Dontavius**	origin unknown
0.1	**Donte**	Latin enduring
0.1	**Donte'**	Latin enduring
0.1	**Dontrell**	newly-created African-American name
0.2	**Dorian**	Celtic stranger
0.9	**Douglas**	Celtic gray; Scottish from the dark water
0.4	**Drake**	Latin dragon
0.1	**Draven**	origin unknown
1.0	**Drew**	English sturdy; Welsh wise, short form of Andrew
0.1	**Dryden**	Welsh last name, broken nose
0.1	**Duane**	Irish little and dark
0.3	**Duncan**	Scottish dark-skinned warrior
2.6	**Dustin**	English brown, stone, the brown rock quarry
0.1	**Dusty**	English brown, stone, the brown rock quarry
0.1	**Dustyn**	English brown, stone, the brown rock quarry
0.3	**Dwayne**	Irish little and dark
0.2	**Dwight**	English modern form of De Witt, which is Flemish blond
6.0	**Dylan**	Welsh the sea
0.1	**Dylon**	Welsh the sea

-E-

0.1	**E**	initial used as a first name
0.2	**Earl**	English nobleman
0.5	**Eddie**	English happy guardian
0.1	**Eddy**	English happy guardian

1.5	**Edgar**	Old English prosperous spearman
0.1	**Edgardo**	Anglo-Saxon spear or javelin
0.1	**Edmund**	Old English prosperous protector
0.3	**Edouard**	English happy guardian
2.1	**Eduardo**	English happy guardian
1.9	**Edward**	English happy guardian
0.9	**Edwin**	English rich friend
0.3	**Efrain**	Hebrew fruitful
0.1	**Efren**	Hebrew fruitful
0.4	**Eli**	Hebrew on, up, high
0.5	**Elias**	German and Dutch form of Elijah: Hebrew Jehovah is God
0.1	**Elie**	Hebrew on, up, high
1.3	**Elijah**	Hebrew Jehovah is God
0.1	**Eliseo**	Hebrew God is my health or salvation
0.1	**Elisha**	Hebrew God is salvation
0.3	**Elliot**	English modern form of Elijah
0.2	**Elliott**	English modern form of Elijah
0.1	**Ellis**	Hebrew God is my salvation
0.1	**Elmer**	Old English of famed dignity
0.1	**Elvis**	Old Norse all wise
0.4	**Emanuel**	Hebrew God is with us
0.1	**Emerson**	Old English son of the industrious leader
0.2	**Emile**	Latin flattering
0.2	**Emilien**	Latin Roman family name, amiable or swollen or industrious
0.3	**Emilio**	Latin flattering
0.7	**Emmanuel**	Hebrew God is with us
0.1	**Emmett**	Old German hardworking and strong
0.1	**Emory**	Old German industrious leader
0.4	**Enrick**	Spanish form of Henry: German ruler of an estate

0.7	**Enrique**	Spanish form of Henry: German ruler of an estate
6.5	**Eric**	Norse honorable ruler
0.1	**Erich**	Norse honorable ruler
0.9	**Erick**	Norse honorable ruler
2.0	**Erik**	Norse honorable ruler
0.1	**Erin**	Gaelic western island
0.2	**Ernest**	English earnest
0.5	**Ernesto**	English earnest
0.1	**Ervin**	Old English lover of the sea
0.4	**Esteban**	Spanish form of Steven: Greek a crown
0.1	**Estevan**	Spanish form of Steven: Greek a crown
1.9	**Ethan**	Hebrew strong, firm
0.7	**Etienne**	French form of Stephen: Greek a crown
0.3	**Eugene**	Greek well-born
2.9	**Evan**	Welsh form of John, young warrior
0.1	**Everardo**	Germanic strong as a wild board
0.2	**Everett**	English strong as a boar
0.1	**Ezekiel**	Hebrew strength of the Lord
0.2	**Ezequiel**	Hebrew strength of the Lord
0.1	**Ezra**	Hebrew strength

-F-

0.5	**Fabian**	Latin bean grower
0.1	**Fabrice**	Latin one who works with hard objects
0.1	**Federico**	Spanish variant of Germanic powerful, peace, rich
0.4	**Felipe**	Greek a lover of horses
0.7	**Felix**	Latin fortunate
1.1	**Felix Antoine**	Felix + Antoine
1.1	**Fernando**	Spanish form of Old German world venturing
0.1	**Fidel**	Latin faithful, loyal
0.1	**Filip**	Greek a lover of horses

0.1	**Floyd**	Welsh gray-haired
0.1	**Forest**	English forest, woodsman
0.5	**Forrest**	English forest, woodsman
0.1	**Francesco**	Latin free man, French man
1.0	**Francis**	Latin free man, French man
1.6	**Francisco**	Latin free man, French man
0.1	**Franco**	Latin free man, French man
0.5	**Francois**	Latin free man, French man
0.3	**Francois Xavier**	Francois + Xavier
1.1	**Frank**	Latin free man, French man
0.2	**Frankie**	Latin free man, French man
0.3	**Franklin**	English free landowner
0.2	**Fraser**	English one who makes charcoal
0.1	**Fred**	German peace, king, ruler
0.1	**Freddie**	German peace, king, ruler
0.3	**Freddy**	German peace, king, ruler
0.5	**Frederic**	German peace, king, ruler
0.5	**Frederick**	German peace, king, ruler
0.5	**Frederik**	German peace, king, ruler
0.2	**Frederique**	German peace, king, ruler
0.2	**Fredrick**	German peace, king, ruler
0.1	**Fredy**	German peace, king, ruler

-G-

0.3	**G**	initial used as a first name
3.8	**Gabriel**	Hebrew God is my strength, devoted to God
0.2	**Gabryel**	Hebrew God is my strength, devoted to God
0.1	**Gael**	name for Celtics of Scotland, Ireland, and the Isle of Man
0.7	**Gage**	origin unknown
0.1	**Galen**	Gaelic bright
0.1	**Garett**	English to watch; with a mighty spear
0.2	**Garret**	English to watch; with a mighty spear
2.3	**Garrett**	English to watch; with a mighty spear
0.1	**Garrison**	Old French a garrison, troops stationed at a fort

0.7	**Gary**	English a spear-bearer, a warrior
0.7	**Gavin**	Welsh little hawk
0.1	**Genaro**	Latin consecrated to God
0.1	**Gene**	Greek well-born
0.3	**Geoffrey**	English gift of peace
0.1	**Geordie**	Hebrew to descend
1.5	**George**	Greek a farmer, a tiller of the soil
0.4	**Gerald**	English a warrior; Latin spear-ruler
0.1	**Gerard**	Old English brave with a spear
0.8	**Gerardo**	Old English brave with a spear
0.2	**German**	Old German warrior
0.2	**Ghislain**	Old French pledge
0.1	**Giancarlo**	Italian form of John + Charles
0.3	**Gilbert**	Old English a man famed for his promise
0.3	**Gilberto**	Spanish form of Gilbert: a man famed for his promise
0.1	**Gino**	Italian form of John: Jehovah has been gracious
0.6	**Giovanni**	Italian form of John: Jehovah has been gracious
0.1	**Giovanny**	Italian form of John: Jehovah has been gracious
0.1	**Giuseppe**	Italian form of Joseph
0.2	**Glen**	Celtic a glen, a dale, a secluded woody valley
0.2	**Glenn**	Celtic a glen, a dale, a secluded woody valley
0.1	**Gonzalo**	Germanic fight, combat
0.2	**Gordon**	English hill of the plains
0.1	**Grady**	Gaelic famous
0.2	**Graeme**	Latin a grain; English the gray home
0.4	**Graham**	Latin a grain; English the gray home
1.2	**Grant**	English to give, to assure; English great

0.2	**Grayson**	Old English son of the local bailiff
0.1	**Gregorio**	Greek vigilant; Latin watchman, watchful
2.2	**Gregory**	Greek vigilant; Latin watchman, watchful
0.3	**Griffin**	mythological animal with body of a lion and head and wings of an eagle
0.2	**Guadalupe**	Arabic valley of the wolf
1.8	**Guillaume**	French form of William: resolute protector
0.5	**Guillermo**	Spanish form of William: English resolute protector
0.1	**Gunnar**	Norse battle army
0.1	**Gurjot**	origin unknown
0.1	**Gurpreet**	Punjabi devoted to guru or prophet
0.1	**Gurvir**	Sikh warrior of the guru
0.6	**Gustavo**	Old Norse staff of the Goths
0.1	**Guy**	English a guide; Hebrew valley

-H-

0.1	**Hakeem**	Ethiopian doctor
0.1	**Hans**	Scandinavian form of John: Hebrew Jehovah has been gracious
0.1	**Hardeep**	Punjabi loves God, devoted to God
0.4	**Harley**	Old English from the meadow of the hare
0.2	**Harold**	Scottish army-ruler; English soldier, short form of Harold
0.1	**Harpreet**	Punjabi loves God, devoted to God
0.7	**Harrison**	English Harry's son; Old English son of the army man
0.2	**Harry**	Scottish army-ruler; English soldier, short form of Harold
0.1	**Harvey**	Old French worthy of battle
0.1	**Harvir**	Sikh warrior of God

0.1	**Hassan**	Arabic handsome
0.9	**Hayden**	Old English from the hedged hill
0.1	**Heath**	English from the heath
1.1	**Hector**	Greek steadfast
1.2	**Henry**	German ruler of an estate
0.1	**Herbert**	Old German glorious soldier
0.2	**Heriberto**	Spanish form of Herbert: glorious soldier
0.1	**Herman**	Old German warrior
0.1	**Hernan**	Germanic to make peace
0.2	**Holden**	Old English a valley
0.1	**Houston**	Anglo Saxon the house in the town
0.2	**Howard**	English watchman
0.5	**Hugo**	German and Dutch form of Hugh: intelligence
0.3	**Humberto**	Old German very brilliant
2.5	**Hunter**	Old English a huntsman
0.1	**Hyrum**	Biblical name borne by a king of Tyre

-I-

2.5	**Ian**	Scottish form of John
0.1	**Ibrahim**	Arabic form of Abraham: Hebrew father of the multitude
0.2	**Ignacio**	Latin ardent, flaming
0.2	**Irvin**	Old Welsh from the white river; also Old English friend of the sea
0.1	**Irving**	Old Welsh from the white river; also Old English friend of the sea
1.7	**Isaac**	Hebrew he will laugh
0.1	**Isai**	Hebrew God's grace
1.0	**Isaiah**	Hebrew God is my salvation
0.2	**Isaias**	Hebrew salvation of the Lord
0.1	**Isiah**	origin unknown
0.1	**Isidro**	Greek gift of Isis
0.4	**Ismael**	Hebrew God will laugh
0.5	**Israel**	Hebrew soldier of the Lord

0.1	**Issac**	Hebrew he will laugh
1.2	**Ivan**	Russian form of John, grace

-J-

0.2	**J**	initial used as a first name
0.1	**Jabari**	newly-created African-American name
0.2	**Jace**	invented name, possibly from initials J and C
1.4	**Jack**	short form of Jacob; nickname for John
0.1	**Jackie**	short form of Jacob; nickname for John
1.0	**Jackson**	Old English son of Jack
13.8	**Jacob**	Hebrew one who holds back another, supplanter
0.1	**Jacoby**	Hebrew one who holds back another, supplanter
0.1	**Jacques**	French form of Jacob: one who holds back another, supplanter
0.1	**Jade**	Spanish jade, a precious stone
0.2	**Jaden**	newly-created African-American name
0.1	**Jaiden**	newly-created African-American name
0.8	**Jaime**	Spanish form of James
0.2	**Jairo**	Hebrew he enlightens
1.9	**Jake**	Hebrew one who holds back another, supplanter
0.3	**Jakob**	Hebrew one who holds back another, supplanter
0.1	**Jaleel**	Arabic majestic
0.7	**Jalen**	origin unknown
0.1	**Jamaal**	Arabic a camel, beauty
0.5	**Jamal**	Arabic a camel, beauty
0.1	**Jamar**	probably a combination of prefix Ja- and suffix -mar
0.1	**Jamarcus**	newly-created African-American name
0.1	**Jamel**	Arabic a camel, beauty

10.4	**James**	English form of Jacob, held by the heel, supplanter
0.1	**Jameson**	son of James
0.5	**Jamie**	English form of Jacob, held by the heel, supplanter
0.1	**Jamil**	Arabic a camel, beauty
0.1	**Jamison**	son of James
0.2	**Jaquan**	newly-created African-American name
0.1	**Jaquez**	origin unknown
2.6	**Jared**	Hebrew to descend, descendent, one who rules
0.1	**Jarod**	Hebrew to descend, descendent, one who rules
0.1	**Jaron**	Hebrew to sing, cry out
0.2	**Jarred**	Hebrew to descend, descendent, one who rules
0.3	**Jarrett**	Hebrew to descend, descendent, one who rules
0.2	**Jarrod**	Hebrew to descend, descendent, one who rules
0.2	**Jarvis**	Old German keen as a spear
0.1	**Jaskaran**	Sikh one who sings praises to the Lord
0.1	**Jaskarn**	Sikh one who sings praises to the Lord
0.2	**Jasmin**	Persian jasmine
4.6	**Jason**	Greek healer
0.1	**Jasper**	Old French stone
0.1	**Javaris**	origin unknown
1.3	**Javier**	Spanish owner of the new house
0.2	**Javon**	Biblical Javan is son of Japheth
0.1	**Javonte**	origin unknown
0.5	**Jay**	English gaius, a bird in the crow family; English blue jay
0.2	**Jayden**	newly-created African-American name
0.2	**Jaylen**	origin unknown
0.1	**Jaylin**	origin unknown
0.1	**Jaylon**	origin unknown

0.2	**Jayson**	Greek healer
0.2	**Jean**	French form of John: Hebrew Jehovah has been gracious
0.3	**Jean Benoit**	Jean + Benoit
2.3	**Jean Christopher**	Jean + Christopher
0.6	**Jean Daniel**	Jean + Daniel
0.3	**Jean David**	Jean + David
0.4	**Jean Felix**	Jean + Felix
3.0	**Jean Francois**	Jean + Francois
0.2	**Jean Gabriel**	Jean + Gabriel
0.1	**Jean Luc**	Jean + Luc
0.2	**Jean Marc**	Jean + Marc
1.8	**Jean Michel**	Jean + Michel
0.3	**Jean Nicolas**	Jean + Nicolas
0.2	**Jean Pascal**	Jean + Pascal
4.4	**Jean Philippe**	Jean + Philippe
0.2	**Jean Samuel**	Jean + Samuel
2.0	**Jean Sebastien**	Jean + Sebastien
0.6	**Jean Simon**	Jean + Simon
0.1	**Jean-Francois**	Jean + Francois
0.1	**Jean-Philippe**	Jean + Philippe
0.1	**Jedediah**	Hebrew beloved of the Lord
0.2	**Jeff**	English gift of peace
0.1	**Jefferson**	Old English son of Jeffery
0.7	**Jeffery**	English gift of peace
2.9	**Jeffrey**	English gift of peace
0.1	**Jeremi**	Hebrew appointed by Jehovah, God will uplift
1.0	**Jeremiah**	Hebrew appointed by Jehovah, God will uplift
0.5	**Jeremie**	Hebrew appointed by Jehovah, God will uplift
4.1	**Jeremy**	Hebrew appointed by Jehovah, God will uplift
0.3	**Jermaine**	Middle English sprout, a bud
0.4	**Jerome**	English of holy name
0.1	**Jerrell**	form of Gerald: English a warrior; Latin spear-ruler
0.1	**Jerrod**	Hebrew to descend, descendent, one who rules
0.7	**Jerry**	nickname for Jerome or Gerald

0.1	**Jess**	Greek wealthy, a gift, God exists
4.5	**Jesse**	Greek wealthy, a gift, God exists
0.5	**Jessie**	Greek wealthy, a gift, God exists
0.2	**Jessy**	Greek wealthy, a gift, God exists
2.9	**Jesus**	Hebrew God will help
0.1	**Jim**	English form of Jacob, held by the heel, supplanter
0.1	**Jimmie**	English form of Jacob, held by the heel, supplanter
0.9	**Jimmy**	English form of Jacob, held by the heel, supplanter
0.2	**Joaquin**	Hebrew God will establish
0.1	**Jocelyn**	German supplanted, substituted
0.5	**Joe**	Hebrew Jehovah adds
1.9	**Joel**	Hebrew God is willing, Jehovah is the Lord
0.4	**Joey**	Hebrew Jehovah adds
9.8	**John**	Hebrew Jehovah has been gracious
1.1	**Johnathan**	Hebrew Jehovah has been gracious
0.4	**Johnathon**	Hebrew Jehovah has been gracious
0.2	**Johnnie**	Hebrew Jehovah has been gracious
0.9	**Johnny**	Hebrew Jehovah has been gracious
0.4	**Jon**	Hebrew Jehovah has been gracious
0.6	**Jonah**	Hebrew dove
0.1	**Jonas**	Hebrew the doer
0.1	**Jonatan**	Hebrew Jehovah has been gracious
9.2	**Jonathan**	Hebrew Jehovah has been gracious
1.0	**Jonathon**	Hebrew Jehovah has been gracious
7.4	**Jordan**	Hebrew to descend

0.1	**Jorden**	Hebrew to descend
0.3	**Jordon**	Hebrew to descend
2.0	**Jorge**	Spanish form of George: Greek a farmer, a tiller of the soil
6.4	**Jose**	Hebrew Jehovah adds; Spanish for Joseph
0.1	**Jose'**	Hebrew Jehovah adds; Spanish for Joseph
0.1	**Josef**	Hebrew Jehovah adds
0.1	**Joseluis**	Jose + Luis
11.1	**Joseph**	Hebrew Jehovah adds
0.1	**Josh**	Hebrew Jehovah saves
14.5	**Joshua**	Hebrew Jehovah saves
0.4	**Josiah**	Hebrew Jehovah supports
0.6	**Josue**	form of Joshua
0.1	**Jovan**	Slavonic form of John: the gift of God
0.1	**Jovani**	variant of Roman god Jove
0.1	**Jovanni**	variant of Roman god Jove
0.1	**Jovanny**	variant of Roman god Jove
0.1	**Jovany**	variant of Roman god Jove
3.8	**Juan**	Spanish form of John: Hebrew God has been gracious
0.1	**Juancarlos**	Juan + Carlos
0.1	**Jules**	Greek youthful and downy-bearded
1.4	**Julian**	Greek soft-haired, light-bearded
0.4	**Julien**	Greek soft-haired, light-bearded
0.7	**Julio**	Spanish form of Julius: Greek youthful and downy-bearded; Latin the god Jupiter
0.2	**Julius**	Greek youthful and downy-bearded
0.1	**Junior**	Latin young
0.2	**Justice**	origin unknown
9.9	**Justin**	Latin just, upright
0.1	**Justyn**	Latin just, upright

0.1	**Juwan**	newly-created African-American name

-K-

0.3	**K**	initial used as a first name
0.1	**Ka**	origin unknown
0.1	**Kade**	origin unknown
0.1	**Kadeem**	an African-American original
0.2	**Kaden**	origin unknown
0.1	**Kahlil**	origin unknown
0.2	**Kai**	Hawaiian ocean; Welsh keeper of the keys
0.1	**Kainoa**	Hawaiian the name
0.6	**Kaleb**	Hebrew a dog, faithful, bold one
0.1	**Kalvin**	Latin bald
0.3	**Kameron**	Celtic bent nose
0.1	**Kamil**	Latin Camillus: old Roman family name
0.1	**Kane**	Gaelic fair; also warlike and tribute
0.1	**Kareem**	Arabic noble, exalted
0.4	**Karl**	German form of Charles: English manly, strong; German farmer
0.2	**Kasey**	Celtic valorous; Irish brave
0.1	**Kayden**	origin unknown
0.2	**Keanu**	origin unknown
0.3	**Keaton**	English one who comes from Ketton
0.4	**Keegan**	Irish little and firey
0.4	**Keenan**	Gaelic little ancient one
1.2	**Keith**	Gaelic the wind; Welsh from the forest
0.3	**Kekoa**	Hawaiian the courageous one
0.1	**Kellen**	German surname
0.2	**Kelly**	English the ship on or near the river; Irish warrior
0.1	**Kelsey**	Old Norse dweller by the water
0.1	**Kelton**	Celtic town

0.4	**Kelvin**	English a friend or lover of ships
0.1	**Ken**	nickname for names beginning with ken
0.1	**Kendal**	Old English from the bright valley
0.4	**Kendall**	Old English from the bright valley
0.1	**Kendarius**	origin unknown
0.3	**Kendrick**	Irish son of Henry; English royal ruler
2.4	**Kenneth**	Scottish comely, handsome; English royal oath
0.3	**Kenny**	Scottish comely, handsome; English royal oath
0.1	**Kent**	Welsh white, bright
0.1	**Kentavious**	origin unknown
0.1	**Kenton**	Old English from the estate of the king
0.1	**Kentrell**	origin unknown
0.1	**Keon**	short form of McKeon: Irish well born
0.1	**Kerry**	Gaelic son of the dark one
0.4	**Keven**	Gaelic handsome, beautiful
8.9	**Kevin**	Gaelic handsome, beautiful
0.1	**Kevon**	Gaelic handsome, beautiful
0.1	**Khalid**	Arabic horse rider; eternal
0.3	**Khalil**	Arabic friend
0.2	**Kieran**	Irish little and dark-skinned
0.2	**Kirk**	Scottish a church
0.5	**Kody**	English a cushion
0.1	**Kolby**	Old English from the black farm
0.2	**Kolton**	Old English from the dark town
0.2	**Korey**	Latin a helmet, from the hollow
0.2	**Kory**	Latin a helmet, from the hollow
0.3	**Kristian**	Greek Christ-bearer
0.1	**Kristofer**	Greek Christ-bearer
0.6	**Kristopher**	Greek Christ-bearer

0.3	**Kurt**	German bold, wise, counsellor
0.3	**Kurtis**	German bold, wise, counsellor
8.9	**Kyle**	Gaelic a hill where the cattle graze
0.4	**Kyler**	American surname

-L-

0.2	**L**	initial used as a first name
0.1	**Ladarius**	origin unknown
0.1	**Laine**	Old English from the narrow road
0.2	**Lamar**	Latin from the sea
0.1	**Lamont**	Scottish lawyer
0.6	**Lance**	Latin a light spear; German land
0.1	**Landin**	Old English from the long hill
0.7	**Landon**	Old English from the long hill
0.5	**Lane**	Old English from the narrow road
0.7	**Larry**	Latin a laurel, a crown
0.1	**Laurence**	Latin a laurel, a crown
0.3	**Laurent**	Latin a laurel, a crown
0.5	**Lawrence**	Latin a laurel, a crown
0.1	**Layne**	Old English from the narrow road
0.1	**Layton**	last name used as a first name, town on the side of a hill
0.1	**Lazaro**	Hebrew God will help
0.4	**Lee**	English field, meadow; short form of Leo, Leon, Leroy, Leslie, Leigh
0.1	**Leland**	Old English from the meadowland
0.2	**Leo**	Latin lion
0.2	**Leon**	Greek form of Leo, lion, French lion-like

0.3	**Leonard**	English form of German, strong as a lion
0.4	**Leonardo**	English form of German, strong as a lion
0.2	**Leonel**	English lion cub
0.1	**Leopoldo**	Germanic bold for people
0.1	**Leroy**	Old French king
0.1	**Leslie**	English small meadow, a dell; Scottish from the gray fortress
0.1	**Lester**	Latin from the camp of the legion
1.1	**Levi**	Hebrew joined to, attendant upon; Hebrew joined in harmony
0.2	**Lewis**	Welsh lionlike, lightning
0.7	**Liam**	Irish form of William: English resolute protector; English to bind, tie
0.1	**Liban**	origin unknown
0.1	**Lincoln**	Old English from the settlement by the pool
0.1	**Lionel**	English lion cub
0.1	**Lloyd**	Welsh gray-haired
2.6	**Logan**	English a felled tree; Irish from the hollow
0.2	**Loic**	origin unknown
0.1	**Lonnie**	nickname for Lawrence: Latin a laurel, a crown
0.1	**Loren**	form of Lawrence: Latin a laurel, a crown
0.5	**Lorenzo**	Spanish and Italian form of Lawrence: a laurel, a crown
0.1	**Louie**	English famous in battle
0.6	**Louis**	English famous in battle
0.7	**Louis Charles**	Louis + Charles
0.2	**Louis David**	Louis + David
2.5	**Louis Philippe**	Louis + Philippe
0.2	**Luc**	English form of Latin Lucius: light
0.1	**Luca**	English form of Latin Lucius: light

2.2	**Lucas**	English form of Latin Lucius: light
0.1	**Lucio**	Latin native of Lucaria
0.4	**Ludovic**	English and Scottish devotee of the Lord
0.3	**Ludovick**	English and Scottish devotee of the Lord
3.4	**Luis**	English famous in battle
0.3	**Lukas**	English form of Latin Lucius: light
2.0	**Luke**	English form of Latin Lucius: light
0.1	**Lyle**	English from the island

-M-

0.2	**M**	initial used as a first name
0.5	**Mackenzie**	Irish son of the wise leader
0.1	**Madison**	Old English son of the mighty warrior
0.1	**Malachi**	Hebrew angel
0.5	**Malcolm**	Arabic a dove
0.6	**Malik**	Arabic king; angel, divine messenger; Punjabi lord or master
0.1	**Manpreet**	origin unknown
0.1	**Manraj**	origin unknown
1.4	**Manuel**	form of Emanuel: Hebrew God is with us
0.1	**Manveer**	origin unknown
0.2	**Manvir**	origin unknown
0.7	**Marc**	Latin warlike; Italian form of Mark
0.5	**Marc Alexandre**	Marc + Alexandre
6.3	**Marc Andre**	Marc + Andre
9.2	**Marc Antoine**	Marc + Antoine
0.3	**Marc Etienne**	Marc + Etienne
2.9	**Marc Olivier**	Marc + Olivier
0.3	**Marc-Andre**	Marc + Andre
0.3	**Marc-Antoine**	Marc + Antoine
0.2	**Marcel**	English short form of Marc and Marcus; Latin little and warlike; Italian form of Marcel

0.1	**Marcelino**	Latin Roman god of war, Mars
1.0	**Marco**	Latin Mars, warlike
0.1	**Marcoantonio**	Marco + Antonio
0.6	**Marcos**	Latin Mars, warlike
2.3	**Marcus**	Latin Mars, warlike
1.3	**Mario**	Latin warlike; Italian form of Mark
3.3	**Mark**	Latin warlike; Italian form of Mark
0.1	**Markanthony**	Mark + Anthony
0.1	**Markel**	newly-created African-American name
0.1	**Markell**	newly-created African-American name
0.2	**Markus**	Latin warlike; Italian form of Mark
0.3	**Marlon**	English little falcon
0.1	**Marquavious**	origin unknown
0.1	**Marques**	French a sign, a mark
0.1	**Marquez**	French a sign, a mark
0.4	**Marquis**	Old French a nobleman
0.2	**Marquise**	Old French a nobleman
0.4	**Marshall**	English steward, horse-keeper
0.1	**Martez**	origin unknown
1.5	**Martin**	English warlike; Latin akin to Marcus
0.5	**Marvin**	Old English famous friend
1.4	**Mason**	English a mason, a worker in store
0.1	**Massimo**	Italian the greatest
0.1	**Mateusz**	Hebrew gift of God
1.0	**Mathew**	Hebrew gift of God
1.8	**Mathieu**	Hebrew gift of God
15.4	**Matthew**	Hebrew gift of God
0.2	**Matthieu**	Hebrew gift of God
0.4	**Maurice**	Latin dark-skinned
0.3	**Mauricio**	Spanish form of Maurice: Latin dark-skinned
0.1	**Maverick**	origin unknown
0.8	**Max**	Latin great, most excellent
0.2	**Maxence**	origin unknown

0.2	**Maxim**	Latin great, most excellent
3.9	**Maxime**	Latin great, most excellent
0.2	**Maximilian**	Latin great, most excellent
0.1	**Maximiliano**	Latin great, most excellent
0.1	**Maximillian**	Latin great, most excellent
0.9	**Maxwell**	Latin great, most excellent
0.2	**Mckade**	origin unknown
0.1	**Mckay**	Scottish son of fire
0.1	**Mckenzie**	Irish son of the wise leader
0.3	**Melvin**	Gaelic polished chief
0.6	**Micah**	Hebrew who is like God
19.5	**Michael**	Hebrew who is like God
0.1	**Michal**	Hebrew who is like God
0.6	**Micheal**	Hebrew who is like God
0.2	**Michel**	Hebrew who is like God
0.2	**Mickael**	Hebrew who is like God
2.3	**Miguel**	Hebrew who is like God
0.1	**Miguelangel**	Michael + Angel
0.2	**Mikael**	Hebrew who is like God
0.2	**Mike**	Hebrew who is like God
0.1	**Mikel**	Hebrew who is like God
0.5	**Miles**	Latin a warrior, a soldier
0.2	**Milton**	Old English dweller at the farmstead of the mill
0.1	**Misael**	Hebrew who is like God (Michael)
0.2	**Mitchel**	Hebrew who is like God (Michael)
2.9	**Mitchell**	Hebrew who is like God (Michael)
0.1	**Mohamad**	Arabic praised
0.2	**Mohamed**	Arabic praised
0.2	**Mohammad**	Arabic praised
0.2	**Mohammed**	Arabic praised
0.4	**Moises**	Spanish form of Moses: Greek drawn from the water
0.1	**Montavious**	origin unknown
0.1	**Montel**	origin unknown
0.1	**Montrell**	newly-created African-American name
0.6	**Morgan**	Celtic one who lives near the sea

0.1	**Moses**	Greek drawn from the water
0.1	**Muhammad**	Arabic praised
0.4	**Myles**	Latin a warrior, a soldier
0.1	**Myron**	Greek fragrant essence

-N-

0.2	**N**	initial used as a first name
5.0	**Nathan**	Hebrew gift of God
0.2	**Nathanael**	Hebrew gift of God
0.2	**Nathanial**	Hebrew gift of God
2.2	**Nathaniel**	Hebrew gift of God
0.1	**Navdeep**	Sikh the ever new light, the new lamp
0.1	**Neal**	English a champion
0.3	**Neil**	English a champion
0.3	**Nelson**	Gaelic son of Neal
0.1	**Nephi**	Hebrew God will aid me in my struggle
0.2	**Nestor**	Greek he remembers
13.2	**Nicholas**	Greek victory of the people
0.1	**Nick**	Greek victory of the people
0.5	**Nickolas**	Greek victory of the people
0.1	**Nico**	Greek victory of the people
1.8	**Nicolas**	Greek victory of the people
0.2	**Nigel**	English night, dark
0.1	**Nikko**	Greek victory of the people
0.1	**Niko**	Greek victory of the people
0.1	**Nikola**	Greek victory of the people
0.3	**Nikolas**	Greek victory of the people
1.2	**Noah**	Hebrew rest, peace
0.3	**Noe**	Spanish quiet peace
0.3	**Noel**	English to be born, the Nativity, born at Christmas
0.6	**Nolan**	Irish famous, noble
0.2	**Norman**	English a man from the North
0.8	**Not**	origin unknown

-O-

0.1	**Octavio**	Latin eight
0.4	**Oliver**	Latin an olive tree

2.6	**Olivier**	French form of Oliver: an olive tree
1.4	**Omar**	Arabic long life, first son, highest, follower of the Prophet
0.1	**Orion**	French the Orient, the East, where the sun rises
0.3	**Orlando**	English from the pointed land
1.7	**Oscar**	Old Norse divine spearman
0.3	**Osvaldo**	Spanish form of Oswald: Old English with power from God
0.1	**Oswaldo**	Teutonic he who governs with the power of God
0.3	**Owen**	Welsh variation of Eugene, well born

-P-

0.4	**Pablo**	Spanish form of Paul: Latin small
0.1	**Paolo**	Latin small
0.1	**Pardeep**	Sikh mystic light
0.1	**Paris**	Greek in legend a king of Troy
0.6	**Parker**	Old English guardian of the park
0.1	**Parmvir**	Sikh the greatest of warriors
0.2	**Pascal**	Italian born at Easter or Passover
0.3	**Patrice**	Latin of noble descent
4.4	**Patrick**	Latin a patrician, a person of noble descent
0.1	**Patryk**	Latin a patrician, a person of noble descent
2.6	**Paul**	Latin small
0.1	**Pawel**	origin unknown
0.2	**Payton**	Old English from the estate of the warrior
1.0	**Pedro**	Spanish form of Peter
0.2	**Perry**	Middle English from the pear tree

2.1	**Peter**	Greek a rock
0.2	**Peyton**	Old English from the estate of the warrior
0.9	**Philip**	Greek a lover of horses
0.1	**Philipe**	Greek a lover of horses
1.2	**Philippe**	Greek a lover of horses
0.2	**Philippe Olivier**	Philippe + Olivier
1.2	**Phillip**	Greek a lover of horses
0.3	**Pier Alexandre**	Pier + Alexandre
0.5	**Pier Luc**	Pier + Luc
0.6	**Pier Olivier**	Pier + Olivier
0.1	**Pierce**	Anglo French form of Peter
0.2	**Pierre**	Greek a rock
0.8	**Pierre Alexandre**	Pierre + Alexandre
0.3	**Pierre Andre**	Pierre + Andre
0.2	**Pierre Etienne**	Pierre + Etienne
3.1	**Pierre Luc**	Pierre + Luc
0.3	**Pierre Marc**	Pierre + Marc
1.9	**Pierre Olivier**	Pierre + Olivier
0.3	**Pierre Yves**	Pierre + Yves
0.1	**Piotr**	origin unknown
0.1	**Prabhjot**	Sikh the light of God
0.7	**Preston**	English from the priest's estate

-Q-

0.4	**Quentin**	Latin fifth; Old English from the estate of the queen
0.2	**Quincy**	Old French from the estate of the fifth son
0.4	**Quinn**	Irish wise
0.2	**Quintavious**	origin unknown
0.1	**Quintavius**	origin unknown
0.1	**Quinten**	Latin fifth
0.2	**Quintin**	Latin fifth
0.4	**Quinton**	Latin fifth

-R-

0.1	**R**	initial used as a first name
0.1	**Raekwon**	origin unknown

0.8	**Rafael**	Spanish form of Raphael: Hebrew God has healed
0.2	**Raheem**	Punjabi God; Arabic kind
0.1	**Rakeem**	origin unknown
0.2	**Ralph**	Old Norse counsel wolf
0.3	**Ramiro**	Teutonic powerful in army
0.5	**Ramon**	Spanish form of Raymond: English wise protection
0.4	**Randall**	English superior protection; English shield-wolf
0.7	**Randy**	English superior protection; English shield-wolf
0.5	**Raphael**	Hebrew God has healed
0.1	**Rashaad**	Arabic guider, wisdom
0.2	**Rashad**	Arabic guider, wisdom
0.1	**Rashawn**	origin unknown
0.1	**Rasheed**	Arabic director, pious
0.9	**Raul**	French form of Randolph: Old English shield wolf
0.3	**Ray**	English wise protection
1.5	**Raymond**	English wise protection
0.2	**Raymundo**	?? Spanish form of English wise protection
0.1	**Reece**	Old Welsh rash, ardent
0.3	**Reed**	English red-haired
0.1	**Reese**	Old Welsh rash, ardent
0.4	**Reginald**	Old English powerful and mighty
0.3	**Reid**	English red-haired
0.2	**Remi**	possibly a form of Roman: Latin a person from Rome
0.3	**Renaud**	Old English powerful and mighty
0.4	**Rene**	English to be reborn, to revive
0.1	**Reuben**	Hebrew behold, a son
0.1	**Reyes**	Latin kings
0.1	**Reynaldo**	Teutonic he commands with intelligence
0.1	**Rhett**	Old English a small stream
0.1	**Rhys**	Old Welsh rash, ardent
1.6	**Ricardo**	English powerful, rich ruler
4.2	**Richard**	English powerful, rich ruler
0.1	**Rick**	English powerful, rich ruler
0.1	**Rickey**	English powerful, rich ruler
0.7	**Ricky**	English powerful, rich ruler
0.1	**Rico**	English powerful, rich ruler
0.2	**Rigoberto**	Teutonic splendid for his wealth
1.1	**Riley**	German, Dutch a small stream; Irish valiant
0.1	**River**	origin unknown
8.8	**Robert**	German bright fame
1.1	**Roberto**	German bright fame
0.2	**Robin**	German bright fame
0.1	**Roch**	Germanic rest
0.1	**Rocky**	Old English rock; the well near the rock
0.2	**Roderick**	German famous ruler
0.5	**Rodney**	English from the island clearing
0.4	**Rodolfo**	Spanish form of Rudolph: famous wolf
0.3	**Rodrigo**	Spanish and Italian form of Roderick: famous ruler
0.3	**Rogelio**	Teutonic he of glorious spear
0.5	**Roger**	English famous, noble warrior
0.1	**Roland**	German from the famous land
0.2	**Rolando**	German from the famous land
0.3	**Roman**	Latin a person from Rome
0.1	**Romario**	Latin a person from Rome
1.0	**Ronald**	Scottish wise, judicious
0.3	**Ronnie**	Scottish wise, judicious
0.1	**Roosevelt**	Dutch field of roses
0.1	**Rory**	Irish red king
0.4	**Ross**	English woods, meadow; English red; Scottish headland
0.4	**Roy**	English king
0.1	**Royce**	Old English song of the king
0.9	**Ruben**	Hebrew behold, a son
0.3	**Rudy**	Old German famous wolf

0.6	**Russell**	English red
11.5	**Ryan**	Irish little king
0.1	**Ryder**	Middle English to clear land
0.1	**Rylan**	English dweller on hill where rye is grown
0.1	**Ryley**	German, Dutch a small stream; Irish valiant

-S-

0.1	**S**	initial used as a first name
0.1	**Sacha**	nickname for Alexander: Greek helper of mankind, protector of man
0.1	**Sage**	origin unknown
0.8	**Salvador**	Latin to be saved
0.1	**Salvatore**	Latin to be saved
0.3	**Sam**	Hebrew God has heard
0.1	**Sammy**	Hebrew God has heard
0.1	**Samson**	Hebrew child of the sun
6.8	**Samuel**	Hebrew God has heard
0.3	**Santiago**	form of Saint Diego (James): held by the heel, supplanter
0.1	**Santos**	Latin sacred, inviolable
0.4	**Saul**	Hebrew asked for
0.1	**Savon**	origin unknown
0.2	**Sawyer**	Middle English one who works with a saw
2.5	**Scott**	English Scotsman
4.2	**Sean**	Irish form of John
0.7	**Sebastian**	Greek venerable
0.9	**Sebastien**	Greek venerable
1.2	**Sergio**	Italian form of Serge: Latin attendant
1.6	**Seth**	Hebrew garment; appointed; Syriac appearance
1.9	**Shane**	Irish form of John
0.2	**Shannon**	Irish small and wise
0.1	**Shaquan**	newly-created African-American name
0.5	**Shaquille**	African-American variation on an Arabic name

0.4	**Shaun**	Irish form of John
1.8	**Shawn**	Irish form of John
0.1	**Shay**	origin unknown
0.1	**Shayden**	origin unknown
0.2	**Shayne**	Irish form of John
0.1	**Shea**	Gaelic ingenious, courteous and regal
0.2	**Shelby**	English from the ledge estate
0.3	**Sheldon**	English protected kill
0.1	**Shelton**	English protected kill
0.1	**Shyheim**	origin unknown
0.2	**Sidney**	short for Saint Denys, derived from Dionysius, the Greek god of wine
0.1	**Silas**	Latin forest dweller
1.0	**Simon**	Latin he heard
0.6	**Simon Pierre**	Simon + Pierre
0.1	**Singh**	Hindi lion
0.3	**Skylar**	Dutch a shelter
0.7	**Skyler**	Dutch a shelter
0.1	**Solomon**	Hebrew man of peace
0.1	**Sonny**	son or boy
2.2	**Spencer**	English steward, administrator, butler
0.3	**Stanley**	English a stony meadow
0.3	**Steeven**	Greek a crown
0.4	**Stefan**	Greek a crown
0.2	**Stephan**	Greek a crown
0.4	**Stephane**	Greek a crown
0.1	**Stephanie**	Greek a crown
3.1	**Stephen**	Greek a crown
0.2	**Stephon**	Greek a crown
0.3	**Sterling**	Old English of value
0.1	**Stetson**	last name, Danish step son
0.5	**Steve**	Greek a crown
5.5	**Steven**	Greek a crown
0.1	**Stewart**	English a steward
0.1	**Storm**	Old English impetuous by nature
0.3	**Stuart**	English a steward
0.1	**Syed**	Arabic master, chief
0.2	**Sylvain**	Latin forest dweller

-T-

0.2	**T**	initial used as a first name
0.1	**Talon**	origin unknown
2.0	**Tanner**	English leather worker
0.1	**Tate**	American Indian windy
0.1	**Tavaris**	origin unknown
0.1	**Tayler**	English tailor
3.0	**Taylor**	English tailor
0.2	**Terence**	Latin smooth
0.4	**Terrance**	Latin smooth
0.3	**Terrell**	German belonging to Thor; martial
0.4	**Terrence**	Latin smooth
0.6	**Terry**	Latin smooth
0.5	**Tevin**	newly-created African-American name
0.1	**Thaddeus**	Greek courageous; Latin praiser
0.4	**Theodore**	Greek divine gift
0.3	**Thierry**	French form of Greek divine gift
6.3	**Thomas**	Hebrew a twin
0.2	**Timothe**	Greek to honor God
4.5	**Timothy**	Greek to honor God
0.1	**Tobias**	Hebrew goodness of God
0.1	**Toby**	nickname for Tobias
0.5	**Todd**	English fox
0.1	**Tom**	Hebrew a twin
0.3	**Tomas**	Hebrew a twin
0.6	**Tommy**	Hebrew a twin
0.1	**Tomy**	Hebrew a twin
0.8	**Tony**	short form for Anthony: Greek flourishing; Latin worthy of praise
0.1	**Tory**	Old English from the tower
0.1	**Trace**	Greek harvester
0.1	**Tracy**	Greek harvester
2.9	**Travis**	Latin crossroads
0.2	**Travon**	newly-created African-American name
0.1	**Trayvon**	newly-created African-American name
0.1	**Tre**	origin unknown
0.1	**Tre'**	origin unknown
0.1	**Tre'von**	newly-created African-American name
0.1	**Tremaine**	Old Cornish from the house of stone
0.5	**Trent**	Latin torrent
0.6	**Trenton**	Latin torrent
0.1	**Trever**	Celtic prudent
0.3	**Trevon**	newly-created African-American name
3.1	**Trevor**	Celtic prudent
0.5	**Trey**	Middle English third born
1.0	**Tristan**	Celtic tumult, noise; Welsh sorrowful
0.3	**Tristen**	Celtic tumult, noise; Welsh sorrowful
0.1	**Tristin**	Celtic tumult, noise; Welsh sorrowful
0.2	**Triston**	Celtic tumult, noise; Welsh sorrowful
1.2	**Troy**	Irish foot soldier
0.3	**Tucker**	Old English one who fulled, teased and burled cloth
0.1	**Turner**	Latin a worker with a lathe
0.5	**Ty**	British a house
13.7	**Tyler**	English maker of tiles
0.3	**Tylor**	English maker of tiles
0.1	**Tyre**	Biblical place name
0.2	**Tyree**	origin unknown
0.1	**Tyrel**	German belonging to Thor; martial
0.2	**Tyrell**	German belonging to Thor; martial
0.4	**Tyrone**	Greek sovereign; Irish land of Owen
0.5	**Tyson**	English firebrand

-U-

0.3	**Ulises**	Greek wrathful
0.1	**Ulysses**	Greek wrathful

| 0.3 | **Uriel** | Hebrew powerful light of God |

-V-

0.1	**Valentin**	Latin strong and healthy
0.1	**Vance**	Middle English from the grain fan
0.1	**Vaughn**	Old Welsh small one
0.1	**Vernon**	Latin spring-like, youthful
0.3	**Vicente**	Spanish form of Vincent: Latin victor, conqueror
2.2	**Victor**	Latin victor, conqueror
2.3	**Vincent**	Latin victor, conqueror
0.1	**Vincenzo**	Latin victor, conqueror

-W-

0.1	**W**	initial used as a first name
0.3	**Wade**	English to wade; from the river crossing
0.1	**Wai**	origin unknown
0.2	**Walker**	Old English one who cleans and thickens cloth
0.5	**Walter**	German powerful warrior
0.1	**Wanya**	origin unknown
0.3	**Warren**	English preserver, defender
0.1	**Waylon**	English from the land by the road
0.3	**Wayne**	English a way; wagoner
1.3	**Wesley**	English the west meadow
0.3	**Weston**	English from the western estate
0.1	**Wilfred**	Old German resolute for peace
0.1	**Will**	English resolute protector
9.5	**William**	English resolute protector
0.4	**Willie**	English resolute protector
0.2	**Wilson**	Old German son of William
0.1	**Winston**	Old English from the friend's town

| 1.2 | **Wyatt** | Old French form of Guy: English a guide; Hebrew valley |

-X-

| 1.2 | **Xavier** | Arabic bright |

-Y-

0.4	**Yan**	Hebrew Jehovah has been gracious
0.4	**Yanick**	origin unknown
0.3	**Yann**	Hebrew Jehovah has been gracious
0.6	**Yannick**	origin unknown
0.4	**Yoan**	origin unknown
0.1	**Yoann**	origin unknown
0.2	**Yohan**	origin unknown
0.3	**Youri**	Greek farmer

-Z-

0.2	**Z**	initial used as a first name
0.3	**Zachariah**	Hebrew the remembrance of the Lord
9.9	**Zachary**	Hebrew the remembrance of the Lord
0.7	**Zachery**	Hebrew the remembrance of the Lord
0.6	**Zackary**	Hebrew the remembrance of the Lord
0.4	**Zackery**	Hebrew the remembrance of the Lord
0.1	**Zakary**	Hebrew the remembrance of the Lord
0.3	**Zane**	form of John: Hebrew Jehovah has been gracious
0.1	**Zechariah**	Hebrew the remembrance of the Lord

Section III —

 # Popular
and Unusual Names

with popularity ratings

Parentheses after a name contains its popularity rating (frequency per thousand).
Names without parentheses have a popularity rating of less than .01 — many of these
names are one in a million, or are unique in North America.

Some larger names have been truncated by the databases which reported the data. As well,
capitalization and punctuation variations may occur due to the nature of the database records.

🔤 Girls Names

-A-

A *(0.08)*
A Brail
A Chante
A Chish
A Daysha
A Driana
A Jeona
A Joya
A Jwana
A Kayla
A Keelah
A Keema
A Keila
A Keiyah
A Kera
A Kilah
A Kira
A Laney
A Lexcia
A Liena
A Liyah
A Neiya
A Nikko
A Quila
A Rie L
A Riyichia
A Shantae
A Shante
A Shanti
A Sheana
A Shia
A Shonti
A Shunti
A Su Sena

A Tashia
A Veryell
A'abrea
A'aliyah
A'bresha
A'breya
A'briahn
A'briana
A'brianna
A'brion
A'briyah
A'caila
A'ceondra
A'dasia
A'dasjah
A'deja
A'dena
A'detria
A'dia
A'dorah
A'dorn
A'drema
A'drianna
A'driarna
A'erica
A'gea-Zhane
A'geno
A'isa-Laie
A'isha
A'isho
A'ja
A'já
A'jah
A'jahnea
A'jai
A'jalyn

A'janae
A'janae Sheniqu
A'janai
A'janea
A'jasah
A'jena
A'jené
A'jenee
A'jhane
A'jhia
A'kasha
A'kayla
A'kecya
A'keila
A'keilah
A'keyah
A'keyla
A'kia
A'kiah
A'kiela
A'kiera
A'kierra
A'kinyele
A'kira
A'kiylah
A'kiyyah
A'kkerria
A'kyra
A'kyshalyn
A'la
A'laayfia
A'ladean
A'laiyah
A'lana
A'landra
A'lanska

A'layah
A'lea
A'leah
A'leaha
A'leea
A'leesia
A'leiya
A'leshia
A'leshial
A'levus
A'lexcyia-Ashana
A'lexis
A'lexiya
A'lexus *(0.01)*
A'lexzia
A'leya
A'leyia
A'licia
A'lintra
A'lisa
A'lisha
A'lissia
A'livia
A'liyah
A'lydia
A'mani
A'mara
A'marah
A'marie
A'marrie
A'maury
A'miya
A'moni
A'mya
A'nasia
A'neezja

A'neisha
A'neitra
A'nessa
A'nesty
A'ngeliqué
A'nia
A'nivia
A'niya
A'niyu
A'nyce
A'nysa
A'nyssa
A'onna
A'quada
A'quaya
A'quilla
A'reaonnia
A'resha
A'rielle
A'risa
A'rrielle
A'sa
A'sade
A'seanti
A'sha
A'shanique
A'shanta
A'shantae
A'shanté
A'shanti
A'shantie
A'shari
A'shauntalle
A'shaunte
A'shawna
A'shyea

A'shyiah
A'sonta
A'stayshavon
A'taisha
A'tanai
A'tanya
A'tese
A'tháasia
A'tika
A'vanti
A'veanna
A'yaivii
A'yesia
A'yonne
A'zhane
A'zharia
A'zhia
A-Oleon
A-Sha
A-Yanna
A-Yaunte
A. *(0.01)*
A. Hawley
Aa'eshah
Aabbee
Aabriella
Aahana
Aahjah
Aahliyah
Aailiyah
Aailyah
Aaisha
Aaishah
Aajanae
Aajenée
Aajneet

Aakanksha	Aalylh	Aarthi	Abbey-Gayle	Aberleigh	Abischa
Aala	Aamani	Aarthiga	Abbey-Mae	Abertine	Abish
Aalaa	Aamber	Aarti *(0.01)*	Abbeygale	Abey	Abisha
Aalaina	Aamena	Aaryana	Abbi *(0.01)*	Abeytu	Abivarshini
Aalaiya	Aami	Aaryhon	Abbi-Marie	Abhilasha	Ablana
Aalayah	Aamina	Aaryka	Abbie *(0.14)*	Abhira	Abonee
Aalayaha	Aaminah	Aaryn	Abbie-Gail	Abhiti	Abony
Aalayjah	Aamir	Aashé	Abbie-Marie	Abhneet	Abou-Nica
Aaléyah	Aamna	Aasha	Abbie-Rae	Abi	Abra
Aalea	Aamnah	Aashima	Abbiegail	Abia	Abraeshea
Aaleah	Aamoli	Aashini	Abbiegayle	Abiah	Abrafi
Aaleaha	Aanchal	Aashka	Abbigael	Abian	Abragail
Aaleasha	Aanika	Aashna	Abbigail *(0.07)*	Abianne	Abrail
Aalecia	Aanisha	Aashni	Abbigal	Abida	Abrar *(0.01)*
Aaleeyah	Aaniyah	Aashya	Abbigale *(0.01)*	Abie	Abratina
Aaleigah	Aanjae	Aasia	Abbigayl	Abiebatu	Abraya
Aaleigha	Aanuoluwa	Aasiana	Abbigayle *(0.01)*	Abiel	Abraysha
Aalexis	Aany	Aasiyah	Abbira	Abiemwese	Abréa
Aalexus	Aanye	Aaste	Abbiramy	Abier	Abrea
Aalexxus	Aaqila	Aasya	Abbott	Abies	Abreale
Aaleyah *(0.01)*	Aaqueelah	Aateka	Abbrionna	Abiffany	Abreana
Aaleyiah	Aaraa	Aatikah	Abbryana	Abigael *(0.02)*	Abreanna
Aaleyyah	Aaraby	Aaushi	Abby *(0.52)*	Abigail *(3.10)*	Abreanne
Aalia	Aaramika	Aaya	Abby Gail	Abigail-Alex	Abree
Aaliah *(0.01)*	Aaran	Aayana	Abby-Kaye	Abigail-Rose	Abreeanna
Aaliahy	Aarandeep	Aaybria	Abby-Lynne	Abigail-Sarai	Abreia
Aaliaya	Aarane	Aayonealya	Abbye	Abigaile	Abreigh
Aaliayah	Aaren	Aayonna	Abbygail *(0.01)*	Abigaill	Abrelyn
Aaliayh	Aareon	Aazia	Abbygale	AbigalAbigale	Abreon Te
Aaliesha	Aareonna	Ab Brecka	Abbygayl	*(0.04)*	Abreona
Aalieyha	Aareyionna	Abaca	Abbygayle	Abigayil	Abreonia
Aalihay	Aarezo	Abagael *(0.01)*	Abbylene	Abigayl	Abri
Aalihya	Aarhianna	Abagail *(0.05)*	Abdirai	Abigayle *(0.05)*	Abria *(0.01)*
Aaliiyiah	Aarian	Abagaile	Abdullah	Abigel	Abriah
Aalijah	Aariana	Abagale	Abedah	Abigial	Abriair
Aalisha	Aarianna	Abagayle	Abeer *(0.01)*	Abigrace	Abrial
Aalissah	Aarica	Abageal	Abeerah	Abiir	Abrian
Aalivah	Aariel	Abaigael	Abeere	Abike	Abriana *(0.04)*
Aaliy'ah	Aarielleevi	Abaigeal	Abeey	Abilana	Abriann
Aaliya *(0.01)*	Aarieonna	Abajah	Abegail *(0.01)*	Abilene	Abrianna *(0.03)*
Aaliyah *(0.56)*	Aarieyana	Abang	Abegaile	Abimbola	Abriannah
Aaliyah Chantel	Aarika	Abarna	Abegale	Abinaa	Abriéa
Aaliyah Chelsey	Aarin	Abasha	Abeir	Abinaiya	Abrieana
Aaliyaha	Aariona	Abashiana	Abeka	Abinaya	Abriel
Aaliyan	Aarionne	Abbagail *(0.01)*	Abel	Abinayan	Abriell
Aaliyanah	Aaris	Abbagale	Abelina	Abiodun	Abrielle *(0.01)*
Aaliyeha	Aariuna	Abbagayle	Abena	Abiola	Abrien
Aaliyha	Aariuna	Abbe	Abenaa	Abir	Abrienna
Aaliysah	Aaron *(0.03)*	Abbea	Abenaya	Abira	Abrienne
Aallayhia	Aarona	Abbegail	Abeni	Abirami	Abril *(0.02)*
Aalleyah	Aaronisha	Abbegale	Abera	Abiramy	Abrilla
Aalliah	Aaronishia	Abbegayle	Aberaa	Abirene	Abrille
Aalliyah	Aaronnesha	Abbeha	Aberah	Abirna	Abrion
Aalyah	Aarreanna	Abbeigh	Aberamy	Abisai	Abrionée
Aalyiah *(0.01)*	Aarronisha	Abbey *(0.21)*	Aberial	Abisatu	Abrionne
	Aarthee				

Abritenzhaye	Acqu'aria	Adanehowan	Adebisi	Ader	Adison *(0.01)*
Abriunna	Acquanette	Adanika	Adebola	Adera	Adisynne
Abrosia	Acsa	Adanma	Adecia	Aderah	Adithi
Abrya	Acura	Adanna	Adedolapo	Aderian	Aditi *(0.01)*
Abryann	Acye	Adaobi	Adedoyin	Adero	Aditi Laksh
Abryanna	Acyre	Adar	Adee	Aderra	Aditti
Abryell	Ada *(0.06)*	Adara *(0.02)*	Adeeba	Aderrika	Adiva
Abryona	Ada-Marie	Adarah	Adeela	Aderyl	Adiza
Abryssa	Adacia	Adarees	Adeena	Adeseraé	Adja
Abshur	Adadra	Adarra	Adeesha	Adesha	Adjanee
Abugail	Adaen	Adarys	Adei	Adeshiá	Adjawan
Aby	Adaeze	Adasha	Adeidre	Adeshpal	Adjiernar
Abygael	Adah	Adashia	Adeja	Adesola	Adjoa
Abygail *(0.01)*	Adaija	Adasia	Adejah	Adessa	Adjowa
Abygale	Adaijah	Adaugo	Adejumoke	Adessia	Adjua
Abygayle	Adair *(0.01)*	Adauré	Adel	Adesuwa	Adjubi
Abyssina	Adaira	Adavia	Adela *(0.05)*	Adetia	Adla
Acacia *(0.06)*	Adaire	Aday	Adelae	Adetokunbo	Adleigh
Acadia	Adaisena	Adaya	Adelaida *(0.01)*	Adetoun	Adlen
Acari	Adaisha	Adayja	Adelaide *(0.03)*	Adewonuola	Adlenamae
Acarie	Adaizha	Adayjah	Adelaine	Adeye	Adleni
Acasha	Adaizhna	Adaysha	Adelait	Adeyinka	Adletic
Acatia	Adajah	Adayshia	Adelayne	Adhara	Adline
Acaya	Adajia	Adazja-Gaye	Adele *(0.05)*	Adhira	Adlyn
Acca	Adajiah	Adazsia	Adeleha	Adi	Adlynn
Accalia	Adal	Adda	Adelena	Adia *(0.01)*	Admyra
Accardia	Adalane	Addae	Adelfa	Adiah	Adna
Accassia	Adalaz	Addah	Adelheid	Adiam	Adnisha
Accoushia	Adalea	Addalyn	Adeli	Adiana	Adoesha
Aceia	Adaleah	Addalynn	Adelia *(0.01)*	Adianes	Adoma
Acelin	Adalee	Addee	Adeliana	Adiasa	Adomaah
Acelyn	Adalena	Addi	Adelie	Adiba	Adomany
Aceonna	Adalene	Addie *(0.04)*	Adelin	Adicia	Adondrea
Acey	Adali	Addie-Michelle	Adelina *(0.03)*	Adienne	Adonia
Aceya	Adalia	Addiekenese	Adeline *(0.05)*	Adijah	Adonica
Achaia	Adalicia	Addis	Adelise	Adila	Adonis
Achala	Adalie	Addisen	Adelita	Adilah	Adonna
Achante	Adalin	Addison *(0.11)*	Adell	Adile	Adonnica
Achanté	Adalina	Addisson	Adella	Adileena	Adora *(0.01)*
Achanti	Adaline	Addlena	Adelle *(0.01)*	Adileh	Adorale
Ache	Adalinn	Addlilziar	Adellena	Adilen	Adore
Acheva	Adalis	Addoris	Adelyda	Adilene *(0.11)*	Adoria
Achievia	Adaliz	Addre	Adelyn	Adileni	Adorn
Achley	Adallis	Addreccia	Adelyne Adenike	Adilenne	Adra
Achline	Adaly	Addrian	Adelynn	Adilia	Adrain
Achma	Adalyn	Addrianna	Adelynne	Adina *(0.04)*	Adrali
Achsah	Adalynn	Addriyanna	Aden	Adinah	Adranne
Achshaya	Adalynne	Addy *(0.01)*	Adena *(0.01)*	Adine	Adraya
Acia	Adalys	Addye	Adene	Adira	Adréona
Acianie	Adam	Addyson *(0.01)*	Adene-Wassie	Adirana	Adrea
Ackley	Adama	Ade	Adenike	Adis	Adrean
Acnadaise	Adamaly	Adéa	Adenla	Adisa	Adreana *(0.01)*
Acoda	Adamma	Adea	Adenna	Adisen	Adreanna *(0.01)*
Acoriana	Adams	Adeala	Adenrele	Adisette	Adreanne
Acoryeeia	Adana	Adeana	Adeola	Adislada	Adreauna

Adreeanna	Adrienne Ynna	Aeliyah	Afke	Agnes *(0.04)*	Ahlana
Adreen	Adrieunna	Aelon	Afnan	Agneshizkam	Ahlandra
Adreena	Adrieva	Aemilia	Afokeoghene	Agnessa	Ahlaya
Adreenah	Adrieyana	Aenah	Afra	Agneta	Ahlea
Adreene	Adrina *(0.01)*	Aenea	Afraa	Agnieszka *(0.01)*	Ahleah
Adreeyana	Adrinanna	Aeneita	Afralakeesha	Agnola	Ahleaha
Adreia	Adrinauna	Aeniesha	Afreen	Agnus	Ahleana
Adreiana	Adrineh	Aeniva	Africa *(0.01)*	Agueda	Ahleese
Adreinna	Adrinne	Aeon	Africa-Jaquan	Aguirre	Ahleeyah
Adreinne	Adrio'na	Aeoris	Africaya	Agustina	Ahleizah
Adrene	Adrion	Aera	Africia	Agwan	Ahlexis
Adrenea	Adriona	Aeran	Africiana	Ah Queen	Ahlexus
Adreona	Adrionna	Aerial *(0.03)*	Afrika *(0.01)*	Ah'jenee	Ahley
Adreonna	Adris	Aerian	Afriqiyah	Ah'keriya	Ahleya
Adrey	Adrith	Aeriana	Afrodita	Ah'niyah	Ahlia
Adri'ana	Adriuna	Aerianna	Afrodite	Ah-Janai	Ahliah
Adri'anna	Adriunna	Aerica	Afrothiti	Ah-Keia	Ahlisabith
Adri-Anne	Adriyana	Aericka	Afroze	Ah-Zhane	Ahliya
Adria *(0.02)*	Adriyanna	Aeriel *(0.01)*	Afsana	Ahanna	Ahliyah
Adrial	Adrya	Aerielle	Afsaneh	Ahanti	Ahlora
Adrian *(0.08)*	Adryan	Aerienra	Afsha	Ahaud	Ahlysa
Adrian Lee	Adryana	Aerieonna	Afshan	Ahbiya	Ahlyssa
Adriana *(1.10)*	Adryane	Aeril	Afsheen	Ahblela	Ahmalia
Adriana-	Adryanna	Aerile	Aftinn	Ahbree	Ahmani
Guadalupe	Adryanne	Aerin *(0.01)*	Afton *(0.01)*	Ahbri	Ahmari
Adriana-Maria	Adryelle	Aeriol	Aftyn	Ahbriel	Ahmaya
Adriana-River	Adtrianna	Aerion	Afua	Ahdauni	Ahmber
Adriananna	Aduesia	Aerionna	Agaisha	Ahdiayah	Ahmed
Adriane *(0.02)*	Adunniade	Aeron	Agaja	Ahdriana	Ahmeena
Adrianeisha	Advelina	Aeronesha	Agaliyah	Ahdyah	Ahmesha
Adriani	Adwoa	Aerrhon	Agalja	Aheesha	Ahmiaha
Adriann	Adyana	Aerrionna	Agalyaa	Ahia	Ahmina Aquilah
Adrianna *(0.40)*	Adyla	Aerryn	Aganetha *(0.01)*	Ahieya	Ahmira
Adrianne *(0.07)*	Adylan	Aery	Aganna	Ahila	Ahmoni
Adriannea	Adyna	Aeryhan	Agaperose	Ahilla	Ahmrae
Adriannia	Adysen	Aeryka	Agapita	Ahiza	Ahmya
Adriatica	Adyson *(0.01)*	Aeryn	Agata	Ahja	Ahmyrah
Adriauna	Adzo	Aesha	Agatah	Ahja'nique	Ahna
Adriaunna	Aecha	Aeshia	Agatha *(0.01)*	Ahjah	Ahna-Elizabeth
Adriayon	Aecia	Aespen	Agathe *(0.01)*	Ahjalah	Ahnahceleh
Adricka	Aegious	Afaf	Ageblah	Ahjalik	Ahnalika
Adriénne	Aegis	Afak	Agedria	Ahjanae	Ahndreah
Adrieanna	Aeia	Afeefa	Ageela	Ahjee	Ahndrianna
Adrieanne	Aeilla	Afeni	Ageir	Ahkaejah	Ahnekqua
Adrieaunna	Aeinab	Aferdita	Ageis	Ahkayla	Ahnesha
Adriel	Aeiral	Affifa	Agenique	Ahkeelah	Ahnesia
Adrielle *(0.01)*	Aeirian	Affiron	Agerá	Ahkeema	Ahnesshia
Adrielli	Aeisha	Affrikah	Agerianna	Ahkeesha	Ahnia
Adrien *(0.01)*	Aejanae	Afhley	Agetha	Ahkirah	Ahnissa Ying
Adrienanna	Aelani	Afi	Aggy	Ahkiya	Ahnjenay
Adriene *(0.01)*	Aeleah	Afia	Aghigh	Ahlaam	Ahnna
Adrienia	Aelexus	Afidah	Agia	Ahlai	Ahntia
Adrienna *(0.01)*	Aeli	Afifah	Aginia	Ahlai-Shea	Ahntoni
Adriennah	Aelia	Afina	Aglaya	Ahlaia	Ahnyae
Adrienne *(0.34)*	Aelicia	Afiya	Agner Gl	Ahlam *(0.01)*	Ahnyiah

Ahofolau	Aida *(0.05)*	Ailini	Aireanah	Aishan	Ajá
Ahraby	Aidaliz	Ailis	Aireanna	Aishane	Aja-Nikohl
Ahran	Aidan *(0.03)*	Ailis-Lee	Airedana	Aishatu	Ajada
Ahrani	Aidasha	Ailish	Aireel	Aisheh	Ajadanielle
Ahraya	Aide *(0.02)*	Ailiyah	Aireka	Aishellyn	Ajaésha
Ahreanna	Aided	Ailjell	Airel	Aishia *(0.01)*	Ajaela
Ahreea	Aidee *(0.01)*	Aillen	Airele	Aishlee	Ajah *(0.01)*
Ahreisha	Aiden *(0.01)*	Ailliyaha	Airelle	Aishlinn	Ajah'
Ahren	Aieral	Ailsa	Airen	Aishwarya	Ajahnae
Ahri	Aierel	Ailsha	Aireona	Aisia	Ajahne
Ahriana	Aieron	Ailwynne	Aireonna	Aisian	Ajahnique
Ahrianna	Aiesha *(0.01)*	Ailya	Aires	Aisis	Ajai
Ahriel	Aieshia	Ailyse	Airesa	Aisjha	Ajaidiyah
Ahris	Aieysha	Aima	Airese	Aisjonée	Ajaiya
Ahrizoo	Aigai	Aime *(0.05)*	Airess	Aislee	Ajak-Angela
Ahsaki	Aignee	Aimé	Aireul	Aisley	Ajala
Ahsan	Aigner	Aimée	Aireus	Aislin	Ajalae
Ahshana	Aihetahna	Aimee *(0.44)*	Aireyonna	Aisling *(0.01)*	Ajaleigh
Ahshyia	Aiiat	Aimee Suzanne	Airi	Aislinn *(0.02)*	Ajalon
Ahsia	Aiiesha	Aimée	Airiale	Aislyn	Ajana
Ahsika	Aiiryel	Aimee-Danielle	Airian	Aislynn *(0.01)*	Ajanaé
Ahslee	Aija	Aimee-Jeanne	Airiana	Aislynne	Ajanae
Ahsleigh	Aijah	Aimee-Lynn	Airianna	Aissa	Ajanaé
Ahsley	Aijalon	Aimet	Airianne	Aissatou-Andra	Ajanahs
Ahsmatu	Aijeleth	Aimey	Airica	Aiste	Ajane
Ahtajhma	Aijia	Aimie *(0.01)*	Airicka	Aitiana	Ajané
Ahtearra	Aijzsa	Aimiende	Airiél	Aitlyn	Ajanee
Ahteea	Aika	Aimilia	Airien	Aitriona	Ajanique
Ahteelah	Aikerion	Aimmé	Airika	Aivan	Ajaniqué
Ahtiana	Aikia	Aimy	Airiona	Aivree	Ajanta
Ahuva	Aikiela	Aina	Airis	Aivy	Ajara
Ahven	Aikiera	Aindrea	Airlecia	Aixa *(0.01)*	Ajare
Ahvia	Aikilah	Aine	Airlen	Aiya	Ajayhla
Ahyana	Aikira	Ainea	Airlia	Aiyah	Ajazz
Ahyetoro	Aiko	Ained	Airn	Aiyana *(0.03)*	Ajce
Ahyris	Aila	Ainee	Airon	Aiyanna *(0.01)*	Aje
Ahzahrie	Ailana	Aingeal	Airrani	Aiyannah	Ajéna
Ahzanae	Ailcey	Ainnes	Airrel	Aiyaunda	Ajea
Ahzeah	Ailee	Ainslee	Airreonna Donni	Aiyesha	Ajee *(0.03)*
Ahzhane	Aileen *(0.10)*	Ainsleigh	Airrerna	Aiyhana	Ajee Tiombe
Ahzita	Aileena	Ainsley *(0.05)*	Airriana	Aiyona	Ajée *(0.01)*
Ahzurée	Aileigh	Ainslie *(0.01)*	Airrion	Aiyonia	Ajeemah
Ai *(0.01)*	Ailemarg	Ainulshfa	Airris	Aiyonna	Ajejandra
Ai Drianna	Ailemis	Ainzley	Airryon	Aiysha	Ajela
Ai Thuy	Ailen	Aionyea	Airyana	Aiyunna	Ajena
Ai'jeanae	Ailene	Air'reonna	Airyanna	Aiza	Ajená
Ai'keyia	Ailesh	Aira	Airyn	Aiza Jonelle	Ajenae
Ai-Vy	Ailet	Airam	Aisa	Aizara	Ajenaé
Aia	Ailey	Airana	Aischa	Aizha	Ajené
Aiah	Aili	Airanisha	Aish-A	Aizhani	Ajessica
Aialyah	Ailia	Airanna	Aisha *(0.18)*	Aizia	Ajeya
Aianna	Ailien	Aire	Aisha Mosaedssa	Aj Zhane	Ajeyah
Aiasha	Ailijah	Aireal	Aishá	Aj'rielle	Ajha
Aicha *(0.01)*	Ailin	Aireale	Aisha-Caroline	Aja *(0.09)*	Ajhane
Aicitel	Ailinh	Aireana	Aishah	Aja Ameena	Ajhanee

Ajhee	Akeema	Akia (0.02)	Akshina	Alaieya	Alanya
Ajhia	Akeemia	Akiá	Akshitha	Alaija	Alanys
Aji	Akeeondra	Akiah	Akua (0.01)	Alaijah	Alanzia
Ajia (0.01)	Akeera	Akiane	Akuabata	Alaina (0.29)	Alaqua
Ajiana	Akeero	Akiaya	Akuah	Alainah	Alaquay
Ajiane	Akeesha	Akiba	Akunna	Alaine	Alara
Ajit	Akeeyá	Akida	Akura	Alaini	Alarica
Ajitha	Akeeye	Akiea	Akuuma	Alainie	Alarious
Ajjia	Akeia	Akiela	Akvile	Alainna	Alasha
Ajla	Akeiba	Akielah	Akwaya	Alair	Alashae
Ajona	Akeidria	Akiera	Akya	Alaira	Alashava
Ajonta	Akeila	Akierra	Akyah	Alaisa	Alashawn
Ajoya	Akeilah	Akieva	Akyaira	Alaisha	Alashaye
Ajsah	Akeira	Akiho	Akyia	Alaishia	Alashia
Ajsanay	Akeisha	Akiko	Akyiah	Alaishyah	Alashná
Ajsha	Akeishia	Akila (0.01)	Akyla	Alaisjah	Alasia
Ajuana	Akeitha	Akilah (0.03)	Akylah	Alaitra	Alasiah
Ajuanne	Akeithia	Akilaih	Akynell	Alaiya	Alaska
Ajula	Akeivia	Akile	Akyra	Alaiyah	Alastria
Ajyani	Akeiya	Akilé	Akyvia	Alaiza	Alathiaalie
Akacia	Akela (0.01)	Akili	Al	Alajah	Alatians
Akadia	Akelah	Akili-Kariamu	Al Junna	Alajandra	Alauna
Akaela	Akelia	Akilia	Al Niece	Alalia	Alaundra
Akaelia	Akeliah	Akilina	Al'lia	Alalyah	Alaura (0.01)
Akaena	Akelina	Akillah	Al'nesha	Alamnesh	Alauren
Akaesha	Akelya	Akim	Al'niqua	Alan	Alavia
Akaiá	Akemi	Akimi	Al'sharaniqua	Alana (0.46)	Alavone
Akaila	Akemmy	Akina (0.01)	Al'tina	Alana Richelle	Alaweya
Akailah	Akena	Akinasi	Al-Anood	Alanae	Alaxandra
Akaisha	Akencia	Akinjaa	Al-Asia	Alanah (0.03)	Alaxandria
Akala	Akendra	Akinyi	Al-Licia	Alanda	Alaxes
Akamdeep	Akenke	Akira (0.03)	Al-Nisaa	Alandra (0.01)	Alaxis
Akamsha	Akeno	Akirah	Al-Qahtani	Alandrea	Alaxna
Akane	Akenya	Akire	Ala	Alandria (0.01)	Alaxzandria
Akansha	Akera	Akiria	Ala Ahmad	Alane	Alaya (0.01)
Akara	Akerah	Akirolyn	Aláa	Alanea	Alayah (0.01)
Akari	Akeria (0.01)	Akirrah	Ala'ysha	Alanenia	Alaychia
Akas	Akeriá	Akisha	Alaa (0.02)	Alaney	Alaycia
Akasha (0.01)	Akerra	Akita	Alaah	Alani (0.01)	Alayeea
Akashpreet	Akerria	Akiva	Alaana	Alania	Alayha
Akasia	Akeshia	Akiya	Alabama	Alanie	Alayia
Akayla (0.01)	Akessah	Akiyá	Alacia	Alanis	Alayiah
Akayla-Alesha	Akevia	Akiyah	Alacyia	Alanjreia	Alayjia
Akaylah	Akeya	Akkila	Alacyn	Alanna (0.29)	Alayla
Akaylia	Akeyhemia	Akon	Aladdin	Alanna-Marie	Alayna (0.13)
Akaysha	Akeyilla	Akosita	Aladriana	Alannah (0.09)	Alaynah
Akebia	Akeyla (0.01)	Akosua	Alae	Alannam	Alayne
Akeda	Akeylah	Akoya	Alaecia	Alannie	Alaynna
Akedra	Akeyrahia	Akreyonna	Alaena	Alannis	Alaysha (0.01)
Akeeá	Akeyri	Akrista	Alaese	Alanoud	Alayshá
Akeecia	Akeyvia	Aksa	Alaesha	Alante	Alayshia
Akeedra	Akhemjinea	Aksana	Alafia	Alanté	Alaysia (0.01)
Akeela	Akhir	Akshara	Alahna	Alantis	Alayson
Akeelah	Aki	Akshay	Alai'zia	Alantra	Alayssia
Akeely	Aki'zhane	Akshaya	Alaia	Alantris	Alaytra

Alazae	Aldyn	Alee	Aleiza	Alesis	Alexandra-Marie
Alazay	Alécia	Aleéa	Aleja	Aleska	Alexandra-Victoria
Alazaya	Aléyah	Aleea *(0.01)*	Alejadera	Alessa *(0.01)*	Alexandrae
Alazayia	Alea *(0.04)*	Aleeah	Alejandra *(1.21)*	Alessandra *(0.13)*	Alexandre *(0.02)*
Alazhe	Aleacia	Aleeanna	Alejandra-De-Laz	Alessandria	Alexandréa
Alazia	Aleacya	Aleece	Alejandria	Alessandro	Alexandrea *(0.19)*
Alba *(0.03)*	Aleada	Aleeceia	Alejandrina *(0.02)*	Alessaundra	Alexandreana
Albana	Aleah *(0.10)*	Aleechia	Alejandro	Alessea	Alexandreia
Albanesa	Aleaha *(0.01)*	Aleecia *(0.01)*	Alejha	Alessi	Alexandri
Albani	Aleahya	Aleeha	Alek	Alessia *(0.04)*	Alexandria *(2.09)*
Albanie	Aleana	Aleema	Aleka	Alesya	Alexandria-Chris
Albanisha	Aleandra	Aleen	Aleksa *(0.01)*	Aleta *(0.01)*	Alexandria-Rose
Albany	Aleandrea	Aleena *(0.04)*	Aleksandra *(0.03)*	Aletea	Alexandrie
Albaro	Aleaner	Aleenah	Aleksandrija	Aletha *(0.01)*	Alexandriea
Alberaneshia	Aleara	Aleene	Aleksandriya	Alethea *(0.01)*	Alexandrieah
Albernisha	Alease	Aleesa *(0.01)*	Aleksey	Aletheia	Alexandrina
Albert	Aleasha *(0.01)*	Aleese	Aleksi	Alethia	Alexandrine *(0.02)*
Alberta *(0.01)*	Aleashae	Aleesha *(0.04)*	Aleksia	Aletia	Alexandrya
Albertina	Aleashea	Aleeshia	Aleksija	Aletka	Alexane *(0.01)*
Albertine	Aleashia	Aleesia	Aleksis	Aletria	Alexann
Albey	Aleasia	Aleesiya	Aleksy	Aletta	Alexanna
Albina	Aleassa	Aleesjah	Alekya	Aleuah	Alexanndrea
Albranee	Aleatha	Aleessa	Alekza	Aleva	Alexanndria
Albré	Aleathea	Aleethia	Aleli	Alewah	Alexanne *(0.02)*
Albrea	Aleayah	Aleetra	Alelssandra	Alex *(0.21)*	Alexas *(0.01)*
Albreanna	Aleaysia	Aleexis	Alely	Alex Ann *(0.01)*	Alexaundrea
Albreona	Alec	Aleeya *(0.01)*	Aleman	Alex Anne *(0.01)*	Alexaundria
Albreonna	Alec'	Aleeyah	Alena *(0.10)*	Alex Sandra	Alexaundrija
Albreyon	Aleccia	Aleeza *(0.01)*	Alencia	Alexá	Alexcai
Albrica	Alece	Alegandra	Alenda	Alex-Andrea	Alexcenah
Albrittney	Alecea	Alegandrina	Alendria	Alex-Andria	Alexci
Alcaid	Aleceea	Aleggrá	Alene	Alex-Andrya	Alexcia *(0.01)*
Alcee	Aleceia	Alegra	Alenea	Alexa *(1.38)*	Alexcia Samantha
Alcia	Alechaia	Alegria	Alenia	Alexa Danielle	Alexcis
Alcida	Alechia	Aleha Koye	Alenjandra	Alexa Odetta	Alexe *(0.01)*
Alda	Alecia *(0.08)*	Alehna	Alenka	Alexa-Antoinette	Alexea
Aldan	Alecia-Marie	Alehtse	Alenna	Alexa-Jennifer	Alexei
Aldea	Aleciya	Aleia *(0.02)*	Alenny	Alexa-Jordan	Alexendra
Aldeana	Aleciyah	Aleiah	Alenya	Alexace	Alexendria
Aldeja	Aleck	Aleicia	Aleona	Alexah	Alexendrine
Alden *(0.01)*	Alecs	Aleida	Aleria	Alexahia	Alexenia
Aldenceise	Alecsandra	Aleidra	Alerion	Alexali	Alexes *(0.01)*
Aldene	Alecsandria	Aleigh	Alerrya	Alexan	Alexess
Aldercy	Alecsis	Aleigha *(0.02)*	Alesa	Alexana	Alexi *(0.07)*
Alderika	Alecsus	Aleighsha	Alesah	Alexanda	Alexia *(0.44)*
Aldesha	Alectra	Aleigiha	Alesandra	Alexander *(0.02)*	Alexia Jewel
Aldeshia	Alecxis	Aleika	Alescia	Alexandera	Alexiá
Aldon	Alecy	Aleina	Alese	Alexanderia *(0.01)*	Alexian
Aldora	Alecya	Aleis	Alesha *(0.09)*	Alexandia	Alexiana
Aldredica	Alecys	Aleisa	Aleshaann	Alexandr	Alexias
Aldrena	Aleczandra	Aleise	Aleshandra	Alexandra *(5.83)*	Alexiauna
Aldreyanna	Aleczandria	Aleisha *(0.05)*	Aleshanee	Alexandra Eliza	Alexica
Aldrian	Aleczina	Aleishka	Aleshia *(0.03)*	Alexandra Joalle	Alexicia
Aldriana	Aleda	Aleiya	Aleshya	Alexandra-Anna	Alexie *(0.03)*
Aldrin	Aledra	Aleiyah	Alesia *(0.03)*	Alexandra-Maria	

Alexiea	Alexus *(0.46)*	Alfredia	Alicyn *(0.01)*	Alisan	Alixsandria
Alexin	Alexus Lapa	Alfreida	Alicynn	Alisandra	Alixus
Alexina	Alexus'	Alfrenisha	Alida *(0.01)*	Alisar	Alixzandria
Alexine	Alexusia	Algeria	Alidia	Alischia	Alixzaundria
Alexious	Alexuss	Algernay	Alie *(0.01)*	Aliscia	Alixzendria
Alexis *(5.81)*	Alexx	Alham	Aliea	Alise *(0.02)*	Aliya *(0.05)*
Alexis Gloria	Alexxa	Alhan	Alieah	Alisea	Aliya Gwendolyn
Alexis Rogdreni	Alexxandra	Alhana	Aliecia	Alisebeth	Aliyah *(0.31)*
Alexis Rysh	Alexxas	Alhanoof	Aliegh	Alisen	Aliyaha
Alexis-Chareece	Alexxia	Alhisa	Alieh	Alisenne	Aliyan
Alexis-Danielle	Alexxis *(0.02)*	Ali *(0.11)*	Alieha	Aliseya	Aliye
Alexis-Eriahna	Alexxiz	Ali'cya	Alieje	Alisha *(0.67)*	Aliyeh
Alexis-Logan	Alexxus *(0.01)*	Ali'ya	Aliena	Alisha Kendra	Aliyha
Alexis-Marie	Alexy	Alia *(0.10)*	Aliena Rhei	Alisha-Dale	Aliyiah
Alexis-Rae	Alexya	Aliah *(0.03)*	Aliesa	Alisha-Marie	Aliysa
Alexisa	Alexyes	Aliah Mae	Aliesha *(0.02)*	Alisha-May	Aliyyah
Alexisanne	Alexyis	Aliah Nyree	Alieshia	Alishakye	Aliz
Alexiscatherine	Alexys *(0.05)*	Aliaha	Aliessi-A	Alishba	Alizé
Alexisfriendly	Alexyscharl	Aliana	Aliexandra	Alishea	Aliza *(0.03)*
Alexisia	Alexyss	Aliandra	Alieya	Alisheia	Alizabeth *(0.01)*
Alexisionnia	Alexzae	Alianna	Alieyah	Alishia *(0.03)*	Alizay
Alexisrose	Alexzallie	Alianne	Alieza	Alishiana	Alize *(0.01)*
Alexiss *(0.01)*	Alexzandera	Aliasists	Alihah	Alishonay	Alize Jeshanti
Alexiunna	Alexzandra *(0.04)*	Aliavah	Alihya	Alisia *(0.03)*	Alizé
Alexius *(0.03)*	Alexzandrea	Aliayah	Aliina	Alisin	Alizee
Alexiy'	Alexzandria *(0.02)*	Alica	Aliisa	Alision	Alizelle
Alexiyanna	Alexzandriah	Alican	Aliisha	Alison *(0.97)*	Alizha
Alexiz	Alexzandrya	Aliccia	Alija	Alison Gail	Aljana
Alexjandra	Alexzanna	Alice *(0.33)*	Alijah	Alisonn	Aljaneke
Alexjandrea	Alexzee	Alice Karolyne	Alijandra	Aliss	Aljanese
Alexnadra	Alexzena	Alicea	Alik	Alissa *(0.44)*	Aljeanae
Alexndra	Alexzianderine	Aliceandra	Alika	Alissandra	Aljexi
Alexondra	Alexzis	Alicee	Alikesha	Alissar	Aljinae
Alexondrea	Aleya *(0.01)*	Aliceeya	Aliki	Alissaya	Aljohara
Alexondria	Aleyah *(0.01)*	Aliceia	Alilia	Alisse	Aljonai
Alexous	Aleyana	Alicelia	Alilla	Alissea	Alkana
Alexsa *(0.01)*	Aleyda	Alicemarie	Alillia	Alissia *(0.01)*	Alkanisha
Alexsandra *(0.03)*	Aleyia	Alicen *(0.01)*	Alima	Alisson	Alkeea
Alexsandria	Aleyiah	Alicenn	Alimat Abisayo	Alissondra	Alkeili
Alexsandro	Aleylani	Alicesohn	Alin	Alissya	Alkyshia
Alexsandy	Aleyna	Aliceson	Alina *(0.23)*	Alistair	Alla
Alexsé	Aleysa	Alichia	Alinah	Alistine	Allaa
Alexses	Aleysha	Alicia *(2.01)*	Alinane	Alisyia	Allacia
Alexshay	Aleysia	Alicia Ann	Alinda	Alisyn *(0.01)*	Allahon
Alexsia	Aleyssia	Aliciá	Alindseya	Alita *(0.01)*	Allain
Alexsiana	Alezé	Aliciaann	Aline *(0.02)*	Alivah	Allaina
Alexsis *(0.03)*	Aleza	Aliciah	Alinna	Alivia *(0.07)*	Allaiya
Alexsiya	Alezandria	Alician	Alintina	Alivia-Jeane	Allakrea
Alexssa	Alezendria	Aliciana	Alira	Alix *(0.07)*	Allan
Alexsus	Alfa	Alicianna	Aliris	Alixandra *(0.02)*	Allana *(0.04)*
Alexsys	Alfair	Alicija	Alisa *(0.22)*	Alixandria *(0.01)*	Allanah *(0.01)*
Alextia	Alfena	Alicja *(0.01)*	Alisa-Ann	Alixandriya	Allandra
Alexuia	Alfoneisha	Alicka	Alisa-Beth	Alixe	Allandrea
Alexuis	Alfranzia	Alicon	Alisabeth	Alixia	Allanie
Alexundria	Alfreda *(0.01)*	Alicya	Alisah	Alixis	Allanna

Allantae	Allessandra	Allisondra	Allysia *(0.01)*	Alnitria	Alsya
Allante	Allesun	Allisone	Allyson *(0.58)*	Alocka	Alsyssa
Allanté	Alletta	Allissa *(0.02)*	Allyson Gail	Alocky	Alta
Allap	Allex	Allissia	Allyson-Nicole	Aloha	Altagracia
Allarie	Allexa	Allisson	Allysondra	Alohalani	Altaira
Allasen	Allexandrah	Allister	Allysonn	Alohna	Altajane
Allassandra	Allexia	Allisther	Allyssa *(0.13)*	Aloma	Altamease
Allauna	Allexis *(0.01)*	Allisun	Allyssah	Alon	Altamese
Allaura	Allexiua	Allisyn *(0.01)*	Allyssar	Alona	Altana
Allaya	Allexius	Allix	Allyssia	Alonda *(0.01)*	Altanna
Allaya-Alicia	Allexus *(0.01)*	Allixandra	Allysson	Alondra *(0.14)*	Altavia
Allayah	Allexx	Allixandria	Allyssyah	Alondrea	Altea
Allayna	Allexys	Allixandrya	Allyx	Alondria	Altenesha
Allaynia	Alley *(0.01)*	Alliya	Allyxandria	Alondriah	Altenika
Allaysha	Alleyah	Alliyah *(0.04)*	Allyxis	Alonequia	Alteria
Alle	Alleyna	Alliyha	Allyyssa	Alonia	Alterria
Alléxius Ra'ch	Alleynah	Alliyia	Allyza	Alonjae	Althea *(0.02)*
Allea	Alleysha	Alliyyah	Alméaiesha	Alonna *(0.01)*	Althea-Jean
Allea'yah	Alleysia	Allonia	Alma *(0.32)*	Alonnah	Althenthea
Alleah	Alleyson	Allontae	Alma Alicia	Alonni	Alther B.
Alleana	Allgood	Allora	Alma Brenda	Alontakeyera	Altiana
Alleara	Alli *(0.02)*	Allorah	Alma Mahura	Alontay	Alticia
Allease	Allia *(0.01)*	Allsion	Alma Rosa	Alonte	Altina
Alleasha	Alliah *(0.01)*	Allssa	Almadelia	Alontia	Altinezha
Alleaya	Alliana	Allsun	Almah	Alontra	Altinique
Allecia	Alliarra	Allura *(0.01)*	Almalydia	Alonya	Altionette
Alleda	Allicea	Ally *(0.03)*	Almanik	Alonyah	Altoneisha
Allee	Alliceson	Allya	Almanique	Alora *(0.05)*	Altonesha
Alleecia	Allicia *(0.01)*	Allyah	Almarina	Alorah	Altonia
Alleen	Allicianna	Allyce	Almarosa	Aloralee	Altoria
Alleesha	Allicson	Allycia	Almarose	Alorha	Altra
Alleesiah	Allicyn	Allycyn	Almarys	Alorie	Altrashonna
Allegra *(0.04)*	Allida	Allyease	Almas	Aloura	Altrenia
Allegria	Allie *(0.24)*	Allyesha	Almber	Alouria	Altson
Alleia	Allie-Eileen	Allyftina	Almeda	Aloxiana	Altyana
Alleigh	Alliea	Allyia	Almeera	Aloyma`	Aluncia
Alleigha	Alliece	Allyiah	Almella	Aloysia	Alundra
Alleigra	Alliegene	Allyiha	Almena	Alpana	Alundria
Alleise	Allieha	Allyisa	Almenia	Alpha	Alunte
Alleiya	Alliesha	Allyn *(0.01)*	Almesha	Alquesha	Aluntrea
Allen	Allieson	Allyn-Marie	Almetrius	Alrena	Alura
Allena	Allijah	Allyna	Almira	Alsace	Alussa
Allená	Allin	Allyne	Almmesty	Alsatia	Aluxus
Allenandra	Allina	Allynn	Almney	Alsea	Alva
Allene *(0.01)*	Allis	Allynna	Almodine	Alsey	Alvada
Allenea	Allisa *(0.02)*	Allyona	Almog	Alshanda	Alvalena
Allenisha	Allisan	Allysa *(0.05)*	Almonetsha	Alshanti	Alvalous
Allenya	Allisandra	Allysah	Almoni'	Alshanti'	Alvaro
Allerim	Allisen	Allysan	Almuqtadir	Alshaqueria	Alvera
Allerine	Allisha *(0.01)*	Allysandra	Alnasha	Alshateck	Alvertina
Allese	Allishia	Allysanne	Alneka	Alshavon	Alvety
Allesha	Allisia	Allyse *(0.01)*	Alnekia	Alshia	Alvika
Allesia	Allison *(3.46)*	Allysen *(0.01)*	Alnesica	Alshica	Alvima
Alleson	Allison-Alfreida	Allysha *(0.02)*	Alnika	Alshribina	Alvina *(0.01)*
Allessa	Allison-Marie	Allyshia	Alnisha	Alston	Alvinae

Alvinesha	Alyn	Alyssandra	Amajah	Amanjit	Amaryllis
Alvinette	Alyna (0.02)	Alysscia	Amajesty	Amanjot (0.01)	Amarys
Alvinia	Alynda	Alysse (0.01)	Amaka	Amanjyot	Amasha
Alvinita	Alyne	Alyssha	Amal (0.04)	Amanllia	Amatahallah
Alvion	Alyneisha	Alyssiá	Amala	Amanpreet (0.01)	Amatealwadood
Alvira	Alynese	Alyssia (0.09)	Amalea	Amanta	Amathis
Alvis	Alynn	Alyssiah	Amaleah	Amanté	Amathy
Alvita	Alynna	Alysson	Amaleny	Amantha	Amatikwa
Alvonna	Alyona	Alysun	Amali	Amanti	Amatullah
Alvonya	Alyra	Alythia	Amalia (0.08)	Amanveer	Amauree
Alwxandra	Alyric	Alytta	Amalia-Sandra	Amany	Amauri
Alwyn	Alyrii	Alyvea	Amalie	Amapola	Amaury
Alx	Alys	Alyvia	Amalié	Amar	Amay
Alxea	Alys'as	Alyx (0.02)	Amalija	Amara (0.06)	Amaya (0.01)
Alxis	Alysa (0.10)	Alyx-Ayn	Amalilia	Amara-Grace	Amayleea
Alxya	Alysah	Alyxa	Amalin	Amarabi	Amaziah
Aly	Alysan	Alyxandra (0.02)	Amalinda	Amarachi	Ambar (0.05)
Alya	Alysandra	Alyxandrea	Amalissa	Amarachukwu	Ambarwina
Alyah (0.01)	Alysar	Alyxandria (0.01)	Amaliya	Amarae	Ambeer
Alyaha	Alyscia	Alyxia	Amalya	Amarah	Amber (5.33)
Alyahial	Alyse (0.06)	Alyxis (0.01)	Aman (0.01)	Amaral	Amber Edith
Alyana	Alysea	Alyxzandrya	Aman'ya	Amaranta	Amber Jo
Alyanna	Alysen	Alyysa	Amana	Amaranth	Amber Lynn
Alyanna Pamela	Alysha (0.26)	Alyz	Amanaa	Amaras	Amber Marie
Alyanna-Aiko	Alysha-Ann	Alyza	Amanada (0.05)	Amaray	Amber Mary
Alyannah	Alysha-Anne	Alyza Grace	Amanat	Amardeep	Amber Yvette
Alyasa	Alysha-Jane	Alyzabeth	Amanbir	Amaree	Amber-Ann
Alyccia	Alyshah	Alyzsa	Amanda (8.34)	Amarée	Amber-Anne
Alyce (0.01)	Alyshea	Alyzza	Amanda Marie	Amareliz	Amber-Brianna
Alycea	Alyshia (0.02)	Alzaria	Amanda-Hoan	Amari (0.02)	Amber-Elizabeth
Alycen	Alyshya	Alzeta	Amanda-Jane	Amari'	Amber-Lee
Alycia (0.13)	Alysia (0.11)	Alzina	Amanda-Jean	Amaria	Amber-Leigh
Alyciah	Alysia-Deanna	Alzora	Amanda-Leigh	Amariah	Amber-Lynn
Alycon	Alysiagh	Am Brea	Amanda-Lyn	Amarialis	(0.01)
Alyda	Alysiah	Am'ber	Amanda-Lynn	Amariann	Amber-Lynne
Alydia	Alysica	Ama	Amanda-Rae	Amarie	Amber-Mae
Alyeah	Alysin	Amaal	Amanda-Rose	Amariell	Amber-Marie
Alyena	Alyson (0.29)	Amaanat	Amandah	Amarii	Amber-Mary
Alyeria	Alyson Michelle	Amabel	Amandajane	Amarilis	Amber-May
Alyesa	Alyss	Amada	Amandalee	Amarily	Amber-Nechole
Alyesha	Alyssa (4.87)	Amadi	Amandalynn	Amarilys	Amber-Nicole
Alyessa	Alyssa Aines	Amadria	Amandee	Amaris (0.05)	Amber-Rae
Alyessea	Alyssa Ashley	Amahni	Amandeep (0.02)	Amarissa	Amber-Rose
Alyeyah	Alyssa Elizabeth	Amaia	Amandia	Amarit	Amber-Tyra
Alyhia	Alyssa Leigh	Amaili	Amandra	Amaritpal	Amberae
Alyi	Alyssa-Ann	Amaily	Amandy	Amariyah	Amberaye
Alyia	Alyssa-Beth	Amaira	Amane	Amarjit	Ambereen
Alyiah (0.01)	Alyssa-Dorthy	Amairaine	Amanee	Amaron	Amberia
Alyica	Alyssa-Jena	Amairan	Amaneet	Amarpal	Amberice
Alyicia	Alyssa-Mae	Amairane	Amaney	Amarpreet	Amberine
Alyisa	Alyssa-Marie	Amairani (0.05)	Amani (0.06)	Amarri	Amberishia
Alyissa	Alyssa-Michelle	Amairanie	Amani'	Amarta	Amberjot
Alyjah	Alyssa-Shanae	Amairany (0.01)	Amania	Amaryah	Amberlain
Alyka	Alyssabeth	Amaiya	Amanie	Amaryla	Amberle
Alymius	Alyssah	Amaiyah	Amanie-Fadda	Amarylis	Amberlea

Amberlee *(0.01)*	Ambria *(0.02)*	Amelia-Fay	Amiellia	Amit	Amoolee
Amberleigh	Ambriah	Amelia-Josephine	Amielue	Amita	Amoon
Amberley *(0.01)*	Ambriana	Amelie *(0.43)*	Amierah	Amitai	Amora
Amberli	Ambrianna	Amelija	Amii	Amitha	Amordai
Amberlie	Ambriel	Amelinda	Amija	Amithyst	Amore
Amberlin	Ambriele	Amellia	Amika	Amitie	Amoré
Amberlina	Ambrielle	Amely *(0.01)*	Amiko	Amitis	Amoree
Amberlly	Ambrill	Amelya	Amiksha	Amitoj	Amoretta
Amberly *(0.05)*	Ambrin	Amen	Amikya	Amity *(0.01)*	Amorette
Amberlye	Ambrine	Amena	Amila	Amiya	Amori
Amberlyn *(0.01)*	Ambrisha	Amenah	Amilah	Amiyah	Amoricka
Amberlyne	Ambriya	Amenda	Amilee	Amjad	Amorie
Amberlynn *(0.01)*	Ambrocya	Amendeep	Amili	Aml	Amorkor
Ambermae	Ambrosha	Amenita	Amilia *(0.01)*	Amleset	Amortia
Ambermarie	Ambrosia *(0.01)*	Amenmaat	Amiliana	Amma	Amory
Ambernique	Ambrozia	Amer	Amilie *(0.01)*	Ammal	Amorya
Amberniqueka	Ambrya	Amera	Amillia	Ammala	Amoshia
Ambernisa	Ambryel	Ameral	Amily	Ammanda	Amoure
Ambernishia	Ambrynn	Amerea	Amilya	Ammany	Amoy
Amberr	Ambuhr	Ameree	Amilyn	Ammarah	Amoya
Amberrose	Ambur	Amerh	Amilynne	Ammaris	Amparo *(0.02)*
Ambershalom	Ambur-Lyne	Ameria	Amina *(0.07)*	Ammber	Ampreal
Ambershay	Ambure	America *(0.06)*	Aminah *(0.01)*	Ammee	Ampreale
Ambes	Ambyr *(0.01)*	Americana	Aminat	Ammerman	Ampriana
Ambika	Ambyre	Americe	Aminat Mary	Ammie	Amran
Ambor	Ame	Amerie	Aminata	Ammiee	Amreen
Ambra *(0.01)*	Amea	Amerika	Aminatu	Ammonie	Amreet
Ambraesha	Amecca	Ameris	Aminda	Ammons	Amreetha
Ambrah	Amecia	Ameritia	Amine	Ammy	Amren
Ambrana	Amecka	Amerlynn	Aminea	Amna *(0.01)*	Amrena
Ambrasia	Amee *(0.01)*	Amery	Aminee	Amnah	Amress
Ambraya	Amée	Amerylis	Amineh	Amnastee	Amri
Ambre	Ameena *(0.01)*	Amesha	Aminh	Amneel	Amria
Ambre-Lynn	Ameenah	Ameshia	Aminia	Amneet	Amrinah
Ambrea	Ameeqa	Amethyot	Aminpreet	Amnesty	Amrit *(0.02)*
Ambreal	Ameera *(0.01)*	Amethyst *(0.02)*	Aminta	Amni	Amrita *(0.02)*
Ambreana	Ameerah	Amethyst-Marie	Amintha	Amninder	Amritha
Ambreanna	Ameesha	Ametria	Amir	Amnit	Amritpal
Ambree	Ameeshia	Ametrias	Amira *(0.05)*	Amogechi	Amritpaul
Ambreem	Ameet	Ametrish	Amiracle	Amol	Amritpreet
Ambreen	Ameeta	Amey	Amirah *(0.01)*	Amola	Amruta
Ambreetta	Amega	Amgelique	Amireer	Amollia	Amrutha
Ambreia	Ameila	Amher	Amiri	Amon	Amry
Ambreial	Ameilia	Ami *(0.04)*	Amiriam	Amoné	Amte
Ambreion	Ameilya	Ami'	Amirical	Amonee	Amthul
Ambrekia	Ameisha	Amia *(0.01)*	Amirita	Amoni	Amtoj
Ambrell	Ameka	Amiah	Amiron	Amoni'	Amtul
Ambresha	Amekia	Amiana	Amirra	Amonie	Amulya
Ambreshia	Amel	Amiaya	Amirrah	Amonique	Amun
Ambret	Amela	Amica	Amirriah	Amonité	Amunique
Ambrey	Amelaine	Amichia	Amirtha	Amonna	Amy *(2.47)*
Ambreya	Amelcka	Amicia	Amirthavarshini	Amonney	Amy-Catherine
Ambri	Ameleigh	Amie *(0.09)*	Amisadai	Amonnie	Amy-Jacqueline
Ambri-Shel	Amelia *(0.60)*	Amiee *(0.01)*	Amisha	Amonyca	Amy-Jo
	Amelia Masumi	Amielle	Amishia	Amonye	Amy-Lee

Amy-Leigh	Ana-Marina	Anaisie	Analysha	Anastaysia	Anderalla
Amy-Lynn	Anab	Anaitte	Analysia	Anastazia (0.01)	Anderanette
Amy-Nicole	Anabel (0.09)	Anaivis	Analyssa	Anastazja	Anderann
Amya	Anabela	Anaiz	Analysse	Anastesia	Andericka
Amye	Anabele	Anaja	Analyssia	Anastia	Anderika
Amyia	Anabelen	Anajah	Anam (0.01)	Anasuya	Anderina
Amyieshia	Anabeli	Anajai	Anamaria (0.01)	Anatasia	Andersa
Amyjah	Anabell	Anajana	Anamarie	Anathea	Andersen
Amyjo	Anabella	Anajeia	Anamarija	Anatia	Anderson
Amylea	Anabelle (0.04)	Anajelly	Anamartin	Anatolia	Andess
Amylee	Anabely	Anajha	Anamary	Anau	Andezha
Amyleigh	Anaberis	Anajia	Anamica	Anauncia	Andi (0.02)
Amylia	Anacaren	Anakah	Anamika	Anaus	Andi-Jo
Amyllia	Anacarolina	Anakaisa	Anampreet	Anavel	Andia
Amyra	Anacary	Anakaren (0.03)	Anan	Anavely	Andie (0.04)
Amyrah	Anaceli	Anakarina	Ananda	Anaya	Andie-Mae
Amyre	Anacelia	Anakarla	Anandhi	Anayah	Andonae
Amythest	Anache	Anakary	Anandjit	Anayele	Andora
Amythist	Anaczia	Anakita	Ananis	Anayeli (0.02)	Andovia
Amythyst	Anadaria	Analaura (0.01)	Ananthigai	Anayely	Andr
An (0.01)	Anadea	Analea	Anaregina	Anayetzi	Andra (0.02)
An Gell	Anadela	Analee	Anareli	Anayid	Andraea
An Jhaelyn	Anadelis	Analeesha	Anarely	Anayiz	Andrai
An Jhanae	Anadi	Analeeze	Anari	Anayliz	Andraique
An'aam	Anadia	Analeigh	Anarmily	Anays	Andraliesha
An'chayla	Anadora	Analeis	Anarosa	Anaysa	Andramada
An'deshi	Anaé	Analeticia	Anaryka	Anaysha	Andrana
An'dia	Anael	Anali (0.02)	Anaset	Anazjia	Andranay
An'drea	Anaeli	Analia	Anasha	Anbarin	Andranequia
An'jerica	Anafusipala	Analice	Anasheia	Anber	Andranice
An'jerika	Anagraviela	Analicia (0.02)	Anashia	Anbrea	Andranika
An'jonai	Anah	Analie	Anashiana	Anbrosha	Andranique
An'quanette	Anahai	Analies	Anasia	Anca	Andranise
An'ya	Anaheeta	Analiese	Anasiya	Ancaria	Andranisieya
An-Novis	Anahi (0.07)	Analillia	Anasja	Anchal	Andraya
Ana (1.12)	Anahid	Analilya	Anassa	Anchala	Andrazia
Ana Alicia	Anahit (0.01)	Analis	Anastacha	Anchevia	Andre
Ana Aurelia	Anahita	Analisa (0.02)	Anastacia (0.04)	Anchu	André
Ana Aurora	Anahiza	Analise (0.02)	Anastacie	Ancurlisha	Andréa (0.01)
Ana Cecilia	Anahy (0.01)	Analisha	Anastagha	Andala	Andréah
Ana Christina	Anai (0.03)	Analisia	Anastaisa	Andaliyaha	Andréanna
Ana Gabriela	Anaia	Analissa	Anastaisha	Andasia	Andréneshia
Ana Karen	Anaiah	Analita	Anastascia	Ande	Andréya
Ana Leza	Anaid	Analiz	Anastasha	Andee (0.01)	Andre-Anne
Ana Lucia	Anaida	Analiza	Anastashah	Andee-Mari	Andrèa
Ana Maria	Anaidi	Analleli	Anastashia	Andeep	Andrea (3.14)
Ana'stiee	Anaiesa	Anallely	Anastasi	Andeisha	Andreá
Ana-Brijida	Anaija	Anallie	Anastasia (0.37)	Andeka	Andrea-Celine
Ana-Carime	Anaile	Analucia	Anastasija	Andela	Andrea-Sheunna
Ana-Celilia	Anairis	Analucy	Anastasja	Andelin	Andrea-Stephanie
Ana-Cristina	Anais (0.10)	Analuz	Anastassia	Andeline	Andreaella
Ana-Emilia	Anais'	Analy	Anastasue	Andelyn	Andreah
Ana-Len	Anais-Nicole	Analysa	Anastasya	Andelynn	Andreaka
Ana-Lisa	Anaisa	Analyse	Anastatia	Andenequia	Andrean
Ana-Maria	Anaise	Analyse-Belle	Anastayshia	Andera	Andreana (0.02)

Andreane *(0.02)*
Andreanet
Andreanna *(0.01)*
Andreanne *(0.17)*
Andreas
Andreaunna
Andreca
Andree *(0.01)*
Andree Ann *(0.01)*
Andree Anne *(0.04)*
Andree-Ann
Andree-Anne
Andreea
Andreena
Andreha
Andreia *(0.01)*
Andreielle
Andreina *(0.02)*
Andreisha
Andreja
Andreka
Andrekah
Andrekia
Andreli
Andrelia
Andrell
Andrelle
Andrellica
Andrelnette
Andrena
Andrenasha
Andrené
Andrenea
Andreneisha
Andrenene
Andrenequa
Andreniece
Andrenique
Andreona
Andrequa
Andres
Andresha
Andretta
Andrew
Andrewetta
Andrewneka
Andreya *(0.01)*
Andreyana
Andreyonna
Andrez
Andrezza
Andri'ynne
Andria *(0.08)*
Andrian

Andriana *(0.02)*
Andrianna *(0.02)*
Andrianná
Andrianne
Andrias
Andricia
Andriel
Andriel'
Andrienne
Andrietta
Andrija
Andrika
Andrikkah
Andrina
Andrinka
Andriona
Andrionna
Andris
Andrisell
Andriss
Andriurkis
Andriyah
Andromahi
Andromeada
Andromeda
Androniki
Andronique
Andrunea
Andrus
Andry
Andrya
Andrzelika
Anduyen
Andy
Andyrea
Ane
Ané
Anéjha
Aneaka
Aneasia
Aneca
Anecia
Aneek
Aneeka
Aneela
Aneeqa
Aneesa *(0.01)*
Aneesha *(0.01)*
Aneeshia
Aneet
Aneeta
Aneeza
Aneicia
Aneila
Aneisa

Aneisha
Aneitha
Aneitra
Aneka
Anekia
Anel *(0.03)*
Anela
Anela'okalani
Anela-O-Kanani
Anelbi
Aneli
Anelie
Aneliese
Anelique
Anelisa
Anelise
Anem
Anephia
Anequia
Aneres
Anerica
Anerlee
Anesa
Anese
Anesha *(0.01)*
Aneshia *(0.01)*
Anesia *(0.01)*
Anessa *(0.02)*
Anessia
Anestacia
Anet
Aneta *(0.01)*
Anetha
Anethia
Anetmarie
Anetra
Anetria
Anetris
Anetta
Anette
Anevia
Anexa
Anexis
Anexy
Aneyele
Aneysha
Aneytraei'
Aneza
Anfaal
Anfal
Anfisa
Anfrenea
Angél
Angailiqua
Angalek

Angaletta
Angali
Angalina
Angalisa
Angam
Angara
Angblique
Ange
Ange Le
Angel *(0.72)*
Angel Marie
Angel-Rita
Angel-Simone
Angela *(1.96)*
Angela Lourdes
Angela Nga
Angela-Lee
Angelaca
Angelann
Angelay
Angelca
Angele *(0.01)*
Angelea *(0.01)*
Angeleah
Angelece
Angelee
Angeleen
Angeleena
Angeleigh
Angeleka
Angelena *(0.01)*
Angelene
Angeles *(0.02)*
Angeli
Angelia *(0.06)*
Angelian
Angelic *(0.03)*
Angelica *(1.45)*
Angelica France
Angelica Marie
Angelica Nicole
Angelica-Evelis
Angelica-Lee
Angelica-Marie
Angelice
Angelicia *(0.01)*
Angelicque
Angelie *(0.01)*
Angeliena
Angeliga
Angeliine
Angelik
Angelika *(0.04)*
Angelike
Angeliki

Angelin
Angelina *(0.45)*
Angelina-Maria
Angelinamarina
Angeline *(0.06)*
Angelinna
Angelinque
Angeliqe
Angelique *(0.24)*
Angelique Alexis
Angelique-Simone
Angelis
Angelisa *(0.01)*
Angelise
Angelisha
Angelissa
Angelisse
Angelita *(0.04)*
Angelita Patricia
Angell *(0.01)*
Angella *(0.01)*
Angellaka
Angelle *(0.01)*
Angelleana
Angellecca
Angellena
Angelli
Angellia
Angellica *(0.01)*
Angellie
Angellina
Angellyia
Angelnisha
Angelou
Angelque
Angelsea
Angelu
Angely
Angelyanne
Angelyca
Angelyce
Angelyn *(0.01)*
Angelyna
Angelynn
Angelys
Angene
Angenette
Angenica
Angeoica
Angerika
Angharad
Anghel
Anghela
Angie *(0.18)*

Angiedina
Angieleen
Angielena
Angielyn
Angiemyr
Angieneth
Angilena
Angilezaall
Angilia
Angilica
Anginae
Anginette
Anginique
Angjela
Angle *(0.01)*
Anglee
Anglena
Anglenia
Anglequie
Anglica
Anglicque
Anglina
Angrea
Angsleka
Angsley
Angu
Anguinisha
Anguyuaq
Angy
Angyalka
Angyl
Angyla
Angynae
Anh *(0.02)*
Anh-Thu
Anh-Tram
Anh-Tu
Anh-Tu Emmeline
Anhar
Anhdang
Anhelika
Anhhong
Anhthu
Ani *(0.02)*
Ani'ya
Ania *(0.01)*
Ania Lauren
Aniah
Anialette
Anias
Aniaya
Anica *(0.01)*
Anices
Anicia
Anick

Anicka	Anisty	Anjene	Ann-Taylor	Annadele	Annalyse
Anidra	Anita (0.22)	Anjené	Anna (3.90)	Annagen	Annalysia
Anieca	Anita-Lynn	Anjernique	Anna Britt	Annagrace	Annalyssa
Aniecia	Anita-Zahari	Anjeska	Anna Gabriella	Annah (0.02)	Annam
Aniedi	Anitamarie	Anjhané	Anna Judite	Annah-Marie	Annamae
Aniela	Anitdra	Anjillina	Anna Katherine	Annahi	Annamari Joset
Aniella	Anite	Anjily	Anna Kathryn	Annahy	Annamaria (0.01)
Anielyn	Anitique	Anjinai	Anna Ki	Annai	Annamarie (0.06)
Aniema	Anitra (0.02)	Anjiya	Anna Kristina	Annaice	Annamary
Aniesa	Anitraous	Anjlee	Anna Lea	Annajillian	Annamica
Aniesha	Anitrea	Anjly	Anna Luisa	Annaka	Annamicca
Aniessa	Anitria	Anjnette	Anna Lynn	Annakaren	Annaneisha
Anietria	Anitta	Anjoilique	Anna Madeline	Annakarent	Annarae
Anieya	Anixa	Anjola	Anna Margaret	Annakarina	Annarosa
Anifa	Aniya (0.01)	Anjoli	Anna Maria (0.01)	Annakiah	Annarose
Anig'	Aniyah	Anjolique	Anna Marie (0.01)	Annalacia	Annaruth
Aniger	Aniysa	Anjonette-Mauric	Anna May	Annalaura	Annas
Anihhya	Aniza	Anju	Anna Ruth	Annalea	Annasha
Anihja	Anizha	Anjuli (0.01)	Anna Teresa	Annaleah	Annastacia
Anija	Anja (0.01)	Anjulique	Anna-Alesia	Annalecia	Annastasha
Anijah	Anja'le	Anjuna	Anna-Alicia	Annalee (0.02)	Annastashia
Anijarae	Anjala	Anjunae	Anna-Brooke	Annaleesa	Annastasia (0.02)
Anik (0.01)	Anjalace	Anjunea	Anna-Christine	Annaleigh	Annastasija
Anika (0.09)	Anjalea	Anjutha	Anna-Jane	Annaleigha	Annastaysia
Anikah	Anjalee	Anka	Anna-Julia	Annaleise	Annastazia
Anike	Anjalena	Ankaria	Anna-Katarina	Annalena	Annasteacha
Anikka	Anjali (0.03)	Ankia	Anna-Katharina	Annalene	Annastel
Aniko	Anjalie	Ankita	Anna-Kristina	Annalese	Annastesia
Anilea	Anjalisa	Ankitha	Anna-Lashae	Annalesia	Annatake
Anilia	Anjana	Ankiyah	Anna-Laura	Annali	Annatasia
Anilu	Anjanae	Ankush	Anna-Lee	Annalia	Annataya
Animah	Anjanai	Anlena	Anna-Leigh	Annalicia	Annavell
Animikiikwe	Anjanea	Anli	Anna-Linn	Annalie	Annber
Anina	Anjanee	Anlondria	Anna-Lisa	Annalie Marie	Anncy
Anine	Anjanette	Anly	Anna-Lise	Annalies	Anndee
Aniqa	Anjani	Anlya	Anna-Liza	Annaliesa	Anndelia
Aniqua (0.01)	Anjanie	Anmari	Anna-Lizzi	Annaliese (0.02)	Annderria
Anique	Anje	Anmarie	Anna-Louise	Annalin	Anndi
Aniqueka	Anjélique	Anmol (0.01)	Anna-Lysa	Annalina	Anndraia
Aniquia	Anjee	Ann (0.33)	Anna-Maria	Annalinda	Anndrea
Anirak	Anjeet	Ann Alyce	Anna-Marie (0.02)	Annalis	Anndria
Aniria	Anjel	Ann Chapin	Anna-Michelle	Annalisa (0.05)	Anne (0.69)
Anisa (0.06)	Anjela (0.01)	Ann Elizabeth	Anna-Nicole	Annalise (0.07)	Anne - Marie
Anisah	Anjele	Ann Julie	Anna-Simone	Annalisha	Anne Catherin
Anise (0.01)	Anjeleek	Ann Margaret	Anna-Sophia	Annalissa	(0.01)
Anisha (0.08)	Anjelica (0.09)	Ann Marie (0.01)	Anna-Stasia	Annalisse	Anne Claire
Anishawfe	Anjelicia	Ann Sarah	Anna-Therese	Annalita	Anne Frederiq
Anishia	Anjelika	Ann Sophie (0.01)	Annabal	Annaliza	Anne Gabriell
Anishuaw	Anjelina	Ann-Carolin	Annabel (0.06)	Annallena	Anne Julie (0.02)
Anisia	Anjella	Ann-Chloe	Annabelie	Annaly	Anne Laurence
Anissa (0.24)	Anjelle	Ann-Dee	Annabell (0.01)	Annalycia	Anne Marie (0.10)
Anissah	Anjellica	Ann-Louise	Annabella (0.01)	Annalyn	Anne Sophie
Anissi	Anjeluca	Ann-Marie (0.01)	Annabelle (0.13)	Annalyn Clare	(0.07)
Anissia	Anjelyka	Ann-Nesha	Annabeth	Annalynn	Anné
Anistacia	Anjenae	Ann-Pauline	Annaclaire	Annalysa	Anne-Barrett

Anne-Caroline	Annet	Annisia	Annyes	Antaisha	Anthea
Anne-Cecilia	Anneta	Annissa (0.03)	Annyssa	Antaleah	Antheayéza
Anne-Dahlie	Annete	Annissia	Anoja	Antalisha	Antheia
Anne-Julie	Annetta	Annistassia	Anonna	Antalya	Anthi
Anne-Lise	Annette (0.14)	Anniston	Anoojie	Antanae	Anthia
Anne-Marie (0.03)	Annette-	Annita	Anoop	Antanasha	Anthonae
Anne-Pascale	Catherine	Annitra	Anoopam	Antanea	Anthonavia
Anne-Phalonne	Anngalina	Anniyah	Anoosha	Antanee	Anthonee
Anne-Sophie	Anngella	Annja	Anora	Antaneka	Anthonella
(0.01)	Anngilee	Annjanette	Anorah	Antanese	Anthonese
Annea	Anngilyn	Annjeanette	Anoree	Antanesha	Anthonesha
Anneasha	Anni	Annjela	Anoriana	Antaneshia	Anthoneshea
Annebelle	Anniéce	Annjelicia	Anoshia	Antanetta	Anthonette
Annecia	Annia	Annjenette	Anouchka	Antanette	Anthoni
Anneciah	Annica	Annjerrica	Anouk (0.02)	Antaneya	Anthonia
Annecy	Annice	Annkatrin	Anquainette	Antangela	Anthonique
Annee	Annicia	Annkeila	Anquaneisha	Antania (0.01)	Anthonisha
Anneece	Annick (0.03)	Annlynne	Anquaneki	Antanica	Anthony (0.01)
Anneelyse	Annicka	Annmaria (0.02)	Anquanequa	Antanil	Anthonyiek
Anneisha	Annie (0.50)	Annmarie (0.05)	Anquanett	Antanina	Anthonysha
Anneiya	Annie Claude	Annne	Anquanette	Antanisha	Anthonyshia
Annejannette	(0.01)	Annoja	Anquania	Antanshaa	Anthoula
Annejulie	Annie Johannah	Annolivia	Anquanisha	Antara	Anti Onna
Anneka	Annie Kim (0.01)	Annora	Anquanita	Antas'zsa	Antia
Anneke (0.01)	Annie Mae	Annquanesha	Anquantis	Antasha	Antiana
Annekiya	Annie Pier (0.01)	Annquanette	Anquicea	Antashay	Antianna
Annel	Annie-Claude	Annquinita	Anquinetta	Antashia	Antiara
Annel-La	Annie-Laurel	Annriya	Anquinette	Antasia	Anticia
Anneleisce	Annie-May	Annslee	Anquneice	Antaver	Antigone
Anneleissa	Annie-Pier	Annsley	Anquneisha	Antavia	Antigoné
Anneli	Annie-Rose	Annslie	Anqunette	Antayvia	Antimesha
Annelia	Annieaque	Anntaesh A	Anqwanette	Ante	Antina
Annelie	Anniebell	Anntaneshia	Anraya	Antea	Antineka
Anneliese (0.03)	Anniecia-Daniel	Anntanya	Anrea	Anteaira	Antinesha
Annelisa	Anniejoy	Anntashamonique	Ansa	Anteasa	Antinet
Annelise (0.04)	Annieka	Anntaylor	Ansajanee	Anteia	Antinia
Anneliza	Annielle	Annteniah	Anseca	Anteisha	Antinique
Annelize	Annieluz	Annteona	Anselynn	Antelica	Antiona
Annell	Anniese	Anntiarra	Anshaleka	Antenesha	Antione
Annella	Anniesha	Anntoinette	Anshanti	Anteneshia	Antionesia
Annelle	Annietra	Anntonette	Anshaunti	Antenia	Antionet
Annellie	Anniina	Anntravea	Anslea	Anteniece	Antionett
Annely	Annik	Anntrece	Anslee	Antenis	Antionette (0.03)
Annelyn	Annika (0.08)	Anntrell	Ansleigh (0.01)	Antenisha	Antionia
Annelyse	Annike	Annudeep	Ansley (0.09)	Antennellia	Antionique
Annemarie (0.05)	Anniken	Annunziata	Anslie	Anteonna	Antionnette
Annemiek	Annikka	Annural	Anslynn	Anteria	Antiqua
Annena	Annilee	Annusa	Ansonia	Anterica	Antiqudra
Anneria	Anninthika	Annushka	Anstasiya	Antericka	Antirra
Annesa	Annique	Annwin	Answa	Anterria	Antisha
Annesha	Annis	Anny (0.01)	Ant'shaquita	Antesha	Antishamonay
Anneshia	Annisa (0.01)	Anny Joyce	Ant'taishia	Antesia	Antitauna
Annesia	Annise	Annya	Antacia	Antezia	Antivione
Annesly	Anniseh	Annyana	Antaesha	Anthania	Antiwonesha
Annessa (0.01)	Annisha (0.01)	Annye	Antaijah	Anthasia	Antje

Antnesha	Antonyse	Antwinique	Anyce	Appolonia	Aquila *(0.01)*
Anto'nia	Antonysha	Antwoinesha	Anycia	Apprentice	Aquilla *(0.01)*
Antoinay	Antoria	Antwoinque	Anyea	Aprael	Aquinas
Antoinda	Antowanette	Antwokeyia	Anyia	Aprésha	Aquinda
Antoiné	Antowanna	Antwonasha	Anyminah	Aprecia	Aquindana
Antoineesha	Antownette	Antwonesha	Anysa	Apreshelle	Aquinette
Antoinel	Antoya	Antwonet	Anysha	Apreshun	Aquinna
Antoinesha	Antoyanisha	Antwonete	Anyshiya	Apriah	Aquira
Antoinet	Antoynette	Antwonett	Anysia	Aprianna	Aquita
Antoinetta	Antquanique	Antwonette	Anysja	Apriel	Aqurah
Antoinette *(0.15)*	Antranae	Antwonika	Anyssa *(0.05)*	April *(1.02)*	Aquria
Antoinic	Antraneice	Antwynek	Anyssa Liyah	April Ann	Aquwona
Antoinique	Antraneshia	Antwynette	Anza	April Sherrie	Aqwauneshay
Antoinisha	Antranette	Antya	Anzalique	April-Danielle	Ar'ian
Antoinnette	Antranice	Antyanna	Anzanetta	April-Marie	Ar'ja
Anton'nae	Antranise	Antycha	Anzhane	April-Summer	Ar'karyia
Antonae	Antravia	Antynique	Anzhané	Aprill	Ar'keria
Antonay	Antravies	Anu	Anzlie	Aprille	Ar'leecia
Antonaya	Antravius	Anugelica	Anzu	Aprilli	Ar'queen
Antone	Antrea	Anuhea	Aoibheann	Aprilyn	Ar'rellya
Antoné	Antreal	Anuhya	Aoife	Aprull	Ar'ricia
Antonea	Antreneck	Anuja	Aolani	Apryl *(0.01)*	Ar'teedra
Antonece	Antrenise	Anule	Aomori	Apsimosis	Ar'temrahs
Antonee	Antreshaye	Anum *(0.01)*	Apache	Apya	Ar'tia
Antoneisha	Antria	Anum-Kausar	Aparna	Apyaya	Ara
Antonela	Antriana	Anumeet	Apearl	Aqbaal	Ara'via
Antonella *(0.01)*	Antrianna	Anupa	Apearre	Aqeela	Araba
Antoneria	Antrice	Anupama	Aperame-Aru	Aqia	Arabe
Antonesha	Antricia	Anupinder	Aphaia	Aqila	Arabel
Antoneshia	Antrickia	Anupkaur	Aphasia	Aqrisha	Arabell
Antonett	Antrinice	Anupreet	Aphelion	Aqsa	Arabella
Antonette *(0.02)*	Antrinique	Anuradha	Aphia	Aquailla	Arabelle
Antonetté	Antrinita	Anureet	Aphra	Aquaisha	Arabi
Antoneya	Antronel	Anuri	Aphracea	Aquala	Arabia
Antoni	Antronette	Anurit	Aphrael	Aqualyn	Arabiah
Antonia *(0.16)*	Antroniqua	Anuruthiya	Aphrah	Aquanala	Aracele
Antonice	Anttanishia	Anusha	Aphrika	Aquandra	Araceli *(0.26)*
Antonie	Antterious	Anushaa	Aphrodisiac	Aquanette	Aracelia
Antoniesha	Anttu	Anusheh	Aphrodite	Aquaria	Aracelis
Antonietta	Antuanette	Anushka	Apinaya	Aquaries	Aracelli
Antoniette	Antuanette-	Anushri	Apinder	Aquarius	Aracely *(0.08)*
Antonija	Charlotte	Anusia	Apiphani	Aquasha	Aracelys
Antonik	Antwainetra	Anusiya	Apiphanni	Aquashá	Aracia
Antonina *(0.01)*	Antwainnette	Anuvir	Apiramy	Aquashia	Aradeli
Antonine	Antwana	Anverlin	Apirita	Aquasia	Aradhana
Antonio	Antwanett	Anvita	Apirrami	Aquavia	Arae
Antonique *(0.01)*	Antwanette	Anvy	Apita	Aqueelah	Arah
Antonise	Antwanic	Anwar	Apolinaria	Aquela	Arahzad
Antonisha *(0.01)*	Antwanika	Anwen	Apolinia	Aquene	Arai'ya
Antonita	Antwanique	Anwesha	Apolonia	Aquenna	Araial
Antoniya	Antwanish	Anwyn	Aponi	Aquesha	Araina
Antonnella	Antwanisha	Anya *(0.06)*	Appalonia	Aquia	Araisa
Antonnette	Antwashaé	Anyae	Apparchia	Aquiana	Araiya
Antonyeisha	Antwéasia	Anyah	Appifany	Aquiel	Araleili
Antonyque	Antwi	Anyai	Apple	Aquielle	Arali

Arali Chardonnay
Araliya
Araly
Aram
Aramalix
Aramina
Aramis
Aranda
Arandeep
Arandeni
Arandy
Arani
Arantxa
Arantza
Aranzazu
Araseli *(0.02)*
Arasely
Arash
Arasha
Arashdeep
Arashpreet
Arathi
Arati
Aravene
Araya *(0.01)*
Arayah
Arayana
Araynia
Arayshea
Araz
Arazi
Arazo
Arbanaé
Arbella
Arbenita
Arberesha
Arbiona
Arbnora
Arbrea
Arbrealle
Arbreana
Arbreasia
Arbrelle
Arbria
Arbriana
Arbrianna
Arbriéanna
Arbrielle
Arbutus
Arcadia
Arcangela
Arcashia
Arcasia
Arcaya
Arcelia *(0.02)*

Archa
Archana
Archangela
Archchana
Archchanna
Archelle
Archer
Archieva
Archinda
Architha
Archna
Arcina
Arcisha
Arcsheria
Arctavia
Arctica
Arcyca
Ardaijah
Ardajah
Ardajahyia
Ardana
Ardea
Ardedra
Ardelaine
Ardell
Ardelle
Ardema
Arden *(0.03)*
Ardena
Ardenesia
Arderia
Ardina
Ardis
Ardo
Ardraya
Ardrina
Ardriyanna
Ardyce
Ardyst
Area
Areal
Areana
Areanna
Areatha
Arecca
Arecia
Arecshiya
Areduna
Areeba
Areej
Areen
Areeqa
Areetha
Arefa
Arei

Areial
Areil *(0.01)*
Areila
Areile
Areion
Areiyen
Areka
Arel
Arelee
Areleesia
Areli *(0.06)*
Areli'
Arelia
Arelica
Areliema
Arelis
Arella
Arelli
Arellia
Arelly
Arellys
Arely *(0.07)*
Arelya
Arelys
Aremi'
Aren
Arena
Arenda
Arenthial
Areon
Areona
Areonna
Aresea
Areshae
Aretha
Areti
Aretta
Areyanna
Areyonna
Areyonne
Arezo
Arfah
Argentina
Argyro
Arhea
Arhema
Ari *(0.01)*
Ari Yana
Ariéus
Ari'l
Ari'onna
Ari'yana
Ari-Chanel
Aria *(0.06)*
Aria'nna

Ariacne
Ariadna *(0.01)*
Ariadne
Ariah *(0.01)*
Ariahna
Ariahnna
Arial *(0.01)*
Ariam
Ariamis
Arian *(0.01)*
Ariana *(0.91)*
Ariana Yvonne
Arianá
Arianah
Ariance
Arianda
Ariandrah
Ariane *(0.19)*
Ariann
Arianna *(0.48)*
Arianna Cind
Ariannah
Arianne *(0.09)*
Arianny
Arianyia
Arias
Ariauna
Ariaunna
Ariayanna
Ariba
Aribella
Arica *(0.02)*
Aricca
Aricela
Aricka
Aricka Dazja
Aridaid
Arie *(0.01)*
Arie L
Arie-Ann
Ariea
Ariea'na
Arieal
Ariealle
Arieana
Arieanna *(0.01)*
Arieanne
Arieauna
Ariege
Ariel *(0.92)*
Ariel Antio
Ariel-Anne
Ariel-Maria
Ariela *(0.01)*
Arielah

Ariele *(0.01)*
Arieliz
Ariell *(0.01)*
Ariella *(0.05)*
Arielle *(0.30)*
Arielle Carina
Arielle Marie
Arielleanne
Arielyn
Arielys
Arielyss
Arien
Ariena
Ariene
Arienna
Arienne
Arieon
Arieona
Arieonna
Arieonté
Arier
Aries *(0.01)*
Ariesdyce
Ariess
Arietta
Arieva
Arieyonna
Ariez
Arifah
Arija
Arijana
Arika *(0.04)*
Arike
Arikiraa
Arikka
Arilyn
Arimalena
Arimie
Arimn
Arin *(0.02)*
Arin-Alexis
Arina
Arinea
Ariniesha
Arinique
Arinna
Arinola
Arinthia
Ariole
Arion
Ariona *(0.01)*
Arionna *(0.01)*
Arionne
Ariqa
Aris

Arisa
Arisara
Arisbet
Arisbeth
Ariselda
Arisendi
Arisha
Arishma
Arishona
Arishta
Arisi
Arisia
Arisleidy
Arismel
Arismenia
Arispa
Ariss
Arissa *(0.02)*
Arisse
Arista
Aristana
Aristen
Aristina
Arisvett
Arith
Aritisha
Aritneese
Aritney
Ariuana
Arius
Ariva
Ariya
Ariyah
Ariyan
Ariyana
Ariyanna
Ariyel
Ariyeona
Ariyon
Ariyonia
Ariyonna
Ariyonne
Ariyuna
Ariza
Arizbeth
Arizona *(0.01)*
Arizz
Arizzona
Arjaena
Arjana
Arjanae
Arjanai
Arjenique
Arjutha
Arkasia

Arkavia	Arlicia	Armirica	Arnisya	Arriele	Artaviauna
Arkayla	Arlidian	Armisa	Arnithia	Arriell	Artavius
Arkea	Arlie	Armisha	Arnitia	Arrielle	Artaysha
Arkeevia	Arliesha	Armisher	Arnitra	Arrien	Artayssia
Arkeia	Arliett	Armita	Arnizhia	Arrienne	Arteisha
Arkeisha	Arlillie	Armon	Arnnitra	Arrin	Arteishara
Arkeithia	Arlim	Armonda	Aron	Arrington	Artemisia
Arkela	Arlin	Armondi	Arondi	Arrinica	Artequa
Arkeni	Arlina	Armoni	Arone	Arrinique	Arteria
Arkenia	Arlincia	Armonti	Aronesia	Arriola	Artesha
Arkeria	Arlinda	Armreel	Aronique	Arrion	Arteshia
Arkeriahe	Arline	Armynda	Arooj	Arrionna	Artesia
Arkerria	Arlis	Arna	Arora	Arris	Artessa
Arkesha	Arlisa	Arnace	Arouj	Arrisa	Arteya
Arkeshia	Arlise	Arnaisa	Aroura	Arrius	Arthea
Arkeya	Arlisha	Arnasha	Aroyn	Arron	Arthel
Arkeyia	Arlisia	Arnasia	Arpa	Arronia	Arthika
Arkeyla	Arliss	Arnasian	Arpil	Arronice	Arthty
Arkeysia	Arliyah	Arnazia	Arpna	Arruniya	Arthur
Arkia	Arlonda	Arnece	Arquavia	Arry	Arti *(0.01)*
Arkilra	Arlonia	Arnecia	Arquisia	Arryan	Artia
Arkira	Arlyann	Arnedra	Arquita	Arryana	Artiana
Arkisha	Arlyn	Arneesha	Arquitta	Arryanna	Artianna
Arkiya	Arlyn Danielle	Arneet	Arranda	Arryn	Articha
Arla	Arlynn	Arneica	Arranka	Arsema	Artie
Arlanda	Armaity	Arneish	Arrashae	Arsemia	Artiera
Arlandra	Arman	Arneisha *(0.01)*	Arrayh	Arsenia	Artiesha
Arlandria	Armanee	Arneishia	Arreal	Arshana	Artiffany
Arlania	Armani *(0.01)*	Arnelda	Arreana	Arshanae	Artisha *(0.01)*
Arleada	Armani'	Arnell	Arreanna	Arshanda	Artisia
Arleah	Armanii	Arnella	Arreashá	Arsharelle	Artkesha
Arlean	Armanis	Arnellda	Arreba	Arshawna	Artlisia
Arleathia	Armanni	Arnelle *(0.01)*	Arreisha	Arshay	Artoria
Arlee	Armauni	Arnereanna	Arrelia	Arshayla	Artrease
Arleen *(0.02)*	Armecia	Arnesa	Arren	Arshbir	Artrece
Arleene	Armeciya	Arnesha *(0.01)*	Arreon	Arshdeep *(0.01)*	Artrell
Arleigh	Armel	Arneshia	Arreonna	Arsheika	Artrese
Arlen	Armelle	Arnesia	Arreva	Arshi	Artresia
Arlena *(0.02)*	Armendy	Arnesse	Arria	Arshica Keyerra	Artresis
Arlene *(0.15)*	Armenter	Arnesta	Arriah	Arshika	Artrevia
Arleny	Armerina	Arnetia	Arrial	Arshiniece	Artrez
Arlesha	Armesha	Arnetria	Arriana *(0.01)*	Arshiya	Artrice
Arleshia	Armesia	Arnett	Arrianna	Arshneel	Artricea
Arlesia	Armetha	Arnetta	Arrianne	Arshontae	Artrinae
Arlessia	Armetra	Arnice	Arrianta	Arshpreet	Artumese
Arlet	Armetrice	Arnicea	Arrianya	Arshvir	Artvenia
Arletha	Armetris	Arnicia	Arrias	Arsiama	Aruba
Arlethea	Armi	Arnie	Arriauna	Arténcia	Aruna
Arlethia	Armig	Arniecia	Arrica	Art'keshia	Arundeep
Arlett	Armijo	Arnieciea	Arricka	Artajia	Aruni
Arlette *(0.01)*	Armincia	Arnika	Arrie	Artameiz	Arunima
Arlexia	Arminda	Arnina	Arrieal	Artana	Arunpreet
Arley	Armindie	Arniquekia	Arrieauna	Artashina	Arunyah
Arli	Armine	Arnisha *(0.01)*	Arriel *(0.01)*	Artasia	Arusa
Arlia	Armirah	Arnissia	Arriela	Artavia	Arusha

Arushana	Asa *(0.01)*	Ashanté	Ashelie	Ashleen *(0.01)*	Ashliana
Arushi	Asabe	Ashant'i	Ashelle	Ashleena	Ashlie *(0.14)*
Arveen	Asafoni	Ashanta	Ashelley	Ashleh	Ashlie Ann
Arvette	Asala	Ashantae	Ashellina	Ashlei *(0.03)*	Ashlie Milinda
Arvina	Asalah	Ashantai	Ashelly	Ashleigh *(0.59)*	Ashliee
Arvind	Asalee	Ashantay	Ashely *(0.07)*	Ashleigh Nicole	Ashliegh *(0.01)*
Arvinder	Asalh	Ashante *(0.02)*	Ashely Hau	Ashleigh-Rae	Ashlih
Arvneet	Asalia	Ashanté *(0.01)*	Ashelyn	Ashleighan	Ashlin *(0.03)*
Arvola	Asami	Ashantee	Ashelynne	Ashleighana	Ashlind
Arvyette	Asanki	Ashanti *(0.10)*	Ashenee	Ashlely	Ashling
Arwa *(0.01)*	Asanoula	Ashanti'	Asher	Ashlen *(0.02)*	Ashlinn
Arwah	Asante	Ashantie	Ashera	Ashlene	Ashlinne
Arwan	Asantewa	Ashantier	Asherah	Ashlenn	Ashliy
Arwen	Asasha	Ashantinika	Asheton	Ashley *(13.56)*	Ashllee
Arwilda	Asasia	Ashantis	Asheyla	Ashley Andrea	Ashlley
Ary	Asata	Ashara	Ashi	Ashley Ann	Ashlly
Aryah	Asaudi'	Ashari	Ashi'ana	Ashley Bernadine	Ashlon
Aryan	Asberry	Asharie	Ashia *(0.03)*	Ashley Breo	Ashlon'
Aryana *(0.02)*	Aschia	Asharma	Ashiana	Ashley Damilola	Ashlun
Aryanah	Aschley	Asharri	Ashijah	Ashley Denise	Ashlunn
Aryane	Aseal	Ashaté	Ashika	Ashley Josephine	Ashly *(0.14)*
Aryann	Aseantia	Ashaun	Ashilei	Ashley Joy	Ashlyan
Aryanna *(0.02)*	Aseanya	Ashauna	Ashilin	Ashley Kate	Ashlye
Aryannah	Aseel	Ashauni	Ashily	Ashley Marie	Ashlyen
Aryanne	Aseelah	Ashaunta	Ashima	Ashley Nicole	Ashlyn *(0.52)*
Aryauna	Aseirie	Ashaunte	Ashington	Ashley T	Ashlyne
Arychez	Asena	Ashaunté	Ashinique	Ashley Yahui	Ashlynn *(0.16)*
Aryel *(0.01)*	Aseneth	Ashaunti	Ashira	Ashley'sue	Ashlynn Joy
Aryelle *(0.01)*	Ash Lee	Ashauti	Ashita	Ashley-	Ashlynne *(0.02)*
Aryenne	Ashá	Ashawna	Ashitha	Alexandrea	Ashma
Aryeris	Ash'leigh	Ashawnti	Ashiyande	Ashley-Ann	Ashmere
Aryes	Ash-Lee	Ashay	Ashiyia	Ashley-Anne	Ashmi
Aryies	Ash-Leigh	Ashaya	Ashjah	Ashley-Elizabeth	Ashmin
Aryion	Asha *(0.12)*	Ashayana	Ashjley	Ashley-Jessie	Ashminder
Aryka	Asha-Kaye	Ashaye	Ashka	Ashley-Josselyn	Ashmini
Arylette	Ashadia	Ashayla	Ashkeia	Ashley-Kristen	Ashna
Aryn *(0.03)*	Ashae	Ashaymarie	Ashkira	Ashley-Kristian	Ashnaa
Aryne	Ashaela	Ashby	Ashla	Ashley-Krystal	Ashney
Arynn	Ashahamdi	Ashd	Ashlan *(0.01)*	Ashley-Lynn	Ashnique
Arynne	Ashai	Ashden	Ashland	Ashley-Maria	Ashnti
Aryona	Ashakela	Ashdon	Ashlann	Ashley-Marie	Asholey
Aryonna	Ashaki	Ashe	Ashlar	Ashley-May	Ashonda
Arys	Ashalin	Ashé	Ashlay	Ashley-Nicole	Ashonique
Arysa	Ashallie	Ashea	Ashlay-Lyne	Ashley-Raye	Ashonta
Arysbet	Ashally	Ashean	Ashle *(0.01)*	Ashley-Symone	Ashontay
Aryssa *(0.01)*	Ashan'ti	Asheaun	Ashléon	Ashley-Victoria	Ashonte
Aryza	Ashana	Ashee	Ashlea *(0.03)*	Ashleyann	Ashonté
Aryzona	Ashanah	Asheera	Ashleah	Ashleyanne	Ashontee
Arze	Ashanday	Asheika	Ashlean	Ashleye	Ashonti *(0.01)*
Arzeen	Ashani	Asheka	Ashleanna	Ashleyh	Ashonti'
Arzeena	Ashaniece	Ashel	Ashlee *(0.69)*	Ashleyn	Ashontis
Arzoo	Ashanik	Ashelae	Ashlée *(0.01)*	Ashleys	Ashonty
Arzu	Ashanique	Ashele	Ashlee-Ann	Ashleytate	Ashontys
As'janaye	Ashanna	Asheleigh	Ashlee-Marie	Ashli *(0.09)*	Ashony
As'liaha	Ashant E	Asheley *(0.01)*	Ashleeh	Ashlian	Ashouraita

Ashourina	Asias	Aspyn *(0.01)*	Aszhaan	Atiene	Atwooki
Ashpreet	Asieona	Aspynn	Aszjeca	Atiera	Atyan
Ashrena	Asifa	Asra	At'lea	Atika	Atyana
Ashrita	Asiha	Asraa	Ataa	Atileti	Atylica
Ashsa	Asila	Asrael	Ataijah	Atima	Atyra
Ashtan	Asilah	Asre	Ataila	Atina	Au Jonae
Ashtar	Asili	Asriel	Atajah	Atinana	Au Kia
Ashten *(0.03)*	Asima	Asrin	Atalain	Atinderpal	Au'bria
Ashti	Asiria	Assadassa	Atalanta	Atinuke	Au'drianna
Ashtin *(0.04)*	Asisa	Assata	Atalanti	Atiqah	Au'lyrics
Ashtine	Asisha	Asseel	Atalaya	Atira	Au'ntranaé
Ashton *(0.39)*	Asiya *(0.01)*	Assel	Atalee	Atiri	Au'sani
Ashtyn *(0.08)*	Asiyah	Asselah	Atalia	Atisa	Au'shanta
Ashtynne	Asiyanna	Assia	Atalie	Atisha	Au'tiana
Ashudee	Asiza	Assiatu	Atalina	Atiya *(0.02)*	Au'tianna
Ashunta	Asizhane	Assira	Atallah	Atiyá	Au'vian
Ashunte	Asja *(0.01)*	Assya	Atanas	Atiyah *(0.01)*	Aubanita
Ashunti	Asjá	Assyria	Atanya	Atiyana	Auber
Ashunti'	Asjah	Asta	Atara	Atiyonna	Auberny
Ashuntis	Asjanae	Astara	Ataraah	Atiyya	Aubery
Ashura	Asjenia	Astaria	Atarah	Atlanta *(0.01)*	Aubony
Ashurina	Asjha	Astarry	Atasha	Atlantis	Aubra
Ashveen	Asjia	Astassia	Atavia	Atlee	Aubrae
Ashvini	Askor	Astazia	Atawjah	Atmiyata	Aubranee
Ashviniy	Aslan	Asteney	Atayah	Atoconia	Aubre
Ashwini	Aslaug	Aster	Atayia	Atoria	Aubré
Ashya *(0.01)*	Aslen	Astera	Atazia	Atoriana	Aubrea
Ashyabibi	Asley	Asthrid	Ateana	Atorria	Aubreana
Ashyana	Aslhley	Asti-Marie	Ateante	Atoshica	Aubreanna
Ashyia	Asli	Aston	Atearia	Atour	Aubree *(0.11)*
Ashykia	Asliene	Astoncia	Atefa	Atra	Aubree Ivo
Ashylie	Aslin	Astoria	Ateiya	Atravia	Aubrée
Ashylnn	Aslinn	Astou	Atejah	Atraya	Aubrei
Ashyna	Aslyn	Astra	Atenas	Atreona	Aubreigh
Ashyuna	Aslynn	Astraea	Athamandia	Atreya	Aubreiona
Ashyveal	Asma *(0.02)*	Astraya	Athanaa	Atriana	Aubren
Ashzia	Asmá	Astri	Athanasia	Atrice	Aubrene
Asia *(0.53)*	Asmaa *(0.01)*	Astria	Athciri	Atrina	Aubretia
Asia Aaliyah	Asmabanu	Astrid *(0.07)*	Athea	Atrionna	Aubrey *(0.45)*
Asia Anissa	Asmae	Astride	Atheena	Atriunna	Aubrey-Anne
Asia Marquise	Asmah	Astry	Atheenia	Atsiri	Aubrey-Lee
Asia-Lea	Asmahan	Astyn	Athelia	Attalah	Aubreyana
Asiaalana	Asmara	Asu	Athen	Attaleigh	Aubreyanna
Asiah *(0.01)*	Asmau	Asucena	Athena *(0.13)*	Attalia	Aubreyanne
Asiana	Asminda	Asuka	Athenas	Attallah	Aubreyena
Asiane	Asmita	Asunique	Athenie	Attasha	Aubreyiá
Asianee	Asmnita	Asusena *(0.02)*	Athenoula	Attessa	Aubreynia
Asianeic	Asmoni	Asvini	Athens	Attirah	Aubreyona
Asianek	Asonta	Aswathy	Athere	Attisyn	Aubreyonna
Asianese	Asontasia	Aswini	Athina *(0.01)*	Attiyah	Aubri *(0.01)*
Asianna *(0.01)*	Aspacia	Asya *(0.02)*	Athirat	Attlah	Aubri'anna
Asianne	Aspasia	Asyá	Athran	Attra	Aubria
Asiannia	Aspen *(0.12)*	Asyah	Athyna	Attya	Aubriana *(0.01)*
Asiantia	Aspenn	Asyata	Atiana	Aturena	Aubriane
Asiaonna	Aspin	Asyia	Atianna	Atusa	Aubriann

Aubrianna *(0.01)*	Audrey Anna	Aukelia	Aunmol	Aurora *(0.16)*	Autumnn
Aubrianne	Audrey Anne	Aukia	Aunna	Aurora Celeste	Autumnstorm
Aubrie *(0.07)*	*(0.07)*	Aula	Aunnalaray	Aurora/Faith	Autunn
Aubrie-Elle	Audrey Maude	Aulana	Aunt'	Aury	Autuum
Aubriea	*(0.01)*	Aulbrie	Auntash	Ausensia	Autym
Aubrieanna	Audrey-Emilia	Auleah	Auntel	Auset	Autymn
Aubrieaunne	Audrey-Lynn	Aulena	Auntiana	Ausha	Auva
Aubriegh	Audrey-Marie	Aulexis	Auntravia	Aushawnda	Auvion
Aubriel	Audreyana	Auli'i	Aunya	Aushéana	Auybriana
Aubrielle *(0.01)*	Audreyanna	Aulicia	Aunyae	Ausheirah	Auystainia
Aubrienne	Audreyauna	Aulisa	Aunyeja	Aushia	Auyuna
Aubriesha	Audreylee	Auliyah	Aunyiea	Aushinett	Auyunna
Aubrion	Audreyona	Aumara	Aunzhanae	Aushiona	Auz'janae
Aubriona	Audri	Aumbrey	Auocean	Aushlynn	Auzainna
Aubrionna	Audria	Auminee	Auquida	Aushunea	Auzaya
Aubriuna	Audriana *(0.02)*	Aun'jelika	Auqurra	Aushzanique	Auzhane
Aubry *(0.01)*	Audrianna *(0.04)*	Aun-Marie	Aura *(0.01)*	Ausia	Auzhaneek
Aubryelle	Audrianne	Auna	Auralee	Ausinikka	Auzna
Aubryn	Audrice	Aunae	Auraleigh	Aussie	Auzsa
Auburey	Audrie *(0.01)*	Aunaleisa	Auralia	Austa	Av
Auburn *(0.02)*	Audriea	Aunalyss	Auralis	Austen *(0.01)*	Av'era
Auburney	Audrienna	Aundi	Aurayla	Austi	Ava *(0.12)*
Aubyan	Audrienne	Aundraea	Aurbriney	Austianna	Ava Linda
Aucia	Audrijean	Aundranay	Aurbyanna	Austin *(0.09)*	Ava-Dawn
Audajiha	Audrina *(0.01)*	Aundraya	Aurdey	Austinah	Ava-Marie
Audasia	Audrinna	Aundréa	Aurdra	Austine	Avah
Aude *(0.01)*	Audrisha	Aundrea *(0.05)*	Aurea	Austraia	Avairee
Audelia	Audrishá	Aundrea-Rehnee	Aureal	Australia	Avaiu
Auden	Audry *(0.01)*	Aundreah	Aureana	Australya	Avalee
Audessie	Audrya	Aundreal	Aureauna	Austrea	Avallone
Audia	Audryanna	Aundreanna	Auree	Austriana	Avalon *(0.04)*
Audissea	Audumn	Aundreia	Aurela-Patrycja	Austyn *(0.02)*	Avalona
Audora	Auguna	Aundrell	Aurelia *(0.03)*	Austynn	Avalyn
Audra *(0.11)*	August *(0.02)*	Aundrena	Aurelie *(0.04)*	Autam	Avan
Audra-Lyn	August-Sierra	Aundria	Aurelis	Autamn	Avanche
Audralee	Augusta *(0.01)*	Aundrianna	Aurena	Autaneak	Avanda
Audralynn	Auguste	Auneesha	Aurenesha	Autasha	Avanel
Audre	Augustia	Auneet	Aureon	Autasia	Avanell
Audré	Augustina	Aunekah	Aureonde	Autaum	Avangelia
Audréonna	Augustine	Aunekqua	Aureonia	Autavia	Avani
Audrea *(0.01)*	Auhsha	Auneshá	Aureonna	Autesha	Avanjelina
Audreana	Auisha	Auneshia	Auria	Autia	Avanté
Audreanna	Auj'nae	Aungela	Auriahna	Autionna	Avante-Marie
Audreanne *(0.01)*	Auja	Aungelica	Aurian	Autri	Avantee
Audree *(0.03)*	Aujahnae	Aungelina	Auriana *(0.01)*	Autry	Avanti
Audreia	Aujamia	Aungelique	Aurianah	Autuam	Avari
Audreianna	Aujana	Aungelle	Aurianna	Autum *(0.03)*	Avarie
Audreihanna	Aujanee	Aunia	Auriel *(0.01)*	Autuma	Avary
Audrelia	Aujanée	Auniece	Aurielia	Autume	Avaya
Audrenique	Aujaun-Nae	Aunika	Aurielle	Autumece	Avayla
Audreona	Aujela	Aunisia	Aurienday	Autumm	Avaz
Audreonna	Aujonae	Aunita	Aurieona	Autumn *(1.19)*	Avazia
Audresha	Aujuanaé	Aunjalique	Auriestela	Autumn Yvon	Avdhi
Audrey *(1.38)*	Aujuané	Aunjuae	Aurita	Autumn-Jade	Ave
Audrey Ann *(0.05)*	Aujunae	Aunjunae	Auritze	Autumn-Rose	Aveance

Avee	Avione	Axelle (0.01)	Ayiesha	Ayonda	Ayzlin
Aveen	Avira	Axelle-Gabriell	Ayina	Ayondria	Az'jinay
Aveena	Avis	Axenya	Ayisat	Ayonna (0.01)	Aza
Aveesha	Avishan	Axis	Ayisha	Ayréona	Azadeh Soghra
Aveeyon	Avita	Ay'anna	Ayishwarya	Ayreael	Azaela
Aveleena	Avital	Ay'dreain	Ayjah	Ayreanna	Azahla
Avelina	Avital-Vicki	Aya (0.04)	Ayjai	Ayreial	Azahria
Aveline	Aviva (0.01)	Ayaan	Ayjshia	Ayreona	Azaija
Avely	Aviyon	Ayaana	Ayla (0.12)	Ayreonna	Azaila
Avemaria	Avla	Ayaat	Ayla Rose	Ayres	Azaina
Aven	Avleigh	Ayah (0.02)	Ayla-Marie	Ayrian	Azalea (0.02)
Avenamar	Avneet (0.02)	Ayahni	Aylah	Ayriana	Azalee
Aveon	Avni	Ayahnna	Aylan	Ayrica	Azalia
Averee	Avnika	Ayaka	Aylassa	Ayrie Bckyll	Azaliah
Averell	Avnit	Ayako	Aylea	Ayrielle	Azalie
Averey	Avnoor	Ayala	Ayleace	Ayrienna	Azaline
Averi (0.02)	Avo	Ayalia	Ayleah	Ayrika	Azamina
Averia	Avoly	Ayan (0.02)	Ayleanna	Ayrione	Azaneth
Averianna	Avona	Ayana (0.10)	Aylee	Ayrionna	Azanethe
Averiauna	Avoni	Ayani	Ayleem	Ayris	Azantae
Averie (0.01)	Avonlea (0.01)	Ayania	Ayleen	Ayriss	Azar
Averil	Avonna	Ayanna (0.12)	Aylene	Ayrmis	Azara
Averinesha	Avonte	Ayannagrace	Aylenne	Ayrn	Azaria (0.02)
Averiona	Avorie	Ayannah	Aylennmaria	Ayron	Azariah
Avery (0.26)	Avory	Ayannia	Ayleshia	Ayrron	Azarial
Averyanna	Avrea	Ayano	Ayli	Ayrssa	Azarra
Averyl	Avreah	Ayantan	Aylien	Aysa	Azarya
Averyneqa	Avree	Ayasha	Ayliesha	Aysan	Azea
Avhlee	Avri	Ayasmine	Aylin	Ayse	Azeb
Avi	Avrie	Ayat (0.01)	Aylinn	Ayseah	Azeema
Avia	Avriel	Ayatt	Aylish	Aysel	Azeemah
Aviana (0.01)	Avrielle	Ayauna	Aylisha	Aysen	Azeen
Avianca	Avril	Ayballin	Aylison	Aysh	Azeeza
Aviance	Avrinder	Aybie	Aylissa	Aysha (0.03)	Azelia
Aviancé	Avrya	Aybriel	Aylla	Ayshe	Azena
Aviane	Avunna	Aydasha	Ayllisia	Ayshea	Azerdi
Avianna	Avvan	Ayde	Aylssa	Ayshia	Azeria
Aviante	Avy	Aydee	Aylwyn	Ayshonna	Azeta
Avie	Avyana	Aydelisa	Aymara	Aysia (0.02)	Azha
Aviel	Avyanna	Ayden	Ayme	Aysiah	Azhana
Aviella	Aw'neisha	Aydrian	Aymed	Ayslan	Azhanae
Avience	Awa	Ayésha	Aymee	Ayslynn	Azhané
Aviendha	Awanda	Ayea	Aymie	Aysriel	Azhanti
Avigail	Awatif	Ayeala	Aymiey	Ayssha	Azhare
Avigayil	Awauaniki	Ayeesha	Ayna	Aysvn	Azhia
Avika	Awawu	Ayeh	Aynea	Aytia	Azhiá
Avila	Awaz	Ayeisha	Aynesha	Ayuanna	Azhree
Avilene	Awbrianna	Ayelet	Aynslee	Ayumi	Azhudrea
Aviley	Awnare	Ayenna	Aynsley	Ayuna	Azia (0.01)
Avilgayle	Awnjana	Ayera	Aynur	Aywak	Azia-Dawn
Avin	Awntranielle	Ayeri	Ayodele	Ayyat	Aziah
Avina	Awnzsa	Ayesha (0.05)	Ayoka	Ayzel	Aziel
Avion	Awo	Ayesha Ahsan	Ayoma	Ayzha	Azierena
Avionce	Awut	Ayeshah	Ayomide	Ayzhia	Azikia
Avioncé Jované	Axa	Ayha	Ayona	Ayzia	Azilee

Azima	B.	Baja	Bao Nhi	Barthibah	Baylee *(0.19)*
Azin	Ba-Adisah	Bakari	Bao Yen	Bartola	Baylee-Anne
Azina	Baanoola	Bakayendel	Bao-Ngoc	Bartow	Baylei
Azinne	Babandeep	Bakeirathy	Bao-Quyen	Bartrecia	Bayleigh *(0.02)*
Aziona	Babetta	Baker	Bao-Tran	Bartresa	Baylen
Azita	Babette	Bakhtawar	Bao-Vi	Basant	Bayley *(0.03)*
Aziza *(0.01)*	Babie	Bakiya	Baotram	Bascha	Bayli *(0.01)*
Azizah	Babneet	Bakiyaa	Baraá	Basha	Bayli Michelle
Azize	Babriela	Balana	Bara'h	Bashaama	Bayli-Anne
Azjah	Bacari	Balaria	Baraa	Bashamah	Baylie *(0.03)*
Azka	Bach	Baldeep	Barah	Bashan	Bayliee
Azlan	Badana	Baleigh *(0.01)*	Baraha	Basheba	Bayliegh
Azley	Badhatu	Balentine	Barakia	Bashée	Baylijo
Azlin	Baek	Baleria	Baranda	Basia	Baylin
Azlyn	Baelee	Baley	Baraniha	Basilhea	Baylor
Azmina	Baeleigh	Bali	Barbara *(0.34)*	Basilisa	Bayly
Azra	Baeley	Balie	Barbara Ann	Basilyne	Bayo
Azraa	Baeli	Baliegh	Barbara Jean	Basima	Bayonne
Azrea	Baeyle	Baljinder	Barbara-Anne	Basirat	Bays
Azrian	Bafleg	Baljit	Barbara-Jean	Basiymah	Be
Azriel	Bah'jey	Baljot	Barbara-Rose	Basma	Béanna
Azsa	Baha	Balkos	Barbarajean	Basmah	Bénisha
Azsane	Bahaar	Ballery	Barbarella	Basro	Bealyn
Azsha	Bahar	Balley	Barbee	Basseema	Beashley
Azsia	Bahareh	Balneerez	Barbera	Bastian	Beata
Aztra	Bahati	Balpreet	Barbi	Basya	Beate
Azucena *(0.05)*	Bahia	Balreet	Barbie	Bata	Beathamae
Azura	Bahirah	Balssam	Barbinder	Batania	Beatitude
Azuravesta	Bahja	Baltej	Barblina	Batelhim	Beatric
Azurdee	Bahlandra	Balwinderjit	Barborah	Bathany	Beatrice *(0.14)*
Azure *(0.01)*	Bai Lee	Bambi	Barbra *(0.01)*	Bathsheba	Beatris *(0.02)*
Azuré	Bai-Leigh	Bambie	Barbra-Jean	Batool *(0.01)*	Beatrix
Azuree	Baiden	Bambizvidi	Barbralyn	Batoul *(0.01)*	Beatriz *(0.24)*
Azurée	Baiky	Bana	Barbrey	Batrice	Beatriz Angelica
Azurelyn	Baila	Banafsheh	Barbriell	Batsheva	Beatty
Azuri	Baile	Banaz	Barby	Battle	Beau
Azurley	Bailea	Bancy	Barcardia	Batul	Beaubolean
Azusena	Bailee *(0.13)*	Bandeep	Barea	Batya	Beaulah
Azuza	Bailée	Bandna	Bari *(0.01)*	Bau	Beauletta
Azwana	Bailei	Bandrea	Bariah	Bauer	Beaunca
Azya	Baileigh *(0.01)*	Baneen	Barieann	Bavyn	Beaunka
Azyah	Bailey *(1.41)*	Baneeskia	Barkha	Bawan	Beautiful
Azyia	Bailey Jo	Baneet	Barkley	Bawneet	Beauty
Azzelyn	Baili *(0.01)*	Baneita	Barkli	Bay	Bebe
Azzhaley	Baili-Ann	Banesa *(0.01)*	Barnhild	Bay-Leigh	Bebecca
Azzie	Bailie *(0.03)*	Baneza	Barrah	Bayaan	Bebesis
Azzra	Baillee	Banika	Barredo	Bayan	Bebhinn
	Bailley	Baninder	Barrett *(0.01)*	Bayanka	Beca
-B-	Bailli	Banne	Barri	Bayann	Becca *(0.03)*
	Baillie *(0.01)*	Banny	Barrie	Bayanna	Beccalynn
B *(0.04)*	Baily *(0.02)*	Bansari	Barrinesha	Baydan	Becka *(0.01)*
B'atriss	Bailye	Banu	Barron	Bayla	Beckey
B'etta	Bailyn	Banuji	Barry	Bayle	Becki
B'onca	Baina	Banushaa	Barsherri	Baylea *(0.01)*	Beckie
B'shara	Bairavi	Bao *(0.02)*	Barshona	Bayleah	Becklin

Becky *(0.05)*	Belquis	Beracah	Berni	Bethanie *(0.02)*	Betzai'
Becky Marie	Belsabel	Berangere	Berni-Lynn	Bethann	Betzaida
Becqua	Belsy	Beranna	Bernice *(0.06)*	Bethanna	Betzayra
Beda	Belti	Berdeisha	Bernice Karon	Bethanne	Betzy
Bedahbin	Belul	Berdine	Bernicia	Bethannie	Beulah
Bedran	Belynda	Berea	Berniesha	Bethanny	Beushaie
Bedriah	Ben'nae	Berean	Bernikkia	Bethany *(1.07)*	Beutty
Bee	Benafsha	Bereanna	Bernisee	Bethany June	Bevan
Beejal	Benay	Bereda	Bernisha	Bethany Michaela	Bevanee
Beena	Benda	Berendina	Bernita	Bethany Rose	Bevel
Beenish	Bene Chevelle	Berenice *(0.15)*	Bernitta	Bethany-Anne	Bevely
Beerat	Benea	Berenis	Beronia	Bethany-Jane	Beven
Beesan	Benedicte *(0.01)*	Berenise *(0.01)*	Beronica	Bethay	Beverley *(0.01)*
Befunei Ma-Y	Beneet	Berenisi	Berquandria	Bethel	Beverley-Anne
Beige	Benesha	Berenisse	Berretta	Bethelle	Beverlly
Beighly	Benetria	Berenitse	Berrey	Bethelyn	Beverly *(0.15)*
Beittany	Benetrice	Bereniz	Berrin	Bethenie	Bevin
Beja	Benevieu	Berenize	Berrion	Betheny	Bevneet
Bekah	Benfsha	Berenizze	Bersabem	Bethia	Beya
Bekcy	Beng	Beretnize	Bershada	Bethie	Beyanka
Bekendrianna	Bengu	Beretta	Bershaun	Bethiel	Beyaunka
Bekka	Beni	Bergen	Berta *(0.01)*	Bethlehem *(0.01)*	Beyleigh
Bektu	Benicia	Beri	Bertevia	Bethlhem	Beyonca
Bela	Benisha	Berit	Bertha *(0.07)*	Bethlyn	Beyonka
Belah	Benita *(0.01)*	Berkeley	Bertice	Bethlynn	Beyonna
Belainesh	Benjamin	Berkley *(0.01)*	Bertina	Bethney	Beyza
Belantha	Benjanee	Berkly	Bertisha	Bethni	Beza
Belcky	Benkely	Berlanne	Bertreice	Bethnie	Bezawit
Belda	Benlie	Berlayna	Berucka	Bethny	Bg
Belecia	Benlina	Berlin	Bervelie	Bethonay	Bhaanurubi
Belen *(0.07)*	Benna	Berlinda	Bervely	Bethsaida	Bhagwanpreet
Belenda	Bennautica	Berline	Berverlie	Bethzabe	Bhakti
Belia	Bennet	Berlisha	Beryl	Bethzael	Bhalwender
Belicia	Bennett	Berlitha	Besa	Betina	Bhanu
Belieff	Bennetta	Berlynda	Besan	Betnay	Bharathi
Belim	Bennie	Berlynn	Besarta	Betquweshia	Bhareh
Belina	Benniesha	Berlynne	Beselot	Betsabe	Bhargavi
Belinda *(0.10)*	Bennika	Bermary	Bess *(0.01)*	Betsaida	Bhavika
Belinda May Mee	Bennita	Bermetra	Bessie *(0.01)*	Betsey	Bhavina
Belinda-Aikee	Bennjamin	Berna	Beste	Betsi	Bhavini
Belise	Benta	Bernadete	Beta	Betsie	Bhavjot
Belkis	Benthe	Bernadett	Betania	Betsua	Bhavna
Belky	Bentleigh	Bernadetta	Betel	Betsy *(0.07)*	Bhavneet
Belkys	Bentley	Bernadette *(0.09)*	Betellhem	Bette	Bhawan
Bella *(0.03)*	Bentli	Bernadine	Beth *(0.15)*	Bette Brook	Bhawandeep
Bellarosa	Bentlie	Bernaé	Beth Ann	Bettey	Bhawanjot
Belle *(0.01)*	Benyetta	Bernaiyya	Beth Anne	Betthany	Bhawna
Belle-Marie	Benyiwenu	Bernara	Beth-Ann	Betti	Bhrea
Belliqwa	Beonca	Bernarda	Beth-Anne	Bettianne	Bhrianna
Bellkeis	Beondra	Bernardette	Bethalin	Bettie	Bhrooke
Bellkiss	Beonica	Bernardine	Bethan	Bettina *(0.01)*	Bhume
Bellona	Beonka	Bernel	Bethanee	Betty *(0.12)*	Bhumi
Bells	Beosha	Bernelle	Bethaney	Betul	Bhumika
Belocet	Ber Nisha	Berneta	Bethani *(0.02)*	Betzabe	Bhupinder
Belquesé	Ber'da'ja-Al'	Bernetta	Bethania	Betzabel	Bhupinderjit

Bi'anncha	Billee	Birgitta	Blayne (0.01)	Bobi Jo	Bowie
Bi'onnie	Billena	Biridiana (0.01)	Blayre	Bobie	Bownie
Biaca	Billi (0.01)	Biridiona	Blaze	Bobo	Bowsmena
Biahna	Billi Jo	Birlyn	Bleida	Bobresha	Boyanna
Biamca	Billi-Jo	Birtha	Blendina	Bobrianna	Boyc
Biana	Billie (0.10)	Birunthaa	Blenna	Bobriona	Boyce
Bianca (1.41)	Billie Ann	Bisa	Blerta	Bobyn	Boydaisha
Bianca Florita	Billie Jean	Bisan	Blessey	Bocephus	Boyoung
Biancá	Billie Joe	Bisma	Blessing	Bocks-Anne	Bozena
Bianca-Elena	Billie Sue	Bismah-A	Blessings	Bodash's	Br'eanna
Bianca-Rose	Billie-Gean	Bisman	Bleu	Bodeok	Bra'dreka
Biancca	Billie-Jean	Bissaya	Blia	Bodour	Bra-Seanda
Biance	Billie-Jo	Bita	Blidgie	Boey	Bracha
Bianchi	Billie-Lee	Bittany	Blinija	Bogues	Brachell
Bianci	Billiejean	Biunka	Blinne	Bohae	Braci
Bianco	Billiejo	Bivaik	Bliss	Boinhi	Bracken
Biandra	Billine	Biviana	Blissonna	Bojana	Brad
Bianet	Billisha	Bj	Blondena	Bojieya	Bradalynn
Bianey	Billqeece	Bjarcalar	Blossom	Bokyria	Bradanielle
Biani	Billy (0.01)	Bjargey	Bloveshlene	Bolton	Bradee
Bianica	Billye	Bladen	Blue	Bomi	Braden
Bianka (0.05)	Billyeta	Bladesh	Bluelamina	Bomy	Bradetta
Biannca	Billyne	Blaeze	Bluma	Bona	Bradey
Bianney	Billysue	Blahnca	Blumie	Bonesha	Bradi
Bianneyh	Bilma	Blaiken	Blyss	Bonetta	Bradie
Biannka	Bilneka	Blaine (0.01)	Blythe (0.02)	Boni	Bradlee
Biarra	Bilqis	Blainedreal	Bo	Bonica	Bradleigh
Biasia	Bina	Blair (0.15)	Bo'nee	Bonifacia	Bradley (0.01)
Biata	Binaebi	Blaire (0.05)	Bo-Yeon	Bonika	Bradley-Nicole
Biatris	Bindhya	Blairquesha	Boatemaa	Bonita (0.01)	Bradlie
Bibanjeet	Bindi	Blaise (0.01)	Boatemah	Bonnelyn	Bradlisia
Bibb	Bindia	Blaize	Bobbe	Bonnesha	Bradlyn
Bibi (0.01)	Bindiya	Blake (0.08)	Bobbi (0.13)	Bonney	Bradrika
Bibiana (0.03)	Bindumalini	Blakelea	Bobbi Jane	Bonni	Brady (0.01)
Bibimariame	Bineeta	Blakelee	Bobbi Jo	Bonnie (0.21)	Bradyn
Bicanca	Bing	Blakeleigh	Bobbi Jo'	Bonnie-Jene	Bradynn
Bich	Binni	Blakeley	Bobbi Unqua	Bonnie-Oi	Brae
Bichtuyen	Binny	Blakeli	Bobbi-Ann	Bonnilee	Braé
Bidalmis	Binta	Blakely (0.01)	Bobbi-Jo	Bonny	Braeanna
Bidisha	Binte	Blakelyn	Bobbi-Lyn	Boone	Braedan
Biencarla	Binty	Blakelynn	Bobbi-Lynn	Bopah	Braedean
Bienda	Binwant	Blaken	Bobbie (0.14)	Borah	Braeden (0.01)
Bijal	Bioleta	Blakley	Bobbie Jo	Boravy	Braedi
Bijancha	Bionca (0.01)	Blakli	Bobbie Jolynn	Boshra	Braedyn
Bijane	Biondina	Blanca (0.25)	Bobbie-Ann	Bosia	Braegan
Bijel	Bionica	Blanca Iris	Bobbie-Jo (0.01)	Bosnia	Braelee
Bijhou	Bionka	Blancaestela	Bobbie-Lea	Boston	Braeleigh
Bilan	Bionnca	Blanche (0.01)	Bobbijean	Bostyn	Braelene
Bilane	Biontina	Blanda	Bobbijo	Bothine	Braelin
Bildora	Biradnika	Blandy	Bobby	Boudicca	Braelle
Bileigh	Biranavi	Blane	Bobby-Jo	Bounavy	Braelon
Bilie	Birara	Blanette	Bobbyann	Bourbon	Braelyn (0.01)
Biliqua	Bird	Blanka	Bobbye	Boushra	Braelynn
Bilisha	Birdie	Blare	Bobbylee	Bouvvea	Braelynne
Bilitis	Bire	Blayke	Bobi	Bovianna	Brahm

Brahna	Brandia	Brasha	Bre Anna *(0.01)*	Breaaunah	Breasha
Braia	Brandice	Brashaé	Bre Antae	Breadan	Breashea
Braiana	Brandie *(0.12)*	Brashai	Bre Asia	Breagan	Breauana
Braianna	Brandie-Lee	Brashawn	Bre Density	Breah *(0.01)*	Breauna *(0.04)*
Braidan	Brandiee	Brashawna	Bre Enna	Breah Ja	Breaunie
Braidee	Brandii	Brashay	Bre Gana	Breahana	Breaunna *(0.01)*
Braiden	Brandilei	Brashea	Bre Ona	Breahanna	Breaunta
Braidey	Brandilyn	Brashell	Bre Onne	Breahna *(0.01)*	Breauon
Braidi	Brandilynn	Brashella	Bre Ozuwaly	Breahnah	Breawanna
Braidie	Brandis *(0.01)*	Brashley	Bre Shondra	Breahnna	Breawna
Braidy	Brandisha	Brashonda	Bre Zall	Breain	Breayana
Braidyn	Brandiss	Brashuna	Bréahn	Breaira	Breayanne
Braigan	Brandit	Braunty	Bréahna	Breaire	Breayonda
Braiji	Brandiwyne	Braven	Bréana *(0.01)*	Breaisha	Breaze
Brailee	Brandize	Braviega	Bréanika	Breale	Brecarea
Brailenn	Brandon *(0.01)*	Bravinna	Bréann	Brealynn	Brecca
Brailey	Brandrika	Brawne	Bréanna *(0.02)*	Brealynne	Brechan
Braili	Brandwyn	Braxine	Bréannah	Breamber	Brechana
Brailyn	Brandy *(0.58)*	Braxten	Bréanne	Brean	Breche
Brainne	Brandy Jo	Braxton *(0.01)*	Bréanné	Breana *(0.27)*	Brechelle
Brakayla	Brandy Maka	Braxtyn	Bréasia	Breana Cecilia	Brechi
Brakia	Brandy-Leigh	Bray'anna	Bréayna	Breanah	Brechrisha
Braleigh	Brandyanne	Brayaden	Bréjhané	Breanca	Brecia
Braley	Brandye	Brayah	Brékolia	Breanda	Breck
Bralyn	Brandywyne	Brayanah	Bréon	Breandra	Breckan
Bralynn	Branée	Brayanna	Bréona *(0.01)*	Breandrea	Breckell
Bran'di	Braneeshia	Brayanne	Bréonca	Breane	Brecken
Brana	Braneisha	Braycee	Bréonna	Breaney	Brecklyn
Brancey	Branesha	Braydee	Bréonne	Breanha	Breckon
Brand'ee	Branid	Brayden	Bréonta	Breania	Breckyn
Brand'i	Branigan	Brayden-Leigh	Bréosha	Breanica	Bree *(0.08)*
Branda *(0.01)*	Branik	Braydn	Brésha	Breanika	Bree Ann
Brandace	Branika	Braydon	Bréshae	Breann *(0.12)*	Bree Anna
Brandale	Branisha	Brayeah	Bréshai	Breanna *(1.90)*	Breéana
Brandalyn	Branislava	Brayenna	Bréshauna	Breanna Franc	Breéanna
Brandalynn	Branka	Brayla	Bréshaunnia	Breanna Marie	Breénet
Brandan	Branlyn	Braylan	Bréshay	Breanná	Bree-Anna
Brandascious	Branna	Braylee	Bréshuna	Breanna-Jean	Bree-Anne
Brande *(0.01)*	Brannan	Brayley	Bréuna	Breannah	Bree-Lynn
Brandé	Brannavy	Braylin	Bréyana	Breannan	Breea
Brandea	Branndais	Braylon	Bréyanie	Breannda	Breeah
Brandee *(0.06)*	Branndi	Braylyn	Bréyanna	Breanne *(0.29)*	Breeahna
Brandell	Branne	Braylynn	Bréyonna	Breannea	Breean
Branden	Brannen	Brayn'	Bréyuna	Breannen	Breeana *(0.05)*
Brandesha	Brannisha	Brayna	Bréyunna	Breanner	Breeana-Lynn
Brandette	Brannon	Brayonna	Bre-Anah	Breanni	Breeanah
Brandey	Branshika	Brayshon	Bre-Anna	Breannia	Breeancá
Brandey-Lee	Brante	Brayton	Bre-Anne	Breannin	Breeann *(0.01)*
Brandhi	Brantesha	Brazeik	Bre-Asia	Breannon	Breeanna *(0.09)*
Brandi *(1.06)*	Brantley	Brazil	Brea *(0.07)*	Breanta	Breeannah
Brandi-Angel	Brantlie	Bre *(0.01)*	Breá	Breaonca	Breeanne
Brandi-Grace	Branwen	Bre A	Brea'nná	Breaoni	Breeaonz
Brandi-Jo	Branyia	Bre Amber	Brea-Ana	Brearia	Breeauna
Brandi-Lee	Braquail	Bre Ana	Brea-Anna	Breariaer	Breece
Brandi-Rae	Braquel	Bre Ann	Breaanna	Brearian	Breechelle

Breecia	Breighlynn	Brendalee	Brennyn	Breshelle	Breyanna *(0.03)*
Breeia	Breight	Brendaly	Brenshir	Breshia	Breyannah
Breein	Breille	Brendalyn	Brent-Lee	Breshna	Breyanne
Breejea	Brein	Brendalynn	Brentae	Breshon	Breyannoina
Breely	Breina	Brendan	Brentan	Breshona	Breyata
Breelyn	Breindia	Brendaria	Brentaysha	Breshonda	Breyauna
Breelynn	Breinne	Brendee	Brentisha	Breshuna	Breyawna
Breena *(0.01)*	Breion	Brendell	Brentleigh	Breshunna	Breydon
Breendsay	Breiona	Brenden	Brentney	Bresley	Breyell
Breene	Breionna	Brendetta	Brentny	Breslin	Breyelle
Breeon	Breiontay	Brendha	Brenton	Bret *(0.01)*	Breyer
Breeona	Breit	Brendi	Brentress	Brethny	Breyhauna
Breeoni	Breiyah	Brendia	Brenttana	Bretia	Breyia
Breeonna	Brejae	Brendjene	Brenttney	Bretle	Breyiana
Breerica	Brejahnia	Brendle	Brenyale	Bretlyn	Breylyn
Breesha	Brejahnna	Brendo	Brenyana	Bretney	Breyna
Breeshia	Brejana	Brendolyn	Brenyettá	Bretni'	Breyo'nta
Breeta	Brejay	Brendy	Brenyia	Breton	Breyon
Breeuna	Breje	Brene	Brenzelle	Bretona	Breyona *(0.01)*
Breeyauna	Brejena	Brenéa	Breoanna	Brett *(0.05)*	Breyonda
Breeyawna	Brejhyla	Brenea	Breon	Brett-Ann	Breyonia
Breeze *(0.01)*	Brejona	Brenecia	Breon'za	Brettagne	Breyonna *(0.01)*
Breezell	Brejuana	Brenee	Breona *(0.04)*	Brettani	Breyrah
Breezi	Brekana	Breneisa	Breonah	Brettanie	Breyunna
Breezianne	Brekea	Breneka	Breonca	Brettany	Breyunnah
Breezy	Brekel	Brenell	Breonda	Brette *(0.01)*	Brezzie
Bregan	Brekell	Brenelle	Breondra	Brettin	Brhe Anne
Breh'ana	Brekeshia	Breneshia	Breoni	Brettlen	Brhea
Brehana	Brekeyda	Brenia	Breonia *(0.01)*	Brettlyn	Brhiannan
Brehanna	Brekha	Breniah	Breonica	Brettne	Bri
Brehannah	Brekita	Brenica	Breonjae	Brettnee	Bri A
Brehlie	Brekka	Brenika	Breonn	Brettney	Bri Ann
Brehna	Brekkan	Brenisha	Breonna *(0.11)*	Breu'ana	Bri Anne
Brehona	Brekke	Brenita	Breonne	Breuhna	Bri Ona
Brehonna	Breland	Breniz	Breonsha	Breuna	Bri Shane
Brei	Breleigh	Brenkaya	Breonyx	Breunah	Bri'an
Brei'ana	Brelin	Brenlée	Breosha	Breunca	Bri'ana
Breia	Brelind	Brenleigh	Breoshni	Breunica	Bri'anna
Breiah	Brella	Brenlene	Brescia	Breunna *(0.01)*	Bri'anne
Breiahna	Brelle	Brenley	Bresha	Breunney	Bri'asia
Breial	Brelyn *(0.01)*	Brenlie	Breshaé	Breunnica	Bri'elle
Breiana *(0.01)*	Brelynn	Brenn	Breshae	Breuntae	Bri'en
Breiane	Brelynne	Brenna *(0.47)*	Breshamte	Breveena	Bri'jae
Breiann	Bremcy	Brennae	Breshanna	Breven	Bri'ona
Breianna *(0.01)*	Brena *(0.01)*	Brennah	Breshaun	Brewer	Bri'onna
Breianne	Brenae	Brennaka	Breshaunda	Breya	Bri'shari
Breichel	Brenaé	Brennalin	Breshaunna	Breyah	Bri'shona
Breigh *(0.01)*	Brenai	Brennalyn	Breshawn	Breyahna	Bri'shonta
Breigh Anne	Brenaldee	Brennan *(0.02)*	Breshawna	Breyahnna	Bri'yana
Breigha	Brenann	Brennea	Breshawnia	Breyan	Bri-A
Breighan	Brenaszha	Brennen	Breshawnna	Breyana *(0.02)*	Bri-A'nna
Breighanah	Brency	Brennesia	Breshay	Breyandra	Bri-Ana
Breighanna	Brenda *(1.44)*	Brennicia	Breshayla	Breyane	Bri-Ann
Breighanne	Brenda Brooke	Brennisha	Bresheah	Breyanka	Bri-Shon
Breighel	Brendal	Brennon	Breshell	Breyann	Bri-Yion

Bria *(0.32)*	Brianná	Briclyn	Brielle *(0.09)*	Briittany	Brinkley
Bria Alexis	Briannaé	Bricola	Briellen	Brija	Brinkli
Briá	Brianna-Jo	Brid	Brielyn	Brijaana	Brinlee
Bria'na	Brianna-Lee	Bridarra	Brielynn	Brijada	Brinleigh
Bria'nna	Brianna-Lynn	Bridaya	Briena	Brijanna	Brinley
Bria'onna	Brianna-Miriah	Briddget	Briená	Brijea	Brinli
Briaana	Briannaa	Bridene	Brienae	Brijhae	Brinn
Briaanna	Briannae	Bridesha	Brienca	Brijida	Brinna
Briadanielle	Briannah *(0.01)*	Bridet	Briene	Brijiun	Brinne
Briah *(0.01)*	Briannan	Bridey	Brienna *(0.02)*	Brijon	Brinnlee
Briah-Am	Brianne *(0.40)*	Bridgeen	Brienne *(0.01)*	Brijonna	Brinnley
Briahna *(0.01)*	Brianné	Bridgeona	Brieon	Brijonnay	Brinnlie
Briahnna	Briannen	Bridget *(0.66)*	Brieona	Brikeisha	Brinny
Briail	Brianni	Bridgete	Brieonna *(0.01)*	Brikkel	Brinslea
Briaira	Briannia	Bridgeth	Brier	Brikki	Brinsley
Briaire	Briannica	Bridgetime	Briere	Brikti	Brintha
Briajah	Briannie	Bridgett *(0.07)*	Brierra	Brilana Dawn	Brio'na
Briajani	Briannis	Bridgette *(0.20)*	Briesha	Brilee	Brion
Briale	Briannon	Bridggett	Brieshette	Briley *(0.01)*	Briona *(0.03)*
Brialle	Brianntay	Bridgid	Briesjenxe	Briley-Ann	Brionah
Brialy	Brianona	Bridgit	Brietta	Brillance	Brionca
Brialynn	Brianté	Bridgitt	Brieun	Brilliana	Brionche
Briamony	Brianta	Bridgitte	Brieya	Brilyn	Brionda
Brian	Briantay	Bridie	Brieyannia	Brilynn	Brione
Brianá	Briante	Bridilene	Brieyona	Brin	Brioney
Briana *(1.97)*	Brianté	Bridish	Brieyonna	Brina *(0.02)*	Brioni
Briana Nicole	Brianth	Briditte	Briez	Brinae	Brionia
Briana-Nicole	Briany	Bridjette	Brigan	Brinaé	Brionica
Brianaca	Briaona	Bridney	Brigee Crystal	Brinaka	Brionka
Brianah	Briar *(0.01)*	Bridnie	Briget	Brinda	Brionna *(0.10)*
Brianan	Briara	Bridon	Brigett	Brindana	Brionnah
Brianca *(0.01)*	Briarna	Bridyet	Brigetta	Brindda	Brionne
Briancah	Briashlon	Brie *(0.03)*	Brigette *(0.05)*	Brindee	Brionta
Brianda *(0.04)*	Briasia	Brie Ann	Brigettee	Brinderdeep	Brionte
Briandra	Briata	Brie Anne	Brigget	Brindi	Briontia
Briandrea	Briatty	Brié	Briggin	Brindisy	Briony
Briane	Briauhna	Briéannah	Briggitte	Brindizi	Brioona
Briané	Briauna *(0.04)*	Brie-Ann	Brighid	Brindl	Briosha
Brianecia	Briaundria	Brie-Anna	Bright	Brindle	Brirah
Brianee	Briaunna *(0.01)*	Brie-Anne	Brighton *(0.01)*	Brindley	Brisa *(0.03)*
Brianeisha	Briawna	Brie-Lynn	Brigid *(0.02)*	Brindsi	Brisa Ariana
Brianell	Briayana	Briea	Brigida	Brindy	Brisaida
Brianesha	Briayle	Brieana *(0.02)*	Brigidd	Brine	Brisareli
Brianeshia	Briayna	Brieann *(0.01)*	Brigidh	Brinea	Briscida
Briani	Brice *(0.01)*	Brieanna *(0.08)*	Brigio	Brineatta	Brise
Brianica	Briceida	Brieannah	Brigit *(0.01)*	Brinesha	Briseida *(0.03)*
Brianie	Bricelee	Brieanne *(0.02)*	Brigita	Brinessa	Briselda
Brianique	Bricelly	Briedget	Brigith	Briney	Brisen
Brianisha	Bricelyn	Briege	Brigitta	Brinia	Briseyda
Briann *(0.02)*	Briceyra	Briehanna	Brigitte *(0.11)*	Briniia	Briseydy
Brianna *(4.77)*	Brichell	Briel *(0.01)*	Brigitte Lyle	Brinika	Brisha
Brianna Elizabeth	Bricia	Brieland	Brihana	Brinique	Brishae
Brianna Martell	Brickeall	Briele	Brihanna	Brinisha	Brishana
Brianna Mirland	Brickell	Briell	Brii	Brinka	Brishani
Brianna My	Brickley	Briella	Briiohn	Brinker	Brishanika

Brishanna	Britice	Brittannia	Brittnée	Brodie-Lynn-Lesl	Brooklynne (0.01)
Brisharri	Britine	Brittannie	Brittnei	Brodry'ona	Brooks (0.01)
Brishauna	Britiney	Brittanny (0.01)	Brittney (1.59)	Brody	Brooksana
Brishawna	Britini	Brittany (8.36)	Brittney Ann	Brogain	Brookshire
Brishia	British (0.01)	Brittany Ann	Brittney Le	Brogan (0.01)	Brooksie
Brishna	Britkni	Brittany Kay	Brittney-Lynn	Brogen	Broolyn
Brishon	Britlee	Brittany Nicole	Brittneylynne	Broghan	Broshannie
Brishonda	Britleigh	Brittany Qi	Brittni (0.12)	Broklyn	Broshawna
Brishunda	Britlyn	Brittany-Amanda	Brittnie (0.05)	Bronaign	Brouklenn
Brisly	Britlynn	Brittany-Amber	Brittnii-Mariah	Bronlynn	Browen
Brismayda	Britnay	Brittany-Ann	Brittny (0.05)	Bronnwyn	Brown
Brison	Britne	Brittany-Brooke	Brittnyeshia	Bronsley	Browyen
Brissa	Britné	Brittany-Jean	Britton (0.01)	Brontae	Bru Chon
Bristal	Britnee (0.02)	Brittany-Lynn	Brittonee	Bronte (0.04)	Bruana
Bristen	Britneigh	Brittany-Madeline	Brittoni	Bronti	Bruce
Bristeyn	Britney (0.43)	Brittany-Nicole	Brittony (0.01)	Bronwen (0.01)	Brucenta
Bristin	Britni (0.06)	Brittany-Rae	Britty	Bronwyn (0.05)	Brukiera
Bristol (0.01)	Britni'	Brittany-Rose	Brittyn	Bronwyn Tumau	Brukieta
Bristy	Britniay	Brittanya	Brittyne	Bronwynn	Bruna
Bristyl	Britnie (0.01)	Brittanyann	Brityn	Bronya	Brunettea
Bristyn	Britnie Ann	Brittanyjean	Britzel	Brook (0.15)	Brunia
Brit	Britny (0.02)	Brittanyliz	Briuana	Brook'len	Brunica
Brit Nai	Britnye	Britte	Briuanna	Brook-Kynne	Brunisha
Brit'ney	Britony	Britten (0.01)	Briuna	Brook-Lyn	Brusha
Brit'ni	Britoya	Brittenay	Briunia	Brook-Lynn	Bruttney
Brita	Britshana	Brittenie	Briunna	Brookayla	Bry'ana
Britain	Britt (0.01)	Britteniegh	Briya	Brookcalled	Bry'toni
Britain Ann	Britt'nee	Britteny (0.02)	Briyana (0.01)	Brooke (2.81)	Bry-Anna
Britaini	Britta (0.02)	Britti	Briyanka	Brooke Ann	Bryah
Britainy	Brittain	Brittian	Briyanna (0.01)	Brooké	Bryahna
Britan	Brittaine	Brittianie	Briyell	Brooke-Asheli	Bryan
Britana	Brittainey	Brittiany (0.02)	Briyelle	Brooke-Ashley	Bryana (0.10)
Britanee	Brittaini	Brittien	Briyid	Brooke-Lin	Bryanika
Britaney	Brittainie	Brittin	Briyit	Brooke-Linn	Bryann
Britani (0.02)	Brittainy	Brittina	Briyon	Brooke-Lyn	Bryanna (0.26)
Britanica	Brittamie	Brittinee	Briyona	Brooke-Lynn	Bryanna Michell
Britanical	Brittan (0.01)	Brittiney	Briyonia	(0.01)	Bryannamari
Britanie (0.01)	Brittana	Brittini (0.01)	Briyonna	Brooke-Lynne	Bryanne (0.02)
Britanie Ann	Brittanae	Brittini-Ann	Briyonne	Brooke-Noel	Bryanni
Britanna	Brittane	Brittinie	Briyunna	Brookel	Bryantae
Britannia	Brittanee (0.01)	Brittinny	Brizah	Brookelin	Bryaonne
Britanny	Brittanei	Brittiny (0.01)	Brizeida	Brookelle	Bryar
Britany (0.08)	Brittaney (0.07)	Brittisha	Brizhe	Brookely	Bryasia
Britanya	Brittani (0.24)	Brittlee	Bro'quazsha	Brookelyn (0.01)	Bryauna
Britashia	Brittani'	Brittley	Brocdricka	Brookelyne	Bryce (0.07)
Britayjuah	Brittania	Brittli	Brocha	Brookelynn (0.01)	Brycelyn
Britazia	Brittanica	Brittlyn	Brochette	Brooklen	Brycen
Briteny	Brittanie (0.11)	Brittlynn	Brock	Brookley	Brychelle
Britesha	Brittanii	Brittmarie	Brockelle	Brooklin (0.01)	Bryden
Brithany	Brittanika	Brittnae	Brodee	Brooklyn (0.35)	Brydijia
Brithney	Brittanise	Brittnany	Brodericka	Brooklyn-	Brye
Brithnie	Brittanna	Brittnay (0.02)	Brodi	Kimberly	Bryéantae
Britian	Brittanney	Brittne	Brodia	Brooklyne (0.01)	Bryea
Britiany	Brittanni	Brittnea	Brodie (0.01)	Brooklynn (0.07)	Bryee
		Brittnee (0.06)	Brodie-Lyn	Brooklynn-Daisy	Bryel

Bryelle	Bryson	Busi	Ca Voni	Cadejá	Cahari
Bryenna	Brystal	Bussma	Ca'andi	Cadeja	Cahjanae
Bryennah	Brystel	Buthaina	Ca'brina	Cadejah	Cahla
Bryer	Brystie	Butler	Ca'che	Cadejia	Cahliah
Bryesha	Brytani	Butool	Ca'desia	Cadely	Cahlina
Brygida	Brytanie	Byan	Ca'maya	Caden	Cahner
Bryhana	Brytanny	Byanca	Ca'rencia	Cadence (0.01)	Cahrizma
Bryiana	Brytany	Byanka	Ca'rinthya	Cadene	Caia
Bryianna	Brytnai	Byer	Ca'shari	Cadentz	Caiana
Bryinna	Brytnee	Byesha	Ca'teria	Cades	Caice
Brylan	Brytnei	Byllie	Ca-Daryl	Cadesha	Caicha
Brylee (0.01)	Brytnie	Bylliee	Caanah	Cadeshia	Caida
Brylei	Brytnn	Byllye	Caasi	Cadesia	Caidyn
Brylene	Bryton	Byneshia	Cabell	Cadesjah	Caiely
Bryley	Bryttanee	Bynisha	Cabraya	Cadey	Caigan
Bryli	Bryttani (0.01)	Byonica	Cabre	Cadi	Caihlan
Brylie	Bryttani Nicole	Byreona	Cabreisha	Cadice	Caila (0.01)
Bryn (0.05)	Bryttanie	Byriana	Cabri	Cadidra	Cailah
Bryna (0.01)	Bryttany (0.01)	Byrione	Cabria	Cadidrea	Cailain
Brynda	Bryttney	Byrleen	Cabrianna	Cadie (0.01)	Cailand
Bryndahl	Bryttni	Byrnae	Cabrina	Cadijah	Caile
Bryndazia	Bryttnie	Byrnese	Cabrinia	Cadijahia	Cailea
Bryndi	Brytton	Byronae	Cabrino	Cadisha	Cailean
Bryndilynn	Bryuna	Byronica	Cacee	Cadiva	Cailee (0.01)
Bryndl	Bryunna	Byronisha	Cacey	Cadlyn	Caileen
Bryndolyn	Bryyonna	Byulee	Cachae	Cadmill	Caileigh (0.01)
Bryneisha	Bryza		Cache (0.01)	Cadora	Cailen
Bryneka	Bu-Jin	**-C-**	Caché	Cadosgi	Cailey (0.05)
Brynelle	Buasavahn		Cachéy	Cady (0.05)	Caili
Brynesha	Bubble	C (0.04)	Cachericia	Cae-Shay	Cailie
Brynette	Bubbledeep	C Quoya Jos	Cachet	Caedra	Cailin (0.06)
Brynisha	Budur	C'aira	Caci	Caehla	Cailleach
Brynitra	Buffie	C'airra	Cacia	Caela (0.01)	Caillean
Brynlee	Buffy	C'alayia	Cacie	Caelainn	Cailleigh
Brynleigh	Bukola	C'aniye	Caclinh	Caelan	Cailley
Brynley	Bulah	C'ara	Cacy	Caeleigh	Caillie
Brynli	Bullock	C'asia	Cada	Caelen	Cailsey
Brynlie	Bunica	C'elsea	Cadacia	Caeley	Cailtin (0.01)
Brynmor	Buon	C'era	Cadaia	Caeli	Cailtyn
Brynn (0.09)	Burgandi	C'erica	Cadance	Caelidh	Caily
Brynna (0.02)	Burgandie	C'erra	Cadasa	Caelie	Cailyn (0.04)
Brynnan	Burgandy	C'iara	Cadashia	Caelin (0.01)	Cailynn
Brynne (0.01)	Burgardy	C'iera	Caddeja	Caelinn	Cailynne
Brynnigan	Burgundee	C'mone	Caddie	Caellaigh	Cailyx
Brynnley	Burgundy	C'nedra	Cade	Caelly	Caiman
Bryona (0.01)	Burina	C'nia	Cadeasha	Caelon	Caimyn
Bryonda	Burkely	C'noria	Cadeashia	Caely	Caina
Bryonna (0.01)	Burkley	C'onna	Cadedra	Caelyn (0.01)	Caipriest
Bryonnia	Burnat	C'priana	Cadee	Caelynn	Caira
Bryony	Burnita	C'quret	Cadeeja	Caesare	Cairece
Bryre	Busbono	C'yanna	Cadeidr'e	Caesarea	Cairn
Brysan	Bushara	C'yhera	Cadeidra	Caetlin	Cairney
Brysen	Bushonda	C. (0.01)	Cadeidre	Cafferty	Cairo
Bryshae	Bushra (0.01)	C.J.	Cadeija	Cage	Cairra
Bryshanaye	Bushraa	Ca Rin	Cadeisha	Cagney	Caisa

Caisee
Caisey
Caisha
Caisie
Caissie
Caissy
Caitelyn
Caitesby
Caitha
Caithlyn
Caithyna
Caitilyn
Caitlaine
Caitlan *(0.02)*
Caitland
Caitlee
Caitlen *(0.01)*
Caitlenn
Caitley
Caitlin *(2.02)*
Caitlind
Caitline
Caitlinn
Caitlinrose
Caitllin
Caitln
Caitlon
Caitlund
Caitlyn *(0.95)*
Caitlyn Bryanna
Caitlyn-Uyen
Caitlynd
Caitlyne
Caitlynn *(0.07)*
Caitlynne *(0.01)*
Caitlynne-Brooke
Caitria
Caitrin
Caitrina
Caitriona
Caityln
Caiya
Caiylen
Caja
Cajiun
Cajsa
Cajuana
Cajza
Cal Nesha
Cala
Calabrian
Calah
Calais
Calandra *(0.01)*
Calandrea

Calandria
Calantha
Calasia
Calaysia
Calea
Caleah
Caleb
Caledonia
Calee *(0.01)*
Caleen
Caleena
Caleeyah
Caleh
Caleigh *(0.05)*
Caleisha
Calen
Calena
Calenda
Calendre
Calene
Calesha
Caleshia
Calesia
Calesta
Caletria
Caley *(0.05)*
Calgary
Calhoun
Cali *(0.06)*
Calia
Calian
Caliana
Calice
Caliche
Calicia
Calico
Calida
Calidora
Calie *(0.01)*
Caliegh
Calierya
Caliey
Calille
Calin
Caline
Calisa
Calisandre
Calisha
Calishia
Calisia
Calista *(0.01)*
Calixta
Caliyah
Calla *(0.01)*
Callah

Callahan
Callan *(0.02)*
Callata
Callaway
Calle
Calleann
Callee
Calleigh
Callen *(0.01)*
Calletana
Calley *(0.01)*
Calleyanne
Calli *(0.04)*
Calliandra
Callianna
Callianne
Callie *(0.34)*
Callieja
Callihan
Callilla
Callin
Callina
Calliope
Callisa
Callise
Callison
Callista *(0.01)*
Callon
Calloway
Callum
Cally *(0.01)*
Callyn
Callyssa
Calmeshia
Calnesha
Calneshia
Calnesia
Calonda
Calre
Calsey
Calsha
Calsi
Caltina
Calub
Caludette
Calvajia
Calvari
Calveasha
Calvieonia
Calvina
Calvinesha
Calvion
Calvisha
Calvo
Calvona

Caly
Calya
Calyi
Calyn *(0.01)*
Calyne
Calynn
Calyope
Calyse
Calyshia
Calyssa
Calysta
Camael
Camantha
Camara *(0.01)*
Camarah
Camari
Camaria
Camarie
Camarin *(0.01)*
Camaro
Camaron
Camary
Camaryn
Camas
Camay
Camaya
Camayia
Camber
Camblyss
Cambray
Cambre
Cambrea
Cambree
Cambreece
Cambreia
Cambreona
Cambri
Cambria *(0.03)*
Cambrianne
Cambridge
Cambrie
Cambriel
Cambriella
Cambrisha
Cambry
Cambryn
Camden *(0.01)*
Camdyn
Cameasha
Camedra
Cameesha
Cameisha
Camekia
Camela
Camelia *(0.02)*

Camella
Camella Krystel
Camellia *(0.01)*
Camen
Cameo *(0.01)*
Cameo'
Camera *(0.01)*
Cameran
Cameren
Cameria
Camerin
Camerina
Cameron *(0.16)*
Cameron C
Camery
Cameryn
Camesa
Camesha *(0.01)*
Cameshaa
Cameshia
Carney
Cameya
Cami *(0.03)*
Camia
Camibella
Camicia
Camie *(0.01)*
Camiel
Camielle
Camiesha
Camil
Camila *(0.05)*
Camile
Camilee
Camilia
Camilia Joycely
Camill
Camilla *(0.07)*
Camilla-Michelle
Camille *(0.99)*
Camille Amelia
Camille Angelina
Camiller
Camillia
Camilya
Camira
Camiran
Camiron
Camisha *(0.02)*
Cammi
Cammi Carmela
Cammie *(0.01)*
Cammilla
Cammy *(0.01)*
Camorah

Camoriae
Campbell *(0.01)*
Campos
Campshakia
Camra
Camrea
Camree
Camren
Camrey
Camri *(0.01)*
Camrie *(0.01)*
Camrin
Camron
Camry *(0.02)*
Camryn *(0.02)*
Camrynn
Camshia
Camy
Camyeshia
Camyle
Camyll
Camylle *(0.01)*
Camyra
Camyrah
Camyrn
Can'dace
Cana *(0.01)*
Canaan
Canacee
Canada
Canadi
Canady
Canara
Candac'e
Candace *(0.46)*
Candace Gill
Candace-Joyce
Candaces
Candaice
Candance *(0.01)*
Candanee
Candas
Candasia
Candaysha
Cande
Candece
Candee
Candeisha
Candela
Candelace
Candelaria *(0.02)*
Candell
Candi *(0.01)*
Candi-Li
Candiace

Candiance	Canvas	Cardasia	Carinah	Carlexis	Carlynn *(0.01)*
Candice *(0.38)*	Canyon	Cardeana	Carinda	Carley *(0.26)*	Carlynne
Candicee	Canyshea	Cardeja	Carine *(0.01)*	Carley Jae	Carlyse
Candida *(0.01)*	Canzella	Cardejah	Carinn	Carley-Marie	Carlysha
Candidace	Cao	Carden	Carinna	Carli *(0.13)*	Carlysheyona
Candids	Caolin	Cardesheia	Carinne	Carli-Voelzing	Carlysle
Candie *(0.01)*	Caora	Cardia	Carino	Carliann	Carlytta
Candies	Capeanne	Cardine	Carintay	Carlianne	Carma
Candis *(0.01)*	Caphleen	Cardisha	Caris	Carlicia	Carmaleda
Candise	Caprésha	Care-Lee	Carisa *(0.01)*	Carlie *(0.18)*	Carmaleta
Candiss	Capreccia	Carea	Carise	Carlie-Anne	Carmalina
Candler	Caprece	Caredean	Carisha	Carlie-Rae	Carmalita
Candra *(0.01)*	Caprecia	Caree	Carisma	Carlie-Sue	Carman *(0.01)*
Candria	Capresha	Careena	Cariss	Carliegh	Carmanah
Candy *(0.07)*	Capri *(0.01)*	Careese	Carissa *(0.39)*	Carlin *(0.02)*	Carmanecia
Candyce *(0.01)*	Capri'nara	Carel	Carisse	Carlina *(0.01)*	Carmean
Candyda	Capria	Careli	Carissia	Carline	Carmeisha
Candylisa	Capriati	Carelle	Carista	Carling *(0.01)*	Carmeka
Candynce	Caprice *(0.02)*	Carely	Carita	Carling-Mary	Carmel *(0.01)*
Candyse	Capricia	Carelyn	Carizmia	Carlisa *(0.01)*	Carmela *(0.03)*
Candyss	Caprielle	Carelys	Carl	Carlise	Carmelia
Caneatra	Capriese	Caren *(0.02)*	Carla *(0.34)*	Carlisha *(0.01)*	Carmelina
Caneel	Caprisha	Carena	Carla Guadalupe	Carlishia	Carmelita *(0.01)*
Caneisaya	Caprishea	Carene	Carla-Grace	Carlisia	Carmell
Caneisha	Caprisheana	Carenina	Carlacea	Carlisle	Carmella *(0.01)*
Caneka	Capry	Carenna	Carlacie	Carlissa *(0.01)*	Carmelle
Canella	Car	Careonia	Carlaine	Carlissah	Carmen *(0.55)*
Canequa	Car'le	Caresea	Carlana	Carlista	Carmen Adriana
Canese	Car'réa	Caress	Carlanna	Carlita *(0.01)*	Carmen Rosario
Canesha	Cara *(0.39)*	Caressa *(0.01)*	Carlannah	Carllee	Carmen-Lyn
Caneshia	Cara Lynne	Caresse	Carlasia	Carllie	Carmen-Marie
Canessa	Cara Mia	Caretha	Carldashion	Carlliesha	Carmencita
Canetra	Cara-Ann	Carew	Carldera	Carlmecia	Carmene
Cania	Cara-Cydney	Carey *(0.03)*	Carle	Carlneshia	Carmenique
Canice	Cara-Leigh	Carhiga	Carlea	Carlonda	Carmenlita
Canicha	Cara-Lyn	Cari *(0.05)*	Carleah	Carlondra	Carmesha
Caniece	Caraee	Cari'	Carleasya	Carlos	Carmia
Caniejrah	Caragh	Cari-Jean	Carlee *(0.14)*	Carlota	Carmia-Syleste
Caniel	Carah *(0.01)*	Caria	Carlee-Marie	Carlotta *(0.01)*	Carmie
Caniesa	Caralee *(0.01)*	Carianne	Carlee-Rae	Carlshyia	Carmieshia
Canieslia	Caraleigh	Carice	Carleen *(0.02)*	Carlteria	Carmila
Caniquia	Caralena	Caridad	Carleh	Carlton	Carmile
Canise	Caraline	Carie	Carleigh *(0.05)*	Carltoneisha	Carmilla
Canisha	Caralissa	Cariel	Carleigha	Carltonia	Carmille
Canisius	Caralyn *(0.01)*	Cariesha	Carleisha	Carltonisha	Carmin
Cannelle	Caralynna	Carigan	Carlen	Carlundia	Carmina *(0.02)*
Canning	Caramene	Carika-Jade	Carlena *(0.01)*	Carly *(1.18)*	Carmina Hearty
Cannon	Caramia	Carilange	Carlene *(0.03)*	Carly Jo	Carmina Janine
Canny	Caran	Carileen	Carlenea	Carly Robin	Carmine
Canon	Caraneisha	Carily	Carlese	Carly-Anne	Carmisha
Cansas	Carashea	Carilyn	Carlesha	Carlya	Carmon
Cansu	Caraycha	Carim	Carlesia	Carlye *(0.02)*	Carneal
Cantey	Carbella	Carin *(0.01)*	Carlessa	Carlyle	Carnease
Cantrece	Cardae	Carin Angel	Carletha	Carlyn *(0.02)*	Carnee
Cantrell	Cardajia	Carina *(0.31)*	Carletta	Carlyna	Carneeka

Carneemah	Carolinn	Carrieann	Caryl	Casia	Cassia *(0.02)*
Carneice	Caroljane	Carriell	Carylee	Casiana	Cassiana
Carneish	Caroll	Carrielle	Caryn *(0.04)*	Casianne	Cassianna
Carneisha	Caroll Ann	Carrieona	Carynn	Casid	Cassianne
Carneissia	Carolle	Carrieonia	Carynne	Casiday	Cassida
Carnell	Carollee	Carriese	Carys *(0.01)*	Casidee	Cassiday
Carnella	Carollyn	Carrigan *(0.01)*	Caryssa	Casidhe	Cassidee *(0.01)*
Carnen	Carolmi	Carrin	Carzenei	Casidi	Cassidee-Ria
Carnequa	Carolneshia	Carrina	Casady	Casidy *(0.01)*	Cassidi *(0.01)*
Carnese	Carolorjane	Carrinda	Casalyn	Casie *(0.04)*	Cassidi-Rae
Carnesha	Carolou	Carrington *(0.01)*	Casan	Casie Ann	Cassidie *(0.01)*
Carneshia	Carolyn *(0.56)*	Carrisa *(0.01)*	Casandera	Casietta	Cassidy *(1.30)*
Carnesia	Carolyn Bet	Carrissa *(0.01)*	Casandr	Casilda	Cassidy Gehazel
Carnesiea	Carolyn-Denise	Carrita	Casandra *(0.24)*	Casimir	Cassidy-Rae
Carnetta	Carolyn-Leigh	Carrlyn	Casandra-Ashley	Casimira	Cassie *(0.36)*
Carnette	Carolyna	Carrol	Casandre	Casja	Cassie Jo
Carney	Carolyne *(0.02)*	Carrolin	Casandrea	Caslon	Cassie-Marie
Carneysha	Carolynn *(0.01)*	Carroline	Casandrey	Caslyn	Cassieann
Carnicia	Carolynne	Carroll	Casanndra	Casmia	Cassiel
Carnique	Caron	Carrolline	Casanon	Casmira	Cassiele
Carnise	Carona	Carrollynn	Casara	Cason	Cassii
Carnisha	Caroylann	Carrolyn	Casarah	Casondra	Cassilly
Carnita	Carquisha	Carry	Casarha	Casondralee	Cassina
Carnitha	Carra *(0.01)*	Carryn	Casaria	Casper	Cassioy
Carnithia	Carradina	Carrysa	Casaundra	Cass	Cassity
Caro	Carrah	Carsen *(0.01)*	Casaurah	Cassa	Casslyn
Carol *(0.21)*	Carramaena	Carsey	Casaurina	Cassaday	Cassondra *(0.06)*
Carol Ann *(0.04)*	Carrel	Carshea	Casee	Cassadee	Cassonia
Carol Anne *(0.02)*	Carren	Carslin	Casei	Cassadey	Casssandra
Carol Jean	Carrena	Carson *(0.10)*	Caseley	Cassadie	Casssidy
Carol Lee	Carrera	Carssily	Casendra	Cassady *(0.02)*	Cassy *(0.02)*
Carol-Ann	Carress	Carsyn	Casey *(1.05)*	Cassalyn	Cassy Jo
Carol-Anne	Carrey	Cartasia	Casey Lynn	Cassamdra	Cassydi
Carola	Carri	Cartazia	Casey-Ann	Cassandera	Castalina
Carolan *(0.01)*	Carri-Ann	Cartéga	Caseylynn	Cassandra *(2.53)*	Castille
Carolane *(0.11)*	Carrial	Carteesiyah	Casha	Cassandra Rebec	Castilleja
Carolann *(0.03)*	Carriann	Carteneka	Cashae	Cassandra-Lee	Caswell
Carolanne *(0.06)*	Carrianna	Carter *(0.03)*	Cashai'	Cassandra-Viola	Casy
Carolawne	Carrianne	Cartera	Cashandria	Cassandrah	Casya
Carole *(0.01)*	Carribean	Cartese	Cashaunda	Cassandramae	Catalena
Carole Ann *(0.01)*	Carrie *(0.40)*	Cartesia	Cashay	Cassandre *(0.02)*	Catalina *(0.13)*
Carole Anne	Carrie Dawn	Carthenia	Cashé	Cassandrea	Catalyn
(0.02)	Carrie Jean	Carthy	Cashea	Cassandria	Catanda
Carole-Anne	Carrie Lynn	Carti	Casheena	Cassanina	Catara
Carolee	Carrie Una	Cartia	Cashenda	Cassanora	Catareana
Caroleena	Carrie-Ann	Cartier	Cashle	Cassara	Catarena
Caroleina	Carrie-Anne	Cartina	Cashmere *(0.01)*	Cassarie	Catarin
Carolena	Carrie-Beth	Cartisha	Cashmire	Cassaundra *(0.03)*	Catarina *(0.04)*
Carolette	Carrie-Charlene	Cartishe	Cashola	Cassdy	Catarina-Raquel
Carolin	Carrie-Lee	Cartney	Cashone	Cassedi	Catashia
Carolina *(0.54)*	Carrie-Lyn	Cartrell	Cashonti'	Cassee	Catasia
Caroline *(1.76)*	Carrie-Lynn	Carvella	Cashsha	Cassel	Cate
Caroline Marie	Carrie-Lynne	Carvetta	Cashshay	Cassela	Catearra
Caroline Rainier	Carrie-Marie	Cary *(0.01)*	Cashunda	Cassey *(0.02)*	Cateesha
Caroline-Marjorie	Carrieana	Caryann	Casi *(0.01)*	Cassi *(0.02)*	Cateland

Catelin *(0.01)*	Cathrine *(0.01)*	Cavossey	Caznika	Cecilea	Ceericka
Cateline	Cathryn *(0.06)*	Cawanda	Cboia	Cecilee	Ceiari
Catelon	Cathryne	Cawanna	Cc'liyah	Cecilely	Ceicley
Catelyn *(0.02)*	Cathrynn	Caya	Cclenahan	Ceciley	Ceidie
Catelyne	Cathy *(0.10)*	Cayachelyn	Ce Nisha	Cecilia *(0.23)*	Ceidre
Catelynn *(0.01)*	Cathyanna	Cayamarie	Céaira	Cecilia Kameish	Ceila
Catendra	Cati	Cayanna	Céandria	Cecilia-Rae	Ceileigh
Catera	Catia *(0.01)*	Cayce *(0.01)*	Cédana	Ceciliann	Ceileighn
Cateresa	Catiana	Caycee	Cédejia	Cecilianna	Ceili
Caterin	Catianna	Caydee	Céerra	Cecilie	Ceilidh *(0.01)*
Caterina *(0.02)*	Catie *(0.01)*	Cayden	Célandria	Cecilie-Ann	Ceilioh
Caterine	Catilin	Caydi	Cénedra	Ceciliy	Ceilo
Caternia	Catilyn	Caydianne	Cénentá	Cecille	Ceinwen
Caterra	Catilynn	Caye	Céotia	Cecillia	Ceira *(0.01)*
Catesa	Catina *(0.01)*	Cayenna	Céquanta	Cecily *(0.06)*	Ceire
Catesby	Catiria	Cayenne	Ceacellia	Cecily Ann	Ceirra *(0.01)*
Catesia	Catisha	Cayla *(0.17)*	Ceaira *(0.01)*	Cecilya	Ceirstan
Catey	Catlin *(0.02)*	Cayla'n	Ceairah	Cecilyn	Ceisaley
Cath'almanda	Catlyn *(0.01)*	Cayla-Don	Ceairra	Ceclie	Cejae
Cathaleen	Catlynne	Caylah *(0.01)*	Ceajay	Ceclynn	Cejay
Catharen	Caton	Caylan	Cealan	Cecoyia	Cekesia
Catharin	Catonya	Cayle	Ceamornia	Cecylia	Cela
Catharina	Catora	Caylea	Ceana	Cedalee	Celandria
Catharine *(0.02)*	Catoria	Cayleanna	Ceandra	Cedani Rose	Celange
Catharyn	Catrecia	Caylee *(0.03)*	Ceandria	Cedar *(0.01)*	Celastine
Cathelina	Catreena	Cayleen	Ceann	Cedara	Celby
Catheline	Catreesha	Cayleigh *(0.01)*	Ceanna *(0.01)*	Cedaria	Celeah
Cathene	Catrelle	Caylen *(0.01)*	Ceara *(0.02)*	Cedbra	Celease
Catherene	Catresa	Caylene	Ceara Silissa	Ceddrina	Celebrindal
Catherie	Catriah	Cayley *(0.02)*	Cearah	Cededra	Celecea
Catherien	Catrice	Cayli *(0.01)*	Cearaha	Cedequa Kellie	Celeen
Catheriene	Catriece	Caylia	Cearden	Cedes	Celeena
Catherin	Catriena	Caylie *(0.02)*	Ceare	Cedilin	Celeene
Catherina	Catrin	Caylin *(0.02)*	Cearea	Cedine	Celeeza
Catherine *(2.39)*	Catrina *(0.07)*	Cayloee	Cearia	Cedlyne	Celena *(0.08)*
Catherine Eliza	Catrine	Caylon	Cearra *(0.01)*	Cednecia	Celene *(0.04)*
Catherine Rose	Catriona *(0.01)*	Caylonna	Cearria	Cedra	Celenge
Catherine Thanh	Catti Brie	Caylor	Ceasha	Cedreaunna	Celenia
Catherine-Ann	Catti-Brie	Caylya	Ceasia	Cedreeka	Celeny
Catherine-Elizab	Cattia	Caylyn	Ceasyn	Cedrena	Celerina
Catherine-Jean	Cattileona	Caylyne	Ceayrra	Cedriahanna	Celes
Catheryn *(0.01)*	Cattleya	Caylynn	Cebonia	Cedriania	Celesia
Catheryne	Cattlin	Cayman	Cebre	Cedrica	Celess
Cathie	Catuta	Caymin	Cebrianna	Cedricionne	Celest
Cathie-Allegra	Caty	Caysa	Cebrina	Cedricka	Celesta *(0.01)*
Cathina	Catyana	Cayshiana	Cece	Cedrika	Celeste *(0.51)*
Cathleen *(0.04)*	Caulene	Caysi	Ceceli	Cedrina	Celesté
Cathleene	Caullette	Cayte	Cecelia *(0.38)*	Cedrionna	Celester
Cathlene	Cauncia	Caytlin	Cecelie	Cedrisha	Celestial
Cathlin	Caurisa	Caytlon	Cecely	Cedriyonna	Celestina
Cathline	Caviare	Caytlyn	Cechia	Cedtara	Celestine *(0.01)*
Cathlyn	Caviness	Cazandra	Ceci	Ceduna	Celestrial
Cathlynn	Cavongela	Caziah	Cecil	Cee	Celestte
Cathren	Cavonna	Cazma	Cecila	Ceejae	Celestyn
Cathrina	Cavonne	Cazmyr	Cecile *(0.01)*	Ceejay	Celestyna

Celexia	Ceniz	Cesilia *(0.02)*	Chabreah	Chahara	Chalai'
Celia *(0.16)*	Cenobia	Cesley	Chabreia	Chahaya	Chalandra
Celian	Centansia	Ceslie	Chabria	Chahayla	Chalandria
Celiana	Centauria	Cessalie	Chabrie	Chai	Chalane
Celicia	Centcha	Cessiley	Chabriel	Chai-Zean	Chalay
Celie	Centennial	Cessily	Chacandace	Chaia	Chalcee
Celiece	Centeria	Cesue	Chacelynn	Chaidez	Chaldees
Celiena	Centhyia	Cetan	Chacey	Chaidrianna	Chalea
Celimar	Centiviya	Cetiva	Chachá	Chaihann	Chalee
Celimary	Centoria	Ceva	Chachat	Chaila	Chalee Breanne
Celin	Centrell	Ceverena	Chachet	Chailenna	Chaleen
Celina *(0.35)*	Cenya	Ceyanna	Chachianna	Chailsey	Chaleigh
Celinda	Ceonna	Ceyanne	Chacia	Chailyn	Chalena
Celine *(0.19)*	Cepetria	Ceyarra	Chacity	Chaimee	Chalena-Jara
Celine Michelle	Cephia	Ceydi	Chacolby	Chaina	Chalene
Celine-Adrienne	Cephra	Ceyley	Chacorrie	Chaina Denisse	Chalesha
Celinna	Cepia	Ceylin	Chacoya	Chainte	Chalet
Celinsong	Cepidee	Ceylon	Chacye	Chaiquila	Chalethia
Celisa	Cepra	Ceyonne	Chad	Chairee	Chaley
Celisia	Cepre	Ceyora	Chadalyn	Chais	Chaleycia
Celissa	Cepresia	Ceyuanna	Chadara	Chaise	Chalfont
Celisse	Ceqouia	Cha	Chadaysha	Chaisity	Chalice
Cellee	Cequoyah	Cha Ia	Chaddam	Chaislyne	Chalicea
Celleen	Cequoyia	Cha Kelsia	Chade	Chaisma	Chalil
Celleigh	Cera *(0.03)*	Cha Kilah	Chadee	Chaisty	Chalina
Cellest	Cera-Rose	Cha Quola	Chadeijha	Chaizly	Chaline
Celleste	Cerecia	Cha Rhonya	Chadell	Chajohnna	Chalini
Celli	Cereena	Cha Vontae	Chadena	Chakaela	Chalis
Cellina	Cerelia	Cha'bria	Chaderrick	Chakara	Chalisa
Cellisa	Cerena	Cha'jadacent	Chadi	Chakari	Chalise
Celsa	Cerenity	Cha'keema	Chadianis	Chakata	Chalissa
Celsey *(0.01)*	Ceres	Cha'kemia	Chadijah	Chakeidra	Chalisse
Celsi	Ceri	Cha'kyra	Chadisty	Chakell	Chalitza
Celum	Ceria	Cha'maine	Chadjah	Chakelle	Challen
Celyn	Cerian	Cha'nel	Chadlyn	Chakema	Challes
Celyne	Cericka	Cha'rae	Chadne	Chakendra	Challese
Celynn	Ceridwen	Cha'relle	Chadnesha	Chakeria	Challie
Celynne	Cerina	Cha'riah	Chadon	Chakethia	Chally
Celyssa	Cerise	Cha'ron	Chadreek	Chakeya	Chalo'n
Cemantha	Cerisia	Cha'sani	Chadsiti	Chakeyra	Chalon
Cemisha	Cerline	Cha'tara	Chae	Chakia	Chalona
Cemone	Cerolayn	Cha'toyah	Chaedra	Chakiba	Chalonda
Cena	Cerra	Cha'uri	Chaedren	Chakiea	Chalonte
Cencera	Cerredia	Cha'vae	Chaela	Chakima	Chalrise
Cendasia	Cerria	Cha'vea	Chaelee	Chakira	Chalsae
Cendi	Cerrice	Cha-Christra	Chaelen	Chakirá	Chalsay
Cendra	Cersten	Chaaliyah	Chaeli	Chakita	Chalse
Cendy	Cerstin	Chabacca	Chaeliana	Chakiya	Chalsea
Cenedra	Cerys	Chabel	Chaella	Chakoya	Chalsey
Cenelia	Cesar	Chabeli *(0.01)*	Chaelsea	Chakra	Chalsy
Cenenté	Cesarah	Chabelly	Chaenel	Chakya	Chaltu
Cenet	Cesi	Chabely	Chaenna	Chakyra	Chaly
Cenia	Cesia	Chablee	Chaezni	Chala	Chalyn
Cenica	Cesiceiea	Chablis	Chaffney	Chalaa	Chalyse
Cenisa	Cesilee	Chaborgan	Chaffon	Chalae	Chalyssa

Chamaine	Chan'terrial	Chandliare	Changlynn	Chansley	Chantelya
Chamara	Chan'teze	Chandlie	Chani	Chansorya	Chantenique
Chamari	Chan-Tam	Chandlier	Chania	Chansreyroatha	Chantera
Chamaria	Chana *(0.04)*	Chandlor	Chanice *(0.01)*	Chanté	Chanterelle
Chamary	Chanacey	Chandlum	Chanicka	Chant'el	Chanteria *(0.01)*
Chamaya	Chanae	Chandlynn	Chanicqua	Chanta	Chanterica
Chamberlynn	Chanai	Chandlyr	Chaniece	Chantá	Chanterie
Chambers	Chanakan	Chandni *(0.01)*	Chanier	Chanta'l	Chanteshia
Chambliss	Chanamarony	Chandny	Chanika	Chantae	Chantesia
Chambrae	Chanaqua	Chandra *(0.06)*	Chanikia	Chantaé	Chantessa
Chambray	Chanara	Chandrae	Chanille	Chantaey	Chanteuse
Chambre	Chanarah	Chandray	Chanin	Chantai	Chantevia
Chambrey	Chanavia	Chandre	Chaning	Chantaia	Chantey
Chambria	Chanaya	Chandre Ett	Chaniqua	Chantail	Chanteyl
Chambrie	Chanbresia	Chandré	Chanique	Chantal *(0.25)*	Chantez
Chaméra	Chancalor	Chandrea	Chanirea	Chantal-Michelle	Chantezes'
Chamea	Chance *(0.02)*	Chandreka	Chanise *(0.01)*	Chantala	Chanthal
Chameel	Chancés	Chandrel	Chanisse	Chantale *(0.01)*	Chanthavy
Chameika	Chancee	Chandri-Dawn	Chanita	Chantalee	Chanti
Chameka	Chancelie	Chandria	Chanitra	Chantall	Chantia *(0.01)*
Chamel	Chancellor	Chandrial	Chaniya	Chantalle *(0.01)*	Chantiá
Chamelea	Chancely	Chandrika	Chanjree	Chantallie	Chantiara
Chamera	Chancery	Chandy	Chanketrice	Chantally	Chantiaria
Chamey	Chances	Chane	Chanla	Chantana	Chantice
Chamika	Chancetta	Chané	Chanlee	Chantanel	Chantiece
Chamikka	Chancey *(0.01)*	Chanél	Chanler	Chantanic	Chantiel
Chamille	Chancie	Chanea	Chanley	Chantasia	Chantiera
Chamisiya	Chancis	Chaneah	Chanlier	Chantavia	Chantiere
Chamiya	Chanclee	Chanece	Channa	Chantavious	Chantika
Chammera	Chancy	Chanee	Channah	Chantavy	Chantil
Chammy	Chanda *(0.02)*	Chaneice	Channal	Chantawry	Chantilée
Chamoah	Chandail	Chaneil	Channay	Chantay	Chantill
Chamomile	Chandale	Chaneka	Channeis	Chantaye	Chantille
Chamonique	Chandaleir	Chanel *(0.26)*	Channel *(0.02)*	Chante *(0.04)*	Chantilly
Champa	Chandana	Chanel'	Channell	Chanté *(0.02)*	Chantinique
Champagne *(0.01)*	Chandandeep	Chanel-Lee	Channelle *(0.01)*	Chantéa	Chantiqua
Champaign	Chandani	Chanele	Channica	Chantél	Chantira
Champaigne	Chandanise	Chanell *(0.02)*	Channing *(0.02)*	Chantear	Chantis
Champaine	Chandanpreet	Chanelle *(0.12)*	Channon	Chantee	Chantise
Champainé	Chandara	Chanelle Kwanna	Channsomarly	Chantée	Chantle
Champale	Chandary	Chanelly	Channtal	Chanteel	Chanto
Champall	Chandee	Chanen	Channtay	Chanteese	Chantoria
Champane	Chandeep	Chanequa	Chanoa	Chanteia	Chantra-Lee
Champange	Chandel	Chanera	Chanoir	Chantel *(0.32)*	Chantranice
Champayne	Chandell	Chanesa	Chanoni	Chantel Monet	Chantreal
Champell	Chandelle	Chanese	Chanpnell	Chantel-Rae	Chantrece
Champelle	Chandesha	Chanesia	Chanpreet	Chantele *(0.01)*	Chantrel
Champree	Chandi	Chanessa	Chanprell	Chantell *(0.05)*	Chantrey
Chamtel	Chandice	Chanet	Chanquenett	Chantell Chanis	Chantrice
Chamy	Chandie	Chanetris	Chanqula	Chantella	Chanttel
Chamyce	Chandine	Chanetta	Chanreyelle	Chantelle *(0.18)*	Chantura
Chamyia	Chandini	Chaney *(0.01)*	Chanrithany	Chantelle Le	Chantyana
Chan	Chandlar	Chaneyll	Chansamone	Chantelle-Lise	Chantyria
Chan'niqua	Chandler *(0.26)*	Chaneyra	Chansie	Chantelle-Vyvyan	Chantyva
Chan'te	Chandler-Marie	Chanez	Chansler	Chantelria	Chantz

Chanun	Chard'ai	Charice *(0.01)*	Charleene	Charlish	Charmonie
Chanutda	Chard'e	Charidan	Charleeon	Charlisha	Charmonique
Chanvia	Charda	Charidee	Charleese	Charlisi	Charmore
Chanya	Chardae *(0.01)*	Charie	Charleigh *(0.01)*	Charlissa	Charmyne
Chanyce	Chardaé	Chariell	Charleisha	Charlita	Charmynne
Chanyia	Chardai	Charielle	Charlekia	Charlite	Charn
Chanz	Chardai'	Chariene	Charlen	Charllote	Charn El
Chanze	Chardaie	Chariety	Charlena	Charllotte	Charna
Chaola	Chardajus	Charika	Charlenae	Charlnae	Charnaé
Chapel	Chardanele	Charionta	Charlene *(0.25)*	Charlo	Charnae
Chapelle	Chardasia	Charionté	Charlene Clairis	Charlondria	Charnaé
Chapin	Charday	Charioty	Charles	Charlotte *(0.62)*	Charnai
Chaporche	Charde	Charis *(0.02)*	Charlesa	Charlotte-Jennifer	Charnasia
Chappelle	Chardé	Charisa	Charlesana	Charlottie	Charnaye
Chapresha	Chardeisha	Charise	Charlese	Charlreese	Charnaza
Chaqouya	Chardeja	Charish	Charlesea	Charlsa	Charne
Chaquan	Chardell	Charisma *(0.02)*	Charlesetta	Charlsea	Charné
Chaquana	Chardelle	Charissa *(0.04)*	Charlesey	Charlsey	Charneal
Chaquandra	Chardelyne	Charisse *(0.01)*	Charlesha	Charlsie	Charnece
Chaquanya	Chardeon	Charisty	Charleshia	Charlsta	Charnee
Chaquara	Chardey	Charita	Charlesia	Charltarrius	Charnée
Chaquawen	Chardie	Charitee	Charlesse	Charlton	Charneillia
Chaque	Chardnay	Chariti	Charlessia	Charlvon	Charneisha
Chaquell	Chardney	Charitie	Charlessley	Charly *(0.01)*	Charneka
Chaquella	Chardon	Charitmy	Charlesy	Charlye	Charnekko
Chaquera	Chardonae	Charity *(0.21)*	Charleszetta	Charlymae	Charnel
Chaquerea	Chardonaé	Charity Blessed	Charleszettia	Charlyn	Charnele
Chaqueria	Chardonai	Charizma	Charlet	Charlyne	Charnell
Chaquinais	Chardonay	Charkel	Charleta	Charlynne	Charnelle *(0.01)*
Chaquita	Chardonaye	Charkeria	Charletabian	Charm	Charnequa
Char	Chardonna	Charkerriah	Charlete	Charmae	Charnesa
Char Dana	Chardonnae	Charkesia	Charleton	Charmagne	Charnese
Char'	Chardonnai	Charkisia	Charlett	Charmaigne	Charnesha
Char'maine	Chardonnay *(0.01)*	Charkita	Charletta	Charmain	Charneshia
Char'meice	Chardonney	Charla *(0.01)*	Charlette	Charmaine *(0.08)*	Charnessia
Char'recca	Chardyne	Charlaceya	Charlexius	Charmane *(0.01)*	Charnetta
Char-Dawna	Charea	Charlaina	Charley *(0.02)*	Charmayn	Charneyce
Char-Lee	Charece	Charlaine	Charli *(0.03)*	Charmayne	Charnice
Chara	Charee	Charlamaigne	Charlia	Charmecia	Charniece
Charadee	Charée	Charlane	Charliann	Charmeine	Charniesha
Charae	Chareece	Charlay	Charlianne	Charmel	Charnika
Charakee	Chareeze	Charlayna	Charlice	Charmeon	Charniqua
Charaki	Charell	Charlayne	Charlicia	Charmese	Charnique
Charamine	Charelle	Charle	Charlie *(0.08)*	Charmesha	Charniqué
Charanbind	Charellé	Charlé	Charlie-Ann	Charmeshia	Charnise *(0.01)*
Charanjit	Charena	Charlea	Charlien	Charmetria	Charnisha
Charanjot	Charese	Charleace	Charliesha	Charmeyon	Charnita
Charann	Charessa	Charlean	Charlika	Charmia	Charnitria
Charaté	Charesse	Charlecia	Charlilyn	Charmian	Charnjot
Charay	Charez	Charlee *(0.03)*	Charlin	Charmiecia	Charnorma
Charaya	Charezka	Charlee Anne	Charline *(0.01)*	Charmin	Charnvir
Charayven	Chari	Charlee-Jean	Charlisa *(0.01)*	Charmine	Charnyqwa
Charbene	Chari's	Charleeann	Charlise	Charminique	Charo
Charbriae	Charia	Charleece	Charliséa	Charmise	Charola
Charbrina	Charian	Charleen *(0.01)*	Charlisea	Charmita	Charolett

Charolette	Charyl	Chassidi	Chauncie	Chavonne	Che Nurul
Charolotte	Charyn	Chassidy (0.03)	Chauncy	Chawana	Che Ron
Charoltte	Charys	Chassie	Chaundele	Chawna	Che Vaughn
Charon	Charyse	Chassiti	Chaundra	Chawntey	Chékayla
Charon'	Charzeda	Chassity (0.01)	Chaundrea	Chawntiel	Chékeyshia
Charona	Chas	Chassity Faith	Chaundrica	Chaya (0.02)	Chékiera
Charonda	Chasady	Chassney	Chaundrise	Chayan	Chéla
Charonn	Chasaity	Chasstidy	Chaunee	Chayana	Chélese
Charosnese	Chasalynn	Chassy	Chauneshia	Chayanne	Chémaiah
Charpele	Chasan	Chasta	Chaunessy	Chaybree	Chémanual
Charqualia	Chasaney	Chastady	Chaunice	Chayce	Chénisha
Charquandra	Chasatee	Chastiana	Chauniece	Chaydin	Che-Ann
Charquiesa	Chasatie	Chastidy	Chaunsay	Chaye	Chea
Charquill	Chasauna	Chastie	Chaunsiqua	Chayiesha	Cheadee
Charquisha	Chasautea	Chastin	Chauntae	Chayla (0.01)	Cheakina
Charquoya	Chasdy	Chastine	Chauntay	Chaylah	Cheala
Charra	Chase (0.02)	Chastiny	Chaunte	Chayle	Chealajuan
Charrae	Chasedy	Chastity (0.06)	Chaunté	Chaylee	Chealmie
Charri	Chaseny	Chastity St	Chauntel (0.01)	Chaylen	Chealse
Charrie	Chasetti	Chastiy	Chauntell	Chaylena	Chealsea
Charrita	Chasety	Chaston	Chauntelle	Chaylene	Chealsey
Charsandra	Chasey	Chasty	Chaunteria	Chayley	Chealsi
Charsenia	Chasha	Chastyn	Chaunti	Chaylie	Chealsie
Charshika	Chasi	Chasya	Chauntiana	Chaylon	Chealtzea
Charsie	Chasidee	Chasyka	Chauntice	Chaylyn	Chealyn
Charta	Chasidée	Chatana	Chauntiia	Chaylynn	Chealynn
Chartaa	Chasidey	Chataqua	Chauntilena	Chayna	Cheandra
Chartace	Chasidie	Chatara	Chauntora	Chaynan	Cheanell
Chartasha	Chasidity	Chatarah	Chauntoria	Chayse	Checotah
Chartasia	Chasidty	Chatavia	Chaunya	Chaysee	Checourria
Chartaun	Chasidy (0.02)	Chataya	Chauricce	Chaystin	Checree
Charteá	Chasika	Chatazia	Chaurice	Chayundra	Chedale
Chartell	Chasima	Chate-Lane	Chauta	Chaz	Chedeline
Chartella	Chasin	Chatel	Chauvondra	Chazah	Chednise
Charter	Chasitee	Chatelaine	Chava	Chazaria	Chedowrian
Charterius	Chasitey	Chatell	Chavá	Chazda	Chee-lab
Chartonia	Chasiti	Chatera	Chavae	Chazemene	Cheeara
Chartoria	Chasitie	Chaterrika	Chavakaye	Chazeray	Cheerokee
Charuga	Chasitiy	Chatia	Chavante	Chazeton	Cheery
Charvae	Chasitty	Chatiaya	Chavanté	Chazide	Cheffon
Charvaé	Chasity (0.22)	Chatika	Chave	Chazite	Chehala
Charveda	Chasity Mar	Chatizah	Chavei	Chazloyn	Chehalie
Charvel	Chasley	Chatnavon	Chaveli	Chazlyn	Cheheyla
Charvella	Chaslie	Chaton	Chavell	Chazmin	Cheila
Charvi	Chaslyn	Chatoria	Chavella	Chazmine	Cheilsey
Charvie	Chasma	Chatrene	Chavelle	Chazmyane	Cheina
Charviell	Chasmin	Chatrice	Chavely	Chazney	Chejai
Charvis	Chasmine	Chattra	Chavenese	Chazrina	Chekale-
Charvona	Chasnee	Chaturah	Chavette	Chazton	Keiondre
Charvonna	Chasntity	Chau	Chavine	Chazz	Chekeal
Charwyna	Chason	Chau-Linda	Chavis	Chazzaré	Chekeshia
Chary	Chassadi	Chaun'céy	Chavon	Che	Chekilla
Charyah	Chassady	Chaunacey	Chavona	Che La	Chekina
Charyea	Chassee	Chaunceia	Chavonda	Che Lon	Chekinna
Charyian	Chassida	Chauncey	Chavondrea	Che Lyn	Chekira

Chekiria	Chelsah	Chemeko	Cheoka	Cherilyn (0.01)	Cherrokee
Chekisa	Chelsalynn	Chemere	Cheonna	Cherilynn	Cherron
Chekoya	Chelsay	Chemetria	Chephirah	Cherima	Cherroneka
Chel'c	Chelse (0.02)	Chemia	Chequania	Cherimi	Cherroyas
Chel'le	Chelséa	Chemika	Chequita	Cherina	Cherry (0.01)
Chel'sea	Chelsea (3.48)	Chemise	Chequoia	Cherinda	Cherrye
Chela	Chelsea Marie	Chemmin	Cheqweia	Cheris	Cherryicucca
Chelaia	Chelsea Symone	Chemonae	Cher	Cherise (0.02)	Cherryl
Chelan	Chelseá	Chen	Cher'ea	Cherish (0.07)	Cherstin
Chelbe	Chelsea-	Chenah	Chera	Cherisha	Cherub
Chelbi	Alexandra	Chenal	Cheraden	Cherisma	Cheryce
Chelbie	Chelsea-Ann	Chenalynn	Cheradin	Cheriss	Cheryl (0.14)
Chelby (0.01)	Chelsea-Anne	Chenari	Cheraevia	Cherissa	Cheryl-Lynne
Chelce	Chelsea-Jo	Chenaya	Cherakee	Cherisse (0.01)	Cherylann
Chelcee	Chelsea-Lyne	Chenayla	Cheralill	Cherissia	Cherylanne
Chelcey	Chelsea-Nycole	Chenda	Cherall	Cheristy	Cherylee
Chelchasity	Chelsea-Rae	Chendandeep	Cheralyn	Cherita	Cherylene
Chelci (0.01)	Chelsea-Rose	Chendra	Cheramesha	Cherith	Cherylethia
Chelcie (0.01)	Chelseah	Chenea	Cherall	Cheriti	Cheryll
Chelcie-Ann	Chelsean	Cheneeta	Chere	Cheritta	Cheryll Joy
Chelcy	Chelseanne	Cheneisha	Cherea	Cherkara	Cherylnn
Cheleah	Chelseay	Cheneka	Chereau	Cherlaine	Cherylyn
Chelean	Chelsee (0.04)	Chenel	Chereaye	Cherleetha	Cherylynn
Cheleana	Chelsée	Chenell	Cherebyum	Cherlene	Cheryse
Cheleas	Chelsei	Chenelle (0.01)	Cheree	Cherli	Cherysh
Chelease	Chelseigh	Chenesa Vina	Cherée	Cherlia	Chesaleo
Chelesa	Chelsey (0.68)	Chenessa	Chereese	Cherlie	Chesanie
Chelese	Chelsey-Jade	Chenett	Cherehan	Cherline	Chesanne
Chelesea	Chelsey-Lynn	Chenetta	Chereis	Cherly	Chesar'e
Chelesey	Chelshy	Chenette	Cherek	Cherlyn	Cheserae
Cheliese	Chelsi (0.09)	Cheney	Cherell	Cherlynn	Chesia
Chelise	Chelsi'	Chenez	Cherelle (0.02)	Chermaine	Chesica
Chelissa	Chelsia (0.01)	Cheng	Cheresa	Chermel	Chesirée
Chell'le	Chelsie (0.26)	Chenia	Cherese (0.01)	Chermin Joy	Cheska Chelsea
Chella	Chelson	Chenicka	Cherety	Chernaira	Cheslay
Chellá	Chelssey	Chenika	Cheri (0.03)	Chernell	Cheslea
Chellby	Chelssie	Chenille	Cherian-D'onn	Chernise	Chesleah
Chellcee	Chelssy	Chenique	Cheriana	Cherokee (0.04)	Chesley
Chellcey	Chelston	Chenisa	Cherianne	Cheron	Chesli
Chelle	Chelsy (0.06)	Chenise	Cherica	Cherrae	Cheslie
Chellie	Chelsy-Lynn	Chenissa	Cherice (0.01)	Cherrel	Chesmand
Chelliney	Chelsye	Chennel	Cherida	Cherrell (0.01)	Chesmeka
Chellini	Cheltea	Chennelle	Cheridan	Cherrelle	Chesna
Chellise	Chelton	Chennine	Cheridon	Cherri (0.01)	Chesnee
Chellsea	Cheltsa	Chenoa (0.01)	Cheridy	Cherriale	Chesney (0.01)
Chellsee	Cheltsey	Chenoah	Cherie (0.05)	Cherrica	Chesnie
Chellsei	Cheltsie	Chenquia	Cherié	Cherrice	Chessa (0.01)
Chellsey	Cheltyn	Chenteel	Cherie-Ann	Cherrie	Chessala
Chellsie	Cheltzie	Chentell	Cheriece	Cherrika	Chessi
Chellsy	Cheltzy	Chentelle	Cheriee	Cherrilaine	Chessica
Chelniece	Chely	Chenyah	Cheriel	Cherrill	Chessie
Chelnise	Chelyn	Chenyier	Cherielynne	Cherrise	Chessly
Chelonte	Chelynn	Chenying	Cherienne	Cherrish	Chessney
Chelsa (0.01)	Chelyse	Chenyrene	Cheriez	Cherrita	Chessy
Chelsae	Chelzee	Chenyse	Cherigmy	Cherrity	Chesteen
				Cherika	

Chestity	Cheylene	Chicyah	Chinenye	Chloe-Joy	Chrisandra
Cheszaré	Cheylo	Chidera	Chineshia	Chloe-Katrine	Chrisann
Chetanpal	Cheylyn	Chidi	Chinetta	Chloediamon	Chrisanne
Cheteigra	Cheylynn	Chidinma	Chineze	Chloee	Chriscinda
Cheterricka	Cheylynn-Erin	Chidumebi	Ching	Chloey	Chrisea
Chetia	Cheyna *(0.01)*	Chie	Chinica	Chloie	Chrisean
Chetstina	Cheyne	Chieko	Chiniquea	Chlorissa	Chriselle
Cheuk	Cheynee	Chielo Jane	Chiniseual	Chlsea	Chriserria
Cheuk-Yin	Cheyney	Chiemeka	Chinna	Chlsey	Chrisfelia
Cheung	Cheynna	Chiemelia	Chinná	Chnuka	Chrisha
Chev'qavia	Cheynne	Chiese	Chinnee	Cho	Chrishá
Chevalia	Cheynoa	Chieshionna	Chinonye	Chobi	Chrishae
Chevanne	Cheyondra	Chiffon	Chinonyerem	Chohnice	Chrishalen
Chevelle *(0.01)*	Cheyteria	Chigozie	Chinook	Chole *(0.01)*	Chrishana
Chevenne	Cheytoya	Chihiro	Chinqua	Cholé	Chrishandal
Chevie-Lee	Chezarae	Chika	Chinquay	Cholena	Chrishandra
Chevon	Cheznee	Chikara	Chinthu	Chon-Ting	Chrishani
Chevona	Chezney	Chikela	Chinthusa	Chona	Chrishanna
Chevonna	Chezzarae	Chikere	Chinwe	Chondra	Chrishanthi
Chevonne	Chhabria	Chikiya	Chinyere	Chonelle	Chrishara
Chevonya	Chi *(0.01)*	Chikodi	Chinzia	Chong	Chrishauna
Chevousia	Chi'ann	Chikyra	Chioma *(0.01)*	Chonkeea	Chrishaunda
Chevy	Chi'nita	Chikyta	Chion	Chonna	Chrishaunna
Chewanah	Chi-Anna	Chila	Chiona	Chonsa	Chrishavona
Chey	Chia	Chilan	Chione	Chontaul	Chrishawn
Chey Anne	Chia Hsin	Childs	Chiquana	Chontavia	Chrishawna
Chey-He-La	Chia-Nian	Chiliyah	Chiquera	Chontaye	Chrishawnta
Cheyaane	Chiaira	Chillet	Chiquira	Chonté	Chrishayla
Cheyalla	Chiaka	Chilneshia	Chiquita *(0.02)*	Chontel	Chrishea
Cheyan	Chiaki	Chilsea	Chiquitta	Chontell	Chrishell
Cheyana	Chiamaka	Chima	Chiqure	Chontia	Chrishelle
Cheyane	Chian	Chime	Chirayil	Chontise	Chrishera
Cheyann *(0.03)*	Chiana	Chimene	Chirihane	Chonyi	Chrishey
Cheyanna *(0.02)*	Chiandra	Chimera	Chirstin	Choquilla	Chrishna
Cheyanne *(0.28)*	Chiane	Chimere	Chisama Ku	Chor	Chrishon
Cheyauntae	Chiangdatarnak	Chimuanya	Chisato	Choran	Chrishona
Cheydene	Chianice	Chin	Chishoua	Chori	Chrishonda
Cheydey	Chiann	China *(0.08)*	Chisom	Chornell	Chrishonte
Cheye	Chianna	China-Brittany	Chitney	Choua *(0.01)*	Chrishuna
Cheyeana	Chianne *(0.01)*	China-Jade	Chitra	Chounlie	Chrisina
Cheyeanna	Chiante	Chinacat	Chiu	Chourtné	Chrisine
Cheyeanne	Chianté	Chinace	Chivante	Choute	Chrisitne
Cheyeene	Chianti	Chinadoll	Chivina	Chrajon	Chrisleen
Cheyena	Chianti'	Chinaelo	Chivon	Chrashauna	Chrislesne
Cheyene *(0.01)*	Chiao	Chinah	Chivonn	Chreasha	Chrislyn
Cheyenee	Chiara *(0.05)*	Chinara	Chivonte	Chrianya	Chrismali
Cheyenen	Chiarina	Chinasaa	Chiyierrja	Chrichna	Chrisna
Cheyenna *(0.01)*	Chiarra	Chinazom	Chizoba	Chrimontrez	Chrisonna
Cheyenne *(1.62)*	Chiave	Chinazor	Chl'e	Chrineicia	Chrisoula
Cheyenne Doris	Chiavi	Chiné	Chleo	Chrinesha	Chrisovalantou
Cheyenne-Alvani	Chiayo	Chinea	Chleo Viselle	Chrinita	Chrissa
Cheyienne	Chibuzo	Chineka	Chlo'e	Chris *(0.01)*	Chrissandra
Cheyla	Chicana	Chinell	Chloe *(1.31)*	Chris'shéa	Chrissey
Cheylan	Chicara	Chinelo	Chloé *(0.03)*	Chris-Shawna	Chrisshelle
Cheyleigh	Chicharlah	Chinemerem	Chloe-Alexandra	Chrisana	Chrisshona

Chrissie (0.01)	Christiani	Christoria	Chrystyn	Chyler	Ciarra-Jo-Anne
Chrissini	Christiania	Christsandra	Chrystyna	Chylicia	Ciarra-Marie
Chrissy (0.02)	Christiann	Christy (0.27)	Chryzel	Chylie	Ciarrah
Christa (0.23)	Christianna (0.03)	Christy Ann	Chu	Chyllane	Cibrian
Christa-Dale	Christianne (0.01)	Christy Tiffany	Chua	Chyloh	Cicelia
Christa-Mattie	Christie (0.14)	Christy Tru	Chudasama	Chylynn	Cicely (0.01)
Christabel	Christie Lynn	Christy-Alexis	Chuder	Chymaiah	Cicerra
Christabell	Christie-Anne	Christyal	Chudney	Chymeia	Cici
Christabelle	Christie-Lee	Christyan	Chuen	Chyna (0.04)	Ciciley
Christafien	Christiean	Christyana	Chuen-Xi	Chyna-Lynn	Cicilia
Christain (0.01)	Christien	Christyanne	Chueqa	Chynel	Cicily
Christaina	Christiena	Christye	Chui	Chynelle	Cid
Christajiah	Christima	Christyl	Chuilin	Chynicua	Cidell
Christal (0.05)	Christin (0.22)	Christyn (0.01)	Chukwunedum	Chynithia	Cidnee
Christal Joyce	Christina (3.39)	Christyna	Chukyi	Chynna (0.03)	Cidney (0.01)
Christalin	Christina Ashle	Christyne	Chulisa	Chynnique	Cidni
Christalina	Christina-Franc	Christynna	Chumany	Chyranda	Cidnie
Christaline	Christina-Khanh	Chrisya	Chun'tia	Chyrell	Cidra
Christalyn	Christina-Sabrina	Chriteria	Chun-Lam	Chyrstin	Cie Rra
Christan (0.01)	Christina-Siham	Chrizar	Chun-Teva	Chytiera	Ciére
Christana	Christina-Vayia	Chrlene	Chundra	Chytissha	Ciérra
Christanda	Christinaa	Chrmaine	Chuneice	Ci Ayra	Cieaira
Christann	Christinaq	Chrquita	Chung	Ci'aira	Cieana
Christanna	Christine (1.43)	Chrustona	Chunille	Ci'anna	Cieanna
Christarra	Christine Lynn	Chryanthi	Chunita	Ci'ara	Cieara
Christasia	Christine Marie	Chryelle	Chunke	Ci'aris	Ciearra (0.01)
Christauna	Christine Mary-E	Chrys	Churee	Ci'era	Ciebiena
Christawna	Christine-Ida	Chrysa	Chutkira	Ci'yasia	Cieera
Christayle	Christine-Tamra	Chrysalis	Chuyita	Cia	Ciel
Christazja	Christine-Van	Chrysan	Chy Ann	Ciaera	Cielo
Christecia	Christinea	Chrysantha	Chy Anne	Ciaira	Ciena
Christee	Christineno	Chrysanthe	Chy-Na	Ciairá	Cienjuan
Christeen	Christineville	Chrysanthy	Chy-Nedia	Ciamara	Cienna (0.01)
Christeena	Christing	Chrysdeanna	Chyah	Cian	Cieon
Christeina	Christini	Chrysen	Chyan	Ciana (0.02)	Ciera (0.24)
Christel (0.01)	Christinia	Chryshana	Chyana	Ciana-Lenae	Ciera Mallié
Christel Fatima	Christinna	Chryshanisse	Chyane	Ciana-Ri	Ciera-Sue
Christele	Christinnah	Chrysilla	Chyann (0.01)	Cianan	Cierah
Christell	Christion	Chrysler	Chyanna	Cianara	Cieran
Christelle (0.02)	Christiona	Chryslin	Chyanne (0.04)	Ciandra	Ciere
Christelle-Jean	Christione	Chryssa	Chyara	Ciani	Cieria
Christelyn	Christionta	Chrysta (0.01)	Chydai	Ciann	Cierika
Christen (0.11)	Christite	Chrystal (0.07)	Chyeana	Cianna (0.01)	Cierra (0.61)
Christen An	Christle	Chrystale	Chyee	Ciante	Cierra S
Christena (0.01)	Christlene	Chrystalla	Chyenn	Cianya	Cierrá
Christene (0.01)	Christline	Chrystallina	Chyenna	Ciar	Cierra-Dallas
Christer	Christly	Chrystalynn	Chyenne (0.03)	Ciara (0.61)	Cierra-Leigh
Christey	Christlyn	Chrystel (0.01)	Chyennee	Ciará	Cierrah
Christi (0.02)	Christmas	Chrystelle	Chykeria	Ciara-Martina	Cierre
Christia	Christobol	Chrystian	Chyla	Ciarah	Cierria
Christia-Ann	Christol	Chrystianna	Chylah	Ciaran	Cierro
Christian (0.25)	Christon	Chrystin	Chylcie	Ciaree	Ciesha
Christiana (0.13)	Christonna	Chrystina	Chyleece	Ciaria	Cieyara
Christiana Maeve	Christony	Chrystyan	Chyleen	Ciarisse	Cigne
Christiane (0.01)	Christopher (0.01)	Chrystyl	Chylene	Ciarra (0.05)	Ciham

Cija	Ciperanna	Claireece	Clarisia	Clayre	Clinetta
Ciji	Cipreona	Clairese	Clarissa (0.44)	Clayresha	Clinique
Cikethia	Cipriana	Clairesse	Clarissa Elizabeth	Clayton	Clinisha
Cikya	Ciprianna	Clairey	Clarissa-Ann	Clénesha	Clintara
Cilea	Ciquoiia	Clairice	Clarissadon	Cléshay	Clintasha
Cileena	Cira	Clairionna	Clarisse (0.01)	Clea	Clintina
Cilena	Circe	Clairisa	Clarisse Courtney	Cleanae	Clintoria
Cilene	Cire	Clairissa (0.01)	Clarita	Cleandra	Clinyse
Cilia	Cirea	Clalissa	Claritsa	Cleanna	Clio
Cilicia	Cireena	Clancey	Clarity	Cleante	Cliotide
Cilki	Cirgida	Clancie	Claritza	Clearencia	Clique
Cilla	Cirié	Clancy (0.01)	Clarivel	Clease	Clishay
Cimantha	Ciristin	Clandra	Clariza	Clein-Wheh	Clissie
Cimber	Cirra	Clania	Clarizza	Cleiry	Clista
Cimberly	Cirrea	Clantija	Clark	Clela	Clitiauna
Cimmeion	Cirri	Clar'aisha	Clarke	Clelia	Clivane
Cimone	Cirsten	Clara (0.30)	Clarneisha	Clemecia	Clodagh
Cina	Cirstie	Clarabelle	Claromanoora	Clemel	Clodia
Cincerae	Cisha	Clarace	Clarque	Clemence (0.02)	Cloe (0.06)
Cinda	Cisile	Clarachrist	Clarrese	Clemencia	Cloei
Cindara	Cissaly	Claraines	Clarrie	Clementina	Cloey
Cindarae	Cissy	Claraissa	Clarrisa	Clementine	Cloie
Cindel	Cistinna	Clarandra	Clarrissa	Clemesha	Cloria
Cinden	Citaly	Clare (0.16)	Clary	Clemetra	Clorisa
Cinderella	Citlali	Clarésha	Clarycia	Clemisha	Clorissa (0.01)
Cindi (0.02)	Citlalin	Clarece	Clarysel	Clemons	Clorissa-Dwan
Cindia	Citlalli	Claremarie	Classie	Clenarsia	Clossena
Cindra	Citlallin	Claren	Classy	Cleo (0.01)	Cloteal
Cindy (0.92)	Citlally	Clarence	Clatie	Cleonna	Clotean
Cindy Cynthia	Citlaly (0.01)	Clarencia	Clattell	Cleontra	Clothilde
Cindy-Anh	Cityana	Clarene	Claude (0.01)	Cleopatra	Clotilde
Cingarkaq	Cityra	Clarenisha	Claudel (0.01)	Clera	Clottymar
Cinjin	Civia	Clareonta	Claudelle	Clerfta	Clover
Cinna	Civiana	Claresa	Claudestene	Clerisa	Clovis
Cinnae	Ciya	Clareshatae	Claudette (0.01)	Clerissa	Cloydia
Cinnammon	Ciyah	Claresia	Claudia (0.95)	Clester	Cly'isha
Cinnamon (0.02)	Ciyanna	Claressa	Claudia Marcela	Cleta	Clyeisha
Cinnamond	Ciyera	Claretha	Claudiana	Cletha	Clyjazia
Cinnimin	Cj	Claretta	Claudiane	Clevayezha	Clylisha
Cinquasha	Cjayna	Clariana	Claudie (0.04)	Cleveland	Clyneisha
Cintdia	Cjeylon	Claribel (0.02)	Claudie-Jade	Clevon	Clyneshia
Cintera	Ckinu	Claribell	Claudin	Clevona	Clytie
Cinteria	Cla'shanna	Claribeth	Claudina	Cleyana	Clyttina
Cinthia (0.09)	Clace	Clarica	Claudine (0.01)	Cleyydys	Cne
Cinthiya	Clacey	Clarice (0.03)	Claudio	Clhoe	Cnee
Cinthya (0.04)	Clacina	Claricia	Claudy	Cliche	Co'asia
Cintia (0.02)	Cladia	Clarie	Claudya	Cliff'teena	Co-Shey
Cintrailia	Clae	Clariece	Claurene	Cliffany	Coartney
Cinzia	Claiborne	Clarielle	Claurine	Clifonda	Cobair
Ciomara	Claice	Clarinda	Claurissa	Clifshaun	Cobb
Cion	Claiire	Clarine	Clavdia	Clifton	Cobbie
Ciona	Clair (0.02)	Clarionta	Clavette	Clijuana	Cobi
Ciondira	Claira	Clarisa (0.12)	Claybrache	Clinasia	Cobie
Ciondra	Claire (1.10)	Clarise	Claylon	Clinesha	Cobrana
Cionna	Clairece	Clarisha	Claylyn	Clinesia	Coby

Cochran	Colleen (0.59)	Connisha	Cora-Lynn	Coree	Corita
Coco	Colleena	Conniver	Coraal	Coreen (0.01)	Coritha
Cocodrie	Colleene	Connlee	Corabeth	Coreena (0.01)	Corithian
Cocosharelle	Collen	Connlesha	Corah	Corei Ana	Coriyalla
Coddie	Collene	Connor (0.04)	Coraima (0.03)	Coreima	Coriyanna
Codee	Collete	Connr	Coraiyma	Coreina	Corkeisha
Codetta	Collett	Conntessah	Coral (0.10)	Coreion	Corla
Codey	Collette (0.02)	Conny	Coralea	Corella	Corlee
Codi (0.05)	Colleyna	Conor	Coralee	Corelle	Corleen
Codi-Lynn	Collice	Conor-Allysia	Coralene	Coren	Corlehdra
Codia	Collida	Conquestieia	Coraley	Corena	Corley
Codie (0.03)	Collie	Conquista	Corali	Corene	Corlisha
Codie-Jo	Collier	Conreliisha	Coralia	Corenisha	Corliss
Codiebeth	Collin	Conshá	Coralie (0.04)	Corenna	Corllette
Cody (0.07)	Collinda	Consiha	Coralin	Corenthea	Corly
Cody-Jo	Colline	Consquela	Coralina	Corenthia	Corlyn
Coekee	Collisha	Consquellia	Coraline	Coresa	Cormella
Coel	Collista	Constadina	Coralisse	Coressa	Cormellia
Coelida	Collnishia	Constance (0.12)	Coraliz	Coretta (0.01)	Cornaie
Coelina	Collyn	Constancia	Corallanne	Corey (0.08)	Corneail
Coeurin	Colt	Constans	Coraly	Corey'an	Corneathea
Cohenisha	Colton	Constanti	Coralynn	Corey-Anne	Cornecia
Cointa	Coluntiya	Constantina	Coralynne	Coreyana	Corneisha
Cojuanna	Colyn	Constanza	Coralys	Coreyanda	Cornelia (0.01)
Cokie	Comekia	Constanze	Coran	Coreyanna	Corneliu
Cola	Comeshia	Constious	Coraya	Coreyneika	Cornelius
Colae	Comfort	Constynse	Corayma	Cori (0.12)	Cornella
Colaina	Comonique	Consuela (0.01)	Corazon	Corian	Cornellia
Colbee	Compassion	Consuela Shantr	Corban	Coriana	Cornequia
Colbey	Comsuelo	Consuella	Corbe	Coriane	Cornesha (0.01)
Colbi (0.01)	Conasia	Consuelo (0.04)	Corbi	Coriann	Corneshia
Colbie (0.01)	Concepcion (0.01)	Conswala	Corbin (0.01)	Corianna	Cornesia
Colby (0.06)	Concetta (0.01)	Conswella	Corby	Corianne	Cornessia
Colby-Lynn	Concetti	Contesa	Corbyn	Coridona	Cornette
Cole	Conchairta	Contessa (0.01)	Corbynn	Corie (0.04)	Cornia
Colee	Conchetta	Contina	Corda	Coriesha	Cornika
Coleen (0.01)	Conchi	Contonia	Cordae	Corika	Corniquia
Coleman	Conchita	Contressa	Cordeghia	Corilla	Cornisha
Colena	Condeaish	Contynse	Cordeja	Corille	Cornithia
Colene	Condwiramurs	Conzuelo	Cordelia (0.02)	Corima	Coroanda
Colesha	Conecia	Cookie	Cordera	Corin (0.01)	Coronda
Coleshea	Coni	Coollan	Cordet	Corina (0.17)	Corra
Coleshia	Coniesha	Cooper (0.01)	Cordia	Corine (0.01)	Correen
Coletta	Coniika	Cooper Nichelle	Cordiaul	Corinisha	Correena
Colette (0.07)	Coniqua	Coortane	Cordie	Corinn	Corren
Colice	Conisha	Coortnae	Cordijah	Corinna (0.05)	Correna
Colin	Conishia	Copeland	Cordilla	Corinne (0.24)	Correnda
Colina	Conley (0.01)	Copely	Cordin	Corino	Correonna
Colisa	Connar	Copelyn	Cordniqua	Corintha	Correy
Colisha	Connay	Copper	Coreá	Corinthea	Corri
Coliss	Conneka	Cora (0.16)	Coreal	Corinthia (0.01)	Corrial
Colissa	Connelly	Cora-Elizabeth	Coreana	Corinthian	Corriana
Colista	Conner (0.02)	Cora-Leah	Coreasha	Corionne	Corriann
Colla	Conni	Cora-Lee	Corecia	Corisa	Corrianna
Collean	Connie (0.20)	Cora-Leigh	Coredaja	Corissa (0.03)	Corrianne

Corriauna	Cortne	Courtland	Cranecia	Criselda	Cristle
Corricka	Cortné	Courtlin	Craneisha	Criselia	Cristlynn
Corrie *(0.05)*	Cortnee *(0.01)*	Courtlyn *(0.01)*	Cranisha	Crisencia	Cristol
Corrie Anne	Cortney *(0.24)*	Courtlynn	Crashawna	Crishana	Criston
Corrie Lyn	Cortni *(0.01)*	Courtnay	Crashawnda	Crishara	Cristy *(0.02)*
Corrie-Ann	Cortnie *(0.01)*	Courtne	Crashunia	Crishawnda	Cristyn
Corrieonna	Cortnie-Anne	Courtné	Cratavia	Crishell	Crittney
Corrigan	Cortny	Courtnee *(0.03)*	Cratia	Crishon	Croix
Corrin *(0.02)*	Cortnye	Courtnée	Craven	Crishonda	Crook
Corrina *(0.07)*	Cortridgra	Courtneelynn	Crawford	Crishonna	Crosbie
Corrinda	Corunn	Courtnei *(0.01)*	Cre Chel	Crisie	Crosby
Corrinder	Corvette	Courtneigh	Crea	Crisla	Crstina
Corrindia	Corvina	Courtney *(5.91)*	Cream	Crislyn	Crusita
Corrine *(0.06)*	Corwin	Courtney Alison	Creasha	Crisna	Cruz
Corrinna	Cory *(0.04)*	Courtney Ann	Creasie	Crisol	Cruzita
Corrinne *(0.01)*	Cory-Lisa	Courtney Elizab	Crecia	Crissa	Crysandra
Corrisa	Cory-Lynn	Courtney Lynn	Cree *(0.01)*	Crissabeth	Crysania
Corrisha	Coryell	Courtney Nicole	Creeana	Crissauna	Cryshel
Corrissa	Coryetta	Courtney-Jeanne	Creeanna	Crissell	Cryshona
Corriyone	Coryl	Courtney-Lynn	Creeanne	Crissey	Crysinthea
Corry	Coryn *(0.01)*	Courtney-Rae	Creedance	Crisseyda	Crysta *(0.03)*
Corryn	Corynn *(0.01)*	Courtney-Shea	Creedence	Crissieanna	Crysta Rain
Corryna	Corynna	Courtney-Victoria	Creeshia	Crissy	Crystabella
Corsanne	Corynne	Courtneyjade	Creiona	Crista *(0.03)*	Crystal *(2.21)*
Corseina	Coryssa	Courtneypag	Crelinia	Cristabel	Crystal Jean
Corsha	Corzet	Courtni *(0.02)*	Crenisha	Cristah	Crystal Sarah
Corshara	Cosandrra	Courtnie *(0.05)*	Crenna	Cristal *(0.23)*	Crystal Sha
Corsica	Cosaundra	Courtnii	Creona	Cristalanna	Crystal Shalon
Cortana	Coscha	Courtny *(0.01)*	Creonne	Cristalinda	Crystal Uyen Vi
Cortani	Cosette *(0.01)*	Courttany	Creosha	Cristallina	Crystal Wadad
Cortanie	Coshawndra	Couryanna	Crescant	Cristalyn	Crystal-Anne
Cortanny	Coshia	Coushatta	Crescent	Cristan *(0.01)*	Crystal-Boatemaa
Cortany	Cosi	Coutlyn	Crescenza	Cristeena	Crystal-Josephine
Cortashia	Cossette	Coutrney	Cresencia	Cristel	Crystal-Leigh
Cortayshia	Costanza	Cova	Cresent	Cristela	Crystal-Lisa
Corteaneishea	Costelle	Covania	Creshauna	Cristen *(0.02)*	Crystal-Lynn
Corteasia	Cotina	Coven	Creshone	Cristena	Crystal-Marie
Cortecca	Coty *(0.01)*	Coventry	Cresline	Cristeresa	Crystal-May
Corteea	Coua	Covyn	Cressa	Cristey	Crystale
Corteisha	Cougar	Coy	Cressida	Cristhy	Crystalee
Corteney	Countess	Coyia	Cressinda	Cristi *(0.01)*	Crystalieen
Cortesa	Countney	Coyja	Creston	Cristia	Crystalis
Cortesha	Courey	Coyote	Cresulia	Cristian *(0.01)*	Crystall
Corteshian	Couriana	Coytashia	Crete	Cristian-Taylor	Crystalle
Cortessia	Courmika	Cozette	Crey	Cristiana *(0.01)*	Crystallynn
Corteze	Courney	Coziena	Cria	Cristiane	Crystallynne
Cortillius	Courntey	Cq'quanda	Cricelda	Cristiara	Crystalon
Cortisha	Courtaney	Crace	Cricket	Cristie	Crystalrose
Cortlan	Courtany	Cradriana	Crickett	Cristin *(0.01)*	Crystalyn
Cortland	Courtenay *(0.02)*	Craig	Crimson	Cristina *(0.62)*	Crystalynn
Cortlandt	Courteney *(0.04)*	Craigea	Crina	Cristina-Michael	Crystan
Cortlin	Courteny	Craineshia	Crinise	Cristine *(0.02)*	Crystani
Cortlinn	Courthey	Cramer	Crisbel	Cristinela	Crystara
Cortlyn	Courtia	Crameshia	Criscia	Cristinia	Crystavia
Cortlynn	Courtiunna	Crandall	Criseld	Cristinita	Crystel *(0.01)*

Crystela	Curry	Cydee Je	Cyndal	Cyresa	D'amour
Crystelle	Cursha	Cydel	Cyndavia	Cyrett	D'ana
Crysthel	Curshala	Cydne	Cyndee	Cyri	D'anae
Crystiana	Curshelle	Cydnee (0.01)	Cyndel	Cyrica	D'ananetia
Crystianna	Curshena	Cydnei	Cyndella	Cyrille	D'andra (0.01)
Crystie	Cursten	Cydney (0.09)	Cyndi (0.01)	Cyrina	D'andre
Crystin	Cursti	Cydni (0.01)	Cyndie	Cyrissa	D'andrea (0.01)
Crystina (0.01)	Curstin	Cydnie	Cyndreka	Cyrstal	D'angela
Crystine	Curstina	Cyeadra	Cyndusty	Cyrstin	D'anjena
Crystl	Curtaeya	Cyearra	Cyndy	Cyrulleann	D'anna
Crystle	Curtangi	Cyena	Cyneia	Cysily	D'annessa Shetar
Crystol	Curtavia	Cyenna	Cynelle	Cystral	D'aqualynn
Crystra	Curtece	Cyera	Cyneshia	Cytabria	D'arcy
Crysty	Curterra	Cyerah	Cynetria	Cythia	D'aria
Crystyl	Curtesha	Cyerra (0.01)	Cynetta	Cytlalik	D'arial
Crystyn	Curteshia	Cyerria	Cynina	Czaina	D'arren
Crystyna	Curtesia	Cyesha	Cynintae	Czarina (0.01)	D'arsiah
Crystyne	Curtia	Cyeshia	Cynise	Czessia	D'asha
Crytal	Curtierra	Cyla	Cynita		D'ashanique
Crytelle	Curtiesha	Cyle	Cynithia	**-D-**	D'ashia
Csaskia	Curtiqua	Cylee	Cynna	D (0.02)	D'ashley
Csenge	Curtis	Cylena	Cynnea	D Aira	D'ashunta
Cseni	Curtisha (0.01)	Cylest	Cynniece	D Ambra	D'asia (0.01)
Csilla	Curtisy	Cylie	Cynoa	D Ambre	D'asijah
Cualonda	Curtizia	Cylieann	Cynritia	D Anca	D'aujanae
Culisa	Curtney	Cylina	Cynta	D Andraneci	D'aundra
Culiyah	Curtnisha	Cyliyah	Cyntanna	D Andrea	D'avara
Cullen	Curtnitra	Cylk	Cyntasia	D Andrei	D'avva
Culver	Curtovia	Cylvia	Cynteria	D Anna	D'awna
Cumbina	Curtrellany	Cylvonia	Cynterya	D Antoinette	D'aysa
Cunthia	Curyna	Cymantha	Cynthia (1.77)	D Ashia	D'ceita
Cuphea	Cushawn	Cymba	Cynthia Michell	D Ashley	D'chantel
Cupid	Cushiera	Cymberli	Cynthiamari	D Asia	D'cora
Cura	Cushun	Cymbie	Cynthiana	D Ijana	D'eja
Curdesia	Cutrina	Cymbre	Cynthis	D Iranique	D'eloquent
Curin	Cuza	Cymbri	Cynthoria	D Lashunta	D'enai
Curina	Cwana	Cymbria	Cynthy	D Metria	D'endrae
Curinna	Cxiatimechay	Cymbrie	Cynthya	D Neacia	D'eona
Curisa	Cy'nashia	Cymeisha	Cyntia (0.01)	D Netria	D'era
Curisma	Cyahna	Cymetria	Cyntina	D Niqua	D'erica
Curissa	Cyairra	Cymira	Cyntonia	D Onna	D'ericka
Curleesha	Cyan	Cymone	Cyntoria	D Shay	D'erika (0.01)
Curleia	Cyana	Cymoné	Cyntrecia	D Tashawua	D'erra
Curlene	Cyandra	Cymoni	Cyntrell	D'acrcy	D'erricka
Curletha	Cyanea	Cymphonie	Cynyatah	D'aeishia	D'essence
Curliah	Cyann	Cymphony	Cyplell	D'ahmari	D'eyoni
Curlida	Cyanna	Cyn-Toria	Cypres	D'aira	D'haysa
Curmesha	Cyantel	Cynamin	Cypress (0.01)	D'airrah	D'iara
Curnesha	Cyara	Cynamon	Cypriss	D'aisha	D'iesha
Curnisha	Cybele	Cynara	Cyprus	D'aja	D'ja
Curran	Cybelle	Cynarra	Cyra	D'ajai	D'jade
Currie	Cybil	Cyncere	Cyré	D'alice	D'jah
Currin	Cybill	Cynchancius	Cyreen	D'alma	D'janet
Currionne	Cycelea	Cyncidia	Cyreese	D'ambria	D'janique
Currisha	Cydavia	Cynda	Cyrena	D'ambri	D'jarah

D'jeriell	D'shawna	Da Shan	Da'naya	Daad	Daejá
D'jonae	D'shaye	Da Shanda	Da'naye	Daaimah	Daejah *(0.01)*
D'juana	D'shonda	Da Shanique	Da'ne	Daaja	Daejah'
D'jue	D'shonna	Da Shaona	Da'near'	Daaminie	Daejanae
D'kaila	D'shonti	Da Sharra	Da'neesha	Daana	Daejia
D'kara	D'stiny	Da Shauna	Da'neisha	Dabasha	Daejon
D'keya	D'uncia	Da Shone	Da'nejah	Dabney	Daejzonna
D'kiva	D'undrea	Da Shonte	Da'nell	Dabratia	Daelee
D'kwona	D'vyn	Da Stacia	Da'nese	Dabreca	Daelene
D'leslie	D'yanna	Da Trina	Da'nesha	Dabresha	Daelyn
D'liyah	D'yante	Da Vine	Da'neshia	Dabria	Daelynn
D'londra	D'yona	Da Vonte	Da'nica	Dabriana	Daemonique
D'lonra	D'yonna	Da'angela	Da'nierra	Dabrielle	Daena
D'lorah	D'zhané	Da'asia	Da'nisha	Dabrisha	Daenesha
D'lynne	D'zhonea	Da'bresha	Da'nishia	Dacaspian	Daenielle
D'maea	D-Azmyn	Da'briel	Da'nitra	Daccari	Daera
D'maia	D.	Da'brielle	Da'nyshia	Daccoda	Daerryal
D'marie	D. Allison	Da'cara	Da'quana	Dacei	Daesa
D'mariyea	Da	Da'coya	Da'quanese	Dacey *(0.01)*	Daeseana
D'metria	Da Isha	Da'dreonna	Da'quesha	Daceya	Daesha *(0.01)*
D'mia	Da Ja	Da'drianna	Da'quise	Dacha	Daeshavon
D'mona	Da Jae	Da'j	Da'quontashiya	Dachanique	Daeshawn
D'mya	Da Jah	Da'ja	Da'rashawn	Dachantay	Daeshinaire
D'nai	Da Jahnea	Da'jae	Da'sadria	Dachawn	Daeshnea
D'najha	Da Jai	Da'jah *(0.01)*	Da'sha	Dacheira	Daeshun
D'nara	Da Janique	Da'jai	Da'shana	Dachelle	Daesy
D'nasia	Da Jarin A	Da'jan	Da'shaney	Dachrista	Daetaeshaia
D'nay	Da Jasni	Da'janae	Da'shaun	Dacia *(0.02)*	Daeza
D'naymi	Da Java	Da'janea	Da'shawna	Dacia-Moreh	Daezha
D'nea	Da Jha	Da'janiqua	Da'shawnda	Daciah	Daffaney
D'neesha	Da Jiaron	Da'janique	Da'sheona	Dacoda	Daffanie
D'neisha	Da Joanae	Da'jauna	Da'shia	Dacota	Daffney
D'nellia	Da Jon	Da'je	Da'shona	Dadavi	Daffodil
D'nesia	Da Jounaise	Da'jinay	Da'shouna	Dadlyn	Dafina
D'nessa	Da Jung	Da'jona	Da'tonya	Dadriana	Dafini
D'nia	Da Juniece	Da'jonae	Da'treanna	Dae	Dafne
D'nidra	Da Juon	Da'jsha	Da'vijah	Dae Aja	Dafney
D'niece	Da Kata	Da'kassha	Da'vina	Dae Shaun	Dafni
D'niesha	Da Kota	Da'keira	Da'vonya	Daéja	Dagan
D'nika	Da Leighici	Da'keisha	Da'wayna	Daéjora	Dagean
D'nisha	Da Lesia	Da'laura	Da'yanna	Daékeria	Dagmar
D'nita	Da Lexus	Da'laysua	Da'zha	Daémonique	Dagmara
D'omini	Da Meka	Da'licia	Da'zohna	Daéneria	Dagne
D'ondra	Da Nae	Da'lona	Da'zzai	Daénique	Dagney
D'ondrea	Da Nai	Da'mashae	Da-Eun	Daéquana	Dagnie
D'ondria	Da Nara	Da'meisha	Da-Johna	Daésha	Dagny *(0.01)*
D'onna *(0.01)*	Da Naya	Da'mon	Da-Lexus	Daeanna	Dah'niera
D'onnal	Da Necia	Da'monica	Da-Nisha	Daeanyra	Dahae
D'ontrinique	Da Neisha	Da'monique	Da-Quavia	Daeca	Dahama
D'quirrah	Da Neshia	Da'moya	Da-Rae	Daecember	Dahana
D'shaela	Da Net	Da'nae	Da-Shawna	Daecy	Dahhia
D'shai	Da Nija	Da'nahja	Da-Tranell	Daedmari	Dahja
D'shanai	Da Niqua	Da'najah	Da-Yona	Daehante	Dahjaney
D'shaunna	Da Nisha	Da'nasha	Daa'iyah	Daeinera	Dahje
D'shaunta	Da Sha	Da'nay	Daa'jzia	Daeja *(0.01)*	Dahli

Dahlia (0.04)	Daijhunai	Daisareneta	Dajá	Dajuana	Dalana
Dahliah	Daijia	Daise	Dajaé	Dajuanay	Dalanda
Dahlya	Daijiah	Daisey (0.01)	Daja'h	Dajuh	Dalanee
Dahlye	Daijo'n	Daiseylee	Dajae	Dajusha	Dalaney
Dahna	Daijon	Daish	Dajaé	Dajva	Dalani
Dahnicka	Daijonaé	Daisha (0.07)	Dajah (0.02)	Dakala	Dalanie
Dahnycka	Daijonique	Daishá	Dajaha	Dakara	Dalanique
Dahnyelle	Daikiyah	Daishae	Dajahnai	Dakaria	Dalanis
Dahrien	Daile	Daishalon	Dajahne	Dakarra	Dalas
Dahshon	Dailea	Daishaneak	Dajahnee	Dakarri	Dalasountez
Dahsn	Dailee	Daishanique	Dajai	Dakasha	Dalayah
Dahyia	Daileigh	Daishauna	Dajala	Dakayla	Dalayla
Dahzhané	Dailen	Daishia	Dajaliette	Dakeena	Dalayna
Dai	Dailey	Daishonna	Dajana	Dakeia	Dalaynee
Dai Ja	Dailia	Daishun	Dajanae	Dakeidra	Dalayni
Dai Jah	Dailin	Daishya	Dajanai	Dakendra	Dalayon
Dai'jah	Dailon	Daishzá	Dajanara	Dakesha	Dalaysha
Dai'jon	Dailyn	Daisi	Dajanay	Daketa	Dalbir
Dai'sha	Dailynn	Daisia (0.01)	Dajane	Dakeya	Dale (0.01)
Dai-Jour	Daimar	Daisie	Dajanea	Dakezjah	Dale-Lee
Dai-Shanique	Daimarin	Daisie-Mae	Dajaneke	Dakia	Daleah
Dai-Zsa	Daimelys	Daisja	Dajaniero	Dakila	Daleaka
Daia	Daimenia	Daislin	Dajaniqu'e	Dakina	Daleashia
Daiajamore	Daimiona	Daissy	Dajanique	Dakira	Dalecia
Daiana	Daina (0.01)	Daisua	Dajarnaée	Dakirah	Daleda
Daianara	Daina-Marie	Daisy (0.95)	Dajasia	Dakita	Daleen
Daianera	Dainaira	Daisy Ray	Dajayla	Dakkota	Daleesha
Daibreeona	Dainara	Daisy-Jo	Daje	Dakmar	Daleia
Daicee	Daine	Daitasha	Dajé	Dakoda (0.01)	Daleigh
Daichelle	Dainee	Daiton	Dajely	Dakohta	Daleisha
Daici	Daineira	Daitral	Dajena	Dakota (0.49)	Dalela
Daicreshia	Dainelle	Daityn	Dajenia	Dakota-Jene	Dalelisha
Daicy	Dainera	Daiunna	Dajeong	Dakota-Leigh	Dalen
Daidra	Dainesha	Daiva	Dajha	Dakota-Rae	Dalena (0.02)
Daidre	Dainiqua	Daiva-Symone	Dajhanae	Dakota-Rain	Dalene
Daienaria	Dainn	Daivonna	Dajhanai	Dakotah (0.03)	Dalericka
Daiennera	Dainora	Daiwa	Dajhay	Dakotah-Lynn	Dales
Daifka	Daione	Daiz'ja	Daji	Dakotea	Dalesha
Daigah	Daiquaisha	Daiza	Dajia	Dakotha	Daleshia
Daihna	Daiquana	Daizee	Dajiané	Dakotia	Daleshka
Daii	Daiquanda	Daizha	Dajinae	Dakotta	Daletha
Daii'quon	Daira	Daizhane	Dajion'e	Dakri	Daletra
Daiiyah	Dairah	Daizhanelle	Dajjah	Dakwaneisha	Dalexandria
Daija (0.04)	Dairany	Daizhauna	Dajoina	Dakydra	Daley
Daijaah	Daire	Daizi	Dajoinnae	Dakyra	Daleyni
Daijah (0.03)	Dairian	Daiziah	Dajon	Dal'	Dalhia
Daijahnaé	Dairien	Daizjha	Dajonay	Dalacy	Dali
Daijanae	Dairiona	Daizsa	Dajone	Dalage	Dalia (0.24)
Daijea	Dairrian	Daizshawn	Dajonique	Dalaina	Dalia Shira
Daijenai	Dairy	Daizy	Dajonna	Dalainee	Daliah
Daijeonna	Dairyan	Daj Enique	Dajonnay	Dalais	Dalial
Daijha	Dairyn	Daj'ah	Dajournay	Dalaisha	Daliana
Daijhah	Dais'ha	Daj'alon	Dajsae	Dalajha	Dalianais
Daijhe	Daisa	Daja (0.03)	Dajsha	Dalal	Daliane
Daijhée	Daisah	Daja Nee	Daju	Dalal Tareq	Daliarubi

Dalica	Dalpreet	Dameia	Damoné	Danavia	Daneshia *(0.01)*
Dalice	Dalshanica	Dameisha	Damonec	Danay	Danessa
Dalicha	Dalton *(0.01)*	Dameka	Damoneke	Danaya	Danesy
Dalicia	Daltrey	Damekia	Damoni'	Danayja	Danethia
Dalien	Daltrica	Damekiah	Damonica	Danayr E	Danetra
Daliesha	Dalveen	Naquan	Damonie	Danayre	Danetracy
Dalila *(0.03)*	Dalvir	Damekwa	Damonik	Danaysha	Danetta
Dalilah	Daly	Dameon	Damonika	Danbi	Danette
Dalin	Dalya	Damerra	Damonique	Dancia	Daneva
Dalina	Dalyce	Damerria	Damonisha	Dancica	Daney
Dalinda	Dalyceeia	Damesha *(0.01)*	Damorria	Dancie	Daneya
Daline	Dalyla	Dameshell	Damthah	Dandra	Daneysia
Dalis	Dalyllah	Dameshia	Damya	Dandrea	Dani *(0.05)*
Dalisa	Dalymar	Dametra	Damyia	Dandria	Dani-Danette
Dalischia	Dalyn	Dametreale	Damyka	Dane	Dani-Jean
Dalise	Dalynette	Dametria	Damysha	Dane Sia	Dani-Marie
Dalisha *(0.01)*	Dalynn	Dametris	Dan	Danéya	Dania *(0.05)*
Dalishea	Dalynrae	Dami	Dan Phuong	Danea	Daniadine
Dalishia	Dalys	Damia *(0.01)*	Dan'deisha	Daneá	Daniah
Dalisia	Dalysha	Damian	Dan'quisha	Daneal	Daniale
Dalisse	Damaiana	Damiana	Dan-Xuan-Spring	Danealle	Danialla
Dalissky	Damaiya	Damica	Dana *(0.72)*	Daneasha	Danialle
Dalita	Damajah	Damicela	Dana-Ann	Daneca	Daniaris
Daliyah	Damajia	Damicia	Dana-Lynn	Danecia	Daniash
Daliz	Damali	Damicka	Dana-Marie	Danee	Danibeles
Daljia	Damalis	Damie	Danae *(0.08)*	Danée	Danica *(0.18)*
Daljie	Daman	Damieka	Danaé	Daneeka	Danicah
Daljit	Damandip	Damielle	Danaee	Daneekah	Danice
Dalkeianna	Damandrea	Damien	Danaeszy	Daneel	Danicia
Dallace	Damani	Damienne	Danah *(0.01)*	Daneen	Danicka
Dallae	Damania	Damijah	Danai	Daneesha	Danicquiwia
Dallana *(0.01)*	Damanique	Damik	Danaia	Daneika	Daniea
Dallas *(0.24)*	Damanise	Damika	Danaice	Daneill	Danieka
Dallason	Damanjit	Damilola	Danaile	Daneille	Daniel *(0.01)*
Dallata	Damanjot	Daminga	Danair	Daneiqua	Daniela *(0.60)*
Dallayna	Damanpreet	Damini	Danaisa	Daneisha *(0.02)*	Daniele *(0.03)*
Dalleis	Damara *(0.01)*	Daminque	Danaisy	Daneishal	Danielia
Dallen	Damaras	Damiona	Danait	Daneisis	Daniell *(0.01)*
Dallena	Damarays	Damioneisha	Danaizhia	Daneka	Daniella *(0.27)*
Dallia	Damari	Damira	Danajá	Danel	Daniella
Dallie	Damaria	Damiracle	Danajah	Danela	Adesuwa
Dallion	Damaris *(0.09)*	Damisa	Danajua	Danell	Daniella-Angeli
Dallis *(0.01)*	Damarius	Damisha	Danaka	Danella	Daniella-Odette
Dallise	Damariz	Damishia	Danakei	Danelle *(0.03)*	Daniellah
Dallus	Damarra	Damita	Danaliz	Danely	Danielle *(5.58)*
Dallyn	Damarshia	Damitreya	Danara	Danena	Danielle Antoin
Dallys	Damary	Damitrya	Danardra	Daneqa	Danielle G
Dalmeka	Damarylin	Damiya	Danaree	Danequea	Danielle Joy
Dalminque	Damarys	Damneet	Danarra	Danera	Danielle Lyn
Dalon	Damascus	Damnika	Danasha	Daneri	Danielle Marie
Dalonda	Damaya	Damny	Danashia	Daneris	Danielle Michelle
Dalondra	Damayra	Damon	Danashius	Danesa	Daniellé
Dalonna	Damazea	Damon Yan	Danasia *(0.01)*	Danese	Danielle-Rae
Daloras	Dambar	Damondra	Danastacia	Danesha *(0.04)*	Danielleanne
Dalores	Damecia	Damondria	Danatha	Danesha's	Daniellia

Daniello	Dannelle	Danyal	Daqueita	Darci *(0.03)*	Dariene
Danielly	Dannesha	Danyale *(0.01)*	Daquesha	Darciana	Darienne *(0.01)*
Daniely	Danneshia	Danyasha	Daquiana	Darcie *(0.02)*	Darijah
Danierra	Dannete	Danyca	Daquila	Darcieda	Darijan
Daniesha *(0.01)*	Dannett	Danyea	Daquilla	Darcy *(0.08)*	Darilyn
Danija	Dannetta	Danyeil	Daquinna	Darcyn	Darin
Danijah	Dannette	Danyel *(0.02)*	Daquiri	Darcys	Darine
Danijela	Danni *(0.02)*	Danyela	Daquisha	Dardacia	Darinee
Danika *(0.18)*	Dannia	Danyele	Daquita	Dare	Darineisha
Danikah	Danniane	Danyelé	Daquona	Darea	Darinesha
Danikha	Dannica *(0.01)*	Danyell *(0.03)*	Daquoya	Dareah	Darinka
Danikia	Dannice	Danyell'	Daqwesha	Darealle	Dariohn
Danila	Dannie	Danyella	Dar	Darean	Darion *(0.03)*
Danile	Danniece	Danyelle *(0.09)*	Dar'mesha	Darece	Dariona
Danilee	Danniel	Danyellé	Dar'nesha	Dareena	Darione
Danille	Dannielle *(0.04)*	Danyelle-Ann	Dar'nishia	Dareese	Darionna
Danillie	Danniellle	Danyetta	Dar'sha	Dareian	Darionne
Danine	Dannieyah	Danyiel	Dar'shanique	Darein	Darisha
Daninira	Dannika	Danyielle	Dara *(0.05)*	Dareion	Darissa
Danioelle	Dannikah	Danyka *(0.01)*	Dara Jane	Dareka	Daritza
Daniqua *(0.01)*	Dannilea	Danyle	Daragh	Darelice	Darius
Daniquae	Dannille	Danylle	Daragina	Darelle	Dariya
Danique	Dannis	Danzel	Darah *(0.01)*	Daren	Dariyan
Danis	Dannisha	Danzig	Daralasha	Darenda	Dariyanne
Danisa	Dannisshiah	Dao	Daraleigh	Dareneque	Dariyn
Danischia	Dannon	Daotpm	Daralie	Dareon	Dariynne
Danise	Danny	Daphaene	Daralina	Daresha	Dariys
Danisela	Dannyeisha	Daphane	Daralnisha	Darhione	Darja
Danish-Wahid	Dannyel	Daphanee	Daralyn	Darhkyelle	Darjenaé
Danisha *(0.03)*	Dannyell	Daphaney	Daranaé	Dari	Darkeisha
Danishia	Dannyontia	Daphanie	Daranie	Daria *(0.04)*	Darkia
Danisia	Dannysha	Daphanie Septim	Daranika	Daria Na	Darkita
Danita *(0.01)*	Danon	Daphany	Daranique	Darian *(0.33)*	Darkota
Danitra	Danova	Daphene	Darany	Darian Alex	Darkqist
Danitrea	Danquisha	Dapheney	Darartu-Tiya	Dariana	Darkresha
Danitria	Danquishia	Daphine	Darashay	Dariane *(0.01)*	Darkus
Danitza	Danqwelia	Daphiney	Daravia	Dariann	Darla *(0.03)*
Daniya	Danrica	Daphlie	Daraya	Darianna *(0.01)*	Darlasha
Danja	Danshay	Daphna	Darbe	Darianne *(0.01)*	Darlayzi
Danjanée	Dansheryal	Daphne *(0.21)*	Darbee	Dariauna	Darlean
Danjela	Dantashia	Daphné	Darbi *(0.02)*	Daric	Darleasha
Danka	Dantasia	Daphnee *(0.09)*	Darbie	Darica	Darlecia
Dankay	Dante	Daphney *(0.01)*	Darby *(0.19)*	Darice	Darlee
Danlynn	Dantezia	Daphnie	Darby Marie	Daricia	Darleen
Danmesha	Dantia	Daphniea	Darby-Reed	Daricka	Darleene
Danna *(0.03)*	Dantoinia	Daphonie	Darby-Rose	Dariea	Darleeseia
Danna-Jean	Danuh	Daphy	Darbye	Dariean	Darleisha
Dannae	Danusha	Daqa	Darcarra	Darieen	Darlena
Dannah *(0.01)*	Danusia	Daqualashun	Darcee	Dariel *(0.01)*	Darlene *(0.15)*
Danne	Danuta	Daquana	Darcel	Darielis	Darlene Jane
Danneca	Dany	Daquanta	Darcell	Dariell	Darlenne
Dannecia Da	Danya *(0.04)*	Daquaria	Darcelle	Darielle *(0.01)*	Darleta
Dannee	Danyae	Daquashia	Darcey	Dariellle	Darletta
Dannell	Danyael	Daquasia	Darche	Dariellys	Darlette
Dannella	Danyaisha	Daquecia	Darchelle	Darien *(0.08)*	Darley

Darlin (0.01)	Darqamber	Darrinisha	Darya (0.01)	Dashawnna	Dasjarea
Darline	Darqrisha	Darrinniesha	Daryan (0.01)	Dashay (0.01)	Dasjhia
Darling	Darquelle	Darrion (0.01)	Darybelle	Dashaya	Daskyra
Darlisha	Darquetta	Darriona	Daryell	Dashaye	Dasmin
Darlla	Darquisa	Darrionna	Daryelle	Dashayi	Dasom
Darly	Darquise	Darris	Daryen	Dashayla	Daspri
Darlyn (0.01)	Darquisha	Darrisa	Daryenne	Dashea	Dassia
Darlynn	Darquisia	Darrisha	Daryia	Dasheana	Dastamara
Darlynne	Darra	Darrlyn	Daryl (0.02)	Dasheel	Dateisha
Darlyze	Darra Lynn	Darron	Daryl-Ann	Dasheka	Datesia
Darmesha	Darragh	Darronique	Darylina	Dashel	Datevia
Darmeshia	Darrah (0.01)	Darry	Daryll	Dashell	Datezia
Darmesia	Darranesha	Darry'll	Darylle	Dashelle	Datia
Darmetria	Darranika	Darryan	Daryllin	Dashene	Datiqauw
Darmeyon	Darrby	Darryanna	Darylnessia	Dashera	Datisha
Darmia	Darrchelle	Darryenne	Darylnique	Dasherik	Datiyana
Darmisha	Darrean	Darryl	Daryn (0.01)	Dasherra	Datona
Darmone	Darrein	Darryl Lynn	Daryne	Dashia (0.01)	Datonya
Darnaizha	Darreishaiye	Darryllynn	Darynne	Dashia'shanice	Datra
Darnay	Darreka	Darryln	Daryon	Dashiah	Datreal
Darnea	Darrel	Darrylneish	Daryona	Dashika	Datreanna
Darneasha	Darrel'lisha	Darrylneka	Daryss	Dashine	Datrell
Darneeaha	Darrell	Darrylynn	Daryztmar	Dashinique	Datrice
Darneh	Darrella	Darryn	Das'ja	Dashiona	Datriesha
Darneicca	Darrellyn	Darrynn	Dasaysha	Dashira	Datrion
Darneisha (0.01)	Darrelwanda	Darseny	Dasché	Dashjia	Datu
Darneishia	Darrelyn	Darsey	Daschel	Dashley	Daun
Darnell	Darrelynn	Darsha	Daschytézinik	Dashline	Dauna
Darnell Ter	Darren	Darshae	Daseur	Dashmeet	Daunte
Darnella	Darrenesha	Darshana	Dasha (0.04)	Dashmy	Dausha
Darnelle	Darrenisha	Darshanae	Dashá	Dashon	Dausharaé
Darnequa	Darreonia	Darshanne	Dashae	Dashona	Daushea
Darnesha (0.01)	Darretta	Darshay	Dashaé	Dashonda	Dava
Darneshea	Darreyon	Darshaya	Dashaireae	Dashonique	Davady
Darneshia	Darri	Darshe	Dashala	Dashonna	Davajia
Darnesia	Darria	Darshea	Dashalla	Dashonne	Davalyée
Darnetta	Darriah	Darsheeka	Dashalonna	Dashontae	Davalyn
Darnica	Darrialle	Darsheena	Dashana	Dashontanae	Davan
Darnice	Darrian (0.06)	Darshell	Dashanae	Dashonte	Davana
Darnicia	Darriana	Darshella	Dashanda	Dashonté	Davanay
Darnie	Darriane	Darshena	Dashane	Dashquan	Davane
Darniesha	Darriann	Darshequa	Dashanique	Dashsa	Davanesha
Darnika	Darrianna	Darshia	Dashannon	Dashuna	Davania
Darniqua	Darrianne	Darshika	Dashante	Dashye	Davanika
Darnique	Darrica	Darshini	Dashaquia	Dasia (0.05)	Davanique
Darnise	Darricka	Darshpreet	Dashaun	Dasiah	Davanna
Darnisha (0.02)	Darriea	Darsi	Dashauna	Dasialyn	Davaria
Darnisheontae	Darriean	Dartanya	Dashaunté	Dasianee	Davasea
Darnita	Darriel	Darun	Dashaval	Dasianera	Davasha
Darnya	Darriell	Darusana	Dashawana	Dasianiera	Davaughnda
Daronda	Darrielle (0.01)	Darvella	Dashawn (0.01)	Dasijah	Davayna
Daroneshia	Darrien (0.02)	Darvelle	Dashawna	Dasinique	Dave
Daroshenna	Darriene	Darvelyn	Dashawnda	Dasja	Davea
Darouny	Darrika	Darvia	Dashawndra	Dasjah	Daveeda
Darpan	Darrikk	Darvonhá	Dashawnia	Dasjaré	Daveen

Daveena	Daviona	Dawnie	Dayessi	Dayoung	Dazhae
Daveisha	Davionna	Dawnielle	Dayia	Dayqana	Dazhane
Daveki	Davionta	Dawnika	Dayinaira	Dayquana	Dazhané
Davelle	Davis	Dawnisha	Dayisha	Dayquanesha	Dazhaneá
Davelynne	Davisa	Dawnita	Dayj'elle	Dayra	Dazhoné
Daven	Davisha	Dawnn	Dayja	Dayrey	Dazhonna
Davena	Davita (0.01)	Dawnna	Dayjah	Daysee	Dazia (0.01)
Davene	Davitta	Dawnnisha	Dayjane	Daysha (0.03)	Dazia Jana
Daveneisha	Daviya	Dawnquinta	Dayjaun	Dayshaa	Daziah
Davenia	Daviyona	Dawnsha	Dayjenae	Dayshalie	Dazirae
Davenise	Daviyone	Dawnshaée	Dayjona	Dayshana	Daziray
Davenna	Davneet	Dawnta	Daykota	Dayshanay	Dazja (0.01)
Daveonshe	Davon (0.01)	Dawntavia	Dayla (0.01)	Dayshanaye	Dazjaa
Davesha	Davon-Rae	Dawnunique	Daylan (0.01)	Dayshanell	Dazjah
Daveshia	Davona	Dawnyalé	Daylana	Dayshanique	Dazjia
Davetria	Davondra	Dawnyéa	Dayle (0.01)	Dayshawnna	Dazmain
Davetta	Davone	Dawnyel	Daylea	Dayshia	Dazmine
Davette	Davonia	Dawnyelle	Daylee	Dayshibreka	Dazmn
Davey	Davonna	Dawonna	Dayleena	Dayshona	Dazmon
Davi	Davonne	Dawson	Daylen	Dayshu	Daznae
Davia (0.01)	Davonnia	Daxanne	Daylene	Dayshundra	Dazniel
Davia-Symone	Davonta	Daxia	Daylia	Daysi (0.02)	Dazreal
Daviahna	Davontae	Daxton	Daylin (0.01)	Daysia	Dazsana
Davian	Davonte	Day Junay	Dayllin	Dayspring	Dazsha
Daviana	Davour	Day'neesha	Dayln	Daysy	Dazy
Davianna	Davronique	Day'sha	Daylon	Dayton (0.01)	Dazzlin
Davicia	Davunda	Day'zhane	Daylyn	Daytona (0.01)	Dazzmin
David (0.01)	Davy	Day-Elis	Daylynn	Daytonia	Da~sha
Davida (0.01)	Davyana	Daya	Daymara	Daytreiona	Dbora
Davidda	Davynn	Dayalin	Dayme	Dayu	Dchunvea
Davidia	Davyon	Dayami	Daymeah	Dayva	Ddandreah
Davidra	Dawan	Dayamy	Daymeanna	Dayvon	De
Davidrez	Dawana	Dayana (0.14)	Daymeia	Daywana	De A'nna
Davie	Dawanda	Dayanaira	Daymin	Dayzá	De Aira
Davie-Ann	Dawanna	Dayanara (0.02)	Daymis	Dayze	De Amore
Daviea	Dawannd	Dayanaris	Daymiyah	Dayzha	De Ana
Davieanna	Dawantay	Dayanelesse	Daymon	Dayzhane	De Anairah
Daviée	Dawauna	Dayanera	Dayna (0.15)	Dayzhane~	De Andrea
Davielle	Dawn (0.14)	Dayaneray	Dayna-Lynn	Dayzi	De Andreia
Daviesha	Dawn-Eve	Dayanerha	Dayna-Marie	Dayzjah	De Andria
Daviey	Dawn-Lee	Dayaneruh	Daynah	Daz'ja	De Angelia
Davika	Dawn-Ming	Dayani	Daynalise	Daz'mine	De Anna
Davilia	Dawna (0.01)	Dayanir	Daynara	Daz'shanae	De Ashley
Davin	Dawnalee	Dayanna (0.02)	Daynarah	Daza	De Asia
Davina (0.05)	Dawnantoni	Dayanne	Dayne	Dazahna	De Asya
Davinder	Dawnasia	Dayanni	Dayneisha	Dazana	De Atyana
Davinder-Kaur	Dawndianna	Dayasha	Daynesha	Dazanic	De Aunduria
Davine	Dawne	Daycie	Dayneshia	Dazarae	De Coyia
Davinesha	Dawnecia	Daydra	Daynie	Dazaray	De Endria
Daviney	Dawnell	Daydria	Daynisha	Dazareh	De Erica
Davinia	Dawnella	Daye	Daynna	Dazasia	De Erin
Davinjit	Dawnelle	Dayel	Daynza-Vo	Dazauh	De Ion
Davinn	Dawnesha	Dayelis	Dayonda	Dazéja	De Ja
Davinna	Dawnetta	Dayelle	Dayonna	Dazemone	De Jah
Davion	Dawneve	Dayenera	Dayosha	Dazha	De Jahnique

De Janai	Déannalisa	Dékishi	Déstini	Deandreia	Deatrice
De Janay	Déannie	Délacha	Désunique	Deandria	Deaujae
De Janira	Déarisha	Délanah	Détorri	Deandriea	Deaujarae
De Jaron	Déasha	Délanna	Détrionna	Deane	Deaujiah
De Jior	Déashya	Délaun	Déundra	Deanekuquia	Deauna
De Juana	Déasia (0.01)	Délease	Dévanta	Deaneria	Deaundra (0.01)
De Laina	Déasiajah	Déledai	Déveisha	Deangala	Deaundria
De Laney	Déasijania	Déleisha	Dévine	Deangalique	Deaunique
De Lena	Déasya	Délisha	Déyonna	Deangela (0.01)	Deaunna
De Leon	Déaubany	Délissa	Dézai'	Deangle	Deaunshay
De Licia	Déaundra	Délonya	Dézhane	Deanie	Deaunzjinay
De Lois	Déauntyana	Délyn	Dézhané	Deanira	Deauteá
De Maiya	Déaushanae	Démarion	Dézhanette	Deanka	Deavan
De Miaya	Déayr	Démetria	De-Asia	Deann (0.01)	Deaven
De Nae	Débrijae	Démiya	De-Chaner	Deanna (0.83)	Deavin
De Naija	Décara	Démonica	De-Erica	Deanna Marie	Deavon
De Nais	Déchambre	Démornay	De-Shaun	Deanna-Lee	Deayisha
De Nequa	Dédriana	Démy'ja	De-Shazma	Deanna-Marie	Deayla
De Nese	Déera	Dénage	Dea	Deanna-Renee	Deayra
De Nishia	Déerica	Dénaysia	Dea'jah	Deannah	Deaysha
De Oinicea	Déericka	Dénee	Dea'niqua	Deanndra	Deazhá
De Qualla	Déerra	Déneja	Deadra	Deanndrea	Deazharia
De Quia	Déessence	Dénekqua	Deadrienne	Deanne (0.02)	Deb'bria Michel
De Sean	Déhja	Déneshia	Deaetta	Deanni	Deba
De Shaun	Déija	Dénijya	Deagega	Deanouenita	Debahi
De Shauna	Déja (0.03)	Dénosha	Deah	Deanshá	Debanee
De Shawn	Déja Monet'	Déona	Deahnna	Deante	Debanée
De Shionana	Déjá	Déondra	Deaiddra	Deanté	Debben
De Shon	Déjae	Déongela	Deaijah	Deantonecia	Debbi
De Shone	Déjah (0.01)	Déonna	Deaira	Deantonise	Debbie (0.10)
De Shontae	Déjah'na	Déquanda	Deairra	Deantré	Debbie-Ann
De Sjonae	Déjahli	Déquandra	Deairyl	Deanye	Debbora
De Unaka	Déjan	Dérajela	Deaisa	Deanyra	Debbra
De Von	Déjana	Déreshé	Deaisha	Deanza	Debbrah
De Vonna	Déjanae	Déronshia	Deaja	Deaonca	Debbresha
De Vykia	Déjanaie	Désean	Deajá	Deara	Debby (0.01)
De Wanna	Déjanera	Déshae	Deajane	Dearay	Debera
De Yanira	Déjanique	Déshananya	Deaje	Dearea	Debeyun
Dé	Déjasnae	Déshanasty	Deajia	Dearicka	Debi
Déadriane	Déjenae	Déshanique	Deajsha	Deariqa	Debonair
Déaiddera	Déjha	Déshanna	Dealiva	Dearra	Debora (0.03)
Déaira	Déjhae	Déshannon	Dealla	Deasa	Deborah (0.31)
Déairra	Déjia	Déshauna	Deamber	Deasha	Deborah-Lynn
Déaja	Déjoi	Déshaunda	Deamie	Deashanique	Debra (0.11)
Déajree	Déjona	Déshaunty	Dean	Deashea	Debra Mae
Déamber	Déjonay	Déshawn	Deana (0.06)	Deashia	Debrah
Déambra	Déjoni	Déshawntae	Deanah	Deashleigh	Debranda
Déana	Déjsa	Déshay	Deanara	Deashley	Debrashia
Déandra	Déjuan	Désheyle	Deanasia	Deashona	Debrauna
Déandre	Déjuonai	Déshona	Deanca	Deasia (0.02)	Debrayah
Déandrea	Déjuonique	Déshondra	Deandra (0.05)	Deasiahonor	Debréona
Déandreas	Déjyila	Déshondria	Deandraneke	Deaspria	Debreail
Déandria	Dékayla	Déshonna	Deandre	Deatira	Debreeanah
Déangela	Dékia	Désia	Deandrea (0.02)	Deatra	Debreyonia
Déanna (0.01)	Dékiera	Déstani	Deandreá	Deatria	Debria

Debriah	Deeanne	Deianira	Deja'ne	Dejianna	Delaini
Debriana	Deeayon	Deiara	Deja'via	Dejon	Delainie
Debrianna	Deeba	Deici	Deja-Ariaha	Dejonae	Delainy
Debrina	Deebica	Deicy	Dejada	Dejone	Delaisha
Debrion	Deedee	Deidra *(0.05)*	Dejadira	Dejonee	Delali
Debrionna	Deedra *(0.01)*	Deidre *(0.04)*	Dejae	Dejonelle	Delan
Debroah	Deedra-Ann	Deidré	Dejah *(0.03)*	Dejour	Delana *(0.02)*
Debron	Deega	Deidre-Ann	Dejahane	Dejreiona	Delancey
Deby	Deeja	Deidrea	Dejahna	Dejuan	Delancia
Deca	Deejae	Deidrianna	Dejahnae	Dejuana	Delandria
Decambry	Deejay	Deidrie	Dejahnea	Dejuanna	Delane
Decardrea	Deekandra	Deidry	Dejahnna	Dejuantashia	Delanea
Decarolyn	Deeksha	Deija	Dejai	Dejuante	Delanee
Decarra	Deelora	Deijha	Dejainé	Dejune	Delaney *(0.32)*
Decarri	Deema	Deilyn	Dejalon	Dejunique	Delaney-Chrisl
Dece	Deemeshia	Deinaira	Dejan'-E	Dejziah	Delani *(0.01)*
December *(0.01)*	Deena *(0.04)*	Deineria	Dejana	Dek'la	Delania
Dechaiah	Deenaalee	Deinte	Dejanae *(0.02)*	Deka	Delanie *(0.06)*
Dechair	Deenesha	Deinyn	Dejanah	Dekara	Delanise
Dechelle	Deep	Deion	Dejanai	Dekarla	Delanjane
Decia	Deepa *(0.01)*	Deion'na	Dejanara	Dekayla	Delann
Deciah	Deepali	Deiona	Dejanay	Dekaylah	Delanna
Decie	Deepalj	Deiondra	Dejane	Dekedrianna	Delanta
Decker	Deepika	Deionna	Dejane T	Dekeeya	Delany
Deckontee	Deepthi	Deionshay	Dejanea	Dekeidra	Delara
Declyn	Deepti	Deiontra	Dejanee	Dekeira	Delaram
Decoda	Deeqo	Deiony	Dejaneira	Dekeisiana	Delashay
Decole	Deericka	Deiosha	Dejaneke	Dekeithia	Delashelle
Deconnie	Deerin	Deira	Dejanerha	Dekelia	Delaycia
Decora	Deesha	Deirdra	Dejanier	Dekendral	Delayna *(0.01)*
Decorria	Deeshannia	Deirdre *(0.03)*	Dejanique	Dekerion	Delayne
Decota	Deesli	Deirdréonna	Dejanira *(0.01)*	Dekerra	Delayney
Decoya	Deetta	Deirra	Dejanna	Dekescia	Delaynie
Dedee	Deeva	Deiryn	Dejannaye	Dekeysa	Delbra
Dedra *(0.01)*	Deevina	Deisel	Dejarenee	Dekhia	Delbrianna
Dedre	Deeyana	Deisha	Dejasha	Dekia	Delbrica
Dedria	Defne	Deishon	Dejau	Dekiah	Delcie
Dedriana	Dega	Deisi	Dejaun	Dekira	Delcora
Dedrica	Degenica	Deisi Nayeli	Dejaunte	Dekiya	Delcoya
Dedricka	Deghan	Deissy	Dejavahn	Dekiyah	Deldrishia
Dedtra	Dehab	Deisy *(0.04)*	Dejavette	Deklan	Deleah
Dee *(0.01)*	Dehanna	Deitra	Deje	Dekonti	Deleaner
Dee Anna	Dehja	Deiva	Dejé	Dekorie	Deleanna
Dee Dee	Dehjua	Deivanne	Dejean	Dekota	Deleasa
Deéanna	Dehlia	Dej	Dejeane	Dekoushe	Delecia
Dee-Ajra	Dehonda	Dej A	Dejenae	Dekyvia	Deleena
Dee-Anna	Dehondra	Dej'asia	Dejhae	Del'cresha	Deleesha
Dee-Anne	Deia	Deja *(0.25)*	Dejhana	Del'lisha	Deleicia
Deeaira	Deiadra	Deja E	Dejhanae	Del'toshio	Deleighla
Deeana	Deiamore	Deja Lynn	Dejhane	Delacée	Deleika
Deeandra	Deianara	Deja Nai	Dejhia	Delaceya	Deleila
Deeandre	Deianaria	Dejá *(0.01)*	Deji	Delaina *(0.01)*	Deleiny
Deeani	Deiandra	Deja' Nay	Dejia	Delaine *(0.01)*	Deleisha
Deeann	Deianeira	Deja'h	Dejiah	Delainee	Deleisia
Deeanna *(0.01)*	Deianiera	Deja'nae	Dejiana	Delainey *(0.01)*	Delena

Delenn	Delmeka	Demaira	Demetriua	Demyshja	Deneja
Deleon	Delmesha	Demajah	Demetrius	Dena *(0.05)*	Deneka
Deleonna	Delmi	Deman	Demetrous	Denaé	Denell
Deleonne	Delmira	Demani	Demetruia	Dena-	Denelle
Deles'han	Delmy *(0.01)*	Demar	Demeyia	Alexsandrea	Denelly
Delesdenier	Delna	Demara	Demi *(0.15)*	Denae *(0.02)*	Denene
Delesha	Delnavaz	Demarcea	Demi-Jo	Denah	Denequa
Deleshia	Delnaz	Demarcia	Demi-Lee	Denai	Denequa Nichelle
Deletria	Delnec'ia	Demari	Demi-Lisa	Denair	Denera
Delexus	Delnecia	Demaria	Demia	Denaira	Deneria
Delfi	Delnelle	Demarie	Demiá	Denaisha	Denesa
Delfina *(0.01)*	Delnesha	Demario	Demiah	Denaj'e	Denesha *(0.02)*
Delgadina	Delnetta	Demaris	Demiana	Denaja	Deneshia
Delhanie	Delnick	Demarje	Demicia	Denajah	Denesia
Deli	Delnisha	Demarra	Demicka	Denajia	Denesse
Delia *(0.07)*	Deloma	Demarria	Demii	Denali *(0.01)*	Denetra
Deliah	Delona	Demarsha	Demika	Denalyn	Denetria
Deliana	Deloná	Demarshay	Demille	Denancy	Denetrice
Delica	Delonda	Demartha	Deminah	Denaria	Denetrics
Delicia *(0.01)*	Delondra	Dematra	Deminica	Denarra	Denetryia
Delicia Ormonie	Delonique	Demauri	Deminique	Denasha	Deneya
Delight	Delora	Demaya	Demirah	Denashawn	Deneydra
Delila	Delorean	Demeachia	Demiral	Denasia	Deni
Delilah *(0.05)*	Delores *(0.03)*	Demeasha	Demiree	Denatcia	Denia
Delilah Vanessa	Deloria	Demecca	Demiria	Denaushre	Deniak
Delilla	Deloris *(0.01)*	Demecia	Demisha	Denaveyen	Denialle
Delimar	Delorse	Demeciah	Demitra	Denavia	Deniara
Delina *(0.01)*	Delouis	Demeisha	Demitria *(0.01)*	Denay	Denica *(0.01)*
Delinda	Deloure	Demeishia	Demitrice	Denaya	Denice *(0.02)*
Delira	Deloyce	Demeka	Demitrus	Denaye	Denicia
Delirio	Delph Tree-	Demereal	Demiyah	Denayé	Deniece
Delis	Flower	Demeri	Demmi	Denby	Denielle
Delisa *(0.01)*	Delpha	Demeria	Demmie	Dendree	Deniesha
Delise	Delphia	Demerija	Demming	Dene	Denijah
Delisha *(0.01)*	Delphina	Demery	Demmisha	Dené	Denika *(0.01)*
Delishia	Delphine *(0.03)*	Demesha *(0.01)*	Demolha	Denea	Denikah
Delisia	Delphinea	Demeshia	Demondrea	Deneá	Denikia
Delissa	Delquishá	Demeshrianna	Demondta	Deneace	Denikqua
Delissia	Delrae	Demesia	Demone	Deneakqa	Denilene
Deliverance	Delray	Demesnia	Demonica	Deneal	Denilyn
Delivia	Delrey	Demestrice	Demonich	Denean	Denim
Delivion	Delrisa	Demeteria	Demonika	Deneane	Denimm
Deliyah	Delroba	Demetra *(0.01)*	Demonisha	Denecia	Deninia
Deliz	Delsa	Demetri	Demonnda	Denecion	Deniqua
Deliza	Delsey	Demetria *(0.06)*	Demontrice	Denecyia	Denique
Delizbeth	Delta	Demetriá	Demorah	Denedra	Deniquea
Delkeyia	Delveta	Demetriana	Demoya	Denee	Deniqwia
Della *(0.02)*	Delvina	Demetrianna	Dempsey	Denée	Denis *(0.01)*
Della'jae	Delvonica	Demetrias	Demra	Deneen	Denisa
Dellanira	Delwar	Demetrice	Demrae	Deneicia	Denise *(0.64)*
Dellarose	Delynn	Demetries	Demrah	Deneika	Denise Laarnie
Dellisa	Delysha	Demetriona	Demri	Deneil	Denise-Susan
Dellisha	Delysia	Demetrionna	Demy	Deneira	Denisea
Dellissta	Delyth	Demetrious	Demyria	Deneisha *(0.01)*	Denisha *(0.12)*
Delmeisha	Dema	Demetris	Demyrice	Deneishea	Denisheya

Denishia	Denzella	Dequita	Deron	Des'tini	Deshanae
Denishion	Deoatious	Dequoyah	Deronique	Des-Rée	Deshanai
Denisia	Deocia	Der'quiona	Derquacia	Desa	Deshanay
Denisica	Deodata	Der'rická	Derra	Desa'ray	Deshandra
Denissa	Deoin	Der'rickiya	Derrashea	Desai	Deshane
Denisse *(0.08)*	Deoisha	Dera	Derreauna	Desair	Deshanee
Denita *(0.01)*	Deojinae	Deranda	Derreion	Desairee	Deshanice
Denitia	Deojinay	Derby	Derreisha	Desandra	Deshanique
Denitra	Deolinda	Derecheaux	Derrell	Desanea	Deshanna
Denitria	Deomni	Derek	Derrenisha	Desanee	Deshanta
Deniyia	Deomoni	Dereka	Derresha	Desanta	Deshantá
Deniz	Deon *(0.01)*	Derekká	Derretha	Desarae *(0.03)*	Deshantae
Denize	Deon'dra	Derelyn	Derreunta	Desaraee	Deshantare
Denman	Deona *(0.01)*	Derenisha	Derri-Anne	Desarai	Deshante
Denna	Deonah	Deresha	Derria	Desarain	Deshanté
Denna Jo	Deonaise	Derexshana	Derrian	Desaray *(0.01)*	Deshantee
Dennard	Deonandreya	Dergin	Derriana	Desaraye	Deshanti
Dennardra	Deonara	Derhonda	Derriane	Desarea	Deshantiana
Denneariah	Deondra *(0.02)*	Deri	Derrica *(0.01)*	Desaree	Deshara
Denneisia	Deondrea	Deri Nique	Derricca	Desarée	Deshari
Dennelle	Deondria	Deria	Derrice	Desareé-Rose	Desharnany
Denney	Deonica	Deriah	Derricia	Desarhea	Desharoah
Denni	Deonna *(0.03)*	Derian *(0.01)*	Derrick	Desaria	Desharra
Dennice	Deonná	Deriana	Derricka *(0.02)*	Desarine	Deshauna
Dennicta	Deonne	Deriane	Derrickka	Desary	Deshaundelyn
Denniel	Deonsha	Derica *(0.01)*	Derriclesha	Deschley	Deshaunmyiaa
Dennielle	Deonshá	Derice	Derriel	Deschone	Deshaunna
Dennietra	Deonta	Dericia	Derrielle	Deseana	Deshaunta
Dennii	Deontae	Dericka	Derrienna	Deseandra	Deshaunte
Dennine	Deonte	Dericka Tatayan	Derrika	Desenae	Deshaunté
Denniqa	Deonté	Deridra	Derrineka	Deserae *(0.02)*	Deshauntel
Dennique	Deontee	Derien	Derrinesha	Deserai	Deshavonda
Dennis	Deontra	Derienne	Derriniquka	Deseraie	Deshawn *(0.01)*
Dennis'sha	Deoshia	Derika	Derrion	Deseray *(0.01)*	Deshawna *(0.01)*
Dennisa	Depali	Deriknesha	Derriona	Deseré	Deshawna-
Dennise *(0.02)*	Depelsha	Derin	Derris	Deserea	Neisha
Dennisé May	Deprise	Derinesha	Derrisha	Deseree *(0.02)*	Deshawnda
Dennisha	Dequana	Derion	Derriyah	Deserée	Deshawndra
Dennishia	Dequanda	Derirae	Derriyell	Deseri	Deshawnna
Dennisse	Dequandelyn	Derise	Derriyle	Deseria	Deshawnta
Denora	Dequandrea	Derisha	Dersiree	Deserrae	Deshawntae
Denotra	Dequania	Derisheka	Derunita	Desery	Deshawntavia
Denre	Dequanna	Derishon	Derval	Desha *(0.01)*	Deshay *(0.01)*
Denton	Dequanshae	Derissa	Derwinisha	Deshadda	Deshaya
Dentrah	Dequanyaii	Derivia	Derya	Deshadrian	Deshayda
Denuja	Dequasha	Deriya	Deryan	Deshae	Deshaye
Denver *(0.01)*	Dequashia	Deriyan	Deryka	Deshai	Deshayla
Denvir	Dequeria	Deriyn	Deryn	Deshaina	Deshaylay
Denya	Dequetta	Derlaina	Des Ja	Deshainae	Deshayne
Denyae	Dequila	Dermany	Des Monique	Deshaira	Deshe
Denys	Dequilla	Dermecia	Des Rae	Deshala	Deshea
Denyse	Dequincia	Derna	Des Ree	Deshambria	Desheka
Denysha	Dequinta	Derneeshia	Des'arae	Deshambrian	Deshelle
Denyzia	Dequira	Dernika	Des'aray	Deshana	Desherrione
Denzel	Dequisha	Dernisha	Des'ree	Deshanaa	Desherrionte

Deshia	Desirrae	Desta	Destiny-Lee	Devanne	Devinne *(0.01)*
Deshiray	Desirre	Desta Nee	Destiny-Star	Devanshi	Devion
Deshon	Desirré	Destainy	Destinydemi	Devansi	Devione
Deshona	Desirrea	Destan	Destiy	Devanté	Devionne
Deshonda	Desirree	Destanae	Destnay	Devany	Devionshay
Deshondra	Desirrée	Destané	Destney	Devarae	Devisha
Deshondrea	Desiryée	Destanée	Destonee	Devaree	Devita
Deshonna	Desitny	Destanee *(0.01)*	Destoni	Devarria	Devitria
Deshonta	Desja	Destanée	Destony	Devasha	Deviya
Deshontae	Desjan	Destaney *(0.01)*	Destree	Devashia	Deviyah
Deshontaviyana	Desjana	Destani *(0.02)*	Destri	Devaughn	Devki
Deshonte	Desjarae	Destanie *(0.02)*	Destrie	Devaune	Devlin
Deshonté	Desjiá	Destanié	Destry	Devaunshae	Devlyn
Deshonti	Deslin	Destannee	Desty	Devauria	Devlynn
Deshuana	Desma	Destany *(0.06)*	Destyn	Devaushanna	Devneet
Deshun	Desmann	Destefany	Destyne *(0.01)*	Deveen	Devni
Deshuna	Desmarais	Destenee	Destyné	Deveena	Devon *(0.35)*
Deshunta-Lakeed	Desmarie	Desteni	Destynee *(0.01)*	Devehn	Devon'ae
Deshylae	Desmayonna	Destenie	Destynée	Deveka	Devon'na
Deshynejdra	Desmesha	Destenii	Destyni *(0.01)*	Deven *(0.01)*	Devona *(0.01)*
Deshyra	Desmine	Desteny *(0.01)*	Destynie	Devena	Devonae
Desi	Desmonee	Destfny	Desy	Devenae	Devonay
Desi'ree	Desmonique	Desti	Desyre	Devenasia	Devonchia
Desia	Desne	Destimona	Deszara	Deveney	Devonda
Desideria	Desneige	Destin *(0.01)*	Desziree	Deveney Don	Devondra
Desie	Desneiges	Destin'ee	Detashé	Deveni	Devone
Desiedra	Desney	Destina	Detasia	Devenine	Devoné
Desile	Desniege	Destinae	Dethena	Devenn	Devonee
Desimone	Desoray	Destinay	Detra	Devenne	Devonée
Desinee	Desorine	Destine *(0.02)*	Detrelle	Devenney	Devoney
Desiney	Despena	Destiné	Detria	Deveousha	Devonha
Desini	Despina *(0.01)*	Destinée	Detriona	Devera	Devoni
Desinuique	Desr'ee	Destinea	Detriyan	Deveri	Devonia
Desir'e	Desrae	Destinee *(0.30)*	Detsis	Devery	Devonie
Desira	Desree	Destinée *(0.01)*	Detta	Deveshia	Devonna *(0.01)*
Desirae *(0.20)*	Desrée	Destinei	Deuanee	Devetra	Devonne
Desirai	Dessa	Destinequa	Deuna	Devi	Devonnie
Desiray *(0.03)*	Dessaire	Destiney *(0.14)*	Deunbra	Devi-Ann	Devonnshea
Desiraya	Dessaly Annette	Destini *(0.13)*	Deundra	Devia	Devonshe
Desiraye	Dessarae	Destini'	Deuntrice	Devian	Devonsheia
Desire *(0.04)*	Dessaree	Destini-Wade	Deuondra	Devika *(0.01)*	Devonta
Desire E	Dessarie	Destinie *(0.06)*	Deuphine	Devin *(0.35)*	Devonte
Desire Emerald	Desserae	Destiniee	Deva	Devin Ann	Devontearra
Desiré *(0.01)*	Desseray	Destinine	Devaca	Devin-Leigh	Devonua
Desirée *(0.01)*	Desserra	Destinique	Devada	Devina *(0.01)*	Devony
Desirea *(0.01)*	Desserrae	Destinny	Devail	Devinae	Devonya
Desireá	Dessica	Destinty	Devan *(0.13)*	Devinder	Devora *(0.01)*
Desireah	Dessie	Destiny *(1.96)*	Devana	Devine	Devorah
Desiree *(0.98)*	Dessiere	Destiny Cha	Devanee	Devinia	Devory
Desiree Puaolen	Dessirae	Destiny Elizabe	Devaney	Devinie	Devorya
Desirée *(0.05)*	Dessiray	Destiny Evon	Devani	Devinione	Devotion
Desireemarie	Dessire	Destiny Rol	Devanie	Devinique	Devoughna
Desirey	Dessiree	Destiny Zhané	Devann	Devinisha	Devounta
Desirée *(0.01)*	Dessirie	Destiny-Ann	Devanna	Devinn	Devra
Desiri	Dest'yne	Destiny-Dawn	Devannae	Devinna	Devrann

Devren	Deysia	Deziree *(0.01)*	Dharsha	Diahnie	Dianecia
Devri	Deysy	Dezirée	Dharshie	Diaja	Dianée
Devron	Deyza	Deziree-Skye	Dharti	Diajah	Dianeka
Devry-Jean	Deyzha	Dezirre	Dhasia	Diajia	Dianela
Devvanae	Dez'mon	Deziyer	Dheepa	Diamand	Dianeli
Devvoy	Dez're	Dezja	Dhekryat	Diamanda	Dianelkis
Devyan	Dez'ree	Dezjah	Dherrian	Diamanesha	Dianelliz
Devyani	Dez'shyra	Dezlyn	Dhesie	Diamanic	Dianelly
Devyn *(0.12)*	Dez-Anise	Dezlynn	Dhesorae	Diamanta	Dianelys
Devyne	Deza	Dezma	Dhestini	Diamante	Dianette
Devynn *(0.01)*	Deza'ray	Dezmonee	Dhestinny	Diamanté	Dianey
Devynne	Dezah	Dezora	Dhi'mon	Diamari	Diangela
Devyon	Dezahré	Dezorai	Dhivya	Diamber	Diani
Dewaina	Dezanequa	Dezoree	Dhounmala	Diamella	Dianiche
Dewana	Dezara	Dezra	Dhrew	Diamin	Dianika
Dewanda	Dezarae *(0.02)*	Dezray	Dhruti	Diamiya	Dianira
Dewanna	Dezarai	Dezree	Dhurata	Diamon *(0.02)*	Dianiris
Dewayna	Dezaray *(0.01)*	Dezrene	Dhuvashiga	Diamond *(0.66)*	Dianjané
Dewhitney	Dezaraya	Dezriell	Dhwani	Diamond Daisy	Dianllela
Dewi	Dezare	Dezstini	Dhyamond	Diamond Mailani	Dianmond
Dewonne	Dezaré	Dezstiny	Dhyana	Diamond Tina	Diann
Dexhiana	Dezarea	Deztine	Di	Diamond'ann	Dianna *(0.11)*
Dexsha	Dezaree *(0.01)*	Deztini	Di Era	Diamond-Emani	Diannah
Dextiny	Dezarée	Deztinie	Di Sheeka	Diamond-Lu'	Dianne *(0.06)*
Dextra	Dezarey	Deztynee	Di'ana	Diamond-Marie	Dianre
Dextress	Dezarhay	Dezuray	Di'anna	Diamonde	Diara *(0.01)*
Dextyna	Dezarra	Dezure	Di'ashley	Diamondique	Diarah
Dey'kida	Dezaye	Dezyana	Di'ashonique	Diamondleve	Diaria
Dey'sha	Deze Ray	Dezyn	Di'asia	Diamondna	Diarra *(0.01)*
Deyadira	Dezeney	Dezyre	Di'chay	Diamondray	Diasha
Deyadra	Dezerae	Dezyree	Di'elle	Diamondrya	Diasia
Deyana	Dezerah	Dezzarae	Di'esha	Diamonds	Diasy
Deyanira *(0.03)*	Dezerai	Dezzaraé	Di'keireayia	Diamondsade	Diauna
Deyanna	Dezeray	Dezzaray	Di'keriya	Diamone	Diavonna
Deyannarah	Dezere	Dezzaré	Di'laine	Diamoné	Diavonni
Deyanti	Dezerea	Dezzeray	Di'mara	Diamonee	Diayne
Deyara	Dezeree	Dezzery	Di'mekyia	Diamonique	Diazha
Deyauna	Dezerny	Dh Creeion	Di'mesha	*(0.01)*	Diazia
Deyauni	Dezerray	Dhakiya	Di'monique	Diamonisha	Diba
Deyci	Dezgrae	Dhalia	Di'ondre	Diamonte	Dibell
Deycy	Dezha	Dhamahi	Di'onna	Diamony	Dichanta
Deyeasia	Dezhanae	Dhaman	Di'or	Diamyn	Dichelle
Deyeen	Dezhane	Dhamar	Dia	Diamynd	Dichiara
Deyel	Dezhanée	Dhana	Dia Jon	Diamynde	Dicia
Deyja	Dezhanile	Dhanella	Dia Mira	Diamynn	Dicy
Deyjah	Dezhanna	Dhaneshia	Dia Nisha	Dian	Didaisha
Deyla	Dezhia	Dhanisha	Dia'mond	Diana *(1.73)*	Didra
Deylaynah	Dezhire	Dhaniya	Dia'na	Diana-Denise	Didreanne
Deymar	Dezi	Dhanroong	Diablo	Dianalyn	Dieanira
Deyona	Deziah	Dhara *(0.01)*	Diadira	Dianca	Dieanna
Deyonka	Deziaray	Dharah	Diadra	Diandra *(0.02)*	Diea~uchaka
Deyonna	Dezira	Dharbi	Diadranaé	Diandrea	*)1)*
Deysha	Dezirae *(0.03)*	Dharia	Diah	Diandria	
Deyshaniek	Deziray *(0.01)*	Dharik⌐	Diahana	₁	
Deysi *(0.01)*	Dezire	Dh⌐	Diahna		

Dieira	Dilara	Dineisha	Dionte	Divine	Dohaa
Dieisha	Dilcia	Dineke	Diontrá	Divinity	Doherty
Diekeeshia	Dilia	Dineliz	Dionysia	Divneet	Dohnnishia
Diella	Dilian	Dinesha (0.01)	Dionzanique	Divora	Dohntaesha
Dielle	Dilianna	Dineshia	Dior	Divpreet	Doireann
Diem (0.01)	Dilini	Dinesstee	Dioselina	Divya (0.02)	Dojshan
Diemlan-Lisa	Dilinila	Dinetra	Diosmery	Divyanshi	Dolcy
Dienae	Diljot	Ding	Diovanna	Diwan	Doleesha
Diendra	Dillan	Dinh	Dipa	Dixan	Dolla
Dienis	Dillania	Dini	Dipaali	Dixiana	Dollesha
Diep	Dillon	Dinia	Dipal	Dixie (0.03)	Dollicia
Diera	Dillyn	Dinisha	Dipali	Dixieanna	Dollie
Dierda	Dilma	Dinishia	Dipanjali	Dixsha	Dollnisha
Dierdra	Dilmeet	Dinjot	Dipika	Diy'mond	Dolly (0.01)
Dierdre	Dilpreer	Dinna	Dipporah	Diya	Dollye
Dierra (0.01)	Dilpreet (0.01)	Dinnah	Diquanna	Diyana	Dolmecia
Diesha	Dilraj	Dinora	Diquiesha	Diyar	Dolores (0.06)
Dieta	Dilruba	Dinora Isamar	Diquisha	Diyasha	Dolphina
Dietrice	Dilshaayee	Dinorah	Direensha	Diyashani	Dolrehonna
Dieu	Diltaj	Dinosha	Direll	Diychele	Domagoja
Dieuwke	Dilva	Dinysha	Diresha	Diyerra	Domanasha
Diezaray	Dilys	Dioanna	Dirshaya	Diyyinah	Domaneik
Diffani	Dima	Diobel	Disa	Dizhané	Domanesha
Diggs	Dimani	Dioccelia	Disarae	Dizion	Domani
Digna	Dimanique	Diojionee	Diseree	Dizzioná	Domaniqua
Digna Vanes	Dimare	Diojjanese	Disha	Dj	Domanique (0.01)
Digonae	Dimari	Diomaris	Dishae	Djaida	Domaniquela
Dihae	Dimary	Diomoyanna	Dishai	Djamah	Domenek
Dihcole	Dimeasha	Dion	Dishana	Djemila	Domenic
Diiamond	Dimeria	Diona (0.01)	Dishane	Djenaba	Domenica (0.01)
Dij'ona	Dimi	Dionade	Dishawna	Djenabe	Domenique (0.01)
Dij-Ani	Dimica	Dionamis	Dishawnte	Djenne	Domeniqué
Dijah	Dimira	Dioncencia	Dishay	Djuana	Domenisha
Dijah-Marie	Dimitiz	Diondnea	Disheba	Dkeiya	Domenteria
Dijan	Dimitra (0.01)	Diondra (0.01)	Disheka	Dlite	Domesha
Dijanai	Dimitri	Diondria	Dishi	Dmazae	Dometria
Dijea	Dimitria	Dione	Dishica	Dmia	Domianna
Dijjonae	Dimon	Dionee	Disney	Dnashai	Domina
Dijon	Dimond	Diongelia	Disney Lenae	Dnasia	Dominae
Dijona Ashley	Dimond Tanisha	Dioni'	Disonisha	Dnay-Sha	Dominck
Dijonae	Dimonica	Dionia	Disraé	Dneisha	Dominésha
Dijonaie	Dimpal	Dionica	Dissneya	Dnia	Domineke
Dijonaise	Dimple	Dionicia	Distiny	Dnima	Domineque
Dijoni'	Dimples	Dionis	Diswaisha	Dnyssa	Dominesha
Dijonnae	Dina (0.09)	Dionisia	Ditesha	Do-Nyal	Dominga
Dijonnaie	Dina-Marie	Dionjanae	Diteshia	Doaa	Domini
Dijonnaise	Dinae	Dionjonae	Ditiffany	Doan	Dominic
Dijonnase	Dinah (0.02)	Dionna (0.05)	Ditra	Doan-Thy	Dominica (0.02)
Dijonnay	Dinah Lee	Dionne (0.02)	Ditrese	Dobie-A	Dominice
Dijuan	Dinah-Leezah	Dionnedra	Diuya	Dobrila	Dominick
Dikeya	Dinahstie	Dionneshaé	Diva	Dockeshia	Dominicka
Dikranouhi	Dinalee	Dionquianesha	Divad	Docqinisheá	Dominiece
Dila	Dinar	Dionsha	Divarche	Dodi	Dominigue
Dilan	Dinécia	Dionshay	Divin	Dodie	Dominik
Dilany	Dineen	Diontae	Divina	Doha	Dominika (0.01)

Dominiqe	Donatella	Donjazase	Donnissa	Donyell	Dorie
Dominiqua	Donato	Donjé	Donnita	Donyelle	Dorielle
Dominique *(1.03)*	Donatta	Donjeea	Donnitta	Donyeta	Dorien
Dominiqué	Donavia	Donjeta	Donnjae	Donyetta	Dorienne
Dominiquea	Donaya	Donjetta	Donnsha	Donysha	Dorin
Dominisha	Donby	Donkeia	Donntá	Donzel	Dorina
Dominke	Donché	Donlandra	Donntenerria	Doolarie	Dorina-Dale
Dominqua	Dondra	Donmika	Donnyqua	Doone	Dorinda *(0.01)*
Dominque *(0.06)*	Dondrea	Donminique	Donquasha	Doonia	Doriona
Dominques	Dondreca	Donmisty	Donquisha	Dor Shea	Dorionne
Dominquie	Dondrika	Donmonique	Donricka	Dor Thea	Doris *(0.07)*
Dominuqe	Dondril	Donn	Donsha	Dora *(0.06)*	Doris Ashley
Dominysha	Donea	Donna *(0.25)*	Donsharell	Dorah	Dorisa
Domique	Donece	Donna Leigh	Donshay	Dorain	Dorisha
Domitilia	Doneisha *(0.01)*	Donna Ti Na	Donshel	Doraina	Dorishay
Dommaneka	Doneishia	Donná	Donshell	Dorali	Dorissa
Domminic	Doneka	Donna-Ann	Donshia	Doralice	Dorissia
Domna	Donekia	Donna-Brittany	Donta	Doralis	Dorista
Domna-Athanasia	Donella	Donna-Jean	Dontaé	Doraliz	Dorjeana
Domnique	Donelle	Donna-Jo	Donta'ja	Doralsha	Dorlena
Domniquwa	Donequa	Donna-Marie	Donta'lisa	Doraluz	Dorleta
Domonic	Donesha *(0.02)*	Donnae	Donta'ya	Doralyn	Dorly
Domonica	Doneshaé	Donnalee	Dontaisha	Doran	Dorma
Domonik'	Doneshea	Donnamae	Dontaisia	Dorance	Dormasha
Domonika	Doneshia *(0.01)*	Donnamaria	Dontanequa	Doranda	Dormekya
Domoniqe	Donesia	Donnanica	Dontanise	Doranely	Dorna
Domoniqu'e	Donetta	Donnashika	Dontasia	Dorann	Dornesha
Domoniqua	Donette	Donnay	Dontavia	Doranna	Dorneya
Domonique *(0.11)*	Doneyll	Donnecia	Dontaya	Dorathy	Dornicia
Domoniqué	Dong-Min	Donneice	Dontazia	Dorathy Aletha	Dornique
Domonitria	Doni	Donneika	Donte	Dorcas *(0.01)*	Dornisha
Domynique	Donia *(0.01)*	Donneisha	Donteria	Dorcus	Doronte
Don	Doniá	Donneka	Donteshia	Dorean	Dorota
Don Dreka	Donia-Jean	Donnel	Dontia	Doreeal	Dorotea
Don Janae	Doniaila	Donnell	Dontice	Doreen *(0.02)*	Dorotha
Don'crita	Donica	Donnella	Dontilisha	Doreisha	Dorothan
Don'ell	Donicha	Donnelley	Dontoria	Dorely	Dorothea *(0.01)*
Don'naesha	Donicia	Donnesha	Dontraelle	Dorena	Dorothee *(0.01)*
Don'nisha	Donide	Donneshaa	Dontrece	Dorene	Dorothi
Don'tay	Doniece	Donnesia	Dontrell	Doresha	Dorothie
Don-Asia	Doniele	Donnetta	Dontresa	Doretha	Dorothilyn
Dona	Doniell	Donnette	Dontrese	Dorethea	Dorothy *(0.20)*
Donae	Donielle *(0.02)*	Donni	Dontrice	Doretta	Dorothy Ann
Donaé	Donika	Donnia-Surya	Dontriniece	Dori *(0.01)*	Dorqueisha
Donah	Donikia	Donnicha	Dontrinique	Doria	Dorraine
Donaizha	Doninique	Donnicia	Donya *(0.01)*	Doriale	Dorrelle
Donaji	Doniqua	Donnie	Donyae	Dorian *(0.03)*	Dorrene
Donaka	Donique	Donnielle	Donyaella	Doriana	Dorreth
Donalda	Doniquéa	Donniesha	Donyal	Doriane *(0.01)*	Dorriane
Donaldine	Donis	Donnieshaw	Donyale	Dorianna	Dorrie
Donaneisha	Donisa	Donnika	Donyalle	Dorianne *(0.01)*	Dorrin
Donarah	Donisha *(0.03)*	Donnikquia	Donye	Dorianza	Dorris
Donasha	Donita	Donniquca	Donyea	Dorica	Dorrit
Donashawa	Donja	Donnis	Donyeal	Doricarmen	Dorsey
Donashay	Donjanea	Donnisha *(0.01)*	Donyel	Doricia	Dorshanique

Dortha	Dréanna	Dria	Dungnhi	Dy Junera	Dyiamend
Dorthia	Drékelia	Driahna	Dunia *(0.01)*	Dy Lana	Dykea
Dorthy	Dréqunna	Driana	Dunja	Dy Monique	Dykerria
Dorthyine	Dréshanna	Drianna	Dunnum	Dy Niecia	Dyketa
Doruthy	Drea	Drieann	Dunte Ya	Dy Onna	Dylaan
Doryan	Drea-Lynn	Driel	Dunya	Dy Reall	Dylaina
Doshae	Drealesha	Drina	Dunyah	Dy'amond	Dylan *(0.07)*
Doshia	Dream	Dristan	Duong Thuy	Dy'anna	Dylana *(0.01)*
Doslidia	Dreama	Dristine	Dupinder	Dy'asia	Dylane
Doticaera	Dreamanne	Drita	Dupreisha	Dy'asmine	Dylanee
Dotriann	Dreamer	Drover	Dupresha	Dy'chell	Dylanie
Dottie	Dreana	Dru	Duquita	Dy'equa	Dylann
Doughty	Dreanalee	Druanne	Duran	Dy'esha	Dylanna
Douglas	Dreanika	Drucelle	Durasia	Dy'lean	Dyleezia
Dougless	Dreanna	Drucilla *(0.01)*	Durati	Dy'lishia	Dylen
Douha	Dreanne	Drue *(0.01)*	Duraysha	Dy'min	Dylencia
Doujsha	Drecia	Drury	Dureshia	Dy'nasia	Dylicia
Doungchan	Dreeann	Druscilla	Durga	Dy'sha	Dylin
Dounia	Dreema	Drusilla	Durham	Dy'shanna	Dyllan
Doura	Dreisha	Dsana	Durkah	Dy'zhane	Dyln
Douteriaei	Drejauna	Dsaree	Durriyyah	Dy-Mond	Dylynn
Dova	Drekara	Dsatohanmwen	Dusha	Dy-Nel	Dymahnn
Dove	Drekia	Du'shonta	Dushika	Dy-Reaka	Dymariz
Doveye	Drelone	Duaa	Dusteen	Dya'mond	Dymaund
Dovi	Drema	Duah	Dusti *(0.01)*	Dyadra	Dymaya
Dovie	Drenda	Duana	Dustie	Dyais	Dymeshia
Dowana	Drenecia	Duanai	Dustin *(0.01)*	Dyala	Dymin
Doya	Dreneisha	Duane	Dustina	Dyamanté	Dyminn
Doyleshia	Dreneshia	Duane-Na	Dustine	Dyamin	Dymon
Doynicia	Drenika	Duanshe	Dusty *(0.02)*	Dyamon	Dymond *(0.03)*
Dquaneice	Drenikia	Duanyaé	Dutcher	Dyamond *(0.01)*	Dymonde
Dr Brandie	Drenna	Duatlanzer	Duvela	Dyamone	Dymone
Drae-Anna	Drennan	Duayna	Duwaah	Dyan	Dymonn
Drake	Dreonna	Dubelsa	Duwen	Dyana *(0.02)*	Dyna
Drakevia	Drerisha	Duc	Dvina	Dyandra	Dyna-Ann
Dralaya	Dresden	Duchess	Dwaisha	Dyani	Dynae
Dralyn	Dresha	Ducy	Dwana	Dyaniqua	Dynasia
Dralynn	Dreshonna	Duenny	Dwanda	Dyanjvay	Dynastee
Dramecka	Dresnee	Duff	Dwaneishia	Dyann	Dynasti
Dramonesha	Dreteria	Dujana	Dwanika	Dyanna *(0.01)*	Dynastie
Draneisha	Drevonna	Dukesika	Dwanisha	Dyanne	Dynasty *(0.02)*
Dranell	Drew *(0.12)*	Dulakshiga	Dwantia	Dyara	Dynecia
Dranira	Drew Ann	Dulca	Dwanyea	Dyasia	Dyneisha
Draren	Drewann	Dulce *(0.19)*	Dwaun	Dychelle	Dynequa
Drashea	Drewcilla	Dulce Anahi	Dwaunika	Dyénisha	Dynesha
Drateasha	Drewcille	Dulcemaria	Dwayna	Dyeashia	Dyneshia
Draven	Drewe	Dulcey	Dwayne	Dyeena	Dynetta
Dravyanna	Drewshadra	Dulcie	Dwayneisha	Dyeisha	Dyniesha
Draxie	Drewsilla	Dulin	Dwhitney	Dyenesha	Dynikki
Drayakka	Drexyn	Dulse	Dwiesha	Dyesha	Dynisha
Drayla	Dreya	Dumanisha	Dwikendra	Dyeshanae	Dynishia
Draylin	Dreyah	Dumetreia	Dwouachanh	Dyeshia	Dyon
Dre Carla	Dreyana	Dumina	Dwuanya	Dyessia	Dyona
Dre Shana	Dreyonna	Dunesha	Dwynesha	Dyeve	Dyonesse
Dréana	Drez	Dung	Dwyronyelle	Dyhann	Dyonika

Dyonna
Dyonnay
Dyonne
Dyqueasha
Dyquisha
Dyqwasha
Dyr'rica
Dyrana
Dyresha
Dysha
Dyshae
Dyshaunna
Dyshawnté
Dyshay
Dyshea
Dysheada
Dysheaka
Dysheka
Dyshekia
Dyshelle
Dyshema
Dysheria
Dyshia
Dysiree
Dysis
Dystanee
Dystaney
Dystani
Dysteni
Dystine
Dystinee
Dystini
Dystiny
Dystonie
Dystyny
Dytia
Dytisha
Dytria
Dyvannya
Dyvoniek
Dywana
Dywoneica
Dyzera
Dzenana
Dzifa
Dziko

-E-

E (0.02)
E Keidra
E Lexus
E Lissa
E Mani
E Shia

E Terica
Éavona
Éceilia
Échanti
Édeisha
Édriana
Édronna
Éjanay Jamirra
Éjustis
Ékala
Élana
Élaserie
Élexis
Élexus
Élicia
Élise
Élishah
Élonte
Élora
Élyse
Élyshia
Émani
Émauney
Émecisa
Émone
Émoni
Émonique
Énasia
Éndaja
Éniya
Éonna
Érijan
Éseanti
Éshauna
Éshonna
Étaija
Étasia
Étaysheuna
Étearrea
Étemad
Évoni
E-Man
E-Qwaina
E.
Ea
Ea'stacia
Eacoa
Eadaoine
Eadelin
Eaden
Eady
Eahgi
Ealeen
Ealeisha
Ealexia

Ealisha
Ealiyah
Eanara
Eandra
Eanna
Earielle
Earin
Earlane
Earlaun
Earldesha
Earlecia
Earlencia
Earlene
Earlesia
Earlexsia
Earlexus
Earlicia
Earline
Earlisha
Earlkelia
Earllonna
Earlmesha
Earlsheika
Early
Earlysha
Earlyssia
Earnestine
Earnicia
Earnisha
Earricka
Earrin
Eartha
Earum
Easten
Easter
Eastin
Easton
Eastyn
Eavan
Eaven
Eavon
Eba
Ebanie
Ebanjelina
Ebany
Ebbeney
Ebbie
Ebelia
Ebelin
Ebelyn
Ebeni
Ebere
Eberechi
Ebizuoye
Ebnoy

Ebomy
Ebon'e
Ebona
Ebone (0.02)
Eboné (0.01)
Eboné-Nycole
Ebonée
Ebonea
Ebonee (0.02)
Ebonée
Eboneshia
Eboney (0.01)
Eboni (0.10)
Eboni'
Eboni-Rai
Ebonick
Ebonie (0.02)
Ebonié
Ebonique
Ebonne
Ebonni
Ebonnie
Ebony (0.39)
Ebony Chone
Ebony-Jean
Ebonyammani
Ebory
Ebrahim
Ebriel
Ebtihal
Ebulalla
Eby
Ebyan
Ebynie
Eccelisha
Ecclesia
Ece
Ecense
Ecezel
Echo (0.02)
Ecko
Ed Driana
Ed'dri'anna
Eda
Edalia
Edan
Edana
Edashinae
Eddel
Eddi
Eddiea
Eddieasia
Eddiesha
Eddisa
Eddisha

Eddonishia
Eddreeka
Eddreka
Eddricka
Eddrina
Eddrinia
Eddwina
Eddy
Eddyrae
Edel
Edelene
Edelmira
Edelmis
Eden (0.17)
Eden Elizabeth
Edend
Edenia
Edenia Cathydia
Edera
Edermis
Edesha
Edessa
Edgar
Edge
Edhit
Edie
Edie-Jane
Edierah
Edijah
Edil
Edina
Edis
Ediselda
Edislen
Edit
Edith (0.27)
Edithanne
Edjeania
Edjuana
Edlawit
Edleisia
Edlexis
Edlira
Edlisha
Edliyah
Edlyn
Edlyne
Edlynn
Edmalena
Edman
Edmarys
Edmee
Edmilen
Edmond
Edmy

Edna (0.05)
Ednah
Ednee Mae
Ednesher
Edneshia
Ednisha
Edome
Edona
Edoné
Edosa
Edquisha
Edreanna
Edreione
Edria
Edriana
Edrianika
Edrianna
Edricka
Edrickey
Edrienne Fae
Edrina
Edrina Christia
Edris
Edrodsye
Edsel
Edtress
Eduardo
Eduleen
Edvelyn
Edwardia
Edwedge
Edwenna
Edwin
Edwina (0.01)
Edwinique
Edwmary
Edwynn
Edyli
Edyn
Edyta
Edyth
Eekima
Eeleyah
Eelisa
Eelje
Eemanhnnie
Een
Eerika
Eerum
Eesha
Eevon
Eeyama
Efehi
Effie (0.01)
Effstathia

Efimia	Eillianna	Elaha	Elaysha	Elekes	Elfi
Efleen	Eilzabeth	Elaida	Elayza	Elektra	Elgie
Efmorfia	Eiman	Elaijah	Elba	Elen	Elgin
Efosa	Eimi	Elain	Elbertha	Elen-Yuan	Elgine
Efrah	Eimly	Elaina *(0.13)*	Elbethel	Elena *(0.45)*	Elham *(0.01)*
Efrasinia	Einajo	Elaine *(0.28)*	Elbia	Elena Maria	Elhana
Efrocini	Eionnah	Elaine Marie	Elbony	Elena-Lee	Eli
Efstathia	Eiphnh	Elaine-Elizabeth	Elbrisha	Elenamarie	Eli Juliet
Eftehia	Eira	Elainea	Elcalena	Eleni *(0.06)*	Eli-Jo
Efthemia	Eirene	Elainée	Elda	Elenie	Elia *(0.04)*
Efua	Eirenée	Elainette	Eldine	Elenita	Eliabeth
Egan	Eirin	Elainey	Eldonia	Elenna	Eliada
Eggla	Eiro	Elaini	Eldora	Elenoa	Eliah
Egheomwanre	Eisel	Elainie	Eldresah	Elenor	Eliahn
Eglindina	Eisele	Elainna	Eldricia	Elenora	Eliamar
Egypt *(0.01)*	Eisha	Elaisha	Eldricka	Eleny	Eliana *(0.08)*
Egypt Alexandria	Eishe	Elaiza Marie	Eldwrian	Eleona	Eliane *(0.04)*
Egyptmarguerite	Eithne	Elan	Eléna	Eleonor	Eliani
Ehi	Eivianna	Elana *(0.06)*	Eleada	Eleonora	Elianis
Ehlana	Eiyauna	Elanaria	Eleah	Eleonore	Elianna
Ehlanna	Eiyesha	Elanda	Eleaine	Eleora	Elianne *(0.01)*
Ehlannah	Ejana	Elandra	Eleana	Eleri	Eliany
Ehli	Ejiemen	Elandria	Eleandra	Elesa	Elibeth
Ehma	Ejigayehou	Elane	Eleanor *(0.22)*	Elese	Elica
Ehren	Ejiro	Elanee	Eleanore *(0.01)*	Elesha *(0.01)*	Elica Jasmin
Ehreni	Ekamjot	Elaney	Eleasa	Eleshea	Elicea
Ehrica	Ekanem	Elangie	Eleasah	Elesia	Elichia
Ehsaan	Ekaterina *(0.01)*	Elani	Elease	Elesiah	Elicia *(0.04)*
Eia	Ekaterine	Elania	Eleasha	Eleskcia	Elicka
Eibhilin	Ekaterini	Elanie	Eleasia	Elesse	Elida *(0.02)*
Eiden	Ekdeep	Elanna	Elecia	Eletia	Elide *(0.03)*
Eieftheria	Ekemini	Elanni	Electa	Eletric	Elided
Eila	Ekenechukwu	Elanor	Electra	Eleutheria	Elidee
Eilane	Ekerria	Elanta	Elecycia	Elexa	Elideth
Eilani	Ekeya	Elantae	Eleecia	Elexandra	Elidia
Eilee	Ekjot	Elanté	Eleen	Elexandria	Elidy
Eileen *(0.16)*	Eknoor	Elantra	Eleena	Elexaray	Elienay
Eileen Marie	Eko	Elany	Eleese	Elexas	Eliese
Eileena	Ekram	Elara	Eleesha	Elexcious	Eliesha
Eileene	Ekran	Elasah	Eleesia	Elexes	Eliessa
Eileesh	Ekraneesha	Elasan	Eleeza	Elexess	Eliett
Eilene	Ekta	Elasha	Eleezia	Elexeya	Eliette
Eiley	Ekua	Elashi	Elefteri	Elexia	Eliezer
Eili	Ekya	Elatise	Elefteria	Elexiah	Elif
Eiliah	El Geiana	Elauna	Eleftheria	Elexis *(0.05)*	Eligoria
Eiliann	El'Iohna	Elaunshae	Elegra	Elexius	Elihana
Eilidh	El'nisha	Elaura	Eleida	Elexous	Elija
Eilie	El-Desicca	Elaxus	Eleigha	Elexsus	Elijah *(0.01)*
Eilina	El-Hannah	Elaya	Eleighna	Elexus *(0.04)*	Elijanna
Eiline	El-Shaddai	Elayah	Eleiha	Elexxus	Elijel
Eilionora	Ela	Elayna *(0.02)*	Eleina	Elexys	Elijha
Eilis	Eladia	Elaynah	Eleindie	Eleyia	Elijhahrel
Eilish *(0.01)*	Elaena	Elayne	Eleisha	Eleyna	Elika
Eilleen	Elah	Elayni	Elejah	Elezebeth	Elila

Elilta	Eliya	Ellaina	Ellinor	Eloise *(0.05)*	Elvina
Elim	Eliyah	Ellan	Elliot	Eloiza	Elvira *(0.04)*
Elimey	Eliyana	Ellana	Elliott	Eloizza	Elvony
Elin	Eliza *(0.19)*	Ellanah	Elliotte	Elon	Elvy
Elina *(0.02)*	Eliza-Marie	Ellania	Elliottnish	Elon'te	Ely
Elinor *(0.01)*	Elizabaeth	Ellanie	Ellis *(0.01)*	Elona	Elya
Elinore	Elizabath	Ellanor	Ellisa *(0.01)*	Elondra	Elyana
Eliodora	Elizabeh	Ellanora	Ellise	Eloni	Elyane *(0.01)*
Eliot	Elizabeht	Ellaricka	Ellisha	Elontra	Elyanna
Eliphia	Elizabel	Ellarie	Ellishia	Elony	Elyaunna
Eliris	Elizaberth	Ellary	Ellisia	Elora *(0.02)*	Elycci
Elirissa	Elizabess	Ellatrice	Ellison *(0.01)*	Elora-Danan	Elyce
Elirosy	Elizabet *(0.02)*	Ellazha	Ellissa	Eloralisa	Elycia *(0.01)*
Elisa *(0.26)*	Elizabete	Elle *(0.06)*	Ellisure	Elorie	Elyemi
Elisa Cissy	Elizabeth *(7.65)*	Ellé	Elliza	Elose	Elyn
Elisa-Marie	Elizabeth Ann	Elleah	Ellizabeth	Eloude	Elynn
Elisabel	Elizabeth Belle	Elleceia	Ellon	Elouise	Elyonna
Elisabet *(0.02)*	Elizabeth Lily	Elleda	Ellora	Eloyza	Elyric
Elisabeth *(0.45)*	Elizabeth-Ann	Ellee	Elloree	Elpida	Elys
Elisabeth Ann	Elizabeth-Gail	Elleigh	Ellouise	Elria	Elysa *(0.01)*
Elisabethe	Elizabethann	Ellen *(0.58)*	Ellvi	Elriana	Elyse *(0.16)*
Elisabetta	Elizabethe	Ellen-Irene	Elly *(0.01)*	Elrica	Elysee
Elisamary	Elizabette	Ellena *(0.01)*	Ellya	Elrielle	Elysha *(0.01)*
Elisapeta	Elizabhet	Ellenar	Ellyana	Elronda	Elyshia
Elisavette	Elizabith	Ellender	Ellyanne	Elsa *(0.11)*	Elysia *(0.02)*
Elise *(0.41)*	Elizah	Ellene	Ellyat	Elsa Marissa	Elysia Joy
Elise-Marie	Elizajo	Elleni	Ellyce	Elsana	Elysia-Rose
Elisea	Elizamar	Elleniqua	Ellycia	Elsasha	Elysian
Elisebeth	Elizane	Ellenmarie	Ellyn *(0.02)*	Elsbeth	Elyssa *(0.07)*
Elisee	Elizaved	Ellenna	Ellynn	Else	Elysse
Elisette	Elizbeth	Ellenor	Ellynne	Elselijn	Elyssé
Elisha *(0.11)*	Elize	Ellerie	Ellysa	Elsha	Elyssia
Elisha-Melissa	Elizebath	Ellery *(0.01)*	Ellyse	Elshadai	Elyvelisse
Elisha.mae	Elizebeth *(0.01)*	Ellesa	Ellysha	Elshandrea	Elyza
Elishah	Elizet	Ellese	Ellyson	Elshane	Elyzabeta
Elishama	Elizete	Ellessa	Ellyssa	Elsi	Elyzabeth
Elisheba	Elizibeth	Ellessea	Elma *(0.01)*	Elsia	Elyzabeth Ann
Elishesa	Elizsa	Ellette	Elmaia	Elsie *(0.07)*	Elyze
Elisheva *(0.01)*	Elizza	Ellexis	Elmeda	Elsien	Elyzibeth
Elishia	Elizzabeth	Ellexus	Elmesha	Elsmiene	Elza
Elishiba	Eljonai	Elli *(0.01)*	Elmeta	Elspeth *(0.01)*	Elzbieta
Elisia *(0.01)*	Elka	Ellia	Elmis	Elssa	Elzypet
Elisian	Elke	Ellian	Elna	Elsy	Ema *(0.02)*
Elissa *(0.11)*	Elkena	Elliana	Elnaaz	Eltianna	Emaan
Elissah	Elkis	Elliann	Elnaz	Elton	Emahni
Elisse	Ell'e	Ellianna	Elnora	Elura	Emailda
Elissha	Ella *(0.14)*	Ellianne	Elodee	Eluxis	Emaje
Elissia	Ella Mae	Ellice	Elodia	Elva *(0.03)*	Emalah
Elita	Ella Marie	Ellicia	Elodie *(0.09)*	Elvalenna	Emalea
Elitanina	Ellá	Ellie *(0.14)*	Elody	Elveen	Emalee *(0.02)*
Elitra	Ella-Anne	Elliese	Eloh	Elverta	Emaleigh *(0.01)*
Elitza	Elladee	Ellina	Eloida	Elvia *(0.05)*	Emali
Elivia	Elladiana	Ellington	Elois	Elvie	Emalie *(0.01)*
Elivsha	Ellah	Ellinna	Eloisa *(0.02)*	Elvin	Emaline

Emally	Emeline (0.01)	Emilie (0.68)	Emlynne	Emmanvelle	Emony
Emaly (0.01)	Emellie	Emilie-Anne	Emma (2.63)	Emmaquin	Emoree
Emalyn	Emelly	Emilie-Justine	Emma Bao Ha	Emmaren	Emorie
Eman (0.01)	Emely (0.05)	Emiliecatharine	Emma Kate	Emmarie	Emory (0.01)
Emanda	Emely-Cindy	Emiliee	Emma Lee	Emmarose	Emperatriz
Emane	Emelye Ann	Emiliene	Emma Lena	Emmary	Empire
Emanée	Emelyn	Emilija	Emma Rose	Emmauella	Emporess
Emani (0.03)	Emelynn	Emiline	Emma Salome	Emme	Emporia
Emanie	Emeral	Emilio	Emma Sandra	Emmelene	Empress
Emann	Emerald (0.12)	Emiliy	Emma-Catherin	Emmeli	Empriest
Emanna	Emeraldann	Emille	Emma-Irene	Emmelie	Emry
Emanual	Emeraldina	Emillea	Emma-Jane	Emmeline (0.01)	Emrye
Emanuel	Emeraude	Emillee	Emma-Jean	Emmely	Emunuelle
Emanuela	Emeri	Emillie	Emma-Kate	Emmelyn	Emy (0.02)
Emanuella	Emerial	Emilly (0.02)	Emma-Lee	Emmerett	Emyia
Emanuelle (0.01)	Emerica	Emilse	Emma-Leigh	Emmeri	Emyle
Emar	Emerida	Emilu	Emma-Lisa	Emmerson	Emylee (0.01)
Emara	Emerie	Emily (11.85)	Emma-Lynn	Emmi	Emylie
Emarald	Emerita	Emily Anne	Emma-Mae	Emmie (0.01)	Emyline
Emaree	Emerlin	Emily Elizabeth	Emma-Marie	Emmiela	Emys
Emarey	Emerlissa	Emily Jo	Emma-Rose	Emmili	En'chante
Emari (0.01)	Emerly	Emily Michele	Emma-Thomas	Emmilie	En'dia
Emarie	Emerlyn	Emily Ngoc	Emmacait	Emmiline	En'dyia
Emarii	Emerson	Emily Susann	Emmah	Emmille	Ena (0.01)
Emarsharae	Emery (0.01)	Emily-Amber	Emmakay	Emmily (0.01)	Enaezia
Emary	Emery-Anna	Emily-Ann	Emmalang	Emminique	Enaika
Emasia	Emeryanna	Emily-Anne	Emmalea	Emmonnie	Enala
Emauni	Emese	Emily-Belle	Emmalee (0.04)	Emmony	Enantroop
Emauntee	Emi	Emily-Bliss	Emmalei	Emmsa	Enas
Emaya	Emia	Emily-Catherine	Emmaleigh	Emmy (0.04)	Enass
Ember (0.02)	Emialee	Emily-Elizabeth	Emmalen	Emmylea	Enasshia
Ember-Leigh	Emian	Emily-Jade	Emmalena	Emmyllye	Enatia
Emberlee	Emicelda	Emily-Jane	Emmalene	Emmylou	Enbar
Emberly	Emicia	Emily-Jayne	Emmaley	Emmylu	Enchancia
Embree	Emie (0.01)	Emily-Jean	Emmali	Emnet	Enchate
Embreyana	Emielia	Emily-Joy	Emmalia	Emni	End'asia
Embrezia	Emigdian	Emily-Marie	Emmalie (0.01)	Emo'nee	Endasha
Embry	Emigo	Emily-Rose	Emmalin	Emoline	Endazha
Eme	Emijah	Emilyann	Emmalina	Emon	Endea
Emebeit	Emika	Emilyanne	Emmaline (0.02)	Emondé	Endejah
Emecca	Emiko	Emilye	Emmalisa	Emone	Enderna
Emecia	Emilce	Emilyjane	Emmalise	Emoné	Endesha
Emeecha	Emile (0.01)	Emilyn (0.01)	Emmaly	Emonee	Endia (0.01)
Emeishia	Emilea	Emilynn	Emmalyn	Emonée	Endicia
Emelea	Emilee (0.26)	Emilyy	Emmalyne	Emonei	Endiya
Emelee	Emilée	Emilze	Emmalynne	Emoney	Endora
Emelen	Emileigh (0.01)	Emina	Emmamarie	Emonfre	Endwovigine
Emelene	Emilene	Emine	Emman	Emoni (0.02)	Endy
Emeley	Emiley (0.02)	Emira	Emmani	Emoni'	Endya
Emeli	Emili (0.01)	Emiren'e	Emmanuel	Emonie (0.01)	Endyia
Emelia (0.03)	Emilia (0.12)	Emity	Emmanuela	Emonié	Endyiana
Emelia-Eden	Emilia Suyapa	Emiya	Emmanuella	Emonnee	Enecia
Emelie (0.02)	Emilialyn	Emiyrose	Emmanuelle (0.09)	Emonnie	Enedina (0.01)
Emelin	Emiliana	Emlea	Emmanuet	Emonté	Eneida
Emelina	Emilianne	Emlyn		Emonuie	Enelida

Eneliz	Enya *(0.01)*	Eriannah	Erin-Lee	Ernecia	Esdras
Enercida	Enyae	Erianne	Erina	Erneikia	Esekel
Enesha	Enyllop	Eriberto	Erinaija	Erneisha	Esence
Enesia	Eola	Eric	Erine	Erneitsha	Esense
Enessicia	Eona	Eric'el	Erinecia	Ernequa	Eseosa
Eneziah	Eowyn	Erica *(2.48)*	Erineesha	Ernercia	Eseta
Enfateria	Eowynn	Erica Daija	Erineisha	Ernesha	Esfer
Enfinity	Ephesia	Erica Monique	Erinfaye	Ernesia	Esha
Engelica	Epic	Erica Octavia	Erini	Ernesta	Eshana
Engelique	Epihany Neferta	Erica Paige	Erinika	Ernestina *(0.01)*	Eshanee
Engelor	Epiphani	Erica-Paulos	Erinique	Ernestine	Eshay
England	Epiphany *(0.01)*	Ericah	Erinisha	Ernisha	Eshayla
Engle	Eponine	Ericajoy	Erinka	Erniya	Eshe
Englesh	Eppelina	Ericca	Erinn *(0.04)*	Erole	Eshé
English	Eppie	Ericha	Erinn'	Eronica	Eshelon
Englishe	Eqilla	Ericia	Erinne	Eronide	Esheta
Engracia	Equana	Ericka *(0.23)*	Erinneshia	Erquail	Eshita
Eni	Equillia	Ericka Lynne	Erinteresa	Erreckra	Eshna
Enia	Equity	Erickah	Eriol	Errian	Eshunzy
Enid	Er Lisha	Erickia	Erion	Erricka	Eshyra
Enidia	Er'shai	Ericsha	Eriona	Errika	Esinam
Enigma	Era	Erida	Erionna	Errin *(0.01)*	Esir
Enika	Eraceena	Eridian	Eriqa	Errinika	Esirae
Eniko	Erah	Erie	Erique	Errionniah	Esiyah
Enilie	Eraina	Erieal	Erirn	Erris	Eskye
Enisa	Erainia	Eriean	Eris	Errollneish	Esli
Enise	Erakeyana	Eriecka	Eriselda	Erron	Esma
Enisha	Eraleigh	Eriekca	Erisha	Erryn	Esme
Enit	Eram	Eriel *(0.01)*	Erisheka	Erum	Esmé
Enita	Eran	Eriell	Erissia	Ervasha	Esmee
Enja	Erana	Erielle	Erith	Erveouna	Esmeralda *(0.37)*
Enjoli	Erandi	Erien	Eritrea	Ervetta	Esmeralde
Enjonae	Erandy	Erienekia	Erittany	Ervina	Esmerelda
Enjunay	Eraneisha	Erienne	Erixcia	Ervion	Esmirhonda
Enna *(0.01)*	Ercilia	Erieyona	Eriyal	Ervonni	Esmirna
Ennesa	Ercla	Eriinda	Eriyana	Eryca	Esna
Ennissa	Erdin	Erik	Eriyasha	Erycka	Esohe
Enola	Erdokia	Erika *(1.73)*	Eriyel	Eryian	Esosa
Enoruwa	Ereca	Erika Sharee	Eriyeni	Eryka	Espana
Enovyar	Ereena	Erika-Leigh	Erjahna	Eryl	Esparanza
Enquine	Eren	Erika-Maria	Erla	Eryn *(0.10)*	Esperansa
Enrayia	Erena	Erikaa	Erland	Eryne	Esperanz
Enrica	Erendida *(0.01)*	Erikah	Erlande	Erynn *(0.01)*	Esperanza *(0.09)*
Enrika	Erendira *(0.02)*	Erikecia	Erlecha	Erynne	Espiony
Enriqueta	Eresarena	Erikha-Lee	Erlin	Erzsebet	Esprit
Enrriqueta	Ereshay	Erikka *(0.01)*	Erlinda	Esa	Esqualondria
Ensenatte	Ereyda	Eriko	Erline	Esabelle	Esquire
Enshala	Erezi	Erilca	Erliscia	Esaysha	Esquite
Enslie	Ergbe-Selam	Erily	Erma *(0.01)*	Esbaide	Esra
Entasia	Eri	Erilyn	Ermelie	Esbeidy	Esraa
Entegrity	Eriaché	Erilysha	Ermelinda	Esbeydi	Essa
Entinne	Erial	Erin *(3.11)*	Erminia	Esbleyde	Essenc
Entiza	Erian	Erin Chantell	Ermite	Esbryana	Essence *(0.13)*
Enuashia	Eriana	Erin Kea	Erna	Escara	Essences
Envie	Erianna	Erin-Jean	Ernalyn	Esdee	Essenchal

Essenes	Estonya	Eugina	Euthemia	Eveleen	Evone
Essenia	Estralla	Eujene	Euvenia	Evelena	Evones
Essense	Estraya	Eujenia	Euzetta	Evelene	Evoni
Essentra	Estrella (0.04)	Eukirah	Eva (0.38)	Evelia (0.01)	Evonjohnae
Essex	Estrellita	Eula	Eva Julia	Evelian	Evonna
Essie	Esty	Eulaida	Eva Mae	Eveliany	Evonne (0.01)
Essilfua	Esveide	Eulala	Eva Nia	Evelin (0.08)	Evontia
Essiline	Esveidie	Eulalee	Eva-Elmira	Evelina (0.01)	Evoyal
Essley	Eswyn	Eulalia	Eva-Helene	Eveline (0.01)	Evropi
Essraa	Esylen	Eulamae	Eva-Jenee	Eveling	Evthoxia
Essynce	Eszter	Euleasia	Eva-Maria	Evelisse	Evva
Esta	Eta	Eulesha	Eva-Marie	Eveliz	Evvey
Estafania	Etaf	Euline	Evada	Evely	Evy
Estafi	Etain	Eulisa	Evadne	Evelyn (0.74)	Evye
Estania	Etana	Eulonda	Evah	Evelyn Karen	Evyn
Estany	Etasha	Eulyncia	Evaleana	Evelyn Margaret	Ewa
Estavia	Etasia	Eumela	Evalina	Evelyn Tiffanie	Ewe
Estavian	Etchnaydine	Eumelia	Evaline	Evelyna	Ewelina
Estee	Eterica	Eun	Evalyn	Evelyne (0.04)	Ewunike
Estefana	Eternity (0.01)	Eun'ganea	Evalynn	Evelynn	Ewura-Ama
Estefane	Eternity-Sade	Eun-Chae	Evan (0.04)	Evelynne	Ewurama
Estefani (0.07)	Ethan	Eun-Ji	Evana	Evenlyn	Ex-Starvia
Estefanîa	Ethel (0.01)	Eunbyi	Evancha	Evensia	Examene
Estefania (0.08)	Ethela	Eunese	Evangel	Eveonna	Excellence
Estefanie	Ethelvina	Eunice (0.11)	Evangelea	Everee	Exie
Estefann	Ethelyn	Eunice Marie	Evangelene	Everette	Exierine
Estefany (0.07)	Ethiana	Eunice-Dayinera	Evangelia	Everleigh	Extasé
Esteicy	Ethil	Eunika	Evangelina (0.03)	Everli	Exzalin
Estel	Ethyah	Euniqa	Evangeline (0.04)	Everlis	Exzarvea
Estela (0.03)	Ethyl	Euniqua	Evangeline Chere	Everly	Ey'tiana
Estella (0.02)	Etia	Eunique	Evangelis	Everlyn	Eyadena
Estella Lataya	Etienne (0.01)	Euniquice	Evangelyn	Everoy-Aspen	Eyana
Estella Marie	Etonica	Eunisha	Evanidia	Everyell	Eyanna
Estellanee	Etoy	Eunishia	Evanisha	Evett	Eydi
Estelle (0.03)	Etoya	Eunita	Evanka	Evette (0.03)	Eyeisha
Estenia	Etrea	Eunnie	Evann	Evey	Eyhanna
Estephani	Etta (0.01)	Eunnycce	Evanna	Eveyln	Eyleah
Estephania	Ettaghenu	Eunyque	Evanne	Evhan	Eyleen
Estephanie (0.03)	Ettia	Eupharzine	Evans	Evi	Eyman
Estephany (0.01)	Etty	Euphemia	Evante	Evian	Eymane
Estephine	Etua	Euphfemea	Evanthia	Eviana	Eymara
Ester (0.04)	Etvania	Eura	Evany	Evie (0.02)	Eymbree
Estera	Eu Nisha	Eurasia	Evarista	Evienia	Eymi
Esterina	Euasion	Eureeka	Evas-Ariel	Evila	Eymon
Esterlina	Eudelia	Eureka	Evatney	Evin	Eynnesha
Esther (0.42)	Eudora	Euricka	Evauna	Evina	Eyona
Esther-Maria	Eudoxia	Euridice	Eve (0.17)	Evinne	Eyonna
Esther-Mary	Eufemia	Eurika	Eve Marie (0.01)	Evita	Eyranique
Esthera	Eugena (0.01)	Euriyka	Eve-Ling	Evlalia	Eyrica
Estherita	Eugene	Europe	Eve-Nana	Evlee	Eyron
Estia Lashanna	Eugenea	Europia	Eveanfia	Evnika	Eyvette
Estina	Eugenee	Eusebia	Eveda	Evon	Eyvol
Estinder	Eugenia (0.03)	Eustacia	Eveena	Evona	Eyvone
Estizer	Eugenie (0.02)	Eustasia	Evelea	Evonda	Ezabel

Ezandra	Fadia	Falasha	Fannieisha	Farishte	Fatia
Ezaniah	Fadra	Falavia	Fanniesha	Fariya	Fatiha
Ezarrah	Fadrea	Falcon	Fanny *(0.11)*	Fariza	Fatim
Ezenwanyi	Faduma	Faleasha	Fannysha	Farizah	Fatima *(0.23)*
Ezequiela	Fadumina	Falechia	Fanshon	Farja	Fatimaa
Ezhane	Fadumo	Faleesha	Fanta0	Farjana	Fatimah *(0.02)*
Ezibel	Fadwa	Faleesia	Fantajah	Farnaz	Fatimata
Ezinwa	Fadymo	Faleisha	Fantanyzha	Farniz	Fatime
Ezleia	Fae	Falencia	Fantasha	Faro	Fatimeh
Ezmeralda	Faebrianna	Falesha	Fantashia	Faron	Fatin
Ezola	Faeeza	Falhad	Fantasía	Farra	Fatma *(0.01)*
Ezra	Faegen	Falicia *(0.01)*	Fantasia *(0.02)*	Farrah *(0.05)*	Fatmah
Ezri	Faellyn	Falicity	Fantasy	Farrahan	Fatmata
Ezria	Faelyn	Faliecia	Fantasya	Farrahn	Fatme *(0.01)*
Ezza	Faemia	Faliesha	Fantaysia	Farran	Fatmeh
	Faeythimani	Falilat	Fantazeon	Farrand	Fatoom
	Faezah	Falin	Fantazia	Farrel	Fatou
-F-	Fahda	Falina	Fantini	Farrell	Fatouma
F	Fahey	Faline	Fany *(0.01)*	Farren	Fatoumat
Fa'agaosa	Fahima	Falisa	Faolan	Farrin	Fatoumata
Fa'já	Fahjr	Falisaty	Fara	Farris	Fatumata
Fa'nise	Fahmeda	Falisha *(0.01)*	Faraci	Farron	Fau
Fa'tima	Fahreen	Falishia	Farah *(0.05)*	Farryne	Faula
Faa'izah	Fahren	Falisity	Faran	Fartoon	Faulk
Faaiu	Fahtima	Falista	Farandia	Farwa	Faunescia
Faanimo	Fai	Fallan	Farathiya	Farwa Fatima	Faustina
Faaria	Faibias	Fallen	Fardowsa	Faryaal	Fauve
Faatema	Faina	Fallon *(0.07)*	Fareaba	Faryal	Fauzia
Faatima	Faiqa	Fallyn	Fareeha	Faryn	Fauziya
Faatimah	Fairahn	Fallyne	Fareen	Farzana	Favda
Fabeha	Fairen	Fallynn	Fareezeh	Farzanah	Faven
Fabian	Fairlane	Falmatuu	Fareha	Farzeen	Faviana
Fabiana *(0.01)*	Fairley	Falon *(0.01)*	Faren	Faseeha	Faviola *(0.05)*
Fabianne	Fairren	Falonda	Fargol	Fashawna	Fawn *(0.01)*
Fabiene	Faisa	Falonia	Farha	Fashia	Fawna
Fabienne *(0.01)*	Faissa	Falyn *(0.01)*	Farhana	Fashon	Fawnna
Fabiola *(0.16)*	Faith *(0.62)*	Falysia	Farhanaz	Fasika	Fawzia
Fabiole	Faith Ashty	Famatta	Farheen	Fassan	Fawziah
Fabion	Faithann	Famia	Farhia	Fasshanta	Fay *(0.01)*
Fabree	Faithe	Fanatisa	Farhio	Fastima	Fayana
Fabrian	Faithlyne	Fancy	Farhiyo	Fatama	Faybriana
Fabriana	Faitia	Fandy	Faria	Fatdricka	Faydra
Fabrianna	Faiyh-Marie	Fane	Fariah	Fateemah	Faye *(0.02)*
Fabriciana	Faiza *(0.01)*	Faneisha	Fariby	Fateenma	Fayemae
Fabriella	Faizah	Faneshia	Farida	Fateiyyah	Fayeth
Fabrizia	Fakiara	Fanessa	Faridy	Fatema *(0.01)*	Fayette
Fabryann	Fakira	Fanfan	Farieza	Fatemah	Fayga
Fabu	Fala	Fang	Fariha *(0.01)*	Fatemah-Iman	Fayla
Fabyana	Falak	Fangufangumana	Farihah	Fatemasughra	Fayleah
Fabyola	Falan	Fangupo	Farilyn	Faten	Fayleen
Fachunda	Falana	Fania	Farin	Fateysha	Faylyn
Fadaa	Falanda	Fanifreda	Faris	Fathia	Faylynn
Fadashia	Falandra	Fanisha	Farisha	Fathima	Fayo
Fadeke	Falanne	Fannie *(0.03)*	Farishta	Fati	Fayola

Fayonda	Felica (0.01)	Fenita	Fierro	Flemmisha	Fnan
Fayrani	Felice (0.01)	Fenley	Fifi	Fleur-Rio	Foenasha
Fayten	Felicha	Fenn	Figrareti	Fleurette	Foever
Fayth	Felichia	Fennessey	Filah	Flisha	Folake
Faythe (0.01)	Felicia (0.72)	Fenton	Filestra	Flishea	Folasade
Faytlin	Felicia Anne	Fenya	Filia	Flissha	Folashade
Fayza	Felicia-Lynn	Feodosia	Filiberto	Flo'nesha	Fonda
Fazeela	Feliciana	Feofaneya	Filisha	Floli	Fontaine
Fazeena	Felicica	Feofania	Filomena	Flomeshia	Fontayne
Fazia	Felicidad	Feojha	Filomena-Cassidy	Flor (0.09)	Fontaysha
Fazila	Felicie	Feon	Filsan	Flora (0.03)	Fontella
Fe Lecia	Felicija	Feray	Fima	Florance	Foos
Fe Lexus	Felicita	Fergie	Fina	Floranisha	Foreesca
Féalia	Felicitaelissa	Ferha	Finau	Flordalia	Forest
Férren	Felicitas	Ferial	Findlay	Florde	Foreste
Fe-Neisha	Felicite	Ferica	Findley	Flordeliza-Marie	Forever
Feagia'i	Felicity (0.05)	Ferlanda	Finehika	Floreen	Forin
Fealicie	Felicya	Ferlisha	Finesse	Floreita	Foroozan
Feancé	Felina	Fermecha	Finey	Floreli'	Forrest (0.01)
Feather	Felipa	Fermeshé	Finia	Florelia	Forreste
Feaven	Felipe	Fermica	Finise	Florence (0.17)	Fortellia
Febe	Felisa (0.01)	Fern (0.01)	Finley	Florencia	Fortrina
Feben	Felisaa	Fernanda (0.08)	Finné	Florencio	Fortune
Febin	Felise	Fernande	Fion	Florendeana	Fosiyo
Febrian	Felisea	Ferne	Fiona (0.14)	Florenia	Foster
February	Felisha (0.07)	Ferniqua	Fionn	Florentina	Fosteriana
Feda	Felishia	Ferra	Fionna	Florette	Fotini
Feddia	Felisia	Ferralita	Fior	Floriana	Founding
Fedeline	Felisita	Ferran	Fiorella	Floriane	Fouziah
Federica	Felisity	Ferrari	Firdaus	Florianne	Fowsia
Fedghyne	Felissa	Ferrarie	Firdausnavdeep	Floribel	Fox
Fedia	Felissya	Ferria	Firdaws	Floricel	Foyg-Marie
Fedine	Felitsa	Ferron	Firdose	Floricela	Fozia
Fedlina	Feliz	Feryal	Fisher	Florida	Fra'shonna
Fedline	Feliza	Feryn	Fitisha	Florida-Mae	Frache
Fedora	Felizita	Feshanee	Fitzroya	Florie	Fraida
Fedoshia	Fellina	Fetima	Fiuna	Florie Lynn	Frakia
Feenicia	Felniqua	Feven	Fiver	Florina	Fran
Fei Xiang	Feltana	Feyonda	Fiyinfoluwa	Florindaersilia	Franca
Feile	Feltisha	Feyth	Fiza	Florine	Francal
Feisty	Felyce	Ffion	Fizza	Floriscel	Franccesca
Feitta	Felycia	Ffyona	Flamica	Florisela	France
Fekissa	Felysha	Fhelicia	Flannery	Florita	Francecesa
Felchia	Felyssia	Fianna	Flauriane	Floritzel	Franceen
Feldmena	Female (0.01)	Fiath	Flavi	Flormaria	Franceene
Feleacia	Femn	Fiavaai	Flavia	Flornell	Francees
Felecia (0.03)	Femy	Fiaza	Flavie (0.02)	Flory	Francel
Feleeza	Fendi	Fidalene	Flavie-Anne	Flossieanna	Francelene
Feleg	Feneisha	Fide	Fleasha	Floticia	Francelynne
Feleisha	Feness	Fidelia	Flecisha	Flowery	Francene
Felena	Fenessa	Fidelina	Fleeta	Floyd	Frances (0.25)
Felesha	Fenica	Fidon	Fleica	Floydisha	Francesa
Feleshia	Fenio	Fielding	Fleicha	Floyesha	Francesca (0.30)
Felestia	Fenisha	Fiera	Fleicia	Flyisha	Francese
Feleysa	Fenishe	Fierra	Fleming	Flynn	Franceska (0.01)

Francesmae
Francessca
Franchassica
Franchel
Franchella
Franchesca (0.05)
Francheska (0.02)
Franchesta
Franchonda
Francia
Francie
Francilia
Francina
Francine (0.05)
Francinia
Francinity
Francis (0.07)
Francisca (0.05)
Franciscá
Francisco
Francise
Franciska
Francoise (0.01)
Francy
Francyne
Francys
Frandine
Frandrika
Franeisha
Franesa
Franesha
Franeshia
Franiqua
Franiquia
Franisha
Franjellica
Franjessica
Franjetta
Frankcheska
Frankdesha
Franke
Frankecia
Frankee
Frankeia
Frankel
Frankesha
Frankevia
Franki (0.01)
Frankia
Frankie (0.07)
Frankisha
Frankita
Franklin
Franknesha
Franky

Frankye
Franmayca
Frannie
Franqolene
Franscesca
Franseka
Franshesca
Fransheska
Franshy
Fransisca
Franslene
Franszyska
Frantasia
Frantoria
Frany
Franzella
Franzinny
Franziska
Fraser
Fraxedy
Frazia
Fraziae
Frazier
Frédaizsha
Frea
Freasia
Frecia
Freda
Fredarleen
Fredcidra
Freddi
Freddie
Freddranique
Freddrica
Freddricka
Freddya
Fredecia
Frederica (0.01)
Fredericka
Fredericke
Frederika
Frederike (0.01)
Frederique (0.21)
Fredesha
Fredi
Fredia
Fredicka
Fredjane
Fredline
Fredozia
Fredreeka
Fredreka
Fredrica
Fredricia
Fredrick

Fredricka (0.01)
Fredriekia
Fredriká
Fredrika
Fredrique
Fredtasia
Free
Freechaeuh
Freeda
Freedia
Freedom (0.01)
Freeland
Freesia
Fregine
Freici
Freida
Fremecia
Frenchelle
Frenda
Frenequa
Frenika
Frenshay
Frenyadda
Freshta
Fresia
Frettina
Freya (0.01)
Freyja
Frezjá
Frica
Frida (0.02)
Friday
Frieda
Friederike
Frietzen
Frindeep
Friney
Frishta
Frithzi
Fritjeana
Fritzanna
Fritzi
Fritzlene
Fritznier
Fritzy
Froiline
Frona
Froncine
Fruma
Fubuki
Fuchsia
Fulvie
Fumika
Fumy
Fur'shanna

Furaisha
Furat
Furgaria
Furnisha
Furwah
Fuschia
Fushia
Futch
Futuria
Fuyuko
Fyla
Fylicity
Fyori

-G-

G
G Era
G Juana
G Nell
G Neque
G Su
G Terrika
G'aria
G'quesia
G'rina
G'teyia
G'vanni
G.
Ga
Ga Nasua
Ga'breesha
Ga'kia
Ga-Alo
Gab
Gab'vonna
Gabbie
Gabbriel
Gabbrielle
Gabbryel
Gabby
Gaberiele
Gaberille
Gabgielle
Gabi
Gabie
Gabina
Gabirelle
Gabraelle
Gabre
Gabreal
Gabreale
Gabrealle
Gabrecia
Gabreila

Gabreill
Gabreille
Gabrella
Gabrelle
Gabrellie
Gabri
Gabri'elle
Gabria
Gabrial
Gabriana
Gabrianna
Gabrieila
Gabriel (0.09)
Gabriela (1.50)
Gabriele (0.03)
Gabriele Cara
Gabrielia
Gabriell (0.01)
Gabriella (0.83)
Gabriella Nicole
Gabriella Victo
Gabriellá
Gabrielle (2.47)
Gabrielle Alexis
Gabrielle Elo
Gabrielle Maxine
Gabrielle Rae
Gabrielle-Anne
Gabrielle-Kathle
Gabriellia
Gabrielly
Gabrilla
Gabrille
Gabrina
Gabriylle
Gabryel
Gabryel-Marysa
Gabryell
Gabryella
Gabryelle
Gaby (0.02)
Gadari
Gade
Gadeer
Gadreal
Gaebreille
Gaebriell
Gaebrielle
Gaelan
Gaeli
Gaelle (0.01)
Gaelyn
Gagan
Gagandeep (0.01)
Gagandip

Gaganjeet
Gaganjit
Gaganjote
Gaganjoyt
Gaganpreet
Gaganveer
Gage
Gagnadeep
Gagndeep
Gagneet
Gagnvir
Gahdeer
Gaia
Gaibrell
Gaige
Gail (0.02)
Gail-Ann
Gailen
Gailon
Gailya
Gailynn
Gaites
Gaitha
Gaitlynn
Gaitri
Gajana
Gal
Gala
Galaa
Galasia
Galaxy
Galdina
Gale
Galen (0.01)
Galesia
Galfreet
Galia
Galicia
Galilea
Galilee
Galina
Galisa
Galissia
Galit
Gallia
Gallila
Galya
Galyn
Galynn
Galyzet
Gamaathige
Gamaleah
Gamarha
Gamesha
Gamia

Gana'sha	Garrinika	Gazzalpreet	Gelemanie	Genée	Genisha
Ganaé	Garrisen	Ge Na	Gelen	Geneia	Genisis
Ganelle	Garrison	Ge Sherra	Geliani	Geneieve	Genita
Ganesa	Garrity	Géashia	Gelice	Geneiva	Geniva
Ganevia	Garshá	Gékeisha	Gelicia	Geneka	Genive
Ganiece	Garth	Gékeyra	Gelila	Genel	Genivieve
Ganika	Gartrina	Géniya	Geline	Genelia	Genmari
Ganneet	Gary	Geah	Gelisa	Genell	Genna (0.02)
Gaoshoua	Garyana	Geahna	Gelise	Genella	Genna Bre
Gaothajying	Garyfalia	Geana	Gelisia	Genelle	Genna-Lynne
Gar	Garyka	Geaná	Gelissa	Genequa	Gennae
Gara	Garyn	Geanelly	Gellakate	Genero	Gennah
Garalea	Garyyonna	Geanette	Gelsey	Generosa	Gennavie
Garanique	Gasaniyosta	Geania	Gelsomina	Genes	Gennaya
Garbeille	Gatanna	Geanna (0.01)	Gem	Genese	Gennea
Garbielle	Gataysiah	Geanné	Gema (0.03)	Genesha	Gennel
Garbo	Gatelle	Geannia	Gemara	Genesia	Gennelle
Garcelle	Gates	Gearldine	Gemari	Genesis (0.40)	Gennene
Garcia	Gatlin	Geavoni	Gemasha	Genesis Yopaxis	Gennesis
Garciela	Gaudelupe	Geborah	Gemeka	Genesis'	Gennesserret
Gardenia (0.02)	Gaudencia	Gebrielle	Gemelin	Genesis-Ibeth	Gennessis
Gardinia	Gauge	Gechelle	Gemima	Genesiss	Gennet
Garenika	Gauri	Geddy	Gemini	Genessa	Gennevi
Garett	Gavi	Geder	Gemintang	Genesse	Gennger
Gargi	Gavin	Gederica	Gemisha	Genessie	Gennia
Gariel	Gavion	Gee	Gemma (0.04)	Genessis (0.01)	Gennice
Gariell	Gavita	Geeanna	Gemmy	Genet	Gennie
Garielle	Gavneet	Geena (0.07)	Gena (0.03)	Genetha	Gennifer (0.01)
Garien	Gavonna	Geerthana	Genae	Genette	Genniflore
Gariesha	Gavrayell	Geerthanna	Genaé	Geneva (0.10)	Gennine
Garima	Gavriela	Geertiga	Genai	Geneve	Gennise
Garine	Gavriella	Geet	Genaise	Genevera	Genny
Garion	Gavrielle	Geeta	Genalynn	Genevi	Genoa
Garionna	Gavy	Geetaj	Genamarie	Genevie	Genova
Garisha	Gavynne	Geetanjly	Genan	Genevieve (0.43)	Genovee
Gariunna	Gayadiri	Geethana	Genara	Genevieve Milix	Genoveva
Gariza	Gayathri	Geethega	Genasee	Genevive	Genriel
Garland	Gayatri	Geethena	Genava	Genevra	Genseska
Garlen	Gaybrial	Geethu	Genaveeve	Genica	Gentelle
Garline	Gaybrianna	Geetika	Genaveve	Genice	Gentian
Garmai	Gaybrielle	Geettana	Genavie	Genicia	Gentiana
Garmen	Gayge	Geetu	Genavieve	Genicis	Gentilissa
Garmikly	Gayla (0.01)	Gehan	Genavive	Genie (0.01)	Gentle
Garnea	Gayle (0.01)	Geimy	Genay	Genien	Gently
Garneet	Gaylen	Geiri	Gendell	Genieveve	Gentrell
Garnet	Gaylene	Geisell	Gendra	Genifer	Gentri
Garoneisha	Gayly	Geissa	Gene	Genika	Gentricia
Garrett	Gaylyn	Gekera	Gené	Genikki	Gentrie
Garri	Gaynelle	Gekeriiya	Genétria	Genina	Gentry (0.01)
Garrido	Gaynisha	Gekeyia	Genea	Genine	Genua
Garriela	Gaynor	Gelasia	Geneca	Geniqua	Genysis
Garrielle	Gaython	Gelcys	Genecei	Genis	Geomara
Garriesha	Gazal	Gelda	Genecia	Genise	Geon
Garrika	Gazhia	Geleen	Genecis	Genises	Geonna

Geonoir	Geovanna *(0.01)*	Germain	Gestine	Gianina	Ginamarie
Geor Qecia	Geovonna	Germaine	Getara	Gianinna	Ginan
Geor'nai	Gequeesha	Germanee	Getasha	Gianna *(0.21)*	Ginasia
Geor'shyla	Ger'kima	Germanek	Getaya	Giannarae	Gindresska
Geordan	Gera	Germani	Geterria	Gianne	Gineen
Geordayne	Gerae	Germanie	Getruda	Giannee	Ginei'ja
Geordeesia	Gerald	Germanié	Getryna	Giannely	Ginell
Georga	Geralda	Germaris	Gevenina	Gianni	Ginelle
Georgann	Geraldda	Germecia	Gewndolyn	Giannie	Ginesha
Georganna	Geraldin	Germeisha	Gexenia	Giannina	Gineska
George-Gina	Geraldina	Germeka	Geyana	Giannis	Ginett
Georgea	Geraldine *(0.05)*	Germesha	Geydy	Gianny	Ginette
Georgeann	Geraldmeka	Germikia	Geysi	Giara	Ginger *(0.04)*
Georgeanna	Geraldneka	Germisha	Geyzi	Giaszmyne	Ginger Mae Jani
Georgeanne	Geraldyne	Gernecia	Gezelle	Giavanna	Gini
Georgeena	Geralin	Gernera	Gezzelle	Giavonna	Ginicia
Georgelle	Geralkeesia	Gernesha	Gha'kora	Giavonni	Ginienashly
Georgena	Geralrisha	Gernika	Ghada	Gibbons	Ginika
Georgenia	Geraltine	Gerniva	Ghadear	Gibron	Ginikach
Georgesula	Geralyn	Gero'ne	Ghadeer	Gibson	Ginikanwa
Georgetta	Geralynn	Gerolyn	Ghadir	Gicela	Ginna
Georgette *(0.02)*	Geranda	Gerquel	Ghalitt	Gicell	Ginnean
Georgfia	Gerardine	Gerra	Ghané	Gidget	Ginnelle
Georggianna	Gerbrialyn	Gerrenee	Ghania	Giedre	Ginnesica
Georgi	Gerda	Gerri *(0.01)*	Ghanwa	Giemilyn	Ginny *(0.01)*
Georgia *(0.19)*	Gereisha	Gerri-Ale	Ghaundra	Gien	Ginnypher
Georgia-May	Gerell	Gerria	Ghayda	Giera	Ginta
Georgialee	Gerelynn	Gerriane	Ghazal	Gierra	Ginthuga
Georgialei	Geresia	Gerrianna	Ghea	Gift	Ginu
Georgiana *(0.01)*	Gerhonda	Gerrica	Gheannieveleen	Giggi	Ginya
Georgiann	Geri *(0.01)*	Gerricá	Ghezal	Gigi *(0.01)*	Gioia
Georgianna *(0.01)*	Geri Keona	Gerricka	Ghina	Gihanny	Gioialina
Georgianne	Geriah	Gerrida	Ghisele	Gikarra	Giolany
Georgie *(0.01)*	Gerian	Gerrie	Ghislaine	Gila	Gionna
Georgieann	Geriana	Gerrika	Ghizal	Gilandria	Gionny
Georgieonna	Geriann	Gerrilee	Ghofran	Gilberte	Giordana
Georgina *(0.09)*	Gerica *(0.01)*	Gerrinisha	Ghoufron	Gilbresha	Giorgia
Georgy	Gericka	Gerrise	Ghufran	Gilda	Giorgianna
Georiamay	Gerika	Gerry	Ghufron	Gilesa	Giorgina
Georja	Gerilene	Gerscel	Gi	Gilian	Giorgio
Georjina	Gerilynn	Gertha	Gi-Yuen	Gilleece	Giori
Georleny	Gerine	Gertie	Gia *(0.01)*	Gillen	Giovana
Georlyci	Gerinelle	Gertruda	Gia Carolin	Gillermina	Giovanna *(0.09)*
Geormika	Gerisha	Gertrude *(0.01)*	Gia'nna	Gillian *(0.14)*	Giovanne
Georna	Geritta	Gertruida	Gialeshia	Gillianne	Giovanni *(0.01)*
Geornée	Gerizma	Gertude	Giana *(0.03)*	Gillis	Giovannica
Georneisha	Gerkaria	Gertyra	Gianaia	Gilma	Giovannina
Geornerika	Gerkeriá	Gervaise	Gianandria	Gilmore	Giovonna
Georrina	Gerkeviá	Geselle	Gianell	Gimarian	Gipsi
Georvon	Gerlicia	Gesika	Gianella	Gimena	Gira
Georvonna	Gerlinde	Gesile	Gianelle	Gina *(0.57)*	Giralda
Geory	Gerlisa	Gessalynn	Gianesha	Gina Maria	Girasol
Geosha	Gerlonda	Gessenip	Giang	Ginai	Girija
Geovana	Gerlynn	Gessica	Giangela	Ginamaria	Girlie

Girolama	Gladys *(0.14)*	Glorya	Grabueka	Gratia	Greyson
Girselda Briunn	Glaire	Gloryah	Grace *(1.43)*	Graviela	Greysyn
Girthamarie	Glayna	Gloryanne	Grace Anne	Gray	Gricelda *(0.02)*
Gisel *(0.02)*	Gléquita	Glorymar	Grace Champa	Grayce *(0.01)*	Gricelle
Gisela *(0.04)*	Gleannan	Glovanna	Grace Lee	Graydon	Gricenia
Giselda	Glecia	Glynda	Grace-Ann	Graysen	Griecharlie
Gisele	Glee	Glyneva	Graceann	Graysie	Grier
Gisell *(0.01)*	Glen	Glynnecia	Graceanna	Grayson *(0.03)*	Griffen
Gisella	Glena	Glynnisha	Graceanne	Grayson-Mhykelti	Griffin
Giselle *(0.18)*	Glenah	Glys	Gracee	Grazel	Grisdelin
Gisemonde	Glenaija	Gnaajwi	Gracela	Grazia	Grisel *(0.02)*
Gislaine	Glenazia	Gnae	Gracelaine	Graziano	Griselda *(0.14)*
Gissel *(0.02)*	Glenda *(0.05)*	Gnanaluxumy	Graceland	Graziela	Grisell
Gissela	Glendalis	Gneshia	Gracelena	Graziella	Griselle
Gissell	Glendaly	Gobriella	Gracelinda	Grénisha	Grishma
Gissella	Glendine	Goddess	Gracely	Greccia	Grismarie
Gisselle *(0.03)*	Glendy	Goddia	Gracelyn *(0.01)*	Grechy	Grissel
Gisun	Glendyz	Godinez	Gracelynn	Grecia *(0.05)*	Grisselda
Gita	Glenesha	Godnela	Gracemarie	Grecia Elizabeth	Grissell
Gital	Glenesia	Godnette	Gracemelly	Greer *(0.01)*	Grizcelda
Gitana	Glenezia	Gofan	Gracen *(0.01)*	Grefaria	Grizel
Gitanjali	Glenis	Gohar	Gracey	Gregkia	Groff
Gitty	Glenise	Goivanna	Gracia	Gregnisha	Gruenetter
Giulana	Glenisha	Golda	Graciana	Gregori	Guada
Giulia *(0.01)*	Glenlinda	Goldamare	Gracianna	Gregoria	Guadalupe *(0.77)*
Giulia Albuquer	Glenn	Golden	Gracie *(0.05)*	Gregory	Guadelop
Giuliana *(0.01)*	Glenna *(0.02)*	Goldie *(0.01)*	Graciela *(0.12)*	Gregory'anna	Guadelupe
Giulianna	Glenne	Golfo	Graciella	Gregoryanti	Guadlupe
Giulliana	Glenneshia	Goli	Gracilia	Gregoryell	Guanesha
Giusepina	Glennia	Golzar	Gracine	Gregoryiana	Guartola
Giuseppina *(0.01)*	Glennis	Gomes	Gracinta	Gregoryonia	Gudalupe
Givana	Glennisha	Gon	Graciona	Greniqua	Guendi
Givedio	Glennora	Gonul	Gracy	Grequcia	Guendis
Givens	Glenshaye	Gonxhe	Gracyn *(0.01)*	Gresalda	Guenevere
Giverny	Glentoria	Gonzalez	Gracynn	Gresha	Guenivere
Givionce	Glenys	Gopena	Graecie	Greshawna	Guerdine
Givonna	Glori	Gopi	Graelyn	Gresheena	Guerland
Giyan	Gloria *(0.45)*	Gopika	Graf	Greshunna	Guerline
Gizan	Gloriana	Gordana	Graham	Greta *(0.04)*	Guerreline
Gizel	Gloriann	Gordina	Graice	Greta Madeline	Guia
Gizela	Glorianna	Gordon	Graicen	Gretalee	Guiliana
Gizele	Glorianne	Goretti	Grainne	Gretchen *(0.09)*	Guillaine
Gizelle *(0.01)*	Glorias	Gorgia	Graison	Gretchin	Guillerma
Gizem	Gloribee	Gorgonia	Graisyn	Gretchyn	Guillermina *(0.01)*
Gizman	Gloribel	Goriann	Graite	Gretel	Guillian
Gjervonna	Glorie	Gorsharen	Gralicia	Greterra	Guinevere
Gla'neita	Glorielle	Gortaejan	Gramolt	Grethel	Guiosmary
Glacia	Glorijanaa	Gorvie	Granada	Gretta *(0.01)*	Guisselle
Gladeana	Glorimar	Goua	Granique	Grettel	Guisset
Gladi	Glorinez	Gourisree	Grant	Gretzchen	Gulap
Gladiola	Gloris	Gowsika	Granville	Grey	Gulcan
Gladis *(0.03)*	Glorisa	Goyesha	Grashonda	Greylin	Guleena
Gladiz	Gloriyia	Grabiela	Grasiela	Greylynn	Gulianna
Glady	Glory *(0.01)*	Grabriela	Grasien	Greyonna	Gulie
Glady's	Glory Anne	Grabrielle	Grasyn	Greysen	Gulnaz

Gulsun	Gurtej	Gyllian	Haddi	Hai	Hakeema
Guneet	Gurtinder	Gynefer	Haddy	Hai-Mi	Hakeeya
Guneetinder	Gurveen	Gynelle	Hadeel (0.01)	Haia	Hakimah
Gungeet	Gurveena	Gyntrelle	Hadelyne	Haicha	Hakira
Gunjan	Gurveer	Gypsie	Haden	Haida	Hala (0.01)
Gunneet	Gurvina	Gypsy	Hadia	Haide	Halah
Gunreet	Gurvinder	Gyriah	Hadija	Haidee	Halaina
Guntash	Gurvir	Gysell	Hadijah	Haidi	Halal
Gupal	Gushonda		Hadil	Haidn	Halan
Gur	Gustavia	**-H-**	Hadir	Haidy	Halana (0.01)
Guramardeep	Gutana		Hadiya	Haidyn	Halance
Gurandeep	Guthrie	H (0.02)	Hadiyah	Haiely	Halbeydi
Gurasees	Guy	H Jaryn Danyel	Hadiyyah	Haifa	Hale
Gurasha	Guya	H'martha	Hadiza	Hailah	Haléna
Gurasis	Guyer	H-Nancy	Hadleigh	Haile (0.01)	Halea
Gurdeep	Guylynn	H-Racel	Hadley (0.03)	Hailea	Haleah
Gurinder	Guymly	H.	Hadli	Hailee (0.17)	Halee (0.05)
Gurjapvir	Guynikka	Ha	Hadlie	Hailee-Lynn	Haleema
Gurjas	Gvensha	Ha Ane	Hadly	Hailee-Marie	Haleena
Gurjeet	Gwashauna	Ha Ani	Hady	Haileevaun	Haleh
Gurjinder	Gwen (0.01)	Ha Eun	Hadyn	Hailei	Halei
Gurjit	Gwenasha	Ha'shida	Hae (0.01)	Haileigh (0.01)	Haleigh (0.23)
Gurjiv	Gwenda	Ha-Young	Haeden	Hailena	Haleigh-Rain
Gurjiven	Gwendalin	Haadia	Haein	Hailey (1.46)	Haleighr
Gurjiwan	Gwendalyn	Haadiah	Haela	Hailey-Ann	Haleliah
Gurjot (0.01)	Gwendalynn	Haadiya	Haelee	Hailey-Lynn	Halema
Gurkamaljot	Gwendelyn	Haafizah	Haeleigh	Haili (0.02)	Halen
Gurkeerat	Gwendelynn	Haala	Haeley (0.01)	Hailie (0.03)	Halena
Gurkiran	Gwendilyn	Haania	Haeli	Hailiegh	Haley (3.84)
Gurkirat	Gwendlyan	Haarika	Haelie	Hailin	Haley Alexandra
Gurleen (0.02)	Gwendolen	Haaya	Haelleigh	Haille	Haley Dawn
Gurlenena	Gwendolin	Habeeba	Haelli	Haillee	Haley Katelynn
Gurmail	Gwendoline	Haben	Haellie	Hailley	Haley-Anne
Gurman	Gwendolyn (0.11)	Haberlin	Haely	Hailli	Haley-Marie
Gurminder	Gwendolynn	Habiba	Haena	Haillie	Haleyanna
Gurmohit	Gweneth	Habibah	Haeun	Hailly	Haleyanne
Gurneet (0.01)	Gwenevere	Habibeh	Haeve	Haily (0.04)	Haleyjean
Gurnimrat	Gwenija	Habon	Haevyn	Hailyn	Haleyna
Gurnisha	Gwenisha	Habone	Haezel	Haimee	Hali (0.09)
Gurnit	Gwenissiea	Habsii	Hafeeza	Haiqa	Halie (0.15)
Gurnoor	Gwenna	Habu	Hafiya	Haisa	Haliegh
Gurpinder	Gwenyth	Hac-Tu	Hafiz	Haiwatha	Haliey
Gurpreet (0.02)	Gwone	Hada	Hafizah	Haizel	Halima (0.01)
Gurprit	Gwyn	Hadar	Hafsa (0.01)	Haja	Halimah
Gurpriya	Gwyndolyn	Hadara	Hafsah	Hajaera	Halimasadia
Gursahiba	Gwyneth	Hadas	Hafza	Hajar (0.01)	Halimatu
Gursangeet	Gwynndolen	Hadasah	Hagan	Hajara	Halimo
Gursawarn	Gwynne	Hadasha	Hagar	Hajer	Halina
Gurshan	Gwynneth	Hadashia	Hagen	Hajera	Halisia
Gursharan	Gyanelin	Hadassa	Hager	Hajir	Haliyah
Gursharn	Gyanna	Hadassah (0.01)	Haggar	Hajira	Hall
Gursharon	Gyasi	Hadaya	Hahlay	Hajjar	Halla (0.01)
Gursimaranjit	Gybe	Haddah	Hahnji	Hajra	Hallah
Gursimran	Gyekyewa	Haddasa	Hahnna	Hajraa	Halle (0.11)
Gursimrat	Gylian	Haddasah	Hahyoung	Hakeem	Hallé

Hallee *(0.01)*	Hananah	Hanny	Harley Danielle	Harsift	Havan
Halleigh	Hananh	Hannyl	Harli *(0.01)*	Harsimarjit	Havana
Halleleyah	Hane	Hansini	Harliann	Harsimran *(0.01)*	Havanna
Halleshia	Hanean	Hanslene	Harlie *(0.05)*	Harsimrat	Havannah
Hallett	Haneda	Hanson	Harlie Antoinette	Harsimrin	Haven *(0.05)*
Halley *(0.06)*	Haneefa	Hanwen	Harlow	Harsimryn	Havilah
Halli *(0.01)*	Haneen *(0.01)*	Hanya	Harlynn	Harsirat	Havird
Hallie *(0.18)*	Haneet	Hanyn	Harmala	Hart	Havyn
Hallima	Haneisha	Hao	Harman	Hartasia	Hawa
Halloran	Hanen	Hao-Anna	Harmandeep	Harte	Hawaa
Hally	Hang	Happi	Harmanjit	Hartemese	Hawalul
Hallye	Hanh	Happie A	Harmanpreet	Hartley	Haweya
Halona	Hanh-Ngoc	Happy	Harmeen	Hartman	Hawkins
Halonah	Hanha	Har'coya	Harmeet *(0.01)*	Haruka	Hawlee
Halpern	Hania	Hara	Harmene	Harveen	Hawleigh
Halsea	Haniesha	Haram	Harmeni	Harveer	Hawley
Halsey	Hanifah	Harbani	Harmin	Harven	Hawn
Halsie	Hanim	Harbir	Harminder	Harvest	Hawo
Halston	Hanin	Harbour	Harmon	Harvinder	Hawra
Haly	Hanine	Hardaijah	Harmonee	Harvir	Hawraa
Halye	Hanisha	Hardeep	Harmonei	Harwinder	Hawthorn
Halyn	Hanita	Harding	Harmoni	Hasanati	Hay
Hamam	Haniya	Hareem	Harmonie	Hasanki	Hay-Mann
Hamamalini	Hanlin	Hareer	Harmony *(0.09)*	Hasanna	Haya *(0.01)*
Hamasha	Hanmar	Harena	Harmony-Sky	Hasanpreet	Hayaat
Hamda	Hanna *(0.57)*	Hargot	Harmorisa	Haseena	Hayat *(0.01)*
Hamdalat	Hanna-Leah	Hariet	Harnanun	Hasel	Hayate
Hamdi *(0.01)*	Hanna-Louisa	Harina	Harneet *(0.01)*	Hashana	Hayatt
Hameet	Hannaa	Harinder	Harneshia	Hashekia	Hayde
Hami	Hannah *(7.60)*	Harini	Harnoor	Hashika	Haydee
Hamida	Hannah Camille	Haripriya	Haroiana	Hashtwana	Haydelis
Hamidah	Hannah Christine	Harishan	Haroline	Hasina	Haydelyn
Hamilla	Hannah Denise	Harjazmin	Harolyn	Hasna	Hayden *(0.06)*
Hamilton	Hannah Grace	Harjeet	Haroneka	Hassana	Haydin
Hamma	Hannah Rae	Harjit	Harpal	Hassna	Haydn
Hamms	Hannah-Grace	Harjiwan	Harper *(0.02)*	Hassona	Haydon
Hamree	Hannah-Jayne	Harjot *(0.01)*	Harpinder	Hassti	Haydy
Hamrin	Hannah-Jo	Harkamal	Harpreet *(0.02)*	Hassuyi	Hayeon
Hamrit	Hannah-Leigh	Harkiran	Harprit	Hasti	Hayes
Hamsa	Hannah-Mae	Harkirat	Harpuneet	Hastina	Hayette
Hamsananthy	Hannah-Marie	Harkirn	Harriet *(0.01)*	Hasumi	Hayhle
Hamsini	Hannah-Michelle	Harkomal	Harriett	Hatara	Hayla
Hamza	Hannah-Rae	Harlan	Harrington	Hatice	Haylan
Han	Hannah-Ruth	Harlea	Harris	Hatin	Hayle *(0.02)*
Han Nan	Hannahniah	Harleah	Harrisia	Hatley	Haylea *(0.02)*
Hana *(0.12)*	Hannalee	Harleanna	Harrison	Hatsal	Haylee *(0.27)*
Hanaan	Hannalore	Harlee *(0.04)*	Harryl	Hatte	Haylee-Ann
Hanadee	Hannan	Harleen *(0.02)*	Harshana	Hatti	Haylei
Hanadi	Hannay	Harleey	Harsharonpreet	Hattie *(0.02)*	Hayleigh *(0.04)*
Hanae	Hanne	Harlei	Harshdeep	Hattilyn	Haylen
Hanah *(0.03)*	Hanneaka	Harleigh *(0.02)*	Harshehnaz	Hau	Hayley *(1.19)*
Hanai	Hannelore	Harlene	Harshika	Haua	Hayleyann
Hanako	Hanni	Harlequine	Harshita	Hauley	Hayli *(0.02)*
Hanamarie	Hannia	Harlequinn	Harshmeet	Haushawn	Hayli-Jean
Hanan *(0.02)*	Hanniah	Harley *(0.32)*	Harshpreet	Hava	Haylie *(0.09)*

Haylin	Heeba	Hellena	Herlinda *(0.01)*	Hidori	Hira-Maja
Haylle	Heela	Hellyn	Herline	Hidri	Hirah
Hayllie	Heelorie	Helmi	Hermandeep	Hidy	Hiral
Hayly	Heema	Helms	Hermeisha	Hiede	Hirangi
Haylyn	Heena *(0.01)*	Heloise *(0.01)*	Hermelinda	Hiedi	Hirari
Haymee	Heer	Helon	Hermenia	Hiediann	Hiren
Hayshia	Heera	Helvi	Hermesha	Hien *(0.01)*	Hiroka
Hayven	Heeral	Helyena	Hermina	Hieneka	Hirokazu
Hazannah	Hei	Helyn	Hermine	Hiep	Hisel
Hazel *(0.07)*	Heide	Hema	Herminia *(0.01)*	Hieu Kathy	Hisha
Hazell	Heidee	Hemakshi	Herminna	Hifa	Hishale
Hazelle	Heidi *(0.50)*	Hemita	Herneisha	Hifsa	Hisnaybi
Hazelynn	Heidi Dawn	Hemna	Herneishia	Hightower	Hitaishi
Hazen	Heidie	Hemwattie	Hernesha	Hikari	Hitomi
Hazlett	Heidy *(0.05)*	Hen'qerriah	Herolia	Hikendrea	Hitzel
Hazmavely	Heighly	Hena	Heron	Hil	Hiu
Hazzell	Heike	Henaa	Herrin	Hila	Hiwot
Hea Mee	Heiley	Henah	Hershell	Hilaire	Hiyawan
Healah	Heili	Hend	Hershini	Hilal	Hizela
Healey	Heilin	Henderson	Hersimran	Hilalo	Hjen
Heallan	Heim	Hendiah	Hersline	Hilari	Hli
Healy	Hein	Hendley	Hervela	Hilaria	Hlima
Heanna	Heisha	Heni	Heshlyn	Hilary *(0.12)*	Hlimah
Heaqther	Helai	Henley	Hesmeralda	Hilary-Anne	Hnai
Heath	Helaina *(0.01)*	Henna *(0.02)*	Hesper	Hilda *(0.07)*	Ho
Heather *(2.96)*	Helaine	Henneiceyah	Hester	Hildelisa	Hoainam
Heather-Ann	Helan	Henneka	Hesther	Hiliary	Hoang
Heather-Lyn	Helana *(0.01)*	Hennessey	Heta	Hilina	Hoang-Anh
Heather-Lynn	Helaná	Hennessy	Hetal	Hilit	Hobie
Heather-Marie	Helania	Henny	Hether	Hill	Hoc
Heatheranne	Helanie	Henrelle	Hettie	Hilla	Hocelyn
Heatherjene	Helda	Henretta	Hetty	Hillachel	Hoda *(0.01)*
Heatherlea	Heldana	Henrietta *(0.01)*	Heustolia	Hillaree	Hodan *(0.01)*
Heatherrenee	Heleana	Henry-Ana	Hevean	Hillarey	Hodazhamaniwin
Heathur	Heleena	Hensherriek	Heven	Hillari	Hoden
Heaven *(0.17)*	Heleine	Hensley	Hevenly	Hillarie	Hodges
Heaven Shantel	Helen *(0.43)*	Henterrika	Hevin	Hillary *(0.20)*	Hodo
Heaven-Leigh	Helena *(0.18)*	Hera	Heyam	Hillery	Hodon
Heavenlee	Helene *(0.05)*	Heran	Heydy	Hilli	Hoffman
Heavenleigh	Helenia	Herandi	Hiba *(0.01)*	Hilliary	Hoi
Heavenley	Helennahae	Herbdricka	Hiba Hisham	Hilluian	Hoi-Lok
Heavenly	Heley	Herbeneisha	Hibah	Hilman	Hok
Heaveny	Helga	Herberta	Hiban	Himali	Hokulani
Heavien	Helgon	Herbnesh	Hibaq	Himani	Holden
Heavin	Helia	Herbrena	Hibatual	Himara	Holeigh
Heavon	Heliana	Herchele	Hibaz	Himika	Holiday
Heavyn	Helicia	Herchran	Hibba	Hin	Holidia
Heba *(0.01)*	Helin	Herékia	Hibbatun	Hina *(0.01)*	Holin
Hebada	Helina	Herendida	Hibbo	Hind	Holladay
Hebah	Helisabet	Herendira	Hibo	Hinda	Holland *(0.02)*
Hedi	Helizabet	Herica	Hicela	Hine	Holleah
Hedwa	Hella	Herjoat	Hicks	Hinna	Hollee *(0.01)*
Hedy	Helle	Herkiran	Hida	Hinsene	Holleena
Hee	Hellen *(0.02)*	Herleen	Hidaya	Hinson	Holleigh
Hee-Yeong	Hellen Hong	Herliene	Hidie	Hira *(0.01)*	Holleonna

Holley *(0.02)*	Hor	Hunter *(0.35)*	Hystri	Iankia	Idalmis
Holley Brooke	Horache	Hunter Danielle	Hyun	Ianlys	Idaly
Holley Grace	Horeisha	Hunter-Lee	Hyun Sue	Iann	Idania
Holli *(0.06)*	Horia	Hunter-Paige	Hyun-Jeong	Ianna	Idara
Holli Lu	Horlisha	Hunter-Pheonix	Hyun-Sook	Iannel	Idarae
Holli-Lyne	Hormon	Huntter	Hyunchung	Iannesha	Idarmis
Holliá	Hornecia	Huong *(0.01)*	Hyunyoung	Ianneysha	Idasha
Hollianne	Hortencia	Huriya		Iantha	Idasia
Holliday	Hortensia	Hurley	**-I-**	Iara	Idaysha
Hollie *(0.11)*	Hosack	Hursula		Iasbella	Idazha
Hollina	Hosaena	Hushaiana	I	Iasia	Ideatrice
Hollis *(0.01)*	Hosanna *(0.01)*	Husna	I Jonnika	Iasmone	Ideesha
Holly *(1.32)*	Hosanne	Husnia	I Keria	Iatiana	Idelande
Holly Delilah	Hoshiahna	Hutchins	I Keshia	Ibanez	Idelis
Holly-Ann	Hosna	Hutton	I Kia	Ibarra	Idella
Holly-Jolene	Hoson	Huxley	I Meshia	Ibeth	Idelys
Holly-Joy	Hossai	Huyana	I Munique	Ibethe	Idesha
Hollyann	Hossana	Huyen *(0.01)*	I Naetra	Ibis	Idette
Hollyanne	Hotonah	Huynh	I Neshia	Ibrei	Idia
Hollyaunj A	Hou	Hwa-Jin	I Tonia	Ibreionna	Idialis
Hollye	Houda *(0.01)*	Hy	I'ecia	Ibreonna	Idil *(0.01)*
Hollyn *(0.01)*	Houra	Hy'keema	I'eisha	Ibriana	Idil-Ardirihanan
Hollynn	Houriah	Hyacinth	I'esha	Ibtihaj	Idman
Holman	Houston	Hyam	I'eshia	Ibtijah	Idna
Holsey	Howel'thea	Hyanet	I'jae	Iccel	Idocia
Holton	Howetha	Hyapatia	I'keisha	Iceala	Idolina
Homa	Hrania	Hyatt	I'leanna	Icealina	Idona
Homaira	Hrisoula	Hyddie	I'mani	Iceiawna	Idraia
Homer	Hristina	Hyde	I'nari	Icela	Idre Anna
Homera	Hristy	Hydea	I'reka	Icelene	Idriana
Homira	Hsin-Hsueh	Hydee	I'saaz	Iceline	Idrissa
Homma	Hubble	Hydeia *(0.01)*	I'sakhiyia	Icelle	Idsiar
Honar	Hubertine	Hydi	I'sha	Ices	Idy
Honbit	Huda *(0.02)*	Hydia	I'sis	Icesis	Iétausjua
Honda	Hudda	Hydie	I'tesia	Icess	Ieasha *(0.01)*
Honeina	Hudson	Hydiea	I'tiauna	Icesse	Ieashe
Honestee	Hue	Hydn	I'tionna	Icey	Ieasher
Honesti	Hufsa	Hye-Jee	I'toina	Ichrisha	Iecha
Honestie	Hufsah	Hye-Soo	I'yana	Icia	Ieesha
Honesty *(0.01)*	Hugo	Hyebinn	I'yanah	Icis	Ieisa
Honesty-Lynn	Hui	Hyett	I'yaunah	Icisist	Ieisha *(0.01)*
Honey	Huida	Hykiesha	I'zanique	Icsel	Ieishia
Honeyzib	Huisun	Hyla	I'zerriya	Icuria	Ieishlia
Hong-Loan	Hulda	Hylan	I-Asia	Icy	Ieman
Honnor	Hulya	Hyleah	I-Won	Ida *(0.04)*	Iemima
Honor	Huma	Hylisha	Ia	Ida-Marie	Iemonei
Honora	Humaira	Hynephia	Iaian	Idah	Ienaisha
Hontur	Humairaa	Hyoeun	Iain	Idahlia	Iera
Hoodo	Humayra	Hyojung	Iaisha	Idalesse	Iesa
Hope *(0.55)*	Humera	Hypacha	Iajaira	Idalia *(0.02)*	Iescha
Hope-Daniel	Hummara	Hyriah	Iakeshia	Idalis *(0.01)*	Iesha *(0.11)*
Hope-Shelia	Humna	Hyrian	Iakira	Idalise	Ieshah
Hopefull	Hun	Hyroop	Ialiyah	Idaliz	Ieshea
Hopeton	Hunar	Hysionna	Ian *(0.01)*	Idallas	Iesheia
Hopkins	Huntar	Hyson	Iana	Idallis	Ieshia *(0.02)*

Ieshora	Ikharia	Iliriana	Imane	Indago	Indygo
Ieshua	Ikhlas	Ilirida	Imané	Indaia	Indyka
Iesla	Ikia	Ilisa	Imane-Amina	Indaita	Ineabelisse
Ieva	Ikiea	Ilish	Imani (0.33)	Indalecia	Ineia
Ieyeshia	Ikierae	Ilisha	Imani Khaliaah	Indanecia	Ineicia
Ife	Ikiia	Ilissa	Imani'	Inde	Ineid
Ifechi	Ikima	Iliza	Imanie	Indéa	Ineikqua
Ifedolapo	Ikina	Ilka	Imanii	Indeah	Ineisha
Ifeoma	Ikjot	Illa	Imara	Indee	Inell
Ifetayo	Ikku	Illanté	Imari (0.03)	Indeep	Ines (0.03)
Ifeyi	Ikra	Illé	Imaris	Indega	Inesha
Ifeyinwa	Ikram	Illeana	Imarra	Indeia	Inesha-S
Ifrah (0.01)	Ikran	Illia	Imaya	Indera	Ineshia
Ifreke	Ikria	Illiana	Imbré	Inderdeep	Inessa
Ignacia	Ikumi	Illianexie	Ime	Inderia	Inetha
Igran	Ila (0.01)	Illianise	Imeelynn	Inderjit	Inez (0.03)
Iguria	Ilaha	Illianna	Imelda (0.03)	Inderpaeet	Infant (0.01)
Ihkaria	Ilaina	Illie	Imeldo	Inderpal	Infiniti (0.01)
Ihnit	Ilaisaane	Illissa	Imely	Inderpreet	Infinitra
Ihonie	Ilaise	Illissia	Imerita	Inderveer	Infinity (0.01)
Ihsan	Ilamae	Illona	Imesha	Indeya	Infinti
Ihuaku	Ilana (0.05)	Illyana	Imihaa	Indhu	Inga
Ihycha	Ilanda	Illyanna	Imin	Indhyra	Inge-Lise
Iiae	Ilaneli	Ilna	Imira	Indi	Ingie
Iiesha	Ilania	Ilona (0.01)	Immaculada	India (0.26)	Ingri
Iimmanni	Ilaria	Ilonna	Immaculee	India Lynn	Ingri-Sofie
Iisha	Ilaya	Ilsa (0.01)	Immere	Indiaella	Ingrid (0.12)
Ijae	Ilce	Ilsari	Immy	Indiah	Ingrid Rainier
Ijahneke	Ilcen	Ilsce	Imo	Indian	Ingris
Ijania	Ilda	Ilse (0.04)	Imogen	Indiana	Inhan
Ijanika	Ilea	Ilse-Marie	Imon	Indianna	Inicity
Ijebusomma	Ileah	Ilsse	Imonee	Indiara	Inida
Ijee	Ileaha	Iluchukwy	Imoni (0.01)	Indica	Inika
Ijeena	Ileana (0.05)	Ilwad	Imonica	Indie	Iniqua
Ijeoma	Ileanna	Ilyasah	Imoniee	Indieya	Inisha
Ijhanea	Ilee	Ilyce	Imperia	Indiga	Initia Queennan
Ijnanya	Ilena	Ilysa	Imrea	Indigo (0.02)	Injeel
Ijuana	Ilene (0.02)	Ilyse	Imrit	Indigo Elizabet	Inkari
Ika	Ilenia	Ilysha	Imrose	Indika	Inkashi
Ikarieyne	Iletha	Ilysia	Imtithal	Indika-Rose	Inkera
Ikea	Ilexis	Ilyssa (0.01)	Imun	Indira	Inkeria
Ikedia	Ileya	Ilyza	Imunique	Indiya	Inkeyra
Ikeea	Ilhaam	Ilze	In	Indoneshia	Inkira
Ikeena	Ilham	Ilzi	Ina (0.02)	Indoneshia	Inna
Ikeia	Ilhan	Ima	Inaeja	Indonesia	Innanna
Ikeisha	Ilia	Ima'ni	Inam	Indonica	Innessa
Ikela	Iliah	Imaara	Inamar	Indra	Innis
Ikera	Iliamna	Imahni	Inanna	Indrani	Innocence
Ikereia	Iliana (0.10)	Imaiya	Inara	Indre	Innocencia
Ikeria	Ilianaris	Imalay	Inari	Indreanna	Innocencia Dy'k
Ikesha	Ilianeth	Iman (0.08)	Inasia	Indria	Inocencia
Ikeurah	Ilianette	Iman Ali	Inasse	Indriya	Insaf
Ikeya	Iliani	Iman-Lemae	Inbal	Induja	Inshallen
Ikeyia	Ilijana	Imana	Inbar	Indy'jah	Intasar
Ikeyla	Ilira	Imanda	Inca	Indya (0.01)	Integrity
				Indya Vashauna	

Inthila	Iressia	Isabel *(0.62)*	Ishawna	Isolina	Ithzel
Inthu	Ireta	Isabel Jean	Ishay	Isolt	Itika
Inthuja	Ireth	Isabel-Marie	Ishe	Isora	Itily
Inthuya	Ireyal	Isabel-Wynne	Ishi	Isouri	Itiyana
Intisar	Ireyele	Isabela *(0.03)*	Ishia	Isra	Itohan
Inya	Ireyone	Isabele	Ishionte	Isrá	Itorria
Inyori	Ireysha	Isabelia	Ishita	Israa *(0.01)*	Itsamar
Ioana	Irhis	Isabell *(0.02)*	Ishiyara	Israel	Itsayana
Ioanna	Irian	Isabella *(0.72)*	Ishjaisaaca	Israelle	Itsel *(0.01)*
Iolanda	Iriana	Isabella-Gabriel	Ishleen	Israh	Itssel
Iona	Iriane	Isabella-Line	Ishma	Israia	Ittika
Ione	Irianna	Isabelle *(0.45)*	Ishmael	Isrial	Itza
Iora	Iricia	Isabelle-Nhu	Ishmeet	Isrielle	Itzallany
Ioyana	Iridian *(0.01)*	Isable	Ishmel	Isryel	Itzamar
Iptisam	Iridiana	Isachey	Ishpal	Issa	Itzayana *(0.03)*
Iqra *(0.01)*	Irie	Isadora *(0.01)*	Ishpreet	Issabella	Itzchel
Iqraa	Irie-Raine	Isaella	Ishrag	Issalze	Itzel *(0.24)*
Iquan	Irieana	Isah	Ishveer	Issam	Itzell
Iquasia	Irieka	Isai-Chai	Ishwary	Issamar	Itzen
Iqueena	Iriel	Isaiah	Ishyia	Issata	Itzia
Iquesha	Irielle	Isaiahei	Ishynite	Issima	Itzlasiwal
Iquila	Irin	Isakia	Isi's	Issis	Itzuri
Ir Eal	Irina *(0.01)*	Isalia	Isia	Issrae	Iuriko
Ira	Irionne	Isaly	Isidora	Istahil	Iva *(0.01)*
Ira Neeka	Iris *(0.24)*	Isalyn	Isidra	Istiana	Ivah
Iraika	Iris Jazmin	Isamar *(0.07)*	Isidre	Istrelia	Ivalee
Irais	Iris Mae	Isamari	Isiha	Isys	Ivalis
Iraiz	Iris-Marie	Isamaria	Isimeme	Isza	Ivan
Iraldy	Irisa	Isanell	Isir	Iszabella	Ivana *(0.08)*
Iram	Irisbeth	Isarel	Isis *(0.08)*	Ita	Ivanah
Iranesha	Irish	Isaria	Isla	Itahi	Ivanaka
Irania *(0.01)*	Irisha	Isata	Islam	Itahiri	Ivanette
Irasema	Irishia	Isatu	Island	Itaisa	Ivaney
Iray	Irismarie	Isaura *(0.02)*	Islay	Ital'tiana	Ivani
Iraya	Irissa	Isavel	Islein	Itali	Ivania
Ireal	Irizema	Isayah	Isles	Italia	Ivanka
Ireena	Irja	Isean	Isley	Italie	Ivanna *(0.03)*
Ireian	Irjaria	Isel *(0.02)*	Islia	Italy	Ivannia
Ireil	Irleen	Isela *(0.05)*	Islonne	Italya	Ivany
Ireka	Irma *(0.10)*	Isenia	Ismaela	Itaska	Ivari
Irelan	Irmeca	Iseona	Ismahan	Itati *(0.01)*	Iveanna
Ireland	Irony	Isha *(0.01)*	Ismaray	Itcel	Ivelisa
Ireli	Iroquois Orenda	Ishaé	Ismari	Itchakomi	Ivelise
Ireliz	Irsia	Isha-Marie	Ismary	Itchel	Ivelisee
Irely	Irum	Ishae	Ismay	Itéa	Ivelisse *(0.01)*
Irelynn	Irvanna	Ishalé	Ismcnia	Iteasha	Ivelys
Iren	Irvinpreet	Ishamere	Ismelda	Iteasia	Iveneet
Irena *(0.01)*	Irydian	Ishamia	Ismenia	Itecka	Ivesha
Irene *(0.33)*	Irys	Ishanaa	Ismeta	Iteiana	Iveshia
Irene-Sophie	Iryssa	Ishanee	Isobel *(0.01)*	Iteonna	Ivester
Irenea	Isa *(0.01)*	Ishani	Isobell	Iternity	Ivet
Irenia	Isa Elena	Ishanna	Isobella	Itesel	Ivett
Irequez	Isaaka	Ishanti	Isobelle	Ithandevhi	Ivette *(0.11)*
Irery	Isabaelle	Ishara	Isoke	Ithati	Ivey *(0.02)*
Iresha	Isabeau *(0.01)*	Isharae	Isolda	Ithiopia	Ivia

Ivian	Iyana *(0.01)*	Izrael	J'nessa	Ja Nesha	Ja'kera
Iviana	Iyanah	Izsharaya	J'nique	Ja Net	Ja'keria
Ivie	Iyanna *(0.01)*	Izumi	J'nisha	Ja On	Ja'kerra
Ivililo	Iyannah	Izumi Ka Hoku	J'niyah	Ja Prentis	Ja'kese
Iviney	Iyannia	Izza	J'nosha	Ja Quanna	Ja'kesha
Ivis	Iyante	Izzabella	J'onna	Ja Quasha	Ja'keshia
Iviss	Iyaona	Izzah	J'quana	Ja Queisha	Ja'keya
Ivneet	Iyauna		J'quanda	Ja R'eika	Ja'keyah
Ivon *(0.03)*	Iyeasha	**-J-**	J'quice	Ja Shanta	Ja'keyiah
Ivona	Iyeniesha		J'quisha	Ja Shay	Ja'kia
Ivondell	Iyesha *(0.01)*	J *(0.04)*	J'quistia	Ja Shaylin	Ja'kieya
Ivone	Iyeshah	J Aime	J'renee	Ja Shonae	Ja'kila
Ivonee	Iyiannah	J Avanti	J'shatai	Ja Tauria D	Ja'kira
Ivonka	Iyland	J Kesia	J'shauna	Ja Tera	Ja'kiria
Ivonne *(0.09)*	Iylish	J Leigh	J'shel	Ja Terrica	Ja'kirreya
Ivonne-Maria	Iyoka	J Lynn	J'shon	Ja Torie	Ja'kita
Ivoory	Iyona	J Mara	J'shonna	Ja Torien	Ja'kwanzaa
Ivori	Iyoná	J Mmy	J'shree	Ja Vonda	Ja'kyra
Ivorica	Iyonawan	J Myrehea	J'tasya	Ja Vonna	Ja'layiah
Ivorie	Iyonna	J Neia	J'uan	Ja Vonne	Ja'lea
Ivory *(0.05)*	Iype	J Neisha	J-Anne	Ja' Coya	Ja'lecia
Ivoryante	Iyron	J Nya	J-Lynn	Ja'andrea	Ja'leeshia
Ivoryione	Iysha	J Shawnna	J.	Ja'auna	Ja'leezia
Ivoryish	Iyslen	J Taisha	J. Jesus	Ja'aundriyah	Ja'lencia
Ivoska	Iyssia	J' Chelle	Ja	Ja'barriyah	Ja'leshia
Ivy *(0.26)*	Iyteisha	J'aira	Ja Brea	Ja'breea	Ja'lexia
Ivy-Jade	Iza	J'alexius	Ja Cayla	Ja'breia	Ja'lexus
Ivy-Lynn	Izabel	J'ana	Ja Christie	Ja'bria	Ja'liecesa
Ivy-Rose	Izabela	J'andra	Ja Courtie	Ja'cara	Ja'lisa *(0.01)*
Ivyann	Izabell	J'anissa	Ja Erica	Ja'cinta	Ja'lisha
Ivyanna	Izabella *(0.03)*	J'arlene	Ja Gail	Ja'coreya	Ja'lishia
Ivyanne	Izabellah	J'den	Ja Kayla	Ja'covia	Ja'liyah
Ivyrose	Izabelle	J'hanna	Ja Kela	Ja'cquel	Ja'lyn
Iwalani	Izabett	J'ira	Ja Kezhua	Ja'cura	Ja'lynn
Iwona	Izamar	J'kandice	Ja Kia	Ja'da	Ja'mani
Ixallana	Izamari	J'kayla	Ja Kiera	Ja'daijah	Ja'mecce
Ixamar	Izamaris	J'kela	Ja Kyra	Ja'daisha	Ja'meeka
Ixchel	Izamary	J'keyah	Ja La Quett	Ja'dawn	Ja'meia
Ixchelle	Izanna	J'kyah	Ja Leah	Ja'de	Ja'meisha
Ixeel	Izaremi	J'la	Ja Lee	Ja'decia	Ja'meka
Ixel	Izat	J'lexxius	Ja Leesha	Ja'deidra	Ja'meria
Ixia	Izaya	J'leyah	Ja Len	Ja'del	Ja'merrian
Ixsel	Izebelle	J'lynn	Ja Lesha	Ja'el	Ja'merron
Ixtel	Izegbuwa	J'lysa	Ja Licia	Ja'fre	Ja'mese
Ixtlily	Izehinomen	J'meisha	Ja Lisa	Ja'kari	Ja'mesh
Ixtzel	Izel	J'meshia	Ja Lissa	Ja'kayla	Ja'mesha
Ixzacil	Izelia	J'myia	Ja Lyn	Ja'kaysia	Ja'meshia
Ixzel	Izermee	J'nae	Ja Mara	Ja'kecia	Ja'mesia
Iy Lonnie	Izhane	J'nai	Ja Marquies	Ja'keczja	Ja'mia
Iya	Izhel	J'nay	Ja Mea	Ja'keeanu	Ja'miaa
Iya'nta	Izia	J'naya	Ja Meisha	Ja'keeyah	Ja'mica
Iyabo	Izma	J'naysha	Ja Meka	Ja'keia	Ja'mika
Iyah	Izobella	J'nel	Ja Mesia	Ja'keiia	Ja'mikka
Iyahana	Izola	J'nell	Ja Monica	Ja'kela	Ja'mila
Iyahanna	Izolde	J'nequa	Ja Nace	Ja'kendria	Ja'mile

Ja'miraka	Ja'shae	Jaboah	Jacenda	Jackleen	Jacoya
Ja'mise	Ja'shai	Jaborah	Jacendia	Jacklena	Jacqeida
Ja'mylia	Ja'shana	Jaboryi	Jacenia	Jacklin	Jacqelyn
Ja'myra	Ja'shatrice	Jabrayla	Jacenta	Jackltnne	Jacqelynn
Ja'na	Ja'shauna	Jabrea (0.01)	Jacey (0.05)	Jacklyn (0.16)	Jacqese
Ja'nadia	Ja'shay	Jabreal	Jacey-Lynn	Jacklyne	Jacqia
Ja'nae (0.01)	Ja'shayla	Jabree	Jachala	Jacklynn (0.01)	Jacqilynn
Ja'nai	Ja'shena	Jabreea	Jachele	Jacklynne	Jacqjeline
Ja'nala	Ja'shier	Jabreena	Jachell	Jackonin	Jacqkenia
Ja'nasia	Ja'taime	Jabrelle	Jachelle	Jackquanna	Jacqline
Ja'nay	Ja'tavia	Jabreona	Jachina	Jackqueline	Jacqlyn
Ja'naye	Ja'tayzha	Jabresha	Jaci (0.02)	Jackquelyn	Jacqlynn
Ja'nea	Ja'terria	Jabri	Jacia	Jackquen	Jacquaisha
Ja'nece	Ja'tia	Jabria (0.02)	Jacianna	Jackquline	Jacquale
Ja'nee	Ja'tiera	Jabriah	Jacie (0.02)	Jackqulyn	Jacqualene
Ja'née	Ja'tora	Jabriana	Jacilyn	Jackson (0.01)	Jacqualin
Ja'neil	Ja'vita	Jabrie	Jacilynn	Jackueline	Jacqualine
Ja'neisha	Ja'von	Jabriel	Jacinda (0.03)	Jackwolyn	Jacqualyn
Ja'neka	Ja'vona Ty'iera	Jabrielle	Jacineth	Jacky	Jacquan
Ja'nell	Ja'vontavia	Jabrienna	Jacinta (0.01)	Jacky-Chrystelle	Jacquana
Ja'nella	Ja'wana	Jabrika	Jacinte	Jackye	Jacquanique
Ja'nelle	Ja'yla	Jabrina	Jacinthe (0.02)	Jackyln	Jacquar
Ja'nese	Ja'zmin	Jabrittany	Jacintia	Jackynn	Jacquarae
Ja'nesha	Ja-Dee	Jabrtia	Jaciona	Jaclare	Jacquay
Ja'neshia	Ja-Korre	Jac'quelene	Jacira	Jaclene	Jacquayla
Ja'nesia	Ja-Lacia	Jac'quinneisha	Jack'kia	Jaclin	Jacquaysha
Ja'nessa	Ja-Leah	Jacala	Jackae	Jacline	Jacquces
Ja'nia	Ja-Lia	Jacalin	Jackala	Jaclisia	Jacque
Ja'nice	Ja-Meshia	Jacalucia	Jackalyn	Jaclyn (0.53)	Jacquee
Ja'nicia	Ja-Mie	Jacalyn (0.01)	Jackalynn	Jaclyne	Jacqueese
Ja'niece	Ja-Nai'	Jacalynn	Jacke	Jaclynn (0.02)	Jacqueisha
Ja'nikqu	Ja-Niqua	Jacandice	Jackee	Jacnaya	Jacqueitta
Ja'niqua	Ja-Quan	Jacara	Jackeisha	Jacnaye	Jacquel
Ja'nise	Ja-Shae	Jacarda	Jackelin	Jacob (0.01)	Jacquelaine
Ja'nisha	Ja-Theron	Jacardia	Jackeline (0.05)	Jacoba	Jacquelann
Ja'nyce	Ja-Tonia	Jacari	Jackelline	Jacobee	Jacquelee
Ja'nyda	Jaa'len	Jacaria	Jackellyn	Jacobi (0.01)	Jacquelena
Ja'nyira	Jaada	Jacaroll	Jackelyn (0.04)	Jacobia	Jacquelene
Ja'onna	Jaairi	Jacarra	Jackenya	Jacoby	Jacquelia
Ja'poria	Jaakia	Jacarrie	Jackey	Jacolby	Jacqueliine
Ja'prela	Jaala	Jacasia	Jackeyria	Jacole	Jacquelin (0.05)
Ja'qeisha	Jaalah	Jacaynlene	Jacki	Jacolyn	Jacquelina
Ja'quan	Jaalan	Jaccarra	Jackie (0.11)	Jacolyné D	Jacqueline (2.41)
Ja'quana	Jaaliyah	Jaccelynn	Jackielee	Jacolynn	Jacqueline Marie
Ja'quanda	Jaamilah	Jacci	Jackielyn	Jaconna	Jacqueline Renee
Ja'quarriah	Jaana	Jaccika	Jackielyn Nicole	Jacora	Jacqueline-Jane
Ja'quasha	Jaanai	Jace	Jackiesha	Jacoreyah	Jacqueline-Yvonn
Ja'quela	Jaandrea	Jacé	Jackillin	Jacori	Jacquelinne
Ja'quele	Jaara	Jaceda	Jackilyn	Jacoria	Jacquell
Ja'quia	Jaas	Jacedy	Jackilyne	Jacorica	Jacquelli
Ja'quiesha	Jaba	Jacee (0.01)	Jackilynn	Jacory	Jacquellin
Ja'quisha	Jabara	Jacée	Jackinie	Jacorya	Jacquellyn
Ja'quita	Jabbriana	Jaceline	Jackirea	Jacotia	Jacquely
Ja'quna	Jaben	Jacelyn (0.01)	Jackisha	Jacovia	Jacquelyn (0.45)
Ja'reisha	Jabira	Jacelynn	Jackita	Jacoy	Jacquelyne (0.01)

Jacquelynn (0.04)	Jadah	Jadzia (0.01)	Jaerie	Jahcelyne	Jahntae
Jacquelynne	Jadahi	Jadzie	Jaerren	Jahdeja	Jahntelle
Jacquenell	Jadajah	Jae	Jaeshon	Jahdem	Jahnyce
Jacquenesha	Jadalyn	Jae Kela	Jaeureka	Jahdiel	Jahnysha
Jacquera	Jadasha	Jaé-Chelle	Jaevian	Jahdziah	Jahnyssia
Jacquerna	Jadayra	Jaéara	Jaevynn	Jahee	Jahquanna
Jacquerra	Jadaysa	Jaéda	Jaewon	Jahfeja	Jahquarsha
Jacques	Jadazia	Jaélynn	Jafara	Jahida	Jahree
Jacquese	Jadda	Jaeana	Jaffa	Jahidah	Jahsaya
Jacquesha	Jadden	Jaeanna	Jaffni	Jahira	Jahshauna
Jacquetta (0.01)	Jade (1.17)	Jaebrielle	Jafia	Jahkevia	Jahsheeba
Jacquette	Jade Renee	Jaecee	Jagana	Jahkia	Jahstece
Jacqui	Jadé	Jaecie	Jagdeep	Jahkyria	Jahsylon
Jacquice	Jade-Alexandra	Jaeda (0.01)	Jagjit	Jahlah	Jahtavia
Jacquie	Jade-Marie	Jaeden	Jagjot	Jahlayia	Jahteka
Jacquiece	Jade-Nicole	Jaedine	Jagmeet	Jahlayna	Jahthiyah
Jacquiline	Jadea	Jaedyn (0.01)	Jagmit	Jahleel	Jahtiana
Jacquilla	Jadeann	Jaedynn	Jagnoor	Jahlia	Jahtisha
Jacquille	Jadedrius	Jaeger	Jaguar	Jahliah	Jahtiya
Jacquilyn	Jadee	Jaeisha	Jah Na	Jahlisa	Jahtonia
Jacquilyne	Jadeen	Jael (0.02)	Jah Ra	Jahliyah	Jahtoyoa
Jacquilynn	Jadeju	Jaela (0.01)	Jah'keanah	Jahmanda	Jahupsa
Jacquinette	Jadelaine	Jaelah	Jah'keya	Jahmarea	Jahvarie
Jacquira	Jadeline	Jaelann	Jah'meeka	Jahmea	Jahvece
Jacquire	Jadell	Jaele	Jah'nae	Jahmeika	Jahveela
Jacquise	Jadelyn (0.01)	Jaelee	Jah'nay	Jahmel	Jahwah
Jacquisha	Jadelyne	Jaeleen	Jah'naye	Jahmela	Jahzelle
Jacquita	Jadelynn	Jaelei	Jah'nessa	Jahmelia	Jahziah Jamie
Jacqul	Jademoné	Jaelen	Jah'nise	Jahmeyka	Jahzmere
Jacqulin	Jaden (0.06)	Jaelene	Jah'niyah	Jahmia	Jahzmine
Jacquline (0.01)	Jadena	Jaelie	Jah'tarius	Jahmiel	Jai (0.01)
Jacqulyn (0.01)	Jadene	Jaelin	Jah'tyra	Jahmila	Jai'
Jacqulyne	Jadera	Jaelinn	Jah'zai	Jahmira	Jai'la
Jacqulynn	Jaderica	Jaelithe	Jah-Lana	Jahn'ne	Jai'lissa
Jacqulynne	Jaderriá	Jaelon	Jah.nice	Jahna (0.01)	Jai'lynique
Jacquoline	Jadey	Jaelun	Jaha	Jahnae	Jai'miya
Jacquoya	Jadeyn	Jaely	Jahaah	Jahnai	Jai'nica
Jacsiry	Jadha	Jaelyn (0.03)	Jahaan	Jahnay	Jai'queisha
Jacslin	Jadi	Jaelyne	Jahada	Jahne	Jai'tyria
Jacueline	Jadia	Jaelynn (0.01)	Jahadrah	Jahnée	Jai'veonne
Jaculyne	Jadian	Jaeme	Jahaila	Jahnee	Jai-El
Jacuquline	Jadie (0.01)	Jaemee	Jahaira (0.01)	Jahneela	Jai-Lyn
Jacy (0.03)	Jadijah	Jaemen	Jahala	Jahneen	Jai-Nadja
Jacyln	Jadin	Jaemian	Jahan	Jahneice	Jai-Quilah
Jacyn	Jadine	Jaemica	Jahana	Jahneiha	Jaia
Jacynda	Jadira	Jaemilene	Jahania	Jahneisha	Jaiá
Jacynta	Jadis	Jaemima	Jahara	Jahnell	Jaiah
Jacyntha	Jadisha	Jaemonique	Jaharah	Jahnelle	Jaiamber
Jacynthe (0.01)	Jadonna	Jaena	Jahari	Jahnesia	Jaiana
Jacyrha	Jadonya	Jaenaeva	Jaharra	Jahnia	Jaianai
Jad'esha	Jadranka	Jaeneisha	Jahauna	Jahnicia	Jaianesha
Jada (0.33)	Jadrian	Jaenelle-Lauren	Jahayla	Jahnie	Jaice
Jada Quanisha	Jady	Jaenieshia	Jahayra	Jahniece	Jaicee
Jadae	Jadyn (0.02)	Jaenna	Jahaziel	Jahnique	Jaicelyn
Jadaé	Jadynn	Jaenne	Jahbria	Jahnisha	Jaici

Jaicie	Jaimie Lou	Jajiba	Jakell	Jaklyne	Jaleesah
Jaiclyn	Jaimie Lyn	Jajonda	Jakelyn	Jakobi	Jaleese
Jaicola	Jaimilyn	Jajuan	Jakelynn	Jakoya	Jaleesia
Jaicy	Jaimin	Jajuanah	Jakelynne	Jakresha	Jaleeya
Jaicyea	Jaimine	Jajuania	Jakenna	Jakwanae	Jaleeza
Jaid *(0.01)*	Jaimisha	Jak-Lyn	Jakenya	Jakwanza	Jaleh
Jaida *(0.02)*	Jaimme	Jakaila	Jakenzie	Jakya	Jaleia
Jaidá	Jaimoni	Jakailynn	Jakera	Jakyla	Jaleida
Jaidah	Jaimy	Jakaira	Jakereya	Jakylia	Jaleigh
Jaidan	Jaimyra	Jakaiya	Jakeria *(0.01)*	Jakyra *(0.01)*	Jaleigha
Jaide *(0.01)*	Jaina *(0.01)*	Jakaiyla	Jakeriya	Jakyrah	Jaleighsa
Jaiden *(0.01)*	Jaina-Brooke	Jakala	Jakerria	Jal'lesa	Jaleika
Jaidey	Jainaba	Jakalah	Jakesha	Jal'raka	Jaleisa
Jaidhe	Jainah	Jakalay	Jakesia	Jala *(0.01)*	Jaleisha
Jaidi	Jainara	Jakalyn	Jakesmine	Jalá	Jaleisya
Jaidin	Jaine	Jakara	Jakessia	Jala'i	Jaleithia
Jaidon	Jainee	Jakaria	Jaketriya	Jalah	Jalela
Jaidyn *(0.01)*	Jaineen	Jakarla	Jakeva	Jalahn	Jalen *(0.02)*
Jaierra	Jaineshia	Jakarra	Jakevia	Jalai	Jalena
Jaihla	Jainisha	Jakarrah	Jakeya	Jalaina	Jalencia
Jaihra	Jaiquel	Jakarri	Jakeyah	Jalan	Jalene *(0.01)*
Jaii	Jaira	Jakarria	Jakeyia	Jalana	Jalenia
Jaikeria	Jairah	Jakarta	Jakeyna	Jalanda	Jalesa *(0.01)*
Jaikia	Jairdin	Jakartra	Jakhari	Jalanea	Jalescia
Jaiknesie	Jairelle	Jakasha	Jakhobi	Jalaney	Jalese
Jaila *(0.01)*	Jairiliz	Jakasmine	Jaki	Jalani	Jalesha
Jailah	Jairiz	Jakaui	Jakía	Jalanie	Jaleshia
Jailee	Jairumie	Jakaura	Jakia *(0.01)*	Jalashá	Jalesia
Jaileen	Jairy	Jakavia	Jakiah	Jalasia	Jalessa *(0.01)*
Jailen	Jaisa	Jakayla *(0.01)*	Jakiana	Jalaunie	Jalessica
Jailene *(0.01)*	Jaisah	Jakaylah	Jakiara	Jalaya	Jaleta
Jailia	Jaisal	Jake	Jakibbia	Jalayah	Jalexia
Jailijah	Jaisalyn	Jakéilah	Jakiela	Jalaydah	Jalexis
Jailin	Jaise	Jakea	Jakiera	Jalayia	Jalexus
Jailine	Jaisea	Jakeah	Jakieria	Jalayla	Jalexxus
Jailiyh	Jaisee	Jakedria	Jakierra	Jalayna	Jaleyne
Jailya	Jaisha	Jakeeda	Jakieyah	Jalayne	Jaleynn
Jailyn *(0.02)*	Jaisie	Jakeem	Jakila	Jalaysha	Jaleyshia
Jaima	Jaisly	Jakeena	Jakilah	Jalea *(0.01)*	Jaleysia
Jaimalyn	Jaisree	Jakeera	Jakilya	Jaleah	Jalia *(0.01)*
Jaimaya	Jaissley	Jakeeria	Jakima	Jaleasa	Jaliah
Jaime *(0.28)*	Jaisyn	Jakeeva	Jakina	Jalece	Jaliaha
Jaime-Lee	Jaitai	Jakeia	Jakira	Jalecea	Jalian
Jaime-Lynn	Jaitel	Jakeiara	Jakirah	Jalecia *(0.01)*	Jalica
Jaimee *(0.07)*	Jaitesha	Jakeiba	Jakiria	Jalee	Jalicia *(0.01)*
Jaimee Daine	Jaitraya	Jakeidra	Jakirya	Jaleea	Jalie
Jaimee-Lynn	Jaiveonna	Jakeina	Jakise	Jaleece	Jalieka
Jaimee-Lynne	Jaivon	Jakeira	Jakita	Jaleecia	Jaliesa
Jaimeela	Jaiyana	Jakeiria	Jakiya	Jaleeda	Jaliessa
Jaimelyn	Jaiyme	Jakeisha *(0.01)*	Jakiyah	Jaleel	Jalil
Jaimeson	Jaiymee	Jakeitha	Jakke	Jaleelah	Jalilah
Jaimey	Jaize	Jakeithia	Jakki	Jaleen	Jalin
Jaimi *(0.01)*	Jaizmeine	Jakela	Jakkia	Jaleena	Jalina
Jaimian	Jaizsa	Jakelin *(0.01)*	Jakklin	Jaleene	Jalincia
Jaimie *(0.11)*	Jajaira	Jakeline	Jaklyn	Jaleesa *(0.02)*	Jaline

Jalinie	Jamaia	Jamecia (0.03)	Jamerika	Jamie Taylor	Jamira (0.01)
Jaliqua	Jamaica (0.01)	Jamecka	Jamerson	Jamiésha	Jamirah
Jaliria	Jamaih	Jamee (0.02)	James (0.01)	Jamie-Ann	Jamiria
Jalisa (0.09)	Jamaika	Jamée	James'e	Jamie-Jean	Jamiria Chantav
Jalise	Jamaiqua	Jameeha	Jamesa	Jamie-Lee (0.01)	Jamirria
Jalisha (0.01)	Jamaiya	Jameeka	Jamesanna	Jamie-Lynn (0.01)	Jamisa
Jalishia Ausher	Jamaka	Jameela (0.01)	Jamescia	Jamie-Marie	Jamisan
Jalishua	Jamal	Jameelah	Jamese (0.01)	Jamiea	Jamise
Jalisia	Jamala	Jameelia	Jameseea	Jamiece	Jamisen
Jalissa (0.04)	Jamalah	Jameera	Jamesena	Jamiee	Jamisha (0.01)
Jalissac	Jamalia	Jameesha	Jamesetta	Jamieka	Jamishi
Jalissau	Jamalin	Jameeshia	Jamesh	Jamiel	Jamiska
Jalissia	Jamaliz	Jamehia	Jamesha (0.06)	Jamiela	Jamison (0.01)
Jalisyia	Jamalla	Jamei	Jameshay	Jamielee	Jamita
Jalita	Jamalliah	Jamei'	Jamesheah	Jamielisse	Jamius
Jaliya	Jamana	Jameia	Jameshia (0.01)	Jamielyn	Jamiya (0.01)
Jaliyah (0.02)	Jamanda	Jameica	Jamesia (0.01)	Jamieneshia	Jamiyah
Jaliz	Jamani	Jameice	Jamesianna	Jamiesha	Jamiyla
Jalizah	Jamaniqua	Jameika (0.01)	Jamesica	Jamieson	Jammaj
Jallaina	Jamantha	Jameila	Jamesina	Jamiha	Jammée
Jalleyah	Jamar	Jameilah	Jameson	Jamii	Jammell
Jalliney	Jamara (0.01)	Jameilla	Jamesse	Jamika (0.03)	Jammen
Jalliyah	Jamarcus	Jameillia	Jamessia	Jamikella	Jammeria
Jallona	Jamarea	Jameilyara	Jamesy	Jamil	Jammes
Jalmedal	Jamaree	Jameira	Jameszetta	Jamil'yah	Jammia
Jalnaisy	Jamareia	Jameisa	Jameta	Jamila (0.09)	Jammie (0.01)
Jalon	Jamari	Jameisha (0.01)	Jametria	Jamila Marie	Jamneisha
Jalonda	Jamaria (0.01)	Jameishan	Jametrice	Jamilabelle	Jamoi
Jalondria	Jamarial	Jameison	Jametta	Jamilah (0.02)	Jamonda
Jaloni	Jamarica	Jameka (0.04)	Jamey (0.02)	Jamile	Jamoni
Jalonica	Jamarie	Jameka-Darrell	Jameya	Jamilee	Jamonica (0.01)
Jalora	Jamarii	Jamekia (0.01)	Jameycia	Jamileh	Jamonicá
Jalyah	Jamarion	Jamekica	Jameyia	Jamiless	Jamonya
Jalycia	Jamarious	Jamekka	Jameyla	Jamilet	Jamorné
Jalyea	Jamarra	Jamela	Jamez	Jamileth	Jamoya
Jalyn (0.04)	Jamarsha	Jamelia (0.01)	Jami (0.10)	Jamilett	Jamselah
Jalyna	Jamarys	Jameliah	Jami'lah	Jamilex	Jamshed
Jalyncia	Jamasia	Jamella	Jami-Lyn	Jamilia (0.01)	Jamsine
Jalyndra	Jamaundi	Jamellah	Jami-Lynn	Jamiliet	Jamy
Jalyne	Jamavia	Jamelle	Jamia (0.03)	Jamilla (0.01)	Jamya (0.01)
Jalynn (0.02)	Jamay	Jamellia	Jamiah	Jamillah (0.01)	Jamyah
Jalynne	Jamaya (0.01)	Jamelsha	Jamiahya	Jamille	Jamye
Jalysa (0.01)	Jamayah	Jamelyn	Jamiane	Jamilya	Jamyia
Jalyse	Jamayca	Jamelynn	Jamiann	Jamilyn	Jamylee
Jalysma	Jamazja	Jamen	Jamica (0.01)	Jamime	Jamyra (0.01)
Jalyssa	Jame	Jamena	Jamica Mahalia	Jamina	Jamyriyale
Jalyssia	Jamé	Jamenethia	Jamicca	Jaminah	Jamyyia
Jama (0.01)	Jaméce	Jamequa	Jamice	Jamine	Jamyyla
Jamaal	Jamea	Jameque	Jamiceia	Jamineca	Jan (0.01)
Jamacaia	Jameah	Jamequillan	Jamicia	Jaminecia	Jan A
Jamachia	Jamear	Jamera	Jamicka	Jaminique	Jan'e
Jamacia	Jamearian	Jamere	Jamie (1.74)	Jaminque	Jan'ée
Jamad	Jameca	Jameria	Jamie Ann	Jamious	Jan'nisha
Jamae	Jamecca	Jamerica	Jamie Myranda	Jamiqua	Jan-Erika
Jamahra	Jamece	Jamerican	Jamie Shantrell	Jamir	Jan-Kirstyn

Jana *(0.12)*	Janci	Janeissa	Janhvi	Janisse	Jannyka
Janaé	Jancillin	Janeisy	Jani *(0.01)*	Janita *(0.01)*	Jannylec
Janaan	Jancinta	Janeiya	Jania *(0.01)*	Janitha	Janoah
Janada	Jancy	Janeiyah	Janiah	Janitza	Janobia
Janae *(0.20)*	Janda	Janeka	Janiana	Janitzza	Janohah
Janae Jordan	Jandalynn	Janekia	Janibe	Janiya	Janon
Janaé *(0.01)*	Jandee	Janekqua	Janica *(0.01)*	Janiyah	Janora
Janaea	Janderi	Janel *(0.07)*	Janice *(0.20)*	Janiyiah	Janorria
Janael	Jandi	Janela	Janicé	Janiza	Janou
Janaesha	Jandilyn	Janelcy	Janicea	Janjay	Janquise
Janah	Jandolyn	Janele	Janiceya	Janki *(0.01)*	Janquisha
Janai *(0.02)*	Jandra	Janeli	Janicia	Janli	Janrae
Janai'	Jandy	Janell *(0.07)*	Janicie	Janlynn	Jansen
Janaiah	Jane *(0.32)*	Janell Olga	Janick *(0.01)*	Janlynne	Jansi
Janaira	Jane T	Janella	Janie *(0.16)*	Janna *(0.09)*	Janssen
Janais	Jane Y	Janelle *(0.43)*	Janie D'nae	Janná	Janssy
Janaisie	Jané	Janelle Maymi	Janiece *(0.01)*	Jannacy	Janta
Janaiya	Janée	Janelli	Janiechia	Jannae	Jantavia
Janajah	Jane-Ellen	Janelly *(0.01)*	Janiecia	Jannah *(0.01)*	Jantel
Janakee	Jane-Louise	Janellyn	Janiecsa	Jannai	Jantera
Janaki	Janea *(0.01)*	Janely *(0.02)*	Janiefer	Jannais	Jantez
Janal	Janeace	Janelys	Janieka	Jannan	Janthal
Janale	Janeae	Janene	Janiel	Jannani	Jantrel
Janalee	Janeah	Janequa	Janielle	Jannathi	Jantzen
Janalyce	Janeakqua	Janequia	Janielyn	Janné	Januari
Janalyn	Janeal	Janerika	Janiesha	Jannea	January
Janalynn	Janean	Janesa	Janieya	Jannece	Janusa
Janamay	Janeanne	Janesca	Janieyah	Jannefer	Janvier
Janan	Janeca	Janese *(0.01)*	Janihya	Janneh	Jany *(0.01)*
Jananee	Janece	Janesea	Janik *(0.01)*	Janneke	Janyca
Janani	Janecia *(0.01)*	Janesha *(0.01)*	Janika *(0.01)*	Jannel	Janyce
Janann	Janeda	Janeshia	Janikia	Jannela	Janyé
Jananni	Janedene	Janesia	Janikqua	Jannelie	Janyla
Janany	Janee *(0.02)*	Janeska	Janikwa	Jannell *(0.01)*	Janys
Janara	Janée	Janess	Janile	Jannella	Janysha
Janaris	Janee-T'shawna	Janessa *(0.17)*	Janilee	Jannelle *(0.01)*	Janyssa
Janasha	Janeeka	Janessa-Lee	Janilet	Jannely	Jaolcy
Janasia	Janeen *(0.01)*	Janessi	Janimar	Jannen	Jaonna
Janasie	Janeese	Janessia	Janina *(0.02)*	Jannery	Jaordana
Janat	Janeesha	Janesza	Janine *(0.12)*	Jannesa	Jaozell
Janaticia	Janeeva	Janet *(0.57)*	Janine Angelika	Janneska	Japaula
Janaur	Janei	Janet Alejandra	Janiqua *(0.01)*	Jannet *(0.03)*	Japernicer
Janautica	Janeia	Janeth *(0.03)*	Janique *(0.01)*	Jannett	Japhena
Janavé	Janeica	Janethea	Janique-Danielle	Jannette *(0.02)*	Japjit
Janaveah	Janeice	Janetje	Janiquia	Janneya	Japonica
Janavi	Janeida	Janetra	Janir	Jannica	Japorya
Janavia	Janeigha	Janetrice	Janira	Jannick *(0.01)*	Japri'
Janaviya	Janeika	Janetsy	Janis *(0.01)*	Jannie *(0.01)*	Japuji
Janay *(0.09)*	Janeil	Janett *(0.02)*	Janisa	Jannifer	Jaqaesa
Janaya *(0.02)*	Janeill	Janetta *(0.01)*	Janise *(0.01)*	Jannika	Jaqeesha
Janayah	Janeille	Janette *(0.13)*	Janisha *(0.01)*	Jannina	Jaqentiline
Janaye *(0.01)*	Janeiri	Janeva	Janishi	Jannis	Jaqera
Janayia	Janeise	Janevia	Janishia	Jannise	Jaqhayla
Janaysia	Janeisha *(0.01)*	Janey *(0.02)*	Janisia	Jannixa	Jaqi
Janazia	Janeisia	Janhelly	Janissa	Janny	Jaqia

Jaqiera	Jaquesta	Jardana	Jarmeisha	Jasandra	Jashione
Jaqiria	Jaqueta	Jarde	Jarmeshia	Jasaria	Jashira
Jaqkeita	Jaquetta (0.01)	Jardin	Jarmiah	Jascelynn	Jashive
Jaqlyn	Jaquette	Jardy	Jarmilya	Jascia	Jashley
Jaqoria	Jaqueya	Jarease	Jarmyesha	Jasdeeb	Jashmini
Jaqua	Jaqueze	Jareatha	Jarná	Jasdeep (0.01)	Jashna
Jaquade	Jaqui	Jarecea	Jarnae	Jasdip	Jashon
Jaquai	Jaquia	Jared	Jarneisha	Jase	Jashona
Jaquail	Jaquia Keosha	Jaree	Jarnelle	Jasega	Jashonda
Jaquaila	Jaquiana	Jareka	Jarnesha	Jaseleen	Jashone
Jaquakea	Jaquice	Jareli	Jarnevia	Jaselle	Jashontaé
Jaquala	Jaquiella	Jarelitzi	Jarnisha	Jaselyn	Jashulynn
Jaqualin	Jaquiesha	Jarell	Jarod	Jaselynn	Jashuna
Jaqualine	Jaquil	Jarely	Jaron	Jasemine	Jashyia
Jaqualla	Jaquila	Jaremey	Jaronda	Jasena	Jashyna
Jaqualya	Jaquilla	Jaren	Jaronsa	Jasenia	Jasi
Jaquan	Jaquillia	Jarena	Jarquavion	Jasenie	Jasia
Jaquaná	Jaquilyn	Jareni	Jarquial	Jaseny	Jasica
Jaquana (0.01)	Jaquilynn	Jareshly	Jarquicia	Jasenya	Jasie
Jaquanda	Jaquina	Jaretta	Jarquis	Jasey (0.01)	Jasiel
Jaquandalynn	Jaquinta	Jarhonda	Jarra	Jasha	Jasika
Jaquandra	Jaquira	Jarhondra	Jarranique	Jashá	Jasilas
Jaquania	Jaquirra	Jari	Jarrany	Jashae	Jasilyn
Jaquanna	Jaquise	Jaria	Jarred	Jashaela	Jasimary
Jaquanta	Jaquisha	Jariah	Jarrell	Jashai'	Jasime
Jaquaria	Jaquita (0.01)	Jarian	Jarren	Jashain	Jasimen
Jaquarious	Jaquite	Jariana	Jarrett	Jashala	Jasimie
Jaquasia	Jaquitta	Jaribeth	Jarria	Jashama	Jasimin
Jaquavia	Jaquittie	Jarica	Jarrica	Jashan	Jasimine
Jaquay	Jaqule	Jaricel	Jarrice	Jashana	Jasimne
Jaquaya	Jaqulene	Jarie	Jarrika	Jashanae	Jasina
Jaquayal	Jaqulia	Jarielle	Jarrin	Jashanda	Jasinia
Jaque	Jaquline	Jarielys	Jarris	Jashandra	Jasinique
Jaquece	Jaqulla	Jarika	Jarron	Jashanea	Jasinta
Jaqueda	Jaqulyn	Jarilee	Jarryn	Jashania	Jasinthe
Jaquei'ah	Jaqunise	Jarima	Jartice	Jashanna	Jasity
Jaqueia	Jaqunza	Jarimet	Jartirra	Jashanta	Jasjuana
Jaqueisha	Jaquoiya	Jarin	Jarvanna	Jashante	Jaskaran
Jaquekera	Jaquonda	Jarinya	Jarvetta	Jashanti	Jaskaren
Jaquel	Jaquonna	Jaris	Jarvicia	Jashara	Jaskarn
Jaquelin (0.04)	Jaquoya	Jarisa	Jaryah	Jasharay	Jaskia
Jaquelina	Jaqwandra	Jarise	Jaryn	Jasharey	Jaskinder
Jaqueline (0.15)	Jar'da	Jarissa	Jas	Jashari	Jaskiran (0.01)
Jaquell	Jara	Jaritsa	Jas'anai	Jashaughna	Jaskiranjit
Jaquella	Jara-Lynn	Jaritza	Jas'lynn	Jashaun	Jaskirat
Jaquelyn (0.02)	Jarae	Jarius	Jas'mi	Jashauna	Jasleen (0.02)
Jaquelynn	Jarah	Jariya	Jas'mine	Jashawn	Jaslene
Jaquelynne	Jaraiesha	Jarkea	Jasa (0.01)	Jashawna	Jaslien
Jaquencia	Jaraka	Jarkelia	Jasalie	Jashawnna	Jaslin
Jaquenia	Jaralyn	Jarkira	Jasalyn	Jashay	Jasline
Jaquentis	Jaralynn	Jarlana	Jasalynn	Jashayla	Jasly
Jaquese	Jaralys	Jarlexia	Jasamine	Jashella	Jaslyn (0.01)
Jaquesha	Jaramie	Jarlisha	Jasamray	Jashima	Jaslynn
Jaqueshia	Jaraysha	Jarlissa	Jasandeep	Jashimara	Jaslynn Janea
Jaquest	Jarcelyn	Jarmeika	Jasandip	Jashine	Jaslynne

Jasma *(0.01)*
Jasmaine *(0.02)*
Jasman *(0.01)*
Jasmandeep
Jasmane
Jasmari
Jasmarie
Jasmaura
Jasmeen *(0.01)*
Jasmeet *(0.01)*
Jasmeia
Jasmen
Jasmend
Jasmene
Jasmere
Jasmi
Jasmia
Jasmica
Jasmide
Jasmien
Jasmiene
Jasmihn
Jasmila
Jasmin *(0.90)*
Jasmin Aida
Jasmina *(0.01)*
Jasminda
Jasminder
Jasmine *(5.67)*
Jasmine Kiera
Jasmine Latrice
Jasmine Marie
Jasmine Nakia
Jasmine Nicole
Jasmine Oneshia
Jasmine Paris
Jasmine Racquel
Jasmine Virginia
Jasminé
Jasminé Aungele
Jasmine-
  Chardonnay
Jasmine-Kadejah
Jasmine-Rae
Jasminejit
Jasminemarie
Jasminepreet
Jasmines
Jasming
Jasminie
Jasminka
Jasminne
Jasmione
Jasmire
Jasmit

Jasmne
Jasmon
Jasmond
Jasmone
Ja3monique
Jasmyhn
Jasmyn *(0.09)*
Jasmyn-Lea
Jasmyne *(0.08)*
Jasmyne-Lee
Jasmynn
Jasmynne
Jasna
Jasnaid
Jasneer
Jasneet
Jasniá
Jasnique
Jasniquio
Jasonia
Jaspe
Jasper *(0.01)*
Jaspinder
Jaspreet *(0.03)*
Jaspring
Jasprit
Jaspriya
Jaspur
Jasraj
Jasreen
Jasreli
Jasrina
Jassa
Jassadi
Jassamine
Jassamyn
Jassandra
Jassanie
Jassaray
Jassari
Jasselyn
Jassica
Jassie
Jassimin
Jassimran
Jassium
Jassleen
Jassman
Jassmin
Jassmine *(0.01)*
Jassminn
Jassmyn
Jastasia
Jasteen
Jastej

Jastelynne
Jastindeep
Jastiney
Jastinne
Jasveen
Jasvinder
Jasvinel
Jasvir
Jaswinder
Jasyman
Jasymine
Jasymn
Jasynn
Jaszanek
Jaszmane
Jaszmin
Jaszmon
Jataé
Jatani
Jatanya
Jatara
Jatasia
Jataura
Jatavia *(0.01)*
Jataya
Jataysia
Jatayviah
Jatea
Jateal
Jateara
Jateasia
Jateia
Jatekia
Jatender
Jateria
Jatericka
Jaterra
Jaterria
Jaterrika
Jatesha
Jatesia
Jathea
Jatia
Jaticisha
Jatina
Jaton
Jatoni
Jatori
Jatoría
Jatoria
Jatouri
Jatoya
Jatoza
Jatricia
Jatu

Jatyra
Jatziry
Jau
Jau-Shay
Jauana
Jaucha
Jaudine
Jauelle
Jauhara
Jaukevia
Jauleesa
Jaune T
Jaunice
Jaunikquaw
Jaunique
Jaunisha
Jauria
Jauteria
Jauwanda
Jauzlin
Javacia
Javae
Javairia X
Javalene
Javan
Javana
Javanda
Javani
Javanique
Javanna
Javanti
Javarah
Javarra
Javaughn
Jave
Javean
Javecia
Javeen
Javelin
Javelina
Javeline
Javen
Javenly
Javeria
Javeta
Javia
Javiana
Javianna
Javicia
Javiel
Javiera
Javin
Javis
Javita
Javon *(0.01)*

Javona *(0.01)*
Javonaé
Javonda
Javondria
Javone
Javoné
Javoni
Javonna *(0.01)*
Javonne
Javonni
Javonta
Javontay
Javonte
Javonté
Javonya
Jawaher
Jawan
Jawana
Jawanda
Jawanna
Jawanza
Jawea
Jawny
Jawrutha
Jawyan
Jaxmin
Jay
Jay'la
Jay'ne
Jay-Lene
Jay-Lynn
Jay-Neash
Jaya *(0.01)*
Jayah
Jayana
Jayann
Jayanna *(0.01)*
Jayanthi
Jayanti
Jayashalini
Jayasheena
Jayashree
Jayassiona
Jaybralis
Jaybrielle
Jaybrioanna
Jaybryana
Jayca
Jayce *(0.01)*
Jaycee *(0.05)*
Jaycelin
Jaycey
Jaycha
Jayci *(0.01)*
Jaycie *(0.02)*

Jaycinda
Jayd
Jayda *(0.04)*
Jayda-Lane
Jayda-Mariene
Jaydah
Jayde *(0.06)*
Jayde-Ann
Jaydee
Jaydeen
Jaydell
Jaydelyn
Jayden *(0.04)*
Jaydene
Jaydia
Jaydin
Jaydira
Jaydn
Jaydon
Jaydrian
Jaye
Jayelisa
Jayelynne
Jayhoner
Jayhua
Jayia
Jayjuana
Jaykeena
Jaykeysha
Jaykiaya
Jaykierria
(0.10) Jayla
Jaylaa
Jaylaan
Jaylaena
Jaylah
Jaylahni
Jaylan
Jayland
Jayle
Jayleana
Jaylee *(0.01)*
Jayleen *(0.01)*
Jayleene
Jaylen *(0.01)*
Jaylene *(0.03)*
Jaylenne
Jaylesia
Jayli
Jaylia
Jayliah
Jaylie
Jaylin *(0.02)*
Jayline
Jaylinn

Jaylisa	Jayra	Jazilyn	Jazreel	Jazzmone	Jean'nae
Jaylise	Jayron	Jazimeon	Jazrie	Jazzmun	Jean-Ann
Jaylissa	Jaysa	Jazimien	Jazriel	Jazzmyn (0.01)	Jean-Grey
Jaylla	Jaysabel	Jaziya	Jazrin	Jazzmyne (0.01)	Jeana (0.04)
Jayln	Jaysea	Jazlee	Jazryn	Jazznee	Jeana Maree
Jaylon	Jaysee	Jazlin	Jazs	Jazzni	Jeanae
Jaylyn (0.03)	Jayseena	Jazline	Jazshey	Jazzqwondolyn	Jeanann
Jaylynn (0.01)	Jaysha	Jazlyn (0.02)	Jazsman	Jazzra	Jeanara
Jaylynne	Jayshauna	Jazlynn (0.01)	Jazsmine	Jazzriel	Jeancarla
Jaylysa	Jaysheena	Jazlynne	Jazsper	Jazzsmine	Jeandra
Jayma	Jayshyia	Jazma	Jazsymin	Jazzy	Jeane
Jayme (0.15)	Jaysia	Jazmaine	Jaztoni	Jazzybelle	Jeaneca
Jayme-Lee	Jaysie	Jazman (0.01)	Jazwanna	JC	Jeanecia
Jayme-Marie	Jayslyn	Jazmane	Jazymin	Je Anne	Jeaneen
Jaymee (0.03)	Jaysma	Jazmanee	Jazymne	Je Aunte	Jeaneiclis
Jaymee-Teaanna	Jaysmine	Jazmarae	Jazz (0.01)	Je Nada	Jeaneil
Jaymeeka	Jayssa	Jazmarie	Jazz-Myne	Je Neisha	Jeanell
Jaymeele	Jaytoria	Jazmeen	Jazza'nique	Je Risha	Jeanelle (0.01)
Jaymeisha	Jayvanni	Jazmein	Jazzae	Jé'	Jeanelly
Jaymelee	Jayveus	Jazmeir	Jazzaliece	Jéana	Jeanelyn
Jaymen	Jayvonna	Jazmeka	Jazzalyn	Jébriesha	Jeanene
Jaymes	Jaywian	Jazmen (0.02)	Jazzamine	Jédrien	Jeanessa
Jaymesha	Jayzah	Jazmena	Jazzanine	Jékeila	Jeanet
Jaymeshan	Jayzmin	Jazmend	Jazzaria	Jékera	Jeanethe
Jaymi (0.02)	Jaz	Jazmene	Jazzee	Jékerra	Jeanetta (0.01)
Jaymie (0.04)	Jaz Mynae	Jazmerie	Jazzelina	Jékhauri	Jeanette (0.25)
Jaymie-Lynn	Jaz'men	Jazmin (0.78)	Jazzelyn	Jélesa	Jeaneva
Jaymiee	Jaz'menda	Jazmin Mariah	Jazzelynn	Jélinn	Jeanevone
Jaymina	Jaz'min	Jazmin'	Jazzeray	Jélissia	Jeanha
Jaymison	Jaz'mine	Jazmina	Jazzeree	Jélyrics	Jeanie (0.02)
Jayna (0.04)	Jaz'mon	Jazmine (0.72)	Jazzi	Jémia	Jeanielle
Jaynah	Jaz'neek	Jazmine-Ashley	Jazzie	Jéna	Jeanifer
Jaynani	Jaz'quya	Jazminn	Jazzietta	Jénae	Jeanine (0.05)
Jaynay	Jaz-Zae	Jazminne	Jazzima	Jénalta	Jeaniqua
Jayne (0.05)	Jazady	Jazmon	Jazziman	Jénay	Jeanique
Jayné	Jazaline	Jazmond	Jazzime	Jénean	Jeanise
Jaynecia	Jazalyn	Jazmone	Jazzimen	Jénese	Jeanisha
Jaynecshia	Jazamine	Jazmonique	Jazzle	Jénetta	Jeankyria
Jaynee (0.01)	Jazan	Jazmun	Jazzlyn (0.01)	Jéni	Jeanmarie
Jaynée	Jazanay	Jazmyn (0.11)	Jazzlynn	Jéquana	Jeanna (0.03)
Jayneisha	Jazandeep	Jazmyne (0.08)	Jazzma	Jéshyia	Jeannae
Jaynell	Jazanee	Jazmyne	Jazzmaen	Jésonja	Jeannail
Jaynese	Jazarai	Deaunsh	Jazzmain	Jétera	Jeanndallen
Jaynessa	Jazekka	Jazmynn	Jazzmaine	Jévaughn	Jeanne (0.09)
Jayney	Jazel	Jazmynne	Jazzman	Je-Stephany	Jeanne B'adgliec
Jayni	Jazell	Jazna	Jazzmane	Je-Taime	Jeannell
Jaynia	Jazelle	Jazne	Jazzmeen	Jea'na	Jeannelle
Jaynice	Jazelyn	Jazné	Jazzmen (0.01)	Jealisa	Jeannemarie
Jaynie (0.01)	Jazeman	Jaznee	Jazzmene	Jealissa	Jeannenazaré
Jayniqua	Jazemea	Jazniun	Jazzmenn	Jealyssa	Jeanneret
Jaynisha	Jazemeka	Jazoya	Jazzmiere	Jeami	Jeannet
Jaynna	Jazemin	Jazper	Jazzmin (0.07)	Jeamis	Jeannetta
Jayoina	Jazemine	Jazpony	Jazzmine (0.06)	Jean (0.07)	Jeannette (0.08)
Jayonna	Jazemyn	Jazpreet	Jazzmon	Jean Nicole	Jeanney
Jayoung	Jazendra	Jazra	Jazzmond	Jean'na	Jeanni Phuo

Jeannia
Jeannice
Jeannicole
Jeannie *(0.04)*
Jeannie-Anne
Jeannie-Rae
Jeannika
Jeannine *(0.02)*
Jeanvielle
Jeany
Jeanyah
Jeaqualyn
Jeaquinta
Jearicka
Jearldine
Jearni
Jeasha
Jeassi
Jeastina
Jeastine
Jeathmaliz
Jeavette
Jeberia
Jebet
Jebrea
Jebria
Jecé
Jecee
Jecelyn
Jecenia
Jecey
Jecika
Jecill
Jecinda
Jecobi
Jecoby
Jecy
Jecynda
Jeda
Jedawn
Jedaya
Jedda
Jedidiah
Jedith
Jee
Jee Min
Jee-Ae
Jee-In
Jeehyun
Jeena
Jeenay
Jeenhy
Jeennifer
Jeeny
Jeerie

Jeerin
Jeessie
Jeevun
Jeeyoon
Jef Feya
Jef'shauna Char
Jeffana
Jefferi
Jefferies
Jefferion
Jefferson
Jeffery
Jeffione
Jeffonya
Jeffre Al
Jeffreana
Jeffresha
Jeffrey
Jeffrica
Jeffta
Jefftina
Jeffy
Jefimija
Jefvonte
Jehad
Jehan
Jehanne
Jeharrah
Jehiica
Jehna
Jehne
Jehnivia
Jehona
Jehvonna
Jei'meka
Jeilene
Jeilyn
Jeimy
Jeintenna
Jeisselle
Jeivanis
Jekata
Jekeia
Jekeira
Jekeire
Jekelle
Jekerra
Jekiah
Jekiera
Jekilah
Jekyia
Jelaci
Jelaina
Jelaine
Jelainy

Jelana
Jelanda
Jelani *(0.01)*
Jelanni
Jelayna
Jelberte
Jelcia
Jeleah
Jeleana
Jelecyee
Jelen
Jelena *(0.01)*
Jelene
Jelesha
Jelessa
Jelexus
Jeliane
Jelianne
Jelica
Jelicia
Jelimar
Jelina
Jelinda
Jeline
Jelisa *(0.01)*
Jelise
Jelissa *(0.01)*
Jelitha
Jelitza
Jeliver
Jellese
Jellice
Jelly
Jelnar
Jelon
Jelyne
Jelynn
Jelynne
Jelysa
Jelyssa
Jem
Jema
Jemara
Jemaraa
Jemaria
Jemayne
Jemecca
Jemeera
Jemeisha
Jemeka
Jemel
Jemeli
Jemensa
Jemesha
Jemesia

Jemetria
Jemi
Jemia
Jemiah
Jemica
Jemika
Jemila
Jemilah
Jemilla
Jemima
Jemiracá
Jemirah
Jemise
Jemisel
Jemisha
Jemiya
Jemiyah
Jemm
Jemma *(0.01)*
Jemmalyn
Jemmi
Jemmy
Jemoria
Jemyca
Jen'tavia
Jen-Ai
Jena *(0.12)*
Jena Deloris
Jena Rene
Jena-Lee
Jena-Molly
Jenacee
Jenade
Jenadre
Jenae *(0.03)*
Jenaé
Jenafir
Jenah
Jenahsea
Jenahya
Jenai
Jenaile
Jenaira
Jenais
Jenakalyn
Jenal
Jenalee
Jenalene
Jenalyn
Jenalysse
Jenamarie
Jenan
Jenann
Jenapher
Jenashia

Jenasie
Jenaveve
Jenavie
Jenavieve
Jenay *(0.01)*
Jenaya *(0.01)*
Jenayah
Jenaye
Jenbrica
Jence
Jencey
Jenci
Jency
Jencyn
Jend
Jendayi
Jene
Jené
Jenéa
Jenea
Jeneá
Jeneal
Jenean
Jeneane
Jeneca
Jenece
Jenee
Jenée
Jeneen
Jeneese
Jeneeth
Jenefer
Jeneice
Jeneicia
Jeneile
Jeneir
Jeneisha
Jeneka
Jenel
Jenel-Ann
Jenela
Jenele
Jenell *(0.01)*
Jenell April
Jenella
Jenelle *(0.05)*
Jenellra
Jenelyn
Jenery
Jenesa
Jenese
Jenesia
Jenesis
Jenessa *(0.05)*
Jenessia

Jenest
Jenet
Jenetra
Jenetta
Jenette *(0.01)*
Jeneva *(0.01)*
Jeneva-Ashley
Jenevieve
Jenevra
Jenevy
Jeney
Jeneya
Jenfay
Jengela
Jenhene
Jeni *(0.01)*
Jenia
Jeniah
Jeniann
Jenica *(0.02)*
Jenicaline
Jenice *(0.01)*
Jenicia
Jenie
Jenieca
Jeniece
Jenielee
Jenien
Jeniesha
Jenieva
Jenife
Jenifer *(0.12)*
Jeniferr
Jeniffer *(0.04)*
Jenika *(0.01)*
Jenikca
Jenikka
Jenikquia
Jenilee
Jenilice
Jenille
Jenilyn
Jenimae
Jenine *(0.01)*
Jenipher
Jenique
Jenis
Jenisa
Jenise *(0.01)*
Jeniseceah
Jenisha
Jenisha-Thomas
Jenishay
Jenissa
Jenisse

Jenita	Jennette	Jennyfer (0.04)	Jer Mesia	Jeriana	Jermeria
Jenitha	Jenneva	Jennylou	Jer Quavia	Jerica (0.05)	Jermesha
Jenivieve	Jennevie	Jennyn	Jer Reka	Jericah	Jermeta
Jenkins	Jennez	Jennypher	Jer'ray	Jericca	Jermetrayha
Jenmeet	Jenni (0.01)	Jenoa	Jer'ronda	Jerice	Jermia
Jenmis	Jennia	Jenodini	Jera	Jericha	Jermiah
Jenn	Jennica (0.02)	Jenoia	Jerae	Jericho	Jermica
Jenna (2.03)	Jennice	Jenoja	Jerah	Jericka (0.01)	Jermicease
Jenna Keisha	Jennie (0.14)	Jenora	Jeraldina	Jerielle	Jermiché
Jenna Paige	Jennie-Mae	Jenri	Jeraldine	Jeriesha	Jermicia
Jenna-Ashley	Jenniece	Jenscena	Jeraldyne	Jerika (0.02)	Jermika
Jenna-C	Jennier	Jensen (0.04)	Jeralee	Jerikai	Jermille
Jenna-Diane	Jenniezes	Jensey	Jeralyn	Jerikka	Jermique
Jenna-Lane	Jennifer (6.79)	Jensine (0.01)	Jeralynn	Jeriko	Jermiria
Jenna-Leah	Jennifer Marie	Jensun	Jerame	Jerilene	Jermisha
Jenna-Lee (0.01)	Jennifer Rose	Jensyn	Jeramie	Jerily	Jermishia
Jenna-Lynn	Jennifer-Afiriyie	Jenta	Jeran	Jerilyn (0.01)	Jermmel
Jenna-Marie	Jennifer-Jade	Jentel	Jeranika	Jerilynn	Jermondia
Jenna-Renee	Jennifer-Lee	Jenteria	Jeranisha	Jerin	Jermonee
Jennaca	Jennifer-Lyn	Jentle	Jeraylin	Jerine	Jermonica
Jennae	Jennifer-Lynn	Jentrey	Jerbraylen	Jerinique	Jermuria
Jennaé	Jennifer-Randi	Jentri	Jerbrea	Jerinn	Jernai
Jennafer (0.01)	Jennifer-Sylvia	Jentrie	Jercora	Jerinsha	Jernasha
Jennah (0.03)	Jennifer-Thao	Jentry	Jere	Jeris	Jernate
Jennai	Jenniferl	Jentzen	Jereaka	Jerissa	Jernay
Jennaka	Jenniferr	Jenuine	Jereca	Jeritza	Jerneca
Jennalee (0.01)	Jenniffer (0.01)	Jenusa	Jerecka	Jerivannece	Jerneisha
Jennalyn	Jennifher	Jenusha	Jeree	Jerkia	Jernerica
Jennamarie	Jennifier	Jenviave	Jerell	Jerlacie	Jernesha
Jennasee	Jennika	Jeny	Jerelle	Jerleshia	Jernika
Jennasia	Jennilee	Jenya	Jerelly	Jerlicia	Jerniqua
Jennasis	Jennilin	Jenyah	Jerelyn	Jerlisa	Jernishia
Jennat	Jennilyn (0.01)	Jenyfer	Jeremeka	Jerlisha	Jernkia
Jennaveve	Jennilynn	Jenyika	Jeremia	Jerlyn	Jernovous
Jennavie	Jennin	Jenying	Jeremiah	Jerlysha	Jernyra
Jennavieve	Jennine	Jenzece	Jeremica	Jermaine	Jeromeisha
Jennaya	Jennings	Jenzel	Jeremicka	Jermaira	Jeromica
Jenne	Jennipher	Jeonna	Jeremisha	Jermaiya	Jeron
Jennea	Jennique	Jeorgia	Jeremy	Jermanay	Jerona
Jenneca	Jennis	Jeorgy	Jerena	Jermanaye	Jeronda
Jennece	Jennise	Jeovanna	Jerenae	Jermanee	Jeronica
Jennedy	Jennisha	Jeovannah	Jerenecia	Jermani	Jerotich
Jennee	Jennissa	Jephina	Jererika	Jermanique	Jerphine
Jennefer	Jennitza	Jephri	Jeresa	Jermante	Jerquanda
Jennefer Ly	Jennivee	Jequa	Jeresha	Jermany	Jerquanna
Jenneka	Jennosha	Jequalla	Jeressa	Jermara	Jerqueisha
Jennel	Jenntte	Jequan	Jereyn	Jermésha	Jerquila
Jennell	Jenny (0.60)	Jequanna	Jergmesá	Jermeasha	Jerquira
Jennella	Jenny Anh Thu	Jequavia	Jerhi	Jermeashia	Jerquis
Jennelle (0.01)	Jenny Jasmine	Jequel	Jeri (0.03)	Jermechia	Jerra
Jenneni	Jenny Lee (0.01)	Jequil	Jeri'	Jermecia	Jerrah
Jennesa	Jenny Rose	Jequisha	Jeri'ca	Jermeia	Jerraka
Jennese	Jenny-Lee	Jequita	Jeri-Alexandria	Jermeisha	Jerraya
Jennessa	Jenny-Marie	Jequoya	Jeri-Lee	Jermeka (0.01)	Jerréneka
Jennet	Jenny-May	Jer Mesha	Jeri-Lyn	Jermekia	Jerree

Jerrela	Jeselica	Jessamyn	Jessica-Rae	Jessye *(0.01)*	Jewelann
Jerrett	Jesen	Jessandra	Jessica-Rai	Jessyka *(0.01)*	Jewelia
Jerri *(0.03)*	Jesenia *(0.07)*	Jessany	Jessica-Rose	Jest'us	Jeweliana
Jerri-Ann	Jesennia	Jessarae	Jessicaa	Jestann	Jeweliann
Jerri-Gail	Jeseray	Jessayca	Jessicaangela	Jestavia	Jewelie
Jerri-Lynne	Jesha	Jessaymn	Jessicaanne	Jestenia	Jewell *(0.03)*
Jerrian	Jeshea	Jessca	Jessicah	Jester	Jewelle
Jerriana	Jeshira	Jesscia	Jessicamari	Jestin	Jewellene
Jerrica *(0.08)*	Jeshona	Jesse *(0.17)*	Jessicca *(0.01)*	Jestina *(0.01)*	Jewelletha
Jerricah	Jeshonda	Jessea	Jessicia	Jestine	Jewellonda
Jerricca	Jesi *(0.01)*	Jesseaca	Jessicka	Jestini	Jeweloni
Jerricha	Jesica *(0.07)*	Jesseca *(0.03)*	Jessico	Jestiny	Jewels
Jerricka	Jesicalyn	Jessee	Jessicsa	Jesty	Jewelyah
Jerrieka	Jesicca	Jesseeca	Jessie *(0.69)*	Jesuana	Jewelyann
Jerrien	Jesie	Jesseeka	Jessie Mara	Jesula	Jewewl
Jerriesha	Jesika *(0.02)*	Jesseica	Jessie Marie	Jesunna	Jewrita
Jerriette	Jesikah	Jessel	Jessie-Ann	Jesus *(0.02)*	Jewyl
Jerrika *(0.01)*	Jesikkah	Jessely	Jessie-Jeanne	Jesus Stephanie	Jeya
Jerrilyn	Jesilea	Jesselyn	Jessie-Joyce	Jesusa	Jeyaseelan
Jerrilynn	Jesilyn	Jessen	Jessie-Lyn	Jesusita	Jeydy
Jerrina	Jesilynn	Jessena	Jessie-Lynn	Jesyca	Jeyleen
Jerrineisha	Jesina	Jessenia *(0.07)*	Jessielynn	Jesyka	Jeymi
Jerrinesha	Jesined	Jesserae	Jessiemae	Jeszybel	Jeynees
Jerriona	Jesirae	Jesseruth	Jessierae	Jeta	Jeyny
Jerrisha	Jeskia	Jessetta	Jessietta	Jetaun	Jeyonna
Jerrissa	Jeskiret	Jessette	Jessika *(0.18)*	Jetavia	Jeza
Jerron	Jeslakilya	Jessey	Jessika Rebe	Jeterra	Jeza'marie
Jerrtta	Jeslene	Jesseya	Jessika-Jaymes	Jetia	Jezabel *(0.01)*
Jerry	Jeslin	Jessi *(0.09)*	Jessilee	Jetlynn	Jezanie
Jerrymi	Jeslyn	Jessi-Ann	Jessilyn *(0.01)*	Jetoinne	Jezarae
Jerseanee	Jeslynn	Jessi-Lee	Jessilynn	Jett	Jezaray
Jersey	Jesmaris	Jessi-Mae	Jessime	Jetta	Jezebel
Jershona	Jesmin	Jessia	Jessina	Jettá	Jezekah
Jertaraia	Jesmina	Jessian	Jessiney	Jette	Jezel
Jertecia	Jesmine	Jessiane	Jessiqua	Jettie	Jezell
Jerterris	Jesneet	Jessic	Jessiquence	Jettylin	Jezenia
Jerusalem	Jesoly	Jessica *(16.60)*	Jessired	Jeuell	Jezmaraya
Jerusha *(0.01)*	Jesreen	Jessica Eliza	Jessiree	Jeulee	Jezmine
Jervasha	Jess	Jessica Elizabeth	Jessita	Jeulie	Jezmone
Jervis	Jess'ca	Jessica Harley	Jesslan	Jeunesia	Jezmyn
Jervona	Jessa *(0.05)*	Jessica Jane	Jesslin	Jeunesse	Jezreal
Jeryka	Jessa Mae	Jessica Lea	Jesslyn *(0.02)*	Jeung	Jezreel
Jeryn	Jessa-Maree	Jessica Marie	Jesslynn	Jeunne Kay	Jezybel
Jerzavyer	Jessabel	Jessica Noelle	Jesslynne	Jevana	Jezzlyn
Jerzy	Jessaca	Jessica Ria	Jessmeet	Jevaney	Jh'anhycia
Jesa	Jessah	Jessica Rose	Jessmere	Jevante	Jh'twoi-N'jai
Jesaca	Jessaka	Jessica Ruth Lo	Jessmyn	Jeviell	Jha'liah
Jesalyn	Jessaka-Toni	Jessica-Anne	Jessola	Jevin	Jha'marica
Jesalynn	Jessakah	Jessica-Faye	Jessolyn	Jevon	Jha'mila
Jescica	Jessalyn *(0.03)*	Jessica-Jean	Jesstine	Jevoné	Jha'nisha
Jescilla	Jessalynn	Jessica-Lee	Jesstineka	Jevonna	Jha'quorsha
Jesdsica	Jessamen	Jessica-Leigh	Jessuca	Jevonne	Jhacobia
Jese	Jessamine	Jessica-Lyn	Jessuly	Jew'licia	Jhacree
Jesénia	Jessamir	Jessica-Lynn	Jessy *(0.07)*	Jewanda	Jhada
Jeseca	Jessamy	*(0.01)*	Jessyca *(0.03)*	Jewel *(0.05)*	Jhaia

Jhailyn	Jhay'lah	Jiani	Jillmary	Jimmilee	Jisala
Jhakala	Jhayde	Jianina	Jillquisha	Jimmillia	Jisel
Jhakia	Jhaymie	Jianna	Jillyan	Jimmisha	Jisela
Jhakielah	Jhazmine	Jiara	Jillyn	Jimmy	Jiselle
Jhakira	Jhelia	Jiat-Wen	Jilysa	Jimmyquia	Jishay
Jhakiya	Jhemyah	Jibré	Jim'mina	Jimoria	Jisoluwa
Jhalena	Jhene	Jie Nise	Jima'rah	Jimrah	Jisoo
Jhalia	Jhenifer	Jiehan	Jimae	Jimta'cha	Jissantt
Jhalyn	Jhenna	Jiemil	Jimaiah	Jimyla	Jissel
Jhamakia	Jhequae	Jierra	Jiman	Jin *(0.01)*	Jissell
Jhamara	Jheran	Jigail	Jimanisha	Jin Hee	Jitia
Jhamby	Jheri	Jigna	Jimber-Nee	Jina *(0.01)*	Jitisha
Jhamecia	Jherica	Jignasha	Jimecia	Jiná	Jivana
Jhamelah	Jherrica	Jihan	Jimecka	Jinada	Jiwanjot
Jhamelia	Jherrika	Jihana	Jimee	Jinai	Jixi
Jhamilah	Jhesica	Jihanna	Jimeka	Jinal	Jiya
Jhamycianna	Jhessica	Jihee	Jimelia	Jinan	Jiyoon
Jhana	Jhi	Jihn'ai	Jimena *(0.02)*	Jinane	Jiyun
Jhanae	Jhiliah	Jikala	Jimeria	Jindra	Jizel
Jhanaé	Jhirmekia	Jikerra	Jimeryl	Jineavea	Jizella
Jhanai	Jho Né	Jil	Jimesha	Jineen	Jizelle
Jhanaisa	Jhoan	Jil-Leesa	Jimetra	Jinelle	Jizyah
Jhanay	Jhoana	Jilaine	Jimeva	Jinette	Jizzmone
Jhance	Jhoanny	Jilan	Jimeyah	Jing	Jjleen
Jhane *(0.01)*	Jhoarea	Jilani	Jimi	Jing-Yin	Jlynn
Jhané *(0.01)*	Jholene	Jilda	Jimia	Jingwen	Jme
Jhanea	Jhon'e	Jilee	Jimiah	Jinhee	Jmie
Jhanelle	Jhona	Jilene	Jimica	Jinia	Jmika
Jhani	Jhoná	Jilesa	Jimicia	Jinikqua	Jna
Jhanik	Jhoniequea	Jilian	Jimie	Jinine	Jna'ishatriyah
Jhaniqua	Jhonikwa	Jiliane	Jimiece	Jinisa	Jnae
Jhanique	Jhonne	Jiliane-Elise	Jimiere	Jinjer	Jnai
Jhann	Jhontrell	Jill *(0.19)*	Jimieshia	Jinju	Jnara
Jhanna	Jhordana	Jill-Marie	Jimilah	Jinna	Jnaye
Jhannel	Jhori	Jillain	Jimille	Jinnelen	Jo *(0.01)*
Jhanneu	Jhubria	Jillana	Jimilyn	Jinnifer	Jo Ana
Jhannon	Jhyairah	Jillayah	Jiminesha	Jinny *(0.01)*	Jo Ann
Jhante	Ji	Jillayne	Jimisha	Jinpreet	Jo Anna
Jhantha	Ji Hye	Jilleen	Jimissa	Jinqua	Jo Ellen
Jhanya	Ji Shena	Jilleesa	Jimita	Jinsyn	Jo Hanna
Jhara	Ji'mara	Jilleigh	Jimiya	Jinyoung	Jo Hannah
Jhardai	Ji'savorya	Jillena	Jimmaka	Jioanna	Jo Kerria
Jharel	Jia	Jillesa	Jimmar	Jioia	Jo Lee
Jharitzi	Jia-Leen	Jilliam	Jimmecia	Jiorgi	Jo Lisha
Jharline	Jiaanna	Jillian *(0.67)*	Jimmeka	Jipcia	Jo Marie
Jharlinne	Jiabella	Jillian Blair	Jimmequa	Jiquaila	Jo Meikya
Jharmela	Jiah	Jillian Renee	Jimmera	Jiquelyn	Jo N'ail
Jharon	Jiahna	Jilliana	Jimmeria	Jiquetta	Jo Nay
Jhasha	Jiahndria	Jilliane	Jimmesha	Jiqueyna	Jo Nea
Jhasmin	Jiaira	Jilliann	Jimmi	Jirah	Jo Neka
Jhasmine	Jialing	Jillianne	Jimmia	Jire L	Jo Nique
Jhasmyne	Jialisa	Jilliela	Jimmiaya	Jireail	Jo Vannee
Jhatashia	Jiameshia	Jillion	Jimmie	Jireh	Jo'anna
Jhavariel	Jian	Jillise	Jimmiéla	Jiriko	Jo'aquen
Jhave	Jianeshiá	Jillissa	Jimmiesha	Jirmika	Jo'esha

Jo'keria	Joanshen	Jocqueisha	Joekeria	Joezi	Johnetra
Jo'lesha	Joany (0.01)	Jocqueline	Joekivia	Jofina	Johnetta (0.01)
Jo'myira	Joaquina	Jocy	Joekyra	Joh'quanna	Johnette
Jo'neeka	Joaquinne	Jocylan	Joel	Joham	Johni
Jo'nesha	Joardan	Jocylen	Joelaine	Johan	Johnica
Jo'nycia	Joarden	Jocylyn	Joele	Johana (0.07)	Johnice
Jo'quandreia	Jobaha	Jod'e	Joeleen	Johanie (0.02)	Johnicia
Jo'selda	Jobana	Joda	Joelene	Johann	Johnie
Jo'shara	Jobany	Jodace	Joelia	Johanna (0.27)	Johniece
Jo'travia	Jobelle	Jodan	Joelie	Johannah (0.03)	Johniera
Jo'vona	Jobenia	Jodanna	Joelisha	Johanne (0.01)	Johniesh
Jo'vonana	Jobeth	Jodeci (0.01)	Joell	Johannie (0.02)	Johniesha
Jo'vonn	Jobi	Jodee (0.01)	Joella	Johanny (0.01)	Johnika
Jo-Ann	Jobie	Jodeja	Joelle (0.19)	Johany	Johnimae
Jo-Anna	Jobita	Jodel	Joellen	Johari	Johniqu'e
Jo-Anne	Jobrea	Jodelle	Joellene	Johbarie	Johniqua
Jo-Annie	Jocalyn	Jodericka	Joelli	Johhna	Johnique
Jo-Dawn	Jocastia	Jodeshia	Joelly	Johlisa	Johnisa
Jo-Meyka	Jocee	Jodesia	Joellyn	Johlonda	Johnise
Jo-Nytranna	Jocefina	Jodesja	Joely	John (0.01)	Johnisha (0.01)
Joacelynne	Jocelanne	Jodey	Joelyn	John'na	Johnishia
Joahlee	Jocelayn	Jodi (0.16)	Joelyne	Johna (0.01)	Johnkeelah
Joahna	Jocelia	Jodi-Ann	Joelynn	Johná	Johnmesha
Joahnna	Jocelie	Jodi-Anne	Joelys	Johnae (0.01)	Johnna (0.04)
Joaja	Jocelin (0.04)	Jodi-Lynn	Joemaricel	Johnaé	Johnná
Joakim	Jocelina	Jodi-Lynne	Joemetria	Johnai	Johnnae
Joali	Joceline (0.02)	Jodia	Joemika	Johnaisha	Johnnaé
Joan (0.06)	Jocelinn	Jodiann	Joemilin	Johnakia	Johnnah
Joana (0.11)	Joceliz	Jodianne	Joen	Johnalyn	Johnnay
Joana Alicia	Jocely	Jodie (0.09)	Joeneicia	Johnalynn	Johnnaye
Joana Rebeca	Jocelyn (1.13)	Jodie-Ann	Joeneisha	Johnana	Johnnedra
Joanadene	Jocelyne (0.08)	Jodie-Leigh	Joeneka	Johnante	Johnneisha
Joanalyn	Jocelynn (0.03)	Jodie-Rose	Joenesia	Johnasha	Johnneka
Joane	Joceyln	Jodiee	Joenessadiana	Johnasia	Johnnell
Joangela	Jochebed	Jodilee	Joenetta	Johnathen	Johnneria
Joani	Jochelle	Jodilyn	Joenicqwa	Johnaura	Johnnesha
Joanie (0.25)	Jochelyn	Jodine	Joeniesha	Johnay	Johnnetta
Joanika	Joci	Jody (0.06)	Joenika	Johnékia	Johnnette
Joanique	Jociana	Jody-Ann	Joenisha	Johnea	Johnnia
Joanise	Jociann	Joe	Joenna	Johneatha	Johnnica
Joanisha	Jocie	Joékara	Joeny	Johnee	Johnnice
Joanize	Jociel	Joél	Joequetta	Johneele	Johnnie (0.02)
Joann (0.06)	Jocilyn	Joe-Dy	Joesakaura	Johneika	Johnnié
Joanna (0.83)	Jocilynn	Joeal	Joesphine	Johneil	Johnnielyn
Joanna Mari	Jocinda	Joeana-Gim-Linh	Joessie	Johneisha	Johnnika
Joanna-Maria	Jockedra	Joeann	Joetashaann	Johneka	Johnniqua
Joanna-Marie	Jocland	Joeanna	Joetta	Johnell	Johnnisa
Joannaashley	Joclyn (0.01)	Joecee	Joette	Johnella	Johnnise
Joannah	Joclynn	Joecindy	Joeveen	Johnelle	Johnnisha
Joanne (0.18)	Joclynne	Joecyln	Joevena	Johnequa	Johnnita
Joannelys	Jocobi	Joedi	Joevontay	Johnese	Johnny
Joanni	Jocobia	Joedy	Joewin	Johnesha (0.01)	Johnnyle
Joannia	Jocolyn	Joee	Joey (0.03)	Johneshia	Johnquetta
Joannie (0.06)	Jocorrea	Joeelis	Joeylyn	Johnesia	Johnquisha
Joanny (0.01)	Jocquale	Joei	Joeyna	Johnetha	Johnsie

Joyrjah	Juan'niqua	Judie	Julesia	Juliet (0.06)	Jummeloh
Joys	Juana (0.14)	Judienne	Juley	Julieta (0.03)	Jumonyse
Joysee	Juana-Inez	Judit	Julhi-Ann	Juliett	Jun'lisa
Joyselle	Juanaceli	Judith (0.25)	Juli	Julietta	Juna
Joysha	Juanalyn	Judith Ann	Juli-Hannah	Juliette (0.10)	Junalee
Joyslin	Juaneikka	Judley	Julia (2.47)	Julihanna	Junaris
Joyti	Juaneiqua	Judlyne	Julia Anne	Julin	June (0.05)
Joytoria	Juanell	Judny	Julia Elizabeth	Julina	Junea
Jozalyn	Juaneshia	Judy (0.13)	Julia Naomi	Juline	Juneisha
Jozée	Juanetta	Judy Ann	Julia-Ann	Julinet	Junel
Jozel	Juaney	Judy-Lynn	Julia-Anne	Julio	Junella
Jozella	Juaniká	Judyt	Julia-Ascenza	Juliona	Junelle
Jozelyn	Juanika	Judyta	Julia-Marie	Julis	Junellie
Jozelynne	Juaniqa	Juel	Julia-Melissa	Julisa (0.03)	Junelly
Jozet	Juaniqua	Juelle	Julia-Rose	Julisha	Junera
Jozette	Juanique	Juells	Julia-Shea	Julisia Jovita	Junessa
Jozi	Juanise	Juenesse	Juliaann	Julissa (0.09)	Juneva
Jozianne	Juanisha	Juesline	Juliaanne	Julita	Juney
Jozie (0.01)	Juanit	Jugjot	Juliafaye	Julius	Jung-Yeon
Jozlyn	Juanita (0.17)	Jugman	Juliah	Juliya	Junia
Jozlynn	Juanita Lea	Jugroop	Julialette	Juliyann	Junie
Jozlynne	Juanneisha	Jugveer	Juliama	Juliza	Junieth
Jozmen	Juannetta	Juhee	Julian (0.01)	Julizza	Juniett
Jozy	Juannia	Juhi (0.01)	Juliana (0.32)	Julle	Junievy
Jozzmyn	Juannissa	Juil	Juliandra	Jullee	Junikka
Jr	Juantanic	Juilanna	Juliane (0.01)	Jullette	Junikqua
Jriselda	Juantazia	Juiliane	Juliane-Marie	Jullian (0.01)	Juniper
Jsane	Juaquina	Juilianna	Julianique	Jullian Mercede	Junique
Jsasmine	Juawanna	Juistine	Juliann (0.03)	Julliana	Junisa
Jshanna	Juayeshia	Jujuanna	Julianna (0.23)	Jullianie	Junisha
Jssi	Jube	Jukala	Julianne (0.21)	Jullianna	Junita
Jtyia	Jubilation	Jukeara	Juliarna	Jullie	Junixsy
Ju	Jubilee (0.01)	Jukendrial	Juliauna	Julliette	Junnicia
Ju Lie	Jubitza	Jukeria	Julie (1.31)	Jully	Juno
Ju Nesha	Juboria	Jukeya	Julie Ann	Julma	Junoet
Ju'hstiz	Jubray	Jukipa	Julie Anne (0.01)	Julonda	Junotta
Ju'keria	Jubria	Jukita	Julie Tram	Julsean	Junshi
Ju'kia	Jubulation	Jula	Julie-Ann	July	Juntrell
Ju'lexius	Jucinda	Julan	Julie-Anne	Julya	Juquala
Ju'lisa La'toya	Judaéa	Julani	Julie-Marie	Julyana	Juquila
Ju'niquetta	Judah	Julann	Juliea	Julyanna	Jur Nae
Ju'nisha	Judalon	Julanne	Julieana	Julyna	Jureá
Ju'wanna	Judashia	Jule	Julieann (0.01)	Julynda	Juri
Ju-El	Jude	Julea	Julieanna (0.01)	Julyne	Juricouria
Ju-Leah	Judea	Juleah	Julieanne	Julysa	Jurie
Jua	Judeah	Julean	Juliece	Julyssa	Jurieka
Jua'neishia	Judeana	Juleann	Julielyn	Jumaanah	Jurika
Juacole	Judejah	Julee (0.01)	Julien	Jumana	Jurissa
Juah Vaun	Judeline	Julee-Ann	Juliena	Jumanah	Juritzi
Juahana	Judeliza	Juleean	Juliene	Jumarrikka	Jurnee (0.01)
Juakota	Judi	Juleeia	Julienn	Jumecia	Jurney
Jualisa	Judia	Juleika	Julienne (0.01)	Jumekia	Jurrena
Juan	Judiah	Julena	Julienne Aira	Jumika	Jurrisa
Juan Qasia	Judibrown	Julenice	Julierose	Jumilyah	Juscintinia
Juan'esh	Judidtsy	Jules	Juliesa	Jumira	Jushawn

Jusilya	Jvonne	Jyssinia	K'nequa	Ka'dija	Ka-Necia
Jusleen	Jwanna	Jywanna	K'ona	Ka'dijah	Ka-Neiya
Juslen	Jwanta	Jywikia	K'osha	Ka'disha	Ka-Raun
Jusmine	Jwbettzy	Jyya	K'sha	Ka'drah	Ka-Ren
Juspreet	Jy'aisha	Jyzzyka	K'shambiá	Ka'la (0.01)	Kaaja
Jussica	Jy'ashia	Jzaibriel	K'shunte	Ka'lani	Kaajalpreet
Justa	Jy'miera	Jzatia	K'tia	Ka'lare	Kaala
Justean	Jy'nisha	Jzayla	K'tianna	Ka'ledrea	Kaalen
Justeen	Jy'raisha	Jzona	K'tonna	Ka'lenna	Kaaliya
Justeena	Jy'tise	Jzordan	K'tris	Ka'lesha	Kaalyah
Justeene	Jy'wuanseia	Jzsa	K'ueen	Ka'liesha	Kaambria
Justeia	Jy-Nee	Jzy'eva	K'vaughn	Ka'llon	Kaamilya
Justena	Jya		K'vonna	Ka'lynn	Kaamran
Justene	Jyaira	**-K-**	K'wmesha	Ka'mia	Kaaren
Justess	Jyairra		K'yauna	Ka'najasha	Kaari
Justi'ce	Jyanette	K (0.08)	K-Ann	Ka'nasia	Kaarle
Justia	Jyella Jakeisha	K Ann	K-Ci	Ka'nechia	Kaarsten
Justice (0.36)	Jyenna	K C	K-La	Ka'neesha	Kaaryn
Justice-Chanté	Jyesha	K C Renée	K-Leigh	Ka'neeshia	Kaatarina
Justicee	Jyfinati'e	K Cee	K-Shaydra	Ka'neisha	Kaathleen
Justie	Jyi	K lera	K.	Ka'nesha	Kaatla
Justiene	Jyianika	K Juana	K.C.	Ka'neshia	Kaatlyn
Justin (0.01)	Jykerria	K Leia	K.C. Lyn	Ka'netra	Kaatrina
Justina (0.14)	Jyl	K Llezia	K.D.	Ka'nia	Kaavya
Justine (0.74)	Jylah	K Lynn	Ka (0.03)	Ka'nice	Kaayla
Justine Nicole	Jylain	K'ahda	Ka Anilee	Ka'nijasha	Kabeera
Justinee	Jylan	K'aisa	Ka Cosa	Ka'nisha	Kabeerah
Justis (0.01)	Jyleah	K'amberia	Ka Darie	Ka'oni	Kabina
Justise (0.01)	Jylece	K'anna	Ka Deejah	Ka'osjah	Kabree
Justiss	Jyllann	K'ayla	Ka Deisha	Ka'phersa	Kabreeha
Justisse	Jyllean	K'briyauna	Ka Deja	Ka'precious	Kabreil
Justitia	Jyllyann	K'cianna	Ka Desia	Ka'quana	Kabrena
Justiz	Jymeshia	K'deja	Ka Lyn	Ka'ra	Kabresha
Justus (0.01)	Jymesia	K'deshia	Ka Prisha	Ka'sandra	Kabretta
Justy	Jymia	K'desia	Ka Shatta	Ka'shauna	Kabri
Justyce (0.01)	Jymie	K'dierea	Ka Sheena	Ka'shawnda	Kabria (0.01)
Justyn	Jymiesha	K'dijah	Ka Teishia	Ka'shay	Kabriana
Justyna (0.01)	Jynai	K'ehleyr	Ka Teyah	Ka'shayla	Kabriani
Justyne (0.01)	Jynay	K'eona	Ka Tomja	Ka'shondre	Kabriann
Justynn	Jynessa	K'erria	Ka Zoua	Ka'shrena	Kabrianna
Justynne	Jynessa-Lyn	K'halia	Ka'alijah	Ka'shun	Kabriea
Justys	Jynette	K'haylah	Ka'briel	Ka'shyra	Kabrielle
Jutai	Jynique	K'ieasha	Ka'cetrya	Ka'tice	Kabrienne
Jutoria	Jynnika	K'leigh	Ka'chandan	Ka'tora	Kabrieshia
Juvana	Jyntill	K'lia	Ka'chel	Ka'tura	Kabrina (0.01)
Juvia	Jyote	K'liyah	Ka'dasha	Ka'vasha	Kabrini
Juvilane	Jyoti	K'loni	Ka'daysha	Ka'waunya	Kabrionna
Juwairyah	Jyotiba	K'ly	Ka'deasia	Ka'yonnah	Kabrityné
Juwan	Jyraca	K'lyn	Ka'dedrah	Ka-Bao	Kabriya
Juwana	Jyralisa	K'lynn	Ka'deidra	Ka-Breauna	Kabura
Juwanna	Jyralyn	K'maia	Ka'deija	Ka-Brittany	Kacaina
Juwaria	Jysha	K'marchai	Ka'desha	Ka-Cyndra	Kacandra
Juwayriyah	Jyshaé	K'mesha	Ka'desia	Ka-Imani'	Kacasiá
Juweria	Jyssica	K'miya	Ka'detria	Ka-Jana	Kacaundra
Juya	Jyssika	K'nayla	Ka'diesha	Ka-Jong	Kace

Kacee (0.02)	Kadedrah	Kadia	Kadylee	Kaen	Kahleisia
Kaceelyn	Kadedria	Kadiah	Kadyn	Kaena	Kahlen
Kaceia	Kadee (0.02)	Kadiane	Kadysha	Kaesey	Kahlena
Kacelyn	Kadeedra	Kadianne	Kadyshia	Kaesha	Kahley
Kacey (0.12)	Kadeeja	Kadiatou	Kae	Kaeshena	Kahli (0.01)
Kachanne	Kadeejah (0.01)	Kadiatu	Kae Ana	Kaeshia	Kahli-Ann
Kachanteau	Kadeejha	Kadidjah	Kae La	Kaesi	Kahlia (0.01)
Kachaundra	Kadeem	Kadidra	Kae Ranisha	Kaeslyn	Kahlie
Kache	Kadeen	Kadie (0.04)	Kae-Lynn	Kaetee	Kahlil
Kachét	Kadeesha (0.01)	Kadiedra	Kae-Shonar	Kaethe	Kahliyah
Kachee	Kadeeshia	Kadieja	Kaeana	Kaethlenn	Kahloni
Kachelé	Kadeesia	Kadiejah	Kaechelle	Kaetlin	Kahlyn
Kachelle	Kadeesiah	Kadiejha	Kaeci	Kaetlyn (0.01)	Kahlyssa
Kachet	Kadeezha	Kadiesha	Kaecia	Kaetlynn	Kahmiah
Kachia	Kadeezia	Kadieshia	Kaede	Kaevin	Kahmina
Kachina	Kadehja	Kadigah	Kaeding	Kaewanee	Kahnasia
Kachine	Kadehjra	Kadighdra	Kaedryn	Kaeylla	Kahneesha
Kachna	Kadeidra (0.01)	Kadihja	Kaedyn	Kaeylla Tawanna	Kahny
Kachtia	Kadeidre	Kadiijha-Simone	Kaehla	Kafela	Kaho
Kaci (0.07)	Kadeidré	Kadija (0.01)	Kaehn	Kafia	Kaho'olanakila
Kacia	Kadeidria	Kadijah (0.13)	Kaeila	Kafiya	Kahra
Kaciann	Kadeija (0.01)	Kadijaha	Kaeja	Kafyebien	Kahrin
Kacie (0.14)	Kadeijah	Kadijeah	Kaela (0.12)	Kagan	Kahrys
Kacii	Kadeisha (0.01)	Kadijesha	Kaelah	Kagelik	Kahshanna
Kacissa	Kadeitra	Kadijh	Kaelah-Arianna	Kagi	Kahtera
Kaclyn	Kadejá	Kadijha	Kaelan	Kagiso	Kahtlyn
Kacondra	Kadeja (0.01)	Kadijiá	Kaelani	Kagla	Kahtool
Kacreasea	Kadejá	Kadijua	Kaelcey	Kaglan	Kahvashea
Kacy (0.05)	Kadejah (0.03)	Kadijuh	Kaelea	Kah'sha	Kahvia
Kacyee	Kadejia	Kadin	Kaeleah	Kahae	Kahyla
Kada	Kadejiah	Kadina	Kaelee (0.01)	Kahalia	Kai (0.03)
Kadaajah	Kadejihia	Kadine	Kaeleen	Kahania	Kai'chea
Kadaijah	Kadejra	Kadira	Kaelei	Kahara	Kai'dra
Kadaja	Kadejsha	Kadisha (0.01)	Kaeleigh (0.01)	Kahdaija	Kai'esha
Kadajah	Kadejuia	Kadishia	Kaeleigh-Lynne	Kahdashia	Kai'ran
Kadajahi	Kadelyn	Kadisia	Kaelen (0.01)	Kahder	Kai'shayla
Kadalya	Kademah	Kadiya	Kaelene	Kahdija	Kai-Anna
Kadara	Kaden	Kadizah	Kaeley (0.01)	Kahdijah	Kai-Lonnee
Kadasha	Kadence	Kadizjah	Kaeli (0.03)	Kahdijahn	Kai-Mailie
Kadashia	Kader	Kadizjhah	Kaelia	Kahdijiah	Kaia (0.02)
Kadastany	Kaderá	Kadj	Kaeliann	Kahea	Kaiah
Kadayjah	Kaderha	Kadjah	Kaelie (0.01)	Kaheema	Kaiala
Kadazia	Kaderion	Kadjia	Kaelii	Kahela	Kaianne
Kaddie	Kadesa	Kadra	Kaelin (0.07)	Kahetonni	Kaicee
Kade	Kadesha (0.03)	Kadre	Kaelina	Kahilah	Kaicierra
Kadeadra	Kadesheia	Kadrea	Kaelinn	Kahisha	Kaida
Kadeah	Kadeshia (0.01)	Kadree	Kaelly	Kahiya	Kaidedra
Kadean	Kadeshjia	Kadria	Kaelon	Kahjasmine	Kaideidra
Kadeasha	Kadesia (0.01)	Kadriah	Kaely (0.01)	Kahla (0.01)	Kaiden
Kadeazsha	Kadessa	Kadrian	Kaelye	Kahlae	Kaidi
Kadecia	Kadetra	Kadsha	Kaelym	Kahlah	Kaidin
Kadedia	Kadey	Kadshia	Kaelyn (0.11)	Kahlan	Kaidra
Kadedra (0.02)	Kadezia	Kady (0.04)	Kaelynn (0.02)	Kahléa	Kaidy
Kadedra Daniell	Kadezjah	Kady-Ann	Kaelynne	Kahlea	Kaidyn
Kadedra Monique	Kadi (0.02)	Kadya	Kaemen	Kahlee	Kaie

Kaiesha	Kainat	Kaitly	Kalahan	Kaler	Kalix
Kaighin	Kainesha	Kaitlyn *(3.51)*	Kalahyn	Kalesha	Kaliya
Kaih	Kainna	Kaitlyn Oli	Kalai	Kaleshia	Kaliyah *(0.02)*
Kaija *(0.01)*	Kaiontay	Kaitlyn-Anne	Kalaia	Kalesia	Kaliyani
Kaijana	Kair'sha	Kaitlyn-Marie	Kalaiah	Kalesianna	Kalkidan
Kaila *(0.28)*	Kaira *(0.01)*	Kaitlynd	Kalainty	Kalessia	Kalla *(0.01)*
Kailagh	Kairee	Kaitlyne *(0.01)*	Kalan *(0.01)*	Kaletia	Kallah
Kailah *(0.02)*	Kairelle	Kaitlynn *(0.33)*	Kalana	Kaley *(0.22)*	Kallalisa
Kailan	Kairi	Kaitlynne *(0.02)*	Kalandria	Kaleya	Kallan
Kailand	Kairstin	Kaitriana	Kalaneshia	Kaleyah	Kallana
Kailani	Kaisa	Kaitryn	Kalani *(0.02)*	Kalhiea	Kallas
Kailanii	Kaise	Kaity	Kalarelyn	Kali *(0.28)*	Kalle
Kailanni	Kaisee	Kaityln	Kalasia	Kali-Ann	Kalleah
Kailash	Kaiser	Kaityn	Kalauna	Kalia *(0.03)*	Kallee
Kailasha	Kaisey	Kaivon	Kalauni	Kaliah *(0.01)*	Kalleena
Kaile *(0.01)*	Kaisha *(0.01)*	Kaiya *(0.01)*	Kalaya	Kaliann	Kallei
Kailea	Kaishá	Kaiyah	Kalayna	Kalianna	Kalleigh
Kailee *(0.13)*	Kaishala	Kaiyia	Kalaysha	Kalianne	Kallen
Kailee Jo	Kaishawn	Kaiyla	Kalcey	Kaliayh	Kalley *(0.01)*
Kaileen *(0.01)*	Kaishela	Kaiylee	Kalcie	Kalicia	Kalli *(0.05)*
Kaileena	Kaisho	Kaiysha	Kalcina	Kalie *(0.10)*	Kalli-Alexis
Kaileh	Kaishon	Kaiythry	Kalea *(0.01)*	Kaliea	Kallie *(0.06)*
Kaileigh *(0.02)*	Kaisie	Kaja	Kaleá	Kaliean	Kallihaja
Kailen *(0.01)*	Kaissidy	Kajá	Kaleah	Kaliecia	Kallin
Kailena	Kaiston	Kajah	Kaleayah	Kaliegh	Kallison
Kailene	Kait	Kajal *(0.01)*	Kaleb	Kaliegha	Kallista
Kailey *(0.31)*	Kaitalin	Kajanée	Kalebra	Kaliene	Kallisti
Kailey-Jenna	Kaite	Kajaniya	Kalecia	Kaliese	Kallon
Kaileyne	Kaitee	Kajauna	Kaledria	Kaliesha	Kally *(0.01)*
Kaili *(0.03)*	Kaitelin	Kajaunza	Kalee *(0.08)*	Kalijah	Kallyn
Kailia	Kaitelyn	Kajavia	Kaleeia	Kalika	Kallysta
Kailiana	Kaitelynn	Kajetha	Kaleel	Kalila	Kalmia
Kailice	Kaitey	Kajhia	Kaleema	Kalilah	Kalneria
Kailicia	Kaithleen	Kajia	Kaleen *(0.01)*	Kalima	Kalo
Kailie *(0.02)*	Kaithlin	Kajill	Kaleena *(0.01)*	Kalimbria	Kalomira
Kailin *(0.01)*	Kaithlyn	Kajlie	Kaleesha	Kalin *(0.02)*	Kalon
Kailina	Kaithynn	Kajohna	Kalei *(0.01)*	Kalina *(0.03)*	Kalona
Kailinh	Kaitia	Kajol	Kalei-O-Ka-Lani	Kalinajay	Kalonda
Kailla	Kaitie	Kajounrei	Kaleia	Kalinda	Kaloni
Kailli	Kaitilyn	Kajri	Kaleibh	Kalindi	Kalonna
Kaillie	Kaitin	Kajsa	Kaleigh *(0.21)*	Kalindra	Kalosha
Kailon	Kaitlan *(0.03)*	Kajsha	Kaleigha	Kaline	Kalottie
Kailtin	Kaitland *(0.01)*	Kajtelyn	Kaleighan	Kalinee	Kalree
Kailtyn	Kaitlee	Kajuan	Kaleiha	Kalinen	Kalsea
Kaily *(0.02)*	Kaitlen *(0.02)*	Kajuana	Kaleinani	Kaliope	Kalsey
Kailya	Kaitlin *(1.56)*	Kajun	Kaleis	Kalisa	Kalsie
Kailyn *(0.10)*	Kaitlinann	Kajuree	Kaleisa	Kalise	Kalthum
Kailynda	Kaitlind	Kakeria	Kaleisha	Kalisha *(0.01)*	Kaltresula
Kailynn *(0.02)*	Kaitlinleig	Kakisha	Kalela	Kalishia	Kaltum
Kaimee	Kaitlinn *(0.01)*	Kako	Kalen *(0.02)*	Kalissa *(0.01)*	Kalulah
Kaimesha	Kaitlinne	Kal-El	Kalena *(0.02)*	Kalissiá	Kalveen
Kaimi	Kaitlon	Kala *(0.14)*	Kalene *(0.02)*	Kalista *(0.01)*	Kalvenia
Kaimila	Kaitlun	Kala Jewel	Kalenea	Kalistia	Kalvina
Kaina	Kaitlun-Kourtne	Kalafornia	Kalenna	Kalistian	Kaly *(0.01)*
Kainan	Kaitlunkour	Kalah *(0.02)*	Kalentia	Kalita	Kalya

Kalyah	Kamauri	Kamesia	Kamonée	Kandis *(0.01)*	Kaniesha
Kalyani	Kamaya	Kametra	Kamoney	Kandis-Lynn	Kanietra
Kalycia	Kamayah	Kametria	Kamora	Kandise	Kanijah
Kalycya	Kamayra	Kameyah	Kamorria	Kandiss	Kanika *(0.01)*
Kalye	Kamber	Kami *(0.05)*	Kampi	Kandlar	Kanikisa
Kalyiah	Kambi	Kami'llah	Kamra	Kandon	Kaniqu'e
Kalyn *(0.11)*	Kambrai	Kami'ya	Kamran	Kandra *(0.01)*	Kanique
Kalyn Caren	Kambrea	Kamia	Kamree	Kandrea	Kanise
Kalyna	Kambree	Kamiah	Kamren	Kandree	Kanish
Kalynah	Kambreia	Kamiaha	Kamrey	Kandria	Kanisha *(0.05)*
Kalynda	Kambrelee	Kamiana	Kamri *(0.01)*	Kanduntrel	Kanishia
Kalyne	Kambren	Kamica	Kamrie	Kandy	Kanita
Kalynn *(0.06)*	Kambreon	Kamie *(0.01)*	Kamrin	Kandyce *(0.01)*	Kanitra
Kalynne	Kambreya	Kamiea	Kamron	Kandyl	Kaniya *(0.01)*
Kalyrics	Kambria *(0.01)*	Kamiel	Kamry *(0.01)*	Kandyse	Kaniz
Kalysha	Kambrie	Kamielle	Kamrye	Kane	Kanna
Kalyssa	Kambriel	Kamiellia	Kamryn *(0.04)*	Kanea	Kannessa
Kalysta	Kambry	Kamijha	Kamrynn	Kaneasha	Kannis
Kam	Kamden	Kamika	Kamseha	Kaneata	Kannusha
Kamae	Kamdian	Kamil	Kamsi	Kaneca	Kanny
Kamaia	Kamea	Kamila *(0.01)*	Kamy	Kanecha	Kanokporn
Kamaila	Kameah	Kamilah *(0.01)*	Kamyia	Kanecia	Kanon
Kamaira	Kameca	Kamilia	Kamyra	Kaneda	Kansar
Kamaiya	Kameceya	Kamill	Kamyris	Kanedra	Kansas *(0.01)*
Kamajhia	Kameeka	Kamilla	Kamysha	Kaneedra	Kanshaun
Kamal	Kameela	Kamillah	Kamyylah	Kaneeka	Kansis
Kamala	Kameelah	Kamille *(0.04)*	Kana	Kaneesha *(0.01)*	Kanté
Kamalani	Kameeria	Kamillia	Kanae	Kaneisha *(0.02)*	Kanteese
Kamaldeep	Kameesha	Kamilliyah	Kanah	Kaneitra	Kanthy
Kamaldip	Kameilah	Kamilya	Kanai	Kanekia	Kantrenia
Kamalei	Kameisha	Kamio	Kanaiza	Kanela	Kanuiokalani
Kamalen	Kameishi	Kamira	Kanako	Kanequah	Kanval
Kamali	Kameita	Kamirea	Kanan	Kanesah	Kanwal
Kamalini	Kameka	Kamirin	Kanani	Kanesha *(0.03)*	Kanya
Kamaljit	Kameko	Kamis	Kanaporn	Kaneshea	Kanyell
Kamalpreet	Kameksha	Kamish	Kanara	Kaneshia	Kanyelle
Kamalvir	Kamela	Kamisha *(0.01)*	Kanaratonkie	Kanessa	Kanyia
Kamaly	Kamelia	Kamita	Kanasha	Kanesyah	Kanyon
Kamani	Kamell	Kamitria	Kanashious	Kaneta	Kanyra
Kamanie	Kamella	Kamiya *(0.01)*	Kanasia	Kanethia	Kanysha
Kamar	Kamelle	Kamiyah	Kanavyss	Kanetia	Kanza
Kamara *(0.02)*	Kamelya	Kamiylah	Kanchan	Kanetra	Kao
Kamarae	Kamen	Kamley	Kanchilyn	Kaney	Kaoie
Kamaray	Kameo	Kamlin	Kancisha	Kaneya	Kaoija
Kamaree	Kamer	Kammala	Kanda	Kaneysha	Kaolin
Kamari *(0.01)*	Kamera	Kammaria	Kandace *(0.07)*	Kani	Kaona
Kamaria *(0.02)*	Kameran	Kammarie	Kandake	Kani-La-Trel	Kaori
Kamariah	Kamerellé	Kammelee	Kandas	Kania	Kaoru
Kamarin	Kameri	Kammi	Kandence	Kaniawa	Kaory
Kamario	Kamerine	Kammie	Kandeshia	Kanica	Kapre
Kamariya	Kameris	Kammilla	Kandi *(0.01)*	Kanice	Kapreá
Kamariyah	Kameron *(0.03)*	Kammira	Kandi-Lee	Kanicka	Kaprece
Kamary	Kameryn *(0.01)*	Kammy	Kandice *(0.05)*	Kaniecia	Kaprecia
Kamarya	Kamesha *(0.01)*	Kammye	Kandichia	Kaniecsa	Kapree
Kamaura	Kameshia	Kamneev	Kandie	Kanieece	Kapreece

Kapreese	Karby	Karenpal	Karion	Karlijl	Karneshi
Kaprese	Karcen	Karent	Kariona	Karlin	Karni
Kapresha	Karchie	Karese	Karis *(0.02)*	Karlina	Karniesha
Kapri *(0.01)*	Kardasha	Karesha	Karisa *(0.03)*	Karlinda	Karnika
Kapria	Kardeidra	Karess	Karise	Karling	Karniqua
Kaprice	Kardia	Karessa	Karisha	Karling-Jo	Karnisha
Kaprii	Kardiá	Karestyn	Karishma *(0.02)*	Karlinna	Karnpreet
Kaprina	Kardija	Karetta	Karisma *(0.01)*	Karlis	Karnyia
Kaprise	Kardijah	Karey *(0.01)*	Karissa *(0.37)*	Karlisa	Karo
Kaprisha	Kardyn	Karharine	Karissa-Ann	Karlisha	Karol *(0.01)*
Kaprishia	Karea	Kari *(0.23)*	Karissa-Lynn	Karlishia	Karol Ann *(0.01)*
Kapryce	Kareah	Kari-Ann	Karisse	Karlisia	Karol Anne
Kar	Kareasha	Kari-Anne	Karissma	Karlisle	Karolan
Kar Dasia	Karecia	Kari-Lea	Karista	Karlissa	Karolane *(0.06)*
Kar Lee	Karee	Kari-Lynn	Karisten	Karlita	Karolann *(0.01)*
Kar-Ying	Kareeka	Karia *(0.01)*	Karita	Karlniesha	Karolanne *(0.02)*
Kara *(0.96)*	Kareem	Kariah	Kariya	Karlotta	Karolen
Kara-Lee	Kareema *(0.01)*	Karialei	Kariyel	Karly *(0.21)*	Karolena
Kara-Marie	Kareemah	Karian	Kariza	Karly-Ann	Karolina *(0.05)*
Karabeth	Kareen *(0.01)*	Kariana	Karizma	Karlyanne	Karoline *(0.02)*
Karaea	Kareena *(0.01)*	Kariane *(0.02)*	Karizse	Karlycia	Karoling
Karagan	Kareesia	Kariann *(0.01)*	Karla *(0.61)*	Karlye	Karoll
Karah *(0.02)*	Karegan	Karianna	Karla Elisabeth	Karlyn *(0.02)*	Karolle
Karah-Jean	Kareigh	Karianne *(0.05)*	Karlaecia	Karlynn	Karollyn
Karahn	Kareinma	Karice	Karlamary	Karlynne	Karolyn *(0.01)*
Karajia	Kareisha	Karicia	Karlandria	Karlyon	Karolyna
Karalea	Kareka	Karie *(0.02)*	Karlayah	Karlyse	Karolynn
Karalee *(0.01)*	Karel *(0.01)*	Kariela	Karlayna	Karlysle	Karolynne
Karaleisa	Kareli	Kariella	Karle	Karma	Karon
Karali	Karelia	Karielle	Karlea	Karma Lee	Karonda
Karalie	Karelise	Kariema	Karleacia	Karmallita	Karra *(0.01)*
Karalina	Karelisha	Karigan	Karleah	Karman	Karrah *(0.01)*
Karaline	Karell	Kariina	Karlee *(0.19)*	Karmayne	Karren
Karalissa	Karelle *(0.01)*	Karilee	Karleen *(0.01)*	Karmecia	Karresa
Karalyn *(0.01)*	Karely *(0.02)*	Kariln	Karleena	Karmeisha	Karri *(0.01)*
Karalynn	Karem	Karilyn *(0.01)*	Karlei	Karmella	Karri Anne
Karam	Karema	Karilynn	Karleigh *(0.04)*	Karmelle	Karri-Anne
Karamae	Kareme	Karim	Karleigh-Ann	Karmen *(0.03)*	Karrianna
Karamah	Karemma	Karima *(0.01)*	Karleikeyá	Karmen Michelle	Karrica
Karamiah	Karen *(1.26)*	Karimah *(0.01)*	Karlen	Karmenjeet	Karrie *(0.03)*
Karamjot	Karen Ann	Karime	Karlena *(0.01)*	Karmia	Karrietta
Karamyn	Karen Denise	Karimeh	Karlene *(0.02)*	Karmila	Karrigan
Karan	Karen Elizabeth	Karin *(0.04)*	Karlenea	Karmilla	Karrin
Karanda	Karen Jeanette	Karina *(1.25)*	Karlenta	Karmilya	Karrina
Karandeep	Karen Marie	Karina Isela	Karlesha	Karmin	Karrine
Karanja	Karen Rosalie	Karina-Elodia	Karleshia	Karmina	Karrington
Karanpreet	Karen-Lynn	Karinda	Karlessa	Karminia	Karrinton
Karanycia	Karena *(0.02)*	Karine *(0.17)*	Karley *(0.15)*	Karmyn	Karrion
Karas	Karená	Karinee	Karli *(0.18)*	Karna	Karris
Karasten	Karenda	Karines	Karli-An	Karnae	Karrisa *(0.01)*
Karastyn	Karendeep	Karington	Karlice	Karnaicia	Karrissa
Karatha	Kareneshia	Karinisha	Karlicia	Karndeep	Karrista
Karatina	Kareney	Karinna	Karlie *(0.19)*	Karneisha	Karrleigh
Karaysha	Karenna	Karinne	Karlie-Lynn	Karnelia	Karrmen
Karaz	Karenno	Karinthia	Karliegh	Karnesha	Karrolle-Ann

Karry	Kasandrajean	Kasheria	Kasina	Kastarja	Katasha
Karryn	Kasane	Kashette	Kasinda	Kasten	Katashia
Karryssa	Kasanita	Kashia	Kasinga	Kasthuri	Katasia
Karsee	Kasara	Kashianya	Kasity	Kastile	Katavia
Karsen (0.01)	Kasaundra (0.01)	Kashifa	Kasjah	Kastin	Kataya
Karsha	Kasawndra	Kashina	Kasla	Kastle	Katayia
Karshana	Kasaye	Kashinda	Kaslen	Kastlin	Katayon
Karshiniquia	Kascee	Kashious	Kaslyn	Kastralin	Kataysia
Karson (0.01)	Kaschell	Kashira	Kasmar	Kasturee	Katazma
Karsten	Kaschelle	Kashja	Kasmeondra	Kasturi	Katchina
Karstin	Kasci	Kashlee	Kasmere	Kasumi	Kate (0.38)
Karstyn	Kascie	Kashley	Kasmierre	Kaswana	Kate Lyn
Karsun	Kasdin	Kashman	Kasmira	Kaswayla	Kate Lyne
Karsyn (0.01)	Kasee	Kashmer	Kasondra (0.01)	Kasweka	Kate Lynn
Kartesha	Kaseena	Kashmere (0.01)	Kassadee	Kaswell	Katélynn
Karthiga	Kaselyn	Kashminder	Kassadey	Kasyera	Kate-Lyn
Karthigaa	Kasen	Kashmir	Kassadi	Kasztan	Kate-Lynn (0.01)
Karthika	Kasenia	Kashmira	Kassadie	Kat Lyn	Kate-Lynne
Karty	Kasenya	Kashmire	Kassady	Kata	Kateal
Karumba	Kasey (0.43)	Kashmiri	Kassalyn	Katah	Kateannia
Karuna	Kasey-Lynn	Kashon	Kassanda	Kataira	Kateara
Karussa	Kash	Kashonda	Kassandera	Katajhreon	Kateasha
Kary (0.01)	Kash'reanna	Kashondra	Kassandra (0.88)	Katalba	Katedra
Karya	Kasha (0.02)	Kashondré	Kassandra Rose	Kataleen	Katee (0.01)
Karyan	Kashae	Kashoni	Kassandra-Lynn	Kataleena	Katée
Karyana	Kashaerie	Kashonna	Kassandrah	Katalena	Kateejia
Karyanna	Kashai	Kashonta	Kassandre (0.01)	Katalin	Kateesha
Karyee	Kashaira	Kashtin	Kassaundra (0.02)	Katalina (0.02)	Kateezia
Karyell	Kashala	Kashton	Kassedi	Katalya	Kateina
Karyl	Kashalya	Kashtyn	Kassedie	Katalyn	Katela
Karylyn	Kashana	Kashuana	Kassee	Katalynda	Katelain
Karyma	Kashanda	Kashuel	Kasserine	Katalynn	Katelan
Karyn (0.03)	Kashanna	Kashun	Kassey (0.01)	Katana (0.01)	Kateland (0.02)
Karyna (0.01)	Kashara	Kashunte	Kassi (0.02)	Katandria	Katelane
Karynda	Kashari	Kashya	Kassia (0.01)	Katani	Katelee
Karyne	Kashari'	Kashyara	Kassiane	Katania	Kateleen
Karynn	Kasharria	Kashyma	Kassiani	Katanna	Katelen
Karynna	Kashaun	Kashyna	Kassianna	Katanni	Katelin (0.19)
Karys	Kashauna	Kashyra	Kassidee (0.01)	Katara (0.01)	Katelind
Karysa	Kashavea	Kasi (0.02)	Kassidey	Katarar	Kateline
Karysa Crystal	Kashawn	Kasi-Lee	Kassidi (0.02)	Katareena	Katelinn
Karysa-Jean	Kashawna	Kasia (0.02)	Kassidie	Katarena	Katella
Karyss	Kashawnda	Kasiah	Kassidy (0.25)	Katariina	Kateln
Karyssa (0.01)	Kashawnna	Kasiaha	Kassidy-Rae	Katarina (0.27)	Katelon
Karzeta	Kashay	Kasian	Kassie (0.06)	Katarina-Anne	Katelund
Kasaa	Kashaya	Kasidee	Kassie Jo	Katarina-Bobana	Kately
Kasacia	Kashayla (0.01)	Kasidi	Kassity	Katarine	Katelyn (2.47)
Kasahra	Kasheana	Kasidy	Kassondra (0.01)	Katarinna	Katelyn Nic
Kasajien	Kasheanna	Kasie (0.04)	Kassondria	Katarinne	Katelynd
Kasak	Kasheeka	Kasieah	Kassundra	Katariya	Katelynde
Kasal	Kasheema	Kasielea	Kassy (0.01)	Katarra	Katelyne (0.01)
Kasan	Kasheena	Kasilda	Kassya	Katarrina	Katelynn (0.51)
Kasanda	Kashella	Kasileigh	Kassydi	Katarriya	Katelynn Vi
Kasandra (0.19)	Kashena	Kasimea	Kassyndra	Kataryna	Katelynne (0.02)
Kasandradee	Kashenda	Kasin	Kasta	Katarzyna (0.02)	Katempra

Katenlyn	Katherine K	Kathyela	Katiya	Katriel	Kaula
Katera (0.01)	Katherine-Ann	Kathylynn	Katiyana	Katrienne	Kauleen
Katerá	Katherine-Anne	Kathyran	Katja (0.02)	Katriina	Kaulen
Katerhine	Katherine-Louise	Kathyrn	Katja-Lauren	Katrika	Kaunstance
Kateri (0.01)	Katherinea	Kathyrne	Katje	Katrin (0.01)	Kaunstince
Kateria (0.01)	Katherinne	Kati (0.04)	Katla	Katrina (0.99)	Kaur (0.01)
Katerin	Kathern	Kati-Lyn	Katlaina	Katrina Grazel	Kauri
Katerina (0.14)	Katherne	Kati-Yureen	Katlan	Katrina Mae	Kaurica
Katerina Abriel	Katheron	Katia (0.07)	Katland	Katrina Marie	Kaurie
Katerina-Alexandra	Katheryn (0.10)	Katiana (0.01)	Katleen	Katrina-Leigh	Kaurtney
Katerine (0.01)	Katheryne (0.01)	Katiann	Katleigh	Katrina-Marie	Kausalya
Katerra	Katherynn	Katianne	Katlen	Katrinalee	Kauser
Katerri	Kathia (0.01)	Katiarina	Katleyn	Katrine (0.02)	Kausha
Katerria	Kathiana	Katiba	Katlin (0.12)	Katrinia	Kaushalya
Katerrya	Kathianne	Katica	Katlina	Katrinka	Kauthar
Kateryn	Kathie	Katie (2.16)	Katline	Katrinna	Kauther
Kateryna	Kathiel	Katie Linn	Katlyn (0.52)	Katrino	Kauuina
Katesha	Kathina	Katie Lynn	Katlynd	Katriona	Kauzhana
Kateshia	Kathique	Katie Lynn Tayl	Katlyne (0.01)	Katrisse	Kavalier
Katesia	Kathlean	Katie Marie	Katlynn (0.09)	Katriunna	Kavana
Katessa	Kathleen (1.21)	Katie Rose	Katlynne	Katryn	Kavanah
Katey (0.03)	Kathleen-Anne	Katiélyn	Katnicha	Katryna (0.01)	Kavanna
Katey-Jo	Kathleen-Christ	Katie-Ann	Katonya	Katryna-Marie	Kavanya
Kateylnn	Kathleena	Katie-Jo	Katora	Katsi	Kavarc'lyn
Kateylynn	Kathleene	Katie-Lee	Katorée	Kattee	Kavassha
Kateyn	Kathlene	Katie-Lyn	Katori	Katti	Kavayanna
Kath'e	Kathlien	Katie-Lynn (0.01)	Katoria	Kattia	Kaveena
Kath-Lynn	Kathlin	Katie-Marie	Katoriana	Kattie (0.02)	Kaveinga
Kathaleen	Kathlina	Katieann	Katorina	Kattierra	Kavelle
Kathalina	Kathllen	Katieanne	Katorria	Kattiya	Kaven
Kathalyn	Kathlyn (0.02)	Katielee	Katoya	Kattren	Kavena
Katharen	Kathlynn	Katielyn	Katoyia	Kattreona	Kaveri
Katharin	Kathrean	Katielynn	Katrea	Kattrina	Kavi
Katharina (0.02)	Kathreen	Katiera	Katreanna	Katty (0.01)	Kavia
Katharine (0.25)	Kathreena	Katiere	Katreasha	Kattyna	Kavina
Katharyn (0.01)	Kathren	Katiesha	Katrece	Kattyria	Kaviona
Kathe	Kathrene	Katiia	Katreec	Katura	Kavita (0.01)
Kathedral	Kathrin (0.01)	Katijo	Katreece	Katurah	Kavitha
Katheen	Kathrina (0.01)	Katijona	Katreen	Katusha	Kavon
Katheine	Kathrine (0.09)	Katil	Katreena	Katy (0.15)	Kavona
Katheleen	Kathrun	Katilda	Katreesia	Katy Rose	Kavonda
Kathelin	Kathrya	Katilia	Katreia	Katya (0.05)	Kavondrea
Kathelon	Kathryn (1.94)	Katilin	Katreina	Katyah	Kavonna
Kathelyn	Kathryn Ann	Katilyn (0.04)	Katrell	Katyana	Kavonne
Katheral	Kathryn Jade	Katilynn	Katrena (0.01)	Katyann	Kavonya
Katheran	Kathryn-Lynn	Katina (0.03)	Katrenia	Katyanna	Kavosia
Katherane	Kathryne (0.03)	Katinna	Katrenna	Katye	Kavoura
Katheranne	Kathryne Lizette	Katira	Katressa	Katylin	Kavrina
Katheren	Kathrynmarie	Katiria	Katria	Katyln	Kavya
Katherene	Kathrynn (0.01)	Katirina	Katriah	Katylynn	Kavyn
Katheri	Kathrynne	Katisha (0.01)	Katriana	Katymarie	Kawaii
Katherin (0.04)	Kathwren	Katiusca	Katrianna	Katyra	Kawain
Katherina (0.01)	Kathy (0.28)	Katiuscia	Katrice (0.01)	Kau'aliyah	Kawaiolele
Katherine (4.40)	Kathya (0.01)	Kativa	Katricia	Kauilah	Kawajalein
	Kathyary	Katiy	Katricka	Kauithaa	Kawana

Kawanda	Kaydeanne	Kaylan *(0.07)*	Kaylie-Ann	Kayry	Kayuana
Kawanna	Kaydee *(0.02)*	Kaylana	Kayliegh	Kaysa	Kayundra
Kawanzaá	Kayden *(0.01)*	Kayland	Kayliene	Kaysandra	Kayva
Kawauna	Kaydene	Kaylani *(0.01)*	Kaylila	Kayse	Kayven
Kawehi	Kaydi	Kaylann	Kaylin *(0.22)*	Kaysea	Kayveshia
Kawena	Kaydie	Kaylar	Kaylina	Kaysee	Kayvin
Kawnejah	Kaydon	Kaylauni	Kaylind	Kaysey	Kayvonda
Kawona	Kaydra	Kaylay	Kayline	Kaysha *(0.01)*	Kayvondra
Kawondra	Kaydran	Kayle *(0.03)*	Kaylinn	Kayshala	Kayzha
Kawonza	Kaydriane	Kaylea *(0.03)*	Kaylis	Kayshan	Kayzia
Kawsar	Kaydrie	Kayleah	Kaylisa	Kayshanna	Kayzie
Kawser	Kaye	Kaylean	Kaylisha	Kayshaunda	Kaza I N Ba
Kawtar	Kayela	Kayleanna	Kayliss	Kayshawna	Kaza're
Kawthar	Kayelah	Kayleata	Kaylissa	Kayshel	Kazandra
Kawther	Kayelan	Kayleb	Kayliyah	Kayshevona	Kazaya
Kaxandra	Kayeland	Kaylee *(1.16)*	Kaylla	Kayshia	Kazden
Kay *(0.03)*	Kayelea	Kaylee Carmen	Kayln *(0.01)*	Kayshonna	Kazh'e
Kay Lee	Kayelee	Kaylee-Anne	Kaylnn	Kaysi	Kazi
Kay Leigh	Kayeleigh	Kaylee-Hope	Kayloa	Kaysia	Kazia
Kay Lyn	Kayelene	Kaylee-Lyn	Kaylon *(0.01)*	Kaysie *(0.01)*	Kaziah
Kay Lynn	Kayeli	Kaylee-Ray	Kaylond	Kayslynn	Kazie
Kay Oshia	Kayelin	Kaylee-Shay	Kayloni	Kaysone	Kazmier
Kay See	Kayely	Kayleejo	Kaylor	Kayte *(0.01)*	Kazmiera
Kay'la	Kayelyn	Kayleen *(0.08)*	Kayly	Kaytee	Kazmira
Kay'zanique	Kayelynn	Kayleen-Marie	Kaylyen	Kayteira	Kazmyre
Kay-Ann	Kayeshawnda	Kayleen-Rose	Kaylyn *(0.22)*	Kaytelin	Kazougher
Kay-Esha	Kaygan	Kayleena *(0.01)*	Kaylyna	Kaytelyn	Kazusa
Kay-Leigh	Kayhlie	Kayleene	Kaylyne	Kaytelynn	Kazzie
Kay-Lyn	Kayiah	Kayleh-Marie	Kaylynn *(0.11)*	Kaytelynne	Kazzmere
Kaya *(0.03)*	Kayiona	Kaylei	Kaylynne *(0.01)*	Kayterrian	Kbreana
Kaya-Marie	Kayisha	Kayleigh *(0.25)*	Kaylyssa	Kaythi	Kbret
Kayah	Kayja	Kayleine	Kayma	Kayti	Kc *(0.01)*
Kayal	Kaykeaona	Kaylen *(0.05)*	Kaymeron	Kayti-Lynn	Kcarli
Kayan	Kayl	Kaylen Marjorie	Kaymi	Kaytie *(0.01)*	Kcee
Kayana	Kayl'n	Kaylena *(0.01)*	Kaymin	Kaytilan	Kchasni
Kayanat	Kayla *(7.81)*	Kaylene *(0.05)*	Kayna	Kaytilyn	Kcin
Kayanda	Kayla Joi	Kaylene Aliyah	Kaynesha	Kaytin	Kcursidey
Kayann	Kayla Kemani	Kaylenn	Kayniscia	Kaytla	Kd
Kayanna *(0.01)*	Kayla Ray	Kayler	Kayon	Kaytlan	Kd'delleya
Kayanne	Kaylá	Kaylesha	Kayona	Kaytland	Kdamond
Kayantoni	Kayla-Anahi	Kayleshia	Kayonda	Kaytlann	Kdijah
Kayauna	Kayla-Ann	Kaylesia	Kayonia	Kaytlen	Ke
Kayawna	Kayla-Anne	Kaylex	Kayonna	Kaytlin *(0.05)*	Ke Aira
Kaybre	Kayla-Ashley	Kayley *(0.11)*	Kayosha	Kaytlyn *(0.06)*	Ke Ana
Kaybrei	Kayla-Leigh	Kayley Ann	Kaypeus	Kaytlyn Tamara	Ke Andrea
Kayce *(0.02)*	Kayla-Lynn	Kayleya	Kayra	Kaytlyne	Ke Anteria
Kaycee *(0.09)*	Kayla-Lynne	Kayli *(0.10)*	Kayray	Kaytlynn *(0.02)*	Ke Ariah
Kaycée	Kayla-Marie	Kayli Ann	Kayreah	Kaytlynne	Ke Ashayann
Kaycei	Kayla-Raquel	Kayli'	Kayree	Kayton	Ke Azia
Kaychia	Kaylaa	Kaylia *(0.01)*	Kayrele	Kaytoya	Ke Chetta
Kayci *(0.01)*	Kayladawn	Kayliah	Kayren	Kaytra	Ke Ebony
Kaycia	Kaylah *(0.07)*	Kayliana	Kayri	Kaytria	Ke Erin
Kaycie *(0.01)*	Kaylajay	Kayliauna	Kayrn	Kaytriana	Ke Joilacia
Kayda	Kaylam	Kaylidh	Kayron	Kaytrina	Ke Juan Te
Kayde	Kaylamarie	Kaylie *(0.20)*	Kayronda	Kaytryna	Ke Ondra

Ke Onnika	Kéondra	Keailea	Kearia	Kebrinna	Keejanae
Ke Shandra	Kéonie	Keaira (0.03)	Kearica	Kebron	Keela
Ke Shanna	Kéonna	Keairah	Keariston	Kecha	Keelan
Ke Shawn	Kéontae	Keairra (0.01)	Kearlisa	Kechawndra	Keelana
Ke Shelle	Kéonya	Keairraca	Kearna	Kecheka	Keelaye
Ke Shia	Kéosha	Keairre	Kearney	Kechelle	Keele
Ke Shyra	Kéoshae	Keaisha	Kearra (0.01)	Kecia (0.01)	Keelee
Ke Spre	Kéoyndra	Keaishia	Kearrha	Keciah	Keelei
Ke Swanis	Késhail	Keake	Kearria	Kecy	Keeley (0.03)
Ke Undra	Késhana	Keala (0.01)	Kearse	Kedan	Keeli
Ke Vangela	Késhanna	Kealan	Kearsha	Kedara	Keelia
Ke Yana	Késhara	Kealani	Kearson	Kedeasha	Keelie
Kéaaron	Késharra	Kealee	Kearsten (0.01)	Kededra	Keelin (0.01)
Kéaira	Késhauna	Kealey	Kearstie	Kededria	Keely (0.10)
Kéairra	Késhaunnia	Kealie	Kearstin (0.01)	Kedeeja	Keelye
Kéala	Késhawn	Kealin	Kearston (0.01)	Kedeisha	Keelyn
Kéamber	Késhawna	Kealoha	Kearstyn	Kedeja	Keena (0.01)
Kéambra	Késhayla	Kealsha	Keasha (0.01)	Kedejera	Keenan
Kéambria	Késhon	Kealy	Keasharrow	Kedesha	Keenanni
Kéana	Késhona	Keamber	Keashia	Kedeshia	Keeneesha
Kéandra	Késhuna	Keambra	Keashley	Kedestiny	Keenen
Kéandrea	Késhyra	Keana (0.07)	Keashonda	Kedijah	Keenia
Kéandreia	Késuana	Keanah	Keasia	Kedisha	Keenya
Kéanna	Késwanna	Keanca	Keasley	Kedishia	Keeoctea
Kéanne	Kétara	Keanche	Keasmin	Kedline	Keeona
Kéara	Kétedra	Keanda	Keather	Kedra	Keeonya
Kéara T'ambria	Kétyria	Keandra (0.02)	Keaton (0.01)	Kedria	Keeosha
Kéaria	Kétyriona	Keandrah	Keatyn	Kedrianna	Keera (0.01)
Kéashia	Kéundra	Keandre	Keaudra	Kedriona	Keerat
Kéashlee	Kévisha	Keandrea	Keauna (0.01)	Kedriyana	Keerati
Kéasia	Kéwania	Keandria	Keauná	Kedron	Keersten
Kéasiajah	Kéwanie	Keandris	Keaundra	Kedyn	Keerstin
Kéasmine	Kéyana	Keaneena	Keaundria	Kee	Keerstyn
Kéatiayana	Kéyanna	Keanha	Keauni	Kee Onie	Keerthana
Kéatte	Kéyata	Keani	Keaunna	Kee Shon	Keerthanaa
Kéauna	Kéyon	Keanisha	Keaura	Keéva	Keerthi
Kéaunah	Kéyonna	Keanitra	Keausha	Keévonda	Keerthiga
Kéaundra	Kéyuana	Keanna (0.08)	Keautishay	Keéyuna	Keerthika
Kéauni	Kéyunna	Keanne	Keavna	Kee-Shawn	Keertiga
Kéautica	Ke-Onna	Keanne Rose	Keavondria	Keeaira	Keesa
Kéchelle	Ke-Shawna	Keannel	Keavonna	Keeajah	Keesehmboh
Kéerah	Kea	Keano	Keavonta	Keeana	Keesha (0.02)
Kéerra	Kea'aundranique	Keante	Keavriauna	Keeann	Keeshá
Kéia	Kea'na	Keanu (0.01)	Keawna	Keeanna	Keeshae
Kélena	Kea'ra	Keanua	Keayla	Keeara	Keeshana
Kélisha	Kea'undretria	Keanue	Keayonna	Keeauria	Keeshanne
Kélonie	Kea-Jane	Keanya	Keayra	Keeba	Keeshawna
Kémaiya	Keadesia	Keaonna	Keazia	Keebler	Keeshawnda
Kémani	Keadra	Keara (0.07)	Keba	Keechina	Keeshonna
Kémaurye	Keaerica	Kearah	Keba Patrice	Keedra	Keeshya
Kémoya	Keagan (0.01)	Kearan	Kebreeya	Keegan (0.02)	Keetley
Kénee	Keah	Kearee	Kebria	Keegen	Keeva
Kéneicia	Keahla	Kearen	Kebriana	Keeghan	Keevia
Kénisha	Keahlani	Keareona	Kebrianna	Keeionna	Keevonna
Kéniya Tarshae	Keahna	Keari	Kebrina	Keeirra	Keeyan

Keeyana	Keichelle	Keimonie	Keishambreyia	Keiyanna	Keleigh *(0.01)*
Keeyanah	Keicheona	Keimya	Keishan	Keiyara	Keleighan
Keeyanna	Keidi	Keina	Keishana	Keiyare	Keleisha
Keeyata	Keidra	Keinaisha	Keishand	Keiynna	Kelen
Keeyatta	Keidrah	Keinekia	Keishanna	Keiyona	Kelena
Keeyona	Keidren	Keinesha	Keishara	Keiza	Keleon
Keeyonna	Keiera	Keinna	Keisharda	Kejana	Kelesey
Kefah	Keierika	Keiombra	Keisharra	Kejonnae	Keleshia
Kefira	Keierra	Keion	Keishaun	Keju'ana	Kelesy
Kegan	Keifawna	Keiona *(0.01)*	Keishauna	Kejuana	Kelexus
Keghouhi	Keifer	Keionah	Keishaundra	Keke	Keli *(0.01)*
Keh	Keigan	Keionda	Keishaunna	Keksey	Kelia *(0.01)*
Keheir	Keighan	Keiondra	Keishawn	Kel'ciay	Keliah
Keheira	Keighla	Keiondria	Keishawna	Kela *(0.01)*	Keliana
Kehla	Keighley	Keione	Keishawnna	Kelaena	Keliane
Kehlee	Keighlyn	Keionia	Keishay	Kelah	Keliayah
Kehli	Keightley	Keionna *(0.01)*	Keisheka	Kelaiah	Kelicha
Kehmyille	Keightlyn	Keionta	Keishell	Kelaisha	Kelicia
Kei	Keihana	Keiosha *(0.01)*	Keishia	Kelana	Kelie
Kei Andra	Keihane	Keioshani'	Keishla *(0.01)*	Kelanah	Keliesha
Kei Odshila	Keihla	Keir	Keishon	Kelane	Keliisa
Kei Waunna	Keihysha	Keir Marie	Keishonda	Kelani	Kelin
Kei'	Keiji	Keira *(0.07)*	Keishonna	Kelani-Leialoha	Kelina
Kei'aisja	Keijuan	Keirá	Keishun	Kelanie	Keline
Kei'andria	Keijuana	Keirah	Keishundria	Kelasha	Kelisa
Kei'anna	Keikahnza	Keiran	Keishunna	Kelbe	Kelisd
Kei'ondra	Keiki	Keirann	Keishyra	Kelbee	Kelisha
Kei'onna	Keiko	Keircen	Keisian	Kelbey	Kelishianna
Kei'yaira	Keila *(0.05)*	Keiretta	Keisjia	Kelbi	Kelison
Kei'yana	Keilah *(0.01)*	Keiri	Keiskiera	Kelbie	Kelissa
Kei-Aira	Keilan	Keirianna	Keisonia	Kelby *(0.01)*	Kelita
Keia *(0.01)*	Keilandra	Keirin	Keissa	Kelcci	Keliyah
Keiah	Keilani *(0.01)*	Keirnan	Keita	Kelce	Kella
Keiaira	Keilanna	Keirra *(0.01)*	Keitera	Kelcea	Kellae
Keiajah	Keilany	Keirrah	Keith'shara	Kelcee *(0.01)*	Kellan *(0.01)*
Keiala	Keilee	Keirre	Keitha	Kelcey *(0.03)*	Kellby
Keiamber	Keiley	Keirria	Keithalyn	Kelci *(0.05)*	Kellci
Keiana *(0.02)*	Keili	Keirrira	Keithleen	Kelcia	Kellcy
Keianda	Keilia	Keirsharra	Keithlethia	Kelcie *(0.06)*	Kelldy
Keiandra	Keilicia	Keirstan	Keithra	Kelcii	Kelle
Keianna *(0.02)*	Keilih	Keirstein	Keithshae	Kelciya	Kellea
Keianná	Keilly	Keirsten *(0.02)*	Keitia	Kelcy *(0.02)*	Kellea-Maria
Keiannah	Keilondria	Keirstin *(0.01)*	Keitisma	Kelda	Kellece
Keianta	Keilsey	Keirston	Keitra	Keldeshia	Kellee *(0.01)*
Keiara *(0.02)*	Keily *(0.01)*	Keirsty	Keiunna	Keldy	Kelleen
Keiarah	Keilyn	Keirstyn *(0.01)*	Keiva	Kele	Kelleher
Keiarra *(0.01)*	Keilynn	Keirstynne	Keivona	Kelea	Kelleigh *(0.01)*
Keiasha	Keilysmer	Keiry	Keivonna	Keleah	Kellen *(0.02)*
Keiashuna	Keima	Keisen	Keivonne	Keleana	Keller
Keiasia	Keimaiya	Keisey	Keivonya	Kelechi	Kelley *(0.19)*
Keiaudra	Keimani	Keisha *(0.14)*	Keivoria	Kelecia	Kelli *(0.40)*
Keiauna	Keimaya	Keisha-Iris	Keiwanna	Kelee	Kelli Ann
Keiaunna	Keimetriana	Keisha-Lee	Keiya	Keleen	Kelli Anne
Keiauntae	Keimiya	Keishaiahna	Keiyah	Kelehear	Kelli-Jo
Keiba	Keimonee	Keishain	Keiyana	Keleia	Kelli-Lyn

Kelli-Mae	Kelseia	Kemberley	Kenah	Kendle	Keneedra
Kellia	Kelseigh	Kemberley Lynne	Kenahri	Kendora	Keneesha
Kellian	Kelsel	Kemberlie	Kenai'	Kendra *(1.16)*	Keneifia
Kelliann	Kelsen	Kemberly	Kenajawa	Kendra Marina	Keneisha *(0.01)*
Kellianne	Kelsey *(4.47)*	Kemberly Sujeir	Kenampoy	Kendra-Cymone	Keneishia
Kelliauna	Kelsey-Ann	Kemble	Kenan	Kendra-Kit	Keneka
Kellie *(0.38)*	Kelsey-Jane	Kembrah	Kenana	Kendra-Lee	Kenequa
Kellie-Rae	Kelsey-Lyn	Kembre	Kenanna	Kendra-Lynn	Keneque
Kellin	Kelsey-Lynn	Kembreia	Kenashia	Kendrah	Kenerly
Kellina	Kelsey-Rose	Kembri	Kenasia	Kendralea	Kenesha *(0.01)*
Kelliona	Kelsey-Scott	Kembria	Kenassa	Kendralia	Keneshay
Kellisha	Kelsha	Kemeesha	Kenay	Kendralyn	Keneshia
Kellisia	Kelsi *(0.19)*	Kemeisha	Kenayana	Kendrana	Kenesia
Kelljanique	Kelsia	Kemelly	Kenberle	Kendranique	Kenessa
Kellniqua	Kelsian	Kemerey	Kenberlin	Kendre	Kenet
Kellsea	Kelsie *(0.48)*	Kemery	Kenberlyn	Kendrea	Kenetia
Kellsei	Kelsie Lee	Kemesha	Kenbria	Kendreah	Kenetra
Kellsey *(0.01)*	Kelssey	Kemi	Kenbrielle	Kendreéa	Kenettrea
Kellsi	Kelsy *(0.06)*	Kemia	Kenchasela	Kendreka	Keneyha
Kellsie *(0.01)*	Kelsye	Kemiah	Kenchelle	Kendrella	Kengi
Kellsie Ann	Kelsyie	Kemika	Kenciah	Kendreonda	Keni
Kelly *(2.35)*	Kelteria	Kemilah	Kency	Kendria *(0.01)*	Kenia *(0.13)*
Kelly Ann *(0.01)*	Kelti	Kemilee	Kenda *(0.01)*	Kendrianna	Kenichia
Kelly Anne *(0.01)*	Keltie	Kemira	Kendadra	Kendrica	Kenicia
Kelly-Ann	Kelton	Kemisha	Kendaesha	Kendrice	Kenide
Kelly-Anne	Keltsey	Kemiya	Kendahl *(0.01)*	Kendrick	Kenidee
Kelly-Eileen	Keltsie	Kemiyah	Kendaisia	Kendricka	Kenidi
Kelly-Marie	Kelty	Kemmesha	Kendal *(0.12)*	Kendrie	Kenidie
Kelly-Regina	Kelvanje	Kemmie	Kendale	Kendriea	Kenidy
Kellya	Kelvélina	Kemna	Kendalie	Kendriece	Keniely
Kellyann	Kelvenna	Kemonda	Kendalin	Kendrika	Keniesha
Kellyanne	Kelvesha	Kemory	Kendall *(0.76)*	Kendrionna	Kenika
Kellybeth	Kelvie	Kemper	Kendalyn *(0.01)*	Kendriuna	Keninna
Kellye	Kelvin	Kemry	Kendalynn	Kendrix	Keniqua
Kellygrace	Kelvina	Kemthia	Kendasha	Kendsey	Kenique
Kellyjo	Kelvisha	Kemwania	Kendashiá	Kendy	Kenisa
Kellylee	Kelvlyn	Kemyatta	Kendebria	Kendyl *(0.05)*	Kenise *(0.01)*
Kellyn *(0.02)*	Kelvonna	Ken Toya	Kendedra	Kendyle	Kenisha *(0.04)*
Kellynn	Kely	Ken'drynea	Kendee	Kendyll *(0.01)*	Kenishia
Kelnesha	Kely-Joan	Ken'esha	Kendeja	Kene	Kenissa
Kelnisha	Kelyanna	Ken'shae	Kendel *(0.01)*	Kené	Kenita
Kelonda	Kelyn	Ken'taja	Kendell *(0.02)*	Kenésha	Kenitha
Kelondra	Kelyné	Ken'terra	Kendelle	Keneasha	Kenithia
Kelonie	Kelysha	Ken'yail	Kendera	Keneathia	Kenitra
Kelsa *(0.01)*	Kelzi	Ken'yanta	Kenderricka	Kenece	Kenitria
Kelsae	Kelzy	Ken'youna	Kendesha	Kenechi	Keniya
Kelsaey	Kema	Ken/taesha	Kendi	Kenechukwu	Keniyra
Kelsay	Kemabri	Kena *(0.01)*	Kendia	Kenecia	Kenj'uana
Kelse	Kemani	Kenadee *(0.01)*	Kendie	Kenedee	Kenja'ah
Kelsea *(0.17)*	Kemari	Kenadi *(0.01)*	Kendiesha	Kenedey	Kenjah
Kelsea-Dawn	Kemarie	Kenadie	Kendijah	Kenedi *(0.01)*	Kenjetta
Kelseann	Kemauri	Kenadii	Kendil	Kenedie	Kenji
Kelseanna	Kemaya	Kenady	Kendilyn	Kenedy	Kenjina
Kelsee *(0.03)*	Kemba	Kenae	Kendis	Kenee	Kenjiya
Kelsei *(0.01)*	Kember	Kenaé	Kendl	Kenée	Kenkeyanna

Kenla	Kenniecia	Kenterria	Kenyoshia	Keontré	Keriana
Kenlee	Kennikki	Kentezia	Kenyota	Keonya	Keriann
Kenleigh	Kennis	Kentilé	Kenyotá	Keonza	Kerianna
Kenley *(0.01)*	Kennisha *(0.01)*	Kentisha	Kenyrra	Keora	Kerianne
Kenli	Kennita	Kentora	Kenysha	Keora Keona	Kerica
Kenlicia	Kennitra	Kentorria	Kenyunna	Keoromunitevy	Keridan
Kenlie	Kennix	Kentoya	Kenyutta	Keosha *(0.03)*	Keridwen
Kenlisha	Kennize	Kentra	Kenza	Keoshae	Kerie
Kenly	Kennola	Kentrá	Kenzea	Keoshamine	Kerieka
Kenlyn	Kenny	Kentrell	Kenzee	Keoshi	Kerigan *(0.01)*
Kenmora	Kennya	Kentrianna	Kenzey	Keoshia	Kerika
Kenna *(0.07)*	Kennyara	Kentrice	Kenzhané	Keosia	Kerilee
Kenna-Sue	Kennyatta	Kentrieyce	Kenzi *(0.01)*	Keourtany	Kerilyn
Kennade	Kennysha	Kenturah	Kenzia	Keousha	Kerin
Kennadee	Kennzie	Kentwana	Kenzie *(0.09)*	Keouta	Kerina *(0.01)*
Kennadi *(0.01)*	Kenora	Kentya	Kenzja	Keoysha	Kerinase
Kennadie	Kenosha	Kentynese	Kenzy	Keplun	Kerington
Kennady *(0.01)*	Kenoshia	Kentzie	Kenzyea	Kepriah	Kerinsa
Kennae	Kenoya	Kenusha	Keoana	Kera *(0.02)*	Keriona
Kenndall	Kenquieana	Kenvosierrah	Keochia	Kerah	Kerione
Kenndel	Kenra	Keny	Keohnna	Kerala	Kerisa
Kenndi	Kenrekea	Kenya *(0.29)*	Keoka	Keralynda	Kerisha
Kenndra	Kenrell	Kenya Vivian	Keokina	Keran	Kerissa *(0.01)*
Kennecia	Kenricca	Kenyada *(0.01)*	Keola	Kerana	Keristen
Kenneda	Kenricka	Kenyah	Keolani	Keranda	Kerith
Kennede	Kensey *(0.01)*	Kenyan	Keombra	Kerani	Keriuna
Kennedee	Kensha	Kenyana *(0.01)*	Keomi	Kerashundria	Keriwin
Kennedée	Kenshara	Kenyanna	Keon	Keratin	Keriya
Kennedey	Kensharie	Kenyar	Keon Dra	Kerbendine	Keriyae
Kennedi *(0.03)*	Kenshauna	Kenyara	Keona *(0.03)*	Kerby	Kerlande
Kennedie *(0.01)*	Kenshawer	Kenyarri	Keonay	Kerdijah	Kerline
Kennedy *(0.45)*	Kenshawna	Kenyata *(0.01)*	Keonda	Kereena	Kerlisha
Kennedy-Marie	Kenshea	Kenyatah	Keondra *(0.03)*	Kereigh	Kerlyn
Kennee	Kenshondra	Kenyatta *(0.05)*	Keondre	Kereina	Kermeshia
Kenneisha	Kenshunna	Kenyatta Cassan	Keondria	Kereisha	Kermiqua
Kenneka	Kenshyia	Kenyattá	Keoni *(0.01)*	Kerel	Kermiria
Kennen	Kensi	Kenyatte	Keonia	Kerem	Kermisha
Kennesa	Kensie	Kenyattia	Keonica	Keren *(0.01)*	Kermita
Kennesha	Kensington	Kenyawtta	Keonikia	Keren-Kalkidan	Kernesha
Kenneshia	Kenslee	Kenyel	Keoniqua	Kerena	Kernisha
Kenneta	Kensleigh	Kenyella	Keonisha	Kerenisa	Keron
Kenneth	Kensley *(0.01)*	Kenyerra	Keonna *(0.03)*	Kerenne	Kerondra
Kennetha	Kenslie	Kenyetta *(0.02)*	Keonnah	Kerensa	Kerr
Kennethia	Kenswan	Kenyette	Keonni	Keresa	Kerra *(0.01)*
Kennethtra	Kensy	Kenyettea	Keonnia	Keresha	Kerragan
Kennetra	Kensye	Kenyia	Keonsha	Keresten	Kerre
Kennetria	Kent	Kenyna	Keonshay	Kereston	Kerren
Kennetta	Kentara	Kenyoda	Keonta	Kereth	Kerretta
Kenni	Kentaria	Kenyon	Keontá	Keri *(0.13)*	Kerri *(0.13)*
Kennia *(0.01)*	Kentasha	Kenyona	Keontah	Keri-Ann	Kerri-Ann
Kennidee	Kentavia	Kenyonia	Keontay	Keri-Anne	Kerri-Anne
Kennidi	Kenteaca Alisha	Kenyoniá	Keontaye	Keri-Lynn	Kerri-Leigh
Kennidy	Kenteria	Kenyonica	Keonte	Keria	Kerri-Lynn
Kennie	Kentericka	Kenyonna	Keontis	Keriakoula	Kerria
Kenniece	Kenterra	Kenyora	Keontra	Kerian	Kerrian

Kerriane	Keryssa	Keshini	Ketilia	Kevionna	Keyani
Kerrianna	Kesa	Keshisha	Ketina	Keviontae	Keyania
Kerrianne	Kesaia	Keshla	Ketley	Kevious	Keyanie
Kerriayle	Kesamber	Keshon	Ketmaly	Kevisha	Keyanna (0.07)
Kerrica	Kesang	Keshona	Ketna	Keviyana	Keyanná
Kerricka	Kesaundra	Keshonda	Ketnari	Keviyuana	Keyannah
Kerrie (0.02)	Keschia	Keshonde	Keto	Kevli	Keyano
Kerrie-Lee	Keseana	Keshondra	Ketondrea	Kevlin	Keyantaye
Kerriel	Kesedria	Keshone	Ketorah	Kevon	Keyara (0.02)
Kerrielle	Keserin	Keshonna	Ketoria	Kevona	Keyarah
Kerrigan (0.01)	Kesey	Keshonta	Ketoura	Kevonciaria	Keyaree
Kerrigen	Kesha (0.02)	Keshowna	Ketra	Kevonda	Keyari
Kerrin (0.02)	Keshadra Chaqui	Keshra	Ketri	Kevonia	Keyaria
Kerrin-Lee	Keshah	Keshrica	Ketria	Kevonna	Keyarra (0.01)
Kerrina	Keshal	Keshun	Ketrin	Kevonne	Keyarria
Kerrine	Keshala	Keshuna	Ketrina	Kevonnie	Keyarrow
Kerrington	Keshan	Keshundria	Ketsia	Kevono	Keyasa
Kerriohna	Keshana	Keshunmyiaa	Ketti	Kevonshay	Keyasha
Kerrion	Keshanda	Keshyra	Ketty	Kevonya	Keyasia
Kerrionna	Keshanna	Kesi	Kettyn	Kevreonda	Keyata
Kerrioyn	Keshanté	Kesia (0.01)	Keturah (0.03)	Kevriel	Keyatta
Kerris	Keshar	Kesiara	Keturia	Kevyana	Keyauna
Kerrisa	Keshara (0.01)	Kesindra	Kety	Kevyannah	Keyaundra
Kerrisha	Keshara K	Kesleigh	Keuana	Kevyn	Keyaunna
Kerrissa	Kesharia	Kesley (0.01)	Keuinia	Kewana	Keyavondra
Kerrith	Kesharra	Kesli	Keuna	Kewanee	Keyayra
Kerry (0.13)	Keshaun	Keslie	Keundra	Kewanna	Keydra
Kerry-Amber	Keshauna	Kess	Keunna	Kewanne	Keyear
Kerry-An	Keshaund	Kessa	Kev-Lyn	Kewanua	Keyelle
Kerryann	Keshaunda	Kessalyn	Keva	Kewau	Keyenna
Kerryanna	Keshaundra	Kessandra	Kevaiya	Kewaun	Keyera (0.01)
Kersee	Keshaunna	Kessia	Kevan	Key'anna	Keyerah
Kersha	Keshauntae	Kessiah	Kevanett	Key'isha	Keyeria
Kershaun	Keshava	Kessie	Kevanna	Key'onna	Keyerra (0.01)
Kershawna	Keshawn	Kessler	Kevanne	Key-Laya	Keyetta
Kershner	Keshawna (0.01)	Kesslie	Kevante	Key-Lee	Keyezmin
Kershondra	Keshawnda	Kestin	Kevasha	Keya	Keyia
Kershonna	Keshawnna	Kestle	Kevbrain	Keyah	Keyiah
Kersta	Keshay	Kestlie	Kevbrisha	Keyahra	Keyiana
Kerstain	Keshaye	Kestrel	Keven	Keyaina	Keyianna
Kerstan	Keshayla	Ketaira	Keverine	Keyaira (0.01)	Keyiara
Kerste	Keshé	Ketarah	Kevia	Keyairai	Keyiarra
Kerstein	Keshea	Ketaria	Keviece	Keyairra	Keyiera
Kersten (0.01)	Keshealla	Ketasha	Kevieth	Keyala	Keyierra
Kersti	Kesheena	Ketasia	Kevin	Keyalmsha	Keyina
Kerstie	Keshele	Ketaurah	Kevina (0.01)	Keyama	Keyionta
Kerstien	Keshell	Ketema	Kevinee	Keyamber	Keyira
Kerstin (0.02)	Keshera	Keteria	Kevinesha	Keyamonie	Keyisha
Kerston	Kesherra	Ketevan	Kevineshia	Keyana (0.07)	Keyla (0.04)
Kersty	Keshia (0.02)	Ketfa	Kevinik	Keyana-Ashley	Keylah
Kerstyn (0.01)	Keshia Denise	Kether	Kevinique	Keyanah	Keylana
Kerstynn	Keshian	Kethia	Kevinisha	Keyanda	Keylantra
Kerswill	Keshiaunna	Kethika	Kevinna	Keyandra (0.01)	Keyle
Kery	Keshila	Kethry	Kevinnesha	Keyandre	Keylee
Kerynn	Keshina	Ketia	Kevion	Keyandrea	Keyleigh

Keylin	Keyshawn	Khadajia	Khadjá	Khalyiam	Kharonsea
Keyly	Keyshawna	Khadasia	Khadjah	Khalyilya	Kharrie
Keymarah	Keyshia	Khaddishia	Khadjak	Khalyn	Kharyl
Keymasha	Keyshla	Khaddra	Khadjeih Oshene	Khalysia	Kharyne
Keymaya	Keyshona	Khadéja	Khadjiah	Khamai	Kharyssa
Keymeca	Keyshonna	Khadedra (0.01)	Khadra	Khamali	Khashini
Keymilee	Keyshunda	Khadeeja (0.01)	Khadreaka	Khamar	Khasity
Keyminey	Keyshunvia	Khadeejah	Khadrijah	Khamara	Khassandria
Keymiya	Keyshyla	Khadeeji	Khadtjah	Khamarii	Khassey
Keyna	Keysi	Khadege	Khadyah	Khambriel	Khatara
Keynia	Keysia	Khadegya	Khaede	Khameisa	Khatasha
Keyoana	Keytondra	Khadeidra	Khaelyn	Khamera	Khatedrah
Keyoca	Keytreona	Khadeijah	Khaetlyn	Khamica	Khateeja
Keyochia	Keyturah	Khadeisha	Khai	Khamila	Khateria
Keyocia	Keyua	Khadeja (0.01)	Khai-Huyen	Khamiya	Khatianna
Keyomba	Keyuana	Khadejah (0.02)	Khaia	Khamya	Khatija
Keyomi	Keyuanna	Khadejha	Khaidijah	Khamyah	Khatol
Keyon	Keyumbra	Khadejia	Khaila (0.01)	Khamyra	Khatona
Keyona (0.05)	Keyuna	Khadesha	Khailah	Khanasai	Khatura
Keyonana	Keyundra	Khadesia	Khailiah	Khandace	Khatyrah
Keyonda (0.01)	Keyundrea	Khadesjah	Khaina	Khandi	Khaudeesha
Keyondra (0.01)	Keyunia	Khadetria	Khainna	Khandice	Khaudejah
Keyondrea	Keyunna	Khadicia	Khairah	Khandilyn	Khawaja
Keyondria	Keyunta	Khadidra	Khairi	Khandis	Khaya
Keyoni	Keyva	Khadidrah	Khairulzani	Khaneethah	Khayla (0.01)
Keyonia (0.01)	Keyvione	Khadigah	Khaja	Khanel	Khaylea
Keyonica	Keyvon	Khadihah	Khaki	Khanesha	Khaylia
Keyonjola	Keyvonna	Khadihaj	Khala (0.01)	Khanette	Khaylian
Keyonna (0.04)	Keywanda	Khadiiah	Khalaan	Khanh	Khaylin
Keyonnia	Keywandra	Khadiija	Khalah	Khania	Khaylla
Keyonnie	Keywaneka	Khadija (0.06)	Khalahjia	Khanidjah	Khayooth
Keyonta	Keyyona	Khadija-Inez	Khalani	Khanijah	Khayreana
Keyontae	Kezhane	Khadijah (0.44)	Khalea	Khanisha	Khayri
Keyonte	Kezia (0.01)	Khadijaha	Khaleah	Khaniyah	Khayriyyah
Keyontel	Keziah (0.01)	Khadijat	Khaleal	Khankeo	Khayyah
Keyonya	Keziga	Khadije	Khalee	Khanner	Khdija
Keyorah	Kezirah	Khadijha	Khaleela	Khansa	Khdijah
Keyosha (0.01)	Kezlyn	Khadijha Royaile	Khalehla	Khantal	Khéshada
Keyoshi	Kezra	Khadijhá	Khalei	Khanya	Khétyiah
Keyoshia	Kh'dajaha	Khadijhia	Khaler	Khaola	Khea
Keyouna	Kha	Khadijia	Khalesia	Khara	Kheana
Keyova	Kha'dejah	Khadijiah	Khali	Khare	Kheari
Keyra	Kha'dijah	Khadijrah	Khalia (0.02)	Kharee	Khedia
Keyron	Kha'lia	Khadijuah	Khaliaah	Khareia	Kheiana
Keyrra	Kha-Ai	Khadira	Khaliah (0.01)	Kharesa	Kheilenn
Keyrva	Kha-Deidra	Khadisah	Khalidda	Khari	Kheily
Keyseana	Kha-Dijah	Khadisha	Khalidha	Kharia	Khelsea
Keysha (0.01)	Khaalidah	Khadishya	Khalie	Kharina	Khelsey
Keyshaee	Khad'maleketh	Khadisia	Khalil	Kharis	Khelsi
Keyshana	Khadadijah	Khadisja	Khalilah (0.01)	Kharisma	Khendra
Keyshanna	Khadaijah	Khadiyah	Khalilaha	Khariya	Khera
Keyshara	Khadaisha	Khadiza	Khaliq	Kharizma	Kheria
Keysharra	Khadaja	Khadizah	Khalisha	Kharizmah	Kheristen
Keysharrah	Khadajah	Khadizha	Khalishia	Kharlise	Kherith
Keyshaunna	Khadajaih	Khadja	Khaliyah (0.01)	Kharlye	Kherra

Kheryn	Khoriana	Khyle	Kia-Louise	Kiania	Kiayna
Khetam	Khorrie	Khyleah	Kiaana	Kianisha	Kiayra
Khey	Khorshid	Khylee	Kiaanna	Kianna *(0.14)*	Kiayuna
Kheyana	Khortazhia	Khyli	Kiaara	Kiannah	Kibben
Kheyany	Khree	Khyliegh	Kiabeth	Kiannakay	Kibreona
Kheyla	Khrichaii	Khynni	Kiabria	Kianne	Kiccarol
Kheyonna	Khrishawda	Khyra	Kiadasha	Kianni	Kichelle
Khia	Khrissa	Khyrstan	Kiaerica	Kiant E	Kichina
Khiah	Khrista	Khyrstyana	Kiaeshia	Kianta	Kichna
Khiala	Khristal	Khyrstyn	Kiah *(0.04)*	Kiantaé	Kichonna
Khiamber	Khristanna	Khysa	Kiaha	Kiante *(0.01)*	Kicki
Khiana *(0.01)*	Khristapher	Khyshenia	Kiahana	Kianté	Kidada
Khianah	Khristen	Ki	Kiahanna	Kiantee	Kiddman
Khiande	Khristerria	Ki Ana	Kiaheshia	Kianti	Kidisha
Khianna	Khristian	Ki Ara	Kiahesia	Kianyá	Kidist
Khianti	Khristiana	Ki Er	Kiahna *(0.01)*	Kianyana	Kidston
Khiara	Khristin	Ki Era	Kiahni	Kiar	Kie
Khiarah	Khristina	Ki Ja	Kiaiara	Kiara *(0.60)*	Kie Asha
Khiasia	Khristine	Ki Jana	Kiair	Kiará	Kiéara
Khiera	Khristlyn	Ki Ona	Kiaira *(0.01)*	Kiarabel	Kiéashia
Khiesha	Khristuana	Ki Onna	Kiairah	Kiarah	Kiéla
Khila	Khristyn	Ki Shawn	Kiaire	Kiari	Kiéra
Khili	Khristyna	Ki Voceya	Kiairra	Kiaria	Kie-'ona
Khimual	Khristyonna	Ki'-Ana	Kiaisha	Kiaris	Kiea
Khinara	Khrizelle	Ki'aira	Kiaja	Kiarisce	Kieaira
Khindra	Khrysha	Ki'am	Kiajah	Kiaron	Kieal
Khiory	Khrysta	Ki'amber	Kiajuana	Kiarra *(0.05)*	Kieana
Khira	Khrystail	Ki'ambra	Kial	Kiarrah	Kieana Rochelle
Khiren	Khrystal	Ki'ana	Kiala	Kiarri	Kieanna *(0.01)*
Khirran	Khrystelle	Ki'andra	Kialee	Kiarria	Kiear
Khirsha	Khrystian	Ki'andrah	Kialey	Kiarrica	Kieara *(0.01)*
Khirstee	Khrystille	Ki'anna	Kiali	Kiarrye Latia	Kiearah
Khirsten	Khrystilyn	Ki'ara	Kialie	Kiarsha	Kiearra
Khirstyn	Khrystina	Ki'asia	Kiama	Kiarstin	Kieawhana
Khiuna	Khrystyn	Ki'ayra	Kiamara	Kiarya	Kiecia
Khiya	Khrystyne	Ki'ena	Kiamber	Kiarytza	Kieffer
Khiyahna	Khrystynna	Ki'erra	Kiamesha	Kiasa	Kiegee
Khiyana	Khubra	Ki'errah	Kiameso-	Kiasha *(0.01)*	Kieisha
Khiylah	Khudija	Ki'jana	⁣ Ndampia-	Kiashani	Kiela
Khiyvon	Khulood	Ki'juana	⁣ Deborh	Kiasia	Kielah
Khlia	Khusbu	Ki'ongela	Kiami	Kiasiniay	Kiele
Khloe	Khushbi	Ki'shandra	Kian	Kiata	Kielee
Khloé	Khushboo	Ki'shauna	Kiana *(0.62)*	Kiattia	Kieley
Khloee	Khushbu	Ki'yana	Kianah	Kiauna *(0.01)*	Kielle
Khloey	Khushmol	Ki'yuana	Kianalynn	Kiaundra	Kiely
Khloie	Khy	Ki'yunia	Kiandra *(0.02)*	Kiauni	Kiena
Khlood	Khya	Ki-Aira	Kiandranae	Kiavany	Kienna
Khloud	Khyala	Ki-Amber	Kiandre	Kiawana	Kienyu
Khlude	Khyan	Ki-Anna	Kiandrea	Kiawanna	Kieomié
Khoi	Khyandria	Ki-Jana	Kiandria	Kiawannah	Kieona
Khole	Khyara	Ki-Juana	Kiane	Kiawna	Kieonna
Kholloed	Khyché	Ki-Yaana	Kianelis	Kiaya *(0.01)*	Kieora
Khoosbu	Khydijah	Kia *(0.09)*	Kianesha	Kiayana	Kier
Khora	Khyla	Kia Vondra	Kiani *(0.01)*	Kiayanna	Kierá
Khori	Khylah	Kia-Ann	Kiani'	Kiayla	Kiera *(0.25)*

Kierah	Kieshona	Kilie	Kimberlin *(0.01)*	Kimise	Kindale
Kieran *(0.01)*	Kiessa	Kiliefia	Kimberlin A	Kimisha	Kindall
Kierany	Kieta	Kilika	Kimberlisa	Kimiya	Kindeep
Kierazlean	Kietra	Kilisa	Kimberliss	Kimjuana	Kindel
Kierca	Kiette	Kilisha	Kimberlly	Kimley	Kindela
Kiercy	Kieu	Killashandra	Kimberln	Kimlynn	Kindeli
Kierea	Kieu Trinh	Killian	Kimberly *(3.81)*	Kimmbria	Kindell
Kieree	Kiev	Killion	Kimberly Beth	Kimmeka	Kindermarie
Kieri	Kieva	Kiloisha	Kimberly Dawn	Kimmeone	Kindi
Kieria	Kieviyonnia	Kiloni	Kimberly Lorhen	Kimmeria	Kindia
Kiericka	Kievonie	Kilston	Kimberly Mae	Kimmerly	Kindle
Kierilyn	Kieyanna	Kilsys	Kimberly Michel	Kimmerlyn	Kindley
Kierin	Kieyarra	Kilty	Kimberly-Ann	Kimmi	Kindolyn
Kieris	Kieyona	Kilwanna	Kimberly-Anne	Kimmie	Kindra *(0.03)*
Kiernan	Kieyuanna	Kilyn	Kimberly-Faye	Kimmika	Kindre
Kierney	Kieyuna	Kim *(0.32)*	Kimberly-Jean	Kimmiya	Kindrea
Kiernon	Kiezia	Kim My	Kimberlyhazel	Kimmy *(0.01)*	Kindred
Kieron	Kiezza	Kim'dretria	Kimberlyn *(0.04)*	Kimneshia	Kindree
Kierra *(0.35)*	Kiffaney	Kim'mecha	Kimberlynn *(0.01)*	Kimone	Kindrina
Kierra Angelika	Kigeria	Kim-Fatima	Kimbernesia	Kimonie	Kindsay
Kierra Mae	Kihana	Kim-Lee	Kimbia	Kimora	Kindsey
Kierrá	Kihara	Kim-Lien	Kimble	Kimothy	Kindyl
Kierrah	Kiheria	Kimahra	Kimbly	Kimowan	Kiné
Kierralyn	Kihewisquew	Kimairi	Kimbra	Kimra	Kinea
Kierranika	Kihewkwun	Kimaiya	Kimbré	Kimsey	Kineasha
Kierre	Kihya	Kiman	Kimbree	Kimshai	Kineisha
Kierree	Kiia	Kimani *(0.01)*	Kimbreia	Kimshaina	Kinerey
Kierren	Kiijuana	Kimara	Kimbrell	Kimtecia	Kinesha
Kierria	Kiiyana	Kimari	Kimbreyana	Kimunna	Kiness
Kierrica	Kiiyona	Kimaria	Kimbreyata	Kimverli	Kineta
Kierroll	Kija	Kimarie	Kimbria	Kimverly	Kinezsha
Kierrs	Kijabre	Kimaura	Kimbriana	Kimwil	Kinfasha
Kiersien	Kijah	Kimaya	Kimbrianna	Kimya	King
Kiersta	Kijai	Kimaye	Kimbriel	Kimyaha	Kinga
Kierstan	Kijana	Kimbell	Kimbrien	Kimyata	Kini
Kiersteen	Kijonna	Kimbelry	Kimbriyona	Kimyatta	Kinikia
Kiersten *(0.18)*	Kijuanna	Kimbelryn	Kimburly	Kimyette	Kinisha
Kiersten Ann	Kike	Kimber *(0.05)*	Kimby	Kimyia	Kinita
Kiersti	Kiki	Kimber-Lea	Kimdeep	Kimyl	Kiniya
Kierstie	Kikilia	Kimber-Lee	Kimdrea	Kimyn	Kinjal
Kierstin *(0.06)*	Kiko	Kimberely	Kimeka	Kimyohnia	Kinjitay
Kierstn	Kil'antá	Kimberl	Kimekio	Kimyona	Kinla
Kierston *(0.01)*	Kila	Kimberland	Kimerley	Kimyri	Kinley *(0.01)*
Kierstyn *(0.02)*	Kilah	Kimberle	Kimerly	Kin	Kinnae
Kierstynn	Kilara	Kimberlea	Kimesha	Kin'tura	Kinnebrew
Kiery	Kilbey	Kimberlee *(0.10)*	Kimi	Kina	Kinnedi
Kieryn	Kilcy	Kimberlei	Kimia	Kinadie	Kinnisha
Kiesance	Kildee	Kimberleigh	Kimiaya	Kinady	Kinny
Kiescha	Kilea	Kimberley *(0.16)*	Kimika	Kinamon	Kinperly
Kieseonna	Kilee *(0.02)*	Kimberley Michel	Kimiko *(0.01)*	Kinari	Kinquana
Kiesha *(0.02)*	Kileia	Kimberley-Ann	Kimilee	Kinay	Kinrecka
Kieshauna	Kileigh	Kimberley-Anne	Kimille	Kinaya	Kinrencia
Kieshawn	Kiley *(0.14)*	Kimberley-Dale	Kimily	Kinberly	Kinsee
Kieshia	Kileyna	Kimberli *(0.01)*	Kiminique	Kindah	Kinsey *(0.08)*
Kieshira	Kili	Kimberlie *(0.01)*	Kimirra	Kindal	Kinshasa

Kinshea	Kiranpreet	Kirshyra	Kishma	Kiya *(0.02)*	Klani
Kinsie	Kiransangeet	Kirsi	Kishon	Kiyah *(0.01)*	Klara *(0.01)*
Kinslee	Kiranveer	Kirsie	Kishona	Kiyale	Klarc
Kinsley *(0.02)*	Kiranvir	Kirski	Kishonna	Kiyameshika	Klarisa
Kinslie	Kirasten	Kirsta	Kishsa	Kiyan	Klarissa *(0.03)*
Kinslyn	Kirastyn	Kirstain	Kishunna	Kiyana *(0.02)*	Klarissica
Kinsten	Kirat	Kirstan *(0.01)*	Kisina	Kiyaná	Klarrissa
Kinswana	Kiratpreet	Kirste	Kisondrea	Kiyandra	Klarrissia
Kintasha	Kirbee	Kirstee	Kissandra	Kiyani	Klaryce
Kintévia	Kirbi	Kirstein	Kissha	Kiyanna *(0.01)*	Klaryssa
Kintira	Kirby *(0.03)*	Kirsten *(0.76)*	Kissiah	Kiyante	Klassic
Kinuthia	Kire	Kirsten Marie	Kissie	Kiyara	Klaudia *(0.01)*
Kinya	Kiree	Kirsten Sharée	Kissqwanna	Kiye	Klaudija
Kinyada	Kirei	Kirstey	Kisten	Kiyenna	Klaudine
Kinyana	Kirelle	Kirsti *(0.01)*	Kiston	Kiyera	Klauren
Kinyarwanda	Kiren	Kirstian	Kisuemi	Kiyerra	Klaya
Kinyatah	Kirena	Kirstie *(0.06)*	Kiswana	Kiyhanna	Klaysha
Kinyatta	Kirenia	Kirstien	Kiswanna	Kiyiah	Klea
Kinyeer	Kirenjit	Kirstin *(0.11)*	Kit	Kiylee	Klein
Kinyetta	Kireon	Kirstine	Kita	Kiylia	Kleiya
Kinyotta	Kiresaa	Kirston	Kitam	Kiylier	Kleopatra
Kinza *(0.01)*	Kiresha	Kirsty *(0.02)*	Kitana *(0.01)*	Kiyome	Klerissa
Kinze	Kirey-Anna	Kirstyn *(0.05)*	Kitanna	Kiyomi	Klesha
Kinzee	Kirhonda	Kirstynn	Kitara	Kiyomi-	Klia
Kinzey	Kiri *(0.01)*	Kirti	Kitauna	Maximilian	Kline
Kinzi	Kiria	Kirtly	Kitavia	Kiyondra	Kliricia
Kinzie *(0.01)*	Kiriahna	Kirtney	Kitch	Kiyonna	Klista
Kinzy	Kiriaki	Kirtrina	Kiteara	Kiyoshi	Kloe
Kioka	Kiriakia	Kirusanthy	Kitera	Kiyoshi'	Kloee
Kioko	Kiriam	Kirutiga	Kithea	Kiyra	Kloey
Kion	Kiriana	Kirya	Kitiana	Kiysha	Klohe
Kiona *(0.02)*	Kirianne	Kirynn	Kitiara	Kiyuana	Klohie
Kiondra	Kirim	Kirzdy	Kitina	Kiyundra	Kloie
Kioni	Kirin	Kis'hana	Kitluka	Kizandra	Klorisa
Kionia	Kirine	Kisa	Kitra	Kizarra	Klover
Kionjra	Kirisa	Kisanet	Kitrina	Kizuwanda	Klowie
Kionna *(0.02)*	Kirissa	Kisha *(0.01)*	Kitsein	Kizzi	Klurisa
Kionte	Kiristan	Kisha-Lynn	Kitshell	Kizzie	Klydie
Kiosha	Kiristen	Kishae	Kittanya	Kizzle	Klylena
Kioshi	Kirita	Kishan	Kitten	Kizzy	Klyn
Kioshia	Kirkhart	Kishana	Kittiya	Kjahna	Klynn
Kiota	Kirkland	Kishanan	Kitty *(0.01)*	Kjanela	Kmaj
Kiquana	Kirklyn	Kishani	Kittyara	Kjatosia	Knadijah
Kira *(0.35)*	Kirktisha	Kishanna	Kitura	Kjersten	Knadriel
Kira-Devon	Kirmika	Kishanne	Kiturah	Kjersti	Knarvie
Kira-Elena	Kirn	Kishanta	Kiuana	Kjerstin	Knatoschia
Kira-Jayne	Kirndeep	Kishara	Kiunta	Kjh-Lajhni	Knautosha
Kirah	Kirnvir	Kishauna	Kiva	Kjirsten	Kneale
Kiralee	Kirra	Kishaunda	Kivanna	Kjirstin	Kneasha
Kiralyn	Kirrah	Kishawna	Kivett	Kk	Knechelle
Kiran *(0.04)*	Kirren	Kishaya	Kivona	Kkandice	Knecole
Kirandeep *(0.01)*	Kirreona	Kishayla	Kiwana	Klaasje	Kneisa
Kiranjeet	Kirri	Kishea	Kiwani	Klair	Kneisha
Kiranjit *(0.01)*	Kirschten	Kishi	Kiwanna	Klaire *(0.01)*	Knekola
Kiranjot *(0.01)*	Kirsha	Kishira	Kiwona	Klancy	Kneosha

Knesha	Koko	Konstadina	Korin *(0.01)*	Koryne	Koy
Knezle	Kokomuneecha	Konstandena	Korina *(0.04)*	Korynn	Koya
Knhojzhee	Kokwi	Konstantina	Korinasue	Korynna	Koyaan
Knieka	Kola	Konstanza	Korine	Korynthia	Koyal
Knighta	Kolbee	Konstanze	Korinn	Kosala	Koyia
Knikole	Kolbey	Konswayla	Korinna	Kosar	Koyote
Knisha	Kolbi *(0.01)*	Koonisha	Korinne *(0.01)*	Kosha	Kquan Dazia
Knoeisha	Kolbie	Kooper	Korinthia	Kosher	Kquienshay
Knoelle	Kolby *(0.01)*	Koos	Korinthian	Koshi	Krachell
Knowosha	Kole	Koosha	Korisa	Kosiga	Kraiton
Knya	Koleen	Kopikaa	Korisha	Kosntantina	Kramer
Knyah	Koleena	Kor	Korissa	Kostantina	Krana
Knyeisha	Koleicia	Kora *(0.01)*	Koriuanna	Kostanto	Krasaunda
Knyelah	Kolene	Korah	Korlyse	Kosumo	Krashonda
Knyishia	Koletta	Koraima *(0.01)*	Kornequa-Genet	Kote	Kre Osha
Knykkia	Kolette	Koral *(0.01)*	Kornesha	Koteeri	Kréshavia
Knyla	Koleytta	Koralee	Korra	Koti	Krea
Koa	Kolina	Koraleigh	Korral	Kotie	Kreanna
Koady	Kolisha	Koralie *(0.01)*	Korren	Kotonya	Kreanne
Koann	Kolkani	Koralyn	Korrey	Kotrney	Kreashia
Kobbi	Kollean	Koran	Korri *(0.01)*	Kotryna	Kreasia
Kobegia	Kolleen *(0.01)*	Korayma	Korrianna	Kottia	Krecedez
Kobena	Kolleicha	Korbee	Korrie	Koty	Krecia
Kobie	Kollena	Korbin	Korriel	Kotysha	Kreena
Kobree	Kolly	Korby	Korrin *(0.01)*	Kountessa	Kreeshia
Koby	Koloud	Korbynn	Korrina	Kourageous	Krehauna
Kocia	Kolynna	Korday	Korrine	Koureteney	Kreisher
Koda	Komako	Kordia	Korrinne	Kourion	Kreneshia
Kodee	Komal *(0.01)*	Kordicha	Korrio	Kournney	Krenshara
Kodey	Komaljot	Kore	Korrisa	Kourri	Kreshauna
Kodi *(0.03)*	Komalpreet	Korea *(0.01)*	Korry	Kourt'ne	Kreshawna
Kodie *(0.01)*	Komari	Koreana	Korryn	Kourtanee	Kreshona
Kodijah	Komeia	Korée	Korryne	Kourtenay	Kresley
Kodilee	Komeisha	Koreen	Korrynne	Kourteney	Kreslyn
Kodjah	Komeka	Koreena	Korshye	Kourtez	Kresta
Kody *(0.01)*	Komel	Koren *(0.01)*	Korsica	Kourtland	Krestina
Kody-Lynne	Komikka	Korena	Korteney	Kourtlyn	Krestlynn
Kodye	Komil	Korenda	Korteria	Kourtnay	Kreston
Koehler	Koncrieta	Korene	Kortland	Kourtne	Krestor
Koey	Konequa	Koresa	Kortnai	Kourtné	Kretessa
Kofi	Koneshiwa	Koresca	Kortne	Kourtnee *(0.01)*	Kria
Kogan	Konesia	Korey *(0.01)*	Kortné	Kourtnei *(0.01)*	Kricket
Koh-Eun	Koney	Koreyell	Kortnée	Kourtneigh	Krickett
Kohar	Kongaydra	Kori *(0.14)*	Kortnee *(0.01)*	Kourtney *(0.25)*	Kridesha
Koharu	Koniee	Kori'lyn	Kortnei	Kourtneyi	Krika
Kohl	Konika	Koria	Kortney *(0.10)*	Kourtni *(0.01)*	Krikett
Kohlie	Konisha	Koriana	Kortney-Lynn	Kourtnie *(0.01)*	Krikland
Kohowye	Konnar	Koriane	Kortni *(0.02)*	Kourtnie-Ann	Krimson
Koi	Konner	Korianna	Kortnie *(0.01)*	Kourtny	Krin
Koia	Konni	Korianne	Kortny	Kourtnyi	Krina
Kojana	Konnie	Korica	Korula	Kouryney	Krineéjua
Kok	Konnisha	Korie *(0.02)*	Kory *(0.01)*	Kouther	Krinysha
Kokenya	Konnor	Korii	Koryanna	Kowsar	Kripa
Koki	Konovia	Korilye	Koryn *(0.01)*	Kowser	Kris
Kokia	Konquitta	Korilyn	Koryna	Kowthar	Kris Denzel

Kris'sandra	Krislyn (0.01)	Kristen-Dawn	Kristun	Kryssha	Krystydna
Kris-Ann	Krislynn	Kristen-Nicole	Kristy (0.25)	Kryssia	Krystyn (0.01)
Krisa	Krisna	Kristen-Taylor	Kristy-Lynn	Kryssiah	Krystyna (0.02)
Krisalyn	Krisney	Kristena (0.01)	Kristyana	Krysta (0.12)	Krystyne
Krisamy	Krisol	Kristene	Kristye	Krystaal	Ksenia
Krisan	Krissa (0.01)	Kristenilycia	Kristyl	Krystah	Ksenija
Krisanda	Krissany	Kristeny	Kristyn (0.13)	Krystail	Ksenja
Krisandra	Krissaundra	Kristhal	Kristyn Michelle	Krystain	Kshara
Krisani	Krisshonda	Kristhina	Kristyna (0.01)	Krystal (0.76)	Kshatriya
Krisann	Krissi	Kristi (0.21)	Kristyne	Krystal Faith	Kshondra
Krisanne	Krissie	Kristi-Anne	Kristynn	Krystal-Ann	Ksinya
Krisantheum	Krissy (0.01)	Kristi-Lynn	Kristyona	Krystal-Anne	Ksonna
Krischell	Krissy-Lynn	Kristia	Kristyonna	Krystal-Lynn	KT
Krischelle	Krissylee	Kristia Leanne	Krisuantha	Krystal-Renee	Ku'ali'i
Kriscia	Krista (0.72)	Kristian (0.10)	Krisy	Krystale	Ku'uipolani
Kriscinda	Krista-Anne	Kristiana (0.05)	Krisztina	Krystalene	Ku'ulei
Kriscynthia	Krista-Lee	Kristiania	Krithika	Krystalin	Ku'wana
Kriseata	Krista-Lynn	Kristiann	Kriti	Krystall	Kuadrika
Krisel	Kristafer	Kristianna (0.02)	Kritika	Krystalle	Kuana
Krisella	Kristagiah	Kristianne	Kritzia	Krystallena	Kuanicia
Krisena	Kristah	Kristians	Kriyundra	Krystallyn	Kubosnia
Krisenda	Kristain	Kristianti	Krizan	Krystalyn (0.01)	Kubra
Krisette	Kristal (0.08)	Kristie (0.10)	Krizia	Krystalynn	Kubria
Kriseyesha	Kristal America	Kristien	Krizma	Krystalynne	Kubryna
Krisha (0.01)	Kristal-Ann	Kristiga	Kriztina	Krystan (0.01)	Kudejah
Krishae	Kristalee	Kristiina	Krizzia	Krystane	Kudiratu
Krishan	Kristalene	Kristijna	Krupa (0.01)	Krysteanna	Kudrat
Krishana	Kristalin	Kristil	Krupali	Krystee	Kuera
Krishanda	Kristallyn	Kristilin	Krushana	Krysteele	Kuersten
Krishandra	Kristalyn (0.01)	Kristilyn	Krustal	Krysteen	Kuheli
Krishanna	Kristalynn	Kristin (1.09)	Krustin	Krystel (0.03)	Kuinn
Krishaun	Kristalynne	Kristin-	Krustun	Krystel Gewel	Kula'aunani
Krishauna	Kristamarie	Shamshoum	Kruti	Krystelle (0.01)	Kulabrea
Krishawn	Kristan (0.04)	Kristina (1.23)	Krutika	Krysten (0.07)	Kulani
Krishawna	Kristana	Kristina-Anne	Kruzkaya	Krystene	Kuldip
Krishawnda	Kristaney	Kristina-Rae	Kry'shala	Krysti	Kulie
Krishawyn	Kristanna	Kristinae	Kryanna	Krysti-Ann	Kuljan
Krisheka	Kristanne	Kristinagiuseppa	Krychelle	Krystian (0.01)	Kuljeet
Krishell	Kristany	Kristine (0.31)	Kryesha	Krystiana	Kuljinder
Krishelle	Kristara	Kristine Mae	Kryn	Krystiana Alexi	Kuljit
Krishion	Kristarra	Kristine May	Krynn	Krystianna	Kullani
Krishma	Kristasha	Kristinne	Krysa	Krystie	Kulquinda
Krishna (0.01)	Kristatyn	Kristinnia	Krysalyn	Krystilynn	Kulsoom
Krishnaveni	Kriste	Kristins	Kryscynthia	Krystin (0.05)	Kulveen
Krishni	Kristean	Kristionna	Krysha	Krystin-Michael	Kulvelee
Krishon	Kristeana	Kristiy	Kryshana	Krystina (0.08)	Kulvir
Krishonda	Kristee	Kristle	Kryshawna	Krystine (0.01)	Kumari
Krishonna	Kristeen	Kristlyn	Kryshawnda	Krystinn	Kundana
Krishtina	Kristeena	Kristoin	Kryshna	Krystle (0.05)	Kuneshia
Krishun	Kristein	Kristolyn	Kryshonna	Krystn	Kungo
Krishuna	Kristeina	Kriston (0.01)	Kryshta	Krystne	Kunique
Krisia	Kristel (0.01)	Kristopher	Krysia	Krystofer	Kunisha
Krisika	Kristell	Kristta	Krysle	Krystol	Kupere
Krisina	Kristelle (0.01)	Kristul	Kryslyn	Kryston	Kuphenyia
Krisitna	Kristen (2.55)	Kristuline	Kryssa	Krystyana	Kura

Kuran	Kwaneshia	Ky'ongela	Kyeanna	Kylee (0.34)	Kymber (0.01)
Kuri	Kwanesia	Ky'ra	Kyeantane	Kyleérayne	Kymberely
Kurin	Kwaneysah	Ky'ri	Kyée	Kylee-Anne	Kymberlee (0.01)
Kurina	Kwani	Ky-Duyen	Kyeesha	Kyleeanna	Kymberleigh
Kurious	Kwanice	Ky-Lia	Kyeisha	Kyleen (0.01)	Kymberli (0.01)
Kurissa	Kwaniesha	Ky-Mesha	Kyela	Kyleer	Kymberlie
Kuristy	Kwanika	Kya (0.03)	Kyelah	Kyleesha	Kymberly (0.03)
Kurneishe	Kwanisha	Kya'mber	Kyelee	Kylei	Kymberlyn (0.01)
Kurnisha	Kwanita	Kya'na	Kyeli	Kyleigh (0.07)	Kymberlynn
Kurrisa	Kwanjai	Kya-Lee	Kyenne	Kyleigha	Kymberlynne
Kursha	Kwankila	Kya-Rochelle	Kyera (0.01)	Kyleisha	Kymbra
Kursheeka	Kwanna	Kyah (0.01)	Kyerha	Kylen	Kymbre
Kurshell	Kwannee	Kyahna	Kyeria	Kylena	Kymbrea
Kurstee	Kwantika	Kyaira	Kyericka	Kylene (0.01)	Kymbreanna
Kursten	Kwanza	Kyairra	Kyerika	Kyler (0.01)	Kymbreia
Kurstian	Kwanzaa	Kyaisa	Kyerra (0.01)	Kylesha	Kymbriana
Kurstin	Kwarnasia	Kyaisha	Kyerstein	Kyley (0.02)	Kymbriell
Kurston	Kwashai	Kyaivah	Kyerstin	Kyli (0.02)	Kymbriona
Kurstyn	Kwashay	Kyala	Kyesh	Kylia	Kymbur
Kurteya	Kwashayla	Kyalamboka	Kyesha (0.01)	Kyliah	Kymeberley
Kurtisha	Kwauntaizja	Kyale	Kyeshia	Kylian	Kymere
Kusaie	Kwayera	Kyana (0.05)	Kyetaronda	Kylie (1.26)	Kymesha
Kusala	Kwayneshia	Kyanah	Kyetra	Kylie Nicole	Kymeshia
Kushaldeep	Kwéqueonna	Kyandra	Kyevin	Kylié	Kymia
Kushanne	Kweisi	Kyandria	Kyhadijah	Kylie-Ann	Kymiesha
Kushonah	Kweli	Kyani	Kyhanná	Kylie-Marie	Kymmery
Kutah	Kwenci	Kyanjala	Kyhia	Kyliee	Kymonee
Kutarha	Kwenessia	Kyann	Kyhla	Kyliegh	Kymonie
Kutira	Kwenette	Kyanna (0.01)	Kyi	Kyliesha	Kymonya
Kutrel	Kweshauna	Kyanne	Kyia (0.01)	Kylii	Kymora
Kuturah	Kwest	Kyanni	Kyiah	Kyliie	Kymyatta
Kuuipo	Kwetana	Kyanté	Kyianna	Kylila	Kyna
Kuulei	Kwijona	Kyantia	Kyiesha	Kylin	Kynachbba
Kuuleimomilani	Kwinci	Kyara (0.02)	Kyieta	Kylina	Kynadee
Kuuleinani	Kwinlyn	Kyarah	Kyiion	Kylinda	Kynara
Kuumakanahiwahiw	Kwok	Kyaria	Kyilah	Kylisha	Kynat
Kuylin	Kwontasia	Kyarie	Kyisha	Kyliyah	Kyndahl
Kuymeisha	Kwristanith	Kyarra	Kyjana	Kylla	Kyndal (0.02)
Kvinde	Kwun	Kyashia	Kyjuana	Kylle	Kyndall (0.02)
Kwa-Weisha	Kwyanna	Kyasia	Kykiana	Kyllie	Kyndalle
Kwachanna	Kwynsee	Kyaszia	Kyla (0.37)	Kyllie Joanne	Kyndel
Kwadasia	Ky	Kyauh	Kyla-Jade	Kyllie Mae	Kyndell
Kwaeshye	Ky Ashia	Kyauna	Kyla-Lee	Kylsie	Kyndelle
Kwai-Fu	Ky Ché	Kyaundra	Kyla-Marie	Kyly	Kyndi
Kwakisha	Ky Ira	Kyavis	Kylah (0.01)	Kylyn	Kyndl
Kwaleyshia	Ky Lunta	Kybria	Kylai	Kylynn (0.01)	Kyndle
Kwamesha	Ky'aira	Kychét	Kylan	Kylysses	Kyndol
Kwamesiha	Ky'airra	Kychelle	Kylar	Kym (0.02)	Kyndra (0.02)
Kwammila	Ky'ana	Kydra	Kylara	Kym Miah	Kyndra Mara
Kwamysha	Ky'anna	Kye	Kylashay	Kymaletha	Kyndrea
Kwan'jai	Ky'ara	Kyéanndre	Kyle (0.03)	Kymani	Kyndree
Kwana	Ky'eisha	Kyédashia	Kylea (0.01)	Kymara	Kyndrian
Kwanae	Ky'esha	Kye-Keya	Kyleah	Kymaria	Kyndsey
Kwaneria	Ky'jha	Kye-Lee	Kyleann	Kymarlyn	Kyneasha
Kwanesha	Ky'miah	Kyeana	Kylecia	Kymbelle	Kynedi

Kyneeshaw	Kyrin	Kyyrie	La Koya	La Tia	La'hazel
Kynesha	Kyrina	Kyzel	La Kysha	La Tieya	La'iesha
Kyneshia	Kyrionne	Kyzie	La Maya	La Tiqua	La'jauntae
Kynetta	Kyrisha		La Naja	La Tisha	La'jerieka Yasa
Kynidi	Kyrissa	**-L-**	La Najha	La Toni	La'joi
Kyniecesha	Kyrolynn		La Naya	La Tonia	La'jsae
Kyniesha	Kyron	L (0.03)	La Nequia	La Tonna	La'justice
Kynisha	Kyronachamp	L Chailyn	La Nisha	La Toya	La'kalveya
Kynishia	Kyronda	L'achelle	La Nyia	La Trina	La'kaya
Kynjari'	Kyrra	L'dedra	La Paris	La Triva	La'kayla
Kynlee	Kyrsa	L'kira	La Porcha	La Troya	La'keavian
Kynsie	Kyrsa-Lee	L'najah	La Porisha	La Verne	La'kedra
Kynslie	Kyrsha	L'neisha	La Porscha	La Vona	La'keela
Kynya	Kyrstal	L'oreal	La Porsche	La Vonne	La'keia
Kynyatta	Kyrstan	L'sha	La Preshous	La Vonzell	La'keisha
Kynyetta	Kyrsten (0.02)	L'shai	La Quarion	La Wanda	La'keitha
Kynzee	Kyrsti	L'shonya	La Quasha	La'angela	La'keithia
Kynzi Amalia	Kyrstiana	L'tanya	La Queenia	La'ashley	La'keivah
Kynzie	Kyrstie	L'tavia	La Quesha	La'asia	La'keivia
Kyo	Kyrstin (0.02)	L-Zhae	La Queshia	La'brenda	La'kellseyia
Kyoka	Kyrstyn (0.01)	L.	La Rajanea	La'bresha	La'kendra
Kyoko	Kysa	La (0.02)	La Raya	La'breya	La'kenya
Kyomi-Celeste	Kysha	La Amie	La Raysha	La'brina	La'keria
Kyona	Kyshalah	La Aongdao	La Ree	La'cambria	La'kerri
Kyondra	Kyshara	La Audurey	La Reginaln	La'cara	La'kerria
Kyondria	Kyshaunda	La Bianca	La Renia	La'carie	La'keshia
Kyonia	Kyshaundra	La Brayia	La Rhonda	La'cayya	La'kesia
Kyonila	Kyshayla	La Brea	La Riah	La'chaia	La'kessia
Kyonna	Kyshelle	La Brittane	La Rica	La'chel	La'ketta
Kyonte	Kyshema	La Brittany	La Risha	La'china	La'kevias
Kyouka	Kysheria	La Cameron	La Rita	La'chonya	La'keya
Kyoung-A	Kyshmah	La Chace	La Rose	La'christa	La'keyera
Kyra (0.33)	Kyshmah Hasonna	La Ché Bennetr	La Shai	La'cole	La'keyta
Kyra Ewatah	Kyshondra	La Christia	La Shall	La'corey	La'keythea
Kyra Lyn	Kyssta	La Daisha	La Shandra	La'crystal	La'ki'etha
Kyra-Ann	Kytana	La Daviery	La Shannie	La'daijah	La'kia
Kyra-Lynn	Kytara	La Dayija	La Shanta	La'daisha	La'kiera
Kyrae	Kytia	La Derwiniq	La Shante	La'danike	La'kimbria
Kyrah	Kytzia	La Dijah	La Shawn	La'darra	La'kita
Kyralyn	Kyu	La Donna	La Shawnda	La'darrica	La'kiya
Kyran	Kyuana	La Faye	La Shay	La'dazha	La'krisha
Kyrda	Kyuana Briana	La Jacqueline	La Shayla	La'denesha	La'kyra
Kyreal	Kyung	La Jeffreca	La Shon	La'destenee	La'la
Kyree	Kyunteh	La Jessica	La Shonda	La'dezha	La'lace
Kyreia	Kyuyoung	La Kayra	La Shontier	La'dietra	La'marah
Kyrena	Kyvin	La Keah	La Shunte	La'dondra	La'mesha
Kyresha	Kywan	La Kedra	La Sonya	La'donna	La'metria
Kyri	Kywana	La Keisha	La Stiuana	La'donte	La'mirah
Kyria	Kywanda	La Kelshe	La Taronette	La'drafius	La'missa
Kyrian	Kywanna	La Kesha	La Tasha	La'dreka	La'monica
Kyriana	Kywauna	La Ketreaus	La Tavia	La'drunca	La'mya
Kyrianna	Kywia	La Keya	La Teia	La'dunsha	La'naisha
Kyrianne	Kyya	La Kia	La Teishia	La'era	La'naviera
Kyrie (0.02)	Kyyah	La Kiara	La Terria	La'farrah	La'naya
Kyrié	Kyyamm	La Kira	La Teysha	La'greggrea	La'neasha

La'neeka	La'sharon	La'vette	Labresha	Lachasity	Lacrecia
La'neisha	La'shawn	La'vita	Labreshia	Lachaun	Lacree
La'nekia	La'shawntae	La'vondia	Labreyah	Lachaunta	Lacreisha
La'nequa	La'shay	La'wanda	Labreyana	Lache	Lacresha
La'nia	La'shayla	La'yeisha	Labri'	Lacheesha	Lacresia
La'niah	La'she	La-Chelle	Labria (0.01)	Lachele	Lacretia
La'nik	La'shé	La-Dana	Labriana	Lachell	Lacreyel
La'nika	La'shea	La-Dawn	Labriania	Lachella	Lacricia
La'nikka	La'sheena	La-Destinna	Labrieana	Lachelle (0.01)	Lacriesha
La'nikque	La'sheka	La-Dreke	Labrina	Lacherri	Lacrisah
La'nisha	La'shell	La-Faye	Labrinna	Lachia	Lacrisha
La'niyah	La'shelle	La-Kaysha	Labrisha	Lachina	Lacrishia
La'nora	La'shena	La-Keesha	Labrittainy	Lachita	Lacrissa
La'nyah	La'shequai	La-Micah	Labrittanii	Lachlan	Lacrysta
La'passion	La'sherimie	La-Nise	Labrittany	Lachon	Lacrystal
La'patra	La'shika	La-Qiesha	Labyra	Lachonda	Lacsy
La'porcha	La'shonda	La-Shawnia	Lacaia	Lachrea	Lacy (0.14)
La'porsha	La'shondra	La-Shona	Lacaila	Lachrisha	Lacye
La'porshe	La'shonna	La-T'yvi	Lacammera	Lachrissa	Lacylee
La'portia	La'shyra	La-Tesha	Lacamra	Lachrista	Lacyn
La'precious	La'stacia	La-Tiffany	Lacandance	Lachristy	Lacynthia
La'presha	La'stella	La-Tisha	Lacandria	Lachun	Ladacia
La'quailla	La'taisha	La-Tya	Lacangy	Lachuntate	Ladaesha
La'qualla	La'tanyá	La-Vanitey	Lacara	Lachyna	Ladaijah
La'quana	La'tarisu	Laaken	Lacarla	Laci (0.05)	Ladaise
La'quaná	La'tasha	Laakini	Lacarliss	Lacia	Ladaisha (0.01)
La'quasha	La'taujae	Laangel'	Lacarrol	Laciann	Ladaishea
La'queena	La'tavia	Laangela	Lacarsha	Lacie (0.08)	Ladaisjah
La'queisha	La'tayshia	Laannabra	Lacasia	Lacie-Ann	Ladaiza
La'quesha	La'teisha	Laantonise	Lacassie	Laciee	Ladaja
La'quiesha	La'tequilla	Laantroshá	Lacathy	Laciey	Ladaja H
La'quis	La'terra	Laashley	Lacaunya	Lacilyn	Ladajah
La'quisha	La'terri	Laasia	Laccey	Lacinda	Ladaje
La'quita	La'terria	Laastreia	Lace (0.01)	Lacitta	Ladan (0.01)
La'raven	La'tessia	Laavanya	Lacé	Laclara	Ladana
La'reá	La'tia	Laavia	Lacea	Laclinta	Ladante
La'rece	La'tiana	Laaysia	Lacedes	Lacola	Ladara
La'reshia	La'tice	Labarbara	Lacedria	Lacole	Ladarby
La'rhonda	La'tisa	Labarcia	Lacee (0.02)	Laconda	Ladaria
La'ricca	La'tisha	Labecca	Lacei	Laconities	Ladarika
La'rikka	La'tondria	Labiba	Lacelle	Lacora	Ladarra
La'ritatajzhawn	La'tori	Labibah	Lacesha	Lacorae	Ladarrá
La'royia	La'toya	Labina	Lacey (0.52)	Lacorah	Ladarral
La'sabre	La'traicia	Labisa	Lacey Tee	Lacoreyia	Ladasha (0.01)
La'sabrea	La'trenica	Labortiya	Lacey-Lynn	Lacorriye	Ladashia
La'saysha	La'tresa	Labosh	Lacey-Rose	Lacosta	Ladashiah
La'sha	La'tressa	Labranica	Lach'e	Lacota	Ladasia
La'shá	La'trice	Labraya	Lacha	Lacoty	Ladava
La'shae	La'tricia	Labrea	Lachae	Lacouia	Ladaveona
La'shai	La'trinati	Labreeska	Lachaela	Lacouresia	Ladavias
La'shaiya	La'trionia	Labreia	Lachanda	Lacourtney	Ladawn
La'shane	La'trisa	Labreka	Lachandra	Lacovya	Ladawna
La'shara	La'troya	Labrenda	Lachanté	Lacoyá	Ladaya
La'sharia	La'tyra	Labrene	Lachara	Lacoyia	Ladayja
La'sharlena	La'veranique	Labreque	Lachariot	Lacramioara	Ladaysha

Ladayshia	Laeeqa	Laiklyn	Lajhonay	Lakeishia	Lakeymeshia
Ladaysia	Laekia	Laikyn *(0.01)*	Lajoan	Lakeishon	Lakeyn
Ladazea	Laekin	Laila *(0.05)*	Lajohnia	Lakeisia	Lakeynata
Ladazja	Laekyn	Lailah	Lajohnica	Lakeita	Lakeyneshia
Laddie	Lael	Lailani	Lajoi	Lakeitha	Lakeysha
Lade Ja	Laelle	Lailanie	Lajoy	Lakeithia	Lakeyshia
Ladedra	Laena	Lailany	Lajoya	Lakeitra	Lakeysia
Ladee	Laesha	Lailoni	Lajoyia	Lakeiya	Lakeystyanna
Ladeidra	Laeshay	Lailonnah	Lajuana	Lakeiyah	Lakhandra
Ladeisha	Laeticia	Laily	Lajuandra	Lakeiyra	Lakhirah
Ladeja	Laetitia	Lailynn	Lajustice	Lakela	Lakhisha
Ladejha	Laettner	Laima	Lakahla	Lakell	Lakia *(0.02)*
Ladejhia	Laeva	Lain	Lakaia	Lakella	Lakiara
Ladejza	Laexandra	Laina *(0.01)*	Lakaisha	Lakelvanesha	Lakiea
Ladell	Lafaiva	Lainah	Lakaiya	Lakely	Lakiesha *(0.01)*
Ladelshia	Lafaysha	Lainamaria	Lakala	Lakelyn	Lakieshia
Ladena	Laflora	Laine *(0.01)*	Lakan	Lakelynn	Lakieta
Ladera	Lafonda	Lainee	Lakanya	Lakema	Lakieva
Ladereka	Lafonté	Lainen	Lakara	Laken *(0.07)*	Lakieya
Laderka	Lafranco	Lainey *(0.03)*	Lakasha	Lakena	Lakiisha
Laderria	Lafreda	Laini	Lakashia	Lakenaisha	Lakil
Laderricka	Lafyette	Lainie	Lakasja	Lakenda	Lakila
Ladesha	Lagae	Lainna	Lakavia	Lakendra *(0.02)*	Lakillia
Ladesta	Lagara	Lairen	Lakawdra	Lakendral	Lakim
Ladetra	Lagarriya	Lairlashay	Lakaya *(0.01)*	Lakendria	Lakimberiya
Ladetria	Lagashia	Laisa	Lakayla *(0.01)*	Lakennthia	Lakimberly
Ladeyah	Lagena	Laisha	Lakayln	Lakentay	Lakimbra
Ladiaha	Lagenia	Laishanquaria	Lakaysha	Lakenya *(0.01)*	Lakimbrea
Ladiamond	Lageorgia K	Laishon	Lakaysia	Lakenzie	Lakin *(0.03)*
Ladiashia	Laghanaé	Laita	Lakaza	Lakeria	Lakindria
Ladie	Lagina	Laitlin	Lakazjah	Lakerra	Lakinya
Ladija	Lagloria	Laitlyn	Lake	Lakerria	Lakioya
Ladinaka	Lah'kia	Laiza	Lakea	Lakesa	Lakira
Ladisha	Lahana	Lajackie	Lakeasha	Lakese	Lakisa
Ladiva	Laharini	Lajada	Lakebia	Lakeseha	Lakise
Ladon	Lahdann	Lajae	Lakechia	Lakesha *(0.02)*	Lakisha *(0.02)*
Ladon Dra	Laheisha	Lajaé	Lakecia	Lakeshia *(0.02)*	Lakita *(0.01)*
Ladonna *(0.02)*	Lahela	Lajaia	Lakeda	Lakesi	Lakitric
Ladonya	Lahini	Lajaiah	Lakedra	Lakesia	Lakitta
Ladora	Lahiqa	Lajaisha	Lakeédra	Laketa	Lakiva
Ladorne	Lahiru	Lajalie	Lakeeda	Laketha	Lakivia
Ladorothy	Lahna	Lajamia	Lakeema	Lakethia	Lakiya *(0.01)*
Ladosha	Lahoma	Lajané	Lakeena	Lakethya	Lakkenn
Ladrea	Lahonna	Lajari	Lakeenya	Laketia	Lakkia
Ladreca	Lahtiana	Lajavia	Lakeesa	Laketionna	Lakniyja
Ladrece	Lahtiesha	Lajayda	Lakeesha	Laketta	Lakoda
Ladreka	Lahunia	Lajaysha	Lakeeshia	Lakeva	Lakohta
Ladrena	Lai	Lajé	Lakeeta	Lakeya *(0.01)*	Lakoshia
Ladrica	Laia	Lajeanesse	Lakeia	Lakeyah	Lakota *(0.02)*
Ladronda	Laiali	Lajefferica	Lakeidra	Lakeyda	Lakotah
Ladsami	Laicon	Lajelcia	Lakeidre	Lakeydra	Lakourtney
Ladwan	Laika	Lajennice	Lakeila	Lakeyesa	Lakoyia
Lady-Guinevere	Laike	Lajerika	Lakeira	Lakeyevette Jac	Lakrecha
Ladye	Laiken *(0.01)*	Lajerrica	Lakeisha *(0.06)*	Lakeyia	Lakreesha
Lae Montesha	Laikin	Lajeune	Lakeisha Rashon	Lakeyla	Lakreisha

Lakresha	Lamaria	Lamoya	Lanéya	Lanikkie	Laporschia
Lakriesha	Lamaris	Lamya	Lanea	Lanina	Laporsha (0.01)
Lakrisha	Lamariya	Lamyra	Laneasha	Laniqua	Laporshe
Lakrishandaé	Lamarjja	Lamyria	Lanecha	Lanique	Laporshia
Lakrissha	Lamarko	Lan	Lanecia	Laniquia	Laporshua
Lakrista	Lamarla	Lan-Anh	Lanee	Lanise	Laportía
Lakrystal	Lamarquesh	Lana (0.10)	Lanée	Lanisha (0.02)	Laportia
Lakrysten	Lamaryia	Lana't	Laneesa	Lanishia	Laprecious
Lakshmi	Lamaya	Lana-Jane	Laneesha	Lanita	Lapresha
Lakundrika	Lambrini	Lanaceya	Lanei	Lanitra	Lapresheanna
Lakwandre	Lamburgenie	Lanadia	Laneika	Lanivea	Lapricia
Lakwayza	Lamea	Lanae (0.01)	Laneisha (0.01)	Laniya	Laprincia
Lakwonda	Lameas	Lanaé	Laneishia	Laniyah	Laqeisha
Lakya	Lameatrice	Lanaea	Laneka	Lanizsha	Laqesha
Lakyan	Lameca	Lanai	Lanekqua	Lanna (0.01)	Laqeshia
Lakyen	Lameceya	Lanaisa	Lanell	Lannah	Laqisha
Lakyia	Lameeka	Lanaisha	Lanelle	Lannay	Laqorsha
Lakyla	Lameesha	Lanaisia	Lanese	Lannette	Laqua-Na
Lakyn (0.02)	Lameika	Lanajha	Lanesha (0.01)	Lanney	Laquacious
Lakyna	Lameisha	Lanara	Laneshea	Lanni	Laquaia
Lakynn	Lameithia	Lanaria	Laneshia	Lannie	Laquaisha
Lakyra	Lameka	Lanasha	Lanesia	Lannikki	Laquala
Lakysha	Lameria	Lanasia	Lanessa	Lannique	Laquan
Lakyshia	Lamese	Lanasjau	Lanetra	Lannisha	Laquana
Lakzisha	Lamesha	Lanay	Lanetrá	Lannon	Laquanda (0.01)
Lalah	Lameshia	Lanaya	Lanett	Lannys	Laquandra
Lalaine	Lametrice	Lanayria	Lanetta	Lanoise	Laquandrea
Lalainia	Lamia (0.01)	Lanaysha	Lanette (0.01)	Lanor	Laquanna
Lalandra	Lamiah	Lanayzia	Lanettea	Lanora	Laquansala
Lalani	Lamichael	Lance	Laneva	Lanorra	Laquanshea
Lalanie	Lamicie	Lancee	Lanexa	Lanoshia	Laquanta
Lalar	Lamija	Lancesha	Laney (0.04)	Lanphuong	Laquantise
Lalaya	Lamika	Lanceshell	Langatotoa	Lansinger	Laquanza
Lalaynia	Lamilriel	Lancey	Langley (0.01)	Lantya	Laquasey
Laleathea	Lamina	Lancy	Langlie	Lanya	Laquasha
Laleena	Laminat	Land	Langston	Lanyce	Laquashia
Laleigh	Laminia	Landan	Lani (0.02)	Lanycea	Laquasia
Lalena	Lamink	Landen	Lania	Lanyea	Laquata
Lalia	Lamira	Lander	Lanice	Lao	Laquavia
Lalique	Lamiria	Landi	Lanicia	Laosha	Laquaya
Lalissia	Lamise	Landie	Lanie (0.02)	Lapaige	Laquazahya
Lalita	Lamisha	Landin	Laniece (0.01)	Lapara	Laque
Lalitha	Lamishia	Landis	Lanieja	Laparis	Laqueasha
Laliyah	Lamiya	Landon (0.01)	Lanielle	Laparish	Laqueatta
Laloni	Lamiyah	Landra	Lanier	Lapassion	Laquecia
Lalyric	Lamonae	Landrá	Laniere	Lapattra	Laqueena
Lam	Lamoni	Landri	Laniesa	Lapaysha	Laqueesha
Lama (0.01)	Lamonica (0.01)	Landria	Laniese	Laperia	Laqueisha
Lamadeline	Lamonika	Landriona	Laniesha	Laphinany	Laqueishia
Lamanda	Lamonjana	Landry	Lanieta	Lapleasure	Laquelle
Lamar	Lamont	Landy	Lanijah	Lapoltina	Laquellia
Lamara	Lamonta	Landyn (0.01)	Lanika	Laporcha	Laquence
Lamara Kawa	Lamontaneice	Landynne	Lanikaka	Laporche	Laquerida
Lamaree	Lamonyca	Lane (0.03)	Lanikka	Laporscha	Laquesha (0.01)
Lamaressa	Lamott	Lane Sha	Lanikki	Laporsche	Laqueshia

Laquestiya	Larane	Larinique	Larrease	Lasandra *(0.01)*	Lasharon
Laqueta	Laranisha	Larinisha	Larrelle	Lasandria	Lasharra
Laquetta	Larasita	Lariona	Larren	Lasara	Lasharri
Laquette	Larauen	Larionia	Larrese	Lasaraca	Lashaun *(0.01)*
Laquevia	Laraven	Larionna	Larresha	Lasasha	Lashauna
Laquia	Laravia	Larionne	Larrhon	Lasaysha	Lashaunda
Laquicia	Laray	Laris	Larri	Lascarlett	Lashaunda-Kierra
Laquiece	Laraya	Larisa *(0.05)*	Larri'keithia	Laschastia	Lashaundra
Laquiesha	Larayn	Larisana	Larriana	Lasean	Lashaunna
Laquil	Laraynna	Larise	Larrianna	Lasena	Lashaunta
Laquill	Laraysha	Larisha *(0.01)*	Larrica	Lasey	Lashauntá
Laquilla	Larcenia	Larissa *(0.38)*	Larricka	Lasha *(0.01)*	Lashaunte
Laquinja	Lareatrica	Larissah	Larriel	Lashada	Lashaunté
Laquinna	Lareb	Larissha	Larriell	Lashade	Lashauntée
Laquinta *(0.01)*	Lareca	Larita	Larrielle	Lashae *(0.02)*	Lashauntia
Laquiria	Larecesa	Laritssa	Larriesha	Lashaé	Lashauntis
Laquirria	Larecia	Laritta	Larrija	Lashaevia	Lashavya
Laquis	Larecka	Laritza	Larrika	Lashai *(0.01)*	Lashawn *(0.03)*
Laquish	Laree	Laritzza	Larrineisha	Lashaia	Lashawna *(0.01)*
Laquisha *(0.03)*	Lareesa	Lariyah	Larrinita	Lashaique	Lashawnda *(0.01)*
Laquita *(0.02)*	Lareese	Larizze	Larrinysha	Lashala	Lashawndra
Laquitia	Lareesha	Lark	Larrion	Lashalle	Lashawndre
Laquitta	Lareika	Larka	Larrisa *(0.01)*	Lashambria	Lashawnia
Laqula	Lareisha	Larkera	Larrisa-Lyn	Lashamonique	Lashawnta
Laqunda	Lareitha	Larkin	Larrisha	Lashan	Lashawnte
Laquntanay	Larell	Larkins	Larrishiana	Lashana	Lashawnté
Laqunya	Laren *(0.01)*	Larkyn	Larrissa *(0.01)*	Lashanae	Lashawnteona
Laquoia	Larena	Larllene	Larrissia	Lashand	Lashawntianna
Laquonna	Larenda	Larmetria	Larrvetta	Lashanda *(0.01)*	Lashay *(0.03)*
Laquontus	Larenn	Larmonica	Larry	Lashandra	Lashaya *(0.01)*
Laquoria	Larenshay	Larna	Larryel	Lashandrea	Lashaye
Laqusha	Laresa	Larnequa	Larryelle	Lashane	Lashayla
Laqusher	Laresha	Larneshia	Larryn	Lashania	Lashaylia
Laqwanda	Lareshia	Larnetra	Larryssa	Lashanik	Lashaylyn
Lar'brina	Laressa	Larnique	Larsen	Lashanique	Lashayna
Lar'kierra	Largime	Larny	Larsharee	Lashanna	Lashaynna
Lara *(0.17)*	Larhee	Larobin	Larshonda	Lashannon	Lashe
Lara Nicole	Larhessia	Larohanda	Larsie	Lashanta	Lashé
Lara-Ella	Larhonda	Laronda *(0.01)*	Larson	Lashantae	Lashea *(0.01)*
Lara-Lyn	Lari	Laronica	Larsyn	Lashante	Lasheá
Lara-Lynn	Laria	Laronna	Lartricia	Lashanté	Lasheaka
Larabe	Lariah	Laronne	Larua	Lashanti	Lashealia
Larae *(0.01)*	Lariana	Larosa	Laruby	Lashantia	Lasheba
Larah	Lariane	Larose	Laruen	Lashantiyon	Lasheemia
Laraia	Larianne	Larosia	Laryn	Lashantrell	Lasheena
Laraib	Larica	Larosie	Larynn	Lashanuntae	Lasheene
Larain	Larice	Laroya	Larysa	Lashara	Lasheerica
Laraine	Laricha	Laroyce	Laryssa *(0.02)*	Lasharah	Lasheila
Laralee	Laricia	Larra	Larz	Lasharay	Lashekia
Laralyn	Laricka	Larrah	Lasabriona	Lashareca	Lashell
Laramey	Lariel	Larraina	Lasada	Lasharee	Lashelle
Laramie *(0.01)*	Lariesha	Larraine	Lasadia	Lashareka	Lashenai
Laramy	Lariisa	Larrann	Lasadie	Lasharia	Lashenequa
Laranda	Larina	Larrayna	Lasalette	Lasharika	Lasheonia
Larandar	Larineisha	Larreanna	Lasanda	Lasharn	Lashera

Lasheree
Lasheria
Lasherre
Lasherrica
Lasherton
Lashey
Lashia
Lashiah
Lashieka
Lashiena
Lashima
Lashiqua
Lashiya
Lashon *(0.01)*
Lashona
Lashonay
Lashonda *(0.03)*
Lashonde
Lashondra *(0.01)*
Lashonea
Lashonia
Lashonna
Lashonnia
Lashonta
Lashonte
Lashonya
Lashounda
Lashown
Lashoynia
Lashun
Lashunca
Lashunda
Lashundra
Lashundria
Lashunna
Lashuntae
Lashuntia
Lashynet
Lashyra
Lasia
Lasie
Lasina
Laskyi
Lasley
Laslie
Lasonda
Lasondra
Lasonia
Lasonja
Lasonya
Lasonyna
Lassie
Lastar
Lastara
Lastarr

Lastashia
Lasteveia
Lasteveion
Lasti'ra
Lata
Latacha
Lataghia
Latahja
Lataia
Lataijah
Lataijah-Ray
Lataisha
Lataiy'jah
Lataiya
Lataja
Latajah
Latajha
Latajia
Latamera
Latanda
Latandria
Latanee
Latangela
Latangie
Latania
Latanique
Latanja
Latanya *(0.01)*
Latanza
Latara *(0.01)*
Lataria
Lataris
Latarra
Latarsha
Latasha *(0.09)*
Latasheona
Latashia *(0.01)*
Latashiana
Latasi
Latasia
Latasma
Latastreia
Latatyana
Lataundra
Lataunya
Latavete
Latavia *(0.02)*
Latavishia
Lataya
Latayasia
Latayiah
Lataylor
Latayna
Lataysha
Latayshia

Latayshya
Lataysia
Latayvia
Latayviya
Latayzia
Latazia
Latda
Lateace
Lateah
Lateairra
Lateasha *(0.01)*
Lateashia
Lateaya
Lateayah
Latecea
Latechia
Latecia
Latedia
Latedra
Lateea
Lateefa
Lateefah
Lateefat
Lateeka
Lateesha *(0.01)*
Latefer
Lateia
Lateidra
Lateiea
Lateisha *(0.01)*
Lateka
Latel
Latena
Latequa
Latequia
Latera
Lateraca
Lateranae
Lateré
Lateri
Lateria
Laterial
Laterica
Laterika
Laterra
Laterria
Laterrica
Latesa
Latese
Latesha *(0.02)*
Lateshia *(0.01)*
Latesia
Latessa
Latessia
Latevia

Lateya
Lateysha
Lathasa
Latheria
Lathia
Lathlyn
Latia *(0.03)*
Latiana
Latiara
Latiasha
Latibias
Latibra
Latica
Latice
Laticia *(0.01)*
Laticiakatrina
Latie
Latieca
Latiena
Latiera
Latierah
Latierra
Latierre
Latiesha
Latifa
Latifah *(0.01)*
Latifay
Latiffa
Latiffany
Latifha
Latiful
Latija
Latijera
Latika
Latilya
Latina *(0.01)*
Latinia
Latipha
Latiqua
Latira
Latisa
Latish
Latisha *(0.10)*
Latisha Alexander
Latishia
Latishya
Latissa
Latitia
Latitiana
Lativia
Latiya
Latiyah
Latoddra
Latoia
Latoisha

Latondra *(0.01)*
Latondria
Latonga
Latonia *(0.01)*
Latonja
Latonnah
Latonya *(0.02)*
Latonyia
Latori
Latoria *(0.01)*
Latorian
Latorrea
Latorrian
Latorsha
Latorya
Latosha *(0.02)*
Latoshia
Latoshya
Latouria
Latoy
Latoya *(0.07)*
Latoyana
Latoyia
Latoyiea
Latra
Latracey
Latracia
Latracy
Latramese
Latranee
Latraveis
Latray
Latrayvia
Latreace
Latreas
Latrease
Latreasea
Latrece
Latrecia
Latreece
Latreese
Latreesha
Latreice
Latreisha
Latrekka
Latrell
Latrella
Latrelle
Latrena
Latrenae
Latresa
Latrese
Latreshanae
Latreshia
Latresia

Latresia-Loren
Latressa
Latressia
Latrevia
Latrial
Latric
Latrica
Latrice *(0.04)*
Latricia *(0.01)*
Latrina *(0.01)*
Latrion
Latrionna
Latrish
Latrisha *(0.01)*
Latrishia
Latrisica
Latronda
Latroy
Latroya
Latroyia-Arttizi
Latsha
Latt
Lattesa
Lattia
Lattiesha
Lattisha
Lattra
Latut'arlee
Latuya
Latwana
Latwonna
Laty'yana
Latya
Latyana
Latychanét
Latyna
Latyoshi
Latyra
Latyran
Latyscha
Latysha
Lauden
Laudia
Laughton
Laugiantaya
Laujuana
Laumanu
Launa
Launja
Laura *(3.26)*
Laura Brook
Laura Elle
Laura Gayle
Laura Mae
Laura-Anna

Laura-Anne	Lauri	Lavargea	Lawonisha	Laysea	Léia
Laura-Ashley	Lauria	Lavasciá	Lawren (0.01)	Layshanique	Lékeia
Laura-Lee	Laurian	Lavaughn	Lawrence	Layshonquie	Lékeisha
Laura-Leigh	Lauriana	Lavaughna	Lawrencenei	Laysie	Lékeishia
Laura-Lynn	Lauriane (0.02)	Lavay	Lawrencia	Layson	Lékendria
Laura-Mae	Laurianne (0.05)	Lavena	Lawrentrice	Layssa	Lékia
Laura-Maria	Laurice	Lavender	Lawresha	Layte	Lékwan
Laurah	Laurie (0.29)	Lavenia	Lawriell	Layten	Lémont
Laurain	Laurie Ann (0.01)	Lavenus	Lawrielle	Layton	Lémorria
Laurajean	Laurie Anne	Lavera	Lawrinda	Lazana	Lénaye
Laural	(0.02)	Lavern	Lawrisha	Lazandera	Lénecia
Lauralee (0.01)	Laurie Eve	Laverne	Lawronica	Lazandra	Léonidia
Lauralei	Laurie-Anne	Lavesha	Lawson	Lazaner	Léreisha
Laurali	Lauriea	Lavetta	Laxavier	Lazara	Léshay
Lauralise	Lauriel	Lavette	Laxhmi	Lazarela	Létara
Lauralyn	Laurielle	Lavida	Laxmi	Lazaria	Léteisia
Lauralynn	Laurien	Lavie	Laxsana	Lazaryia	Létequia
Lauran (0.01)	Laurilee	Lavimia	Laxshana	Lazavia	Léterria
Laurana	Laurin (0.01)	Lavin	Laxshna	Lazelda	Létia
Lauranda	Laurinda	Lavina (0.01)	Laya (0.01)	Lazeria	Létitia
Laurann	Laurine	Lavine	Layah	Lazette	Léya
Lauranna	Laurine Lorrain	Lavinia (0.01)	Layal (0.01)	Lazia	Le-Ann
Lauranne	Laurisa	Lavionne	Layalee	Lazzandra	Le-Rica
Laurasia	Laurisa-Lee	Lavisa	Layan	La~shunda	Le-Shawn
Lauray	Laurisha	Lavissa	Layanda	Le (0.01)	Le-Shawne
Laure	Laurissa (0.01)	Lavita	Layanna	Le Andra	Le-Vondria
Laure-Alissa	Laurisson	Lavodia	Layce	Le Ann	Lea (0.20)
Laureanne (0.01)	Laurlee	Lavon	Laycee	Le Ashley	Lea Ann
Lauree	Laurn	Lavona	Layci	Le Cola	Lea Audrey
Laureen	Laurna	Lavonda	Laycia	Le Daja	Lea Marie (0.01)
Laureena	Laursa	Lavonia	Laycie	Le Ellis	Lea'trice
Laurel (0.24)	Laurtina	Lavonicá	Laydavea	Le Jeuenek	Leaana
Laurell	Laury (0.01)	Lavonise	Layden	Le Johntria	Leaandrea
Laurella	Lauryl	Lavoniya	Laydi	Le Kia	Leaann
Laurelle	Lauryn (0.12)	Lavonjah	Layeli	Le Nee	Leaanna
Lauren (6.54)	Laurynn	Lavonjay	Laykelin	Le Neir	Leach
Lauren Ann	Lauryssa	Lavonna	Layken	Le Reine	Leacy
Lauren'	Lausanne	Lavonnda	Laykin	Le Ronika	Leaghan
Lauren-Ashle	Lausususga	Lavonne (0.01)	Laykon	Le Shae	Leah (1.34)
Lauren-Ashley	Lautice	Lavontrice	Laykyn	Le Shanta	Leah Feona
Lauren-Frances	Lautwanese	Lavonzia	Layla (0.12)	Le Shay	Leah Jo
Lauren-Zoe	Lauve	Lavoya	Laylah	Léamesha	Leah-Ann
Laurena	Lauvece	Lavra	Laylana	Léandra	Leah-Anne
Laurence (0.38)	Lauw-Ya Singing	Lavren	Laylanie	Léanesha	Leah-Camille
Laurencia	Lavada	Lawadjia	Layli	Léanna	Leah-Christine
Laurene	Lavados	Lawan	Layllah	Léanndra	Leah-Craig
Laurenlee	Lavaisha	Lawanda (0.02)	Layna	Léarea	Leaha
Laurenne	Lavallie	Lawanna	Layne (0.04)	Léasia	Leahana
Laurens	Lavana	Lawantay	Laynee	Léchell	Leahsharie
Laurent	Lavanche	Lawavia	Laynett	Léchena	Leahya
Laurentana	Lavandria	Lawden	Layney	Léchey	Leaigh
Laurentina	Lavania	Lawes	Layni	Léderica	Leaira
Laureta	Lavanja	Lawna	Laynie	Lédeshian	Leaisha
Lauretta (0.01)	Lavanna	Lawnice	Laynisi	Lédréla	Leala
Laurette	Lavanya	Lawonda	Layota	Léessence	Leamber

Leamsi	Lecreesha	Leeman	Leigh Ann	Leizle	Lemya
Lean	Lecretia	Leen	Leigh Anne	Lejana	Len'ae
Leana *(0.02)*	Lecsi	Leena *(0.04)*	Leigh-Ann	Lejayah	Len'nesha
Leanaida	Lectisia	Leenan	Leigh-Anna	Lejeinez	Len'terria
Leanda	Lecy	Leeneisha	Leigh-Anne	Lejla	Lena *(0.21)*
Leandera	Leda	Leenikia	Leigha *(0.06)*	Lejna	Lena-Ann
Leandra *(0.09)*	Ledaysha	Leenisha	Leighan	Lekaelin	Lena-Gabrielle
Leandraniq	Ledbetter	Leenoy	Leighandra	Lekala	Lenae
Leandré	Lede	Leenza	Leighann *(0.01)*	Lekana	Lenaea
Leandrea	Ledeisha	Leeonna	Leighanna *(0.01)*	Lekayla	Lenah
Leandrecia	Ledejia	Leer	Leighanne *(0.01)*	Lekecia	Lenamae
Leandria	Ledia	Leerra	Leighara	Lekeisha *(0.01)*	Lenara
Leane	Ledisha	Leesa *(0.01)*	Leighellen	Lekelci	Lenardria
Leanetta	Lednac	Leese	Leighia	Lekembria	Lenasha
Leanette	Ledonna	Leesena	Leighila	Lekenyia	Lenaya
Leangela	Ledora	Leesha *(0.01)*	Leighla	Lekeria	Lency
Leanie	Lee *(0.05)*	Leeshunna	Leightavia	Lekesha	Lendell
Leann *(0.07)*	Lee Ann	Leesly	Leightaylor	Lekeshiya	Lendra
Leanna *(0.20)*	Lee Anna	Leesun	Leighton	Leketha	Lendsay
Leanna-Marie	Lee Morgan	Leetha	Leihua	Leketta	Lendsi
Leanndra	Leéal	Leetonya	Leiie	Lekeya	Lendsy
Leanne *(0.21)*	Leéhannah	Leetta	Leikela	Lekiah	Lendzi
Leanora	Leéquesha	Leette	Leikina	Lekir	Lene
Leanza	Leéshora	Leevonda	Leila *(0.12)*	Lekira	Lené
Leara	Lee-Ana	Leevonne	Leilah *(0.01)*	Lekita	Lenea
Learae	Lee-Ann	Leeya	Leilani *(0.10)*	Lekiya	Lenecher
Learesi	Lee-Anna	Leeyah	Leilani Ho'oika	Lekoa	Lenecia
Learia	Lee-Anne	Leeza *(0.03)*	Leilany	Lekora	Lenedra
Learria	Lee-Nisha	Lefay	Leileiya	Lekuria	Leneika
Learta	Leea *(0.01)*	Legaci	Leiliany	Lekyia	Leneise
Learyn	Leeah	Legan	Leiloni	Lel'shadda	Leneisha
Leasa	Leeajah	Legase	Leilony	Lela *(0.02)*	Leneitta
Leashai	Leeana	Legeena	Leimomi	Lelah	Lenequia
Leashaun	Leeandra	Legend	Leina	Lelaina	Lenesa
Leasia	Leeandrea	Legenia	Leinaala	Lelan	Lenesha
Leasley	Leeann *(0.05)*	Legiovanni	Leinys	Lelana	Leneta
Leaslie	Leeanna *(0.02)*	Lehanka	Leiona	Leland	Lenetrius
Leassa	Leeanne *(0.01)*	Lehar	Leionna	Lelani	Lenette
Leat	Leeanne-Rose	Lehennie	Leiran	Lelavadee	Leni
Leather	Leeannena	Lehilda	Leirra	Lelia *(0.01)*	Lenia
Leatherwood	Leeara	Lehla	Leisa *(0.01)*	Leliah	Lenice
Leauna	Leearaha	Lehualani	Leisel	Lelicia	Lenicia
Leaundra	Leeasa	Lei	Leisha *(0.01)*	Lelin	Leniegh
Leavell	Leeasha	Lei'laun	Leishla	Lelisha	Leniesha
Leaysha	Leecy	Leia *(0.02)*	Leisley	Lelyan	Lenieshia
Leba	Leeda	Leia-Ta	Leisli	Lemeisha	Leniesia
Lechante	Leedonna	Leiah	Leissa	Lemia	Leniessia
Leché	Leeellen	Leiana	Leita	Lemiah	Lenina
Lechelle	Leeesther	Leianna	Leithia	Lemicka	Leniqah
Lechong	Leeetta	Leiannia	Leitia	Lemikka	Lenique
Lechreshia	Leeha	Leicy	Leitumalosalega	Lemondra	Lenisa
Leci	Leekiash	Leida	Leiya	Lemonica	Lenise
Lecia	Leela	Leidi	Leiyah	Lemorá	Lenisha
Lecie	Leelan	Leif	Leizel	Lempsely	Lenishá
Leclee	Leelannee	Leigh *(0.10)*	Leizl	Lemy	Lenishka

Lenita	Leonie (0.03)	Lesaundra	Lesslie	Levante	Lexxie
Lenka	Leoniqua	Lesdy	Lessly	Levashia	Lexxis
Lenna	Leonisha	Leseana	Lestacia	Levator	Lexxus (0.01)
Lennea	Leonitra	Leselle	Lester	Levatt	Lexxy
Lennejah	Leonna (0.01)	Lesette	Lestlee	Levena	Lexy (0.01)
Lennet	Leonne	Lesha	Lestreonia	Levenia	Lexyngton
Lennin	Leonor (0.02)	Leshae	Lesvia	Levera	Lexyss
Lennise	Leonora	Leshai	Lesvy	Levi	Leya
Lennisha	Leonore	Leshanna	Leta	Levie	Leyah
Lenniyah	Leonsa	Leshante	Letaja	Levina	Leyanis
Lennon	Leonshay	Leshaundra	Letajah	Levondra	Leyanna
Lennox	Leonti	Leshawn	Letavia	Levondreia	Leyanne
Lenoja	Leony	Leshawna	Lete-Medhin	Levonna	Leyauna
Lenora (0.01)	Leonya	Leshawner	Letecia	Levonne	Leycei
Lenore	Leor	Leshay	Leterius	Levrick	Leyda
Lenox	Leora (0.01)	Leshayla	Letesa	Lewai	Leydi
Lensey	Leore	Leshea	Letesha	Lewam	Leydi Mari
Lenshia	Leorina	Lesheanna	Leteshia	Lewis	Leykon
Lensy	Leoshia	Lesheda	Letha	Lewnna	Leyla (0.01)
Lentia	Leotie	Leshelle	Letia	Lex-Ann	Leylanni
Lenyia	Leotra	Leshem	Letiana	Lexa	Leyli
Lenyn	Leovanna	Leshon	Letice	Lexa-Rae	Leymoon
Lenys	Leporschia	Leshonda	Leticha	Lexah	Leyna (0.01)
Lenysha	Leprea	Lesia	Leticia (0.32)	Lexandra	Leyshla
Lenyx	Leprecious	Lesicca	Letisha (0.01)	Lexandria	Leyton
Lenzee	Leqaa	Lesili	Letishia	Lexanna	Leyxus
Lenzi	Leqi	Leslea	Letisia	Lexas	Leza
Lenzie	Lequanza	Leslee (0.01)	Letissa	Lexce	Lezah
Lenzy	Lequeen	Leslei	Letita	Lexcia	Lezari
Leocia	Lequenda	Lesleigh (0.01)	Letitia (0.02)	Lexcidia	Lezlee
Leokadia	Lequesha	Lesley (0.12)	Letitia-Lynn	Lexcie	Lezli-Ann
Leola	Lequeshalina	Lesley-Ann	Letizia	Lexee	Lezlie
Leolani	Lequisha	Lesley-Anne	Letoria	Lexes	Lezza
Leoma	Lequisho	Lesleyanne	Letorin	Lexey	Lhakpa
Leomaris	Lequita	Lesli (0.02)	Letorrian	Lexi (0.10)	Lhanze
Leon'dra	Lequsha	Leslianne	Letra	Lexi-Jo	Lhear
Leona (0.04)	Lera	Leslie (1.05)	Letreil	Lexia	Li
Leona Eizabeth	Lerae	Leslie Ann	Letrell	Lexie (0.10)	Li Diannette
Leonadia	Leranie	Leslie-Ann	Letresha	Lexiene	Li'angela
Leonae	Leray	Leslie-Anne	Letrianna	Lexiie	Li'khyri
Leonanie	Leriany	Leslie-Jo	Letrice	Lexin-Kae	Li'quisha
Leonarda	Lerika	Leslie-Nicole	Letricia	Lexine	Lia (0.08)
Leonashia	Lerissa	Leslieann	Lettetia	Lexington	Lia-Monet
Leonda	Leronda	Leslieanne	Letticcia	Lexis (0.06)	Liah
Leondra (0.01)	Leroya	Leslimar	Letticia	Lexius	Liahnni
Leondrea	Leroyia	Lesline	Lettie	Lexous	Liaina
Leondria	Lersonda	Leslley	Lettina	Lexsey	Liaja
Leone	Les Lea	Lesly (0.07)	Letty	Lexsie	Liakiasha
Leonela	Lesa (0.01)	Leslye (0.01)	Letxa	Lexsis	Lial
Leonella	Lesabia	Leslyn	Letycia	Lextavia	Liam
Leonetta	Lesabra	Leslyne	Leunora	Lextoria	Liamari
Leoni	Lesabre	Lessa	Leunshé	Lexus (0.16)	Lian (0.01)
Leonia	Lesadre	Lessia	Levada	Lexuss	Liana (0.12)
Leonica	Lesandra	Lessie	Levan	Lexxeus	Liandra
Leonicia	Lesanna	Lesslee	Levana	Lexxi	Liandy

Liane *(0.02)*
Lianet
Lianetxis
Liann
Lianna *(0.04)*
Lianne *(0.02)*
Liannette
Lianny
Liaric
Liat
Liatasha
Liatrice
Liauna
Liav
Liban
Libanos
Libbey
Libbie
Libby *(0.04)*
Liberdee
Liberia
Liberti
Libertie
Liberty *(0.03)*
Liberty-Ann
Libery
Libi
Libia
Libier
Libna
Libni
Libny
Librada
Libri'
Libya
Lica
Licete
Liceth
Lichelle
Licia
Lida *(0.01)*
Lida-Louise
Liddya
Lidea
Lidelia
Lideny
Lidia *(0.10)*
Lidiana
Lidija
Lidise
Lidya
Lidybet
Lieanna
Lieanne
Lieghton

Lieisha
Liekita
Liel
Liela
Liemena
Lien *(0.01)*
Lienna
Lienza
Lieren
Lierin
Lierra
Liesa
Liese
Liesel *(0.01)*
Lieshia
Liesl
Liethandra
Lieza
Liezel
Liezl
Lifase
Ligia
Liia
Liisa
Lija
Liji
Lijuria
Lika
Likelsya
Likeyal
Likiana
Lil Sandra
Lil'china
Lil.miracle
Lila *(0.06)*
Lilac
Lilah *(0.01)*
Lilamarie
Lilandra
Lilane
Lileana
Liley
Lili *(0.02)*
Lilia *(0.08)*
Liliam
Lilian *(0.08)*
Liliana *(0.46)*
Lilianda
Liliane *(0.02)*
Liliann
Lilianna
Lilianne
Lilias
Lilibeht
Lilibelle

Lilibeth *(0.02)*
Lilien
Lilika
Lililia
Lilina
Liline
Lilinoe
Lilith
Lilith Sarah
Liliuokalani
Liliya
Lilja
Lilla
Lillah
Lillan
Lillanann
Lillea
Liller
Lilley
Lilli
Lilli-Anne
Lillia
Lilliam
Lillian *(0.38)*
Lillian Eli
Lilliana *(0.03)*
Lilliane
Lilliann
Lillianna *(0.01)*
Lillianne
Lillie *(0.05)*
Lillielle
Lilliilona
Lillith
Lilly *(0.07)*
Lillyan
Lillyann
Lilqueen
Lilwa
Lily *(0.35)*
Lily Kathryn
Lily-Anne
Lilyan
Lilyana
Lilyann
Lilyanna
Lilyen
Lilyn
Lilza
Lima
Limairy
Limary
Limbana
Limesha
Limiteti

Limnyuy
Limor
Lin
Lin Da
Lina *(0.09)*
Linaea
Linaya
Lincoln
Lincy
Linda *(0.60)*
Linda Edith
Linda Oasis
Linda Sue
Linda Violeta
Linda-Danielle
Linda-Noel
Linda-Thuy
Lindahong
Lindaluz
Lindasy
Linday
Linddsay
Linde
Lindee
Linden
Linder
Linderia
Lindey
Lindi
Lindie
Lindijo
Lindita
Lindiwe
Lindley
Lindra
Lindsae
Lindsay *(1.41)*
Lindsay-Marie
Lindsdey
Lindsea
Lindsee *(0.01)*
Lindsei
Lindsey *(2.07)*
Lindsi *(0.01)*
Lindsie *(0.01)*
Lindsway
Lindsy *(0.02)*
Lindy *(0.03)*
Lindzay
Lindze
Lindzee
Lindzey
Lindzy
Lineesa
Linesha

Linessa
Linet
Linete
Lineti
Linette *(0.01)*
Ling-Ling
Linh *(0.03)*
Linhyen
Lini
Linitria
Linley *(0.01)*
Linn
Linna
Linnae
Linnaea
Linnajha
Linnea *(0.07)*
Linneah
Linnell
Linnessa
Linnet
Linnette
Linney
Linnie
Linniece
Linnzi
Linoria
Linqua
Linsa
Linsay
Linse
Linsea
Linsee
Linsey *(0.06)*
Linshia
Linshima
Linsi
Linsie
Linsley
Linsy
Lintsey
Liny
Linye
Linzee *(0.01)*
Linzey
Linzi
Linzie
Linzy *(0.01)*
Linzzi
Lionesha
Lionia
Lionisha
Lionna
Lionnetta
Lionor

Lior
Liora
Liphania
Lipi
Liqa
Liquila
Liqwana
Liran
Liraz Vasht
Liria
Liriana
Liriangel
Lirio
Lirise
Lirobya
Liron
Lirona
Lironda
Lis
Lisa *(1.25)*
Lisa Chanel
Lisa Maria
Lisa Marie *(0.01)*
Lisa-Ann
Lisa-Marie
Lisaani
Lisaann
Lisabelle
Lisabet
Lisabeth
Lisacha
Lisalia
Lisamarie
Lisan
Lisandra *(0.01)*
Lisandre
Lisanne *(0.01)*
Lisavette
Lisay
Lisbed
Lisbeidy
Lisbet *(0.01)*
Lisbeth *(0.05)*
Lischelle
Lisde
Lise
Lise-Anne
Lise-Marie
Lisebet
Lised
Liseht
Lisel
Liseldy
Liselle
Lisendy

Lisenette	Livleen	Llaquelin	Loine	Lonya	Lorelie
Lisenia	Livya	Llarely	Lois (0.04)	Lonyá	Lorell
Lisesett	Liw	Llarismel	Lois Sarah	Lonyaé	Lorelle
Liset (0.02)	Liwam	Llasmin	Lojen	Lonyay	Lorelli
Lisete	Liwiza	Lleona	Lok	Lonyea	Lorellin
Liseth (0.01)	Lixamary	Llerfines	Lok-Yee	Lonzella	Loremi
Lisett	Lixania	Llesenia	Lokadia	Loomis	Loren (0.14)
Lisette (0.09)	Liya	Llewellyn	Lokenya	Loonan	Loren-Ashley
Lisha (0.01)	Liyah (0.01)	Lleyna	Lokiesa	Lopa	Lorena (0.36)
Lishah	Liyang	Lliabeth	Lokmeet	Lopriela	Lorenda
Lishan	Liyanis	Llora	Lola (0.01)	Loquessnie	Lorene (0.01)
Lishawna	Liz (0.03)	Lloy Dejá	Lola Leana	Loquisha	Lorenea
Lishay	Liza (0.08)	Lloyd	Lolade	Loquitia	Loreneke
Lishayll	Lizabel	Lloydann	Lolah	Loquitte	Lorenia
Lisheil	Lizabeth (0.02)	Lloynisha	Loleta	Lora (0.06)	Lorenn
Lishelle	Lizaida	Lloytifah	Lolita (0.01)	Lora-Ann	Lorenna
Lisie	Lizandra (0.01)	Lludit	Loma	Lora-Lee	Lorenne
Lismore	Lizanne	Lluiza	Lon'naysha	Lorae	Lorenza
Lissa (0.01)	Lizarain	Llunuen	Lon'quisha	Lorain	Lorenzia
Lissamarie	Lizatt	Lluri	Lon'ya	Loraina	Lorenzo-Taylor
Lissan	Lizbed	Lluridia	Lon'ya Dénaye	Loraine	Loreon
Lissandra	Lizbeidi	Lluvia	Lona	Lorainna	Loresa
Lisset (0.02)	Lizbelly	Llyric	Lonching	Loral	Loreta
Lissete	Lizberania	Llysa	Londa	Loralee	Loretha
Lissethe	Lizbet (0.02)	Lndsay	Londayjah	Loralei	Loretta (0.05)
Lissett	Lizbeth (0.26)	Lo'deja	Londen	Lorali	Lorettajean
Lissette (0.09)	Lizet (0.06)	Lo'gen	London (0.06)	Loralie	Lorette
Lissy	Lizeth (0.10)	Lo'real	London Cleste	Loralyn	Loreya
Listala	Lizett (0.01)	Lo-Richama	London Jenesta	Loramae	Lori (0.19)
Listi	Lizette (0.15)	Loagen	Londra	Loran	Lori-Ann
Listina	Lizia	Loalisha	Londun	Loranda	Lori-Anne
Lisvet	Lizibeth	Loan	Londy	Lorane	Lori-Lee
Lisy	Lizl	Lobba	Londyn	Lorann	Loria
Liszet	Lizli	Lochelle	Loneka	Lorantiya	Loriale
Lisztgn	Lizquindra	Lockie	Lonette	Lorcan	Lorian
Lita (0.01)	Lizsandra	Loden	Loney	Lordasia	Loriana
Litafah	Lizvet	Lodisha	Longerie	Lordumie	Loriann
Lital	Lizvett	Loegan	Loni (0.02)	Lorea	Lorianne (0.01)
Litekiah	Lizy	Loewe	Loniqua	Lorea L	Loriauna-Maree
Litha	Lizz	Logan (0.41)	Lonisha	Loreal (0.01)	Loriay
Lithette	Lizza	Logan-Leigh	Lonita	Loreal'	Loribeth
Litia	Lizzet (0.01)	Logann	Lonna (0.01)	Lorean	Loribethe
Litisha	Lizzeth	Loganne	Lonnae	Loreanna	Lorica
Littaney	Lizzette (0.01)	Logen	Lonnece	Loreatha	Lorie (0.02)
Little Iva	Lizzie (0.01)	Loghan	Lonneisha	Loredana	Lorieal
Littlestar	Lizzieann	Logia	Lonnesha	Loredona	Loriel
Litzi	Lizzy	Logun	Lonnette	Loree	Loriele
Liv	Ljiljana	Logyn	Lonnia	Loreen	Lorielle
Liva	Lladeris	Logynn	Lonnie	Loreena	Lorien
Livei	Lladra	Lohgunn	Lonniece	Loreese	Loriescha
Livesay	Llajana	Lohithasindhupa	Lonniesha	Loreica	Lorijoy
Livia (0.02)	Llandess	Loi	Lonquille	Loreisa	Lorilani
Livida	Llaned	Loida	Lontaisha	Lorelea	Lorilei
Liviert	Llani	Loie	Lontina	Lorelei (0.01)	Lorilynn
Livinia	Llanie	Loilette	Lony	Loreli	Lorimae

Lorimar	Loshaveon	Louren	Luana	Lucke	Lukia
Lorin *(0.03)*	Loshonda	Louria	Luandra	Luckia	Lukiya
Lorina	Losika	Lourie	Luann	Luckie	Lukka
Lorinda	Lossie	Lousha	Luanna	Luckshi	Lukki
Lorine	Lot	Lousia	Luanne	Lucky	Lukonde
Loring	Loteshia	Loutena	Luba	Luckya	Lukrisha
Lorion	Lothlorien	Loutilia	Lubaina	Lucnise	Lul
Lorionna	Lotina	Loutori	Lubana	Lucoya	Lula
Lorisa	Lotis	Loutricia	Luberth	Lucquettia	Lulamae
Lorisha	Lotnita	Louvenia	Lubna	Lucrece	Lule
Lorissa *(0.02)*	Lotoshia	Louvertta	Lubnah	Lucreshia	Lulia
Lorissia	Lotoya	Lov'anna	Lubomyra	Lucretia *(0.01)*	Lulline
Lorita	Lotoyoria	Lov'tia	Lubov	Lucricia	Lulu
Loriza	Lott	Lovaida	Luca	Lucrisha	Lulwah
Lorlyn	Lottie *(0.01)*	Lovanda	Lucas	Lucy *(0.28)*	Luly
Lorna *(0.03)*	Lottieyunah	Lovda	Lucca	Lucyana	Luma
Lorna-Lee	Lotus	Love *(0.01)*	Luccia	Lucyanna	Lumesha
Lorne	Lou	Lovedeep	Luceeanne	Lucyanne	Luminne Marie
Lornna	Lou Racheal	Lovejoy	Luceldy	Lucyhelena	Lumiya
Lorra	Louann	Lovejuan	Luceli	Lucyjean	Luna *(0.03)*
Lorrai	Louanne	Lovelee-Lou	Lucelle	Lucynda	Lunden
Lorraina	Loubeth	Loveleen	Lucely	Lucyta	Lundin
Lorraine *(0.10)*	Loucinda	Loveley	Lucerito	Luczy	Lundon
Lorrainea	Loudney	Loveline	Lucero *(0.15)*	Luderia	Lundsey
Lorrane	Louella	Lovell	Luceroto	Ludibina	Lundy
Lorrayne	Lougena	Lovella	Lucetta	Ludie	Lundyn
Lorre	Louisa *(0.04)*	Lovelle	Lucette	Ludis	Lunelly
Lorreal	Louisa Aracely	Lovely *(0.01)*	Lucey	Ludithe	Lunia
Lorree	Louise *(0.05)*	Lovely Mystique	Luchiana	Ludmila	Lunicel
Lorren	Louisee	Loveminda	Luchiona	Ludmilla	Lunika
Lorrena	Louisena	Lovey	Luchyna	Ludy	Lunita
Lorrene	Louisiana	Lovianshé	Luci *(0.01)*	Ludys	Lupe *(0.02)*
Lorresha	Louisiane	Lovie	Lucia *(0.21)*	Luella	Lupelele
Lorretta	Louisiette	Lovika	Lucia-Maria	Luereainda	Lupi
Lorri	Louissa	Lovina	Lucian	Lueretta Jasmine	Lupita *(0.05)*
Lorrie *(0.01)*	Louiza	Lovine	Luciana *(0.01)*	Luerne	Luppi
Lorriel	Louizza	Lovona	Luciann	Luesther	Luqesha
Lorrin	Loujain	Lovpreet	Lucianna	Luette	Luquandrá
Lorrisa	Loukeria	Lovye	Lucidia	Luevina	Luquecia
Lorrissa	Loukicha	Lowell	Lucie *(0.01)*	Luilia	Luquetta
Lorriza	Loukya	Lowrie	Lucie-Amelie	Luis	Luquoria
Lorron	Loulwa	Lowsa	Lucienne	Luisa *(0.08)*	Lura
Lorryn	Loumeekqwa	Loy	Luciera	Luisacarolina	Lurachel
Lortea	Louna	Loyal	Lucija	Luise	Lurah
Lortolana	Lounah	Loyce	Lucila *(0.02)*	Luiseach	Luralyn
Lory *(0.01)*	Louneet	Loyda	Lucile	Lujain	Lurd
Lorybeth	Louniesha	Loyola	Lucilia	Lujaine	Lurdes
Loryn *(0.01)*	Lounikka	Loysha	Lucilla	Lujane	Luria
Lorysa	Loura	Loza	Lucille *(0.05)*	Lujayna	Luriel
Loryssa	Louraine Christ	Lozana	Lucimar	Luka	Lurina
Losa	Lourden	Lozen	Lucina	Luke	Luris
Losehina	Lourdes *(0.11)*	Lu Ana	Lucinad	Lukeia	Lurissa
Losha	Lourdes Amelia	Lu Anna	Lucinda *(0.04)*	Lukeisha	Lurlee
Loshaina	Lourdine	Lua	Lucine	Lukendra	Lurlene
Loshanah	Lourdline	Luan	Lucirely	Lukevia	Lusajo

Lusera
Luserito
Lusero
Lushia
Lusia
Lusiana
Lusila
Luskiana
Lustria
Lustrina
Luther
Luticia
Lutisha
Lutricia
Luv
Luvenia
Luvleen
Luvy
Luwam
Luwanda
Luxanaa
Luxchica
Luxchiga
Luxmi
Luxshiani
Luxuary
Luyen
Luz *(0.16)*
Luz Cecilia
Luz Elena
Luz Maria
Luzalina
Luzana
Luzcyreliz
Luzelena
Luzelly
Luzinda
Luzmari
Luzmaria *(0.01)*
Luzviminda
Lwam
Lwanda
Lwaxana
Ly *(0.01)*
Ly'rica
Ly'shawina
Lyadsay
Lyaia
Lyaire
Lyan
Lyana
Lyann
Lyanna
Lyanne
Lyanneth

Lyannette
Lyannis
Lyarresa
Lyasia
Lybertie
Lycah Charlene
Lychelle
Lyda
Lydaris
Lydea
Lydean
Lydi'ann
Lydia *(0.79)*
Lydia-Ann
Lydiah
Lydian
Lydiana
Lydianna
Lydianne
Lydie
Lydmar
Lyeissha
Lyesha
Lyeshia
Lyhua
Lyia
Lyisha
Lykeisha
Lykendra
Lykiaira
Lyla *(0.02)*
Lyla-Marie
Lylah
Lylai
Lyleann
Lyles
Lyliana
Lylla
Lyllian
Lyly
Lylybell
Lymaries
Lymyah
Lyn
Lyn Shandra
Lyna
Lynae *(0.01)*
Lynai
Lynardia
Lynardra
Lynasheia
Lynasia
Lynaya
Lynda *(0.05)*
Lyndah

Lyndal
Lyndall
Lyndasy
Lyndci
Lynde
Lyndee *(0.01)*
Lyndel
Lynden
Lyndey
Lyndi *(0.02)*
Lyndia
Lyndie *(0.01)*
Lyndin
Lyndlee
Lyndoll
Lyndon
Lyndreanna
Lyndsay *(0.09)*
Lyndsea
Lyndsee *(0.01)*
Lyndsey *(0.20)*
Lyndsi
Lyndsie *(0.01)*
Lyndsy *(0.01)*
Lyndy
Lyndz
Lyndzee
Lyndzey
Lyndzi
Lyndzie
Lyne
Lyneaha
Lynée
Lyneece
Lyneera
Lyneesa
Lyneise
Lyneisha
Lynejia
Lynell
Lynella
Lynelle
Lynesha
Lynesia
Lynett
Lynetta
Lynette *(0.08)*
Lynh
Lynhda
Lynika
Lynisa
Lynisha
Lynissa
Lynita
Lynitra

Lynjenaé
Lynjosha
Lynlee
Lynleigh
Lynley
Lynn *(0.12)*
Lynn Thuy
Lynn-Chian
Lynn-Dora
Lynna *(0.01)*
Lynnae *(0.01)*
Lynnale
Lynnann
Lynnasia
Lynnaya
Lynncie
Lynndee
Lynndel
Lynndsay
Lynndsey
Lynndsie
Lynne *(0.01)*
Lynnea *(0.01)*
Lynneashie
Lynnell
Lynnelle
Lynnesia
Lynness
Lynnesse
Lynnet
Lynnetta
Lynnette *(0.01)*
Lynnetter
Lynnisha
Lynnlee
Lynnox
Lynnsea
Lynnsey
Lynnsie
Lynnsley
Lynnya
Lynnyana
Lynnze
Lynnzi
Lynnzie
Lynsay
Lynsee
Lynsey *(0.06)*
Lynsi
Lynsie *(0.02)*
Lynsy
Lyntaeya
Lyntaria
Lyntrell
Lynya

Lynz
Lynzai
Lynze
Lynzee *(0.01)*
Lynzey
Lynzi
Lynzie *(0.01)*
Lynzy
Lyon'netta
Lyqueisha
Lyquita
Lyra
Lyrex
Lyric *(0.08)*
Lyrica
Lyrical
Lyrics
Lyrie
Lyrik
Lyrinika
Lyriq
Lyrissa
Lysa *(0.01)*
Lysadra
Lysandra *(0.01)*
Lysandre *(0.01)*
Lysanne *(0.01)*
Lysbel
Lysbeth
Lysette *(0.01)*
Lyshae
Lyshel
Lyshun
Lysia
Lysialette
Lysiya
Lyska
Lysle
Lysondra
Lyssa *(0.01)*
Lyssandra
Lyssette
Lysvette
Lyteisha
Lythasha
Lythesia
Lytia
Lytiasia
Lytice
Lytori
Lyttia
Lyubov
Lyudmila
Lyvia
Lyvonda

Lyza
Lyzbeth

-M-

M *(0.07)*
M Elise
M Ghan
M Nilda
M Shanna
M'cayla
M'chaela
M'cheyla
M'elia
M'iquelle
M'isha
M'kaila
M'kailah
M'kayla
M'kaylah
M'kenna
M'kenzie
M'khala
M'kiela
M'linka
M'lissa
M'ria
M'rittani
M'tumesha
M-Sauvea
M. *(0.01)*
M. Brstila
M. Magdalena
Ma
Ma Corina
Ma Eisha
Ma Guadalupe
Ma Kaela
Ma Kaelie
Ma Kala
Ma Kaya
Ma Kayla *(0.01)*
Ma Kenna
Ma Kenzie
Ma Kesha
Ma Lee
Ma Lia
Ma Rhonda
Ma Rissa
Ma Shayla
Ma''
Ma'ata
Ma'isha
Ma'kayla
Ma'kazsha

Ma'kenzi
Ma'kia
Ma'kira
Ma'kla
Ma'lon
Ma'loni
Ma'quari
Ma'quisha
Ma'quita
Ma'shaveous
Ma'shawnda
Ma'shea
Ma'ya
Ma'ye
Ma-Kaela
Ma.
Maacah
Maacha
Maackenzie
Maag
Maaia
Maaike
Maajidah
Maala
Maaliyah
Maani
Maansi
Maany
Maaref
Maari
Maaria
Maariah
Maartje
Maaya
Maayan
Maayke
Mabel (0.03)
Mabeli
Mabelin
Mabella
Mabelynne
Mabinty
Mable
Mabri
Mabry
Mac
Mac Kayla
Mac Kenzie (0.01)
Macada
Macady
Macae
Macaela (0.01)
Macahlia
Macail
Macaila

Macailey
Macailia
Macaiyyah
Macala
Macalah
Macaleigh
Macaley
Macalie
Macall
Macallan
Macalley
Macara
Macarena
Macari
Macarra
Macartney
Macaul
Macaulay
Macauley
Macayla (0.02)
Macaylaa
Macaylah
Macaylan
Macayle
Macayli
Maccallum
Maccayla
Macchelle
Maccie
Macdamise
Macee (0.01)
Macelisa
Macella
Macelyn
Macen
Macenzie
Macenzy
Macey (0.10)
Macgregor
Machae
Machael
Machaela (0.01)
Machaelah
Machaelie
Machaella Kiarra
Machaiah
Machaila
Machal
Machala
Machalia
Machalyn
Machatta
Machéla
Macheala
Macheka

Machela
Machele
Machell
Machelle
Machenzie
Macheya
Machi
Machiela
Machinza
Machishia
Machyas
Maci (0.06)
Macia
Macie (0.09)
Maciel
Macielle
Macire
Mackaela
Mackanzie
Mackarie
Mackaulie
Mackayla (0.01)
Mackayla-May
Mackayla-Rose
Mackayley
Mackeel
Mackeever
Mackeisha
Mackelle
Mackena
Mackencie
Mackenize
Mackenizie
Mackenna (0.01)
Mackensey
Mackensie (0.01)
Mackenze
Mackenzea
Mackenzee
Mackenzey
Mackenzi (0.02)
Mackenzie (1.74)
Mackenzie-
  Megan
Mackenzie-Rae
Mackenzy (0.01)
Mackenzye
Mackia
Mackie
Mackiel
Mackienze
Mackinley
Mackinnley
Mackinsey
Mackinsie

Mackinze
Mackinzee
Mackinzey
Mackinzi
Mackinzie
Mackyiah
Mackynley
Mackynze
Maclaine
Macoyá
Macquel
Macqueleigh
Macquelyn
Macrae
Macrena
Macuse
Macy (0.27)
Macye
Macylin
Macyn
Mada
Madahi
Madai
Madail
Madailein
Madaisha
Madaja
Madala
Madalaine
Madalana
Madalayne
Madaleen
Madaleine
Madalen
Madalena
Madalene
Madali
Madalin
Madalina
Madaline (0.01)
Madalon
Madalyn (0.12)
Madalyn Jane
Madalyne
Madalynn (0.01)
Madalynne
Madame
Madasen
Madason
Madasyn
Madavy
Madawi
Maday
Maddalena
Maddalene

Maddaline
Maddalyn
Madday
Maddelaine
Maddelena
Maddelina
Maddeline
Maddelynn
Madden
Maddeysen
Maddi
Maddie (0.01)
Maddilyn
Maddilynn
Maddisan
Maddisen (0.01)
Maddison (0.19)
Maddisson
Maddisyn
Maddox
Maddy
Maddyson
Madeeha
Madeel
Madeena
Madeha
Madeine
Madeira
Madel
Madelaina
Madelaine (0.08)
Madelane
Madelayne
Madelein
Madeleina
Madeleine (0.56)
Madelen
Madelene (0.02)
Madeleyne
Madeli
Madeliene (0.01)
Madelilne
Madelin (0.01)
Madelina
Madeline (1.79)
Madeline Sage
Madelinej
Madelinn
Madelion
Madelle
Madellin
Madelline
Madellyn
Madelon
Madelsar

Madelyn (0.27)
Madelyna
Madelyne (0.03)
Madelynn (0.03)
Madelynne (0.01)
Madena
Madera
Madesen
Madesia
Madessa
Madesyn
Madge
Madgei
Madgina
Madhumita
Madhuri
Madi
Madia
Madicen
Madicyn
Madie
Madiesther
Madigan
Madighen
Madiha
Madihah
Madilen
Madiline
Madilyn (0.03)
Madilyne
Madilynn (0.01)
Madina
Madinah
Madira
Madisan
Madisen (0.07)
Madisin
Madison (4.04)
Madison-Anne
Madisson (0.02)
Madissyn
Madisun
Madisyn (0.03)
Madisynn
Madisynne
Madiya
Madjina
Madlean
Madlen
Madlena
Madlene
Madlin
Madlina
Madlon
Madlson

Madlyn (0.01)	Maeleisha	Magdulin	Mahaley	Mahria	Maika (0.01)
Madoka	Maelene	Magean	Mahalia (0.01)	Mahriah	Maika'la
Madolan	Maeley	Magella	Mahalia Dorissa	Mahrissa	Maikala
Madolin	Maeli	Magen (0.03)	Mahaliah	Mahriya	Maiken
Madoline	Maelin	Magenta	Mahalie	Mahroop	Maikiya
Madolyn (0.01)	Maelis	Maggali	Maham	Mahrukh	Maikka
Madolyne	Maelle	Magge	Mahanika	Mahrun	Maikue
Madolynn	Maeloni	Maggee	Maharrey	Mahryah	Maila
Madolynne	Maelyn	Maggen	Mahasin	Mahsa	Maile (0.03)
Madonna	Maelyne	Maggi (0.01)	Mahayla (0.01)	Mahsheed	Mailee
Madoree	Maelynn	Maggid	Mahaylah	Mahta	Maileen
Madraye	Maemi	Maggie (0.52)	Mahaylia	Mahtab	Mailei
Madronica	Maenishia	Maggie-Mae	Mahdi	Mahtap	Maileka
Madsy	Maeola	Maggie-May	Mahdiah	Mahum	Mailen
Madumita	Maeonna	Maggie-Me	Mahdyeh	Mahveen	Maili
Mady	Maeping	Maggieann	Mahee	Mahyla	Mailia
Madya	Maeryl	Maggineese	Maheen	Mai (0.08)	Mailie
Madylan	Maesa	Maggy (0.02)	Mahek	Mai Hoa	Mailin
Madylann	Maeson	Maghan (0.01)	Mahelat	Mai Pachia	Maily
Madylon	Maeva	Maghann	Mahelet	Mai'asia	Mailyn
Madylynne	Maeve (0.04)	Maghen	Maher	Mai'ya	Maimee
Madyra	Maevelyn	Magi	Mahera	Mai-Han	Maimoona
Madysan	Maevis	Magie	Mahesha	Mai-Jan	Maimouna
Madysen (0.01)	Mafalda	Magin	Maheyla	Mai-Keyah	Main
Madyson (0.04)	Mafanta	Maginda	Mahgan	Mai-Khanh	Maina
Madysun	Mafaz	Magna	Mahi	Mai-Lan	Mainor
Mae (0.02)	Mafu	Magneilia	Mahilet	Mai-Phuong	Maira (0.16)
Mae Ellen	Magali (0.09)	Magnelenda	Mahin	Mai-Sia	Maircaidez
Mae Zoana	Magalie (0.03)	Magnolia (0.01)	Mahisha	Maia (0.08)	Maire (0.01)
Maeah	Magally	Magon	Mahiya	Maia-Margaret	Mairead (0.01)
Maebell	Magaly (0.09)	Maguire	Mahkala	Maiaalicia	Mairedith
Maebeth	Magan (0.03)	Magun	Mahkalay	Maiadah	Mairen
Maebh	Magaret	Magy	Mahkayla	Maiah (0.01)	Mairene
Maeceedes	Magaretha	Maha (0.02)	Mahkia	Maianh	Mairi
Maecy	Magarita	Mahabba	Mahlan	Maiben	Mairi-Gabrielle
Maeda	Magda (0.01)	Mahadevi	Mahlaya	Maica	Mairiana
Maedla	Magdala	Mahadia	Mahlayshia Orian	Maicee	Mairibeth
Maee	Magdaleen	Mahagani	Mahlea	Maicey	Mairiel
Maeetta	Magdalen (0.01)	Mahagany	Mahlet (0.01)	Maici	Mairin
Maefrie	Magdalena (0.13)	Mahagony	Mahlia	Maicie	Mairis
Maegan (0.17)	Magdalene (0.02)	Mahah	Mahlissa	Maida	Mairyn
Maegan Rose	Magdalene Jo	Mahaila	Mahna	Maidaliz	Maisa
Maegen (0.01)	Magdalene-Makai	Mahailah	Mahnoor	Maidely	Maise
Maeghan (0.02)	Magdali	Mahailey	Maho	Maie	Maisey (0.01)
Maegin	Magdaline	Mahaileygh	Mahockie	Maiesha	Maisha (0.01)
Maeisy	Magdalyn	Mahaillie	Mahoganey	Maigan (0.01)	Maishara
Maeja	Magdalynn	Mahailya	Mahogani	Maigen	Maishunda
Maejean	Magdelaine	Mahajanea	Mahoganie	Maighdlin	Maisie (0.02)
Maekala	Magdelane	Mahak	Mahogany (0.02)	Maigie	Maison (0.01)
Maekayla	Magdelena	Mahal	Mahoghani	Maigold	Maisoon
Maekena	Magdelene	Mahala (0.01)	Mahoghany	Maigra	Maisy
Maekenzie	Magdeline	Mahalah	Mahogney	Maih	Maite (0.01)
Maelani	Magdelyn	Mahaleigh-Anne	Mahola	Maiha	Maitlan
Maeleah	Magdelynn	Mahaleja	Maholley	Maija (0.01)	Maitland (0.01)
Maelee	Magderly	Mahalet	Mahreen	Maijura	Maitlyn

Maitlynn	Makailan	Makeba	Makeysia	Makynlee	Malazia
Maitreyi	Makailee	Makeda *(0.02)*	Makhaila	Makynzey	Malcayla
Maively	Makailey	Makedja	Makhala	Makyra	Malcilra
Maiwah	Makaili	Makeeba	Makhayla	Mal An	Maléika
Maiya *(0.03)*	Makailla	Makeedah	Makheya	Mal'kesia	Malea *(0.01)*
Maiyá	Makaillah	Makeeko	Makhisza	Mala	Maleah *(0.01)*
Maiya'-Deja	Makaily	Makeelah	Makhya	Mala Jah	Maleaha
Maiyah	Makailye	Makeena	Maki	Malace	Malee
Maiyahnahjaée	Makaira	Makeese	Makia *(0.01)*	Malachia	Maleék
Maiysha	Makaishea	Makeesha	Makiá	Malacia	Maleea
Maizee	Makaiya	Makeeta	Makiah *(0.01)*	Malacie	Maleeha
Maizey	Makala *(0.06)*	Makeeva	Makiala	Maladh	Maleehah
Maizie	Makalae	Makehla	Makiba	Malaika *(0.01)*	Maleeka *(0.01)*
Maja *(0.01)*	Makalah	Makeila	Makida	Malaikah	Maleekah
Majam	Makalai	Makeilah	Makieya	Malaina *(0.01)*	Maleekia
Majarrie	Makalea	Makeisha	Makiko	Malaishá	Maleena *(0.01)*
Majeda	Makalee	Makeiva	Makila	Malajae	Maleenia
Majel	Makaleh	Makela	Makilah	Malajah	Maleeqa
Majelle	Makaleigh	Makelah	Makilia	Malak *(0.02)*	Malees
Majenta	Makaleigha	Makele	Makima	Malaki	Maleeya
Majerae	Makaley	Makell *(0.01)*	Makimbe	Malakiya	Maleeyah
Majerle	Makalia	Makella	Makina	Malaky	Maleha
Majeska	Makalie	Makelle *(0.01)*	Makinlee	Malana	Malehia
Majesta	Makall	Makellia	Makinley	Malanda	Maleia
Majestic	Makalya	Makena *(0.03)*	Makinna	Malanee	Maleigh
Majestie	Makalynn	Makendie	Makinsee	Malani	Maleigha
Majhone	Makandra	Makendra	Makinsey	Malanie	Maleika
Maji	Makanna	Makendrick	Makinzee	Malanka	Maleikah
Majida	Makara	Makenize	Makinzi	Malare	Maleisha
Majidah	Makare	Makenly	Makinzie	Malari	Maleka *(0.01)*
Majorie *(0.01)*	Makarenyeny	Makenna *(0.14)*	Makisha	Malarie	Malekia
Majory	Makari	Makennah	Makisicha	Malashia	Malekwa
Majoy	Makaria	Makense	Makita *(0.01)*	Malasia	Malen
Majureka	Makasha	Makensey	Makitah	Malathi	Malena *(0.01)*
Mak Kieda	Makasini	Makensie *(0.01)*	Makitha	Malaun	Malencia
Maka	Makatlyn	Makenya	Makiya *(0.01)*	Malaurie	Malenda
Makaala	Makaya	Makenze	Makiyah	Malavika	Malene
Makacie	Makayalla	Makenzee *(0.01)*	Makiyra	Malay	Maleni
Makae	Makayela	Makenzey	Makkah	Malaya *(0.01)*	Malenia
Makael	Makayia	Makenzi *(0.02)*	Makkasia	Malaya Louisa	Maleny
Makaela *(0.03)*	Makayla *(0.80)*	Makenzie *(0.26)*	Maklun	Malayaa	Malequa
Makaelah	Makayla Jewel	Makenzy	Maklyn	Malayah	Maleri
Makaelee	Makayla-Lynn	Makenzye	Maklynn	Malayaisha	Malerie *(0.01)*
Makaelin	Makaylah *(0.01)*	Makeria	Mako	Malayasia	Malesha
Makaella	Makaylan	Makeshia	Makoya	Malayca	Maley
Makaely	Makayle	Makesia	Maksuda	Malayisa	Malgorzata *(0.01)*
Makaelynn	Makaylee *(0.01)*	Maketria	Makya	Malayna	Mali
Makaenne	Makayleigh	Maketta	Makyah	Malaynia	Malia *(0.13)*
Makagbe	Makayli	Makeveria	Makyera	Malayra	Maliah *(0.01)*
Makahla	Makaylia	Makeya	Makyia	Malaysha	Maliaka
Makai	Makaylla	Makeyah	Makyiah	Malayshia	Malialani
Makaiah	Makaylyn	Makeycia	Makyla *(0.02)*	Malaysía	Maliana
Makail	Makda	Makeyla	Makylah	Malaysia *(0.03)*	Malibu
Makaila *(0.04)*	Makea	Makeyla-Abrie	Makylee	Malaysiah	Malica
Makailah	Makealah	Makeylee	Makyna	Malayssa	Malichi

Malicia	Mallisa	Mamyiye	Maneesia	Manprit	Mar Triell
Malick	Mallison	Man *(0.01)*	Maneisha	Manpriya	Mar'chelle
Malie	Mallissa	Man-Fong	Manekque	Manquetta	Mar'kecia
Malieka	Mallissia	Mana	Manelle	Manreet *(0.01)*	Mar'keisha
Maliha	Malliyah	Manaal	Manely	Manroop	Mar'kelia
Malihe	Mallora	Manada	Manerian	Manrose	Mar'kesha
Malihka	Malloray	Manaesha	Manesha	Mansata	Mar'keshia
Malijah	Malloreah	Manahel	Manessa	Mansi	Mar'kia
Malik	Malloree	Manahil	Mang	Manssa	Mar'kiana
Malika *(0.07)*	Mallorey	Manaie	Manguntaas	Manton	Mar'kisha
Malikah *(0.01)*	Malloreye	Manaje	Manhattan	Mantza	Mar'leshia
Malikee	Mallori *(0.01)*	Manajia	Mania	Manu	Mar'naysha
Malikha	Mallorie *(0.04)*	Manal *(0.01)*	Maniahjeea	Manuala	Mar'qessia
Maliki	Mallory *(0.71)*	Manali	Manica	Manuela *(0.03)*	Mar'queeta
Malikia	Mallory Ana	Mananeel	Manie	Manuelita	Mar'quel
Malin	Mallory Kaitlyn	Manar *(0.01)*	Maniesha	Manuella	Mar'quiesha
Malina *(0.03)*	Mallory-Dalto	Manasa	Manijeh	Manuelle	Mar'quisha
Malinda *(0.03)*	Mally	Manasha	Manika	Manuir	Mar'rhea
Maline	Malon	Manasi	Maninder	Manujaa	Mar'shall
Maling	Malona	Manasseh	Manise	Manuri	Mar'shay
Malini	Malondra	Manasseha	Manisha *(0.03)*	Manuthisaa	Mar'shaye
Malinneum	Malone	Manbir	Manisher	Manveer	Mar'sheiona
Maliny	Maloni	Manbit	Manit	Manvir *(0.01)*	Mar'teece
Maliqua	Maloree	Manchari	Manivanh	Manya	Mar'tezia
Malique	Maloreigh	Mancini	Maniya	Manyara	Mar'trina
Maliry	Malori *(0.01)*	Mancy	Manizha	Maoli	Mar-Kisha
Malisa *(0.02)*	Malorie *(0.03)*	Manda	Manjari	Maoloisa	Mara *(0.14)*
Malisah	Malory *(0.03)*	Mandalee	Manjevan	Maple	Mara Jhozel
Malisha	Maltida	Mandalin	Manjinder	Maplyn	Mara-Joanne
Malissa *(0.04)*	Malucci	Mandaline	Manjot *(0.01)*	Maqiala	Mara-Paige
Malita	Maluvae	Mandalya	Manjote	Maqila	Marabel
Malitza	Malvina	Mandalyhna	Manju	Maquavia	Marabelle
Maliya	Maly	Mandalyn	Mankaran	Maquayla	Marabia
Maliyah *(0.01)*	Malya	Mandalynn	Mankeeran	Maque	Maracle
Maliza	Malyah	Mandalynne	Mankiran	Maqueda	Marada
Malka	Malycca	Mande	Manleen	Maquee	Maradeth
Malka Pearl	Malyéa	Mandee *(0.01)*	Manmeet *(0.01)*	Maquel	Maradyn
Malkah	Malyea	Mandeep *(0.01)*	Manmit	Maquela	Marae
Malkeet	Malyka	Mandelyn	Manna	Maquell	Maraea
Malkeevia	Malyn	Mandi *(0.04)*	Mannah	Maqueneze	Maragret
Malketta	Malyna	Mandi Jo	Mannal	Maquiesha	Marah *(0.02)*
Malkia	Malynda	Mandie *(0.01)*	Mannesha	Maquila	Maraha
Malkie	Malynia	Mandilyn	Manniyah	Maquilia	Marahi
Mallak	Malynn	Mandip	Mannveet	Maquinta	Maraia
Mallan	Malynne	Mandisa	Manoela	Maquisa	Maraiha
Mallari	Malyra	Mandolin	Manohar	Maquisha	Maraika
Mallarie	Malysha	Mandolyn	Manoia	Maquita	Maraina
Mallary	Malyshia	Mandolynn	Manolya	Mar	Marainna
Malleri	Malyssa *(0.01)*	Mandria	Manon *(0.01)*	Mar Kaylen	Marajanae
Mallerie	Mame	Mandy *(0.14)*	Manouchca	Mar Keisha	Marajhe
Mallery	Mami	Mandymae	Manouchka	Mar Kevia	Maraki
Malley	Mamie *(0.01)*	Mandze	Manoush	Mar Lesha	Maral
Mallice	Mammie	Manecheia	Manouska	Mar Quaea	Maralee
Mallie	Mammyiye	Maneeka	Manoutcka	Mar Ryha	Maralis
Mallika	Mamye	Maneesha	Manpreet *(0.04)*	Mar Tenesha	Maralisa

Maralys	Marcelle *(0.01)*	Marconna	Mareshia	Margina	Maria-Antonia
Maram	Marcellene	Marcqui	Maressa *(0.01)*	Marginer	Maria-Cleusa
Maramawit	Marcellette	Marcquila	Marete	Margit	Maria-Estela
Maran	Marcellia	Marcquishia	Marett	Margo *(0.03)*	Maria-Giovanna
Maran Angeli	Marcelline	Marcquita	Maretta	Margorie	Maria-Ines
Maranatha	Marcellis	Marcquitta	Maretza	Margot *(0.04)*	Maria-Jose
Maranda *(0.26)*	Marcello	Marcresha	Mareya	Margoth	Maria-Katrina
Marandia	Marcellous	Marcus	Marfel	Margreet	Maria-Maria
Marangaby	Marcellus	Marcy *(0.03)*	Marfelia	Margret *(0.01)*	Maria-Peter
Marangalie	Marcelnia	Mardaina	Marg	Margrete	Maria-Stephanie
Marangela	Marcelo	Marde	Marga	Margretta	Maria-Teresa
Marangeline	Marcenia	Mardeceia	Margareet	Margrette	Maria-Zenovia
Marangeliz	Marcesha	Mardee	Margaressa	Marguarite	Mariac
Marangelly	Marceshia	Mardeen	Margaret *(1.28)*	Marguerita	Mariaceleste
Maranllely	Marcey	Mardessa	Margaret	Marguerite *(0.07)*	Mariadejesus
Maranna	Marceyan	Mardester	Elizabeth	Marguertte	*(0.01)*
Marannda	March	Mardi	Margaret Marie	Marguitia	Mariadela
Maranuely	Marchae	Mardianna	Margaret Mary	Margurette	Mariae
Maraquita	Marchanda	Mardocha	Margaret Rose	Margurite	Mariaelana
Marasha	Marchayla	Mardochee	Margaret-Claire	Margy	Mariaelena *(0.02)*
Marashia	Marche	Maré-Shia	Margaret-Joyce	Marheena	Mariaelvira
Marasia	Marché	Marea	Margaret-Kaye	Marhia	Mariafe
Marassa	Marchel	Mareana	Margareta	Marhiya	Mariafeliz
Maraushanik	Marchela	Maredie	Margarete	Mari *(0.08)*	Mariagrazia
Maray	Marchele	Maredith	Margareth	Mari Charles	Mariaguadalu
Maraya *(0.02)*	Marchell	Maree	Margaretha *(0.01)*	Mari Mar	*(0.02)*
Marayjcia	Marchell'	Mareen	Margarethe	María	Mariaguadalupe
Marayna	Marchella	Mareena *(0.01)*	Margarett	Mari'ce	Mariah *(2.14)*
Marayvia	Marchellae	Mareena-Anne	Margaretta	Mari-Celia	Mariah Agnes
Marbel	Marchelle *(0.01)*	Mareesa	Margarette	Mari-Kate	Mariah Angelica
Marbelia	Marcher	Mareesha	Margarida	Maria *(3.22)*	Mariah Jade
Marbelin	Marcherie	Mareeyana	Margarit *(0.01)*	Maria Adelina	Mariah Reigine
Marbella *(0.02)*	Marcheta	Mareial	Margarita *(0.24)*	Maria Bianca	Mariah Summer
Marbelly	Marcheyell	Marek	Margarita France	Maria Charito	Mariah-Katherin
Marc'el	Marchieta	Marel	Margarite	Maria Christina	Mariah-Nichole
Marca	Marci *(0.01)*	Mareli	Margart	Maria Crist	Mariaha
Marcadies	Marcia *(0.05)*	Mareling	Margary	Maria Cristina	Mariahe
Marcatie	Marciane	Marelis	Margaux *(0.01)*	Maria De Jesus	Mariahliz
Marcayla	Marcianna	Mareliza	Margaux Nadine	Maria Del	Mariahrae
Marcaylah	Marcianne	Marell	Margeaux	Maria Del Carme	Mariaisabel
Marce	Marciara	Marella	Margel	Maria Del Rosari	Mariajesus
Marcea	Marcides	Marelle	Margelle	Maria Del Socorr	Mariajose
Marcede	Marcideze	Marely	Margeraé	Maria Elizabeth	Mariajuana
Marcedes *(0.01)*	Marcie *(0.02)*	Marelyn	Margeret	Maria Eugenia	Marial
Marcedis	Marcielynn	Marelys	Margert	Maria Guadalupe	Marialaine
Marcee	Marcilyn	Maren *(0.04)*	Margery	Maria Louise Ab	Marialejandra
Marcel	Marcina	Marena *(0.03)*	Marget	Maria Luisa	Marialena
Marcela *(0.09)*	Marcine	Marenda	Margeta	Maria Michelle	Marialexis
Marcelene	Marcissa	Marene	Marggie	Maria Monserrat	Mariali
Marcelina *(0.02)*	Marckala	Marenna	Marggiestell	Maria Nicole	Marialice
Marceline	Marckel	Marenth	Margharita	Maria Venicia	Marialicia
Marcelisha	Marckiya	Mareon	Margherita	Maria'h	Marialina
Marcell	Marcline	Maresa *(0.01)*	Margherite	Maria-Adriana	Marially
Marcella *(0.08)*	Marco	Maresha	Margi	Maria-Angela	Marialuisa
Marcella Anne	Marcoisha	Mareshah	Margie *(0.01)*	Maria-Angeli	Marialyce

Marialynn
Marialys
Mariam *(0.15)*
Mariam-Catherin
Mariama *(0.01)*
Mariamawit
Mariamercedes
Mariamme
Marian *(0.06)*
Marian Elizabet
Marian-Alexandr
Mariana *(0.31)*
Marianá
Mariane *(0.03)*
Marianela
Marianella
Marianely
Mariangel
Mariangela
Mariangelica
Mariangely
Mariangie
Marianin
Marianita
Mariann *(0.01)*
Marianna *(0.07)*
Marianne *(0.23)*
Mariant
Marianthi
Marianthy
Mariany
Mariapaula
Mariaraphael
Mariasol
Mariateresita
Mariay
Mariaye
Maribel *(0.26)*
Maribelisabel
Maribell
Maribella
Maribelle
Maribeth *(0.01)*
Marica *(0.01)*
Maricandy
Maricar
Maricarmen *(0.02)*
Maricela *(0.14)*
Mariceli
Maricelia
Maricella
Maricely
Maricia
Marick
Mariclaire

Maricle
Maricris
Maricruz *(0.06)*
Maride
Marideth
Maridith
Marie *(0.66)*
Marie Andree
  (0.02)
Marie Anne *(0.03)*
Marie Antoniette
Marie Audrey
Marie Camille
Marie Catheri
Marie Chantal
  (0.01)
Marie Christi
  (0.04)
Marie Clair
Marie Claire *(0.01)*
Marie Claude
  (0.04)
Marie Elaine
  (0.01)
Marie Eve *(0.28)*
Marie France
  (0.02)
Marie Frederi
Marie Gabriel
Marie Helene
  (0.03)
Marie Jeanne
  (0.02)
Marie Joelle *(0.02)*
Marie Josee *(0.01)*
Marie Julie
Marie Kim *(0.01)*
Marie Kris
Marie Laurenc
  (0.03)
Marie Lee
Marie Lou *(0.04)*
Marie Louise
  (0.01)
Marie Maude
  (0.01)
Marie Michele
  (0.03)
Marie Michell
  (0.02)
Marie Noelle
  (0.01)
Marie Paige
Marie Paloma

Marie Pascale
  (0.01)
Marie Perle
Marie Philipp
  (0.02)
Marie Pier *(0.27)*
Marie Pierre *(0.02)*
Marie Rose
Marie Soleil *(0.06)*
Marie Sophie
  (0.01)
Marie-Adele
Marie-Andree
Marie-Angela
Marie-Ann
Marie-Anne
Marie-Antoine
Marie-Blanda-
  Dominique
Marie-Chanel
Marie-Chantal
Marie-Claire
Marie-Claude
  (0.01)
Marie-Danielle
Marie-Dominique
Marie-Elise
Marie-Eve *(0.02)*
Marie-France
Marie-Gabrielle
Marie-Gil
Marie-Ginette-
  Gabriell
Marie-Helene
Marie-Josee
Marie-Lee
Marie-Louise
Marie-Lyne
Marie-Lyne-
  Frederique
Marie-Melanie
Marie-Michelle
Marie-Nicole
Marie-Noelle
Marie-Pascale
Marie-Pier *(0.02)*
Marie-Reine
Marie-Soleil
Marie-Xiarhina
Mariecatherine
Marieclaire
Mariedith
Marieena
Marieh
Mariejane

Marieka
Marieke
Mariel *(0.08)*
Mariel Therese
Mariela *(0.17)*
Marielena *(0.03)*
Marieli
Marielie
Marielisa
Mariell
Mariella *(0.01)*
Marielle *(0.06)*
Marielle Consta
Mariellen
Mariely
Marielys
Mariem
Marien
Mariena
Mariesa
Mariesha
Marieshka
Mariessa
Mariestela
Marietta *(0.01)*
Mariette
Marieugenia
Marieve *(0.01)*
Marifa
Marife
Marifel
Marigalay
Marigny
Marigold
Marigrace
Marih
Mariha *(0.01)*
Mariha-Mae
Marii
Mariirene
Marija *(0.01)*
Marijana
Marijane
Marije
Marijhá
Marijka
Marijke
Marijo
Marika *(0.07)*
Marikah
Marikar
Marikate
Marike
Marikka
Mariko *(0.01)*

Marilara
Marilaura
Marilee
Marileidi
Marileina
Marilen
Marilena
Marili
Marilia
Mariliana
Marilie *(0.01)*
Marilin
Marilis
Marilisa
Marilla
Marilleona
Marilou *(0.10)*
Marilu *(0.02)*
Mariluna
Marily *(0.01)*
Marilyn *(0.26)*
Marilyne *(0.01)*
Marilynn *(0.02)*
Marilyssa
Marimar *(0.03)*
Marin *(0.02)*
Marina *(0.68)*
Marinae
Marinah
Marinajoe
Marinda *(0.01)*
Marine *(0.01)*
Marinee
Marinel
Marinette
Marinez
Marini
Marinia
Marinicole
Marinn
Marinna *(0.01)*
Marino
Mario
Mario-Pia
Mariola
Mariom
Marion *(0.06)*
Marion Herr
Marionii
Marionna
Mariquisha
Marirae
Marirose
Maris *(0.02)*
Marisa *(0.93)*

Marisa-Jean
Marisabel
Marisah
Marisalee
Marisalyne
Marisanne
Marise
Marisel
Marisela *(0.12)*
Marisella
Mariselle
Marish
Marisha *(0.02)*
Marishka
Mariska
Marislea
Marisoe
Marisol *(0.37)*
Mariss
Marissa *(2.70)*
Marissa Denise
Marissa Georgee
Marissa Le
Marissa Lynnette
Marissa Melanie
Marissa-Jean
Marissah
Marissela
Marissia
Marissiah
Marisso
Marista
Marit
Marita *(0.01)*
Maritaz
Marite
Marithza
Maritona
Maritsa *(0.02)*
Maritssa
Maritza *(0.28)*
Maritza Noemi
Marium
Marival
Marivel *(0.02)*
Marivelle
Mariwa
Mariweir
Marixell
Mariya *(0.01)*
Mariyah *(0.01)*
Mariyam
Mariyan
Mariyana
Mariyanna

Mariye	Markeah Christin	Markeyah	Marlaina *(0.01)*	Marlisa *(0.01)*	Maronda
Mariyum	Markeala	Markeyha	Marlaine	Marlise	Marone
Mariza *(0.01)*	Markeasha	Markeyia	Marlainna	Marlisha	Maronna
Marize	Markecia	Markeyonna	Marlana *(0.02)*	Marlissa	Marosa
Marizel	Markeda	Markeysha	Marlania	Marlisse	Marowa
Marizela	Markedia	Markeysia	Marlayna *(0.01)*	Marlissia	Marqasia
Marizi	Markedleine	Markeyta	Marlea	Marliyah	Marqee
Marizol	Markee	Markeytha	Marleana	Marlli	Marqesha
Marizza	Markeeisha	Markham	Marlee *(0.09)*	Marlo *(0.01)*	Marqetah
Marja	Markeela	Markheira	Marleen *(0.02)*	Marlon	Marqi
Marjahnee	Markeema	Marki *(0.01)*	Marleena	Marlonika	Marqia
Marjai	Markeemia	Markia *(0.02)*	Marleene	Marlori	Marqieta
Marjaié	Markees	Markiá	Marleeni	Marlotte	Marqita
Marjan	Markeesa	Markiah	Marleesha	Marlow	Marquail
Marjana	Markeesia	Markian	Marleigh *(0.01)*	Marlowe	Marquaja
Marjani	Markeeta	Markida	Marleina	Marly *(0.01)*	Marquajah
Marjeke	Markeeya	Markie *(0.03)*	Marleise	Marlyana	Marquaneka
Marjhonique	Markeia	Markiee	Marleisha	Marlyatou	Marquasha
Marjim	Markeida	Markierra	Marlen *(0.07)*	Marlyn *(0.04)*	Marquashae
Marjinnette	Markeidra	Markiesa	Marlena *(0.09)*	Marlyna	Marquashaun
Marjoarishell	Markeil	Markiesha	Marlene *(0.31)*	Marlynda	Marquashia
Marjolaine *(0.01)*	Markeisa	Markieta	Marleni	Marlynna	Marquashianna
Marjolene	Markeisha *(0.02)*	Markijo	Marlenie	Marlys	Marquasia
Marjon	Markeisia	Markila	Marlenn	Marlyse	Marquavia
Marjonia	Markeita	Markina	Marlenne	Marlyss	Marquazha
Marjonna	Markeitha	Markiria	Marleny *(0.01)*	Marme	Marque
Marjori	Markeithia	Markisa	Marlesa	Marnae	Marqué
Marjorie *(0.13)*	Markeitta	Markisha *(0.02)*	Marlesha	Marnasha	Marquésha
Marjorieann	Markela	Markisia	Marlesia	Marne	Marquee
Marjornia	Markele	Markissa	Marlet	Marnee	Marqueeta
Marjory	Markelia	Markissia	Marleth	Marneesha	Marqueisha
Marjulys	Markell *(0.01)*	Markita *(0.03)*	Marlett	Marneiquia	Marquel
Marjury	Markella	Markitta	Marlexus	Marneisha	Marquela
Mark	Markelle *(0.01)*	Markivia	Marley *(0.10)*	Marnell	Marquell
Mark'issa	Markelsia	Markiya	Marleyna	Marnequea	Marquella
Marka	Markemia	Markiyah	Marleysha	Marnequia	Marquelle
Markae	Markenna	Markiyon	Marlhy	Marnesha	Marquenique
Markail	Markenya	Markiysha	Marli	Marneshia	Marquesa
Markaila	Markesa	Markje	Marlicia	Marnette	Marquesha *(0.01)*
Markala	Markesh	Markley	Marlie *(0.01)*	Marney	Marqueshia
Markale	Markesha *(0.01)*	Markqueeta	Marliena	Marni *(0.01)*	Marquesia
Markaleh	Markeshá	Markqueisha	Marlies	Marnie *(0.02)*	Marquessa
Markanesha	Markeshia *(0.01)*	Markquel	Marliese	Marniecha	Marquet
Markaria	Markesia	Markquetta	Marliesha	Marnika	Marqueta
Markariote	Markeska	Markquita	Marlii	Marnika Marshea	Marquetia
Markasia	Markessa	Marks	Marlin *(0.01)*	Marniqua	Marquetta *(0.01)*
Markatta	Marketa *(0.01)*	Marktika	Marlina *(0.01)*	Marnique	Marquette
Markay	Marketah	Markya	Marlinda	Marnisha *(0.01)*	Marquevias
Markaya	Markethia	Markyra	Marline	Marnishia	Marquez
Markayel	Marketta	Markysha	Marlini	Marnita	Marqueze
Markayla *(0.01)*	Markeva	Markyshia	Marlinka	Marnoucheka	Marquia
Markayzia	Markevia	Marla *(0.07)*	Marlinn	Marnuice	Marquiana
Markchene	Markey	Marlae	Marlinne	Marny	Marquianda
Marke	Markeya	Marlaena	Marliqua	Marnye	Marquiann
Markea	Markeyá	Marlaia	Marlis	Marob	Marquica

Marquicha	Marrylyn	Marshjé	Martiana	Marvilyn	Mary Therese
Marquida	Marryssa	Marshon	Martianna	Marvina	Mary Virginia
Marquie	Marsadees'	Marshona	Martica	Marvyn	Mary'alexis
Marquiese	Marsades	Marshonda	Martice	Marwa (0.02)	Mary'k
Marquiesha	Marsadies	Marshonna	Marticia	Marwah	Mary-
Marquila	Marsal	Marshundrea	Martie	Marwo	Mary-Agnes
Marquilla	Marscella	Marstejia	Martiees	Mary (3.39)	Mary-Alice
Marquinesha	Marsea	Marta (0.06)	Martiena	Mary Agnes	Mary-Alyssa
Marquiria	Marseana	Martai'jha	Martika (0.02)	Mary Alexis	Mary-Ana
Marquis (0.01)	Marseanna	Martaj	Martiki	Mary Allene	Mary-Angelyn
Marquisa	Marsela	Martajah	Martikia	Mary Alynda	Mary-Ann
Marquise (0.01)	Marselina	Martanesha	Martilya	Mary Angelica	Mary-Anna
Marquisha (0.03)	Marsella	Martanic	Martin	Mary Ann (0.01)	Mary-Anne
Marquisha Lasho	Marsella-Antonia	Martaniece	Martina (0.12)	Mary Beth	Mary-Ashley
Marquisia	Marsha (0.03)	Martanique	Martinaene	Mary Brent	Mary-Ashlin
Marquisicia	Marshá	Martashá	Martine (0.03)	Mary Caroline	Mary-Aurelia
Marquisse	Marshae (0.01)	Martasia	Martine-Claudette	Mary Catherine	Mary-Beth
Marquita (0.05)	Marshaé	Martavia	Martinez	Mary Cathrine	Mary-Caitlin
Marquitta (0.01)	Marshai	Martayja	Martinicel	Mary Christine	Mary-Catherine
Marquivia	Marshaila	Martaysha	Martinique	Mary Claire	Mary-Elise
Marquiya	Marshal	Marteaka	Martink	Mary Clare	Mary-Elizabeth
Marquoise	Marshala	Martee	Martinna	Mary Donna	Mary-Hannah
Marquretia	Marshall	Marteea	Martino	Mary Eileen	Mary-Jane
Marra	Marshan	Marteeka	Martinque	Mary Elizabeth	Mary-Jo
Marrah	Marshana	Marteen	Martisa	Mary Ella	Mary-Joann
Marrakech	Marshane	Marteena	Martise	Mary Ellen	Mary-Kaitlyn
Marranda	Marshanese	Marteesa	Martisha (0.01)	Mary Emma	Mary-Kate (0.01)
Marren	Marshareka	Marteia	Martishia	Mary Eve	Mary-Katherine
Marrerh	Marshariea	Marteil	Martisia	Mary Frances	Mary-Kathryn
Marresa	Marshauna	Marteisha	Martita	Mary Grace	Mary-Kelly
Marresha	Marshauntie	Marteja	Martiyah	Mary Helen	Mary-Lynn
Marriah (0.01)	Marshavia	Marteka	Martiza	Mary Jane	Mary-Marae
Marrial	Marshawe	Martekah	Martrece	Mary Jean	Mary-Margaret
Marriam	Marshawn	Martena	Martrelle	Mary Jo	(0.01)
Marriana	Marshawna	Martenana	Martrese	Mary Joy	Mary-Mcneil
Marriani	Marshawnda	Marteniece	Martrice	Mary Kate (0.01)	Mary-Michaelene
Marriann	Marshawnna	Martenique	Martricé	Mary Katherine	Mary-Morgan
Marrianna	Marshay (0.01)	Martenya	Marty (0.01)	(0.01)	Mary-Payton
Marrie	Marshayda	Martes'sha	Martyka	Mary Kathleen	Mary-Paz
Marrielle	Marshe	Martesha	Martyna	Mary Kathrine	Mary-Rhine
Marrin	Marshé	Marteshia	Martyne	Mary Kathryn	Mary-Rose
Marrinna	Marshea	Martesia	Martynia	Mary Kay	Marya
Marris	Marsheba	Martha (0.43)	Marueisha	Mary Kelly	Maryah (0.01)
Marrisa (0.02)	Marshée	Martha Caroline	Marui	Mary Kristen	Maryallyn
Marrisah	Marsheeka	Martha Elena	Marusha	Mary Lee	Maryam (0.06)
Marrisha	Marshei	Martha Yaneth	Marva	Mary Lilly	Maryama
Marrissa (0.03)	Marshekia	Martha-Lene	Marvel	Mary Lou	Maryan (0.01)
Marrissa-Ann	Marsheley	Marthalee	Marvela	Mary Lynn	Maryana
Marrit	Marshell	Marthalicia	Marvella	Mary Magdalen	Maryann (0.06)
Marriun	Marshella	Marthaluz	Marvellena	Mary Margaret	Maryanna
Marron	Marshelle	Marthana	Marvelous	Mary Marie	Maryanne (0.03)
Marroz	Marsherry	Marthia	Marvetta	Mary Raene	Maryanron
Marry-Kate	Marsheta	Marthianne	Marvi	Mary Rose	Marybel
Marryann	Marshetta	Marti (0.01)	Marvia	Mary Teresa	Marybella
Marryanna	Marshiana	Martia (0.01)	Marviana	Mary Theresa	Marybelle

Marybeth (0.01)	Marynell	Masiat	Mathilde-Bherer	Matthania	Maurie
Maryca	Marynelle	Masie	Mathison	Matthea	Mauriel
Marycait	Marynicole	Masiha	Mathlusha	Matthew (0.01)	Maurika
Marycarmen	Maryon	Masika	Mathura	Matthews	Maurina
Marycatherine	Maryorie	Masina	Mathushea	Matti	Maurine
Maryclare	Maryper	Masini	Mathuvany	Mattia	Maurisa
Marycolleen	Maryrica	Maskeen	Mathy	Mattie (0.08)	Maurisamay
Marycruz (0.02)	Maryrose	Maslyn	Matia	Mattie-Jean	Maurisha
Marydeth	Marys	Mason (0.02)	Matiana	Mattiera	Maurishia
Marye	Marysa (0.01)	Masoon	Maticen	Mattilyn	Maurissa (0.01)
Maryea	Marysah	Masouna	Matija	Mattilynn	Maurita
Maryel	Maryse (0.02)	Masride	Matilda (0.02)	Mattingly	Maurkeva
Maryelizabeth	Marysia	Massey	Matilde	Mattisen	Maurkiesha
Maryellen (0.01)	Marysol	Massie	Matilyn	Mattison (0.01)	Maurlicia
Maryem	Maryssa (0.04)	Massiel	Matilynn	Mattox	Maurnece
Maryemma	Marysue	Massimo	Matina	Matty	Maursharee
Maryesler	Marytalynn	Massyl	Matisha	Maty	Maursheka
Maryeva	Marytza	Masteska	Matison	Matya	Maury
Maryglen	Maryuana	Masuda	Matisse	Matyra	Maurya
Marygrace	Maryum	Masy	Matiya	Matyri	Mauryssa
Maryhelen	Maryun	Masyn	Matiyaa	Matyriah	Mausherri
Maryiah	Maryuri	Masyra	Matkia	Matyson	Mausum
Maryion	Marza	Mat	Matlin	Mau'kesha	Mautrice
Maryjane (0.02)	Marzaree	Mata	Matlyn	Maud	Mavalin
Maryjean	Marzela	Matacious	Matney	Maude (0.47)	Mavana
Maryjo (0.01)	Marzella	Mataina	Matou	Maude Emilie	Mavanee
Maryjoe	Marzjohnnie	Matalin	Matozzerra	Maudie	Mavell
Maryk	Masako	Matalyn	Matraca	Maudilee	Maven
Maryka	Masami	Matana	Matrace	Maudline	Maverick
Marykate (0.01)	Maschel	Matanya	Matracia	Maulene	Mavi
Marykatherine	Masen	Matari	Matreonia	Maunia	Mavia
Marykathryn	Masey	Mataria	Matresa	Mauntris	Mavielhen
Marykelly	Masha	Matavia	Matreta	Maur'teisha	Mavis (0.01)
Marykza	Mashaal	Mataya (0.01)	Matreya	Maura (0.11)	Mavity
Marylaine	Mashaelia	Matayah	Matrica	Maurah	Mavrine
Marylane	Mashaie	Matayia	Matrice	Maurana	Mavuna
Marylauren	Mashaila	Matea	Matrika	Maurasia	Mawadda
Marylee	Mashal	Mateea	Matrina	Maurcine	Mawish
Maryleen	Mashana	Mateenah	Matta	Maure	Mawuena
Marylene (0.01)	Masharie	Mateja	Mattaline	Maureen (0.12)	Mawusi
Marylin (0.01)	Mashashe	Materia	Mattalyn	Maureena	Max
Maryline	Mashawna	Matesja	Mattawana	Maurekia	Max Sandra
Marylisa	Mashay	Matesse	Mattaya	Maurella	Maxanie
Marylou (0.04)	Mashayla (0.01)	Mateya	Matte	Maurelle	Maxcine
Marylouise	Mashaylah	Matgorzata	Mattea (0.02)	Mauren	Maxee
Marylu	Mashea	Matha	Matteah	Mauresha	Maxey
Maryluz	Masheika	Mathanega	Matteasha	Maurgan	Maxi
Marylyn	Mashell	Mathasha	Mattecia	Mauri	Maxie
Marylynn	Mashelle	Mathea	Mattelyn	Mauriah	Maxime (0.02)
Marymar	Mashia	Matheetha	Mattelynn	Mauriana	Maximiliana
Marymargare	Mashiah	Mathew	Mattes	Maurianna	Maximina
Marymargaret	Mashira	Mathi	Mattesha	Maurica	Maxine (0.10)
Marymargret	Mashitah	Mathieu (0.01)	Mattesia	Mauriceyia	Maxsie
Maryn (0.01)	Mashonda	Mathilda	Matteson	Mauricia (0.01)	Maxtonie
Maryna	Masi	Mathilde (0.06)	Mattey	Mauricio	Maxwell

Maxx	Maylana	Maytee	Mccay	Mckeever	Mckya
Maxyne	Maylasia	Maythe	Mccayla	Mckeil	Mckyaella
May *(0.04)*	Maylat	Maytlin	Mcclendon	Mckel	Mckyla
May Lieng	Mayleah	Mayu	Mccormack	Mckell *(0.02)*	Mckylie
May Rose	Maylee	Mayuana	Mccormick	Mckelle	Mckyna
May-A'neece	Mayleen	Mayumi	Mccoy	Mckena *(0.01)*	Mckynna
May-Lannie	Mayleesa	Mayumijoy	Mccray	Mckendra	Mckynze
Maya *(0.54)*	Mayleigh	Mayuna	Mccrea	Mckenian	Mckynzie
Maya-Ann	Maylen	Mayuri	Mcdonald	Mckenize	Mclaine
Mayah *(0.01)*	Maylena	Mayzie	Mcghee	Mckenlee	Mclane
Mayai	Maylene	Maza	Mcguire	Mckenley	Mclaren
Mayakala	Mayleth	Mazbal	Mckady	Mckenna *(0.39)*	Mclayne
Mayakoda	Mayli	Mazella	Mckae	Mckennah	Mclean
Mayalisa	Maylia	Mazey	Mckaela *(0.01)*	Mckennen	Mcleod
Mayan	Maylin	Mazi	Mckaelie	Mckennlee	Mclynn
Mayanna	Maylinna	Mazie	Mckaella	Mckennly	Mcmillon
Mayar	Maylisa	Mazna	Mckaely	Mckennzie	Mcneely
Maybee	Maylo	Mazy	Mckahle	Mckensee	Mcpherson
Maybella	Mayloni	Mazzarie	Mckaila *(0.01)*	Mckensey *(0.01)*	Mcquaela
Maybelle	Maylsia	Mazzi	Mckailah	Mckensi	Mcrae
Maybelline	Maylyn	Mc *(0.01)*	Mckailey	Mckensie *(0.01)*	Mcsandra
Maybre	Maylynn	Mc Caela	Mckaily	Mckensy	Mcshane
Maycala	Maylynne	Mc Call	Mckaiya	Mckenze	Mcverlynn
Mayce	Mayme	Mc Callister	Mckala *(0.01)*	Mckenzee *(0.01)*	Me Kaila
Maycee *(0.01)*	Maymun	Mc Caulie	Mckale	Mckenzey	Me Kayla
Maycey	Maymuna	Mc Cayla	Mckaleigh	Mckenzi *(0.02)*	Méatia
Mayci	Maymunah	Mc Kae	Mckaler	Mckenzie *(0.72)*	Méchele
Maycie	Mayna	Mc Kailie	Mckaley	Mckenzii	Méchelle
Maycin	Mayola	Mc Kayla	Mckali	Mckenzy *(0.01)*	Méita
Mayda	Mayoly	Mc Kayleigh	Mckalia	Mckenzye	Méka
Maydevi	Mayora	Mc Kenna *(0.02)*	Mckalii	Mckeya	Mékell
Maydli	Mayorga	Mc Kenzi	Mckall	Mckhale	Mékhai
Maye	Mayquele	Mc Kenzie *(0.02)*	Mckalla	Mckierlyn	Mélanice
Mayela	Mayra *(0.64)*	Mc Kinsey	Mckalynn	Mckinaly	Mélicia
Mayelene	Mayraalejand	Mc Kinsie	Mckanna	Mckindle	Méshae
Mayelin	*(0.01)*	Mcail	Mckanzie	Mckinlay	Méyon
Mayelisa	Mayralejandra	Mcalla	Mckay	Mckinlee	Mea
Mayella	Mayranely	Mcallison	Mckaya	Mckinleigh	Meá
Mayelyn	Mayranyellys	Mcara	Mckayala	Mckinley *(0.02)*	Meabh
Mayes	Mayree	Mcauley	Mckaye	Mckinley-Lynne	Meachia
Mayetta	Mayreliz	Mcavion	Mckayla *(0.19)*	Mckinlie	Meadow *(0.01)*
Maygan *(0.01)*	Mayrin	Mcayla	Mckaylah	Mckinna	Meaga
Maygan-Rose	Maysa *(0.01)*	Mccaela	Mckaylan	Mckinnah	Meagan *(0.76)*
Maygen *(0.01)*	Maysee	Mccaffrey	Mckayle	Mckinney	Meagan-Helen
Mayghan	Maysen	Mccaila	Mckaylee *(0.01)*	Mckinnley	Meagen *(0.01)*
Maygn	Maysha	Mccala	Mckayleh	Mckinnon	Meaghan *(0.36)*
Maygon	Mayshonna	Mccall *(0.02)*	Mckayleigh	Mckinsey	Meaghan-Lee
Maygra	Maysia	Mccalla	Mckayli	Mckinsley	Meaghann
Mayiah	Mayson	Mccallah	Mckaylia	Mckinze	Meaghen
Mayim	Maysoon	Mccallen	Mckaylie	Mckinzea	Meagkan
Maykayla	Mayssa	Mccalli	Mckayln	Mckinzee	Meagon
Maykelly	Mayssan	Mccallister	Mckaylyn	Mckinzi	Meagyn
Maykiae	Maytal	Mccants	Mckaysha	Mckinzie *(0.02)*	Meah
Mayla	Mayte *(0.02)*	Mccarley	Mckee	Mckinzy	Meah Morgan
Maylah	Mayteana	Mccauley	Mckeeda	Mckoy	Meahgyn

Meahway	Meelandra	Meghan *(1.43)*	Meikaylah	Mekiella	Melea *(0.01)*
Meambershin	Meeli	Meghana	Meikelle	Mekieshia	Meleah *(0.01)*
Meana	Meelony	Meghann *(0.03)*	Meilani	Mekila	Meleaha
Meandra	Meena *(0.01)*	Meghanne	Meilanie	Mekine	Meleana
Meannia	Meenakshi	Meghen	Meilee	Mekinna	Meleane
Meara *(0.01)*	Meenu	Meghin	Meileeta	Mekinzee	Meleanee
Meari	Meenuva	Meghna	Meili	Mekinzi	Meleanie
Meata	Meera *(0.01)*	Meghyn	Meilina	Mekira	Meleanne
Mecaila	Meerah	Megin	Meina	Mekita	Meleasa
Mecamesly	Meeranda	Megkinize	Meira	Mekka	Meleashia
Mecayla	Meeresa	Megna	Meiren	Mekkah	Melecca
Mecca *(0.02)*	Meesa	Megon	Meisel	Mekkena	Melece
Meccah	Meesha *(0.01)*	Megumi *(0.01)*	Meisen	Meklit	Meleena
Meccasia	Meetali	Megyn	Meish	Meko	Meleesa
Mecede	Meetra	Meh-Jabine	Meisha *(0.01)*	Mekole	Meleessa
Mecenzie	Meeyah	Meha	Meishaun	Mekyelle	Meleeza
Mechaela	Mefah	Mehaf	Mejia	Mekyla	Meleia
Meche	Meg *(0.03)*	Mehak	Mejoan	Mekynzee	Meleigha
Mechel	Meg'n	Mehanie	Meka *(0.01)*	Mel	Meleika
Mechele	Megahn	Meharban	Mekael	Melady	Meleka
Mechell	Megala	Meharjot	Mekaela	Melah	Melekoula
Mechelle *(0.01)*	Megan *(7.91)*	Mehartaj	Mekahla	Melaia	Melena
Mechon	Megan Elizabeth	Mehdiya	Mekahlia	Melaina *(0.01)*	Melena Lyn
Meckael	Megan Lee	Mehek	Mekaila	Melaine	Melenda
Meckennah	Megan-Jade	Meher	Mekailah	Melainie	Meleni
Meckenzee	Megan-Joy	Meheret	Mekala	Melan	Melenia
Meckenzie	Megan-Juanita	Mehgan	Mekalah	Melana	Melenie
Mecker	Megan-Marie	Mehgen	Mekaliah	Melandie	Melenthia
Meco	Megan-Rose	Mehitabel	Mekall	Melane	Meleny
Medaline	Megana	Mehjabeen	Mekayla *(0.03)*	Melanee	Melesa
Medea	Megane *(0.05)*	Mehki	Mekaylia	Melanesia	Meleshe
Medelia	Meganf	Mehneek	Mekdara	Melaney *(0.01)*	Meleshia
Medeliz	Meganie	Mehnoor	Mekdes	Melangll	Melesia
Medgina	Meganj	Mehreen	Mekeda	Melani *(0.01)*	Melesilika
Medgyne	Meganlyn	Mehret	Mekedes	Melani-Renee	Melesiu
Medha	Megann *(0.01)*	Mehrin	Mekeha	Melania	Melessa
Medici	Meganna	Mehron	Mekeida	Melanie *(1.41)*	Melexis
Mediha	Meganne *(0.01)*	Mehru	Mekel	Melanie-Ann	Melia *(0.03)*
Medina *(0.01)*	Megason	Mehry	Mekela	Melaniece	Meliah
Medinah	Megau	Mehtab	Mekelit	Melaniese	Meliange
Medjeen	Megdalyn	Mehtaj	Mekella	Melanija	Melicia
Medjina	Megdelawit	Mehvish	Mekendra	Melanna	Melida
Medjy	Megean *(0.01)*	Mei *(0.01)*	Mekenna	Melannie *(0.01)*	Meliena
Medley	Megee	Mei'asia	Mekensie	Melantha	Melika
Medora	Megen *(0.01)*	Mei-Jun	Mekenzi	Melany *(0.02)*	Melike
Medows	Meggan *(0.03)*	Mei-Kei	Mekenzie *(0.01)*	Melanye	Melild
Medrion	Meggee	Meia	Mekesha	Melat	Melina *(0.25)*
Medusha	Meggen	Meicco	Mekeya	Melaun	Melinda *(0.32)*
Mee	Meggie *(0.02)*	Meicha	Mekhala	Melaya	Melinda-Lee
Meéchelle	Meggin	Meichelle	Mekhia	Melayna	Melinez
Meecha	Meggy *(0.01)*	Meidje	Meki	Melaysia	Melinna
Meeda	Meggyn	Meigan	Mekia	Melba	Melira
Meegan	Megh	Meighan	Mekiayla	Melbreena	Melis
Meeghan	Megha *(0.01)*	Meika	Mekiel	Meldoy	Melisa *(0.10)*
Meeka	Meghaen	Meikala	Mekiela	Mele *(0.02)*	Melisande

Melisca	Mellonee	Memarie	Meranda Rae	Meredith *(0.50)*	Merita
Melise	Melly	Memori	Merandah	Meredith-Dawn	Merium
Melise-Isabelle	Mellyn	Memorie	Merandia	Meredyth	Meriwether
Melish	Melneisha	Memories	Merannda	Meredythe	Meriya
Melisha	Melniekque	Memory	Merari *(0.01)*	Merehedy	Merkenide
Melishai	Melodee	Memphis	Meraris	Mereissa	Merland
Melishia	Melodey	Memry	Merary	Merel	Merle
Melissa *(4.75)*	Melodi	Mena	Mercades *(0.01)*	Merelin	Merleen
Melissa Estelle	Melodi-Bahar	Menachem	Mercadez	Merella	Merlin
Melissa Mere	Melodie *(0.10)*	Menajah	Mercadi	Merely	Merline
Melissa Nicole	Melody *(0.38)*	Menaka	Mercadies	Merena	Merlinn
Melissa-Ann	Melody Ann	Menatallah	Merccedes	Merenda	Merlou
Melissa-Anne	Melody Christin	Mende	Merce	Merete	Mermyla
Melissa-Escano	Melody-Dawn	Mendez	Merceades	Merey	Merna
Melissa-Gianina	Melondie	Mendy	Merced	Mereysel	Merny
Melissa-Lynn	Melondy	Menelene	Mercede *(0.01)*	Merhan	Meron
Melissa-Marie	Meloney	Menesha	Mercedés	Meri	Merone
Melissa-Nicole	Meloni	Mengting	Mercedee	Meria	Meronin
Melissa-Rosita	Melonie *(0.01)*	Meni	Mercedees	Meriah *(0.01)*	Meronin
Melissa-Savannah	Melony	Menielle	Mercedeez	Meriam	Merranda *(0.01)*
Melissa.laura	Melora	Menika	Mercedes *(0.69)*	Merian	Merrea
Melissah	Melorie	Menina	Mercedes	Merianda	Merrell
Melissandra	Melpina	Menique	Ambroz	Meriane	Merren
Melissavet	Melpomenie	Menisha	Mercedese	Merianna	Merretta
Melissia	Melquana	Menlie	Mercedeshelene	Merica	Merri
Melissqa	Melrose	Menna	Mercedez *(0.04)*	Merical	Merria
Melita	Melshayla	Mennlee	Mercedezs	Mericia	Merriah
Melitia	Melsi	Menta	Mercedi	Mericoh	Merriam
Melitta	Meltem	Mentasia	Mercedie	Merida	Merrica
Meliyah	Meltia	Menucha	Mercedies	Meriden	Merrick
Meliz	Meltrecia	Menvir	Mercedis	Merideth	Merrideth
Meliza	Meltrika	Menwooe	Mercedrs	Meridian	Merridy
Meliza-Selina	Melva	Menyata Elexas	Merceds	Meridith *(0.01)*	Merrie
Melizabeth	Melvalicia	Meochia	Mercedz	Meridy	Merriel
Melizza	Melvalisha	Meona	Merceedes	Meriel	Merril
Melkeata	Melveda	Meonaka	Mercees	Merielle	Merrill
Melkesha	Melvesha	Meondra	Mercer	Merien	Merrill-Lee
Mellanease	Melveshia	Meoniée	Mercerdes	Merighan	Merrily
Mellaneshia	Melvia	Meonna	Merci	Merika	Merrin
Mellanie	Melviena	Meosha	Mercia	Meril	Merrion
Mellany	Melvina	Meoshae	Mercie	Merilee	Merrisa
Mellea	Melvinea	Meoshia	Mercilia	Merilyn *(0.01)*	Merrisah
Melleah	Melvinna	Meozha	Mercina	Merina *(0.01)*	Merrissa
Melleka	Melvisha	Mepa	Mercury	Merina-Lynn	Merrit
Mellena	Mely Yaritza	Mequashia	Mercy *(0.02)*	Merinda	Merritt *(0.01)*
Mellia	Melyce	Mequilla	Mercyann	Merine	Merry *(0.01)*
Melliah	Melyn	Mera	Mercydys	Merinn	Merryhelen
Mellicent	Melyna *(0.02)*	Meradyth	Mercyla	Meris	Merryll
Mellis	Melynda *(0.01)*	Merae	Merdedes	Merisa *(0.01)*	Mersade
Mellisa *(0.03)*	Melyndia	Meraida	Merdina	Merisena	Mersadees
Mellisha	Melyne	Meraises	Merea	Merisha	Mersadeez
Mellissa *(0.03)*	Melyssa *(0.04)*	Meralis	Merecedes	Merissa *(0.08)*	Mersadeis
Mellissea	Melyssa Ann	Meran	Merecedie	Merissa-Lynn	Mersades
Melliza	Melyssande	Merana	Meredeth	Merissha	Mersadez
Mellody	Mema	Meranda *(0.07)*	Meredidth	Merit	Mersadi

Mersadie	Meshi	Mfon-Obong	Miaja	Micayah	Michallia
Mersadies	Meshia	Mhairi	Miajhya	Micayala	Michand
Mersadiez	Meshiah	Mhakia	Miakah	Micayla (0.05)	Michanda
Mersadize	Meshil	Mharee	Miami	Micayle	Michandra
Mersaede	Meshil'le	Mhari	Miana (0.01)	Micaylee	Michann
Mersaides	Meshinque	Mharie	Mianca	Micbeth	Michanna
Mersal	Meshonda	Mharlove	Miangel	Micca	Michanne
Mersaydeez	Meshonna	Mhegan	Mianimar	Miceala	Michaonya
Mersaydez	Meshunda	Mhina	Mianiqua	Mich'e	Michara
Mersedez	Mesnayda	Mhyesha	Mianna	Micha (0.01)	Micharlenta
Mersedies	Messalina	Mi	Miante	Michaélla	Michaya
Mershon	Messel	Mi Kayla	Miara	Michaalah	Michayla (0.03)
Mershontay	Messellah	Mi Mi	Miarah	Michae	Michaylah
Merticka	Messiah	Mi Shai	Miaraha	Michaé	Miche
Mertina	Messianna	Mi Shana	Miarra	Michaeila	Micheai
Mertis	Mesuun	Mi Tram	Miasa	Michael (0.05)	Micheal
Meruna	Meta	Mía	Miasean	Michaela (1.45)	Micheal-Jane
Merve	Metallica	Mi'angel	Miasha	Michaelá	Micheala (0.04)
Merveille	Metallya	Mi'ara	Miasia	Michaelah	Michealla
Merveline	Metaxia	Mi'asia	Miata (0.01)	Michaelann	Michealle
Meryana	Meteja	Mi'aysha	Miatha	Michaele	Micheba
Meryeil	Methma	Mi'chael	Miavanni	Michaelea	Micheila
Meryem	Metia	Mi'chel	Miavictoria	Michaelee	Micheisha
Meryl (0.01)	Metica	Mi'chele	Miaya (0.01)	Michaelene	Michel (0.02)
Meryl-Lynn	Metiya	Mi'chelle	Miayaloni	Michaeli	Michel Le
Merylin	Meto	Mi'eshiah	Miayan	Michaelia	Michela (0.04)
Meryll	Metosha	Mi'isha	Miayasu	Michaelina	Michelah
Meryn	Metra	Mi'jai	Mibsam	Michaeline	Michele (0.23)
Meryssa	Metria	Mi'kalah	Mic'quell	Michaell	Michelea
Merzaya	Metuschelah	Mi'kayla	Mica (0.02)	Michaella (0.07)	Michelena
Merzedes	Meuy	Mi'kea	Micaeala	Michaelle	Michelina (0.01)
Mesa	Mevisha	Mi'kel	Micaela (0.26)	Michaely	Micheline (0.01)
Mesan	Mey Ta	Mi'kerria	Micaeleigh	Michaelya	Michell (0.03)
Meseret	Meya	Mi'kesa	Micaella	Michaelyn	Michell'e
Meserhet	Meyahna	Mi'keyia	Micaelyn	Michaelynn	Michella
Mesgana	Meyail	Mi'kia	Micagla	Michah	Michelle (4.38)
Mesha (0.01)	Meyanna	Mi'oshia	Micah (0.12)	Michaiah	Michelle Elyse
Meshadae	Meyasha	Mi'shyra	Micah Ruth	Michaila (0.01)	Michelle Guadal
Meshaila	Meyata	Mi'tonyá	Micaha	Michaila-Rae	Michelle Mae
Meshal	Meyauna	Mi-Kerria	Micahalah	Michailey	Michelle Star
Meshalae	Meyci	Mia (0.39)	Micahia	Michailia	Michelle Thao
Meshalanna	Meydy	Mia Nani	Micahla	Michajla	Michellé
Meshalay	Meyer	Mia Rasa	Micaiah (0.01)	Michal (0.02)	Michelle-Ann
Meshale	Meygan	Mia Teresa	Micaila (0.01)	Michala (0.04)	Michelle-Lynn
Meshan	Meyia	Miá	Micailah	Michalah	Michelle-Maria
Meshandra	Meyke	Mia'chanel	Micajah	Michale	Michelle-Shelly
Meshanquil	Meykia	Mia-Beeslee	Mical	Michalea	Michellea
Meshanthini	Meylin	Mia-Marie	Micala (0.01)	Michaleen	Michellene
Meshawn	Meymuna	Miaa	Micalah	Michaleh	Michellepauline
Meshay	Meyon	Miachea	Micale	Michalia	Michellett
Meshayla	Meyonda	Miada	Micalea	Michalic	Michelli
Meshel	Meyonia	Miah (0.02)	Micalena	Michalina	Michellie
Meshell	Meyonsha	Miaiesha	Micalyn	Michalla (0.01)	Michelline
Meshellay	Meyoshi	Miairah	Micarah	Michalle	Michellw
Meshelle	Mfodwaa	Miaisha	Micay	Michallé	Michelly

Michelsea	Mickewa	Miha	Mikali	Mikeita	Mikiayla
Michelyn	Mickey	Mihaela	Mikalia	Mikel *(0.01)*	Mikidra
Michema	Mickeya	Mihalia	Mikalin	Mikela *(0.01)*	Mikiko
Michena	Micki	Mihan	Mikalla	Mikelah	Mikilani
Micherlynne	Micki-Lani	Miharelys	Mikalley	Mikelia	Mikinea
Michesha	Mickia	Mihcaela	Mikaly	Mikeline	Mikinley
Micheyla	Mickie	Mihelle	Mikalya	Mikelita	Mikinna
Michi	Mickinze	Mihesha	Mikalyla	Mikell	Mikinzee
Michiah	Mickinzie	Mihika	Mikalyn	Mikella	Mikinzi
Michica	Mickinzy	Mihira	Mikalynn	Mikellá	Mikinzie
Michigan	Micky	Mihkeyera	Mikan	Mikelle *(0.01)*	Mikinzy
Michiho	Mickyzjha	Mihlanie	Mikar	Mikelyn	Mikiquesha
Michiko	Micole *(0.01)*	Miho	Mikara	Mikenda	Mikirra
Michkaela-Lyn	Micqa-Sa	Miiauna	Mikarah	Mikenly	Mikisha
Michkayla	Micquala	Miika	Mikasa	Mikenna *(0.01)*	Mikita
Michla	Micqualyn	Miisha	Mikaweelches	Mikenya	Mikiya
Michlynn	Micquaya	Miiya	Mikaya	Mikenzee	Mikiyah
Michol	Micqueala	Miiyon	Mikayah	Mikenzi	Mikiyela
Michole	Micquel	Mijah	Mikayela	Mikenzie *(0.01)*	Mikjá
Michon	Micquella	Mijail	Mikayiah	Mikeondra	Mikka *(0.01)*
Michquel	Midah	Miji	Mikayla *(0.94)*	Mikequana	Mikkah
Michue	Mide	Mijken	Mikayla-Jayde	Mikeria	Mikkayla
Michyla	Midelis	Mijo	Mikayla-Raie	Mikeriea	Mikkealla
Miciah	Midge	Mik'quasha	Mikaylah	Mikeriya	Mikkel
Miciha	Midia	Mika *(0.03)*	Mikayle	Mikerra	Mikkela
Micinze	Midian	Mika'yla	Mikaylea	Mikesa	Mikki *(0.01)*
Micita	Midori	Mikael	Mikaylee	Mikesha *(0.01)*	Mikki-Taylor
Mickael	Mie	Mikaela *(0.43)*	Mikaylei	Mikeshia	Mikkia
Mickaela *(0.01)*	Mieana	Mikaelah	Mikayli	Mikesiaya	Mikkie
Mickaeli	Mieasha	Mikaele	Mikaylia	Mikessa	Mikkira
Mickaella	Mieisha	Mikaeli	Mikaylie	Mikey	Mikko
Mickail	Mieka	Mikaelia	Mikaylin	Mikeya	Miklin
Mickaila	Miekael	Mikaella	Mikaylla	Mikeycia	Miko
Mickailynn	Miekayla	Mikaelyn	Mikaza	Mikeyia	Mikole
Mickala *(0.01)*	Mieke	Mikaeyla	Mikéa	Mikeyla	Mikosz
Mickalah	Miekia	Mikah *(0.01)*	Mikéal	Mikeysa	Mikoyia
Mickale	Miekle	Mikahelia	Mikévia	Mikeysha	Miku
Mickalin	Mieko	Mikahla	Mike-Keyejauh	Mikhael	Mikuella
Mickayla *(0.04)*	Mielle	Mikahyalah	Mikea	Mikhaela *(0.01)*	Mikwan
Mickaylaa	Miellyn	Mikai	Mikeá	Mikhaele	Mikyah
Mickaylea	Mieola	Mikaila *(0.06)*	Mikeal	Mikhaella	Mikyaila
Mickaylie	Mierale	Mikaila-Jade	Mikeala *(0.01)*	Mikhaila *(0.01)*	Mikyla *(0.01)*
Mickee	Mierra	Mikailah	Mikeale	Mikhala *(0.01)*	Mikylah
Mickeisha	Mieshá	Mikaile	Mikeara	Mikhalea	Mikyle
Mickel	Miesha *(0.04)*	Mikailla	Mikedra	Mikhayla *(0.02)*	Mikynna
Mickela	Mieshel	Mikako	Mikee	Mikhea	Mikysha
Mickell	Mieshia	Mikal *(0.01)*	Mikeedra	Mikheala	Mila *(0.01)*
Mickella	Mieysha	Mikala *(0.12)*	Mikeela	Mikhela	Milaany
Mickelle	Migdalia	Mikalah *(0.01)*	Mikeera	Mikhiael	Milady
Mickenna	Migdalis	Mikalaha	Mikeesha	Miki	Milagro
Mickensie	Migina	Mikale	Mikeh	Mikia *(0.01)*	Milagros *(0.01)*
Mickenzee	Mignon	Mikalea	Mikeia	Mikiaela	Milaheya
Mickenzi	Miguel	Mikalee	Mikeila	Mikiah	Milahna
Mickenzie *(0.01)*	Miguelisa	Mikaleh	Mikeisha	Mikiana	Milahne
Mickenzy	Miguiel	Mikaleigh	Mikeishia	Mikiara	Milaina

Milaine	Milisa	Mindy *(0.13)*	Miquella	Mireli	Mirsa
Milaka	Milisha	Mine	Miquelle	Mirella *(0.03)*	Mirta
Milan *(0.02)*	Milishia	Mineko	Miqueria	Mirelle	Mirtha
Milana *(0.01)*	Milissa	Minelda	Miqula	Mirellise	Miru
Milanda	Militsa	Minerva *(0.03)*	Miquonia	Mirelsa	Mirya
Milande	Milka	Minesha	Miqweshia	Mirely	Miryah
Milandria	Millacyne	Mineve	Mira *(0.03)*	Miresha	Miryam *(0.02)*
Milane	Millandra	Ming	Mira Marie	Mireya *(0.08)*	Miryan
Milanne	Millany	Ming-Yu	Miraal	Mireyda	Miryka
Milaun	Millat	Mingxue	Mirabai	Mireysa	Misa
Milaya	Millay	Minh	Mirabel	Mirfina	Misae
Milayla	Millee	Minh-Nguyet	Mirabella	Mirhonda	Misael
Milbrey	Millenie	Minh-Phuc	Miracah	Miri	Misaki
Milca	Miller	Minh-Tam	Miracle *(0.08)*	Miria	Misako
Milcah	Millesha	Minh-Thi	Miracle Ray	Miriah *(0.03)*	Misandy
Milchelle	Millicent *(0.01)*	Minha	Miraclé	Miriahvivian	Misato
Milda	Millie *(0.02)*	Minhaz	Miracles	Mirial	Misba
Mildalia	Millinda	Minica	Mirae	Miriam *(0.41)*	Misbah
Mildred *(0.03)*	Millisent	Minisha	Mirage	Miriam Lisbeth	Misbeth
Mildreed	Millissia	Minita	Miragha	Miriam-Ariana	Mischa
Mildreka	Millveen	Minjee	Mirah *(0.01)*	Mirian *(0.04)*	Mischele
Mildrena	Milly	Minji	Miraha	Mirianna	Miscia
Milea	Milnaira	Minjung	Miraje	Miricale	Misha *(0.03)*
Mileah	Milon	Minka	Miraka	Mirielle	Misha-Lee
Milecia	Milouse	Minley	Mirakle	Miriham	Mishaal
Miledy	Milto	Minna	Miral	Mirijam	Mishae
Mileena *(0.02)*	Miltoneisha	Minnah	Mirale	Mirika	Mishael
Mileibi	Milva	Minnesa Darrian	Miralee	Mirilina	Mishaela
Mileidi	Milvia	Minnetta	Mirallyne	Mirina	Mishaele
Mileidy	Milya	Minnette	Miran	Mirinda	Mishaelia
Milen	Milyka	Minni	Mirand	Mirisa	Mishaila
Milena *(0.02)*	Milyra	Minnie *(0.01)*	Miranda *(2.52)*	Mirisah	Mishal
Milenda	Milyric	Minnie-Lee	Miranda'rae	Mirissa	Mishala
Milene	Milyssa	Minniesha	Mirandah	Mirita	Mishanty
Milenna	Mimeau	Minnika	Mirandi	Mirjam	Mishari
Mileny	Mimi *(0.04)*	Minnisha	Mirandy	Mirjana	Mishaun
Milesha	Mimian	Minori	Mirannda	Mirka	Mishawn
Mileta	Mimidoo	Minsiss	Miranti	Mirkiyya	Mishawna
Miletha	Mimma	Minta	Miraquelle	Mirley	Mishay
Milexus	Mimosa	Mintha	Mirashia	Mirlianb	Mishaye
Miley	Min	Mintie	Mirasol	Mirline	Mishayla
Mileya	Min-Yan	Minuet	Miraya	Mirlyne	Mishé Aleigh
Mileydis	Mina *(0.08)*	Minuette	Mirchime	Mirna *(0.04)*	Mishea
Milgaros	Mina Ellen	Minyon	Mircle	Mirna Fabiola	Misheila
Milia	Minae	Minyoung	Miréyna	Miroslava	Mishel
Miliany	Minahs	Mio	Mirea	Mirra	Mishela
Milica	Minal	Mion	Mireha	Mirracle	Mishele
Milicca	Minami	Miona	Mireia	Mirramoni	Mishell
Milie	Minan	Miosha	Mireida	Mirranda *(0.01)*	Mishella
Milieania	Minarei	Miosotys	Mireille *(0.04)*	Mirrca	Mishelle
Milika	Minchew	Miozotis	Mireille Margue	Mirriah	Misheon
Milin	Minda	Miquael	Mireja	Mirriam	Mishika
Milina	Minda-Maria	Mique	Mirel	Mirrisa	Mishka
Milinda	Mindi *(0.01)*	Miquel	Mirela	Mirrissa	Mishla
Milinoris	Mindie	Miquela *(0.01)*	Mirelda	Mirronda	Mishma

Mishon	Mityra	Moddrika	Molisa	Monaye	Monice
Mishou	Mityrra	Modell	Molissie	Monce	Monichia
Mishri	Mitza	Modenise	Molitor	Moncerrad	Monicia
Mishyara	Mitzi *(0.04)*	Modesta	Molle	Monche	Monico
Misi	Mitzie	Modesty	Mollee	Monche L	Monida
Miska	Mitzy *(0.01)*	Modhura	Molleena	Monchelle	Monie
Miski	Miuniba	Modista	Molleigh	Moncia	Moniek
Mislady	Mixie	Modisti	Molley	Moncine	Monier
Misoa	Mixtli	Modita	Molli *(0.02)*	Mondala	Monifa
Mispha	Mixtly	Modupé	Mollianne	Mondina	Monigue
Miss Keith	Mixy	Moe	Mollie *(0.17)*	Mondrea	Monika *(0.16)*
Missie	Miya *(0.03)*	Moét	Mollie-Rose	Mondy	Monikka
Missollie	Miyá	Moeina	Mollissika	Mone	Monikue
Missouri	Miyah *(0.01)*	Moeko	Molly *(1.42)*	Mone I	Monina
Missourie	Miyaka	Moeniesha	Molly Ann	Mone T	Moniqca
Missy *(0.01)*	Miyako	Moenisha	Molly-Jane	Moné	Moniqu'e
Mistaya	Miyaletha	Moepreet	Molly-Kate	Monéleeke	Moniqua *(0.01)*
Misti *(0.02)*	Miyan	Moeshae	Molly-Lyn	Monét	Moniquah
Mistic	Miyana	Moet	Molly-Lynn	Moneá	Moniquca
Mistie *(0.01)*	Miyanna	Mogene	Mollyanne	Moneaka	Monique *(0.82)*
Mistii	Miyatta	Mohagony	Mollye	Moneasha	Moniqué
Mistika	Miyeah	Mohamed	Mollykate	Moneay	Monique-Raelyn
Mistina	Miyeko	Mohena	Mollymae	Moneca	Monique-Rose
Mistiree	Miyha	Mohibo	Molyte	Monée	Moniqueka
Mistralle	Miyka	Mohika	Mom	Moneek	Moniquia
Misturat	Miyo	Mohima	Momana	Moneeka	Moniquica
Misty *(0.19)*	Miyoko	Mohini	Momena	Moneet	Moniquie
Misty-Le	Miyon'	Mohna	Momenah	Monehra	Monisa
Misty-Marie	Miyona	Mohneet	Momina	Moneisha *(0.01)*	Monise
Misty-Sierra	Miyonette	Mohogany	Mominatu	Moneisia	Monisha *(0.02)*
Misty-Skye	Miyonna	Moi	Momoko	Moneka	Monishá
Mistyann	Miyu	Moiché	Mon'dieu	Monekia	Monishay
Mitajah	Miyuki	Moinesha	Mon'et	Monell	Monishia
Mitali	Mizel	Moinque	Mon'i	Moneque	Monisola
Mitasha	Mizetta	Moir	Mon'téne	Monerah	Monita
Mitchaela	Mizlon	Moira *(0.04)*	Mon'terri	Monese	Moniz
Mitchee	Mizuha	Moire	Mona *(0.05)*	Monesha	Monjai'
Mitchell	Mizuki	Mojgan	Mona Lisa	Moneshia	Monkia
Mitchelle	Mjnira	Mojisola	Mona Mohamed	Monet *(0.05)*	Monnazjea
Mitchshaneka	Mkaela	Mojohnay	Mona'y	Monet'	Monnekiya
Miteisha	Mkaul	Mokihana	Mona-Antonia	Monetria	Monnette
Mitena	Mkayla	Moknysia	Mona-Sherjinka	Monette	Monnica
Mitheha	Mkya	Mokunfayo	Monaca	Money	Monnie
Mithella	Mleen	Molana	Monadae	Mong	Monnika
Mithra	Mmelissa	Molanie	Monae *(0.02)*	Moni'ya	Monnisha
Mithuna	Mnar	Moleca	Monaé	Monia	Monqiue
Mithura	Mniha	Molena	Monaeka	Monic	Monquaishia
Mithuya	Mo'nae	Molette	Monah	Monica *(1.97)*	Monquie
Mitilaa	Mo'nay	Moli	Monai	Monica Brianna	Monquisha
Mitra	Mo'nique	Molica	Monalaisa	Monica Christina	Monrissa
Mitsu	Mo-Nae	Molie	Monalisa	Monica Frae	Monrit
Mitsy	Moah	Molika	Monalissa	Monica Josephin	Monroe
Mittie	Moana	Molin	Monasha	Monica Victoria	Monserad
Mittisha	Mobashira	Molina	Monawar	Monica-Ri	Monserat
Mittithyah	Mobina	Molinda	Monay	Monican	Monserrat *(0.04)*

Monserrath	Montiquá	Morelle	Morlisa	Moulan	Mureena
Monsesca	Montique	Morene	Mormadina	Mouly	Muriah
Monsha	Montiqwa	Moreshia	Morna	Moumina	Murial
Monshaé	Montisha	Moressa	Mornae	Mouna	Muriame
Monshay	Montissha	Morgahn	Morning	Mounique	Muriana
Monshaya	Montoya	Morgaine	Morning Star	Mounlady	Muriel *(0.01)*
Monshell	Montrayal	Morgan *(4.75)*	Morning-Song	Mowery	Murielle
Mont'eah	Montrea	Morgan Ashley	Morningstar	Moya	Murita
Montaasia	Montrece	Morgan Cierra	Moronica	Moyi	Murline
Montagia	Montreel	Morgan Shea	Moronke	Moyosore	Murouge
Montaijah	Montrell	Morgan-Anne	Morra	Moyra	Murphy *(0.01)*
Montaiju	Montrelle	Morgan-Breanne	Morranda	Mozelle	Murraya
Montajia	Montrese	Morgan-Jayde	Morreonté	Mrgan	Murrell
Montana *(0.19)*	Montrice	Morgan-Kara	Morrigan	Mriah	Murrthah
Montana-Lee	Montricia	Morgan-Lea	Morrighan	Mrittney	Mursal
Montanez	Montrina	Morgan-Marley	Morrisa	Mrnalini	Musetta
Montanna *(0.01)*	Montrise	Morgan-Rose	Morrisha	Mrranda	Musette
Montara	Montserat	Morgana	Morrishia	Mrrwa	Musfara
Montariel	Montserrat	Morgane *(0.01)*	Morrishka	Mrunal	Mushawnia
Montarra	Monya	Morganlea	Morrison	Mrunmayi	Music
Montashia	Monyaé	Morgann *(0.01)*	Morrissa	Mrysa	Muska
Montasia	Monyai Kenya	Morganna	Morrissey	Ms Rasheika	Mustika
Montavia	Monye	Morganne *(0.03)*	Morrneisha	Mshael	Musu
Montclair	Monyette	Morgayne	Morrow	Muamnkaujligzoo	Mutahira
Monte	Monyque	Morgen *(0.03)*	Morsal	Mubarakah	Mutsumi
Monte Lynn	Monyra	Morggan	Morshai	Mudsaya	Muuno
Montecia	Monzerath	Morghaine	Morssal	Muhubo	Muzzammil
Monteen-Alyse	Monzeratte	Morghan *(0.02)*	Mortega	Mujan	Mwaaya
Monteesha	Monzerrat	Morghen	Morticia	Mukarrah	Mwija
Montegomery	Moody	Morghin	Mortika	Mukelti	My *(0.01)*
Monteia	Moona	Morghyn	Morton	Mulak	My A
Monteiya	Moonisaha	Morgien	Mortoria	Mulki	My Duyen
Montelia	Moqaddasa	Morgin	Moryia	Mulunesh	My Esha
Montellia	Moquet	Morgon	Mosadi	Mum	My Hanh
Montenee	Mor'queishia	Morgunn	Mosangi	Mumina	My Huyen
Montera	Mora	Morgwn	Mosella	Mumtaj	My Kayla
Monterey	Mora-Devi	Morgyn *(0.01)*	Moses	Mun-Lene	My Kethia
Monteria	Morae	Morgynn	Moshá	Muna *(0.02)*	My Kieu
Montesha	Moraea	Morgynne	Moshai	Munaya	My Lynh
Monteshea	Morag	Mori	Moshanay	Muneca	My'angel
Monteshia	Moragan	Moria	Moshanique	Muneera	My'asia
Montgomery	Moragh	Moriah *(0.21)*	Moshawquie	Muneet	My'chelle
(0.01)	Moraima	Moriah Sheree	Moshe	Munira *(0.01)*	My'eisha
Montha	Morales	Moriam	Moshé	Muniya	My'esha
Monti'sia	Moran	Moricka	Moshika	Munkiran	My'iesha
Montia	Moranda	Moriel	Mosie	Munoz	My'ifsha
Montiá	Moranne	Morigan	Motanna	Munpreet	My'isha
Montica	Morayo	Morika	Motayvea	Munro	My'kail
Monticia	More	Morina	Motezía	Munsa	My'keese
Montietta	Moreen	Morissa	Motina	Munsaka	My'keia
Montika	Moreena	Moriya	Mouang	Muntaha	My'kiara
Montina	Moregan	Moriza Mae	Moudane	Murabalie	My'kiela
Montinice	Morel	Morjan	Moufida	Muranda	My'kiera
Montiniqua	Morelia	Morjana	Mouhoubo	Murcedes	My'leshia
Montinique	Morella	Morla	Mouk	Murdena	My'lethia

My'neisha	Mydaijha	Mykalie	Mylaica	Myqnesha	Myrranda
My'nisha	Mydaisha	Mykalin	Mylan	Myquel	Myrthe
My'osha	Mydazia	Mykarah	Mylana	Myra *(0.10)*	Myrtie
My'qyeirra	Mydearia	Mykaya	Mylanie	Myra Shay	Myrtika
My'tanja	Mydelle	Mykayl	Mylann	Myra'nur	Myrtis
My-An	Mydia	Mykayla *(0.03)*	Mylashia	Myracle	Myrtle
My-Anh	Mydisa	Mykaylla	Mylaya	Myrah	Myryam
My-Duyen	Mydresha	Mykéla	Mylaysia	Myraja	Mysean
My-Hanh	Mydrisha	Mykeah	Mylea	Myrakle	Mysha
My-Kim	Myésha	Mykeal	Myleah	Myralee	Myshae
My-Linh	Myeasha	Mykecia	Mylecia	Myranda *(0.12)*	Myshala
Mya *(0.04)*	Myeda	Mykeeia	Mylee	Myrandah	Myshaundra
Myada	Myeekedra	Mykehla	Myleen	Myrandia	Myshawn
Myah *(0.02)*	Myeesha	Mykeia	Myleigh	Myrannda	Myshaya
Myaih	Myeha	Mykeilla	Myleika	Myraven	Myshayla
Myaikasha	Myeisha *(0.02)*	Mykeisha	Myleka	Myrcades	Myshea
Myaja	Myeishia	Mykel *(0.01)*	Mylelia	Myrcedez	Myshel
Myalai	Myeka	Mykela	Mylena	Myrcleine	Myshell
Myale	Myekayla	Mykelah	Mylene *(0.06)*	Myrda	Myshella
Myalisa	Myelle	Mykelin	Myles	Myrdine	Myshia
Myan	Myembree	Mykell	Mylesha	Myreah	Myshona
Myana	Myers	Mykelle	Mylesia	Myreeka	Mysia
Myangel	Myesha *(0.05)*	Mykelti	Mylie	Myreekole	Mystaya
Myani	Myesha Tiangela	Mykelya	Mylika	Myreel	Mysteek
Myann	Myeshia *(0.01)*	Myken	Mylin	Myreia	Mystelle
Myanna	Myessia	Mykenna	Mylinda	Myreille	Mysteri
Myara	Myesthia	Mykenzee	Mylinh	Myrelia	Mystery
Myasia	Myetta	Mykenzie	Mylinn	Myrell	Mysti
Myauh	Myeung	Mykera	Myliqua	Myrella	Mystic
Myazia	Myfanwy	Mykeria	Mylissa	Myrendie	Mystic Rune
Myca	Myghan	Mykerria	Mylles	Myresha	Mystica
Mycaela	Myhia	Mykeya	Mylon	Myretha	Mystie
Mycah *(0.01)*	Myhuyen	Mykeyah	Mylyn	Myreya	Mystique
Mycaila	Myi'tia	Mykeyla	Myna	Myria	Myta'sha
Mycala	Myia *(0.02)*	Mykhayla	Mynda	Myriah *(0.04)*	Mytaijah
Mycalah	Myiah	Mykia *(0.01)*	Myndi	Myriaha	Mytam
Mycethia	Myicia	Mykiah	Myneesha	Myriam *(0.30)*	Mytaneia
Mycha	Myiea	Mykiea	Myneisha	Myriame	Mytchellcole
Mychael	Myieasha	Mykiece	Mynesha	Myrian	Mytesha
Mychaela *(0.01)*	Myiesha *(0.02)*	Mykierra	Myneshia	Myrianne	Mytia
Mychal	Myieshia	Mykiesha	Mynesia	Myrica	Mytintie
Mychala	Myilin	Mykiha	Mynia	Myrical	Mytra
Mychall	Myisha *(0.02)*	Mykil	Mynica	Myrick	Mytriavieate
Myche	Myissa	Mykila	Myniesha	Myridian	Myuana
Mychea	Myji	Mykilah	Mynisha	Myrieal	Myuramy
Mycheal	Myka *(0.01)*	Mykiria	Mynita	Myriesha	Myuri
Mychel	Mykael	Mykisha	Myona	Myrina	Myya
Mychele	Mykaela *(0.01)*	Mykissinee	Myondra	Myrionne	Myyah
Mychelle	Mykah	Mykkal	Myone-Lea	Myris	Myza
Myckaela	Mykaila *(0.01)*	Mykla	Myonia	Myrissa *(0.01)*	Mzriah
Myckaila	Mykal	Mykle	Myonka	Myrka	
Myckel	Mykala *(0.03)*	Mykyah	Myonni	Myrlaine	
Myckenzie	Mykale	Mykyla	Myonshia	Myrlena	**-N-**
Myckla	Mykalei	Myla	Myosha	Myrna *(0.02)*	N *(0.01)*
Myda	Mykalia	Mylah	Myoshia	Myrnaliz	N Dea

N'ala	Na'ela	Naamee	Nadaya	Naelin	Nai'ka
N'brisha	Na'ila	Naashiya	Nadea	Naella	Naia
N'cyontia	Na'imah	Naasia	Nadean	Naemah	Naibla
N'dca	Na'jae	Naastasiah	Nadeen (0.01)	Naemie	Naicora
N'dea	Na'jah	Naatalie	Nadege	Naemo	Naida (0.01)
N'deia	Na'jee	Naayma	Nadeia	Naeroby	Naidalyz
N'dera	Na'jhaé	Naba	Nadeige	Naetrice	Naidy
N'dia	Na'keisha	Nabeeha	Nadejda	Naeve	Naieemah
N'diaza	Na'kera	Nabeela	Nademeh	Naeysha	Naieme
N'digo	Na'kia	Nabeelah	Naden	Nafatali	Naieysha
N'diia	Na'kiana	Nabeha	Nadene	Nafees	Naifeh
N'dya	Na'loni	Nabiha	Nadera	Nafeesa	Naiha
N'jemilé	Na'quasha	Nabihah	Nadesna	Nafeesaa	Naihla
N'kae	Na'quavia	Nabila (0.01)	Nadesta	Nafeesha	Naija
N'kai	Na'quesha	Nabilaa	Nadezhda	Nafis	Naijah
N'kayla	Na'quvia	Nabilah	Nadhiena	Nafisa (0.01)	Naijir
N'keiah	Na'resha	Nabreesha	Nadia (0.39)	Nafisah	Naijja
N'kia	Na'sha	Nabreet	Nadia Marie	Nafisha	Naika
N'kieta	Na'shara	Nabresha	Nadiah	Nafiso	Naikeitha
N'kole	Na'shayla	Nabria	Nadica	Nafissa	Naikeycia
N'nah	Na'sheba	Nabrisha	Nadieska	Nafiza	Naikwandra
N'shyka	Na'shelle	Nabriska	Nadigna	Nagad	Naila
N'taezha	Na'shonda	Nabta	Nadiia	Nagar	Nailah (0.02)
N'yah	Na'stalgia	Nacala	Nadija	Nagela	Nailea
N'ydea	Na'tahasha	Nacarri	Nadijah	Naghem	Naillil
N'zinda	Na'tajah	Naccacia	Nadika	Naghmeh	Naima (0.01)
N'zinga	Na'talya	Nacenya	Nadin	Nagie	Naimah
N.	Na'tasha	Nachanti	Nadina	Nagine	Naimey
Na	Na'tashae	Nachaye	Nadine (0.17)	Nagjije	Naimo
Na Carra	Na'tashianna	Nachebia	Nadini	Nagtha	Naina
Na Cosha	Na'tavia	Nachelle	Nadira	Nagwa	Naiomi
Na Jamie	Na'teara	Nachole	Nadirah	Nagwah	Naiomme
Na Jarae	Na'teasha	Nacina	Nadiri	Nah-Dira	Naipha
Na Kayla	Na'terika	Nacine	Nadison	Nahal	Naira
Na Kia	Na'tesha	Nacirema	Nadiya	Nahall	Naire
Na Kiera	Na'tessia	Nacoal	Nadiyah (0.01)	Nahanni	Nairelle
Na Kiya	Na'tezha	Nacoala	Nadj	Nahdia	Nairim
Na Kya	Na'thia	Nacocha	Nadja (0.01)	Naheen	Naisha (0.01)
Na Shawn	Na'tori	Nacole	Nadjae	Naheer	Naishma
Na Tisha	Na'toria	Nacona	Nadjah	Nahgdea	Naitre
Ná	Na'tosha	Nacorea	Nadjeda	Nahia	Naitsha
Na'aram	Na'triell	Nacoshia	Nadlene	Nahid	Naivasha
Na'asia	Na'twand	Nacqusha	Nadley	Nahida	Naivitsi
Na'aujah	Na-Keia	Nacrisha	Nadra	Nahila	Naivondra
Na'aysha	Na-Quan	Nacy	Naduah	Nahjae	Naiya (0.01)
Na'breanna	Na-Talya	Nada (0.02)	Nadya (0.01)	Nahjah	Naiyana
Na'bria	Naa	Nadacia	Nadzhe	Nahjala	Naiyear
Na'casey	Naadia	Nadaijah	Naechelle	Nahjisa	Naiyelle
Na'chell	Naadirah	Nadaisha	Naedia	Nahketha	Naiyma
Na'ciya	Naadiya	Nadaleen	Naeehma	Nahla	Naja (0.01)
Na'coleone	Naadra	Nadali	Naeema	Nahld	Najaah
Na'deja	Naafiah	Nadaly	Naeja	Nahomi	Najae
Na'dia	Naairah	Nadalynn	Naekeara	Nahtalya	Najaé
Na'eema	Naama	Nadash	Naela	Nahyeera Shanti	Najah (0.02)
Na'eisha	Naamah	Nadasha	Naelia	Nai	Najai

Najama	Nakawe	Nakia *(0.07)*	Nali	Nanda	Naquesheaun
Najare	Nakay	Nakiah *(0.01)*	Nalia	Nanda-Devi	Naquesia
Najarel	Nakaya	Nakiaya	Nalicia	Nande	Naquessa
Najaria	Nakaycha	Nakiba	Nalijah	Nandee	Naquila
Najaun	Nakayla *(0.01)*	Nakie	Nalini	Nandele	Naquille
Najavia	Nakaylia	Nakiea	Nalis	Nandi *(0.02)*	Naquion
Najaza	Nakazi	Nakiel	Nalisa	Nandia	Naquisha
Najazemin	Nakea *(0.01)*	Nakiella	Nalisha	Nandini	Naquita
Najda	Nakeadlia	Nakienah	Naliya	Nandita	Naqunsha
Najea	Nakearah	Nakiesha *(0.01)*	Naliyah	Nandy	Naquonda
Najee *(0.01)*	Nakearian	Nakieya	Nallah	Nandzy	Naquria
Najée	Nakechia	Nakika	Nalleli	Naneisha	Nar'leshia
Najeé Jeneil	Nakeda	Nakilla	Nallely *(0.05)*	Nanette *(0.01)*	Nara *(0.01)*
Najeea	Nakedra	Nakilyyah	Nalonee	Naniko	Naraly
Najeeah	Nakedria	Nakimya	Nalorin	Nanita	Naranda
Najeeba	Nakeéa	Nakina	Nalumaga	Nanna	Naray
Najemah	Nakeebia	Nakira	Nalungia	Nannette	Narcessa
Najera	Nakeeria	Nakiria	Naly	Nansi	Narchadille
Najerai	Nakeesha	Nakisa	Nalyssa	Nanya	Narcharlette
Najeray	Nakeeta	Nakisha *(0.01)*	Nam	Nanyamka	Narchelle
Najeria	Nakeethia	Nakishewa	Nam-Cam	Nao	Narcika
Najetta	Nakeeva	Nakishia	Namara	Naoko	Narcissa
Najh	Nakeeya	Nakiska	Namarion	Naoky	Narcisse
Najha	Nakeia *(0.01)*	Nakita *(0.03)*	Namaryia	Naome	Narcy
Najhctet	Nakeidra	Nakitra	Namaudi	Naomee	Narda
Najibah	Nakeisha *(0.02)*	Nakiya *(0.01)*	Nami	Naomh	Nardeep
Najieh	Nakeita	Nakiyah	Namibia	Naomi *(0.64)*	Nardia
Najina	Nakeitha	Nakkia	Namiesha	Naomia	Nardy
Najiya	Nakeitra	Nakkita	Namika	Naomie *(0.04)*	Narea
Najiyyah	Nakel	Nako	Namira	Naomy *(0.01)*	Nareeka
Najja	Nakela	Nakoa	Namita	Naon	Nareen
Najla *(0.01)*	Nakelah	Nakori	Namitha	Naphaterria	Narel
Najma *(0.01)*	Nakelya	Nakosha	Namra	Naphina	Narges
Najmah	Nakema	Nakota	Namrata	Naphtali	Nargis
Najmi	Nakena	Nakotah	Namrataa	Napier	Narhalee
Najna	Nakendra	Nakouisha	Namrit	Naporscha	Nari
Najocelyn	Nakenja	Nakyah	Namrita	Naporsha	Naria
Najshae	Nakenya	Nakyala	Nan	Naporshia	Nariah
Najshea	Nakeria	Nakyera	Nana *(0.01)*	Napualani	Narianna
Najtoria	Nakerra	Nakyia	Nanaama	Naqasha	Nariateresa
Najuma	Nakescha	Nakyobe	Nanake	Naqavia	Narie
Najwa	Nakesha *(0.01)*	Nakyra	Nanaki	Naqia	Nariea
Najwan	Nakeshia	Nakysha	Nanako	Naqima	Nariessa
Najyá	Naketa	Nakyzia	Nanami	Naqoyah	Narika
Nakacia	Naketah	Nala *(0.01)*	Nanayaá	Naquaia	Nariko
Nakahri	Naketris	Nalah	Nancee	Naquailla	Narina
Nakai	Nakeva	Nalahn	Nancey	Naquajha	Narine
Nakail	Nakeya *(0.01)*	Nalanda	Nanci *(0.03)*	Naquan	Narinpon
Nakailla	Nakeyah	Nalani *(0.01)*	Nancie	Naquanda	Narisa
Nakairá	Nakeyda	Nalashia	Nancy *(1.13)*	Naquandra	Narise
Nakala	Nakeyia	Nalayah	Nancy Lee	Naquanta	Narisha
Nakaria	Nakeysha	Nalaysia	Nancy Lyn	Naquasha	Narissa *(0.01)*
Nakarri	Nakeyta	Naleisa	Nancy-Ann	Naquasia	Narjes
Nakasha	Naki	Nalesia	Nancydiane	Naquavia	Narjis
Nakasia	Naki-Aki	Nalexia	Nancys	Naquesha	Narkelia

Narlischwa	Nashe	Nastajia	Nataliya	Natausha	Nathifa
Narmany	Nashé	Nastalgia	Nataliyah	Natavia	Nathika
Narmeen	Nashea	Nastasha	Natalka	Natavion	Nathima
Narmin	Nasheema	Nastasia (0.01)	Natallea	Natavya	Nathina
Narmina	Nasheena	Nastasja	Natallia	Nataya (0.01)	Nathley
Narmisha	Nashelle	Nastassia	Natallie	Natayia	Nathmaulynna
Narmy	Nashely	Nastassja (0.01)	Natally	Natayle	Nathmoulich
Narnia	Nashema	Nastazia	Nataly (0.13)	Nataylia	Nathyelli
Narolin	Nashera	Nasteho	Natalya (0.02)	Natayne	Natia
Naromie	Nasheta	Nastia	Natalyn	Nataysha	Natiá
Narqusha	Nasheye	Nastofia	Natalynn	Natazeia	Natiah
Narrekia	Nashia	Nastrashia	Nataná	Natazha	Natiaha
Narruilyn	Nashine	Nasya (0.01)	Natane	Natazia	Natiaira
Narsha	Nashira	Nasyah	Natani-Lynn	Natazzja	Natialya
Narsheika	Nashiyah	Nasyitah	Natania	Nate	Natiana
Narshena	Nashiyat	Nasynia	Natanya	Naté	Natianna
Narsherika	Nashjam	Naszreen	Natara	Natea	Natibidad
Nartica	Nashlee	Nata Jah	Natari	Nateasha	Natice-Dina
Narumi	Nashley	Natacha (0.04)	Nataria	Natecia	Natichsha
Narusha	Nashlyn	Natacia	Natariel	Natedine	Naticia
Nary	Nashlyne	Natacsha	Natarsha	Nateena	Natiera
Naryman	Nashmeyah	Natahnee	Natarshia	Nateesha	Natiesha
Nasanin	Nashonda	Nataia	Natasa	Natehia	Natifa
Nasara	Nashonica	Nataija	Natasah	Nateisha	Natifah
Nasasha	Nashonta	Nataisha	Natasala	Natekerria	Natih
Nasaundria	Nashreen	Nataja	Natascha (0.01)	Natelie	Natijah
Nascha	Nashwa	Natajah	Nataschia	Natercia	Natika
Nasea	Nashya	Natajia	Natascia	Nateria	Natiki
Naseana	Nashyra	Natajoin	Natash	Naterra	Natilee
Naseeb	Nasi	Natajsha	Natasha (1.41)	Naterria	Natilie
Naseem	Nasia	Nataki	Natasha Joy	Natesha (0.01)	Natilli
Naseera	Nasiasia	Natal	Natasha	Nateshia	Natily
Nash	Nasieda	Natale	Labrenda	Nateya	Natilya
Nasha	Nasiem	Natalee (0.05)	Natasha Maria	Nathalee	Natima
Nashaba	Nasiha	Nataleh	Natasha Rachel	Nathali	Natina
Nashabreá	Nasim	Nataleigh	Natasha-Lee	Nathalia (0.03)	Nationn
Nashae	Nasina	Nataley	Natasha-Rae	Nathalie (0.24)	Natisha (0.01)
Nashala	Nasiyah	Natali (0.05)	Natashal	Nathalie Ta	Natisna
Nashali	Naslie	Natalia (0.36)	Natashalyn	Nathalin	Natita
Nashall	Nasonavo	Natalia Carmesh	Natashea	Nathaline	Nativiad (0.01)
Nashalyn	Nasondra	Natalie (3.08)	Natashia (0.02)	Nathalis	Natividad Caitl
Nashan	Nasra (0.01)	Natalie Cat Tuon	Natashiana	Nathaly (0.05)	Natiya
Nashana	Nasreen (0.01)	Natalie Dieneis	Natashja	Nathalya	Natiyah
Nashanda	Nasrin	Natalie Nicaule	Natashua	Nathan	Natjassia
Nashandra	Nasrine	Natalie-Ann	Natashya	Nathania	Natjjaé
Nashante	Nasro	Natalie-Anne	Natasia (0.01)	Nathaniel	Natlie
Nashantre	Nassaundra	Natalie-Chantal	Natasja	Nathanya	Natly
Nashara	Nasseem	Natalie-Marie	Natasjha	Nathanyel	Natondra
Nashaun	Nassia	Nataliee	Natassa	Nathasa	Natondrá
Nashauwna	Nassim	Natalija	Natassia (0.01)	Nathasha	Natori (0.02)
Nashawn	Nassrin	Natalin	Natassja (0.01)	Nathasia	Natoria
Nashawnda	Nasstaja	Natalina	Natassje	Nathchell	Natorian
Nashay	Nasstasja	Nataline	Natassjia	Natheana	Natorica
Nashayla	Nastaja	Natalis	Natasza	Natheena	Natorious
Nashda	Nastajah	Natalise	Natatie	Nathia	Natorrie

Natory	Nauti'ca	Nawal	Nazareth	Neala	Neeasia-Taylor
Natosha (0.02)	Nautica (0.02)	Naween	Nazareth-Jean	Nealchae	Neeca
Natoshia	Nautica Aisha	Nawell	Nazarin-I	Nealee	Neecha
Natoshya	Nautikah	Nawincia	Nazcha	Neali	Needaá
Natoya (0.01)	Nava	Naxehlix	Nazdar	Nealy	Needea
Natoyria	Navada	Naya	Nazel-Ann	Neamber	Needra
Natozha	Navah	Nayaab	Nazgol	Neandra	Neeha
Natravia	Navaira	Nayab	Nazia	Neanet	Neeka
Natrecia	Navaisha	Nayade	Naziba	Neanila	Neeki
Natrelle	Navalya	Nayalee	Nazie	Neanna	Neela
Natrice	Navante	Nayambi	Nazifa	Nearie	Neelam (0.01)
Natrinia	Navarra	Nayana	Nazik	Nearyrath	Neelem
Natriona	Navarre	Nayanna	Nazira	Neasa	Neelema
Natroya	Navarria	Nayantara	Nazirah	Neasau	Neeley
Natsha	Navasha	Nayantra	Naziroh	Neasha	Neeli
Natsuko	Navdeep (0.01)	Nayari	Nazish	Neasia	Neelika
Natsumi (0.01)	Navdip	Nayaset	Naziya	Neastacia	Neelkiran
Nattalie	Navea	Naycole	Nazje	Neatia	Neelofer
Nattaly	Navedeep	Nayeasha	Nazlah	Neawana	Neelufar
Nattassia	Naveen (0.01)	Nayeli (0.11)	Nazli	Neaysha	Neely
Nattie	Navera	Nayelia	Nazly	Nebal	Neena (0.02)
Nattoriyah	Navey	Nayelli	Nazmeen	Nebat	Neenah
Natural	Navi	Nayelly (0.01)	Nazneen	Nebia	Neeoshee
Nature	Navia	Nayely (0.03)	Nazra	Nebiha	Neera
Naturel	Navidia	Nayha	Nazsane	Nebila	Neeraja
Natusha	Navie	Nayia	Nazurah	Nebilah	Neesa
Natwanda	Naviesha	Nayiesha	Nazya	Nebraska	Neeshaa
Natwiya	Navijha	Nayirah	Nazzula	Nebreiagh	Neeshma
Natyare	Navila	Nayla	Nbarbara	Nebridga	Neeta
Natyeli	Navinder	Nayla Xochitl	Nchekwube	Nebrina	Neethu
Natyja	Navit	Naylea	Ncroc	Nechama	Neeti
Natyra	Navita	Naylynn	Nda	Nechbedije	Neetu
Natysia	Navjeet	Nayna	Ndia	Nechelle	Neeva
Natyssja	Navjhot	Nayomi	Ndidi	Nechoal	Neeve
Nau'tica	Navjit	Nayomie	Ne Sharri	Nechol	Neeyah
Naudeep	Navjot (0.01)	Nayosha	Né Cohl	Nechoma	Neeyi
Naudia (0.01)	Navjoyt	Nayra	Néamber	Necia	Nefer
Naudie	Navkarn	Nayrah	Néasia	Necoius	Nefertari
Naudtia	Navkiran	Naysa	Nékayla	Necole	Nefertary
Naudtica	Navkiranjit	Naysha	Nékedra	Necoli	Nefertia
Naukasha	Navleen	Nayshon	Nékeisha	Nectaly	Nefertirri
Naula	Navlpreet	Nayshonda	Nékendria	Neda (0.02)	Nefertiti
Nauncé	Navneet (0.02)	Nayshya	Nékia	Neda-Z	Nefertri
Naundi	Navneetkaur	Nayshyla	Néosha	Nedaa	Nefeteria
Naundy	Navnit	Naysla	Néquel	Nedaara	Nefeterria
Naupreet	Navondra	Naytaya	Néshonda	Nedah	Nefferitti
Naura	Navpreet (0.01)	Naytese	Néssa	Nedda	Neffertia
Naureen	Navreen	Naytoshia	Néteria	Nedeljka	Neffertti
Naureesha	Navreet	Naz	Ne-Ne-	Nedgee	Nefia
Naurice	Navroop	Naza	Ne-Shay	Nedia	Nefratiria
Nausha	Navrose	Nazaneen	Nea	Nedly	Nefretiri
Nausiccaa	Navroup	Nazanine	Neah	Nedra	Neftali
Naut'ica	Navsurkamal	Nazaree	Neaha	Nedria	Neftali'
Nautasha	Navy	Nazareen	Neajha	Nedrianna	Neftaly
Nauteshé	Nawah	Nazaret	Neaka	Neeah	Negan

Negar	Neketa	Nema	Nerisa	Netika	Ngozi
Negat	Neketrice	Nemah	Nerissa (0.01)	Netisha	Nguatem
Negeen	Neketriz	Nemaris	Nerissa Jane	Netoya	Nguyen (0.01)
Neggin	Nekeya	Nemi	Nerita	Netsanet	Nguyet
Negin	Nekeysha	Nemisha	Nerittza	Netta	Nha
Neha (0.05)	Nekia (0.01)	Nemma	Nerivnea	Nettie	Nha-Khuyen
Nehal	Nekiara	Nena (0.01)	Nerlande	Nettiesh	Nhama
Nehali	Nekisha	Nena-Estelle	Nerlene	Netuan	Nhan
Nehan	Nekiya	Nency	Nerlie	Neubian	Nhandi
Nehanda	Nekiyah	Nenna	Nerline	Neva (0.01)	Nhaomi
Nehcmi	Neko	Nenorita	Nerlita	Nevada (0.02)	Nharseria
Nehemie	Nekoda	Nenzie	Nerly	Nevadria	Nhat
Nehemy	Nekol	Neokia	Neroobha	Nevarda	Nhatey
Nehmat	Nekya	Neokya	Nerriah	Neve	Nhavan
Nehtia	Nekyhra	Neolla	Nerrisa	Neveen	Nhawndie
Nehushta	Nekyia	Neombi	Nery	Nevetha	Nhi (0.02)
Neia	Nela	Neomi	Nesa	Neveyan	Nhi-Thuc
Neiah	Nelani	Neomia	Nesana	Nevia	Nhiya
Neialette	Nelanie	Neon	Nesby	Neville	Nhooph
Neica	Nelanthi	Neona	Neschelle	Nevin	Nhu (0.01)
Neicia	Nelcy	Neondra	Nese	Nevonne	Nhu Teresa
Neicy	Nelda	Neoni	Nesha	Nevyat	Nhu-Mai
Neida (0.01)	Nele	Neonila	Neshara	Newborn	Nhu-Y
Neidasha	Neli	Neosha	Neshari	Newtondrea	Nhung
Neidi	Nelida	Nepeya	Neshawn	Newtori	Nhya
Neidy	Nelisa	Nephateria	Neshay	Nexxis	Nhydaisha
Neiibra	Nelisha	Nephatoria	Neshayla	Ney Shae	Nhyrico
Neijia	Nelissa	Nephewteirie	Neshca	Neya	Ni Cara
Neikoo	Nelka	Nephititi	Neshea	Neyah	Ni Eisha
Neila	Nell (0.01)	Nephratiti	Neshia	Neyambah	Ni Gena
Neilah	Nella	Nephtali	Neshiyqah	Neyasha	Nía
Neilia	Nellande	Nephtalie	Neshon	Neyata	Ni'acqua
Neily	Nelle	Nephtaly	Nesmah	Neyda	Ni'asha
Neima	Nelleen	Nephthali	Nesreen	Neydia	Ni'asia
Neimath	Nellie (0.03)	Neqiynah	Nesrien	Neydin	Ni'chelle
Neina	Nellis	Nequa	Nesrin	Neyesia	Ni'cosha
Neira	Nellissa	Nequandria	Nesrine	Neyha	Ni'eisha
Neisa	Nellofer	Nequia	Nessa	Neykare	Ni'eshia
Neisa Soledad	Nelly (0.06)	Nequiesha	Nessaya	Neysa (0.01)	Ni'geria
Neisha (0.01)	Nelmar	Nequila	Nessenta	Neysha	Ni'jala
Neitalia	Nelsa	Nequoyah	Nessreen	Neyshaliz	Ni'kira
Neiya	Nelsade	Nereida (0.03)	Nestor	Neyshana	Ni'nesha
Nejal	Nelsha	Nereira	Neta	Neyshia	Ni'ree
Nejane	Nelson	Nereliz	Netae	Neyshmelys	Ni'shawnda
Neka	Nelssie	Nerelys	Netali	Nezariel	Ni'terica
Nekailyah	Nelsy	Nereyda (0.01)	Netalia	Nezerena	Ni'ya
Nekane	Nelteisha	Nereyida	Netania	Nezia	Ni'yana
Nekayah	Neltha	Nergez	Netanya (0.01)	Ng'endo	Ni'yelle
Nekayla	Nelufar Nicky	Nergis	Netasha	Nga	Ni-Jette
Nekecia	Nelufer	Neria	Netasia	Ngaire	Nia (0.17)
Nekeeta	Nelvy	Neriah	Netaya	Ngalula	Nia Gal
Nekeisha	Nely	Neriangela	Neteyah	Ngan	Nia Kedra
Nekela	Nelyda	Nerica	Nethania	Ngar	Nia'jay
Nekelia	Nelzina	Nerida	Nethaum	Ngoc (0.02)	Nia'keya
Nekesha	Nelzy	Nerin	Nethmi	Ngoc-Dung	Nia-Marie

Nia-Mercedes	Nichaela	Nickolet	Nidedra	Nijara	Niketa
Nia-Nicole	Nichalette	Nickolette	Nidhi	Nije	Niketta-Lynn
Nia-Symoné	Nicheal	Nickota	Nidia (0.02)	Nijee	Nikeya (0.01)
Niaa	Nicheala	Nickovia	Nidiathamayra	Nijel	Nikeyairra
Niab	Nichée	Nickta	Nidirah	Nijessica	Nikeyla
Niabi	Nichele	Nicku	Nidja	Nijheria	Nikeyna
Niachea	Nichell	Nicky (0.01)	Nieara	Nijima	Nikeysha
Niah	Nichelle (0.06)	Nicky-Lee	Nieca	Nijintra	Nikeyshia
Niairelle	Nichelle Carly	Nicle	Niecele	Nijired	Nikha
Niaja	Nichoal	Nicloe	Nieceshay	Nijma	Nikhaule
Niakita	Nichol (0.01)	Nico	Niecha	Nijra	Nikhia
Niala	Nichola	Nico'le	Niechia	Nijzah	Nikhita
Nialah	Nicholas (0.01)	Nicoe	Nieesha	Nijzha	Nikhito
Niall	Nichole (0.49)	Nicol	Niegera	Nik Kayla	Niki (0.07)
Nialla	Nichole Alexsan	Nicola (0.07)	Niegi	Nik'quasha	Nikia (0.02)
Niam	Nicholett	Nicolas (0.01)	Nieka	Nika (0.03)	Nikiah
Niamah	Nicholette (0.01)	Nicolasa	Niekia	Nikada	Nikiara
Niamat	Nicholetti	Nicole (7.48)	Niela	Nikael	Nikiawonda
Niamb	Nicholin	Nicole Elise	Nielia	Nikaela	Nikie
Niambi (0.01)	Nicholla	Nicole Kikiula	Nielofer	Nikaila	Nikiea
Niambre	Nicholle (0.03)	Nicole Marie	Nielsy	Nikala	Nikierra
Niamey	Nichollette	Nicolé	Niema	Nikalia	Nikika
Niamh (0.01)	Nicholson	Nicole-Anne	Niemah	Nikalla	Nikila
Niana	Nick-Esther	Nicole-Bess	Niemat	Nikara	Nikima
Nianahlisa	Nickale	Nicole-Lucia	Nienke	Nikarra	Nikimah
Niandra	Nickay	Nicole-Stephanie	Niesa	Nikashinna	Nikina
Niandre	Nickayla	Nicoleen	Niesha (0.01)	Nikaya	Nikira
Niani	Nickdreka	Nicolemarie	Nieshia	Nikaya-Lee	Nikiraya
Niaquanda	Nickee	Nicolena	Nieszka	Nikayah	Nikisha
Niara (0.01)	Nickeela	Nicolenne	Nieve	Nikayla (0.02)	Nikita (0.09)
Niari	Nickeia	Nicolet	Nieves	Nikayla-Lee	Nikitah
Niaria	Nickeisha	Nicoleta	Nifeesa	Nikaysha	Nikitha
Niasbey	Nickeita	Nicolett	Nigea	Nike	Nikitia
Niasha	Nickeitra	Nicoletta	Nigel	Nikea	Nikitra
Niashia	Nickelle	Nicolette (0.31)	Nigela	Nikeaira	Nikitrius
Niasia	Nickeria	Nicolina (0.01)	Nigeria (0.01)	Nikeashay	Nikitta
Niaterra	Nickesha	Nicoline	Nigerria	Nikeba	Nikiya
Niatikqua	Nicketa	Nicollai	Niha	Nikecia	Nikiyah
Niaya	Nickey	Nicolle (0.07)	Nihara	Nikeeta	Nikka
Niayla	Nickeya	Nicollete	Niharika	Nikeia	Nikkaye
Niaz	Nickhera	Nicollette (0.03)	Nihchelle	Nikeille	Nikkea
Nibria	Nicki (0.02)	Nicolshia	Nihiemah	Nikeisa	Nikkemma
Nibyré	Nickia	Nicolya	Nihkea	Nikeisha	Nikkeria
Nica	Nickiah	Nicolyn	Nii Lante	Nikekia	Nikketa-Marie
Nicaella	Nickie (0.01)	Nicona	Niina	Nikel	Nikketta
Nicalette	Nickira	Nicosha (0.01)	Niisa	Nikela	Nikkeya
Nicara	Nickitta	Nicoshil	Niisii	Nikelie	Nikkhia
Nicarra	Nickkia	Nicoya	Niiyobinesiik	Nikelle (0.01)	Nikki (0.33)
Nicayla	Nickkole	Nicqualya	Nijá	Nikena	Nikki Hien
Nicca	Nickky	Nicte-Ha	Nija (0.01)	Nikeona	Nikki Thuy
Nicco	Nickol	Nictel	Nija Ebonique	Nikera	Nikki-Anne
Niccole	Nickola	Nida (0.01)	Nijaa	Nikeria	Nikki-Lynn
Niccolette	Nickolas	Nidavah	Nijae	Nikeriya	Nikki-Nancy
Nicele	Nickole (0.02)	Nidda	Nijah (0.01)	Nikerria	Nikkia (0.01)
Nicha	Nickolena	Nideara	Nijai	Nikesha	Nikkiah

Nikkialexa	Nile	Ninna	Niromi	Nita	Niykeyá
Nikkie	Nileen	Ninnetta	Nirosha	Nita Rae	Niyla
Nikkiesha	Nilema	Ninochka	Niroshi	Nitai	Niyoki
Nikkii	Nilena	Ninorta	Niroshitha	Nitalia	Niyoksa
Nikkila	Nili	Ninoshka	Nirruba	Nitanis	Niyomi
Nikkilya	Nilima	Ninoska	Niruba	Nitara	Niz
Nikkirra	Nilmarie	Ninozzka	Nirujaa	Nitasaa	Niza
Nikkisha	Niloojini	Ninpha	Nirujah	Nitasha	Nizandra
Nikkita *(0.01)*	Niloufar	Ninthuya	Nirujiga	Nitasia	Nizharé
Nikkitta	Nilsa	Ninu	Nirusha	Nitaya	Nizhay
Nikkiya	Nilseen	Ninundria	Nirusika	Nitha	Nizhone
Nikko	Nilufa	Ninveh	Nirvana	Nitharshana	Nizhoni
Nikkole *(0.01)*	Nilufar	Niobe	Nirvaná	Nitharsiga	Nizhonie
Nikkolet	Nilufer	Niobi	Nisa *(0.02)*	Nithusa	Nizza
Nikkolette	Nilufur	Nioca	Nisaa	Niti	Nizziria
Nikkya	Nilvia	Niocca	Nisan	Nitia	Njera
Nikkyia	Nilyah	Nioka	Nisana	Nitianna	Njeri
Niko	Nilze	Niombe	Nisany	Nitika	Njvon
Nikoa	Nima	Niome	Nisbeth	Nitisha	Nkao
Nikoda	Nimali	Niomi	Nisean	Nitori	Nkechinyere
Nikohl	Nimaliny	Niomie	Nisede	Nitra	Nkeiruka
Nikol	Nimao	Niondra	Nisga	Nitshell	Nkem
Nikola	Nimara	Nioxsha	Nisha *(0.04)*	Nittan	Nkenge
Nikolai	Nimat	Niozjia	Nishalic	Nitu	Nkolika
Nikole *(0.07)*	Nimata	Nipaporn	Nishan	Nitya	Nlersadies
Nikoleta	Nimeaga	Nipawset	Nishana	Nitzabel	Nneamaka
Nikoletta	Nimeh	Niqasha	Nishani	Nitzel	Nneka *(0.01)*
Nikolette *(0.01)*	Nimenesha	Niquay	Nishanne	Niulka	Nnenna
Nikolia	Nimkii-	Niquea	Nishara	Niurka	Nneoma
Nikolina *(0.01)*	Waasmokwe	Niquel	Nishat	Niusha	Nnijah
Nikolle	Nimmesia	Niquela	Nishauntae	Niva	Nnkechika
Nikomia	Nimmi	Niquelle	Nishay	Nivaashinyi	Noa
Nikoo	Nimmy	Niquesna	Nishayla	Nivany	Noaf
Nikota	Nimo	Niquetta	Nisheba	Nivatha	Noah *(0.01)*
Nikoya	Nimotalai	Niquila	Nishedra	Nivea	Noahamin
Nikquila	Nimra	Niquisha	Nisheika	Nivedita	Noam
Nikté	Nimrah	Niquita	Nisheka	Nivetha *(0.01)*	Noami
Nikxi	Nimrat	Nira	Nishelle	Nivethaa	Noamie
Nikya	Nimret	Nirali *(0.01)*	Nishi	Nivette	Noar
Nikyia	Nimrit	Niranda	Nishin	Nivia	Noarhan
Nikyla	Nimrta	Nirba	Nishita	Nivin	Noatik
Nikyra	Nin	Nireca	Nishkala	Nivitha	Noble
Nil	Nina *(0.47)*	Nireeka	Nishma	Nivra	Nobuko
Nila *(0.01)*	Nina Jasmine	Nireka	Nishon	Niwekhaa	Nocole
Nilaanie	Nina Ni	Nirelle	Nishonda	Nixcee	Nocona
Nilah	Nina-Francesca	Nirenda	Nishtha	Niya *(0.02)*	Nodaca
Nilaiss	Ninaellen	Niriesha	Nisia	Niyá	Nodeeia
Nilaja	Ninah	Nirisha	Nisma	Niya-Shavon	Nodekah
Nilajah	Ninakupenda	Nirjiga	Nisreen	Niyah *(0.01)*	Nodia
Nilam	Ninamarie	Nirlap	Nisrene	Niyailieka	Nodja
Nilani	Ninel	Nirma	Nisrine	Niyara	Nodrecka
Nilda	Ninesha	Nirmal	Nissa *(0.01)*	Niyati	Noe
Nildamaris	Nineveh	Nirman	Nissandle	Niyia	Noehly
Nildia	Ninfa	Nirmeen	Nissma	Niyika	Noehmi
Nildjah	Nini	Nirobiá	Nissy	Niyirah	Noel *(0.09)*

Noela	Noltavia	Norianna	Nou *(0.01)*	Nunca	Ny-Quisha
Noelain	Nolvia	Norianne	Nouche	Nuntaya	Ny-Shel
Noelani *(0.01)*	Noma	Noribelle	Nouf	Nunzia	Nya *(0.02)*
Noelcy	Nomblé	Noricell	Noufar	Nuquita	Nya-She
Noele	Nomie	Norida	Nouha	Nur *(0.01)*	Nyaa
Noeli	Nona *(0.01)*	Norie	Nouhad	Nur Kamilah	Nyachombanyathi
Noelia *(0.01)*	Noneka	Noriko	Nour *(0.03)*	Nura	Nyadah
Noelie	Nonely	Norine	Nour Al-Houda	Nurah	Nyadoar
Noelina	Noni	Norisha	Noura	Nuran	Nyah *(0.01)*
Noell	Nonica	Norisma	Noureen	Nurce	Nyahlette
Noella *(0.01)*	Nonieann	Norissa	Nova *(0.01)*	Nureaka	Nyaijha
Noelle *(0.24)*	Nonik	Norjoria	Novalene	Nurell	Nyaisha
Noelle Dayshara	Nonika	Norkaa	Novaly	Nureshá	Nyajah
Noelle Eve	Nonisja	Norkeya	Novamarie	Nurey	Nyakia
Noelle-Renee	Nonna	Norlande	Novanna	Nuri	Nyambi
Noelly	Nontobeko	Norlin	Novara	Nuria	Nyamekye
Noeloni	Noon	Norlyn	Novella	Nuria Maria	Nyana
Noely *(0.01)*	Noor *(0.05)*	Norma *(0.21)*	Novelle	Nuribeth	Nyanaka
Noema	Noor-Ul-Aeen	Norma-Mary	Novelte	Nuris	Nyanda
Noemi *(0.22)*	Noora	Norma-Rae	November	Nurisha	Nyangore
Noemi Angeli	Noorah	Normady	Noveneet	Nursel	Nyani
Noemie *(0.34)*	Nooran	Normalee	Novia	Nurul	Nyara
Noemy *(0.05)*	Nooranne	Norman	Novice	Nury	Nyaria
Noessy	Noorey	Normandi	Novjoot	Nusayba	Nyarika
Nogah	Noorie	Normandie	Nowree	Nusaybah	Nyarko
Nogoye	Nophe	Normayda	Nowrin	Nusheen	Nyaruot
Noha	Nora *(0.24)*	Normekia	Noyani	Nushelle	Nyasa
Nohadra	Nora May	Normendie	Noyica	Nushmeen	Nyasha
Nohal	Noraa	Normesha	Nozania	Nushrat	Nyashe
Nohelany	Noraann	Normice	Nozomi	Nusirat	Nyasi
Noheli *(0.01)*	Norah *(0.01)*	Norquida	Nsheika	Nuvea	Nyasia *(0.01)*
Nohelis	Noral Huda	Norrell	Nshwah	Nuvi	Nyasiah
Nohely *(0.09)*	Noraleen	Norriana	Nsibisi	Nuvia	Nyat
Nohemi *(0.02)*	Noralisia	Norrie	Nsren	Nuvneet	Nybora
Nohemie	Norandria	Norriesha	Ntoh	Nuwani	Nybriah
Nohemy	Norangely	Norrisa	Ntosake	Nuwar	Nycale
Nohrwafi	Norann	Norshell	Ntumba	Nwal	Nycara
Nohwlia	Noranna	Nortaisha	Nu	Nwanna	Nychelle
Noilen	Norasha	Nortana	Nuah	Nwanyinna	Nycole *(0.01)*
Noirá	Norasia	Nortecia	Nub	Nwoye	Nycolette
Nojod	Norchelle	Nortee	Nubia *(0.03)*	Ny Jarika	Nycolle
Nokeyia	Noreem	Norteshia	Nucola	Ny'asia	Nyda
Nokia	Noreen *(0.02)*	Nortice	Nuer	Ny'eekquia	Nydézsa
Nokomis	Noreena	Norwood	Nuesha	Ny'esha	Nydeshia
Nola *(0.01)*	Noreene	Nosagie	Nuha	Ny'ira	Nydia *(0.02)*
Nolan	Norela	Noshaba	Nuiok	Ny'jeri	Nydiana
Nolande	Norelle	Nosita	Nujai	Ny'jia	Nydrah
Nolani	Norely	Noslein	Nujeema	Ny'keara	Nyeama
Nolawit	Norena	Nosybah	Nukea	Ny'keira	Nyeasha
Nolbia	Norene	Not *(0.01)*	Nukeisha	Ny'keisha	Nyedoar
Noldine	Norgyn	Notasha	Nukisha	Ny'kerria	Nyeelah
Nolette	Norhan	Nothyna	Nukiya	Ny'kia	Nyeema
Nolia	Nori	Notichia	Nukolla	Ny'kira	Nyeemah
Nolisha	Noriah	Notra	Numa	Ny'quandra	Nyeeshia
Nolle	Noriam	Notrusley	Numera	Ny-Jai	Nyeisha *(0.01)*

Nyeja	Nykesia	Nyreisher	O'keefe	Obiamaka	Odette *(0.01)*
Nyeka	Nykessia	Nyrel	O'kellia	Obianuju	Odile
Nyekia	Nykeya	Nyri	O'kema	Obichukwu	Odilia
Nyema	Nykeyah	Nyriah	O'kera	Obikwelu	Odina
Nyema'sha	Nykhol	Nyrie	O'kevia	Obna	Odinaka
Nyemah	Nykia *(0.02)*	Nyrmari	O'lecia	Obrianna	Odira
Nyemia	Nykiah	Nyrra	O'leya	Occendra	Odita
Nyenda	Nykiana	Nysa	O'lissa	Occo	Odranae
Nyende	Nykiara	Nysha	O'livia	Occonelle Prehu	Odyssey
Nyera	Nykiel	Nyshá	O'malley	Ocea	Odyssey-
Nyesha *(0.01)*	Nykijah	Nyshae	O'meisha	Ocean *(0.02)*	Dominique
Nyeshia	Nykimmie	Nyshaleena	O'najma	Oceana *(0.01)*	Odzhane
Nyger	Nykira	Nyshara	O'neal	Oceananna	Ofaq
Nygera	Nykisha	Nyshequa	O'nealsha	Oceane *(0.01)*	Ofelia *(0.03)*
Nygeria	Nykita	Nyshia	O'neesha	Oceania	Oferina
Nyheisha	Nykkayta	Nyshira	O'neisha	Oceanna	Ofracina
Nyia *(0.01)*	Nykki	Nysrete	O'nesha	Oceanne	Ogasso
Nyiá	Nykkoel	Nyssa *(0.02)*	O'neysha	Oceaonna	Ogbazghi
Nyiah	Nykkole	Nystrand	O'nyia	Oceon	Ogechukwu
Nyiara	Nykol	Nytajha	O'quasha	Ochelle	Ogeeda
Nyiazia	Nykole	Nytasha	O'reilly	Ochitsukanai	Oglacia
Nyibol	Nykyria	Nyteka	O'reshia	Ocia	Ohara
Nyiesa	Nykyta	Nytessia	O'rhyan	Ocianna	Ohinninyia
Nyiesha	Nyla *(0.02)*	Nytessja	O'seannesi	Ocie	Oijah
Nyikisha	Nylah	Nytevea	O'sha	Ocina	Oivia
Nyindia	Nylar	Nytia	O'shae	Ociri	Oixiusu
Nyisha	Nylasha	Nytiasha	O'shan	Ocquianna	Oja'nique
Nyishia	Nyle	Nytina	O'shaylee	Oct'cavious	Ojané
Nyivy	Nyleena	Nytisha	O'sheauna	Octabia	Ojania
Nyja	Nyleka	Nytisia	O'tasia	Octasia	Ojel
Nyjae	Nyler	Nywana	O'tavya	Octavia *(0.09)*	Ojiugo
Nyjah	Nylesha	Nywanna	O'tesha	Octaviah	Okeema
Nyjia	Nylicia	Nyya	O'tisha	Octaviais	Okeemah
Nyjustice	Nymesha	Nyzell	O'tishia	Octavio	Okevia
Nykayla	Nymma	Nyzhé	O'tisjah	Octavious	Okeya
Nykea	Nyna	Nzadi	O-Shay	Octavya	Okeyia
Nykeadra	Nynaih	Nzinga	Oacia	Octese	Okie
Nykecia	Nynisha	Nzingha	Oadiah	Octivia	Okima
Nykee	Nyoka		Oakima	October	Okkishiq
Nykeelah	Nyokee	**-O-**	Oaklee	Octrana	Okom
Nykeemah	Nyome		Oakleigh	Ocyanna	Oksana *(0.02)*
Nykeesha	Nyomee	O	Oakley	Odair	Oksanasharon
Nykeevah	Nyomi	O Meshia	Oakli	Odaisha	Oksanna
Nykeidra	Nyomie	O Neischa	Oaklie	Odalis	Okwuchi
Nykeidria	Nyonna	O Nesius	Oaklynne	Odaliz	Ola *(0.01)*
Nykeisha	Nyosha	O Sona	Oamil	Odaly	Oladunni
Nykela	Nyqueasha	O Tisha	Oana	Odalys	Olajumake
Nykendra	Nyqueisha	O'ashiya	Oanh *(0.01)*	Odashia	Olanike
Nykera	Nyquelle	O'dellshalah	Oasha	Odeh	Olanta
Nykeria	Nyquesha	O'derricka	Oasia	Odell	Olantha
Nykerian	Nyquiah	O'dessa	Oasis	Odella	Olashae
Nykerria	Nyquisha	O'donya	Obdulia	Odesha	Olayinka
Nykeseia	Nyra	O'eshia	Obession	Odessa *(0.02)*	Olcay
Nykesha	Nyree	O'hara	Obiageli	Odessia	Olden
Nykeshia	Nyreeshia	O'jaznae	Obiageriaku	Odeth	Oldyne

Olecpeeka	Olonna	Omeirah	Onessa	Ophelie *(0.01)*	Orleana
Oleena	Olubusola	Omeisha	Onessia	Ophia	Orlena
Oleesha	Oluchi	Omelia	Onethia	Ophir	Orlenda
Oleishia	Olukemi	Omesha	Onevious	Opra	Orlesia
Oleisly	Olumayomide	Omeshia	Oneyda	Opral	Orlexiah
Olena *(0.01)*	Olumide	Omi	Oni	Oquéshá	Orli
Olenczuk	Olumuyiwa	Omily	Onica	Oquisha	Orlinda
Olenna	Oluremi	Omirah	Oniesha	Or Rion	Orlinda Jewel
Olesha	Oluseyi	Omnae	Onika	Or'tessiana	Orly
Olesia	Olutomilade	Omnia	Onisha	Ora *(0.01)*	Orlysha
Olesya	Oluwabusayo	Omniké	Oniss	Ora'lisa	Ormanee
Oleta	Oluwabusayo	Omnineisha	Onistee	Orah	Ornella
Oletha	Abim	Omo	Onita	Orali	Ornelle
Olevey	Oluwafunmike	Omolabake	Onitisha	Oralia	Orpah
Olevia	Oluwajuwon	Omolara	Onjanae	Oralynn	Orpha
Olga *(0.11)*	Oluwakemi	Omotola	Onjelee	Oranesha	Orrinisha
Olga Elena	Oluwami	Omoyele	Onjenaé	Orchid	Orsalia
Olga-Alycea	Oluwapa	Omoyeni	Onkari	Oreanna	Orsolya
Olgadel	Oluwasemilore	Omuwa	Onna	Oreen	Ortavia
Olgadilia	Oluwaseyi	Omy	Onnah	Oreionne	Ortiz
Olice	Oluwashayo	Omyah	Onnally	Orelle	Ortrice
Olicia	Oluwatamilore	Omyni	Onnastayzea	Oren	Oruba
Olimpia	Oluwatitomi	Omyra	Onnica	Orena	Orule
Olinda	Oluwatobi	Omyrii	Onnie	Oreoluwa	Oryan
Olinga	Oluwatoni	On Dontranique	Onnilee	Oreon	Oryarna
Olisa	Oluwatosin	On Jonae	Onsha	Oresta	Orysa
Olisha	Oluwatoyin	On'drea	Ontario	Oretha	Osa
Olishia	Oluwatunmise	Ona *(0.01)*	Ontaya	Oretiana	Osahenrumwen
Oliva	Olwyn	Ona-Sophia	Onteona	Orezime	Osana
Olive	Olympia *(0.01)*	Onai	Onteria	Oria	Osaretin
Olivea	Olysia	Onalise	Onterra	Oriah	Osarugue
Oliveia	Olyvia *(0.01)*	Ondene	Onterria	Orian	Osaserer
Oliveira	Olyvia Shan'tel	Ondi	Onticha	Oriana *(0.03)*	Osayuki
Oliver	Olyvia-Marie	Ondina	Ontiona	Orianna	Osaze
Olivera	Oma	Ondine	Ontirria	Oriannah-	Osazomon
Olivi	Omadevi	Ondra	Ontisha	Josaphienne	Osbeida
Olivia *(3.30)*	Omaima	Ondraya	Ontitnia	Orieana	Osbelia
Olivia Fran	Omaira	Ondrea *(0.01)*	Ontoria	Oriel	Osbeyda
Olivia Irene	Omajaé	Ondreana	Ontrael	Oriell	Osbie
Olivia Marie	Omalia	Ondria	Ontraneka	Orien	Oscar
Olivia Rae	Omana	Ondrianna	Onya	Oriette	Oscelia
Olivia-Marie	Omar	Oneasha	Onyae	Orilis	Oschelle
Olivia-Rose	Omarah	Oneida	Onyeka	Orina	Oseremi
Olivier	Omarangelys	Oneidalis	Onyi	Orinda	Osha
Olivir	Omari	Oneika	Onyinyechi	Oriole	Oshakeiya
Olivvya	Omaria	Oneisa	Onyka	Orion	Oshakia
Olivya	Omarra	Oneisha *(0.01)*	Onyx *(0.01)*	Orisha	Oshameria
Olizabeth	Omarricka	Oneisia	Onzeka	Orishamola	Oshani
Olla	Omaya	Oneissa	Ooma	Oritsesgbubemi	Oshanique
Ollanecy	Omayra	Oneitha	Oomalaq	Orla	Oshawn
Ollie *(0.01)*	Omayya	Oneka	Oona	Orlandia	Oshea
Ollie-Anna	Ombréa	Onequa	Ooyuan	Orlandra	Osheena
Ollisa	Omega *(0.01)*	Onesha	Opal *(0.01)*	Orlandria	Osheiauna
Ollisha	Omegea	Oneshia	Opheli	Orlashia	Oshera
Olna	Omeika	Onesia	Ophelia *(0.01)*	Orlean	Oshian

Oshiana	Oyuki	Paigelin	Pamela Mercedes	Pardip	Parsha
Oshianna	Oyuky	Paigen	Pamela-Ann	Pardis	Parthavi
Oshien	Ozlem	Paighton	Pamella	Parece	Paru
Oshinac	Ozodinobi	Paiglyne	Pamesha	Pareen	Parva
Oshiona	Ozra	Paiglynn	Pamila	Pareesa	Parvaneh
Oshla	Ozsana	Paije	Pamima	Pareesha	Parveen (0.01)
Osiris	Ozuronye	Pailge	Pamjit	Pares	Parveer
Ositee	Ozziana	Pairrys	Pamla	Paresha	Parvir
Osjha		Paishia	Pamninder	Parge	Parvyn
Osjlen	**-P-**	Paislay	Panagiota (0.01)	Pari S	Parwinder
Oskana		Paislee	Panagota	Pari's	Parys
Oskary	P (0.01)	Paisley (0.03)	Panagoula	Paria	Parysse
Osma	P.	Paiten	Panathida	Paridhima	Pascal
Osmara	Pa (0.02)	Paitha	Panayiota	Parie	Pascale (0.09)
Osmari	Pa Ia	Paiton (0.01)	Panayoda	Pariesa	Pascalle
Osmin	Pa'shea	Paitra	Panayota	Parijat	Pascha
Osna	Pa'sion	Paityn	Pandi	Parion	Pasche
Ososese	Paage	Paityne	Pandora	Paris (0.24)	Pascuala
Ossie	Paam	Paiuline	Pandorá	Paris Larae	Paseanna
Osunkemi	Paaton	Paiyton	Paneet	Paris'	Pasha
Otavia	Pacha	Paizlei	Pang (0.01)	Parisa (0.01)	Pashae
Otcione	Pache	Paizleigh	Pangdi	Parise	Pashaé
Oteria	Pachence	Paizley	Pannell	Parish	Pashal
Oterrion	Pachion	Paizsa	Pansy	Parisha	Pashe
Otesha	Pachionetta	Pajas	Pantera	Parishian	Pashell
Otey	Pacia	Paje	Panuja	Parishya	Pashence
Otia	Pacome	Pajenai'	Pany	Pariss	Pasheuna
Otilia	Pacquita	Pajeria	Panya	Parissa	Pashion
Otionna	Padea	Pak	Paola (0.38)	Parisse	Pashionaé
Otis	Padee	Pakasutha	Paola Sarai'	Parita	Pashk
Otisha	Padeedeh	Pakou	Paola Vanessa	Pariz	Pashonne
Otisia	Padein	Palacios	Paolaandrea	Pariz'	Pashuntz
Otissare	Paden	Palaire	Paoli	Parizad	Pasia
Otteisha	Padgett	Palak	Paolina	Park	Pasion
Otti	Padideh	Palakiiya	Papouleh	Parke	Paskale
Ottiana	Padmanie	Palevi	Paquina	Parker (0.03)	Pasley
Ottie	Padreona	Paley	Par'is	Parkin	Passhania
Otyanna	Paelle	Palin	Par'ris	Parlee	Passia
Oucelina	Paeton	Pallas	Para	Parmeet	Passion (0.02)
Oula	Paetra	Pallavi	Parabhleen	Parmel	Passion'e
Ouma	Paetyn	Pallovy	Paradice	Parminder	Passionaé
Oumamah	Paevia	Palmer (0.01)	Paradise (0.01)	Parmpreet	Passionate
Ourtney	Pagan	Palmer-Hollan	Paradisha	Parneet	Passionette
Ova	Page (0.04)	Palmira	Paramjit	Parneisha	Pastora
Ovelia	Pagie	Palolo	Parandeep	Parnell	Pat
Oveyaa	Pagon	Paloma (0.08)	Paranjot	Parnevia	Pat'dreka
Ovidia	Paha	Paluma	Parashika	Paroma	Patara
Ovies	Pahola	Palvi	Paraskevi	Parria	Patatricia
Ovijah	Pahoua (0.01)	Palvir	Parastoo	Parrias	Patchouli
Owen	Pahue	Palwinder	Parastwo	Parris (0.02)	Patcy
Owenda	Paichá	Pamala	Paratie	Parrise	Patdriana
Oxanna	Paicience	Pamaletta	Parbeen	Parrish	Pateesha
Oxenia	Paige (2.55)	Pamela (0.45)	Parbhjot	Parrisha	Paten
Oyinkansola	Paige-Ashli	Pamela Bale	Parchi	Parrys	Pateng
Oyshi	Paige-Marie	Pamela Cerria	Pardeep	Parrysh	Paterra

Pathriencé
Patia
Patiance
Patice
Paticia
Patience (0.07)
Patient
Patina
Patince
Patishia
Patlada
Patra (0.01)
Patrais
Patraneka
Patrece
Patreece
Patreeka
Patreena
Patreese
Patreia
Patria
Patrial
Patrica
Patricana
Patrice (0.08)
Patrice Anquane
Patricea
Patrich
Patrichea
Patricia (1.19)
Patricia Colleen
Patricia Jean
Patriciacatherine
Patriciana
Patricianna
Patrick
Patricka
Patriece
Patrierra
Patrina (0.01)
Patriona
Patrique
Patrisha (0.01)
Patrishia
Patrisia
Patrisic
Patrissa
Patrizia
Patrricia
Patryce
Patrycia
Patrycja (0.01)
Patrycza
Patshawn
Patshunce

Patsi
Patsia
Patsy (0.03)
Patsy-Jane
Patti
Pattiann
Pattice
Pattie
Patton
Patty
Pau Shonique
Pau'sha
Pauala
Paul
Paul-Anndra
Paula (0.29)
Paula Marie
Paule
Pauleanna
Paulena
Paulencia
Paulene
Paulenia
Paulet
Paulett
Pauletta
Paulette (0.02)
Pauli
Pauliana
Paulianne
Paulicia
Paulie
Paulien
Paulin
Paulina (0.22)
Pauline (0.11)
Paulisha
Paulita
Paulla
Paullaine
Paullena
Paullett
Paulletta
Pauly
Paulyna
Paulynn
Paulysha
Paushana
Paustine
Pavan
Pavandeep
Pavanee
Pavaneet
Pavanjot
Pavanpreet

Pavanvir
Paveenaa
Paven
Pavena
Pavendeep
Pavi
Pavielle
Pavin
Paviter
Pavithra
Pavitura
Paviya
Pavleen
Pavlina
Pavlita
Pavneet (0.01)
Pavol
Pavyna
Pawandeep
Pawanjit
Pawanjot
Pawlina
Pax'tn
Paxtin
Paxton (0.03)
Paxtynn
Payal (0.01)
Payden
Paydon
Payge (0.01)
Payge Diana
Payje
Payne
Payshance
Payson
Paytan
Payten (0.01)
Paytin
Paytn
Payton (0.26)
Paytton
Paz
Pazia
Pazley
Pédreshia
Pégysia
Peace
Peaches
Peachlyn
Peachtreanna
Pearl (0.06)
Pearla
Pearlá
Pearle
Pearlie

Pearlina
Pearlisha
Pearlittier
Pearllani
Pearly
Pearlyn
Pearson
Peary
Pebbels
Pebbles (0.01)
Peccola
Pecies
Pecky
Pecola
Peden
Pedra
Pedraza
Pedrinisha
Peetrylia
Pegah
Pegan
Peggi
Peggie
Peggy (0.04)
Pei
Peichanda
Peige
Peigelyn
Peighton (0.01)
Pekolia
Pela
Pele
Pelissar
Pember
Pemricka
Penelope (0.06)
Penifea
Penina
Penina Geral
Penlyn
Penney
Pennie (0.01)
Penny (0.03)
Penoy
Peony
Peorreya
Pepbles
Pepper
Pepsi
Pequitta
Perchell
Percia
Percila
Percilla
Percy

Pereasha
Peregrine
Pereijah
Perez
Peri (0.02)
Peris
Perisha
Perkell
Perkins
Perkoshia
Perla (0.21)
Perlamassiel
Perlamelissa
Perlin
Perlisha
Permalice
Permeen
Permelia
Pernell
Perniecee
Pernisha
Perralyn
Perre
Perrette
Perri (0.01)
Perría
Perrié
Perriel
Perrilyn
Perrilynn
Perrin
Perrinishi
Perry (0.02)
Perry'unna
Perryanna
Perryion
Perscilla
Persephanie
Persephany
Persephone
Persephonie
Persia
Persis
Pertrice
Perye
Peryonna
Peshelley
Pesi
Petals
Peter
Peterice
Petert
Petiola
Petra (0.04)
Petralin

Petralyn
Petranella
Petrevious
Petrice
Petrina
Petrona
Petronella
Petula
Peydon
Peygan
Peyten
Peyton (0.21)
Peyton-Ann
Peytyn
Pfae
Pfeacia
Pfeiffer
Pha'trece
Phabiola
Phadacia
Phadra
Phaedra
Phairyn
Phaivanh
Phalaine
Phalandia-Rose
Phalen
Phalistine
Phallan
Phallon
Phalyn
Pham
Phamyscha
Phan
Phania
Phantasia
Phantessia
Phantom
Phaquasha
Phaquira
Phara
Pharoah
Pharrah
Pharyn
Phatejá
Phatema
Phaydra
Phaylor
Phebe (0.01)
Pheben
Pheby
Phedra-Lyn
Pheerica
Phelishia
Phenaidra

Phenelope	Phoenix *(0.03)*	Pierreline	Pooja *(0.06)*	Prabhjot	Préchaye
Phenicia	Phoenyk	Pierrette	Poojadeep	Prabhjyot	Preacious
Phenisha	Phoenyx	Pieta	Poonam *(0.01)*	Prabhkiran	Preandra
Phenix	Phoi	Pik	Poornika	Prabhleen	Preanna
Phennie	Phone	Pilar *(0.03)*	Poorva	Prabhrit	Precelia
Phenomenal	Phonesavanh	Pillar	Poorvi	Prabhroop	Prechynthia
Pheobe	Phonethip	Pily	Poppy	Prabiat	Preciaus
Pheonix	Phong	Pina	Por'trait	Prabjit	Precila
Phethmany	Phree	Pinar	Porcha *(0.02)*	Prabjot	Precilla
Phetpalansy	Phuc	Pinderjit	Porchae	Prabjyot	Precillinn
Phi-Uyen	Phuc Hau	Pinkerton	Porche *(0.01)*	Prabpreet	Precioues
Phia	Phung	Pinkie	Porché	Prabsimran	Precious *(0.27)*
Phianie	Phuong *(0.01)*	Pinky	Porcher	Prabsimrin	Precious Angel
Phidiana	Phuong-Cat	Piny	Porchia *(0.01)*	Prachee	Precious Jasmine
Phierica	Phuong-Chan	Piper *(0.04)*	Porcia	Prachi	Preciouse
Phil Ja	Phuong-Dong	Piphani	Porcsha	Pracilla	Precisha
Phil'leshia	Phy'jaé	Pippa	Poresha	Pracious	Precti
Philaira	Phyera	Piramiya	Poria	Pradeega	Precyous
Philana	Phyl-Kia	Pirasha	Porisha	Praelle	Predenxia
Philandrea	Phylandra	Pirathahini	Porn	Pragina	Preesha
Philanna	Phyleia	Piraveena	Pornghamoln	Prairie *(0.01)*	Preet
Philbertha	Phylesha	Piraveenah	Porscha *(0.02)*	Praise	Preeta
Philecia	Phylica	Piravena	Porschah	Praiselyn	Preetha
Philencia	Phylicia *(0.02)*	Pistal	Porsche *(0.02)*	Praize	Preethi
Philenia	Phylicity	Piya	Porsché	Prakruti	Preeti
Philesha	Phylinda	Piyamon	Porschea	Praksha	Preetinder
Philiama	Phylis	Piyanka	Porschela	Pramachandiran	Preety
Philicha	Phylisha	Pjrathanya	Porschella	Pranavi	Preeya
Philicia *(0.01)*	Phyliss	Platonida	Porschia	Praneet	Preia
Philicity	Phylissa	Pleasant	Porschia Debra	Pranisha	Preimere
Philicity-Joy	Phyllicia	Pledneashia	Porsha *(0.06)*	Pranita	Prekiya
Philieza	Phyllis *(0.02)*	Pleshett	Porshá	Pranvera	Prema
Philineshia	Phyllis-Caitlyn	Pleshette	Porshana	Prarin	Prema-Vanya
Philinisha	Phyllisha	Plessa	Porshanetta	Prartana	Premiere
Philip	Phyllissa	Plina	Porshanna	Praryya	Prencella
Philippa	Phyllyza	Pliny	Porshaona	Prasanthi	Prenecia
Philisha	Phyneshia	Plivia	Porshay	Prascilla	Prenisha
Phillis	Phynola	Pnina	Porshe	Prasha	Prenna
Phillisa	Pia *(0.01)*	Poéetic	Porshé	Prashana	Prennay
Phillisha	Pia-Christina	Poetrie	Porshea	Prathna	Prentice
Phillistina	Pia-Zoe	Poetry	Porshette	Prathyusha	Prentiss
Phillyis	Piaget	Polagea	Porshia	Pratibha	Preochia
Philomena	Piandria	Polena	Porter *(0.01)*	Praticia	Preona
Philshala	Piara	Polina	Portia *(0.03)*	Pratika	Prerna
Philtaria	Piasia	Polinia	Portiashla	Pravdeep	Presada
Phina	Picabo	Poljanka	Porticia	Praveena	Prescence
Phineas	Picabo-Siera	Pollard	Portley	Pravena	Prescilla
Phinesha	Picarra	Polly *(0.02)*	Portrait-Cympho	Pravetha	Prescious
Phiphacksa	Pich	Pollyanna	Pouline	Pravina	Preshauna
Phlecia	Pieadra	Pologne	Pounds	Pravitha	Preshious
Phlisha	Pier	Polokala	Powell	Pravleen	Presilla
Phocien	Pier Ann *(0.01)*	Poniesha	Prabh	Praxton	Presious
Phoebe *(0.12)*	Pier-Anne	Ponina	Prabhdeep	Prayona	Preslea
Phoebe-Ann	Pierra	Ponthip	Prabhjit	Praysheyanna	Preslee
Phoenicia	Pierre	Pontic	Prabhjoit	Prayther	Preslei

Presleigh	Priscilia	Pryscylla	Qenzel	Quachelle	Quanda
Presley *(0.07)*	Priscilla *(0.70)*	Psalm	Qetuwrah	Quadaisha	Quandashai
Presli	Priscillia	Ptashi	Qhadijah	Quadaishia	Quandaysia
Preslie	Prisda	Pualani	Qhasia	Quadajah	Quandra
Presly	Prisha	Puentes	Qhyonni	Quadasha	Quandrá
Preslye	Prishay	Pui	Qia	Quadasia	Quandranic
Prespa	Prishonna	Puja *(0.01)*	Qiana *(0.01)*	Quadayshia	Quandranikia
Pressie	Prishtina	Pulak	Qiana Neferpiti	Quadaza	Quandranique
Pressilia	Prisila	Pulcheria	Qianna	Quadeisha	Quandrea
Pressley	Prisilla	Puneet *(0.01)*	Qianyuan	Quadejah	Quane
Presslie	Prisina	Pura	Qiara	Quadellanecia	Quaneaka
Pressly	Prisma	Purdy	Qiauna	Quadesha	Quaneasa
Presteyien	Prissila	Purim	Qierra	Quadeshia	Quanece
Prestige	Pristine	Purneisha	Qiluya	Quadiasha	Quanecia
Prestina	Pritha	Purshall	Qing	Quadigah	Quaneesha
Prestini'	Priti	Purva	Qinshalia	Quadijah	Quaneice
Prestique	Pritiga	Purvasha	Qionta	Quadira	Quaneisha *(0.01)*
Preston	Pritika	Putrease	Qirrat	Quadjat	Quaneka
Pretoria	Pritty	Putthamany	Qiuana	Quadrea	Quanekka
Pretti	Prityauna	Pyana	Qiyuan	Quadreka	Quaneria
Prettisha	Priya *(0.07)*	Pykari	Qourtasia	Quadrenna	Quanerra
Preya	Priyaben	Pyne	Qoydasha	Quadriia	Quanesha *(0.02)*
Preyavanee	Priyadeep	Pyneeta	Qrayesia	Quaesha	Quaneshaia
Preyona	Priyadharshini	Pyper	Qrnes	Quahnah	Quaneshia
Prezevia	Priyajeet	Pyrave	Qrunisha	Quailar	Quanesia
Pria	Priyajit	Pyravi	Qrystal	Quaineya	Quanessa
Prianka	Priyajot		Qu Neal	Quainjanique	Quanessia
Priceous	Priyal		Qu Nequi	Quainta	Quanice
Pricila	Priyana	**-Q-**	Qu'daisha	Quairra	Quanicya
Pricilla *(0.04)*	Priyanga		Qu'shel	Quaisha	Quaniece
Pricsilla	Priyanika	Q Ianna	Qu'taisha	Quakiiya	Quanielle
Prima	Priyanka *(0.05)*	Q Wanna	Qu'teria	Qualicia	Quaniesha
Primativa	Priyankaben	Q'dijah	Qu'vanda	Qualiesha	Quaniex
Primitiva	Priyoshi	Q'mia	Qua	Qualisha	Quanika
Princes	Priythma	Q'wadreana	Qua Asia	Qualiter	Quaniqua
Princesa	Prizzi	Q-Erica	Qua'daija	Quameca	Quaniqual
Princess *(0.09)*	Proffitt	Qa'hnesha	Qua'dasha	Quamecia	Quanisha *(0.06)*
Princess Fergie	Proma	Qa'shandanique	Qua'daysha	Quameisha	Quanishia
Princess Nyosha	Promila	Qa'shay	Qua'desha	Quamesha	Quanita
Princess-Beth	Promis	Qadaysha	Qua'desia	Quameshia	Quanitra
Princess-Sharro	Promise *(0.01)*	Qadirah	Qua'dijia	Quamica	Quanjanieka
Princesswakeeta	Promiss	Qahira	Qua'keidra	Quamyesha	Quanjeroina
Princetta	Promys	Qaila	Qua'naija	Quan	Quanna
Princia	Promyse	Qaitlin	Qua'nika	Quan'nesha	Quannesha
Princina	Prophecy	Qamar	Qua'shaiila	Quan'nisha	Quanneshia
Prineet	Providenza	Qaneisha	Qua'sheba	Quan'nita	Quannezia
Prineisha	Provvidenza	Qanta	Qua'shonna	Quan'tageah	Quannilla
Prineta	Prubjot	Qarina	Qua'taisha	Quan'toya	Quanrika
Prinsélena	Prudence	Qasas	Qua'tavia	Quan-Tevia	Quansha
Printha	Prudens	Qasia	Qua'vyana	Quanae	Quanshae
Prionna	Pruneet	Qasim	Qua-Tasia	Quanallarie	Quanshay
Prisca *(0.01)*	Prutha	Qassye	Quaaniesha	Quanasha	Quanshaydria
Priscela	Prycinthia	Qaundrika	Quachandra	Quanashia	Quanshe
Priscella	Pryian	Qayima	Quachasity	Quanasia	Quanshé
Priscila *(0.03)*	Pryrika	Qeelin	Quachell	Quanciana	Quantaisha
		Qeianna			

Quantaneice	Quashayla	Qudsia	Quenncha	Quianah	Quindaijah
Quantaneka	Quashea	Quédasha	Quennisha	Quianda	Quindeija
Quantania	Quasheda	Quédonia	Quenntaija	Quiandra	Quindolyn
Quantanishia	Quasheka	Quéerris	Quensha	Quiane	Quineisha
Quantara	Quashiaviai	Quéshonda	Quenshella	Quiani	Quineka
Quantarius	Quashikula	Quéyamonique	Quenswayla	Quianita	Quinella
Quantasha	Quashima	Queana	Quentanet	Quianna (0.01)	Quinequoi
Quantasia	Quashon	Queandria	Quentara	Quianné	Quinesha (0.01)
Quantavia	Quashonda	Queanta	Quentaria	Quianoa	Quineshia
Quantayi	Quashondria	Quearahnisha	Quentasia	Quiantae	Quinessa
Quantaza	Quashyna	Quebalea	Quentavia	Quiante	Quinessia
Quanteasia	Quasia	Quebec	Quentaya	Quianti	Quinetta
Quantedia	Quasiah	Queen (0.02)	Quentella	Quiara (0.01)	Quinette
Quanteria	Quasondra	Queen Isis	Quenterica	Quiarra	Quinhoja
Quantesha	Quataijah	Queen Montic	Quenterrious	Quiateesha	Quinidra
Quantessence	Quatarius	Queen Travita	Quentia	Quiatessa	Quiniece
Quantezia	Quatavia	Queena	Quentiera	Quiaudry	Quiniesha
Quanthavia	Quatazia	Queenasia	Quentillia	Quiaunna	Quinika
Quantia	Quateisha	Queency	Quentin	Quibulah	Quinine
Quantiesha	Quatera	Queenesha	Quentina	Quichea	Quininshea
Quantinae	Quateria	Queenetta	Quentisha	Quichelle	Quinisa
Quantineasha	Quatesha	Queenice	Quentishia	Quidaesha	Quinisha (0.01)
Quantinna	Quatesia	Queenie (0.01)	Quentoria	Quiena	Quinishia
Quantiona	Quatesion	Queenisha	Quentyn	Quienish	Quinita
Quantisha	Quatevia	Queenkhadij	Quentyshia	Quientera	Quinitra
Quantrella	Quatia	Queenlaunity	Queon	Quiera	Quiniya
Quantrice	Quatiaa	Queenmecca	Queona	Quierah	Quinlaine
Quanykisha	Quatiah	Queennetta	Queonqua	Quiere	Quinlan
Quanzetta	Quatiesha	Queenointa	Queonshay	Quieria	Quinlaw
Quar'neka	Quatisha	Queenteria	Queosha	Quierra	Quinlyn
Quardashy	Quatoria	Queentesa	Quereshia	Quieshana	Quinlyn-Skye
Quardayja	Quatreta	Queentessa	Querida	Quieshia	Quinlynne
Quareka	Quatti	Queentoria	Querstin	Quiettina	Quinn (0.09)
Quarenisha	Quauna	Queerra	Quesha	Quima	Quinna
Quarla	Quauné	Queheir	Queshaana	Quimby	Quinndolyn
Quarmell	Quavadis	Queidi	Queshala	Quin	Quinne
Quarnetta	Quavetria	Queilla	Quesheika	Quin'asia	Quinnesha
Quarteisha	Quavett	Queisha	Queshia	Quin'neisha	Quinneshia
Quartevia	Quawanna	Quelatifah	Queshunda	Quina	Quinnett
Quartisha	Quawnea	Quele	Questeara	Quinadra	Quinnetta
Quartnee	Quawnlindreia	Quelena	Quetasia	Quinae	Quinnice
Quartney	Quayci	Quelexus	Quetiana	Quinana	Quinnikka
Quasha	Quaycianna	Quen'tavia	Quetora	Quinara	Quinnisha
Quashai	Quaylana	Quenata	Quetta	Quinasia	Quinnlan
Quashallia	Quayneicia	Quenci	Quevette	Quinby	Quinnlyn
Quashana	Quayneshia	Queneesha	Queyenna	Quincavia	Quinnshell
Quashaná	Quaysha	Queneidra	Queyona	Quincee	Quinnyae
Quashane	Quayshia	Quenelle	Queyonna	Quincella	Quinnyatta
Quashanna	Quayzaih	Quenesha	Queysha	Quincentra	Quinque
Quashannon	Quazella	Quenetta	Queznay	Quincey (0.01)	Quinquie
Quashara	Qubanaé	Quenette	Qui Wan	Quinchelle	Quinsetta
Quashawn	Qubilliah	Queniqua	Qui'ana	Quinci	Quinsha
Quashawna	Qudajah	Quenisha (0.01)	Qui'anna	Quincia	Quinshawta
Quashawnique	Qudasha	Quenita	Quiambra	Quincie	Quinshay
Quashay	Qudashua	Quenitra	Quiana (0.04)	Quincy (0.03)	Quinshayla

Quinshea	Quiraira	Qurratulann	Qyleshia	Ra'lyn	Rachaell
Quinshell	Quirez	Qurston	Qymberli	Ra'lynn	Rachail
Quinsy	Quirina	Qurteria	Qynaya	Ra'mesha	Rachal (0.01)
Quinta	Quirine	Qusala Damb	Qynicha	Ra'mona	Rachalia
Quintacia	Quiristen	Qushanda	Qyxiaan	Ra'myia	Rachalle
Quintaesha	Quirnechia	Quston		Ra'na	Rachana
Quintaesia	Quishana	Quteria	**-R-**	Ra'neija	Rachanda
Quintaeyu	Quishanté	Qutia		Ra'neshia	Rachane
Quintainque	Quishauna	Qutina	R (0.02)	Ra'nya	Rachanna
Quintana	Quishenae	Quvasha	R Iyani	Ra'quelle	Rachante
Quintara	Quishunna	Quwanna	R Neeca	Ra'quiesha	Rachara
Quintarea	Quisqueya	Quyanna	R'achaela	Ra'shanae	Rache
Quintaria	Quissana	Quyashona	R'shonda	Ra'shanda	Racheal (0.13)
Quintasha	Quitayvia	Quyen	R'wanda	Ra'shawn	Racheal Jo
Quintashia	Quitella	Quyia	R-Janai	Ra'sheia	Racheal-Anne
Quintasia	Quitney	Quymekia	R.	Ra'shel	Racheel
Quintava	Quivia	Quynci	Ra	Ra'shon	Rachel (7.59)
Quintavia	Quiyana	Quynh	Ra Jaznee	Ra'tearea	Rachel Bethany
Quintavie	Quiynteria	Quynh Nhu	Ra Jel	Ra'van	Rachel Marie
Quintaysha	Quizariah	Quynh-Huong	Ra Jon	Ra'ven	Rachel Marilyn
Quintcey	Qukwanni	Quynh-Phuong	Ra Miriam	Ra'veona	Rachel-Elizabet
Quinteesha	Qulinda	Quynhnhu	Ra Neisha	Ra'vequayana	Rachel-Elizabeth
Quinteetia	Qulyndreia	Quynn	Ra Neshia	Ra'zene	Rachel-Lynne
Quinteka	Qumani	Quynterra	Ra Nijia	Ra-Tese	Rachel-Rose
Quintela	Qumeisha	Quyovvne	Ra Shawn	Raabya	Rachelann
Quintella	Qundesha	Quysharra	Ra Zon	Raagavi	Rachele (0.02)
Quintera	Quneasha	Qve Lyn	Ra' Shayla	Raagavy	Rachell (0.02)
Quinteria	Qunetta	Qwa'shay	Ra'ann	Raakel	Rachella
Quinterra	Qunica	Qwache	Ra'chele	Raamiah	Rachelle (0.33)
Quinterria	Qunidresha	Qwame	Ra'chelle	Raanee	Rachelmary
Quinterrica	Qunika	Qwameesia	Ra'daisha	Raanika	Rachelnicho
Quinterrick	Qunisha	Qwameshia	Ra'dasja	Raashaida	Rachelyn
Quintesa	Quntazesha	Qwan'janée	Ra'dina	Raashauna	Racheya
Quintesha	Quo Charicq	Qwandreka	Ra'eshia	Raashyda	Rachhana
Quintessa	Quoc	Qwanechia	Ra'gein	Raazeem	Rachielle
Quintessia	Quoin'da	Qwanesha	Ra'gene	Rabacca	Rachita
Quintia	Quomesha	Qwanessia	Ra'giean	Rabbiyah	Rachle
Quinticia	Quon Nessa	Qwanisha	Ra'gine	Rabecca (0.01)	Rachlyn
Quintina	Quonesha	Qwantasha	Ra'hel	Rabecka	Rachna
Quintisha	Quonisha	Qwantearia	Ra'isha	Rabeeah	Rachonda
Quintivia	Quonnisha	Qwantesé	Ra'ja	Rabeka	Rachpaul
Quinton	Quontaza	Qwatavia	Ra'jahnee	Rabekah	Rachuel
Quintoria	Quornika	Qwatrice	Ra'janeen	Rabía	Rachwel
Quintosha	Quortasia	Qwendolyn	Ra'janique	Rabia (0.01)	Rachyia
Quintrelle	Quortni	Qweyana	Ra'jaun	Rabiah	Rachyl
Quintrice	Quortnie	Qwillyn	Ra'jean	Rabiga	Racine
Quintus	Quoshane	Qwinsee-Lah	Ra'jien	Rabiya	Racio
Quinyana	Quoshia	Qwinterria	Ra'kale	Rabiyan	Rackel
Quinyauna	Quotisha	Qwintonja	Ra'kejah	Rabsha-Keh	Racnel
Quinzola	Qura-Tul-Ann	Qwisun	Ra'ketah	Racara	Racqual
Quiona	Quran	Qwshanda	Ra'kim	Racel	Racquel (0.05)
Quionna	Qurani	Qy-Asia	Ra'kira	Racelle	Racquell
Quionté	Quratul	Qydasha	Ra'kya	Rachae	Racquelle
Quiosha	Qurina	Qydasia	Ra'layzia	Rachael (1.13)	Racquia
Quiotte	Qurorshena	Qylci	Ra'lesha	Rachael-Anne	Racquille

Racqule	Rae-Shawna	Raelicia	Raezhine	Rahiel	Raija
Racyne	Raea	Raelin	Rafa	Rahila	Raijean
Rada	Raeaja	Raelinda	Rafael	Rahima	Raijeana
Rada-Karina	Raean	Raelise	Rafaela *(0.01)*	Rahisha	Raijen
Radaisha	Raeana	Raelisha	Rafaella	Rahissa	Raijon
Radaja	Raeann *(0.04)*	Raelle	Rafaelle *(0.01)*	Rahjainee	Raijuenea
Radasia	Raeanna *(0.03)*	Raelyn *(0.04)*	Rafeeia	Rahjita	Raikel
Radasza	Raeannah	Raelynb	Rafeona	Rahkel	Raikyia
Radazaih	Raeanne *(0.02)*	Raelynda	Raffaella	Rahma	Raileena
Radeenah	Raebecca	Raelyne	Raffinee Angeli	Rahmah	Raileigh
Radeja	Raechael	Raelynn *(0.04)*	Rafi	Rahmeish	Railen
Radeka	Raechal	Raelynne	Rafia	Rahmeisha	Railene
Radericka	Raechanze	Raemi	Rafina	Rahnae	Railey
Radha	Raechel *(0.03)*	Raemyra	Raga	Rahne	Raili
Radheesha	Raechele	Raena *(0.01)*	Ragan *(0.01)*	Rahnecia	Raimatia
Radhia	Raechell	Raenah	Ragavey	Rahnell	Raimee
Radhija	Raechell May	Raeneek	Ragavi	Rahnesha	Raimi
Radhika *(0.01)*	Raechelle *(0.01)*	Raeneisha	Ragda	Rahniqua	Raimona
Radhiya	Raechyl	Raenelle	Rage	Rahnisha	Rain *(0.02)*
Radiance	Raedah	Raenen	Ragean	Rahnuma	Raina *(0.07)*
Radijah	Raedawn	Raenessia	Rageane	Rahquel	Rainah
Radisha	Raeesa	Raenia	Rageen	Rahsaana	Rainai
Radiyah	Raeesah	Raenie	Ragen *(0.01)*	Rahshedah	Rainbow
Radja	Raegan *(0.06)*	Raenika	Ragene	Rahshonda	Raine *(0.02)*
Radojka	Raegen	Raeniqua	Rageni	Rahterika	Rainea
Radshida	Raegene	Raenisha	Ragenna	Rahuf	Rainee *(0.01)*
Rae *(0.05)*	Raegima	Raenna	Raggan	Rahvin	Raineisha
Rae Ann	Raegime	Raeonda	Ragghantti	Rahwa	Rainell
Rae Anna	Raegina	Raeonna	Ragha	Rahyké	Rainen
Rae Anne	Raegine	Raequana	Raghad	Rahyven	Rainer
Rae Claire	Raeginelle	Raeshan	Raghani	Rai Deisha	Raines
Rae Jean	Raegyn	Raeshanna	Raghd	Rai'gean	Rainesha
Rae Lyn	Raeinna	Raeshauna	Ragin	Rai'jeen	Rainey *(0.01)*
Rae Lynn	Raeisha	Raeshawn	Ragina	Rai'ne	Rainforest
Rae Lysa	Raejaiene	Raeshawna	Ragine *(0.01)*	Rai'nysha	Raini *(0.01)*
Rae Shaun	Raejean	Raesheann	Raginee	Rai'shell	Rainie
Rae Ven	Raejene	Raesheena	Ragon	Rai'shelle	Rainika
Raé Jaena	Raejine	Raeshell	Ragpal	Raia	Rainslee
Raéanne	Raejiné	Raeshelle	Raguelin	Raiahnna	Raintree
Raéchelle	Raejona	Raesheyana	Rah Jrchess	Raian	Rainy *(0.01)*
Raégene	Raekqwuana	Raeshon	Rah'lesha	Raianna	Raion
Raéshonia	Rael	Raessa	Raha	Raichel	Raionda
Raésonia	Raela	Raetta	Rahaf	Raidah	Raisa *(0.01)*
Raéven	Raelani	Raevaughn	Rahasia	Raiden	Raisah
Raévin	Raele	Raeven *(0.01)*	Rahat	Raiell	Raise
Raévon	Raeleah	Raevin	Rahcel	Raiesha	Raisha
Rae-Ann	Raelee	Raevion	Raheal	Raigan	Raishelle
Rae-Anna	Raeleen	Raevonna	Raheem	Raigaysha	Raishoundria
Rae-Anne	Raeleia	Raevyn	Raheema	Raigene	Raissa
Rae-Chelle	Raeleigh	Raevynne	Rahel	Raighel	Raivan
Rae-Elle-Antonett	Raelein	Raewyn	Rahela	Raign	Raiven
Rae-Lee	Raelene *(0.02)*	Raewynne	Rahelyn	Raigyn	Raivin
Rae-Lynn	Raelennia	Raeyauna	Rahema	Raihaana	Raivo
Rae-Mischel	Raeley	Raeyn	Rahema-Nasreen	Raihan	Raivyn
Rae-Neisha	Raeli	Raeyonna	Rahfen	Raihana	Raiya

Raiyana	Rakaiya	Raman Preet	Ramza	Ranesha *(0.01)*	Raphaella
Raiza	Rakala	Ramanda	Raná	Raneshia	Raphaelle *(0.04)*
Raizaan	Rakayla	Ramandeep	Ran'disha	Ranessa	Rapinder
Raizel	Rakbe	*(0.02)*	Ran'nay	Ranessia	Rapture
Raj	Rakea	Ramaneek	Rana *(0.03)*	Ranette	Raqchel
Raja	Rakeah	Ramanjit	Ranada	Raney	Raqhel
Raja Lynn	Rakeal	Ramanjot	Ranadra	Raneycia	Raqiyah
Raja Ne	Rakeea	Ramanpreet	Ranae	Rangina	Raqkell
Raja'nee	Rakeese	Ramariah	Ranase	Rani *(0.01)*	Raquael
Raja-Nee	Rakeia	Rame	Ranasha	Rania *(0.01)*	Raquana
Raja-Nique	Rakeisha	Ramea	Ranay	Rania Virginia	Raquandra
Rajaah	Rakeishah	Ramealia	Rand	Ranice	Raqueal
Rajae	Rakel	Rameccia	Randa *(0.02)*	Ranicka	Raqueia
Rajaé	Rakell	Rameisha	Randajah	Ranie	Raquel *(0.53)*
Rajah *(0.01)*	Rakelle	Rameka	Randal	Raniesha	Raquel Jane
Rajai	Rakelsha	Ramekia	Randalee	Ranika	Raquel-Del
Rajanae	Rakemah	Ramekquia	Randalin	Ranikqua	Raquele
Rajandeep	Rakena	Ramen	Randall	Raniqua	Raqueli
Rajane	Rakendra	Ramena	Randalyn	Ranise	Raqueline
Rajanée	Rakeria	Ramendeep	Randasha	Ranisha *(0.01)*	Raquell
Rajanea	Rakesha	Ramesha	Randazia	Ranita	Raquelle *(0.01)*
Rajanece	Rakesia	Rameshia	Rande	Ranitra	Raquerria
Rajanee	Raketta	Rametra	Randecia	Ranjini	Raquesha
Rajanée	Rakevia	Ramey	Randee *(0.01)*	Ranjit	Raquia
Rajani	Rakeya	Rami	Randee-Lee	Rankani	Raquicia
Rajaniah	Rakeyla	Ramia	Randeen	Rankierra	Raquita
Rajavi	Rakhim	Ramiah	Randeep	Rankin	Raquiyah
Rajdeep	Rakia *(0.01)*	Ramicqua	Randeisha	Ranko	Raquiyia
Rajean	Rakiesha	Ramie	Randenny	Ranndi	Raquyyahha
Rajeen	Rakieta	Ramina	Randesha	Ranndom	Rarecelee
Rajell	Rakira	Ramique	Randi *(0.28)*	Ranndy	Rasa
Rajena	Rakisha	Ramisa	Randi-Lea	Rannee	Raschele
Rajene	Rakita	Ramisha	Randi-Lynn	Rannette	Raschell
Rajia	Rakiya	Ramita	Randie *(0.01)*	Ranni	Raschella
Rajina	Rakiyah	Ramitashini	Randikay	Rannie	Raschelle
Rajine	Raktima	Ramla	Randilee	Rannika	Rasean
Rajkiran	Ralanda	Ramlah	Randilyn	Rannisha	Raseandra
Rajmeen	Ralea	Rammya	Randin	Ranodia	Rasela
Rajmeet	Ralecia	Ramndeep	Randis	Ransheá	Rasha *(0.01)*
Rajnay	Raleiah	Ramndip	Randisha	Ranteria	Rashaana
Rajnea	Raleigh *(0.01)*	Ramneek	Randishia	Ranusha	Rashada
Rajneet *(0.01)*	Ralen	Ramneet *(0.01)*	Randy	Ranushini	Rashae
Rajnit	Ralencia	Ramnik	Randyll	Ranvir	Rashael
Rajpreet	Raley *(0.01)*	Ramolda	Raneame	Ranvon	Rashai
Rajsha	Ralisa	Ramona *(0.06)*	Ranecia	Ranya *(0.01)*	Rashaila
Rajveena	Ralisha	Ramonda	Ranee	Ranyah	Rashal
Rajveer	Ralph	Ramondria	Raneem	Ranzaya	Rashala
Rajvi	Ralpheella	Ramonica	Raneen *(0.01)*	Ranzie	Rashalian
Rajvir	Ralyn	Ramot	Raneesha	Raolat	Rashan
Rajwinder	Ralynn	Ramsey *(0.01)*	Raneisha *(0.01)*	Raoud	Rashana
Raka	Rama	Ramsha	Ranekea	Raphael	Rashanae
Rakael	Ramada	Ramsi	Ranell	Raphaela	Rashanah
Rakahia	Ramae	Ramsie	Ranelle	Raphaela Carmela	Rashanda *(0.01)*
Rakaia	Ramah	Ramya	Ranen	Raphaele	Rashane
Rakaila	Raman *(0.01)*	Ramyaa			Rashanique

Rashanise	Rashon	Ravena	Raychael	Raylyn	Rayshawnna
Rashanita	Rashonda *(0.01)*	Ravendawn	Raychel *(0.01)*	Raylynn *(0.01)*	Raysheeka
Rashanna	Rashondria	Ravene	Raychele	Raylynne	Rayshell
Rashante	Rashonna	Ravenn	Raychell	Rayma	Rayshelle
Rashantta	Rashumba	Ravenna	Raychelle *(0.01)*	Raymanda	Rayshena
Rashara	Rashunae	Ravenne	Raychil	Rayme	Rayshina
Rashaun	Rashunda	Raveon	Raydale	Raymee	Rayshine
Rashauna	Rashyannah	Ravern	Raydeen	Raymesha	Rayshona
Rashaunda	Rashyia	Raveyana	Raydein	Raymi	Rayshonda
Rashaune	Rashyla	Raveyn	Rayden	Raymie	Rayshunna
Rashavia	Rashylah	Ravhen	Raydience	Raymima	Raytavia
Rashawda	Rasia	Ravia	Raydisha	Raymin	Rayuka
Rashawn *(0.01)*	Rasika	Ravin *(0.01)*	Raydus	Raymona	Rayvan
Rashawna	Rasio	Ravina *(0.01)*	Raye	Raymonda	Rayvana
Rashawnda *(0.01)*	Rasje	Ravinder	Raye-Marie	Raymondi	Rayvein
Rashawnna	Rasline	Ravinne	Rayeal	Raymonique	Rayven *(0.02)*
Rashay	Rasmal	Ravion	Rayeann	Rayn	Rayvenne
Rashaye	Rasmamdeep	Ravleen	Rayeanna	Rayna *(0.07)*	Rayveona
Rashéyarna	Rasmine	Ravneet *(0.01)*	Rayegine	Rayna Marie	Rayvin
Rasheal	Rasya	Ravon *(0.01)*	Rayel	Raynah	Rayvon
Rasheda *(0.01)*	Raszhane	Ravyn *(0.02)*	Rayel Eliza	Raynasha	Rayvonia
Rashee	Ratanjot	Ravynn	Rayelle *(0.01)*	Rayne *(0.03)*	Rayvonsha
Rasheed	Ratasia	Rawan *(0.01)*	Rayena	Rayne-Marie	Razan
Rasheeda	Ratchel	Rawnak	Rayenne	Rayneicia	Razanne
Rasheedah	Rathai	Rawniesha	Rayesha	Rayneisha	Razeem
Rasheeka	Rathani	Ray	Rayessa	Raynekiaqua	Razeen
Rasheema	Rathna	Ray Junay	Raygan	Raynell	Razeena
Rasheena	Ratia	Ray Neisha	Raygen	Raynelle	Razelle
Rasheka	Ratika	Ray'keyah	Raygene	Rayner	Razette
Rashel *(0.01)*	Ratinna	Ray'neisha	Rayghan	Raynesha	Razhane
Rashele	Ratizha	Ray'niveah	Raygin	Rayneshia	Razhané
Rashell *(0.01)*	Ratnasingam	Ray'shene	Rayha	Raynia	Razhene
Rashella	Ratyana	Ray'tysha	Rayhana	Raynida	Razhoun
Rashelle *(0.01)*	Raujua	Ray'von	Rayia	Raynie	Razia
Rashema	Raulliean	Ray-Lynn	Rayiana	Raynie Indianna	Raziel
Rashena	Raulshema	Ray-Lynne	Rayion	Raynika	Razin
Rashenia	Raunie	Raya *(0.01)*	Rayjeem	Rayniqua	Raziya
Rashenna	Rauqelle	Rayael	Rayjheen	Raynisha *(0.01)*	Razja
Rashenne	Rauzimi	Rayah	Raykeema	Raynita	Razshonée
Rashetá	Rava	Rayahna	Raykeivia	Rayola	Re Al
Rasheya	Ravadee	Rayal	Rayla *(0.01)*	Rayona	Re Becca
Rashi	Ravali	Rayalan	Raylan	Rayonda	Re Gine
Rashia	Ravan	Rayan *(0.01)*	Raylandria	Rayonée	Re Jon
Rashida *(0.02)*	Ravanna	Rayana	Raylea	Rayonia	Re Kita
Rashidah	Ravdeep	Rayane	Rayleana	Rayonna *(0.01)*	Re Neisha
Rashieka	Raveen *(0.02)*	Rayann *(0.01)*	Raylee *(0.01)*	Rayquana	Réann
Rashiele	Raveena *(0.03)*	Rayanna *(0.03)*	Rayleen *(0.01)*	Rayquell	Rédashia
Rashiemah	Raveenn	Rayanne *(0.02)*	Rayleigh	Raysel	Régena
Rashika	Raveka	Rayannen	Raylena	Raysha	Régene
Rashina	Raven *(0.79)*	Rayasha	Raylene *(0.04)*	Rayshakia	Régina
Rashinae	Raven Denelle	Rayat	Rayli	Rayshanna	Régine
Rashlin	Raven-Angel	Rayauna	Raylin	Rayshari	Réjana
Rashma	Raven-Dawn	Rayca	Raylinn	Rayshaun	Réjean
Rashmeen	Raven-Kristen	Rayce	Raylisha	Rayshauna	Réjeane
Rashmi	Raven-Si	Raycela	Raylonna	Rayshawn	Réjene

Réjon
Réneekyia
Réneisha
Réneshay
Rénishá
Réonna
Réshona
Rétaija
Révan
Réven
Réyana
Re-Aee
Re-Neisha
Rea
Rea-Anna
Rea-Lynne
Reaco
Reagan *(0.11)*
Reagen
Reaghan
Reagine
Reah
Reaham
Reahanne
Reahliey
Reaia
Reajean
Realisa
Reality
Ream
Rean
Reana
Reanayla
Reandra
Reann
Reanna *(0.10)*
Reannah
Reannda
Reanne *(0.01)*
Reannen
Reannon
Rease
Reashea
Reashema
Reasia
Reassa
Reatha
Reatta
Reauna
Reaunte
Reaushon
Reba *(0.05)*
Reba Marie
Rebaca
Rebacca

Rebajo
Rebakah
Rebba
Rebbeca
Rebbecca *(0.01)*
Rebbecka
Rebbeka
Rebbekah
Rebbekka
Rebeca *(0.16)*
Rebecah
Rebecca *(5.20)*
Rebecca Gin
Rebecca Jane
Rebecca Lynn
Rebecca-Alish
Rebecca-Ann
Rebecca-Anne
Rebecca-Beryl
Rebecca-Joann
Rebecca-Marina
Rebecca-Melissa
Rebecca-Sylvia
Rebeccah *(0.01)*
Rebeccajean
Rebecka *(0.06)*
Rebeckah *(0.01)*
Rebeka *(0.03)*
Rebekab
Rebekah *(0.88)*
Rebekah-Rose
Rebekahlee
Rebekan
Rebekar
Rebekha
Rebekka *(0.02)*
Rebekkah *(0.02)*
Rebel
Rebell
Reberca
Rebicca
Rebie
Rebirtha
Rebka
Rebra
Rebuka
Rececca
Rechael
Rechel
Rechelle
Recia
Recka
Red
Redate
Redez

Redha
Rediate
Reeann
Reeanna
Reeanne
Reeba
Reeca
Reece
Reecha
Reecy
Reed *(0.01)*
Reede
Reegan
Reeghan
Reeia
Reeja
Reem *(0.03)*
Reema *(0.02)*
Reena *(0.02)*
Reenie
Reenika
Reeno
Reeny
Reeona
Rees
Reesa
Reese
Reesha
Reeshale
Reeta
Reetika
Reetinder
Reetu
Reeva
Reeve
Reeves
Reeya
Reezaly
Reg Jarnae
Regal
Regam
Regan *(0.16)*
Regane
Regatu
Regeena
Regeine
Regelle
Regena
Regene
Regenea
Regenique
Regeria
Reggene
Reggi
Reggie

Regginae
Regginay
Reggineka
Regginisha
Reghan *(0.01)*
Regi
Regia
Regiann
Regianna
Regiene
Regime
Regin
Regina *(0.25)*
Regina Marie
Regina Nicole
Reginae
Reginai
Reginald
Reginale
Reginay
Regine *(0.06)*
Regine Sarah
Reginé
Reginee
Reginia
Reginique
Reguina
Regzine
Rehab
Reham
Rehana
Rehanna
Reheema
Rehema
Rehindia
Rehmat
Rehobath
Rehtaeh
Rei
Reia
Reiana
Reianna
Reice
Reid *(0.01)*
Reighan
Reigna
Reigne
Reiko
Reilana
Reilee
Reileigh
Reiley
Reili
Reilleékah
Reilley

Reilly *(0.03)*
Reily
Reilyn
Reina *(0.09)*
Reinah
Reinbo
Reine
Reinie
Reinna
Reione
Reise
Reisen
Reisha
Reita
Reiuna
Rejae
Rejanée
Rejaney
Rejanne
Rejeana
Rejeane
Rejina
Rejine
Rejinée
Rejoice
Reka
Rekala
Rekayla
Rekeda
Rekeenya
Rekeesha
Rekeiah
Rekeisha
Rekendria
Rekensha
Rekesha
Reketa
Rekha
Rekisha
Rekyia
Rekyndra
Rel Aneshia
Relanda
Relane
Rella
Rema
Remani
Reme
Remeal
Remedios
Remegia
Remekia
Remeshia
Remetria
Remi *(0.01)*

Remi'
Remia
Remica Jhen
Remie
Remilekun
Remilou
Remina
Reminesha
Remingtn
Remington *(0.02)*
Reminissa
Remmington
Remneeka
Remney
Remon
Remona
Remonda
Remonia
Remonica
Remontara
Remy *(0.03)*
Remysarai
Ren
Ren'niqua
Rena *(0.05)*
Rená
Renaca
Renad
Renada
Renae *(0.07)*
Renaie
Renaja
Renajae
Renajo
Renalda
Renaqua
Renarta
Renasha
Renasia
Renat
Renata *(0.03)*
Renate
Renatta
Renauda
Renay
Renazya
Renda
Rende
Rendi
Rene *(0.05)*
René
Renée
Renéqua
Renea *(0.01)*
Reneasha

Renecca	Reonia	Revah	Rhagan	Rheonna	Rhyan *(0.01)*
Renece	Reonka	Revathi	Rhagen	Rhesa	Rhyann
Renecha	Reonna	Revati	Rhaimey	Rhett	Rhyanna *(0.01)*
Renee *(0.50)*	Reonshaye	Revé	Rhaine	Rhetta	Rhyanne
Renee Marie	Reonte	Reveka	Rhaja	Rheya	Rhyannon
Renée *(0.02)*	Repeka	Reven	Rhajá	Rheyana	Rhye
Renee-Claude	Requel	Reverie	Rhajine	Rheza	Rhyelle
Renee-Lyne	Requisha	Reverna	Rhakyria	Rhi'kearia	Rhykeisha
Reneigh	Requita	Revi	Rhana	Rhi'ya	Rhylee
Reneisa	Resa	Revina	Rhandedra	Rhia	Rhylie
Reneisha *(0.01)*	Rescha	Revlon	Rhandi	Rhian	Rhyma
Reneizha	Reschika	Revonna	Rhandy	Rhiana *(0.01)*	Rhymer
Renelle *(0.01)*	Resha	Revyn	Rhani	Rhiana-Hsu	Rhynecia
Renelyn	Reshaani	Rexanna	Rhanie	Rhianan	Rhys
Renena	Reshae	Rexford	Rhanna	Rhiandra	Rhyse
Renequa	Reshai	Rey	Rhanne	Rhiann	Rhythm
Renes	Reshaka	Reya	Rhapsody	Rhianna *(0.07)*	Ri
Renesha *(0.01)*	Reshamah	Reyahnna	Rhaquel	Rhiannah	Ri Yanna
Renessa	Reshauna	Reyan	Rhasha	Rhiannan	Ri'jae
Renetta	Reshaunda	Reyana	Rhasha'nae	Rhianne	Ri'niká
Renette	Reshaundra	Reyann	Rhasheka	Rhiannen	Ri-Keydra
Reni	Reshawan	Reyanna	Rhatika	Rhiannoa	Ria *(0.01)*
Reni'cia	Reshawntay	Reychell	Rhaven	Rhiannon *(0.20)*	Riah
Renia	Reshay	Reychelle	Rhavin	Rhiannon Marie	Riahanna
Renica	Reshayla	Reyielle	Rhaya	Rhianon	Riajah
Renice	Reshea	Reykaela	Rhayna	Rhiki	Riako
Renie	Resheá	Reylena	Rhe Ma	Rhiley	Rian *(0.02)*
Reniece	Resheema	Reymie	Rhea *(0.04)*	Rhima	Riana *(0.03)*
Renieka	Resheen	Reyna *(0.18)*	Rheachal	Rhina	Rianah
Reniesha	Resheka	Reyna Lynn	Rhead	Rhiniqua	Rianda
Renika	Reshelle	Reynada	Rheagan	Rhionna	Riane *(0.01)*
Renina	Resherle	Reynalda	Rhealene	Rhita	Riani
Reniqua	Reshika	Reyne	Rheallytee	Rhoanisha	Riann
Renique	Reshma	Reynell	Rheana	Rhoda *(0.01)*	Rianna *(0.05)*
Renisha *(0.01)*	Reshnu	Reynett	Rheann	Rhodelene	Riannan
Renita *(0.01)*	Reshona	Reyni	Rheanna *(0.02)*	Rhodessa	Rianne *(0.01)*
Reniyah	Reshwnna	Reynisha	Rheanne	Rhoketta	Riannon
Renji	Resi	Reynna	Rheannin	Rholda	Riansy
Renna	Resia	Reynolds	Rheannon *(0.01)*	Rhona	Riasia
Rennasia	Resita	Reynosha	Rheanon	Rhonda *(0.07)*	Riauna
Rennay	Ressa	Reyshah	Rheaona	Rhonda-Lee	Riawna
Renne	Resse	Reythe	Rhebeka	Rhondelle	Riby
Renni	Ressina	Reyuna	Rhecie	Rhondolyn	Ric-Quanda
Rennie	Restaycia	Rezan	Rhee	Rhoneasha	Rica
Rennisha	Reta	Rhadeijah	Rheeannah	Rhonelle	Ricajanee
Reno	Retha	Rhadijah	Rheema	Rhonesha	Ricara
Renotta	Rethea	Rhaégine	Rhegan	Rhoni	Ricardia
Renuka	Retisha	Rhaea	Rheid	Rhonie	Ricardo
Reny	Retivia	Rhaeann	Rhema	Rhonni	Ricari'
Renyanne	Retonya	Rhaedawn	Rhema-Breanna	Rhonnie	Ricarra
Reo	Retrina	Rhaegan	Rheme	Rhonshay	Ricarria
Reolsha	Retta	Rhaejean	Rhemechia	Rhontoney	Ricasha
Reon	Reuneisha	Rhael	Rhemekiya	Rhozel	Ricaya
Reona	Reut	Rhaelyn	Rhenda	Rhueshedia	Ricca
Reonda	Reva *(0.02)*	Rhaeven	Rheo	Rhya	Riccayah

Ricci *(0.01)*
Riccole
Riccy
Ricdrakia
Ricdreka
Ricela
Rich
Richa *(0.01)*
Richaé
Richada
Richae
Richalynn
Richan
Richana
Richanda
Richara
Richard
Richarda
Richarnee
Richarr
Richarykah
Richaura
Richayla
Riche
Richea
Richel
Richela
Richele
Richelina
Richelle *(0.08)*
Richenda
Richetta
Richi
Richie
Richika
Richlyn
Richmond
Richonda
Richshama
Richshell
Richshond
Richshunda
Richyra
Rici
Ricia
Riciel
Rick'e
Rick'el
Rickael
Rickal
Rickala
Rickara
Rickayonna
Rickcanna
Rickea

Rickeahas
Rickee
Rickeesha
Rickeetta
Rickeisha
Rickeisiya
Rickel
Rickela
Rickell
Rickelle *(0.01)*
Rickena
Rickeshia
Rickesia-Anne
Ricketa
Ricketta
Rickeva
Rickey
Rickeya
Rickeyona
Rickhia
Rickhiya
Rickhuria
Ricki *(0.09)*
Ricki-Lee
Ricki-Lynn
Rickia *(0.01)*
Rickia Centrel
Rickiá
Rickie *(0.01)*
Rickie-Lee
Rickiea
Rickieda
Rickiesha
Rickieta
Rickilee
Rickima
Rickinah
Rickira
Rickisha
Rickishia
Rickita
Rickki
Ricklove
Ricknesha
Ricknisha
Rickoria
Rickquana
Rickshell
Ricky
Rickyá
Rickyah
Rickyma
Rickyna
Ricney
Rico

Ricoh
Ricola
Ricole
Ricolía
Ricquejha
Ricquel
Ricqueria
Ricquiah
Ricquonda
Ricshae
Rida
Ridda
Riddhi
Riddhini
Ridgely
Ridgena
Ridha
Ridhi
Ridhima
Ridle
Ridley
Ridwaanah
Rieanna
Riegen
Rieka
Rieki
Riel
Rieland
Rielee
Rieley
Rielle
Rielly
Riely
Riena
Rienell
Riesa
Rieta
Rietrje
Rifat
Rigina
Riham
Rihana
Rihannah
Rihanni
Riho
Rihya
Riian
Riikee
Riikka
Riiko
Rija
Rijanye
Rika
Rikara
Rikaya

Rikayla
Rikecia
Rikeema
Rikeia
Rikeishia
Rikel
Rikelle
Rikeria
Rikeshia
Riki *(0.01)*
Riki-Lee
Rikia
Rikilee
Rikili
Rikira
Rikita
Rikitiana
Rikka
Rikke
Rikkel
Rikkell
Rikketa
Rikki *(0.16)*
Rikki-Ann
Rikki-Cynda
Rikki-Lee
Rikki-Leigh
Rikki-Lyncoln
Rikki-Lynn
Rikkia
Rikkiann
Rikkie
Rikkilinn
Riko
Rikquel
Riku
Rikyah
Rikyia
Rileah
Rilee *(0.02)*
Rileigh *(0.01)*
Rilene
Rilesia
Riley *(0.41)*
Rileyann
Rilie
Rilla
Rilynn
Rim *(0.01)*
Rima *(0.01)*
Riman
Rimineet
Rimneet
Rimpal
Rimpi

Rimsha
Rina *(0.02)*
Rinayah
Rindelle
Rindi
Rine
Rinelle
Rinequa
Rinia
Rinku
Rinky
Rinnah
Rino
Rinsa
Rinya
Rio *(0.01)*
Rioanne
Rion
Riona
Riondra
Rionna
Rionna-Ronné
Rionne
Riordan
Riorose
Rioux
Ripal
Ripan
Riplee
Ripley
Riqie
Riqua
Riquel
Riquelle
Riqueza
Riquina
Riquita
Rirdasha
Risa *(0.03)*
Risaira
Risako
Risalee
Rischan
Rischelle
Risé
Riselle
Risha
Rishah
Rishan
Rishanda
Rishara
Rishawnta
Risheena
Rishell
Rishetta

Rishina
Rishma
Rishon
Risica
Risie
Risikat
Rissa
Riste
Rita *(0.16)*
Rita-Ashley
Ritaann
Ritacia
Ritah
Ritalyn
Ritanna
Ritche
Ritha
Rithem
Rithly
Ritia
Ritika
Ritney
Ritsza
Ritta
Rittana
Rittie
Rittu
Ritu
Ritza
Ritzhielle
Riva
Rivanna
River *(0.01)*
River-Dawn
Rivers
Riviera
Riviera Joanna
Rivierra
Rivka
Rivkah
Rixie
Rixing
Riya
Riyadh
Riyael
Riyah
Riyan
Riyanna
Riyasha
Riyokuho
Riz
Riza
Rizia
Rizka
Riztine

Rizza	Robindawn	Rockaycielle	Rodniqua	Rojen	Rometra
Rmeisha	Robine	Rockee	Rodnique	Rojia	Romi
Rneshia	Robinette	Rockel	Rodniquia	Rojiene	Romia
Ro Nikkiya	Robiniki	Rockele	Rodnisha (0.01)	Rokeisha	Romiatia
Ro Zanna	Robinique	Rockell	Rodnita	Rokeith	Romicia
Ro'asia	Robinn	Rockelle	Rodnora	Rokell	Romie
Ro'chelle	Robinque	Rockia	Rodqueria	Rokera	Romina
Ro'janae	Robinson	Rockie	Rodra	Rokesha	Romita
Ro'quesha	Robisa	Rockiera	Rodreama	Rokeyla	Romke
Ro'quil	Robkeisha	Rockne	Rodreka	Rokhaya	Romney
Ro'shae	Robkeshia	Rocquail	Rodrica	Rokhsane	Romniesha
Ro'shanno	Robneshia	Rocquel	Rodricka	Rokia	Romolla
Ro'shaunda	Robnetta	Rocquia	Rodrika	Rokianda	Romona
Ro'shawna	Robreesha	Rocy	Rodriqua	Rokira	Romonia
Ro'shontay	Robreshia	Rod' Reona	Rodrisha	Rokiya	Romorreau
Ro-Knesha	Robretia	Rod'nee	Rodsalan	Roksana	Romy (0.01)
Roaisha	Robria	Roda	Rodshanik	Rokshana	Romykia
Roanne	Robricha	Rodacia	Rodshay	Roksolana	Ron Aka
Roastanna	Robrieal	Rodaciá	Rodshea	Rola	Ron Derica
Roayasha	Robrielle	Rodashia	Rodsheeda	Rolanda (0.02)	Ron Jerica
Rob'shaunda	Robriyion	Rodaysha	Rodsheena	Rolande	Ron Nae
Roba	Robtresia	Roddashia	Rodsheka	Rolando	Ron Taje
Robann	Robtrice	Rodedra	Rodtavia	Rolaunda	Ron'kitea
Robberica	Robvena	Rodeisha	Rodterriauna	Roleesha	Ron'kyesha
Robbi (0.01)	Roby	Rodell	Rodtesha	Rolena	Ron'nequah
Robbi-Lynn	Robyance	Rodelle	Roeann	Rolesha	Ron'nesha
Robbie (0.01)	Robyn (0.38)	Rodenisha	Roechelle	Rolexis	Ron'nisha
Robbie-Lynn	Robyn-Asia	Roderica	Roelisha	Rolicia	Ron'tavia
Robbin	Robyn-Lee	Roderico	Roelyn	Roliesha	Rona (0.01)
Robby	Robyne	Rodesha	Roenea	Rolinda	Rona-Jean
Robbye	Robynette	Rodesia	Roesha	Rolita	Ronaca
Robbyn	Robynn (0.01)	Rodessa	Rofeo	Rollene	Ronae
Robbynn	Robynn Claire	Rodika	Roga	Rolonda (0.01)	Ronaé
Robdreka	Robynne	Rodisha	Rogan	Roma	Ronaesha
Robeen	Rocci	Rodishah	Rogean	Romai	Ronaeshá
Robekka	Rocclaysion	Rodjae	Rogeana	Romaine	Ronajah
Roben	Rocelle	Rodjzae	Rogelia	Romalysia	Ronald
Robena	Rocelyn	Rodkeisha	Rogelio	Romana	Ronaldine
Robernae	Rochallene	Rodkeysha	Rogelle	Romania	Ronaldo
Robernecia	Rocheal	Rodline	Rogena	Romanick	Ronalyn
Robernique	Rochealle	Rodneayna	Rogene	Romany	Ronangri
Robersha	Rocheelle	Rodneca	Roger Finne	Romaya	Ronasia
Roberson	Rochel (0.01)	Rodnecia	Rogeria	Romdnet	Ronata
Robert (0.01)	Rochele	Rodneisha (0.01)	Rogers	Rome	Ronayshia
Roberta (0.05)	Rochelina	Rodneiyka	Rogina	Romeca	Ronaysia
Robertniece	Rochell	Rodneka	Rohane	Romeche	Ronda (0.01)
Robertnisha	Rochella	Rodnequea	Rohanié	Romecia	Rondasha
Roberto	Rochelle (0.23)	Rodnesha (0.01)	Roheen	Romeika	Rondaysha
Robey	Rochelle Dawn	Rodneshia	Rohina	Romeisia	Rondesia
Robi	Rochellene	Rodney	Rohini	Romeka	Rondi
Robia	Rocheney	Rodneycia	Roikiesha	Romel	Rondie
Robiane	Rochun	Rodneysha	Roisheen	Romelia	Rondisha
Robiauna	Rocio (0.24)	Rodni	Roisin (0.01)	Romer	Rondorian
Robin (0.37)	Rocita	Rodnicka	Roja	Romesha	Rondraell
Robina	Rockaai	Rodnika	Rojda	Romeshia	Rondreka

Rondrell	Ronna'y	Roquesha	Rosamay	Rosella *(0.01)*	Roshicka
Rone	Ronnae	Roquie	Rosamelia	Roselle	Roshiga
Roneacia	Ronnay	Roquira	Rosamond	Rosellen	Roshilsa
Roneasha	Ronneca	Rori	Rosana *(0.01)*	Rosellian	Roshin
Ronecia	Ronnee	Rorie	Rosandra	Rosely	Roshna
Ronedisa	Ronneicia	Roro	Rosangel	Roselyn *(0.02)*	Roshnee
Ronee	Ronneisha	Rory *(0.01)*	Rosangela	Roselyne	Roshni *(0.01)*
Roneesha	Ronneka	Rosa *(0.60)*	Rosangelica *(0.01)*	Roselynn	Roshny
Roneika	Ronnekia	Rosa Avelina	Rosangelly	Rosemari	Roshonda *(0.01)*
Roneique	Ronnesha	Rosa Maria	Rosanise	Rosemarie *(0.07)*	Roshowna
Roneisha *(0.01)*	Ronneshia	Rosa-Altesa	Rosanna *(0.03)*	Rosemary *(0.17)*	Roshuma
Roneishala	Ronnetta	Rosa-Victoria	Rosanne *(0.01)*	Rosemely	Roshumba
Roneka	Ronney	Rosaalva	Rosarah	Rosemeyer	Roshunda *(0.01)*
Ronel	Ronni *(0.03)*	Rosabelia	Rosaria	Rosemond	Roshy
Ronelle	Ronni'	Rosabella	Rosarie	Rosemund	Roshyian
Ronequa	Ronnica	Rosabeth	Rosario *(0.08)*	Rosend	Rosi
Ronese	Ronnie *(0.03)*	Rosaele	Rosary	Rosenda	Rosia
Ronesha *(0.01)*	Ronniesha	Rosaelvira	Rosauara	Rosenna	Rosibel
Roneshia *(0.01)*	Ronnika	Rosaelys	Rosaugrua	Rosenne	Rosida
Roneshina	Ronnise	Rosagloria	Rosaura *(0.02)*	Rosenni	Rosie *(0.07)*
Ronesia	Ronnisha *(0.01)*	Rosaida	Roschine	Roseryn	Rosie Lee
Ronessia	Ronnita	Rosaidi	Rose *(0.36)*	Rosetrina	Rosiebel
Ronetta	Ronnitra	Rosaisela	Rose Ann	Rosetta *(0.01)*	Rosieeather
Ronette	Ronntasia	Rosajean	Rose Anne	Rosette	Rosiekia
Roni *(0.01)*	Ronny	Rosalana	Rose Marie *(0.02)*	Rosey	Rosiland
Ronia	Ronnyece	Rosaland	Rose Mary	Rosezetta	Rosimer
Ronica *(0.01)*	Ronquaya	Rosalba *(0.03)*	Rose-Anick	Roshae	Rosina
Ronicia	Ronquayla	Rosalea	Rose-Anna	Roshan	Rosindee
Ronie	Ronquel	Rosalee *(0.01)*	Rose-Anne	Roshana	Rosine
Ronieka	Ronsha	Rosaleen	Rose-Laure	Roshanaa	Rosio *(0.05)*
Ronielle	Ronshana	Rosaleigh	Rose-Lynda	Roshanda	Rosita *(0.02)*
Roniesha	Ronshaunda	Rosaleina	Rose-Marie	Roshani	Rosivel
Ronika *(0.01)*	Rontaisha	Rosalene	Rose-Mary	Roshann	Rosland
Ronina	Rontaria	Rosaleta	Rosea	Roshanna	Rosley
Roniqua	Rontasja	Rosalexa	Roseabelle	Roshanti	Roslin
Ronique *(0.01)*	Rontavia	Rosaley	Rosealee	Roshaun	Roslyn *(0.02)*
Ronise	Rontisha	Rosali	Rosealeen	Roshauna	Roslynn
Ronisha *(0.04)*	Rontrice	Rosalia *(0.04)*	Rosealie	Roshaund	Rosmari
Ronisha-Veniqua	Ronturria	Rosalie *(0.17)*	Roseann	Roshaunda	Rosmarie
Ronit	Ronya	Rosalin	Roseanna *(0.01)*	Roshawn	Rosmery
Ronita	Ronyá	Rosalina *(0.02)*	Roseanne *(0.01)*	Roshawna	Rosmita
Ronitra	Ronye	Rosalind *(0.02)*	Rosebud	Roshawnda	Rosmun
Roniya	Ronyea	Rosalinda *(0.07)*	Roseelise	Roshayla	Rosolen
Ronja	Ronyiek	Rosaline	Roselaine	Roshea-Lee	Ross
Ronjae	Roohi	Rosaliss	Roseland	Rosheda	Rossana
Ronjanique	Roopa	Rosalva *(0.02)*	Roselande	Rosheeda	Rossi
Ronkay	Roopdip	Rosalyan	Roselani	Rosheena	Rossie
Ronkeia	Rooseline	Rosalyn *(0.04)*	Roselba	Rosheika	Rossina
Ronkeiria	Root	Rosalynd	Roselee	Rosheka	Rosslyn
Ronkeria	Ropafadzo	Rosalynde	Roselene	Roshel	Rossmary
Ronkia	Roquaysia	Rosalyne	Roseli	Roshell	Rossnelly
Ronkresha	Roquel	Rosalynia	Roselie	Roshelle	Rostella
Ronksiha	Roquell	Rosalynn	Roseline *(0.01)*	Roshely	Rostina
Ronmia	Roqueri	Rosamaria *(0.02)*	Roselious	Roshenika	Rosvin
Ronna *(0.01)*	Roquesan	Rosamarie	Rosell	Rosherry	Rosy *(0.02)*

Rosylin	Roya *(0.02)*	Ru'ja	Rukhma	Russlyn	Ryda
Roszaliyn	Royal	Ruaa	Rukhsaar	Rusti	Rydel
Roszanna	Royalandra	Ruanne	Rukhsana	Rustin	Rydell
Rotasha	Royale	Ruba *(0.01)*	Rukhsar	Rusty	Rydricka
Rotcia	Royaliesha	Rubab	Rukia	Rut	Rye
Rotesha	Royalty	Rubal	Rukiat	Ruta	Ryee
Rothavy	Royan	Rubbie	Rukiya	Ruth *(0.36)*	Ryeema
Rotisha	Royce	Rubby	Rukmini	Ruth Deirdre	Ryeisha
Roubnide	Roychelle	Rubee	Ruksana	Ruth-Elizabeth	Ryelee
Rouby	Roydasha	Rubeena	Ruksha	Ruth-Joy	Ryeley
Rouel	Royelle	Ruben	Rula	Ruthann	Ryelie
Rouen Roz	Roykevia	Rubeni	Ruleigh	Ruthanna	Ryelynn
Roukaya	Roylene	Rubenisha	Ruley	Ruthannah	Ryen
Roula	Royneisha	Rubi *(0.06)*	Ruma	Ruthanne	Ryene
Rounaq	Royneka	Rubianna	Rumana	Ruthchama	Ryenice
Roury	Roynerah	Rubicela	Rumeet	Ruthell	Ryequira
Roussna	Roynisha	Rubicelia	Rumer	Ruthie *(0.01)*	Ryesha
Rovianie	Roynita	Rubicilia	Rumeysa	Ruthlyn	Ryessa
Rowa	Royqueshia	Rubid	Rumneet	Ruthy	Ryeza
Rowan *(0.05)*	Royshan	Rubie	Rumor	Ruun	Rygent
Rowana	Roysheka	Rubiela	Rumsha	Ruvi	Ryianna
Rowayda	Royshika	Rubiera	Rumya	Ruvicela	Ryin
Rowdee	Royshyya	Rubina	Runa	Ruviela	Ryinne
Rowe	Royunna	Rubini	Rund	Ruvinder	Rykayla
Rowela	Roz	Rubis	Runeka	Ruvinka	Rykel
Rowelena	Roz Che	Ruby *(0.49)*	Runeshi	Ruweida	Ryken
Rowen	Roza	Ruby Belen	Runisha	Ruxandra	Rykenshia
Rowena	Rozalin	Ruby-Mae	Runquia	Ruyny	Rykeria
Rowey	Rozalind	Rubyselia	Ruo-Ying	Ruyra	Rykia
Rowkayah	Rozaly	Ruchama	Rupal	Ruza	Rykiana
Rowley	Rozalyn	Ruchdia	Rupali	Ruzan	Rykie-Lee
Rowmel	Rozana	Ruchelle	Rupika	Ruzha	Rykki
Rownna	Rozeena	Ruchi	Rupinder *(0.01)*	Rwan	Ryla
Rowyn	Rozel	Ruchika	Rupleen	Rwanda	Rylah
Rox-Anne	Rozell	Ruchsdia	Rupneet	Rwonda	Rylan
Roxan	Rozelli	Rudi	Ruqayya	Ry Leah	Ryland
Roxana *(0.16)*	Rozelyn	Rudrecia	Ruqayyah	Ry Nesha	Rylann
Roxana-Marisol	Rozena	Rudsel	Ruquesha	Ry'keita	Rylea
Roxane *(0.05)*	Rozetta	Rudy	Ruscia-Lea	Ry'nesha	Rylee *(0.15)*
Roxann	Rozhaana	Ruel	Rush	Rya	Rylei
Roxanna *(0.07)*	Rozheen	Ruelle	Rusha	Ryah	Ryleigh *(0.02)*
Roxannah	Rozia	Ruemor	Rushai	Ryalli	Ryles
Roxanne *(0.51)*	Rozina	Ruffa	Rushane	Ryan *(0.14)*	Ryley *(0.02)*
Roxanne Alexis	Rozlin	Rufina	Rushawna	Ryan-Michelle	Ryli
Roxayn	Rozlyn	Ruhammah	Rusheena	Ryana	Rylie *(0.06)*
Roxe	Rozlynn	Ruhie	Rushnie	Ryane *(0.01)*	Rylin
Roxie *(0.01)*	Rozza	Ruindia	Rushpa	Ryann *(0.07)*	Rylisha
Roxie-Lyn	Rozzie	Ruis	Rusla	Ryanna *(0.01)*	Rylleigh
Roxmara	Rrachel	Ruiying	Ruslana	Ryanne *(0.02)*	Ryly
Roxmery	Rraeanna	Rujia	Russ	Ryatt	Rym
Roxolana	Rrayven	Rukan	Russanalee	Rybeca	Ryneisha
Roxsana	Rregan	Rukayah	Russelle	Rybecca	Ryneqa
Roxy *(0.01)*	Rrogan	Rukayat	Russhay	Rybeckah	Ryner
Roxyn	Rroya-Rae	Rukeih	Russhonica	Rycal	Rynesha
Roxzann	Rryla	Rukeya	Russia	Rychada	Ryneshia

Rynessa	Sa'nyah	Saben	Sabrine-Shelley	Sadécia	Saemin
Rynisha	Sa'poria	Sabena	Sabrinia	Sadea	Saesha
Rynnelle	Sa'qura	Saber	Sabrinna	Sadedria	Saeti
Rynnionsha	Sa'ron	Sabersy	Sabrinsarai	Sadee *(0.01)*	Safa *(0.01)*
Rynshaila	Sa'taitshia	Sabeth	Sabriya	Sadeeqa	Safaa
Ryoisha	Sa'toria	Sabetta	Sabroya	Sadeisya	Safafina
Ryonna	Sa-Reyiah	Sabey	Sabrunia	Sadeja	Safaray
Rysa	Sa-Tiya	Sabha	Sabryee	Sadelle	Safari
Rysah	Saa'idah	Sabhah	Sabryna *(0.03)*	Sadena	Safaria
Rysha-Rae	Saabirah	Sabian	Sabrynna	Sadequa	Safarrah
Ryshanna	Saabria	Sabiha	Saby	Sadera	Safarrie
Ryshay	Saachi	Sabija	Sabyl	Saderia	Safeeya
Ryshea	Saada	Sabin	Sacajawea	Sadey	Saffa
Ryshelia	Saadet	Sabina *(0.05)*	Sacauya	Sadhana	Saffiyah
Ryshell	Saadi	Sabine *(0.01)*	Saccid	Sadhika	Saffron *(0.01)*
Ryshenna	Saadia	Sabitha	Saccora	Sadi *(0.01)*	Safi
Ryshi'ma	Saadiha	Sabiyah	Saceyon	Sadia *(0.01)*	Safia *(0.01)*
Ryveen	Saadiqah	Sable *(0.01)*	Sacha *(0.02)*	Sadiah	Safiah
Ryver	Saadiya	Saboreyah	Sacharia	Sadie *(0.41)*	Safilina
Ryvkah	Saadya	Saboyce	Sache	Sadie Anne	Safira
Ryzhel	Saafir	Sabra *(0.02)*	Sachelle	Sadiecia	Safire
	Saahel	Sabrah	Sachely	Sadielynn	Safiya *(0.01)*
	Saakshi	Sabrar	Sachi	Sadies	Safiyah
-S-	Saalehah	Sabrayia	Sachia	Sadiey	Safiyyah
	Saalihah	Sabre	Sachiko	Sadilynn	Safonya
S *(0.06)*	Saambavy	Sabrea	Sachine	Sadina	Safoora
S Me	Saandra	Sabreah	Sacia	Sadisleidy	Safra
S Tesha	Saara	Sabreanner	Sacie	Sadiya	Safraa
S'einna	Saarah	Sabree	Sacora	Sadiyah	Safron
S'mantha	Saasha	Sabreea	Sacordia	Sadiyyah	Saga
S'mia	Saatema	Sabreen *(0.01)*	Sacori	Sadlene	Sagal *(0.01)*
S'nicca	Saayd	Sabreena *(0.01)*	Sacoria	Sadney	Sagan
S'noviah	Saba *(0.02)*	Sabrena *(0.01)*	Sacorra Ren	Sadona	Sagana
S'quana	Sabaah	Sabrene	Sacorya	Sadondria	Sagarika
S.	Sabah	Sabreona	Sacouya	Sadora	Sage *(0.13)*
S. Patton	Sabai	Sabrey	Sacoya	Sadra	Sagel
S. Rachel	Sabal	Sabreyon	Sacred	Sadreal	Sagesse
Sa	Sabana	Sabri	Sacresha	Sadrena	Saghar
Sa Quana	Sabar	Sabria *(0.01)*	Sacuesta	Sadricka	Sagina
Sa Sha	Sabarina	Sabriah	Sadá	Sadrina	Sagrario
Sa'brina	Sabariz	Sabrian	Sad'e	Sady	Sagry
Sa'brinna	Sabatinie	Sabriana	Sada	Sadya	Sagun
Sa'briyah	Sabba	Sabrianna	Sadá	Sadye	Sah'quandra
Sa'coya	Sabbath	Sabriarra	Sada'sha	Sadyia	Sah'quita
Sa'daziah	Sabbatina	Sabrie	Sadaf *(0.01)*	Sae	Sahaana
Sa'de	Sabbitha	Sabriea	Sadaff	Sae-Lynn	Sahab
Sa'dedria	Sabdanaa	Sabrielle	Sadalia	Saeah	Sahaira
Sa'dia	Sabdie	Sabrien	Sadara	Saeda	Sahajbir
Sa'keena	Sabe	Sabriena	Sadari	Saedee	Sahala
Sa'lena	Sabeeha	Sabrina *(2.00)*	Sadaryle	Saeeda	Sahale
Sa'leste	Sabeen	Sabrina Anne	Sadasia	Saeema	Sahalya
Sa'loyal	Sabeina	Sabrina Mae	Saddia	Saeghan	Sahana
Sa'mara	Sabel	Sabrinah	Saddie	Saeko	Sahar *(0.04)*
Sa'metrice	Sabela	Sabrinca	Sade *(0.10)*	Sael	Sahara *(0.03)*
Sa'miya	Sabella	Sabrine *(0.01)*	Sadé *(0.02)*	Saelynn	Saharah
Sa'mone					

Sahari	Saipriya	Sakshi	Salishia	Samantha *(10.65)*	Sami *(0.01)*
Saheedat	Saiquan	Sakura	Salissa	Samantha Jo	Sami Jo
Saheer	Saira *(0.04)*	Sakya	Salista	Samantha Rae	Sami-Jo
Saheli	Saira Banu	Sakyiwaa	Salita	Samanthá	Samia *(0.01)*
Saher *(0.01)*	Saira-Naaz	Sakyra	Sallee	Samantha-Anne	Samiah *(0.01)*
Sahib	Sairaf	Sala	Sallene	Samantha-Hei	Samiaia
Sahibah	Sairah	Salaam	Sallianne	Samantha-Jo	Samiat
Sahibpreet	Sairaya	Salafina	Sallie *(0.01)*	Samantha-Lynn	Samienta
Sahilaja	Sairi	Salah	Sallie-Joe	Samantha-Maja	Samiera
Sahina	Saisa	Salaha	Sallina	Samantha-Maria	Samiesha
Sahira	Saisha	Salai	Sally *(0.19)*	Samantha-Marie	Samiha
Sahla	Saja	Salal	Sally-Kay	Samantha-Nicole	Samijo
Sahlaha	Sajaa	Salam	Sally-Sue	Samantha-Phuon	Samila
Sahndrea	Sajada	Salama	Sallyan	Samantha-Rose	Samina
Sahr	Sajah	Salamasina	Sallye	Samanthah	Samir
Sahra *(0.01)*	Sajal	Salanta	Salma *(0.02)*	Samanthan	Samira *(0.06)*
Sahrah	Sajani	Salathea	Salome *(0.01)*	Samanthe	Samira Carmen
Sahrang	Sajda	Salathia	Salomi	Samanthia	Samirah
Sahraya	Saje	Salayh	Salon	Samar *(0.01)*	Samire
Sahreena	Sajeana-Lee	Saldy	Saloni	Samar-Omar	Samiria
Sahrina	Sajeda	Saleana	Salonica	Samara *(0.07)*	Samirora
Sahsa	Sajedah	Saleema	Salonje	Samarah *(0.01)*	Samirra
Sahsha	Sajia	Saleemah	Salote	Samari	Samita
Sahvanna	Sajida	Saleen	Salsabil	Samaria *(0.02)*	Samitra
Sahyanna	Sajil	Saleena *(0.01)*	Salu	Samariah	Samiya *(0.01)*
Sahyli	Sakaana	Saleesha	Salud	Samarian	Samiyah
Sai	Sakah	Saleeta	Salwa	Samarie	Samiyyah
Sai-Sawn	Sakalya	Saleh	Saly	Samariel	Sammantha *(0.05)*
Saible	Sakara	Saleha	Salyna	Samarra	Sammary
Saida	Sakari	Salehah	Salynn	Samarrea	Sammatha
Saidah	Sakeena	Salem *(0.01)*	Sam	Samarys	Sammeah
Saide	Sakemia	Salena *(0.08)*	Sama	Samatha *(0.03)*	Sammi *(0.01)*
Saidee	Sakena	Salene	Sama'ria	Samauria	Sammi-Jo
Saidey	Sakendra	Salenna	Samaa	Samay	Sammibelle
Saidi	Sakendria	Saleria	Samadhi	Samaya	Sammie *(0.01)*
Saidia	Sakenna	Saleshia	Samadi	Samayia	Sammiyah
Saidie	Sakera	Salesta	Samah *(0.01)*	Samayntha	Sammy *(0.01)*
Saidy	Sakeria	Saleta	Samahir	Samderla	Samneethea
Saieesha	Sakesia	Salexis	Samaira	Sameca	Samntha
Saiegra	Sakeya	Saleya	Samairra	Sameen	Samoan
Saiena	Sakeyna	Salgado	Samaiya	Sameena	Samoane
Saige *(0.03)*	Sakhena	Salia	Samaiyah	Sameera	Samolia
Saigh	Sakhet	Salice	Samaly	Sameha	Samon
Saiida	Sakia	Salicia	Saman	Sameika	Samona
Saij	Sakile	Salida	Samana	Sameisha	Samone *(0.02)*
Saila	Sakina *(0.01)*	Saliem	Samanatha *(0.01)*	Samejah	Samoné
Sailor	Sakinah	Salihah	Samanda	Sameka	Samonia
Sailys	Sakira	Salima	Samandeep	Samelia	Samora
Saima	Sakiricka	Salime	Samandip	Samella	Samorra
Saimila	Sakirra	Salin	Samaneha	Samelli	Samotá
Saimyl	Sakisha	Salina *(0.13)*	Samanntha	Samentha	Sampavi
Saint Claire	Sakita	Salinah	Samanta *(0.03)*	Samera	Samquette
Saint-Anne	Sakiya	Salinda	Samantah	Sameria	Samra
Saintalise	Sakiyna	Salisa	Samantan	Samesha	Samrah
Saintaneria	Sakondra	Salisha	Samanth	Sametria	Samrath

Samrawit	Sandemetrica	Sangita	Santeala	Saporia	Sarabeth
Samree	Sanderica	Sangora	Santeda	Saporsha	Sarabhjot
Samreen	Sandhya	Sangwon	Santerica	Sapphira	Sarabi
Samril	Sandi (0.02)	Sania	Santerri	Sapphire (0.02)	Sarabia
Samriti	Sandia	Sanica	Santerria	Sapphitah	Sarabie
Samsam	Sandiamond	Sanice	Santese	Sapphron	Sarabjoat
Samshyra	Sandibel	Sanika	Santesha	Sapria	Sarabpreet
Samsona	Sandie	Saniqua	Santessa	Saprina	Saracelia
Samtha	Sandijah	Sanisha	Santeyanna	Saqiah	Sarada
Samtonia	Sandilyn	Sanissa	Santhi	Saqoia	Saradiane
Samuel (0.02)	Sandina	Sanithe	Santhiya	Saqouah	Sarae
Samuela	Sandip	Saniya	Santhosia	Saquan	Saraeli
Samuella	Sandisha	Sanja	Santia	Saquanna	Saraellen
Samuelle (0.01)	Sandiya	Sanjana	Santiana	Saquasha	Sarafina (0.01)
Samunique	Sandonna	Sanje	Santiara	Saquavia	Sarah (11.68)
Samya	Sandra (1.00)	Sanjeevani	Santierra	Saqueenia	Sarah Alexandra
Samychia	Sandra Leticia	Sanjel	Santiesha	Saquella	Sarah Ann (0.01)
Samyra	Sandra Nika	Sanjida	Santina (0.01)	Saqui	Sarah Anne (0.01)
Samyria	Sandra-Lee	Sanjit	Santisia	Saquia	Sarah Elise
Samyuktha	Sandra-Lynn	Sanjitha	Santonea	Saquita	Sarah Elizabeth
San	Sandraliz	Sanjna	Santonika	Saquoia	Sarah Eve (0.02)
San Juana	Sandré	Sanjog	Santonya	Saquoya	Sarah Jade
San Juanita	Sandrea	Sanjot	Santoria	Saquoyah	Sarah Jane (0.02)
San Tanna	Sandreak	Sanjuana	Santoya	Saqwess Joanne	Sarah Jeanne
San"dria	Sandreana	Sanjuanita	Santrece	Sar	(0.01)
San'netrisha	Sandrene	Sankarrious	Santremica	Sar'dia	Sarah Jo
San'torria	Sandria	Sankeria	Santrese	Sara (3.30)	Sarah Katherine
San'tyera	Sandrianna	Sanmika	Santria	Sara Ann	Sarah Kim
San-Beria	Sandrica	Sanna (0.01)	Santrice	Sara Eve (0.01)	Sarah Marie (0.01)
San-My	Sandrice	Sannarey	Santrisca	Sara Grace	Sarah Maude
Sana (0.04)	Sandricka	Sanne	Santrise	Sara Jane (0.01)	(0.03)
Sana-Shaheed	Sandriea	Sannie	Santryvia	Sara Jean	Sarah Micaela
Sanaa	Sandrina	Sannon	Santwanisha	Sara Joe	Sarah Nicole
Sanaa-Walid	Sandrine (0.10)	Sanora	Sanvir	Sara Marie	Sarah Rebecca
Sanaah	Sandtrice	Sanova	Sanya	Sara Maude (0.01)	Sarah Rose
Sanae	Sandy (0.31)	Sanovia	Sanyia	Sara Nayeli	Sarah Scott
Sanah	Sandya	Sanpreet	Saod	Sara Tamar	Sarah Tarek
Sanam	Sandybell	Sanquana	Saoli	Sara Wolf	Sarah Taylor
Sanamtha	Sanea	Sanquanita	Saori	Sara-Amanda	Sarah Victoria
Sanantha	Saneh	Sanquita	Sapan	Sara-Ann	Sarah-Ann
Sanara	Saneitra	Sansaesha	Sapana	Sara-Anne	Sarah-Anne
Sanatra	Saneiya	Sanskriti	Sapaphenea	Sara-Irene	Sarah-Ashlie
Sanaya	Saneka	Santa	Sapena	Sara-Jane	Sarah-Beth
Sanaye	Sanela	Santana (0.06)	Sapfo	Sara-Jean	Sarah-Bly
Sanaz	Sanella	Santanese	Sapha	Sara-Jo	Sarah-Elizabeth
Sanbria	Sanequa	Santania	Sapheria	Sara-Kate	Sarah-Grace
Sancha	Sanericka	Santanna (0.01)	Saphire (0.01)	Sara-Lee	Sarah-Gwendoly
Sanchesta	Sanerrika	Santannaé	Saphron	Sara-Michelle	Sarah-Jane
Sanchi	Sanessa	Santannah	Saphronia	Sara-Ray	Sarah-Jean
Sanchia	Sanetra	Santara	Saphyr	Sara-Rene	Sarah-Jo
Sanchita	Sanford	Santasha	Saphyra	Sara-Rose	Sarah-Joy
Sanda	Sang	Santasia	Saphyre	Sara-Vanesa	Sarah-Katie
Sanddii	Sangai	Santavia	Sapir	Saraah	Sarah-Laurie
Sandee	Sangeeta	Santaya	Sapiria	Saraalicia	Sarah-Lilly
Sandeep (0.01)	Sangeetha	Santé	Sapna (0.01)	Sarabelle	Sarah-Lynn

Sarah-Mae	Sarasha	Sariya	Sashea	Saturn	Savantha
Sarah-May	Sarasija	Sariyah	Sasheeka	Satveer	Savara
Sarah-Nicole	Sarathel	Sarmija	Sashelle	Satvinder	Savaria
Sarah-Rose	Saratho	Sarmila	Sashera	Satvir	Savasia
Sarah-Theresa	Saravy	Sarmin	Sashey	Satwant	Savasja
Saraha	Saray *(0.02)*	Sarmina	Sashi	Satwinder	Savaughna
Sarahann	Saraya	Sarmla	Sashia	Satya	Savaunnah
Sarahanna	Sarayh	Sarnia	Sashira	Sau	Savaya
Sarahbeth	Sarayha	Saroeum	Sashlee	Saubrenna	Saveah
Saraheve	Sarayna	Sarojani	Sashya	Saucha	Saveon
Sarahfina	Sarban	Sarom	Saskia *(0.01)*	Sauchi	Savera
Sarahgin	Sarbjit	Saron	Saskya	Saudee	Savett
Sarahi *(0.03)*	Sarbjot	Sarona	Sasshanae	Saudi	Saveyonna
Sarahina	Sardai	Saroya	Sasshay	Saudia	Savhana
Sarahjane	Sare	Saroyo	Sasshena	Saudia Aradia	Savhanna *(0.01)*
Sarahkate	Saredo	Sarquetta	Sassille	Saudiah	Savhannah
Sarahlyn	Saree	Sarra *(0.01)*	Sassy	Saufeeya Bint	Savilla
Sarahlynn	Sareena	Sarrah *(0.02)*	Sasy	Sauitre	Saville
Sarahmarie	Sareka	Sarrahmindel	Saszha	Saul	Savin
Sarahn	Sarel	Sarrauh	Satai	Saumya	Savina
Sarahy	Saren	Sarren	Satandra	Sauna	Savine
Sarai *(0.13)*	Sarena *(0.04)*	Sarrie	Satania	Saunabria	Savinee
Sarai'	Sarenatée	Sarrina	Satara	Saundra *(0.01)*	Savinya
Saraida	Sarenna	Sarron	Satchel	Saundria	Savita
Saraii Paola	Sarese	Sarronda	Satchell	Saung	Savitri
Saraileigh	Sarethia	Sarscha	Sateeva	Sauntasia	Savneet
Saraisabel	Saretta	Sarswattie	Satelyn	Saurina	Savnnah
Sarait	Sarette	Sarussa	Satera	Sauscha	Savon
Saraj	Sareya	Sarvenaz	Saterdae	Sausha	Savona
Sarajane	Sargentina	Sarvin	Sateria	Sauzray	Savonna
Sarajayne	Sarha *(0.01)*	Sarvnaz	Saterica	Sava	Savonnah
Sarajean	Sari *(0.01)*	Sarwary	Satia	Savacia	Savonne
Sarajo	Saria *(0.01)*	Sary	Satia Darrell	Savahana	Savoria
Saralee	Sariah *(0.02)*	Saryane	Satie	Savahanna	Savoury
Saralena	Sarian	Saryn	Satierhia	Savahna	Savoy
Saralin	Sariann	Saryna	Satieva	Savana *(0.07)*	Savoya
Saralita	Sarianna	Sas	Satin	Savanah *(0.19)*	Savreen
Saraliz	Sarie	Sasa	Satinae	Savanah-Lia	Savtaj
Saraly	Sariem	Sascha	Satinka	Savanaha	Savun
Saralyn *(0.01)*	Sarika	Sasha *(0.30)*	Satiqua	Savanha	Sawlehah
Saralyn Si	Sarilda	Sasha Davyo	Sativa *(0.01)*	Savanna *(0.43)*	Sawnicia
Saralynn	Sarin	Sashá	Satomi	Savanna-Lee	Sawsan
Saramaria	Sarina *(0.11)*	Sasha-Parisa	Satonia	Savannah *(2.19)*	Sawyar
Saran	Sarina-Cheryl-	Sashae	Satore	Savannah Jo	Sawyer *(0.02)*
Sarana	Lynn	Sashah	Satori	Savannah	Sawyor
Saranah	Sarinaty	Sashai	Satoria	Kathlee	Saxon
Saranda	Sarine	Sashalee	Satoya	Savannah-Jade	Saxony
Saranjit	Sarinna	Sashaly	Satranina	Savannah-Lynne	Saya
Saranki	Sarinthea	Sashamarie	Satrasha	Savannah-Rose	Sayah
Saranne	Sarish	Sashana	Satrina	Savannahche	Sayahda
Saranya	Sarisha	Sasharan	Satsuki	Savannahh	Sayaka
Saranyah	Sarissa	Sashary	Sattia	Savannan	Sayanikka
Saraphina	Sarit	Sashaunna	Sattoria	Savannha	Sayde *(0.01)*
Saraphine	Sarita *(0.01)*	Sashawna	Sattyadeep	Savannhah	Saydee *(0.01)*
Sararose	Saritta	Sashay	Satuki	Savanpreet	Saydi

Saydia
Saydie
Saydy
Sayer
Sayge
Sayira
Sayla
Saylah
Saylor
Sayma
Sayna
Saynab
Sayo
Sayoa
Sayona
Sayra *(0.01)*
Sayrah
Sayre
Sayri
Saysa
Saysha
Saysheon
Sayumi
Sayuri
Sayury
Sayvana
Sayvanna
Sayvon
Sayward
Sayyid
Sazeda
Sazurae
Sbeen
Scarlene
Scarlet *(0.03)*
Scarleth
Scarlett *(0.12)*
Scarlett Tara
Scarlette
Scarlit
Scarlly
Scarly
Scego
Scenthuri
Sch
Sch'nisha
Sch'vannia
Schae
Schae-Lynne
Schaenelle
Schafer
Schaffer
Schalee
Schaleenah
Schalyce

Schalyn
Scham
Schamona
Schanae
Schanael
Schanavia
Schandellyn
Schaneekiya
Schanelle
Schanice
Schaniece
Schaniya
Schantell
Schantrice
Schaquonda
Scharah
Schari
Scharlee
Scharlet
Schataé
Schatyanna
Schayla
Schdreqa
Schea
Scheherazade
Scheherzade
Schekinah
Schelby
Schemyrda
Schenera
Schenice
Schenina
Schenita
Scheper
Scherezade
Schericka
Scherlynn
Scherry
Schicarée
Schinae
Schmera
Schmonia
Schnea
Schniqua
Schnique
Schnorra
Schoenstatt
Schrader
Schranda
Schuyler *(0.01)*
Schwanna
Schylar
Schyler *(0.02)*
Schylla
Schymira

Scierra
Scikea
Sciler
Scintavia
Scinteria
Scolaysha
Scolisha
Scot'esha
Scotia
Scotisha
Scotland
Scotlin
Scott
Scottahja
Scotti
Scottice
Scottie
Scottlyn
Scotty
Scout *(0.01)*
Scoutt
Scycyly
Scyla
Se Quayla
Se Quoia
Sé
Séasia
Sédreana
Sékedra
Séqualia
Sérress
Sésha
Se-Won
Sea
Sea-Wai
Seacret
Seaera
Seaira *(0.01)*
Seairra *(0.01)*
Seairya
Sealena
Seamas
Sean *(0.03)*
Seaná
Seana *(0.02)*
Seana-Lee
Seanasea
Seandjasia
Seandra
Seandre
Seandrea
Seanei
Seaneka
Seanell
Seanese

Seanicia
Seanie
Seanique
Seanisha
Seaniya
Seanna *(0.03)*
Seannah
Seannan
Seanne
Seanneka
Seannequal
Seanquéria
Seansai
Seanta
Seantá
Seantae
Seante
Seantel
Seantell
Seantelle
Seanteria
Seantique
Seantona
Seantwanese
Seantyana
Seanzell
Seaoni
Seara
Searci
Seare
Searis
Searra *(0.01)*
Season
Seasons
Seataesca
Seaton
Seattle
Seau
Seavhanna
Seayra
Sebahat
Sebastian
Sebastiana
Sebastiane
Sebastien
Sebika
Sebione
Sebre
Sebrena
Sebrenna
Sebria
Sebriana
Sebrina *(0.01)*
Sec'queria
Secdrian

Secelia
Sechivir
Secilia
Secily
Seconcea
Secoquia
Secora
Secori
Secoro
Secorri
Secoya
Secoyia
Secret *(0.01)*
Secrett
Secrit
Secylia
Seda
Sedatia
Seddy
Sedelia
Sedenia
Sedera
Sederia
Sedia
Sedienta
Sedina
Sedona *(0.01)*
Sedonia
Sedonte
Sedora
Sedra
Sedreana
Sedrecka
Sedricka
Sedrika
Sedrion
Sedryona
See *(0.01)*
Seela
Seely
Seema *(0.01)*
Seemal
Seemeen
Seena
Seendy
Seerie
Seeta
Seetha
Seetran
Seferina
Sefon Obong
Sefra
Sefrah
Segane
Segirra

Segovia
Sehaj
Seham
Sehar
Sehdia
Seher
Sei
Seiara
Seidi
Seidy
Seifon
Seihla
Seikia
Seiko
Seiloni
Seilyn
Seinab
Seini
Seinimili
Seinna
Seira
Seirra *(0.02)*
Seirria
Seivan
Sejal *(0.01)*
Sejha
Seji
Sekani
Sekayi
Sekayia
Sekeena
Sekel
Sekethia
Sekia
Sekina
Sekinah
Sekne
Sekoya
Sekoyah
Sekwen
Sela *(0.01)*
Selaem
Selah *(0.01)*
Selaha
Selajah
Selali
Selam
Selamawit
Selana
Selasie
Selaya
Selby
Selden
Seléna
Selea

Seleah	Selwa	Senequa	September *(0.01)*	Serenidy	Sessilia
Seleana	Selyna	Senequae	Septisha	Serenitee	Sessily
Seleena	Selynne	Senequai	Seqioa	Serenitey	Sessy
Selema	Sem	Seneque	Seqoiyia	Sereniti	Sestina
Selemawit	Sema	Senesa	Seqouyia	Sereniti'	Setaira
Selen Lluvin	Semaj *(0.01)*	Senetra	Seqoya	Serenitiy	Setanyette
Selena *(0.60)*	Semaj'	Senetrea	Sequana	Serenity *(0.06)*	Setarem-Michelle
Selena-Lee	Semajé	Senettie	Sequanna	Serenna	Setavia
Selenah	Semajia	Seng	Sequayah	Sereno	Setayesh
Selene *(0.10)*	Semantha	Sengaroun	Sequea	Seresa	Seteeva
Seleni	Semar	Sengmanee	Sequence	Serese	Setel
Selenia	Semara	Senia	Sequenis	Seretha	Seterria
Selenie	Semaran	Seniay	Sequia	Serevan	Seteyah
Selenna	Semariah	Senica	Sequiah	Serfil	Seth
Selens	Semba	Senika	Sequintá	Sergedricka	Sethlee
Seleny	Sembra	Senina	Sequioa	Sergeline	Seti
Seles	Semele	Seniorita	Sequioah	Sergina	Seton
Selesa	Semetrius	Seniqua	Sequita	Seri	Setra
Selesha	Semhal	Senise	Sequitta	Seria	Setreace
Selesia	Semhar	Senita	Sequoi	Seriah	Setsuko
Seleste *(0.01)*	Semharr	Senite	Sequoia *(0.05)*	Seriann	Seung
Selethel	Semia	Senitra	Sequoiah	Serife	Seuquanyia
Seletute	Semiah	Senna	Sequoria	Serii	Sevan
Selfa	Semika	Sennaia	Sequoya *(0.01)*	Serin	Sevana
Seli	Semira	Sennethia	Sequoyah *(0.01)*	Serina *(0.07)*	Sevannah
Selia	Semmler	Sennia	Sequoyha	Serine	Sevastiana
Seliah	Semone	Senora	Sera *(0.01)*	Serinity	Sevda
Seliana	Semonika	Senovia	Serafina	Serisa	Sevde
Selica	Semplece	Senri	Serah *(0.01)*	Serissa	Severa
Selicia	Semra	Sensaisha	Seraiah	Serita	Severia
Selida	Sen	Sentaiya	Seraie	Sermira	Sevillia
Seliene	Sena *(0.01)*	Sentara	Seraina	Sermon	Sevina
Selika	Sena'ah	Senterria	Seralda	Sernquia	Sevita
Selim	Senada	Senthura	Seralyn	Serra	Sevon
Selima	Senaida	Sentisha	Serana	Serrá	Sevrina
Selin *(0.01)*	Senait	Sentoree	Seraphim	Serrabi	Sevy
Selina *(0.31)*	Senaka	Sentoyha	Seraphima	Serrea	Sevyn
Selinda	Senandra	Sentrail	Seraphina	Serreana	Sewheat
Seline	Senaqwila	Sentral	Seraphine	Serreena	Sexeya
Selinia	Senatra	Sentrayle	Serapia	Serrenna	Sextoneriya
Selisha	Senay	Seolin	Seraya	Serrennity	Seychelle
Selita	Senaya	Seona	Serayah	Serria	Seydi
Sellam	Senayet	Seondra	Sercie	Serrina	Seyla
Selleka	Senayit	Seonna	Serea	Serrisa	Seylia
Selleste	Sencerae	Seoyoung	Sereen	Servannha	Seymon
Sellina	Senclair	Sephara	Sereena	Seryca	Seymone
Selly	Sender	Sepharra	Sereina	Seryna	Seymorer
Selma *(0.01)*	Sendi	Sephirah	Seren	Seselia	Seymouria
Selome	Sendie	Sephora	Serena *(0.37)*	Sesiley	Seynabo
Selona	Sendy	Sephorah	Serena Alexis	Sesilia	Seynabou
Seltic	Seneca *(0.01)*	Sephra	Serenah	Sesimani	Seyyedeh
Selva	Senedra	Sephrah	Serenatea	Sesley	Seza
Selvi	Seneka	Sephrenia	Serene *(0.02)*	Sesly	Sh Terrian
Selvie	Senem	Sepideh	Serenea	Sessalie	Sh Terrica
Selvije	Senenté	Seprela	Serenia	Sessili	Sh'darian

Sh'keeyah	Sha'corra	Sha'nale	Sha'tiareni	Shabina	Shacorey
Sh'kell	Sha'corya	Sha'nee	Sha'tone	Shabitha	Shacori
Sh'kevin	Sha'crea	Sha'neese	Sha'tonia	Shabnam	Shacoria
Sh'keyah	Sha'daria	Sha'neka	Sha'toniá	Shabnum	Shacorri
Sh'kyra	Sha'dayhna	Sha'nell	Sha'torrea	Shabonda	Shacorria
Sh'lace	Sha'dehzah	Sha'nelle	Sha'torria	Shaboz	Shacota
Sh'lre	Sha'dia	Sha'nequia	Sha'tyra	Shabre	Shacotah
Sh'nika	Sha'doriun	Sha'nice	Sha'tyri	Shabré	Shacourtney
Sh'ron	Sha'drea	Sha'nicia	Sha'uri	Shabrea	Shacoya (0.01)
Sh'tara	Sha'dresha	Sha'nigua	Sha'von	Shabreail	Shacoyá
Sh'terrion	Sha'ebonie	Sha'niqua	Sha'vonne	Shabree	Shacoyia
Sh'tyra	Sha'ereka	Sha'nita	Sha'voria	Shabreeka	Shacoyla
Sh-Kiyrah	Sha'fiah	Sha'pa	Sha-Breia	Shabreka	Shacquetta
Sha	Sha'garrian	Sha'quala	Sha-Dasha	Shabrelia	Shacrysta
Sha Brecia	Sha'garyia	Sha'quan	Sha-Davia	Shabrell	Shacura
Sha Brittan	Sha'ivory	Sha'quana	Sha-Karia	Shabreya	Shad'dericka
Sha Brittney	Sha'jouria	Sha'quanda	Sha-Keah	Shabreyona	Shada
Sha Cyllia	Sha'kara	Sha'quanna	Sha-Kenya	Shabri	Shadá
Sha Dae	Sha'kayvia	Sha'quanta	Sha-Kira	Shabria (0.01)	Shadadren
Sha Darius	Sha'kedra	Sha'quari	Sha-Lania	Shabriana	Shadae
Sha Darry L	Sha'keela	Sha'quasia	Sha-Lynn	Shabrica	Shadaé
Sha Derria	Sha'keila	Sha'quica	Sha-Myia	Shabriel	Shadai
Sha Destiny	Sha'keilya	Sha'quiel	Sha-Neisha	Shabrielle	Shadaia
Sha Harold	Sha'keira	Sha'quila	Sha-Niece	Shabrika	Shadaisa
Sha Kayla	Sha'keisha	Sha'quilla	Sha-Nika	Shabrina	Shadaisha
Sha Keesa	Sha'kelia	Sha'quira	Sha-Nikiya	Shabritney	Shadaja
Sha Kella	Sha'kera	Sha'quiza	Sha-Quan	Shabrittany	Shadajah
Sha Kenya K	Sha'kerra	Sha'quoia	Sha-Raye	Shabron	Shadajhia
Sha Keria	Sha'kevia	Sha'quoria	Sha-Ron	Shabryia	Shadale
Sha Khiry	Sha'keyla	Sha'qwanna	Sha-Tina	Shabryian	Shadalya
Sha Lundria	Sha'keylia	Sha'ray	Sha-Tyra	Shabunda	Shadanah
Sha Melba	Sha'keyvia	Sha'rece	Sha=wna	Shacambria	Shadaniel
Sha Nazy	Sha'khari	Sha'rell	Shaa	Shacandra	Shadanny
Sha Neal	Sha'kiea	Sha'renée	Shaadie	Shacara	Shadarean
Sha Neisha	Sha'kimbreya	Sha'rhonda	Shaahidah	Shacari	Shadari
Sha Nel	Sha'kira	Sha'rise	Shaailyah	Shacari'	Shadaria
Sha Quay	Sha'kirah	Sha'ron	Shaaista	Shacarla	Shadarian
Sha Quelle	Sha'kym	Sha'ronda	Shaakira	Shacarra	Shadarien
Sha Quory	Sha'kyra	Sha'ronna	Shaakirah	Shacarrha	Shadaris
Sha Raven	Sha'lacey	Sha'ryl	Shaakurah	Shacarri	Shadarl
Sha Shawna	Sha'leah	Sha'seanna	Shaamini	Shachel	Shadarricka
Sha Terrika	Sha'lena	Sha'taea	Shaana	Shachole	Shadarryl
Sha Torie	Sha'lynn	Sha'tara	Shaanta	Shacia	Shadaryl
Sha Yvon Ja	Sha'maindra	Sha'taura	Shaareem	Shacira	Shadasha
Shá	Sha'mara	Sha'tea	Shaarmi	Shackina	Shadashia
Sha'-Quila	Sha'marri	Sha'tearia	Shaarmini	Shaclare	Shadavia
Sha'andrea	Sha'marria	Sha'teeva	Shaata	Shacobi	Shadaviah
Sha'aniqua	Sha'mekia	Sha'tekée	Shabana	Shacobia	Shadawanda
Sha'bre	Sha'mekqua	Sha'tera	Shabanee	Shacohya	Shaday
Sha'bree	Sha'mika	Sha'terra	Shabanna	Shacola	Shadaya
Sha'bria	Sha'miriam	Sha'terria	Shabarea	Shacole	Shadayna
Sha'camberia	Sha'miya	Sha'terrica	Shabbli'	Shacondra	Shadaysa
Sha'caria	Sha'monica	Sha'terriel	Shabi	Shaconna	Shaddan
Sha'clara	Sha'mony	Sha'terris	Shabiena	Shacony	Shaddar
Sha'cola	Sha'myia	Sha'tia	Shabiha	Shacora	Shaddin

Shade *(0.01)*	Shadreka	Shaevon	Shahrazade	Shaila *(0.02)*	Shaiteice Ann
Shadea	Shadriana	Shaeye	Shahrzad	Shailah	Shaiteria
Shadeana	Shadricka	Shaeyla	Shahtava	Shailaja	Shaitha
Shadee	Shadrieka	Shafae	Shahtilé	Shailec	Shaitiana
Shadeh	Shadrika	Shafak	Shahwahnekzhihk	Shailee *(0.01)*	Shaitiba
Shadeidrion	Shady	Shafali	Shahykhila	Shaileen	Shaitiona
Shadeigha	Shadya	Shafari	Shahzadi	Shailen	Shaitonya
Shadeja	Shae *(0.09)*	Shafaris	Shai *(0.01)*	Shailey	Shaitria
Shadejha	Shaélah	Shaffer	Shai'	Shaili	Shaityea
Shadeka	Shaéonna	Shaffira	Shai'ann	Shailie	Shaityonna
Shadela	Shaéquanna	Shafi	Shai'anté	Shailiene	Shaiy-Ane
Shadell	Shae-Alexis	Shafia	Shai'keria Keyo	Shailion	Shaiya
Shaden	Shae-Dawn	Shafina	Shai'ma	Shailja	Shaiyan
Shadena	Tanees	Shafreda	Shai'mel	Shailla	Shaiyana
Shadene	Shae-Dee	Shafreena	Shai'rocka	Shailley	Shaiyann
Shadentra	Shae-Lee	Shafrin	Shai'zer	Shaily	Shaiyanne
Shaderia	Shae-Leigh	Shagana	Shai-Ann	Shailyn *(0.01)*	Shaiyena
Shaderica	Shae-Lyn	Shaganaa	Shai-Anne	Shailynn *(0.01)*	Shaiyla
Shaderrica	Shae-Lynn *(0.01)*	Shagari	Shai-Aparnecia	Shaima	Shajada
Shaderricka	Shae-Lynne	Shagaryca	Shai-Keesa	Shaimaa	Shajerrika
Shaderrika	Shaeada	Shageria	Shai-Lee	Shaimece	Shajiah
Shadese	Shaeane	Shaghaeygh	Shai-Liah	Shaimeisha	Shajicaa
Shadesha	Shaeanna	Shagini	Shai-Linn	Shaimen	Shajitha
Shadesia	Shaeanne	Shagira	Shai-Neequah	Shaimere	Shajuan
Shadesmon	Shaedan	Shagiya	Shaian	Shaina *(0.18)*	Shajuana
Shadestinee	Shaedee	Shagufta	Shaiana	Shainalea	Shajuandi
Shadeveney	Shaeden	Shagun	Shaiandra	Shaindel	Shajuann
Shadey	Shaedyn	Shahada	Shaiane	Shaindia	Shakaana
Shadi	Shaeffer	Shahaela	Shaiann	Shaine	Shakaela
Shadia *(0.01)*	Shaeina	Shahaila	Shaianna	Shainea	Shakail
Shadiaman	Shael	Shahala	Shaianne *(0.01)*	Shaineshia	Shakaila
Shadiamond	Shaela *(0.01)*	Shahaley	Shaiasia	Shaini	Shakailee
Shadie	Shaelagh	Shahaly	Shaibrean	Shainice	Shakaira
Shadijah	Shaelah	Shahamaling	Shaibreka	Shainiec	Shakal
Shadiqua	Shaelaine	Shahana	Shaibrielle	Shainita	Shakala *(0.01)*
Shadiya	Shaelan	Shahanna	Shaida	Shainna	Shakanna
Shadoe	Shaelanie	Shahannah	Shaide	Shainne	Shakara *(0.01)*
Shadolaya	Shaelanna	Shahara	Shaiderius	Shainoor	Shakaren
Shadomicken	Shaelea	Shahayla	Shaidrea	Shainqua	Shakari *(0.01)*
Shadon	Shaelee *(0.01)*	Shahbano	Shaidrequa	Shainy	Shakaria
Shadonna	Shaeleigh	Shahbrea	Shaieley	Shainyce	Shakarie
Shadonnika	Shaelene	Shahd	Shaienne	Shaiona	Shakasuwian
Shadonte	Shaeley	Shaheem	Shaiesha	Shaiqeisha	Shakavia
Shadonya	Shaeli	Shaheen	Shaifali	Shaiqiyonna	Shakavious
Shadora	Shaelice	Shaheerah	Shaikeara	Shaiquale	Shakaydra
Shadorian	Shaelie	Shahida	Shaikee	Shaiquita	Shakayla *(0.03)*
Shadorie	Shaelin	Shahina	Shaikeira	Shaira	Shakaylen
Shadoris	Shaely	Shahiqa	Shaikeise	Shairá	Shakayvia
Shadow *(0.01)*	Shaelyn *(0.04)*	Shahirah	Shaikela	Shairell	Shakea
Shadowe	Shaelyne	Shahirrie	Shaikerra	Shairika	Shakeah
Shadowlynne	Shaelynn *(0.02)*	Shahla	Shaikeyah	Shais	Shakeana
Shadowna	Shaelynne	Shahnaz	Shaikha	Shaisha	Shakeara
Shadra	Shaena *(0.01)*	Shahnnon	Shaikia	Shaista	Shakeba
Shadreeka	Shaeneno	Shahnoor	Shaikious	Shaitave	Shakedra
Shadrejah	Shaetara	Shahrazad	Shaikira	Shaitaya	Shakeea

Shakeeda	Shakesha	Shakiya	Shalan	Shalen	Shallyne
Shakeela	Shaketa	Shakiyah	Shalana	Shalena *(0.01)*	Shalom
Shakeelah	Shakethia	Shakiyla	Shalanda *(0.01)*	Shalene *(0.01)*	Shaloma
Shakeema *(0.01)*	Shakeva	Shakola	Shalandra	Shaleny	Shalon *(0.01)*
Shakeena	Shakevia	Shakona	Shalandrea	Shaleria	Shalona
Shakeera	Shakeya *(0.01)*	Shakoofa	Shalandria	Shalesa	Shalonda *(0.03)*
Shakeerah	Shakeyah	Shakora	Shalane	Shalese	Shalondra
Shakeeria	Shakeydra	Shakori	Shalanee	Shalesha	Shalondria
Shakeesha	Shakeyera	Shakoria	Shalanta	Shalessa	Shalone
Shakeeta	Shakeyia	Shakorian	Shalanthya	Shaleta	Shalontay
Shakeeva	Shakeyla	Shakoriell	Shalaressa	Shaletha	Shalonte
Shakeevia	Shakeyra	Shakorya	Shalarria	Shaletta	Shaloree
Shakei	Shakeyria	Shakota	Shalatta	Shalexis	Shalquilla
Shakeia	Shakeyta	Shakoya	Shalauna	Shalexus	Shalu
Shakeida	Shakhera	Shakri	Shalay	Shalexusia	Shalun
Shakeidrian	Shakhia	Shakria	Shalaya	Shaley	Shaluntia
Shakeima	Shakhila	Shakthigah	Shalayah	Shaleyza	Shalyah
Shakeina	Shakhirra	Shakti	Shalaye	Shali	Shalyce
Shakeira	Shakhyjah	Shakuana	Shalayia	Shalia *(0.01)*	Shalyea
Shakeirra	Shakhyra	Shakuel	Shalayla	Shaliah	Shalyia
Shakeita	Shakia *(0.02)*	Shakur	Shalayna *(0.01)*	Shalice	Shalyn *(0.02)*
Shakeitha	Shakia Rayna	Shakur-Nique	Shalayne	Shalicia	Shalynceia
Shakeithia	Shakiá	Shakura	Shalayné	Shalida	Shalyndrea
Shakeithya	Shakiah	Shakuria	Shalaynna	Shalie	Shalynn *(0.02)*
Shakeiva	Shakiara	Shakurria	Shalaysha	Shaliece	Shalynne *(0.01)*
Shakeiya	Shakiba	Shakurya	Shalbe	Shaliene	Shalyric
Shakel	Shakicia	Shakwajalyn	Shalbie	Shalijah	Shalyse
Shakela *(0.01)*	Shakiedra	Shakwanza	Shale	Shalil	Sham'payne
Shakelby	Shakiela	Shakwayla	Shalé	Shalimar	Shama
Shakell	Shakiella	Shakya	Shalea	Shalimora	Shamad
Shakelya	Shakiera *(0.01)*	Shakyla	Shaleacia	Shalin	Shamae
Shakema	Shakierra	Shakyler	Shaleah	Shalina	Shamai
Shakembria	Shakija	Shakyra *(0.03)*	Shaleaha	Shalinda	Shamaia
Shakemia	Shakikka	Shakyria	Shalebra	Shaline	Shamaila
Shakemiya	Shakil	Shakyrrha	Shalece	Shalini *(0.01)*	Shamaine
Shakemmion	Shakila *(0.01)*	Shala *(0.01)*	Shalecia	Shalinna	Shamaiya
Shakena	Shakilah	Shalaana	Shaledra	Shalisa *(0.01)*	Shamaiye
Shakenda	Shakilla	Shalace	Shalee *(0.01)*	Shalise	Shamala
Shakendra	Shakilra	Shalae	Shaleece	Shalisha	Shaman
Shakendria	Shakim	Shalaetne	Shaleedra	Shalishea	Shamana
Shakenia	Shakima *(0.01)*	Shalagh	Shaleeka	Shalissa	Shamanda
Shakente	Shakimbria	Shalah	Shaleen *(0.01)*	Shalita	Shamane
Shakenya *(0.01)*	Shakimma	Shalai	Shaleena	Shaliyah *(0.01)*	Shamaneek
Shakera *(0.03)*	Shakina	Shalaila	Shaleesha	Shalla	Shamangela
Shakerah	Shakinah	Shalain	Shaleeza	Shallan	Shamani
Shakeria *(0.03)*	Shakinnah	Shalaina-Marie	Shalei	Shallandra	Shamanice
Shakeriah	Shakir	Shalaine	Shaleia	Shallanté	Ragine
Shakerious	Shakira *(0.09)*	Shalaka	Shaleigh	Shalleena-Kay	Shamantha
Shakeriyahae	Shakirah	Shalakius	Shaleigha	Shallen	Shamar
Shakerra *(0.01)*	Shakirea	Shalakyisha	Shaleisha	Shalley	Shamara *(0.01)*
Shakerral	Shakiria	Shalala	Shaleiyah	Shallie	Shamare
Shakerri	Shakirra *(0.01)*	Shalalah	Shalek'qua	Shallon	Shamareá
Shakerria *(0.01)*	Shakisha	Shalamar	Shaleka	Shallu	Shamaree
Shakerya	Shakita *(0.01)*	Shalame	Shalela	Shally	Shamarée
Shakeryia	Shakitric	Shalamiesha	Shalem	Shallyn	Shamari *(0.01)*

Shamaria (0.01)	Shameke	Shammaree	Shanacie	Shandan	Shanease
Shamariah	Shamekia	Shammron	Shanada	Shandann	Shaneatra
Shamaris	Shamel	Shamnice	Shanadiá	Shandaria	Shaneba
Shamarius	Shamelia	Shamon	Shanae (0.01)	Shandasha	Shanece (0.01)
Shamariya	Shamell	Shamona	Shanaé	Shandee	Shanecia
Shamarow	Shamelle	Shamone	Shanafrica	Shandel (0.01)	Shanecka
Shamarri	Shamequa	Shamonica (0.01)	Shanah	Shandelaina	Shanecqua
Shamas	Shamequia	Shamonicka	Shanahl	Shandelina	Shaneda
Shamauri	Shamera	Shamonie	Shanai	Shandell	Shanedel
Shamauria	Shamerah	Shamonja	Shanaia	Shandelle (0.01)	Shanee (0.01)
Shamay	Shamerca	Shamonraie	Shanaira	Shandellia	Shaneece
Shamaya	Shamere	Shamontae	Shanakka	Shanderica	Shaneeda
Shamayne	Shameria	Shamora	Shanale	Shanderlier	Shaneeka
Shamazay	Shamerial	Shamoray	Shanali	Shandesa	Shaneekah
Shambavi	Shamerica	Shamori	Shanalle	Shandestiny	Shaneen
Shamber	Shamerriz	Shamorriah	Shanalynn	Shandi (0.01)	Shaneequa
Shambera	Shamese	Shamorris	Shanan	Shandi'rae	Shaneeque
Shamberika	Shamesha	Shampagne	Shananda	Shandie	Shaneesa
Shamberlynn	Shametria	Shampaigne	Shanandoah	Shandiin	Shaneesha
Shambrae	Shametrias	Shampaine	Shanandra	Shandler	Shaneetra
Shambray	Shametris	Shampaliante	Shanara	Shandn	Shaneez
Shambreca	Shamgail	Shampange	Shanará	Shandole	Shaneia
Shambreea	Shamia (0.01)	Shampel	Shanardra	Shandon	Shaneice (0.01)
Shambreka	Shamiah	Shampri	Shanarion	Shandoria	Shaneik'quia
Shambrekia	Shamica	Shamra	Shanarra	Shandra (0.01)	Shaneika (0.01)
Shambrel	Shamice	Shamralee	Shanasia	Shandrana	Shaneika-Ann
Shambrelle	Shamick	Shamray	Shanata	Shandraya	Shaneikah
Shambreya	Shamicka	Shamria	Shanavea	Shandre A	Shaneikqua
Shambria (0.01)	Shamiece	Shamrock	Shanavia	Shandrea	Shaneikwa
Shambria Nashay	Shamier	Shamseen	Shanay	Shandreá	Shaneil
Shambrica	Shamiga	Shamus	Shanaya (0.01)	Shandree	Shaneila
Shambriea	Shamika (0.02)	Shamya	Shanaye	Shandreia	Shaneill
Shambrika	Shamikka	Shamyah	Shanayne	Shandreika	Shaneiqua
Shambryia	Shamiko	Shamyeh	Shanaz	Shandreka	Shaneisha
Shame	Shamil	Shamyia	Shanazia	Shandrel	Shaneka (0.03)
Shamea	Shamila	Shamyiah	Shanbreá	Shandrell	Shaneka's
Shameace	Shamima	Shamylia	Shanbreka	Shandrenae	Shanekia
Shameaka	Shamini	Shamyra (0.01)	Shanbria	Shandrese	Shanekqua
Shameakah	Shamique	Shan	Shanbriel	Shandria (0.01)	Shanekquah
Shameca	Shamir	Shan Terric	Shanbril	Shandrica	Shanekque
Shamecca	Shamira (0.01)	Shan Tiera	Shance	Shandrice	Shanel (0.02)
Shamecciaa	Shamiracle	Shan'bria	Shance-Samarah	Shandrika (0.01)	Shanel'
Shamecia	Shamirea	Shan'i	Shancia	Shandryn	Shaneli
Shamecqua	Shamiria	Shan'qualcia	Shancobius	Shandy	Shanelia
Shameeca	Shamirkle	Shan'quese	Shanda (0.02)	Shandylier	Shanell (0.04)
Shameeka	Shamirra	Shan'tana	Shandae	Shandyn	Shanelle (0.08)
Shameela	Shamise	Shan'taniqua	Shandaira	Shane (0.02)	Shanellé
Shameema	Shamisha	Shan'téera	Shandaja	Shané	Shanen
Shameera	Shamiska	Shan'tearra	Shandal	Shanea (0.01)	Shanena
Shameerah	Shamiso	Shan'tel	Shandale	Shaneace	Shanene
Shameesha	Shamitha	Shan'tia	Shandalia	Shaneah	Shaneqa
Shameeza	Shamitra	Shan'toriana	Shandalier	Shaneal	Shanequá
Shameika	Shamiya (0.01)	Shan-Dréa	Shandalin	Shanean	Shanequa (0.02)
Shameira	Shamiyah	Shan-Qunesha	Shandalria	Shaneaqua	Shanequia
Shameka (0.04)	Shammai	Shana (0.17)	Shandalyn	Shanearia	Shanequiá

Shanequwa
Shanera
Shaneria
Shanerika
Shanery
Shanes
Shanese *(0.01)*
Shanesé
Shanesha
Shaneshia
Shanetal
Shanethea
Shanether
Shanethia
Shanetika
Shanetra
Shanetria
Shanetris
Shanett
Shanetta
Shanette
Shaney
Shaneyre
Shangaree
Shangela
Shanghavy
Shani *(0.02)*
Shani-Dawn
Shania *(0.28)*
Shania Li
Shaniah *(0.02)*
Shanica
Shanice *(0.26)*
Shanicea
Shanicesha
Shanick
Shanicka
Shanické
Shanico
Shanicquia
Shanida
Shanie *(0.01)*
Shaniea
Shanieca
Shaniece *(0.04)*
Shaniedra
Shanieka
Shaniel
Shanielle
Shanience
Shaniequa
Shaniera
Shaniese
Shanik
Shanika *(0.05)*

Shaniká
Shanikia
Shanikki
Shanikqa
Sł.anikqua
Shanikque
Shanikwa
Shanil
Shanila
Shanille
Shanin
Shanina
Shanine
Shaniqa
Shaniqia
Shaniqua *(0.08)*
Shaniqua Cierra
Shaniquah
Shaniqual
Shanique *(0.02)*
Shaniquequa
Shaniquia
Shaniquwa
Shaniqwa
Shanira
Shanirea
Shanirqua
Shanisa
Shanise *(0.02)*
Shanisha
Shanisia
Shanissa
Shanisse
Shanita *(0.02)*
Shanitique
Shanitra
Shanitta
Shanittra
Shaniya *(0.01)*
Shanja
Shankeitha
Shankeria
Shankerria
Shankethia
Shanketia
Shankeya
Shankia
Shankierra
Shankija
Shankika
Shankilria
Shankiyah
Shankria
Shankwa
Shankyria

Shanlee
Shanlen
Shanley
Shanlie
Shanmisha
Shanna *(0.14)*
Shanna-Dale
Shannae
Shannaé
Shannah *(0.02)*
Shannai
Shannalee
Shannan *(0.02)*
Shannany
Shannara
Shannay
Shannaya
Shannaz
Shannea
Shannece
Shannel *(0.01)*
Shannell
Shannelle
Shannen *(0.06)*
Shannes
Shannesa
Shannesha
Shannet
Shannette
Shanneya
Shanni
Shannia
Shannica
Shannice
Shannie
Shanniece
Shanniele
Shannika
Shanniko
Shannikquia
Shannin
Shanniqa
Shannise
Shannleigh
Shannoah
Shannon *(2.32)*
Shannon Gale
Shannon Samant
Shannon-Lee
Shannon-Leigh
Shannon-Morgan
Shanntae
Shanntellee
Shanny *(0.01)*
Shannyce

Shannyn
Shanoah
Shanobia
Shanola
Shanon *(0.02)*
Shanora
Shanovia
Shanovon
Shanpelle
Shanqua
Shanquale
Shanquan
Shanquaneta
Shanque
Shanquela
Shanquella
Shanquenel
Shanqueria
Shanquerria
Shanquesha
Shanqueta
Shanquetta
Shanquette
Shanquice
Shanquiette
Shanquil
Shanquila
Shanquilla
Shanquirra
Shanquise
Shanquisha
Shanquita
Shanqula
Shanqulle
Shanquon
Shanqutia
Shanqwa
Shanqwesha
Shanra
Shanrail
Shanrée
Shanriel
Shanshatara
Shanté
Shanta *(0.02)*
Shantá
Shantabia
Shantabrea
Shantae *(0.01)*
Shantaé
Shantaeshia
Shantaeviya
Shantaga
Shantai
Shantaina

Shantaira
Shantaiva
Shantaja
Shantajah
Shantal *(0.02)*
Shantall
Shantallice
Shantalya
Shantameika
Shantana
Shantanae
Shantane
Shantané
Shantanea
Shantaneese
Shantaneka
Shantanell
Shantanes
Shantanese
Shantania
Shantanic
Shantaniece
Shantanika
Shantanique
Shantanise
Shantanna
Shantannah
Shantaqua
Shantara
Shantaria
Shantasha
Shantashia
Shantasia *(0.01)*
Shantava
Shantavia *(0.01)*
Shantavious
Shantavis
Shantay
Shantaya
Shantaysha
Shantazia
Shante *(0.04)*
Shanté *(0.02)*
Shantél
Shantea
Shanteá
Shantearia
Shantease
Shanteavia
Shantee
Shanteedra
Shanteia
Shanteisa
Shantel *(0.16)*
Shantel'

Shantel-Ann
Shantele
Shantelé
Shantelia
Shantell *(0.05)*
Shantella
Shantelle *(0.03)*
Shantellis
Shantellius
Shantena
Shanteneshi
Shantenik
Shantenique
Shantenise
Shantequa
Shantera
Shanteria *(0.02)*
Shanterica
Shanterika
Shanteris
Shanteriyonce
Shanterra
Shanterria *(0.01)*
Shanterrian
Shanterrica
Shanterrie
Shanterrika
Shanterris
Shantese
Shantesha
Shantesia
Shantevia
Shanteya
Shantez
Shanteze
Shantezja
Shanthana
Shanthi
Shanti *(0.01)*
Shantia *(0.02)*
Shantiana
Shantiara
Shantice
Shantiel
Shantierra
Shantika
Shantil
Shantilacy
Shantillie
Shantilliya
Shantima
Shantina
Shantinese
Shantinique *(0.01)*
Shantinque

Shantiqua	Shanyla	Shaquanda *(0.02)*	Shaqueza	Shaquora	Sharasmine
Shantiquá	Shanyn	Shaquandey	Shaquia *(0.01)*	Shaquorae	Sharaven
Shantique	Shanyna	(0.01)	Shaquice	Shaquoter	Sharay
Shantira	Shanynn	Shaquandra	Shaquida	Shaquoya	Sharaya
Shantiria	Shanyque	Shaquandria	Shaquiel	Shaquoyah	Sharayah *(0.01)*
Shantirrea	Shanyra	Shaquania	Shaquiera	Shaqura	Sharayha
Shantisa	Shanyria	Shaquanna *(0.01)*	Shaquil	Shaqurah	Sharayl
Shantiwa	Shanyse	Shaquansa	Shaquila *(0.01)*	Shaquri	Sharaymond
Shantoiria	Shanythia	Shaquanta	Shaquilah	Shaqurian	Sharaza
Shantoneeka	Shanytra	Shaquantae	Shaquile	Shaqusia	Sharazade
Shantonette	Shanza	Shaquantay	Shaquill	Shaquta	Sharazazi
Shantonia	Shanzay	Shaquante	Shaquilla *(0.02)*	Shaquwn	Sharbriel
Shantonishelle	Shanzenyetta	Shaquanya	Shaquillah	Shaquyia	Sharcorya
Shantora	Shanzi	Shaquara	Shaquilldrea	Shaqwana	Sharda *(0.01)*
Shantorace	Shaolin	Shaquari	Shaquille *(0.01)*	Shaqwanda	Shardae *(0.01)*
Shantoria *(0.01)*	Shaona	Shaquaria	Shaquillia	Shaqwanna	Shardaé
Shantorria	Shaoor	Shaquarionna	Shaquin	Shaqwareya	Shardaeijah
Shantoya	Shapassion	Shaquaris	Shaquinas	Shaqweisha	Shardai
Shantral	Shaphyn	Shaquarius	Shaquinda	Shaqwitta	Shardaisha
Shantravious	Shapleigh	Shaquarra	Shaquindilyn	Shaqwonda	Shardanea
Shantrece	Shapna	Shaquasia	Shaquindoly	Shar Tan	Shardara
Shantrecia	Shaporche	Shaquata	Shaquinn	Shar'nay	Shardasia
Shantrel	Shapraya	Shaquavea	Shaquinta	Shar'nese	Shardavia
Shantrell *(0.01)*	Shapree	Shaquavia	Shaquionna	Shar'quan	Sharday
Shantrelle	Shaprina	Shaquavious	Shaquira *(0.01)*	Shar'quayla	Shardazia
Shantrese	Shapromise	Shaquawn	Shaquirah	Shar'tia	Sharde
Shantress	Shapuria	Shaquay	Shaquire	Shar-Darnay	Shardé
Shantrezia	Shaqanna	Shaquaya	Shaquirra	Shar-Kel	Shardea
Shantria	Shaqauna	Shaquayla	Shaquise	Shar-Nia	Shardena'y
Shantrial	Shaqavious	Shaquayle	Shaquisha	Shara *(0.02)*	Shardesha
Shantrice *(0.01)*	Shaqeeta	Shaque	Shaquita *(0.03)*	Sharadha	Shardeya
Shantricia	Shaqeria	Shaquéshia	Shaquithea	Sharae	Shardez
Shantriel	Shaqika	Shaquea	Shaquitta *(0.01)*	Sharaé	Shardha
Shantrina	Shaqira	Shaqueel	Shaquiva	Sharaequa	Shardia
Shantris	Shaqirha	Shaqueena	Shaquivia	Sharah	Shardinai
Shantrisse	Shaqkwela	Shaqueesha	Shaqukell	Sharaha	Shardiné
Shantry	Shaqolah	Shaqueia	Shaqula	Sharai'	Shardisa
Shantuala	Shaqonda	Shaquel	Shaqulla	Sharaiah	Shardivia
Shantwaniqua	Shaqoria	Shaquelia	Shaquna	Sharajha	Shardonae
Shantwanique	Shaqorie	Shaquell	Shaqunda	Sharalyn	Shardonay
Shantyl	Shaqoya	Shaquella	Shaqunia	Sharalynn	Shardonnai
Shantyle	Shaqrece	Shaquelle	Shaqunita	Sharan	Shardonnay
Shantyle Arlene	Shaqua	Shaquenda	Shaqunté	Sharana	Shardreka
Shanu	Shaquadra	Shaquendra	Shaquoa Mic	Sharanda	Shardyne
Shanuce	Shaquadria	Shaquenta	Shaquocora	Sharandeep	Sharea
Shanvelles	Shaquail	Shaquenthia	Shaquoia	Sharandip	Shareace
Shany *(0.01)*	Shaquaille	Shaquera	Shaquon	Sharane	Sharebra
Shanya	Shaquaiu	Shaqueria	Shaquona	Sharanea	Sharece
Shanyaa	Shaquaja	Shaquese	Shaquoncia	Sharaneya	Sharee *(0.01)*
Shanyah	Shaqual	Shaquesha	Shaquonda	Sharanga	Sharee-Razjnees
Shanyaida	Shaquala	Shaquesia	Shaquondra	Sharanjit	Shareece
Shanyal	Shaqualia	Shaqueta	Shaquondria	Sharanvir	Shareedah
Shanyce *(0.01)*	Shaqualla	Shaquetta *(0.01)*	Shaquonnie	Sharanya	Shareefa
Shanyeya	Shaquan *(0.01)*	Shaquette	Shaquontus	Sharareh	Shareefah
Shanyia	Shaquana *(0.02)*	Shaquevia	Shaquonza	Sharasha	Shareeka

Shareen	Sharine	Sharmeen	Sharniquea	Sharronda	Shatalia
Shareena	Sharion	Sharmeka	Sharnise	Sharry	Shatamber
Shareese	Shariona	Sharmel	Sharnjit	Shartal	Shatamea
Shareice	Shariqua	Sharmela	Sharnki	Shartasha	Shatana
Shareika	Sharisa	Sharmell	Sharno	Shartavia	Shatangela
Shareka *(0.01)*	Sharise	Sharmetrea	Sharnpreet	Shartavious	Shatangi
Sharekia	Sharish	Sharmica	Sharnyah	Shartay	Shatania
Sharel	Sharissa *(0.01)*	Sharmietra	Sharokeena	Sharterria	Shatanise
Sharell *(0.01)*	Sharisse	Sharmika	Sharola	Shartese	Shatanja
Sharelle	Sharita *(0.01)*	Sharmila	Sharolt	Shartesia	Shatanya
Sharen	Sharitee	Sharmin	Sharolyn	Shartiara	Shatara *(0.02)*
Sharena	Sharitha	Sharmine	Sharome	Shartisha	Shataraica
Sharene	Shariya	Sharmini	Sharon *(0.39)*	Shartria	Shatarea
Sharenna	Shariza	Sharminy	Sharon-Bethany	Sharu	Shatari
Sharese	Sharke	Sharmon	Sharona	Sharunte	Shataria
Sharesse	Sharkee	Sharmontez	Sharonda *(0.03)*	Sharva	Shatarise
Sharessia	Sharkeevia	Sharmora	Sharondra	Sharvae	Shatarra
Sharetha	Sharkena	Sharn	Sharondrea	Sharvasia	Shatarrius
Sharetta	Sharkethia	Sharna	Sharone	Sharvay	Shatasha
Sharey	Sharkira	Sharná	Sharonica	Sharvell	Shatashia
Shareyah	Sharla *(0.01)*	Sharnae	Sharonik	Sharvera	Shatasia
Sharezza	Sharlean	Sharnaé	Sharonjeet	Sharvika	Shataslyn
Sharhaiah	Sharlecia	Sharnaee	Sharonna	Sharvisha	Shataun
Sharhe	Sharleen *(0.01)*	Sharnasia	Sharontay	Sharwan	Shatauqua
Sharhia	Sharlena	Sharnay	Sharoyal	Sharwina	Shatavea
Sharhonda	Sharlene *(0.03)*	Sharnaye	Sharq'uetta	Shary	Shatavia *(0.02)*
Shari *(0.05)*	Sharlenne	Sharndeep	Sharquala	Sharyce	Shataviá
Shari-Marie	Sharless	Sharnecia	Sharquaveia	Sharyn	Shatay
Shari-Nicole	Sharleta	Sharnee	Sharquavia	Sharzae	Shatayia
Sharia	Sharlette	Sharnée	Sharqueesdia	Sharzay	Shateal
Shariah *(0.01)*	Sharley	Sharneekquia	Sharquel	Shasana	Shateanna
Shariale	Sharley Rae Deb	Sharnei	Sharquilla	Shase	Shateara
Sharian	Sharlie	Sharneice	Sharra	Shasha	Shatearya
Shariana	Sharlimagne	Sharneicia	Sharrafti	Shashah	Shateia
Sharica	Sharlin	Sharneisha	Sharrah	Shashamane	Shateidra
Sharice *(0.02)*	Sharlina	Sharneka	Sharraine	Shashan	Shateka
Sharidan	Sharlinda	Sharnell *(0.01)*	Sharrann	Shashana	Shatell
Sharie	Sharlini	Sharnelle	Sharras	Shashaunie	Shatelle
Shariea	Sharliqua	Sharnequa	Sharreile	Shashawna	Shateonna
Shariece	Sharlisa	Sharnese	Sharrel	Shashona	Shatequa
Sharieka	Sharlonda	Sharnesha	Sharrell	Shashony	Shatera
Shariel	Sharlton	Sharneshia	Sharren	Shasia	Shateria *(0.01)*
Sharielle	Sharly	Sharnesia	Sharreon	Shaska	Shaterian
Shariesse	Sharlyne	Sharnesse	Sharresse	Shaslin	Shaterica
Sharifa	Sharlynn	Sharnest	Sharri	Shasmine	Shaterical
Sharifah Syahir	Sharma-Qeni	Sharneta	Sharrica	Shassadie	Shaterr
Shariha	Sharmae	Sharnetta	Sharrice	Shasta *(0.03)*	Shaterra *(0.01)*
Sharik	Sharmaine *(0.02)*	Sharnevia	Sharricka	Shasta-Dawn	Shaterri
Sharika	Sharmane	Sharney	Sharrie	Shastell	Shaterria
Sharikka	Sharmanie	Sharnia	Sharriel	Shastin	Shaterrica
Sharilyn	Sharmaniqua	Sharnicca	Sharrin	Shastina	Shaterricka
Sharilynn	Sharmaya	Sharnice *(0.01)*	Sharrington	Shastity	Shaterryca
Sharimar	Sharmayne	Sharnicia	Sharrion	Shastyla	Shateyah
Sharin	Sharmayra	Sharniece	Sharrisse	Shataja	Shatha
Sharina *(0.01)*	Sharmean	Sharniqua	Sharron *(0.01)*	Shataka	Shathea

Shathelma
Shathem
Shatia *(0.01)*
Shatianna
Shatice
Shatienna
Shatievia
Shatigra
Shatika
Shatikka
Shatilya
Shatina
Shatiqua
Shatiquia
Shatira
Shatirah
Shatire
Shatirra
Shatisha
Shatishia
Shativa
Shativia
Shatiya
Shatiyuna
Shatoga
Shatoi
Shaton
Shatona
Shatondra
Shatoney
Shatoni
Shatonia
Shatonna
Shatonya
Shatora
Shatorea
Shatori
Shatoria *(0.01)*
Shatorica
Shatorrey
Shatorri
Shatorria
Shatorryia
Shatory
Shatosha
Shatoya *(0.01)*
Shatravious
Shatrevia
Shatrice
Shatwala
Shatya
Shatyra
Shatyre
Shatyria
Shau'niqua

Shauanne
Shaude
Shaudeishia
Shaughnessey
Shaughnessy
Shaugnassey
Shaula
Shaulin
Shaumere
Shaumithri
Shaun *(0.01)*
Shauna *(0.16)*
Shauna-Enza
Shauna-Marie
Shaunacee
Shaunacy
Shaunan
Shaunaste
Shaunasty
Shauncee
Shauncei
Shaunda
Shaundaius
Shaundale
Shaundé
Shaundén
Shaundee
Shaundeen
Shaundel
Shaundelyn
Shaundra
Shaundrea
Shaundreka
Shaundrel
Shaundria
Shaune
Shaunecie
Shaunecishia
Shaunee
Shauneece
Shaunel
Shauneque
Shaunese
Shaunessy
Shaunetra
Shaunetta
Shauney
Shaunglazer
Shauni
Shaunia
Shaunice *(0.01)*
Shaunie
Shauniese
Shaunika
Shaunisha

Shaunjanae
Shaunmaine
Shaunna *(0.02)*
Shaunnay
Shaunnie
Shaunquella
Shaunquie
Shaunquise
Shaunsey
Shaunta
Shauntaé
Shauntae *(0.01)*
Shauntal
Shauntalle
Shauntana
Shauntanique
Shauntanyse
Shauntaria
Shauntasha
Shauntasia
Shauntav
Shauntavia
Shauntavius
Shauntay
Shaunte
Shaunté
Shauntea
Shaunteise
Shauntel *(0.01)*
Shauntell
Shauntelle
Shauntené
Shauntera
Shaunteria
Shaunterica
Shauntese
Shauntey
Shauntia
Shauntiara
Shauntiarra
Shauntice
Shauntinique
Shauntiqua
Shauntrayah
Shauntreana
Shauntrell
Shauntria
Shauntrice
Shauntricia
Shauny
Shaunya *(0.01)*
Shaunyce
Shauquaney
Shauqunna
Shaurdasia

Shaurema
Shaurice
Shaurie
Shautiqua
Shauwonna
Shauya
Shavah
Shavana
Shavanna
Shavannah
Shavanni
Shavantá
Shavantae
Shavanté
Shavanyae
Shavarious
Shavaris
Shavaughn
Shavaughn'ya
Shavaughnte
Shavaun
Shavayla
Shavéla
Shaveeka
Shaveeta
Shavel
Shavelle
Shavelli
Shavena
Shavencia
Shavenia
Shaveya
Shavia
Shavika
Shavillyia
Shavion
Shavionne
Shavita
Shavitta
Shavoci
Shavon *(0.04)*
Shavon'
Shavona
Shavonda *(0.01)*
Shavondalynn
Shavondria
Shavone
Shavonia
Shavonica
Shavonn
Shavonna *(0.01)*
Shavonne *(0.02)*
Shavonnia
Shavonnie
Shavonta

Shavontá
Shavontae
Shavontay
Shavonte
Shavontré
Shavor
Shavosia
Shavunia
Shavyvonta
Shaw
Shawaa
Shawaenica
Shawaina
Shawan
Shawana *(0.01)*
Shawanda
Shawanna *(0.01)*
Shawanté
Shawaylan
Shawaynea
Shawdee
Shawell
Shawentela
Shawight
Shawika
Shawkia
Shawmiyah
Shawn *(0.04)*
Shawn C.
Shawn'drekka
Shawn-Lynn
Shawn-Marie
Shawna *(0.36)*
Shawna-Lee
Shawna-Lei
Shawna-Mae
Shawna-Marie
Shawnacie
Shawnacy
Shawnae
Shawnakay
Shawnalee
Shawnalie
Shawnarika
Shawnasee
Shawnasty
Shawnay
Shawnd
Shawnda *(0.01)*
Shawndahleigh
Shawndaia
Shawnday
Shawndee
Shawndel
Shawndell

Shawndericka
Shawndi
Shawndra
Shawndra-Lyn
Shawndrea
Shawndria
Shawndricka
Shawndrika
Shawne
Shawnea
Shawneasha
Shawnece
Shawnee *(0.06)*
Shawneea
Shawneen
Shawneeshea
Shawneis
Shawneisha
Shawneka
Shawnelle
Shawneller
Shawnequa
Shawnese
Shawnessy
Shawnette
Shawney
Shawni
Shawni-Marie
Shawnia
Shawnic
Shawnice
Shawnicé
Shawnicee
Shawnie
Shawnie-Marie
Shawnie-Rae
Shawniece
Shawnika
Shawnique
Shawnise
Shawnisha
Shawnissia
Shawnita
Shawnkia
Shawnmere
Shawnna *(0.01)*
Shawnnaé
Shawnnay
Shawnneatri
Shawnneshia
Shawnnon
Shawnqwillerie
Shawnsali
Shawnta *(0.01)*
Shawntá

Shawntae	Shawuna	Shaylandria	Shaynna	Shérida	Shecamry
Shawntaine	Shay *(0.07)*	Shaylayna	Shaynne	Shévika	Shecara
Shawntal	Shay Lynn	Shayle	Shayona	She-Kerria	Shechaniah
Shawntana	Shay'auna	Shaylea	Shayonee	Shea *(0.12)*	Shechinah
Shawntarian	Shay'ele	Shayleah	Shayonika	Shea-Lea	Shecoria
Shawntarrica	Shay'la	Shaylece	Shayonna	Shea-Linn	Shecosta
Shawntas	Shay'trese	Shaylee *(0.08)*	Shayquana	Shea-Lyn	Shedna
Shawntasia	Shay-La	Shayleece	Shayquandria	Shea-Lynn	Shedrickia
Shawntasna	Shay-Lynn	Shayleen *(0.01)*	Shayquann	Sheaffer	Sheeana
Shawntavest	Shaya *(0.01)*	Shayleena	Shayra	Sheajhanna	Sheefa
Shawntavia	Shayah	Shaylei	Shayréll	Sheakeeba	Sheel
Shawntavious	Shayal	Shayleigh	Shayrena	Sheakevia	Sheela
Shawntay	Shayan	Shayleina	Shayrome	Sheakeyna	Sheelagh
Shawnte	Shayana	Shaylen *(0.01)*	Shayron	Sheal	Sheelah
Shawnté	Shayann	Shaylena	Shayrun	Sheala	Sheema
Shawntea	Shayanna	Shaylene *(0.03)*	Shaysa	Shealagh	Sheena *(0.08)*
Shawntearia	Shayannah	Shayler	Shayterria	Shealan	Sheenah
Shawntee	Shayanne *(0.01)*	Shaylesa	Shayterrius	Shealee	Sheenakaye
Shawntekia	Shayanutha	Shayley	Shaytisha	Shealeen	Sheenal
Shawntel *(0.01)*	Shayarra	Shayli *(0.01)*	Shayvahna	Shealeigh	Sheene
Shawntell	Shayauna	Shaylicia	Shayvionta	Shealene	Sheeneh
Shawntelle	Shayauni	Shaylie *(0.01)*	Shayvon	Sheali	Sheenika
Shawnteria	Shayawna	Shaylin *(0.02)*	Shayvone	Shealin	Sheeniqua
Shawnterria	Shaybrielle	Shaylin Kal	Shayvontae	Shealisa	Sheenka
Shawnterya	Shaycara	Shaylina	Shayvonya	Shealy	Sheeonia
Shawntes	Shayda	Shaylinn	Shaywan	Shealyn *(0.01)*	Sheer
Shawntia	Shayde	Shaylise	Shaza	Shealynn	Sheerah
Shawntiana	Shaydee	Shaylissa	Shazadeh	Shealynne	Sheeré
Shawntiara	Shaydel	Shaylla	Shazavia	Sheana	Sheereen
Shawntina	Shaydelynn	Shayln	Shazeda	Sheanah	Sheetal
Shawntinique	Shayden	Shaylon	Shazema	Sheanalee	Sheevang
Shawntiva	Shaydreonda	Shaylonda	Shazeya	Sheandra	Shefa
Shawntonese	Shaye *(0.02)*	Shaylr	Shazia	Sheani	Shefali
Shawntora	Shayébria	Shaylyn *(0.03)*	Shaziana	Sheanita	Shefat
Shawntoria	Shayeera	Shaylynn *(0.02)*	Shaziya	Sheanna	Shegal
Shawntory	Shayele	Shaylynne	Shazlyn	Sheanne	Shehan
Shawntrea	Shayeley	Shaymaa	Shazma	Sheante	Shehina
Shawntrece	Shayelle	Shaymaa	Shazmeena	Sheanun	Shehnaz
Shawntrell	Shayena	Mohamed	Shazmin	Sheaphia	Shehnila
Shawntrese	Shayenne	Shayn	Shazmine	Sheara	Shehnoor
Shawntrice	Shayera	Shayna *(0.26)*	Shazmyn	Shearabia	Shehreen
Shawny	Shayesta	Shaynah	Shazna	Shearies	Shei'nell
Shawny E	Shayina	Shaynanna	Shaztada	Sheatelia	Shei'tika
Shawnyce	Shayisha	Shayne *(0.04)*	Shazzneque	Sheather	Sheida
Shawnyra	Shayjunna	Shaynece	Shchey	Sheaundra	Sheila *(0.17)*
Shawon	Shaykeria	Shaynecia	Shdline	Sheavel	Sheilagh
Shawonda	Shaykota	Shaynee	She Askkie	Sheay	Sheilisa
Shawontez	Shaykura	Shayneka	Shéante	Sheayanna	Sheilla
Shawonuka	Shayla *(0.40)*	Shaynel	Shédara	Sheba	Sheily
Shawqi	Shayla Mae	Shaynell	Shédavia	Shebani	Sheima
Shawqweisha	Shayla-Ann	Shayney	Shékyrrah	Shebia	Sheina
Shawryell	Shaylah *(0.01)*	Shaynie	Shélise	Shebraska	Sheinah
Shawtá	Shaylan	Shayniece	Shémetra	Shebreanna	Sheinnera
Shawtric	Shaylana	Shaynique	Shénice	Shebria	Sheirra
Shawun	Shayland	Shaynise	Shéparc	Shebritta	Shejia

Shekaija	Shelbern	Shelisa *(0.01)*	Shelyntay	Sheneal	Shenterrica
Shekanah	Shelbey *(0.03)*	Shelise	Shema'n	Shenece	Sheny
Shekayla	Shelbi *(0.14)*	Shelisha	Shema-Meream	Shenecia	Shenya
Shekayle	Shelbi Roje	Shelisia	Shemae	Sheneen	Shenyce
Shekeera	Shelbiann	Shelisse	Shemaiah	Sheneh	Sheon
Shekeia	Shelbie *(0.12)*	Shelita	Shemarcel	Sheneil	Sheon'ta
Shekeitha	Shelbie-Lin	Sheliz	Shemariah	Sheneilla	Sheona
Shekeja	Shelby *(3.42)*	Sheliza	Shemaya	Sheneka	Shepeara
Shekela	Shelby Cheyenne	Shella	Shemayah	Shenekqua	Shephard
Shekelia	Shelby Jess	Shellaine	Shemeika	Shenel	Sheporia
Shekema	Shelby Lee	Shellandra	Shemeka	Shenell *(0.01)*	Shequan
Shekendra	Shelby-Ann	Shellbi	Shemekia	Shenella	Shequana
Shekenté	Shelby-Gail	Shellbie *(0.01)*	Shemeria	Shenelle *(0.01)*	Shequavia
Shekera	Shelby-Irene	Shellby *(0.01)*	Shemerik	Shenequa	Shequeena
Shekeria	Shelby-Lee	Shelleen	Shemerria	Shenerica	Shequel
Shekerra	Shelby-Lyn	Shellen	Shemesshia	Shenese	Shequelle
Shekerria	Shelby-Lynn	Shellene	Shemeta	Shenesha	Shequeria
Shekesha	Shelby-Sierra	Shellese	Shemetria	Shenethia	Shequetta
Sheketia	Shelbye	Shellesea	Shemeya	Shenetrius	Shequila
Sheketria	Shelbyjo	Shelley *(0.08)*	Shemia	Sheng	Shequilla
Shekeya	Shelcie	Shelleyann	Shemiah	Shenia	Shequita
Shekeyvia	Shelda	Shelleyrae	Shemica	Sheniah	Shequitta
Shekhadeep	Sheldesa	Shellfna	Shemieah	Shenica	Shequittia
Shekia	Sheldina	Shelli	Shemika *(0.01)*	Shenice *(0.01)*	Shequore-Janzel
Shekila	Sheldine	Shellia	Shemiko	Shenie	Shequoya
Shekima	Sheldon *(0.01)*	Shellian	Shemina	Sheniece	Sher'raevion
Shekina	Sheldreka	Shellie *(0.01)*	Shemir	Shenika *(0.01)*	Sher'risa
Shekinah *(0.03)*	Sheldrika	Shellinder	Shemira	Shenikwa	Sher'ron
Shekiniah	Sheldrina	Shellis	Shemirah	Shenina	Sher-Shawna
Shekira	Sheldyn	Shellisa	Shemita	Shenine	Shera
Shekita	Shelea	Shellneithia	Shemiya	Sheniqua *(0.01)*	Sherae
Shekkinah	Sheleah	Shellsea	Shemko	Shenique	Sheraé
Shekqua	Sheleana	Shelly *(0.11)*	Shemmiah	Sheniquia	Sherah
Shekrell	Shelece	Shelly-Ann	Shemone	Sheniqwa	Sherai
Shekria	Sheleeda	Shellye	Shen	Shenisa	Sheraine
Shekyel	Sheleigh	Shellyn	Shena *(0.01)*	Shenise *(0.01)*	Sherall
Shekyrea	Shelelia	Shelonda	Shenada	Shenisha	Sheralyn
Shela	Shelena	Shelondra	Shenadra	Shenita	Sherandrika
Shelacco	Shelene	Shelora	Amallak	Sheniya	Sheraven
Shelacey	Shelenna	Shelove	Shenae *(0.01)*	Sheniyah	Sheravia
Sheladria	Shelesa	Shelquinay	Shenaé	Sheniyia	Sheray
Shelagh	Shelese	Shelrae	Shenah	Sheniz	Sheraya
Shelah	Sheletha	Shelsea *(0.01)*	Shenail	Shenna	Sherbosnia
Shelaine	Sheley	Shelsey	Shenandoah	Shennae	Sherdarrel
Shelan	Sheleyse	Shelsie	Shenandoah-Lee	Shennah	Sherdes
Shelana	Shelgeza	Shelsy	Shenarah	Shennell	Sherdine
Shelandria	Sheli	Shelta	Shenarra-Lee	Shennen	Shere
Shelane	Shelia *(0.01)*	Shelter	Shenay	Shennia	Shereack
Shelantra	Sheliah	Shelton	Shenaya	Shennille	Sherean
Shelaya	Shelica	Sheltoria	Shenaz	Shennondoah	Sherebia
Shelayne	Shelice	Shelvi	Shendaia	Shenoa	Sherece
Shelbbie	Shelina	Shelvie	Shendri	Shenoll	Sheree *(0.02)*
Shelbe *(0.01)*	Sheline	Shelvy	Shene	Shenqule	Shereece
Shelbea	Sheliqua	Shely	Shenea	Shentel	Shereeka
Shelbee *(0.01)*	Shelique	Shelynn	Sheneaka	Shentelle	Shereemer

Shereen *(0.01)*	Sherkeial	Sherreka	Sheryl *(0.04)*	Sheyonna	Shieda
Shereena	Sherkell	Sherrell *(0.01)*	Sheryll	Sheyquon	Shiela
Sherees	Sherkenye	Sherrelle	Sheryllyn	Sheza	Shiely
Shereese	Sherkia	Sherren	Sheryn	Shezza	Shiena
Shereice	Sherkivia	Sherrena	Sheryne	Shgloria	Shiene
Shereka	Sherlee	Sherri *(0.03)*	Sheryra	Shh'kyia	Shienea
Sherel	Sherlene	Sherri-Anne	Sheshia	Shi *(0.01)*	Shieneka
Sherell *(0.01)*	Sherley *(0.01)*	Sherria	Shesniqua	Shi Quandra	Shienna
Sherelle *(0.01)*	Sherlin	Sherriah	Shesrnae	Shi'anne	Shiera
Sheren	Sherlina	Sherrian	Shetavia	Shi'gregorie	Shierine
Sherena	Sherlinda	Sherriann	Shetavis	Shi'kerria	Shiesha
Sherene	Sherline	Sherriayn	Shetelia	Shi'kesha	Shietell
Sheresa	Sherlisa	Sherrica	Sheteria	Shi'liyah	Shifa
Sherese	Sherll	Sherrice	Sheterica	Shi'mere	Shifarica
Sheretta	Sherlun	Sherrick	Sheterra	Shi'niqua	Shiffon
Sherharris	Sherly	Sherridan	Sheterrian	Shi'nitra	Shifra
Sherhonda	Sherlyn	Sherridon	Sheterrica	Shi'tavia	Shigeko
Sheri *(0.02)*	Sherlyne	Sherrie *(0.01)*	Shetonya	Shi'teria	Shihan
Sheri-Anne	Sherlynn	Sherriell	Shetoria	Shi'tierria	Shihanne
Sheri-Marie	Shermain	Sherril	Sheundra	Shi-Dazusha	Shihara
Sheria	Shermaine *(0.01)*	Sherrill	Sheureka	Shi-Teria	Shiho
Sherian	Shermakia	Sherrilyn	Sheva	Shi-Yon	Shihyan
Sherica *(0.01)*	Shermanda	Sherrilynn	Shevalle	Shia	Shiina
Sherice *(0.01)*	Shermane	Sherrina	Shevallini	Shiadavia	Shijonna
Sherices	Shermeen	Sherrise	Shevaugh	Shiadaysh	Shika
Shericia	Shermesia	Sherrity	Shevaun	Shiakera	Shikaira
Shericka	Shermia	Sherrlandus	Shevelle	Shiakia	Shikara
Sherida	Shermichael	Sherron *(0.01)*	Shevon	Shiala	Shikari
Sheridan *(0.08)*	Shermin	Sherronda	Shevonna	Shian *(0.01)*	Shikaria
Sheridane	Shermona	Sherronia	Shevonne	Shian Ne	Shikeira
Sherideen	Shernae	Sherry *(0.11)*	Shevonte	Shiana *(0.01)*	Shikeita
Sheriden	Shernavia	Sherry-Lynn	Shevyion	Shianah	Shikera
Sheridian	Shernay	Sherry-Vy	Shewanda	Shianahra	Shikeria
Sheridon	Shernell	Sherryce	Shewit	Shianbriel	Shikerra
Sherie *(0.01)*	Shernelle	Sherrye	Shey	Shiandra	Shikeya
Sherika *(0.01)*	Shernette	Sherryl	Sheyan	Shiane *(0.01)*	Shikha *(0.01)*
Sheril	Shernice	Sherrylyn	Sheyane	Shiané	Shikia
Sherilann	Sherokee	Sherrylynn	Sheyann	Shiann *(0.02)*	Shikim
Sherill	Sherol	Sherteria	Sheyanna	Shianna *(0.01)*	Shikira
Sherilyn *(0.01)*	Sherolin	Sherterra	Sheyannah	Shiannah	Shikirah
Sherilynn	Sheron	Sherthea	Sheyanne *(0.01)*	Shianne *(0.07)*	Shikiya
Sherin	Sherona	Shertresia	Sheyene	Shianne-Nicole	Shikiyah
Sherina *(0.01)*	Sheronda	Sheruneda	Sheyenne *(0.03)*	Shiany	Shikria
Sherine	Sheroug	Shervani	Sheyetta	Shianyia	Shiksha
Sherinett	Sherquita	Shervecia	Sheyika	Shiarah	Shikulia
Sherinthia	Sherra	Shervondney	Sheykena	Shiasia	Shikyra
Sherion	Sherracia	Shervontae	Sheykira	Shiayla	Shila
Sherionna	Sherrah	Sherwanda	Sheyla *(0.02)*	Shiayna	Shilah *(0.01)*
Sherisa	Sherrai	Sherwin	Sheylah	Shiceera	Shilea
Sherise	Sherraine	Sherwina	Sheylin	Shickelle	Shileah
Sherissa	Sherral	Sherwine	Sheylinn	Shidaysha	Shilee
Sherisse	Sherranda	Sherwrika	Sheylyn	Shidira	Shiley
Sherita *(0.01)*	Sherre	Shery	Sheymoney	Shie	Shiliza
Sheritta	Sherrece	Sherydan	Sheyna	Shieana	Shilkara
Sherityn	Sherree	Sherye-Ann	Sheynita	Shieanne	Shilo *(0.01)*

Shiloah	Shinora	Shirlena	Shiyla	Shondina	Shonquwull
Shiloah Brook	Shinthigia	Shirlendy	Shizana	Shondise	Shonta (0.01)
Shiloe	Shinthu	Shirlene	Shizuka	Shondora	Shontae (0.01)
Shiloh (0.04)	Shinthujah	Shirlethia	Shizuna	Shondra	Shontaé
Shilon	Shiny	Shirlett	Shkeisha	Shondralique	Shontai
Shilpa (0.01)	Shinyoung	Shirlette	Shkela	Shondranique	Shontal
Shilpi	Shinyse	Shirley (0.18)	Shkendje	Shondrea	Shontalene
Shilyn	Shion	Shirley-Anne	Shkila	Shondrekia	Shontana
Shilynne	Shiona	Shirleyshia	Shleana	Shondrell	Shontanice
Shima	Shionell	Shirlie	Shleby	Shondria	Shontaniese
Shimaa	Shionta	Shirlinda	Shlena	Shondriana	Shontaniqua
Shimari	Shiori	Shirlisa	Shlomit	Shondrika	Shontarria
Shimeah	Shiphrah	Shirlvetta	Shlonequia	Shone	Shontassia
Shimeka	Shiqi	Shirly	Shmyra	Shonée	Shontaveya
Shimera	Shiquan	Shirlyn	Shnae	Shoneisa	Shontavia (0.01)
Shimetra	Shiquana	Shirlynn	Shnequa	Shonekka	Shontavious
Shimika	Shiquel	Shirlyric	Shnicquar	Shonele	Shontay
Shimira	Shiquestta	Shirmaine	Shniquie	Shonell	Shontaye
Shimizu	Shiquindalyn	Shirmece	Shntae	Shonere	Shontayzia
Shin	Shiquirrah	Shirmeen	Shoba	Shonese	Shonte (0.01)
Shin-Fang	Shiquisha	Shirmel	Shobana	Shonesha	Shonté
Shina	Shiquita	Shirquanica	Shobha	Shoneshia	Shontél
Shinade	Shiquite	Shirrell	Shobitha	Shonessey	Shontea
Shinae	Shiquitta	Shirriah	Shobnom	Shonesty	Shonteadria
Shinal	Shir	Shirron	Shoei	Shonetavia	Shonteaira
Shinay	Shira (0.02)	Shirtavia	Shohreh	Shonetta	Shonteallé
Shinayla	Shirah	Shirvantes	Shola	Shonette	Shontel (0.01)
Shince	Shiralay	Shisharay	Sholaine	Shonice	Shontell (0.01)
Shindawia	Shiran	Shishi	Sholanda	Shonie	Shontella
Shinea	Shiran Frieda L	Shistine	Shoma	Shoniece	Shontelle
Shinedeep	Shirani	Shitanya	Shomanique	Shonieka	Shonteonna
Shinedle	Shiranna	Shitera	Shomari	Shoniqua	Shontera
Shineen	Shiray	Shiuntay	Shombia	Shonique	Shonteria
Shineese	Shiraya	Shiunte	Shombria	Shoniquea	Shontericka
Shineice	Shiraz	Shiva	Shomonique	Shonita	Shonterra
Shineka	Shirean	Shivajini	Shon	Shonkevia	Shonterri
Shinel	Shiree	Shivali	Shon'drekia	Shonkia	Shonterrian
Shinelle	Shireen (0.02)	Shivaly	Shon'tara	Shonkira	Shonterricka
Shinenette	Shirel	Shivam	Shon'tasia	Shonlanda	Shontese
Shinequa	Shirell	Shivana	Shon'telle	Shonna (0.01)	Shontevia
Shineque	Shirelle	Shivangi	Shon'toya	Shonnah	Shonthini
Shinera	Shireon	Shivani (0.05)	Shona (0.01)	Shonnece	Shontía
Shinese	Shirey	Shivanie	Shonacee	Shonnel	Shontia (0.01)
Shinett	Shiri	Shivanna	Shonae	Shonnell	Shontice
Shinetta	Shiriah	Shivawn	Shonagh	Shonnelle	Shontielle
Shinia	Shirin	Shivay	Shonah	Shonnequa	Shontierra
Shinice	Shirina	Shivhan	Shonal	Shonnie	Shontika
Shiniecia	Shirine	Shivika	Shonbria	Shonnika	Shontina
Shinika	Shirl	Shivonne	Shonda (0.02)	Shonnita	Shontinae
Shinikque	Shirlan	Shiwani	Shondaketa	Shonnon	Shontinique
Shiniqua	Shirlana	Shiyanda	Shondaria	Shonora	Shontique
Shinique	Shirlea	Shiyandra	Shonday	Shonquarius	Shontiquea
Shinnéa	Shirlecia	Shiyane	Shondedria	Shonquell	Shontira
Shinniah	Shirlee	Shiyenne	Shondell	Shonqueta	Shontisha
Shinnomon	Shirleen	Shiyetta	Shondelle	Shonquita	Shontita

Shontivia	Shrarre	Shumirra	Shurell	Shydae	Shyleisha
Shontodra	Shravya	Shun	Shureza	Shydasha	Shylene
Shontoria	Shrémica	Shunay	Shuriah	Shydra	Shyler
Shontra	Shrecca	Shunda	Shurkuan	Shye	Shyleshia
Shontrail	Shree	Shunderika	Shurlyn	Shye-Ann	Shyletra
Shontranae	Shreen	Shundiin	Shuron	Shyeeda	Shylexis
Shontranice	Shreena	Shundina	Shurperial	Shyel	Shyley
Shontrell	Shreese	Shundra	Shuruthy	Shyelle	Shyli
Shontreonia	Shreya (0.01)	Shundrea	Shutaro	Shyene	Shylia
Shontrice	Shrika	Shundreka	Shutayah	Shyenique	Shylie
Shontyonna	Shrina	Shundrey	Shutell	Shyenna	Shylieca
Shontyria	Shrinell	Shundrika	Shuvonna	Shyenne (0.01)	Shyliesha
Shonya	Shringala	Shuneece	Shwanda	Shyera	Shylin
Shonyce	Shristi	Shunes	Shwanna	Shyesha	Shylina
Shonyell	Shrita	Shunez	Shweta	Shyeshia	Shylo (0.01)
Shonzara	Shriya	Shunica	Shwonda	Shyesta	Shyloe
Shopikaa	Shronda	Shunice	Shy (0.01)	Shyetia	Shyloh
Shora	Shrook	Shunie	Shy Nuishua	Shyheim	Shylon
Shori	Shrouk	Shunika	Shy'anne	Shyi'metrius	Shylyn
Shorok	Shrreya	Shuniqua	Shy'brea	Shyianne	Shylynn
Shorouq	Shruthi	Shunise	Shy'deshia	Shyien	Shyma
Shorraine	Shruti (0.01)	Shunjustice	Shy'dreika	Shyja	Shymaine
Shortara	Shrylle	Shunkentha	Shy'ela	Shyjuana	Shymari
Shortora	Shrymika	Shunquarria	Shy'keria	Shykéma	Shymecca
Shoruke	Shryundra	Shunquill	Shy'liyah	Shykedon	Shymehika
Shoshana (0.03)	Shterna	Shunta	Shy'na	Shykeea	Shymeira
Shoshanah	Shu	Shuntae	Shy'nika	Shykeena	Shymequa
Shoshanna	Shu Min	Shuntaneque	Shy'nne	Shykeila	Shymiera
Shoshannah	Shu Terria	Shuntaria	Shy'tiqua	Shykela	Shymiesha
Shoshaunah	Shu'derricka	Shuntarious	Shy'tise	Shykelia	Shymiracle
Shoshawna	Shua	Shuntavia	Shy-An-Storm	Shykeria	Shymonicqia
Shosheah	Shuana	Shuntavius	Shy-India	Shykerria	Shymonté
Shoshona	Shuang	Shuntecia	Shy-Kira	Shykeya	Shymyra
Shoshone	Shuanise	Shuntel	Shy-Kym	Shykeyla	Shynarra
Shoshonee	Shuann	Shunteled	Shy-Lynn	Shykia	Shynea
Shoshoney	Shuanna	Shuntell	Shy-Reif	Shykiera	Shyneace
Shoshoni	Shubana	Shuntelle	Shy-Von	Shykila	Shynece
Shoteria	Shubha	Shuntera	Shyah	Shykwayla	Shyneece
Shoterricka	Shubhashri	Shunterrica	Shyair	Shykylla	Shyneice
Shottees	Shubohe	Shuntesia	Shyal	Shyla (0.09)	Shyneicka
Shounda	Shuchi	Shuntia	Shyale	Shyla-Marie	Shyneiquah
Shounette	Shuet-Ching	Shuntiara	Shyan (0.01)	Shylah	Shyneise
Shoupra	Shugofa	Shuntina	Shyana	Shylamis	Shyneisha
Shovkeira	Shugri	Shuntrell	Shyandra	Shylan	Shyneka
Shovonté	Shuk	Shunya	Shyane	Shylasiá	Shynekia
Shovvanah	Shukaia	Shunydra	Shyanee	Shylaura	Shynekwa
Shownyea	Shukayla	Shuojia	Shyann (0.08)	Shylayah	Shynel
Shoyia	Shukri	Shupora	Shyanna (0.02)	Shylayna	Shynele
Shpresa	Shukriyyah	Shuquanda	Shyanne (0.14)	Shylayne	Shynequa
Shquan	Shukura	Shuquita	Shyanyne	Shyle	Shynequia
Shquanda	Shukurat	Shuqunna	Shyara	Shyleah	Shyneqwa
Shqueena	Shulara	Shuranda	Shyasha	Shylece	Shynesa
Shqueta	Shumaila	Shureeka	Shyaz	Shylee	Shynessa
Shquittia	Shumara	Shureha	Shybria	Shyleen	Shynethia
Shradha	Shumarion	Shureka	Shybriona	Shyleeni	Shynetra

Shynetrice	Si	Siddika	Sierrah-Mae	Silvie	Sims
Shynette	Si'aira	Siddiqua	Sierralynn	Silvija	Simya
Shynia	Si'ara	Siddney	Sierrea	Silvuna	Sin
Shyniaya	Si'coi	Siddrah	Sierria	Silvya	Sina
Shynice	Si'diyia	Sidiga	Sierriana	Sima	Sinai
Shynickwa	Si'erika	Sidionie	Siesha	Siman	Sinaka
Shyniece	Si'erra	Sidne	Siet	Simantha	Sinay
Shynika	Si'mone	Sidnee *(0.01)*	Sietta	Simardeep	Sinclair *(0.01)*
Shyniqua	Si'moune	Sidnei	Sieu	Simarié	Sinclaire *(0.01)*
Shynisha	Si-Ya	Sidnequia	Sieve	Simarjeet	Sindhura
Shynkalia	Si-Yun	Sidney *(0.32)*	Sifa	Simarjot	Sindi
Shyntel	Sia	Sidney-Rae	Siga	Simarnjeet	Sindia
Shynyce	Siadiea	Sidneya	Sighe	Simarron	Sindora
Shyona	Siah	Sidni	Signe	Simaya	Sindu
Shyoné	Siahna	Sidnie *(0.01)*	Signey	Simba	Sindujah
Shyonna	Siaja	Sidny	Signora	Siméon	Sindy *(0.03)*
Shyqence	Siamari	Sidnye	Signy	Simedar	Sine
Shyquanda	Siamoyia	Sidonae	Sigourney	Simek	Sinead *(0.02)*
Shyquanné	Sian	Sidonia	Sigrid	Simer	Sinedu
Shyquayciar	Siana	Sidonie	Sigurast	Simera	Sinem
Shyqueenia	Sianae	Sidra *(0.01)*	Siham	Simerjot	Sinensis
Shyquita	Sianai	Sidrah	Sihera	Simi	Sinfany
Shyra *(0.01)*	Sianey	Sidreaka	Siiri	Similolu	Sinfonia
Shyrae	Sianna *(0.01)*	Sidrean	Sijam	Simira	Sing
Shyrah	Siannah	Sidrha	Sikari	Simjera	Singer
Shyrai	Sianne	Sie Sia	Sikéra	Simmet	Singiza
Shyrece	Sianni	Sieanna	Sikenya	Simmi	Sinh
Shyreif	Sianny	Sieara	Sikesia	Simmone	Sini
Shyrelle	Siany	Siearra	Sikira	Simmret	Sinia
Shyrica	Siao	Siedah	Sila	Simmrin	Sinika
Shyrice	Siara *(0.02)*	Siefora	Silas	Simmy	Sinji
Shyrie	Siarah	Sieglinde	Silathia	Simna	Sinjun
Shyro	Siarra *(0.01)*	Siejah	Sile	Simoane	Sinneva
Shyrose	Siarrah	Sieko	Silena	Simogne	Sinnthia
Shytaijah	Siasia	Siemaj	Silepa Carmynn	Simoma	Sinora
Shytasha	Siaw	Siena *(0.03)*	Silesia	Simon	Sinteria
Shytasia	Siba	Siendrra	Silia	Simona *(0.02)*	Sinthia
Shytavia	Sibel	Sienna *(0.08)*	Silian	Simondria	Sinthiya
Shyteeka	Sibell	Sienna-Marie	Silicia	Simone *(0.28)*	Sinththura
Shyteona	Sibella	Sientiya	Silina	Simoné	Sinthu
Shytequa	Siberia	Siephanie	Silkan	Simone-Alyse	Sinthuha
Shyteraquist	Sibet	Siera *(0.05)*	Silke	Simoneka	Sinthuja
Shyteria	Sibil	Sierah	Silkeisha	Simonne	Sinthura
Shyteriah	Sibley	Sieralyn	Silken	Simplicia	Sintia *(0.01)*
Shyterikia	Sibrina	Sierha	Sillisa	Simraaj	Sintian
Shyterra	Sibyl	Sieriah	Siloam	Simran *(0.03)*	Sintique
Shytia	Sicely	Sierra *(2.42)*	Silone	Simrandeep	Sintril
Shytiauna	Siciida	Sierra Kesh	Siloni	Simranjit	Siobahn
Shytina	Sicilia	Sierra Marie	Silpa	Simranveer	Sioban
Shyuana	Sicily	Sierra Mercedes	Silpsupha	Simrat	Siobel
Shyun	Sicora	Sierra Nora	Silva	Simren	Siobhan *(0.08)*
Shyvette	Sicorra	Sierra Rain	Silvana *(0.01)*	Simrin	Siobhon
Shyvondra	Sicoya	Sierrá	Silver *(0.01)*	Simrit	Siobion
Shyvonna	Sidaadza	Sierra-Rose	Silveria	Simrith	Siomara
Shyyne	Sidanna	Sierrah *(0.02)*	Silvia *(0.19)*	Simrun	Siomora

Sion	Siv	Skyesha	Smaragdo	Sogol	Solvi
Siouxsie	Siva	Skyi	Smaranjit	Sogourner	Soly
Siouxzana	Siva Siobhainsw	Skyia	Smaria	Soha	Solymar
Siqouya	Sivaani	Skyirea	Smarjesse	Sohad	Solyna
Siquoya	Sivadra	Skykila	Smilie	Sohaiba	Soma
Sira	Sivahaame	Skyla *(0.04)*	Smita	Sohaila	Somaia
Sirah	Sivakaami	Skyla-Jo	Smith	Sohana	Somala
Siran	Sivan	Skylae	Smriti	Sohanie	Somalia
Siraniha	Sivana	Skylair	Smyrna	Sohany	Somalley
Sirat	Sivane	Skyland	Sneela	Soharra	Somaly
Siraylafa	Sivani	Skylania	Sneha *(0.01)*	Sohdanie	Somane
Sireesha	Sivannah	Skylar *(0.28)*	Snehaa	Sohila	Somara
Sirell	Sive	Skylar Danyelle	Snejana	Sohini	Somaya
Sirena *(0.04)*	Sivia	Skylee	Snelayne	Sohni	Somenta
Sirene	Sivonyia	Skylen	Snezana	Sohvana	Somer *(0.02)*
Sirenia	Sixta	Skylend	Snibree	Soibhan	Somerlyn
Sirenity	Siyobhan	Skylene	Snigdha	Soila	Somerrain
Sirey	Sjabreiah	Skyler *(0.19)*	Snimerdeep	Sojourner	Somersby
Siri *(0.01)*	Sjada	Skylet	Snober	Sojourney	Somerset
Siriah	Sjadaya	Skylett	Snoor	Sok	Somerville
Siriena	Sjohn'taye	Skyli	Snostorm	Sokchanta	Somher
Sirila	Sjolin	Skylia	Snow	Sokjaney	Somie
Sirina	Sjona	Skylia Lexi	Snowfeather	Sokuen	Somier
Sirisha	Skai	Skyliana	Snowflake	Sol	Sommar
Sirleny	Skarsheema	Skylie	Snowie	Solaire	Sommayria
Sirlyn	Skaye	Skylin	Snyden	Solana *(0.01)*	Sommer *(0.08)*
Sirolyn	Skeena	Skylka	Snyder	Solanche	Sommers
Sirrenahdi	Skenikwa	Skyllah	So	Solange *(0.01)*	Sommy
Sirrenthia	Skevi	Skyllar	So Eun	Solanikia	Somoleyah
Sirria	Ski	Skylor	So'yun	Solara	Somolia
Sirusha	Skiblu	Skylyn	Soad	Solcil	Somon
Sisalee	Skidasha	Skylynn	Soana	Soleda	Somone
Sisely	Skie	Skylyr	Soanya	Soledad *(0.03)*	Somotochukwu
Siska	Skii	Skymarie	Sobia	Soleia	Somsaiya
Sisley	Skiler	Skyonee	Sobitha	Soleil *(0.01)*	Somya
Sisndy	Skishae	Skyquilya	Sobrina	Soleille	Somyiah
Sissaley	Skky	Skysis	Soccora	Solene	Son
Sissell	Skotlyn	Skytaviia	Soccorro	Solenne	Sona
Sissy	Skue	Skytia	Socheata	Solette	Sonacia
Sister	Skwlax	Skyunae	Socheta	Soleya	Sonada
Sistinas	Sky *(0.05)*	Skyy *(0.01)*	Sochil	Solimar	Sonae
Sita	Sky'leigh	Skyylar	Socoia	Solinda	Sonal
Sitaara	Sky'toria	Slack	Socoria	Solitaire	Sonalee
Sitara	Skya	Slade	Socorro *(0.02)*	Solmari	Sonali
Sitara-Lyn	Skyann	Slavia	Sodny	Solmaria	Sonaly
Sitera	Skyanna	Slayten	Soemi	Solmayra	Sonam
Siterria	Skyanne	Sli Shaun	Sofea	Solmy	Sonara
Sithara	Skye *(0.16)*	Sloan *(0.02)*	Soffia	Solnett	Sonata
Siti	Skye-Lee	Sloand	Sofhua	Solome	Sonceré
Siti Hajar	Skyela	Sloane *(0.02)*	Sofia *(0.29)*	Solomia	Sonchell
Sitia	Skyelar	Sloanne	Sofie *(0.01)*	Solomita	Sondira
Sitona	Skyelee	Slobhan	Sofija	Solomiya	Sondos
Sittesha	Skyeler	Smaila	Sofiya	Solomon	Sondra *(0.02)*
Siu-Lan	Skyelur	Smanatha	Sofonie	Solona	Sondra-Joan
Siuyen	Skyemarie	Smantha	Sofya	Solvei	Sondrea

Sondrine	Soobin	Soryia	Sparkyl	Staciann	Starcey
Sonds	Sook	Sosan	Spawn	Stacie *(0.12)*	Starchia
Sondya	Soomin	Sosena	Spe-Chaelle	Stacie-Ann	Starcie
Sonette	Soona	Sosha	Spechal	Stacielyn	Starcy
Song	Soozee	Soshana	Spechele	Stacimarie	Stardacia
Songa	Sopeak	Sossi	Spechelle	Staciona	Stariel
Songhai	Sopha	Sossina	Spechyl	Stacy *(0.36)*	Starjus
Sonia *(0.43)*	Sophal	Soteara	Special *(0.01)*	Stacy Anne	Starkaye
Sonica	Sophamany	Sotera	Specious	Stacy-Ann	Starkea
Sonielle	Sophar	Sotheavy	Spencer *(0.07)*	Stadie	Starkeesha
Sonieya	Sophea	Sotherd	Spenceria	Staeria	Starkela
Soniff	Sophi	Sotirea	Spenser *(0.01)*	Staesha	Starkeria
Sonika	Sophia *(0.86)*	Sotoria	Speranca	Stafford	Starkeshia
Soniquia	Sophia-Ermelinda	Sotrionna	Spero	Stafonia	Starkila
Sonita	Sophia-Rosana	Souad	Spesyal	Staisha	Starks
Sonite	Sophie *(0.56)*	Souadou	Sphie	Stajia	Starla *(0.02)*
Sonitra	Sophie Stephani	Souha	Spirit	Stakaya	Starlea
Soniya	Sophie-Ann	Souhair	Splendid	Stalexus	Starlee
Sonja *(0.07)*	Sophie-Anne	Souhiela	Spring *(0.01)*	Staley	Starleena
Sonjaneke	Sophie-Francois	Soukayna	Spring Sage	Stalissia	Starlen
Sonjay	Sophilia	Souknapha	Spryng	Stamatia	Starlena
Sonje	Sophit	Souksakhone	Spyncer	Stamatiki	Starlene
Sonjela	Sophiya	Souktyda	Sr'derra	Stana	Starlet
Sonjia	Sophonie	Soulee	Sraddha	Stanaelle	Starlett
Sonjineke	Sophronia	Souleik	Srah	Stanaisha	Starley
Sonna	Sophy	Soulona	Sraiya	Stanazisha	Starlight
Sonné	Sopie	Soumaya	Sravya	Standasha	Starlina
Sonnet	Sopirinye	Soumetha	Srey	Standfill	Starling
Sonnia	Sopmone	Soumeya	Sreynita	Standrea	Starlisa
Sonnie	Soqueisha	Soumiya	Sri Radha	Stanecia	Starlit
Sonny	Sora	Soumya	Sri'lanka	Staneda	Starlitt
Sonnya	Sorah	Sounita	Srijana	Staneet	Starlove
Sonora	Soraida	Souphansa	Srijesa	Stanella	Starly
Sonová	Soraiyah	Souraya	Srilakshmi	Stanesha	Starlyn *(0.01)*
Sonovia	Soraya *(0.02)*	Souriya	Srishti	Stangela	Starlyne
Sonquilla	Soraya-Corine	Sourya	Srisuda	Stania	Starlynn
Sonsaray	Sorayma	Sousan	Srita	Stanise	Starnecia
Sonseeahray	Sorca	Southern	Srividya	Stanisha	Starnesha
Sonseriya	Sorcha	Souvany	Sriya	Stanita	Starneshia
Sonsha	Sorcia	Souzanne	Srujal	Stanley	Starnisha
Sonteona	Soreeytti	Sovannary	Ssahar	Stantezya	Starquette
Sontia	Soren	Sovanny	Ssavanah	Stanton	Starquoia
Sontisha	Sorenna	Sovary	St	Stantoria	Starr *(0.03)*
Sontorya	Soreya	Sovaya	Sta'vesha	Stanze	Starr-Lorene
Sontosha	Sorina	Sow	Stacean	Staphanie	Starr-Lynn
Sontrece	Sorita	Soy	Stacee *(0.01)*	Staphany	Starr-Quasia
Sontreon	Soriyah	Soyara	Stacey *(0.41)*	Star *(0.02)*	Starr-Sierra
Sonu	Soriyia	Soyine	Stacey Nicole	Star Shawn	Starre
Sonya *(0.17)*	Soroosh	Soyinkayobi	Stacha	Star-Lynn	Starriann
Sonyae	Sorovsha	Soyla	Stachia	Stara	Starris
Sonyanita	Soroya	Soyoung	Staci *(0.07)*	Staraisa	Starrla
Sonyasha	Sorrel	Spandana	Staci Alayi	Starashia	Starrletta
Sonyeasha	Sorriyah	Spane	Staci Rae	Starasia	Starsha
Soo	Sorsha	Sparkle *(0.01)*	Stacia *(0.03)*	Starbright	Starsheima
Soo-Jin	Sortori'	Sparkles	Stacia Shay	Starbrina	Starsterria

Startaesha	Steffanee	Stephanie-Nicol	Stevenise	Strawberry	Sueidaliz
Startavius	Steffaney	Stephanie-Silken	Stevetta	Streeana	Suejean
Startia	Steffani *(0.01)*	Stephanine	Stevey	Streisanne	Suelena
Startricia	Steffanie *(0.02)*	Stephanique	Stevi *(0.01)*	Stronjé	Sueling
Starwanda	Steffany *(0.03)*	Stephanni	Steviana	Strowbridge	Suellen
Starzie	Steffé	Stephannie *(0.01)*	Stevie *(0.13)*	Strunj'ee	Suemaya
Stasey	Steffee	Stephany *(0.24)*	Stevie-Anne	Stu Yan	Suendus
Stasha *(0.01)*	Steffi *(0.01)*	Stephany Susett	Stevie-Lee	Stuart	Suesan
Stasia *(0.01)*	Steffie	Stephanye	Stevie-Lynn	Stuartt	Suet
Stasie	Steffney	Stephen	Stevierose	Styles	Suet-Sum
Stasja	Steffsanie	Stephenee	Stevionna	Stylisha	Suevyann
Staten	Stefhanie	Stepheney	Steviree	Su	Sueyen
Statham	Stefhany	Stepheni	Stevmesha	Su Rhin	Suezan
Statia	Stefiany	Stephenie *(0.04)*	Stevonie	Su'ad	Suezanne
Statrell	Stefini	Stephenny	Stevonté	Sua	Suezzette
Statyn	Stefinie	Stepheny	Stevvona	Suaad	Sufey
Staunzie	Steflyn	Stephien	Stewart	Suad	Sufia
Stausha	Stefnee	Stephiene	Steyana	Suad Sabrina	Suganija
Stavna	Stefoni	Stephine *(0.01)*	Sthefanie	Suannah	Suganya
Stavroula *(0.01)*	Stefonia	Stephinie	Sthephanie	Suanne	Sugar
Stayana	Stefvany	Stephnae	Stillborn	Suany	Sugeetha
Staycee	Stefy	Stephney	Stinson	Suashia	Sugeiri
Staycha	Stehanie	Stephnie	Stirio	Suavae	Sugeiry
Stayleen	Stelecia	Stephny	Stirling	Subanki	Sugita
Staysha	Stella *(0.07)*	Stephonee	Stobhan	Subanya	Sugueidy
Staziah	Stella Ann	Stephonya	Stojanka	Subaya-Osman	Suha
Stévasha	Stella-	Stephy	Stone	Subeyda	Suhail
Steacy	Stellanne	Stephyanie	Stonebria	Subhadra	Suhani
Steadasha	Stellera	Stepvoni	Stoneisha	Subhah	Suhasini
Steante	Stello	Ster	Stoney	Subhneet	Suhier
Steaven	Steohanie	Ster'quandria	Stonie	Subia	Suhua
Steavie	Steona	Sterlicia	Storee	Subin	Suhur
Stecoria	Stepanie	Sterlin	Storey	Subreen	Sui
Stedson	Stepfanie	Sterling *(0.03)*	Stori	Subreena	Sujal
Steedra	Stephaie	Sterlissia	Storie	Subreinia	Sujanna
Steele	Stephaine *(0.01)*	Sterlondria	Storm *(0.03)*	Subrena	Sujany
Steely	Stephana	Sterly	Storm-Brianne	Subrina	Sujaytha
Steevee	Stephane	Sterlyn	Storme	Suchi	Sujean
Steevi	Stephanee	Sterra	Stormee	Suchita	Sujey
Steevondra	Stephanely	Sterwing	Stormey	Suchjot	Sujicaa
Stef'nie	Stephaney	Steshawna	Stormi *(0.02)*	Sucoya	Sujitha
Stefa-Anne	Stephani *(0.05)*	Stesi	Stormie *(0.04)*	Sudanisis	Sujurijahara
Stefana	Stephani'sue	Stetson	Stormii	Sudduth	Suk
Stefane	Stephania *(0.01)*	Steva	Stormm	Sudie	Sukaina
Stefanee	Stephanianna	Stevahna	Stormy *(0.08)*	Sudney	Sukanya
Stefani *(0.07)*	Stephanie *(7.38)*	Stevana	Stormy Lyn	Sue *(0.02)*	Sukari
Stefania *(0.02)*	Stephanie Ann	Stevanaa	Story	Sue A	Sukayna
Stefanie *(0.25)*	Stephanie Anne	Stevangela	Stpehanie	Sue-Ann	Suke
Stefanie Faith	Stephanie Marie	Stevanna	Stracy	Sue-Jin	Sukeina
Stefanni	Stephanie Patri	Stevanne	Strajah	Sueann	Sukhbina
Stefanny	Stephanie-	Stevee	Strajée	Suede	Sukhbir
Stefany *(0.05)*	Claudette	Stevefany	Strang	Suefie	Sukhdeep *(0.01)*
Stefanya	Stephanie-Kira	Steven	Strang'e	Sueha	Sukhdip
Stefawn	Stephanie-Leah	Steveni	Strangé	Suehelen	Sukhjeevin
Stefenie	Stephanie-Lynn	Stevenie	Strawbarry	Suehier	Sukhjinder

Sukhjit	Sumaire	Sumyr	Sunshine *(0.02)*	Suruthi	Suzann
Sukhjot	Sumaita	Sun-Sierra	Sunshyn	Suruthy	Suzanna *(0.07)*
Sukhleen	Sumaiya	Suna	Sunshyne	Sury	Suzannah *(0.02)*
Sukhman	Sumaiya-Sadik	Sunaina	Sunsieah	Surya	Suzanne *(0.19)*
Sukhmani	Suman	Sunali	Sunsire	Susada	Suze
Sukhmankaur	Sumana	Sunamita	Sunsiree	Susan *(0.43)*	Suzelle
Sukhmanprit	Sumandeep	Sunanda	Suntanna	Susan-Elisabeth	Suzenji
Sukhmeet	Sumanpreet	Sunantha	Suntavia	Susana *(0.28)*	Suzenna
Sukhmin	Sumar	Sunasia	Suntiah	Susanah	Suzett
Sukhminder	Sumathi	Sunceray	Sunveer	Susane	Suzette *(0.03)*
Sukhmit	Sumati	Sundae	Sunya	Susann	Suzi
Sukhpal	Sumaya *(0.01)*	Sundai	Suong	Susanna *(0.09)*	Suzie *(0.02)*
Sukhpreet *(0.01)*	Sumayah	Sundal	Supal	Susannah *(0.06)*	Suzlevia
Sukhraj	Sumayya	Sundas	Supanee	Susanne *(0.01)*	Suzy
Sukhreet	Sumayyah	Sunday *(0.01)*	Supaya	Susej	Suzzanna
Sukhveer	Sumble	Sundeep	Superia	Suselix	Suzzie
Sukhvir	Sumeet	Sundjata	Suphany	Susette	Svaja
Sukina	Sumeetha	Sundos	Supharem	Sushani	Svanna
Sula	Sumeka	Sundrina	Suphronia	Sushanna	Svava
Sulakha	Sumen	Sundus	Supor	Sushannah	Svea
Sulamie	Sumer *(0.02)*	Sunee	Supreen	Sushine	Sveena
Sulamita	Sumera Soorma	Suneet	Supreet *(0.01)*	Sushmita	Sveina
Sulamithe	Sumerlyne	Sunena	Supreya	Susie *(0.04)*	Svenja
Sulayma	Sumeya	Sunera	Supriya	Susie Dixie	Svenna
Sulaymi	Sumeyye	Sunevra	Suquanna	Susie-Monique	Sveta
Suleika	Sumi	Sunflower	Suquey-Amparo	Susieann	Svetlana *(0.01)*
Suleima *(0.01)*	Sumika	Suni	Sura	Susmita	Svjetlana
Suleima Yasmin	Sumiko	Sunia	Surabhi	Sussan	Svonne
Suleiman	Sumiya	Sunianne	Surah	Sussette	Swafiya
Suleka	Summar	Sunicia	Suraiya	Sussin	Swain
Sulekha	Summer *(0.95)*	Sunishia	Suramiya	Susy	Swainthesia
Sulema	Summer-Jane	Sunita	Suraya	Sutamas	Swan
Sulemita	Summer-Lee	Sunita-Kumari	Surayah	Sutikshna	Swan'daysa
Sulemma	Summer-Leigh	Sunjidah	Surayya	Sutton	Swan'tyiesia
Suleq	Summer-Lily	Sunjot	Surayyah	Suvana	Swana
Suleyma *(0.01)*	Summerann	Sunkiya	Surbhi	Suvanna	Swantice
Sulinda	Summerine	Sunmeet	Sureaga	Suvarna	Swapna
Suling	Summerlin	Sunmi	Sureanna	Suvarnalatha	Swarna
Sulivone	Summerlyn	Sunnah	Sureel	Suvathe	Swarnali
Sulleen	Summerlynn	Sunney	Sureetha	Suvatheka	Swasey
Sulli	Summers	Sunni	Sureimy	Suvathika	Swathi
Sullivan *(0.01)*	Summiah	Sunnie	Sureka	Suveethy	Swathy
Sullivette	Summiarn	Sunnisha	Surekga	Suvie	Swati
Sullyann	Summie	Sunniva	Surekha	Suvina	Swaylana
Sulma	Summit	Sunny *(0.03)*	Surelle	Suvluuraq	Swayzie
Sulochana	Summre	Sunny Bryanna	Surelys	Suwaida	Sweden
Sultan	Summré	Sunnyshine	Suren	Suwan	Sweeney
Sultana	Summyr	Sunora	Surena	Suwanda	Sweet
Sultanat	Sumner	Sunries	Suria	Suwilangi	Sweta
Sulty	Sumone	Sunrise	Surima	Suxein	Swetha
Suluama	Sumonia	Sunserae	Surina	Suyapa	Sy
Suly	Sumorya	Sunserrae	Suriya	Suzahn	Sy-Kerria
Sum-Err	Sumre	Sunset	Surmetria	Suzan *(0.01)*	Sya
Suma	Sumrina	Sunsharé	Surrayya	Suzana *(0.01)*	Syad
Sumaira	Sumun	Sunshea	Suruchi	Suzane	Syaila

Syaira	Syilvana	Symphanie	Syteria	T'ayra	T'nia
Syana	Sykeriah	Symphany	Sytia	T'ea	T'nisha
Syandene	Sykira	Symphonée	Sytianna	T'eil	T'niyah
Syann	Sykoyia	Symphoni	Sytira	T'ekeyah	T'nya
Syanne	Syl'quala	Symphonie	Sytoria	T'era	T'oinne
Syannia	Syla	Symphony *(0.01)*	Syvanna	T'eria	T'onna
Syara	Sylanie	Symplicity	Syvannah	T'erica	T'onnie
Syarrah	Sylbina	Synammon	Syveah	T'ericka	T'osha
Sybel	Syleen	Synanta	Syxx	T'erika	T'oshe
Sybelle	Syleica	Synclair	Szascha	T'erra	T'quana
Sybellen	Sylence	Synclare	Sze	T'erre	T'quay
Sybil *(0.01)*	Sylenthia	Syndey	Sze-Kei	T'essence	T'quoshai
Sybley	Sylia	Syndi	Szeja	T'evin	T'sai
Sybrea	Sylicia	Syndia	Szipporah	T'iana	T'shawna
Sybria	Sylina	Syndney	Szofia	T'iara	T'shona
Sybrina	Sylisha	Syndy	Szor'danner	T'iarra	T'shurah
Sybrisha	Sylken	Syneba	Szu-Aun	T'iera	T'sung
Syd	Sylla	Synethia		T'ierra	T'uana
Sydali	Sylmari	Synetra		T'kasha	T'yana
Syday	Sylmarie	Synetria	**-T-**	T'keeyah	T'yana Leita Mar
Sydel	Sylvana	Synia		T'keia	T'yanca
Sydelle	Sylvanah	Syniah	T *(0.03)*	T'kendra	T'yanna
Sydenie	Sylvania	Synnamon	T Aira	T'kenya	T'yawne
Sydeny	Sylvanna	Synnove	T Asia	T'keya	T'yiece
Sydequa	Sylver	Synobyia	T Erica Tri	T'keyah *(0.04)*	T'yona
Sydne *(0.01)*	Sylvera	Synovia	T Erika	T'keyah-Ll'chelle	T'yonna
Sydnea	Sylvi	Synphne	T Gloria	T'keyan	T-Ania
Sydnee *(0.12)*	Sylvia *(0.28)*	Synquasha	T Iara	T'keyea	T-Anna
Sydnei *(0.01)*	Sylvia-Anne	Synquawna	T Joni	T'keyha	T-Keiah
Sydney *(2.98)*	Sylvian	Synques	T Kaya	T'keyhia	T-Yona
Sydney-Alexis	Sylvianne *(0.01)*	Synquest	T Kelyah	T'keyiah	T.
Sydney-Alyson	Sylvie *(0.02)*	Synquis	T Keyah	T'keyra	T.C.
Sydney-Desiree	Sylvina	Synthia *(0.01)*	T Kia	T'keyuh	Ta
Sydney-Lee	Sylvonah	Syntierra	T L Jones	T'kia	Ta Cheyanna
Sydney-Nicole	Sylvonia	Syntonia	T Mirraw	T'kieya	Ta Chiana
Sydney-Rain	Sylvonna-Ying	Syntoria	T Oine	T'krya	Ta Dreyan
Sydney-Taylor	Sylvy	Syona	T Shayla	T'kyah	Ta Ja
Sydneyjo	Sylwia *(0.01)*	Syonie	T Shyla	T'kyra	Ta Jah
Sydni *(0.10)*	Sylycia	Sypress	T Ya	T'lacy	Ta Janique
Sydni'	Syma	Syrah	T'ahshay	T'layah	Ta Keitha
Sydnie *(0.10)*	Symantha *(0.01)*	Syreeta	T'aira	T'leah	Ta Kisia
Sydny	Symantha P	Syrena *(0.01)*	T'airra	T'lesha	Ta Kynya
Sydnye	Symara	Syrenia	T'aja	T'lisha	Ta Leesia
Sye	Symba	Syretha	T'akeyah	T'lissa	Ta Lesha
Syeasha	Symiah	Syretta	T'andra	T'liyah	Ta Lissia
Syed	Symira	Syri	T'andreus	T'mara	Ta Maira
Syeda *(0.01)*	Symmantha	Syriah	T'andria	T'meya	Ta Mara
Syedda	Symmeon	Syriana	T'ang	T'meyah	Ta Marcus
Syedh	Symmieona	Syrina	T'angela	T'mia	Ta Nacia
Syera	Symmone	Syringa	T'anna	T'miyah	Ta Neisha
Syerra *(0.01)*	Symona	Syrinthia	T'ara	T'nai	Ta Nikqua
Syerrah	Symond	Syrlena	T'arra	T'naya	Ta Niyah
Syhréna	Symone *(0.07)*	Syrrah	T'ashlee	T'neisha	Ta Quadra
Syidah	Symoné	Syrrita	T'asia	T'nerra	Ta Relle
Syietta	Symonne	Systerlaine	T'ausia	T'nesha	Ta Shawn

Ta Tiana	Ta'lasha	Ta'tashia	Tabbittha	Tacheiaa	Taelyr
Ta Tyana	Ta'leah	Ta'teona	Tabby	Tachena	Taemurni
Ta Tyania	Ta'lecia	Ta'teyana	Tabbytha	Tachet	Taeneshia
Tá	Ta'leesha	Ta'tiana	Tabea (0.01)	Tachiana	Taera
Ta'brea	Ta'lisa	Ta'tianna	Taben	Tachiara	Taesha
Ta'bria	Ta'liyah	Ta'tiara	Taber	Tachina (0.01)	Taeshawna
Ta'cara	Ta'llyah	Ta'tiyana	Tabetha (0.03)	Tachirara	Taeshia
Ta'carol	Ta'losha	Ta'tyana	Tabia	Tachiyra	Taesjona
Ta'charia	Ta'mar	Ta'tyanna	Tabiatha	Taci	Taesoo
Ta'cheona	Ta'mera	Ta'vea	Tabish	Tacianna	Taetiana
Ta'chianna	Ta'mia	Ta'za	Tabita	Tacinda	Taevosha
Ta'china	Ta'naji	Ta'zhae	Tabitha (0.57)	Tacobi	Taeylar
Ta'coreia	Ta'nari	Ta'zhania	Tabitha Avery	Tacolya	Taeylor
Ta'corra	Ta'nayiah	Ta-Che-Anna	Tabitha Rochell	Tacora	Tafaya
Ta'darron	Ta'neasha	Ta-Janay	Tabitha Sha	Tacorea	Tafeequa
Ta'daysha	Ta'nedra	Ta-Keishiya	Tabitha-Ann	Tacoria	Taffani
Ta'dedra	Ta'neisha	Ta-Kelya	Tabitha-Lee	Tacorra	Taffany
Ta'djanique	Ta'nesha	Ta-Lice	Tabithia	Tacorrie	Taffanye
Ta'drae	Ta'neshia	Ta-Raya	Tableah	Tacorya	Taffin
Ta'drianna	Ta'nia	Ta-Shara	Tabra	Tacoya	Taffy
Ta'ericka	Ta'nice	Ta-Shaun	Tabran	Tacreshia	Tagan
Ta'hedia	Ta'nika	Ta-Shauna	Tabreacia	Tacy	Tagaria
Ta'ina	Ta'nisa	Ta-Sheana	Tabreea	Tadaejah	Tagen
Ta'ja	Ta'nisha	Ta-Taneshia	Tabreka	Tadaisha	Tagenn
Ta'jahe	Ta'niya	Ta-Tanishia	Tabresha	Tadasha	Tagera
Ta'jai	Ta'nya	Ta-Teana	Tabria (0.01)	Tadasia	Taglera
Ta'jamican	Ta'ondria	Taa	Tabrianna	Tadatha	Tah'sherria
Ta'jana	Ta'quala	Taa'liah	Tabrieah	Tadausha	Tah-Jahnek
Ta'jeare	Ta'queria	Taaha	Tabrieal	Tadaysha	Tah-Shiekqua
Ta'jhea	Ta'quiia	Taahira	Tabriel	Tadeidra	Tahalia
Ta'kaiya	Ta'rah	Taahirah	Tabrielle	Tadeja	Tahani
Ta'kala	Ta'rayia	Taaj	Tabrina	Tadesha	Tahanie
Ta'kara	Ta'rena	Taajvir	Tabriya	Tadia	Tahanni
Ta'karsha	Ta'resha	Taalyiah	Tabura	Tadijiah	Tahany
Ta'keira	Ta'rhea	Taanna	Tabutha	Tadira	Tahara
Ta'keisha	Ta'seana	Taarani	Tabytha (0.01)	Tadisha	Taharath
Ta'keiya	Ta'sha	Taarna	Tacahna	Tadrianna	Tahaveen
Ta'keiyah	Ta'shara	Taashera	Tacaia	Tadrieka	Tahayshia
Ta'kena	Ta'shauna	Taasia	Tacalia	Taélor	Taheelah-Marie
Ta'kera	Ta'shaunda	Tabaitha	Tacamjula	Taéneequa	Taheera
Ta'keria	Ta'shaundra	Taban	Tacara	Taea	Taheerah
Ta'kerra	Ta'shawn	Tabara	Tacarmen	Taegan	Tahely
Ta'keta Sty'lex	Ta'shawnna	Tabarak	Tacaro	Taehlor	Tahera
Ta'ketria	Ta'shay	Tabasia	Tacarra	Taeisha	Tahere
Ta'kevia	Ta'shayia	Tabassum	Taccar	Taejah	Taherri
Ta'keya	Ta'shayla	Tabata	Taccarra	Taejanay	Tahesha
Ta'keyah	Ta'sheionya	Tabatha (0.14)	Tacee	Taelar (0.01)	Taheshia
Ta'keyha	Ta'shericka	Tabatha-Lynn	Tacey	Taelehs	Tahgmah
Ta'keyla	Ta'shiauna	Tabatha-Rae	Tachae	Taeler (0.01)	Tahiara
Ta'kiala	Ta'shika	Tabathia	Tachara	Taeli	Tahillah
Ta'kira	Ta'shyra	Tabbata	Tacharia	Taelin	Tahina
Ta'kiyah	Ta'sia	Tabbatha (0.01)	Tache	Taellor	Tahira
Ta'kreisha	Ta'sommer	Tabbetha	Taché	Taelor (0.05)	Tahirah
Ta'laesha	Ta'taneasha	Tabbi	Tacheana	Taelore	Tahireh
Ta'laiah	Ta'tanysha	Tabbitha (0.01)	Tacheanna	Taelynn	Tahirih

Tahitia	Tai Janae	Tailyr	Taja *(0.01)*	Tajyeiah	Takerria
Tahj	Tai Jasmine	Taima	Tajá	Tajza	Takesha *(0.01)*
Tahj Uwon	Tai Sha	Taima-Lynn	Taja'aunna	Tajzhe	Takeshia
Tahja	Tai Shana	Taimane	Tajada	Tajzhona	Takesia
Tahjai	Tai Shianna	Taimi	Tajae	Tak'ira	Taketa
Tahjai'	Tai'asious	Taimia	Tajaé	Takaará	Taketia
Tahjanai	Tai'jah	Taina	Tajah *(0.01)*	Takaila	Takevia
Tahjanea	Tai'leone	Tainaisha	Tajahnae	Takaiya	Takeviá
Tahjanyqué	Tai'quirrer	Tainaj	Tajahné	Takako	Takeya *(0.01)*
Tahjiana	Tai'sha	Taineesha	Tajai	Takala	Takeyah
Tahjire	Tai'yanna	Taiontay	Tajai'	Takalia	Takeyceya
Tahjiza	Tai'ylor	Taiquana	Tajana	Takalra	Takeyla
Tahjma	Tai-Lena	Taiqueisha	Tajanae	Takami	Takeyra
Tahkara	Tai-Lyn	Taira *(0.01)*	Tajanaé	Takaneshia	Takeysha
Tahkehiah	Taia	Tairanique	Tajanai	Takara *(0.01)*	Takeysheonna
Tahkiya	Taiah	Tairra	Tajane	Takarah	Takezia
Tahleah	Taiann	Tairrah	Tajanee	Takaria	Takhamrri
Tahleia	Taibat	Tairyn	Tajanée	Takarra	Takhera
Tahlia *(0.02)*	Taibtha	Taisa	Tajani	Takasha	Takhiya
Tahlor	Taicha	Taisha *(0.01)*	Tajania	Takaya	Takhye
Tahlyr	Taichée	Taishana	Tajanique	Takayah	Takia *(0.03)*
Tahmaira	Taidra	Taishanee	Tajanise	Takayia	Takiah
Tahmarrah	Taidria	Taishaun	Tajara	Takayla *(0.01)*	Takiara
Tahmaya	Taiesha	Taishawn	Tajarée	Takayler	Takiela
Tahmina	Taigan	Taishea	Tajarei	Takayli	Takiera
Tahmya	Taige	Taisheena	Tajarirah	Takayra	Takierah
Tahnal	Taigen	Taishia	Tajashanique	Takéa	Takierra
Tahnayee	Taighen	Taishiana	Tajay	Takeara	Takierria
Tahne	Taighlor	Taishira	Tajaye	Takeba	Takiesha
Tahneal	Taihler	Taishonna	Tajayna	Takecia	Takieshia
Tahnee	Taihlin	Taisia	Tajenae	Takeema	Takievea
Tahneshia	Taiilor	Taisley	Tajh'neik	Takeena	Takieya
Tahni	Taij	Taisly	Tajha	Takeenya	Takiijah
Tahnisha	Taija *(0.01)*	Tait	Tajhai	Takeera	Takila
Tahnya	Taijah	Taitana	Tajhan	Takeesha	Takilah
Tahoni	Taijahna	Taite	Tajhané	Takeia *(0.01)*	Takilya
Tahonna	Taijan	Taitiana	Tajhia	Takeidria	Takima
Tahreem	Taijana	Taitianna	Tajhzna	Takeila	Takina
Tahriana	Taijanae	Taitumn	Taji	Takeira	Takira *(0.01)*
Tahrima	Taijhel	Taityana	Tajia	Takeirah	Takirah
Tahsena	Taijiana	Taityanna	Tajiana	Takeisha	Takiria
Tahsezah	Taijuan	Taiva	Tajianna	Takeitha	Takirra
Tahshelle	Taikina	Taiveyuana	Tajieana	Takel	Takisha *(0.01)*
Tahsin	Taiksha	Taiwana	Tajier	Takela	Takita
Tahsis	Taila	Taiya	Tajinder	Takelia	Takiya *(0.01)*
Taht'yanna	Tailah	Taiyler	Tajjanee	Takemma	Takiyah *(0.01)*
Tahtiana	Tailar	Taiylor	Tajmeen	Takendria	Takizea
Tahtianna	Tailer *(0.01)*	Taiylore	Tajon	Takenna	Taknisha
Tahtiona	Tailesha	Taiyon	Tajonea	Takenya	Takobia
Tahtiyana	Tailia	Taiz	Tajpreet	Takenyah	Takojah
Tahvi	Tailiah	Taiza	Tajruba	Takera	Takoma
Tahyana	Taillor	Taize	Tajuana	Takeri	Takonderia
Tahyeka	Tailor *(0.01)*	Taizonique	Tajuanna	Takeria *(0.01)*	Takora
Tahylor	Taily	Taj	Tajunique	Takerian	Takoria
Tai *(0.01)*	Tailyn	Taj Chene	Tajya	Takerra	Takosha

Takoya	Talena *(0.01)*	Talleila	Taman	Tambree	Tamie
Takoyia	Talencia	Talley	Tamana	Tambresha	Tamieka
Takshaka	Taler	Tallia	Tamand	Tambria	Tamiel
Takweyla	Talesa	Tallie	Tamanda	Tambricha	Tamiera
Takwona	Talese	Tallis	Tamanik	Tambrie	Tamika *(0.06)*
Takya	Talesha *(0.01)*	Talliyah	Tamanna	Tambrietta	Tamika-Renee
Takyah	Taleshia	Tallulah	Tamar *(0.03)*	Tambry	Tamikah
Takyia	Talesia	Tallundrea	Tamara *(0.58)*	Tamburlyn	Tamike
Takyla	Talesshia	Tally	Tamara-Lynn	Tame	Tamikia
Takylia	Taletha	Tallya	Tamara-Rose	Tamea	Tamil
Takyra	Talethe	Tallyn	Tamarae	Tameca	Tamila
Takyrra	Talethia	Talmadgeria	Tamarah *(0.01)*	Tamecia	Tamile
Tal	Taleur	Talnisha	Tamaral	Tameeka	Tamille
Tala *(0.01)*	Talexis	Talon *(0.01)*	Tamarcia	Tameekah	Tamim
Talaciya	Taleya	Talonda	Tamare	Tameesha	Tamina
Talaia	Taleyah	Talondre	Tamareka	Tamei'sha	Taminder
Talaina	Taleyha	Talonna	Tamaren	Tameica	Tamir
Talainia	Tali	Talor *(0.01)*	Tamaria *(0.01)*	Tameicia	Tamira *(0.02)*
Talaiya	Talia *(0.26)*	Talore	Tamariah	Tameika	Tamiracle
Talala	Taliah *(0.01)*	Talsianna	Tamarial	Tameira	Tamirae
Talana	Taliana	Talvanisha	Tamarian	Tameisha *(0.01)*	Tamirah
Talar	Talibah	Talvir	Tamariel	Tameiya	Tamiraw
Talasha	Talibra	Talwinder	Tamarii	Tameka *(0.03)*	Tamircle
Talasia	Talicia	Taly	Tamarika	Tameká	Tamiria
Talathea	Talie	Talya *(0.01)*	Tamarin	Tamekia *(0.01)*	Tamirra
Talatu	Taliea	Talya Tra'keyla	Tamarin-	Tamela *(0.01)*	Tamisha *(0.02)*
Talaya *(0.01)*	Taliesin	Talyah	Alexandrea	Tamelia	Tamitha
Talayah	Talieya	Talyaha	Tamarind	Tamera *(0.09)*	Tamiwa
Talayia	Talija	Talyaneke	Tamarion	Tameran	Tamiya *(0.01)*
Talayla	Talijiaha	Talye	Tamaris	Tameria	Tamiyah
Talayna	Talika	Talyia	Tamarishia	Tamerick	Tamiyha
Talayne	Talikeyah	Talyn	Tamariya	Tamerly	Tamka
Talayshia	Talina *(0.01)*	Talyndria	Tamarow	Tamerra	Tamkia
Talaysia	Talinda	Talynn	Tamarra *(0.01)*	Tamerras	Tamla
Talbot	Taline	Talysa	Tamarrah	Tameryal	Tamlyn
Talbryn	Taliria	Talysha	Tamarria	Tamesha *(0.02)*	Tammam
Talea *(0.01)*	Talisa *(0.02)*	Talysia	Tamarrion	Tameshá	Tammara
Taleah *(0.01)*	Talise	Talyssa	Tamary	Tameshetta	Tammaria
Taleaha	Talisha *(0.02)*	Tam	Tamarya	Tameshia *(0.01)*	Tammariah
Taleana	Talishia	Tama	Tamaryn	Tameshya	Tammassha
Taleatha	Talisia	Tamacia	Tamarys	Tamesia	Tammea
Talecia	Talissa *(0.01)*	Tamader	Tamasha	Tametra	Tammera
Taleea	Talita	Tamadj	Tamashe	Tametres	Tammesha
Talees	Talitah	Tamadja	Tamasheaun	Tametris	Tammeshia
Taleesa	Talitha *(0.02)*	Tamadrionna	Tamasin	Tameyah	Tammi
Taleese	Talivia	Tamaesha	Tamasyn	Tami *(0.01)*	Tammicka
Taleesha	Taliya	Tamaica	Tamatra	Tamia *(0.01)*	Tammie *(0.01)*
Taleia	Taliyah *(0.02)*	Tamaijanay	Tamaura	Tamiah	Tammika
Taleinna	Talizia	Tamaira *(0.01)*	Tamauriance	Tamiak	Tammiko
Taleisha	Talja	Tamaiya	Tamaya	Tamian	Tammisha
Taleita	Talkea	Tamaja	Tamber	Tamiay	Tammra
Taleiya	Tallah	Tamajuna	Tamberlynn	Tamica	Tammy *(0.14)*
Talejah	Tallas	Tamaka	Tambie	Tamicah	Tammy-Lynn
Taleka	Tallayah	Tamala	Tambra	Tamice	Tammylee
Talen	Talleha	Tamam	Tambranesha	Tamicka	Tamona

Tamonica
Tamonika
Tamonique
Tamorah
Tamoya
Tamra *(0.03)*
Tamrah
Tamrien
Tamrion
Tamrit
Tamriyonna
Tamron
Tamry
Tamsan
Tamsha
Tamsin *(0.01)*
Tamsun
Tamsyn
Tamundia
Tamur
Tamura
Tamy
Tamya
Tamyaa
Tamyah
Tamyka
Tamyra *(0.01)*
Tamyria
Tamyrra
Tamytrice
Tamzen
Tamzin
Tan
Tan'nieshia
Tan-Nishia
Tana *(0.03)*
Tanacia
Tanaciá
Tanae
Tanaeja
Tanaejah
Tanaeya
Tanah
Tanai
Tanaia
Tanairi
Tanairy
Tanaisa
Tanaisha
Tanaiya
Tanaja
Tanajah
Tanajia
Tanajoa
Tanaka

Tananda
Tanangela
Tanara
Tanasha
Tanashia
Tanasia *(0.01)*
Tanaundra
Tanay
Tanaya *(0.01)*
Tanayah
Tanayalyn
Tanayga
Tanayia
Tanayisha
Tanaysa
Tanaysha
Tanaysja
Tanaz
Tanbir
Tance
Tanche
Tancie
Tandaekah
Tandarae
Tandaway
Tandeep
Tandi
Tandia
Tandice
Tandis
Tandlandya
Tandra *(0.01)*
Tandrea
Tandreona
Tandria
Tandy
Tane
Tané
Tanésha
Tanea *(0.01)*
Taneah
Taneal
Taneasha
Tanecia
Taneda
Tanedra
Tanee
Taneeka
Taneen
Taneesa
Taneesha *(0.01)*
Taneesheia
Taneeshia
Taneeshjot
Taneeza

Taneia
Taneidra
Taneigha
Taneika
Taneil
Taneira
Taneisha *(0.02)*
Taneishia
Taneiya
Tanejah
Taneka *(0.01)*
Tanekea
Tanekia
Tanekque
Tanekquie
Tanela
Tanell
Tanelle
Tanequa
Tanequia
Tanera
Tanesa
Tanesha *(0.06)*
Taneshia
Taneshya
Tanesia
Tanesiá
Taneskea
Tanessa
Tanesy
Tanetra
Tanetta
Taney
Taneya
Taneysha
Tang
Tanganekia
Tanganika
Tanganiqua
Tanganique
Tanganyika
Tangee
Tangela *(0.01)*
Tangelia
Tangeneka
Tangenia
Tangerae
Tangeria
Tangernekia
Tangi *(0.01)*
Tangie *(0.02)*
Tangiélica
Tangier
Tangileaq
Tangilene

Tangineka
Tanginicqua
Tangray
Tangueray
Tangy
Tanha
Tani
Tani'
Tania *(0.39)*
Tania Areli
Tania Valeria
Tania-Mba
Taniah
Tanica
Tanice
Tanicha
Tanicia
Tanicka
Tanider
Tanidra
Tanieka
Taniel
Taniesha *(0.01)*
Tanig
Tanija
Tanijah
Tanika *(0.04)*
Tanikka
Tanikqua
Tanille
Taniqua *(0.01)*
Tanique
Taniquea
Tanis *(0.02)*
Tanisa
Tanise
Tanish
Tanisha *(0.24)*
Tanisha-Jade
Tanishia
Tanishie
Tanisia
Tanissha
Tanita
Tanitha
Tanitia
Tanitra
Taniya *(0.01)*
Taniyah
Tanj Elque
Tanja *(0.01)*
Tanjá
Tanjaléna
Tanjanequa
Tanjanique

Tanjenay
Tanjeria
Tanji
Tanjunique
Tankey
Tankia
Tanmra
Tanna *(0.01)*
Tannah
Tannaka
Tannayah
Tannaz
Tanneh
Tanner *(0.03)*
Tannette
Tannew
Tannia
Tannie
Tanniguar
Tannija
Tannika
Tanniqula
Tannis *(0.01)*
Tannisha
Tannishtha
Tannor
Tannsinee
Tannya
Tannyann
Tannyr
Tanotzin
Tanova
Tanoya
Tanpreet
Tanquaria
Tanquera
Tanquisia
Tanquvious
Tansha
Tanshell
Tansy
Tantaleia
Tantaneia
Tantaneice
Tantiana
Tanu
Tanu'neka
Tanul
Tanuraj
Tanveer
Tanvi
Tanvir
Tanya *(0.40)*
Tanya-Ann
Tanyail

Tanyal
Tanychee
Tanycia
Tanye
Tanyelle
Tanyesha
Tanyhya
Tanyia
Tanyin
Tanyjah
Tanyr
Tanys
Tanysha
Tanza
Tanzana
Tanzaneá
Tanzania *(0.01)*
Tanzeela
Tanzeelah
Tanzenia
Tanzia
Tanzie
Tanzima
Tanzinia
Tanznea
Tanzy
Tanzzie
Tao
Taofo
Tapainga
Tapanga
Tapangha
Tapassion
Tapazia
Taphanie
Tapina
Taporshia
Taportia
Taprée
Tapu
Taq'uisa
Taqera
Taqeshia
Taqiyyah
Taqoya
Taqqeéa
Taquaela
Taquaisha
Taqualla
Taquana
Taquanda
Taquane
Taquanjria
Taquanna
Taquanta

Taquanya	Taraneh	Tarkessa	Tarynn	Tashaunna	Tashina *(0.02)*
Taquasjah	Taraneka	Tarkethia	Tarynn-Dawn	Tashavia	Tashionea
Taquavia	Taranjit	Tarkia	Taryon	Tashawn	Tashiquiona
Taquaviana	Tarannum	Tarlecia	Tasa	Tashawna *(0.01)*	Tashira
Taquayla	Taranpreet	Tarlexus	Tasa'ma	Tashawnda	Tashiraliz
Taquaysha	Tarasha	Tarlisha	Tasaddaq	Tashawnna	Tashiya
Taque	Tarashea	Tarmarra	Tasana	Tashawnnia	Tashiyana
Taqueeria	Tarasiana	Tarmeldria	Tasanee	Tashay *(0.01)*	Tashiyionna
Taqueeshallyn	Taraya	Tarmim	Tasbeh	Tashaybrea	Tashjae
Taqueeva	Tarayja	Tarndeep	Tasca	Tashayla *(0.01)*	Tashleena
Taquella	Tarayshia	Tarnecia	Tascha	Tashaylar	Tashlya
Taqueria	Tarazia	Tarneda	Tasché	Tashe	Tashmekka
Taqueshia	Tardasha	Tarneshia	Tasciana	Tashé	Tashna
Taquesta	Tardazia	Tarnetta	Taseana	Tashéauna	Tashney
Taquienca	Tarélia	Tarnisha	Taseanna	Tashea	Tasho'shua
Taquiesha	Tareasia	Tarnjeet	Tasenia	Tasheá	Tashon
Taquila	Tareca	Tarnjit	Tasey	Tasheana	Tashona
Taquilla	Taree	Tarnpreet	Tasfia	Tasheante	Tashonda
Taquinta	Tareesha	Tarnyeshia	Tasha *(0.24)*	Tasheara	Tashonda-Lynn
Taquinya	Tareikah	Tarolyn	Tasha Jo	Tasheba	Tashonia
Taquira	Taren *(0.01)*	Tarolynne	Tasha-Lee	Tashee	Tashonna
Taquirra	Tarena	Taroniquahe	Tasha-Ria	Tasheeana	Tashowna
Taquisha	Tarerria	Tarquiana	Tashada	Tasheema	Tashoya
Taquita	Taresa	Tarquitta	Tashadow	Tasheena *(0.01)*	Tashpreet
Taquiya	Taresha	Tarra *(0.01)*	Tashae	Tasheiba	Tashqua
Taqulia	Tareshia	Tarrah *(0.01)*	Tashael	Tasheika	Tashraiel
Taqundra	Taressa	Tarran	Tashaela	Tasheka	Tashrica
Taqunisha	Tareya	Tarras	Tashaera	Tashekia	Tashrondra
Taquonna	Tareylon	Tarrell	Tashai	Tashela	Tashua
Taqusha	Tari	Tarren	Tashai'	Tashelia	Tashuana
Taqwa	Taria	Tarreshia	Tashakay	Tashell	Tashuanna
Tara *(0.90)*	Tariah	Tarri	Tashal	Tashelle	Tashuna
Tara Lynn	Tariana	Tarria	Tashala	Tashema	Tashunda
Tara-Ann	Tarianna	Tarrica	Tashalica	Tashemia	Tashundra
Tara-Anne	Tarica	Tarrie	Tashalle	Tashena *(0.01)*	Tashunna
Tara-Ashleigh	Taricka	Tarrin	Tashamarie	Tashennia	Tashyana
Tara-Lea	Tariel	Tarron	Tashambra	Tasheona	Tashyanna
Tara-Lee	Tarielle	Tarry	Tashan	Tashera	Tashyla
Tara-Lynn	Tarika	Tarryn *(0.01)*	Tashana *(0.01)*	Tasherey	Tashyra
Tara-Lynn-Denise	Tarilyn	Tarsha	Tashana-Cheryl	Tasheri	Tashyria
Tara-Marie	Tarin *(0.01)*	Tarshaée	Tashanice	Tasherica	Tasi
Tarachel	Tarina	Tarshica	Tashanique	Tasherion	Tasia *(0.03)*
Taradawn	Tarinyce	Tarshua	Tashanna	Tasherit	Tasian
Tarae	Taris	Tartesha	Tashanta	Tasherra	Tasiana
Tarah *(0.05)*	Tarisa	Tartiana	Tashar	Tashi	Tasitá
Taraija	Tarisha	Taru	Tashara *(0.02)*	Tashia *(0.01)*	Tasja
Taraisha	Tarissa	Tarvarshay Anita	Tasharah	Tashiana *(0.01)*	Tasjah
Tarajee	Tariva	Tary'ale	Tasharia	Tashianna	Tasjane
Taral	Tariya	Tarya	Tasharna	Tashiara	Tasjay
Taralee	Tariyn	Taryelle	Tasharra	Tashida	Tasjenee
Taralyn *(0.01)*	Tariyona	Taryn *(0.31)*	Tasharricka	Tashie	Tasjia
Taralynn	Tarja	Taryn-Lee	Tashauna *(0.01)*	Tashieka	Taskina
Taran *(0.01)*	Tarjenay	Taryn-Marie	Tashaundra	Tashiena	Tasleem
Tarandeep	Tarjoyt	Taryne	Tashauni	Tashiera	Tasleema
Taranee	Tarkera	Tarynesha	Tashaunie	Tashika	Taslima

Taslin	Tateyonia	Tatyana *(0.19)*	Taveraché	Tay'shunda	Tayllor
Tasline	Tatezick	Tatyanah	Tavey	Tay'veonna	Tayllore
Tasmee	Tathiana	Tatyani	Taveyana	Tay-Niqkia	Tayloer-Anne
Tasmeea	Tathianna	Tatyanna *(0.03)*	Tavi	Tay-Quéla	Tayloir
Tasmia	Tathya	Tatyannah	Tavia *(0.02)*	Taya *(0.02)*	Taylon
Tasmin	Tatiahna	Tatyarah	Tavica	Taya-Tybrie	Taylor *(10.12)*
Tasmine	Tatiana *(0.54)*	Tatyiana	Tavie	Tayacia	Taylor Ann
Tasmyn	Tatianá	Tatyiona	Tavion	Tayah	Taylor Ashl
Tasne	Tatiani	Tatyna	Taviona	Tayajia	Taylor Cheyann
Tasneam	Tatiania	Tatyona	Tavione	Tayan	Taylor Cullayne
Tasneem *(0.01)*	Tatianna *(0.08)*	Tatyonna	Tavis	Tayana *(0.01)*	Taylor Lean
Tasneema	Tatianya	Tatyuana	Tavita	Tayania	Taylor Marie
Tasneembibi	Tatiara	Tau'toya	Tavleen	Tayanna	Taylor Rae
Tasniel	Tatiauna	Tauba	Tavneet	Tayaqua	Taylor Symone
Tasnim	Tatiayana	Taucia	Tavnoor	Tayatta	Taylor'ann
Tassann	Tatiera	Taudra	Tavoa	Tayce	Taylor-Alexandra
Tasseowna	Tatierra	Taughnee	Tavon	Tayci	Taylor-Ann
Tassia	Tatiianna	Tauheedah	Tavona	Tayde	Taylor-Anne
Tassie	Tatijana	Tauja	Tavonasha	Tayden	Taylor-Danielle
Tassneem	Tatijanna	Tauna	Tavondra	Taye	Taylor-Diane
Tassyana	Tatinesha	Taunda	Tavonna	Tayeba	Taylor-Elise
Tastie	Tatinia	Tauni	Tavoria	Tayele	Taylor-Jane
Tasya	Tatiniya	Taunia	Tavyn	Tayelor	Taylor-Lee
Taszmere	Tationa	Taunie	Tawahna	Tayesha	Taylor-Marie
Tat'era	Tationia	Taunjanika	Tawaii	Tayestaday	Taylor-Nicole
Tat'yanna	Tationna	Taunjear	Tawakalitu	Tayhler	Taylor-Rae
Tatam	Tatityana	Tauntania	Tawan	Tayia	Taylorann
Tatamione	Tatiuna	Taunya	Tawana *(0.01)*	Tayina	Tayloranne
Tataneisha	Tatiunna	Taunyae	Tawanda	Tayira	Tayloranne-Brook
Tataneshia	Tatiyana *(0.02)*	Taura	Tawanna	Tayisha	Taylore *(0.01)*
Tatania	Tatiyanna	Taurae	Tawanya	Tayja	Taylornicolé
Tataniesha	Tatiyon	Taure	Tawanza	Tayjah	Taylorr
Tatanina	Tatiyona	Taurelle	Tawasha	Tayla *(0.08)*	Taylour *(0.01)*
Tatanisha	Tatiyonna	Taurena	Tawayna	Taylah	Tayloure
Tatanna	Tatiyumma	Tauri	Tawiah	Taylan	Taylr
Tatanya	Tatiyuna	Tauria	Tawnaja	Taylana	Taylre *(0.01)*
Tatayana	Tatjana *(0.01)*	Taurian	Tawnee *(0.01)*	Taylar *(0.04)*	Taylur
Tatayanna	Tatjhana	Taurie	Tawney *(0.01)*	Taylare	Taylyn
Tatayna	Tatjiana Paulin	Taury	Tawney-	Tayleah	Taylynn
Tatchiana	Tatonisha	Tausha	Cassandra	Taylee	Taymaria
Tatchiyana	Tatreeanna	Tausherriaye	Tawney-Leigh	Tayleigh	Tayna
Tate *(0.01)*	Tatreeonia	Tausoa	Tawni *(0.03)*	Taylen	Taynah
Tatea'na	Tatrina	Tautiana	Tawnia	Taylene	Taynaya
Tateana	Tatshyana	Tautianna	Tawnie *(0.01)*	Tayler *(0.38)*	Tayneisha
Tateanna	Tatshyanna	Tava	Tawniel	Tayler-Rae	Taynia
Tateeyachta	Tatsiana	Tavaceau	Tawnisha	Tayler-Threnea	Taynikua-
Tatelyn	Tatsy-Ana	Tavana	Tawnnie	Taylesha	Carmelle
Tatem	Tatti-Ann	Tavangela	Tawny *(0.05)*	Taylhor	Tayola
Tatenesha	Tattiana	Tavani	Tawnya *(0.01)*	Taylie	Tayon
Tatenga	Tattianna	Tavarian	Tawonna	Tayliesha	Tayona
Tatenisha	Tattyanna	Tavarie	Tawry	Taylin	Tayonandra
Tateona	Tatum *(0.06)*	Tavéunshae	Tawwney	Taylinn	Tayonia
Tateonia	Tatunna	Tavelyn	Taxiarhia	Taylir	Tayonna
Tateonna	Taty'ana	Tavena	Tay Jaha	Tayllar	Tayra
Tateyana	Tatya-Na	Taveonda	Tay'na	Tayller	Tayrin

Tayrn	Tazsha	Télese	Teague	Tearah	Tediah
Taysha	Tazue	Télesha	Teah (0.01)	Tearani	Tedra
Tayshana	Tazuri	Télor	Teahl	Tearanie	Tedrianna
Tayshawn	Tazuria	Télur	Teahlyn	Tearanye	Tedricia
Tayshe	Tazyana	Ténaj	Teaion	Teareya	Tedy
Tayshia	Tazzijah	Ténara	Teaira (0.02)	Teari	Tee
Tayshonkivia	Tazzjia	Ténesha	Teaireus	Tearia	Tee Ira
Tayshunna	Tazzy	Téniya	Teairra (0.01)	Teariea	Tee-Andra
Taysia	Tc'yana	Téohnna	Teairre	Tearika	Teea
Tayt	Tcheyana	Téona	Teairria	Tearinee	Teeahna
Tayte	Te	Téondra	Teaisa	Tearinie	Teeaira
Taytiana	Te Aeria	Téondria	Teajae	Tearney	Teeaja
Taytum	Te Andrea	Téonja	Teajha	Tearra (0.01)	Teeare
Tayvada	Te Angela	Téosha	Teaka	Tearraney	Teegan
Tayvaunna	Te Keiya	Téoshia	Teakesha	Tearria	Teeira
Tayvea	Te Kendria	Téquana	Teakre	Tearrin	Teeja
Tayven	Te Keyarial	Téquanna	Teal (0.02)	Tearsa	Teeka
Tayvia	Te Kiyah	Téquece	Teala (0.01)	Teasa	Teekira
Tayviah	Te Ko A	Téquesta	Tealandria	Teasha (0.01)	Teel
Tayvila	Te Lisa	Téquria	Tealane	Teashan	Teela (0.01)
Tayvionna	Té	Tércia	Tealauna	Teashiela	Teelexcious
Tayvonnia	Té Mequeiion	Térica	Teale	Teashla	Teema
Tayyna	Téaaron	Téricko	Tealeigh	Teasia (0.01)	Teena (0.01)
Tayzia	Téacah	Térika	Tealle	Teasja	Teenisha
Tayzsha	Téaira	Téron	Tealle-Marie	Teatrice	Teera
Taz	Téairra	Tésha	Tealnéjia	Teauna	Teerica
Tazahi	Téambria	Téshanna	Tealor	Teaundra	Teerika
Tazaneika	Téana	Téshara	Teamber	Teaunna	Teersa
Tazania	Téandra	Téshera	Teamicka	Teauynna	Teertsah
Tazaria	Téandria	Téshira	Tean	Teava	Teesa
Tazeen	Téangel	Téshon	Teana (0.01)	Teavanisha	Teesha (0.01)
Tazha	Téaquwa	Tésia	Teanah	Teawna	Teeshawnta
Tazhae	Téarra	Téteyonia	Teanca	Teawnna	Teeshondra
Tazhané	Téasha	Téuna	Teandie	Teayana	Teevia
Tazhanek	Téashia	Téviana	Teandra	Teayra	Teeya
Tazhia	Téasia	Téyannah	Teandré	Teayrra	Teeyaa
Tazhon	Téasion	Téyonna	Teandrya	Teaysha	Teeyvonna
Tazia	Téaundra	Te-Ana	Teangela	Teaysia	Teffany
Taziana	Téeaira	Te-Anna	Teanicha	Tebreshia	Tefna
Tazianna	Téerica	Te-Coria	Teanika	Techawna	Tegan (0.04)
Taziyana	Téerika	Tea	Teann	Techemia	Tegen
Tazjah	Téerinn	Teá	Teanna (0.02)	Tecoma	Teggan
Tazjaye	Téiara	Tea'sheala	Teannah	Tecora	Teghan
Tazjeré	Téjae	Teaaina	Teanndra	Tecoria	Tegra
Tazjia	Téjah	Teacen	Teanne	Tecumseh	Tegwyn
Tazlina	Tékaya	Teachan	Teanqua	Tedazia	Tegyn
Tazmeen	Tékedra	Teadra	Teantae	Teddarinia	Teh'shanti
Tazmin	Tékela	Teaerra	Teante	Tedde	Teha
Tazmine	Tékeya	Teagahn	Teanya	Tedde-Shahara	Tehanna
Taznasha	Tékeyah	Teagan (0.05)	Teaona	Teddi (0.01)	Teharra
Tazney	Tékeyha	Teage	Teaoni	Teddie	Tehaynish
Tazondra	Tékia	Teagen	Teaonna	Teddricka	Tehetena
Tazra	Tékira	Teaghan	Teaonnia	Teddy	Tehila
Tazrenia	Télayea	Teaghanne	Teaqua	Tedesa	Tehilalla
Tazsara	Téleisha	Teagin	Teara (0.01)	Tedi (0.01)	Tehina

Tehran	Teju	Telaij	Temara	Tenasia	Tenise (0.01)
Tehreem	Tejuana	Telan	Temarah	Tenauche	Tenisha (0.04)
Tehri'	Tejumade	Telana	Temarée	Tenay	Tenishia
Tehya (0.01)	Tejumola	Telanna	Temarie	Tenaya (0.01)	Tenita
Teia (0.01)	Tejvir	Telar	Tembi	Tencia	Teniya
Teiaira	Teka	Telare	Temeaka	Tenciea	Tenley
Teialana	Tekah	Telaya	Temedria	Tenéa	Tenli
Teianna	Tekaiyah	Telecia	Temeisha	Tenésha	Tenna
Teiarea	Tekal	Teleena	Temeka	Tenea	Tennaya
Teiarria	Tekalya	Teleesha	Temeker	Teneah	Tenneh
Teiasonta	Tekara	Teleia	Temekia	Teneal	Tennell
Teice	Tekari	Teleise	Temelro	Teneasha	Tennesha
Teicorah	Tekayha	Telelia	Temera	Tenecia	Tennessee
Teidra	Tekayla	Telena	Temeral	Tenee	Tennet
Teiera	Tekeia	Telenia	Temeria	Teneeka	Tennicia
Teigan	Tekeila	Telesa	Temerria	Teneel	Tennie
Teige	Tekeira	Telesha	Temetris	Teneia	Tennille
Teigha	Tekeisha	Teleshia	Temia	Teneika	Tenniqua
Teighan	Tekeiya	Teletha	Temika	Teneil	Tennisa
Teighlor	Tekeiyah	Telfer	Temikia	Teneill	Tennise
Teighn	Tekela	Teli	Temiladeife	Teneille	Tennisha
Teighyana	Tekelsha	Telia	Teminder	Teneisha	Tennley
Teija	Tekendra	Teliah	Temira	Teneishia	Tenny
Teika	Tekenna	Telica	Temirra	Teneka	Tennyesha
Teikia	Tekenya	Telicia	Temisha	Tenekwa	Tennyson
Teila (0.01)	Tekera	Teliea	Temitayo	Tenel	Tenosha
Teileisha	Tekeshionna	Telina	Temitope	Tenell	Tensa
Teiler	Tekeu O Teau Ra	Telisa	Temiwunoluwa	Tenelyn	Tensi
Teilor	Tekeva	Telisha (0.01)	Temiya	Tenequa	Tensia
Teilsha	Tekevia	Telisia	Temkia	Teneqwa	Tensiha
Teina	Tekeya	Telissa	Temoriae	Tenerra	Tenverlie
Teiona	Tekeyiah	Telisse	Tempel	Teneseya	Tenya
Teira (0.01)	Tekeyla	Telitha	Temper	Tenesha (0.02)	Tenyang
Teirany	Tekeyonna	Telivia	Temperance	Teneshia	Tenysha
Teirney	Tekeysta	Tella	Tempest (0.01)	Tenessa	Tenzin
Teirra (0.01)	Tekia (0.01)	Telli	Tempesta	Tenessia	Tenzin-Tara
Teirsa	Tekiah	Tellie	Tempeste	Tenethia	Teodora
Teiryn	Tekiesaine	Tellier	Tempestt (0.01)	Tenetta	Teombi
Teisa	Tekilia	Tellisa	Tempia	Teneya	Teon
Teisaa	Tekilla	Tellisha	Tempist	Teni	Teona (0.01)
Teisha (0.01)	Tekilyah	Telma	Temple	Tenía	Teoná
Teiunna	Tekima	Telmesha	Temprestt	Tenia	Teonca
Tej	Tekira	Telmisha	Tempriest	Teniá	Teondra
Teja'	Tekirah	Telnisha	Temra	Teniah	Teonesha
Tejal	Tekisha	Telondra	Temre	Tenicar	Teoni
Tejana	Tekiuh	Telorr	Temri	Tenichia	Teonia
Tejas	Tekiyah	Telsa	Temyia	Tenicia	Teonie
Tejasvi	Tekkar	Telsey	Tena	Teniea	Teonjai
Tejaswi	Tekla	Telsheá	Tenacia	Tenielle	Teonjewlniqu
Tejay	Tekoa	Telsi	Tenaézhe	Teniesha	Teonna (0.02)
Tejia	Tekoria	Telya	Tenaiya	Tenijah	Teonney
Tejianna	Tekuam	Telysa	Tenal	Tenika (0.01)	Teonnia
Tejinder	Tekyra	Tem'mi	Tenariah	Tenikqua	Teonnie
Tejnoor	Tela	Temag	Tenarian	Tenille (0.01)	Teonshay
Tejpreet	Telah	Temage	Tenarrea	Teniquiana	Teosha (0.01)

Teoshia	Terasena	Teriel	Terranesha	Terrionna	Teshayla
Tepetrious	Teraya	Terigbola	Terraneshia	Terriron	Tesheika
Tephanie	Terayan	Terika *(0.01)*	Terranika	Terris	Tesheira
Teporsha	Terayia	Terikeyia	Terranique	Terrish	Tesheka
Tequana	Terazia	Terilyn	Terranisha	Terrisha	Teshekeia
Tequanna	Tercel	Terilynn	Terranne	Terrissa	Teshell
Tequanza	Tercia	Terina	Terrcyn	Terriyana	Teshelle
Tequara	Tercoria	Terinay	Terreah	Terriyonna	Teshena
Tequaria	Tere	Terineisha	Terrell	Terriyunna	Tesheya
Tequasia	Terea	Terineka	Terrella	Terrnika	Teshia
Tequeca	Tereasa	Terinesha	Terrelle	Terrnisha	Teshianni
Tequecia	Terecita	Teriney	Terrena	Terronesha	Teshima
Tequella	Teree	Teriny	Terrencia	Terronia	Teshina
Tequera	Tereesa	Teriomas	Terrene	Terronica	Teshona
Tequesta	Tereian	Terion	Terrenesha	Terronika	Teshree
Tequia	Tereise	Teriona	Terreona	Terry *(0.03)*	Tesi
Tequiara	Terell	Terisa	Terresa	Terry-Lynn	Tesia *(0.02)*
Tequicawann	Terella	Terisha	Terresha	Terryana	Tesiyna
Tequila *(0.01)*	Teren	Terissa	Terressa	Terryann	Tesla *(0.04)*
Tequilia	Terena	Teriyan	Terrey	Terryauna	Tesla-Louise
Tequilla *(0.01)*	Terence	Teriyon	Terrez	Terryelle	Teslah
Tequiria	Terenecka	Terizzah	Terri *(0.11)*	Terryl	Teslem
Tequisha	Terenieka	Termarald	Terri-Ann	Terrylyn	Teslin
Tequlia	Terenna	Termesha	Terri-Joe	Terryn *(0.01)*	Teslyn
Tequoia	Terericka	Termeshia	Terri-Lee	Terryona	Teslynn
Ter'quasia	Teresa *(0.53)*	Termicia	Terri-Lyn	Terryone	Tesneem
Ter'shawnda	Teresa Akua	Terneisha	Terri-Lynn	Terryonn	Tess *(0.22)*
Tera *(0.04)*	Teresa Dawn	Ternesha	Terria *(0.01)*	Terryonna	Tessa *(0.58)*
Teraann	Teresa-Lynn	Ternezia	Terria'nna	Tersa	Tessa-Lee
Terace	Teresana	Terni	Terriah	Tersea *(0.01)*	Tessah
Teracina	Teresann	Ternin	Terriahana	Tershe	Tessahh
Teraesa	Terese *(0.01)*	Ternovia	Terriahn	Tertia	Tessaka
Terah *(0.01)*	Teresea	Teron	Terrian	Terumi	Tessalin
Terai	Teresia	Teronika	Terriana *(0.01)*	Teryan	Tessalynn
Teraion	Teresina	Terquanderl	Terriance	Teryl	Tessamae
Terajaá	Teresita *(0.03)*	Terra *(0.10)*	Terrianna	Teryn *(0.01)*	Tessandra
Teraleigh	Teressa *(0.01)*	Terra Sienna	Terriauna	Teryn-Reona	Tessé
Teralonna	Teressia	Terra'nique	Terrica *(0.01)*	Terynee	Tessence
Teralyn	Teretha	Terrace	Terricca	Terynn	Tessi
Teralynne	Teretsa	Terradys	Terricka *(0.01)*	Tes	Tessia *(0.01)*
Teran	Terez	Terrae	Terrie *(0.01)*	Tesa *(0.01)*	Tessica
Terance	Tereza	Terrah *(0.01)*	Terriell	Tesah	Tessie *(0.01)*
Teraneal	Tereze	Terrain	Terrielle	Tesaira	Tessla *(0.01)*
Teranee	Teri *(0.05)*	Terrainey	Terrika *(0.01)*	Tesara	Tesslia
Teraneika	Teri Jana	Terraka	Terrilisha	Tesaray	Tesslyn
Teraneisha	Teri-Lee	Terralneka	Terrill	Teschina	Tesslynn
Teranejah	Teri-Lyn	Terralyn	Terrilyn	Tese	Tessy
Teraneka	Teri-Lynn	Terralynn	Terrilynn	Teseana	Tetandianocee
Teranisha	Teria *(0.01)*	Terran	Terrin *(0.01)*	Tesha *(0.01)*	Tetatyana
Teranishia	Teriah'	Terrana	Terrina	Teshanna	Tetreanna
Teranni	Teriana	Terrance	Terrinee	Tesharla	Tettambel
Teraquisha	Terianna	Terrane	Terrinesha	Teshaun	Tetyana
Terar	Terica *(0.01)*	Terranecia	Terrinisha	Teshauna	Teundra
Terarial	Terica Shal	Terranee	Terrion	Teshaundria	Teundria
Terasa	Tericka	Terraneka	Terriona *(0.01)*	Teshawna	Teunna

Teva	Th Loria	Thanisha	Thelams	Thi Thu Thans	Thonjené
Tevanna	Thacia	Thannujah	Thelea	Thi Thu Thuy	Thora
Tevenia	Thaddnesha	Thanusha	Thelisa	Thia	Thorlonda
Tevin	Thaddricka	Thanuzgha	Thelma (0.03)	Thiaja	Thoshana
Tevondria	Thadia	Thanya	Thelrietta	Thiana	Thresa
Tewanda	Thadijah	Thao (0.02)	Thema	Thianna	Thrisha
Tewasa	Thadneisha	Thao Thu	Themis	Thiare	Thrmiga
Tewentenhawiht	Thadryanne	Thaomy	Theniesha	Thiaren	Thu (0.01)
ha	Thadshagini	Thaqundra	Thenuga	Thida	Thu Truc
Tewsdae	Thaeann	Thara	Thenuja	Thidalack	Thu-Nguyet
Texanna	Thahera	Tharakie	Thenusha	Thien	Thu-Tracy
Texas	Thai	Tharane	Theodora (0.02)	Thien-An	Thuan Rosal
Texie	Thai Janee	Tharaneetharan	Theodora-	Thien-Ann	Thuc
Tey'erra	Thai'ler	Tharani	Catharina	Thien-Thu	Thuc-Uyen
Teya (0.01)	Thailand	Tharaniya	Theodorarose	Thiffany	Thulasi
Teyah	Thailor	Tharankiny	Theodore	Thiishia	Thuong
Teyahma	Thais (0.01)	Tharmiga	Theodoria	Thilani	Thuraya
Teyaira	Thaiya	Tharmitha	Theodorian	Thilini	Thurcya
Teyaji	Thaiyana	Tharnea	Theodra	Thinaja	Thurga
Teyakoti	Thaiza	Tharsa	Theondra	Thingoe	Thurkka
Teyana (0.01)	Thaksa	Tharsha	Theondria	Thinom	Thurshonda
Teyanah	Thaksayini	Tharshalah	Theora	Thipeekaa	Thurstina
Teyanna (0.01)	Thakza	Tharshika	Theorian	Thipika	Thusani
Teyannah	Thalassa	Tharshni	Theosha	Thirsha	Thusany
Teyaqua	Thalia (0.19)	Tharsiga	Theoshia	Thisha	Thushara
Teyara	Thaliane	Tharsika	Thequita	Thiviga	Thushika
Teyawna	Thalie	Thashing	Thera	Thivija	Thushya
Teyerra	Thalissa	Thashira	Theran	Thiviya	Thusika
Teyese	Thalja	Thashni	Therarat	Thivya	Thusita
Teyha	Thallya	Thasneem	Thereana	Thivyaa	Thuvaraka
Teyhani	Thalon	Thata'nisha	Theresa (0.45)	Thivyah	Thuy (0.02)
Teyharia	Thalya	Thatiana	Theresa Taylor	Thoa	Thuy Linh
Teyia	Tham	Thaviny	Theresa-Lynn	Thobi	Thuy Phuong
Teylah	Thamar	Thavisah	Theresa-Marie	Thoebe	Thuy Trang
Teylar	Thamara	Thayne	Therese (0.05)	Thomais	Thuy-An
Teylene	Thamaraa	Thayz	Therese Frances	Thomas	Thuy-Mi
Teylia	Thamarrah	The	Theresia	Thomasin	Thuy-Vy
Teylia-Rey	Thamera	Thélisia	Thereza	Thomasina	Thuyduong
Teylor (0.01)	Thamicha	Thea (0.03)	Therica	Thomasine	Thuyen
Teyniquah	Thamina	Thea Emerita	Therie	Thomassecia	Thy
Teyola	Thamitchlard	Theadora (0.01)	Therinesha	Thomasson	Thyana
Teyona (0.01)	Thamiyia	Theadosia	Therisa	Thomea	Thyatira
Teyondra	Thana	Theander	Therissie	Thomeasha	Thyesha
Teyoni	Thanairy	Theanna	Therlisha	Thomeisha	Thyeshia
Teyonna	Thanayry	Theannah	Theron	Thomeka	Thyisha-Cholene
Teysha	Thandi	Theano	Theronisha	Thomesha	Thyla
Teyuana	Thandiwe	Theara	Thesa	Thomia	Thylia
Teyundra	Thanemany	Thearvy	Thesawana	Thomiesha	Thyme
Tezley	Thanh (0.01)	Theasia	Thesha	Thomika	Thyna
Teznisha	Thanh Hien	Theavee	Thessalonia	Thomilla	Thyra
Tezra	Thanh Tham	Thecla	Thessly	Thomiqua	Ti
Tezrah	Thanh-Thuy	Theda	Theta	Thomisha	Ti Almbrae
Tezrika	Thanh-Truc	Thedra	Theteryia	Thompson	Ti Amber
Tezriyona	Thania (0.02)	Theediga	Theyma	Thomrika	Ti Ana
Tezzy Rebeca	Thanie	Theita	Thi (0.02)	Thoni	Ti Anna

Ti Ara	Tia-Marie	Tianah	Tiaunna	Tiel	Tifeleeyah
Ti Asity	Tia-Tiara	Tianalynn	Tiausha	Tiela	Tiferet
Ti Erra	Tiaamber	Tianay	Tiawamara	Tieler	Tiffané
Ti Esha	Tiabreshia	Tianca	Tiawana	Tielisha	Tiffanee
Ti Jeanae	Tiaca	Tianda	Tiawanda	Tien	Tiffaney *(0.01)*
Ti Kandra	Tiachantel	Tiandra *(0.01)*	Tiawanna	Tiena	Tiffani *(0.22)*
Ti Re Elle	Tiadie	Tiane	Tiawanne	Tienna	Tiffani Anne
Ti Taniesha	Tiaerra	Tianea	Tiawna	Tiequashia	Tiffani-Amber
Ti'airea	Tiah	Tianee	Tiaya	Tier	Tiffani-Bea
Ti'airus	Tiahja	Tiangela	Tiayanna	Tiera *(0.07)*	Tiffanie *(0.08)*
Ti'alrea	Tiahna	Tiani *(0.01)*	Tiayna	Tierah	Tiffanie Joyce
Ti'amber	Tiahnna	Tianicia	Tiayonna	Tieranae	Tiffanie Mon
Ti'anah	Tiahra	Tianika	Tiayra	Tierani	Tiffanie-Jean
Ti'andra	Tiaina	Tianise	Tiazha	Tieranie	Tiffanney
Ti'ann	Tiaira *(0.01)*	Tianka	Tibreeshai	Tieranni	Tiffanni
Ti'anna	Tiaira Donquani	Tianmei	Tibria	Tierany	Tiffannie
Ti'ara	Tiairra	Tiann	Tiburcia	Tierhavahnna	Tiffanny
Ti'arra	Tiairria	Tianna *(0.28)*	Tical	Tiericka	Tiffany *(3.33)*
Ti'asia	Tiaja	Tianna-Jae	Ticara	Tiernan	Tiffany Amber
Ti'china	Tiajaia	Tianna-Lynn	Ticarion	Tiernee	Tiffany Anna
Ti'eishea	Tiajauna	Tiannah	Ticarra	Tierney *(0.04)*	Tiffany Huy
Ti'erce	Tiajee	Tianne	Ticasey	Tierny	Tiffany Marie
Ti'ericka	Tiajha-Rae	Tianni	Tichai	Tierra *(0.34)*	Tiffany'
Ti'erra	Tiajiah	Tianshae	Tichanti	Tierra Ayana	Tiffany-Amber
Ti'esha	Tiajuana	Tiantae	Tichara	Tierra Tylisa	Tiffany-Anne
Ti'geria	Tiajunai	Tiantay	Ticharla	Tierrah	Tiffany-Jean
Ti'kera	Tiajwanda	Tiante	Tichian	Tierralin	Tiffany-June
Ti'keyha	Tiajwanna	Tianté	Tichin	Tierre	Tiffany-Lynne
Ti'lisea	Tiakesha	Tiaquesha	Tichina *(0.02)*	Tierria	Tiffany-Rae
Ti'liyah	Tiakohl	Tiaquionna	Tichinia	Tierrra	Tiffanyamber
Ti'mea	Tiakya	Tiaquonna	Tichinia Tyishi	Tierson	Tiffanye
Ti'mika	Tiala	Tiara *(0.48)*	Tichira	Tiersten	Tiffeni
Ti'nasha	Tialani	Tiara Audreanna	Ticiena	Tierya	Tiffeny
Ti'nishaul	Tialayh	Tiará	Tico'le	Tieryan	Tiffianie
Ti'qwesha	Tialiaa	Tiarah	Ticynn	Tierza	Tiffiany
Ti'shan	Tialina	Tiarahjean	Tida	Tiesa	Tiffine
Ti'shauntea	Tialynn	Tiare *(0.01)*	Tidari	Tiesha *(0.03)*	Tiffiney
Ti'tana	Tiam	Tiarea	Tidaysha	Tieshah	Tiffini *(0.01)*
Ti'tania	Tiamaelani	Tiareah	Tiéaesha	Tieshawn	Tiffini-Marie
Ti'teanna	Tiamani	Tiari	Tiénair	Tieshay	Tiffiny
Ti-Anna	Tiamanna	Tiaria	Tiea	Tieshea	Tiffney *(0.01)*
Ti-Mara	Tiamara	Tiarion	Tieanna	Tieshia	Tiffni
Ti-Shai	Tiamarie	Tiarra *(0.08)*	Tieara *(0.01)*	Tiessa	Tiffny
Ti-Yana	Tiamarra	Tiarrah	Tiearis	Tiet	Tiffony
Ti-Yanna	Tiamasha	Tiasha	Tiearra	Tieu	Tiffonya
Tia *(0.47)*	Tiambra	Tiashae	Tieasha	Tieuna	Tifney
Tiá	Tiamera	Tiashay	Tieese	Tieyuonna	Tigne
Tia'asia	Tiamira	Tiashia	Tiegen	Tiezhané	Tiguidanke
Tia'ja	Tiamonda	Tiasia	Tieggan	Tifa	Tihamy
Tia'kanecia	Tiamonté	Tiasyah	Tieghan	Tifani *(0.01)*	Tihana
Tia'rah	Tian	Tiaterra	Tiehina	Tifanie	Tihane
Tia-Elizabeth	Tian Janae	Tiauna *(0.01)*	Tieisha	Tifanni	Tihanna
Tia-Liis	Tiana *(0.45)*	Tiauná	Tieka	Tifanny	Tihesha
Tia-Lin	Tianá	Tiaunah	Tieki	Tifany	Tihira
Tia-Lynn	Tiana-Jo	Tiaunia	Tiekyia	Tifarah	Tiia

Tiina	Tilley	Timira	Tinara	Tionté	Tirthna
Tija	Tillia	Timiri	Tinavery	Tionya	Tirza
Tijah	Tillie	Timiria	Tinaya	Tiosha	Tirzah (0.01)
Tijana	Tillisa	Timisha	Tinchina	Tiousha	Tisa
Tijanae	Tilly	Timishia	Tinéqua	Tip'awanna	Tisay
Tijaun	Tilor	Timitria	Tinea	Tipenga	Tisché
Tijauna	Tilynn	Timiya	Tineá	Tiphanee	Tischina
Tijema	Tim Ayrah	Timiyah	Tineisha	Tiphani	Tiseana
Tijer	Tim O'nae	Timlisha	Tineka	Tiphanie (0.01)	Tish
Tijuana	Tim Yanna	Timmara	Tinelle	Tiphanie-Nicole	Tisha (0.03)
Tijuanica	Tim'ara	Timmarica	Tinequa	Tiphany	Tishaa
Tijunna	Tim'mena	Timmatha	Tinerra	Tipmanie	Tishadoan
Tijwanese	Tim'mesha	Timmea	Tinesa	Tiqarah	Tishana
Tika	Tima	Timmeree	Tinesha (0.01)	Tiqira	Tishanay
Tikara	Timandria	Timmery	Tineshia	Tiquana	Tishandi
Tikayla	Timara (0.01)	Timmesha	Tinessa	Tiquanna	Tishani
Tikearra	Timari	Timmetria	Tinia	Tiquarerah	Tishanna
Tikeisha	Timarie	Timmi	Tiniah	Tiquaya	Tishara
Tikel	Timariel	Timmiar	Tiniel	Tiqueisha	Tishauna
Tikenya	Timarius	Timmie	Tiniesha	Tiquenia	Tishaunda
Tikera	Timarshay	Timminy	Tinieshia	Tiquera	Tishauni
Tikeria	Timashly	Timmisha	Tinika	Tiquesha	Tishawn
Tikeyah	Timaya	Timmons	Tiniqua	Tiquinesha	Tishawna
Tikeyia	Timber (0.01)	Timmyra	Tinisha (0.01)	Tiquinneesha	Tishay
Tiki	Timberlee	Timna	Tinishia	Tiquisha	Tishayla
Tikia	Timberlie	Timneka	Tinishya	Tiqura	Tishema
Tikiaa	Timberly	Timnique	Tiniyah	Tiqusha	Tisherneria
Tikiera	Timberlyn	Timoné	Tinka	Tira	Tishiana
Tikira	Timbra	Timony	Tinnie	Tiraneka	Tishina (0.01)
Tikiria	Timbreia	Timoshanae	Tinnielle	Tirani	Tishinia
Tikita	Timbresha	Timothea	Tinnill	Tiranie	Tishira
Tikiya	Timbriah	Timotheia	Tinsley	Tiranique	Tishonda
Tikkri	Timbriana	Timothia	Tinta	Tirannie	Tisi
Tikora	Timea	Timothy	Tinuviel	Tirara	Tisia
Tikoya	Timeca	Timoya	Tiny	Tirath	Tislease
Tikvah	Timeeka Louveni	Timple	Tinysha	Tirayana	Tiss
Tikya	Timeeshah	Timples	Tioman	Tirayshia	Tissierra
Tikyra	Timeka (0.01)	Timreyona	Tiombe	Tireanna	Tita
Tila	Timera	Timryl	Tiombé	Tireashia	Titana
Tilah	Timerra	Timurée	Tiommi	Tireisha	Titania
Tilahya	Timesha (0.01)	Timy	Tiona (0.02)	Tirene	Titawanna
Tilana	Timeshia	Timya	Tionda	Tirené	Titayna
Tilani	Timetha	Timyia	Tiondra	Tiressa	Titayona
Tilar	Timetra	Timyiah	Tiondre	Tiriana	Titeanna
Tilea	Timetrea	Timyra	Tioné	Tiriel	Titeona
Tileen	Timetria	Timysha	Tionette	Tirinika	Titerrera
Tilen	Timeyha	Tin	Tioni	Tiris	Titha
Tilese	Timi	Tin-Po	Tionia	Tirra	Titia
Tilesha	Timia (0.01)	Tina (0.36)	Tionie	Tirrany	Titiana (0.01)
Tilhenn	Timiah	Tina Marie	Tionja	Tirrea	Titianay
Tilia	Timichia	Tina Tuyen	Tionn'e	Tirrell	Titania
Tilisha	Timicia	Tina-Marie	Tionna (0.03)	Tirria	Titianna
Tilissa	Timika	Tinael	Tionnah	Tirsa	Titiayana
Tilla	Timikwa	Tinai	Tionne (0.01)	Tirsh	Titilayo
Tillery	Timir	Tinamari	Tionshé	Tirsia	Titilola

Titionia	Tneil	Toja	Tomisha	Toné	Tonisty
Titiyana	Tnicia	Toka	Tomiya	Tonea	Tonita
Titiyanna	Tniya	Tokaj	Tommecka	Tonecia	Toniyah
Titty	Tnyia	Tokeyo	Tommeria	Toneil	Tonizea
Tityana	Tnysha	Tokilupe	Tommesha	Toneish	Tonja
Tiuana	To	Tokina	Tommi *(0.01)*	Toneisha *(0.01)*	Tonjaneika
Tiuanna	To'laura	Tokora	Tommi-Nikole	Toneka	Tonjanique
Tiva	To'neisha	Tola	Tommia	Tonekqua	Tonjia
Tivia	To-Thi	Toles	Tommie *(0.01)*	Toneseya	Tonna
Tiviana	Toba	Tolesha	Tommieka	Tonesha *(0.01)*	Tonnett
Tivinia Alexis	Tobey	Tollie	Tommy	Toneshia	Tonnette
Tivona	Tobi *(0.01)*	Tolliesha	Tommyka	Toneta	Tonni
Tiwana	Tobie	Tolofi	Tommysha	Tonetria	Tonnie
Tiwanna	Tobie-Lynn	Tolora	Tomnetria	Tonetta	Tonnisha
Tiy'esha	Tobiha-A'lexus	Tolu	Tomoka	Tonette	Tonnitha
Tiya	Tobin	Tolulope	Tomoko	Toney	Tonocka
Tiya-Toonse	Tobria	Toluwa	Tomomi	Toneya	Tonoka
Tiyah	Tobrika	Toluwaleke	Tomoo	Toneysha	Tonore
Tiyan	Toby	Toluwalope	Tomorrow	Toneyshia	Tonquesha
Tiyana *(0.01)*	Tobyn	Tomaira	Tomorrw	Tongelah	Tonrasha
Tiyani	Tocarro	Tomaneisha	Tomoyo	Toni *(0.37)*	Tonshayia
Tiyania	Toccara	Tomanika	Tomrel	Toni Amelie	Tonshica
Tiyanna *(0.01)*	Toccola	Tomanita	Tomya	Toni-Ann	Tonteanna
Tiyannes	Tociana	Tomantha	Ton Taja	Toni-Anne	Tony
Tiychina	Tockeema	Tomara	Ton-Yae	Toni-Lyn	Tonya *(0.12)*
Tiye	Todd	Tomaris	Tona	Toni-Lynn	Tonyan
Tiyeesha	Toddasia	Tomarjhai	Tonae	Toni-Marie	Tonyana
Tiyera	Toddeshia	Tomarrow	Tonaé	Tonia *(0.02)*	Tonye
Tiyesha	Toddy	Tomasa	Tonaesha	Toniah	Tonyea
Tiyonda	Toddymay	Tomasha	Tonah	Toniann	Tonyelle
Tiyonna	Todesha	Tomasina	Tonaia	Tonianne	Tonyia
Tiyquasha	Todjiana	Tomeacia	Tonaj'ah	Tonice	Tonyika
Tiyquila	Todne	Tomeastarr	Tonakia	Tonie *(0.01)*	Tonykea
Tiyrah	Todnisha	Tomecko	Tonalaya	Tonie Grace	Tonysha
Tiysha	Toenell	Tomeeka	Tonancy	Toniea	Tooa
Tiyunna	Tofoya	Tomeisha	Tonanikka	Tonieadra	Tooba
Tizarat	Tofuola	Tomeka	Tonantzin	Toniee	Toobah
Tiziana	Togafiti	Tomekia	Tonara	Tonieka	Topacio
Tizja	Tohri	Tomekyia	Tonasia	Toniesa	Topanga
Tizjee	Toi *(0.01)*	Tomella	Tonay	Toniesha	Topaz
Tjahane	Toiana	Tomenetta	Tonaya	Tonik	Topazz
Tjia	Toianá	Tomeria	Tondalaya	Tonika *(0.01)*	Topeka
Tjork	Toiannah	Tomeric	Tondalia	Tonikqua	Topez
Tjuana	Toiaun	Tomesha	Tondanisha	Tonilia	Topi
Tjyia	Toieka	Tomeshea	Tondayoka	Tonilin	Tora
Tkeya	Toijah	Tomeshia	Tonde	Tonilynn	Torah
Tkeyah *(0.01)*	Toileana	Tomesia	Tondelaya	Tonimarie	Toral
Tkeyha	Toilyn	Tomi *(0.01)*	Tondi	Toninesha	Torameshia
Tkeyia	Toinee	Tomia	Tondi'	Toniq	Torazae
Tkeymah	Toineika	Tomicar	Tondia	Toniqua	Torbjor
Tlarissa	Toinell	Tomie	Tondra	Tonique	Torchia
Tlell	Toinette	Tomii	Tondrea	Toniquea	Tordijah
Tmiyah	Toini	Tomika	Tondri A	Tonise	Tore
Tna'sheo	Toisha	Tomikia	Tondria	Tonisha *(0.03)*	Toreasha
Tneasha	Toiya	Tomiko	Tone	Tonisia	Toree *(0.01)*

Torei	Torrencisa	Totiyanna	Tracey (0.09)	Tramika	Trastacia
Toreian	Torreona	Totonya	Trachele	Tramira	Traujaé
Toreion	Torrey (0.02)	Totrece	Trachella	Tramiya	Travae
Toreka	Torreylynn	Totteanna	Trachelle	Tramura	Travala
Toren	Torri (0.07)	Tottiana	Traci (0.08)	Tran (0.01)	Travanna
Torey (0.02)	Torria	Tottiyonna	Traci-Jo	Tranaci	Travea
Tori (0.87)	Torrianna	Tottyanna	Tracia	Tranae	Traveanna
Tori Lee	Torrica	Totyana	Traciann	Tranaijah	Travena
Tori'	Torrie (0.04)	Touba	Tracie (0.05)	Tranash	Traveshia
Tori'ayunna	Torrin	Toukie	Tracie-Deanna	Tranay	Traveya
Tori-Laine	Torrina	Touobamana	Traciee	Tranaya	Travia
Tori-Lyn	Torrion	Toure	Traclyn	Tranece	Traviana
Tori-Lynn	Torrionna	Tourei	Tracnise	Tranecia	Travina
Toria (0.02)	Torriuna	Tourriana	Tracsha	Tranee	Traviona
Toriah	Torroncia	Tova (0.01)	Tracy (0.31)	Traneesheia	Travionna
Torian	Torry	Tovah	Tracy-Joy	Traneice	Travis
Toriana (0.01)	Torrye	Tovara	Tracy-Tania	Traneika	Travisana
Toriane	Torryonna	Tovi	Tracylee	Traneisha	Travisha
Toriann	Torsha	Toviea	Tradacia	Tranell	Travisia
Torianna	Torshe	Toviyah	Tradaé	Tranequa	Travisitée
Toriante	Torvonna	Tovya	Tradasha	Tranequia	Traviyon
Toriauna	Tory (0.07)	Towai	Tradawnya	Tranese	Travon
Torica	Tory-Lynn	Towana	Tradeisha	Tranesha	Travonda
Torie (0.04)	Toryanica	Towanna	Tradesha	Traneshia	Travondia
Torieesha	Toryce	Towannia	Tradeya	Tranetta	Travonette
Toriel	Torye	Townsend	Traea	Trang (0.02)	Travonna
Toriell	Toryell	Townzena	Traeann	Tranice	Travonshay
Torielle	Toryian	Toya	Traeline	Traniece	Travyann
Torien	Toryn	Toyan	Traelyn	Tranieka	Tray'neccia
Toriesha	Tosal	Toye	Traevena	Traniesha	Tray'quana
Toril	Tosca	Toyesheekia	Traicedes	Tranija	Traya'na
Torilyn	Toscane	Toyia	Traicen	Tranika	Trayan
Torin	Toseana	Toyiesha	Traisha	Tranina	Trayana
Torina	Tosha (0.03)	Toylicia	Traiya	Tranique	Trayanna
Torine	Toshaela	Toynesha	Trakalyn	Tranise	Trayca
Torinne	Toshanna	Toynetta	Trakeyna	Tranisha	Traycee
Torion	Toshay	Toyono	Tralen	Tranishia	Traychell
Torionna	Toshekia	Toyriel	Traliah	Tranna	Trayci
Torionne	Toshia	Tr'oneshia	Tralin	Tranquility	Trayeon
Toris	Toshiba	Tr'zandra	Tralini	Traonna	Trayia
Torishiara	Toshihika	Tra	Tralisa	Traquita	Traykevia
Torissa	Toshika	Tra Donna	Tralyce	Trarella	Traylashe
Torista	Toshima	Tra Ona	Tralynn	Traryshia	Traylen
Toriyanna	Toshina	Tra'kera	Tram (0.01)	Trashae	Trayln
Torlin	Toshivia	Tra'kissa	Tram-Anh	Trashaia	Traymar
Torlonda	Toshiya'na	Tra'nesha	Tramaila	Trashan	Trayneisha
Tornay	Toshona	Tra'nicia	Tramaine	Trashana	Traynesha
Torneisha	Toshua	Tra'shaniq	Tramara	Trashauna	Traynesia
Tornisha	Toshunia	Tra'sheema	Tramauh	Trashawn	Trayona
Torquicea	Tosja	Tra'virra	Tramecia	Trasheena	Trayonis
Torran	Tossiana	Tra'von	Tramella	Trashekia	Trayonna
Torre	Tossiyana	Tra-Kedrian	Tramenka	Trashell	Traysha
Torree	Toteauna	Trabreka	Tramesha	Trashon	Trayshauna
Torreece	Totiana	Tracee	Trameshia	Trashunda	Trayshell
Torrencia	Totionna	Tracendia	Tramia	Trasina	Traytavia

Trayvia	Tredaija	Trenavira	Tressa (0.03)	Tri Keyel	Trineese
Trayvonna	Tredijah	Trenay	Tressi	Tri'anna	Trineesha
Trazia	Treena	Trenda	Tressia	Tri'nell	Trineka
Trazjon	Treenshia	Trené	Tressicia	Tri-Nekkia	Trinell
Tre	Treian	Trenece	Tressie	Tria	Trinese
Tre Shawna	Treillani	Trenecia	Tresslyn	Tria'le	Trinesha
Tréana	Treina	Trenee	Trestney	Triana (0.01)	Trinesia
Tréandria	Treion	Trenée	Treundas	Trianna	Trinetra
Tréanna	Treiona	Treneice	Treva (0.01)	Triannalynn	Trinetta
Tréauna	Treisha	Treneika	Trevanna	Triawna	Trinette
Tréisha	Treishae	Treneisa	Trevar	Trica	Trinh
Trékyria	Trekessa	Treneishia	Trevaris	Trichele	Trinha
Trélisa	Trekeya	Trenell	Trevell	Trichell	Trini (0.01)
Trémasicia	Trekisa	Treneria	Trevena	Trichelle	Trinia
Trémeeka	Trekisha	Trenese	Treveon	Tricia (0.10)	Trinica
Trémoyne	Trekyla	Trenesha	Trevia	Tricilla	Trinice
Trénayah	Trelaná	Trenesia	Treviana	Tricina	Trinicia
Trénea	Trelani	Trenetria	Treviel	Tricya	Trinidad (0.02)
Trénicia	Trelanni	Trenett	Trevien	Trida	Trinidy
Tréniece	Trelby	Trenette	Trevin	Trida-Simone	Trinie
Trénisha	Treles	Treneya	Trevina	Tridedria	Triniece
Tréonna	Treleshia	Treneyce	Trevion	Triechelle	Trinierose
Trésaun	Trelissa	Trenice	Trevivory	Triel	Trinina
Tréshauna	Treliyah	Treniecia	Trevon	Trienietiy	Triniqua
Tréshell	Trellace	Trenika	Trevona	Trier	Trinise
Tréshivette	Trellanni	Trenikia	Trevonia	Triesha	Trinisha
Tréshun	Trellany	Trenise	Trevonna	Trieste	Trinita
Trésline	Trellen	Trenisha	Trevonne	Trieu	Trinite
Trésura	Trelleni	Trenisia	Trevonye	Triev	Trinitee
Tréveona	Trelles	Trenite	Trevor	Triffawna	Triniti
Trévon	Trellina	Trenity	Trevva	Trikeria	Trinity (0.13)
Tre-Lexia	Trellini	Trenius	Trevyna	Trikheshurna	Trinty
Tre-Meia	Trelloni	Trenna	Trey On	Trikina	Triona
Trea	Trelon	Trent	Trey Shekia	Trilaijah	Trionna
Treabreanna	Trelyn	Trenterica	Treyada	Trilby	Trisa
Treacy	Trelynn	Trentina	Treyana	Trilene	Trisann
Treaja	Tremaine	Treona	Treyanna	Trilesia	Trisden
Treamika	Tremanda	Treonna	Treyannah	Trillium	Triseugeni
Treana	Tremara	Treontes	Treyawna	Trillus	Trish
Treanna	Tremayne	Trequair	Treylynn	Trima	Trisha (0.19)
Treasa	Tremeciya	Tres	Treynika	Trimaine	Trisha-Gay
Treasur	Tremelia	Tres'or	Treyonna	Trimeka	Trisha-Lynn
Treasure (0.05)	Tremesha	Tresa	Treysheana	Trimone	Trishala
Treasuré	Tremetria	Tresean	Treyuna	Trina (0.07)	Trishana
Treasury	Tremia	Treseme	Treyvia	Trinade	Trishanna
Treava	Tremiecia	Tresemme	Trez'ja	Trinadee	Trishanpreet
Trebora	Tremika	Tresha	Trezayah	Trinadie	Trishanya
Trebrina	Tremishia	Treshain	Trezhay	Trinady	Trishaun
Trece	Tremiya	Treshala	Trezher	Trinae	Trishauna
Treceanna	Tremoneshia	Treshaun	Trezhure	Trinchelle	Trishawn
Trecha	Tremyia	Treshawn	Trezur	Trinda	Trishele
Trechell	Trena	Treshequa	Trezure	Trinea	Trishell
Trechelle	Trenae	Treshiya	Trezzure	Trinee	Trishelle
Trechia	Trenaé	Tresina	Trhona	Trinée	Trishia
Trecia	Trenasha	Treslyn	Tri Jay	Trineen	Trishia Kathreen

Trishina	Trona	Tsedal	Tunisia	Twanya	Ty'keisha
Trishon	Troshone	Tsedaye	Tunyia	Twen	Ty'kema
Trishona	Troutman	Tshanda	Tuong	Twesdae	Ty'keona
Trishonda	Trovana	Tsharre	Tupou	Twila	Ty'kera
Trishsa	Trovanda	Tshavia	Tupper	Twilight	Ty'keria
Trishta	Troy *(0.01)*	Tsion	Tupray	Twilla	Ty'keya
Trishtina	Troya	Tsubasa	Tuquita	Twin	Ty'keyah
Trisiah	Troyann	Tsun-Ching	Tura	Twin A	Ty'keytah
Triska	Troyanna	Tsurumi	Tureka	Twin B	Ty'kiran
Trisna	Troyce	Tsya	Turia	Twionette	Ty'lein
Trissa	Troyelle	Tsylor	Turiya	Two-Million	Ty'ler
Trista *(0.07)*	Troyia	Tsz	Turlisha	Twonisha	Ty'lisa
Trista-Renee	Troylena	Tu	Turner	Twyana	Ty'londa
Tristah	Troylisa	Tu Trinh	Turnpreet	Twyla *(0.01)*	Ty'meesha
Tristain	Troyneisha	Tu'aijah	Turquoia	Twylia	Ty'meisha
Tristan *(0.11)*	Troyneshia	Tu-Sharia	Turquois	Twylla	Ty'misha
Tristane	Troynique	Tua	Turquoise	Twylyte	Ty'neisha
Tristanni	Troynisha	Tuawna	Tuscany	Twyneisha	Ty'nesia
Tristany	Tru	Tuba	Tusdai	Twynesia	Ty'nisha
Tristen *(0.07)*	Tru'becka	Tuccoa	Tushana	Twynisha	Ty'ocea
Tristene	Truc	Tuchi	Tusharia	Txintlaly	Ty'owna
Tristessa	Trudel	Tucker	Tushaundra	Ty *(0.01)*	Ty'quanesha
Tristi	Trudesha	Tuere	Tushawn	Ty Bree	Ty'quanisha
Tristian *(0.01)*	Trudi	Tueria	Tushena	Ty Era	Ty'quasha
Tristiana	Trudy *(0.01)*	Tuesdae	Tusneem	Ty Esha	Ty'quina
Tristin *(0.04)*	Trudy-Ann	Tuesday *(0.02)*	Tusonnie	Ty Janique	Ty'quisha
Tristina	Trudye	Tuesdea	Tuta	Ty Quincia	Ty'qwasia
Tristine	True	Tuesdee	Tutonda	Ty Riance	Ty'raina
Tristinye	Truitt	Tuffesha	Tuula	Ty Shaé	Ty'rena
Tristn	Trulésia	Tuffina	Tuuli	Ty Vonna	Ty'ria
Triston *(0.01)*	Trulee	Tugce	Tuwana	Ty Wanna	Ty'sha
Tristony	Trulie	Tujuana	Tuwanna	Ty'amber	Ty'shae
Tristyn *(0.01)*	Trulinda	Tula	Tuyen	Ty'ara	Ty'shana
Triteecia	Truly	Tulasi	Tuyet *(0.01)*	Ty'arrah	Ty'shanna
Tritney	Trung	Tule	Tuyet-Mai	Ty'asia	Ty'shara
Tritny	Trunikqu	Tuleash	Tuyet-Nhi	Ty'aurah	Ty'shauna
Trittiany	Truong	Tuler	Tuyet-Son	Ty'azsha	Ty'sheanna
Triva	Trupti	Tuleshia	Tuyetbang	Ty'che	Ty'shian
Trivani	Trusterria	Tulika	Tuyethoa	Ty'chetta	Ty'shon
Trivena	Trya	Tulina	Tuyetnhung	Ty'china	Ty'shyree
Triveni	Trycia *(0.02)*	Tulip	Tvega	Ty'darier	Ty'sonia
Trivette	Tryhston	Tulisa	Twa'shayvia	Ty'eika	Ty'sonya
Trivia	Tryllian	Tulonda	Twainnesha	Ty'eisha	Ty'tana
Trivon	Tryna	Tulsa	Twana	Ty'era	Ty'teanna
Trixie	Trynady	Tulsi	Twanae	Ty'esha	Ty'teannie
Trixy	Tryneisha	Tumaini	Twanda	Ty'eshia	Ty'tiana
Triyana	Trysha	Tumarra	Twaneka	Ty'hesha	Ty'tianna
Triyata	Trystan *(0.01)*	Tumiah	Twanesha	Ty'iesha	Ty'tionna
Triyona	Trysten	Tumu	Twaneshia	Ty'ionna	Ty'yana
Triyuna	Trystin	Tunézha	Twaniesha	Ty'jhai	Ty'yanni
Tro'niqua	Trystyn	Tunekwah	Twanisha	Ty'keara	Ty'yauna
Troi	Tryzana	Tunequaka	Twanishia	Ty'keejah	Ty-Ais
Troia	Tsadhe	Tunesia	Twanja	Ty'keeria	Ty-Bria
Troiauna	Tsara	Tung	Twanshun	Ty'keiah	Ty-Jena
Troiya	Tse	Tunisha *(0.01)*	Twantius	Ty'keira	Ty-Keisha

Ty-Keria	Tybria	Tyerice	Tyjuan	Tylandria	Tylynn
Ty-Kerria	Tybriá	Tyerra	Tyjulante	Tylann	Tymairia
Ty-Kia	Tybriana	Tyerra-Nichelle	Tykara	Tylar *(0.02)*	Tymana
Ty-Kiera	Tybrice	Tyesa	Tykayla	Tylar Samantha	Tymanika
Ty-Neasha	Tybrii	Tyesha *(0.07)*	Tykea	Tyleace	Tymara
Ty-Quan	Tybrishia	Tyeshá	Tykeama	Tyleah	Tymasha
Ty-Shayla	Tybriyona	Tyeshai	Tykeara	Tylean	Tymber
Ty-Shica	Tyceishu	Tyesheka	Tykearine	Tylece	Tymbria
Ty-Yonna	Tychanna	Tyeshia *(0.01)*	Tykearria	Tylecia	Tyme
Tya	Tyche	Tyeshira	Tykecia	Tylee	Tymea
Tya-Lyn	Tychelle	Tyeya	Tykeela	Tyleen	Tymecia
Tyaa	Tychena	Tyfanee	Tykeema	Tyleena	Tymeika
Tyadrian	Tychia	Tyfanie	Myonana	Tylehvia-Theatre	Tymeisha
Tyah	Tychiara	Tyffani	Tykeesha	Tyleigh	Tymeka
Tyahna	Tychina	Tyffanie	Tykeesiana	Tyleigha	Tymekia
Tyaira	Tyciana	Tyffany	Tykeeya	Tyleisha	Tymeri
Tyaisa	Tycoshia	Tygan	Tykeia	Tylekquois	Tymesh
Tyaisha	Tycresha	Tygeanna	Tykeiciunna	Tylene	Tymesha
Tyaler	Tycuria	Tygeonna	Tykeidra	Tylenthia	Tymeshia
Tyall	Tydaisha	Tyger	Tykeira	Tyler *(0.41)*	Tymia
Tyalliah	Tydazia	Tyggra	Tykeirah	Tyler Marie	Tymika
Tyalor	Tydesha	Tyha	Tykeisa	Tyler-Ann	Tymira
Tyana *(0.02)*	Tydra	Tyhana	Tykeisha *(0.01)*	Tylerann	Tymiree
Tyance	Tydreana	Tyhera	Tykeishia	Tylere	Tymisha
Tyandra	Tydreisha	Tyhesha	Tykelia	Tylerr	Tymmiesha
Tyandrea	Tydreka	Tyhesia	Tykema	Tylesha	Tymneyshia
Tyaneka	Tydrika	Tyhessia	Tykendria	Tyleshia	Tymomeshia
Tyanesia	Tye	Tyhisha	Tykendrionn	Tylesia	Tymone
Tyanha	Tyéesha	Tyhrenesha	Tykera *(0.01)*	Tyletha	Tympest
Tyanka	Tyétenyá	Tyia	Tykereiah	Tyleur	Tymple
Tyann *(0.01)*	Tye-Kerri	Tyiana	Tykeria *(0.01)*	Tylexus	Tyna
Tyanna *(0.03)*	Tye-Tiana	Tyiasha	Tykeriah	Tylha	Tynae
Tyanna-Paix	Tyea	Tyiechia	Tykeriha	Tyli	Tynan
Tyannah	Tyeas	Tyiesh	Tykerria	Tylia	Tynardra
Tyanne	Tyease	Tyiesha *(0.01)*	Tykesha	Tylicia	Tynasia
Tyannia	Tyeasha	Tyikeyonna	Tykeya	Tylie	Tyndall
Tyannicia	Tyecha	Tyina	Tykeyah	Tyliegh	Tyne
Tyara	Tyeeka	Tyionna	Tykeyia	Tyliesha	Tynea
Tyarra	Tyeesha *(0.01)*	Tyira	Tykeyra	Tylii	Tyneal
Tyasha	Tyeha	Tyirissa	Tykeysha	Tylika	Tyneaqua
Tyashia	Tyeicha	Tyisha *(0.02)*	Tykia *(0.01)*	Tylimah	Tyneasha
Tyasia *(0.01)*	Tyeirra	Tyishea	Tykiera	Tylin	Tyneashia
Tyasiah	Tyeisha *(0.03)*	Tyishia	Tykierra	Tylina	Tynecia
Tyauanna	Tyeishia	Tyiskia	Tykiesha	Tylisa	Tyneda
Tyauna	Tyeleicha	Tyissa	Tykiria	Tylisha	Tyneesha
Tyaunah	Tyeler	Tyissha	Tykirra	Tylissa	Tyneeshi
Tyawna	Tyelynne	Tyja	Tykita	Tyller	Tyneisha *(0.01)*
Tyayla	Tyena	Tyjah	Tykiya	Tyllie	Tyneisia
Tybee	Tyenesha	Tyjana	Tykoi	Tylliyah	Tyneka
Tybie	Tyenika	Tyjanae	Tykura	Tylo	Tynekia
Tybreambra	Tyeona	Tyjané	Tykweyzha	Tylona	Tynekka
Tybreia	Tyeonia	Tyje	Tyla *(0.03)*	Tylor *(0.01)*	Tynella
Tybreisha	Tyequiere	Tyjenea	Tylah	Tylor-Lynn	Tynequa
Tybresha	Tyequira	Tyjia	Tylan	Tylr	Tynequia
Tybreshia	Tyera	Tyjii	Tylana	Tylyn *(0.01)*	Tynesa

Tynese	Tyqueisha	Tyreisha	Tyroneka	Tyshekia	Tyuana
Tynesha (0.02)	Tyqueishia	Tyreka	Tyronica	Tyshell	Tyunia
Tyneshia (0.01)	Tyquela	Tyrell	Tyronika	Tyshelle	Tyva
Tynesia	Tyqueria	Tyrelle	Tyroniqua	Tyshem	Tyvesha
Tynesiá	Tyquesha	Tyren	Tyronique	Tyshema	Tyviontae
Tynessia	Tyqueshia	Tyrena	Tyroniza	Tyshemia	Tyvonda
Tynetta	Tyquiecha	Tyrenia	Tyronna	Tyshena	Tyvonna
Tynia	Tyquila	Tyrenika	Tyronni	Tysheona	Tywan
Tynica	Tyquincia	Tyrenza	Tyronnya	Tyshequa	Tywana
Tynice	Tyquinda	Tyreona	Tyronzie	Tysherika	Tywanescia
Tynichia	Tyquinica	Tyreonia	Tyrra	Tysherra	Tywasha
Tynicia	Tyquisha	Tyresa	Tyrrah	Tysherricka	Tywneisha
Tynicqua	Tyquita	Tyrese	Tyrrion	Tyshia	Tywon
Tyniesha	Tyquoia	Tyresha (0.01)	Tyrynysha	Tyshiana	Tywona
Tynijha	Tyquoya	Tyreshe	Tyrza	Tyshianna	Tyya
Tynika (0.01)	Tyrá	Tyreshia	Tysandra	Tyshiaun	Tyyanna
Tynille	Tyra (0.16)	Tyress	Tyschell	Tyshiba	Tyzah
Tyniqua	Tyra Anne	Tyresse	Tyseana	Tyshibbi	Tyzeara
Tynisa	Tyra Neasha	Tyressia	Tyseli Ya	Tyshida	Tyzeeka
Tynise	Tyrá	Tyreyun	Tysen	Tyshiera	Tyzelia
Tynisha (0.02)	Tyra-Alexandra	Tyrhem	Tysha	Tyshika	Tyzhanay
Tynishi	Tyra-Danae	Tyri'	Tyshabrea	Tyshira	Tyzhane
Tynitra	Tyraa	Tyria	Tyshae	Tyshoná	Tyziera
Tynka	Tyrae	Tyrian	Tyshaé	Tyshonia	Tzarafina
Tynneal	Tyrah (0.01)	Tyriana	Tyshai	Tyshonna	Tze
Tynnetta	Tyraina	Tyriane	Tyshaila	Tyshonya	Tze-Yan
Tynyshua	Tyran	Tyrianna	Tyshala	Tyshunda	Tzefiraél
Tynyvia	Tyranee	Tyrianne	Tyshana	Tyshunna	Tzipora
Tyona	Tyraneika	Tyrica	Tyshanae	Tyshyre	Tzippy
Tyonda	Tyraneisha	Tyrie	Tyshane	Tyson	Tzirel
Tyonde	Tyraneka	Tyrieka	Tyshanna (0.01)	Tysondra	Tzitziyunue
Tyondra	Tyranesha	Tyriel	Tyshara	Tysonya	Tzivia
Tyonia	Tyranie	Tyrielle	Tysharianna	Tystashia	Tzu
Tyonna (0.01)	Tyranika	Tyriesa	Tyshaun	Tytana	Tzuria
Tyonne	Tyranique	Tyriesha	Tyshauna	Tytanna	
Tyonshay	Tyranisha	Tyrika	Tyshaunda	Tytéanna	
Typanga	Tyranny	Tyrin	Tyshawn	Tyteana	**-U-**
Typhanie	Tyrany	Tyrina	Tyshawna	Tyteanna	
Typhany	Tyrashae	Tyrinae	Tyshawnah	Tyteaonna	U Lessa
Typheny	Tyrayanna	Tyrine	Tyshawnda	Tytearyia	U'kera
Tyqiesha	Tyrdian	Tyrion	Tyshawnna	Tytejuana	U'neqa
Tyquailia	Tyréonna	Tyrione	Tyshawnnan	Tyteonia	U'niq
Tyquajah	Tyrea	Tyrionia	Tyshay	Tyteyana	U'nique
Tyqualia	Tyreasha	Tyrionna	Tyshaya	Tyteyonna	U-La
Tyquana	Tyreatha	Tyrionne	Tyshayla	Tyti'anna	Ubah
Tyquanda	Tyreauna	Tyrisa	Tyshayna	Tytia	Uchechi
Tyquandra	Tyrecca	Tyrisha (0.01)	Tyshéa	Tytiana (0.02)	Uchefuna
Tyquandria	Tyrece	Tyrissa	Tyshea	Tytianna (0.01)	Uchenna
Tyquanesha	Tyree (0.01)	Tyrmiha	Tysheann	Tytianni	Udashia
Tyquania	Tyreen	Tyrnnon	Tysheanna	Tytiiyana	Udoka
Tyquanna	Tyreena	Tyronda	Tysheema	Tytionna	Ufuoma
Tyquanya	Tyreesha	Tyroné	Tysheena	Tytiyana	Ugarie
Tyquasha	Tyreeshá	Tyronee	Tysheia	Tytiyanna	Ugbaad
Tyquasia	Tyreika	Tyroneesé	Tysheika	Tytyana	Ugbad
Tyqueelaah	Tyreion	Tyroneisha	Tysheka	Tytyauna	Ugochi
					Ugochinyere

Ugoma	Un'neka	Urrica	Vakerria	Valincea	Vanecha
Uini	Una	Ursa	Vala	Valincia	Vanecia
Uinta	Unalee	Urshulla	Valacia	Valire	Vaneequa
Uju	Unam	Ursina	Valaine	Valisa	Vaneeshia
Ukari	Undréanna	Ursuala	Valancia	Valisia	Vaneeta
Ukegco	Undrea	Ursula *(0.02)*	Valancy	Valisite	Vaneice
Ukette	Undreya	Ursular	Valaria	Valisity	Vaneisha
Ukeyco	Undria	Urvi	Valarie *(0.05)*	Valissa	Vanekia
Ukiah	Unecia	Urwah	Valbarnie	Valissia	Vanela
Ula	Uneek	Usaamera	Valbona	Valiyah	Vanely
Ulalume	Unehqua	Usera	Valdarea	Valkiria	Vanenteen
Ulanda	Unequa	Usesike	Valean	Valkyrie	Vaneola
Ulani	Uneshia	Usha	Valeana	Vallah	Vanequa
Ulania	Uniah	Ushekqua	Valeane	Vallan	Vanesa *(0.11)*
Ulesha	Unicka	Ushna	Valeata	Vallarie	Vanesha
Ulexia	Unik	Usra	Valecia	Vallary	Vaneshah
Ulexius	Unika *(0.01)*	Uswatte	Valeda	Vallerie	Vanesia
Ulexus	Unikqua	Utona	Valeiria	Valley	Vaneska
Ulia	Uniqá	Utonna	Valen	Vallie	Vaness
Uliana	Uniqia	Utopia	Valena	Vallori	Vanessa *(3.39)*
Ulika	Uniqua *(0.01)*	Uyen	Valencia *(0.05)*	Vallory	Vanessa Ariana
Ulineya	Unique *(0.08)*	Uyennhi	Valendina	Valmeika	Vanessa Cristal
Uliya	Unique Angel	Uymu	Valene	Valmire	Vanessa Lynn
Ulku	Uniqué	Uyvonna	Valenecia	Valoice	Vanessa Nicole
Ulma	Unique-A	Uzel	Valenteen	Valonda	Vanessa-Marie
Ulmary	Uniqueka	Uzetta	Valentena	Valori	Vanessa-Vedana
Uloma	Uniquequa	Uzharia	Valentina *(0.09)*	Valorie *(0.01)*	Vanesse
Ulrika	Uniquia	Uzkah	Valentine	Valri	Vanessia
Ulukilupetea	Uniquoa	Uzma	Valenya	Valry	Vanetta
Ulunma	Uniqwia	Uzoamaka	Valenzcia	Valsamyn	Vanezja
Ulyana	Unity		Valera	Valune	Vangi
Ulyssa	Unjoli	**-V-**	Valere	Valvanuz	Vania *(0.04)*
Ulyssia	Untonia		Valeree	Valydia-Anne	Vanice
Uma	Unzel	V *(0.01)*	Valeri	Valynn	Vanicia
Umadevi	Upasna	V.	Valeria *(0.34)*	Valynsia	Vanida
Umai	Uqba	Va Sha	Valeria Casandra	Van *(0.01)*	Vaniece
Umaima	Uquasiemana	Va'shanna	Valeria Daniell	Van-Zhar	Vanika
Umairoh	Uquinta	Vaasiny	Valerica	Vana	Vanina
Umal-Khayr	Urania	Vaccaro	Valerie *(1.27)*	Vanae	Vaniqua
Umama	Urara	Vacelia	Valerie-Anne	Vanaja	Vanique
Umani	Ure	Vacheffia	Valeriee	Vanasa	Vanise
Umarah	Ureka	Vachel	Valeros	Vance	Vanisha *(0.01)*
Umay	Urena	Vachelle	Valery *(0.04)*	Vanda	Vanishia
Umber	Uria	Vada *(0.01)*	Valesca	Vanda-Lee	Vanissa
Umbrosia	Uriah	Vadadrian	Valeshia	Vandana	Vanita
Umbul	Urid	Vaden	Valeshka	Vandella	Vanitcha
Umdah	Uriel	Vahola	Valeska *(0.01)*	Vandelora	Vaniti
Umeka	Urina	Vaishali	Valex	Vanderia	Vanity *(0.01)*
Umeshia	Urmee	Vaishnave	Valexis	Vanderly	Vaniya
Umkulthoom	Urmiben	Vaishnavi	Valexus	Vandevi	Vanja
Ummama	Urmish	Vaishnavy	Valezca	Vandna	Vanjelica
Ummarah	Urooba	Vaithiga	Valicia	Vandy	Vanka
Umme	Urooj	Vakala	Valida	Vanea	Vanlena
Umme Hanie	Uroojnisa	Vakeena	Valin	Vaneashia	Vanna *(0.01)*
Ummekulsoom	Uroosa	Vakeria	Valina	Vaneatria	Vannari

Vannasia	Vashaun	Veladria	Vennee	Verna *(0.01)*	Vertie
Vanndy	Vashawnda	Velana	Venness	Vernae	Vertonda
Vannell	Vashé	Velda	Vennessa	Vernard	Vertrice
Vannesa *(0.03)*	Vasheria	Velecity	Vennetta	Vernarda	Vertueuse
Vannesha	Vashon	Velen	Vennie	Vernazia	Veruschka
Vannessa *(0.03)*	Vashondra	Velencia	Vennugha	Verncial	Veshimabeth
Vannia	Vashti *(0.01)*	Velheena	Venocia	Verneatrice	Veshon
Vannie	Vashty	Velia	Venotha	Vernecia	Vesley
Vanniece	Vashunda	Velina	Ventoura	Verneesha	Vesna
Vannika	Vasia	Velinda	Ventrise	Verneice	Vessa
Vannis	Vasilia	Vellareatha	Ventura	Verneisha	Vessna
Vanny	Vasilike	Vellatina	Venus *(0.02)*	Vernell	Vesta
Vanobia	Vasiliki *(0.01)*	Velma *(0.01)*	Venusha	Vernenis	Vestana
Vanora	Vasilikia	Velnique	Venya	Vernesha	Vestiny
Vanshikha	Vassalisa	Veloryun	Veola	Verneshia	Veta
Vanssa	Vassiliki	Velsaida	Veonia	Verneshua	Vetahya
Vanssena	Vasthi	Velva	Veonna	Vernessa	Vethania
Vantashá	Vasti	Velvanique	Veora	Vernetta	Vetisha
Vantashia	Vasudha	Velvet	Vequera	Vernette	Vetta
Vantasia	Vasuki	Ven'toyia	Ver'lexus	Vernettia	Vetthya
Vanthalay	Vatoria	Vena	Vera *(0.04)*	Vernice	Veva
Vantonise	Vaughn	Venassa	Veracia	Vernicia	Vevean
Vantoria	Vaun	Vencina	Veraliz	Vernie	Veyla
Vantressa	Vaunni	Vendala	Veranique	Verniece	Veyondra
Vantrice	Vawessa	Vendela	Verba	Vernika	Vhairi
Vanuya	Vayalit	Vendré	Verberi	Verniqua	Vhari
Vanya	Vayana	Venecia *(0.01)*	Verchelle	Vernise	Vhonyea
Vaqesha	Vayda	Veneese	Verdakay	Vernisha *(0.01)*	Vi
Vaquaila	Vaytta	Veneica	Veremis	Vernissia	Viahnely
Vaquesha	Vazhia	Veneice	Verena	Vernita	Vian
Varda	Véesha	Veneicia	Verenice *(0.03)*	Vernitra	Viana Shanénes
Varen	Véneesha	Venesa	Verenis	Vernoda	Viana'y
Varia	Vénettea	Venese	Verenise	Vernoica	Vianca *(0.02)*
Varicillica	Veaira	Veneshia	Vereniz	Vernonica	Viancca
Varie	Veannessa	Venesia	Verenya	Vernordra	Vianelli
Varinderjeet	Vearna	Venessa *(0.04)*	Vergie	Verona	Vianely
Varlina	Vearnshé	Venetia *(0.01)*	Verhonda	Veronic *(0.01)*	Vianet
Varnecia	Veathini	Venezia *(0.01)*	Verika	Veronica *(1.40)*	Vianey *(0.04)*
Varoneck	Veatris	Venia	Verita	Veronica Sarah	Viangelid
Varonica	Veda *(0.01)*	Venice *(0.01)*	Verity *(0.01)*	Veronicia	Vianka
Varquadreonnia	Vedika	Venicésia	Verjinder	Veronik	Vianna
Varrion	Vedrana	Venicia	Verla	Veronika *(0.02)*	Viannesi
Varsha	Vedya	Veniciya	Verlanda	Veronique *(0.22)*	Vianney *(0.01)*
Vartine	Vee	Veniece	Verlena	Veronisounsoun	Viany
Varvara	Veeda	Venikia	Verlesa	Verranesha	Viara
Vasean	Veen	Veniqua	Verletta	Verronica	Viashana
Vasena	Veena	Venique	Verlinda	Versha	Viasia
Vasey	Veenaya	Venir	Verline	Vershae	Vibesha
Vasha	Veeona	Venisa	Verlisa	Vershanta	Vibiana
Vashae	Veeran	Venise	Verliscia	Vershauna	Vicario
Vashanique	Veerpal	Venisha	Verlissa	Versie	Vicelle
Vashanti	Vega	Venissa	Verlyssa	Verstel	Vicenta
Vashara	Vegas	Venita	Vermecia	Verswonna	Vicente
Vasharia	Vegas-Bean	Venitra	Vermekia	Vertasha	Vicera
Vashati	Veiry-Jean	Venkiria	Vern	Vertessia	Vichanta

Vichell
Vichina
Vichna
Vichnou
Vichon
Vicie
Vickery
Vickey
Vicki *(0.05)*
Vickie *(0.04)*
Vickie Quaterri
Vicktoria
Vicktory
Vicky *(0.23)*
Vicmarily
Vicotira
Victgoria
Victioria
Victoia
Victorhea
Victori
Victoria *(5.76)*
Victoria Angeli
Victoria Cristi
Victoria Du
Victoria Lee
Victoria Sally
Victoria-Ann
Victoria-Anne
Victoria-Brooke
Victoria-Ellen
Victoria-Florice
Victoria-Katarzyna
Victoria-Lyn
Victoria-Lynn
Victoria-Marie
Victoria-Marta
Victoria-Thuy
Victorialyn
Victoriamaria
Victoriana
Victorianna
Victoriatori
Victorie
Victorieya
Victorija
Victorina
Victoriya
Victorria
Victorriah
Victory *(0.01)*
Victorya
Victouria
Victoya

Victravia
Victraya
Vicy
Vida
Vidalia
Vidhi
Vidhita
Vidhu
Vidisha
Vidonica
Vidorian
Vidrine
Vidusaa
Vidya
Vien
Viengmaly
Vienna *(0.01)*
Viennetta
Vieno
Viergelane
Viergella
Vierra
Viershanie
Vigginarro
Viithushaa
Vijay
Vijaya
Vijayalakshmi
Vijayita
Viji
Vijil
Vika
Vikeadia
Vikeisha
Vikendrea
Viki
Vikia
Vikise
Vikki *(0.01)*
Vikky
Viktoria *(0.02)*
Viktoria Gorene
Viktoria-Marie
Viktorija
Viktoryia
Viky
Vilaphone
Vilate
Vilena
Vilencia
Vilia
Vilija
Vilma
Vilmary
Vilte-Ruta

Vimala
Vimalprett
Vimani
Vimarilyn
Viminder
Vin'cerra
Vina
Vinadies
Vinaeja
Vinashini
Vinceena
Vinceletta
Vincella
Vincent *(0.01)*
Vincenteja
Vincentoyria
Vincenza
Vincenzia
Vincenzina
Vincesha
Vincetrayvia
Vincietta
Vincy
Vindella
Vindra
Vinecia
Vinedgy
Vinelly
Vinesha
Vinessa
Vinetta
Vinette
Vinettia
Vinh
Viniciah
Vinisha
Vinissa
Vinita
Vinittha
Vinlisha
Vinnie
Vinnii
Vinoi
Vinola
Vinquisha
Vinsanna
Vinsia
Vintasia
Vinteria
Vinterica
Vintiesha
Vintonisha
Vintoya
Vinuja
Vinz-Erl

Viola *(0.01)*
Violet *(0.08)*
Violeta *(0.04)*
Violetta *(0.01)*
Vionise
Vionna
Vionne
Vionshay
Vipali
Vipan
Vipuya
Vira
Viraagna
Virada
Viraj
Viral
Viraphanh
Virdaijah
Virdis
Vireka
Virgen
Virgil
Virgimiah
Virgina
Virginia *(0.43)*
Virginia An
Virginia-Len
Virginie *(0.12)*
Virginnia
Viridiana *(0.11)*
Viringa
Viririana
Virleasha
Virnesha
Vironeca
Vironnica
Virtasia
Viry
Virydianna
Visa
Visal
Visetana
Vishaka
Vishala
Vishanna
Vishay
Vishishya
Vishnusha
Visruti
Vista
Vita
Vithika
Vithucha
Vithursha
Vithurshini

Vithusha
Vithya
Vittoria *(0.01)*
Vitumbiko
Viva
Vivacious
Vivan
Vivana
Vive
Viveca
Viveka
Vivekananthan
Vivi
Vivia
Vivian *(0.53)*
Vivian-Muse
Viviana *(0.28)*
Viviane *(0.02)*
Viviane-Anita
Viviann
Vivianna *(0.02)*
Vivianne *(0.01)*
Vivica
Vivieca
Vivien *(0.01)*
Vivienne
Viwaycka
Vixen
Vixey
Viyada
Viyanah
Viyanka
Vizma
Vjosa
Vladelle
Vladislav
Vlora
Vlyncia
Vneeta
Vo'nique
Vocinell
Voctoria
Vollica
Von
Von'sha
Voncella
Vonchay
Vonchelle
Voncia
Vonda
Vondalynn
Vondaniqua
Vondell
Vonderia
Vonea

Vonecia
Vonedtera
Vonessia
Vonetta
Vonica
Vonice-Elizabet
Vonicia
Voniisa
Vonikke
Vonisha
Vonkeria
Vonkeyla
Vonna
Vonneisha
Vonnie
Vonnisha
Vonny
Vonquese
Vonquesha
Vonquis
Vonshae
Vonshé
Vonshell
Vonta
Vontaejha
Vontajha
Vontashia
Vontasia
Vontavia
Vontavius
Vontaysha
Vonteja
Vonterrica
Vontese
Vontesia
Vontisha
Vontravia
Vontrice
Vontricia
Vorri
Voussra
Vranda
Vreni
Vrunda
Vsalerie
Vu
Vu-Vi
Vubao
Vudbir
Vunchasheia
Vuong
Vy *(0.01)*
Vyctorya
Vyen
Vyktoria

Vylet
Vynique
Vynteria
Vyridyana
Vyrl
Vyshnavey
Vyshnavi
Vyveen
Vyvian
Vyvy
Vyvyan
Vyvyana

-W-

W
Wa
Wa'ad
Wa'kyessia
Wa'neisha
Wa'nya
Waasegeeshgookwe
Wachita
Wachovia
Wadad
Wadejah
Wadeline
Wader
Wadline
Wadsana
Wafa
Wafaa
Wafiyyah
Wages
Wagha
Waheeda
Wahida
Wahnetah
Wai (0.01)
Wai-Kay
Wailana
Wailani Malie
Waileia
Wajdan
Wakaa
Wakaha
Wakako
Wakana
Wakeelah
Wakkirea
Waláa
Walá
Wala
Wala Ahmad
Walaa

Waldon
Waleska
Waletta
Walicia
Walida
Waline
Walker (0.01)
Walkiria
Walla
Wallace
Wallica
Wallis
Wallisha
Walls
Walnatia
Walnika
Walquita
Walta
Waltasia
Walterine
Walterlette
Walternesha
Walterria
Waltierra
Waltkita
Wana
Wanda (0.03)
Wandah
Wandie
Wandria
Wandy
Waneaka
Waneesa
Waneita
Waneka
Waneshia
Wang-Kit
Wania
Wanice
Wanicka
Wanisha
Wanita
Wanja
Wanjiru
Wannah
Wanning
Wanya
Wanyá
Wapun
Waqeelat
Ward
Warda
Wardah
Wardeh
Wardeisha

Wardena
Wardenia
Wardesha
Wardisha
Wardrika
Wardsha
Wareen
Wariel
Warin
Warnakulasuriya
Warner
Warrenisha
Warrine
Washington
Wasylena
Watahskwanan
Water
Waters
Wateshia
Watisha
Wauchope
Wava
Waveney
Waverley
Waverli
Waverly (0.02)
Wavierlee
Wawa-Vafon
Wawijah
Wayana
Waylow
Wayneesha
Wayneisha
Waynesha (0.01)
Waynetta
Waynie
Waynisha
Wayonna
Wazha
Wéchika
Weaam
Wealyn
Weanna
Weatherly
Weaver
Wedad
Wedline
Wednesday (0.01)
Weerawarna
Weesam
Wegaheta
Wei
Wei-Ling
Weijian
Weini
Weiwen

Wejdan
Weldon
Weldontiana
Welela
Welisha
Wells
Wellsley
Wen
Wen'nyse
Wenah
Wency
Wendalyn
Wendalynn
Wendasha
Wenddy
Wendelisha
Wendelle
Wendes
Wendi (0.02)
Wendianne
Wendie
Wendoline Haide
Wendolyn
Wendy (0.58)
Wendyjo
Wendyth
Wenetta
Weng
Wenkie
Wenly
Wenndy
Wennie
Wennilyn
Wenny
Wenonah
Wensday
Wensy
Wenunah
Wenzday
Werdah
Werner
Weslee
Wesleigh
Wesley (0.01)
Wesli
Weslie
Weslyan
Weslyn
Wessal
Wessam
Wessie
Westin
Weston
Wethonia
Whakaiann

Whan
Wheeler
Whenekia
Whetanay
Whinpurr
Whinter
Whinthany
Whisenhut
Whisper (0.01)
Whisper Alyssa
Whissper
Whitaker
White
Whitknie
Whitlee
Whitleigh
Whitley (0.06)
Whitlie
Whitne
Whitnee (0.01)
Whitnei
Whitney (1.32)
Whitney Halle
Whitney-Le
Whitneyanne
Whitni (0.01)
Whitnie (0.01)
Whitnisha
Whitny
Whittaney
Whittanie
Whittany
Whitteny
Whitti
Whittley
Whittnay
Whittnee
Whittney (0.02)
Whittni
Whittnie
Whuckara
Whyishnave
Whytni
Widad
Widdalys
Widline (0.01)
Widlyne
Widmiria
Widneen
Widney
Wijdan
Wil Leisha
Wil'niscia
Wil-Daysa
Wilanda

Wilandria
Wilbelner
Wilda
Wildaline
Wildine
Wilena
Wilene
Wilesha
Wiletta
Wiley
Wilhelmena
Wilhelmina (0.01)
Wilhemina
Wilhermina
Wilhite
Wilia
Wilisha
Wilkeha
Wilkeria
Wilkeydra
Will Ell
Will Nesha
Will Netria
Will'mesha
Willa (0.02)
Willanette
Willen
Willena
Willene
Willequa
Willesha
Willeshia
Willesia
Willette
William (0.01)
Williamina
Williams
Willicea
Willicia
Willie
Williejo
Williemae
Willinda
Willine
Willis
Willisa
Williseiua
Willisha
Willishia
Willmesha
Willnesha
Willnide
Willnisha
Willo
Willoe

Willondra	Winstana	Wyeshya	Wytincia	Xeina	Xoschill
Willontae	Winta	Wyimesha	Wytinsea	Xel'ha	Xotchil
Willorine	Wintana	Wykatelyn	Wytisha	Xela	Xotchitl
Willough	Winter (0.05)	Wykeisha	Wytney	Xemena	Xrisoula
Willow (0.05)	Wintergrace	Wykeisha Ikaved	Wytona	Xena (0.02)	Xristina
Willowcahill	Wintress	Wykenda	Wyvenne	Xenaida	Xsavier
Willuse	Wisdom	Wykeria		Xenea	Xuan
Wilma (0.01)	Wishnekha	Wykeshia	**-X-**	Xenia (0.03)	Xuan My
Wilmarie	Wislande	Wyketa		Xenya	Xuanngoc
Wilmary	Wisline	Wykiesha	X Zalyn	Xeregha	Xue
Wilmeisha	Wisper	Wykisa	X'lanna	Xevia	Xuxa
Wilna	Wisteria	Wyldier	X'zahvielle	Xhama	Xyesha
Wilneisha	Withnine	Wyleisha	X'zavia	Xhanaya	Xykeiriua
Wilnequa	Witley	Wyliah	Xa'quaila	Xhenet	Xykira
Wilnesha	Witney	Wylie	Xabria	Xia	Xyla
Wilneshia	Witni	Wylisa	Xabryia	Xia-Kéla	Xylena
Wilnetra	Witnie	Wylquinta	Xaena	Xiamara	Xylene
Wilnide	Wittie	Wynashia	Xaillii	Xian	Xylia
Wilonda	Witty	Wyndi	Xaine	Xiana	Xylina
Wilsandley	Wiza	Wyndsor	Xaishia	Xiandia	Xylondrea
Wilshaé	Wláa	Wyneisha	Xakeeia	Xiantria	Xzabria
Wilsie	Wlfrano	Wynekia	Xallae	Xiao	Xzabrionna
Wilson	Wolfe	Wynema	Xamaris	Xiao-Yin	Xzariya
Wiltiece	Wolinda	Wynerpher	Xana	Xiaquana	Xzavia
Wimberly	Won'deefoe	Wynesha	Xandi	Xiclalis	Xzaviara
Win-Lok	Wonda	Wyneshia	Xandra	Xiedani	Xzherieh
Wincy	Wongani	Wynetta	Xandria (0.01)	Xien	
Winderia	Wongee	Wynika	Xandria Sai'tha	Xienna	**-Y-**
Windermere	Wonya	Wyninzia	Xania	Xierra	
Windi	Woodberrie	Wynn	Xanna	Xiet	Y
Windie	Woodelyn	Wynnaura	Xante	Ximena (0.01)	Y Aron
Windsor	Wooden	Wynne (0.01)	Xantha	Xinia	Y Svanni
Windy (0.01)	Woodlyne	Wynniekka	Xanthe	Xiola	Y Tavia
Winea	Woodnisha	Wynnter	Xaranda	Xiomanely	Y Toria
Wing (0.01)	Wooten	Wynomie	Xaria	Xiomara (0.08)	Y'ana
Wing-Hei	Worth	Wynona	Xarina	Xiomaris	Y'anika
Wing-Ton	Wotay	Wynonna (0.01)	Xaris	Xiomayra	Y'breka
Wing-Yan	Would	Wynstoria	Xasha	Xion	Y'donia
Wingkie	Wraeshaun	Wyntavia	Xatanna	Xitlali	Y'esha
Wingsee	Wraia	Wynter (0.03)	Xatayia	Xitlalic	Y'evette
Winifred	Wray	Wynteria	Xaun	Xitlaly	Y'kemia
Winnefred	Wraya	Wynthia	Xaveia	Xiu	Y'laysha
Winney	Wren	Wyomi	Xaveria	Xiveria	Y'nicha
Winni	Wrigley	Wyomie	Xaverie	Xixochitl	Y'saka
Winnie (0.04)	Wuantekica	Wyoming	Xavia	Xochil	Y'vondria
Winnifred	Wuteh	Wyona	Xavian	Xochilt (0.03)	Y'vonié
Winnona	Wy Lece	Wyqueill	Xaviena	Xochilth	Y'vonne
Winnter	Wy'meisha	Wysdom	Xavier (0.01)	Xochiquetzali	Y-Nhi
Winny	Wy-Anne	Wysheka	Xaviera (0.01)	Xochithl	Y-Nhu
Winoa	Wyanda	Wyshekia	Xavieria	Xochiti	Ya
Winona (0.02)	Wyatt	Wyshika	Xayana	Xochitl (0.05)	Ya Stacious
Winonna	Wyatte	Wytavia	Xaykevia	Xochiyollotl	Ya'chasity
Winsdy	Wycazsia	Wytencia	Xaylia	Xoicha Alexus	Ya'kerria
Winslow	Wyeisha	Wyteria	Xaymaca	Xora	Ya'keysha
Winsor	Wyesha	Wyterria	Xcenia	Xorla	Ya'kira

Ya'nikia	Yailyn	Yamely	Yanelli	Yaoska	Yasenia
Ya'quisha	Yaima	Yamesha	Yanely *(0.01)*	Yaqqirah	Yasha
Ya'shavia	Yaimara	Yamesse	Yanelys	Yaquelin *(0.02)*	Yashanti
Ya'sheika	Yaimy	Yamia	Yaneries	Yaquisha	Yashara
Ya'zmine	Yainerys	Yamiaya	Yaneris	Yara *(0.02)*	Yasheda
Ya-Launi	Yainet	Yamika	Yanesi	Yarah	Yasheria
Yaalini	Yainslie	Yamil	Yanessa	Yarahi	Yashica
Yaashika	Yaisha	Yamila	Yanet *(0.04)*	Yaraseht	Yashika
Yaazmin	Yaitiare	Yamile	Yanete	Yarasel	Yashima
Yabrianna	Yaiza	Yamilet *(0.01)*	Yaneth *(0.01)*	Yarden	Yashira
Yacinia	Yajaira *(0.09)*	Yamileth	Yanethe	Yare	Yashman
Yacklin	Yajara	Yamiletsy	Yanette	Yareli *(0.03)*	Yashna
Yacoryia	Yajayra	Yamilette	Yanexis	Yarelis	Yashoda
Yacqueline	Yajhaira	Yamilex	Yaney	Yarely *(0.02)*	Yasika
Yadasia	Yajiara	Yamiley	Yangchen	Yarelyz	Yasim
Yadelis	Yakeen	Yamilez	Yanhet	Yaremi	Yaskara
Yadira *(0.19)*	Yakeina	Yamina	Yani	Yaremy	Yaslin
Yadirah	Yakeisha	Yaminah	Yanibet	Yareni	Yasmaine
Yadirha	Yakeitha	Yamini	Yanice	Yaretsi	Yasmari
Yadisha	Yakeiva	Yamiqua	Yanicka	Yareun	Yasmary
Yadlin	Yakelin	Yamisha	Yaniece	Yaricelle	Yasmean
Yadpreet	Yakemia	Yamit	Yanika	Yaricelys	Yasmeem
Yadyra	Yakeria	Yamiyah	Yanikka	Yarida	Yasmeen *(0.10)*
Yadyrah-Lyzbet	Yakerra	Yammel	Yanina	Yaridza	Yasmeena
Yae	Yaki Ra	Yammonika	Yanine	Yarielix	Yasmen *(0.01)*
Yael *(0.01)*	Yakia	Yamnah	Yanique	Yarikssa	Yasmene
Yaeshul	Yakierra	Yamylex	Yaniquewa	Yarileah	Yasmeni
Yaevin	Yakima	Yan	Yanira *(0.05)*	Yarileeza	Yasmenne
Yaffa	Yakimia	Yan-Lin	Yaniri	Yariliss	Yasmery
Yafyute	Yakina	Yan-Ni	Yaniris	Yarilyn	Yasmi
Yagahira	Yakini	Yana	Yanirys	Yarilynn	Yasmien
Yah	Yakinya	Yanae	Yanisa	Yarima *(0.02)*	Yasmiin
Yahaida	Yakira *(0.01)*	Yanaile	Yanisleidis	Yarimar	Yasmika
Yahaira *(0.03)*	Yakiria	Yanali	Yanisliet	Yarionne	Yasmin *(0.26)*
Yahara	Yaklyn	Yanay	Yanissa	Yarisamar	Yasmina *(0.01)*
Yahayra	Yaktavia	Yanayce	Yanisse	Yarisel	Yasminder
Yaheniece	Yalaina	Yanaye	Yanitza	Yarisma	Yasmine *(0.20)*
Yahira	Yalakesen	Yancee	Yanixa	Yarissa	Yasmini
Yahmea	Yalanda	Yancey	Yaniz	Yarithza	Yasminne
Yahn'tea	Yalda	Yanchia	Yankel	Yaritsa	Yasmith
Yahna	Yale	Yanci	Yankia	Yaritssa	Yasmon
Yahné	Yalene	Yancy	Yanlin	Yaritza *(0.10)*	Yasmoné
Yahontas	Yalexix	Yandria	Yanna	Yaritzamar	Yasnei
Yahoska	Yalini	Yaneczka	Yannerik	Yarixsa	Yassah
Yahreah	Yalinie	Yaned	Yannerin	Yarlesha	Yasslin
Yaidelin	Yalitza	Yaneeka	Yannery	Yarmayne	Yassmeen
Yaidelis	Yalonda	Yaneile	Yannet	Yarmoni	Yassmen
Yaidid	Yalontae	Yaneira	Yanneth	Yas'mine	Yassmin
Yaile	Yalyssa	Yaneisi	Yannette	Yasaman	Yasuary
Yaileen	Yamaliz	Yanel Itzayana	Yanni	Yasamin	Yatavia
Yailen	Yamara	Yanela	Yannique	Yasamine	Yathrib
Yailene	Yameka	Yaneli *(0.03)*	Yanory	Yasee	Yati
Yailin	Yamela	Yanelis	Yansy	Yaseenah	Yatil
Yailis	Yamelex	Yaneliz	Yantia	Yasemeen	Yatri
Yailixxa	Yamelix	Yanelle	Yanuka	Yasemin *(0.01)*	Yaveli

Yavonda	Yelba	Yesifin	Yifta	Yoanna	Yonica
Yavonka	Yelda	Yesika	Yik	Yoannelis	Yonna
Yaylim	Yeldah	Yesiko	Yikera	Yobana	Yonnae
Yayline	Yeléna	Yesinia	Yikeria	Yobani	Yonnahana
Yayma	Yelena	Yesleni	Yikevia	Yocelin (0.01)	Yonnie
Yaysha	Yelenda	Yeslien	Yikira	Yoceline	Yonnise
Yaz'mine	Yelisa	Yesly	Yilda	Yocelyn (0.01)	Yonquita
Yazaira	Yelitza	Yesmen	Yilen	Yocelyne	Yonyace
Yazamin	Yelizaveta	Yesmia	Yilismi	Yocheved	Yoojin
Yazell	Yellenis	Yesmin	Yillianne	Yodahet	Yoon
Yazil	Yelli	Yesminn	Yin-Yin	Yodit	Yoon-Joo
Yazira	Yemani	Yesmizel	Yinett	Yoditt	Yoonah
Yazjae	Yemaya	Yesseli	Ying	Yoglisha	Yordanos
Yazmarie	Yemima	Yessenia (0.14)	Yingting	Yohana (0.02)	Yorelis
Yazmeen	Yemisi	Yessenya	Yini Uni	Yohanan	Yorelle
Yazmene	Yemmonté	Yesseria	Yinyin	Yohandri	Yori
Yazmilette	Yen (0.01)	Yessi	Yiomara	Yohanna	Yoridia
Yazmin (0.13)	Yency	Yessica (0.08)	Yisel	Yoidelys	Yorlando
Yazmine (0.02)	Yendis	Yessiel	Yiseli	Yojaira	Yorleny
Yazmyn	Yendy	Yessika	Yisell	Yoko	Yosali
Yazmyne	Yenefer	Yessy	Yismen	Yokwanza	Yosan
Yazzmien	Yeneiri	Yestine	Yismenia	Yola	Yoselim
Yazzmin	Yenesis	Yetta	Yiyera	Yolanda (0.22)	Yoselin (0.06)
Yazzmine	Yenessa	Yetunde	Yizel	Yolande Asongwe	Yoseline (0.01)
Yazzmyn	Yenessis	Yetzaveli	Yizmelkis	Yolando	Yoselyn (0.01)
Ydalis	Yeney	Yetzy	Ykeisha	Yolandra	Yosemite
Ye	Yeni	Yevania	Ykeshia	Yolanthe	Yosha
Yeashia	Yenia	Yeven	Yleahn	Yoledie	Yoshaka
Yeceliana	Yenic	Yevette	Ylena	Yolessya	Yoshamoria
Yecenia (0.03)	Yenifer (0.01)	Yevgeniya	Ylenciá	Yolesvi	Yosheena
Yecica	Yenis	Yevnika	Ylenia	Yolexis	Yoshema
Yedekong	Yenisa	Yewande	Ylexia	Yoliane	Yoshika
Yedolapo	Yenisia	Yewobdar	Yliana	Yolie	Yoshiondra
Yee	Yenith	Yexenia	Yliani	Yoliet	Yosimar
Yeekoyah	Yeniva	Yeylin	Ylisha	Yolina	Yosko
Yeganeh	Yeniz	Yezabel	Yliza	Yolinda	Yosmari
Yehosheba	Yennhi	Yezenia	Ymaday	Yolitzin	Yosselin
Yehryn	Yennifer	Yezet	Ymahn	Yollanda	Yosseline
Yehudis	Yenny	Yezzare	Ymani	Yolnicte	Yosselyn
Yehuie	Yensil	Yhane	Yminh	Yolonda (0.01)	Yotaeccia
Yehunen	Yeny	Yhanique	Ymisa	Yolondria	Yottie
Yeilem	Yeou	Yholanda	Yneikia	Yolotzy	You
Yeilin	Yer (0.02)	Yhontrice	Ynes	Yomaira	Youbenta
Yeilth Gah Koo	Yeraldin	Yhumiko	Ynette	Yomara	Youlonda
Yeimi	Yerelyn	Yi	Ynez	Yomarie	Youn-Mi
Yeine	Yeritza	Yi-Sha	Yngrid	Yomina	Young
Yeini	Yes'enia	Yianna	Ynisha	Yomira	Youngblood
Yeinil	Yeseily	Yiannys	Ynssea'h	Yomna	Younica
Yeira	Yeselin	Yiasha	Yo'honna	Yomnna	Younique
Yeisdania	Yesely	Yiccel	Yo'nara	Yona	Younkyoung
Yeiveliz	Yesendy	Yiczel	Yo-Ceéna	Yonah	Yousine
Yejidé	Yesenia (0.89)	Yida	Yoali	Yoneidy	Yousra
Yekaterina	Yeseniss	Yidalmis	Yoamdelis	Yonella	Yousrasabrina
Yelande	Yesennia	Yidiany	Yoana (0.04)	Yongela	Yovana
Yelanny	Yesica (0.05)	Yiedra	Yoandra	Yongyong	Yovani

Yovanna	Yukiha	Yuriah	Yvet	Zabrienna	Zahkeya
Yowana	Yukiko	Yuriana	Yveta	Zabrina	Zahn
Yoznia	Yukimi	Yuribia	Yvett	Zacara	Zahna
Yquyen	Yukino	Yurico	Yvetta	Zacarra	Zahnaya
Yra	Yuko	Yuridany	Yvette (0.28)	Zacarri	Zahnea
Yraida	Yulamy	Yurideysi	Yviana	Zacchea	Zahneka
Yrainy	Yulander	Yuridia (0.01)	Yvlalia	Zacchia	Zahnyia
Yraiz	Yuleidys	Yuridiana	Yvlyn	Zachariah	Zahquillyah
Yrline	Yuleismy	Yuridy	Yvon	Zacharriya	Zahráa
Ysabel	Yulenia	Yurielle	Yvonda	Zachary (0.01)	Zahra (0.05)
Ysabella	Yuli	Yuriem	Yvonna	Zachecia	Zahraa
Ysanne	Yulia	Yurikkanikol	Yvonnah	Zacheria	Zahraia
Ysatis	Yuliana (0.03)	Yuriko	Yvonne (0.27)	Zachyra	Zahreh
Ysena	Yuliani	Yurima	Yvonne Thao	Zackeira	Zahri
Ysenia	Yulidaisy	Yuris	Yvonnia	Zackeisha	Zahria
Ysheia	Yulidiana	Yurisbeth	Yvonnie	Zackeria	Zahrra
Yshia	Yulie	Yurist	Yvonshaye	Zackerria	Zahtwon
Ysobel	Yulinda	Yuritsi	Yxis	Zacobia	Zahyria
Yssencé	Yulisa	Yuritza	Yyanah	Zacora	Zai'kerria
Ytati	Yulissa	Yuritzi	Yzabel	Zacorene	Zaib
Ytia	Yulix	Yuritzy	Yzarely	Zacouya	Zaibaa
Ytrenda	Yuliza	Yurixsi	Yzejma	Zacoya	Zaicha
Yu (0.01)	Yulmi	Yurixzi	Yzmari	Zada	Zaida (0.02)
Yu'landa	Yulya	Yurniece		Zadah	Zaidanelly
Yu-Chyn	Yuma	Yushela	**-Z-**	Zaddie	Zaide
Yu-Li	Yumaka	Yusleidi		Zadia	Zaidee
Yualanda	Yumi	Yusmary	Z	Zadiamond	Zailey
Yuandrika	Yumiha	Yusmin	Z Bearrea	Zadie	Zaily
Yuanxia	Yumika	Yusnely	Z Kehia	Zadrea	Zain
Yuarys	Yumiko	Yusr	Z Kya	Zadria	Zaina (0.01)
Yuasonia	Yumna	Yusra	Z Leasha	Zadtress	Zainab (0.03)
Yubelka	Yun	Yusran	Z'ashé	Zady	Zainah
Yucera	Yun-Jae	Yut	Z'hana	Zaebriana	Zainar
Yudi	Yun-Lei	Yutina	Z'hane	Zaena	Zaineb
Yudid	Yuna	Yuting	Z'keria	Zaeria	Zainib
Yudit	Yuneisha	Yuuki	Z'quoya	Zaeronycia	Zainna
Yudith	Yunfai	Yuval	Za Fira	Zafirah	Zainub
Yuditt	Yung	Yuvit	Za Kelia	Zah	Zaira (0.03)
Yudondria	Yuniesky	Yuvontiko	Za'keadra	Zah'kia	Zaira Mari
Yudy	Yuniqua	Yuwen	Za'keira	Zah'nay	Zaire (0.01)
Yudys	Yunique	Yuzmely	Za'keyah	Zah'quayvia	Zairea
Yue	Yunjia	Yuztine	Za'kuria	Zahara	Zairrea
Yuen	Yunkyung	Yva	Za'netta	Zaharra	Zaisha
Yuen-Man	Yunn	Yvana	Za'noah	Zahava	Zaita
Yuet	Yunoka	Yvanna	Za'quantanekia	Zaheda	Zajara
Yuh-Rong	Yunsu	Yvannette	Za'queisha	Zahedah	Zakahayah
Yui	Yunuen	Yvaunda	Za'querah	Zaheya	Zakai
Yuiko	Yuquaysha	Yvaunna	Za'wa'di	Zahiah	Zakaria
Yujin	Yurany	Yveline	Zaahidah	Zahiara	Zakariah
Yuk	Yurdagul	Yvelinne	Zaakira	Zahida	Zakarrah
Yuka	Yuree	Yvelis	Zaakirah	Zahira	Zakarri
Yukana	Yureli	Yvelisse	Zaara	Zahiran	Zakayla
Yukeba	Yurelit	Yvena	Zabdi	Zahiyah	Zakaylie
Yukeyra	Yurelkis	Yves	Zabrea	Zahjona	Zakea
Yuki	Yuri (0.03)	Yves-Nola	Zabrelle	Zahkaya	Zakedra

Zakeeya	Zalonzia	Zani	Zaraya	Zaviere	Zehidy
Zakeia	Zamaira	Zania	Zarea	Zawadi	Zehra
Zakeiha	Zamani	Zanib	Zareea	Zayanna	Zeida
Zakeira	Zamantha	Zanielle	Zareeka	Zayarie	Zeila
Zakel	Zamara	Zaniisha	Zareen	Zaybreann	Zeimab
Zakeria	Zamari	Zanil	Zareena	Zaybrienne	Zeina *(0.01)*
Zakerra	Zambia	Zaniqua	Zareh	Zayda	Zeinab *(0.03)*
Zakerria	Zambrana	Zanise	Zarela	Zayhill	Zeinah
Zaketa	Zambria	Zanisha	Zarena	Zayla	Zeinel
Zakevya	Zameena	Zanita	Zareya	Zayle	Zeja
Zakeya	Zameeya	Zaniya	Zarhria	Zaylin	Zeke
Zakeycia	Zamella	Zaniyah	Zari *(0.01)*	Zayn	Zekeia
Zakeyia	Zamesha	Zanna	Zaria *(0.02)*	Zayna *(0.02)*	Zekera
Zakeyionia	Zamesse	Zanná	Zariah	Zaynab *(0.01)*	Zekeya
Zakeyyah	Zametria	Zannia	Zariel	Zaynah *(0.01)*	Zekiara
Zakia *(0.01)*	Zamika	Zannie	Zarin	Zayneb	Zekigha
Zakiá	Zamone	Zannon	Zarina	Zayonna	Zekilya
Zakiah	Zamora	Zanobia	Zarinah	Zayra *(0.01)*	Zelda
Zakieh	Zamorria	Zanocia	Zarionne	Zaysha	Zelena
Zakiera	Zamyia	Zanoria	Zarisa	Zayteonia	Zelesa
Zakierra	Zamzam	Zanovia	Zarith	Zayuri	Zeletha
Zakila	Zamzama	Zanqia	Zariya	Zayury	Zelie
Zakira	Zan'tyese	Zanquandria	Zarki'sa	Zéaira	Zelina
Zakirah	Zana *(0.07)*	Zanquayvia	Zarkia	Zékia	Zella
Zakiria	Zana'ya	Zanqueania	Zarmina	Zéleah	Zelma
Zakiriya	Zanae	Zanquesha	Zarna	Zétyia	Zelmira
Zakivya	Zanah	Zanqueshia	Zarnay	Zea	Zelphia
Zakiya *(0.02)*	Zanaida	Zanquisha	Zarnia	Zea'laous	Zelvonia
Zakiyaa	Zanay	Zantelia	Zaroohi	Zeaira	Zemnobia
Zakiyah	Zanazgia	Zanteria	Zaroya	Zeana	Zemoria
Zakiyya	Zanbria	Zanterrikca	Zarquisha	Zeandria	Zemphira
Zakiyyah	Zandalee	Zanthia	Zarria	Zeanese	Zen
Zakkiyya	Zanderland	Zantina	Zarriene	Zeanka	Zena *(0.03)*
Zakkiyyah	Zandesha	Zantonia	Zarrin	Zeanna	Zenab
Zakkyyah	Zandi	Zantrea	Zarsheema	Zeba	Zenabra
Zaklina	Zandilee	Zantrece	Zaryian	Zebedee	Zenadia
Zakoria	Zandle	Zantrice	Zarysa	Zebib	Zenae
Zakya	Zandra *(0.01)*	Zanur	Zasia	Zebnah	Zenah
Zakyia	Zandrea	Zanyah	Zasmane	Zebrena	Zenaida *(0.01)*
Zakylia	Zandreal	Zanyra	Zasmine	Zebrina	Zenani
Zakyra	Zandria *(0.01)*	Zaporia	Zatae	Zechariah	Zenarra
Zalayca	Zandy	Zaporria	Zatalya	Zecharian	Zenatra
Zaleese	Zane	Zaqoya	Zatara	Zecil	Zenaya
Zalei	Zané	Zaquarya	Zatariana	Zed	Zenayda
Zaleigh	Zaneb	Zaquetta	Zataya	Zeda	Zenda
Zaleisha	Zanebia	Zaquiante	Zates'e	Zedekiah	Zenea
Zaleká	Zanée	Zar	Zatonya	Zee	Zenetta
Zalessia	Zaneh	Zara *(0.02)*	Zatwhyia	Zeelena	Zenettie
Zalexxa	Zaneil	Zarabel	Zaunah	Zeena	Zenia *(0.02)*
Zalia	Zaneisha	Zarah *(0.01)*	Zavanna	Zeenat	Zeniqua
Zalicia	Zaneka	Zarahanne	Zavdi El	Zeenathul	Zenisha
Zalie	Zanele	Zarahi	Zavenda	Zeesy	Zenissa
Zalika	Zanesha	Zarai	Zavia	Zeeyaan	Zenita
Zalina	Zaneta	Zaralexus	Zaviana	Zeeyawnah	Zenna
Zalisha	Zanetta	Zaray	Zavien	Zefferine	Zennah

Zennia	Zhaliah	Zhi'keila	Zindziswa	Zoelle	Zotanique
Zenny	Zhalyn	Zhiakeba	Zinéshea	Zoeminique	Zoua
Zenobia *(0.01)*	Zhan'e	Zhidajha	Zineshia	Zoeniche	Zouie
Zenobie	Zhan'ea	Zhionyelle	Zinet	Zoerina	Zovig
Zenobria	Zhana *(0.01)*	Zhjlexxus	Zinia	Zoey *(0.08)*	Zowe
Zenora	Zhanae	Zhnarya	Zining	Zofia *(0.01)*	Zowey
Zenova	Zhanaé	Zhoma	Zinna	Zografia	Zowie
Zenovia	Zhanaria	Zhonae	Zinneatra	Zoha	Zoya *(0.01)*
Zensha	Zhanay	Zhonice	Zinnia *(0.01)*	Zohal	Zoya-Aleah
Zentilya	Zhanaya	Zhy'ana	Zinthya	Zohaniya	Zoye
Zeny	Zhane *(0.08)*	Zhyra	Ziomaira	Zohr	Zoyi
Zenya	Zhané *(0.03)*	Zhyzel	Ziomari	Zohra	Zqurrai
Zephanie	Zhanea	Zi	Ziomaris	Zoi	Zranda Moriena
Zepher	Zhanee	Zi Era	Zion	Zoia	Zrinka
Zephinah	Zhaneisha	Zi'mara	Ziporah	Zoida	Zsa Necia
Zephra	Zhanel	Zi-Wei	Zippora	Zoie *(0.03)*	Zsa'da
Zephria	Zhanell	Zia *(0.01)*	Zipporah *(0.01)*	Zoie-Anne	Zsa-Zsarea
Zepporah	Zhanelle	Zian	Zipporia	Zoie-Breanna	Zsahné
Zequayá	Zhanesha	Ziana	Zipporoh	Zoikee	Zsakeria
Zequoya	Zhanessa	Zianb	Ziquetta	Zoila *(0.02)*	Zsakira
Zera Kyla	Zhaney	Zianna	Ziquitria	Zoilan	Zsanae
Zerah	Zhani	Zianne	Zirree	Zoili	Zsanelle
Zeraphina	Zhaniah	Ziara	Zirrena	Zoilita	Zsanielle
Zeriah	Zhanice	Ziare	Zissel	Zokara	Zsanique
Zerika	Zhaniece	Zibiah	Zita	Zola	Zsazmyn
Zerlisa	Zhaniqua	Zibonai	Ziterria	Zoleiry	Zsintaya
Zerricka	Zhanique	Zica-Varie	Zitlalic	Zolene	Zsofia
Zerwanika	Zhanise	Zicara	Zitlaly	Zolexi	Zsuzsanna
Zeskia	Zhanna	Zicheria	Ziumara	Zollisca	Zubrina
Zeta	Zhannée	Zieaira	Ziva	Zomora	Zucaru
Zetseat	Zhanneta	Zieneb	Zj Nette	Zon	Zugey
Zettanya	Zhanquanice	Zierra	Zjaih	Zona	Zuhdieh
Zeva	Zhantiya	Ziimeria	Zjani	Zondranika	Zuheily
Zevenia	Zhaqueira	Zikella	Zjardae	Zondria	Zuhra
Zeyla	Zhaquondalée	Ziketra	Zjhaydriea	Zonesian	Zulaini
Zeynab	Zhara	Zikiya	Zlaine	Zonia	Zulay
Zeynep	Zharenee	Zilandra	Zlaire	Zontravia	Zuleica
Zeyri	Zhari	Zilane	Znastasha	Zoo	Zuleidys
Zh'ane	Zharia	Zilla	Zoa	Zooey	Zuleika
Zha'nera	Zharnée	Zillah	Zoal	Zoolaka	Zuleima *(0.03)*
Zha'quasha	Zhatara	Zilphia	Zobia	Zophyah	Zulema *(0.03)*
Zhadaa	Zhate	Zima	Zochil	Zora	Zuleyca
Zhade	Zhatora	Zimani	Zoe *(0.82)*	Zoraida	Zuleyka
Zhaedria	Zhaukiah	Zimaria	Zoe Isabela	Zorana	Zuleyma *(0.02)*
Zhakaysha	Zhaune	Zimika	Zoe Virginia	Zorea	Zulia
Zhakeeria	Zhavia	Zimikia	Zoé	Zoretta	Zulianna
Zhakeria	Zhay	Zimri	Zoé'	Zori	Zulika
Zhakia	Zhayna	Zina *(0.01)*	Zoéria	Zorian	Zulima
Zhakiaya	Zhaytria	Zinab	Zoe-Alanah	Zoriana	Zulimar
Zhakila	Zhenel	Zinah	Zoe-Nicole	Zorra	Zulissa
Zhakirah	Zhenia	Zinahedia	Zoee	Zorria	Zullay
Zhalee	Zhenna	Zinaie	Zoeella	Zorrieal	Zully
Zhaleesa	Zhequita	Zinat	Zoei	Zorrina	Zullymar
Zhaleh	Zhi Naki	Zinaya	Zoel	Zorylis	Zulma *(0.01)*
Zhaleigha	Zhi Xiang	Zindzi	Zoella	Zosia	Zulmarie

Zulu	Zurisadai	Zy'kea	Zyi Kecra	Zylkia	Zyquona
Zuly	Zurisaddai	Zy'kerea	Zykarah	Zymeisha	Zyra
Zumara	Zury	Zyaille	Zykeetria	Zynder	Zyrae
Zunara	Zuryzaday	Zyaira	Zykera	Zyneathia	Zyrah
Zuny	Zutaevia	Zyaire	Zykeria	Zyneshia	Zyreasha
Zurelys	Zuwena	Zyanya	Zykerria	Zynia	Zyricca
Zureya	Zuzanna	Zybiah	Zykeya	Zynisha	Zyriel
Zureyma	Zuzel	Zycheria	Zykia	Zyniya	Zyrina
Zuri *(0.02)*	Zuzu	Zyeasha	Zykiare	Zyporya	Zytlaly
Zurianna	Zvany	Zyeleika	Zykima	Zyquaria	
Zurie	Zvleykha	Zyeria	Zykira	Zyquenthia	

🅰️ Boys Names

-A-

A *(0.05)*
A B
A Darian
A Darien
A Dolphus
A Donta
A J
A Keen
A Shauntey
A'basa
A'darius
A'darrion
A'darrius
A'daunte
A'derise
A'dez
A'dré
A'driene
A'jee
A'jen
A'keem
A'kei
A'lamar
A'lique
A'martinez
A'moris
A'ngel
A'quane
A'quil
A'ron
A'sante
A'shad
A'shanté
A'shon

A'sim
A'sjon
A'taraus
A'vante
A'vion
A'vondré
A'vonté
A'zhae
A-Chai'a Harim
A-Jaun
A-Men
A. *(0.01)*
A. J.
A. Michael
A.J.
Aaaron
Aabid
Aadam
Aaden
Aadesh
Aadil
Aadyn
Aahlijah
Aahron
Aaidan
Aakash *(0.02)*
Aakeem
Aakif
Aalan
Aalim
Aalin
Aaliyah
Aalok
Aamahd
Aamer
Aamir *(0.01)*

Aamir
   Mohammad
Aanand
Aansu
Aanthony
Aaran *(0.01)*
Aaranvir
Aaraon
Aarav
Aaren
Aareon
Aaric
Aarick
Aarik
Aarin
Aarion *(0.01)*
Aaroh
Aaron *(6.11)*
Aaron Dale
Aaron Devon
Aaron Emanu
Aaron Frederick
Aaron Jeffrey
Aaron Joachim
Aaron Joseph
Aaron Jr
Aaron Lee
Aaron Lesney
Aaron Patrick
Aaron Paul
Aaron Timothy
Aaron Willi
Aaron-Cecil
Aaron-James
Aaron-Kyle
Aaron-Lee

Aaron-Lynton
Aaron-Matthew
Aaron-Pio
Aaron-Rey
Aarondip
Aaronjames *(0.01)*
Aaronjeet
Aaronn
Aaronraj
Aaronton
Aarow
Aarren
Aarreon
Aarron *(0.02)*
Aarum
Aarun
Aarush
Aaryk
Aaryn *(0.01)*
Aaryon
Aash
Aasheed
Aashish
Aasim
Aasin
Aaustin
Aavan
Aaver
Aavry
Ab
Aba'si
Ababiya
Abad
Abanob
Abanoub
Abasi

Abass
Abayomi
Abayouni
Abbaas
Abbas *(0.01)*
Abber
Abbey
Abbie
Abbigail
Abbishan
Abbott
Abbran
Abby
Abd
Abd Allah
Abd-Al-Wahab
Abdal-Hakim
Abdalaziz
Abdalbast
Abdalla
Abdallah
Abdeem
Abdel
Abdel-Jaffar
Abdel-Kader
Abdel-Karim
Abdel-Majid
Abdel-Malik
Abdel-Rahman
Abdelhamed
Abdelilah
Abdeljami
Abdelmajed
Abdelmajid
Abdelrahim
Abdelrahman

Abdelraouf
Abdelrazak
Abdelrhman
Abdelsalam
Abderrahmane
Abdi *(0.01)*
Abdi-Aziz
Abdiahman
Abdias
Abdiasis
Abdiel *(0.01)*
Abdifatah
Abdifatam
Abdihakim
Abdihamid
Abdikabir
Abdikarem
Abdikarim
Abdikhalaq
Abdil
Abdilafatah
Abdilkhaliq
Abdimagid
Abdinasir
Abdirahin
Abdirahman
   (0.02)
Abdirashid
Abdirauf
Abdirehman
Abdirezak
Abdirisaq
Abdirizak
Abdisalam
Abdishakur
Abdiwahab

Abdo	Abdull	Abhijit	Abrahaim	Achal	Adarin
Abdon	Abdulla	Abhijot	Abraham *(0.51)*	Achilleas	Adarion
Abdou	Abdullah *(0.05)*	Abhinav *(0.01)*	Abrahame	Achilles	Adarius *(0.01)*
Mohammed	Abdullahi *(0.01)*	Abhinay	Abrahan *(0.02)*	Achim	Adarrius
Abdoulay	Abdullahi-Amir	Abhir	Abraheem	Achish	Adarro
Abdoulaye	Abdullatif	Abhiram	Abrahem	Achitoi	Adarruis
Abdouli	Abdullaziz	Abhishek *(0.01)*	Abrahim	Achyut	Adarryl
Abdoulie	Abdullha	Abhjit	Abrahm	Acie	Adarsh
Abdriel	Abdulmajeed	Abi Turab	Abraian	Ackeal	Adarsh Kumar
Abdu	Abdulmalik *(0.01)*	Abiah	Abraim	Acob	Adarsha
Abdu-Raheem	Abdulmunim	Abid	Abram *(0.07)*	Acquilla	Adarshjit
Abduala	Abdulnaser	Abidan	Abram John	Acquindas	Adaruis
Abduallah	Abdulqadir	Abideen	Abran *(0.01)*	Acqwon	Adaryll
Abdul *(0.05)*	Abdulquadir	Abie	Abrar	Acree	Adauris
Abdul Aziz	Abdulrahman	Abiel	Abraxa	Acrey	Adaven Joseph
Abdul Basith	*(0.01)*	Abijah	Abree	Actavious	Adavian
Abdul Hadi	Abdulrasul	Abilaashan	Abreion	Acue	Adayrl
Abdul Karee	Abdulrazak	Abilash	Abren	Ad	Adazio
Abdul Khader	Abdulwahab	Abile	Abreon	Ad'e	Addae
Abdul Mutinih	Abdur	Abillash	Abrham	Ada	Addam *(0.02)*
Abdul Wahab	Abdur-Rahman	Abima Amimael	Abrian	Adaero	Addarren
Abdul-Aziz	Abdur-Rasheed	Abimael *(0.01)*	Abrie	Adair	Addarryll
Abdul-Baasith	Abdurahman	Abin	Abriel	Adal	Addeil
Abdul-Bari	Abdurraahman	Abinaa	Abrien	Adalberto *(0.04)*	Adden
Abdul-Ghani	Abdurrahman	Abinanth	Abril	Adale	Adderly
Abdul-Hakeem	Abdus-Samad	Abiodun	Abrium	Adalexander	Addie
Abdul-Haqq	Abdyrrahim	Abir	Abrun	Adalles	Addiel
Abdul-Hayu	Abe *(0.01)*	Abiram	Absalaam	Adalverto	Addil
Abdul-Jabar	Abed	Abiran	Absalon	Adam *(5.19)*	Addim
Abdul-Jamal	Abed Al Fattah	Abisael	Abselon	Adam Austin	Addis
Abdul-Kareem	Abed Elrazik	Abisai	Abshar	Adam Bradley	Addisen
Abdul-Khaaliq	Abed-Alhamed	Abisay	Abshir	Adam Ellis Mcilm	Addison *(0.15)*
Abdul-Khalid	Abed-Allah	Abisayo	Absolum	Adam Ezekiel	Addissiaan
Abdul-Malik	Abedel Kare	Abishaiah	Absulwahab	Adam Franklin	Addisun
Abdul-Qadir	Abednego	Abishek	Abtin	Adam Rene	Addonios
Abdul-Rahmaan	Abedrauof	Abishua	Abu	Adam West	Addonis
Abdul-Rahman	Abeenesh	Abisshek	Abubakar	Adam-Alexandr	Addres
Abdul-Rawoof	Abeid	Abiyé	Abubaker	Adam-Ali	Addyson
Abdul-Wa	Abejide	Abjeet	Abubakr	Adam-Joseph	Ade
Abdulahad	Abel *(0.26)*	Ablakely	Abubeker	Adam-Masud	Adéasim
Abdulahi	Abela	Able	Abul	Adama	Adeal
Abdulalrhman	Abelardo *(0.03)*	Abmir	Abyamoi	Adamadios	Adebayo
Abdulazim	Abelino	Abner *(0.02)*	Acari	Adamm	Adebowale
Abdulaziz	Abelito	Aboinasir	Acasio	Adamma	Adedamola
Abdule	Aben	Abokor	Accari	Adamo	Adedapo
Abdulfatah	Abenayan	Abon	Ace *(0.02)*	Adamos	Adedayo
Abdulha	Abener	Aboubacar	Acea	Adams	Adedeji
Abdulhadi	Abenet	Aboubakar	Acee	Adamson	Adedesi
Abdulhakim	Abernathy	Aboubaker	Acelin	Adan *(0.17)*	Adedoyin
Abdulhamid	Abeselom	Aboul	Acemark	Adanan	Adeeb
Abduljabbar	Abey	Aboulla	Acen	Adanel	Adeel *(0.01)*
Abdulkadir	Abhay	Aboullah	Acevado	Adante	Adeem
Abdulkareem	Abhi	Aboullahi	Acey	Adanté	Adefemi
Abdulkarem	Abhideep	Aboyonis	Achaebe	Adareus	Adegboyega
Abdulkariem	Abhijeet	Abraan	Achaias	Adarias	Adehkeem

Adekoyejo	Adny	Adrianne	Afeez	Aharonn	Ahren
Adel *(0.01)*	Ado	Adrianno	Afefi	Ahasuerus	Ahriya
Adelabu	Adock	Adrianno-Ocean	Affan	Ahed	Ahron
Adelaido	Adolf	Adriano *(0.02)*	Affrat	Aheem	Ahsaan
Adelbert	Adolfo *(0.14)*	Adriantaé	Afi	Ahilan	Ahsaas
Adelfino	Adolis	Adric	Afif	Ahir	Ahsaiya
Adelfo	Adolph	Adrick	Afnan	Ahisar	Ahsan
Adeliado	Adolpho	Adriean	Afolabi	Ahjae	Ahsen
Adell	Adolphus *(0.01)*	Adriel *(0.04)*	Afolayan	Ahjanee	Ahshawn
Adem	Adom	Adriel Justyn	Afrah	Ahjuan	Ahson
Ademar	Adon	Adrien *(0.06)*	Afrik	Ahkeal	Ahsten
Aden *(0.02)*	Adonai	Adriene	Afroze	Ahkeel	Ahsun
Adeniran	Adonas	Adrienne	Afsar	Ahkeem *(0.01)*	Ahvier
Adenis	Adonay	Adrihnclay	Afshin	Ahkeen	Ahzerik
Adeqla	Adones	Adrin	Afton	Ahkeim	Ai
Aderemi	Adoni	Adrina	Afzal	Ahkien	Ai'keem
Aderius	Adonia	Adrion	Agalyan	Ahkit	Aian
Adero	Adoniace	Adrionn	Agamemnon	Ahlian	Aidan *(0.43)*
Aderola	Adonias	Adrionne	Agapito	Ahlohn	Aidan-Gregory
Adesegun	Adonijah	Adrisha	Agartuu	Ahmaad	Aiden *(0.08)*
Adessio	Adonis *(0.06)*	Adron	Agaru	Ahmad *(0.18)*	Aidin
Adetokunboh	Adonisce	Adryan	Agassi	Ahmad Myles	Aidon
Adewale	Adonnia	Adryn	Agatino	Ahmad Tillman	Aidyn
Adewumi	Adonnis	Adul	Agenord	Ahmad-Adam	Aikeem
Adeyami	Adonous	Adulah	Agerico	Ahmad-Hussien	Aiken
Adeyemi	Adontay	Adwin	Agharius	Ahmad-Reza	Aiki
Adeyinka	Adonte	Adyson	Agim	Ahmad-Roy	Aiklen
Adham	Adontis	Aedan	Agis	Ahmadd	Ailama
Adhante	Adonus	Aeden	Agit	Ahmadfahim	Ailex
Adharsh	Adony	Aedion	Agiyl	Ahmadré	Ailey
Adi	Adonys	Aemone	Agnus	Ahmadreza	Ailton
Adian	Adoré	Aene As	Agon	Ahmadshah	Aimal
Adib	Adrain	Aeneas	Agostino	Ahmadzia	Aiman
Adiel	Adrainyon	Aengus	Agrene	Ahmam	Aimen
Adil *(0.02)*	Adre Yon	Aennifer	Agron	Ahmani	Aimir
Adilio	Adréveon	Aenri	Aguan	Ahmao	Aimun
Adin	Adrean	Aeon	Aguinaldo	Ahmar	Ainharan
Adio	Adreinne	Aeran	Agunwa	Ahmari	Ainsley
Adirian	Adrekis	Aereon	Agustin *(0.14)*	Ahmati	Ainslie
Adisak	Adrel	Aerian	Agustine *(0.01)*	Ahmauree	Ainsloey
Adisen	Adrell	Aeric	Agustis	Ahmaury	Ainsworth
Adisha	Adren	Aerick	Agusto	Ahmed *(0.16)*	Air'rion
Adison *(0.01)*	Adres	Aerion	Agustus	Ahmed-Nur	Airamis
Adisson	Adrey	Aeris	Agustust	Ahmed-Tayyib	Airees
Adithya	Adria	Aero	Ah	Ahmedrae	Aireon
Aditya *(0.01)*	Adriaan	Aeron	Ah'jhzae Diamon	Ahmer	Aires
Adjetey	Adrian *(1.83)*	Aerro	Ah'keem	Ahmet	Aireus
Adjua	Adrian Gilberto	Aerron	Ah-Heem	Ahmir	Airick
Adlai	Adrian James	Aeryk	Ahad	Ahmod	Airies
Adler	Adrian Luke	Aesha	Ahamad	Ahmodjatai	Airin
Adley	Adrian Winston	Aetagan	Ahamad-Shakil	Ahmon	Airion
Adly	Adriana	Aethne	Ahamed	Ahnaf	Airius
Admir	Adriancarl	Afamefune	Ahamefula	Ahnann	Airon
Adnan *(0.03)*	Adriane	Afanasy	Ahand	Ahned	Airran
Adni	Adriann	Afdhal	Aharon *(0.01)*	Aholiab	Airri

Airrick	Ajirioghene	Akhilesh	Akot	Alaan	Alayn
Airrion	Ajit	Akhtar	Akota	Alac	Alazae
Airrishaun	Ajith	Aki	Akram *(0.01)*	Alack	Alazai
Airvae	Ajiththan	Akia	Akrem	Aladdin	Alazar
Airyc	Ajitpal	Akiah	Akren	Aladean	Alazion
Airyn	Ajlal	Akian	Akrin	Aladin	Alba
Aisan	Ajmaal	Akiarah	Akrom	Alafanso	Alban
Aisea	Ajmain	Akicita	Aksel	Alah	Albanie
Aish	Ajmal	Akie	Aksell	Alahji	Albano
Aislinn	Ajmer	Akiel	Akshaj	Alahn	Albar
Aissa	Ajuanito	Akiem	Akshar	Alain *(0.05)*	Albara
Aithan	Ajule	Akieva	Akshay *(0.03)*	Alain-Phillipe	Albaro *(0.01)*
Aiub	Ajuthan	Akif	Akshaya	Alajah	Albee
Aivings	Ajvinder	Akiff	Akshayan	Alajauah	Albeit
Aiyden	Ajyeman	Akifumi	Akshdeep	Alajawon	Alben
Aizaz	Akaal	Akihiko	Akshveer	Alajuwan	Alber
Aj *(0.01)*	Akaash	Akihiro	Akuamoah	Alajuwon	Alberdo
Aj Alan	Akail	Akiim	Akul	Alak	Alberendi
Aja	Akaiyan	Akikuni	Akumpal	Alam	Alberiano
Aja Blue	Akanni	Akil *(0.03)*	Akwaee	Alamgir	Albert *(0.60)*
Ajabu	Akarshan	Akila	Akwasi	Alamjyot	Albert Cameron
Ajae	Akash *(0.04)*	Akilah	Akwiraron	Alampartap	Albert Lee
Ajai	Akashdeep	Akile	Akxel	Alan *(1.02)*	Alberta
Ajala-Ernest	Akashdip	Akili *(0.01)*	Akyis	Alan-Jack	Albertini
Ajalain	Akasho	Akilian	Akyl	Alan-Michael	Alberto *(0.63)*
Ajalon	Akashvir	Akilies	Al *(0.03)*	Alande	Alberto Enrique
Ajami	Akatzin	Akim	Al Barak	Alandis	Albi
Ajan	Akba Asad	Akimas	Al Elijah	Alando	Albie
Ajani	Akbar *(0.01)*	Akimby	Al Malik	Alandre	Albino
Ajanth	Akeakamai	Akimeyon	Al Shun	Alandus	Alburn
Ajap	Akeal	Akimma	Al'donté	Alang	Albury
Ajaveun	Akean	Akin	Al'juwon	Alann	Alby
Ajax	Akease	Akin-Kamal	Al'kwazi	Alanson	Alce
Ajay *(0.04)*	Akeaz	Akinfemi	Al'malik	Alantae	Alcedia
Ajaybir	Akee	Akinkawon	Al'quaves	Alante *(0.01)*	Alcide
Ajaye	Akeedein	Akinloye	Al'twon	Alanté	Alcido
Ajayi	Akeel	Akinniran	Al-Ameen	Alanzo	Alcimy
Ajaymeet	Akeele-Fabian	Akinola	Al-Anthony	Alaor	Alcindor
Ajaypal	Akeem *(0.07)*	Akintayo	Al-Faisal	Alari	Aldahir
Ajayveer	Akeen	Akintomide	Al-Hasan	Alaric *(0.01)*	Aldair *(0.02)*
Ajayvir	Akeer	Akinyemi	Al-Hassan	Alarick	Aldaith
Ajé	Akeeva	Akio	Al-Hussein	Alarik	Aldale
Ajéjuan	Akeil	Akir'en	Al-Kheem	Alasdair	Aldan
Ajee	Akeilus	Akira *(0.01)*	Al-Penyo	Alastair *(0.01)*	Aldarius
Ajeej	Akembo	Akisch	Al-Qasim	Alaster	Aldayr
Ajeet	Akenson	Akito	Al-Rahim	Alatier	Aldean
Ajeev	Akera	Akiva *(0.01)*	Al-Tadarius	Alatin	Alden *(0.05)*
Ajene	Akerei	Akiva Tzvi	Al-Tavon	Alaungta	Alder
Ajenthan	Akereous	Akkad	Al-Terik	Alaunta	Aldevonte
Ajepan	Akeriyhn	Akkilise	Al-Teryke	Alawi	Aldin
Ajeshajuan	Akeru	Akmal	Al-Wakeel	Alawnzo	Aldin-James
Ajethan	Akheem	Akmed	Ala	Alax	Aldius
Ajevan	Akhenaten	Ako	Aláa	Alaxandar	Aldo *(0.08)*
Ajibola	Akhenaton	Akono	Alaa *(0.01)*	Alaxander	Aldo Paul
Ajinkya	Akhil *(0.01)*	Akosa	Alaaddine	Alaxandir	Aldon

Aldonte	Aleksandor	Alexander-	Alexzandr	Alice	Alixzander
Aldre	Aleksandr *(0.02)*	William	Alexzandyr	Alicia	Alize
Aldreaon	Aleksas	Alexanderic	Alexzay	Alicio	Alizé
Aldred	Aleksei	Alexandor	Aleyeh	Alick	Aljahmond
Aldrek	Aleksey	Alexandr *(0.01)*	Alezzandro	Alidanish	Aljahnon
Aldren	Aleksi	Alexandra *(0.01)*	Alf	Alidjah	Aljakwan
Aldrian	Aleksis	Alexandre *(1.34)*	Alfargo	Alie	Aljandro
Aldric	Alekxander	Alexandré	Alfaz	Aliek	Aljen
Aldrich	Alekxzander	Alexandre-Low	Alffredi	Alieu	Aljhemon
Aldrick	Alekzander *(0.01)*	Alexandrew	Alfie	Alif	Aljohn
Aldrickus	Alekzandr	Alexandria	Alfonce	Aligah	Aljohnel
Aldrid	Alelxander	Alexandrio	Alfonso *(0.25)*	Aligiery	Aljone
Aldrik	Alem	Alexandro *(0.08)*	Alfontain	Aligul	Aljouh
Aldrin *(0.01)*	Alema	Alexandros *(0.01)*	Alfonte	Alija	Aljour
Aldron	Alen *(0.01)*	Alexandru	Alfonté	Alijah *(0.01)*	Aljovan
Aldus	Alend	Alexaner	Alfonza	Alijajuan	Aljun
Aldwin	Aleni	Alexanore	Alfonzo *(0.02)*	Alijha	Alkan
Ale	Aleph	Alexanre	Alfonzon	Alijhiah	Alkean
Alec *(1.38)*	Ales	Alexanthony	Alford	Alijuan	Alkebu
Alecander	Alesandre	Alexas	Alfra	Alijuwon	Alkebu-Lan
Alecc	Alesandro	Alexe	Alfred *(0.20)*	Alijzah	Alkeem
Aleck *(0.01)*	Alesandros	Alexé	Alfrederick	Alik	Alkeen
Alecs	Alesk	Alexee	Alfredo *(0.50)*	Alika	Alkendrick
Alecsai	Alessandre	Alexeev	Alfredrick	Aliko	Alkesh
Alecsander	Alessandro *(0.08)*	Alexei *(0.01)*	Alga	Aliksa	Alkimiss
Alecxis	Alesseo	Alexendar	Algee	Aliksander	Alkis
Alecxiss	Alessio	Alexendre *(0.01)*	Algen	Alikzander	Alladin
Aleczander *(0.01)*	Alethea	Alexes	Alger	Alim *(0.01)*	Allah
Aleczandr	Alex *(3.50)*	Alexey	Algeria	Alimahdi	Allaheem
Alee	Alex Michael	Alexhander	Algernon	Alimohammad	Allahjah
Aleeda	Alex Zachary	Alexi *(0.03)*	Algeron	Alims	Allai-Al-Dein
Aleem *(0.01)*	Alex'andre	Alexiaus	Algia	Alin	Allal
Alegamdro	Alex-Andrew	Alexie	Algin	Alindrea	Allan *(0.30)*
Alegandro	Alex-Hoy-Yum	Alexio	Alha	Aliou	Allan Joseph
Aleice	Alex-John	Alexious	Alhaji	Alioune	Allan Jr
Aleika	Alex-Joseph	Alexis *(0.79)*	Alhassan	Alipeti	Allan'te
Aleister	Alex-Michael	Alexisia	Alhona	Aliraza	Allan-Michael
Aleix	Alexa	Alexiz	Alhondo	Alireza	Allan-Micheal
Alejandio	Alexabder	Alexjá	Ali *(0.30)*	Alisack	Allan-Peter
Alejandra	Alexai	Alexlander	Ali Akbar	Alisandro	Allanc
Alejandre	Alexanda	Alexnader	Ali Alex	Alisdair	Allanray
Alejandro *(1.81)*	Alexandaer	Alexogiender	Ali Mohamad	Alisha	Allanson
Alejanoro	Alexandar *(0.01)*	Alexon	Ali Shan	Alishah	Allanta
Alejndre	Alexandder	Alexphuoc	Ali'ikai	Alishan	Allante *(0.01)*
Alejo	Alexandee	Alexsander *(0.01)*	Ali-Akbar	Alishia	Allante Montrell
Alejondro	Alexandeer	Alexsandre	Ali-Millad	Alison	Allanté *(0.01)*
Alejos	Alexander *(9.92)*	Alexsandro	Ali-Rasheed	Alissa	Allazuwon
Alejrando	Alexander H	Alexsis	Aliadon	Alistair *(0.02)*	Allden
Alek *(0.05)*	Alexander Joe	Alexsus	Aliak	Alistar	Alldonn
Alek'j	Alexander	Alexus	Aliano	Alister	Allec
Alekh	Thomas	Alexus Dion	Alias	Alivn	Alleem
Aleks	Alexander-	Alexx	Alias-Dakota	Alix *(0.01)*	Alleister
Aleksa	Michael	Alexxis-Esdras	Aliazar	Alixander *(0.01)*	Allejandro
Aleksandar *(0.02)*	Alexander-Ray	Alexy *(0.01)*	Alibasha	Alixandre	Allen *(0.67)*
Aleksander *(0.02)*	Alexander-Thoma	Alexzander *(0.03)*	Alic *(0.01)*	Alixandru	Allen Hao

Allen Jeffery	Alonso-Ramon	Altaveious	Alwin	Amanuallah	Amear
Allen Ray	Alontae	Altavious	Alwxander	Amanuel	Amechi'
Allen-Michael	Alontaé	Altavius	Alx	Amanullah	Amed
Allenson	Alontay	Altawn	Alxander	Amanveer	Amedee
Allesandro	Alonte	Altay	Aly	Amanvir	Amedeo
Allex	Alonté	Altaz	Aly-Khan	Amanze	Amee
Allexander	Alontez	Altereque	Alyas	Amar *(0.03)*	Ameed
Allezzandro	Alontia	Alteric	Alycya	Amaran	Ameen *(0.01)*
Alli	Alontre	Alterik	Alyer	Amarandeep	Ameer *(0.03)*
Allic	Alonza *(0.01)*	Altez	Alyjha	Amarcus	Ameet
Allie	Alonzo *(0.18)*	Althavia	Alykhan *(0.01)*	Amardeep	Ameetpaul
Allijerus	Alouso	Althoney	Alyndrick	Amardo	Ameil
Allin	Aloycius	Althony	Alys	Amare	Ameir
Allingham	Aloyis	Altidor	Alysha-Lynn	Amaree	Ameko
Allinson	Aloysius	Altigo	Alyssa	Amareet	Amel
Allis	Alp	Altin	Alyx	Amaren	Amelia
Allison	Alpacino	Altman	Alzaad	Amari *(0.02)*	Amelio
Allison-Reynold	Alpatrick	Alton *(0.07)*	Alzavin	Amaris	Amellio
Allistair	Alper	Altonio	Amaad	Amaritpal	Amen
Allistar	Alpesh	Altonye	Amaan	Amarjat	Amen-Re
Allister *(0.01)*	Alpha	Altorio	Amaar	Amarjeet	Amenaghawon
Allix	Alphaeus	Altovise	Amaceo	Amarjit	Amend
Allonte	Alphanso	Altraruis	Amad	Amarjot	Amer *(0.01)*
Allonté	Alphe-Gregory	Altravious	Amadeo	Amaro	Amer Uddin
Allott	Alphee	Altreveon	Amadeu	Amarpal	Amerdeep
Allreza	Alphonse *(0.01)*	Altron	Amadeus	Amarpreet	Amere
Allson	Alphonso *(0.03)*	Altteriek	Amadeusz	Amarprit	Americo
Allston	Alphonsus	Altwain	Amadi	Amarran	Americus
Allton	Alphonza	Alula	Amadian	Amarri	Amerigo
Allvince	Alphonzo	Alun	Amado *(0.01)*	Amarrion	Amerjoet
Ally	Alpichon	Alundre	Amador *(0.02)*	Amarveer	Amerson
Allyn	Alprentice	Alunta	Amahd	Amarvir	Amerus
Allynn	Alquavious	Aluntae	Amahdi	Amassa	Amet
Alma	Alquawn	Alunté	Amahdre	Amati	Ametrice
Almahdy	Alrayaan	Alunzo	Amahni	Amatto	Ameya
Almamy	Alrick	Alva	Amal	Amatya	Amezy
Almando	Alrik	Alvado	Amalin	Amaurd	Amfenee
Almani	Alrvon	Alvah	Aman *(0.03)*	Amauri	Amgad
Almarius	Alryk	Alvan	Amancio	Amaury	Amhad
Almeida	Alshamque	Alvante	Amanda *(0.01)*	Amaziahi	Amiel
Almetric	Alshinard	Alvanté	Amandeep *(0.02)*	Ambassador	Amier
Almir	Alshon	Alvara	Amando	Amber *(0.01)*	Amiin
Almis	Alson	Alvarez	Amanee	Ambers	Amiir
Almon	Alsone	Alvaro *(0.17)*	Amanel	Ambi	Amil
Almond	Alstair	Alvee	Amani *(0.01)*	Ambriz	Amilcar *(0.01)*
Almondo	Alston *(0.03)*	Alveno	Amanindervir	Ambrocio	Amili
Almus	Alstun	Alvin *(0.25)*	Amanj	Ambrose *(0.01)*	Amilio
Alnesh	Altaf	Alvin Éshaun	Amanjeet	Ambrosio	Amilkar
Alofa	Altaine	Alvino *(0.01)*	Amanjot	Ambrue	Amin *(0.02)*
Alois	Altair	Alvis *(0.01)*	Amanpreet *(0.01)*	Ambryone	Aminadab
Alok	Altamash	Alvonest	Amanprit	Ambswill	Amine *(0.01)*
Alon	Altamont	Alvonta	Amansio	Ambus	Amious
Alonate	Altan	Alvonte	Amante	Amde-Michael	Amir *(0.12)*
Alondra	Altaquan	Alvonté	Amanté	Amdi	Amir-Drakkar
Alonso *(0.08)*	Altario	Alwalie	Amantre	Ame	Amir-Ehsan

Amir-Hesam	Amoral	Ananth	Andraes	Andrew Larry	Anesh
Amir-Qua	Amorce	Ananthan	Andrake	Andrew Marco	Anestis
Amiraj	Amory	Anantvir	Andranik	Andrew Maurice	Aneudy
Amirdon	Amos *(0.05)*	Anari	Andras	Andrew Miguel	Aneudys
Amire	Amose	Anas *(0.02)*	Andravious	Andrew-Blake	Anexcis
Amiri	Amoses	Anasinti Iheonu	Andray	Andrew-	Aney
Amirius	Amparo	Anass	Andre *(0.90)*	Christopher	Anfernee *(0.06)*
Amirmahdi	Ampateishan	Anastacio	Andre Gille	Andrew-Delvin	Anferney
Amirsan	Amr *(0.01)*	Anastacios	Andre Keith	Andrew-Jason	Anfernie
Amirul	Amraj	Anastas	Andre Xavier	Andrew-Jerrid	Anferny
Amish	Amram	Anastasio	André *(0.09)*	Andrew-John	Anfim
Amit *(0.04)*	Amrathal	Anastasios *(0.01)*	Andréas	Andrew-Joseph	Anfranee
Amitabha	Amre	Anastasios	Andrés	Andrew-Kenneth	Anfrene
Amitej	Amrest	Tommy	Andréus	Andrew-Peter	Anfrenee
Amith	Amrik	Anathony	Andréz	Andrews	Angad
Amitjot	Amrinder	Anatol	Andre-Anthony	Andrey *(0.02)*	Angadpal
Amitoj	Amrinderpal	Anatole	Andre-Philippe	Andrey'	Ange
Amitosh	Amrinjeet	Anatoley	Andrea *(0.02)*	Andrez *(0.01)*	Angel *(1.66)*
Amitpal	Amrit *(0.03)*	Anatoli	Andreá	Andrian *(0.01)*	Angel Xavier
Amitpaul	Amritpal *(0.01)*	Anatoliy	Andrean	Andriane	Angela
Amjad	Amritpartap	Anaxis	Andreani	Andrice	Angeldavid
Amjed	Amritpaul	Ancel	Andreas *(0.08)*	Andrick	Angeldejesus
Ammad	Amritveer	Ancil	Andreavious	Andrico	Angeleo
Ammahd	Amritvir	Andargatchew	Andreaz	Andricus	Angelieco
Amman	Amro	Andarious	Andredi	Andriel	Angelina
Ammanuel	Amrue	Andarius	Andredus	Andrieu	Angeline
Ammar *(0.01)*	Amsey	Andarrio	Andree	Andriguez	Angelino
Ammer	Amsony	Anddy	Andrée	Andrij	Angelito
Ammon *(0.03)*	Amund	Andel	Andrees	Andrija	Angell
Amndeep	Amuon	Anden	Andreew	Andrijko	Angello
Amndip	Amville	Ander	Andrei *(0.02)*	Andrik	Angelo *(0.29)*
Amner	Amy	Anderick	Andreios	Andrix	Angelos
Amnie	Amzie	Anderius	Andreius	Andriy	Angelus
Amninder	An *(0.02)*	Anders *(0.04)*	Andrej	Andro	Angeshdeep
Amo	An Taius	Andersen	Andreja	Andron	Anget
Amogh	An Twan	Anderson *(0.07)*	Andrejs	Andros	Angle
Amol	An'fernee	Anderue	Andrel	Andru *(0.01)*	Anguel
Amollie	An'qavion	Anderw	Andrell	Andrue *(0.01)*	Angus *(0.07)*
Amon *(0.01)*	An'ton	Andes	Andrella	Andrus	Anh *(0.01)*
Amon Kai-Ben	An'torion	Andi	Andrelle	Andrw	Anh-Tu
Amon'	An-Khé	Andie	Andrenos	Andrzej *(0.01)*	Anhthy
Amond	Anabayan	Andivar	Andres *(0.94)*	Anduele	Anias
Amonda	Anacleto	Andnan	Andres-Daniel	Andus	Anibal *(0.02)*
Amondo	Anaji	Andnesio	Andressa	Andy *(0.62)*	Aniceto
Amondre	Anakin	Andolino	Andreu	Andy Gustavo	Aniel
Amoni	Anamul	Andom	Andreus	Andzie	Aniello
Amont	Anand *(0.01)*	Andoni *(0.01)*	Andrevs	Aneal	Anik
Amonta	Anandu	Andonios	Andrew *(12.27)*	Aneel	Anil *(0.01)*
Amontae	Anandveer	Andonis	Andrew Austin	Aneesa	Anilj
Amontay	Anane	Andonny	Andrew Demans	Aneesh	Aniljit
Amonte	Ananeli	Andquone	Andrew H	Aneil	Animkii
Amonté	Ananh	Andr'e	Andrew Isaac	Aneke	Aninder
Amontea	Ananjan	Andra *(0.01)*	Andrew Jason	Anel	Aniq
Amontré	Ananse	Andrade	Andrew Joseph	Anem	Anir
Amor	Anant	Andrae *(0.01)*	Andrew Junior	Anerrnee	Anirud

Aniruddha	Anosh	Antawan	Anthron	Antonus	Antwaun *(0.01)*
Anirudh	Anothony	Antawin	Anthuan	Antony *(0.12)*	Antwhon
Anis	Anouluck	Antawn	Antimo	Antonyo *(0.01)*	Antwian
Anis-Andrew	Anouromthayv	Antawne	Antinino	Antonyo Lam	Antwin
Anisan	Anousack	Antawon	Antino	Antoreo	Antwine
Anish *(0.02)*	Anousone	Ante *(0.01)*	Antion	Antori	Antwione
Anisha	Anpherne	Antearion	Antione *(0.03)*	Antorious	Antwoine *(0.01)*
Anishpal	Anphony	Antefernee	Antionio	Antorius	Antwon *(0.05)*
Anit	Anquan	Antelmo	Antionne	Antos'	Antwon Dmala
Anita	Anquavius	Anten	Antiono	Antoun	Antwone *(0.01)*
Anival	Anquell	Antenee	Antisus	Antovius	Antwonn
Anizor	Anquen	Anterio	Antiwan	Antowaine	Antwoun
Anjan	Anqueon	Anternee	Antjuan	Antowan	Antwuan
Anjarvous	Anquini	Antero	Antjuane	Antowaun	Antwun
Anjawon	Anquion	Anterrio	Antoi	Antowine	Antwyné
Anjel	Anquivious	Anterrion	Antoine *(0.49)*	Antown	Antwyon
Anjelo	Anray	Anterrious	Antoinédamor	Antowne	Antwyone
Anji'	Anri	Antershun	Antoineio	Antoyne	Antyonne
Anjo	Anrinque	Antez	Antoini	Antquan	Anuar
Anjomar	Anrontá	Antfernee	Antoinio	Antramico	Anubad
Anjuvachi	Ansab	Anthan	Antoinne	Antran	Anuel
Ankeithvious	Ansar	Anthany *(0.01)*	Antoino	Antranik	Anuj *(0.01)*
Ankhang	Ansel *(0.01)*	Antheny	Antoio	Antraveno	Anuja
Ankhekas	Ansell	Anthine	Antolin	Antravier	Anujan
Ankish	Anselm	Anthney	Antolino	Antravious	Anuje
Ankit *(0.01)*	Anselmo *(0.01)*	Anthnone	Antomo	Antravyon	Anujen
Ankoni	Ansen	Anthoine	Anton *(0.14)*	Antrawn	Anujn
Ankur *(0.01)*	Ansh	Anthoino	Anton Fredric	Antrayves	Anukate
Ankush	Anshawn	Anthon	Anton'	Antré	Anup
Ankwonsé	Anshon	Anthone	Antone *(0.01)*	Antreas	Anupjot
Anmol *(0.01)*	Anshul	Anthonee	Antoneio	Antrell	Anuraag
Anmole	Anshuman	Anthoney *(0.01)*	Antoneo	Antrevis	Anurag
Anna	Anshun	Anthoni	Antoneque	Antrevius	Anurai
Annan	Ansio	Anthoni'	Antoney	Antrivle	Anuraj
Annas	Anslem	Anthonia	Antoni *(0.01)*	Antroin	Anusan
Anndy	Ansley	Anthonie *(0.01)*	Antonia *(0.01)*	Antron	Anushen
Anne	Anson *(0.03)*	Anthonio	Antonie	Antrone	Anuson
Anneeka	Ansonio	Anthony *(9.27)*	Antonieo	Antroy	Anuvir
Annil	Anstacio	Anthony David	Antonies	Antti	Anvil
Annison	Ant'won	Anthony Hoa	Antonijo	Antton	Anwar *(0.01)*
Annoj	Antaevyon	Anthony II	Antonin	Anttonio	Anya
Annown	Antanas	Anthony Jerald	Antonine	Antuan	Anyeslian
Annuel	Antanee	Anthony Jr	Antonino *(0.01)*	Antuane	Anyhony
Annuja	Antanie	Anthony Kyle	Antonio *(1.88)*	Antuann	Anyi
Annujan	Antar	Anthony Michael	Antonio Allen	Antuaun	Anyon
Anochen	Antario	Anthony Ryan	Antonio'	Antuwan	Anzacerous
Anointed	Antarious	Anthony-	Antonio-Lamar	Antuwn	Anzhu
Emanuel	Antarius	Alexander	Antoniodejesus	Antuwon	Anzio
Anoj	Antarnio	Anthony-Jack	Antonion	Antwain *(0.01)*	Anzl
Anojan	Antarus	Anthony-Jaseph	Antonios *(0.01)*	Antwainn	Anzy
Anojh	Antaun	Anthony-John	Antonious	Antwan *(0.09)*	Aodhan
Anold	Antaune	Anthony-Joseph	Antonius *(0.01)*	Antwan'	Aodiy
Anonh	Antavious *(0.01)*	Anthony-Robert	Antonn	Antwane *(0.01)*	Aody
Anoojan	Antavius	Anthonyan	Antonne	Antwann	Aouled
Anoop *(0.01)*	Antawain	Anthonyh	Antontio	Antwanne	Aparicio

Apeeram	Ar Mand	Archibald	Ares	Arion *(0.01)*	Arkell
Aphujk	Ar Matar	Archie *(0.03)*	Aresman	Arione	Arkelle
Apiiran	Ar Treal	Archille	Arevious	Ariq	Arkevious
Apiram	Ar'keem	Archinald	Areya	Arique	Arkido
Apirana	Ar'monte	Archis	Areyan	Aris	Arkie
Apisith	Ar'reon	Archnell	Argel	Arisai	Arkim
Apolinar *(0.01)*	Ar'tayvious	Arcillious	Argelio	Arismendy	Arkin
Apollo	Ar'teus	Arda	Argenis *(0.01)*	Arisneil	Arkinell
Apollos	Ar-Keno	Ardalan	Argeniz	Arisnel	Arkirios
Apollyon	Ara *(0.01)*	Ardale	Argent	Arissen	Arkyo
Apolonio	Arab	Ardan	Arham	Aristarchus	Arlan
Apostolos	Aracin	Ardante	Arhaun	Aristedes	Arland
Appolinar	Arais	Ardarius	Arheem	Aristeed	Arlandes
Appollo	Araivinth	Ardarrius	Arhmad	Aristeo *(0.01)*	Arlandis
Appolloce	Aram *(0.02)*	Ardases	Arhmand	Aristide	Arlando
Apprentance	Aramando	Ardavien	Arhum	Aristides	Arlandor
Apprentice	Aramar	Ardel	Ari *(0.07)*	Aristidis	Arlandre
Aprentice	Aramis *(0.01)*	Ardell	Ari Gaer	Aristo	Arlem
April	Aran *(0.01)*	Arden *(0.01)*	Ari'	Ariston	Arlen *(0.02)*
Apriles	Arandeep	Ardene	Aria *(0.01)*	Aristotle	Arlexander
Aprim	Aranjit	Arderious	Arian *(0.03)*	Arites	Arley *(0.01)*
Aprinus	Ararad	Ardest	Ariana	Aritra	Arliandro
Aqavion	Aras	Ardi	Ariane	Aritrell	Arlie
Aqeel	Arash *(0.02)*	Ardian	Ariann	Arius	Arlik
Aqib	Arashdeep	Ardie	Arianne	Ariya'n	Arlin
Aqil	Arashi	Ardin	Arias	Ariyan	Arlinn
Aqiyl	Arashvir	Ardis	Aric *(0.07)*	Arizona	Arlis
Aqondius	Arasp	Ardise	Aric'	Arizthya	Arlo *(0.01)*
Aqqaluk	Arata	Ardjan	Arich	Arjan	Arlonzo
Aquaelin	Arath	Ardn	Arick *(0.01)*	Arjav	Arlyn
Aquan	Aravienth	Ardon	Aridam	Arjay	Armaan *(0.01)*
Aquanis	Aravind	Ardoni	Arie *(0.01)*	Arjen	Armad
Aquarian	Aravinth	Ardreal	Arieanwn	Arjin	Armahd
Aquarius	Araz	Are	Arieh	Arjoon	Armahn
Aquartae	Arazas	Arec	Ariek	Arju	Armaine
Aquavious	Arbari	Arecial	Ariel *(0.17)*	Arjumand	Arman *(0.04)*
Aquavius	Arbarnado	Areck	Ariell	Arjun *(0.06)*	Armand *(0.05)*
Aquayveon	Arbaz	Aree	Arien	Arjuna	Armand Jules
Aquendius	Arben	Areeb	Aries	Arjune	Armand-Nareg
Aqueous	Arber	Areef	Aries Jojo	Arjunraj	Armanddo
Aquil	Arbert	Areem	Aries'	Arjveer	Armandeep
Aquila	Arbry	Aref	Arieth	Arkadiusz	Armando *(0.61)*
Aquilas	Arbur	Arek	Arif	Arkadiy	Armando Jr
Aquileo	Arcadio *(0.01)*	Arekel	Arihant	Arkady	Armando Jr.
Aquiles	Arcainia	Areli	Arij	Arkame	Armani *(0.06)*
Aquilino	Arcane	Arelious	Arijit	Arkan	Armann
Aquille	Arcangel	Arelius	Arik *(0.02)*	Arkarson	Armanpreet
Aquinndus	Arcelius	Aremus	Arikay	Arkee	Armante
Aquino	Arcenio	Aren *(0.01)*	Arilaus	Arkeel	Armanti
Aquintis	Arch	Arend	Arild	Arkeem	Armatheo
Aquire	Archel	Arendeep	Arile	Arkeem Devu	Armaun
Aquon	Archelaus	Arenta	Arin *(0.02)*	Arkeih	Armaund
Aqwavious	Archelle	Arental	Arinzia	Arkeim	Armeen
Ar	Archer	Arenzo	Ario	Arkeith	Armel
Ar Davisus	Archesia	Areon	Ario'n	Arkelcius	Armelio

Armen *(0.02)*	Arnoldo *(0.03)*	Arsal	Artemio *(0.02)*	Artyom Vladimir	Asaf
Armend	Arnoldson	Arsalaan	Artemis	Arudhir	Asahara
Armer	Arnon	Arsalan	Artemus	Arul	Asai
Armie	Arnou	Arsanios	Arterius	Arulmenan	Asam
Armier	Arntay	Arsante	Arterrious	Arulshon	Asan
Armik	Arnulfo *(0.05)*	Arsany	Artese	Arum	Asanni
Armin *(0.01)*	Aron *(0.12)*	Arsean	Artez *(0.01)*	Arun *(0.01)*	Asante
Armin-Micheal	Arondae	Arsell	Arthavan	Arundeep	Asanté
Arminav	Arondii	Arseme	Arthell	Arunjit	Asanti
Arminder	Aronis	Arsen	Arther	Aruo	Asazuh
Armiro	Arontrez	Arsenio	Arthithyen	Arusanth	Asberry
Armit	Aroon	Arseny	Artho	Arush	Ascarra
Armo	Arotro	Arsh	Arthonn	Aruthur	Ascel
Armon *(0.01)*	Arpan	Arsha	Arthur *(0.53)*	Aruun	Ascencio
Armond *(0.02)*	Arpin	Arshá	Arthur Chris	Arvand	Ascencion
Armondez	Arpit	Arshaad	Arthur Omondi	Arveen	Ascension
Armondo	Arquan	Arshaaud	Arthur T.G.	Arveer	Aseanté
Armoné	Arquavious	Arshad	Arthur-Daniel	Arvel	Aseeb
Armoni	Arquavius	Arsham	Arthurlee	Arvell	Aseem
Armonie	Arquayalaus	Arshan	Artie	Arvellis	Aseer
Armonio	Arquel	Arshano	Arties	Arvencole	Aseesman
Armonn	Arquez	Arshaun	Artiest	Arvene	Aseespaul
Armonni	Arquimides	Arshawn	Artim	Arvid	Asef
Armonta	Arquise	Arshbir	Artimeyo	Arville	Asem
Armontae	Arquonnis	Arshdeep *(0.01)*	Artimon	Arvin *(0.03)*	Asencion
Armonte	Arram	Arshia	Artimus	Arvind *(0.01)*	Aser
Armonté	Arran	Arshli	Artin	Arvinder	Ash Shaket
Armonti	Arrandeep	Arshmin	Artis *(0.01)*	Arvinderjit	Ash'len
Armony	Arrar	Arshod	Artish	Arvonjai	Ashaan
Armour	Arravinth	Arshon	Artist	Arwill	Ashad
Armstong	Array	Arshpal	Artists	Arwin	Asham
Armundo	Arreis	Arshpreet	Artius	Arwinder	Ashan
Arnaldi	Arrek	Arshveer	Artorio	Arwyn	Ashani
Arnaldo *(0.01)*	Arren	Arshvir	Artorious	Ary	Ashante
Arnandez	Arri	Arsim	Artraevion	Arya *(0.01)*	Ashanté
Arnaud *(0.03)*	Arrian	Arslan	Artravious	Aryamehr	Ashantee
Arnav	Arric	Arsoni	Artravis	Aryan *(0.01)*	Ashanth
Arnay	Arrick	Arstell	Artre	Aryas	Ashanti *(0.01)*
Arndola	Arrien	Arstviaes	Artrell	Arye	Ashaqwan
Arne	Arrieus	Artadis	Artrency	Aryeh *(0.01)*	Ashar
Arnel	Arrin	Artago	Artrevius	Aryivon	Asharious
Arnele	Arrington	Artaivius	Artreze	Aryk	Ashaund
Arnelious	Arrion	Artan	Artrico	Aryn *(0.01)*	Ashaunte
Arnell	Arris	Artavian	Artriel	Aryo	Ashawn
Arnelle	Arrison	Artavious	Artrieo	Aryon	Ashby
Arness	Arrix	Artavis	Artrinious	Aryues	Ashdon
Arnett	Arrmond	Artavius	Artrix	Arzack	Ashe
Arnetta	Arron *(0.08)*	Artay	Artshawnde	Arzhang	Asher *(0.05)*
Arni	Arrow	Artchie	Artun	Asa *(0.07)*	Ashereli
Arnie	Arrow-Spirit-Bear	Arteis	Artur *(0.01)*	Asaa	Ashes
Arniel	Arroyn	Arteiz	Arturio	Asaad	Asheton
Arno *(0.01)*	Arroyo	Artell	Arturo *(0.49)*	Asaaru	Ashford
Arnol	Arrun	Artelle	Arturo De Jesus	Asad *(0.02)*	Ashhad
Arnold *(0.11)*	Arry-La	Artem	Arty	Asadeke	Ashi
Arnoldas	Arryn	Artemi	Artyom	Asael *(0.01)*	Ashif

Ashil	Asiantii	Athanasios (0.01)	Atul	Augman	Aurren
Ashiq	Asibayo	Athanasius	Atwoun	Augmon	Aurth
Ashir	Asibolah	Atharva	Atys	August (0.08)	Aurthur
Ashish (0.01)	Asier	Athavan	Au'donte	Augusta	Ausar
Ashjin	Asif (0.01)	Athavhan	Au'keem	Auguste	Ausby
Ashkaan	Asim	Atheer	Au'mau'vion	Augustin (0.02)	Ausencio
Ashkan (0.01)	Asion	Athen	Au-Kanai'i	Augustinas	Aushantea
Ashkon	Asish	Athiban	Aubary	Augustine (0.04)	Aushim
Ashlan	Askia	Athiththan	Aubie	Augustino	Ausin
Ashland	Aslam	Athitthan	Aubin	Augusto	Ausitn (0.01)
Ashlee	Aslan	Athon	Aubjit	Augustus (0.06)	Austadillion
Ashleigh	Aslim	Athri	Aubré	Auja	Austan
Ashlen	Asmarr	Athyun	Aubree	Aulanh	Austen (0.21)
Ashley (0.05)	Asmerom	Atian	Aubrée	Aulston	Austin (11.61)
Ashley-Scott	Asnel	Atiao	Aubreii	Aumani	Austin Blake
Ashlyn	Asonti	Atiba	Aubrey (0.10)	Aumindu	Austin David
Ashlynd	Aspen (0.02)	Atif	Aubrey-Lee	Aumio	Austin Jay
Ashmad	Assaad	Atila	Aubreylee	Aumkaaran	Austin Kyle
Ashmaly	Assad	Atilla	Aubrie	Aumkar	Austin Lee
Ashmeet	Assem	Atinderpaul	Aubrien	Aumri Akule	Austin Ron
Ashneel	Assis	Atish	Aubry	Aumyo	Austin-Hunter
Ashneet	Assyria	Atkeem	Auburn	Aundrae	Austin-James
Ashneil	Astafa	Atkins	Aubyn	Aundraveious	Austin-Jay
Ashnel	Astelyn	Atlan	Aucha	Aundray	Austin-Jordan
Ashney	Asten	Atlas	Auctavian	Aundre (0.01)	Austin-Joseph
Ashodrick	Asti	Atlee	Audaris	Aundré	Austin-Lee
Ashok	Astin	Atley	Auddy	Aundrea	Austin-Michael
Ashon	Astley	Atmiya	Audel	Aundrey	Austin-Roman
Ashor	Aston (0.01)	Atmore	Audelio	Aundry	Austin/hien
Ashpal	Astrit	Atom	Audell	Aunricco	Austine
Ashpen	Astro	Atonio	Auden	Aunrillius	Austinio
Ashquan	Astul	Atonio Atonio J	Audensio	Auntron	Auston (0.07)
Ashraf (0.01)	Astyak	Atorian	Audi	Auntwan-Da	Auston-Alan
Ashraff	Asuka	Atoris	Audie	Aunyis	Auston-Rylie
Ashray	Asuten	Atour	Audifas	Auob	Austreberto
Ashruf	Aswad	Atraveion	Audiffred	Auono	Austrum
Ashtan	Aswan	Atravius	Audin	Auquan	Austsin
Ashten (0.01)	Aswin	Atrayu	Audis	Auraham	Austun
Ashtian	Ata	Atrayue	Audithya	Aurangzeb	Austyn (0.09)
Ashtin (0.01)	Atalo	Atrell	Audla	Aurel	Austyne
Ashtion	Atanacio (0.01)	Atreyu	Audley	Aurele	Autavis
Ashton (0.34)	Atarprit	Atreyue	Audon	Aureliano (0.01)	Autavius
Ashtonn	Atavion	Atridad	Audra	Aurelien	Autham
Ashtun	Atavis	Atrun	Audre	Aurelio (0.04)	Author
Ashtyn	Atavius	Atsushi	Audrea	Aurellio	Author Alle
Ashuma	Atay	Attabiq	Audream	Aureo	Authorlee
Ashunti	Atchuthan	Attah	Audrex	Aurese	Authur
Ashur	Ateendriya	Attal	Audrey (0.01)	Aurey	Autinero
Ashvin	Atekel	Atthen	Audric	Auri	Autreal
Ashwan	Atem	Atticus (0.01)	Audrick	Auria	Autrey
Ashwath	Atemnkeng	Attikis	Audrik	Auric	Autry
Ashwin (0.02)	Atera	Attila	Audrius	Auriel	Autstin
Asiakare	Atere	Attilio	Audry	Auriniko	Autumn
Asian	Atha	Attison	Audy	Aurius	Autura
Asianon	Athan	Attorian	Auftin	Aurlin	Auturo

Auviance	Aviair	Avrohom	Ayo	Azharul	Bader
Auvitar	Avial	Avrom	Ayobami	Azhaun	Badereddin
Auxtin	Avian	Avrom Benjamin	Ayodeji	Azher	Badger
Avadh	Aviance	Avy	Ayodele	Aziah	Badhasa
Avagelos	Avidan	Avyion	Ayokunle	Azib	Badir
Avalton	Aviel	Avyn	Ayooluwa	Aziel	Badpullah
Avan	Avigdor	Avyon	Ayotemide	Azim	Badr
Avand	Avin	Aw-Wab	Ayoub	Azir	Badre
Avandre	Avinaash	Awais	Ayren	Aziz	Bady
Avanish *(0.01)*	Avinash *(0.01)*	Awale	Ayrik	Azjhon	Baeden
Avantae	Avinder	Awan	Ayrinton	Azjuan	Baeshawn
Avante	Avineet	Award	Ayron	Azmar	Baha
Avanté	Avinesh	Awat	Ayrron	Azmi	Bahai
Avantéd'quarion	Avinil	Awbrey	Ayrthon	Azor	Bahari
Avanthony	Avinjit	Awestin	Ayrton *(0.01)*	Azrael	Bahkiyia
Avanti	Avinn	Awidan	Ayrton-James	Azraful	Bahlal
Avanti'	Avio	Awsten	Aysar	Azriel	Bahman
Avary	Avion	Awtwain	Ayshad	Azrith	Bahram
Avas	Aviraj	Awwad	Ayshaun	Azrockay	Bahran
Avaté	Avis	Axeimar	Ayssar	Azubike	Bahta
Avdeep	Avishai	Axel *(0.08)*	Aytan	Azuka	Bahy
Avdi	Avishek	Axiver	Ayub *(0.01)*	Azuree	Bahzad
Ave	Avitaj	Axl *(0.01)*	Ayube	Azzad-Avi	Baian
Aveary	Avitej	Axle	Ayud	Azziel	Baibiran
Aveion	Avitesh	Axton	Ayumu		Baijun
Aveir	Aviv	Axvier	Ayush	**-B-**	Bailee
Avel	Avjeet	Axyle	Ayuz		Bailey *(0.25)*
Avelarto	Avkash	Axzavier	Ayyaub	B *(0.04)*	Bailie
Avelino	Avnash	Aya	Ayyoud	B. *(0.01)*	Baily
Aven	Avneet	Ayaan	Ayyub	B. J.	Bailye
Aveneil	Avner	Ayaaz	Ayzia Adrie	B.J.	Baine
Avenir	Avnider	Ayanle	Azaam	B.L.	Baird
Aveon	Avninder	Ayanleh	Azaan	B.R.	Bairhett
Aveonce	Avnish	Ayanth	Azab	Ba	Bajah
Aver	Avnit	Ayash	Azad	Ba'che	Bajawar
Avere	Avnoop	Ayaz	Azadvir	Baalis	Bajon
Averee	Avon	Aydan	Azalee	Baasit	Bakari *(0.02)*
Averell	Avondre	Aydeam	Azam	Babafemi	Bakarie
Averett	Avondré	Aydean	Azan	Babajide	Bakeem
Averey	Avontá	Ayden *(0.02)*	Azara	Babak	Baker *(0.01)*
Averi	Avontae	Aydin	Azari	Babar	Bakhshi
Averick	Avontaé	Aydriien	Azariah	Babatunde	Bakhtiyar
Averie	Avontai	Ayele	Azarias	Babe	Bakir
Averiel	Avonte	Ayham	Azarik	Babithan	Bakorey
Averil	Avonté	Ayime	Azarius	Babyrlak	Bakr
Averill	Avory	Ayinde	Azavia	Bacardi	Bal
Averion	Avraam	Ayindé	Azay'	Bacari	Bala
Avery *(0.48)*	Avraham *(0.01)*	Aykam	Azchary	Baccarani	Balage
Averyian	Avrahom	Aylan	Azeem	Baccari	Balakrishnan
Averyl	Avram	Ayman *(0.01)*	Azeez Folorunso	Bacchus	Balal
Averyon	Avren	Aymen	Azeivier	Bacelis	Baland
Averyrichard	Avrey	Aymeric	Azell	Bachdang	Balarama
Avetis	Avriel	Aymin	Azeza	Bacilio	Balavikash
Aveus	Avril	Aymir	Azhaé	Badar	Balazs
Avi *(0.02)*	Avrin	Ayndru	Azhar	Baden	Balcari

Baldan	Banny	Barrion	Batir	Beaumont	Benajamin
Baldasaro	Banoub	Barron *(0.02)*	Batista	Beauregard	Benamin
Baldassano	Banton	Barrow	Battle	Beaux	Benancio
Balde	Banvir	Barry *(0.13)*	Baudellio	Bebe	Benard
Baldeep	Bao *(0.01)*	Barry-James	Baudoin	Becca	Benarius
Baldemar	Bao An	Bart *(0.01)*	Bauer	Bechenito	Benben
Baldev	Baqi	Bartek	Baur	Beck	Bendarrius
Baldip	Baqur	Bartholemus	Baveenth	Becker	Benden
Baldo	Bara	Bartholmew	Bavithiran	Beckett	Bendino
Baldomero *(0.01)*	Baráa	Bartholomew	Bawand	Beckton	Bendrick
Baldric	Baraa	*(0.01)*	Baxter *(0.01)*	Bedens	Benedek
Baldwin	Barak *(0.01)*	Bartley	Bay	Bedford	Benedetto
Balel	Baraka	Bartlomiej	Bayan	Bediako	Benedick
Baley	Barakat	Bartlyn	Bayard	Bedr	Benedict *(0.02)*
Balihar	Baraket	Bartolo	Bayardo	Bee *(0.01)*	Benedict-Zam
Balin	Barath	Bartolome	Bayden	Beecher	Benedicto
Balint	Barbaro	Barton *(0.01)*	Baydon	Beelah	Benedikt
Baljeet	Barcarri	Bartosz	Bayjn	Beemnet	Bener
Baljinder	Barck	Bartu	Baylee *(0.01)*	Beernder	Benet
Baljit	Barden	Baru	Bayleigh	Befford	Benett
Baljodh	Bardia	Baruch	Baylen	Befrantz	Benette
Baljor	Bardley	Barzelais	Bayler	Behal	Beneyam
Baljot	Bardolph	Basal	Bayley *(0.01)*	Behansin	Bengamin
Baljyot	Bardomiano	Basam	Baylie	Behzad	Bengt
Balkaar	Barento	Bascal	Baylin	Beige	Bengy
Balkaran	Barfi	Basel	Baylon	Beigh	Benham
Balkarn	Barhett	Basem	Baylor *(0.01)*	Beiwen	Benheart
Balke	Bari	Bashar	Bayly	Bejamin	Beniam
Balkit	Barichel	Bashari	Baymon	Bekalu	Beniamin
Ballard	Barinder	Basheer	Bayne	Bekim	Beniamino
Balmoris	Barinderjeet	Basher	Baynn	Bela	Benigno
Balmyr	Barion	Basherahmad	Bayron *(0.01)*	Belaal	Benijah
Balpreet	Baris	Bashir	Baysean	Belafonte	Benino
Balraj *(0.01)*	Bariso	Bashiru Adisa	Bayshaaun	Belal *(0.01)*	Benis
Balsim	Barjinder	Bashon	Bayshawn	Belall	Benisha
Balsimran	Barkari	Bashonnon	Baytar	Belarmino	Benito *(0.07)*
Baltaj	Barkley	Basil *(0.02)*	Bayton	Belay	Benjahmin
Baltazar *(0.03)*	Barnabas	Basile	Bazel	Beldon	Benjam
Baltej	Barnabi	Basilio *(0.01)*	Bazelais	Belen	Benjaman
Balthazzar	Barnaby	Basim	Bb	Belgin	Benjamen *(0.03)*
Bamikole	Barnard	Basir	Beactrice	Bell	Benjamin *(6.09)*
Ban	Barney	Basit	Bean	Bellamy	Benjamin Crosby
Banave	Baron *(0.03)*	Bass	Bear	Belloir	Benjamin Jr
Bandar	Baron Orion	Bassam	Bearitt	Belmon	Benjamin Kalib
Bander	Baroque	Bassel	Bearley	Beloved	Benjamin Kyle
Bandon	Barr	Bassem	Beatriz	Belrive	Benjamin Luis
Bane	Barrazza	Bassey	Beau *(0.25)*	Belton	Benjamin
Bang	Barrell	Bassirou	Beau-Alexander	Belton Dillon	Wadswo
Banipal	Barret *(0.01)*	Bassit	Beaubrun	Beltron	Benjamin-Gary
Banjamin	Barrett *(0.07)*	Bastian	Beauchesne	Bemajedareki	Benjamin-Joseph
Bankole	Barretta	Bastien *(0.02)*	Beaudan	Bemedict	Benjamin-Joshua
Banks	Barrick	Bastion	Beaudean	Ben *(0.14)*	Benjamine
Bankston	Barrie	Baswell	Beaudee	Ben-Gregorio	Benjaminn
Banner	Barrin	Bates	Beaudoin	Ben-Moshe	Benjamyn
Bannie	Barrington *(0.01)*	Batinder	Beaudry	Benaiah	Benjamynn

Benjeet	Ber'tram	Bershawn	Bhavanpreet	Billydean	Blaid
Benjemin	Berach	Bert (0.01)	Bhavdeep	Billye	Blaide
Benjerman	Beraldo	Bertel	Bhavesh	Billyjoe	Blaik
Benjermen	Beran	Bertell	Bhavik	Billyray	Blaike
Benjermin	Berat	Berthold	Bhavin	Bilmer	Blain (0.02)
Benji	Berchman	Bertin	Bhavjot	Bilwood	Blaine (0.20)
Benjie	Berdaro	Berton	Bhavneet	Bily	Blaine Jr
Benjiman (0.01)	Berekel	Bertrae	Bhavraj	Binepaul	Blair (0.10)
Benjimen	Bereketabe	Bertraim	Bhinderjeet	Bing	Blair Charles
Benjimin	Berend	Bertram (0.01)	Bhisham	Bingamin	Blaire
Benjimon	Berenson	Bertrand	Bhoke	Binghorng	Blais
Benjmain	Berent	Bertraum	Bhrett	Binh	Blaise (0.04)
Benjy	Berge	Bertron	Bhupinder	Binhan	Blaize (0.01)
Benley	Bergen	Bertwin	Bhupinderjeet	Binish	Blake (2.11)
Benly	Berhan	Bervince	Bhushan	Bink	Blake Benjamin
Benmark	Beric	Beryn	Bhyran	Bino	Blakeley
Benmur	Berish	Berzeracque	Bhyren	Bintu	Blakelin
Benn	Berk	Besart	Biagio	Binyam	Blakely (0.01)
Bennario	Berkan	Besher	Biahik	Binyamin	Blakelyn
Benner	Berkano	Besim	Bianca	Biola	Blaken
Bennet	Berkeley	Besnik	Bianluca	Bipanpreet	Blakeslee
Bennete	Berkely	Bessan	Biash	Biranavan	Blaketon
Bennett (0.11)	Berkley (0.01)	Betim	Bichtar	Birannan	Blakley
Bennette	Berle	Beto	Bide	Birch	Blakney
Bennie (0.04)	Berlie	Betram	Bieardo	Birdell	Blal
Bennison	Berlin	Betzalel	Bien	Birdsong	Blanca
Bennjamin	Berlyn	Beua	Bigfoot	Birhan	Bland
Bennon	Berman	Beuben	Bijal	Birihane	Blandon
Benny (0.09)	Bernabe (0.01)	Beullyn	Bijan (0.02)	Birinder	Blane (0.02)
Benoise	Bernabed	Beum	Bijhan	Birjot	Blanne
Benoit (0.11)	Bernadette	Bevan	Bijhon	Birk	Blanton
Benold	Bernadou	Bevante	Bijon	Bishop (0.03)	Blaqu'e
Benortha	Bernard (0.17)	Bevendra	Biko	Bishoy	Blare
Benott	Bernard Jr	Beveto	Bikram	Bishup	Blas (0.02)
Bensan	Bernardin	Bevin	Bikramdeep	Bisma	Blase
Bensen	Bernardino (0.01)	Bevon	Bikramjeet	Bismar	Blashford
Benson (0.03)	Bernardo (0.08)	Bevontae	Bikramjit	Bismark	Blass
Bent	Bernarius	Beya	Bilaal	Bitaal	Blathan
Bentavious	Bernateau	Bg	Bilal (0.06)	Bitahwa	Blaux
Benthony	Bernell	Bhaag	Bilal-Fawzi	Bivens	Blawal
Bentley (0.01)	Berney	Bhagatvir	Bilale	Bivins	Blay
Benton (0.04)	Bernhard	Bhagwant	Bilawal	Biya	Blayke (0.01)
Bentrail	Bernhardt	Bhakti	Bile	Biyan	Blayn
Bentrez	Bernie (0.01)	Bhancha	Bilel	Bj	Blayne (0.04)
Bentson	Beronte	Bhanu	Bilen	Bjarne	Blaytin
Benuel	Berrach	Bhanwar	Bilien	Bjorn (0.02)	Blayton
Benvir	Berrett	Bharat	Bill (0.05)	Bjorn-Erik	Blayz
Benyam	Berric	Bharath	Billaal	Bjorn-James	Blayze (0.01)
Benyamin	Berrick	Bhart	Billah	Bladden	Blayzz
Benz	Berrie	Bhaskar	Billal	Blade (0.03)	Blaze (0.05)
Benzel	Berrik	Bhaumik	Billee	Bladen	Blazen
Benzell	Berrit	Bhautik	Billie (0.01)	Bladimer	Blazer
Benzo	Berron	Bhavan	Billingsley	Bladimir (0.01)	Bless
Beosker	Berry (0.01)	Bhavandeep	Billy (0.44)	Bladon	Blessed
Beplaier	Bershan	Bhavanjit	Billy-John	Bladyn	Blessing

Bleu	Bogdon	Bosco	Bradden	Brahma	Branden Michael
Bleyke	Boggs	Bosheem	Braddly	Brahmjeevan	Brandene
Blois	Bogosibotsile	Bosie	Braddock	Brahmjit	Brandi
Blow	Boh	Bossit	Braddock-James	Brahveen	Brandin *(0.04)*
Blu	Bohdan	Boston *(0.02)*	Bradell	Braian	Brandine
Blue	Bohden	Botrus	Braden *(0.46)*	Braidan	Brando *(0.01)*
Bluewater	Bohdi	Boudy	Braden Leroy	Braiden *(0.04)*	Brandom
Blyth	Bohishan	Boulos	Bradeon	Braidon *(0.01)*	Brandon *(13.74)*
Bo *(0.08)*	Bohn	Bounkong	Bradey *(0.01)*	Braidy	Brandon Christo
Bo Bozidar	Boisie	Bounmy	Bradford *(0.09)*	Braidyn	Brandon Hieu
Bo Garrett	Bojan	Bounthavy	Bradi	Braie	Brandon James
Boakai	Bojesse	Bourbon	Bradie	Braielon	Brandon Kyle
Boanerges	Bokeim	Bouten	Bradin	Braigen	Brandon Lee
Boaz	Bolade	Bouvair	Bradius	Brailon	Brandon Leonard
Boazie	Bolaji	Bouwe	Bradlee *(0.03)*	Brain *(0.01)*	Brandon Michael
Bob *(0.01)*	Bolawa	Bouziane	Bradlee-Scott	Brainard	Brandon Nichola
Boback	Bolden	Bowday	Bradleigh	Braiqued	Brandon-Allan
Bobak	Bolis	Bowdey	Bradley *(2.32)*	Braivon	Brandon-Chase
Bobbi	Bolivar	Bowdie	Bradley J	Braiylaun	Brandon-David
Bobbie *(0.01)*	Bolman	Bowdien	Bradley-Wayne	Braiyten	Brandon-Dean
Bobby *(0.48)*	Boltin	Bowdrie	Bradlie	Braize	Brandon-Glenroy
Bobby Joe	Bomani	Bowe	Bradly *(0.10)*	Braj'on	Brandon-Jayvee
Bobby Joseph	Bomanley	Bowen *(0.02)*	Bradly-Dean	Braken	Brandon-Jeffrey
Bobby Jr	Bomario	Bowie	Bradlyn	Brakken	Brandon-Lee
Bobby-Joe	Bomiriyage	Bowles	Bradnaro	Bralan	Brandon-Michael
Bobbye	Bomun	Bowman	Bradney	Bralen	Brandon-Niles
Boboy	Bon	Bowna	Bradnon	Braley	Brandon-
Bobzavious	Boncana	Boy *(0.01)*	Bradon *(0.02)*	Bralin	Raymond
Bocephus	Boni	Boyan	Bradrick	Bralon	Brandon-Terry
Bockarie	Bonie	Boyce	Bradshaw	Bralyn	Brandonlee
Boddie	Bonifacio	Boyd *(0.02)*	Bradston	Bram *(0.01)*	Brandonlen
Bode	Bonifasio De	Boyer	Bradusjames	Bramdon	Brandonn
Bodé	Bonner	Boylante	Bradway	Brame	Brandrais
Bodee	Bonny	Boysequan	Bradwell	Bramlitt	Brandt *(0.04)*
Boden	Bonritt	Boysie	Bradwick	Bramwell	Brandtley
Bodene	Bontreal	Bozorgmehr	Brady *(0.71)*	Bran-Lon	Brandtly
Bodey	Bony	Bra'shun	Bradye	Branagan	Brandton
Bodhendra	Booker *(0.01)*	Bra-Shad	Bradyn *(0.02)*	Branan	Brandy *(0.01)*
Bodhi *(0.01)*	Boomer	Braché	Bradynne	Branashio	Brandyn *(0.10)*
Bodhisattva	Boone *(0.01)*	Brack	Brae	Branavan	Brandynn
Bodi	Boots	Bracken	Braé	Brance	Branford
Bodie *(0.02)*	Bora	Brackin	Braedan *(0.01)*	Brancen	Branic
Bodin	Borahan	Brackon	Braeden *(0.10)*	Branch	Branigan
Bodisapha	Boram	Brackstin	Braedin	Brand'on	Branimir
Bodizofa	Boramey	Brackston	Braedon *(0.05)*	Brandall	Branin
Bodrew	Boray	Brackus	Braedyn *(0.01)*	Brandan *(0.11)*	Branislav
Bodrey	Borden	Bracky	Braelen	Brandaniel	Branko
Bodyne	Boren	Bracque	Braelin	Brandden	Brannan
Boe	Boricamarack	Bracy	Braelyn	Branddon	Branndan
Boedi	Boris *(0.04)*	Brad *(0.16)*	Braemen	Branddy	Branndon
Boedy	Borivoje	Brad Lee	Braeson	Branded	Brannen *(0.01)*
Boeing	Borna	Brad-Anthony	Brage	Brandeis	Brannigan
Boen	Boruch	Bradach	Bragoin	Brandel	Brannon *(0.06)*
Bogan	Bory	Bradan	Braham	Brandell	Branon
Bogdan	Borys	Bradd	Brahm	Branden *(0.49)*	Bransen *(0.01)*

Bransford
Branson *(0.05)*
Branston
Brant *(0.05)*
Brantavis
Brante
Brantez
Brantford
Brantley *(0.03)*
Brantly *(0.01)*
Branton *(0.01)*
Branyan
Brarick
Brasen
Brashad
Brashard
Brashawn
Brass
Braton
Brauli
Braulio *(0.05)*
Brauliuo
Braun
Braunsen
Braunson
Braveen
Braven
Bravik
Bravon
Brawley
Brax
Braxdon
Braxston
Braxten
Braxtin
Braxton *(0.22)*
Braxton Jason
Braxxton
Bray *(0.01)*
Brayam
Brayan *(0.04)*
Braydan
Brayden *(0.35)*
Braydn
Braydon *(0.09)*
Braydoon
Braydyn
Braye
Brayland
Brayle
Braylen
Braylin
Braylon *(0.02)*
Braylyn
Brayman

Braymer
Brayn
Brayon
Brayson
Brayston
Brayten
Brayton *(0.01)*
Brayvon
Brayzen
Braz
Brazel
Brazen
Brazil
Brazin
Brazir
Brazz
Bre Shaun
Bréandre
Bréon
Bréonte
Bréshaun
Bréshawn
Breadon
Breagan
Breagan Lou
Brealand
Breanainn Loret
Breandan
Breandon
Breanna
Breannan
Breanne
Breante
Breaun
Breaunté
Breayon
Brecan
Brechaun
Brecht
Breck
Breckan
Brecken
Breckenridge
Breckin
Breckinridge
Breckke
Breckonridge
Breckyn
Bredan
Bredensen
Bredesen
Bredesin
Bredndan
Bredon
Bredt

Breedlinn
Breen
Breenan
Breeon
Breet
Breeze
Bregt
Brehdan
Brehon
Breickner
Breidyn
Breighton
Breion
Breitner
Brek
Brekarri
Brekeithon
Brekenta
Brel
Brelain
Brelan
Breland
Brelonn
Brelyn
Bremer
Bren
Brenae
Brenagan
Brenan
Brenard
Brence
Brenda
Brendan *(1.45)*
Brendanmichael
Brenden *(0.36)*
Brendin *(0.01)*
Brendon *(0.29)*
Brendon James
Brendon Michael
Brendonis
Brendt
Brendyan
Brendyn *(0.01)*
Brenen *(0.01)*
Brenham
Brenin
Brenit'azé
Brenn
Brenna
Brennan *(0.42)*
Brennann
Brenndan
Brennden
Brenndon
Brennen *(0.12)*

Brenner *(0.01)*
Brennon *(0.05)*
Brennor
Brennyn
Breno
Brenon
Brenquese
Brenquez
Brenshad
Brensley
Brent *(0.71)*
Brentavious
Brente
Brenté
Brenten *(0.01)*
Brentez
Brentford
Brenth
Brentin
Brentlee
Brentley *(0.01)*
Brently
Brenton *(0.13)*
Brentt
Brentten
Brentton
Brentyn
Brenyn
Brenz
Breon *(0.04)*
Breondon
Breone
Breonn
Breonta
Breonte
Breontr E
Breshawn
Breslin
Bret *(0.17)*
Bretin
Bretley
Bretlin
Breton *(0.01)*
Brett *(1.81)*
Brett James
Brett-Anthony
Brett-Darren
Brettan
Brette
Bretten
Brettlyn
Bretton *(0.02)*
Brevan
Brevard
Brevin

Brevion
Brevon
Brewan
Brewer
Brexton
Brey
Breyan
Breyan-Thomas
Breydale
Breydan
Breyden
Breydon
Breyleigh
Breylin
Breylon
Breylund
Breyon *(0.01)*
Breyontae
Breyton
Brezdan
Brhon
Bri'onn
Bri'quarius
Briam
Brian *(4.78)*
Brian Justin
Brian Keith
Brian Patrick
Brian Tan
Brian Walter
Brian-Anthony
Brian-Edward
Brian-James
Brian-Keith
Brian-Michael
Briana
Briandarious
Briandell
Briandrick
Briane
Briann
Brianna
Brianne
Briant
Briaonte
Briar *(0.04)*
Briason
Briaun
Briayan
Bric
Brica
Brice *(0.14)*
Bricen
Briceson
Briceton

Brich
Brick
Bricker
Bricklen
Bricklin-Styles
Brickman
Bricsen
Bridell
Bridge
Bridger *(0.04)*
Bridget
Bridgetta
Bridney
Bridon
Briean
Briece
Briel
Brielle
Brien *(0.01)*
Brienden
Brient
Brieon
Brier
Brierly
Brieson
Brieton
Brieuc
Brieyice
Brig
Brigg
Briggs
Brigham *(0.02)*
Bright
Brightin
Brighton *(0.01)*
Brigido
Brigitte
Briheem
Brijen
Brijesh
Brik
Brikeystein
Briklin
Briley
Brillanté
Brillarius
Brimaldi
Brin
Brindar
Brindin
Brindley
Brink
Brinkley
Brinnell
Brinnon

Brinson
Brinston
Brintezz
Brinthan
Brinton
Brinttlee
Brion (0.02)
Brione
Brionn
Brionne
Briontay
Brionte
Briot
Briquavious
Briscoe
Brisen
Brishadd
Brishan
Brishawn
Brishen
Brishon
Brisley
Brison (0.01)
Bristen
Bristol
Brit (0.01)
Britain
Britavian
Briten
Britian
Britin
British
Briton (0.01)
Britt (0.01)
Brittain
Brittainie
Brittan (0.01)
Brittany
Britten (0.01)
Brittian
Brittin
Brittney
Britton (0.05)
Brivaughn
Briyonna
Brjen
Broadie
Broadies
Broadon
Broadway
Broady
Broc (0.02)
Brocce
Broch
Brock (0.38)

Brocke
Brockington
Brocklin
Brockman
Brockston
Brockton (0.01)
Brockway
Brocston
Brodan
Brodderick
Brodderrick
Broddrekcus
Broddrick
Brode
Broden (0.01)
Broderic
Broderick (0.05)
Broderrick
Brodey
Brodi
Brodic
Brodie (0.09)
Brodik
Brodis
Brodix
Brodri C
Brodric
Brodrick (0.02)
Brody (0.30)
Broedi
Broedy
Brogan (0.02)
Brogen
Broghan
Broghen
Brok
Brokey
Brokston
Brolan
Brolyn
Bromekis
Bromen
Bromley
Bron
Bronco
Bronquel
Bronsan
Bronsen
Bronson (0.09)
Bronsyn
Bronte
Brontel
Bronton
Bronwyn
Bronx

Bronxton
Bronzell
Brook (0.01)
Brooke (0.01)
Brooker
Brookes
Brooklyn
Brooklyne
Brooklynn
Brooks (0.10)
Broox
Bror
Brose
Broudrick
Brougher
Brouklyn
Browdy
Brown
Browning
Brownyango
Browyn
Broxlin
Broy
Brpan
Bru'shoud
Bruce (0.34)
Bruce Michael
Bruce Willi
Bruce-Lee
Brucedathsman
Brucelee
Bruin
Bruk
Bruno (0.09)
Brunson
Brunthaan
Brunzil
Brushod
Bry'drick
Bry-Lin
Bryacce
Bryam
Bryan (2.47)
Bryan
  Christopher
Bryan Patrick
Bryan-Rizal
Bryana
Bryand
Bryandeep
Bryanden
Bryanjit
Bryann
Bryant (0.64)
Bryant Jr

Bryar (0.01)
Brycan
Bryce (1.07)
Bryce James
Bryce Jr
Brycedon
Bryceland
Brycen (0.02)
Bryceson
Brycetin
Bryceton
Brycon
Brydan
Bryden (0.01)
Brydon (0.01)
Brye
Bryéshawn
Bryen
Bryeon
Bryer (0.01)
Bryeton
Bryhan
Bryin
Bryjhon
Brykael
Brylan
Bryland
Brylee
Brylen
Bryler
Bryley
Brylon
Bryn (0.02)
Brynar
Bryndan
Brynden
Bryndon
Bryne
Bryneigh
Bryner
Brynle
Brynley
Brynn
Brynne
Brynton
Bryntt
Bryon (0.05)
Bryone
Bryontae
Bryor
Brysan
Brysen (0.01)
Bryshard
Bryshaun
Bryshawne

Bryson (0.25)
Brysten
Bryston
Brysun
Brysyn
Brytan
Bryten
Brython
Brytin
Bryton (0.07)
Brytten
Brytton
Bryviin
Bryvontá
Bu-Wan
Buaku
Bubakarr
Bubba
Buchanan
Buck (0.01)
Buckie
Buckinson
Bucky
Bud
Budd
Buddie
Buddy (0.02)
Buford
Bugsianta
Bui
Buket
Bukkapatnam
Bukr
Bulfrano
Bullard
Bulmaro
Bunchhaya
Bungeet
Bungha
Buntan
Bunyamin
Bunyan
Bunyon
Buoth
Bupinder
Bura
Burgess
Burghley
Burhan
Burke (0.01)
Burkhardt
Burkley
Burl
Burles
Burley

Burlin
Burlrando
Burnam
Burnard
Burneal
Burnell
Burnett
Burnice
Burns
Burora
Burrell
Burritt
Burrous
Burt
Burton (0.01)
Bush
Buster
Buta
Butch
Buthler
Butler
Butterscotch
Buzz
Bwahwire
Byagie
Byars
Bycha
Bydrick
Byheem
Bykejzeron
Bylan
Bynum
Byram
Byran (0.01)
Byrant
Byrce
Byrd
Byren
Byrn
Byron (0.28)
Byronjovi
Byrson
Byrtron
Byung-Ho
Byung-Hwa
Byvon

-C-

C (0.06)
C J (0.01)
C L
C Lane
C Ron
C'andre

C'anthony	Cadonis	Caine *(0.02)*	Calim	Calyx	Camry
C'jei	Cadonovan	Cainen	Calin *(0.01)*	Cam *(0.01)*	Camryn *(0.01)*
C'nard	Cady	Caio	Calin Peppard	Camalot	Camrynn
C'quwan	Cadyn	Caiquawh	Calinte	Camaran	Camuel
C'rique	Caeden	Cairan	Calio	Camarcus	Camus
C-Jay	Caedmon	Cairo	Calip	Camaren	Camyar
C-Ryuss	Caedon	Cairon	Caliph	Camari	Camyn
C. *(0.01)*	Caeil	Caison	Calis	Camaron *(0.01)*	Can
C. Bevin	Caelan *(0.03)*	Caitlen	Calistro	Cambell	Cana
C.J.	Caelb	Caitlin	Call	Cambrian	Canaan *(0.02)*
Ca Darrius	Caelem	Caius	Callaghan	Cambron	Canan
Ca'darious	Caelen	Caj	Callahan *(0.01)*	Camden *(0.09)*	Canard
Ca'darius	Caelin	Cajewl	Callajeno	Camdon	Candaimeond
Ca'doreon	Caellin	Cajun	Callan *(0.01)*	Cameli	Candaus
Ca'hari	Caellum	Cal *(0.02)*	Callander	Camelle	Cande
Ca'ra'n	Caelon	Calab	Callaway	Camen	Candelario *(0.01)*
Ca'toine	Caelum	Calabe	Calleia	Cameo	Canden
Caameron	Caelyn	Calagio	Callen *(0.01)*	Cameorn	Candi
Caanan	Caesar	Calahan	Calletano	Cameran	Candice
Caballero	Caesarae	Calan *(0.01)*	Callis	Cameren *(0.01)*	Candido *(0.01)*
Cabbien	Caesars	Calby	Callob	Camerin	Candler
Cabe	Caesear *(0.01)*	Calculus	Callon	Camero	Candre
Cabell	Caeser	Calden	Calloyd	Camerom	Cane
Cabet	Caetano	Calder *(0.01)*	Callum *(0.05)*	Cameron *(3.63)*	Caneil
Cable	Cagan	Caldon	Callyn	Cameron-Andrew	Canen
Cabot	Cage	Caldré	Calm	Cameron-Miles	Caneron
Cabryn	Cager	Cale *(0.05)*	Calmetrius	Cameroun	Canes
Cacey	Cagle	Caléb	Calob	Camerron	Cannen
Cache	Caharri	Calean	Calogero	Camerson	Cannin
Cachjuan	Cahauri	Caleb *(2.72)*	Calon	Camerun	Cannon *(0.02)*
Caci	Cahil	Caleb Alexa	Calton	Cameryn	Canny
Cadan	Cahlee	Caleb Andrew	Calub	Camian	Canon *(0.01)*
Cadaris	Cahli	Caleb Wayne	Calueb	Camile	Cansas
Cadarius	Cahlil	Caleb'	Calum *(0.02)*	Camille *(0.02)*	Cantabile
Cadarrius	Cai	Calebbeh	Calvary	Camillo	Canteze
Cadarrow	Caiaphas	Calebh	Calveion	Camillus	Cantonese
Cadarus	Caid	Caled	Calven	Camilo *(0.03)*	Cantrell
Cadasen	Caiden *(0.01)*	Caledin	Calvert	Camion	Canute
Caddeem	Caige	Calee	Calvertis	Camiron	Canyen
Caddence	Caigen	Caleigh	Calvery	Cammalen	Canyon *(0.01)*
Caddon	Cail	Caleigha	Calvester	Cammern	Caolan
Cade *(0.15)*	Cailas	Calel	Calvien	Cammeron	Capedro
Cadeem	Cailean	Calem	Calvin *(0.81)*	Cammrin	Capel
Cadell	Caileb	Calen *(0.02)*	Calvin Chuo	Cammron	Caper
Caden *(0.10)*	Cailen	Calenta	Calvin James	Camon	Caperton
Cadenas	Cailer	Calentá	Calvin Thomas	Campbell *(0.02)*	Caponi
Cadence	Cailin	Calentae	Calvin-Khang	Campion	Cappy
Cadeyrn	Cailum	Calet	Calvintarius	Camran	Caprice
Cadian	Cailun	Caley	Calvlier	Camre	Caprie
Cadien	Cailyn	Calhoun	Calvon	Camreise	Captain
Cadillac	Caiman	Calhoune	Calvonta	Camren *(0.02)*	Capus
Cadin	Caimen	Caliah	Calvonte	Camreon	Carac
Cadis	Cain *(0.05)*	Calib *(0.01)*	Calvyn	Camrin *(0.01)*	Caramon
Cadisen	Cainaen	Calieb	Calyb	Camrom	Caravian
Cadon	Cainan	Calif	Calyn	Camron *(0.08)*	Caraymeon

Carby	Carlante	Carmelin	Carsen *(0.01)*	Casey	Casuga
Carcellius	Carlas	Carmello	Carsi	Christopher	Caswell
Cardairo	Carlathius	Carmelo *(0.02)*	Carsino	Cash *(0.02)*	Casy
Cardan	Carlderis	Carmen *(0.02)*	Carson *(0.45)*	Cash Money	Cataldo
Cardaniel	Carlee	Carmen-	Carson William	Cash'lynn	Catalino
Cardarian	Carleeto	Alexander	Carsten *(0.01)*	Cash'mere	Catarino
Cardarion	Carlen	Carmeron	Carston	Cashell	Catdrell
Cardarius	Carleo	Carmichael	Cartacious	Cashemere	Cater
Cardarrius	Carleon	Carmin	Cartaveus	Cashie	Cates
Cardaryl	Carles	Carmine *(0.01)*	Cartavian	Cashius	Cathal
Cardazz	Carlester	Carmor	Cartavius	Cashmeire	Cathan
Cardeale	Carlet	Carnail	Carteis	Cashmere	Catherine *(0.01)*
Cardell *(0.01)*	Carleton *(0.01)*	Carnealius	Carter *(0.39)*	Cashon	Catlen
Carden	Carley	Carneilius	Cartez	Cashous	Catlin *(0.01)*
Cardenas	Carlheem	Carnelius	Carthric	Cashton	Catlyn
Carder	Carlheim	Carnell *(0.01)*	Cartier	Cashus	Cato
Carderius	Carli	Carnellius	Cartious	Casiano	Catravious
Cardet	Carlie	Carnethus	Cartis	Casidy	Catrell
Cardeus	Carlile	Carney	Cartouche	Casie	Caul
Cardiá	Carlin *(0.02)*	Carnilious	Cartrayvis	Casimere	Caulan
Cardinal	Carlise	Carnord	Cartrell	Casimir	Caulden
Cardon	Carlisle	Caro	Cartrixton	Casimir-Bradley	Caulen
Caree	Carlisle-Aaron	Carol	Carv'nnie	Casimiro	Cauley
Careem	Carlisle-Jelani	Carolina	Carvaughn	Casin	Caulin
Carell	Carlisstos	Caroline	Carveal	Casino	Caullen
Carenzo	Carlito *(0.01)*	Carols	Carvel	Casio	Caulter
Careron	Carlitos	Carolyn	Carvell	Casnio	Causta
Careton	Carlius	Carom	Carvelle	Cason *(0.02)*	Caustin
Carew	Carllon	Caroman	Carvellius	Cason Jonath	Cavaheri
Carey *(0.03)*	Carlmichael	Caron	Carver *(0.01)*	Casper *(0.01)*	Cavan *(0.01)*
Careyton	Carlnell	Carondeontre	Carvin	Cass *(0.01)*	Cavanaugh
Carez	Carlneus	Carpino	Carvinski	Cassady	Cavarik
Cari	Carlo *(0.08)*	Carpio	Carvion	Cassalle	Cavarri
Carif	Carlon	Carr	Carvon	Cassandra	Cavarsier
Carig	Carlondon	Carraig	Carvontate	Cassanova	Cavasiia Ca
Carim	Carlos *(2.44)*	Carray	Carwin	Cassaries	Cavell
Carina	Carlos Devo	Carre	Cary *(0.04)*	Cassavous	Caven
Cario	Carlos Jr.	Carree	Carygan	Cassell	Cavin *(0.01)*
Carionte	Carlos Mateo	Carrell	Caryl	Cassey	Cavisia
Caris	Carlos Xavier	Carren	Carzhey	Casshawn	Cavon
Carl *(0.68)*	Carlos's	Carrett	Cas	Cassidy *(0.05)*	Cavontae
Carl Angelo	Carlos-Mario	Carrick	Cas-Mine	Cassini	Cavonte
Carl Eric	Carlous	Carrie	Casady	Cassius *(0.01)*	Cavonté
Carl Erwin	Carlsel	Carrigan	Casaebian	Casson	Cavoszyéa
Carl Olivier	Carlson	Carrigen	Casai	Cassy	Cawajalin
Carl Raymond	Carltez	Carrille	Casan	Castella	Cawl
Carl-Antoine	Carlton *(0.15)*	Carrington *(0.03)*	Casaris	Caster	Cawoun
Carl-David	Carltrell	Carris	Cascade	Castilla	Cayce
Carl-Edward	Carlus	Carroil	Cascadean	Castille	Cayde
Carl-Olivier	Carly	Carrol	Case *(0.01)*	Castillo	Cayden *(0.02)*
Carl-Stephen	Carlyle *(0.01)*	Carroll *(0.01)*	Caselll	Castin	Caydin
Carlan	Carmain	Carron	Casen	Caston	Cayetano
Carlandis	Carmaine	Carry	Caseton	Castro	Caylais
Carlandus	Carman	Carse	Caseus	Castulo	Caylan *(0.01)*
Carlans	Carmel	Carsell	Casey *(1.13)*	Casual	Caylans

Cayle	Ceddrick	Cepheus	Chacobrian	Chakestein	Chanceler
Cayleb	Cedeanio	Cequan	Chacuntay	Chakib	Chanceller
Caylebb	Cederic (0.01)	Cequari'	Chad (1.18)	Chakilan	Chancellor (0.02)
Caylen	Cederick	Cera	Chad Joshua	Chakinzi	Chancelor (0.02)
Caylib	Cederrick	Ceril Matheo	Chad Michael	Chakote	Chancely
Caylin	Cedie	Cerles	Chad'darius	Chakree	Chancen
Caylob	Cedomir	Cerlondo	Chad-Alan	Chale	Chancer
Caylon	Cedré	Cerontae	Chadanee	Chalem	Chancey (0.01)
Caylor	Cedric (0.43)	Cerrano	Chadarius	Chalen	Chanchez
Cayman (0.01)	Cedrick (0.11)	Cerulean	Chadd (0.02)	Chales	Chancie
Caymen	Cedriel	Cervando	Chaddler	Chalif	Chancler
Caymin	Cedrik (0.03)	Cervonjai	Chaddley	Chalin	Chanclin
Caymon	Cedrith	Cerwin	Chaddrick	Chalis	Chancy
Cayn	Cedur	Cesar (0.90)	Chaddwick	Challas	Chandale
Caynan	Cedveon	Cesar Antonio	Chade	Challen	Chandan
Cayne	Cee	Cesar Favio	Chaderic	Challen-Dakota	Chandandeep
Cayon	Ceejay	Cesar Jr	Chadford	Challenge	Chandar
Caysaan	Cefar	Cesar-Emilio	Chadham	Challian	Chandel
Cayse	Ceighln-Derrel	Cesare	Chadi	Challis	Chandelar
Cayson	Ceilleon	Cesareo	Chadler	Challon	Chandell
Cayton	Ceishawn	Cesay	Chadley	Challum	Chandlar
Caytron	Cejay	Cesilio	Chadli	Chalmers	Chandler (0.53)
Cayus	Celby	Cessar	Chadoe	Chalon	Chandler Gregor
Caz	Celeo	Cestmir	Chadohl	Chaloni	Chandlier
Cazarian	Celestin	Cetan-Ishta	Chadquan	Chalres	Chandlin
Cazimir Douglas	Celestine	Cethan	Chadrack	Chalton	Chandlor
Cazzie	Celestino (0.01)	Cevein	Chadric	Chalvin	Chandlyr
Cazzy	Celestino-Vicen	Ceveon	Chadrick (0.01)	Chalyn	Chandon
Ca~ron	Celine	Cevin	Chadshawn	Chamane	Chandos
Cdsey	Cellik	Cevon	Chadwick (0.08)	Chamar	Chandra
Ce Ce	Celly	Cevone	Chadwin	Chamara	Chandresh
Ce Darrian	Celone	Cevonte	Chadwyck	Chamarius	Chandripal
Ce Detrick	Celsey	Cevonté	Chae	Chamaun	Chandy
Ce Jay	Celso (0.01)	Ceygan	Chaeden	Chamberlin	Chane
Cé-Ce	Celton	Ceylor	Chaes	Chambers	Chaney (0.01)
Céangelo	Cem	Ceyonte	Chaff	Chameron	Chang
Céquan	Cemaron	Ceyston	Chaffee	Chamois	Chang In
César	Cemberlyn	Cezar (0.01)	Chaffin	Chamond	Chang-Jin
Cévon	Cenquez	Cezil	Chafin	Chamorru	Chang-Lin
Cean	Cenqunn	Cezly	Chagil	Champe	Change
Ceanté	Cenric	Ceznary	Chai	Champion	Changhee
Ceaph	Centel	Cezrick	Chaim (0.01)	Chan (0.01)	Changiz
Ceasar (0.02)	Centonia	Cha	Chainephong	Chan-Crisna	Changyong
Ceaser	Centory	Cha Shaun	Chainey	Chanakan	Chanh
Ceason	Centraveuz	Cha'qwan	Chais	Chanan	Chanito
Ceaton	Centravious	Cha-Khia	Chaise (0.01)	Chananya	Chanjot
Cebastian	Centrell	Cha-Von	Chaisen	Chanarkeno	Chanjyot
Cebastien	Centrelle	Chaas	Chaison	Chanaujee	Chanler
Cecil (0.06)	Centrivious	Chaaz	Chaitanya	Chanbert	Chanmeet
Cecilio (0.01)	Cenyon	Chabasco	Chaitin	Chance (0.58)	Channarith
Ced'kevious	Ceolamar	Chacarion	Chaivan	Chance-Cj	Channell
Ced'quan	Ceon	Chace (0.04)	Chak	Chance-Justice	Channen
Cedar (0.01)	Ceondré	Chache	Chaka	Chancee	Channer
Cedarian	Ceonia	Chachi	Chakaris	Chancelar	Channin
Cedarius	Cephas Mychaela	Chachovar	Chaker	Chanceleor	Channing (0.02)

Channon	Charell	Charlz	Chastan	Chay	Cheermer
Chano	Charels	Charlzell	Chasten	Chaya	Chefonne
Chanoch	Charenzo	Charmel	Chasthan	Chayann	Chehab
Chanpreet	Charick	Charmere	Chastin	Chayanne (0.01)	Chehade
Chanraj	Chariel	Charmhad	Chastinn	Chayce (0.01)	Cheick
Chanreksmey	Chariss	Charmonte	Chaston	Chayden	Chekille
Chans	Charity	Charmorro	Chasty	Chaydon	Chekotah
Chanse (0.02)	Charkeem	Charna	Chasvion	Chayee	Chela
Chanselor	Charkie	Charndeep	Chasz	Chayeh	Chelau
Chansey	Charkille	Charnique	Chatar	Chaylen	Cheldin
Chanslor	Charkues	Charnjeev	Chatarious	Chaylin	Chelon
Chansophanna	Charla	Charnjit	Chatavis	Chaylon	Chelsea
Chanston	Charlance	Charnpreet	Chatchay	Chaynce	Chelsen
Chant	Charlant	Charnvir	Chaten	Chayne	Chelsey
Chantal	Charle	Charome	Chatez	Chayne	Chelsie
Chantani	Charlee	Charon	Chatfield	Haunuuhau	Chelton
Chantavious	Charlemagne	Charquez	Chathan	Chayse (0.01)	Chemar
Chanté	Charles (3.66)	Charquille	Chathurthan	Chaysea	Chemaya
Chantel	Charles Alexa	Charrada	Chatlin	Chaysen	Chemel
Chantez	(0.01)	Charrarles	Chatto	Chayson	Chemir
Chanthakhard	Charles Andre	Charrelle	Chatwoine	Chaysten	Chemon
Chanticlair	(0.01)	Charrles	Chau	Chayton (0.01)	Chen
Chantler	Charles Andrew	Charron	Chaucer	Chayvon	Chen-Hau
Chantry	Charles Antoi	Charsavian	Chaudrey	Chaz (0.13)	Chenaniah
Chants	(0.04)	Chartavious	Chaum	Chaz Levi	Chenaniahu
Chantz (0.02)	Charles Emile	Chartell	Chauman	Chazaray	Chenard
Chantztavio	(0.01)	Charu	Chaun	Chazarus	Chenceler
Chanvir	Charles Eric (0.02)	Charvas	Chaunce	Chazden	Chene
Chanz	Charles Etien	Charves	Chauncey (0.05)	Chaze	Chenel
Chanze	(0.02)	Charvez	Chauncy (0.01)	Chazerae	Cheney
Chao	Charles Jaw	Charvill	Chaunecy	Chazeray	Cheng (0.01)
Chaos	Charles Jeffrey	Charviz	Chaunsey	Chaziere	Chentez
Chapan	Charles Joseph	Charvonte	Chaunszi	Chazjuan	Cheong
Chapelle	Charles Jr	Charvoris	Chauscey	Chazmen	Chequan
Chapen	Charles Olivi	Charzelle	Chavares	Chazmon	Cheran
Chapin	(0.01)	Chas (0.01)	Chavari	Chazney	Cherez
Chaplin	Charles Samuel	Chasden	Chavaris	Chazrick	Cheric-Jean
Chapman (0.01)	Charles-Alexis	Chase (1.64)	Chavarre	Chaztin	Cherine
Chaquail	Charlese	Chase-Anthony	Chavaz	Chazton	Cherlon
Chaquan	Charleskadrick	Chasean	Chaven	Chazworth	Chernel
Chaquille	Charleston (0.01)	Chaselyn	Chavers	Chazy	Cherno
Char'quez	Charleton	Chasen (0.03)	Chaves	Chazz (0.02)	Cherod
Charalambos	Charlette	Chaseton	Chavez (0.01)	Che (0.01)	Cherokee (0.01)
Charan	Charley (0.02)	Chasez	Chaveze	Ché	Cheronn
Charanjit	Charli	Chasid	Chavierr	Chéfon	Cherrakee
Charanjot	Charlie (0.23)	Chasik	Chavies	Chélorenz	Cherrod
Charankan	Charlies	Chasinn	Chavis (0.01)	Chéron	Cherrode
Charanpreet	Charlo	Chaskae	Chavis'	Chea	Cherron
Charbel	Charloe	Chaskai	Chavius	Cheaney	Cherubel
Charcelle	Charlsen	Chaske	Chavon	Cheatham	Cherusan
Chard	Charlston	Chasmen	Chavone	Checotah	Chervez
Chardarius	Charlton (0.02)	Chason (0.01)	Chavontae	Ched	Cherwin
Chardon	Charlton Sebasti	Chass	Chavonte	Chee (0.01)	Cherwly
Chardriq	Charly (0.01)	Chasse	Chawki	Chee-Fung	Ches
Chareles	Charly Dat	Chassidy	Chawn	Cheerag	Chesed

Chesh	Chi-Hang	Chinghsuan	Chozey	Christhian	Christone
Chesley	Chia	Chinh	Chrasean	Christhopher	Christonia
Cheslie	Chia Ger	Chinmay	Chrestien	Christi	Christopehr
Chess	Chiante	Chinnon	Chri'shawn	Christiaan	Christoper (0.01)
Chessmen	Chianthony	Chintan	Chris (0.18)	Christian (5.59)	Christoph (0.01)
Chesten	Chianti	Chinua	Chris-Anthony	Christian D	Christophe (0.12)
Chester (0.06)	Chiantia	Chinwuba	Chrisangel	Christian Dane	Christopher
Chestin	Chibley	Chioke	Chrisbryan	Christian Danie	(15.46)
Cheston (0.01)	Chibueze	Chionesu	Chrischen	Christian Jerard	Christopher Ant
Chet (0.02)	Chibuike	Chip	Chrisdtopher	Christian Lee	Christopher Ash
Chet Jr	Chibunna	Chipper	Chrisean	Christian Miles	Christopher Cody
Cheta	Chibuzo	Chiquan	Chrishan	Christian Olive	Christopher Jam
Chetan	Chicago	Chiquita	Chrishaud	Christian Omar	Christopher Jame
Chett	Chicano	Chiquon	Chrishaun	Christian Rey	Christopher Rey
Chette	Chico	Chirag	Chrishawn	Christian Samuel	Christopher Step
Cheuk	Chicoby	Chiran	Chrishod	Christian-Blair	Christopher Vin
Cheval	Chidera	Chirjeet	Chrishon	Christian-Javar	Christopher-
Chevaris Déqwa	Chidi	Chirshawn	Chrishona	Christian-Joel	Andrew
Chevaughn	Chidiebere	Chirstain	Chrishtian	Christian-Kyle	Christopher-Gor
Chevayon	Chidlet	Chirstopher	Chrislandric	Christian-Le	Christopher-Jam
Chevelle	Chidubem	Chisdai	Chrisna	Christian-Mckay	Christopher-Joh
Chevey	Chiduo	Chisholm	Chrisnell	Christian-Tyler	Christopher-John
Chevez	Chidurum	Chislon	Chrisophel	Christiane	Christopher-Jon
Cheveze	Chief Seattle	Chisom	Chrisopher	Christiann	Christopher-
Chevi	Chiem	Chisper	Chrisotpher	Christianna	Olivier
Cheviay	Chiemezie	Chisterpherlee	Chrispher	Christianno	Christopher-Roy
Cheviez	Chievy	Chistopher	Chrisphor	Christiano	Christopher-Se
Chevious	Chieze	Chitao	Chrispin	Christiansen	Christopherj (0.01)
Chevis	Chiffon	Chiu-Peng	Chrissean	Christianwarren	Christophes
Chevon	Chihiro	Chiv	Chrisshawn	Christie	Christophor
Chevonté	Chijioke	Chivarsky	Chrisshun	Christien (0.01)	Christophoros
Chevy (0.02)	Chika	Chivass	Christ	Christienne	Christophr
Chewek	Chikanayo	Chivez	Christa	Christifer	Christophre
Chewy	Chikaodinaka	Chizitara	Christafer	Christiful	Christophyer
Chey	Chike	Chizobam	Christafur	Christin (0.01)	Christophyr
Cheyane	Chikesie	Chloe	Christain (0.03)	Christina	Christos (0.02)
Cheydon	Chiko	Chlorissa	Christallon	Christine	Christos Lucas
Cheyeenne	Chilion	Cho	Christan (0.01)	Christino	Christos-
Cheyene	Chilleung	Choi	Christane	Christion	Theodoros
Cheyenne (0.05)	Chillton	Choice	Christapher (0.01)	Christipher	Christovell
Cheylayne	Chilton	Choicée	Christaun	Christjan	Christpher
Cheyne (0.02)	Chima	Chois	Christaven	Christman	Christphor
Cheyney	Chiman	Chole	Christavious	Christmas	Christron
Cheyunshi	Chimary	Chomrong	Christavius	Christnel	Christropher
Chez	Chimezie	Chon	Christavon	Christo	Christroy
Chezaray	Chin	Chong (0.01)	Christchan	Christobal	Christum
Chezera	Chin-Yeung	Chonner	Christdonaldo	Christof	Christus
Chezere	China	Chontay	Christefor	Christofer (0.04)	Christy
Chezquan	Chinaru	Chontray	Christein	Christoffer (0.01)	Christyan
Chfone	Chinedu	Chonzy	Christen (0.01)	Christofher	Christyon
Chhalrachhorn	Chinedum	Choo	Christensen	Christofred	Chritian
Chhanbunli	Chineme	Chord	Christepher	Christoher	Chritopher
Chi (0.01)	Chinenyeudo	Chou	Christerfer	Christohoros	Chronicle
Chi' Ali'	Ching	Choung	Christerpher	Christol	Chrsitopher
Chi-Alexander	Ching-Yeu	Choy	Christgen	Christon	Chrydavrius

Chrysostom	Ciaran *(0.02)*	Clardy	Clayton *(1.01)*	Clienton	Coba
Chrystian	Ciarre	Clare	Clayton Ray	Clif	Cobain
Chrystien	Ciarren	Claren	Clayton Vaughn	Cliff *(0.01)*	Cobby
Chrystofer	Cibrian	Clarence *(0.18)*	Claytor	Cliff-Richard	Coben
Chryston	Cicero	Clarence Joseph	Clayviousyae	Cliffert	Cobern
Chrystopher	Cidderius	Clarey	Clayvon	Cliffond	Cobert
Chrystopher-	Cideri	Clarissa	Claywon	Clifford *(0.16)*	Cobey
Jacek	Ciderriean	Clark *(0.13)*	Clésean	Cliffton	Cobi *(0.01)*
Chu	Cidny	Clarke *(0.02)*	Clévon	Cliford	Cobia
Chu-Chu	Cidriyll	Clarkson	Clea	Clift	Cobie
Chuck	Cidronio	Claro	Cleandré	Cliftion	Cobin
Chuckeel	Cielo	Claron	Clearion	Clifton *(0.10)*	Coburn
Chuckey	Cieon	Claronté	Cleatis Keyshawn	Clifton Donell	Coby *(0.06)*
Chuckie	Cieron	Clarque	Cleatus	Climeal	Coda
Chuckwuemeka	Cihan	Clarrissa	Cleavon	Clin	Codarius
Chuddy	Cikidi	Claton	Clebert	Clinard	Coday
Chue *(0.01)*	Cilian	Claud	Clebourn	Cline	Coddrick
Chuej Fue	Cillian	Claude *(0.06)*	Cledante	Clinique	Coddy
Chuen	Cina	Claude-Michel	Cleigh	Clinon	Codea
Chueyee	Cinard	Clauderius	Cleighton	Clint *(0.15)*	Codee
Chuks	Cincinnatis	Claudeson	Cellan	Clinten	Codey *(0.08)*
Chukura	Cindy	Claudey	Clem	Clintion	Codey Jacob
Chukwudi	Cinnamon	Claudi	Clemarion	Clinton *(0.25)*	Codi *(0.05)*
Chukwuebuka	Cinnkota	Claudie	Clemens	Clintrell	Codi Jacob
Chukwuemeka	Cinque	Claudin	Clement *(0.02)*	Clio	Codi'
Chukwuma	Cinwon	Claudio *(0.05)*	Clemente *(0.02)*	Cliphane	Codi-Allen
Chukwuneke	Ciprian	Claudio Vicente	Clemon	Cliston	Codiac
Chun *(0.01)*	Cipriano	Claudis	Clemons	Clite	Codie *(0.07)*
Chun-Wan	Cir-Jaso	Claudius	Clemson	Clive	Codv
Chun-Yi	Ciré	Claudonneson	Clen	Clivon	Cody *(7.64)*
Chun-Yip	Cirey	Claudtavius	Clenard	Clonel	Cody Anthony
Chuncey	Ciriaco	Claudy	Clentaevias	Cloom	Cody Dean
Chuncy	Cirilo *(0.01)*	Clausy	Clenten	Cloud	Cody Duong
Chung-Kei	Ciro *(0.01)*	Clauvelt	Cleo *(0.01)*	Cloutier	Cody Jordan
Chung-Yan	Cirron	Clavin	Cleomin	Clovis *(0.01)*	Cody Lee
Chuong	Cisco *(0.01)*	Clavion	Cleon	Clowdell	Cody Quynh
Churchill	Civilize	Clavon	Cleontaé	Cloy	Cody-Arthur
Chutimun	Cj *(0.01)*	Clavone	Cleophas	Clyatt	Cody-Emmanual
Chutiphon	Cjay	Clavonta	Cleotis	Clyde *(0.06)*	Cody-James
Chyan	Ck Kyle	Clavontae	Clerenzo	Clydele	Cody-Joe
Chyance	Ckjuan	Claxton	Cless	Clydrea	Cody-John
Chyenne	Ckristian	Clay *(0.27)*	Clester	Clydrick	Cody-Lane
Chyheem	Clae	Clay O'brien	Clete	Clynce	Cody-Lee
Chyler	Claeb	Claybon	Cletis	Clyton	Cody-Michael-
Chyles	Claibern	Clayborn	Clevaun	Clyvon	Edmund
Chylo	Claiborn	Clayborne	Cleve *(0.01)*	Cmichael	Cody-Ray
Chyma	Claiborne	Claybourn	Cleveland *(0.03)*	Cneri	Codylee
Chynelle	Claibrone	Claybourne	Cleves	Co Larroes	Coe
Chynung	Clair	Clayburne	Clevlis	Coachie	Coelton
Chyrone	Claire	Clayne	Clevon	Coadi	Coen
Cian *(0.01)*	Clancey *(0.01)*	Claysen	Clevonn	Coady *(0.01)*	Coewan
Cianan	Clancy *(0.01)*	Clayshade	Clevontay	Coal	Cofer
Ciante	Clantavon	Clayte	Clevonte	Coalter	Cohan
Cianté	Clara	Clayten	Cleyandre	Coalton	Cohath
Ciara	Claran	Claytiana	Cleyton	Coan	Cohdey

Cohen *(0.01)*
Cohl
Cohyn
Coi
Coke
Cokenya
Colan
Colanda
Colane
Colar
Colbert
Colbey *(0.01)*
Colbi
Colbie
Colbin
Colborne
Colbourne
Colbrey
Colburn
Colby *(0.59)*
Colby Lee
Colden
Cole *(1.80)*
Cole-Alexander
Cole-Allen
Coleb
Colebee
Coleby
Colee
Colegedo
Coleman *(0.14)*
Colemann
Colen *(0.01)*
Coleon
Coles
Coleson *(0.01)*
Coleston
Coleten
Coleton *(0.05)*
Coletyn
Coley *(0.01)*
Colgan
Colie
Colin *(1.34)*
Colin Dow
Colin Michael
Colin-James
Colin-Matthew
Colinn
Collan
Colland
Colleary
Collen *(0.01)*
Collette Sherard
Collian

Collie
Collier *(0.01)*
Colliln
Collin *(0.89)*
Collins *(0.01)*
Collis
Collos
Collyer
Collyn
Colm
Colman *(0.01)*
Cologeno
Cologne
Colon
Colony
Colorado
Colous
Colsen
Colson
Colston
Colt *(0.08)*
Coltan *(0.01)*
Coltar
Colte
Colten *(0.15)*
Colter *(0.05)*
Coltin *(0.03)*
Coltinn
Coltn
Colton *(1.46)*
Colton Hunter
Colton James
Colttan
Coltton
Coltun
Coltyn *(0.01)*
Coltyne
Colum
Columbia
Columbus
Colval
Colvin
Coly
Colyn *(0.01)*
Commodore
Compton
Con
Conagher
Conal
Conall
Conan *(0.01)*
Conar
Conary
Concepion
Concetto

Condarias
Condarius
Condarrius
Condone
Condra
Condredge
Conelius
Conely
Coner
Coney
Conic
Conlan *(0.01)*
Conley *(0.01)*
Conlin
Conlon
Conly
Conn
Connaire
Connal
Connar *(0.01)*
Connard
Connary
Conneer
Connel
Connell *(0.01)*
Connelly
Connen
Conner *(0.62)*
Connery
Connie
Connley
Connner
Connoe
Connoer
Connolly
Connon
Connor *(3.34)*
Connor Francis
Connor Roy
Connor Wesley
Connord
Connory
Connyr
Conor *(0.39)*
Conor Antony
Conor Riley
Conour
Conrad *(0.15)*
Conrado *(0.01)*
Conradt
Conroy
Conrradino
Consess
Constadinos
Constandine

Constantin
Constantine *(0.02)*
Constantino *(0.01)*
Constantinos
Conston
Contavis
Contee
Conterrion
Conterrius
Contrail
Contravious
Contravis
Contrell
Contrevious
Contreyl
Conway *(0.01)*
Conyilouse
Coolie
Cooper *(0.25)*
Copache
Copeland
Copper
Cor'rez
Cor'teze
Cor'von
Cora
Coradell
Coran
Corandise
Corans
Coray
Corban *(0.01)*
Corbbitt
Corben *(0.01)*
Corbert
Corbet
Corbett *(0.01)*
Corbette
Corbin *(0.24)*
Corbitt
Corbon
Corbrian
Corby *(0.01)*
Corbyn
Corchez
Cord *(0.01)*
Cordairo
Cordal
Cordale
Cordall
Cordao
Cordaral
Cordarde
Cordarell
Cordarelle

Cordario
Cordarion
Cordarious
Cordarius *(0.01)*
Cordaro
Cordarrell
Cordarris
Cordarrius
Cordarro
Cordarrowe
Cordarus
Cordaryl
Corday
Cordéll
Cordea
Cordeflo
Cordeil
Cordel *(0.01)*
Cordele
Cordell *(0.11)*
Cordelle
Cordelral
Cordelriu
Corder
Cordereous
Corderias
Corderious
Cordero *(0.01)*
Corderral
Corderrick
Corderro
Corderryn
Corderus
Cordie
Cordierre
Cordin
Cordjel
Cordliss
Cordney
Cordoran
Cordre
Cordré
Cordrell
Cordric
Cordual
Corduan
Coredale
Coree
Corelelle
Coren
Corentez
Corenzo
Coreon
Coreontae
Corey *(2.16)*

Corey Antonio
Corey James
Corey Jr
Corey Lee
Corey'ontae
Coreyian
Coreylee
Coreyon
Corgan
Cori *(0.01)*
Coria
Corian
Coriante
Corie *(0.01)*
Coriélle
Corin *(0.01)*
Corinth
Corinthian
Corinthius
Corion
Corionte
Corithian
Corjée
Corlan
Corlandis
Corlantis
Corlenza
Corleone
Corley
Corlin
Corlis
Corliss *(0.01)*
Corlos
Cormac *(0.01)*
Cormack
Cornealis
Corneil
Corneilius
Corneilous
Corneilus
Cornel
Cornelia
Cornelias
Cornelio
Cornelious
Cornelis
Corneliu
Cornelius *(0.11)*
Cornell *(0.04)*
Cornellious
Cornellius
Cornelous
Corneluis
Cornelus
Corniélius

Cornies	Corveyle	Coulten	Craigory	Cris	Cruz (0.08)
Cornlius	Corvez	Coulter (0.01)	Craijion	Crisanto	Cruz-Hermilo
Corny	Corvis	Coulton (0.01)	Cramer	Crisfer	Cruze
Corodon	Corvon	Couney	Crance	Crishaun	Cruzeto
Coron	Corvonte	Countrell	Crandel	Crishawn	Cruzito
Coronado	Corvontist	Country	Cranford	Crishna	Cruzko
Corrado	Corwan	Courage	Crannel	Crishneil	Crysostomos
Corrani	Corwin (0.03)	Courman	Cranston	Crishon	Crystal
Correll	Corwinthony	Cournelius	Crash	Crisoforo	Crystapher
Correlle	Corwyn	Cournelyous	Crashawn	Crisp	Crystian (0.01)
Corrence	Corwynn	Courson	Crason	Crispien	Crystifer
Correnth	Corwynne	Court	Cravawn	Crispin	Csaba
Correy	Cory (1.33)	Courten	Craver	Crispinus	Cshane
Correyanté	Cory Demar	Courtenay	Crawford (0.01)	Criss	Cuauhtamoc
Corrick	Cory Jr	Courtenez	Cray	Crist	Cuauhtemoc
Corrie	Cory Michael	Courtes	Craymond	Cristal	(0.02)
Corrigan	Cory-Dane	Courtez	Crayson	Cristan	Cuba
Corrin	Cory-Davhontae	Courtlan	Crayton	Cristapher	Cubalyn
Corris	Cory-Deon	Courtland (0.04)	Créon	Cristean	Cube
Corry (0.01)	Cory-Lee	Courtlandt	Creavon	Cristen	Cuditnarine
Corsair	Corydon	Courtlin	Credale	Cristgen	Cudy
Corsen	Corye	Courtlind	Credence	Cristhian	Cue
Corsha	Coryell	Courtlon	Crederius	Cristhofer	Cuedell
Corsini	Corylee	Courtnee	Cree	Cristiam	Cuhlainn
Corson	Corynn	Courtney (0.10)	Creed (0.01)	Cristian (1.31)	Cuhong
Cort (0.01)	Corzay	Courvoiser	Creede	Cristian-Alejan	Cuillaume
Cortaveion	Corzaylan	Courvoisier	Creedon	Cristiano	Culbert
Cortavian	Coshawn	Courvoisier'	Creek	Cristien	Culkin
Cortavion	Cosimo	Coury	Creg	Cristifer	Cullan (0.01)
Cortavious	Cosme (0.01)	Couvasier	Cregan	Cristin	Cullandane
Cortavis	Cosmin	Covaney	Cregg	Cristo (0.01)	Cullen (0.14)
Cortavius	Cosmo (0.01)	Cove	Creid	Cristobal (0.06)	Culley
Cortaz	Costa	Covéae	Creigh	Cristofaro	Cullin
Corte	Costantino	Coven	Creighton (0.01)	Cristofe	Cullum
Corteco	Costantinos	Cover	Creigren	Cristofer (0.02)	Cully
Corteece	Costas	Coverdale	Creigs	Cristofher	Culton
Cortell	Costeen	Coviliano	Cremson	Cristoforo	Culver
Cortes	Costello	Covin	Crenzel	Cristopher (0.08)	Cuma
Cortez (0.11)	Costie	Cowan	Crescencio	Cristoval	Cunningham
Cortis	Costin	Cowen	Cresencio	Cristovio	Cuong
Cortize	Costner	Cowentay	Creshad	Cristyan	Cuoy
Cortlan	Coston	Cox	Creshaun	Criswell	Cupertino
Cortland (0.02)	Costonzo	Coy (0.03)	Creshawn	Croey	Cupid
Cortlen	Cote	Coyan	Creshon	Croft	Cur'twon
Cortley	Cotey	Coydric	Cressie	Crofton	Curan
Cortlin	Cothran	Coye	Cresson	Croix	Curaton
Cortlyn	Coti	Coyote	Crest	Crosby	Curdarius
Cortne	Cotie	Cozy	Creston	Crosce	Curles
Cortney (0.01)	Cotton	Cpensor	Creth	Crosland	Curley
Corum	Cottrell	Cragin	Crew	Crosley	Curon
Corum-Orion	Cotus	Cragun	Crews	Cross	Curran (0.01)
Corvel	Coty (0.11)	Craig (0.61)	Creyton	Croy	Curren
Corvell	Cotye	Craige	Crhisst	Croydon	Curri
Corvette	Cotyjo	Craigh	Criag	Cruistofer	Currie
Corveuan	Coulson	Craighton	Crimet	Crusito	Currin

Curry (0.01)	Cyress	D Marqus	D'antrae	D'lante	D'onte
Cursante	Cyric	D Michael	D'antre	D'lario	D'ontea
Curshaun	Cyril (0.01)	D Miran	D'aquino	D'lawrence	D'ories
Cursteeve	Cyrill	D Montrae	D'arcy (0.01)	D'lisa	D'orrin
Curstin	Cyris	D Morgan	D'areio	D'londre	D'quan (0.01)
Curt (0.01)	Cyriss	D Ondre	D'aries	D'loren	D'quane
Curtaveous	Cyron	D Quan	D'arington	D'lorian	D'quann
Curtavious	Cyrus (0.10)	D Quavon	D'arius	D'maja	D'quantius
Curtez	Cyruss	D Quayvius	D'armond	D'mantiz	D'quavion
Curtice	Cytravious	D Quin	D'arnaz	D'marco (0.01)	D'quon
Curtis (0.99)	Czaja	D Quincy	D'arrion	D'marcus (0.01)	D'qwuan
Curtis John		D Ravion	D'artagnan (0.01)	D'marea	D'ratio
Curtiss (0.01)	**-D-**	D Schwadraa	D'artangan	D'mareae	D'reyl
Curtland		D Shaun	D'artangnan	D'mareiya	D'ron
Curtron	D (0.06)	D Shundrick	D'artemus	D'mari	D'rone
Curvin	D Aaron	D Trevis	D'aubray	D'mario	D'ronnie
Cushman	D Ajuin	D Untay	D'aundra	D'marius	D'sean
Cushsure	D Andre (0.01)	D Unte	D'aundre	D'markaus	D'shan
Custis	D Andre Kar	D Vante	D'avanté	D'markus	D'shannon
Cutberto	D Andrea	D Vaun	D'carlos	D'marreo	D'shaun
Cutler	D Angelo	D Vine	D'chaun	D'marté	D'shaunn
Cutter (0.01)	D Anglo	D Vonta	D'cory	D'mazei'	D'shawn
Cuyler (0.01)	D Ante	D Vontae	D'eara	D'meko	D'shawne
Cy (0.01)	D Antea	D Vonte	D'edmond	D'meric	D'shea
Cy Ree	D Anterrius	D Wayne	D'eldrick	D'metrius	D'shon
Cyan	D Anthony	D Yon	D'emario	D'metrus	D'terriyian
Cyarrin	D Antoine	D'aarien	D'eonte	D'michael	D'torien
Cycil	D Antonio	D'aaron	D'equawn	D'mil	D'treveian
Cydrick	D Antrae	D'adrian	D'eric	D'mirist	D'undre
Cyite	D Arrian	D'adris	D'erick	D'mitri	D'undré
Cylas	D Arrieus	D'aire	D'errick	D'mitry	D'vante
Cyle (0.03)	D Arsey	D'aireon	D'esmond	D'mon	D'vanté
Cyleb	D Artagnan	D'ajanai	D'evans	D'mondre	D'varis
Cyler	D Aundrey	D'ali	D'evanté	D'montaye	D'varius
Cyles	D Auntre	D'alluntae	D'evon	D'monte	D'vaughandre
Cylik	D Avion	D'alonte	D'finest	D'montra	D'vaughn
Cylil	D Chauncey	D'amonte	D'iamonta	D'montre	D'vaureo
Cylis	D Eric	D'amonté	D'imari	D'montrell	D'viere
Cylor	D Hayden	D'amonti	D'issac	D'montrio	D'von
Cylus	D Jonh	D'andrae	D'ja	D'mtri'	D'vond
Cymin	D Jonterrio	D'andray	D'jahri	D'myrion	D'vone
Cynan	D Joseph	D'andre (0.07)	D'jaris	D'nadre	D'vonn
Cynard	D Juan	D'andré	D'jhyria	D'naja	D'vonta
Cynnequi	D Kerion	D'andres	D'jimon	D'narus	D'vontae
Cynquavious	D Kevin	D'andrez	D'jon	D'nasha	D'vonte (0.01)
Cynryc	D Kota Jewu	D'andrick	D'juan (0.01)	D'nautica	D'vornnial
Cynthia	D Kwavious	D'angelio	D'kambui	D'nerio	D'waine
Cypres	D L	D'angelo (0.03)	D'karas	D'nico	D'wan
Cypress	D Lundarius	D'anglo	D'kartes	D'nikis	D'waun
Cyprian	D Mairan	D'antae	D'kemon	D'omonté	D'wayne
Cyprien	D Marcus	D'antay	D'kente	D'on Leonard	D'whon
Cyree	D Marea	D'ante (0.01)	D'kieren	D'ondre	D'xtra
Cyrel	D Mario	D'anté	D'koda	D'onta	D'yanté
Cyrell	D Markis	D'anthoni	D'kwon	D'ontae	D-Angelo
Cyrenus	D Marlin	D'anthony (0.01)	D'land	D'ontay	D-Artagnan

D-Asjay	Da'kavion	Da'rius	Daanbir	Daé	Daevontey
D-Margio	Da'kelin	Da'ron	Daanial	Daéjon	Daezon
D-Mikal	Da'kierrian	Da'ronce	Daanish	Daéquan	Dafranco
D-Onest	Da'kqwone	Da'sean	Daanyaal	Daéron	Dafredrick
D-Sean	Da'kuan	Da'shae	Daaron	Daéshawn	Dafyd
D.	Da'kwon	Da'shan	Daaronta	Daévonn	Dafydd
D.J.	Da'leon	Da'shauan	Daavid	Dae-Han	Dagan (0.01)
Da	Da'lyn	Da'shaun	Dabarrious	Dae-Shawn	Dagen
Da Cota	Da'ma'jía	Da'shawd	Daben	Dae-Trayun	Dageon
Da Juan	Da'mahzhai	Da'shawn (0.01)	Dabid	Daedrian	Dager
Da Keithan	Da'maj	Da'shawnn	Dabir	Daegan	Dagiem
Da Marco	Da'mar	Da'shay	Dabranton	Daegon	Dagobert
Da Marcus	Da'marcus	Da'shon	Dabrent	Daehon	Dagoberto (0.02)
Da Marqus	Da'mari	Da'shonce	Dabrion	Daeja	Dagoberto Jr
Da Mirian	Da'mario	Da'shone	Dabtavious	Daejon	Dagon
Da Monta	Da'marion	Da'shoun	Dabuvous	Daejuan	Dagua
Da Montraz	Da'markus	Da'shun	Dac	Daekwaun	Dahans
Da Myron	Da'marr	Da'travious	Dacano	Daekwon	Dahavean
Da Nautica	Da'marron	Da'trel	Dacari	Dael	Dahaven
Da Quan (0.01)	Da'maruis	Da'treyon	Dacarius	Daelan	Daher
Da Quay	Da'mekio	Da'va'y	Dacarliuss	Daelen	Dahir
Da Rashio	Da'metrius	Da'vahne	Dacarr	Daelin	Dahji
Da Rell	Da'meyl	Da'vante	Dace	Daelon	Dahleon
Da Ron	Da'mion	Da'vario	Dacen	Daelyn	Dahlin
Da Sean	Da'mir	Da'varis	Dacey	Daelyne	Dahlon
Da Shawn	Da'mon	Da'vaughn	Dachary	Daemean	Dahlton
Da Shon	Da'moni	Da'veon	Dacian	Daemeon	Dahmar
Da Travius	Da'montae	Da'veontae	Dacien	Daemeunt	Dahmon
Da Varius	Da'monte	Da'vhon	Dacious	Daemianmichael	Dahquan
Da Vaun	Da'monté	Da'vid	Dack	Daemien	Dahrian
Da Veed	Da'montre	Da'vion	Dackota	Daemin	Dahrion
Da Vel	Da'montré	Da'voh	Dacoda (0.01)	Daemion	Dahryl
Da Von	Da'narius	Da'von (0.01)	Dacodah	Daemishia	Dahud
Da Vonta	Da'neill	Da'vonnétae	Dacolden	Daemon (0.01)	Dahvone
Da Vonte	Da'ontre	Da'vonta	Dacorey	Daenin	Dahvriel
Da Vorius	Da'qaun	Da'vontae	Dacoreya	Daequan (0.01)	Dahwood
Da'brock	Da'quadraous	Da'vonte	Dacorrick	Daequane	Dai Dreon
Da'cameron	Da'quahn	Da'voughn	Dacory	Daequon	Dai'
Da'cor	Da'quain	Da'wan	Dacota (0.01)	Daequone	Dai'ajani
Da'corion	Da'quan (0.04)	Da'wuan	Dacotah (0.01)	Daeqwan	Dai'juan
Da'delveon	Da'quarn	Da'zaris	Dacotta	Daeron	Dai'kuis
Da'drick	Da'quelle	Da'zhawn	Dacquan	Daesean	Dai'one
Da'jaquan	Da'quian	Da'zhawnté	Dacrius	Daeshad	Dai'quan
Da'jawan	Da'quice	Da-An	Dacy	Daeshaun	Dai'quann
Da'jhaun	Da'quintin	Da-Juan	Daddmus	Daeshawn	Dai'quarrius
Da'jian	Da'quon	Da-Marea	Dade	Daeshon	Dai'qwan
Da'john	Da'quwan	Da-Marius	Daden	Daeshun	Dai'shan
Da'johntai	Da'qwan	Da-Marqus	Dadly	Daetona	Dai'von
Da'jon	Da'qwandre	Da-Quan	Dadrian	Daetrigo	Dai-Sean
Da'jonte	Da'qwaun	Da-Quane	Dadrick	Daeus	Daichi
Da'jour	Da'qwon	Da-Ron	Dadrien	Daevion	Daigan
Da'juan	Da'rel	Da-Shawn	Dae	Daevohn	Daige
Da'juanta	Da'rell	Da-Ud	Dae Jon	Daevon (0.01)	Daigen
Da'juantay	Da'reonday	Da-Veaun	Dae Quone	Daevonne	Daign
Da'junn	Da'rion	Da-Yu	Dae Von	Daevonte	Daij'on

Daijha	Dairus	Dakari (0.01)	Daldric	Daltyn	Damarie
Daijion	Daisean	Dakarri	Dale (0.28)	Daluciano	Damarino
Daijo'in	Daishaun	Dakarries	Daleeyon	Dalvacqio	Damario (0.01)
Daijohn	Daishawn	Dakavion	Dalek	Dalvanta	Damarion
Daijon	Daishon	Dakcota	Dalemone	Dalvas	Damarious
Daikan	Daishoun	Dakeem	Dalen (0.02)	Dalven	Damaris
Daiki	Daisuke	Dakeil	Daleon	Dalvin (0.04)	Damarius (0.01)
Dailan	Daisy	Dakelon	Dalequintin	Dalvinder	Damariya
Dailen	Daiton	Daken	Dalerian	Dalvinear	Damarjé
Dailis	Daitron	Dakendrick	Dalerick	Dalvir	Damarjeza
Daillobe	Daityn	Dakevilian	Daletavious	Dalvis	Damark
Dailon	Daivain	Dakevious	Dalevecchio	Dalvise	Damarkco
Dailyn	Daivd	Dakevis	Daley	Dalvon	Damarkis
Daiman	Daivid	Dakhari	Dalice	Dalvontae	Damarko
Daimari	Daivion	Dakheyvis	Dalin (0.01)	Dalvonte	Damarkus (0.01)
Daimario	Daivon (0.01)	Daki	Dalis	Dalvontrea	Damarkwiss
Daimean	Daivonn	Dakil	Daljinder	Dalvyn	Damarquan
Daimeon	Daivonte	Dakin	Daljit	Dalwinder	Damarques
Daimeyon	Daivonté	Dakkota	Daljot	Daly	Damarquez
Daimian	Daiwan	Dakoa	Dallan (0.01)	Dalyan	Damarquis
Daimien	Daiyaan	Dakoda (0.07)	Dallance	Dalyn (0.01)	Damarrco
Daimin	Daiz	Dakodah	Dallante	Dalynte	Damarre
Daimion	Daizhon	Dakodas	Dallas (0.65)	Damaccion	Damarrea
Daimon (0.01)	Daizon	Dakooa	Dallas Emerson	Damacus	Damarrion
Daimone	Dajae	Dakota (2.61)	Dallen (0.02)	Damadre	Damarrious
Daimoniau	Dajarvis	Dakota Micheal	Dalles	Damaien	Damarrius
Dain (0.01)	Dajaun	Dakota-James	Dallevante	Damain (0.01)	Damarvian
Daine	Dajé	Dakota-John	Dallie	Damaine	Damaryo
Dainel	Dajean	Dakotah (0.08)	Dallin (0.10)	Damaion	Damarzha
Dainentae	Dajhmere	Dakotah-James	Dallis (0.01)	Damal	Damascus
Dainer	Dajiawn	Dakotia	Dallon (0.01)	Daman (0.01)	Damasio
Dainon	Dajin	Dakotta	Dallvin	Damandeep	Damaun
Daion	Dajion	Dakottah	Dallyn (0.01)	Damani (0.01)	Damaureon
Daionta	Dajn	Dakoven	Dalmar	Damaninder	Damauri
Daiontae	Dajohn	Dakoyta	Dalmo	Damanjit	Damaurius
Daiouijus	Dajon (0.02)	Dakquan	Dalmontae	Damanjot	Damayon
Daiqone	Dajonae	Dakshan	Dalon (0.01)	Damanni	Damazeo
Daiqua	Dajour	Dakuan	Dalonny	Damanpreet	Damcshon
Daiquan (0.02)	Dajoure	Dakuari	Dalonta	Damantae	Damean
Daiquane	Dajourr	Dakwan	Dalonte	Damante	Damecius
Daiquavious	Dajouvan	Dalaan	Dalonté	Damar (0.01)	Dameekion
Daiquawn	Dajreaun	Dalajiwuan	Dalontiá	Damarann	Dameian
Daiquez	Dajshon	Dalamar	Dalonzo	Damarco (0.01)	Dameieon
Daiquiri	Dajuan (0.02)	Dalan (0.01)	Dalphe-Joseph	Damarcue	Damein (0.01)
Daiquon	Dajuante	Dalane	Dalrois	Damarcus (0.03)	Dameion (0.01)
Daiqwan	Dajuanye	Dalantae	Dalshawn	Damare	Damekion
Daiqwon	Dajwan	Dalante	Dalson	Damaré	Damekius
Dair	Dajwoun	Dalarrine	Dalston	Damarea	Dameko
Dairal	Dajzon	Dalarrion	Daltan	Damareea	Damel
Dairean	Dakairi	Dalas	Dalten	Damaren	Damele
Daireonté	Dakaota	Dalaton	Daltin	Damareus	Damemian
Dairion	Dakar	Dalaun	Dalton (1.84)	Damarez	Damen (0.02)
Dairn	Dakarai (0.02)	Dalaveon	Dalton John	Damari	Damenion
Dairo	Dakarai Tavonte	Dalbir	Daltrey	Damaria	Dameon (0.03)
Dairon	Dakaraia	Daldashawn	Daltron	Damarick	Damerial

Damerick	Dammion	Danaé	Daniel Angel	Dannesh	Dantrey
Dameris	Dammond	Danaiel	Daniel Charles	Danney	Dantrez
Damerius	Dammy	Danaio	Daniel	Danni	Dantril
Damerjian	Damnit	Danakus	Christopher	Dannial	Dantyrell
Dameron	Damodar	Danan	Daniel Colle	Dannick *(0.02)*	Dantzleer
Damerrian	Damoddre	Danard	Daniel Emanuel	Dannie *(0.02)*	Dantzler
Dametre	Damoio'n	Danardo	Daniel II	Danniel *(0.02)*	Danual
Dametri *(0.01)*	Damom	Danarious	Daniel IV	Danniele	Danushan
Dametries	Damon *(0.39)*	Danarius	Daniel Jay	Dannin	Danute
Dametrik	Damon Xavier	Danato	Daniel Jose	Dannis	Danvell
Dametrious	Damon-William	Danaum	Daniel Lee	Dannish	Danvon
Dametrius *(0.01)*	Damond *(0.02)*	Danavian	Daniel Lionel	Dannon *(0.01)*	Danvon'ta
Damiam	Damonde	Danavite	Daniel Phillip	Danny *(0.68)*	Danvonte
Damian *(0.58)*	Damondrae	Danavon	Daniel Quindo	Danny Dinhg	Dany *(0.09)*
Damian'dra	Damone *(0.01)*	Danay	Webber	Dannylee	Dany'el
Damian-Alexande	Damoni	Danbee	Daniel Salva	Dannyqual	Dany-Pierre
Damian-Chris	Damonic	Danboba	Daniel Wade	Danon	Danya
Damian-Jamal	Damonjah	Dandi	Daniel-Anthony	Danorius	Danyaal
Damiane	Damonjay	Dandley	Daniel-Gerard	Danotria	Danyal
Damiano	Damonl	Dandraze	Daniel-Gia	Danovan	Danyale
Damias	Damonni	Dandre *(0.02)*	Daniel-James	Danqavous	Danyan
Damichael	Damonshay	Dandreius	Daniel-Paul	Danquan	Danyck
Damico	Damont	Dandrick	Daniel-Peter	Danquavious	Danyel
Damidrick	Damonta *(0.01)*	Dandy	Daniel-Ray	Danquavis	Danyell
Damiel	Damontá	Dane *(0.23)*	Danielar	Danquiel	Danyl
Damiem	Damontae	Daneal	Daniele *(0.01)*	Danquil	Danylo
Damien *(0.39)*	Damontai	Daneez	Danielk	Danqune	Danyo
Damien Charles	Damontay	Daneil	Daniell	Danrey	Danyon
Damien-Xavier	Damontayé	Danek	Danielle *(0.02)*	Danrick Vince	Danzel *(0.01)*
Damienne	Damontaze	Danel	Danielo	Danshawn	Danzell
Damientae	Damonte *(0.01)*	Danell	Danier	Danso	Danziel
Damieon	Damonté	Danelle	Daniil	Dantá	Danzig
Damier	Damontez	Danen	Danijel	Dantae *(0.01)*	Danzik
Damiere	Damontray	Danerius	Danik *(0.01)*	Dantaé	Danzil
Damiion	Damontre	Danerrian	Danika	Dantavion	Danzinger
Damiko	Damontré	Danert	Danil	Dantavious	Danzria
Damilola	Damontreal	Danesh	Danila	Dantavius	Dao
Damin *(0.01)*	Damordre	Danevin	Danile	Dantay	Daon
Damine	Damoris	Daney	Danilo *(0.02)*	Dante *(0.24)*	Daony
Damion *(0.17)*	Damoriss	Danez	Danilo Joseph	Danté *(0.05)*	Daoud
Damionne	Damorje	Danford	Danin	Dantee	Dapinder
Damionte	Damound	Danforth	Danique	Dantel	Dapree
Damiquel	Damount	Dang *(0.01)*	Danish *(0.01)*	Danterious	Daptne
Damir	Damoyne	Dang-Khoa	Daniul	Danterrio	Daq'uan
Damiri	Damun	Dangelo *(0.01)*	Danius	Danterrious	Daqabius
Damiroquan	Damus	Dangielo	Daniyal	Danterrius	Daqice
Damitnus	Damyan	Danh	Daniyel	Dantevious	Daqjuan
Damitri	Damyn	Dani	Danjerlek	Dantevius	Daqon
Damitric	Dan *(0.08)*	Danial *(0.04)*	Danjero	Dantez	Daquaci'
Damitrie	Dan Dre	Danick *(0.04)*	Danjot	Danthony	Daquadrea
Damitrious	Dan Joseph	Danie	Danley	Danton *(0.01)*	Daquain
Damiyan	Dan'ta	Danieal	Dannel	Dantraveon	Daquaine
Damiyon	Dan'varius	Danieko	Dannell	Dantré	Daquame
Damjan	Dan-Gabriel	Daniel *(13.02)*	Dannelle	Dantrel	Daquan *(0.14)*
Dammean	Dana *(0.09)*	Daniel Alexandr	Danner	Dantrell *(0.03)*	Daquan Shaquell

Daquan'	Dara *(0.01)*	Darian-Alexander	Darkeem	Darquelle	Darron *(0.03)*
Daquandre	Darahtae	Darian-James	Darkken	Darquez	Darroun
Daquandrey	Darain	Darianne	Darkmon	Darquille	Darrow
Daquane *(0.01)*	Daraj	Dariante	Darko	Darquise	Darrowing
Daquann	Daraja	Darias	Darkon	Darraevious	Darroyl
Daquantae	Darall	Daric	Darl	Darragh	Darrtel
Daquantas	Daran	Darice	Darley	Darraie	Darrus
Daquante	Darango	Darick *(0.01)*	Darling	Darrail	Darrw
Daquarion	Darante	Darico	Darlus	Darral	Darry
Daquarius *(0.01)*	Dararod	Daricus	Darlye	Darrall	Darryan
Daquarri	Daraun	Darie	Darmacus	Darran	Darryck
Daquarrius	Daravichiey	Dariea	Darman	Darrayle	Darryis
Daquarus	Daray	Dariean	Darmani	Darree	Darryk
Daquaun	Darayco	Darieck	Darmar	Darreian	Darryl *(0.27)*
Daquaveá	Darayjel	Dariek	Darmarcus	Darrein	Darryl Anth
Daquavian	Daraymein	Dariel *(0.01)*	Darmarius	Darreion	Darryle
Daquavion	Darby *(0.02)*	Darielle	Darmarjeá	Darrek	Darryll
Daquavious	Darbyn	Darien *(0.19)*	Darmarkis	Darrel *(0.04)*	Darrylreal
Daquavis	Darcae	Darieon	Darmawan	Darrell *(0.27)*	Darryn *(0.01)*
Daquawn	Darcell	Daries	Darmez	Darren *(0.67)*	Darryon
Daquel	Darcey	Darieus	Darmontai	Darren K	Darryus
Daquell	Darcy *(0.03)*	Darik *(0.01)*	Darnail	Darrenisha	Darsan
Daquennis	Dardell	Darikell	Darnaine	Darreon	Darschae
Daquez	Darden	Darin *(0.11)*	Darnall	Darreus	Darsh
Daquin	Daré	Darindra	Darnay	Darreyen	Darshan *(0.01)*
Daquincy	Darérick	Daring	Darneal	Darrial	Darshaun
Daquine	Darean	Dario *(0.09)*	Darneil	Darrian *(0.07)*	Darshawn
Daquis	Dareche	Darion *(0.13)*	Darnel *(0.01)*	Darric	Darshon
Daquon *(0.01)*	Dareck	Dariontae	Darnell *(0.19)*	Darrice	Darshvinder
Daquone	Dareel	Darios	Darnelle *(0.01)*	Darrick *(0.04)*	Darshy
Daquonnzie	Dareen	Darious *(0.02)*	Darnesha	Darricus	Darsikan
Daquory	Dareginald	Dariousz	Darnez	Darriel	Dartagnan
Daquota	Dareil	Dariq	Darntriele	Darrien *(0.07)*	Dartainous
Daquqne	Darein	Darique	Darnyell	Darrik	Dartanian
Daquvious	Dareion	Daris *(0.01)*	Darnyll	Darrin *(0.12)*	Dartaniel
Daquwon	Darek *(0.01)*	Darium	Darocha	Darringer	Dartanion
Daqwain	Darel	Dariun	Darol	Darrington	Dartanious
Daqwan	Darell *(0.02)*	Darius *(0.84)*	Darold	Darrio	Dartanya
Daqwane	Darelle	Darius Lee	Daroll	Darrion *(0.09)*	Dartanyan
Daqwann	Daremen	Darius Willie	Daron *(0.05)*	Darrion Cody	Dartanyon
Daqweise	Daren *(0.05)*	Darius-Jordan	Daronaté	Darrione	Dartavious
Daqwoinne	Darence	Darius-Wesley	Darond	Darrious *(0.01)*	Dartavis
Daqwon	Darentae	Dariuse	Darone	Darris *(0.01)*	Dartavyous
Daqwond	Darenzy	Dariush	Daronn	Darriun	Dartayous
Daqwone	Dareon *(0.01)*	Dariush-Javad	Daronta	Darriunte	Darteez
Dar Ion	Darerein	Dariuss	Darontae	Darrius *(0.13)*	Dartel
Dar'ion	Darese	Dariusz	Darontay	Darriuss	Dartemius
Dar'ius	Dareum	Darivan	Daronte	Darriyun	Darterious
Dar'kwan	Dareus	Darivs	Daronté	Darrly	Darterrius
Dar'nell	Darewood	Dariyan	Daroyl	Darro	Dartez
Dar'nesio	Darez	Dariyn	Darp	Darrocques	Dartezeon
Dar'rick	Darhon	Dariyone	Darquavion	Darroen	Darth
Dar'ryck	Daria	Darjay	Darquavious	Darrol	Dartrell
Dar'shawn	Dariaan	Darkarius	Darqué	Darrold	Daruice
Dar-Jon	Darian *(0.30)*	Darkecé	Darquel	Darroll	Daruis

Darvarius	Dashjon	Dattmon	Davaris (0.01)	David-Anthony	Davon-Tae
Darvel	Dashle	Datus	Davarius	David-Edward	Davoncié
Darvell (0.01)	Dashon (0.02)	Datwan	Davariyoun	David-Emmanuell	Davond
Darvelle	Dashonnie	Datwon	Davaron	David-Hayk	Davondray
Darveon	Dashonte	Dau'an	Davarrius	David-Huy	Davondrick
Darvez	Dashuan	Daud	Davarus	David-Jacob	Davone
Darvian	Dashun	Daudi	Davasyia	David-James	Davonn
Darvielle	Dashure	Daudre	Davaughn (0.01)	David-Joel	Davonne
Darvin (0.01)	Dashwan	Daughlton	Davaune	David-Jonathan	Davonné
Darvis	Dasia'n	Daularrius	Davawn	David-Kenny	Davonnte
Darvon	Dasil	Daulton (0.06)	Dave (0.17)	David-Luke	Davonta (0.03)
Darvonte	Dasio	Daumauriá	Davérnere	David-Michael	Davontá
Darvonté	Dasion	Daumonz	Dave-Yon	David-Micheal	Davontaé
Darvoris	Dasjuan	Daune	Daveantae	David-Ngoc	Davontae (0.02)
Darwil	Dasmin	Daunja	Daved-James	David-Oleg	Davontaé
Darwin (0.06)	Dasmine	Dauntae	Davee	David-Owusu	Davontah
Darwing	Dasmond	Dauntavious	Daveed	David-Royce	Davontai
Darwyn	Dasmone	Daunte	Daveion	Davidadriaan	Davontay (0.01)
Dary	Dason	Dauntee	Davel	Davidanthon	Davontaye
Daryan	Dassan	Daunyel	Davell	Davide	Davonte (0.08)
Daryel	Dastin	Dauphin	Davelle	Davidian	Davonté (0.02)
Daryeon	Dat (0.01)	Daury	Daven (0.02)	Davidlee	Davonté Montré
Daryk	Dat-Hung	Dausen	Davendra	Davids	Davontea
Daryl (0.16)	Dataevius	Daut	Daventry	Davidson (0.01)	Davontee
Daryl Thomas	Datan	Dauvee	Daveon (0.02)	Daviean	Davonthay
Daryle (0.01)	Datania	Dauven	Daveoon	Daviel	Davonti
Daryll	Datari	Dauwn	Davequan	Davielle	Davonti'
Darylwood	Datarie	Dauwood	Daveras	Davien	Davontra
Daryn (0.01)	Dataurean	Davacea	Davere	Davieon	Davontre
Daryon	Datavion	Davad	Daverian	Davierre	Davor
Darythe	Datavious	Davadre	Daverin	Daviet	Davorin
Daryus	Datavis	Davaey	Daverio	Davikiyo	Davoris
Darza	Datavius	Davahnté	Daveron	Davin (0.07)	Davorius
Dasan	Datetion	Davaid	Daveton	Davinder	Davos
Dasante	Dathan (0.01)	Davalous	Davevon	Davindra	Davoun
Dasean (0.01)	Dathian	Davan	Davey (0.02)	Daviné	Davriel
Dash	Dathon	Davanand	Daveyon	Davinus	Davrin
Dasha	Datjuan	Davaniel	Davi	Davion (0.08)	Davron
Dashab	Daton	Davanta	Daviaire	Davionce	Davuhn
Dashae	Datravious	Davantay	Davian (0.01)	Davione	Davvid
Dashamone	Datrayvus	Davante (0.04)	Daviarl	Davionne	Davvinique
Dashan	Datreion	Davanté (0.01)	Davic	Davis (0.28)	Davvion
Dashane	Datrell	Davantray	David (11.38)	Davish	Davy (0.01)
Dashante	Datrelle	Davar	David Alexander	Davison	Davy Aun
Dasharian	Datren	Davara	(0.01)	Daviss	Davyd
Dashaud	Datreon	Davarae De	David Anthony	Davius	Davyn
Dashaun (0.02)	Datrevias	Davard	David Chi-Rei	Daviyon	Davyon
Dashaunte	Datrian	Davares	David Daniel	Daviyonta	Dawan (0.01)
Dashawn (0.08)	Datrice	Davareus	David IV	Davl	Dawann
Dashaye	Datrin	Davarez'	David Jr	Davlin	Dawante
Dashean	Datrion Xavier	Davarian	David Marcel	Davmir	Dawashon
Dasheed	Datron	Davarien	David Michael	Davo'n	Dawaun
Dashel	Datruan	Davario	David Patrick	Davodrique	Dawavn
Dasheme	Datta	Davarion	David-Alexandre	Davon (0.15)	Dawayne
Dashiell (0.01)	Dattir	Davarious	David-Allen	Davon'e	Dawes

Dawid *(0.01)*	Dayin	Daytron	De Aunte	De Va'rious	Déantwon
Dawiel	Dayjion	Daytwan	De Auntrey	De Vacques	Déarcey
Dawing	Dayjuan	Dayvéon	De Drick	De Vantae	Déardis
Dawit *(0.01)*	Daykice	Dayveion	De Edrich	De Vante *(0.01)*	Déaries
Dawlson	Daykota	Dayvell	De Edward	De Vanté	Déarione
Dawlton	Daylan *(0.02)*	Dayven	De Eldrick	De Vanti	Déaris
Dawn	Dayle	Dayveon	De Garyton	De Vaughn	Déarius
Dawnavin	Daylen *(0.01)*	Dayvin	De Gregory	De Vaun	Déarris
Dawon	Daylend	Dayvion	De Ion	De Visea	Déarrius
Dawone	Daylin *(0.01)*	Dayvon *(0.01)*	De Jon	De Von	Déarron
Dawood	Daylon *(0.03)*	Dayvonn	De Joun	De Von Tate	Déartavius
Dawoon	Daylun	Dayzon	De Jour	De Vondré	Déatrius
Dawson *(0.10)*	Daylyn	Daz	De Juan	De Vonta	Déaubrey
Dawsyn	Daymayne	Daz'uan	De Kerry	De Vontae	Déaudre
Dawton	Daymen	Daz-Jon	De Keveon	De Vonte	Déaundra
Dawud	Daymeon	Dazai	De Koria	De Vonté	Déaundre
Dawud Nasiyr	Daymere	Dazarious	De La Blanch	De Wayne	Déauntay
Dawvd II	Daymian	Dazell	De Lon	De Will	Déavis
Dawven	Daymiane	Dazeman	De Lynn	De Wuan	Déavonta
Dawyne	Daymien	Dazhawn	De Marco	Dé	Déavonte
Dawyonne	Daymin	Dazhon	De Marcus *(0.01)*	Dé Jon	Déayrus
Dawyun	Dayminn	Dazhor	De Marius	Dé Wan	Débarus
Dax *(0.03)*	Daymion	Dazhoun	De Marquiez	Dé-Sean	Débreon
Daxius	Daymn	Dazia	De Martavio	Déaaris	Débryan
Daxon	Daymon *(0.01)*	Dazjontae	De Michael	Déadric	Décarlo
Daxter	Daymond *(0.01)*	Dazjoun	De Micheal	Déaire	Décarlos
Daxton *(0.01)*	Daymont	Dazmaine	De Mond	Déaires	Décarrio
Daxx	Dayn	Dazmen	De Mondre	Déallen	Décedric
Day	Dayna	Dazmend	De Monte	Déamonte	Décole
Day Sean	Daynan	Dazmon	De Montrey	Déandra	Décoliéon
Day'ion	Dayne *(0.04)*	Dazmond	De Mun	Déandrae	Décorey
Day'lyn	Daynel	Dazon	De Naireo	Déandray	Dédin
Day'quan	Dayon	Dazreial	De Ohn Ja	Déandre *(0.06)*	Déeric
Day'travon	Dayoné	Dazvon	De Ohndre	Déandrea	Déerrol
Day'vaughn	Dayoni	Dazze	De Onta	Déandrew	Dégshan
Day'vid	Dayquain	Dazzell	De Onte	Déandru	Déhari
Day'von	Dayquale	Dazzie	De Priest	Déanfernee	Déiontez
Day-Jhon	Dayquan *(0.01)*	De *(0.03)*	De Quan	Déangello	Déjaun
Day-Quan	Dayquawane	De Amonta	De Quandre	Déangelo *(0.01)*	Déjaundrell
Dayal	Dayquin	De Amphrany	De Quavieus	Déanglis	Déjavonte
Dayam	Dayqwan	De Andra	De Rrell	Déanglo	Déjhan
Dayan	Dayrell	De Andre *(0.01)*	De Rudre	Déanndre	Déjion
Dayauntae	Dayron	De Andre De	De Sean	Déantae	Déjohn
Dayawn	Daysean	De André	De Seandre	Déantayious	Déjon *(0.01)*
Dayce	Daysen	De Andrea	De Shane	Déante	Déjonvaris
Daycen	Dayshaun	De Andres	De Shanta	Déanteau	Déjoun
Daychawn	Dayshawn *(0.01)*	De Andrew	De Shaughn	Déanthany	Déjshon
Dayden	Dayshon	De Angelo	De Shawn	Déanthius	Déjua
Daydree	Dayson	De Ante	De Shea	Déanthony *(0.01)*	Déjuan
Daydrien	Daythan	De Anté	De Shon	Déantoine	Déjuanne
Daye-Quan	Daython	De Anthony	De Tarius	Déantra	Dékeenan
Dayen	Dayton *(0.11)*	De Antre	De Taurus	Déantre	Dékendrick
Dayhige	Daytona *(0.01)*	De Antré	De Tavion	Déantré	Dékeveyon
Dayhon	Daytonn	De Antres	De Troit	Déantron	Dékevion
Dayi'on	Daytreon	De Antwane	De Untrez	Déantuane	Dékiran

Dékory	Démonta	Déshaud	Dézhon	Deams	Deanu
Dékovan	Démontae	Déshaun *(0.01)*	Dézjaun	Deamun	Deanvo
Dékriston	Démonte	Déshawa	De-Andrea	Dean *(0.35)*	Deaonsy
Dékwan	Démontre	Déshawn *(0.02)*	De-Andrio	Dean Austin	Deaonte
Dékwuan	Démontrell	Déshod	De-Ante	Dean Christopher	Deaquan
Dél	Démorie	Déshon	De-Anthony	Dean-Gabriel	Dearcey
Délajuwon	Démyn	Déshone	De-Armus	Dean-Malcolm	Dearentá
Délamar	Dénarius	Déshun	De-Eric	Dean-Osvaldo	Dearery
Délavonte	Dénautica	Détarius	De-Fonte	Deana	Dearian
Délawn	Déolajuwon	Détavaius	De-Iontez	Deandra *(0.01)*	Dearick
Déleon	Déonbre	Détay	De-Jean	Deandrae	Dearies
Délerenzo	Déondre	Déterrion	De-La Quone	Deandray	Dearion
Délon	Déondrick	Détonio	De-Lorenzo	Deandre *(0.37)*	Dearis
Délon'dre	Déonshé	Détorreion	De-Mallon	Deandré *(0.03)*	Dearius
Délonta	Déonta	Détorrion	De-Marcus	Deandrea *(0.01)*	Deark
Délontae	Déontae	Détray	De-Quan	Deandres	Dearon
Délonzo	Déontay	Détrez	De-Ron	Deandress	Dearrious
Démaine	Déonte *(0.01)*	Détrezz	De-Shaun	Deandrew	Deartae
Démaja	Déontez	Détroy	De-Shun	Deandrey	Dearthur
Démar	Déouandre	Détwain	De-Vante	Deandrez	Deasten
Démarco	Dépree	Détwon	De-Vekyo	Deandriss	Deaton
Démarcus *(0.01)*	Déqaveon	Déunta	De.errik	Deane	Deatrin
Démaria	Déquaci	Déuntae	Dea'quan	Deaney	Deaubrey
Démarian	Déquan *(0.02)*	Déuntrese	Dea'szure	Deange	Deaudis
Démario	Déquandrae	Dévadrae	Deaareon	Deangel'o	Deaudre
Démarion	Déquandre	Dévan	Deaaron	Deangelio	Deaudric
Démarious	Déquann	Dévanta	Deacon	Deangello	Deaudrick
Démaris	Déquanne	Dévantavious	Deacquinn	Deangelo *(0.08)*	Deaugelo
Démarius	Déquanta	Dévante *(0.01)*	Deadrian	Deangilo	Deaundray
Démarkis	Déquante	Dévanté	Deadrick	Deangleo	Deaundre *(0.01)*
Démarko	Déquantye	Dévanti	Deadron	Deanglo	Deaundré
Démarkquis	Déquarius	Dévauntae	Deagan	Deangulo	Deaundrez
Démarkus	Déquariyez	Dévell	Deagen	Deanjay	Deaundry
Démarkuz	Déquarrius	Dévian	Deago	Deanmatthew	Deaunta
Démarna	Déquarus	Dévin	Deaire	Deanna	Deauntae
Démarquaveus	Déquas	Dévon *(0.02)*	Deaires	Deano	Deaunte
Démarquez	Déquavion	Dévon-Tay	Deairrus	Deanta	Deaunté
Démarquis	Déquavious	Dévonce	Deairus	Deantá	Deauntiquam
Démarquise	Déquavis	Dévone	Deaji'	Deantae	Deauntre
Démarqus	Déquavius	Dévonta *(0.01)*	Deajon	Deantai	Deauntrey
Démarrio	Déquawn	Dévontae	Deajuan	Deantay	Deaurburn
Démarswan	Déquay	Dévontaé	Deakin	Deante *(0.03)*	Deautry
Démartic	Déquez	Dévontay	Deal'trae	Deanté *(0.01)*	Deauvre
Démartravious	Déquille	Dévonte *(0.01)*	Dealexandra	Deantée	Deavan
Démarvin	Déquis	Dévonté	Deallen	Deantez	Deaven *(0.01)*
Démaureo	Déquise	Dévontray	Deallo	Deanthony *(0.04)*	Deaveon
Démauriá	Déquon	Dévoreaux	Deallon	Deanthus	Deavis
Démetrase	Déqwan	Dévréountre	Dealte	Deantonio	Deavius
Démetric	Déqwon	Déwattia	Deamanté	Deantrai	Deavon
Démichael	Déreka	Déwayne	Deamarcus	Deantre	Deavone
Démicheal	Dérianté	Déwillis	Deamin	Deantré	Deavonta
Démitrieus	Dérome	Déyon	Deamon	Deantré Rae-Sha	Deavrrio
Démon	Déron	Déyonce	Deamonta	Deantrell	Deawnté
Démond	Désanchez	Dézaune	Deamontae	Deantwain	Deaz
Démondré	Désean *(0.01)*	Dézhan	Deamonte	Deantwuan	Deazjon

Deazsha	Dectrick	Deginald	Dejason	Deklan	Delarnas
Deban	Deddrick	Deguan	Dejaun	Dekobe	Delarrian
Debastian	Dederick	Deh'juan	Dejaunte	Dekoby	Delarrion
Debeion	Dedjaline	Dehaven	Dejean	Dekoda	Delarwance
Debinere	Dedrek	Dehavian	Dejeon	Dekodda	Delasandro
Debonair	Dedreko	Dehrich	Dejerion	Dekota (0.02)	Delashaun
Debonaire	Dedrell	Dei	Dejerius	Dekoven	Delasio
Debony	Dedric (0.01)	Dei Shawn	Dejerrion	Dekoyae	Delasse
Deborah	Dedrick (0.04)	Dei'mikell	Dejion	Dekwalon	Delatavious
Deboyce	Dedrrick	Dei'vontrick	Dejoesph	Dekwan	Delatten
Debrian	Dee	Deiamontae	Dejohn	Dekwante	Delaun
Debrick	Dee Antre	Deighton	Dejohntae	Dekwanté	Delaunte
Debron	Deeandra	Deikwan	Dejohnté	Dekwesi	Delauren
Debryn	Deeandre	Deillbi	Dejon (0.04)	Del (0.01)	Delavon
Debyron	Deed	Deinco	Dejonte	Del Marcus	Delavonta
Dec'quin	Deedar	Deine	Dejordan	Del Monte	Delawnd
Decalveron	Deedrick	Deion (0.15)	Dejore	Del'fontia	Delawno
Decari	Deedward	Deion Tre	Dejsuan	Del'monte	Delawrence
Decarious	Deejay	Deion'dre	Deju'an	Del'rashaun	Delayno
Decarlo	Deeka	Deiondray	Dejuan (0.04)	Del'shaunte	Delband
Decarlos (0.01)	Deekota	Deiondre (0.01)	Dejuane	Del-Vonte	Delbert (0.02)
Decarrio	Deelen	Deiondré	Dejuanta	Delaan	Delcoala
Decephus	Deellison	Deiondrick	Dejuante	Delacey	Delcory
Decesse	Deelyn	Deione	Dejurnett	Delacy	Deldan
Dechaun	Deen	Deionta	Dejwaun	Delafeyette	Deldric'
Dechaune	Deep	Deiontae	Dejzon	Delaine	Deldrick
Deche	Deepak (0.01)	Deiontavious	Dekada	Delainey	Deldridge
Dechristeon	Deepan	Deiontay	Dekareya	Delaion	Deldrin
Dechuan	Deepesh	Deionte (0.01)	Dekari	Delan	Deldrine
Decian	Deepinder	Deionté	Dekario	Delana	Dele
Decio	Deepkaran	Deiontei	Dekarius	Delancea	Delene
Decker (0.01)	Deepta	Deionti	Dekarlo	Delancius	Deleno
Declan (0.05)	Deepu	Deiontre	Dekarlos	Deland	Deleon
Decobe	Deeran	Deiontré	Dekavian	Delandace	Deleoni
Decoco	Deerion	Deiontreil	Dekeeven	Delandan	Deleonté
Decoda	Deeshawn	Deionyos	Dekeevious	Delandis	Delerious
Deconcini	Deevann	Deir	Dekel	Delando	Delexun
Decondia	Deevid	Deisreal	Dekeliaus	Delandré	Delferd
Decopeland	Deevon	Deitrich	Dekemba	Delandry	Delfine
Decordia	Deezjuan	Deitrik	Dekendrick	Delane	Delfino (0.01)
Decorea	Defenson	Deivin	Dekendrix	Delaney (0.01)	Delfonic
Decorey	Deferian	Deivon	Dekerrian	Delang	Delfontay
Decoreyon	Deffick	Deivy	Dekerrie	Delanio	Delfonzo
Decorian	Defonta	Deivyn	Deketric	Delann	Delfred
Decoris	Defonte	Deiyn	Dekevin	Delano (0.02)	Delgene
Decorius	Deford	Deja	Dekevion	Delantá	Delias
Decorrius	Deforest	Deja'n	Dekevious	Delantae	Delietric
Decorrous	Degamarri	Dejae	Dekevius	Delante (0.01)	Delijah
Decoryon	Degan	Dejah	Dekeyun	Delanté	Delin
Decota	Degarian	Dejahzh	Dekhari	Delaon	Delinine
Decovan	Degarius	Dejai	Dekietrich	Delaone	Deljavontay
Decovia	Degarrious	Dejamel	Dekimbe	Delarenta	Deljie
Decovon	Degaryi'o	Dejan	Dekion	Delarintae	Deljon
Decown	Degas	Dejarius	Dekishon	Delarion	Delk
Decree	Degen	Dejarvis	Dekker	Delarius	Dell (0.01)

Dellan	Delquez	Demarciee	Demarre	Demethi	Demilade
Dellanis	Delquist	Demarcio	Demarrea	Demetirus	Demilo
Dellano	Delray	Demarcis	Demarreis	Demetius	Demilton
Dellanté	Delreco	Demarcius	Demarri	Demetorius	Demion
Dellen	Delrico	Demarco (0.06)	Demarrio	Demetray	Demique
Delleon	Delriece	Demarcos	Demarrius	Demetre (0.01)	Demir
Dellil	Delrio	Demarcus (0.12)	Demarriusse	Demetree	Demiracle
Dellion	Delron	Demarcuse	Demarshay	Demetrée	Demiro
Dellis	Delroy	Demarea (0.01)	Demarte	Demetrei's	Demisck
Dellmonta	Delsean	Demareá	Demartiea	Demetreius	Demitre
Dellshaun	Delshawn (0.01)	Demaree	Demartiz	Demetrey	Demitri (0.02)
Delltre	Delshon	Demareo	Demaruice	Demetrez	Demitric
Dellvon	Delsin	Demareus	Demarus	Demetri (0.03)	Demitrice
Delman	Delson	Demargo	Demarvin	Demetri'	Demitrick
Delmar (0.01)	Delten	Demari	Demarvious	Demetria	Demitrie
Delmarco	Delton (0.01)	Demaria	Demarx	Demetriae	Demitries
Delmare	Deltyn	Demariá	Demaryia	Demetrian	Demitrious
Delmario	Deltyra	Demariae	Demarzio	Demetrias	Demitris
Delmarr	Deluis	Demariaé	Demasceion	Demetriaus	Demitrius (0.03)
Delmeko	Delvan	Demariay	Demashawn	Demetric (0.01)	Demitrus
Delmer	Delvante	Demarié	Demasi	Demetrica	Demitry
Delmes	Delvarrion	Demariea	Demaurces	Demetrice (0.01)	Demmon
Delmetrice	Delvaughn	Demarien	Demaurea	Demetrich	Demmy
Delmika	Delvecchio	Demariez	Demaureo	Demetrick (0.01)	Demoddrick
Delmirrio	Delvechio	Demario (0.04)	Demauria	Demetricus	Demodric
Delmody	Delvekyo	Demarion (0.01)	Demaurian	Demetrie	Demoinez
Delmon	Delveron	Demarious (0.01)	Demaurice	Demetries	Demon (0.01)
Delmond	Delvian	Demaris	Demaurie	Demetriez	Demoncia
Delmont	Delvin (0.03)	Demarius (0.02)	Demauriea	Demetrik	Demond (0.04)
Delmonta	Delvionte	Demariuz	Demaurio	Demetrio (0.02)	Demondre (0.01)
Delmonte	Delvis	Demark	Demauriyah	Demetrion	Demondré
Delmonté	Delvon (0.02)	Demarkco	Demazi	Demetrios (0.01)	Demondrea
Delmos	Delvonta	Demarkeo	Demeatrice	Demetrious (0.02)	Demondreo
Delmus	Delvontá	Demarkeon	Demeatrik	Demetrique	Demondtay
Delnore	Delvontae	Demarkis	Demeatruis	Demetris (0.02)	Demone
Deloice	Delvontaé	Demarkiyo	Demecco	Demetrise	Demoné
Deloin	Delvonte (0.01)	Demarko (0.01)	Demeche	Demetriua	Demonique
Delon (0.01)	Delvonté	Demarkos	Demechico	Demetriues	Demonn
Deloncé	Delvron	Demarkus (0.02)	Demecko	Demetrius (0.38)	Demons
Delone	Delwin	Demarlo	Demecus	Demetrius Shere	Demont
Deloni	Delwyn	Demarlon	Demeitri	Demetron	Demont'rae
Delonne	Dema	Demarlyn	Demeko	Demetruis (0.01)	Demonta (0.01)
Delonta	Demaacus	Demarous	Demel	Demetrus	Demontae (0.01)
Delontae	Demaal	Demarqual	Demenyon	Demetry	Demontareo
Delontay	Demahn	Demarquan	Demeon	Demettrius	Demontarious
Delonte	Demain	Demarquavus	Demereice	Demeturis	Demontavious
Delonté	Demaine	Demarqueon	Demerest	Demiah	Demontay
Delorean	Demairo	Demarques	Demerez	Demian	Demontaz
Deloren	Demaninder	Demarquez	Demerick	Demichael	Demontaze
Deloria	Demanté	Demarqui	Demerio	Demichealo	Demonte (0.02)
Deloss	Demantez	Demarquis (0.01)	Demerith	Demico	Demonté (0.02)
Delphine	Demar (0.01)	Demarquo	Demerius	Demiel	Demonterio
Delquan	Demarcco	Demarquon	Demery	Demien	Demonterius
Delquavius	Demarceo	Demarqus	Demeshio	Demietrius	Demontez
Delqueese	Demarces	Demarrain	Demesseo	Demiko	Demontio

Demontrá	Denali	Dennise	Deoin	Deontea	Dequa
Demontrae	Denard (0.01)	Dennison	Deojawann	Deontee	Dequacius
Demontrail	Denarie	Dennon	Deojunique	Deonteya	Dequaghn
Demontravious	Denario	Denny (0.05)	Deolandis	Deonteye	Dequam
Demontray	Denaris	Dennys (0.01)	Deon (0.19)	Deontez	Dequamar
Demontre (0.01)	Denariss	Deno	Deon Dré	Deontia	Dequan (0.08)
Demontré	Denarius	Denolius	Deon'dre	Deontiaz	Dequan'
Demontrea	Denarrius	Denon	Deon'shaye	Deontoe	Dequana
Demontreal	Denby	Denone	Deon'ta	Deontra	Dequandra
Demontrel	Dencel	Denonte	Deon'taye	Deontrá	Dequandre
Demontreon	Dene	Denorise	Deon'te	Deontrae (0.01)	Dequandré
Demontrey	Dené	Denorris	Deonadre	Deontrais	Dequandric
Demontrez	Denea	Denoshn	Deonandra	Deontravious	Dequandrick
Demontri	Denearrius	Denovion	Deonatá	Deontray (0.01)	Dequane
Demontrial	Deneb	Denpota	Deonavon	Deontre (0.02)	Dequann
Demontriez	Deneil	Denray	Deonbre	Deontré	Dequansh
Demontrion	Denel	Densi	Deonce	Deontrea	Dequanta
Demonyé	Denell	Denson	Deonche	Deontrel	Dequante (0.01)
Demoraya	Denerick	Denta	Deoncoe	Deontrell	Dequanté
Demoraye	Denerio	Dentario	Deondary	Deontrey	Dequantez
Demoreah	Denerver	Dentavius	Deondr'e	Deontrez	Dequantie
Demoria	Denesh	Dentell	Deondra (0.01)	Deontrez'	Dequantis
Demorian	Denevin	Dentez	Deondrá	Deontreze	Dequari
Demornay	Denevious	Denton (0.02)	Deondrae	Deontrius	Dequaries
Demorra	Denezra	Dentory	Deondray	Deontrus	Dequarion
Demorrian Dion	Denford	Dentral	Deondre (0.07)	Deontte	Dequarious
Demorris	Denham	Dentrale	Deondré (0.01)	Deontya	Dequarius
Demory	Denic	Dentravious	Deondrea	Deonuteris	Dequaun
Demothenese	Denicholas	Dentravius	Deondree	Deonvis	Dequavahn
Demound	Denico	Dentrell	Deondrei	Deonzae	Dequavaugh
Demoy	Deniel	Dentrey	Deondrey	Deopatt	Dequaven
Demoyne	Denikko	Dentrez	Deondric	Deorpheus	Dequaves
Demoz	Deniko	Denval	Deondrick	Deotray	Dequavious
Dempsey (0.01)	Denim	Denver (0.06)	Deone	Deotré	Dequavis
Dempsie	Denin	Denvil	Deonis	Deoun	Dequavius (0.01)
Demry	Denis (0.07)	Deny	Deonita	Deounta	Dequavon
Demsel	Denise	Denyke	Deonn	Deounté	Dequavous
Demteius	Denish	Denzal	Deono	Deovaunie	Dequawn
Demteruis	Denishan	Denzale	Deonquez	Depak	Dequawn'ta
Demtré	Denishanth	Denzall	Deont E	Depaul	Dequay
Demtri	Denishno	Denzel (0.26)	Deontá	Depert	Dequaylin
Demtria	Denison	Denzeljamal	Deonta (0.05)	Dephen	Dequayveon
Demtrius	Deniz (0.01)	Denzell (0.04)	Deontá (0.01)	Depinder	Dequayvious
Demune	Denley Michael	Denzelle	Deontaé	Deprez	Dequaz
Demunquise	Denn	Denzer	Deontae (0.04)	Depri	Dequentin
Demuntre	Dennard	Denzial	Deontaé	Deprii	Dequenton
Demykal	Dennes	Denziel	Deontai	Deqane	Deques
Demylo	Dennez	Denzil (0.01)	Deontarius	Deqarius	Dequeszman
Demytri	Dennico	Denzle	Deontate	Deqavious	Dequetin
Den'zeill	Dennie	Denzsel	Deontavis	Deqavius	Dequevius
Den'zelle	Dennikson	Denzyel	Deontavius	Deqawn	Dequey
Dena'z	Dennin	Denzyl	Deontay (0.02)	Deqienton	Dequez
Denadré	Dennis (0.75)	Deoante	Deontaye	Deqindre	Dequian
Denairio	Dennis Jay	Deobray	Deonte (0.13)	Deqjuan	Dequiandrick
Denairo	Dennis Michael	Deodrick	Deonté (0.06)	Deqourious	Dequin

Dequince	Derekque	Derrald	Deryk *(0.01)*	Deshion	Desy
Dequincy	Derekta	Derran	Deryl	Deshjion	Desylvia
Dequindel	Derel	Derraun	Deryll	Deshod	Deszmann
Dequinderick	Derele	Derreck *(0.01)*	Deryn	Deshombi	Deszmne
Dequindrae	Derell	Derreion	Deryon	Deshon *(0.03)*	Detabian
Dequindre	Derelle	Derrek *(0.04)*	Des	Deshondre	Detadnan
Dequine	Deremy	Derrel	Des Marquis	Deshone	Detalion
Dequinn	Deren	Derrell *(0.02)*	Des'mon	Deshonn	Detarious
Dequion	Deresh	Derreon	Des'tine	Deshonte	Detavian
Dequivus	Dereshean	Derreonte	Des'tri	Deshonté	Detavion
Dequntez	Derex	Derri	Desante	Deshontei	Detavis
Dequoin	Derez	Derrian *(0.01)*	Desaray	Deshontez	Detavius
Dequon	Derian *(0.01)*	Derric *(0.01)*	Desayvion	Deshun *(0.01)*	Detayveion
Dequonce	Deric *(0.05)*	Derrice	Desbrien	Deshunn	Detcria
Dequonta	Derice *(0.01)*	Derrick *(0.90)*	Descartes	Deshy	Deterian
Dequonte	Derices	Derrick Lat	Deschaun	Desi *(0.01)*	Deterion
Dequris	Derick *(0.16)*	Derrick-Anthony	Desean *(0.03)*	Desimon	Deterraice
Dequrontez	Derico	Derrickk	Deseandre	Desimoral	Deterrious
Deqvarrea	Deriek	Derricks	Deseante	Desjuan	Deterris
Deqwan	Derien	Derrico	Deseantez	Desman	Deterrius
Deqwandre	Derieus	Derrid	Desert	Desmand	Dethumus
Deqwantaris	Derigus	Derriel	Desha	Desmane	Detienne
Deqwon	Derik *(0.04)*	Derrien	Deshaad	Desmen	Detirick
Deqwone	Derik Lee	Derrik *(0.03)*	Deshae	Desmin	Detler
Der Undrae	Derikk	Derrike	Deshain	Desmine	Detorion
Der'verz	Derimi	Derrin	Deshalone	Desmon *(0.01)*	Detrae
Derail	Derion *(0.01)*	Derring	Deshan	Desmond *(0.27)*	Detrale
Derak	Derious	Derrion *(0.01)*	Deshandra	Desmonnd	Detravious
Derald	Deris	Derrionte	Deshane	Desmonte	Detravius
Deraldon	Derise	Derrionté	Deshann	Desmound	Detravon
Deralle	Deritez	Derriontre	Deshannon	Desmund	Detred
Deran	Derius *(0.01)*	Derrious	Deshanté	Desmyn	Detrek
Deranden	Derivian	Derris	Deshaon	Desontae	Detrel
Derante	Derk	Derrit	Deshario	Desramond	Detrell
Derar	Derland	Derriton	Desharious	Desron	Detrells
Derashé	Derly	Derrius *(0.02)*	Deshasian	Desronique	Detreon
Deratio	Dermaine	Derrius D	Deshaude	Dessen	Detreveon
Deraven	Dermarius	Derrix	Deshaudrik	Destan	Detrevon
Derayon	Dermarquis	Derriz	Deshaughn	Desten	Detri
Dercell	Dermerick	Derron *(0.01)*	Deshaun *(0.06)*	Dester	Detric
Dereas	Dermetriuss	Derron'ta	Deshaunta	Destin *(0.06)*	Detrice
Derec	Dermot	Derrrick	Deshauntre	Destine	Detrich
Derece	Dermott	Derryck	Deshavion	Destined	Detrick *(0.01)*
Dereck *(0.05)*	Dernard	Derryel	Deshawn *(0.21)*	Destiny	Detrii
Dereece	Dernell	Derryk	Deshawn Devon	Deston	Detrik
Dereese	Dernis	Derryl	Deshawntae	Destoniq'	Detrion
Dereiko	Deroderick	Dertaevia	Deshawnte	Destony	Detrius
Dereikus	Derol	Dervan	Deshawon	Destri	Detrix
Dereis	Deron *(0.02)*	Dervell	Deshay	Destrie	Detroit
Derek *(2.39)*	Derondre	Derwin *(0.01)*	Deshayn'dye	Destron	Detron
Derek Edward	Deronja	Derwood	Deshayne	Destry	Detroy
Derek Jr	Deronne	Derwounte	Deshazier	Destyn	Detryienne
Derek Tawn	Derontae	Dery	Deshazo	Desuan	Detten
Derek-James	Derontay	Deryan	Deshé	Desvlice	Detwan
Derekk	Deronte	Deryck *(0.01)*	Desheanon	Deswann	Detwon

Detwuane	Devarche	Devern	Devon-Allen	Devontreal	Dewean
Deuel	Devari	Deveron	Devon-Levesque	Devontrez	Dewell
Deunandrea	Devarian	Deveroux	Devon-Te	Devonttaie	Dewey *(0.01)*
Deundrae	Devarié	Deverrick	Devonae	Devonyae	Dewhitt
Deundre	Devaris	Deverton	Devonair	Devoreaux	Dewight
Deundré	Devarius *(0.01)*	Devery	Devonaire	Devorian	Dewine
Deundrea	Devarne	Devetric	Devonare	Devorion	Dewitt
Deundrey	Devaron	Devetrick	Devonceia	Devorius	Dewon
Deunquez	Devarous	Deveyn	Devonche	Devoshay	Dewone
Deunta	Devarri	Devez	Devondra	Devoshia	Dewoyne
Deuntae	Devarryl	Devhin	Devondrae	Devountae	Dex
Deuntay	Devarsious	Deviaire	Devondray	Devoy	Dexavier
Deunte	Devarta	Devian	Devondre	Devozeá	Dexray
Deunté	Devarus	Devianté	Devone *(0.01)*	Devrajsinh	Dextavious
Deunterrious	Devashay	Deviante	Devoni	Devran	Dexter *(0.14)*
Deuntravius	Devassia	Deviare	Devonio	Devree	Dexter-Charles
Deunza	Devatte	Devid	Devonita	Devren	Dexteroy
Deutsche	Devaugh	Devieon	Devonjae	Devrett	Dexton
Dev	Devaughlv	Devihn	Devonjé	Devric	Dextor
Dev'ante	Devaughn *(0.04)*	Deville	Devonlee	Devrick	Dextrel
Devá	Devaughntaé	Devilyn	Devonn	Devron *(0.01)*	Dextyn
Devaan	Devaughnte	Devin *(2.71)*	Devonnair	Devrone	Dey'quan
Devael	Devaul	Devin Austin	Devonne *(0.01)*	Devronte	Dey'shawn
Devaente	Devaun *(0.01)*	Devin Devon	Devonntae	Devryn	Dey'vontae
Devahntau	Devaunte	Devin Karta	Devonquez	Devualle	Deya
Devail	Devay	Devin'	Devonsha	Devuan	Deyan
Devain	Deveal	Devin-Anthony	Devont'ae	Devun	Deyante
Devajee	Devean	Devinare	Devonta *(0.09)*	Devunte	Deyanté
Devajia	Deveche	Devincey	Devontá *(0.01)*	Devven	Deyanun
Devale	Deveil	Devinci	Devontaé	Devvin	Deydrych
Devalin	Devein	Devindra	Devontae *(0.06)*	Devvon	Deyen
Devan *(0.30)*	Deveion	Devine *(0.01)*	Devontaé	Devvonne	Deylin
Devan'te	Devek	Devinere	Devontaé Deond	Devyin	Deylon
Devance	Devell *(0.01)*	Devinn	Devontai	Devyn *(0.11)*	Deymar
Devanchey	Develle	Devinta	Devontarius	Devyn-Lee	Deyne
Devandre	Deven *(0.14)*	Devion *(0.01)*	Devontas	Devynn	Deyon
Devane	Deven'er	Devionce	Devontate	Devynne	Deyondre
Devanere	Devendra	Devionte	Devontavious	Devyontae	Deyonne
Devanle	Devenn	Devis	Devontavius	Dew	Deyonta
Devann	Devenskye	Devita	Devontay *(0.02)*	Dewain	Deyontae
Devansh	Deventae	Devlan	Devontaye	Dewaine	Deyontavis
Devanta *(0.01)*	Deventay	Devlen	Devonte *(0.28)*	Dewal	Deyonte *(0.01)*
Devantá	Devente	Devlin *(0.02)*	Devonté *(0.08)*	Dewalt	Deyonté
Devantae	Deveohn	Devling	Devonte-Moshe	Dewan *(0.01)*	Deyontre
Devantaé	Deveon *(0.01)*	Devlon	Devontea	Dewandtez	Deyshawn
Devantay	Deveone	Devlyn *(0.01)*	Devontee	Dewane	Deython
Devante *(0.22)*	Deveonta	Devn	Devontel	Dewanya	Deyvon
Devante E	Deveontae	Devo'nta	Devontez	Dewanye	Dezanté
Devanté *(0.07)*	Deveonte	Devocio	Devonte~	Dewarren	Dezarah
Devantés	Dever	Devohn	Devonti	Dewaun	Dezarian
Devantée	Deveraux	Devoisier	Devontia	Dewaune	Dezarrus
Devantez	Devere	Devon *(1.46)*	Devontrá	Deway'nn	Dezavieus
Devanty	Devereaux	Devon'	Devontravious	Dewayen	Dezbee
Devar'te	Devereux	Devon't	Devontray	Dewayne *(0.05)*	Dezerri
Devarae	Deverick	Devon'te	Devontre	Dewaynmond	Dezhane

Dezhawn	Di Juan	Diante *(0.02)*	Dietsch	Dilqule	Dinisio
Dezhean	Di Kerry	Dianté *(0.01)*	Dieu	Dilraj	Dino *(0.02)*
Dezjuan	Di Zuan	Diantel	Dieubenit	Dilrajbir	Dinoshan
Dezmalik	Di'andre	Diantey	Diggory	Dilsewak	Dinoth
Dezman	Di'antre	Diantré	Diijon	Dilshaan	Dinshaw
Dezmand	Di'jon	Diaquan	Diivan	Dilshant	Dinu
Dezmen	Di'jonn	Diara	Dij-Juan	Dilson	Dinujan
Dezmer	Di'joun	Diareece	Dijamone	Diltaj	Dio
Dezmin	Di'keist	Diaron	Dijaun	Dilun	Dioblo
Dezmon *(0.02)*	Di'kquawn	Diarra	Dijhon	Dilyan	Diodrick
Dezmond *(0.02)*	Di'mond	Diarronow	Dijion	Dilyn	Diogenes
Dezon	Di'quan	Diarte Arkeith	Dijohn	Dilynn	Diogenese
Dezrell	Di'quawn	Diashawn	Dijon *(0.03)*	Dimaggio	Diogo
Deztin	Di'rell	Diatrae	Dijonn	Dimante	Dion *(0.16)*
Dezzamik	Di'rico	Diatré	Dijoun	Dimarco	Dion Jhir
Dezzel	Di'shan	Diavaunte	Dikari	Dimario	Dion'tay
Dhaakir	Di'shawn	Diavis	Dikembe	Dimaris	Dion'te
Dhaikembie	Di-Ren	Diavon	Dikembé	Dimarkis	Dionadre
Dhakota	Di-Shon	Diavonte	Dikendre	Dimas *(0.01)*	Diondra
Dhakotah	Dia	Diavonté	Dikeos	Dimeris	Diondrae
Dhalathan	Dia'nte	Diaz	Dikota	Dimero	Diondre *(0.02)*
Dhamaa-Barre	Diaa	Dicarious	Diksan	Dimetri	Diondré
Dhamarrio	Diaa Aldin	Dicarlo	Dil	Dimetric	Diondrey
Dhan	Diab	Dice	Dilan *(0.03)*	Dimetrice	Dione *(0.01)*
Dhanelt	Diafuka	Dick	Dilbag	Dimetrius	Dionel
Dhanesh	Diahnté	Dickenzy	Dilber	Dimici	Dionell
Dhanveer	Diajanique	Dickerson	Dildeep	Dimitiri	Dioneté
Dhaquan	Dialin	Dickson *(0.01)*	Dilen	Dimitri *(0.12)*	Dionicio *(0.01)*
Dharai	Diallo *(0.01)*	Diclecis	Dilesh	Dimitric	Dionis
Dhariel	Dialon	Dicqtric	Dilgeer	Dimitrije	Dionisio
Dharius	Diam'ond	Dictavion	Dilian	Dimitrio	Dionjay
Dharmesh	Diaman	Dictron Marquel	Dilin	Dimitrios *(0.02)*	Dionkwe
Dharrieus	Diamanta	Didier *(0.02)*	Dilip	Dimitrios-George	Dionn
Dharsan	Diamante *(0.01)*	Didymus	Diljot	Dimitrious	Dionne *(0.01)*
Dhash	Diamanté	Diedrich	Dilkamalpreet	Dimitris	Dionnetá
Dhaval	Diameyan	Diega	Dilkaranjot	Dimitrius *(0.01)*	Dionntae
Dhavaughn	Diamond *(0.03)*	Diego *(0.63)*	Dillan *(0.12)*	Dimitriy	Diono
Dhavinder	Diamonds	Diegoberto	Dillando	Dimitrus	Dionsay
Dheeran	Diamonique	Diel	Dillanger	Dimitry	Dionsius
Dheia	Diamonta	Dienny	Dillard	Dimond	Diont E
Dheric	Diamonte *(0.01)*	Diente	Dillen *(0.01)*	Dimonic	Dionta *(0.01)*
Dhia	Diamonté	Dieon	Dillian *(0.01)*	Dimonta	Diontá
Dhilan	Diamontel	Dieonisio	Dillin *(0.01)*	Dimontae	Diontaé
Dhillon	Diamontrell	Dieonnte	Dillinger	Dimonte	Diontae *(0.01)*
Dhiren	Diamund	Dieonzea	Dillion *(0.08)*	Dimples	Diontae Jevonne
Dhiviyan	Diamysei	Diequan	Dillon *(1.38)*	Dimytric	Diontaé
Dhiya	Dian	Diermo	Dillon Antonio	Dimytro	Diontavious
Dhorian	Diana	Dieron	Dillpreet	Dinari	Diontavius
Dhruv	Diandre *(0.01)*	Dierre	Dillvon	Dinera	Diontay *(0.01)*
Dhruva	Diandré	Dierrian	Dillyn *(0.01)*	Dinesan	Diontaye
Dhyeya	Diandrew	Diese	Dilmeet	Dinesh	Dionte *(0.05)*
Dhylan	Diangelo	Diesel	Diloe	Dineshan	Dionté *(0.02)*
Di Andre	Diangleo	Dieter	Dilon	Dineth	Diontea
Di Antrée	Diango	Dietrich *(0.01)*	Dilonté	Dinh	Diontravious
Di Jon	Diantae	Dietrick	Dilpreet	Dinh-Hy	Diontray

Diontre	Divaunté	Dmarko	Domanicko	Dommeliq	Donavint
Diontré	Diven	Dmetriy	Domanik	Domminic	Donavo
Diontrey	Divennci	Dmitri *(0.02)*	Domaniq	Domminick	Donavon *(0.04)*
Dionysios	Divesh	Dmitrik	Domanique	Domnic	Donavyn
Dionysis	Divianté	Dmitrius	Domanque	Domnick	Donaye
Dionysius	Divine	Dmitriy	Domarius	Domnique	Donbosco
Dionyssios	Divinian	Dmitry *(0.01)*	Domaykius	Domonic *(0.02)*	Donbray
Dionysus	Divirio	Dmonté	Domeneque	Domonic'	Donche
Diop	Divoc	Dmontre	Domenic *(0.07)*	Domonick *(0.01)*	Donchevell
Diorian	Divon	Dmonyae Qua	Domenick *(0.01)*	Domonik	Dondago
Diormetis	Divonnie	Dnaiel	Domenico *(0.02)*	Domoniq	Dondarian
Diory	Divontá	Dnatriuz	Domenik	Domonique *(0.03)*	Dondavid
Dios	Divontae	Do	Domeniq	Domonnick	Dondell
Diovan	Divontay	Do Vontay	Domenique	Domonquie	Dondi
Diovonni	Divontaye	Do'mar	Domenque	Domonta	Dondiego
Dipatrimarki	Divonte	Do'rrell	Domick	Domqiue	Dondra
Dipesh	Divonté	Doan	Domiere	Domunique	Dondrae
Dipinder	Divontea	Doc	Domigabriel	Don *(0.12)*	Dondrakus
Dippen	Divya	Dock	Dominac	Don Allen	Dondray
Diqawan	Divyanthan	Dockery	Dominador	Don Juan	Dondrayas
Diqawn	Divyaraj	Doctavius	Dominance	Don'dre	Dondre *(0.04)*
Diquan *(0.03)*	Divyen	Doctor	Domineck	Don'jhae	Dondré *(0.01)*
Diquane	Divyesh	Docy	Domineek	Don'tarius	Dondrea
Diquanté	Diwan	Dodge *(0.01)*	Dominek	Don'te	Dondreai'l
Diquavious	Diwanis	Dodley	Domineque	Don'terrio	Dondrell
Diqueel	Diwight	Doe	Domingo *(0.03)*	Don'trell	Dondrick
Diquez	Diwon	Doeke	Dominic *(1.25)*	Don'ya	Dondrikious
Diquize	Dixie Ray	Doewin	Dominic'	Don-Huy-Bui	Done
Diquoine	Dixon *(0.02)*	Dofort	Dominica	Don-Kirk	Donearl
Direk	Dixters	Dogan	Dominick*(0.31)*	Dona Metriu	Doneco
Direll	Diyamonte	Dohnaven	Dominick-John-	Donaciano	Doneel
Dirk *(0.03)*	Diyar	Dohron	Dominicko	Donae	Donehoo
Dirrell	Diyon	Dokda	Dominico	Donahue	Doneil
Dirrick	Diyonte	Dokota	Dominik *(0.06)*	Donail	Donel
Dirriell	Diyuante	Dokotea	Dominiko	Donal	Doneld
Dirul	Dj *(0.01)*	Dolan *(0.01)*	Dominiq	Donald *(1.02)*	Donele
Dirusan	Djakwan	Dolapo	Dominique *(0.42)*	Donald III	Donell *(0.01)*
Dirvonte	Djama	Dolf	Dominique Monte	Donald Lee	Donelle
Disco	Djasarri	Dolfus	Dominiqué	Donaldlee	Donelly
Dishan	Djash	Dolin	Dominique-	Donaldo *(0.01)*	Doner'e
Dishawn	Djavan	Dollard	Roland	Donaldson	Donevan
Dishon	Djavon	Dollen	Dominiquetric	Donangelo	Dong
Dishun	Djemsson	Dollton	Dominiquie	Donardto	Dong-Huyn
Dismar	Djimitri	Dolmokio	Dominko	Donarich	Dong-Hyuk
Ditalion	Djimon	Dolon	Dominnick	Donarius	Dong-Sik
Diterrious	Djon	Dolores	Domino	Donatas	Dongho
Divad	Djordje	Dolph	Dominq'ue	Donate	Donghoon
Divagar	Djordjo	Dolphis	Dominque *(0.06)*	Donathan	Donhenry
Dival	Djuan *(0.01)*	Dolphus	Dominyck	Donathon	Donian
Divanni	Dlast	Doltin	Dominyk	Donato *(0.01)*	Donicio Jeanpaul
Divante	Dm	Dolton	Domion	Donavan *(0.09)*	Doniel
Divanté	Dmaray	Dom	Domique	Donavehn	Donielle
Divantez	Dmarco	Domaco	Domishek	Donaven	Donille
Divarius	Dmarcus	Domanic *(0.01)*	Domisi	Donaver	Donimic
Divaunce	Dmarius	Domanick	Domitilo	Donavin *(0.01)*	Donique

Doniqué	Donquarius	Dontayue	Dontrelle	Doriante	Dovee
Donithan	Donqueá	Dontayves	Dontrellis	Doriaus	Dovid *(0.01)*
Donivan *(0.01)*	Donquece	Dontayvis	Dontrevious	Doriel	Dovin
Donja	Donquell	Dontaz	Dontrey	Dorien *(0.01)*	Dovonta
Donjae	Donquelos	Donte *(0.09)*	Dontrez	Dorieon	Dovontae
Donjai	Donques	Donté *(0.05)*	Dontrial	Dorin	Dovuntai
Donjohrae	Donquevious	Dontévius	Dontrice	Dorion *(0.01)*	Dow
Donjour	Donquez	Dontea	Dontriel	Doriun	Dow-Hsuan
Donjudis	Donquiel	Dontee	Dontriell	Dorjan	Dowdy
Donkevius	Donquis	Dontel	Dontrise	Dorjon	Dowl
Donkiethen	Donqus	Dontell	Donvante	Dormarian	Dowlin
Donley	Donquvious	Dontelle	Donvelle	Dormonshae	Downy
Donminic	Donraél	Dontellis	Donvito	Dornell	Dowson
Donminique	Donregus	Dontelvius	Donvontae	Dorninick	Doy
Donn	Donrell	Donteria	Donvonte	Doron	Doyal
Donnavan	Donriko	Donteriay	Donwyck	Doroteo	Doyle *(0.02)*
Donnavin	Donseyia	Donterio	Dony	Dorquarius	Dozhaven
Donnavon	Donsha	Donterious	Donya	Dorrell	Dozie
Donncha	Donshae	Donterius	Donyae	Dorren	Doziem
Donneal	Donshay	Donterri	Donyah	Dorrese	Dquane
Donnel	Donshé	Donterrio	Donyaih	Dorri'an	Dquann
Donnele	Donshea	Donterrious	Donye	Dorrian *(0.01)*	Dquantae
Donnell *(0.06)*	Donshel	Donterrius	Donye A	Dorriel	Dquayvion
Donner	Donshi	Dontese	Donyea	Dorrin	Dquincey
Donnerick	Donta *(0.02)*	Dontev	Donyel	Dorringtin	Dra'quane
Donnesh	Dontá	Dontevious	Donyell *(0.01)*	Dorrion	Dra'von
Donnevan	Donta'veous	Dontez *(0.02)*	Donyle	Dorron	Dracar
Donneze	Dontac	Dontia	Donzal	Dorryl	Drace
Donnial	Dontae *(0.04)*	Dontiea	Donzay	Dorsey	Draco
Donnick	Dontaé	Dontives	Donze	Dorsie	Dradelle
Donnie *(0.07)*	Dontaevin	Dontonio	Donzeil	Dortavius	Draden
Donnie-Joseph	Dontaevis	Dontonious'	Donzel	Dortez	Drae
Donnis	Dontaivan	Dontorius	Donzell *(0.01)*	Dortione	Draeland
Donnivan	Dontaivous	Dontorrie	Donzelle	Dorval	Draesen
Donnovan	Dontal	Dontorriyon	Donzello	Dory	Draeshawn
Donnoven	Dontanyull	Dontory	Doominik	Doryan	Draevin
Donnovohn	Dontare	Dontra	Doorga	Doss	Drafton
Donnte	Dontarian	Dontrae	Dora	Dostell	Dragan
Donntrel	Dontario	Dontraevion	Dorai	Doston	Dragann
Donny *(0.02)*	Dontarious *(0.01)*	Dontraga	Dorain	Doua	Drago
Donnyell	Dontarius *(0.01)*	Dontraie	Doral	Doug *(0.01)*	Dragomir
Dono	Dontarrion	Dontrail	Doran *(0.01)*	Dougem	Dragon
Dono'von	Dontarrius	Dontral	Dorante	Dougie	Drahcir
Donoval	Dontarvis	Dontrall	Doranty	Dougkevis	Draigan
Donovan *(0.48)*	Dontas	Dontravell	Dorbin	Douglas *(0.85)*	Draikharn
Donovan-James	Dontau	Dontraveous	Dorceau	Douglass *(0.01)*	Drajoin
Donovane	Dontaveis	Dontraveun	Dordell	Doulton	Drakaar
Donoven	Dontavias	Dontravious	Dorell	Doumervil	Drakarius
Donovin	Dontavion	Dontravis	Doremus	Dounn	Drake *(0.36)*
Donovon *(0.01)*	Dontavious *(0.03)*	Dontravius	Doren	Dounte	Drake James
Donqavius	Dontavis *(0.01)*	Dontray *(0.01)*	Dorenton	Dov	Drake-Tyler
Donqua	Dontavius *(0.02)*	Dontre *(0.01)*	Doreon	Dovantay	Drakkar
Donquail	Dontay *(0.02)*	Dontreal	Dorey	Dovante	Dralen
Donquarions	Dontaye	Dontrel	Dori'n	Dovas	Dralon
Donquaris	Dontayre	Dontrell *(0.05)*	Dorian *(0.18)*	Dovber	Dramel

Dranson	Dréshawn	Dreton	Dshawn	Dumaka	Durrant
Draon	Dréune	Dreu	Dta-Wahn	Dumarkus	Durreese
Draper	Drévon	Dreuntae	Du Shuan	Dumauri	Durrel
Draqquarius	Drévonte	Drevan	Du Vonta	Dumauria	Durrell (0.01)
Draquan	Dréylon	Drevaughn	Du'jaun	Dumebi	Durreon
Draquine	Dre-Shawn	Drevaun	Du'juan	Dumetre	Durrett
Drasean	Drea	Dreven	Du'pre	Dumond	Durron
Drashaun	Dreadnell	Drevin	Du'quan	Dunavon	Durugshan
Drashawn	Dreagen	Drevion	Du'shawn	Duncan (0.26)	Durvonta
Drason	Dreagn	Drevon (0.01)	Du'won	Dundee	Durwin
Drasten	Dreaton	Drevone	Du-Un Justin	Dunel	Dusan (0.01)
Draughn	Drecarlos	Drevonte	Dual	Dung	Dusean
Dravaughn	Drecki	Drew (0.82)	Duale	Dunindu	Dushad
Draven (0.05)	Dred	Drewey	Duan	Dunn	Dushai
Dravian	Dredarious	Drewnard	Duan'e	Dunovan	Dushan
Dravin	Dredarius	Drewry	Duane (0.09)	Dunstan	Dushane
Dravion	Dredon	Drexel	Duanté	Dunston	Dushaun
Dravis	Dredrion	Drexler	Duante	Duntrez	Dushawn (0.01)
Dravius	Dreelle	Drexston	Duard	Dunuwilage	Dushon
Dravon	Drego	Drey (0.01)	Duayne	Dunzell	Dushun
Dravone	Drei	Dreyden	Dubar	Duone	Dushyanth
Dravyn	Dreighson	Dreydon	Dubem	Duong	Dusk
Dray	Dreighton	Dreyke	Dublin	Duoth	Dusstin
Drayan	Drekalo	Dreylan	Dubois	Duovontae	Dustain
Drayce	Drekarrie	Dreyon	Duboris	Dupree	Dustan (0.01)
Draydan	Drekeivius	Dreysen	Duc (0.01)	Duquan	Duste
Draydarrius	Drelan	Dreyson	Duce	Duquane	Dusten (0.01)
Drayden	Drelyn	Dreysyn	Duclam	Durad	Dusti
Drayfus	Dremian	Dreyton	Duco	Duramous	Dusti-Ann
Draygen	Dremone	Dreyvin	Ducquan	Duran (0.01)	Dustie
Draylene	Dremont	Dreyvon	Dudley (0.01)	Durance	Dustin (2.64)
Draylon	Dremontay	Drezden	Dudsen	Durand	Dustin Jr
Draysen	Dremonte	Dric	Duey	Durango	Dustin-James
Drayshawn	Drenard	Driggers	Dufferin	Durant	Dustin-Steven
Drayson	Drendan	Driscol	Duffy	Durante	Dustin.
Draytan	Dreneco	Driss	Dufrantz	Duranté	Dustinderpal
Drayton (0.02)	Drenell	Drissel	Dufray	Duray	Dustine
Drayven	Drennan	Dristin	Dugan (0.01)	Duree	Dustion
Drazen	Dreon	Driston	Dugan'grant	Dureese	Duston (0.01)
Dre (0.01)	Drequan (0.01)	Dritan	Duggan	Durekias	Dusty (0.07)
Dre Ion	Drequante	Driton	Duglas	Durell (0.01)	Dustyn (0.07)
Dre Vian	Drequell	Drnell	Duguawn	Dureyl	Dustynn
Dré	Drequone	Drondell	Duguez	Durga	Duszan
Drékardo	Dreqwuane	Dru (0.01)	Duhshon	Durham	Dutch (0.01)
Drékaris	Dreren	Dru'mond	Duillaume	Durian	Dutt
Drémarques	Dresaan	Druce	Duje	Durias	Duvahn
Drémon	Dresdan	Drue (0.01)	Dujuan (0.01)	Duriel	Duval
Drémonte	Dresden	Druex	Dujuane	Durin	Duvall
Drémonté	Dreshard	Druid	Duke (0.03)	Durius	Duvante
Dréon	Dreshaun	Drummond	Dukens	Durmario	Duvaughn
Dréquan (0.01)	Dreshawn (0.01)	Drury	Dukensley	Durnell	Duvaun
Dréquantae	Dreshod	Drustan	Dulan	Duro	Duvon
Dréquawn	Dreshon	Druw	Dullavinh	Durojaiye	Duvonta
Drésean	Dreshown	Dryden (0.01)	Dulton	Duron (0.01)	Duvuri
Dréshaun	Dreston	Dryln	Dumah	Durrae	Duwan

Duwane
Duwaun
Duwayne
Duy *(0.02)*
Dvion
Dvon
Dvonta
Dvonte
Dwain
Dwaine
Dwan *(0.01)*
Dwane
Dwania Jenard
Dwaun
Dwawn
Dwaylne
Dwaylon
Dwayne *(0.23)*
Dwayne-Jerome
Dwaynete
Dwhuan
Dwight *(0.13)*
Dwigth
Dwon
Dwoyn
Dwuan
Dwuane
Dwumo
Dwune
Dwyane
Dwyatt
Dwyene
Dwyer
Dy On
Dy Qwun
Dy Real
Dy'kerian
Dy'lan
Dy'nesius
Dy'quan
Dy'quarius
Dy'ron
Dy'taven
Dy'twan
Dyal
Dyalann
Dyaln
Dyami
Dyan
Dyanie
Dyarius
Dyéjuan
Dyéquan
Dyemonte
Dyeon

Dyer
Dyhar
Dyiriell
Dyjan
Dyjion
Dykerius
Dykese
Dyla
Dylan *(5.82)*
Dylan Isaac
Dylan Jonah
Dylan Léroce
Dylan Rae
Dylan-James
Dyland
Dylane
Dylanger
Dylann
Dylante
Dyle
Dylen
Dylian
Dylin *(0.01)*
Dyllan *(0.05)*
Dyllen
Dyllian
Dyllin
Dyllion
Dyllon *(0.03)*
Dyllyn
Dylon *(0.07)*
Dylyn
Dymaggio
Dyman
Dymari
Dymaris
Dymintion
Dymond
Dyon
Dyone
Dyontá
Dyonte
Dyorlen
Dyquan
Dyquanté
Dyquawen
Dyquez
Dyran
Dyre
Dyreck
Dyreece
Dyreek
Dyreis
Dyrek
Dyrell

Dyren
Dyresse
Dyriece
Dyrome
Dyron
Dyrone
Dyrontae
Dysean
Dyshaun
Dyshaune
Dyshawn
Dysheik
Dyshon
Dyshone
Dyshorn
Dyshown
Dyshun
Dyson *(0.01)*
Dystin
Dytaneon
Dytarian
Dytwan
Dytwon
Dyvion
Dyvon
Dywan
Dywayne
Dywon
Dywone

-E-

E *(0.01)*
E Derius
E Kealen
E Shawn
Édareon
Édonis
Élearn
Élontay
Émari
Émon
Émondra
Émonta
Émontae
Émonyea
Équan
Éqwon
Ésha
Éshawn
Éshon
Étarian
Évonta
Évonte
E-Quan

E. *(0.01)*
E. Christian
E. Ian
Eagle
Eagle Boy
Eagle Son
Eahab
Eain
Eajei
Eaman
Eamon *(0.03)*
Eamonn *(0.01)*
Ean *(0.03)*
Eareon
Earick
Earkins
Earl *(0.13)*
Earl Anthony
Earl Randall
Earl-Brovis
Earlandis
Earle
Earlie
Earljah
Earlvonté
Early
Earmon
Earnell
Earnest *(0.04)*
Earnie
Earon
Earrick
Earrious
Eartie
Earvin
Easam
Easley
Eason
Easten
Eastico
Eastin
Eastman
Easton *(0.06)*
Eastton
Eathan
Eathen
Eathon
Eavan
Eayon
Ebaad
Eban
Ebb
Ebed
Eben
Ebenezer

Eber *(0.01)*
Eberardo *(0.01)*
Ebere
Eberth
Ebighe
Ebin
Ebon *(0.01)*
Ebony
Ebrahim
Ebrima
Ebuka
Ecaree
Echan
Echeva
Echo
Ecion
Ecliserio
Eco
Ecstacey
Ecton
Ector
Ed *(0.01)*
Ed Quinn
Ed'quan
Ed'treon
Edain
Edan *(0.01)*
Edarious
Edarius
Edbert
Edbrion
Eddell
Eddgar
Eddie *(0.41)*
Eddieberto
Eddieion
Eddies
Eddison
Eddiw
Eddixia
Eddrain
Eddreon
Eddric
Eddrick
Eddson
Edduar
Eddy *(0.07)*
Edédius
Edel
Edell
Edeluis
Eden *(0.02)*
Edeno
Eder *(0.03)*
Edgar *(1.17)*

Edgar Daniel
Edgar David
Edgar James
Edgard *(0.02)*
Edgardo *(0.07)*
Edgardo-Inigo
Edge
Edgie
Edguard
Edhino
Edi
Edian
Ediberto
Edie
Edilberto *(0.01)*
Edin *(0.01)*
Edinam
Edio
Edir
Edis
Edison *(0.02)*
Edisto
Edjuan
Edmand
Edmando
Edmar
Edmaund
Edmil
Edmilan
Edmon
Edmond *(0.05)*
Edmondo
Edmondson
Edmun
Edmund *(0.07)*
Edmundo *(0.01)*
Edmuradam
Ednan
Edner
Ednet
Edoardo
Edon
Edosa
Edouard *(0.03)*
Edquandre
Edquon
Edralin
Edraul
Edrawin
Edrean
Edrees
Edrek
Edrese
Edress
Edrewns

Edrian Paul	Eemi	Eion	Elba	Elia	Eliodoro
Edric *(0.01)*	Eerik	Eiquan	Elbert *(0.01)*	Eliab *(0.01)*	Elioebed
Edric Johnathan	Eerion	Eirc	Elberto	Eliah	Elion
Edrick	Eero	Eireion	Elbis	Eliakim	Eliot *(0.02)*
Edrico	Eeron	Eirion	Elbren	Elian	Eliott
Edrienne	Eesh	Eirk	Elby	Elias *(0.41)*	Eliphete
Edrin	Efetobore	Eiron	Elced	Eliasar	Eliquel
Edris	Efezino	Eirtis	Elcee	Eliazar *(0.02)*	Elis
Edrisa	Effrey	Eisbell	Elchan	Eliazer	Elisabeth
Edrise	Efiong	Eisenhower	Elchonon	Eliceio	Elisaha
Edriss	Efraim	Eissa	Eldan	Eliceo	Elisaj
Edruige	Efrain *(0.17)*	Eisuke	Elden *(0.01)*	Elidah	Elisara
Edsel	Efran	Eita	Elder *(0.01)*	Elidel	Elisber
Edsell	Efrayin	Eitan *(0.01)*	Elderick	Elie *(0.03)*	Elisei
Edsen	Efrem	Eithan	Eldie	Elie Antoine	Eliseo *(0.07)*
Edshard	Efrem Zimbalis	Eiton	Eldin	Eliel	Eliset
Edson *(0.03)*	Efren *(0.08)*	Eitzaz	Eldon *(0.01)*	Elier	Elisha *(0.08)*
Edsteve	Efrian	Eivaan	Eldon Steven	Eliesel	Elishah
Edtwan	Efson	Ej	Eldred	Elieser	Elishama
Edu	Efstathios	Ejay	Eldredge	Eliezer *(0.03)*	Elishia
Eduard *(0.01)*	Efton	Ejazz	Eldren	Elifonso	Elishua
Eduardo *(1.66)*	Egal	Ejemia	Eldrick	Elifronsi	Elisiah
Eduardo Luis	Egale	Ejiroghene	Eldridge *(0.01)*	Eliga	Elisio
Eduardo-Davel	Egan *(0.01)*	Ejonte	Eldrien	Eligah	Elison
Edurdo	Egbert	Ekamjot	Eldwin	Eligh	Elitah
Eduvie	Egeh	Ekaphon	Eleanor	Eligha	Eliu
Eduyt	Egen	Ekaum	Eleasar	Elighjah	Eliud
Edvardo	Egerton	Ekelemchi	Eleazar *(0.04)*	Eligia	Elivd
Edvertis	Eghosa	Ekindu	Elefitherios	Eligio	Eliver
Edvin	Egil	Ekjot	Elejandro	Elih	Eliyah
Edwan	Egon	Ekrem	Elek	Elihu	Eliyahou
Edward *(1.79)*	Ehab	El	Eleki	Elija	Eliyahu *(0.01)*
Edward Gabriel	Ehan	El Dominus	Eleno	Elijah *(1.27)*	Eliyahu-Yosaif
Edward III	Ehizogie	El Lavonta	Eleodoro	Elijah Isiah	Eliyas
Edward Robert	Ehmer	El Vonte	Elerenzo	Elijah J.	Elizabeth *(0.01)*
Edward	Ehmisshii	El'ad	Elesey	Elijah-Jerel	Elizah
Tamogin A	Ehren	El'gin	Elester	Elijah-Wa	Elizeré
Edwardanthony	Ehsan	El'gun	Eletharios	Elijaha	Eljarai
Edwardo *(0.02)*	Ehud	El'hajj	Eleuterio	Elijahelan	Eljay
Edwards	Ehven	El'rico	Elevonta	Elijahjuan	Eljireh
Edwardzo	Eian *(0.01)*	El-Harsh	Elex	Elijahuan	Eljuan
Edwen	Eicca	Ela	Elexir	Elijahwon	Elkanah
Edwin *(0.80)*	Eid	Ela'n	Elexsa	Elijaquan	Ell-Jay
Edwin Guadalupe	Eiden	Elad	Elexus	Elijas	Ella
Edwins	Eifrane	Eladio *(0.01)*	Elfago	Elijha *(0.01)*	Ellan
Edwis	Eiji	Elahu	Elfanzo	Elijiah	Ellasha
Edwon	Eilajh	Elaja	Elfego	Elijio	Ellerum
Edwyn	Eileen	Elam	Elfren	Elijuah	Ellery *(0.01)*
Edxael	Eili	Elan *(0.03)*	Elga	Elijza	Ellett
Edy	Eimad	Elante	Elgee	Elikem	Ellias
Edzel Kyle	Ein	Elanté	Elgin *(0.01)*	Elimelec	Ellie
Eean	Einar	Elanteyz	Eli *(0.36)*	Elin	Elligha
Eeathen	Eine	Elasah	Eli'jah	Elinse	Ellijah
Eelynne	Einn	Elaunte	Eli'sha	Elinzo	Ellington
Eemer	Einstein	Elazar	Eli-Dan	Elio *(0.01)*	Elliot *(0.24)*

Elliot James	Elven	Emerich	Emmerich	Eno	Equriea
Elliott (0.21)	Elvens	Emerick	Emmerson	Enoc (0.01)	Er'ron
Elliott-Val	Elver	Emeril	Emmet (0.02)	Enoch (0.04)	Eraclio
Elliotte	Elverne	Emerson (0.06)	Emmett (0.07)	Enock	Erafe
Elliotter	Elvert	Emery (0.03)	Emmette	Enol	Eraldo
Ellis (0.07)	Elvin (0.04)	Emerycharles	Emmit	Enorris	Eram
Ellison	Elvir	Emet	Emmitt (0.02)	Enos	Eran
Ellizah	Elvis (0.10)	Emeterio	Emmott	Enox	Eranest
Ello	Elviz	Emethius	Emmual	Enrice	Erasmo (0.01)
Ellonté	Elvys	Emetrius	Emmuell	Enrick (0.01)	Erasmus
Ellshaun	Elwin	Emett	Emo N	Enricka	Erasto
Ellsworth	Elwood	Emidio	Emon	Enricky	Erdem
Ellwood	Elwyn	Emiel	Emondo	Enrico (0.03)	Erec
Elm	Ely (0.02)	Emielio	Emoni	Enricque	Erek (0.01)
Elmer (0.09)	Elya	Emil (0.04)	Emonie	Enriqe	Erel
Elmerto	Elyakim	Emil Cristo	Emonté	Enrique (0.51)	Eren
Elmi	Elyas	Emile (0.11)	Emontré	Enrique IV	Erenst
Elmis	Elyes	Emileo	Emory (0.03)	Enriquez	Erez
Elmore	Elyie	Emilian	Emorye	Enrrique (0.01)	Erfan
Eloah	Elyjah	Emiliano (0.03)	Emporia	Enrry	Erhan
Eloi (0.01)	Elyse	Emilien (0.01)	Emraan	Enshar	Eri
Eloise	Elyser	Emilija	Emre	Enumah	Eri'c
Elon (0.01)	Elyses	Emilio (0.26)	Emric	Enveer	Eribaldo
Elondrae	Elysha	Emilio Antonio	Emrick-Julio	Enver	Eriberto (0.04)
Elontae	Elzbieta	Emilio	Emrique	Enyelbert	Eric (6.05)
Elonte	Elzie	Christopher	Emron	Enyi	Eric Allen
Elonté	Emaad	Emillio	Emrose	Enzio	Eric Jr
Elontrae	Emad (0.01)	Emily (0.01)	Emry	Enzo (0.01)	Eric Lavon
Elonza	Emael	Eminel	Emsion	Eo	Eric Michael
Eloy (0.04)	Emaje	Emir	Emzie	Eoan	Eric Nguyen
Elpas	Eman (0.01)	Emirhan	Emzy	Eody	Eric Nowell
Elpi	Emancio	Emit	En'rekez	Eoghan	Eric Sinclair
Elpidio (0.01)	Emandi	Emite	Enaji	Eoin (0.01)	Eric Tionte
Elric	Emaney	Emitt	Enauld	Eolin	Eric-Elijah
Elric Alexander	Emani	Emke	Encarnacion	Eon	Eric-James
Elrick	Emaniel	Emllio	Ender	Eontaé	Eric-Michael
Elrico	Emannual	Emma	Enderson	Eonte	Eric-Santiago
Elridge	Emannuel	Emmahnuel	Endicott	Eorey	Erica
Elroy	Emanual	Emmai	Endre	Eorn	Ericc
Elryck	Emanueal	Emmanel	Ends	Eoseph	Erice
Elshdye	Emanuel (0.30)	Emmanual	Endy	Eowan	Ericen
Elsio-Jose	Emanuele	Emmanueal	Enes	Ephesian	Ericesteban
Elson	Emanuell	Emmanuel (0.66)	Engel	Epheson	Erich (0.07)
Elston	Emanuelle	Emmanuel	Engin	Ephraim (0.02)	Erick (0.79)
Elswood	Emari	Gregory	English	Ephram	Erick David
Elteno	Emarion	Emmanuel Nana-	Enguelver	Ephriam	Erick-Antoni
Elthon	Emarri	Y	Eniel	Epifanio (0.01)	Erick-Michael
Elton (0.03)	Emaujai	Emmanuel-	Eniggel	Epigmenio	Erickson (0.01)
Eltonia	Emba	Cedric	Eniko	Eppes	Erickzon
Eluan	Embra	Emmanuel-	Enique	Equa'n	Erico
Eluis	Embrose	Michael	Enjamo	Equan	Erics
Eluith	Embry	Emmanuell	Enki	Equantz	Ericson
Elva	Emeka	Emmanuelle	Enkisns	Equardo	Ericsson
Elvan	Emerardo	Emmanus	Enmanuel (0.01)	Equille	Eridian
Elvane	Emeric	Emmerek	Ennis	Equnn	Erie

Erien	Ernell	Eryan	Essik	Etiel	Evan-Michael
Eriesse	Ernesha	Eryberto	Essilfie	Etien	Evance
Eriic	Ernest (0.20)	Eryck	Essirie	Etienne (0.28)	Evander
Erij	Ernesto (0.39)	Eryk (0.01)	Essix	Etienné	Evandro
Erijovhan	Ernesto Jr	Eryn	Essu	Etnan	Evangelo
Erik (1.73)	Ernestor	Es'tavon	Estaban	Etoh	Evangelos (0.01)
Erik Christian	Erney	Esa	Estader	Etston	Evanle
Erik Daniel	Ernie (0.03)	Esaac	Estafano	Ettien	Evanmichael
Erik Jr	Ernon	Esai (0.01)	Estalim	Ettore	Evann
Erik Manuel	Ernst	Esaias	Estanislao	Etu	Evans (0.01)
Erik Ruben	Erny	Esam	Estarling	Etyel	Evanston
Erik-Alexandre	Erol	Esau (0.01)	Esteban (0.28)	Etzaire	Evanti
Erik-Lee	Erold	Esaul	Esteban Francis	Eu Darriyun	Evar
Erika	Eroll	Esaum	Esteben	Eual	Evaristo (0.02)
Erikcel	Eromon	Escada	Estefan	Euan	Evarts
Erike	Eron (0.01)	Eschol	Estefano	Euangelos	Evasio
Erikson	Eros (0.01)	Esdon	Estefen	Euclid	Evban
Erikzzon	Erpallure	Esdras (0.01)	Esten	Eudell	Eve Luis
Erin (0.07)	Erran	Esequicl	Estephan	Eugen	Evean
Eriner	Errand	Esequiel (0.02)	Estephén	Eugene (0.26)	Eveart
Erio	Erren	Esgar (0.02)	Estephen	Eugenio (0.03)	Evel
Erion	Erric	Esgardo	Ester	Eugui	Evelio
Erionne	Errick (0.01)	Eshaan	Estes	Eulalio (0.01)	Evelyeen
Erious	Errict	Eshaka	Estevan (0.09)	Eulises (0.01)	Evelyn
Eriq (0.01)	Errik	Eshanyl	Estevan Ash	Eulogia	Even
Eriqson	Errin	Eshawn	Esteven (0.01)	Eulogio	Evencio
Erique	Erringhton	Eshmael	Estevon	Eulojio	Evender
Eriqué	Errion	Esho	Estifanos	Eulsa	Evens
Eris	Erris	Eshton	Estill	Eunique	Evensio
Erist	Errius	Eshwar	Estin	Eurdis	Evenson
Erius	Errol (0.02)	Esian	Estip	Euriah	Ever (0.02)
Eriverto	Erroll	Esiderio	Estiven	Euric	Everado
Erkinson	Erron (0.01)	Eskandar	Estix	Euron	Everardo (0.05)
Erland	Erroyl	Eskender	Eston	Eurskin	Everest
Erlangga	Ersen	Esli	Estrale	Eurvonn	Everet
Erlee	Ershad	Esly	Estron	Eusebio (0.01)	Everett (0.13)
Erlin	Erskin	Esmail	Estuardo (0.01)	Eusebiu	Everette (0.01)
Erlis	Erskind	Esman-Kenan	Estus	Euseph	Everhett
Erliss	Erskine	Esmer	Estvardo	Eustace	Everitt
Erlito	Erthales	Esmeraldo	Esvamy	Eustacio	Everrett
Erly	Ertman	Esmond	Eswar	Eustaquio	Everson
Erman	Erubey	Esnef	Eswarasukumar	Eustin	Evert
Ermelandro	Ervens	Esnock	Etamo	Euston	Evertett
Ermelindo	Ervey	Espen	Etan	Eustorgio	Everton (0.01)
Ermenildo	Ervin (0.05)	Espideecy	Etavius	Eustrice	Evgeni
Ermias	Ervina	Espy	Ethaen	Euva	Evi
Ermiase	Ervine	Esquiel	Ethan (1.91)	Euvonte	Evian
Ermin	Erving	Esquire	Ethan Christian	Euzebio	Eviean
Ermine	Ervon	Esrah	Ethan Daniel	Eva	Evik
Erminio	Erwan	Esrail	Ethan-John	Evaine	Evile
Ermiyas	Erwign	Esrom	Ethanial	Evains	Evin (0.02)
Ermon	Erwin (0.05)	Essa	Ethaqn	Evajia	Evinn
Ernaan	Erwin Joseph	Essel	Ethen (0.01)	Evale	Evins
Ernan (0.01)	Erwing	Essex	Ethian	Evan (2.75)	Evisabel
Ernel	Erxhan	Essic	Ethridge	Evan Lawrence	Evodio

Evon *(0.01)*	Ezara	Facundo	Falcon	Faron *(0.01)*	Fayad
Evonta	Ezavier	Fadal	Falema'o	Faronta	Fayaz
Evonte	Ezavin	Fadarius	Falen	Faronté	Faye
Evonti	Ezavine	Fadarrian	Fallasha	Farooq	Fayez
Evraj	Ezavis	Fadarryl	Fallon	Faroque	Fayne
Evrim	Ezeckiel	Faddy	Faly	Faross	Faysal
Evron	Ezekeil	Fade	Famous	Farouk	Fayson
Evyn *(0.01)*	Ezekeyial	Fadeel	Fanandez	Farra	Fayyaz
Ewald	Ezekial	Fadel	Fanchley	Farrad	Fazle
Ewan	Ezekiel *(0.12)*	Fadey	Fane	Farrakhan	Fazon
Ewani	Ezekiel John	Fadhi	Fanezbais	Farrean	Fékerrius
Eward	Ezekielle	Fadi *(0.02)*	Fanfan	Farrell	Féron
Ewart	Ezel	Fadi-Michael	Fangailesau	Farren	Fearghas
Ewell	Ezell	Fadie	Fanongonongo	Farret	Fearley
Ewen	Ezequias	Fadil	Fanonte	Farriest	Fearro
Ewer	Ezequiel *(0.11)*	Faelan	Fanso	Farrin	Feather
Ewing	Ezer	Fagan	Faquan	Farris	Febian
Exavian	Ezetris	Fago	Faquonn	Farroah	Fedale
Exaviar	Ezguard	Fahaad	Faraan	Farron	Fedarius
Exavier *(0.01)*	Ezie	Fahad *(0.01)*	Faraaz	Faruq	Fedele
Exavion	Ezio	Fahbryss	Farad	Farzad	Fedeno
Exavior	Ezoá	Fahd	Farah	Farzam	Federed
Exel	Ezra *(0.10)*	Faheem	Farahman	Farzan	Federico *(0.05)*
Exequiel	Ezrah	Faheem-Ali	Faraiji	Fasal	Federio
Exie	Ezrin	Fahey	Faran	Faseeh	Fednel
Exil	Ezry	Fahim	Faraseldin	Fasely	Fedor
Exon	Eztevan-De	Fahir	Faraz *(0.01)*	Fasil	Feendor
Expavious		Fahiym	Farbod	Fatah	Fei
Exree	**-F-**	Fahmeer	Fardowsa	Fatahi	Feigenbaum
Exso		Fahmi	Fareed	Fate	Feim
Extavien	F *(0.01)*	Fahmiad	Fareen	Fatem	Feisal
Exvonte	F.	Fahraan	Fareh	Faterry	Fela
Exzavier	Fa	Faid	Faren	Fathi	Felandis
Exzavious	Fa Ron	Fain	Farentino	Fathil	Feleti
Exzavis	Fa'asaoina	Fairlieah	Farentto	Fatjon	Feliberto
Exzell	Fa'avevela	Fairreon	Fares	Fatme	Felice
Exziaver	Fa'heim	Faisal *(0.02)*	Farhaad	Fatouma	Feliciano *(0.01)*
Ey	Fa'shun	Faisel	Farhaan	Faud	Feliks
Eyad	Faaris	Faison	Farhaaz	Faudy	Felinquist
Eyan	Faasisila	Faith	Farhad	Faulkon	Felipe *(0.26)*
Eyan Zachary	Faayeque	Faithin	Farhan *(0.01)*	Faurest	Felipe Diego
Eyassu	Fabain	Faiyaz	Farhankhan	Fauscar	Felise
Eyasu	Fabbio	Faiz	Farhaz	Faush	Felix *(0.59)*
Eyby	Fabein	Faizal	Farhin	Faustino *(0.02)*	Felix Antoine *(0.04)*
Eyob	Fabian *(0.35)*	Faizan *(0.01)*	Fari	Fausto *(0.02)*	Felix Olivier *(0.01)*
Eyobe	Fabiano	Faize	Farice	Favain	Feliz
Eyoel	Fabien *(0.02)*	Faizi	Farid	Favian *(0.02)*	Fellini
Eyosas	Fabin	Fakher	Fariez	Favio	Fellony
Eyosias	Fabio *(0.05)*	Fakruddin	Farimang	Favyen	Felman
Eyou-Ab	Fabion	Faladin	Farin	Fawaaz	Felmontae
Eytan	Fabrice *(0.02)*	Falah	Faris *(0.01)*	Fawad	Felton *(0.01)*
Eythan	Fabricio	Falando	Farley	Fawazo Olakite	Feltorious
Eyuel	Fabrizio	Falandus	Farman	Fawwaz	Fenel
Eyvind	Fabyan	Falaniko	Farnardo	Fawzi	Fenell
Ezakeil	Fabyen	Falco	Faro	Fawzi-Geries	Fenell

Feng-Jyh	Fian	Firmin	Fonteau	Francis Phuoc-L	Fransz
Fenner	Fiaz	Firssamuel	Fontray	Francis-Vu	Frantrell
Fenny	Ficna	Fischer *(0.01)*	Ford *(0.02)*	Francisco *(1.35)*	Frantz *(0.01)*
Fenold	Fidel *(0.09)*	Fisher *(0.01)*	Fordham	Francisco Javier	Frantz-Michel
Fenton	Fidelernesto	Fitim	Forest *(0.10)*	Francisco Jr	Frantzdy
Fentress	Fidelis	Fitzbert	Forestt	Francisco Xavier	Frantzky
Fentry	Fidell	Fitzgerald	Forice	Franciscojav	Franz *(0.01)*
Fenwick	Fidelmar	Fitzloy	Foriom	*(0.01)*	Franz-Joseph
Ferando	Fidencio *(0.01)*	Fitzpatrick	Forlando	Franciscus	Franza
Feras	Fieandre	Fitzroy	Fornzcia	Franciskus	Franzie
Ferdarious	Field	Fizavian	Forrell	Francklen	Franzt-Hebert
Ferdinand *(0.01)*	Fielding	Flabio	Forresst	Francklin	Fraser *(0.03)*
Ferdinando	Fields	Flagan	Forrest *(0.49)*	Francky	Frasier
Ferdows	Fievel	Flash	Forrest Tyler	Franco *(0.05)*	Fraz
Ferenc	Figrag	Flavio *(0.02)*	Forrestar	Francoi	Frazer *(0.01)*
Ferghus	Fihussein	Flavius	Forrester	Francois *(0.17)*	Frazier *(0.01)*
Fergie	Fil	Flecher	Forrestt	Francois Xavi	Fred *(0.11)*
Fergus	Filadelfo	Fleetwood	Forris	*(0.01)*	Fredarius
Ferhat	Filakosky	Flem	Forté	Francoise	Fredd
Ferlandes	Filamir	Flemas	Fortino *(0.01)*	Francyllen	Fredde
Ferlin	Filander	Fleppine	Fortune	Frandier	Fredderick
Ferman	Filandros	Fletcher *(0.04)*	Foryst	Frandlie	Freddi
Fermi	Filemon	Flint *(0.01)*	Foshua	Frandy	Freddie *(0.09)*
Fermin *(0.04)*	Filiberto *(0.02)*	Flio	Foster *(0.04)*	Frane	Freddrick *(0.01)*
Fernand	Filimon	Florance	Fostin	Frank *(0.96)*	Freddy *(0.15)*
Fernandez	Filip *(0.03)*	Flordave	Fotios-Phillip	Frank Josephrol	Frederic *(0.31)*
Fernando *(0.86)*	Filip-Amdixej	Florencio *(0.02)*	Fotis	Frank Minh	Frederich
Fernando Andres	Filipe	Florent	Fouad	Frankchard	Frederick *(0.44)*
Fernando Angelo	Filipo	Florent Dean	Fouche	Franke	Frederico
Fernandoandres	Filippo	Florentino *(0.02)*	Foundling	Frankevious	Fredericus
Fernanza	Filis	Flores	Fountane	Frankey	Frederik *(0.09)*
Fernendo	Fillip	Florian	Fourthaddius	Franki	Frederique *(0.01)*
Fernese	Fillup	Floriberto	Fowzi	Frankie *(0.12)*	Frederrik
Ferney	Filmon	Florideo	Fox *(0.01)*	Franklen	Fredi *(0.02)*
Fernie *(0.01)*	Fin	Florim	Foxx	Franklin *(0.28)*	Fredick
Feron	Finesse	Flory	Foxzio	Franklin-Ambrose	Fredis
Feronte	Finest	Floyd *(0.07)*	Foyesade	Franklyn *(0.01)*	Fredlee
Ferrance	Finian	Floye	Fracisco	Franklynn	Frednerson
Ferrante	Finie	Flynn *(0.01)*	Fraderick	Franko	Fredreick
Ferrari	Finlay	Flynt	Fradreico	Frankqueto	Fredrell
Ferrell	Finley	Foaad	Frainc	Franktonny	Fredrequis
Ferrial	Finn *(0.01)*	Foel	Frampton	Franky *(0.02)*	Fredric
Ferrin	Finn-Olaf	Folarin	Francarlo	Franly	Fredrick *(0.14)*
Ferris *(0.01)*	Finnen	Folds	Francarlos	Frano	Fredricklee
Ferroid	Finnian	Follad	France	Franquana	Fredricknathan
Ferron	Finsley	Fololo-Yomo	Frances	Franquez	Fredricks
Ferry	Fintan	Foluke	Francesca	Franqui	Fredrico
Feryixsso	Finton	Fon	Francesco *(0.08)*	Franquise	Fredricus
Fester	Fion	Fon-Joseph	Francesco-	Franqulyn	Fredrik
Fetched	Fiore	Fondanius	Emanuele	Frans	Fredry
Feticite	Firai	Fonsy	Francescoly	Franshawn	Fredson
Feylon	Firas *(0.01)*	Fonta	Francewau	Franshon	Fredtavious
Fharhaad	Firat	Fontanaé	Franchesk	Fransico	Fredterrius
Phillip	Firdaus	Fontavious	Francies	Fransisco *(0.02)*	Fredy *(0.05)*
Fiacro	Firman	Fontavis	Francis *(0.83)*	Fransysco	Freederico

Freedom
Freeman *(0.01)*
Freemin
Freemon
Fregner
Freitas
French
Frenchon
Frendli
Frenky
Frenshaniel
Freston
Freyquill
Freysen
Friandy
Fricardo
Fridey
Friedrich
Friedryk
Friendly
Frinswan
Frisco *(0.01)*
Fritz *(0.01)*
Fritzbert
Fritzerald
Fritzlin
Fritzner
Fritznol
Froilan *(0.01)*
Frontez
Froylan *(0.01)*
Fu Qua
Fu'darius
Fuad
Fue
Fuhad
Fukwang
Fulgencio
Fuli
Fuller
Fulton *(0.01)*
Fumiaki
Fung
Funtezes
Fuquan
Furgason
Furious
Furiouse
Furjaad
Furlando
Furnell
Furqan
Furquan
Fushia
Fuxing

Fylmon
Fynn
Fyodor
Fysal

-G-

G *(0.01)*
G Everett
G Quan
G Quincy
G'ante
G'michael
G'qwon
G'vonte
G'yeon
G-Elen'te
G.
G.J.
G.T.
Ga
Ga Terrius
Ga'juane
Ga'maya
Ga'quawn
Gaagge
Gaant-Cannon
Gabari
Gabariele
Gabe *(0.02)*
Gaberal
Gaberial
Gaberiel
Gaberil
Gabiel
Gabin
Gabino *(0.03)*
Gabirel
Gable
Gabor
Gabrael
Gabraiel
Gabreal
Gabreil
Gabrel
Gabrell
Gabriael
Gabrial *(0.01)*
Gabriélito
Gabrieal
Gabriel *(3.39)*
Gabriel Alexander
Gabriel Fernando
Gabriel Gal
Gabriel-Adrian

Gabriel-Francois
Gabriel-Patrick
Gabriela
Gabriele *(0.01)*
Gabriell
Gabriella
Gabrielle *(0.01)*
Gabrile
Gabrino
Gabryalle
Gabryel *(0.01)*
Gad
Gaden
Gadge
Gadiel
Gadison
Gadkathe
Gaebril
Gaebryal
Gaebryl
Gaeden
Gaege
Gael *(0.01)*
Gaelan
Gaelen
Gaelin
Gaelyn
Gaeta
Gaetan
Gaetano
Gagan *(0.01)*
Gagandeep *(0.02)*
Gagandip
Gaganjit
Gaganpal
Gaganpreet
Gaganveer
Gage *(0.59)*
Gagé
Gaggan
Gagian
Gagundeep
Gaibriel
Gaige *(0.04)*
Gaige William
Gaij
Gaileh
Gailen
Gaillard
Gaines
Gains
Gaired
Gairet
Gairey
Gairitd

Gairy
Gaitlin
Gaivon
Gajan
Gaje *(0.01)*
Gajuan
Gal
Galal
Galan
Galata
Gale
Galeand
Galen *(0.08)*
Galey
Galfato
Galileo
Galiz
Gallegos
Galli
Galma
Galontre
Galovert
Galveston
Galvin *(0.01)*
Galyn
Gamachu
Gamal
Gamaliel *(0.01)*
Gaman
Gamandeep
Gamba
Gamble
Gamealle
Gamel
Gamerry
Gamieysa
Gamil
Gamliel
Gammon
Gamoise
Gana
Ganbriele
Gandhar
Gandhi
Ganesh
Ganga
Gangani
Gangelo
Ganguist
Gani
Ganit
Ganiu-Babajide
Gannan
Gannen
Gannon *(0.02)*

Gant
Gantt
Gaovoni
Gaqvan
Gar
Garad
Garald
Garan
Garany
Garard
Garbiel
Garbriel
Garcell
Garcia
Gardiner
Gardner
Gardy
Gared
Garek
Garen *(0.01)*
Garence
Garet *(0.02)*
Gareth *(0.04)*
Garett *(0.08)*
Garette
Garey
Garfield
Garhett
Garick
Garid
Gariello
Garik
Garin *(0.01)*
Garion *(0.01)*
Garison
Garisson
Garit
Garitt
Garland *(0.02)*
Garlen
Garlyn
Garmiel
Garna'y
Garnall
Garnell
Garner *(0.01)*
Garnet *(0.01)*
Garnett *(0.01)*
Garnishion
Garon
Garrantz
Garrat
Garrek
Garrell
Garren *(0.02)*

Garret *(0.16)*
Garreth
Garreton
Garrett *(2.11)*
Garrett-Adam
Garrette
Garrettethan
Garrhett
Garri
Garric
Garrick *(0.04)*
Garrid
Garridan
Garrie
Garrin
Garringthon
Garrion
Garris
Garrison *(0.07)*
Garrit
Garrith
Garritt
Garrity
Garriun
Garrnett
Garrod
Garrok
Garron
Garry *(0.07)*
Garshen
Garth *(0.02)*
Garthan
Garthner
Gartick
Gartrell
Garven
Garvey
Garvin
Garvy
Garwyn
Gary *(0.70)*
Gary Antoni
Gary III
Gary Jr
Garylee
Garyn
Garyon
Garyt
Gasey
Gashaw
Gasmier
Gaspar *(0.01)*
Gaspard
Gaspare
Gaspari

Gastaun
Gaston (0.02)
Gastonguay
Gasun
Gaten
Gates
Gatlen
Gatlin (0.02)
Gatlon
Gatlyn
Gatre
Gauge (0.01)
Gauin
Gaulvan
Gaurab
Gaurav (0.01)
Gautam
Gautham
Gauthaman
Gavan
Gavargo
Gavarius
Gaven (0.01)
Gavin (0.57)
Gavino (0.01)
Gavn
Gavneet
Gavohn
Gavon
Gavontay
Gavriel
Gavyn (0.01)
Gavynn
Gawen
Gawlen Jr
Gawtam
Gay
Gayanjit
Gayen
Gaylan
Gayle
Gaylen
Gaylin
Gaylon (0.01)
Gaylord
Gayron
Gays
Gazi
Gbadebo
Gchild
Géarius
Gémaal
Géquarrius
Géquille
Gétoddrick

Gévelve
Ge-Hsiang
Ge-Vontae
Geames
Gearld
Gearrin
Geary
Geauni
Geba
Gebahet
Gebrill
Gecole
Geddes
Geddy
Gedeon
Gee
Geejuan
Geerrtthan
Geerthan
Geesu
Geevithan
Geevon
Geffen
Geffery
Geffrey
Gehn
Gehret
Gehric
Gehrig
Gejuan
Gekill
Gelasio
Gelaxson
Gelin
Gelly
Gelon
Gelson
Gemabri
Gemaine
Gemal
Gemar
Gemaude
Gemel
Gemelle
Gemico
Gemini
Gemiran
Gemon
Gen
Genard
Genaro (0.05)
Genat
Genava
Genc
Gend

Gene (0.08)
Gene Michael
Gene-Paul
Genelro
General
Genereo
Genero
Generson
Genesis (0.01)
Genessa
Genevieve
Genevon
Genhel
Genico
Genie
Genin
Genis
Genki
Gennahan
Gennaro
Genner
Geno (0.02)
Genosh
Genovis
Genri
Gentel
Gentina
Gentrey
Gentri
Gentry (0.01)
Century
Geo
Geo'vante
Geo-Voni
Geofery
Geoff
Geoffery (0.02)
Geoffrey (0.29)
Geoffrie
Geoffroy
Geoffry
Geofrey-George
Geomarey
Geon
Geontae
Georabner
Georbec
Geordan (0.01)
Geordi
Geordian
Geordie (0.01)
Geordin
Geordon
Geordy
Georell

Georffrey
Georganne
George (1.39)
George IV
George Joseph
George Josiah
George Peter
George-Michael
George-Nikolay
Georges (0.01)
Georges-Etienne
Georgesharbel
Georgia
Georgian
Georgie
Georgineo
Georgio
Georgios (0.01)
Georgy
Geory
Geosh
Geovani (0.01)
Geovanne
Geovannhi
Geovanni (0.03)
Geovanni'
Geovanny (0.03)
Geovanthony
Geovany (0.01)
Geovany De Jesus
Geovontaé
Gequan
Gequavius
Gequion
Ger (0.01)
Ger'quan
Geraciea
Gerad
Geraden
Gerael
Geraght
Geraid
Geraint
Geral
Gerald (0.39)
Gerald-Garrett
Gerald-Rene
Geraldo (0.02)
Geraldsa
Geraldy
Gerami
Geramiah
Geramie
Geramy

Geran
Gerard (0.07)
Gerard Micheal
Gerard Paul
Gerard-Kyle
Gerardo (0.65)
Gerardo Jr
Geraud
Gerayn
Gerber
Gercon
Gerd
Gerdarius
Gered
Gerell
Geremiah
Geremias
Geremy (0.01)
Gerene
Gergens
Gerhard
Gerhardi
Gerhardt
Gerhart
Gerhort
Gerian
Geric
Gerick
Gerico
Gerihun
Gerik
Geritol
Gerlad
Germaias
Germain (0.01)
Germaine (0.01)
Germall
German (0.11)
Germarlo
Germe Anthony
Germirrio
Germod
Germontrae
Gernard
Gerod
Geroge
Geroge-Albert
Gerold
Gerome (0.01)
Geromiah
Geromino
Geron
Geronia
Geronimo (0.01)
Gerord

Geroy
Gerquan
Gerrad
Gerrald
Gerrard
Gerraud
Gerred
Gerrel
Gerrell
Gerremy
Gerren
Gerret
Gerrett
Gerrick
Gerrid
Gerriel
Gerriell
Gerriet
Gerris
Gerrit (0.02)
Gerritt
Gerrod (0.01)
Gerrode
Gerrold
Gerron
Gerry (0.02)
Gerryn
Gersan
Gershawn
Gerso'n
Gerson (0.04)
Gerus
Gervacio
Gervais
Gervaise
Gervan
Gervante
Gervarus
Gervase
Gervonte
Gervy
Geryn
Gesler
Geson
Getavious
Getavius
Geterri
Geterrian
Gethin
Getro
Geva N
Gevacia
Gevarian
Gevarro
Gevon

Gevonis	Giannii	Gillis	Giovon	Glasco	Gohar
Gevork *(0.01)*	Giannini	Gillom	Giovonni	Glass	Gohn
Geyson	Giannis	Gilman	Giovonnia	Glavenski	Gokul
Geywade	Giannos	Gilmar	Giovonnie	Gleb	Gokulan
Gezim	Gianpaolo	Gilmer	Girandi	Gleeson	Golam
Ghadi	Gianpiero	Gilmour	Girard	Glem	Golden *(0.01)*
Ghaith	Gianrobert	Gilo	Giraud	Glen *(0.15)*	Goldie
Ghajan	Gianvito	Gilsell	Gireh	Glenaj	Gollie
Ghalen	Giavanni	Gilson	Giries	Glenardo	Gomer
Ghalib Bin	Gibb	Gilton	Girishanth	Glenda	Gomez
Ghanan	Gibbar	Gilverto	Girishna	Glendale	Gonffa
Ghaneah	Gibraan	Gimae	Girolamo	Glendinning	Gonsalo
Ghani	Gibram	Gimael	Giscard	Glendon *(0.01)*	Gonzalo *(0.10)*
Ghanim	Gibran *(0.01)*	Gimetrius	Giselle	Glendrick	Gonzelee
Ghannon	Gibraun	Gimond	Gishok	Glendy	Gonzolo
Ghassan	Gibriil	Ginard	Git	Glenford	Good
Ghawn	Gibron	Ginno	Githson	Glengolf	Goodee
Ghay'len	Gibson *(0.01)*	Gino *(0.09)*	Giulano	Glenmore	Gooding
Ghazala	Gibsonly	Ginson	Giuliano *(0.02)*	Glenn *(0.21)*	Gopal
Ghazi	Gidd	Ginthujan	Giulino	Glennard	Goran
Ghejuan	Giddel	Ginyor	Giulio	Glenndale	Gordan
Gheremi	Giddeon	Gio	Giulizno	Glennden	Gorden
Ghikhan	Giddiani	Gioacchino	Giulliano	Glenniell	Gordens
Ghilmaan	Gideon *(0.05)*	Giobani	Giusephi	Glennon	Gordick
Ghislain *(0.01)*	Gidvanni	Giobensky	Giuseppe *(0.06)*	Glennshawn	Gordie
Ghiyath	Gie	Giobin	Giuseppe Jo	Glenrick	Gordon *(0.21)*
Ghulam	Giel	Gionni	Giuseppi	Glensen	Gordon-Steven
Ghunnar	Giftson	Giontos	Giusseppe	Glentavius	Gordonn
Ghussan	Gihan	Giordan	Giustino	Glenton	Gordonvion
Gia	Gikonyo	Giordano *(0.01)*	Givan	Glenvin	Gorey
Giacinto	Gil *(0.02)*	Giordano-Antonio	Givanté	Glenwood	Gorge *(0.01)*
Giaco	Gilad	Giordin	Givawn	Gleyder	Gorgie
Giacomino	Gilau	Giorgi	Giveckio	Gligor	Goriel
Giacomo *(0.01)*	Gilber	Giorgio *(0.01)*	Givinchy	Gloda	Gorjan
Giagien	Gilbert *(0.21)*	Giorgios	Givonni	Gloria	Gorje
Giam	Gilberto *(0.22)*	Giormelo	Givonte	Glory	Gorki
Giampietro	Gilberto-Elias	Giosue	Givyn	Gloster	Gorman
Gian *(0.02)*	Gilchrist	Giovahann	Giwisay	Glover	Gorsieur
Gian-Carlo	Gildardo *(0.01)*	Giovan	Giyoun	Glyn	Gortez
Gian-Francesco	Gilderoy	Giovane	Gizel	Glyndwr	Gosafat
Gian-Luca	Gilead	Giovani *(0.03)*	Gjaiheem	Glynn *(0.01)*	Goss
Gian-Michael	Giles *(0.01)*	Giovanie	Gjaimeir	Glynnis	Gouilloume
Gianan	Gilford	Giovann	Gjergj	Glynon	Gouled
Giancarlo *(0.06)*	Gilfred	Giovannais	Gjervon	Gnyanesh	Goushikan
Giancarlos	Gilibaldo	Giovanni *(0.54)*	Gjon	Goamar	Govan
Gianfranco *(0.01)*	Gill	Giovanni Gustav	Gjovalin	Gobind	Govani-De
Giani	Gillan	Giovanni-Paolo	Gladdie	Gocean	Govanny
Gianluc	Gillen	Giovannie	Glade	Godbless	Govendra
Gianluca *(0.03)*	Gillermo	Giovannii	Gladimiro	Godfred	Govind
Gianmarco *(0.01)*	Gilles *(0.01)*	Giovannte	Gladmar	Godfrey *(0.01)*	Govinda
Gianmario	Gilli	Giovanny *(0.06)*	Gladstone	Godofredo	Govindh
Gianncarlo	Gilliam	Giovante	Gladymir	Godwin	Gow
Gianne	Gillian	Giovantia	Glamorr	Godwins	Gowri
Gianne Lawrence	Gillie	Giovany *(0.01)*	Glandson	Goel	Gowthaam
Gianni *(0.03)*	Gilligan	Giovaughn	Glardon	Gogulan	Gowtham

Gowthaman	Graydan	Greyland	Guijeffrey	Gunn	Gurlall
Gowthamm	Grayden	Greylin	Guilbert	Gunnar *(0.12)*	Gurley
Gowthen	Graydon *(0.02)*	Greysen	Guildford	Gunner *(0.06)*	Gurlov
Grabiel	Graydyn	Greyson *(0.04)*	Guile	Gunnjot	Gurman
Gracen	Graye	Greysten	Guilford	Gunntas	Gurmeet
Graciano	Grayeme	Grier	Guilherme	Gunter *(0.01)*	Gurmehar
Gracjan	Grayham	Grifen	Guiliano	Gunther *(0.01)*	Gurmehtab
Gradalupe	Graylan	Griff	Guillaume *(0.41)*	Gunvir	Gurmick
Graddie	Graylin *(0.01)*	Griffen *(0.01)*	Guille	Guo-En	Gurmohit
Graden	Grayline	Griffeth	Guilleaume	Gur	Gurmukh
Grady *(0.09)*	Graylyn	Griffin *(0.30)*	Guillem	Gurale	Gurnak
Gradys	Graym	Griffith *(0.01)*	Guillermito	Guramrit	Gurnasib
Graeham	Graynold	Griffon	Guillermo *(0.32)*	Gurarjan	Gurneak
Graehme	Grayon	Griffyn	Guillerno	Gurarman	Gurneet
Grael	Graysen	Grifynn	Guillerrmo	Gurbakash	Gurneil
Graem	Grayson *(0.23)*	Grigor *(0.01)*	Guilllermo	Gurbandhan	Gurneill
Graeme *(0.07)*	Grayton	Grigore	Guilmer	Gurbar	Gurney
Graene	Graziano	Grigori	Guimel	Gurbax	Gurnish
Graeson	Gre	Grigorios	Guinness	Gurbaz	Gurniwaz
Graff	Grea	Grigory	Guion	Gurbinder	Gurnoor
Grafton	Greason	Grilman	Guiovani	Gurbir	Gurpal
Graham *(0.37)*	Great-Sun	Grimek	Guiovanni	Gurbishan	Gurpartap
Graham Lee	Grechaun	Grira	Guiseppe	Gurcharn	Gurpaul
Grahame	Greer	Grisha	Guiseppi	Gurdeep *(0.01)*	Gurpavan
Grahamme	Greet	Gritsana	Guiseppie	Gurdir	Gurpinder
Grahm	Greg *(0.06)*	Grizwald	Guisman	Gurdit	Gurpreet *(0.03)*
Graig	Gregary	Groffrey	Guisseppe	Gurditt	Gursahej
Graigory	Gregaunte	Grover	Guitemberg	Gureet	Gursajan
Graison	Gregdrick	Gruprit	Guivens	Gurgir	Gursavick
Graline	Gregery	Gryphon	Gujaun	Gurinder *(0.01)*	Gursean
Gram	Gregg *(0.02)*	Grzegorz	Gujwonde	Gurinderpal	Gursehej
Grame	Greggery	Gsabriel	Gulaid	Gurjaap	Gursev
Gramm	Greggory *(0.03)*	Guabeon	Gulam	Gurjaipal	Gursewak
Grand	Gregoire	Guadalope	Guled	Gurjant	Gurshakti
Grandar	Gregor	Guadalupe *(0.11)*	Guleed	Gurjap	Gurshan
Granderson	Gregorey	Guage	Gulett	Gurjas	Gursharan
Granger	Gregorg	Gualberto	Gulianni	Gurjeet	Gursharanjit
Granson	Gregorie	Guan	Guliano	Gurjeev	Gursharn
Grant *(1.14)*	Gregorio *(0.07)*	Gubaryee	Gulled	Gurjinder	Gurshawn
Grant Michael	Gregory *(2.03)*	Gudelio	Gulleed	Gurjit	Gursher
Grante	Gregory Michael	Guenaro	Gulraj	Gurjivan	Gursimran
Grantham	Gregory-Wayne	Guerandgy	Gulshan	Gurjiwan	Gurtaj
Grantland	Gregorz	Guerby	Gulshandeep	Gurjodh	Gurtaran
Grantley	Gregrey	Guerchom	Gumane	Gurjosh	Gurtej
Granton	Gregtazis	Guerlett	Gumaro	Gurjot *(0.01)*	Gurtejvir
Grantonio	Gregvontay	Guero	Gumberto	Gurkamal	Gurter
Granville	Grehgory	Guerry	Gumeet	Gurkaran	Gurukarn
Granzy	Greigor	Guerson	Gumildo	Gurkarmjit	Gurulove
Grashaun	Greigroe	Guest	Gun	Gurkarn	Guruparan
Grason	Greogry	Guevara	Gunbir	Gurkeerit	Guruparshad
Gratavious	Gresham	Gui	Gundrum	Gurkeert	Guruprasad
Grattan	Greville	Guiancarlo	Gunenion	Gurkevin	Gurvaj
Graves	Grey *(0.01)*	Guibens	Guner	Gurkiran	Gurveer *(0.01)*
Gravson	Greyden	Guido	Gunes	Gurkirat *(0.01)*	Gurvind
Gray *(0.02)*	Greydon	Guigi	Gunesh	Gurlal	Gurvinder

Gurvir *(0.01)*	Haakon	Haille	Hamdan	Hanif	Hardie
Gurwainder	Haaris	Haim	Hamdee	Haninimakohilai	Hardik
Gurwen	Haaroon	Haim-Elias	Hamden	Hanji	Hardil
Gurwinder	Haashim	Haime	Hamdi	Hank *(0.03)*	Hardin
Gus *(0.01)*	Haashir	Haiming	Hamdy	Hanko	Hardly
Guscenie	Habacuc	Haimish	Hamed *(0.01)*	Hanlei	Hardy
Gusmaro	Habeeb	Hair	Hamedo	Hanley	Hareen
Gust	Habel	Hairl	Hamedoulah	Hanna *(0.01)*	Hareish
Gustabo	Haben	Haitai	Hamee	Hanna-John	Harel
Gustav	Habib *(0.01)*	Haitham	Hameed	Hannah *(0.01)*	Harell
Gustava	Habibur	Haitrieu	Hameet	Hannan	Haresh
Gustave	Habil	Hajime	Hami-Lisa	Hannel	Harfateh
Gustavo *(0.48)*	Habraham	Hakam	Hamid *(0.01)*	Hannibal	Hargenio
Gustavus	Habtom	Hakar	Hamidullah	Hanno	Hargobind
Gustin	Hackett	Hakeem *(0.09)*	Hamill	Hannon	Hargopal
Gustine	Hadden	Hakeem	Hamilton *(0.04)*	Hannu	Hargunjot
Gustisse	Haddon	Olajuwon	Hamin	Hanon	Hari
Gustus	Haddyness	Hakeemsan	Hamir	Hans *(0.07)*	Harian
Gusty	Hadee	Hakeen	Hamish	Hans-Fredrik	Harichand
Gustyn	Haden *(0.04)*	Hakem	Hamisi	Hans-Joachim	Harichy
Guthrie	Hadi *(0.01)*	Hakhan	Hamlin	Hansel *(0.01)*	Haridas
Guun	Hadin	Hakiem	Hammaad	Hansell	Hariharan
Guutu	Hadiya	Hakim *(0.01)*	Hammad	Hansen *(0.01)*	Harikajah
Guy *(0.09)*	Hadiyana	Hakiym	Hammond	Hanser	Harim
Guy D'larrius	Hadley *(0.01)*	Haklia	Hamond	Hansol	Harin
Guy-Lawrence	Hadrian	Hakop *(0.01)*	Hamp	Hanson *(0.01)*	Harinam
Guyaume	Hadrien	Hal	Hampton *(0.01)*	Hanspaul	Harinder *(0.01)*
Guyden	Hady	Halan	Hampus	Hansung	Harinderjit
Guyllaume *(0.01)*	Hadyn	Halbert	Hamraj	Hantz	Haris *(0.01)*
Guyron	Hae Sung	Halcy	Hamraz	Hanyu	Harish
Guyto	Haeden	Haldan	Hamsan	Hanz	Harison
Guyton	Haejune	Halden	Hamud	Hanzel	Harith
Gwang	Haemhin	Hale	Hamza *(0.05)*	Hao	Harjaan
Gwayne	Haessler	Halee	Hamza-	Haracio	Harjaap
Gwdion	Hafeez	Halen *(0.01)*	Mohammed	Harahn	Harjan
Gwindell	Hafid	Haley *(0.01)*	Hamzah *(0.01)*	Haralamb	Harjas
Gwungai	Hafiz	Halfredo	Hamze	Haralambos	Harjatin
Gwyot	Hagan *(0.01)*	Halid	Hamzeh	Haraldo	Harjeet
Gyasi	Hagen *(0.01)*	Halil	Hamzia	Haraldur	Harjeevan
Gybran	Hagop *(0.01)*	Halill	Han *(0.01)*	Haran	Harjinder
Gynius	Hahangwivhawe	Halim	Hanad	Haraujhe	Harjit
Gyrsharan	Hahkeem	Halique	Hanamel	Harb	Harjodh
	Hahsson	Halley	Hanan	Harbinder	Harjot *(0.02)*
-H-	Hai *(0.01)*	Halliburton	Hanandis	Harbir	Harjot-Singh
	Haidar	Halliday	Hananyah	Harbor	Harjun
H *(0.01)*	Haiden *(0.01)*	Hallie	Hanceneau	Harce	Harjunt
H'ian	Haider *(0.01)*	Hallowed	Handley	Hardagree	Harkamal
H.	Haidyn	Halston *(0.01)*	Handsome	Hardampaul	Harkaran
H.B.	Haig	Halton	Handy	Hardarsh	Harkaranjit
Ha	Haik	Haltron	Haneef	Hardeep *(0.01)*	Harkarn
Ha Ane	Haikal	Hamaad	Hanes	Hardeesh	Harkeert
Ha'keem	Haikeem	Hamadi	Hang	Harden	Harkin
Ha'keeme	Haikem	Haman	Hangassa	Hardepjit	Harkirat
Ha'sheem	Haile	Hamar	Hani	Hardian	Harkit
Ha-Keem	Hailey *(0.01)*	Hamd	Haniel	Hardick	Harkomal

Harlan *(0.03)*
Harland *(0.01)*
Harlee
Harlem
Harleme
Harlen
Harlend
Harley *(0.33)*
Harley David
Harley Dean
Harley III
Harley-James
Harlin
Harlington
Harlis
Harlon
Harlos
Harlow
Harly
Harlyh
Harm
Harman *(0.03)*
Harmanbir
Harmandeep
Harmanjit
Harmanjot
Harmanpreet
Harmeet
Harmen
Harmenpreet
Harminder
Harmit
Harmon
Harnaik
Harnaldo
Harnam
Harneet
Harneil
Harnek
Harniel
Harnit
Harnoldo
Harnoor
Harol
Harold *(0.20)*
Haron
Haron Nathanial
Haroon *(0.01)*
Haroun
Harout
Haroutiun
Harpal
Harpaul
Harper
Harpinder

Harpreet *(0.01)*
Harras
Harrell
Harresh
Harreson
Harrigan
Harrington
Harris *(0.05)*
Harrish
Harrison *(0.66)*
Harrisson
Harrod
Harrsan
Harrun
Harry *(0.21)*
Harsahib
Harsh
Harsha
Harshan
Harshana
Harsharanjeet
Harshavinder
Harshdeep
Harsher
Harshil
Harshul
Harshyam
Harsim
Harsimar
Harsimran
Hart
Hartaj
Harteg
Hartej
Harter
Hartlee
Hartley
Hartmut
Haruki
Harun
Harut
Harutyun *(0.01)*
Harvard
Harveer
Harveland
Harveltz
Harvette
Harvey *(0.07)*
Harviell
Harvier
Harvind
Harvindar
Harvinder
Harvir *(0.01)*
Harvonne

Harwin
Harwood
Haryug
Hasaamnj
Hasaan *(0.01)*
Hasah
Hasan *(0.04)*
Hasani *(0.01)*
Hasanni
Hasaun
Haseeb
Haseen
Hasham
Hashame
Hashaun
Hashawn
Hasheem
Hashem
Hashema
Hashi
Hashim *(0.01)*
Hashmatali
Hasib
Hasibullah
Hasin
Haskell
Hasmeed
Hasmeet
Hasnain
Hasnan
Hasnus
Hason
Hasram
Hassam
Hassan *(0.10)*
Hassani
Hasseltine
Hassen
Hassin
Hassnain
Hasson
Hastings
Hastolfo
Haston
Hatef
Hathum
Hatim
Hau
Haung Roy
Haussan
Hauston
Hausun
Hava
Haven *(0.01)*
Havey

Havis
Haviv
Hawad
Hawes
Hawk *(0.01)*
Hawke
Hawkin
Hawkins
Hawzua
Hayata
Hayato
Hayd'n
Haydah
Haydan
Haydeh
Hayden *(0.83)*
Hayden Robert
Hayden Todd
Haydenn
Haydn *(0.02)*
Haydon *(0.01)*
Hayel
Hayes *(0.01)*
Haylen
Hayley
Hayli
Hayon
Hays
Hayse
Haytham
Hayward
Haywood
Hayzen
Hazael
Haze
Hazell
Hazem
Hazen *(0.01)*
Hazikiah
Hazim
Haziq
He-Lo
He-Lush-Ka
Headley
Healy
Heart
Hearthan
Heath *(0.10)*
Heather
Heathman
Heaven
Heber *(0.01)*
Hebert
Heberto
Hector *(0.87)*

Hector Aaron
Hector Jr
Hectorluis
Heder
Hedgar
Hedilio
Hedrick
Heera
Heeray
Heeren
Heertanan
Heerththan
Heevi
Hefer
Heigo
Heiko
Heimar
Heinok
Heinreich
Heinrich *(0.01)*
Heinz
Heith
Hekmat
Heladio
Helaman
Helbert
Helcyn
Helder
Heled
Heleman
Helen
Heli
Helio
Helios
Helmi
Helminio
Helmuth
Helom
Hemal
Hemanshu
Hemant
Hemanth
Hemanuel
Hemel
Hemrico
Hemza
Hendarius
Henderson *(0.01)*
Hendrick *(0.01)*
Hendrik
Hendrik-Jan
Hendrix
Henemias
Henery
Henk

Henning
Henock
Henok
Henri *(0.03)*
Henri-Christopher
Henrick
Henrico
Henrik
Henrri
Henrry
Henry *(1.13)*
Henry Allen
Henry-Michael
Henryk
Hensley
Henson
Hentoruis
Hephestion
Heraclio
Heralal
Herald
Herandez
Herben
Herberson
Herbert *(0.09)*
Herbie
Herby
Herchel
Hercules
Heriberto *(0.10)*
Herin
Herlando
Herlindo
Hermaan
Herman *(0.08)*
Herman Dominic
Herman Vincent
Hermandez
Hermann
Hermeet
Hermenegildo
Hermenejildo
Hermes
Hermilo
Herminio
Hermino
Hermon
Hermy
Hern-Luo
Hernaldo
Hernan *(0.07)*
Hernando
Herness
Herno
Herold

Heron	Hien	Hiramabiff	Hoi	Hornsby	Hubertson
Herrick	Hieronymus	Hiran	Hoin	Hornson	Hudhaifah
Herron	Hieu *(0.02)*	Hirel	Hokan	Horton	Hudson *(0.05)*
Herschel	Hieu-Nhut	Hiren	Hoke	Horus	Hue
Hersey	Hifzurrahaman	Hiro	Hokuto	Hosaam	Huehoua
Hersh	Highboy	Hiroaki	Hola	Hosam	Huel
Hershal	Higinio	Hiroki	Holani	Hosberto	Huell
Hershall	Hijinio	Hiromichi	Holcombe	Hosea *(0.01)*	Huey
Hershel *(0.01)*	Hijiri	Hironobu	Holdan	Hosey	Huffie
Hersimren	Hikal	Hiroshi	Holden *(0.13)*	Hosh	Hugan
Herson	Hikaru	Hirotaka	Holdon	Hoshe	Huggins
Hertis	Hikeem	Hirrie	Holdyn	Hoshea	Hugh *(0.07)*
Herty	Hikene	Hirsi	Holland *(0.01)*	Hosie	Hugh-Gene
Herve	Hikevian	Hirton	Holland Isaiah	Hosim	Hughes
Hervey	Hikmat	Hiruy	Holliday	Hossain	Hughie
Hervie	Hikmatullah	Hisaaki	Hollie	Hossam	Hughon
Hesam	Hilaan	Hisani	Hollin	Hossein	Hugo *(0.40)*
Hesen	Hilair	Hisham *(0.01)*	Hollis *(0.01)*	Hostiin	Hugo Armando
Heseny	Hilaire	Hite	Hollon	Hosvaldo	Hugo Cesar
Hesham	Hilal	Hitesh	Holly	Hou	Hugohumberto
Heshan	Hilario *(0.02)*	Hiteshkumar	Holmes	Houghton	Hugues *(0.01)*
Hesston	Hilbert	Hitoshi	Holt	Houlder	Hugunda
Hesteban	Hildebrando	Hiu	Holten	Houssein	Hui
Heston	Hildegardo	Hivan	Holton	Houssin	Huibert
Hetash	Hilding	Hiwad	Homam	Housten	Huissien
Hethel	Hildred	Hiyab	Homan	Houstin	Hullur
Hevante	Hill	Hiyaw	Homar *(0.01)*	Houston *(0.11)*	Hulon
Hever	Hillard	Hizer	Homaree	Hovannes	Hulton
Hevin	Hillary	Hmoad	Homer *(0.01)*	Hovsep	Humaam
Hevon	Hillel	Hmzh	Homero *(0.02)*	How-Dan	Humayun
Hevron	Hiller	Ho *(0.01)*	Hon	Howard *(0.14)*	Humbert
Hewad	Hilliard	Ho-Chun	Honah	Howatdrick	Humberto *(0.17)*
Hewitt	Hilmi	Ho-Min	Honami	Howatnick	Humble
Hewson	Hilmur	Hoa	Hondo	Howell	Humfrey
Hewy	Hilson	Hoai	Hondra	Howie	Humphrey
Hexadore	Hilton *(0.01)*	Hoai-Phuong	Hondray	Howjeen	Humza *(0.01)*
Hey	Hilyard	Hoainam	Honey	Howreeson	Humzah
Heydon	Himal	Hoang *(0.02)*	Hong	Hoyas	Hun
Heytor	Himalay	Hoang Micha	Honman	Hoyle	Hunaan
Hezeki'as	Himanshu	Hoang Phi	Honor	Hoyman	Hunduma
Hezekiah *(0.01)*	Himasa	Hoang-Anh	Honoray	Hoyt	Hung *(0.01)*
Hezekyah	Himat	Hoang-Phong	Honore	Hozalfa	Hunjin
Hezikiah	Himesh	Hoang-Yen	Honorio	Hozell	Hunner
Hezikyah	Himlley	Hobart	Honrek	Hrag	Hunter *(2.45)*
Hezron	Himmat	Hobbs	Hood	Hridray	Hunter-Wayne
Hezzie	Hin	Hobert *(0.01)*	Hooks	Hrishikesh	Huntington
Hi-Keem	Hinds	Hobie *(0.01)*	Hooton	Hristo	Huntley
Hiawatha	Hines	Hobikh	Hoover	Hrushikesh	Huntur
Hibiki	Hinesh	Hobin	Hope	Hsun	Hunverto
Hicham	Hinman	Hobs	Hopeton	Hu	Huossein
Hichem	Hinton	Hoby	Horace *(0.02)*	Hua	Hurandon
Hicks	Hipolito *(0.01)*	Hodari	Horacio *(0.04)*	Huactemo	Hurao
Hidehito	Hira	Hoddie	Horatio	Huamin	Hurbert
Hideo	Hiral	Hogan *(0.01)*	Horato	Huber	Hurdel
Hideori	Hiram *(0.02)*	Hogin	Horland	Hubert *(0.04)*	Hurel

Hurgo
Huriel
Hurley
Huron
Hurquan
Hursh
Hurshel
Huruy
Husain
Husam
Husandeep
Husein
Husien
Husnan
Husni
Husnija
Hussain *(0.01)*
Hussam
Hussan
Hussayn
Hussein *(0.04)*
Hussien *(0.01)*
Hussin
Hussnain
Hussonn
Hustafa
Hustin
Huston *(0.01)*
Hutch
Hutchinson
Hutere
Hutton
Huu
Huver
Huxley
Huy *(0.03)*
Huy Lucas
Huy Zachary
Huynh
Huynh Duc
Huzaifa
Huzaifah
Huzaifahkham
Huzdovich
Huzeir
Hyacinthe
Hyatt
Hyawatha
Hyden
Hyder
Hydrick
Hyeonki
Hyginino
Hykame
Hykeam

Hykeem
Hykein
Hylan
Hyland
Hyler
Hyllis Jr
Hyman
Hymetheus
Hymie
Hyo
Hyrum *(0.02)*
Hysan
Hyssam
Hytham
Hyuk-Joong
Hyun
Hyun Woo
Hyundong
Hyung Woo
Hyung-Man
Hyungeun
Hyvan

-I-

I
I Kheem
I Kiel
I Ra
I'an
I'kee
I'saac
I'zarious
I-Keem
I-Lin
Iacca
Iahuchanan
Iaian
Iain *(0.03)*
Iakannak
Ialen
Iam Jan
Iaman
Ian *(2.38)*
Ian Bernardo
Ian Charles
Ian David
Ian Lee
Ian Michael
Ian Richard
Ian Takuya
Ian Vasco
Ian-Christopher
Ian-Kendall
Ian-Marcus

Ian-Michael
Ian-Paul
Ian-Seph
Ian-Thomas
Ian-Yves
Iane
Ianerondre
Iann
Iannick
Iannis
Ianthius
Iash
Ibad
Iban *(0.01)*
Ibidamola
Ibn
Ibn Yahya
Ibrahaim
Ibraham
Ibraheem
Ibrahem
Ibrahiem
Ibrahiim
Ibrahim *(0.10)*
Ibrahim Luigi
Ibrahim
  Suleyman
Ibrahmim
Ibukun
Ibukunoluwa
Icarus
Ichapooran
Ichtys
Icquorious
Icshon
Icy
Idael
Idan
Idean
Idelgardo
Idelias
Iden
Ideo
Idiong
Ido
Idon
Idorico
Idrease
Idrees
Idres
Idress
Idreus
Idriece
Idris *(0.02)*
Idrissa

Idurono
Ieremia
Iesey
Ieti
Ieuan
Ifaa
Ifeanacho
Ifeanyichukwu
Ifrain
Iftikhaar
Igassi
Ignacio *(0.14)*
Ignacy
Ignatios
Ignatius
Ignazio
Igner
Igor
Igrahim
Ihab
Ihechi
Ihlan
Ihquan
Ihrieon
Ihsan
Iian
Iijama
Ij
Ijael
Ijaz
Ijeoma
Ijlaal
Ikai'ka
Ikaika
Ikdeep
Ike *(0.01)*
Ikeba
Ikechukwu
Ikee
Ikeel
Ikeem *(0.01)*
Ikeia
Ikenna
Ikequintez
Ikerien
Ikhal
Ikheem
Ikiem
Iking
Ikira
Ikjot
Ikram
Ikuna
Ikuya
Ilan *(0.01)*

Ilandis
Ilarino
Ilario
Ildaphonse
Ildefonso
Ilder
Ilia
Ilias
Ilija
Iliodor
Ilir
Iliya
Illan
Illia
Illias
Illya
Ilon
Ilya *(0.01)*
Ilyas *(0.01)*
Ilyes
Ilzas
Imaan
Imad *(0.01)*
Imad Junior
Imaje
Iman *(0.01)*
Imani *(0.01)*
Imanjit
Imanni
Imannu
Imanpal
Imanuel
Imara
Imari
Imbert
Imeer
Imel
Imen
Imer
Imhotep
Imier
Imley
Immanual
Immanuel *(0.04)*
Immar
Imoh
Imond
Imontaye
Imperial
Imraan
Imraj
Imram
Imran *(0.03)*
Imrandeep
Imranjit

Imroze
Imzan
In-Seo
In-Young
Ina
Inaam
Inarsama
Incferce
Indalecio
Inder
Inder-Paul
Inderbir
Inderdeep
Inderious
Inderjit
Inderpal
Inderpaul
Inderpreet
Inderraj
Inderveer
Indervir
Indi
Indiana *(0.01)*
Indica
Indo
Indonesia
Indrajvir
Indraneel
Indravar
Indy
Indyka
Ines
Inez
Infant
Infinite
Infiniti
Ing
Ingemar
Ingersoll
Ingmar
Ingoo
Iniego
Iniko
Iniquez
Injae
Inmar
Inmer
Innes
Ino
Inoke
Inoli
Inosente
Inri
Inricka
Inrico

Insa	Irshad	Isamar	Isidoro *(0.01)*	Itrez	Izak *(0.01)*
Insaf	Irsham	Isami	Isidoros	Ittai	Izavian
Insik	Irsyad	Isamil	Isidro *(0.07)*	Ityce	Izavier
Inthujan	Irtiza	Isamu	Isik	Itzhak	Izavion
Intisar	Irvandeep	Isamuel	Isis-Nashé	Iuta	Izavious
Intwydamalia	Irven	Isau	Iskander	Ival	Izaya
Inu	Irvin *(0.11)*	Isauro	Islam *(0.01)*	Ivan *(0.99)*	Izayah
Inuganti	Irvincent	Isayah	Ismachiah	Ivan De Jesus	Izayaih
Inveer	Irvine	Isbah	Ismael *(0.32)*	Ivan Joseph	Izayiah
Inverpal	Irving *(0.08)*	Isbrandt	Ismael Jon	Ivann *(0.01)*	Izayus
Inyota	Irvinn	Iseiah	Ismail *(0.02)*	Ivannovich	Izeal
Ioakimo	Irvon	Isey	Ismat	Ivano	Izec
Ioan	Irvynle	Iseyed	Ismiel	Ivari	Izel
Ioannis *(0.01)*	Irwin *(0.02)*	Isfrain	Isnel	Ivas	Izel John
Iokepa	Irwing	Ish	Isom	Iveenluis	Izell
Ionathan	Iryan	Ishaac	Ison	Ivel	Izeyah
Iorrany	Is' Real	Ishaan	Israél	Iven	Izeyha
Iosefo	Isa *(0.01)*	Ishak	Israel *(0.41)*	Ivendeep	Izhak
Iosif	Isaac *(1.52)*	Ishakeem	Israel Alejandro	Ivenel	Izhar
Iou-Ren	Isaac Babatunde	Ishan *(0.01)*	Israhel	Iver	Iziah
Ipolito	Isaac Jamarl	Ishandeep	Isreal *(0.03)*	Iverson	Izick
Ippei	Isaac-Abimael	Ishaq	Isrell	Ivey	Izig
Iqbal	Isaac-Joshua	Ishaud	Isrieal	Ivica	Izik
Iqbaul	Isaac-Ross	Ishaun	Isrrael	Ivin	Izmir
Iqbir	Isaacisaac	Ishdeep	Issa *(0.01)*	Ivine	Izrael
Iqpaldeep	Isaack	Ishiah	Issac *(0.12)*	Ivjot	Izvor
Iqram	Isaacs	Ishin	Issacc	Ivo	Izzak
Iquan	Isaak *(0.03)*	Ishion	Issael	Ivon	Izzamon
Ira *(0.04)*	Isaaq	Ishkaran	Issaiah	Ivonte	Izzan
Irael	Isabel	Ishma'iyl	Issaic	Ivonté	Izzat
Iraj	Isabella	Ishmael *(0.04)*	Issak	Ivoon	Izzeldeen
Iram	Isabelle	Ishmaiah	Issam	Ivor	Izzy Severin
Iran	Isac *(0.02)*	Ishmail	Issara	Ivory *(0.01)*	
Irarimam	Isacc *(0.01)*	Ishmale	Issau	Ivos	**-J-**
Irbin	Isacce	Ishman	Issavior	Ivraj	
Irbyn	Isacha	Ishmeal	Issaw	Ivram	J *(0.14)*
Ire	Isadore	Ishmeet	Issay	Ivry	J Alan
Ireal	Isael *(0.01)*	Ishmeil	Issey	Ivy *(0.01)*	J Alexander
Iredia	Isagani	Ishmel	Isshu	Ivyn	J Angel
Iren	Isahc	Ishmiel	Issiah *(0.01)*	Iwitchnaldy	J B
Irenaeus	Isai *(0.07)*	Ishmil	Issiaha	Ixavier	J C
Irene	Isai'	Ishpaul	Issicc	Iya	J Cole
Irfaan	Isaiah *(0.92)*	Ishpreet	Issmeal-Ali	Iyana	J Corri
Irfan *(0.01)*	Isaiah Didym	Ishraq	Istanbul	Iykiemie	J Cruz
Irian	Isaiahs	Ishshon	Isura	Iyon	J Devin
Irie	Isaian	Ishtiaque	Isvinder	Iyonzi	J Don
Irineo *(0.01)*	Isaias *(0.10)*	Ishua	Iswaz	Izaac *(0.01)*	J Donald
Iris	Isaic	Ishuael	Itai	Izaah	J Dwight
Irish	Isaih *(0.01)*	Ishwan	Ital	Izaak *(0.01)*	J Ezra
Irison	Isaiha	Ishwar	Itamar	Izac	J Guadalupe
Irlee	Isak	Isiac	Itami	Izahia	J Horacio
Irmar	Isak J	Isiah *(0.11)*	Itaru	Izai	J Jesus
Irmon	Isaku	Isiaih	Ithemas	Izaiah	J Karus
Iron	Isalah	Isiash	Itoh	Izaic	J Khourri
Irsen	Isamael	Isidor	Itoro	Izail	J Khoury

J Marcus	J'quane	Ja Davion	Ja'drian	Ja'monty	Ja'veaz
J Michael	J'quaris	Ja Hune	Ja'far	Ja'mouri	Ja'veer
J Nathan	J'quarvis	Ja Juan	Ja'hbrien	Ja'muan	Ja'veon
J Nicolas	J'quavious	Ja Karl	Ja'heem	Ja'mundy	Ja'vion
J Nor	J'quayveon	Ja Khel	Ja'hmel	Ja'nathan	Ja'vohn
J P	J'quis	Ja Koren	Ja'hope	Ja'neal	Ja'von (0.01)
J Pablo Nicolas	J'qwan	Ja Loney	Ja'juan (0.01)	Ja'nique	Ja'vonn
J R	J'remy	Ja Lyn	Ja'kane	Ja'ovannie	Ja'vonta
J Shane	J'rome	Ja Malco	Ja'karee	Ja'quail	Ja'vontae
J T	J'ron	Ja Mar	Ja'kari	Ja'quain	Ja'vontae D'ant
J Terrius	J'ryeil	Ja Marcus	Ja'keace	Ja'quan (0.02)	Ja'vontai
J Trel	J'sean	Ja Marrio	Ja'keel	Ja'quar	Ja'vonte
J Vante	J'shonn	Ja Mere	Ja'keem	Ja'quavias	Ja'vonté
J Vin	J'son	Ja Michael	Ja'kei	Ja'quavion	Ja'vontea
J Von	J'uan	Ja Micheal	Ja'kel	Ja'quavious	Ja'voris
J Vont E	J'vante	Ja Miracle	Ja'kevin	Ja'quavis	Ja'won
J W	J'vanté	Ja Myrian	Ja'kevious	Ja'quawn	Ja'wuan
J'ael	J'vaughn	Ja Norris	Ja'khari	Ja'quay	Ja-Bez
J'air	J'von	Ja Okee	Ja'kwan	Ja'quayvion	Ja-I'-Rus
J'andre	J'vonte	Ja Qualan	Ja'kwon	Ja'ques	Ja-Juan
J'anté	J'waun	Ja Quan	Ja'larce	Ja'quez	Ja-Keim
J'aquane	J'woin	Ja Quavis	Ja'lee	Ja'queze	Ja-Kyle
J'aun-Aaron	J'yaire	Ja Quawn	Ja'leer	Ja'quial	Ja-Mar
J'dale	J-Anthony	Ja Quintas	Ja'leil	Ja'quil	Ja-Marcus
J'darius	J-Juan	Ja Quon	Ja'len	Ja'quin	Ja-Monée
J'dee	J-Sean	Ja Ron	Ja'lil	Ja'quivs	Ja-Quan
J'ihad Aakhir	J-Shun	Ja Taurus	Ja'lin	Ja'qwan	Ja-Raun
J'juan	J-Vance	Ja Taveon	Ja'lon	Ja'qwon	Ja.vonte
J'kein	J-Von	Ja Terious	Ja'lyn	Ja'recus	Jaacob
J'khari	J. (0.01)	Ja Vante	Ja'mace	Ja'reginald	Jaadn
J'khary	J. Cruz	Ja Varjeh	Ja'mal	Ja'rel	Jaafar
J'khaylaughn	J. Eduardo	Ja Von	Ja'mar	Ja'riel	Jaak
J'kimbe	J. Guadalupe	Ja Vontae	Ja'marcus (0.01)	Ja'rion	Jaakko
J'koby	J. Isabel	Ja Vonte	Ja'marea	Ja'rius	Jaalam
J'kori	J. Lance	Ja Vonté	Ja'mari	Ja'rod	Jaalen
J'kyrei	J. Ramiro	Ja Wann	Ja'mariay	Ja'roderick	Jaamond
J'lan	J. Stephen	Ja Wauntez	Ja'mario	Ja'ron	Jaan
J'laney	J.B.	Já	Ja'marion	Ja'rue	Jaanesh
J'lexus	J.C.	Ja' Varian	Ja'markus	Ja'sean	Jaante
J'lin	J.Carmen	Ja'boris	Ja'marlon	Ja'shaun	Jaanthony
J'lohn	J.D.	Ja'brell	Ja'marri	Ja'shawn	Jaared
J'lovfonte	J.J.	Ja'carey	Ja'marrie	Ja'shon	Jaaron
J'mane	J.Jesus	Ja'cari	Ja'maurice	Ja'son	Jaarrett
J'marcus	J.Miles	Ja'caspainderone	Ja'maury	Ja'tarius	Jaason
J'mario	J.R.	Ja'colbeye	Ja'meek	Ja'tarrio	Jaavaid
J'markus	J.T.	Ja'colby	Ja'mel	Ja'tavian	Jaaved
J'maul	Ja (0.01)	Ja'corey	Ja'mes	Ja'tavious	Jaaziel
J'maurian	Ja Bryant	Ja'cori	Ja'miah	Ja'tavus	Jaba'ri
J'metri	Ja Cardo	Ja'coris	Ja'micah	Ja'tori	Jabahri
J'mokenteeyahta	Ja Cari	Ja'cory	Ja'michael	Ja'tri	Jabahrie
J'myra	Ja Cobi	Ja'cquez	Ja'michal	Ja'vahn	Jabain
J'nodrick	Ja Coby	Ja'darius	Ja'micheal	Ja'vaius	Jabali
J'ontae	Ja Colby	Ja'darren	Ja'mod	Ja'vante	Jabar
J'ovontae	Ja Corey	Ja'del	Ja'mon	Ja'varius	Jabarae
J'quan (0.01)	Ja Counstus	Ja'deremy	Ja'monte	Ja'vaun	Jabare

Jabaree	Jabroskii	Jacinto *(0.01)*	Jacoda	Jacquese	Jadon *(0.03)*
Jabarei	Jabryant	Jack *(1.33)*	Jacodie	Jacquess	Jadrian
Jabari *(0.07)*	Jabulani	Jack Allen	Jacody	Jacquett	Jadriel
Jabarie	Jac	Jack-Daniel	Jacoel	Jacquevius	Jadrien
Jabarise	Jac'quan	Jackaran	Jacola	Jacquevs	Jadwinder
Jabarri	Jac'quel	Jackcob	Jacolbi	Jacquez *(0.02)*	Jady
Jabarrie	Jac'ques	Jackeil	Jacolby *(0.01)*	Jacqui	Jadyn *(0.01)*
Jabarti	Jac-Quan	Jackenson	Jacopo	Jacquil	Jadyne
Jabarus	Jacab	Jackey	Jacoran	Jacquill O'nea	Jae *(0.01)*
Jabary	Jacade	Jackie *(0.08)*	Jacorei'	Jacquille	Jae Tarius
Jabazz	Jacairr	Jackka	Jacorey *(0.02)*	Jacquin	Jaélin
Jabbar	Jacan	Jacknelson	Jacori	Jacquinn	Jaéson
Jabbaree	Jacar'rie	Jackob	Jacoria	Jacquior	Jaévon
Jabbari	Jacarey	Jackquan	Jacorian	Jacquis	Jae-Hyun
Jabborah	Jacari *(0.01)*	Jackque	Jacorie	Jacquise	Jae-Re
Jabe	Jacarier	Jackquez	Jacoris	Jacqulyn	Jaecob
Jabeorn	Jacarious	Jackquise	Jacorius	Jacquon	Jaeden *(0.01)*
Jaber	Jacaris	Jacksen	Jacorrey	Jacqutavian	Jaedon *(0.01)*
Jabes	Jacarius	Jacksin	Jacorrien	Jacquza	Jaedwin
Jabez	Jacarl	Jackson *(0.94)*	Jacorry	Jacqwese	Jaedyn
Jabian	Jacarlos	Jacky *(0.05)*	Jacorvis	Jacub	Jaee
Jabiari	Jacarre	Jaclyn	Jacorvius	Jacupe	Jaegar
Jabias	Jacarri	Jaco	Jacory *(0.01)*	Jacvan	Jaeger
Jabien	Jacarri'	Jacoab	Jacoshia	Jacwane	Jaeho
Jabier	Jacarrus	Jacob *(14.19)*	Jacouri	Jacy *(0.01)*	Jaehoon
Jabin	Jacarus	Jacob Anthony	Jacourie	Jad *(0.01)*	Jaeid
Jaboc	Jacary	Jacob	Jacourtney	Jada	Jaeirre
Jabon	Jacasino	Christopher	Jacoy	Jadaleral	Jaekob
Jabori	Jacaubré	Jacob Daniel	Jacq	Jadan	Jaekwon
Jaborian	Jacaure	Jacob David	Jacqe	Jadarian	Jael
Jaborie	Jacauri	Jacob Raymond	Jacqius	Jadarien	Jaelan
Jaboris	Jacbo	Jacob Richard	Jacqori	Jadarin	Jaelan-Lee
Jaborris	Jaccar	Jacob Ryan	Jacquain	Jadarious	Jaeland
Jaboukie	Jaccari	Jacob Thomas	Jacqualeon	Jadarius *(0.01)*	Jaelaun
Jabr'e	Jaccheus	Jacob-Allen	Jacquan *(0.01)*	Jadarrius	Jaelen *(0.01)*
Jabrail	Jaccob *(0.01)*	Jacobb	Jacquan'e	Jadavienne	Jaelin *(0.01)*
Jabran	Jaccori	Jacobbe	Jacquar	Jadavion	Jaelon *(0.01)*
Jabre	Jace *(0.17)*	Jacobe *(0.01)*	Jacquareis	Jadd	Jaelyn
Jabré	Jaceden	Jacobé	Jacquavin	Jaddon	Jaemal
Jabree	Jacee	Jacobeau	Jacquavius	Jade *(0.10)*	Jaemon
Jabreel	Jacek *(0.01)*	Jacobee	Jacquawn	Jade-Draven	Jaeon
Jabreian	Jacen *(0.01)*	Jacobey	Jacquay	Jadee	Jaequan
Jabrel	Jaceon	Jacobi *(0.02)*	Jacqub	Jadeen	Jaequon
Jabrell	Jaceson	Jacobi'	Jacque *(0.01)*	Jadeesuan	Jaerard
Jabrelle	Jacey *(0.01)*	Jacobie	Jacque Qua'va	Jaden *(0.18)*	Jaeron
Jabreon	Jach	Jacobii	Jacquece	Jadenn	Jaeroop
Jabreyon	Jachari	Jacoblee	Jacqueel	Jadeon	Jaesean
Jabri	Jachawn	Jacobmichael	Jacquel *(0.01)*	Jader	Jaeson
Jabrial	Jachin	Jacobo *(0.03)*	Jacquenci	Jaderius	Jaeten
Jabrie	Jachob	Jacobs	Jacquer	Jaderrick	Jaetuan
Jabriel	Jachobi	Jacobsen	Jacquere	Jadie	Jaevawn
Jabrielle	Jachun	Jacobsin	Jacques *(0.07)*	Jadiel	Jaevin
Jabril *(0.02)*	Jacie	Jacobson	Jacques'	Jadin	Jaevon
Jabrille	Jaciel	Jacobus	Jacques'west	Jadis	Jaevontae
Jabrion	Jacinta	Jacoby *(0.06)*	Jacques-Eliazar	Jadlin	Jaewan

Jaewon	Jah'nell	Jahkilah	Jahon	Jaicee	Jairdan
Jafar (0.01)	Jah'qavis	Jahlal	Jahondre	Jaicob	Jaire
Jafari	Jah'quez	Jahlani	Jahonn-Darrieon	Jaid	Jaired
Jafaris	Jah'rotic	Jahlanie	Jahquarrius	Jaidan	Jairek
Jafarius	Jah'varr	Jahleel (0.01)	Jahquez	Jaide	Jairen
Jafarsadek	Jah'von	Jahleel Jam	Jahquiele	Jaideep	Jairion
Jafet	Jah-Bari	Jahliek	Jahquil	Jaiden (0.02)	Jairius
Jaffer	Jah-Foday	Jahliel	Jahquille	Jaidon	Jairmey
Jaffery	Jah-Khan	Jahlil (0.01)	Jahquis	Jaidyn	Jairn
Jafontaé	Jah-Mel	Jahlil'khalif	Jahrah	Jaie	Jairo (0.12)
Jafontay	Jah-O	Jahlon	Jahray	Jaigail	Jairon
Jafur	Jah-Paul	Jahloni	Jahred	Jaiger	Jairrin
Jafus	Jah-Quan	Jahmaal	Jahree	Jaii	Jairus (0.02)
Jag	Jah-Quille	Jahmad	Jahreek	Jaijawun	Jairuxson
Jagady	Jah-Reign	Jahmaj	Jahrell	Jaikab	Jairyn
Jagannatha	Jahaad	Jahmal (0.01)	Jahret	Jaikeem	Jairzinhio
Jagar	Jahaan	Jahmaliq	Jahrhon	Jaikel	Jaisaac
Jagat	Jahad	Jahmall	Jahrme	Jaikob	Jaisan
Jagbir	Jahakeem	Jahmallé	Jahron	Jailan	Jaise
Jagdeep (0.01)	Jahal	Jahmani	Jahron-Jaekwon	Jailani	Jaisen
Jagdeesh	Jahan	Jahmar	Jahshua	Jaileen	Jaishiv
Jager	Jahangeer	Jahmare	Jahson	Jailen (0.01)	Jaishon
Jaggar	Jahangir	Jahmari	Jahtavius	Jailon	Jaishun
Jagger (0.04)	Jahanne	Jahmarian	Jahthane	Jailond	Jaison (0.01)
Jagjeet	Jahara	Jahmarl	Jahtsa	Jailyn	Jaitavius
Jagjeevin	Jahard	Jahmarr	Jahuan	Jailynn	Jaiuan
Jagjit	Jahari	Jahmé	Jahue	Jaimal	Jaivanté
Jagjot	Jaharie	Jahmeal	Jahvae	Jaime (0.63)	Jaivas
Jagmeet (0.01)	Jaharis	Jahmeel	Jahvahka	Jaimecion	Jaiven
Jagminder	Jaharri	Jahmeil	Jahvan	Jaimee	Jaives
Jagmit	Jahaud	Jahmel	Jahvante	Jaimée	Jaivion
Jagnoor	Jahayed	Jahmelle	Jahvar	Jaimeer	Jaivon (0.01)
Jagon	Jahaziel (0.01)	Jahmer	Jahvarris	Jaimen	Jaivonté
Jagpaul	Jahbaar-Alomar	Jahmez	Jahveeal	Jaimer	Jaiwon
Jagpreet	Jahbreel	Jahmezz	Jahvon (0.01)	Jaimes	Jajaun
Jagr	Jahbrel	Jahmiah	Jahvonta	Jaimeson	Jajay
Jagraj	Jahcobey	Jahmian	Jahvory	Jaimet	Jajcob
Jagroop	Jahdai	Jahmil	Jahvoy	Jaimie	Jajhirien
Jagsir	Jahdon	Jahmir	Jahvys	Jaimin	Jajuan (0.03)
Jagtar	Jaheart	Jahmon	Jahwaan	Jaimon	Jak
Jagtger	Jahen	Jahmyka	Jahwon	Jaimonté	Jaka
Jaguar	Jahfari	Jahmyl-Tyrel	Jahyam	Jaimson	Jakab
Jagveer	Jahffer	Jahmyree	Jahyra	Jaimy	Jakahari
Jagvir	Jahi (0.01)	Jahn	Jahzael	Jaimz	Jakai
Jagvits	Jahii	Jahn'tae	Jahzeel	Jaineet	Jakaire
Jagwinder	Jahiro	Jahna	Jahziel	Jainil	Jakal
Jah	Jahkari	Jahnaniy	Jai (0.02)	Jainish	Jakalen
Jah Marque	Jahkay	Jahnard	Jai Dev	Jaipal	Jakalyn
Jah'hiness	Jahkeal	Jahnathan	Jai'kir	Jaipaul	Jakar
Jah'lani	Jahkeem	Jahnay	Jai'quan	Jaipreet	Jakaray
Jah'lil	Jahkell	Jahnick	Jai'rus	Jaiqaun	Jakari (0.01)
Jah'me	Jahkendrick	Jahniey	Jai'shon	Jaiquan (0.01)	Jakarie
Jah'meil	Jahki	Jahnmon	Jai'tavies	Jair (0.02)	Jakarious
Jah'myl	Jahkiem	Jahno	Jai'yar	Jairam	Jakarius
Jah'neal	Jahkieme	Jahnyi	Jaicarious	Jairay	Jakarl

Jakarre	Jakita	Jalean	Jamacan	Jamariea	Jamauri
Jakarri	Jakiv	Jalee	Jamacio	Jamarieai	Jamaurius
Jakarus	Jakkar	Jaleek	Jamad	Jamarii	Jamaury
Jakaun	Jakkarius	Jaleel *(0.10)*	Jamae	Jamario *(0.01)*	Jamaya
Jakavian	Jakke	Jaleel J'quan	Jamael	Jamarion	Jamaz
Jakavon	Jakkrit	Jaleel-Jaramaya	Jamahd	Jamarious *(0.01)*	Jamazé
Jakaya	Jako	Jaleell	Jamahl *(0.01)*	Jamaris *(0.01)*	Jame
Jakaye	Jakob *(0.26)*	Jaleen *(0.01)*	Jamahree	Jamarius *(0.02)*	Jamé
Jakayle	Jakob-James	Jaleer	Jamaia	Jamarius Ch	Jameal
Jakayo	Jakobe	Jalees	Jamail	Jamariya	Jamearl
Jake *(1.66)*	Jakobi	Jaleil	Jamaile	Jamark Quin	Jameason
Jake-Taylor	Jakobian	Jalel	Jamaine *(0.01)*	Jamarkees	Jameco
Jakeal	Jakobus	Jalen *(0.62)*	Jamair	Jamarkeus	Jamed
Jakeb *(0.01)*	Jakoby	Jalen Damon	Jamairis	Jamarkio	Jamee
Jakedric	Jakolbi	Jalen Qu Te	Jamaka	Jamarkis	Jameek
Jakee	Jakor	Jalen-Isaiah	Jamal *(0.47)*	Jamarkus *(0.01)*	Jameel *(0.02)*
Jakeel	Jakorbin	Jalend	Jamal Moham	Jamarl	Jameer
Jakeem *(0.01)*	Jakorey	Jalene *(0.01)*	Jamal-Andrew	Jamarlee	Jameil
Jakeen	Jakori	Jali	Jamala	Jamarlin	Jameion
Jakeenan	Jakory	Jalian	Jamalcom	Jamarlon	Jameko
Jakeese	Jakosh	Jalijah	Jamale *(0.01)*	Jamaro	Jamel *(0.09)*
Jakeil Déshunn	Jakota	Jalil *(0.02)*	Jamalius	Jamarol	Jamel Preet
Jakeim	Jakrit	Jalima	Jamall *(0.01)*	Jamaroquai	Jamele
Jakeith	Jakson	Jalin *(0.02)*	Jamall Marice	Jamarqese	Jamelia
Jakel	Jakub *(0.02)*	Jaline	Jamalle	Jamarqueis	Jamell *(0.02)*
Jakeland	Jakup	Jalkim	Jaman	Jamarques	Jamelle
Jakell	Jakwaun	Jallan	Jamane	Jamarquez	Jamelvin
Jaken	Jakwon	Jallante	Jamani	Jamarquian	Jamelyn
Jakendrea	Jakxon	Jallen	Jamanne	Jamarquios	Jamems
Jakendrick	Jakyle	Jalmer	Jamaorian	Jamarquis	Jamen *(0.01)*
Jakennius	Jakytho	Jalon *(0.02)*	Jamar *(0.11)*	Jamarquist	Jamer
Jakeob *(0.01)*	Jakziri	Jalondre	Jamara	Jamarqus	Jamere
Jakeub	Jal	Jalone	Jamaras	Jamarr *(0.01)*	Jamerico
Jakeup	Jala	Jaloni	Jamaraus	Jamarre	Jamerio
Jakeus	Jalaal	Jalonte	Jamarce	Jamarrea	Jameriyo
Jakevian	Jalaan	Jalonzo	Jamarchay	Jamarreá	Jameron
Jakevius	Jalaen	Jalou	Jamarcheon	Jamarree	Jamerrell
Jakezmin	Jalahni	Jalquan	Jamarcio	Jamarri	Jamerrio
Jakhai	Jalain	Jalun	Jamarcis	Jamarries	Jamerron
Jakhari	Jalal *(0.01)*	Jalvin	Jamarco	Jamarrion	Jamerson
Jakhaury	Jalalahmad	Jalvis	Jamarcus *(0.05)*	Jamarrius	James *(10.54)*
Jakheem	Jalan *(0.01)*	Jalyck	Jamare *(0.01)*	Jamarsa	James Alexander
Jakhi	Jaland	Jalyn *(0.02)*	Jamarea	Jamarsai	James Austin
Jakhm	Jalandus	Jalynn	Jamaree *(0.01)*	Jamartae	James Brandel
Jakhory	Jalane	Jalynne	Jamarée	Jamartavion	James Brandon
Jaki	Jalané	Jam'al	Jamareh	Jamarui	James Byron
Jakiah	Jalango	Jama'al	Jamareo	Jamaruz	James Christoffer
Jakib	Jalani	Jamaée	Jamarhi	Jamarvis	James
Jakiel	Jalanie	Jamaad	Jamari *(0.05)*	Jamarya	Christopher
Jakiell	Jalann	Jamaah	Jamari'	Jamarye	James Dalton
Jakieren	Jalante	Jamaal *(0.07)*	Jamaria	Jamason	James Dean
Jakii	Jalaska	Jamaan	Jamariá	Jamau	James Edward
Jakil	Jalaun	Jamaar	Jamarian	Jamaul *(0.01)*	James Elliot
Jakin	Jaléan	Jamaari	Jamarico	Jamaun	James Ewell Bro
Jakirea	Jaleal	Jamabi	Jamarie	Jamauni	James Garbiel

James George	Jamille	Jamory	Jandolph	Jantsen	Jaquaious
James II	Jamin *(0.02)*	Jamour	Jandrew	Jantson	Jaqual
James IV	Jamin-David	Jamoy	Jane	Jantwan	Jaqualen
James Jaquéll	Jaminski	Jamquani	Janeesh	Jantzén	Jaqualion
James Jr	Jamion	Jamroquan	Janeil	Jantzen *(0.01)*	Jaqualone
James Kevin	Jamionn	Jamse	Janeiro	Januel	Jaquam
James Matthew	Jamir *(0.01)*	Jamshaid	Janek	Janus	Jaquan *(0.16)*
James Wilson	Jamirakwa	Jamshed	Janell	Janusz	Jaquandre
James Zachary	Jamiraquon	Jamsheed	Janelle	Januthen	Jaquandric
James-Dryden	Jamire	Jamual	Janerio	Janvetá	Jaquane
James-Jeffrey	Jamiree	Jamuel	Janessa	Janvier	Jaquané
James-Joshua	Jamiro'quan	Jamuga	Janette	Janvuar	Jaquann
James-Levi	Jamiron	Jamul	Jang-Hyun	Jany	Jaquanne
James-Michael	Jamis	Jamun	Jango	Janzen	Jaquanta
James-Paul	Jamisen	Jamurphy	Janiah	Jaomin	Jaquante
James-Thomas	Jamison *(0.09)*	Jamy	Janicento	Jaone	Jaquantis
Jameskelly	Jamitchell	Jamye	Janiel	Jaoronta	Jaquanza
Jamesmichae	Jamiyha	Jamyes	Janier	Jaovontae	Jaquanzi
Jameson *(0.10)*	Jammal	Jamyko	Janieral	Japaul	Jaquar
Jametavious	Jammar	Jamyn	Janigel	Japdeep	Jaquare
Jametric	Jammarrius	Jamyra	Janik	Japeth	Jaquari
Jametrious	Jamme	Jamyron	Janile	Japhee	Jaquarious
Jametrius	Jammeran	Jamyson	Janilo	Japheel	Jaquaris
Jamey *(0.01)*	Jammere	Jamze	Janine	Japhet	Jaquarius *(0.01)*
Jameycia	Jammerin	Jan *(0.05)*	Janit	Japheth	Jaquarvius
Jamez *(0.01)*	Jammerio	Jan Carlos	Janith	Japhia	Jaquashaun
Jameze	Jammie	Jan Te	Janke	Japhuon	Jaquaun
Jami	Jammiko	Jan-Carlo	Jankiel	Japhy	Jaquavas
Jamia	Jammy	Jan-Hendrik	Janko	Japinder	Jaquaveis
Jamiah	Jamoeah	Jana	Janly	Japjeet	Jaquaveius
Jamian	Jamoge	Janadrick	Jann	Japjit	Jaquaveon
Jamicael	Jamohad	Janae	Jannagan	Japjot	Jaquaveous
Jamicheal *(0.01)*	Jamohn	Janagan	Jannese	Japnaam	Jaquavias
Jamid	Jamol	Janairs	Jannesie	Japnam	Jaquavien
Jamie *(0.46)*	Jamon *(0.03)*	Janak	Jannon	Japreet	Jaquavion
Jamie Lee	Jamond *(0.01)*	Janal	Jannus	Japrinceton	Jaquavious *(0.01)*
Jamie Martin	Jamone	Janalt	Janny	Japtej	Jaquavis *(0.01)*
Jamiee	Jamoni	Janam	Jano's Vincent	Japul	Jaquavius *(0.01)*
Jamiel	Jamont	Janan	Janoi	Jaqari	Jaquavus
Jamiele	Jamonta	Jananan	Janorris	Jaqaun	Jaquawn *(0.01)*
Jamien	Jamontaé	Janar	Janos	Jaqavies	Jaquay
Jamieon	Jamontae	Janard	Janoshan	Jaqavious	Jaquayle
Jamier	Jamontay	Janaree	Janoy	Jaqavius	Jaquayvas
Jamiere	Jamonte	Janarie	Janquais	Jaqawan	Jaquaz
Jamies	Jamonté	Janarkus	Janquan	Jaqille	Jaqueasé
Jamieson *(0.02)*	Jamontel	Janaro	Janroop	Jaqoun	Jaqueel
Jamieun	Jamontray	Janarro	Jansen *(0.02)*	Jaqua	Jaqueis
Jamik	Jamontrel	Janarth	Jansin	Jaquaan	Jaquel
Jamika	Jamor	Janarvis	Janson *(0.01)*	Jaquade	Jaquelin
Jamil *(0.07)*	Jamoree	Janathan	Janssen	Jaquadis	Jaquelius
Jamil-Ayoub	Jamori	Janaun	Jansun	Jaquadvias	Jaquell
Jamilah	Jamorie	Janavous	Jantaé	Jaquae	Jaquelle
Jamile	Jamorius	Jancarlos	Jantaruis	Jaquail	Jaqueob
Jamill	Jamorrio	Jance	Jante	Jaquain	Jaquerian
Jamillah	Jamorris	Jander	Jantine	Jaquaio	Jaquerius

Jaquerus	Jarah-Shamere	Jariel	Jaron *(0.13)*	Jarrison	Jasaya
Jaques	Jaraine	Jarien	Jarone	Jarriss	Jasbeet
Jaques'	Jaran *(0.01)*	Jaries	Jaronn	Jarrit	Jascinto
Jaquese	Jarard	Jarik	Jarontaé	Jarrius *(0.01)*	Jasdeep *(0.03)*
Jaquestin	Jaras	Jarin *(0.01)*	Jarontay	Jarrod *(0.17)*	Jase *(0.02)*
Jaqueus	Jarathon	Jarion	Jaronte	Jarroit	Jase-Wainaina
Jaquez *(0.02)*	Jaraud	Jarious	Jaroslaw	Jarron *(0.02)*	Jasean
Jaqueze	Jaray	Jariq	Jaroslov	Jarrot	Jasegan
Jaqui	Jarbar	Jaris	Jarot	Jarru	Jaselle
Jaqui's	Jarbin	Jarit	Jarqavus	Jarry	Jasem
Jaquial	Jarbis	Jarith	Jarquae	Jarryd *(0.01)*	Jasen *(0.03)*
Jaquian	Jarcie	Jarius *(0.02)*	Jarquan	Jarryn	Jasey
Jaquice	Jardan	Jarivs	Jarquavios	Jarson	Jash
Jaquie	Jarden	Jarkeice	Jarquavious	Jartavious	Jashaad
Jaquiel	Jarderis	Jarkell	Jarquavis	Jartavis	Jashan
Jaquievis	Jardin	Jarkese	Jarquavius	Jartavius	Jashandeep
Jaquil	Jardon	Jarkevious	Jarqueese	Jarunte	Jashaque
Jaquille *(0.01)*	Jare	Jarkevius	Jarquel	Jarushaan	Jashaud
Jaquin	Jareal	Jarkievious	Jarquell	Jarvael	Jashaun
Jaquinn	Jareau	Jarkkar	Jarques	Jarvanta	Jashawn *(0.01)*
Jaquinta	Jareb	Jarl	Jarquest	Jarvaris	Jasher
Jaquinten	Jarec	Jarlath	Jarquez	Jarvarius	Jashinthan
Jaquinton	Jared *(2.53)*	Jarmaine	Jarquis	Jarvas	Jashion
Jaquis	Jared John	Jarmal *(0.01)*	Jarquise	Jarvasity	Jashmin
Jaquise	Jared Raymond	Jarman	Jarqulla	Jarvézz	Jashon
Jaqulen	Jared Schaeffer	Jarmane	Jarrad *(0.01)*	Jarvesé	Jashper
Jaqune	Jaredd	Jarmar	Jarrae	Jarvez	Jashua *(0.01)*
Jaquob	Jareem	Jarmarco	Jarrah	Jarvie	Jashun
Jaquoin	Jareid	Jarmarcus *(0.01)*	Jarrain	Jarvierre	Jashy
Jaquon *(0.01)*	Jarek *(0.01)*	Jarmari	Jarral	Jarvin	Jasiah
Jaquone	Jarel *(0.01)*	Jarmario	Jarran	Jarvios	Jasias
Jaquonta	Jarell *(0.03)*	Jarmarious	Jarrard	Jarvious	Jasiel
Jaquonté	Jarelle	Jarmarqez	Jarratt	Jarvirus	Jasik
Jaquori	Jarem	Jarmel	Jarred *(0.22)*	Jarvis *(0.14)*	Jasim
Jaquorie	Jaremie	Jarmen	Jarredd	Jarvis Deshaun	Jasin
Jaquvis	Jaremy	Jarmey	Jarree	Jarvius	Jasinder
Jaquze	Jaren *(0.05)*	Jarmire	Jarrel	Jarvize	Jasiri
Jaqwade	Jarenz	Jarmis	Jarreld	Jarvoius	Jasjeet
Jaqwam	Jareo	Jarmonte	Jarrell *(0.03)*	Jarvon	Jasjit
Jaqwan	Jaresiah	Jarmonté	Jarren *(0.02)*	Jarvontae	Jasjot
Jaqwon	Jaret *(0.02)*	Jarmor'e	Jarres	Jarvor	Jaskamal
Jaqyoune	Jareth *(0.01)*	Jarmore	Jarret *(0.04)*	Jarvoress	Jaskaran *(0.03)*
Jar Craig	Jarett *(0.04)*	Jarmoris	Jarreth *(0.01)*	Jarvus	Jaskarandeep
Jar Vez	Jarette	Jarnail	Jarrett *(0.25)*	Jarwara	Jaskaren
Jar'marus	Jarez	Jarnell	Jarrett Jr	Jaryd *(0.01)*	Jaskarn *(0.01)*
Jar'vees	Jarezz	Jarnelle	Jarrette	Jaryia	Jaskin
Jar'vis	Jari	Jarobi	Jarrhette	Jaryn *(0.01)*	Jaskiran
Jar-Marcus	Jariah	Jarod *(0.07)*	Jarriad	Jarynn	Jaskirat
Jara	Jarian	Jarodd	Jarrian	Jaryon	Jaskirt
Jaraad	Jaric	Jaroge	Jarric	Jas	Jaslee
Jarad *(0.02)*	Jarice	Jaroid	Jarrick	Jasabian Quanja	Jasleen
Jarae	Jarick	Jarol	Jarrid *(0.02)*	Jasan	Jasley
Jaraed	Jarico	Jarold	Jarriel	Jasandeep	Jaslin
Jarael	Jarid *(0.02)*	Jarom *(0.01)*	Jarriett	Jasanpreet	Jasman
Jarah	Jarie	Jarome	Jarrin	Jasaun	Jasmanie

Jasmanjit	Jaswant	Jauantez	Javarian	Javiell	Javorris
Jasmeer	Jaswinder	Jauawan	Javarias	Javien	Javorse
Jasmeet *(0.01)*	Jasyn	Jauha'd	Javarick	Javier *(1.09)*	Javoskie
Jasmez	Jasze	Jaulani	Javarie	Javier Alfredo	Javotay
Jasmin *(0.03)*	Jaszel	Jaulon	Javaries	Javier Jr	Javoun
Jasmine	Jatane	Jaumal	Javarin	Javies	Javraj
Jasmit	Jatanna	Jaumar	Javarious *(0.01)*	Javin *(0.02)*	Javrest
Jasmon	Jatarius	Jaun	Javaris *(0.02)*	Javion *(0.01)*	Javron
Jasmond	Jatarvis	Jaune	Javarius *(0.01)*	Javionne	Javuan
Jasneal	Jataurean	Jaunoi	Javarous	Javious	Javunte
Jasneet	Jatavein	Jaunyaé	Javarreis	Javis *(0.01)*	Javunté
Jasod	Jatavion	Jaunyé	Javarri	Javius	Javy
Jason *(4.32)*	Jatavious	Jauquatzion	Javarris	Javod	Javyn
Jason Allen	Jatavis	Jauquez	Javarro	Javoeontea	Jawaan
Jason Christopher	Jatavius	Jauquon	Javarski	Javog	Jawad *(0.01)*
Jason Damian	Jateen	Jaureese	Javarus	Javohn	Jawain
Jason Earl	Jaterius	Jaurice	Javary	Javohnta	Jawan *(0.02)*
Jason-Adrian	Jaterrance	Jauron	Javaseah	Javolkee	Jawane
Jason-Alexander	Jaterrick	Jaurvis	Javaugh	Javon *(0.17)*	Jawanis
Jason-Allen	Jaterries	Jaushua	Javaughn *(0.01)*	Javon'	Jawann
Jason-Johnathan	Jaterrious	Jauvon	Javaughnte	Javon'sh	Jawanza *(0.01)*
Jason-Kao	Jaterrius	Jauwaun	Javaun	Javon'te	Jawanzie
Jason-Ron	Jatez	Jauwn	Javauntae	Javon-Michael	Jawara
Jasondeep	Jathan *(0.01)*	Jav'on	Javavaier	Javonate	Jawarren
Jaspal	Jathaniel	Java	Javawn	Javondric	Jawaski
Jaspar	Jatheeshwhar	Javaas	Javayd	Javone *(0.01)*	Jawaun *(0.01)*
Jaspartap	Jathisan	Javad	Javeal	Javoni	Jawaylon
Jaspaul	Jathniel	Javae	Javeale	Javonn	Jaweed
Jasper *(0.11)*	Jathon	Javah	Javed	Javonne	Jawell
Jasper Jade	Jathusan	Javahn	Javeil	Javonni	Jawhan
Jaspinder	Jati	Javai	Javein	Javonnie	Jawid
Jaspreet *(0.02)*	Jatinder *(0.01)*	Javairius	Javeion	Javonnte	Jawill
Jaspyn	Jatniel	Javaka	Javel	Javonshay	Jawon *(0.01)*
Jasraj	Jatodd	Javakiel	Javell *(0.01)*	Javont E	Jawon'
Jasrel	Jaton	Javalais	Javelle	Javonta *(0.01)*	Jawonn
Jasroop	Jatony	Javale	Javen *(0.02)*	Javontá	Jawontaé
Jasryan	Jatoreon	Javan *(0.03)*	Javeno	Javontae *(0.02)*	Jawonte
Jass	Jatoris	Javanis	Javeon *(0.01)*	Javontaé	Jawoski
Jassa	Jatorrious	Javanni	Javeous	Javontai	Jawuan *(0.01)*
Jassee	Jatory	Javantae	Javer	Javontaveious	Jawun
Jassel	Jatrel	Javantai	Javere	Javontay *(0.01)*	Jawwad
Jassem	Jattvon	Javante *(0.01)*	Javerius	Javontaye	Jawyan
Jassen	Jatuan	Javanté	Javern	Javonte *(0.06)*	Jax
Jasshan	Jatuporn	Javantée	Javerri	Javonté *(0.02)*	Jaxen
Jassiel	Jatvius	Javantez	Javery	Javontee	Jaxier
Jassin	Jatwan	Javanthony	Javetz	Javonteh	Jaxom
Jasson *(0.01)*	Jatwane	Javanti	Javeyan	Javontes	Jaxon *(0.04)*
Jasten	Jatwi'	Javanus	Javez	Javontey	Jaxsen
Jastin	Jatwind	Javaon	Javhon	Javontre	Jaxson *(0.01)*
Jastinder	Jau'an	Javar *(0.01)*	Javian *(0.01)*	Javontres	Jaxsun
Jaston	Jau'marl	Javaras	Javiar	Javorian	Jaxton
Jasuan	Jau'skil	Javare	Javid	Javoriea	Jaxun
Jasveer	Jauan	Javaree	Javie	Javorious	Jay *(0.43)*
Jasvin	Jauane	Javares	Javiean	Javoris	Jay Henry
Jasvinder	Jauanta	Javari *(0.01)*	Javiel	Javorius	Jay Jay

Jay Kumar	Jayesh	Jayms	Jayvion	Je Vaun	Jean Gabriel
Jay Lon	Jayfrey	Jaymz *(0.01)*	Jayvohn	Je Vontae	*(0.01)*
Jay Ont	Jaygar	Jaynald	Jayvon *(0.03)*	Je Waun	Jean Luc *(0.01)*
Jay Ven	Jayhad	Jaynesh	Jayvone	Jéan	Jean Marc *(0.01)*
Jay W	Jayir	Jaynique	Jayvonn	Jéavan	Jean Mathieu
Jay'corey	Jayjay	Jayon	Jayvontay	Jéavon	Jean Maxime
Jay'deemeko	Jayjuan	Jayon'e	Jayvonte	Jédarius	Jean Michel *(0.06)*
Jay'len	Jayke	Jayonne	Jaywan	Jédon	Jean Nicolas
Jay'leon	Jayke Ahlen	Jayonta	Jaywaun	Jéjuan	*(0.01)*
Jay'lin	Jaykeem	Jaypee	Jaywin	Jékarr	Jean Pascal *(0.01)*
Jay'lon	Jaykob	Jayqaun	Jayzhoné	Jéken	Jean Paul
Jay'montrez	Jaykota	Jayqavious	Jaz *(0.01)*	Jékeri	Jean Philip *(0.01)*
Jay'quan	Jaykumar	Jayqon	Jaz'quan	Jélani	Jean Philippe
Jay'qulin	Jaykwan	Jayquan *(0.01)*	Jazarus	Jélen	*(0.15)*
Jay'vares	Jaykwantay	Jayquawn	Jazaun	Jémar	Jean Pierre
Jay'von	Jaykwon	Jayqunn	Jazavier	Jémarcus	Jean Rene
Jay-Inder	Jayla	Jayre	Jazeel	Jémario	Jean Samuel
Jay-Quan	Jaylaan	Jayrell	Jazel	Jémarr	*(0.01)*
Jay-R	Jaylan *(0.03)*	Jayro *(0.01)*	Jazerrick	Jémel	Jean Sebastien
Jay-Thomas	Jayland *(0.01)*	Jayron	Jaziel	Jénorman	*(0.07)*
Jay-Tyler	Jayle	Jayrus	Jazlyn	Jéquan	Jean Simon *(0.02)*
Jayaleo	Jaylee	Jaysa'n	Jazman	Jéquantaé	Jean-Antoine
Jayalyn	Jayleen	Jaysal	Jazmayne	Jéquays	Jean-Baptiste
Jayant	Jaylen *(0.15)*	Jayse	Jazmine	Jéquayus	Jean-Benoit
Jayanthony	Jaylend	Jaysean	Jazmond	Jérell	Jean-Carlo
Jayarr	Jayleon	Jaysel	Jazmyne	Jéron	Jean-Cedric
Jaybee	Jaylian	Jaysen *(0.02)*	Jazon	Jéshaun	Jean-Charles
Jaybraham	Jaylin *(0.06)*	Jayshaun	Jazreal	Jétory	Jean-Christian
Jayc	Jayline	Jayshawn *(0.01)*	Jazten	Jétoryann	Jean-Christop
Jayca	Jayln *(0.01)*	Jaysheel	Jazz *(0.01)*	Jétravius	Jean-Christophe
Jayce *(0.04)*	Jaylon *(0.07)*	Jayshod	Jazz Jc	Jétwan	Jean-Clare
Jaycee	Jaylund	Jayshon	Jazzariah	Jévarreo	Jean-Claude
Jaycen	Jaylyn *(0.02)*	Jayshun	Jazzdon	Jévaughn	*(0.01)*
Jaycey	Jaylynd	Jaysn	Jazzib	Jévin	Jean-Claudel
Jayciff	Jaylynn	Jayson *(0.20)*	Jazzman	Jévon	Jean-Daniel
Jaycion	Jaylynne	Jayson-Frank	Jazzmond	Jévontae	Jean-David
Jaycob *(0.02)*	Jaymar	Jaystin	Jazzy	Jéwani	Jean-Denis
Jaycub	Jaymarlon	Jayston	Ja~quez	Jeadrian	Jean-Elie
Jayd	Jayme *(0.02)*	Jaysun	Jb	Jeager	Jean-Eric
Jaydan	Jaymel	Jaytee	Jc	Jean *(0.18)*	Jean-Felix
Jayde *(0.01)*	Jaymen	Jayth	Jd	Jean Alexandr	Jean-Francois
Jaydee	Jaymeo	Jaythan	Jden	Jean Anton Nikko	*(0.01)*
Jaydeep	Jaymeon	Jaython	Jdenny	Jean Baptiste	Jean-Gabriel
Jayden *(0.16)*	Jaymes *(0.02)*	Jaythus	Je	Jean Benoit *(0.01)*	Jean-Guillaume
Jaydenpaul	Jaymeson	Jayton	Je Andrus	Jean Christophe	Jean-Luc *(0.03)*
Jaydin	Jaymic	Jaytwan	Je Dedrick	*(0.08)*	Jean-Marc *(0.01)*
Jaydn	Jaymie	Jayvan	Je Drick	Jean Daniel *(0.02)*	Jean-Marcel
Jaydon *(0.02)*	Jaymin	Jayvantay	Je Juan	Jean David *(0.01)*	Jean-Mari
Jaydrian	Jaymis	Jayvaughn	Je Khari	Jean Denis *(0.01)*	Jean-Max
Jaye *(0.01)*	Jaymison	Jayveious	Je Lantis	Jean Eliezer	Jean-Michael
Jayed	Jaymon	Jayven	Je Marcus	Jean Erik	Jean-Michel
Jayel	Jaymonie	Jayvens	Je Mareyon	Jean Felix *(0.01)*	Jean-Patrick
Jayendra	Jaymontey	Jayvian	Je Men	Jean Francois	Jean-Paul *(0.01)*
Jayeon	Jaymore	Jayvie	Je Terrius	*(0.10)*	Jean-Philip
Jayequan	Jaymorea	Jayvin	Je Varis	Jean Frederic	

Jean-Philippe *(0.02)*	Jecole	Jeffone	Jekel	Jemontae	Jeoffrey
Jean-Phillipe	Jecori	Jeffory	Jekhari	Jemonte	Jeomari
Jean-Phillippe	Jed *(0.04)*	Jeffquan	Jekoyree	Jemson	Jeon
Jean-Pierre *(0.01)*	Jedadiah	Jeffre	Jelaen	Jemuel	Jeonard
Jean-Ralph	Jedaiah	Jeffree	Jelan	Jen	Jeong
Jean-Roc	Jedarius	Jeffreon	Jelani *(0.05)*	Jenahaian	Jeovahny
Jean-Sebastie	Jedarrien	Jeffress	Jelanie	Jenaire	Jeovan
Jean-Sebastien	Jedd	Jeffrey *(2.73)*	Jelaun	Jenapthanan	Jeovantay
Jean-Simon	Jeddediah	Jeffrey Jr	Jelber	Jenard	Jeovany
Jean-Sylvainson	Jeddore	Jeffrey Scott	Jelena	Jenaro	Jephthah
Jean-Thomas	Jedediah *(0.02)*	Jeffreys	Jelienne	Jene	Jephthe
Jean-Victor	Jedekiah	Jeffrie	Jeloni	Jener	Jeptha
Jeanatan	Jederie	Jeffries	Jelsema	Jenero	Jeqarius
Jeancarlo	Jederrious	Jeffry *(0.03)*	Jemaal	Jenerro	Jeqaun
Jeancarlos	Jediah	Jeffson	Jemail	Jenes	Jequan *(0.01)*
Jeancotey	Jedidiah *(0.05)*	Jefftayvious	Jemaine	Jenesis	Jequann
Jeandre	Jedidiyah	Jeffton	Jemal *(0.01)*	Jenezes	Jequarius
Jeane	Jedidrah	Jefre	Jemale	Jenias	Jeque
Jeaneal	Jedmaine	Jefri	Jemane	Jenielle	Jequell
Jeanedlet	Jedonté	Jefry	Jemar	Jenier	Jequelle
Jeanette	Jedric	Jefte	Jemaran	Jenilee	Jequis
Jeangat	Jedziel	Jefty	Jemarco	Jenior	Jequon
Jeanluc *(0.01)*	Jee	Jeger	Jemarcus	Jenis	Jer Quavius
Jeannot	Jeefchan	Jeh'juan	Jemare	Jenkins	Jer'hazzia
Jeano	Jeelel	Jeh'morie	Jemari	Jenna	Jer'maurri'
Jeanot	Jeeno	Jehad	Jemarian	Jenneffer	Jer'mell
Jeanpaul *(0.01)*	Jeet	Jehan	Jemario	Jenner *(0.01)*	Jer'quannzie
Jeanpierre *(0.01)*	Jeevan *(0.01)*	Jehiel	Jemarion	Jennifer *(0.01)*	Jera
Jearlon	Jeevanjee	Jehmiah	Jemarkus	Jenning	Jerabs
Jearold	Jeeven	Jehoiada	Jemarrain	Jennings	Jeracole
Jeauar	Jeevesh	Jehojada	Jemasse	Jennison	Jerad *(0.03)*
Jeavil	Jeevin	Jehon	Jemaun	Jennorris	Jerael
Jeavin	Jeewan	Jehonadad	Jemayne	Jennrecus	Jerah
Jeavonte	Jeewanjot	Jehonatan	Jemeal	Jenny	Jerahn
Jeb *(0.02)*	Jef	Jehosafat	Jemedrius	Jeno	Jerak
Jebadiah	Jefaris	Jehosaphat	Jemehl	Jenorris	Jeraki
Jebadieh	Jeferson	Jehoshaphat	Jemel	Jenovin	Jeral
Jebari	Jeff *(0.12)*	Jehoshua	Jemell	Jenri	Jerald *(0.05)*
Jebb	Jeff Lenard	Jehovah	Jemelle	Jenrri	Jerall
Jebediah *(0.01)*	Jeff Ryan	Jehsuam	Jemello	Jenry	Jeralquion
Jebel	Jeff'on	Jehu	Jemerico	Jens *(0.01)*	Jerame
Jeberequias	Jeff-Robert	Jehu'	Jemerio	Jense	Jeramee
Jebidiah	Jeffari	Jehvon	Jemerrio	Jensen *(0.02)*	Jeramey *(0.01)*
Jebrall	Jeffary	Jehwon	Jemiah	Jenson	Jerami
Jebrian	Jeffenson	Jeiel	Jemile	Jenson Jacob	Jerami'
Jebriel	Jeffer	Jeiele	Jemiriquan	Jenssen	Jeramiah *(0.02)*
Jebryon	Jefferey *(0.02)*	Jeihman	Jemmario	Jentavious	Jeramian
Jebson	Jefferie	Jeison	Jemme	Jentrey	Jeramias
Jeby	Jefferrey	Jeisson	Jemmerio	Jentri	Jeramie *(0.01)*
Jecari	Jefferson *(0.10)*	Jejuan	Jemmett	Jentry	Jeramy *(0.03)*
Jecaurius	Jeffery *(0.60)*	Jekaiden	Jemmott	Jentz	Jeran
Jecie	Jeffery Scott	Jekari	Jemmrio	Jentzen	Jerandom
Jeck	Jeffin	Jekario	Jemmy	Jenuz	Jerante
Jecoda	Jeffly	Jekeen	Jemond	Jenvy	Jerard
	Jeffon	Jekeil	Jemone	Jeodfrey	Jerardo *(0.02)*

Jeratez	Jeremy-Joel	Jermainechristop	Jerneal	Jerret *(0.01)*	Jervai
Jeraun	Jeremy-Li	her	Jernell	Jerreth	Jervarious
Jeravonn	Jeremyah	Jermainie	Jernerio	Jerrett *(0.01)*	Jervarius
Jerayle	Jeren *(0.01)*	Jermal *(0.01)*	Jernone	Jerri	Jervarous
Jerbrod	Jerenian	Jermall	Jernorris	Jerrian	Jervell
Jercarl	Jeret	Jermalsmond	Jeroan	Jerrice	Jerver
Jercoby	Jereth	Jerman	Jeroboam	Jerrick *(0.02)*	Jervezz
Jerdair	Jerett	Jermancito	Jerocko	Jerrico	Jervin
Jerdil	Jereyleus	Jermane	Jerod *(0.04)*	Jerricoh	Jervis-Myles
Jere	Jerhiame	Jermanne	Jerode	Jerrid *(0.01)*	Jervon
Jereal	Jerhico	Jermany	Jerodius	Jerrie	Jervond'e
Jerece	Jerhvon	Jermarco	Jerodrick	Jerrik	Jervonne
Jereck	Jeri	Jermarcus	Jeroen	Jerrill	Jervontae
Jered *(0.03)*	Jeriad	Jermari	Jeroid	Jerriminco	Jervonte
Jerediah	Jeriah	Jermario	Jerold *(0.01)*	Jerrimy	Jervonté
Jereed	Jeriamie	Jermarion	Jerom	Jerrin *(0.01)*	Jervontiá
Jereeka	Jerian	Jermarry	Jerome *(0.37)*	Jerrion	Jerwin
Jereem	Jeric *(0.01)*	Jermarshea	Jerome James	Jerrious	Jerwkin
Jeregniald	Jeric Sean	Jermaurious	Jerome Travis	Jerris	Jerwon
Jerek	Jerical	Jermaus	Jeromee	Jerrise	Jery
Jereko	Jericho *(0.04)*	Jermayne	Jeromejustin	Jerrish	Jeryd
Jerel *(0.02)*	Jerick *(0.01)*	Jermeco	Jeromeyo	Jerrit	Jeryl
Jerell *(0.01)*	Jerico *(0.01)*	Jermeel	Jeromie	Jerritd	Jeryle
Jerelle	Jerid *(0.01)*	Jermekus	Jeromija	Jerritt	Jeryn
Jerem	Jeriel	Jermel *(0.01)*	Jeromy *(0.03)*	Jerrius	Jerzey
Jeremah	Jerien	Jermell *(0.01)*	Jeron *(0.02)*	Jerrll	Jerzia
Jeremaih	Jeriet	Jermerrio	Jerondon	Jerrmon	Jerzy
Jeremaine	Jerijah	Jermery	Jerone	Jerrod *(0.08)*	Jes
Jereme *(0.02)*	Jerikoe	Jermey *(0.02)*	Jeronico	Jerrohn	Jesaiah
Jeremé	Jerim	Jermez	Jeronimo *(0.01)*	Jerrol	Jesal
Jeremee	Jerimah	Jermia	Jerooen	Jerrold *(0.01)*	Jesaun
Jeremey *(0.01)*	Jerimani	Jermiah *(0.01)*	Jerosem	Jerrome	Jese
Jeremi *(0.03)*	Jerimia	Jermicah	Jerquail	Jerron *(0.01)*	Jesean
Jeremi'ah	Jerimiah *(0.02)*	Jermichael	Jerquale	Jerrone	Jesel
Jeremia	Jerimy	Jermicheal	Jerquan	Jerronta	Jesen
Jeremiah *(0.89)*	Jerimyah	Jermie	Jerquavious	Jerry *(0.66)*	Jeseph
Jeremiah Francis	Jerin	Jermil	Jerquis	Jerry Jr	Jeshaun
Jeremiah-Ciezer	Jeriod	Jermine	Jerr	Jerry Lee	Jeshawn
Jeremiaih	Jeriq	Jermmario	Jerrack	Jerryco	Jeshod
Jeremial	Jeris	Jermmerio	Jerrad *(0.02)*	Jerryd	Jeshua *(0.02)*
Jeremias *(0.01)*	Jerisen	Jermocio	Jerrade	Jerryl	Jeshuah
Jeremie *(0.22)*	Jerith	Jermol	Jerraine	Jerryn	Jesi
Jeremih	Jeritt	Jermon	Jerrald	Jerryson	Jesiah
Jeremiha	Jerjuan	Jermone	Jerran	Jersain	Jesie
Jeremy *(3.82)*	Jerkell	Jermoney	Jerrand	Jersey	Jesimiel
Jeremy Daniel	Jerkenzi	Jermonta	Jerrard	Jershon	Jesimon
Jeremy Donnie	Jerkhari	Jermonte	Jerray	Jerson *(0.01)*	Jesinthan
Jeremy Ives	Jerkwan	Jermonté	Jerre	Jertavius	Jesjeet
Jeremy Jim	Jerlane	Jermony	Jerred *(0.02)*	Jerterious	Jesman
Jeremy Jon	Jermah	Jermore	Jerrel	Jertorris	Jesmar Joseph
Jeremy Jr	Jermahl	Jermy	Jerrell *(0.04)*	Jeru	Jesmon
Jeremy Marco	Jermail	Jermyia Dontae	Jerremy	Jeruebe	Jesnin
Jeremy Marcus	Jermaile	Jermyis	Jerren	Jeruel	Jesob
Jeremy-Daniel	Jermain *(0.01)*	Jermyll	Jerrenn	Jerufus	Jeson
Jeremy-James	Jermaine *(0.22)*	Jernard	Jerreon	Jerusalem	Jesop

Jesper	Jester	Jevic	Jhacory	Jhett	Jiar'e
Jesrael	Jestin (0.01)	Jevin (0.01)	Jhad	Jhevon	Jib
Jess (0.07)	Jeston	Jevion	Jhaévon	Jhi	Jibben
Jesse (4.24)	Jestoni	Jevius	Jhahid	Jhiar	Jibin
Jesse Devan	Jesu	Jevoaghn	Jhair	Jhilial	Jibran
Jesse Garret	Jesua	Jevon (0.06)	Jhajuany	Jhireiqu	Jibreel
Jesse James	Jesup	Jevon-Joshua	Jhakari	Jhmari	Jibriel
Jesse Lee	Jesus (2.23)	Jevone	Jhakedric	Jhmeer	Jibril
Jesse Ray	Jesus Alan	Jevonn	Jhakee	Jhoacim	Jibu
Jesse William	Jesus Alberto	Jevonne	Jhaki	Jholman	Jickson
Jesse-Bolivar	Jesus Armando	Jevonnie	Jhalen	Jhon (0.01)	Jicorey
Jesse-Dean	Jesus Cruz	Jevons	Jhalil	Jhonatan	Jid
Jesse-Lee	Jesus Gregory	Jevonta	Jhalma	Jhonathan (0.01)	Jie
Jesse-Matthew	Jesus Manuel	Jevontá	Jhamaal	Jhonathon	Jiewon
Jesse-Ray	Jesus Mario	Jevontae	Jhamani	Jhonavan	Jiff
Jesse-Reeve	Jesvin	Jevontaé	Jhamari	Jhonny (0.01)	Jigar
Jessea	Jeswic	Jevontaye	Jhamel	Jhonray	Jigme
Jessee (0.03)	Jeswil	Jevonte	Jhamele	Jhontae	Jiha'd
Jesseee	Jesy	Jevonté	Jhames	Jhonterryun	Jihad (0.02)
Jessel	Jesyn	Jevor	Jhamil	Jhony	Jihari
Jesselee	Jet-Yasin	Jevorris	Jhamonte	Jhoon	Jihong
Jessen	Jeter	Jevuann	Jhan	Jhor	Jihree
Jessenia	Jeterrence	Jewaun	Jhané	Jhordan	Jiiyan
Jessep	Jethro	Jewel	Jhanel	Jhordyan	Jikean
Jesseray	Jethro John	Jewell	Jhani	Jhordyn	Jikim
Jesses	Jethroe	Jewelle	Jhanluis	Jhorvi	Jikori
Jessey (0.03)	Jethron	Jewels	Jhaqie	Jhory	Jilberto
Jessi (0.03)	Jethroshavez	Jewlian	Jhaquelle	Jhosae	Jiles
Jessiah	Jetinder	Jewyane	Jharae	Jhoslyn	Jill
Jessic	Jeton	Jey-T	Jhari	Jhovany	Jillian
Jessica (0.01)	Jetrihcc	Jeya	Jhariel	Jhshod	Jim (0.09)
Jessico	Jett (0.02)	Jeyan	Jharmee	Jhuleon	Jim Patrick
Jessie (0.50)	Jett Jay	Jeyarajaratnam	Jharnemus-Jack	Jhulian	Jimal
Jessie James	Jetun	Jeyaram	Jharquise	Jhunyae	Jimar
Jessie-James	Jetuwr	Jeydier	Jharyld	Jhustyn	Jimaré
Jessie-Lee	Jetwon	Jeyland	Jhaun	Jhusva	Jimares
Jessie-Pandeli	Jetzael	Jeylil	Jhavares	Jhyrede	Jimari
Jessie-Ray	Jetziel	Jeylon	Jhavarious	Jhywon	Jimaris
Jessika	Jeulen	Jezael	Jhavell	Ji	Jimaul
Jessilyn	Jeulien	Jezani	Jhavonte	Ji'marrius	Jimél
Jessmar	Jeulius	Jezekiel	Jhawn	Ji'quel	Jimear
Jessmervin	Jeusf	Jezer	Jhaylen	Ji're	Jimel
Jesson	Jevai	Jeziah	Jhazmin	Ji'ron	Jimell
Jessop	Jevan	Jeziel	Jhazmon	Jia	Jimeric
Jesspal	Jevante	Jezrael	Jhcolbi	Jia'vanté	Jimero
Jessphraim	Jevanté	Jezray	Jhelen	Jiabrinte	Jimetriez
Jessten	Jevara	Jezreel	Jhemari	Jiahid	Jimi (0.01)
Jesstin	Jevari'on	Jezzroy	Jhems	Jiaire	Jimie
Jesston	Jevaris	Jghakarie	Jherald	Jiamante	Jimill
Jessup	Jevarius	Jh'avon	Jherell	Jiame	Jimique
Jessus	Jevaughn	Jh'keric	Jheren	Jiamyl	Jimjoel
Jessy (0.17)	Jevaun	Jha'mier	Jherome	Jian	Jimka
Jessye	Jevell	Jhaarid	Jheromyl	Jianko	Jimkenny
Jessyie	Jeven	Jhacob	Jherrion	Jianni	Jimm
Jesten	Jevethan	Jhacobien	Jherris	Jianwei	Jimmario

Jimmarius	Jippsey	Jo'von	Joc'qui	Joedayle	Johannah
Jimmell	Jiquese	Jo-Ceph	Jocabe (0.01)	Joedell	Johannan
Jimmelle	Jiquies	Jo-El	Jocelyn (0.01)	Joedin	Johannes (0.01)
Jimmere	Jiquive	Jo-Nathan Nathan	Joceri	Joedy	Johannus
Jimmi	Jirad	Jo-Vuan	Jock	Joee	Johansen
Jimmie (0.09)	Jirair	Joab	Jockel	Joeff	Johanson
Jimmie Ray	Jirani	Joabe	Jockquaren	Joehanes	Johanthan
Jimmiel	Jirardo	Joaby	Jocktavious	Joehienze	Johanthin
Jimmielee	Jirdeh	Joachim	Jocoabi	Joejeevan	Johany
Jimmil	Jireh	Joachin	Jocob	Joel (1.66)	Johari
Jimmiray	Jiren	Joah	Jocobb	Joel 2:2	Joharri
Jimmon	Jirl	Joahua	Jocobia	Joel Jesus	Johathan (0.01)
Jimmy (0.80)	Jirriane	Joakeim	Jocolby	Joel Jr	Johathon
Jimmy Khai	Jirrus	Joal	Jocquail	Joel'	Johawn
Jimmy Lee (0.01)	Jisung	Joallen	Jocque	Joell	Johensen
Jimmy-Alan	Jitesh	Joamichael	Jocquel	Joelle	Johenson
Jimmy-James	Jittralakvong	Joan (0.02)	Jocques	Joellee	Johious
Jimmye	Jittreaun	Joan-Christophe	Jocquez	Joellic	Johkez
Jimmyjohn	Jiu	Joanah	Jocqui (0.01)	Joellyes	Johlahn
Jimon	Jiunn-Yiing	Joanathan	Jocquievous	Joemaka	Johmal
Jimontae	Jivan	Joanattan	Jocquince	Joeman	Johmarcus
Jimoy	Jivara	Joangelo	Jocquis	Joemar	John (9.83)
Jimqavious	Jivaundre	Joani	Jocquise	Joemichael	John Albert
Jimson	Jiwan	Joanna	Jocquivious	Joemil	John Aldrich
Jimtavis	Jiwanjot	Joannes	Jocsan	Joen	John Anthony
Jimuan	Jj	Joanni	Joctan	Joenathan	John Cameron
Jimvonta	Jj Anthony	Joanthony	Jodacee	Joerell	John Carlo
Jimy	Jl	Joao (0.02)	Jodahn	Joerion	John Carlos
Jimyhl	Jlanni	Joao-Paulo	Jodat	Joery	John Christophe
Jin (0.02)	Jlyn	Joaquan	Jodeci (0.01)	Joes	John Christopher
Jin Ho	Jm	Joaqui'n	Jodecy	Joeseph (0.02)	John David
Jin-Seok	Jmal	Joaquin (0.13)	Jodee	Joesh	John Dominique
Jin-Sung	Jmari	Joaquin-Jason	Jodel	Joesph (0.04)	John Gabriel Bl
Jinabu	Jmaya	Joar	Joden	Joesy	John Gregory
Jinel	Jmen	Joas	Joderick	Joetavious	John II
Jinender	Jn	Joash	Jodhbir	Joevany	John III
Jinesh	Jna	Joassaint	Jodhua	Joevarious	John Isaac
Jing	Jo	Joasu	Jodi	Joevon	John Jacob
Jingwa	Jo El	Joathan	Jodian	Joevonta	John James
Jinho	Jo Juan	Joave	Jodie	Joevonte	John Jaseph
Jinhyuk	Jo Mar	Joavis	Jodius	Joewel	John Jr
Jinn	Jo Von	Job (0.02)	Jodon	Joey (0.36)	John Lee
Jinnay	Jo Vonte	Joba	Jodran	Joey Phuong	John Lloyd
Jino	Jo'dari	Joban	Jody (0.06)	Joffrion	John Marc
Jinoth	Jo'el	Jobani	Jody-Gilles	Jofray	John Marcus
Jinwoo	Jo'kwanzaa	Jobanjit	Jody-Nesta	Jogie	John Mark
Jio	Jo'nae	Jobanny	Joe (0.38)	Jogpaul	John Michael
Jiovani	Jo'nallie	Jobarri	Joe Marr	Johah	John Patrick
Jiovanie	Jo'quari	Jobe	Joe Vaughn Mario	Johahn	John Paul (0.01)
Jiovann	Jo'quee	Joben	Joél	Johan (0.04)	John Ricky
Jiovanni	Jo'son	Jobias	Joévontá	Johandry	John Robert
Jiovannie	Jo'terriez	Jobie	Joe-Anthony	Johane	John Scott
Jiovanny	Jo'vanti	Jobin	Joe-Pierre	Johanes	John Tavious
Jiovany	Jo'vaughn	Jobson	Joeby	Johanh	John Te
Jiovoni	Jo'vawn	Joby (0.01)	Joecicario	Johann (0.03)	John'

John'el	Johnar	Johnpatrick (0.01)	Johvonne-	Jon'than	Jonathona
John'tavious	Johnary	Johnpaul (0.03)	Christopher	Jon-Alden	Jonathun
John'trel	Johnas	Johnquan	Johvontaé	Jon-Carlo	Jonathyn
John-Aaron	Johnatan	Johnquavious	Joi	Jon-Carlos	Jonatrhan
John-Ali	Johnath	Johnquavis	Joiner	Jon-Christopher	Jonaus
John-Angus	Johnathan (1.04)	Johnquelle	Joji	Jon-Claude	Jonavan
John-Anthony	Johnathan-Allen	Johnquez	Jojo	Jon-Dalton	Jonavery
John-Brendon	Johnathan-Cole	Johnquis	Jojohn	Jon-David	Jonavin
John-Dale	Johnathan-Paul	Johnray	Jojuan	Jon-Kellie	Jonavon
John-Daniel	Johnathann	Johnscott	Jokeidric	Jon-Kjell	Jonclare
John-David	Johnathen (0.02)	Johnsie	Jokorey	Jon-Kyle	Joncolby
John-Davide	Johnathn	Johnson (0.05)	Jokschan	Jon-Luc	Jondale
John-Douglas	Johnathon (0.39)	Johnson-Minh	Jokwan	Jon-Luke	Jondell
John-Elam	Johnathon	Johnston	Jolan	Jon-Mark	Jondre
John-Eric	William	Johnt	Jole	Jon-Michael (0.01)	Jone
John-Gregory	Johnathony	Johnta	Jolen	Jon-Mycal	Joneil
John-Henry	Johnathyne	Johntá	Jolene	Jon-Paul	Jonel
John-Jerome	Johnaton	Johntae	Joliet	Jon-Pierre (0.01)	Jonell
John-Joseph	Johnavin	Johntaé	Jolito	Jon-Reilly	Jones (0.01)
John-Kyle	Johnaxe	Johntarius	Jollil-Hamid	Jon-Taylor	Joness
John-Lee	Johnayhan	Johntavian	Jollyce	Jon-Thomas	Jonethen
John-Logan	Johncurtis	Johntavier	Jolten	Jon-Vincent	Jonethyn
John-Luc	Johndaniel	Johntavious	Joma	Jon-Wesley	Jong
John-Luke	Johndell	Johntavis	Jomal	Jona	Jong-Hyun
John-Mark	Johne	Johntavius (0.01)	Jomall	Jonah (0.59)	Jong-Sun
John-Marshall	Johneal	Johntavous	Jomandi	Jonahs	Jongmin
John-Martin	Johnel (0.01)	Johntay	Jomar (0.02)	Jonahtan	Jongsong
John-Micah	Johnell	Johntaye	Jomar Jim	Jonan	Jonh
John-Michael	Johnes	Johnte	Jomarcus	Jonanthony	Jonha
(0.01)	Johnethan	Johnté	Jomari	Jonard	Jonhneton
John-Mikeal	Johnfrancis	Johntell	Jomarie	Jonardo	Jonhny
John-Morgan	Johnhaven	Johnterius	Jomark	Jonas (0.10)	Jonhy
John-Oliver	Johnie (0.01)	Johnterriou	Jomarri	Jonass	Joni
John-Palmer	Johnie-Lee	Johnterrius	Jomel	Jonat	Jonilo
John-Patrick	Johniel	Johnthan (0.01)	Jomichael	Jonat'an	Jonis
John-Paul (0.01)	Johnille	Johntray	Jommy	Jonatan (0.05)	Jonluc
John-Richard	Johnivan	Johntrel	Jomo	Jonath	Jonluca
John-Robert (0.01)	Johnkerious	Johntye	Jomon	Jonathan (8.70)	Jonluke
John-Ross	Johnkita	Johnvontan	Jomoze	Jonathan Andrew	Jonmarc
John-Ryan	Johnlery	Johny (0.02)	Jomund	Jonathan Avery	Jonmel
John-Scott	Johnmark	Johnzell	Jon (0.36)	Jonathan Brian	Jonmichael
John-Tay	Johnmert	Johnzelle	Jon Christo	Jonathan Charle	Jonn
John-Thomas	Johnmichael	Johon	Jon Jr	Jonathan Cl	Jonnareise
John-Tuan	(0.01)	Johonath	Jon Kia	Jonathan He	Jonnathan (0.01)
John-Wesley	Johnmirean	Johonny	Jon Marques	Jonathan Hi	Jonnathon
John-Wessley	Johnn	Johovas'	Jon Michael	Jonathan Michae	Jonnathun
John-William	Johnnathan	Johsberd	Jon Paul	Jonathan Michael	Jonnee
Johna	Johnnell	Johsua	Jon Taylor	Jonathan-Craig	Jonnel
Johnad	Johnney	Johsue	Jon Taz	Jonathan-Hansun	Jonnie
Johnae	Johnni	Johtae	Jon Trell	Jonathan-Joon	Jonny (0.02)
Johnalbert	Johnnie (0.11)	Johua	Jon'kevious	Jonathan-Peter	Jononta
Johnandrew	Johnniethan	Johuan	Jon'quil	Jonathen (0.01)	Jonothan (0.01)
Johnangelo	Johnny (0.84)	Johvan	Jon'ta	Jonathin	Jonothon
Johnanthan	Johnothan	Johvon	Jon'tavis	Jonathon (0.86)	Jonovan
Johnanthony	Johnotis		Jon'tel	Jonathon Jesus	Jonpatrick

Jonpaul	Joost	Jorden (0.08)	Jorrell	Josea	Joseppe
Jonqavyous	Jophiel	Jordhan	Jorrett	Josealfredo (0.01)	Joses
Jonquale	Joplin	Jordi (0.01)	Jorrian	Josean	Joseth
Jonquavian	Joqualian	Jordian	Jorrie	Joseane	Josevan
Jonquavious	Joquan	Jordie (0.01)	Jorte	Joseangel	Josevicente
Jonquavis	Joquavion	Jordin (0.02)	Jorven	Joseantonio (0.01)	Josey (0.01)
Jonquel	Joquavius	Jordo'n	Jorvis	Joseba	Josh (0.08)
Jonquell	Joquawn	Jordon (0.27)	Jory (0.04)	Josedejesus (0.02)	Josh Christian
Jonquevalone	Joquil	Jordun	Joryan	Josee	Josh-Alexander
Jonquez	Joquin	Jordy (0.03)	Josa	Joseeon	Josha
Jonquil	Joquize	Jordyn (0.03)	Josabeth	Josef (0.09)	Joshan
Jonquill	Joqunn	Jorean	Josael	Josef-Michael	Joshand
Jonqurias	Joquon	Joree	Josaet	Josefat	Josharon
Jonreall	Jor-El	Joreg	Josafat	Josefernando	Joshashwun
Jonrell	Jorad	Jorel	Josafath	Joseff	Joshau
Jonscot	Jorah	Jorell (0.01)	Josaiah	Josefices	Joshaua
Jonson	Joral	Jorelle	Josan	Josefino	Joshauah
Jonta	Joram	Joren (0.01)	Josard	Joseguadalup	Joshaun
Jontae	Joran	Jorens	Josas	(0.01)	Joshawa (0.01)
Jontaé	Joravir	Jorey (0.01)	Josber	Joseh	Joshawael
Jontah	Jorawar	Jorgan	Josdeph	Joseias	Joshawn
Jontarius	Jord	Jorge (1.59)	Jose (5.26)	Joseiko	Joshemiah
Jontavais	Jordaan	Jorge Alberto	Jose Alejandro	Josejuan	Joshia
Jontavious (0.01)	Jordain	Jorge Carlos	Jose Alfredo	Josel	Joshiel
Jontavis	Jordale	Jorge Jr	Jose Andres	Joselito	Joshim
Jontavius	Jordan (7.33)	Jorge Luis	Jose Antonio	Joseluis (0.05)	Joshimar
Jontayvious	Jordan John	Jorge Manuel	Jose Daniel	Josemanuel (0.02)	Joshmar
Jonte (0.01)	Jordan Kimb	Jorge Michael	Jose De	Joseph (10.88)	Joshmine
Jonté	Jordan Ray	Jorge Ricardo	Jose De Jesus	Joseph Benedicy	Joshoa
Jonteryus	Jordan Roman	Jorgé	Jose De Juesus	Joseph Clerance	Joshon
Jontez	Jordan-Alexande	Jorgeluis (0.01)	Jose Filiberto	Joseph Edward	Joshoua
Jonthan (0.01)	Jordan-Anthony	Jorgen (0.01)	Jose Guadalupe	Joseph	Joshua (14.72)
Jonthon	Jordan-Daniel	Jorgio	Jose Hector	Emmanuel	Joshua Ahmad
Jontravious	Jordan-Douglas	Jorgue	Jose Ignacio	Joseph James	Joshua Allan
Jontray	Jordan-Felix	Jorhem	Jose Inacio Juni	Joseph Joshua	Joshua Angelbert
Jontre Clau	Jordan-Immanuel	Jori	Jose Jesus	Joseph Jr	Joshua Arnold
Jontreeal	Jordan-Kamal	Jorian	Jose Juan	Joseph Michael	Joshua Caleb
Jontrel	Jordan-Lee	Jorie	Jose Luis	Joseph Norbert	Joshua Cesar
Jontrell	Jordan-Nathaniel	Joris	Jose Manuel	Joseph Patrick	Joshua Ishmael
Jontrelle	Jordan-Peter	Jorje (0.01)	Jose Paolo	Joseph Rene	Joshua James
Jontrey	Jordan-Thomas	Jorma	Jose Ramon	Joseph Thomas	Joshua Jan
Jontua	Jordan-Troy	Jormam	Jose Thomas	Joseph Wade	Joshua Karl
Jontylar	Jordan-Winston	Jorman	Jose Victor	Joseph-Austin	Joshua Lawrence
Jonuel	Jordane	Jormars	José (0.05)	Joseph-Barry	Joshua Lee
Jonvante	Jordani	Jormnap	José Pablo	Joseph-Elysee	Joshua Michael
Jonvonte	Jordaniel	Jorn	José-Luis	Joseph-Raif	Joshua Nicholas
Jony	Jordanio	Jornell	Joséluis	Joseph-Samuel	Joshua Steven
Joo	Jordann	Joron	Jose-Ann	Josephh	Joshua Travon
Joon	Jordanny	Jorquores	Jose-Armand	Josephheo	Joshua-Alexandre
Joonbum	Jordano	Jorran	Jose-Carlos	Josephine	Joshua-Caleb
Joonha	Jordany	Jorrance	Jose-Daniel	Josephnhan	Joshua-Cody
Joonsung	Jordayne	Jorrdan	Jose-Gaddi	Josephous	Joshua-Daniel
Joonwhi	Jorde	Jorrdin	Jose-Guy	Josephs	Joshua-Dennis
Joonwoo	Jordel	Jorre	Jose-Luis	Josephus	Joshua-Derryll
Joonyoung	Jordell	Jorrel	Jose-Roberto	Josepoh	Joshua-Jean

Joshua-Lee	Josue *(0.51)*	Jovanni *(0.04)*	Joymare	Juan-Giovanni	Juchan
Joshua-Lucas	Josue Samaniego	Jovannie	Joyous	Juan-Marquis	Jucksir
Joshua-Michael	Josué	Jovanny *(0.05)*	Jozef *(0.01)*	Juanantonio	Jucorie
Joshua-Phillip	Josuecalerbe	Jovanpreet	Jozeff	*(0.01)*	Juda
Joshua-Ryan	Josuel	Jovanté	Jozell	Juancamilo	Judah *(0.03)*
Joshua-Steven	Josuer	Jovanta	Jozeph	Juancarlito	Judas
Joshuaa	Josuet	Jovantae	Jozey	Juancarlos *(0.05)*	Judd *(0.01)*
Joshuadaniel	Josuf	Jovantaé	Joziah	Juancruz	Jude *(0.04)*
Joshuah *(0.02)*	Josuha	Jovante *(0.01)*	Jozsef	Juandaniel *(0.01)*	Jude Archimede
Joshual	Josuwa	Jovanti	Jquan	Juandedios *(0.01)*	Jude Benedict
Joshuan	Josvanny	Jovantis	Jr *(0.01)*	Juanderious	Judes
Joshuanayri	Josvany	Jovanvir	Jr Edward	Juandiaz	Judge
Joshue *(0.01)*	Josve	Jovany *(0.05)*	Jr Jose	Juandre	Judkin
Joshuea	Josyia	Jovaris	Jr.	Juane	Judnard
Joshuia	Joszef	Jovaugh	Jrayden	Juaneloy	Judson *(0.02)*
Joshun	Jotavious	Jovaughn	Jrdon	Juanez	Judston
Joshura	Jotham	Jovaun	Jreau	Juani	Judy
Joshuwa	Jothman	Jovazae	Jred	Juanito *(0.01)*	Juei-Chung
Joshuwell	Jotis	Jovel	Jreis	Juanivan	Juelian
Joshven	Jotrey	Joven	Jremy	Juanjé	Juensung
Joshwa	Jotte	Joveris	Jsai	Juanjose *(0.01)*	Juergen
Joshwinder	Jottny	Jovez	Jsalaante	Juanluis	Jugdeep
Joshyua	Jou	Jovhany	Jscob	Juanmanuel	Jugien
Josi'ah	Jouany	Jovi	Jsohua	*(0.02)*	Jugjit
Josia	Joudeh	Jovian	Jsone	Juannis	Jugmeet
Josia's	Joudvince	Jovid *(0.01)*	Jt	Juanpablo	Jugpreet
Josiah *(0.38)*	Joue	Jovin	Ju	Juanquin	Jugveer
Josiah-Corey	Jouette	Jovindeep	Ju Lian	Juantavies	Juhan
Josiah-Isaac	Jouiquwan	Jovinder	Ju Marcus	Juantavius	Juharold
Josian	Joules	Jovo'n	Ju Von	Juantonio	Juhmal
Josias *(0.01)*	Jouney	Jovon *(0.02)*	Ju Wan	Juantravious	Juhman
Josie	Jounior	Jovone	Ju Wann	Juantrelle	Juhmanie
Josif	Jouquin	Jovoni	Ju'cquese	Juanya	Juhmelle
Josimar	Jourdain	Jovonie	Ju'juan	Juanyae	Juhvonnie
Josinacio	Jourdan *(0.02)*	Jovonne	Ju'mario	Juanyai	Jui-Hsi
Josip	Jourden	Jovonni	Ju'micael	Juanyé	Juilien
Josiv	Jourdin	Jovonta	Ju'quavis	Juaqin	Juillard Lee
Josiyah	Jourdon	Jovontae	Ju'toine	Juaqine	Juiluan
Joslin	Jourdyn	Jovontay	Ju'vante	Juaquin	Jujuan *(0.01)*
Josmar	Jourien	Jovonte	Ju'wan	Juaren	Jujuane
Jospeh	Journee	Jovonté *(0.01)*	Ju'wuan	Juarez	Jukilo
Jospeph	Journey	Jovontez	Ju-Young	Juarrezz	Jukurious
Josph	Jousef	Jovony	Juacane	Juashua	Jukwan
Jospreet	Jousha	Jowan	Juahn	Juavon	Jul
Joss	Jova	Jowaun	Juan *(3.11)*	Juawan	Jul'yan
Jossaiah	Jova N	Jowel	Juan Antonio	Juawane	Julamon
Jossiah	Jovahn	Jowell	Juan Carlos *(0.01)*	Juawann	Julance
Jossmen	Joval	Jowonis	Juan Darius	Juawn	Jule
Jossua-Paul	Jovan *(0.10)*	Jowuan	Juan Eduardo	Jubal *(0.01)*	Julean
Jossue	Jovan Terrell H	Jox'queze	Juan Jose	Jubaugh	Julelian
Josten	Jovana	Joy	Juan Pablo	Jubenal	Julen
Jostin	Jovane	Joy-Jermain	Juan Pedro	Jubier	Julendy
Joston	Jované	Joyan	Juan Sergio	Jubilee	Jules *(0.03)*
Josua	Jovani *(0.05)*	Joye	Juan Travio	Jubril	Jules Boniface
Josuan	Jovann	Joylin	Juan-Carlos	Jucarlos	Julia

Julian *(1.21)*	Jun-Kyu	Juriel	Justin-Luke	Juwand	Jysal
Julian Anthony	Jun-Wen	Jurien	Justin-Matthew	Juwane	Jyson
Julian Rafael	Juna	Jurikas	Justin-Morgan	Juwann	Jyvontée
Julianna	Junaid *(0.01)*	Jurlando	Justin-Paul	Juwanza	Jywana
Julianne	Junaluska	Jurmain	Justin-Peter	Juwaun	
Juliano *(0.01)*	Junard	Jurmale	Justin-Thomas	Juwell	**-K-**
Julie	Junayd	Jurnee	Justin-Tyler	Juwhann	
Julien *(0.32)*	June	Jurney	Justina	Juwil	K *(0.03)*
Julien-Elie	Juneau	Juron	Justinderpal	Juwon *(0.01)*	K C
Juliene	Juned	Jurrell	Justine *(0.03)*	Juwonn	K D
Julienn	Juneho	Jury	Justine-Eve	Juwuan	K Darius
Julienne	Junel Westly	Jus'tn	Justingregory	Juwuane	K Lavelle
Julies	Junell	Jusdave	Justinhoai	Juwvan	K Mohne
Juliesus	Junenarri	Jushua	Justinian	Juyan	K Sean
Juliet	Jung	Jusin	Justiniano	Juyung	K Treion
Julijs	Jungbahadur	Jusitn	Justinlee	Jvon	K'aelle
Julil	Jungroan	Jusiya	Justinn	Jvonta	K'andre
Julio *(0.56)*	Jungsup	Juslus	Justino *(0.01)*	Jvontae	K'aron
Juliocesar *(0.01)*	Juni	Jusneel	Justis *(0.04)*	Jvonte	K'aunté
Julion	Juniase	Jusnel	Justise	Jwan	K'awan
Julious	Juniel	Juspin	Justiz	Jwon	K'cey
Julirous	Junil	Jussie	Justlin	Jy'aire	K'darius
Juliun	Junio	Just	Justo	Jy'mond	K'eon
Julius *(0.15)*	Junior *(0.09)*	Justace	Juston *(0.02)*	Jy'polie	K'eoni
Julius Anthony	Junior Jose	Justan *(0.01)*	Justson	Jy'quez	K'evonta
Julius Desh	Junious	Justarius	Justun	Jy'shawn	K'hadree
Jullian *(0.01)*	Junius	Justavin	Justus *(0.06)*	Jyah	K'hari
Jullien	Juniver	Justavus	Justuze	Jyahdin	K'juawn
Jullin	Junji	Justen *(0.06)*	Justyc	Jyaire	K'krissharr
Jullium	Junor	Justi Juan Angel	Justyce	Jyeir	K'lan
Jullius	Junorise	Justian	Justyn *(0.08)*	Jyerick	K'leb
Julon	Junquavis	Justic	Justyne	Jykeem	K'lia
Julse	Junrid	Justice *(0.23)*	Justynn	Jykerum	K'linn
Jultin	Junseo	Justice Franqui	Justyse	Jylan	K'lynn
Juluis	Junwoo	Justicé	Jusuf	Jyle	K'myré
July	Junya	Justin *(9.79)*	Jusufu	Jyler	K'nell
Jumaane	Juoquin	Justin Bern	Jute	Jyles	K'ontis
Jumaani	Juozas	Justin Bryant	Jutin	Jyles Lorenzo	K're
Jumacey	Jupiter	Justin Carlos	Juvan	Jylon	K'ren
Jumal	Juprée	Justin Cassidy	Juvante	Jylor	K'ron
Jumani	Juquacion	Justin Christia	Juvareya	Jymmyee	K'rondis
Jumanne	Juquan *(0.01)*	Justin Christop	Juvaun	Jyoji	K'saun
Jumar	Juqueai	Justin Clark	Juvenal *(0.02)*	Jyquis	K'schaun
Jumarcus	Jurassic	Justin Evan	Juvenal Jr	Jyquonn	K'shaun
Jumaun	Jurastic	Justin Jan	Juvencio	Jyraun	K'shawn
Jumel	Jurdel	Justin Kenedy	Juventino *(0.01)*	Jyreese	K'twan
Jumha	Jure	Justin Michael	Juvnit	Jyrell	K'von
Jummy	Jureca	Justin Paulo	Juvon	Jyren	K'vonne
Jumon	Jurek	Justin Tronie	Juvone	Jyriah	K'vonte
Jumond	Jurell	Justin-Clyde	Juvonte	Jyrius	K'wan
Jumonte	Jurelle	Justin-Fate	Juvreet	Jyrome	K'wani
Jumsher	Juren	Justin-James	Juvuan	Jyrone	K'waun
Jumuel	Jurez	Justin-James-Patrick	Juwaan	Jyrum	K'yeon
Jun *(0.01)*	Jurgan	Justin-Joe	Juwain	Jyrunn	K-Ci
Jun-Ho	Jurgen *(0.01)*		Juwan *(0.10)*	Jyrus	K-Ishawn

K-Von	Kabe	Kaden (0.15)	Kaene	Kahlia	Kailab
K.	Kabeer	Kaden-Chance	Kaenen	Kahlid	Kailan
K.C.	Kabel	Kadence	Kaenin	Kahlie	Kaileb
Ka (0.01)	Kaben	Kader	Kaenyn	Kahlieb	Kailem
Ka Cey	Kabier	Kaderin	Kaesar	Kahliel	Kailen
Ka Derrious	Kabil	Kaderious	Kaesawn	Kahlige	Kailer
Ka Derrius	Kabilan	Kaderius	Kaese	Kahlil (0.07)	Kailik
Ka How	Kabilesan	Kadesh	Kaeshaun	Kahlil Quetavio	Kailin
Ka Raun	Kabine	Kadia	Kaeshwan	Kahlo	Kailis
Ka Ron	Kabir (0.01)	Kadiim	Kaesy	Kahlon	Kailli
Ka Trevious	Kabiseba	Kadin (0.01)	Kaetwon	Kahmal	Kailob
Ka Yen	Kable	Kadir	Kaevon	Kahmis	Kailon
Ka'darion	Kabori	Kadison	Kaewon	Kahmron	Kailop
Ka'daron	Kaborre	Kadon	Kaeyan	Kahn	Kailor
Ka'darrius	Kabrell	Kadrian	Kaeylin	Kahnan	Kailub
Ka'deem	Kabreuan	Kadric	Kafea	Kahner	Kailum
Ka'i	Kabrian	Kadrick	Kafele	Kahnner	Kailund
Ka'jai	Kabrin	Kadrie	Kafi	Kahree	Kailyn
Ka'jerik	Kabrion	Kadrin	Kafil	Kahreem	Kailyp
Ka'lyn	Kace	Kadrius	Kagan (0.01)	Kahrel	Kaiman
Ka'maran	Kacee	Kadron	Kage	Kahri	Kaimen
Ka'nard	Kaceris	Kaduan	Kagen	Kahron	Kaimon
Ka'patrick	Kacey (0.03)	Kady	Kagerald	Kahruann	Kaimyn
Ka'quan	Kacey-Eric	Kadyn	Kaghen	Kahsaan	Kain (0.03)
Ka'ron	Kacher	Kae	Kagisano	Kahtan	Kain El
Ka'shaun	Kaci	Kae V'en	Kah'lil	Kahtravious	Kainan
Ka'shawn	Kacper	Kaec	Kah'ni	Kahvik	Kainda
Ka'shon	Kacy (0.01)	Kaedem	Kah-Shen	Kahvorkian	Kaine (0.02)
Ka'tell	Kadaijah	Kaeden (0.01)	Kahali'ihaulani	Kahydron	Kaine Manuel
Ka'torey	Kadairious	Kaedin	Kahan	Kai (0.15)	Kainen
Ka'vaseo	Kadan	Kaedon	Kaharai	Kai Alexander T	Kaineyon
Ka'vasieá	Kadane	Kaedretis	Kahari (0.01)	Kai Douglas	Kainin
Ka'vauscea	Kadarian	Kaedyn	Kaharie	Kai'shaun	Kaino
Ka'von	Kadarin	Kaegan	Kahdeem	Kai-Jahn	Kainoa (0.03)
Ka'vonte	Kadarious	Kaege	Kahdrell	Kai-Jana	Kainoa-Clarke
Ka-An	Kadaris	Kael	Kaheel	Kai-Shuen	Kainoah
Ka-Chai	Kadarius (0.02)	Kaelam	Kaheem	Kaialii	Kainon
Ka-Fai	Kadarrell	Kaelan (0.03)	Kahfeel	Kaid (0.01)	Kaioh
Ka-Ho	Kadarrion	Kaeland	Kahhende	Kaidan	Kaion
Ka-Jana	Kadarrius	Kaeleb (0.01)	Kahhri	Kaide	Kaique
Ka-Jo	Kadarryl	Kaelem	Kahiem	Kaiden (0.01)	Kaire
Ka-Ken	Kadarus	Kaelen (0.01)	Kahiye	Kaiden Christop	Kairee
Ka-Kit	Kadarvis	Kaelestis	Kahl	Kaidrian	Kairi
Ka-Runn	Kadarvya	Kaelib	Kahlan	Kaie	Kairon
Ka-Wai	Kadavion	Kaelim	Kahle	Kaiea	Kairos
Ka-Wing	Kadavius	Kaelin (0.04)	Kahleal	Kaiel	Kais
Kaaihue	Kaddarrius	Kaelob	Kahlee	Kaigan	Kaisen
Kaalab	Kaddiamm	Kaelon (0.01)	Kahleei	Kaige	Kaiser
Kaalin	Kade (0.11)	Kaelyb	Kahleek	Kaighn	Kaishawn
Kaalon	Kade Edward	Kaelyn	Kahleel	Kaihea	Kaishun
Kaan	Kadedrick	Kaeman	Kahleil	Kaiheem	Kaisiem
Kaare	Kadeem (0.05)	Kaemen	Kahlen	Kaii	Kaisman
Kaarhion	Kadeen	Kaemin	Kahler	Kaijah	Kaisten
Kaarin	Kadein	Kaemon	Kahless	Kaije	Kaitell
Kaarun	Kadell	Kaenan	Kahli	Kail	Kaiten

Kaither	Kaleb Alexander	Kalliber	Kamandip	Kammari	Kanghoon
Kaitlin	Kalebh	Kallin	Kamani	Kammeren	Kani
Kaitlyn	Kaled	Kallion	Kamanie	Kammeron	Kaniel
Kaito	Kaledrick	Kallon	Kamar	Kammin	Kanika
Kaius	Kaleef	Kallum	Kamarai	Kammron	Kanin
Kaivan	Kaleel *(0.01)*	Kalman	Kamarcus	Kamnayochukwu	Kanine
Kaiven	Kaleem	Kalo	Kamaren	Kamo	Kanir
Kaivon	Kaleema	Kalob *(0.02)*	Kamari *(0.01)*	Kamon	Kanisavon
Kaiwan	Kaleffa	Kaloc	Kamaria	Kamoni	Kanishkan
Kaiwo	Kaleh	Kaloeb	Kamarie	Kamonti	Kanjah
Kaiywon	Kalehal	Kalon *(0.01)*	Kamario	Kamonze	Kankejan
Kaizen	Kaleigh	Kalone	Kamarious	Kamoris	Kannen
Kaizer	Kaleiohao	Kalongi	Kamarius	Kamoryn	Kannon *(0.01)*
Kaj *(0.01)*	Kalell	Kalongki	Kamaron	Kampris	Kanoa
Kajah	Kalem *(0.01)*	Kalonji	Kamarr	Kamran *(0.02)*	Kanoderick
Kajan	Kalen *(0.06)*	Kalonn	Kamarre	Kamrein	Kanodrique
Kajanth	Kaleo	Kalonté	Kamashon	Kamren *(0.01)*	Kanon
Kajaun	Kaleo Peter	Kalope	Kamau *(0.01)*	Kamrin	Kansas
Kajavion	Kaleob	Kalston	Kamau-Uhuru	Kamron *(0.03)*	Kansten
Kaje	Kalep	Kalton	Kamayni	Kamrun	Kant
Kajeanth	Kalev	Kalub	Kamber	Kamryn *(0.01)*	Kanten
Kajeeban	Kaley	Kalujge	Kambralus	Kamyar	Kanton
Kajeen	Kalhid	Kalum *(0.01)*	Kambriel	Kamyn	Kantrall
Kajen	Kali	Kalup	Kambron	Kamyu	Kantrell
Kajeric	Kalib *(0.01)*	Kalvan	Kambrone	Kan-Fu	Kantriel
Kaji	Kalibe	Kalven	Kamden *(0.01)*	Kanaan *(0.01)*	Kantrill
Kajipan	Kalic	Kalvin *(0.06)*	Kamdon	Kanaar-Romane	Kanwal
Kajira	Kalid	Kalvin Czar	Kaméron	Kanad	Kanwalnain
Kajona	Kalieb	Kalvinjohn	Kameel	Kanan	Kanwalpal
Kajuan *(0.01)*	Kalieem	Kalvir	Kamel *(0.01)*	Kanard	Kanwar
Kajvan	Kaliel	Kalvis	Kamen *(0.01)*	Kanardo	Kanwarbir
Kaka	Kalif *(0.01)*	Kalvon	Kamenn	Kanari	Kanwardeep
Kakendrick	Kalifa	Kalvonte	Kameo	Kanarie	Kanwarpal
Kakisahawk	Kaliil	Kalvyn	Kameon	Kanaris	Kanyia
Kal	Kalil *(0.01)*	Kalwaski	Kameran	Kanarriso	Kanyon *(0.01)*
Kala	Kalillé	Kalyb	Kameren	Kanarus	Kanyonn
Kalab	Kalim	Kalyen	Kamerin	Kanathishan	Kao *(0.01)*
Kalabe	Kalin *(0.04)*	Kalyjah	Kamerion	Kanawha	Kaolin
Kalaep	Kalinik	Kalyle	Kameron *(0.24)*	Kanayo	Kaontee
Kalai	Kalio	Kalym	Kamerron	Kanbreale	Kaoru
Kalam	Kalip	Kalyn *(0.01)*	Kamerun	Kandace	Kaos
Kalan *(0.01)*	Kaliq	Kalyne	Kameryn	Kandarius	Kapil
Kalane	Kalis	Kalynn	Kamhad	Kandler	Kapilan
Kalani *(0.01)*	Kalishia	Kam	Kamhani	Kane *(0.12)*	Kapioloni
Kalanioku	Kaliso	Kam-Ren	Kamichael	Kane Luke	Kapress
Kalaniuvalu	Kalium	Kamaal	Kamichi	Kane Lynden	Kapri
Kalauti	Kalius	Kamahri	Kamico	Kaneel	Kaprice
Kalavious	Kaljeevan	Kamakanikailial	Kamiin	Kanei	Kaprix
Kaldon	Kaljinder	Kamal *(0.02)*	Kamil *(0.03)*	Kaneii	Kar
Kale *(0.06)*	Kallan	Kamaldeep	Kamilah	Kaneil	Kara
Kalé	Kallb	Kamali	Kamili	Kaneith	Karac
Kaleaf	Kalle	Kamaljeet	Kamiljon	Kaneja	Karaig
Kaleahl	Kalleb	Kamaljot	Kamin	Kanen *(0.01)*	Karaka
Kaleal	Kallem	Kamalveer	Kamion	Kanetis	Karam
Kaleb *(0.55)*	Kallen	Kaman	Kamm	Kang	Karamat

Karamjit	Karin	Karndeep	Karvall	Kashtin *(0.01)*	Katon
Karamo	Karina	Karndey	Karvardus	Kashton	Katorius
Karamoko	Karique	Karnealus	Karver	Kashus	Katorvin
Karamveer	Karis	Karnell	Karvon	Kashwaun	Katravius
Karan *(0.04)*	Karisma	Karniliy	Karwarren	Kashyap	Katrea
Karanbeer	Karl *(0.35)*	Karnjit	Karwayne	Kasimir	Katrel
Karanbir	Karl Anton	Karnjiv	Kary	Kasin	Katrell
Karandal	Karl June	Karnjot	Karyan	Kasinie	Katrez
Karandeep *(0.01)*	Karl Michael	Karno	Karyl	Kasmier	Katrin
Karandip	Karl-Frederick	Karnpreet	Kas	Kasmuri	Katron
Karanjeet	Karl-Heinz	Karnveer	Kasaan	Kason *(0.01)*	Katsumasa
Karanji	Karl-Jon	Karnvir	Kasaar	Kaspar	Katsumi
Karanjit	Karl-Oskar	Karod	Kasai	Kaspellis	Katum
Karanjot	Karla	Karog	Kasal	Kasper	Katwan
Karann	Karlan	Karol *(0.01)*	Kasaun	Kasra	Kaul
Karanpaul	Karlen	Karoly	Kasay	Kass	Kaulins
Karanpreet	Karleton	Karon *(0.01)*	Kascell	Kassam	Kaullen
Karanuir	Karleyun	Karonda	Kasche	Kassan	Kaum
Karanveer *(0.01)*	Karlheinz	Karone	Kasdan	Kassandra	Kaunte
Karanver	Karliff	Karonn	Kase	Kasseem	Kaunvir
Karanvir *(0.01)*	Karlin	Karrdarius	Kaseam	Kassem *(0.01)*	Kauron
Karar	Karlinol	Karree	Kasean	Kassem-Ali	Kaushik
Karast Hekura S	Karlis	Karreim	Kaseb	Kassen	Kaustav
Karaun	Karlo	Karrell	Kasee	Kassey	Kavaine
Karbiel	Karlo's	Karrick	Kaseem	Kassidy *(0.01)*	Kavan *(0.01)*
Karch	Karlo-Branimir	Karrieal	Kasei	Kassim	Kavanagh
Kardai	Karlon	Karrieam	Kaseler	Kassius	Kavanaugh
Kardashian	Karlonte	Karriem	Kasem	Kasson	Kavandeep
Kardell	Karlos *(0.01)*	Karrien	Kasen *(0.01)*	Kassra	Kavante
Kardo	Karloss	Karrington	Kasene	Kasten	Kavares
Kardokh	Karloz	Karron	Kasenet	Kasyn	Kavari
Kardon	Karlrick	Karrson	Kaseon	Kaszab	Kavaris
Kare	Karlson	Karrun	Kasey *(0.13)*	Katakey	Kavarres
Karee	Karlsten	Karsen *(0.01)*	Kash	Katareo	Kavasiá
Kareem *(0.11)*	Karlsu	Karshe	Kashad	Katarino	Kavaugn
Kareem Abdul	Karltez	Karson *(0.03)*	Kashain	Katarn	Kaveem
Kareen	Karlton *(0.01)*	Karstan	Kashajuan	Katavious	Kaveer
Karel *(0.01)*	Karltrell	Karsten *(0.04)*	Kashan	Kate	Kaveera
Karelius	Karlus	Karston	Kashard	Katelin-Bradley	Kaveh
Karell	Karlvontae	Kartan	Kasharé	Katelyn	Kaven *(0.01)*
Karem	Karly	Kartar	Kashaun	Kater	Kaveo
Karen	Karm	Karteau	Kashawn *(0.01)*	Katerina	Kaveon
Karene	Karma	Karter	Kashay	Katez	Kaveonta
Karestiah	Karmaine	Kartez	Kashe	Katharina	Kaveron
Karey	Karman	Kartheegan	Kashen	Kathen	Kavethan
Karez	Karmanveer	Karthigan	Kashese	Katherine	Kavi
Kari	Karmen	Karthik *(0.01)*	Kashev	Kathrein	Kavielle
Karian	Karmin	Kartier	Kashi	Kathrine	Kavier
Karie	Karmjeet	Kartik	Kashief	Kathryn	Kavin *(0.02)*
Karieem	Karmpal	Kartrell	Kashif	Kathy	Kavindeep
Karielle	Karmpaul	Karum	Kashka	Katia	Kavintham
Karif	Karmveer	Karumbe	Kashmeel	Katie	Kavion
Karigan	Karmvier	Karun	Kashmere	Katisha	Kavion Kimano
Karil	Karmvir	Karunvir	Kashmir	Katlin	Kavious
Karim *(0.05)*	Karn	Karuta	Kashon	Kato	Kavirathan

Kavish	Kaygen	Kayvan *(0.01)*	Kéambre	Ke-Ron	Keanue
Kavithan	Kayhan	Kayveond	Kéandre *(0.01)*	Ke-Shawn	Keanuray
Kavon *(0.03)*	Kayin	Kayviah	Kéandré	Ke-Von	Keaone
Kavond	Kayjay	Kayvon *(0.01)*	Kéane	Ke-Vonta	Keaph
Kavone	Kayl	Kaywon	Kéangelo	Kea'ndre	Kearan
Kavontae	Kayla	Kaywood	Kéardrick	Keaaren	Keari
Kavonte	Kaylab	Kayz	Kéarius	Keaaris	Kearin
Kavonté	Kaylan *(0.01)*	Kayzon	Kéatre	Keabrae	Kearion
Kavoris	Kayland	Kaza	Kédarien	Keadrick	Kearius
Kavozeia	Kaylane	Kazadi	Kédarious	Keagan *(0.04)*	Kearkius
Kavya	Kayle *(0.01)*	Kazami	Kédarius	Keagean	Kearnard
Kavyon	Kayleb *(0.01)*	Kazarian	Kédarrus	Keagen	Kearney
Kaw-Liga	Kaylee	Kazden	Kédarryl	Keaghan	Kearon
Kawaine	Kaylef	Kazeem	Kéentrae	Keagyn	Kearston
Kawaljit	Kaylem	Kazem	Kéeric	Keahi	Keary
Kawan	Kaylen *(0.01)*	Kazian	Kéhandre	Keahn	Keaston
Kawanis	Kaylep	Kazie	Kéjaun	Keahnan	Keatan
Kawanta	Kaylib	Kazim	Kéjuan	Kealan	Keaten
Kawantis	Kaylim	Kazimierz	Kélen	Keale	Keath
Kawaun	Kaylin *(0.01)*	Kazimir	Kélyn	Kealin	Keathan
Kawaune	Kayln	Kazlo	Kélynn	Kealo	Keatin
Kawe	Kaylob	Kazmier	Kémari	Kealob	Keatlin
Kawika	Kaylon *(0.02)*	Kazon	Kémarquez	Kealoha	Keaton *(0.22)*
Kawika James	Kaylon Nich	Kazu	Kémarrius	Kealon	Keator
Kawika Ryan	Kaylop	Kazual	Kémarvin	Kealyb	Keatron
Kawliga	Kaylor	Kazuhiko	Kémontae	Kealyn	Keats
Kawlin	Kaylos	Kazuhiro	Kémoze	Kean *(0.01)*	Keatton
Kawon	Kaylp	Kazuki	Kénon	Keanan *(0.01)*	Keatyn
Kawsu	Kaylub	Kazutaka	Kéondra	Keanarii	Keaujay
Kawuan	Kaylum	Kazuto	Kéonte	Keanda	Keaun
Kawun	Kaylyn	Kazuya	Kérian	Keande	Keaun'
Kawyski	Kaylynn	Kazwhun	Késean	Keandra	Keaunis
Kay	Kayman	Kazzmir	Késhandon	Keandray	Keauntae
Kay-Deann	Kaymen	Kc *(0.02)*	Késhane	Keandre *(0.02)*	Keaunté
Kaya	Kaymon	Kcajun	Késhaun	Keandré	Keauntra
Kaya Abbott	Kaymore	Kcee	Késhawn *(0.01)*	Keandree	Keavan
Kayan	Kaynan	Kcharles	Késhon	Keandrell	Keaven
Kayano	Kayne *(0.03)*	Kcim	Késhun	Keandrick	Keavis
Kayben	Kaynen	Ke	Kétez	Keane *(0.01)*	Keavo
Kaybrin	Kaynon	Ke Ali I	Kéundra	Keaneau	Keavon
Kayce	Kayo	Ke Andre	Kévaugh	Keanen	Keawe
Kaycee	Kayode	Ke Darrius	Kévaughntré	Keaneu	Keayan
Kayd	Kayon	Ke Juandre	Kével	Keani	Keb
Kayde	Kayoto	Ke Jwan	Kévon	Keanna	Kebar
Kaydee	Kaypounyers	Ke Onte	Kévonta	Keanno	Keboa
Kayden *(0.04)*	Kayro	Ke Ontra	Kévontay	Keano *(0.01)*	Kebrin
Kaydin	Kayron	Ke Shaun	Kévonte	Keanon	Kebroshia
Kaydn	Kaysaun	Ke Shun	Kévyn	Keant-E	Kebure
Kaydon	Kaysawn	Ke Tori	Kéwon	Keantavious	Kechan
Kaydrian	Kaysen	Ke Vante	Kéwuan	Keantay	Kedaar
Kaydron	Kaysey	Ke Vaughn	Kéwyone	Keante	Kedar *(0.01)*
Kaye	Kayson	Ke Werenton	Kéyundre	Keanté	Kedarrias
Kayed	Kaythen	Ke Yon	Ke-Darreon	Keanu *(0.14)*	Keddie
Kayel	Kaytreon	Ke Yon Ke A	Ke-Koa Auinalaho	Keanu Lee	Keddy
Kayeon	Kayum	Kéadre	Ke-Marius	Keanu'	Keden

Kederer	Keenma	Kehtric	Kein	Keithen *(0.01)*	Keldric
Kederick	Keennan	Kei	Keinan	Keitheon	Keldrick *(0.01)*
Kederrickius	Keeno	Kei Fred	Keino	Keithlin	Keldrid
Kedesh	Keenon *(0.01)*	Kei Von	Keinor	Keithon	Keldron
Kedevyn	Keenoy	Kei Waun	Keinthorn	Keithren	Kele
Kedna	Keenu	Kei'lan	Keinun	Keithric	Kelechi *(0.01)*
Kedreen	Keeny	Kei'on	Keion *(0.03)*	Keithton	Keleian
Kedrek	Keeon	Kei'shawn	Keionda	Keitm-Martin	Kelem
Kedreus	Keeondae	Kei-Yeon	Keiondra	Keiton	Kelev
Kedreyon	Keeontae	Keian	Keiondraé	Keitrey	Kelevi
Kedric *(0.01)*	Keeoyn	Keiandre	Keiondre	Keitron	Kelf
Kedrick *(0.01)*	Keer	Keiandre E	Keioni	Keiunta	Kelford
Kedron	Keeran	Keiantae	Keionta	Keiuntrae	Kelhn
Kedryn	Keerat	Keiave	Keiontae	Keivan	Kelian
Kee	Keeros	Keibreon	Keiontaviouse	Keiven	Kelii
Kee Yontey	Keerstin	Keice	Keiontaye	Keivne	Kelijah
Keéshawn	Kees	Keidaisha	Keionte	Keivon	Kelile
Keéuntae	Keeshadrick	Keiden	Keionté	Keivone	Kelin
Keévin	Keeshaun	Keidre	Keionus	Keivonnis	Keliss
Keévon	Keeshawn	Keidren	Keir *(0.01)*	Keivontae	Kelius
Kee-Aun	Keeshon	Keidric	Keiran *(0.01)*	Keivontay	Keljin
Kee-Fung	Keeshond	Keidrick	Keire	Keiw'an	Kell
Keean	Keeshton	Keidron	Keirnan	Keiwan	Kellagh
Keeano	Keestin	Keifer *(0.04)*	Keiron	Keiwane	Kellam
Keeanu	Keeston	Keiffer	Keirran	Keiwuan	Kellan *(0.02)*
Keeban	Keet	Keifon	Keirstyn	Keiyon	Kellar
Keebrion	Keetan	Keiford	Keiryn	Keiyonte	Kelle
Keefe	Keeth	Keifran	Keisean	Keizar	Kellee
Keefer	Keeton	Keigan *(0.01)*	Keiser	Kejah	Kellen *(0.08)*
Keegan *(0.36)*	Keetwon	Keighan	Keishaun	Kejairis	Keller
Keeghan	Keevan	Keighen	Keishawn	Kejana	Kelley *(0.02)*
Keegon	Keeven	Keigo	Keishay	Kejay	Kelli
Keegun	Keevin	Keihew	Keishea	Kejiva	Kellie
Keehan	Keevis	Keijmaree	Keishi	Kejon	Kellin
Keeion	Keevon *(0.01)*	Keijon	Keishiro	Kejuan *(0.01)*	Kellon
Keejuan	Keevy	Keijuan	Keishod	Kejuana	Kelly *(0.19)*
Keel	Keewan	Keiki	Keishon	Kejuantae	Kelly Thomas
Keelan *(0.02)*	Keewannie	Keil	Keishone	Kekai	Kellyn
Keeland	Keewaun	Keilah	Keishum	Kekoa *(0.02)*	Kelmin
Keelen	Keewin	Keilan *(0.01)*	Keishunn	Kekuewa	Kelmontay
Keeler	Keeya	Keiland	Keislyn	Kelab	Kelob
Keeley	Keeyan	Keileen	Keistan	Kelabe	Kelse
Keeli	Keeyon	Keilen	Keiston	Kelan *(0.01)*	Kelsea
Keelin	Kefer	Keiler	Keisuke	Keland	Kelsey *(0.08)*
Keely	Keffer	Keili	Keita	Kelantae	Kelsi
Keelyn	Kefton	Keilin	Keitaro	Kelbi	Kelsie
Keemo	Kegan *(0.05)*	Keillene	Keitarus	Kelbin	Kelso
Keen	Kegen	Keillyn	Keith *(1.09)*	Kelby *(0.05)*	Kelson *(0.01)*
Keena	Keghan	Keilon	Keith The II	Kelcey *(0.01)*	Kelston
Keenan *(0.31)*	Kegon	Keilon'tae	Keith-Michael	Kelci	Kelsy
Keenau	Kehaku	Keilus	Keith-Ronald	Keldaishia	Kelten
Keene	Kehan	Keilynn	Keitha	Keldan	Keltevious
Keenen *(0.02)*	Kehdairus	Keimon	Keitham	Kelden	Kelth
Keener	Kehinde	Keimoni	Keithan	Keldon *(0.01)*	Keltin
Keenin	Kehlan	Keimontae	Keithdrick	Keldowen	Kelton *(0.07)*

Keltric	Kemontre	Kenderrick	Kenin	Kennith *(0.02)*	Kentavius
Kelty	Kemonty	Kenderrion	Kenino	Kennlius	Kentavous
Keltyn	Kemori	Kenderyious	Kenion	Kennon *(0.01)*	Kentell
Kelvan	Kemorvion	Kendhal	Kenishi	Kennorris	Kenten
Kelvarious	Kemp *(0.01)*	Kendior	Kenith	Kennovia	Kenterius
Kelven	Kemper *(0.01)*	Kendle	Kenjae	Kennsel	Kenterree
Kelveonte	Kempha	Kendo	Kenjamen	Kenntori	Kenterrius
Kelvin *(0.30)*	Kempton	Kendon	Kenjhana	Kenny *(0.29)*	Kentirius
Kelvis	Kemron	Kendorian	Kenji *(0.02)*	Kenny-Br	Kentlee
Kelviyon	Kemuel	Kendra	Kenjiro	Kennyan	Kento
Kelvon	Ken *(0.08)*	Kendrae	Kenkevin	Keno	Kenton *(0.07)*
Kelvontá	Ken Darius	Kendrall	Kenky	Kenoh	Kentorai
Kelvonta	Ken Derrick	Kendrawn	Kenlaw	Kenoiya	Kentory
Kelvontae	Ken Jr	Kendre	Kenledjuan	Kenon	Kentrahl
Kelvonté	Ken'dall	Kendré	Kenley *(0.01)*	Kenorris	Kentrail
Kelvy	Ken'dre	Kendrea	Kenlontae	Kenosha	Kentral
Kelvyn	Ken'drea	Kendrece	Kenly	Kenosohn	Kentravious *(0.01)*
Kelwin	Ken'niqu	Kendred	Kenmar	Kenpal	Kentravius
Kelyn	Ken'tayvious	Kendrel	Kenmone	Kenric *(0.01)*	Kentray
Kelynd	Ken-Dell	Kendrell *(0.01)*	Kenna	Kenrick *(0.01)*	Kentrayl
Kelynn	Ken-Jah	Kendrez	Kennady	Kenrico	Kentraylus
Kem	Ken-Yattá	Kendric *(0.01)*	Kennan *(0.01)*	Kenrie	Kentrayveis
Kemahn	Ken-Yi	Kendrich	Kennard *(0.01)*	Kenron	Kentraza
Kemal	Kenai	Kendrick *(0.24)*	Kennari	Kenroy	Kentre
Keman	Kenan *(0.03)*	Kendrick-Kenyle	Kenndrick	Kenrry	Kentré
Kemani	Kenaniah	Kendricson	Kennebon	Kenrud	Kentreal
Kemanni	Kenard *(0.01)*	Kendrik	Kennedy *(0.06)*	Kenry	Kentrel
Kemar	Kenari	Kendris	Kenneith	Kensean	Kentrell *(0.02)*
Kemarcio	Kenata	Kendriun	Kennel	Kenshaun	Kentrelle
Kemari	Kenaz	Kendrius	Kennen	Kenshiro	Kentreon
Kemarie	Kenber	Kendrize	Kenner	Kenshon	Kentreylus
Kemario	Kenbritt	Kendryck	Kennesaw	Kenshun	Kentrez
Kemarr	Kenda	Kendryn	Kenneta	Kensilver	Kentro
Kemartré	Kendahl	Kendtron	Kennetch	Kenslee	Kentron
Kembrick	Kendaja	Kendul	Kenneth *(2.22)*	Kensley	Kentson
Kembro	Kendal *(0.06)*	Kendy	Kenneth Brian	Kenslo	Kentton
Kemdirim	Kendale *(0.01)*	Kendyl	Kenneth Bryan	Kensloe	Kentucky
Kemeron	Kendall *(0.34)*	Kendyll	Kenneth Jr	Kenson	Kentwain
Kemery	Kendan	Kene	Kenneth William	Kensson	Kentwan
Kemett	Kendarious	Kenedrick	Kenneth-Mark	Kenstin	Kenty
Kemish	Kendarius *(0.01)*	Kenedy	Kenneth-Michael	Kenston	Kenuel
Kemm	Kendarrious	Keneen	Kenneth-Tyrée	Kensuke	Kenute
Kemmo	Kendarrius	Keneil	Kennetha	Kensy	Kenvante
Kemmye	Kendavious	Kenelia	Kennethy	Kent *(0.12)*	Kenvir
Kemo	Kendeal	Kenen	Kennett	Kenta *(0.01)*	Kenwan
Kemon	Kendedrick	Kenesaw	Kenney	Kentá	Kenwick
Kemond	Kendel *(0.01)*	Keneth	Kenni	Kentae	Kenwin
Kemondre	Kendell *(0.04)*	Keng	Kennic	Kentais	Kenwoski
Kemondré	Kendelle	Kengo *(0.01)*	Kennidee	Kentarius	Keny
Kemone	Kenden	Kengy	Kennie	Kentaro	Kenya *(0.02)*
Kemonita	Kenderek	Keni	Kennieth	Kentaryea	Kenyad
Kemonta	Kenderick	Kenia	Kennin	Kentaveus	Kenyada
Kemontae	Kenderious	Kenichi	Kenning	Kentavien	Kenyae
Kemontavious	Kenderius	Kenidy	Kennington	Kentavious *(0.01)*	Kenyaette
Kemonte	Kenderkis	Kenigan	Kennis	Kentavis	Kenyahri

Kenyal	Keonntay	Kermil	Kesey	Keunte	Kevn
Kenyale	Keono	Kermit	Kesha	Keuntray	Kevo
Kenyan *(0.01)*	Keonta *(0.01)*	Kermit-James	Keshad	Keuntrey	Kevokiouse
Kenyana	Keontá	Kermiton	Keshan	Keuontea	Kevon *(0.06)*
Kenyar	Keontae *(0.01)*	Kermitt	Keshanan	Kevan *(0.02)*	Kevondae
Kenyari	Keontaé	Kermontae	Keshandre	Kevandre	Kevondra
Kenyarie	Keontavious	Kern	Keshane	Kevano	Kevondre
Kenyata	Keontay	Kernell	Keshardat	Kevanta	Kevondric
Kenyatae	Keontaye	Kerney	Keshaun *(0.01)*	Kevantae	Kevondrick
Kenyatee	Keonte *(0.02)*	Kerns	Keshav	Kevante	Kevone
Kenyatta *(0.03)*	Keonté *(0.01)*	Kernveer	Keshawn *(0.04)*	Kevanté	Kevonne
Kenyattee-Deter	Keontez	Keroh	Keshayne	Kevantée	Kevonta
Kenyatter	Keontia	Kerollin	Keshion	Kevarious	Kevontae *(0.01)*
Kenyatti	Keontis	Kerome	Keshon *(0.01)*	Kevarius	Kevontay
Kenyen	Keontrae	Keron *(0.01)*	Keshone	Kevaro	Kevonte *(0.01)*
Kenyha	Keontre	Keronte	Keshun *(0.01)*	Kevashia	Kevonté
Kenyon *(0.04)*	Keontré	Keronté	Kesin	Kevatsinh	Kevontee
Kenyonté	Keontres	Kerr	Kesine	Kevaughn	Kevontra
Kenyotis	Keontrey	Kerrei	Kesler	Kevaun	Kevontre
Kenyotta	Keonty	Kerrel	Kesley	Kevedric	Kevork
Kenyroe	Keonwoo	Kerrell	Kesly	Keveen	Kevorkian
Kenysen	Keony	Kerri	Kesman	Keven *(0.27)*	Kevotá
Kenyth	Keonyon	Kerrian	Kesnel	Kevence	Kevoyn
Kenzavious	Keough	Kerrick *(0.01)*	Kesniel	Keventh	Kevran
Kenzel	Keountay	Kerrie	Kesomi	Keveon	Kevrick
Kenzell	Kepa	Kerriem	Kessawi	Keveyonte	Kevrie
Kenzie *(0.01)*	Kephren	Kerrigan	Kessler	Kevian	Kevrin
Kenzley	Keqyane	Kerrin	Kesten	Kevien	Kevyn *(0.03)*
Kenzo	Kera	Kerrington	Kestian	Kevin *(8.23)*	Kevyon
Kenzy	Kerbey	Kerrion	Kestin	Kevin Abron	Kewadin
Keo	Kerbiah	Kerrionte	Keston	Kevin Alexander	Kewan *(0.01)*
Keod	Kerbie-Steffon-T	Kerron	Kestyn	Kevin David	Kewane
Keodrick	Kerby	Kerry	Kesyon	Kevin Estuardo	Kewatino
Keohn	Kerderius	Kerry-Tucker	Ketavious	Kevin James	Kewaun
Keoki	Kerdrick	Kershaun	Ketawun	Kevin Jayson	Kewaune
Keon *(0.09)*	Kereem	Kershawn	Kete	Kevin Jon	Kewetin
Keon Shane	Kerell	Kershel	Keteen	Kevin Lancelot	Kewon *(0.01)*
Keon Te	Kerem	Kershun	Kethan	Kevin Luis	Kewone
Keon'ta	Keren	Kertaivous	Ketius	Kevin Michael	Kewoné
Keon'te	Kerente	Kertiss	Ketlin	Kevin Minh	Key'jwan
Keon'tia	Kergan	Kerushan	Ketnel	Kevin-Alosius	Key'on
Keon'tre	Keri	Kervens	Keto	Kevin-Jay	Key'yon
Keonandrea	Kerian	Kervi	Ketonte	Kevin-Ravendra	Key-Anthony
Keonaté	Keric	Kervich	Ketrell	Kevin-Suede	Key-Wan
Keondez	Keril	Kervin *(0.01)*	Ketrick	Kevin-Vinh	Keyago
Keondra	Kerim	Kervince	Ketro	Kevin-Yessai	Keyairis
Keondrae	Kerin	Kervins	Ketton	Kevindeep	Keyan *(0.01)*
Keondray	Kerington	Kerwin	Kettrell	Kevinion	Keyana
Keondre *(0.01)*	Kerion	Kerwyn	Kettrick	Kevinlee	Keyandre
Keondré	Keris	Keryl	Ketwan	Kevinn	Keyangalio
Keondrick	Keriston	Kes	Ketwion	Kevins	Keyano
Keone	Kerjuan	Kesajan	Keundrick	Kevinsly	Keyanta
Keonente	Kerk	Kesav	Keunta	Kevion *(0.01)*	Keyanté
Keoni *(0.04)*	Kerly	Kesava	Keuntae	Kevis	Keyantée
Keonne	Kermichael	Kesean	Keuntay	Kevlin	Keyari

Keybin	Keyonte *(0.01)*	Khabeer	Khalib	Khapri	Khian
Keybo	Keyonté	Khachik *(0.01)*	Khalid *(0.10)*	Khar'e	Khiandre
Keydrick	Keyontea	Khadane	Khalid Haakim	Khareem	Khiaya
Keydrum	Keyontrez	Khadar	Khalid-Abdul	Khari *(0.05)*	Khidari
Keyen	Keyonvate	Khadari	Khalief	Khari Eric	Khidhar
Keyeon	Keyperrios	Khade	Khaliel	Khari Tyshawn	Khidhr
Keyerin	Keyrian	Khadeem	Khalif *(0.02)*	Kharim	Khiel
Keyes	Keyron	Khadeen	Khalifah	Khario	Khiem
Keyford	Keyshan	Khader	Khalih	Khariun	Khilan
Keyin	Keyshaun	Khadijah	Khalihl	Kharlil	Khiler
Keyion	Keyshawd	Khadir	Khalija	Kharlin	Khilyd
Keyion'ta	Keyshawn *(0.01)*	Khadman	Khalik	Kharlston	Khione
Keyionta	Keyshon	Khadre	Khalil *(0.29)*	Kharn	Khirae
Keyison	Keyshun	Khae-Varre	Khalil Déquan	Kharon	Khirbie
Keyjuan	Keyston	Khagesh	Khalil Devo	Khary	Khiree
Keykwon	Keyswan	Khahari	Khalili	Khasiem	Khirey
Keylan	Keytavius	Khaheem	Khalill	Khatai	Khirron
Keyland	Keyton *(0.01)*	Khahlil	Khalim	Khateeb	Khiry *(0.01)*
Keyle	Keytric	Khai *(0.01)*	Khalin	Khatib	Khiyal
Keylen	Keytwan	Khai-Sun	Khalind	Khaulyl	Khiyle
Keyleo	Keyuntá	Khailfani	Khalio	Khaun	Khizar
Keyleon	Keyunte	Khailil	Khalipha Margid	Khauri	Khizer
Keylin	Keyunté	Khailin	Khaliq	Khavante	Khleef
Keylion	Keyur	Khailyl	Khalis	Khavir	Khlia
Keylon	Keyvan	Khair	Khalise	Khavoizea	Khliel
Keylon Javo	Keyvante	Khairi	Khalleal	Khawaski	Khlynd
Keymani	Keyvaun	Khairie	Khallid *(0.01)*	Khay	Khmarkis
Keymel	Keyvon	Khaiser	Khallifah	Khayam	Khoa *(0.02)*
Keymon	Keyvonta	Khajhklil	Khalob	Khayber	Khoa Viet
Keymond	Keyvonte	Khajuan	Khalon	Khaylon	Khodr
Keymoni	Keywa	Khakenia	Khalyd	Khayman *(0.01)*	Khody
Keymonnie	Keywine	Khalad	Khalyn	Khaymen	Khoi
Keymonte	Keywon	Khalade	Kham	Khayree	Khoja
Keymonty	Keywonta	Khalaf	Khaman	Khayri	Khol
Keyn	Keywuan	Khalan	Khamar	Khays	Kholby
Keynan *(0.01)*	Keywunis	Khalani	Khamara	Khedrahn	Khole
Keynen	Kez	Khaldoon	Khamari	Kheelan	Kholtyn
Keynnard	Kezhun	Khaldoun	Khamaul	Khelad	Khomo
Keynne	Keziah	Khaleah	Khambrel	Khelben	Khord
Keynon	Kezlow	Khaleb	Khambrell	Khelvin	Khorel
Keyo	Kezmon	Khaled *(0.03)*	Khambriel	Kheman	Khori
Keyoba Ladell	Kezra	Khalede	Khamel	Khemarin	Khorvon
Keyokoy	Kezrin	Khaleed	Khameron	Khemaurius	Khory
Keyon *(0.05)*	Kezwan	Khaleef	Khames	Khentavious	Khoury
Keyon-Dre	Kh'alil	Khaleel *(0.01)*	Khamis	Kherington	Khris
Keyondae	Kh'ron	Khaleeq	Khamren	Kherwin	Khrishann
Keyondre	Kha Lil	Khaleif	Khamron	Kheshawn	Khrishon
Keyondrick	Kha'darius	Khaleigh	Khan	Khesly	Khrishtian
Keyonna	Kha'lil	Khaleil	Khaneil	Khevon	Khristan
Keyonne	Khaadim	Khalen	Khang *(0.01)*	Kheyan	Khristian *(0.02)*
Keyonta *(0.01)*	Khaalib	Khalfani	Khanh	Kheyjuan	Khristin
Keyontá	Khaalid	Khali	Khani	Kheyll	Khristofer
Keyontae	Khaaliq	Khalia	Khanner	Kheynan	Khriston
Keyontaé	Khaari	Khalial	Khanse	Khi'lon	Khristophar
Keyontay	Khabar	Khalian	Khapil	Khial	Khristopher *(0.03)*

Khrystian	Ki-Ree	Kieffer *(0.01)*	Kihilil	Kimber	Kinley
Khrystopher	Ki-Shaun	Kiefor	Kihilis	Kimberly	Kinman
Khuong	Ki-Shawn Tyreek	Kiegan	Kihisis	Kimbert	Kinnay
Khuram	Ki-Shon	Kieherran	Kihleal	Kimble	Kinnen
Khurban	Kia	Kieko	Kihry	Kimdrey	Kinnet
Khurram	Kiafaja	Kiel *(0.03)*	Kiiahno	Kimeth	Kinney
Khushal	Kiahnu	Kielan	Kiiefer	Kimiai	Kinnon
Khushdeep	Kiahoush	Kieler	Kiimaa	Kimiyaki	Kinny
Khushkaran	Kiak	Kiell	Kiimar	Kimjuan	Kino
Khushpreet	Kial	Kielman	Kijana *(0.01)*	Kimo	Kinon
Khushvir	Kialer	Kiemo	Kijaun	Kimodi	Kinquashawn
Khustinder	Kiambre	Kiemone	Kijon	Kimon	Kinser
Khwyntarius	Kiamte	Kien	Kijona	Kimoni	Kinsey *(0.01)*
Khy'ree	Kian *(0.02)*	Kienan *(0.01)*	Kijuan	Kimonte	Kinshon
Khyan	Kian An	Kienda	Kikunia	Kimonté	Kinsler
Khye	Kian Michael	Kienen	Kilani	Kimothy	Kinsley
Khyentse	Kiana	Kiente	Kilbert	Kimougo	Kinson
Khyiah	Kiandre	Kienuwa	Kilby	Kimoy	Kinston
Khyl	Kiandrei	Kieon	Kile *(0.01)*	Kimplov	Kintavious
Khyle	Kiantae	Kieondric	Kilean	Kimsear	Kintavius
Khyler	Kiante *(0.01)*	Kieontae	Kilee	Kimyatta	Kinte
Khylil	Kianté	Kier *(0.01)*	Kilen	Kin	Kinton
Khymere	Kiantia	Kieran *(0.16)*	Kiley *(0.01)*	Kinan	Kintrayveious
Khyre	Kiantre	Kierden	Kili	Kinap	Kintrell
Khyree *(0.01)*	Kianu	Kieren *(0.01)*	Kilian	Kinarious	Kinuanta
Khyri	Kiara	Kierian	Kilien	Kincade	Kinuthia
Khyrice	Kiarah	Kierien	Kilil	Kincaid	Kinwin
Khyrie	Kiarash	Kierin	Killen	Kinch	Kinyarda
Khyrii	Kiari	Kiernan *(0.01)*	Killian *(0.05)*	Kind	Kinyatae
Khyrin	Kiaron	Kiernen	Killian Marshal	Kindal	Kinyatta
Khyron	Kiarri	Kiero	Killiean	Kindell	Kinyon
Khyrstoffer	Kiarron	Kieron *(0.01)*	Killion	Kinder	Kinyua
Khyver	Kias	Kierr	Killy Joe	Kindle	Kinze
Ki *(0.01)*	Kiaun	Kierre	Kilmiel	Kindley	Kinzell
Ki Jana	Kiaunce	Kierron	Kilo	Kindred	Kinzer
Ki Shion	Kiaundric	Kiersin	Kilron	Kindrell	Kinzie
Ki Von	Kiaunte	Kiersten	Kilton	Kindrey	Kio
Ki'airre	Kiavik	Kiersty	Kilty	Kindrick	Kion *(0.01)*
Ki'an	Kiawel	Kiesh	Kilvhonntae	Kindt	Kiondre
Ki'ana	Kiayvonnti	Kieson	Kim *(0.05)*	Kineo	Kiondrick
Ki'andre	Kibwe	Kiestan	Kim Joseph	King *(0.02)*	Kione
Ki'ante	Kice	Kiet	Kim Nam	King Obadiah	Kionie
Ki'jana	Kichinosuke	Kieth	Kima	Kingbol	Kionne
Ki'juan	Kidane	Kiethen	Kimaal	Kingeon	Kionnta
Ki'onte	Kidd	Kiethon	Kimajdre	Kinglsley	Kiontae
Ki're	Kidean	Kiev	Kiman	Kings	Kiontai
Ki'shaun	Kidman	Kievan	Kimane	Kingsley *(0.01)*	Kionte
Ki'yon	Kidson	Kievian	Kimanee	Kingsly	Kiontrae
Ki-Jana *(0.01)*	Kie	Kievon	Kimani *(0.02)*	Kingston *(0.01)*	Kioselong
Ki-Janá	Kie-Aire	Kievone	Kimarco	Kingwood	Kiossy
Ki-Janna	Kieandre	Kiewaan	Kimari	Kingzlee	Kiowa
Ki-Jon	Kieanu	Kiffer	Kimbal	Kinh Tai	Kip *(0.01)*
Ki-Jonté	Kiedale	Kiflando	Kimball *(0.01)*	Kinji	Kipling
Ki-Jun	Kief	Kifton	Kimbel	Kinkade Lee	Kipp *(0.01)*
Ki-Ré	Kiefer *(0.05)*	Kiger	Kimbell	Kinkaid	Kippen

Kipper	Kirti	Kiwahn	Knali	Kody-Lee	Koleby
Kiptis	Kirtis	Kiwan	Knesi	Kodye	Koleman
Kipton	Kirtland	Kiwane	Knicholas	Kodyjames	Kolemann
Kiquan	Kirtley	Kiwian	Knickerbocker	Kodyn	Kolemen
Kira	Kirtus	Kiwond	Knickolas	Koebryn	Kolen
Kiram	Kirubel	Kiwuan	Knighe	Koelby	Koletin
Kiran *(0.01)*	Kirushnth	Kix	Knight	Koen	Koleton
Kirano	Kirwin	Kiyan	Knighten	Koert	Kolia
Kirass	Kiry	Kiyana	Knijele	Koessler	Kolin *(0.01)*
Kiratdeep	Kiryan	Kiyandre	Knoah	Kofe	Kolin James
Kirby *(0.06)*	Kisaun	Kiyante	Knoble	Kofi *(0.01)*	Kolja
Kire	Kiseop	Kiyl	Knolan	Kogul	Kollbei
Kirée	Kiser	Kiyle	Knolys	Kogylan	Kollean
Kireem	Kiseuk	Kiyohito	Knowl	Kohan	Kolleh
Kireet	Kish	Kiyon	Knowledge	Kohdy	Kollen
Kireeti	Kishabapenace	Kiyoshi	Knowlton	Kohei	Kollin *(0.01)*
Kiren	Kishan *(0.02)*	Kiyosumi	Knox *(0.01)*	Kohen	Kollyn
Kiret	Kishanraj	Kizmel	Knoxsom	Kohl *(0.04)*	Kolson
Kiriakos	Kishaun	Kjartan	Knut	Kohlbe	Kolston
Kirian	Kishawn	Kjeisten	Knyeem	Kohlby	Kolt *(0.01)*
Kiriazis	Kishen	Kjel	Ko	Kohle	Koltan *(0.01)*
Kiril	Kisho	Kjell	Ko'shawn	Kohler	Kolte
Kiril-Alexander	Kishon	Klahhaab	Koa	Kohlmann	Kolten *(0.03)*
Kirill	Kishor	Klane	Koal	Kohlton	Kolten-Keith
Kirishnan	Kishore	Klarence	Koalby	Kohner	Kolter
Kiristen	Kishoth	Klark	Koaltin	Kohnor	Koltin *(0.01)*
Kiriyak	Kisione	Klarke	Koapaka	Kohon	Koltn
Kirk *(0.17)*	Kisman	Klas	Kobaine	Kohulann	Kolton *(0.10)*
Kirk Trey	Kison	Klassen	Koban	Koi	Koltyn *(0.01)*
Kirkham	Kisora	Klathan	Kobby	Koichi	Kolva
Kirklan	Kissim	Klaus *(0.01)*	Kobe	Koji	Kolwyn
Kirkland *(0.04)*	Kiswahili Jamal	Klay *(0.01)*	Kobey	Kojiro	Kolya
Kirklen	Kit *(0.01)*	Klayton *(0.02)*	Kobi *(0.01)*	Kojo	Kolyn
Kirklin *(0.01)*	Kitawan	Kleber	Kobia	Kojo-Frimpong	Kom
Kirklind	Kitch	Klee	Kobie	Kojuan	Koman
Kirkline	Kitchener	Klein	Kobina	Kokayi	Komisi
Kirkloun	Kitchidahwa	Klen	Kobinnaw	Koki	Kon Trayve
Kirklun	Kitchrik	Klenton	Kobisan	Kokie-Dwuan	Kona
Kirklyn	Kitekeiaho	Klever	Kobly	Kokil	Konane
Kirklynd	Kiteley	Klevlin	Kobra	Kokkie	Konar
Kirklynn	Kito	Kleysen	Koby *(0.02)*	Kokul	Koner
Kirkpal	Kitrik	Kliff	Kocking	Kol	Kong *(0.02)*
Kirktis	Kitron	Klifford	Koda	Kolade	Kongmeng *(0.01)*
Kirkwood	Kitt	Kline	Kodaah	Kolan	Kongzong
Kiro	Kitt-Donti	Klint	Kode	Kolani	Konin
Kiron	Kittredge	Klinton	Kodee	Kolawole	Konlin
Kirpal	Kittrell	Kloub	Kodeelane	Kolbe	Konnen
Kirpaul	Kitwana	Klyde	Kodey *(0.01)*	Kolbey	Konner *(0.03)*
Kirron	Kiu-Sun	Klye	Kodi *(0.04)*	Kolbi	Konnick
Kirsch	Kiva	Klyon	Kodiak *(0.02)*	Kolbie	Konnor *(0.03)*
Kirshaan	Kiven	Klyve	Kodie *(0.02)*	Kolbin	Konor
Kirsten	Kivon	Km	Kodijo	Kolby *(0.09)*	Konrad *(0.03)*
Kirstopher	Kivontae	Kmarr	Kody *(0.48)*	Kolden	Konraed
Kirt *(0.01)*	Kivonté	Kmen	Kody Julian	Kole *(0.06)*	Konstadine
Kirtan	Kiwa	Knakya	Kody-Claude	Kolebe	Konstandino

Konstantine	Korre	Kouichirou	Kreesan	Krissan	Kruize
Konstantinos	Korrellon	Koujirou	Kreg	Krisstopher	Krunal
(0.01)	Korrey	Kouki	Kregan	Krist	Krusa'n
Konstantyn	Korri	Kounty	Kreggan	Krista	Kruse
Konstatino	Korrick	Kounver	Kreid	Kristafer	Krush
Konyong	Korrie	Kouper	Kreig	Kristain	Krushanthan
Koo	Korrigan	Kourdon	Kreigh	Kristan	Kruz
Koob	Korrun	Kourey	Kreighten	Kristapher	Kruze
Koobhmoov	Korry	Kourjuan	Kreighton	Kristaps	Kryeil
Koochie	Korrye	Kourt	Kreisler	Kristen *(0.01)*	Kryreon
Koon	Korseta	Kourtez	Krel	Kristepher	Krys
Koontz	Kort	Kourtland	Kren	Krister	Krys"tofer
Kooper	Kortavien	Kourtlin	Krenar	Kristerfer	Kryshaun
Kor	Kortavius	Kourtney	Krenwick	Kristerpher	Krystal
Korah	Kortayveon	Koury	Kresimir	Kristian *(0.25)*	Krystefor
Koran	Kortez	Koushal	Kress	Kristian Ariel	Krystian *(0.01)*
Korban	Kortlan	Koushawn	Kresten	Kristian David	Krystie
Korben	Kortland	Koushik	Krey	Kristian Deyb	Krystien
Korbin *(0.03)*	Kortlend	Kouta	Kreyton	Kristian-Lee	Krystin
Korby	Kortlon	Koutaro	Kri'shaw	Kristien	Krystofer
Korbyn	Kortney *(0.01)*	Kouvaris	Kri'shawn	Kristifer	Krystopher *(0.01)*
Kord	Kortni	Kovann	Krieg	Kristijan	Krysztof
Kordaryl	Kortrell	Kovarius	Krieger	Kristin	Kryton
Kordavion	Korvel	Kovas	Kriisan	Kristina	Krzysztof *(0.01)*
Kordaye	Korvon	Kove	Krikor	Kristine	Krzysztow
Kordd	Kory *(0.16)*	Koveh	Krinn	Kristinn	Ksaiah
Kordel	Kory-Morgan	Koven	Kris *(0.03)*	Kristion	Ksean
Kordell *(0.01)*	Korya	Kovington	Kris Martin	Kristjan *(0.01)*	Kshawn
Kordy	Koryen	Kowante	Kris-Anthony	Kristof	Kson
Kore	Kosai	Kowen	Kris-Ley	Kristofer *(0.11)*	Kszmon
Koreal	Kosalan	Koy	Krisanthan	Kristofer E	Kthan
Korean	Koschine	Koya	Krise	Kristoff *(0.01)*	Ktwan
Korede	Kosh	Koyei	Krisel	Kristoffer *(0.04)*	Ku'derian
Koree	Koshin	Koyzell	Krishan *(0.02)*	Kristofo	Kuade
Korei	Koshiro	Kozak	Krishanni	Kristofor	Kuarich
Korein	Kosisochukwu	Kozmo	Krishanth	Kristofyr	Kuba
Koren	Kosta	Kpaul	Krishaun	Kriston *(0.01)*	Kubasa
Korey *(0.14)*	Kostadino	Kpody	Krishawn	Kristopher *(0.59)*	Kudret
Korey'on	Kostadinos	Kquadem	Krishel-Kanin	Kristopher-	Kuemeel
Kori *(0.02)*	Kostandino	Kqué	Krishen	Michael	Kuincie
Korick	Kostandinos	Kquindeyl	Krishna *(0.01)*	Kristopheroy	Kuinton
Korie *(0.01)*	Kostantino	Kr	Krishnan	Kristophor	Kuiokalani
Korii	Kostas	Kragen	Krishneel	Kristopoher	Kuke
Korin	Kostijn	Kraig *(0.02)*	Krishner	Kristorpher	Kulbaj
Korion	Kosuke	Kralen	Krishon	Kristosanthony	Kulbir
Korlan	Kosy	Kramer *(0.01)*	Krishoth	Kristufer	Kuldeep
Korleone	Kosygin	Krantz	Krishtin	Kristy	Kule
Korley	Kota	Krash	Krishun	Kristyn	Kuljeet
Korlie	Kote	Krashawn	Krisiastine	Krisztian	Kuljinder
Korlin	Koti	Krashon	Krisitan	Kritivath	Kuljit
Korliss	Kotohiko	Kraven	Krisjan	Krittin	Kullen *(0.01)*
Korneil	Koty *(0.01)*	Kray	Krisjot	Kron	Kullins
Kornelius	Kou *(0.01)*	Krayg	Krisna	Krstopfer	Kullon
Kornell	Kouda Ben Hal	Krayton	Krisoth	Krue	Kulnain
Koron	Kougar	Kree	Kriss	Kruise	Kulvir

Kulwant	Kusal	Kwanza	Kya'relle	Kyle-Alan	Kyntrell
Kumani	Kush *(0.01)*	Kwanzaa	Kyael	Kyle-Alexander	Kynyasa
Kumar	Kushaiah	Kwanzee	Kyair	Kyle-Jon	Kynyurie
Kumarrie	Kushal *(0.01)*	Kwanzi	Kyaire	Kyle-Lynn	Kyohei
Kumayl	Kushiah	Kwanzie	Kyal	Kyle-Michael	Kyol
Kumen	Kutadah	Kwanzie-	Kyall	Kylee	Kyondre
Kumoski	Kutis	Geronimo	Kyan	Kyleen	Kyong
Kun.va	Kutter	Kwashaun	Kyanno	Kyleke	Kyoni
Kunaal	Kuvia	Kwashen	Kyano	Kylelee	Kyontae
Kunal *(0.02)*	Kuvin	Kwashon	Kyantae	Kylen *(0.01)*	Kyonte
Kunawat	Kuwan	Kwashon Sluth	Kyantrae	Kylend	Kyonté
Kunjan	Kuwayne	Kwasi *(0.01)*	Kyari	Kyleo	Kyra
Kuno	Kuwhan	Kwasie	Kyazi	Kyleorlando	Kyraly
Kunta	Kuyler	Kwata	Kydavion	Kyler *(0.32)*	Kyran *(0.01)*
Kunvarjeet	Kvian	Kwateze	Kyden	Kyles	Kyrawn
Kunyri	Kvodiyah	Kwatin	Kye *(0.02)*	Kylesh	Kyrce
Kuper	Kvon	Kwaun	Kyegar	Kyley	Kyre
Kurby	Kwabena	Kwaune	Kyel	Kylhill	Kyré
Kurdiston	Kwadarius	Kwaunterius	Kyelen	Kylian	Kyrece
Kurdt	Kwade	Kwazzi	Kyen	Kylic	Kyree *(0.02)*
Kurel	Kwadwo	Kweise	Kyenan	Kylie	Kyrée
Kuri	Kwaelon	Kweisi	Kyenté	Kylief	Kyreece
Kuriakis	Kwafo	Kweku	Kyeon	Kylil	Kyreem
Kurk	Kwaishon	Kwen	Kyeran	Kylin	Kyrel
Kuro	Kwajah	Kwentin	Kyeric	Kyline	Kyrell
Kurosh	Kwajuan	Kwenton	Kyesheem	Kyll	Kyren *(0.01)*
Kuroshe	Kwaka	Kwesi	Kyetrévius	Kylle *(0.01)*	Kyri
Kurran	Kwaku	Kwin	Kyham	Kylo	Kyri'
Kurri	Kwaleek	Kwinlon	Kyharee	Kylon	Kyriacos
Kurrick	Kwali	Kwinn	Kyheem	Kyloné	Kyriakos
Kurry	Kwamaine	Kwinten	Kyhmanhe	Kylor *(0.01)*	Kyrian
Kurshaun	Kwamane	Kwinton	Kyhree	Kylsie	Kyriante
Kursten	Kwamar	Kwmay	Kyile	Kylum	Kyric
Kurt *(0.26)*	Kwame *(0.02)*	Kwok	Kyimon	Kylun	Kyrick
Kurtavious	Kwamé *(0.01)*	Kwome	Kyirii	Kylund	Kyrie
Kurtavius	Kwamén	Kwong	Kyius	Kym	Kyriee
Kurtes	Kwamein	Kwong-Sing	Kyj	Kyma	Kyrillos
Kurtez	Kwamen	Kwuan	Kyjahri	Kymahn	Kyrin
Kurthan	Kwami	Kwun	Kyjon	Kyman	Kyrio
Kurtice	Kwan *(0.01)*	Kwymaine	Kyjuan	Kymani	Kyriq
Kurties	Kwan-Chi	Kwymente	Kyla	Kymir	Kyris
Kurtis *(0.28)*	Kwandarius	Kwyn	Kylaar	Kymmond	Kyrise
Kurtis Alexande	Kwando	Kwynn	Kylan *(0.03)*	Kymmothy	Kyrome
Kurtis-Lucien	Kwandre	Kwyntero	Kyland	Kymon	Kyron *(0.03)*
Kurtiss	Kwane	Ky *(0.01)*	Kylar *(0.01)*	Kymond	Kyrone
Kurtland	Kwanez	Ky André	Kylash	Kymoni	Kyrton
Kurtlin	Kwang	Ky Drien	Kyle *(8.67)*	Kymontae	Kysa
Kurtlyn	Kwanmaine	Ky Marion	Kyle 'K.C.'	Kynan *(0.01)*	Kysean
Kurtlynd	Kwanta	Ky'anthony	Kyle Alexan	Kyndal	Kysen
Kurtorious	Kwantaj	Ky'dorien	Kyle Brett	Kyndall	Kyser
Kurtravias	Kwantareus	Ky'lon	Kyle Jr	Kyndel	Kysha
Kurtrell	Kwantez	Ky'ondre	Kyle Michael	Kyndell	Kyshaun
Kurtt	Kwantrel	Ky'onn	Kyle Robert	Kynderious	Kyshaw
Kurtus	Kwantreyviyas	Ky'onte	Kyle Steven	Kyndle	Kyshawn
Kurtys	Kwantrez	Ky'sheem	Kyléanthony	Kynon	Kysheed

Kyshon	La Daris	La'dontae	La'vonta	Lachoy	Ladel
Kyshun	La Darius	La'dontai	La'vontae	Lachristoph	Ladell *(0.01)*
Kysien	La Darren J	La'dontay	La'vonte	Lachristophe	Ladereck
Kyson	La Darrien	La'donte	La'wuane	Lachristopher	Laderic
Kytan	La Darrius	La'dontre	La'zerick	Lacody	Laderion
Kytrell	La Darriuss	La'dwight	La-Darrious	Lacondo	Laderius
Kyu-Hyun	La Derrick	La'george	La-Ken	Lacordeon	Laderrian
Kyundre	La Don	La'jon	La-Marcus	Lacorey	Laderrick *(0.01)*
Kyunte	La Donovan	La'keista	La-Quon	Lacori	Laderricks
Kyus	La Donta	La'keith	La-Sean	Lacorian	Laderrion
Kyusou	La Dorian	La'kendall	La-Tray	Lacorrian	Laderrious
Kyuss	La Dravious	La'ketric	Laaundre	Lacory	Laderris
Kyuyoung	La Jarvous	La'kice	Laavian	Lacoya	Ladirus
Kyvan	La Kiethian	La'marcus	Laban	Lacray	Ladon *(0.01)*
Kyvaun	La Mandres	La'mon	Labaren	Lacy *(0.01)*	Ladonis
Kyven	La Markez	La'mondrey	Labaron	Laczarus	Ladontaé
Kyvias	La Markus	La'monte	Labarren	Lad	Ladontay
Kyvon	La Michael	La'monté	Labarrius	Ladade	Ladonte
Kywon	La Mon Te	La'montez	Labarron	Ladae	Ladonté
Kywontae	La Mot	La'montia	Labearon	Ladahvian	Ladre
Kywynn	La Nard	La'monty	Laben	Ladale	Ladson
Kyya	La Nigel	La'quan	Labib	Ladalvin	Laduan
Kyzlar	La Quan	La'quandrick	Labon	Ladamien	Ladwon
	La Quontia	La'quanlies	Laboria	Ladantia	Ladwyne
	La Reese	La'quann	Laboris	Ladarence	Lael
-L-	La Roderick	La'quez	Labou	Ladarian *(0.01)*	Laemont
	La Ron	La'quindrick	Labra	Ladarick	Laeon
L *(0.02)*	La Royce	La'quinton	Labradford	Ladarien	Laeroc
L C	La Runté	La'quoia	Labrahn	Ladarin	Laertes
L James	La Sean	La'ral	Labrandon	Ladarion	Lafaibian
L Kendrick	La Terious	La'ray	Labray	Ladarious	Lafarrell
L Nard	La Tevion	La'raymond	Labreal	Ladaris	Lafarrin
L'andre	La Trae	La'reco	Labree	Ladarius *(0.05)*	Lafayette *(0.02)*
L'darien	La Tuan	La'ron	Labrelle	Ladarrel	Laferrick
L'don	La Vonte	La'roy	Labrentta	Ladarrell	Lafette
L'donta	La Vonté	La'shaun	Labrian	Ladarren	Laffyette
L'keith	La'andre	La'shawn	Labrielle	Ladarrian	Lafisu
L'michael	La'belvin	La'terrance	Labritish	Ladarrias	Lafitani
L'tre-Shon	La'bront	La'tez	Labroderick	Ladarrick	Laflavious
L-David	La'bryant	La'travious	Labron	Ladarrien	Lafrancis
L.C.	La'chil	La'travius	Labryce	Ladarries	Lafredrick
L.D.	La'clifford	La'tre	Lac	Ladarrin	Lagan
L.G.	La'dale	La'treell	Lacari	Ladarrion	Lagari
L.J.	La'dalvin	La'trel	Lacario	Ladarrious	Lagarion
L.V.	La'darien	La'trell	Lacarlton	Ladarrius *(0.01)*	Lagarius
La *(0.01)*	La'darious	La'tron	Lacarreone	Ladaryl	Lagarrian
La Barion	La'daris	La'vante	Lacarvia	Ladauris	Lagarrion
La Bruce	La'darius *(0.01)*	La'var	Lacedric	Ladavion	Lagrant
La Cardo	La'darren	La'various	Lacedrick	Ladavious	Lagraryis
La Chance	La'darrian	La'varius	Lacell	Ladavius	Laguna
La Chris	La'darryll	La'vedrick	Lacey	Ladaytrick	Lagunan
La Coda	La'davius	La'vell	Lachaston	Ladd	Lahcene
La Damien	La'daz	La'velle	Lachavis	Laddie	Laheem
La Damion	La'dell	La'veras	Lacherro	Ladeboe	Laherman
La Dante	La'don	La'von	Lachlan *(0.01)*	Ladejo	Lahius
La Darion					

Lahraj	Lakendrick	Lamarkus	Lan	Lanial	Laquavius
Lai-Him	Lakenrick	Lamarque	Lanair	Laniel	Laquavon
Lai-Rida	Lakentae	Lamarquise	Lanaldre	Lanier	Laquawn
Laidin	Laketon	Lamarr (0.01)	Lanard	Lanis	Laquawne
Laif	Lakevin	Lamarté	Lanardo	Lankesh	Laquayle
Laighton	Lakevrick	Lamartez	Lanberto	Lannelle	Laqueivian
Laiikn	Lakeyo	Lamartra	Lance (0.49)	Lannes	Laquell
Laike	Lakhan	Lamarvin	Lanceley	Lanney	Laquent
Laiken	Lakhdeep	Lamassio	Lancelot	Lannis	Laquentin
Laiklin	Lakhjot	Lambert	Lancen	Lannix	Laquez
Laikon	Lakhver	Lamberto	Lancent	Lannon	Laquille
Laimar	Lakhwinder	Lamel	Lancer	Lanny	Laquin
Laimon	Lakiis	Lametri	Lancine	Lanon	Laquincy
Lain (0.01)	Lakim	Lametrrius	Lancinet	Lanord	Laquindrick
Laine (0.02)	Lakimeson	Lamichael	Lancton	Lanoris	Laquinn
Laird	Lakin	Lamikeal	Landaeu	Lanorris	Laquinta
Lairn	Lakoda	Lamin	Landan (0.01)	Lanre	Laquinten
Lairs	Lakordo	Lamique	Landarius	Lansana	Laquinton
Laith (0.01)	Lakorri	Lamisitoni Mich	Landas	Lansing	Laquisha
Laithe	Lakota (0.02)	Lammert	Landell	Lanson	Laquita
Laithon	Lakrahn	Lamon (0.01)	Landen (0.04)	Lante	Laquiton
Lajamale	Lakshay	Lamond	Landenn	Lantrell	Laqun
Lajames	Laksumon	Lamondaryl	Lander (0.01)	Lanty	Laquon
Lajamian	Lakwang	Lamonde	Landers	Lantz	Laquone
Lajarrett	Lakwante	Lamondo	Landie	Lanushan	Laquonté
Lajarrius	Lalark	Lamondra	Landin (0.01)	Lap	Laquris
Lajarvis	Laleen	Lamondre	Landing-Eagle	Lap-Man	Laqwan
Lajavia	Lalit	Lamondrio	Landis (0.01)	Laparis	Laqwon
Lajavius	Lalldon	Lamont (0.10)	Landon (0.58)	Lapas	Laqwuane
Lajay	Lally	Lamonta	Landrew	Lapaul	Lar Wayne
Lajaylen	Lalo	Lamontá	Landrin	Lapeer	Lara
Lajerriun	Lam (0.01)	Lamontae	Landrius	Laperial	Laracio
Lajhaun	Lama'cion	Lamontas	Landru	Laperry	Larado
Lajobie	Lamacio	Lamontate	Landrum	Laphonso	Laraib
Lajon	Lamael	Lamontavius	Landry (0.01)	Laphonzo	Larami
Lajonte	Lamain	Lamontay	Landus	Laprentice	Laramie
Lajuan (0.01)	Lamaine	Lamonte (0.02)	Landy	Laqawan	Laramy
Lajuante	Lamaja	Lamonté	Landyn	Laqjuan	Larance
Lajyrish	Lamalcolm	Lamontez	Lane (0.39)	Laqquaries	Larancion
Lakaine	Lamandres	Lamonto	Lane-Bey	Laquad	Laranté
Lakan	Lamanuel	Lamontra	Lane-Michael	Laquain	Laranzo
Lakane	Lamar (0.12)	Lamontray	Laneka	Laquallys	Laraque
Lakari	Lamara	Lamontre	Lanel	Laquan (0.02)	Laray
Lakas	Lamarco	Lamontrey	Lanell	Laquandra	Larbie
Lakavien	Lamarcus (0.02)	Lamonttez	Lanelle	Laquandrea	Laredo
Lakaymine	Lamariantaye	Lamonty	Laneython	Laquandrick	Lareen
Lake (0.03)	Lamariay	Lamonyette	Lanford	Laquann	Lareginald
Lakee	Lamario (0.01)	Lamordre	Lang (0.01)	Laquanta	Larell
Lakeem	Lamarion	Lamorris	Langdon (0.01)	Laquantae	Laremy
Lakeir	Lamarious	Lamount	Lange	Laquante	Laren
Lakeith (0.01)	Lamaris	Lamour	Langipuna	Laquardia	Larence
Lakeithin	Lamarius	Lampreia	Langley	Laquarious	Larenta
Lakeland	Lamark	Lamry	Langston (0.03)	Laquarius	Larentc
Laken	Lamarkese	Lamson	Lanh	Laquavian	Larenté
Lakendric	Lamarko	Lamy	Lani	Laquavious	Larento

Larenz *(0.01)*	Larsn	Lataye	Latrese	Lavanesen	Lavorius
Larenza	Larson *(0.01)*	Lataze	Latrevioun	Lavanndre	Lavozier
Larenzo *(0.01)*	Larsson	Lateef	Latrevious	Lavanta	Lawal
Laresse	Lartabrius	Latenza	Latrey	Lavante	Lawan
Lareston	Larue	Laterrance	Latreyveon	Lavantee	Lawand
Laricky	Larusso	Laterrence	Latrez	Lavar *(0.01)*	Laward
Larico	Larvell	Laterrion	Latrielle	Lavaries	Lawath
Larik	Larvis	Laterrious	Latron	Lavaris	Lawaun
Larinsky	Larvontae	Laterrius	Latroy	Lavarius	Lawayne
Larion	Larz	Laterrus	Latu	Lavarsky	Lawenza
Larison	Larzarus	Latesian	Latuan	Lavarus	Lawerance
Larizrick	Larzo	Latevius	Latwan	Lavaski	Lawerence *(0.01)*
Lark	Lasaba	Latez	Latwon	Lavaughn	Lawfton
Larkin	Lasabrion	Lathairio	Latye	Lavaun'te	Lawilliam
Larmont	Lasal	Latham	Latyson	Lavaunte	Lawkies
Larnell	Lasalle	Lathan *(0.01)*	Lau	Lavdeep	Lawon
Larnelle	Lasam	Lathaniel	Lauchlan	Lavel	Lawrance *(0.01)*
Larny	Lasaun	Lathikhone	Lauchlin	Lavele	Lawren
Laro	Lasaura	Lathusan	Laud	Lavell *(0.02)*	Lawrence *(0.49)*
Larobert	Lascelles	Latif	Laude	Lavelle *(0.01)*	Lawrence Carlo
Larod	Lasean	Latiif	Lauden	Laven	Lawsen
Laroderick	Lash	Latimer	Laudie	Lavenski	Lawson *(0.03)*
Larodney	Lasha	Latino	Laughlin	Laventres	Lawton *(0.01)*
Larome	Lashaad	Latitus	Laumberto	Laventrius	Lawuun
Laron *(0.03)*	Lashae	Latodd	Lauphael	Lavern	Lawyer
Larond	Lashan	Laton	Laura *(0.01)*	Laverne	Laxavier
Larone	Lashane	Latone	Lauran	Lavernon	Laxigan
Laronn	Lashaud	Latori	Laurance	Lavers	Laxshan
Laront'ae	Lashaun *(0.01)*	Latorious	Laureano	Laversay	Layan
Laronz	Lashawa	Latorrance	Lauren *(0.01)*	Lavert	Laycon
Laronze	Lashawn *(0.02)*	Latorries	Laurence *(0.07)*	Lavez	Laydon
Laroy	Lashay	Latoska	Laurent *(0.08)*	Lavictor	Laylyn
Laroyce	Lashedric	Latrae	Laurent-Philippe	Laviere	Laymon
Larrel	Lashelle	Latraé	Laurentino	Lavion	Laymondt
Larrell	Lashodd	Latrai	Laurentz	Lavish	Layn
Larrenté	Lashon	Latraivion	Laurenz	Lavoisier	Layne *(0.08)*
Larrentis	Lashone *(0.01)*	Latrale	Laurenzo	Lavon *(0.01)*	Laynee
Larreon	Lashun	Latraven	Lauri	Lavondre	Layquaun
Larrimius	Lasinto	Latraveus	Lauriano	Lavone	Layson
Larrish	Lasly	Latravion	Laurice	Lavonn	Layten
Larron	Lasney	Latravious	Laurier	Lavonndis	Layth
Larroquette	Last	Latravis	Lauris	Lavonne	Laythan
Larry *(0.61)*	Lastan	Latravius	Lauro *(0.01)*	Lavont	Laython
Larry Corelisus	Lastar	Latray	Laury	Lavonta	Layton *(0.04)*
Larry Marcel	Laszlo	Latray'vius	Lauterion	Lavontá	Layvon
Larry Thomas	Lat	Latraye	Lauviance	Lavontae	Lazandious
Larry-Curtis	Lataevious	Latrayvious	Lavahn	Lavontaé	Lazar *(0.01)*
Larry-Wallace	Latannie	Latrayvous	Lavail	Lavontai	Lazareth
Larryll	Latarious	Latraz	Laval	Lavontay	Lazarian
Larrymikeal	Latarius	Latre	Lavalle	Lavonte *(0.01)*	Lazarius
Larryon	Latarus	Latreal	Lavan	Lavonté *(0.01)*	Lazaro *(0.06)*
Lars *(0.04)*	Lataurse	Latreil	Lavance	Lavontell	Lazarrus
Lars-Erik	Latavin	Latrel	Lavanda	Lavontez	Lazarus *(0.01)*
Larsen	Latavious	Latrell *(0.04)*	Lavander	Lavord	Lazavier
Larshae	Latavius	Latrelle	Lavane	Lavoris *(0.01)*	Lazavion

Laze	Lémarvin	Leath	Leealan	Leigon	Lemontá
Lazederick	Lémichael	Leathan	Leeander	Leihm	Lemontay
Lazeec	Lémonté	Leatrice	Leeandre	Leilan	Lemonte
Lazereo	Léobie	Leavelle	Leebory	Leimas	Lemonté
Lazeric	Léon	Leavester	Leelan	Leinon	Lemontray
Lazerick	Léontrell	Lebaan	Leeland	Leite	Lemontrez
Laziah	Léquinten	Leban	Leeman	Leith	Lemoyne
Lazin	Léray	Lebbeb	Leenarcus	Leiv	Lemskey
Lazo	Léron	Lebon	Leenard	Lejaimen	Lemuel (0.01)
Lazorus	Léshawn	Leborio	Leenell	Lejerico	Lemun
Lazuwaun	Léshon	Leboris	Leequille	Lejohn	Lemy
Lazyrick	Lésteven	Lebradford	Leeran	Lejon	Len
Lazzaro	Létaurus	Lebrandon	Leeren	Lejuan	Lenae
Lc	Létrea	Lebron	Leeron	Lekan	Lenair
Le (0.01)	Létrell	Lebyron	Leeroy	Lekari	Lenale
Le Aires	Létrey	Lecarl	Leeshai	Lekeif	Lenard (0.01)
Le Alan	Létroy	Lecarlo	Leeshawn	Lekeith	Lenathan
Le Andrew	Lévelle	Lecedrick	Leeson	Lekem	Lenax
Le Anthony	Lévictor	Lecharles	Leet	Lekenry	Lendal
Le Broderic	Lévont	Lechon	Leetreze	Lekevis	Lendall
Le Christia	Lévontae	Leckson	Leevaris	Lekota	Lendarius
Le Darius	Lévonte	Lecky	Leevi	Lekun	Lendell
Le Darvis	Le-Jordan	Lecornus	Leevie	Lelan	Lendeverett
Le Derien	Le-Monta	Lecount	Leevion	Leland (0.07)	Lendie
Le Derrick	Le-Shaun	Ledaniel	Leevontae	Lelando	Lendon
Le Jeri'	Le-Tazorius	Ledante	Lefanoga	Lelen	Lendy
Le Maun	Leaaron	Ledario	Lefear	Lelend	Lendyn
Le Michael	Leach	Ledarion	Lefontae	Leliz	Lenear
Le Quan	Leadrian	Ledariun	Lefonz	Lelund	Leneil
Le Roy	Leagan	Ledarius (0.01)	Lefonzo	Lelvin	Lenell
Le Ryan	Leah	Ledarren	Legans	Lemadire	Lenford
Le Terrick	Leaire	Ledarrious	Legend	Lemance	Leng (0.01)
Le Vance	Leajune	Ledarrius	Legette	Lemand	Leni
Le Zerrick	Lealon	Ledarryl	Leglenta	Lemanuel	Leniel
Lé Marcus	Leaman	Ledell	Legrand	Lemar	Lenier
Léaaron	Leamon	Lederick	Legreggernal	Lemarco	Lenijoe
Léandre	Leanard	Lederious	Leh	Lemarcus	Lenin (0.01)
Léandrew	Leanda	Lederrick	Lehauli	Lemario	Lenine Froisard
Léantre	Leanddrow	Lederris	Lehi	Lemark	Lenise
Léarthur	Leander (0.01)	Ledet	Lehm	Lemarquis	Lennard
Léchade	Leandre (0.03)	Lediner	Lehman	Lemeer	Lennart
Lédale	Leandro (0.02)	Ledon	Lehmon	Lemel	Lennie (0.01)
Lédamien	Leandrus	Ledonte	Lehton	Lemere	Lennin
Lédarius	Leanne	Ledrae	Lehtou	Lemeriun	Lennis
Léderrick	Leanord	Ledre	Lehuri	Lemeul	Lennix
Lédon	Leansi	Ledson	Lei	Lemicah	Lennon (0.01)
Léglenn	Leante	Lee (0.37)	Leicester	Lemichael	Lennorris
Léjarius	Leanthoney	Lee Mario	Leif (0.05)	Lemijah	Lennox
Léjuan	Leanthony	Lee Porter	Leife	Lemil	Lenny (0.02)
Lékendrick	Leantoine	Lee Roy	Leifson	Lemmanuel	Leno
Lékeyven	Leantonio	Leévantay	Leigh	Lemmar	Lenon
Lékivo	Leantwone	Lee-Jerson	Leigh Pascual	Lemmie	Lenor
Lékraig	Lear	Lee-Jesus	Leigh-Joseph	Lemoine	Lenord
Lémar	Leartis	Lee-Michael	Leighman	Lemond	Lenore
Lémarcus	Leary	Lee-Shawn	Leighton (0.05)	Lemont	Lenorris

Lenox	Leonté	Lessard	Levester	Leyton	Lil Herman
Lenroy	Leontée	Lessie	Levi (0.96)	Leyvi	Lil John
Lens	Leonterrious	Lestat	Levi Joshua	Lezar	Lil Richard
Lensford	Leonza	Lester (0.08)	Levi-Austin	Lezerick	Lil'
Lentavius	Leopold	Lester Ray	Leviathyn	Lezlie	Lil'david
Lenterious	Leopoldo (0.05)	Lestermagne	Levico	Lezzerrick	Lil'earnest
Lentoli	Leor	Leszek	Levictus	Lhonita	Lil-Robert
Lentrell	Leosvaldo	Letavian	Levie	Li Eroi	Lilal
Lentrick	Leotis	Letcher	Levii	Li Song	Lilbert
Lenus	Leovardo	Leterrian	Levin (0.01)	Li'al	Lilburn
Lenwood	Leovigildo	Leth	Levine	Li'james	Lildavid
Lenworth	Leovins	Lethaniel	Levion	Li'keith	Liles
Lenys	Leoz	Lethon	Levirt	Li'marr	Lilly
Lenzel	Lepaez	Lethrell	Levis	Li-Dunn	Lilroy
Lenzell	Lepaul	Letrail	Levitacus	Li-On	Lilton
Lenzer	Lepone	Letravius	Leviticus	Li-Wey	Limmie
Leo (0.22)	Lepreece	Letre	Levon (0.02)	Lia	Limvano
Leo John	Lequan	Letreal	Levond	Liad	Linard
Leo'ntay	Lequane	Letrel	Levondra Malcol	Liah	Linc
Leo-Quan	Lequeint	Letrell	Levonne	Liam (0.64)	Lincoln (0.08)
Leobardo (0.03)	Lequentae	Letrelle	Levonta	Liam Onyx	Linda
Leocadio	Lequete	Letreyvious	Levontae	Liam-Alexander	Lindahl
Leocardo	Lequez	Letroy	Levontay	Liam-Dimitri	Lindan
Leodan	Lequwon	Lett	Levonte (0.01)	Lian	Lindberg
Leodegario	Lereldo	Letty	Levonté	Liana	Lindel
Leomar	Lerenta	Leucio	Levontre	Liandro	Lindell
Leomarcos	Lerenzo (0.01)	Leutrim	Levonza	Liang	Linden (0.02)
Leon (0.21)	Leri	Lev	Levonzy	Liangyuan	Lindley
Leon'dre	Lerin	Levaante	Levoyd	Libaan	Lindol
Leonance	Lernard	Levan	Levy	Liban (0.02)	Lindon
Leonard (0.24)	Leron (0.02)	Levander	Lewai/a	Libbren	Lindros
Leonard Joseph	Leronté	Levandis	Lewcus	Libert	Lindsay (0.01)
Leonardo (0.30)	Leronzo	Levante	Lewerik	Liborio	Lindsay II
Leoncio	Leroy (0.11)	Levar	Lewey	Librado	Lindsey (0.01)
Leondo	Leroyce	Levarious	Lewis (0.17)	Licharezz	Lindsie
Leondous	Lerrell	Levaris	Lewrenzo	Licinio	Lindsy
Leondrá	Lerrick	Levaron	Lex (0.01)	Lidareeius	Lindzy
Leondray	Les	Levaughan	Lexcel	Lidarius	Linear
Leondre (0.01)	Lesean	Levaughn	Lexie	Lidell	Linebarger
Leondrew	Leseray	Leveland	Lexington	Lidi	Linel
Leondris	Leshan	Levele	Lexis	Lieban	Linest
Leone	Leshaun	Levell	Lexius	Liem (0.01)	Linford
Leonel (0.15)	Leshawn (0.01)	Levelle	Lexson	Lieon	Ling
Leonell	Leshea	Levelly	Lextius	Lifaite	Lingo
Leonia	Leshivias	Leven	Lexus (0.01)	Lige	Lingston
Leonid	Leshun	Levente	Lexva	Lightnin	Lingyu
Leonidas	Leshurn	Leveon	Lexx'zaveir	Lightning	Linh Peter
Leonides	Lesidney	Levere	Lexxus	Lightwalker	Lininell
Leonis	Leslee	Leverenzel	Leyber	Lijah	Link
Leonna	Lesley	Leverette	Leye	Lijimmy	Linken
Leonnard	Lesli	Levern	Leyion	Lijo	Linlamont
Leonta	Leslie (0.09)	Leverne	Leyland	Likenson	Linn
Leontae	Leslie III	Leversus	Leyogi	Lil	Linnel
Leontaé	Lesly	Levert	Leyotn	Lil Benjamin	Linnell
Leonte	Leson	Levertis	Leytan	Lil Eddie	Linniell

Linnon	Llequell	Logyan	Loquan	Lou *(0.01)*	Lovett
Lino *(0.03)*	Llewellyn	Logyn	Lor'renzo	Louay	Loville
Linterrius	Llewlyn	Lohgan	Lorado	Loubens	Lovin
Linton	Lliam	Loic *(0.02)*	Loral	Loucas	Lovise
Linus	Llogan	Lojtao	Lorale	Louden	Lovjit
Linval	Llohandry	Lok	Loran *(0.01)*	Loudon	Lovro
Linward	Llovan	Lokbondo	Lorance	Loudrige	Lowell *(0.02)*
Linwood *(0.01)*	Lloyd *(0.11)*	Loki	Lorantz	Louell	Lowell Brecken
Linzell	Lloyd Kevin	Lokkan	Lorca	Louey	Lowen
Linzie	Llunas	Lokotah	Lord	Louidor	Lowrence
Linzy	Llywellynn	Lolo	Lordjemark	Louie *(0.05)*	Lowrenza
Lion	Lmichael	Lomaj	Lorénzo	Louies	Lowrenzo
Lional	Lo	Lomarian	Loreal	Louis *(0.57)*	Loxley
Lionardo	Lo'qwoyn	Lomayani	Lorel	Louis Alexander	Loy
Lionel *(0.07)*	Loagan	Lon	Loren *(0.08)*	*(0.01)*	Loyal
Lionell	Loagen	Lon'dexter	Lorena	Louis Charles	Loyall
Liony	Loagon	Lon'drelle	Lorenso	*(0.02)*	Loyan
Lior	Loajan	Lonald	Lorent	Louis David *(0.01)*	Loyd
Liprtial	Loanis	Londale	Lorentz	Louis Mathieu	Loyie
Liquaze	Loanne	Londarius	Lorenz	*(0.01)*	Loyldell
Liric	Lobelio	Londel	Lorenz Romel	Louis Philipp	Lu
Liron	Loc	Londell	Lorenza *(0.01)*	*(0.09)*	Lu'roy
Lisa	Loch	Londen	Lorenzo *(0.39)*	Louis Vincent	Luai
Lisandro	Lochlan	Londgray	Lorenzo Antonio	Louis Xavier	Luan
Lisette	Lochlin	London *(0.04)*	Lorenzo Luis	*(0.01)*	Luang
Lisley	Lochsley	Londro	Lorenzo Miguel	Louis-Andreas	Luay
Lismar	Locke	Londyn	Lorenzo Robert	Louis-Claude	Lubinson
Lisolomon	Locklynn	Lonell	Lorez	Louis-Keanan	Luc *(0.08)*
Liston	Locksley	Long *(0.02)*	Lori	Louis-Philipp	Luc-Henri
Lithedath	Lockwood	Loni	Lorin *(0.01)*	Louise	Luca *(0.06)*
Litorren	Lodarious	Lonie	Lorinc	Louistemp	Lucais
Litrum	Loden	Lonn'trez	Loring	Loukas	Lucan
Little	Loderick	Lonneill	Lorinza	Loukerby	Lucand
Little Eagle	Lodi	Lonnel	Loris	Lourdriano	Lucane
Little Joseph	Lodone	Lonnell	Lorman	Lourenzo	Lucano
Little Lawr	Loeden	Lonnelle	Lormar	Loutwan	Lucas *(2.08)*
Little Wind	Loel	Lonney	Lorne *(0.02)*	Louvell	Lucas Abrahamju
Littleton	Loeloe	Lonni	Lornzeo	Louverture	Lucas-Robbie
Littrayton	Loewan	Lonnie *(0.11)*	Lorrance	Louvier	Lucasallen
Liu	Loewen	Lonnie Jr	Lorrnzo	Louvin	Lucata
Liuman	Loften	Lonny *(0.01)*	Lorron	Louviskii	Lucaus
Livell	Loftin	Lonsard	Lorus	Louvonte	Lucca
Livingston	Lofton	Lonshone	Lorvince	Louzandro	Luccas
Livingstone	Loga	Lontarius	Lorzeno	Lovay	Luccus
Livio	Logan *(2.69)*	Lontavius	Losand	Love	Luces
Livonn	Logan-Kyle	Lontravious	Losang	Love-Preet	Luchannel
Liwaa	Logan-Michael	Lontray	Loshane	Lovedeep	Luchiano
Liyahsha	Logann	Lontre	Losson	Lovejot	Luchmoch
Lizandro	Logen *(0.01)*	Lontrell	Lotanna	Lovelean	Lucian *(0.01)*
Lizardo	Loggan	Lonyel	Lotfi	Lovell *(0.01)*	Lucian Blue
Lizbeth	Loghan	Lonzell	Lotharrio	Lovelle	Luciano *(0.05)*
Ljay	Login	Lonzo	Lotravious	Lovelyn	Lucien *(0.02)*
Ljupco	Logn	Loomis	Lott	Loveneet	Lucifer
Llamar	Logun	Lopa	Lottiereo	Loventas	Lucino
Llaser	Logunn	Lopez	Lotus	Lovepreet	Lucio *(0.04)*

Lucio De Jesus
Lucious
Lucis
Lucius *(0.01)*
Luckas
Luckee
Luckie
Luckner
Luckshan
Luckshmon
Luckson
Lucksson
Luckunes
Lucky *(0.02)*
Lucner
Lucny
Lucson
Lucus *(0.02)*
Ludgerus
Ludgi
Ludin
Ludner
Ludomir
Ludovic *(0.04)*
Ludovick *(0.01)*
Ludvelt
Ludwig
Ludwin
Ludyn
Luea
Lugam
Lugene
Lugman
Lui
Luidjy
Luiggi
Luigi *(0.03)*
Luigui
Luigy
Luii
Luinn
Luis *(2.80)*
Luis Albert
Luis Alberto
Luis Alfred
Luis Andres
Luis Angel
Luis Anthony
Luis Antonio
Luis Arturo
Luis David
Luis Enrique
Luis Esteban
Luis Fernando
Luis Jose

Luis-Daniel
Luis-Gilberto
Luis-Miguel
Luisa
Luisalberto *(0.01)*
Luisangel *(0.01)*
Luisantonio *(0.01)*
Luisdavid
Luisenrique *(0.01)*
Luisernie
Luiz *(0.03)*
Luiz Erlaine
Luiza
Luk
Luka *(0.02)*
Lukais
Lukas *(0.27)*
Lukash
Lukasz *(0.01)*
Lukaus
Lukayus
Luke *(1.95)*
Luke Jedidia
Luke Theodore
Luke-Avery
Luke-Robert
Luken
Lukenson
Lukess
Lukeus
Luki
Lukis
Lukiyan
Lukkas
Lukman
Lukoda
Lukus *(0.02)*
Luman
Lumier
Lunceford
Lunden
Lundon
Luner
Luntze
Lupe
Luqas
Luqman
Luquavian
Luquentas
Luquentine
Luras
Lurel
Lurenzo
Lurville
Lusean

Lushawn
Luson
Lut
Lute
Lutena
Lutfie
Luther *(0.04)*
Luther III
Luu
Luv
Luv'anias
Luveaches
Luvpunit
Luwen
Luxan
Luxjan
Luxman
Luxsaan
Luxssun
Luxzon
Luyanda
Luyando
Luyz
Luz
Luzarus
Lvis
Lwis
Ly Delle
Ly-Nell
Lyall
Lyam
Lyatray
Lydarian
Lydell
Lyden
Lydia
Lyfe
Lyle *(0.07)*
Lyle II
Lyle Jr
Lyman
Lymon
Lyn
Lynbyrd
Lyncoln
Lynda'll
Lyndal
Lyndale
Lyndall
Lyndan
Lyndarrius
Lyndel
Lyndell
Lynden *(0.01)*
Lyndon *(0.05)*

Lyndrick
Lyndsay
Lyneld
Lynell
Lynerio
Lynes
Lynesha
Lynette
Lynk
Lynken
Lynn *(0.02)*
Lynnell
Lynnen
Lynnquithis
Lynwood
Lynx
Lyol
Lyon
Lyon Jr
Lyonal
Lyonel
Lyons
Lyracee
Lyron
Lysander
Lyshiem
Lysuan
Lyttle
Lywoyn
Lyzander

-M-

M *(0.04)*
M Erik
M Mitchell
M'salla
M. *(0.01)*
M.C.
Ma Lik
Ma Quan
Ma'dre
Ma'kell
Ma'lachi
Ma'lik
Ma'queale
Ma'shon
Ma-Lik
Maagd
Maahi
Maahir
Maajid
Maake
Maalek
Maaliek

Maalik *(0.01)*
Maan
Maanas
Maaquise
Maarken
Maarten
Maathusan
Maaz *(0.01)*
Mabiala
Mabrey
Mabry
Mac *(0.01)*
Mac Kinnen
Mac-Livane
Macabe
Macaelin
Macahlly
Macail
Macaleb
Macalin
Macalister
Macall
Macallan
Macallen
Macallum
Macalvin
Macario *(0.01)*
Macarlon
Macarthur
Macartney
Macaruthur
Macaulay
Macaulee
Macauley
Macaully
Macauly
Macaven
Maccauley
Macdaniel
Macdonald
Mace
Macen
Maceo *(0.01)*
Maceyo
Macgreggor
Macgregor *(0.01)*
Macgyver
Machalah
Macharia
Machel
Machenry
Machias
Machlin
Machuan
Macie

Maciej *(0.01)*
Maciek
Macieo
Macinnon
Macintyre
Macio
Mack *(0.04)*
Mackauly
Mackay
Mackenize
Mackenna
Mackenry
Mackenson
Mackensy
Mackenze
Mackenzey
Mackenzi
Mackenzie *(0.46)*
Mackenzy *(0.01)*
Mackie
Mackinaw
Mackinley *(0.01)*
Mackinnley
Mackinnly
Mackinnon
Mackinsey
Mackinson
Mackinzie
Macklem
Macklin *(0.01)*
Macks
Mackson
Macky
Maclachlan
Maclain *(0.01)*
Maclaine
Maclane
Maclay
Maclean *(0.01)*
Macleod
Maclin
Maclovio
Maclyn
Macolley
Macolohn
Macon *(0.01)*
Macoy
Macpheden
Macquan
Macquell
Macray
Macson
Mactori
Macualay
Macy

Madala	Mahamedamin	Maira	Makishi	Malesela	Mana
Madamesire	Mahammad	Maisam	Makleen	Malgib	Manas
Madan	Mahammed	Maisan	Makmille	Maliak	Manases
Madani	Mahamoud	Maison *(0.01)*	Makoana	Maliak-X	Manasseh
Madar	Mahamud	Maitland	Makonnen	Malic	Manasses
Madarius	Mahan	Maiwand	Makoto	Malica	Manavtar
Madarren-Trevon	Maharshi	Maize	Makoy	Malicah	Manbeer
Madavy	Mahartaha	Majd	Makray	Malichi	Manbir
Maddison	Mahcallum	Majde	Maksim *(0.01)*	Malick	Mancil
Maddox	Mahde	Majdi	Maksimir	Malicke	Mandalacittahari
Maddux	Mahdee	Majdy	Maksym	Maliek *(0.01)*	Mandeep *(0.01)*
Madeira	Mahdi *(0.01)*	Majed *(0.01)*	Maksymilian	Maliik	Mandeep-Singh
Madeline	Mahdiyar	Majeed	Maktoom	Malik *(0.59)*	Manden
Madhav	Mahdy	Majeevan	Makye	Malik-Amin	Mandeze
Madiba	Mahek	Majesti	Makylan	Malik-Tabari	Mandheer
Madisen	Mahendra	Majid *(0.01)*	Mal	Malik-Troy	Mandhir
Madison *(0.12)*	Maher *(0.01)*	Major *(0.02)*	Malaak	Malikahi	Mandley
Madisson	Mahera	Majuran	Malacat	Malike	Mando
Madisyn	Mahesh	Makade	Malachai	Maliki	Mandreion
Madjer	Mahi	Makagen	Malachi *(0.11)*	Malil	Mandrell
Madkenson	Mahin	Makahl	Malachi'ly	Malinda	Mandy
Madley	Mahinanda	Makai	Malachia	Maliq	Maneesh
Madreik	Mahindra	Makail	Malachiah	Malique *(0.01)*	Maneet
Madrid	Mahir	Makalani	Malachy	Malitt	Manelic
Madsen	Mahit	Makale	Malaci	Maljhum	Manene
Maduke	Mahlan Jr	Makana	Malaehi	Malka	Manesh
Maea	Mahler	Makani	Malak	Malkiat	Manfred *(0.01)*
Maen	Mahliek	Makarios	Malakai *(0.01)*	Malkiel	Manfret
Maeson	Mahlik	Makay	Malake	Malkolm	Mang
Maetron	Mahlon *(0.01)*	Makeba	Malaki	Malkom	Mango
Mafi	Mahmmoud	Makeen	Malan	Malksa	Manh
Magadian	Mahmood	Makei	Malaquias	Malkum	Mani
Magan	Mahmoud *(0.02)*	Makeldrik	Malay	Mallek	Manicko
Magas	Mahmud	Makell	Malcalm	Mallik	Maniferd
Magaye	Mahmuod	Makena	Malclom	Mallory	Manik
Magdaleno	Mahmut	Makenna	Malcohm	Malo Tumau	Maninder *(0.01)*
Magdi	Mahogany	Makennah	Malcolm *(0.43)*	Malon	Maninderdeep
Magdiel	Mahom	Makennen	Malcom *(0.04)*	Malone	Maninderjit
Maged	Mahomy	Makensie	Malcom-Jamal	Malonté	Maninderpal
Magen	Mahoney	Makenson	Malcomb	Malshawn	Manindurjit
Mager	Mahonri	Makenzie *(0.01)*	Malcome	Malvick	Maninita
Maghandi	Mahren	Makenzy	Malcomn	Malvin	Manish
Magic	Mahrke	Makeson	Malcon	Malwood	Manja
Magid	Mahrubius	Makewin	Male *(0.01)*	Malyk	Manjeet
Magno	Mahtoska	Makez	Maleak	Malykai	Manjinder
Magnum	Mahyak	Makhale	Maleaque	Malykia	Manjit
Magnus *(0.01)*	Mahyar	Makhil	Maleek *(0.01)*	Malyq	Manjot *(0.01)*
Magquise	Maichel	Maki	Maleel	Malyra	Manjoth
Maguel	Maikel	Makia	Maleik	Malyyk	Manjyot
Magwes	Mailahn	Makibren	Malek *(0.02)*	Malyzsha	Mankanwar
Mahad *(0.01)*	Maile	Makiesa	Maleka	Mamadou	Mankaran
Mahadis	Mailik	Makil	Maleke	Mamquel	Mankarn
Mahamad	Maimonides	Makin	Maleno	Man	Mankerat
Mahamed	Mainor	Makinley	Maleq	Man-Ho	Manley
Mahamed Ali	Maiontay	Makis	Malerie	Man-Hong	Manmeet

Manmohan	Manvir (0.02)	Marc Etienne (0.01)	Marcelo (0.05)	Marcquel	Marianne
Manning	Manwinder	Marc Eugene	Marcelous	Marcquellis	Mariano (0.05)
Manntavious	Many	Marc Olivier (0.10)	Marcelouse	Marcques	Maric
Mannual	Manyale	Marc Paul	Marcelus	Marcquet	Marice
Mannute	Manyari	Marc Ulysses	Marceon	Marcquis	Marichail
Manny (0.01)	Manza	Marc'quail	Marcese	Marcquise	Marichal
Manny-Gene	Manzel	Marc-Alexandre	Marcetti	Marcravio	Maricio
Manoach	Maor	Marc-Andre (0.03)	March	Marcredus	Marico
Manoah	Maquan	Marc-Andree	Marchael	Marcthespis	Maricus
Manoj	Maquel	Marc-Anthony	Marchaun	Marcues	Marie
Manojan	Maquille	Marc-Antoine (0.03)	Marchavis	Marcuis	Marielle
Manolo	Mar	Marc-Antony	Marche	Marcus (2.12)	Marieo
Manpal	Mar Kio	Marc-Daniel	Marchell	Marcus Gavin	Marijan
Manpreet (0.01)	Mar Quese	Marc-Eli	Marchello	Marcus Jama	Marilynn
Manprit	Mar'chay	Marc-Eric	Marchetti	Marcus Jeffrey	Marin
Manquarvious	Mar'chris	Marc-Etienne	Marchie	Marcus Jr	Marina
Manraj (0.01)	Mar'darius	Marc-Henry	Marchus	Marcus-Allen	Mariner
Manrajpal	Mar'keal	Marc-Olivier (0.01)	Marcial (0.01)	Marcus-Anthony	Marino (0.01)
Manreet	Mar'kee	Marc-Paul	Marcie	Marcus-Antonio	Marinos
Manrik	Mar'kees	Marc-Quail	Marciel	Marcus-Lemorris	Marinterio
Manriques	Mar'keith	Marcal	Marcielo	Marcus-Shayne	Marinus
Manrit	Mar'kel	Marcal Deon	Marcilino	Marcuss	Mario (1.13)
Manroop	Mar'kesie	Marcanthony (0.01)	Marcillo	Marcuus	Mario Antony
Mansa	Mar'kess	Marcantonio	Marcin (0.01)	Marcux	Mario Ferone
Mansfield	Mar'kheyvian	Marcar	Marcio	Mard	Marioadel
Mansford	Mar'kial	Marcarious	Marcion	Mardarius	Marioel
Mansini	Mar'kway	Marcarius	Marcius	Mardarreius	Marion (0.02)
Manson	Mar'kyes	Marcas	Marck	Marday'shajuan	Marion Fitz
Mansoor	Mar'quane	Marcaus	Marck-Andrew	Mardell	Marion Lyle
Mansour	Mar'quell	Marcco	Marckendy	Mardie	Marion'
Mansur	Mar'quez	Marcdavid	Marckenley	Mardig	Marionte
Mantaj	Mar'quincio	Marcea	Marckenson	Mardio	Marious
Mantarius	Mar'quis	Marcearrow	Marckenzie	Mardo	Mariquis
Manteco	Mar'quise	Marcei	Marckenzy	Mardoche	Maris
Mantej	Mar'shaun	Marceis	Marckese	Mardrecus	Marisela
Manthan	Mar'tavis	Marcel (0.15)	Marckinson	Mardrel	Marish
Mantonio	Mar'tell	Marcel Najee	Marcko	Mardy	Marissa
Manu	Mar-Ki	Marceleno	Marckos	Mareese	Marius (0.01)
Manual	Mar-Quan	Marcelias	Marckus	Marek (0.03)	Mariusz
Manuale	Mar-Sean	Marceliers	Marclay	Marel	Marjan
Manucheher	Marair	Marcelin	Marco (0.89)	Marelluis	Marjavius
Manuel (1.16)	Marando	Marcelino (0.05)	Marco Antonio	Maren	Marjolaine
Manuel Antonio	Marash	Marcelis	Marco Jr.	Mareo	Mark (3.12)
Manuel De Jesus	Marben	Marcelius	Marco Polo	Mareon	Mark Alexander
Manuel Jamar	Marc (0.61)	Marcell (0.03)	Marco Vito	Margaret	Mark Alexian
Manuel Julius	Marc Ace	Marcellas	Marco-Louie	Margarito (0.02)	Mark Anthony (0.01)
Manuel-Alfredo	Marc Alexandr (0.02)	Marcelle	Marcoantonio (0.03)	Margrell	Mark Christian
Manuelle	Marc Allen	Marcellino	Marcoli	Margues	Mark Douglas
Manus	Marc Andre (0.21)	Marcellis (0.01)	Marconi	Marguis	Mark II
Manvar	Marc Anthony	Marcello (0.03)	Marcor	Margus	Mark James
Manveer (0.01)	Marc Antoine (0.31)	Marcellous (0.01)	Marcorino	Maria	Mark Lawrence
Manveet	Marc Christian	Marcellus (0.04)	Marcos (0.51)	Mariah	Mark'el
Manvel			Marcous	Marial	Mark-Anthony
Manvinder			Marcquan	Mariam	Mark-Donovan
Manvinderjit				Marian	

Mark-Jr.	Markennon	Markos *(0.01)*	Marqail	Marqueal	Marquion
Mark-Krzysztof	Markentz	Markous	Marqauvis	Marqueavious	Marquios
Mark-Lange	Markenys	Markqes	Marqavia	Marquece	Marquirius
Mark-William	Markenzie	Markquan	Marqavious	Marquee	Marquirus
Markael	Markenzy	Markque	Marqavius	Marquees	Marquis *(0.38)*
Markahl	Markeon	Markquel	Marqeeye	Marquel *(0.04)*	Marquis'
Markail	Markerius	Markques	Marqeicusa	Marquelis	Marquise *(0.21)*
Markal	Markes	Markquese	Marqel	Marquell *(0.02)*	Marquisé
Markalan	Markese *(0.02)*	Markquil	Marqese	Marquelle	Marquisee
Markale	Markesé	Markquis	Marqesse	Marquellis	Marquish
Markanthony	Markess	Markquise	Marqevis	Marquelltrévon	Marquiss
(0.02)	Markesse	Markrecus	Marqez	Marquentin	Marquist
Markas	Markest	Markrin	Marqeze	Marquerious	Marquithe
Markavius	Markethe	Markson	Marqhuan	Marques *(0.07)*	Marquiues
Markcus	Markeveous	Marktavious	Marqi	Marquese *(0.02)*	Marquiveon
Marke	Markevian	Markton	Marqise	Marquese Tr	Marquives
Markéce	Markevion	Markuieast	Marqua	Marquesé	Marquivias
Markél	Markevious	Markuis	Marqua'veous	Marqueslin	Marquivis
Markea'l	Markevis	Markuisten	Marquadius	Marquess	Marquiz
Markeal	Markevius	Markus *(0.16)*	Marquai	Marquesse	Marquize
Markeas	Markevus	Markus Christian	Marquaice	Marquest	Marqukis
Markease	Markey	Markvirgil	Marquail	Marquet	Marqule
Markeast	Markeyce	Marky	Marquaise	Marquett	Marqulies
Markeavous	Markeyes	Markyee	Marqual	Marquette *(0.01)*	Marquon *(0.01)*
Markece	Markeys	Markyle	Marquall	Marquevas	Marquonsa
Markedron	Markeyse	Markys	Marqualyn	Marquevious	Marquos
Markee	Markez *(0.01)*	Marl	Marquan *(0.02)*	Marquevius	Marqus *(0.01)*
Markeeas	Markeze	Marlan	Marquane	Marquevus	Marquse
Markeece	Markham	Marland	Marquante	Marquez *(0.06)*	Marqutte
Markeem	Marki	Marlek	Marquantis	Marquez'	Marquvious
Markeen	Markian	Marlen	Marquaries	Marqueze	Marquwan
Markeeon	Markice	Marley *(0.02)*	Marquarius	Marqui	Marquyse
Markees	Markie	Marlin *(0.04)*	Marquaruis	Marqui S	Marquze
Markeese	Markiem	Marliss	Marquas	Marqui'	Marqwan
Markei	Markiese	Marlo *(0.01)*	Marquaveius	Marqui's	Marqwel
Markeice	Markiesé	Marlom	Marquaves	Marquian	Marqwell
Markeil	Markiest	Marlon *(0.20)*	Marquavian	Marquiaz	Marqwez
Markeis	Markime	Marlone	Marquavias	Marquiaze	Marqwon
Markeise	Markion	Marlos	Marquavice	Marquice *(0.02)*	Marqwyn
Markeith *(0.02)*	Markirkis	Marlow *(0.01)*	Marquavieous	Marquie	Marqys
Markeithdri	Markis *(0.01)*	Marlowa	Marquavieus	Marquiece	Marréll
Markeithon	Markise	Marlowe	Marquavion	Marquiel	Marrece
Markeivius	Markiss	Marly	Marquavious	Marquies *(0.01)*	Marrell
Markel *(0.07)*	Markist	Marlyn	*(0.01)*	Marquiez	Marrhew
Markelius	Markistan	Marnesha	Marquavis	Marquil	Marrick
Markell *(0.06)*	Markivis	Marnier	Marquavius *(0.01)*	Marquiles	Marrico
Markelle	Markku	Marno	Marquavon	Marquill	Marrino
Markelo	Markkus	Maro	Marquay	Marquille	Marrio
Markelor	Markle	Marof	Marquaze	Marquilleon	Marrion
Markenan	Marklester	Marokus	Marquazionne	Marquillus	Marrkus
Markendall	Markley	Maroof	Marquces	Marquin	Marroquin
Markendas	Marklin	Marouf	Marque *(0.01)*	Marquincio	Marsai
Markendel	Marklow	Marq	Marque L	Marquinn	Marsaint
Markene	Marko *(0.04)*	Marq'ue	Marquél	Marquinton	Marsalino
Markenley	Markolvy	Marq-Twoine	Marqués	Marquinyelle	Marsalis *(0.01)*

Marsalius	Martellos	Martravius	Mary	Maszaba	Mathulan
Marsallis	Martellus	Martre	Maryan	Mat	Mathurhaen
Marsden	Marten	Martréail	Marzell	Matan	Mathushan
Marsean	Martenez	Martrévian	Marzet	Matao	Mathushanan
Marselino	Martenis	Martrévis	Marzette	Matas	Mathyis
Marsellis	Marterio	Martrel	Marzhon	Matayo	Mati'as
Marsellius	Marterious	Martrell (0.01)	Masaaki	Mate	Matia
Marsellus	Marterrius	Martrelle	Masaalih	Mateen	Matial
Marsh	Martes	Martreveus	Masafumi	Matei	Matias (0.02)
Marshae	Martese (0.01)	Martrevez	Masaharu	Mateius	Matiel
Marshaine	Marteus	Martrey	Masahiro	Matej	Matieu
Marshal (0.04)	Marteusz	Martrez	Masai	Matekitonga	Matija
Marshall (0.36)	Martevian	Martti	Masakala	Mateo (0.04)	Matin
Marshall Calvin	Martevias	Marttin	Masaki	Materion	Matison
Marshaun (0.01)	Martevious	Martwan	Masami	Materna	Matisse
Marshauwn	Marteyus	Martwane	Masamusa	Mateus	Matisyahu
Marshaw	Martez (0.04)	Martwon	Masan	Mateusz (0.02)	Matiwos
Marshawn (0.03)	Marteze	Marty (0.05)	Masao	Matewas	Matiza
Marshay	Marthony	Martyce	Masato	Matey	Matravius
Marshean	Marti	Martyn (0.01)	Masauo	Mateya	Matrevian
Marsheid	Marti'n	Martynas	Masaya	Math=thew	Matriez
Marsheylyn	Martial	Marucs	Masayasu	Matheau	Matrix
Marshon (0.01)	Martian	Maruice	Masayoshi	Mathen	Mats
Marshood	Martice (0.01)	Marun	Masayuki	Mathepan	Matsen
Marshun	Martie	Marv	Mascud	Matherin	Matson
Marston	Martiece	Marvale	Maseeh	Matheson	Matt (0.04)
Marsus	Martiese	Marvante	Masellious	Matheu	Mattay
Martae	Martiez	Marvcus	Masen	Matheus	Mattays
Martail	Martimion	Marveal	Mashad	Mathew (0.87)	Matteen
Martain	Martimus	Marvel (0.01)	Mashal	Mathew Dylan	Matteo (0.03)
Martaiveus	Martin (1.31)	Marvell (0.01)	Mashama	Mathew John	Matteson
Martaize	Martin De Jesus	Marvelous	Mashaud	Jose	Mattew (0.01)
Martan	Martin Jericho	Marven	Mashaun	Mathew Ray	Mattews
Martarvious	Martin John	Marvens	Mashawn	Mathew-	Mattha
Martatious	Martina	Marves	Mashile	Alexander	Matthaei
Martaveon	Martine	Marvette	Mashiya	Mathew-Chi	Matthaeus
Martavian	Martineau	Marvey'o	Mashucci	Mathew-Minh	Matthan
Martavious (0.01)	Martines	Marviaun	Masiaih	Mathews	Matthaus
Martavis	Martinez (0.01)	Marvie	Masios	Mathewtodd	Matthen
Martavius (0.01)	Martinique	Marvin (0.41)	Masiyah	Matheww	Mattheos
Martavous	Martino (0.01)	Marvin Joseph	Maskwa	Mathhon	Matthes
Martay	Martinous	Marvins	Maslin	Mathias (0.05)	Mattheu (0.01)
Martaz	Martinque	Marvion	Maso Ta Yepsako	Mathias-	Mattheus
Martaze	Martinus	Marvis	Mason (1.38)	Alexander	Matthew (15.58)
Marte	Martious	Marvn	Mason Lafayette	Mathiela	Matthew A.
Martéz	Martique	Marvon	Massey	Mathieli	Matthew Angelo
Martée	Martirs	Marvonte	Massimiliano	Mathieu (0.72)	Matthew Edlar
Marteese	Martise	Marvus	Massimo (0.02)	Mathieux	Matthew III
Martein	Martize	Marvyn	Masson	Mathiew	Matthew Jr
Marteko	Marton	Marvyns	Massoud	Mathis (0.01)	Matthew Mark
Martel (0.02)	Martonio	Marwan (0.01)	Masteal	Mathison	Matthew
Martele	Martopi	Marwin	Master	Mathius	Tmarcus
Martelius	Martraé	Marwo	Masumi	Mathoni	Matthew Tyler
Martell (0.03)	Martravian	Marwuis	Masun	Maththew	Matthew-Cole
Martellis	Martravious	Marxey	Masyn	Mathue	Matthew-David

Matthew-Jan	Maurie	Maximiliam	Mayshaunt	Mcdaniel	Mckiel
Matthew-Michael	Mauriece	Maximilian *(0.13)*	Mayson *(0.01)*	Mcdonnell	Mckinely
Matthew-Mina	Maurilio *(0.01)*	Maximiliano	Mayur	Mcegan	Mckinley *(0.04)*
Matthew-Yat	Maurin	(0.06)	Mayuran	Mcgabraels	Mckinnley
Matthews	Maurion	Maximilien *(0.01)*	Mayushaan	Mcgarrett	Mckinnon
Matthgew	Maurios	Maximillan	Maywand	Mcgee	Mckinzie
Matthias *(0.04)*	Mauriq	Maximillano	Mazahni	Mcgill	Mcklayne
Matthieu *(0.05)*	Maurisio	Maximilliam	Mazarius	Mcgiver	Mckoy
Matthieu-Marc	Maurius	Maximillian *(0.07)*	Mazatl	Mcgowan	Mckuen
Matthieus	Maurizio *(0.01)*	Maximillien	Mazdak	Mcgraw	Mckuhla
Matthiew	Maurkice	Maximillion	Mazen	Mcgregor	Mcky
Matthu	Mauro *(0.03)*	Maximino *(0.01)*	Mazhar	Mcgrew	Mckylin
Matthuew	Maurqise	Maximo *(0.02)*	Mazi	Mcguire	Mclain
Matthwe	Maurrie	Maxinder	Mazin	Mcguyre	Mclane
Matthys	Maurtavius	Maxine	Mazzi	Mcguyver	Mclaren
Matti	Maurtice	Maxis	Mazziah	Mchale	Mclean
Mattia	Maury	Maxmilian	Mazzin	Mcherrey	Mcleod
Mattias *(0.01)*	Mavdeep	Maxmillian	Mbangira	Mcilwain	Mcmillan
Mattieu	Maverick *(0.07)*	Maxo	Mbimba-Esli	Mcintosh	Mcmillian
Mattingly	Maverik	Maxsim	Mc	Mcisaac	Mcneal
Mattison *(0.01)*	Maveryke	Maxson	Mc Kabe	Mcivor	Mcneil
Mattnew	Mavis	Maxston	Mc Kenna	Mckade *(0.01)*	Mcnevin
Mattrell	Mavkenzie	Maxten	Mc Kenzie	Mckae	Mcniel
Mattrhew	Mavric	Maxton	Mcalister	Mckai	Mcpherson
Mattrick	Mavrick	Maxum	Mcaliston	Mckain	Mcquade
Mattson	Mawaldi	Maxwel	Mcariel	Mckale	Mcquinn
Mattwo	Mawleed	Maxwell *(0.79)*	Mcarthur	Mckalyn	Mcreynolds
Matty	Mawuega	Maxwell	Mccabe	Mckay *(0.06)*	Mcspadden
Matuesz	Mawuko	Alexanda	Mccade	Mckayden	Mcthanial
Matusala	Mawunya	Maxx *(0.02)*	Mccaffrey	Mckaydyn	Md.hamidul
Matyas	Mawunyo	Maxximillian	Michael	Mckayla	Me Kota
Mau	Max *(0.70)*	Maxximillion	Mccain	Mckeith	Médine
Mauarice	Max David	Maxxwell	Mccall	Mckel	Mégail
Maucerio	Max Frederick	Maxyme *(0.01)*	Mccallum	Mckell	Méquavious
Mauhdi	Max Phisk	Maxyon	Mccalob	Mckellar	Méquell
Maulana	Maxali	May	Mccamey	Mckenan	Méshawn
Maulik	Maxam	Maya	Mccarthy	Mckencie	Mead
Maunltry	Maxamealian	Mayan	Mccartney	Mckendry	Meade
Maunttearreis	Maxamilian	Mayande	Mccarty	Mckendy	Meaghan
Mauquarius	Maxamillian	Mayank	Mccauley	Mckenize	Meaon
Mauquon	Maxamillion	Mayco	Mccenzie	Mckenley	Mecca
Mauran	Maxamillium	Mayer	Mcclain	Mckenly	Mechech
Mauray	Maxamos	Mayhew	Mcclaran	Mckenna *(0.01)*	Mechel
Maurece	Maxel	Mayid	Mcclean	Mckennan	Mechell
Maurelle	Maxem	Mayim	Mcclellan	Mckennen	Mechul
Maurgan	Maxence *(0.01)*	Maylon	Mcclintock	Mckennley	Meckeal
Mauriao	Maxene	Maylove	Mccomb	Mckennon	Meco
Mauriccio	Maxfield *(0.01)*	Maynald	Mcconnell	Mckenny	Medardo
Maurice *(0.37)*	Maxie	Maynard	Mccord	Mckennzie	Mederic *(0.01)*
Mauriceo	Maxililian	Mayne	Mccormick	Mckensie	Medgar
Mauriceo'	Maxillian	Maynor *(0.01)*	Mccoy *(0.01)*	Mckenson	Medhane
Mauricio *(0.19)*	Maxim *(0.09)*	Mayowa David	Mccoya	Mckenzi	Medwin
Mauricio'	Maxime *(0.86)*	Mayrol	Mccrae	Mckenzie *(0.06)*	Meechael
Maurico	Maximiano	Maysa	Mccray	Mckenzy	Meeko
Mauricus	Maximili	Maysara	Mccully	Mckeyra	Meenan

Meenhaj	Mekyle	Melvin-Gray	Merick	Meyikie	Michael Bra
Meeran	Mel	Melvis	Merico	Meynard	Michael
Meeshak	Mel'vontae	Melvon	Merik	Mezar	Christopher
Meeuwis	Melad	Melvontae	Merilang	Mezhar	Michael Dam
Megael	Melad Alexander	Melvonte	Merit	Mezmure	Michael Daniel
Megal	Melak	Melvyn	Merle *(0.01)*	Mfoniso	Michael Ger
Megale	Melanie	Melward	Merlin *(0.01)*	Mgizi	Michael Henry
Megan *(0.01)*	Melbi	Memar	Merlin Wolfgang	Mhar	Michael Hope
Megerssa	Melcasadek	Membrish	Merlinous	Mhommed	Michael Isiah
Megeulle	Melchi	Memet	Merlyn	Mhyhm	Michael James
Megh	Melchisedec	Mena	Meron	Mi Quan	Michael Joseph
Megha	Melchisedek	Menachem *(0.02)*	Merquise	Mi'jon	Michael Jr
Meghan	Melchor *(0.01)*	Menachen	Merrell	Mi'kael	Michael Lucian
Mehad	Melcom	Menageia	Merric	Mi'keal	Michael Myrick
Meharkaviraj	Meldevon	Menard	Merrick *(0.02)*	Mi'keith	Michael Patrick
Mehde	Meldrick	Menasha	Merril	Mi'kel	Michael Quintra
Mehdi *(0.01)*	Melecio	Menashe	Merrill *(0.01)*	Mi'quel	Michael Thomas
Meherab	Meleeke	Mencari	Merritt *(0.01)*	Mi'quon	Michael William
Mehmed	Meleike	Mencius	Mert	Mi-Quan	Michael-Allen
Mehmer	Melek	Mendel	Merthyr	Miachel	Michael-Anthony
Mehmet *(0.01)*	Meleki	Mendez	Mervin *(0.02)*	Miami	Michael-Brian
Mehmood	Melenio	Mendoza	Mervin Josh	Mian	Michael-Bryan
Mehran	Melesio	Menelaos	Mervins	Miante	Michael-Dean
Mehranullah	Melet	Menelik	Mervyn	Miatece	Michael-Edward
Mehron	Meliance	Menes	Mervyon	Miazé	Michael-Eston
Mehul	Melic	Menfes	Merwin	Mibelson	Michael-George
Meighen	Meliek	Meng *(0.01)*	Merwyn	Mic	Michael-Jack
Meih	Melik	Mengesha	Meryk	Mic Keal	Michael-James
Meiko	Meliksah	Menhefen	Meryland	Mic Trevion	Michael-Jay
Meileik	Melique	Menico	Mesa	Mic'ko	Michael-John
Meir *(0.01)*	Melissa	Menno	Meschac	Mica	Michael-Jon
Meisen	Meliton	Menok	Mesfin	Micadam	Michael-Joseph
Meisha	Meljefvic	Menson	Mesgana	Micade	Michael-Justice
Meishan	Mell	Mentréz	Meshach *(0.01)*	Micael *(0.01)*	Michael-Leo
Meiyako	Mellad	Menzell	Meshal	Micaeleb	Michael-Louis
Mekael	Melnor	Meonte	Meshary	Micah *(0.53)*	Michael-Thomas
Mekalon	Melohn	Meonté	Meshawn	Micah-Joel	Michael-Vinh
Mekeal	Meloy	Meqhuan	Meshon	Micah-Vincent	Michaela
Mekeil	Melphord	Meqontae	Mesiah	Micahel	Michaeladriano
Mekel	Melquan	Meraj	Messejah	Micaiah *(0.01)*	Michaelalfred
Mekey	Melquavius	Merari	Messiah	Micajah	Michaelangel
Mekhai	Melquian	Merasha	Mesud	Mical	*(0.01)*
Mekhail	Melquicedec	Meraz	Meteya	Mical-Ivan	Michaelantho
Mekhale	Melquin	Merced	Methew	Micalan	*(0.01)*
Mekhi	Melquise	Mercedese	Methusaan	Micale	Michaele
Mekiah	Melquisedec	Mercelles	Metin	Miceale	Michaelon
Mekilo	Melquon	Mercer	Metkel	Micha	Michaelsonny
Mekiye	Melrenso	Mercurio	Metrelle	Michae;	Michaelthomas
Mekko	Melroy	Mercury	Metro	Michaeal	Michah
Meklane	Melton	Mercusol	Metta	Michaek	Michaiah
Meklo	Melville	Mercy-Dez	Mevontre	Michael *(19.47)*	Michak
Meko	Melvin *(0.27)*	Meredith	Mewan	Michael Ant	Michal *(0.04)*
Mekonen	Melvin Alexander	Merek	Meyale	Michael Antho	Michale *(0.01)*
Mekquan	Melvin Cheyenne	Meren	Meyer	Michael Atilio	Michall
Mekuez	Melvin Jr	Meric	Meyhad	Michael Bao	Michau

Michaul	Mickey (0.05)	Mijuelangel	Mikit	Milon	Miran
Michayal	Mickeyl	Mika	Mikita	Milorad	Miranda
Michea	Mickhale	Mikaeel	Mikito	Milos	Mirco
Micheail	Micki	Mikael (0.12)	Mikiyale	Milos-Sean	Mircuice
Micheal (0.57)	Mickie	Mikael-Paul	Mikka	Milosh	Mirek
Micheal David	Mickim	Mikaele	Mikkel (0.01)	Milous	Miresh
Micheal-Anthony	Micklo	Mikah (0.01)	Mikki	Milovan	Miriam
Michealan	Micko	Mikahl	Mikko (0.01)	Milt	Mirkana
Michee	Mickolas	Mikaielh	Miklo	Milthon	Mirko
Micheel	Micky	Mikail (0.01)	Miklos	Miltiades	Miron
Micheil	Mickyle	Mikal (0.04)	Miko	Milton (0.12)	Miroslaw
Michel (0.10)	Miclain	Mikalani	Mikol	Min (0.01)	Mirsaad
Michel-Andre	Miclaude	Mikale	Mikolai	Min-Ho	Mirsad
Michel-Olivier	Micmillan	Mikalyn	Mikolaj	Mina	Mirza
Michelangelo	Mico	Mikanor	Mikos	Mince	Misae
Michele (0.01)	Micole	Mikanzis	Mikquel	Mindaugas	Misael (0.07)
Michell	Micquavious	Mikaylo	Mikray	Mine	Misbah
Michelle	Micqueel	Mike (0.14)	Mikul	Mineo	Mischa
Michelline	Micquel	Mikékale	Mikyael	Minesh	Mischael
Michello	Micquell	Mike-Dylan	Mikyle	Ming	Mischawn
Michelo	Micrin	Mikeael	Mila	Minge	Misha (0.01)
Michelson	Mictavius	Mikeal (0.01)	Milaan	Mingo	Mishad
Michener	Micthanyo	Mikeice	Milad	Minh (0.03)	Mishael
Michiah	Mid	Mikel (0.06)	Milagro	Minh-Duc	Mishatona
Michial	Midas	Mikele	Milan (0.03)	Minh-Nam	Mishawn
Michiel	Middleton	Mikell (0.01)	Milandeep	Minh-Tri	Mishayla
Michigan	Midian	Mikelle	Milando	Minh-Truong	Mishko
Michisuke	Mieczyslaw	Mikelous	Milanjot	Minh-Vien	Mishon
Michl	Miengun	Mikelund	Milano	Minha	Mishquazewan
Michmyel	Mier	Miken	Milap	Minhaz	Mishuan
Michol	Miercoles	Mikenson	Milas	Minhquang	Mishwar
Micholas	Migal	Mikenzie	Milder	Minhyuk	Misike
Michon	Migeal	Mikeonta	Mile	Minkyu	Miso
Michqual	Migel (0.01)	Mikequan	Mileak	Minor	Missael (0.01)
Michuel	Migelanjel	Mikese	Mileek	Minoru	Mister (0.01)
Michzael	Migueal	Mikesh	Milen	Mintha	Mistic
Miciah	Miguel (1.99)	Mikeson	Milenko	Minthan	Mistral
Miciyah	Miguel Angel	Miketavious	Miles (0.41)	Minwoo	Misty
Mick (0.01)	Miguel Isagani	Miketerrio	Miles Damien	Miongon-Tay	Mital
Mick-Bonscott	Miguel-José	Mikeven	Miles Edward	Miquail	Mitavius
Mickael (0.08)	Miguelangel (0.06)	Mikevious	Mileszell	Miquale	Mitch (0.03)
Mickaele	Miguelito	Mikey (0.01)	Milford	Miquan	Mitchael
Mickaila	Miguerson	Mikhael (0.01)	Miligan	Miquavis	Mitchal
Mickaiyel	Miguil	Mikhail (0.03)	Milik	Miquayle	Mitchall
Mickal	Mihai	Mikhale	Milique	Mique L	Mitcheal
Mickale	Mihailo	Mikhall	Milka	Miqueal	Mitchel (0.20)
Mickayle	Mihajlo	Mikhel	Milko	Miqueas	Mitcheli
Mickeal	Mihalis	Mikhelvin	Millad	Miquel (0.01)	Mitchell (2.65)
Mickel (0.01)	Mihaly	Mikia	Millar	Miquon	Mitchell Austin
Mickell	Mihcael	Mikiail	Millard	Mir	Mitchell Derric
Mickelson	Mihir	Mikias	Milledge	Mira	Mitchell-Lee
Mickenson	Miika	Mikie	Miller (0.01)	Miracle (0.01)	Mitchell-Mackenz
Mickenze	Mija	Mikieal	Millo	Mirahmad	Mitchelldenis
Mickenzie	Mijael	Mikil	Mills	Miraj	Mitchelle
Mickenzy	Mijel	Mikinley	Milo (0.03)	Miralem	Mitchem

Mitchil
Mitchum
Mitesh
Mithcell
Mithin
Mithoojan
Mithujon
Mithun
Mithuran
Mithyran
Mitionne
Mitra
Mitran
Mitrell
Mitreon
Mitsuyoshi
Mittony
Mitul
Miyagi
Miyesh
Mizael *(0.01)*
Mizani
Mizel
Mizell
Miztli
Mizuki
Mj
Mjamo
Mnan
Mo-Sha
Moaad
Moab
Moad
Moaid
Moana
Moargen
Moataz Bellah
Moawiah
Moayed
Mobahil
Mobeen
Mobin
Mobley
Mochael
Moctavian
Moctezuma
Modesto *(0.01)*
Moeen
Moein
Moesaeah
Moez
Mofeed
Mogen
Mohak
Mohamad *(0.06)*

Mohamad-Ali
Mohamad-
   Hamon
Mohamd
Mohamed *(0.18)*
Mohamed Ali
Mohamed-
   Ameen
Mohamed-Hussin
Mohamedsadiq
Mohamedsalah
Mohameed
Mohammad *(0.17)*
Mohammad
   Hussei
Mohammad
   Mustaf
Mohammed *(0.16)*
Mohammed
   Kareem
Mohammed-Ali
Mohammed-
   Amin
Mohammed-
   Naafe
Mohammed-Saad
Mohammmed
Mohammud
Mohamoud
Mohamud
Mohan
Mohanad
Mohannad
Mohathir
Mohdm
Mohenoa
Mohib
Mohideen
Mohit *(0.01)*
Mohjevanjeet
Mohmad
Mohmed
Mohmmad
   Tawfeeq
Mohmoud
Mohnish
Mohomad
Mohsen
Mohsin
Mohummed
Moices
Moise *(0.01)*
Moises *(0.31)*
Moises Antoni
Moises Daniel

Moishe
Moja Wya
Mojahed
Mojave Peyote
Mojeed
Mok-Sun
Mokece
Mokell
Mokhtar
Moktar
Molefe
Molefi
Molik
Moliki
Molly
Molson
Momcilo
Momen
Momin
Mon'ray
Mon'trae
Monarch
Monchen
Monchez
Moncure
Mondale
Mondarious
Mondarius
Mondavian
Mondavion
Monday
Mondeyl
Mondrago
Mondre
Mondrea
Mondreko
Mondrekus
Mondrell
Mondrevious
Mondricus
Mondy
Monel
Monele
Moner
Mong Ye Chun
Mongzong
Moni
Monica
Monico
Moniel
Monier
Moniko
Monil
Moninder
Moninderpal

Monir
Monish
Monit
Monix
Monjarius
Monjobuis
Monnavuis
Monorail
Monphithack
Monqavious
Monquale
Monquantis
Monquavious
Monquayvious
Monque
Monquel
Monquell
Monquez
Monquiariou
Monroe *(0.01)*
Monshadrik
Monsoor
Mont
Mont'ae
Monta
Montae
Montaé
Montagius
Montagne
Montague
Montaius
Montana *(0.07)*
Montaniel
Montanique
Montanna
Montario
Montarius
Montas
Montate
Montaurius
Montavier
Montavion
Montavious *(0.02)*
Montavis
Montavius *(0.01)*
Montavous
Montay
Montayvious
Montaze
Montchello
Monte *(0.04)*
Monte Lee
Monté
Montévius
Montea

Monteco
Montee
Montego
Montegomery
Monteice
Monteigaus
Montel *(0.05)*
Montele
Montell *(0.01)*
Montelle
Montellomarr
Montellous
Montelrius
Montenegro
Monteria
Monterial
Monterio *(0.01)*
Monterious
Monterius
Monterrell
Monterreo
Monterrious
Monterris
Monterrius
Monterro
Montese
Montevious
Montez *(0.03)*
Montez'
Montezz
Montford
Montgomery
   (0.02)
Monti
Montico
Montie
Montivenus
Montoi
Montoris
Montoya
Montra
Montrae
Montrail
Montral
Montrale
Montralius
Montravious
Montravius *(0.01)*
Montray
Montrayl
Montraz
Montre
Montré
Montrél
Montreal *(0.01)*

Montreall
Montreizes
Montrel *(0.01)*
Montrelas
Montrele
Montrell *(0.04)*
Montrelle
Montres
Montrese
Montrevious
Montrevius
Montrey
Montrez *(0.01)*
Montrez'
Montreze
Montrezl
Montrial
Montrice
Montrieze
Montrio
Montrose
Monty *(0.02)*
Montyce
Monuell
Monyai
Monye
Monyea
Monzaz
Monzel
Monzell
Moody
Moon
Mooneer
Moonyose Neeko
Moore
Mooresse
Mooretalon
Moosa
Mooseop
Mor
Mor'shai
Morad
Morale
Moras
Mordachai
Mordechai *(0.01)*
Mordie
Morelle
Morelli
Morelson
Moreno
Morentie
Morey
Morgan *(0.59)*
Morgen *(0.01)*

Morghan	Mosses	Mubarak	Mulham	Muschy	Mychire
Morgin	Mossy	Mubashar	Mulik	Muse	Mycial
Morgon	Mostafa	Mubasher	Mulland	Mushaun	Myckel
Morgunn	Mostapha	Mubashir	Mullen	Musheer	Myeka
Morgwn	Mostfa	Mubin	Mumin	Mushfiq	Myelle
Morgyn	Motasem	Mucahit	Mumtaaz	Mushtak	Myels
Mori	Motekiai	Muchell	Munaf	Mushtaq	Myengun
Moriael	Motez	Mudasar	Munashe	Musie	Myer
Moriah	Moti	Mudassher	Munassar	Muslim	Myers
Moriel	Motoharu	Mudassir	Munasser	Musliu	Myeterius
Morihiro	Mott	Mudzimu	Mundarius	Mussa	Myhan
Moris	Mouad	Muefaqu	Mundteah	Mussab	Myhre
Moritz	Moubin	Muenchow	Muneeb	Musse	Myka
Morley	Mouchettee	Muerrick	Muneer	Mustaf	Mykael
Mornas	Moufadhil	Mufasa	Munehiro	Mustafa *(0.05)*	Mykah
Morning	Mouhamad	Mugeesh	Muneshwer	Mustafa Bur	Mykail
Moroni	Mouhamadou	Mugunthan	Munib	Mustafaa	Mykal *(0.01)*
Moronkie	Mouhamed *(0.01)*	Muhaimen	Munir	Mustafe	Mykari
Morquise	Mouhammed	Muhaimin	Munish	Mustaffa	Mykeem
Morrafoum	Mouhiodine	Muhamad	Munryan	Mustafo	Mykeeno
Morrel	Moultrie	Muhamed	Munsir	Mustang	Mykel *(0.03)*
Morrell	Moumin	Muhamedali	Munyaradzi	Mustapha *(0.01)*	Mykele
Morrese	Mounear	Muhammad *(0.06)*	Muoarrab	Mustapha-Shah	Mykell
Morrie	Mounir	Muhammad	Mupaarag	Mustoffa	Mykelti
Morris *(0.04)*	Mountaga	Daniel	Muqaddar	Mustofo	Mykeon
Morrise	Mountavius	Muhammad	Muqari	Musumba	Mykerson
Morrison	Mourad	Hanif	Muqqz	Mutabazi	Mykhal
Morry	Mouri	Muhammad-Ahid	Mura'sha	Mutasem	Mykil
Morshawnquis	Mouricio	Muhammad-	Muraad	Mutasim	Mykita
Mortadah	Mousa *(0.01)*	Jawwaad	Murad	Mutaz	Mykle
Mortaze	Moussa	Muhammadali	Murat	Mutez	Mykol
Morte	Moustafa	Muhammed *(0.03)*	Murdock	Muthoka	Mykolas
Morteza	Moustapha	Muhammed-	Mures	Muzamel	Mykuan
Morton	Moutasem	Faruq	Murkeil	Muzamir	Mykwan
Mory	Moutaz	Muhannad	Murone	Muzammil	Myl
Morya	Mouwlid	Muhd	Murphy *(0.02)*	Muzayyan	Mylan
Morye	Mowafak	Muhib	Murray *(0.02)*	Mwbashir	Mylando
Moryelle	Mowgli	Muhiedin	Murrel	Mweene	Myle
Mosab	Mownjgan	Muhit	Murrell	Mxolisi	Myleack
Mose	Moya	Muhmmad	Murry	My	Myleak
Moses *(0.12)*	Moyces	Muhsen	Mursal	My Quan	Myleek
Mosese	Moyses	Muhsin	Murtadi	My'kevius	Mylek
Moshawn	Mozark	Muhtade	Murtajiz	My'trez	Myleke
Moshe *(0.02)*	Mozell	Muhyidin	Murtaza	My-King	Myles *(0.34)*
Moshea	Mrwon	Muizz	Murtessa	Mya	Mylez
Mosheh	Msédangelo	Mujaahid	Murtuza	Myah	Mylick
Moshiu	Msema	Mujahid	Murugan	Myan	Mylik
Mosi	Mshtak	Mujahideen	Musa	Myatt	Mylikk
Mosiah	Mtume Dhiresh	Mujahio	Musaab	Mycah	Mylles
Mosic	Mu'min	Mujally	Musab	Mycal	Myllo
Mosie	Muaadh	Mujeeb	Musahib	Mychael *(0.01)*	Mylo
Mosin	Muad	Mukhtar	Musashi	Mychah	Mylon *(0.01)*
Moslait	Muaiad	Mukthi	Musaver	Mychal *(0.02)*	Mylynn
Moss	Muath	Mukund	Musavvir	Mychall	Mylz
Mossa	Muaz	Mukunth	Musbau	Mycheal	Mynor *(0.02)*

Myon	Na'terrius	Nagel	Najgi	Namiah	Nareshkumar
Myontae	Na-Eem	Nagith	Naji	Namir	Narin
Myooran	Na-Il	Nagrup	Naji-Joseph	Namit	Narine
Myquan	Naader	Nah Lee	Najib	Namjoon	Narish
Myqueal	Naaman	Nahaid	Najib-Abdullahi	Namon	Narjodh
Myquel	Naava	Nahakeem	Najiee	Nan	Narkey
Myran	Naazim	Nahalo	Najih	Nana *(0.01)*	Narles
Myrbene	Nabeeh	Nahaniel	Najiib	Nana-Danso	Naro
Myrese	Nabeel *(0.01)*	Naheem	Najja	Nana-Yaw	Naronne
Myriam *(0.01)*	Nabhila	Naheim	Najjo	Nanayakkarawasam	Narquise
Myrian	Nabi	Nahel	Najmi	Nancy	Narrell
Myrick	Nabih	Nahid	Najum	Nanda	Narsia
Myrion	Nabil *(0.03)*	Nahkia	Nakai	Nandan	Narson
Myro	Nabont E	Nahoh	Nakarin	Nandish	Narvel
Myron *(0.07)*	Nabritt	Nahom	Nakedo	Nangwaya	Narvell
Myrone	Nacari	Nahome	Nakedrick	Nantambu	Naryan
Myrul	Nacarius	Nahqueal	Nakee	Nantarius	Nasah
Myseed	Nacarlos	Nahshon *(0.01)*	Nakeem	Nanthan	Naseeb
Myshawn	Nachga	Nahtan	Nakehko	Naod	Naseem
Myshay	Nachman	Nahthaniel	Nakeia	Naoki	Naseen
Mytae	Nachor	Nahu	Nakeil	Naonta	Naseer
Mytchel	Nachum	Nahuel	Nakeitheus	Naor	Naseimm-Ahlei
Mytchell	Nacobia	Nahum *(0.02)*	Nakendrick	Naoto	Naser
Mythanial	Nada	Nai	Nakenya	Naoya	Nash *(0.02)*
Mythcel	Nadairal	Naiah	Nakharie	Naphtali	Nashad
Myung	Nadarian	Naib	Nakhle	Napier	Nashara
Myung-Rho	Nadarius	Naif	Naki	Napolean	Nashat
Myuran	Nadav *(0.01)*	Naijé	Nakia *(0.01)*	Napoleon *(0.01)*	Nashawn
	Nadeem *(0.01)*	Naim	Nakiah	Napu	Nashe
-N-	Nadege	Naime	Nakial	Naqawn	Nasheed
	Nader *(0.02)*	Nain	Nakian	Naqiya	Nasher
N *(0.02)*	Nader Mahmoud	Nainesh	Nakias	Naquain	Nashid
N'como	Naderricus	Nainoa	Nakii	Naquan *(0.01)*	Nashon
N'dejé	Nadim	Naiquan	Nakim	Naquave	Nashten
N'dere	Nadin	Nairobi	Nakio	Naquavious	Nashton
N'dikho	Nadine	Naitaalii	Nakir	Naquavius	Nashua
N'dri	Nadir	Naithan	Nakita	Naqué	Nasi
N'gall	Nadis	Naizjal	Nakoah	Naquen	Nasir *(0.01)*
N'ghai	Naditus	Najae	Nakoda	Naquille	Nasir-Gaddisa
N.	Nadonion	Najael	Nakoma	Naquincy	Nasiruddin
Na	Nadr	Najah	Nakosi	Naquirra	Nason
Na Quian	Nadrew	Najahwan	Nakota	Naquon	Nasr
Na'anthony	Naeandre	Najai	Nakul	Naqwell	Nasri
Na'darius	Naeem *(0.01)*	Najam	Nakye	Nara	Nasruddin
Na'eem	Nael	Najamon	Nalberto	Narain	Nasrudin
Na'ees	Naem	Najarri	Naldré	Naramseen	Nasser *(0.01)*
Na'el	Naethan	Najawhan	Nalec	Naramsin	Nasser-Youssef
Na'giere	Naethane	Najdat	Nalon	Narcis	Nassier
Na'im	Nafees	Najea Immanuel	Nalson	Narciso	Nassim
Na'jee	Nafeez	Najee *(0.04)*	Nam *(0.02)*	Narcisse	Nassir
Na'kendrick	Nafis	Najée	Nam Justin	Nardarrion	Nassor
Na'quan	Naftali	Najeeb	Namah	Nareg	Nasuayaaq
Na'quante	Nagantie	Najeem	Naman	Narek	Natahj
Na'qwan	Nage	Najei	Nambinh	Naren	Natale
Na'shawn	Nagee	Najep	Namerius De Ont	Naresh	Natalie

Natalio	Natnak	Navkarn	Nchiiwat	Neeshanth	Nekorey
Natan	Natobian	Navkeeret	Nciholas	Neewar	Neldon
Natanael *(0.01)*	Natori	Navneel	Ndahiro	Neewin	Nell
Natanel	Natorious	Navneet	Ndemi	Nefchievous	Nella
Nataniel	Natorius	Navneeth	Ndjaiye	Nefertari	Nelleon
Natas	Natravis	Navnish	Ndrew	Neff	Nello
Natasha	Natrell	Navon	Ndue	Neftali *(0.02)*	Nels
Natavain	Natrevious	Navonta	Nduka	Neftaly	Nelsen
Natavian	Natrion	Navotni	Ndukwe	Negal	Nelson *(0.31)*
Natavis	Natron *(0.01)*	Navpreet	Néjuann	Negash	Nelson IV
Nate *(0.01)*	Natrone *(0.01)*	Navraj	Néquan	Negele	Nelson Jr
Natee	Natsuki	Navreet	Neacko	Nehad	Nelson-Aaron
Nateli	Nattasith	Navroze	Neako	Nehanda	Nelsory
Naten	Natthew	Navtej	Neal *(0.11)*	Nehaz	Nelvi
Naterien	Natu	Navyodh	Neale	Nehemiah *(0.04)*	Nelvin
Naterius	Natwan	Nawaf	Neall	Nehemias	Nema
Nathainel	Naud	Nawar	Nealon	Nehemie	Nemanya
Nathan *(4.80)*	Naujua	Naweed	Nealsaun	Nehemijel	Nemer
Nathan Daniel	Naum	Nawfal	Nealy	Nehemyah	Nemia
Nathan Kumar	Nauman	Nawid	Neander	Neheriah	Nemias
Nathan Ray	Naun	Nawin	Neaqué	Nehimiah	Nemo
Nathan Sai	Naunihal	Nayan	Nearest	Nehme	Nemorio
Nathan-Denis	Naureet	Nayati	Neari	Nehmia	Nenad
Nathanael *(0.18)*	Naurin	Naybu	Neashy	Nehmson	Nene
Nathanal	Nautas	Naydeep	Neathin	Nehumi	Nenet
Nathaneal *(0.01)*	Nauticia	Nayee	Neav	Neidermeirer	Neno
Nathaneal Ian	Navada	Nayeem	Nebai-Emanuel-	Neiia	Nenson
Nathaneil	Navaniel	Nayef	Aforki	Neijel	Neon
Nathanel	Navantre	Nayely	Nebal	Neiko	Neosho
Nathanial *(0.13)*	Navar	Nayib	Nebeyu	Neil *(0.31)*	Nephi *(0.01)*
Nathaniel *(2.13)*	Navaraj	Nayith	Nebi	Neil Alan	Nephorditees
Nathaniel-Calvin	Navari	Nayland	Nebiyu	Neil Jason	Nephus
Nathaniel-David	Navarrio	Naylor	Neckerson	Neilan	Neq'uan
Nathanil	Navdeep *(0.01)*	Nayquan	Necko Kwadrack	Neilay	Nequa
Nathanile	Navdip	Nayqwan	Necksen	Neill	Nequall
Nathanio	Naveathadshan	Nayroop	Neco	Neilsen	Nequan
Nathanual	Naveed *(0.01)*	Nayrough	Necole	Neilson	Nequel
Nathanuel	Naveen *(0.01)*	Nayshard	Ned *(0.01)*	Neima	Nequon
Nathanyal	Naveenan	Naythan	Nedal	Neiman	Neri
Nathanyl	Navees	Naythn	Nedarrius	Neimann	Neriah
Nathean	Naven	Nayulk	Nedjy	Neimon	Neric
Nathen *(0.05)*	Naverro	Nazar	Nedol	Neino	Neris
Nathenial	Navesh	Nazareth	Neénahjah	Neivedan	Neriyah
Nathian	Navid *(0.01)*	Nazario	Neeco	Neiwah	Nermin
Nathianiel	Navid Ulises	Nazariy	Neel *(0.01)*	Neka	Nero
Nathieu	Navied	Nazeeh	Neelan	Nekari	Nerojen
Nathin	Navier	Nazeel	Neelanand	Nekethan	Nerquaye
Nathis	Naville	Nazeem	Neelanjan	Neki	Nerton
Nathniel	Navin *(0.01)*	Nazeer	Neelay	Nekko	Nerujan
Nathon *(0.01)*	Navinkumar	Nazer	Neelesh Troy	Neko	Nery *(0.01)*
Nathyn	Navithan	Nazerene	Neelix	Nekoda	Nesandthan
Nation	Navjit	Nazerine	Neely	Nekol	Nesby
Natividad	Navjot	Nazieh	Neema *(0.01)*	Nekolay	Neshal
Natnael	Navjoth	Nazim	Neenef	Nekoliah	Neshaun
Natnaele	Navjyot	Nazzar	Neeraj	Nekoreale	Nesho

Nesim	Nhat-Khai	Nichloas	Nickelus	Nicolai *(0.01)*	Niguel
Nesley	Nhia	Nichlos	Nickers	Nicolaj	Nihaal
Nesly	Nhia Kou	Nichlous	Nickesh	Nicolas *(1.56)*	Nihal
Neson	Nhiamke	Nichoas	Nickey	Nicolas David	Nihar
Nesta	Nhien	Nichol	Nickhales	Nicolaus *(0.01)*	Nihkee
Nester	Nhishzell	Nichola	Nickholas	Nicolay	Nihreer
Nestor *(0.14)*	Nhixxel	Nicholaas	Nicki	Nicole *(0.01)*	Nii
Nestor-Jake	Nhlanhla	Nicholaes	Nickia	Nicolei	Nii-Kotei
Neta	Nhowahisaac	Nicholai *(0.01)*	Nickie	Nicolelus	Niico
Netanel	Nhu	Nicholaos	Nickiel	Nicoles	Niilo
Netaniel	Ni Quonne	Nicholas *(12.84)*	Nickilas	Nicolette	Nijah
Nethan	Ni'im	Nicholas	Nickilous	Nicoli	Nijal
Nethanel	Ni'jamel	Alexander	Nickita	Nicolia	Nijan
Nethaniel	Ni'quai	Nicholas Avery	Nickjan	Nicolis	Nijee
Nethanyel	Nia	Nicholas Ha'ale	Nicklas *(0.03)*	Nicollo	Nijel
Nethersand	Niachece	Nicholas Maurice	Nicklaus *(0.05)*	Nicolo *(0.02)*	Niji
Neuauda	Niaeem	Nicholas Michae	Nicklauss	Nicolus	Nik
Neulysis	Niage	Nicholas Thinh	Nicklise	Nicomos	Nikal
Neuman	Niah	Nicholas Willia	Nickloes	Nicona	Nikalai
Neumis	Nial	Nicholas-Devon	Nicklos	Nicoras	Nikalas
Nevada *(0.01)*	Niall *(0.02)*	Nicholas-Hai	Nicklous	Nicquarious	Nikalis
Nevade	Niam	Nicholas-James	Nicklus	Nicquell	Nikalous
Nevan	Niamiah	Nicholas-John	Nicknas	Nicquon	Nikalus
Nevanier	Niamke	Nicholas-Omar	Nicko	Nictavious	Nikario
Nevean	Niamonze	Nicholas-Toan	Nickoeye	Nicula	Nikay
Neven	Niandre	Nicholase	Nickolai	Nidhal	Nike
Nevethan	Niar	Nicholasw	Nickolaos	Nidre	Nikeem
Nevil	Niaria	Nicholaus *(0.04)*	Nickolas *(0.49)*	Nieckeo	Nikeer
Neville	Niaujan	Nicholes *(0.01)*	Nickolas Everett	Nieco	Nikel
Nevin *(0.05)*	Niayre	Nicholi	Nickolaus *(0.02)*	Niegel	Nikell
Nevonte	Nibal	Nicholias	Nickoles	Nieholas	Nikesh
Nevyn	Nibel	Nicholii	Nickoli	Nieko	Niket
Newberry	Nibeyu	Nicholis *(0.01)*	Nickolia	Niel	Niketas
Newel	Nicalas	Nichollas	Nickolie	Niels	Nikhil *(0.04)*
Newell	Nicalor	Nicholos *(0.01)*	Nickolie Jr	Nielsen	Nikhilesh
Newlove	Nicanor	Nicholous	Nickolis *(0.01)*	Niem	Nikholas
Newman	Nicasio	Nichols *(0.01)*	Nickolos	Nieman	Niki
Newport	Niccho	Nicholsa	Nickolus *(0.01)*	Nien	Nikia
Newt	Nicco *(0.01)*	Nicholson	Nickolys	Nienkel	Nikidemis
Newton *(0.01)*	Niccolas	Nicholus	Nickoulas	Niesanthan	Nikiel
Ngabo	Niccolino	Nichplas	Nickquavies	Nietzche	Nikifor
Ngai	Niccolo *(0.01)*	Nichquolas	Nickry	Nieves	Nikilis
Ngandi	Nich0las	Nichulas	Nickson	Nigal	Nikin
Ngawang	Nichaeo	Nick *(0.09)*	Nickuan	Nigale	Nikit
Nghia	Nichalas	Nick-Aldo	Nicky *(0.01)*	Nigash	Nikita *(0.01)*
Nghia-Tommy	Nichalaus	Nickadamos	Niclas	Nige L Jama	Nikka
Ngoc *(0.01)*	Nichales	Nickademus	Nico *(0.10)*	Nigeanya	Nikkai
Nguyen *(0.01)*	Nichalos	Nickalas *(0.01)*	Nicodemius	Nigel *(0.21)*	Nikki *(0.01)*
Nguyen Samuel	Nichalous	Nickalaus	Nicodemus	Nigele	Nikki Jacob
Nguyen-Nhat	Nichaolas	Nickalis	Nicohles	Nigell	Nikkie
Nhaba	Nichelas	Nickalos	Nicoholas	Nigelm	Nikkita
Nhadi	Nichkolas	Nickalous	Nicol	Nighkey	Nikko *(0.06)*
Nhan	Nichlas	Nickalus *(0.01)*	Nicola *(0.03)*	Nigiel	Nikkoda
Nhat	Nichlaus	Nickelas	Nicolá	Nigil	Nikkolas
Nhat-Dzu	Nichle	Nickelous	Nicolaas *(0.01)*	Nigle	Nikkolaus Isaac

Niklaas	Nimi	Nishwone	Noaha	Noor-Ahmad	Novell
Niklas *(0.02)*	Nimo	Nissan	Noahie	Noor-E-Alam	Novian
Niklaus	Nimrod	Nisshanee	Noal	Noorahmed	Novisa
Niko *(0.09)*	Nimschi	Nissin	Noam	Noordeen	Nowel
Nikoals	Nimshi	Nisson	Noaman	Nooreldeen	Nowell
Nikoda	Nina	Niszanth	Noble *(0.01)*	Noorullah	Nowfal
Nikodem	Nino *(0.01)*	Nitahji	Noboru	Nooy	Nowland
Nikodemious	Ninort	Nitaino	Nobpon	Nor	Nowruss
Nikodim	Ninos	Nitan	Nobuhiro	Nor'mane	Noyan
Nikoe	Ninous	Nitchel	Nobuyuki	Nora	Nozim
Nikola *(0.04)*	Ninzey	Nitesh	Nochum	Norah	Nozomi
Nikolaas	Niocholas	Nithan	Nocona	Norayr	Nsilo
Nikolai *(0.04)*	Niola	Nithaniel	Nodin	Norbert *(0.01)*	Nsimbi
Nikolaj	Nipin	Nitharsan	Noe *(0.18)*	Norberto *(0.03)*	Ntai
Nikolajs	Nipun	Nitharshan	Noe Aldair	Nore	Nu
Nikolaos *(0.01)*	Nipuna	Nithin	Noé	Noreiyea	Nua
Nikolas *(0.28)*	Niquae	Nithushan	Noel *(0.21)*	Norel	Nukona
Nikolaus *(0.04)*	Niquill	Nitin	Noell	Norland	Numa
Nikolay	Niquo	Nitish	Noer	Norman *(0.15)*	Numair
Nikolee	Nirad	Niton	Nofel	Norman Michael	Numan
Nikoli	Niraj	Nitram	Noha	Normand	Numen
Nikolino	Niral	Niv	Nohe	Normil	Nuno
Nikolis	Nirav	Nivaethan	Nohea	Norquavious	Nuntigorn
Nikolo	Nirjan	Nivake	Noire	Norris *(0.02)*	Nuntreae
Nikoloas	Nirmal	Nivash	Noisy	Norris Hals	Nunzi
Nikolos	Niro	Nived	Nokomis	Norry	Nur
Nikolus	Niroesan	Nivethan	Nokosh	Norsalus	Nuradin
Nikoly	Niroj	Nivil	Nolan *(0.56)*	Norshawn	Nurdeen
Nikos	Nirojan	Nivith	Noland	Norshiaron	Nuredin
Nikota	Niron	Nivontae	Nolande	North	Nuri
Nikoyea	Nirosh	Nivram	Nolando	Northcliff	Nuridin
Nil	Niroshan *(0.01)*	Nixan	Nolane	Northstar	Nuruddin
Nila	Niroshian	Nixon *(0.01)*	Nolasco	Nortori	Nury
Nilanth	Nirris	Nixson	Nolberto	Nortorious	Nusret
Nilaxsan	Nirsan	Nizam	Noldain	Nortré	Nustafa
Nilay	Niru	Nizamodeen	Nolden	Norval	Nuu
Nile *(0.02)*	Niruban	Nizar	Nole	Norvan	Nuutupu
Nilen	Nirushan	Nizell	Nolen *(0.01)*	Norvel	Ny
Niles *(0.02)*	Nisaanth	Njaja	Nolin	Norvell	Ny Kee
Nilesh	Nisanth	Njeri	Nollie	Norverto	Ny'jarie
Nilijah	Nisar	Nkadi	Nolyn	Norvyn	Ny'jario
Nilo	Nisarg	Nkem	Nomaan	Norwin	Ny'rico
Nilon	Nischant	Nkemakonam	Nomamien	Norwood	Ny-Shawn
Niloshan	Nishaal	Nkhanle	Noman	Not *(0.01)*	Nyah
Nilovan	Nishad	Nkile	Nomar	Notay	Nyal
Nils *(0.01)*	Nishahan	Nkosi	Nomeer	Notorious	Nyan
Nilson	Nishal	Nkquasaun	Nomelee	Notorius	Nyang
Nilton	Nishan	Nnaduzie	Noname	Nouphyl	Nyarko
Nilushan	Nishant *(0.01)*	Nnaemeka	Nonathan	Nour *(0.01)*	Nycholas
Nima *(0.01)*	Nishanth	Nnaji	Nonoa	Noure-Allah	Nycholis
Nimai	Nishanthan	Nnamdi	Nonoy	Nouriddean	Nycire
Nimar	Nishat	Noach-Lotan	Nonyeia	Nouvella	Nye
Nimekno	Nishil	Noah *(1.15)*	Noojan	Novdeep	Nyeem
Nimer	Nishith	Noah-Joseph	Noor *(0.01)*	Noveen	Nyembo
Nimesh	Nishon	Noah-Michael	Noor Aldin	Novejote	Nygee

Nygel	O Neil	Oakley *(0.01)*	Octavus	Ohmar	Olanrewaju
Nyguel	O Qwaandre	Obaamiri	October	Ohshay	Olaolu
Nyh-Kwquan	O Sharra	Obada	Octobiano	Ohusegum-Junior	Olaoluwa
Nyheem	O Shay	Obadiah	Octravia	Ohuwatomi	Olatunde
Nyhemah	O Shea	Obaid	Ocue	Oi	Olatunji
Nyigel	O Shon	Obaida	Oczavius	Oichentka	Olaujawon
Nyikadzino	O Tarius	Obaidullah	Odai	Oilavon	Olav
Nyjah	O Terraius	Obalet	Odanny	Oisin	Olawale
Nyjil	O Terrius	Oban	Odara	Oj	Olawoyin
Nyjja	O'brian	Obasi	Odarrius	Oji	Olayinka
Nyjuan	O'brien	Obassi	Oday	Oji-Moyo	Olbinett
Nykaji	O'bryant	Obatula	Oddie	Okechuku	Olden
Nykalas	O'darius	Obayda	Oddis	Okechukwu	Oldruntobi
Nykeed	O'daron	Obdallah	Odean	Okeen	Oleg
Nykeem	O'deon	Obdulio	Odeh	Okeeve	Olegario
Nykei	O'donell	Obed *(0.03)*	Odell *(0.01)*	Okera	Oleh
Nykel	O'keefe	Oberen	Odem	Okevious	Olen *(0.01)*
Nykey	O'keeth	Obey	Oden	Okey	Olgan
Nykhi	O'lajawan	Obi	Oderah	Okiemute	Olijahawon
Nyko	O'lando	Obiajulu	Oderin	Okimi	Olin *(0.01)*
Nykola	O'mair	Obie	Oderra	Okis	Olinson
Nykolahs	O'mar	Obied	Odessa	Okle	Oliseh
Nykolas	O'mare	Obinna *(0.01)*	Odeyi	Okley	Oliva
Nykolus	O'mari	Obrain	Odge	Okoi	Olivea
Nykotimathe	O'mario	Obria	Odiel	Okori	Oliver *(0.33)*
Nyle *(0.01)*	O'marte	Obriel	Odili	Okoye	Oliver Scott
Nyles	O'neail	Obsaa	Odilon	Oksana	Oliver-Pascal
Nylind	O'neal	Obtin	Odin *(0.01)*	Oktavian	Oliverio
Nyll	O'neil *(0.01)*	Obumneme	Odinakachukinu	Okwuosha	Olivia
Nyo	O'neill	Oc	Odinald	Ola Juwon	Olivier *(0.53)*
Nyquan	O'nellus	Ocean *(0.02)*	Odionikhere	Olabode	Olivo
Nyquel	O'rian	Oceanist	Odirachukwumma	Oladipo	Ollie *(0.01)*
Nyralda	O'russell	Oceanus	Odis	Olaf	Ollis
Nyrarere	O'ryan	Ocey	Odisan	Olaja'won	Olly
Nyree	O'sama	Ocie	Odisho	Olajade	Olmedo
Nyrell	O'sha	Ociel *(0.01)*	Odney	Olajajuan	Olnick
Nyrryk	O'shaa'ne	Ocoriye	Odon	Olajawon	Olon
Nyshan	O'shae	Ocsar	Oem	Olajawun	Olondo
Nyshaun	O'shan	Ocshun	Ofelio	Olajowuan	Olorin
Nyshawn	O'shaun	Octavain	Ofentse	Olajuan	Olorunfemi
Nytorius	O'shawn	Octavaius	Offeyette	Olajuanne	Olsen
Nytrellis	O'shay *(0.01)*	Octavé	Official	Olajuawon	Olson
Nyzeil	O'shaye	Octaveous	Ogagaoghene	Olajunti	Olu
Nzila	O'shayne	Octaveus	Ogbemudia	Olajuwa	Olubunmi
	O'shea *(0.01)*	Octavia	Ogbogu	Olajuwan	Olufemi
	O'shey	Octavian	Ogbonnia	Olajuwon *(0.02)*	Olufunmilayo
-O-	O'tario	Octaviano	Ogden	Olakunle	Olufunto
	O'teenie	Octavias	Oger	Olalekan	Olurotimi
O	O'trell	Octaviaus	Ogie	Olamide	Oluseni
O Brian	O'vesta	Octavio *(0.09)*	Ognjen	Olan	Oluseun
O Bryan	O.T.	Octavious *(0.02)*	Oguz	Oland	Olushakin
O C	Oadie	Octavis *(0.01)*	Oh'vere	Olanders	Olutayo
O Darrius	Oak	Octavius *(0.03)*	Ohad	Olandes	Olutimilehin
O Lanjerwan	Oaker	Octavous	Ohan	Olando	Oluwa Segun
O N	Oaklee	Octavtion	Ohene	Olanipekun	Oluwabukunm
O Neal					

Oluwafemi	Omonteez	Oolon	Orlandenez	Osbel	Osvaldo Martin
Oluwagbemi	Omontre	Opeoluwa	Orlandes	Osborn	Osveli
Oluwagbemiga	Omoro	Opeti	Orlandis	Osborne	Osvil
Oluwamide	Omotayo	Ophni	Orlando (0.26)	Osbourne	Oswald
Oluwaseun	Omoteniola	Opie	Orlandos	Oscar (1.42)	Oswaldo (0.05)
Oluwashina	Omotoyosi	Opjot	Orlandrius	Oscar Adrian	Osxea
Oluwatobi	Omri	Oquan	Orlawn	Oscar Antonio	Otavious
Oluwatomi	Omri'	Oquavion	Orlean	Oscar Ramiro	Otavius
Oluwatomisi	Omundez	Oquavious	Orlin	Osceola	Otereo
Oluwatosin	On	Oquendo	Orlis	Oscie	Oterious
Oluwawemimo	On Trell	Or'darious	Orman	Osdy	Otez
Oluwolé	On Zjá	Or'shon	Ormande	Osei	Otha
Olvan	Onaldo	Ora	Ormond	Osei-Yaw	Othel
Olvier	Onassis	Ora'rashun	Ornaldo	Osemekhian	Othello
Olvin	Onazia	Oracio	Ornan	Osgood	Othman
Olvio	Ondarius	Orake	Oronde	Oshá	Othnell
Olyde-Starr	Ondelee	Oral	Orosmel	Oshae	Othni
Olyn	Onderious	Oran (0.01)	Orpheus	Oshai	Othniel
Oma	Ondiek	Orav	Orrain	Oshalone	Othnil
Omadi	Ondra	Orazio	Orren	Oshane	Othon
Omaha	Ondraz'e	Orbelin	Orri	Oshawnesy	Othoniel
Omair (0.01)	Ondre	Orbith	Orrick	Oshay (0.01)	Othra
Omajjé	Ondrea	Orchard	Orrie	Oshaye	Oti
Oman	Ondrey	Orchsley	Orrin (0.01)	Oshe	Otilio
Omandi	Oneal	Ordelius	Orris	Oshea (0.01)	Otis (0.06)
Omanie	Oneeb	Orden	Orry (0.01)	Osheon	Otise
Omar (1.21)	Oneil	Order	Orsam	Oshri	Otisrajan
Omar Oliver	Onel	Ordley	Orson	Oshun	Otivio
Omar-Moises	Onelio	Oree	Orsy	Osias	Otivisit
Omar-Muktar	Onias	Oreido	Ortavia	Osiel (0.01)	Otniel
Omare	Oniel	Oreion	Ortez	Osiris (0.01)	Otoniel (0.01)
Omaree	Onix	Orel	Ortiz	Ositadinma	Otrey
Omarey	Onkar	Oren (0.02)	Orval	Osjuan	Ott
Omari (0.04)	Onkardeep	Orenthial	Orvel	Oskar (0.01)	Ottavious
Omari-James	Onni	Orenthian	Orvelin	Oskarlos	Ottis
Omari-Tor	Onofre	Orentho	Orvie	Osley	Otto (0.03)
Omarilee	Onofrio	Orest	Orvil	Oslind	Ottoman
Omaris	Onorato	Orfanel	Orville (0.01)	Osmal	Ottoway
Omarius	Onoriode	Orfil	Orvin	Osman (0.03)	Otty
Omarr (0.01)	Onrionte	Ori	Orwa	Osman-Shariff	Ou'bey
Omarsharey	Onslo	Oriam	Orwren	Osmar (0.02)	Oudhay
Omeed	Ontario (0.01)	Orian	Ory	Osmel	Oudone
Omeer	Ontarion	Orie	Oryan	Osmi	Ouinten
Omer (0.02)	Ontawon	Orien	Oryn	Osmin	Oumesh
Omer-God	Ontay	Oriental	Orynn	Osmundo	Ourian
Omero	Ontayveis	Orieon	Osadebamwen	Ossama	Ousamoh
Omesh	Onterion	Orin (0.01)	Osagie	Ossian	Oushon
Omid (0.01)	Ontrel	Oriniree	Osahon	Ossice	Oussama
Omied	Ontreze	Orinthid	Osama (0.01)	Ossie	Ovais
Omiles	Ontroy	Orinthus	Osamu	Ostan	Oval
Omkar	Onur	Orion (0.07)	Osamudiamen	Ostin	Ovas
Ommran	Onyshius	Oris	Osarense	Osualdo	Ovel
Omogbolahan	Onyx	Orkun	Osaze	Osue	Ovell
Omondi	Onyxx	Orlan	Osbaldo (0.03)	Osung	Overstolz
Omonte	Onzel	Orlandas	Osbalto	Osvaldo (0.18)	Overstreet

Overton
Ovidio
Ovie
Owace
Owais
Owamtarrius
Owen *(0.28)*
Owen Jr
Owens
Owsley
Owusu
Oxlee
Oxzavian
Oya
Oyedamola Paul
Ozavin
Ozee
Ozell
Oziel
Ozoemenam
Ozric
Ozvie
Ozzie
Ozziel
Ozzy *(0.01)*
Ozzy-James
Ozzy-Michael

-P-

P *(0.01)*
P Angelo
P J
P M
P'are
P.
P.J.
Pa
Pa-Alusene
Paarsa
Paarth
Paarusjit
Pabeerthan
Pablito
Pablo *(0.36)*
Pac Samay
Paccqi
Pace
Pacer
Pachara
Pacifico
Packer
Paco
Pactrick
Padden

Paddi
Paddington
Paddles
Paden *(0.02)*
Padraic *(0.01)*
Padraig
Padraigh
Padre
Padreic
Padriac
Paeris
Page *(0.01)*
Pagel
Pahisi
Pahl
Pahlev
Pahul
Paige *(0.01)*
Paimon
Paine
Painter
Paixing
Pajman
Pak
Pakarai
Pake
Pal
Palak
Palani
Palen
Palenapa
Palise-Jor'd
Palle
Palmer *(0.02)*
Palmez
Palmo
Paloma
Palvinder
Palvir
Pambbjot
Pamomodu
Pan
Panagioths
Panagiotis
Panagis
Panah
Panajotis
Panayiotis
Panayoti
Panayotis
Pancho
Panfilo
Panipal
Panou
Pantelee

Panveer
Paola
Paolo *(0.04)*
Paolo Adrian
Papa
Paradise
Parag
Paramjot
Parampreet
Paramvee
Paramveer
Paramvir
Paras
Parash
Paraskevas
Parathan
Pardeep *(0.01)*
Pardip
Paree
Parelle
Parent
Pares
Parese
Paresh
Pargat
Pargiat
Parhalad
Parham
Paricien
Parie
Parin
Paris *(0.09)*
Parish *(0.01)*
Paritath
Parixit
Parizen
Parjot
Park
Park-Wah
Parkar
Parke
Parker *(0.55)*
Parko
Parks
Parley
Parley Gage
Parman
Parmbir
Parmdeep
Parmeet
Parmer
Parminder
Parmjit
Parmpal
Parmpreet

Parmveer
Parmvir *(0.01)*
Parnell *(0.01)*
Parnvir
Parogio
Parrése
Parren
Parrick
Parrihun
Parris *(0.01)*
Parrish *(0.03)*
Parry
Parrysh
Parsa
Parseram
Parshva
Parth *(0.03)*
Partha
Partheban
Parthey
Parthiv
Parul
Parus
Parvesh
Parvez
Parvinder
Parvir
Parviz
Parys
Pascal *(0.11)*
Pascale
Paschhur
Pasco
Pascual *(0.01)*
Pascul
Pasha
Paskall
Pasmnstmeregsfml
Pasqual
Pasquale *(0.01)*
Pasquali
Pastor
Pat
Patazikivaa
Patch
Patchek
Pate
Patek
Patel
Paten
Pathma
Pathos
Pathum
Patick
Patin

Patrcik
Patreck
Patrek
Patrell
Patrez
Patric *(0.04)*
Patrice *(0.05)*
Patricia
Patricio *(0.02)*
Patrick *(4.12)*
Patrick Ale
Patrick Thomas
Patrick-James
Patrickjohn
Patrickk
Patrik *(0.01)*
Patrion
Patrique
Patriwck
Patrizio
Patrtick
Patryck
Patryk *(0.02)*
Patterson
Patton
Pattrick
Patxi
Paublo
Paul *(2.40)*
Paul Andre
Paul Brandon
Paul Christian
Paul Justin
Paul Steven
Paul William
Paul-Andre
Paul-Dylan
Paul-Eugene
Paul-Francis
Paul-Jacob
Paul-John
Paul-Joseph
Paul-Martin
Paul-Silas
Paul-Stephen
Paulandrew
Pauldeep
Paulemile
Paulemy
Pauley
Paulharvey
Pauli
Paulino *(0.01)*
Paulito
Paulius

Paulo *(0.03)*
Paulon
Paulron
Paulsen
Paulson
Paulthanael
Paulus
Pavan
Pavandeep
Pavanjit
Pavanjot
Pavanpreet
Pavanvir
Pavel *(0.02)*
Paven
Pavenjeet
Pavenjot
Pavhan
Pavilon
Pavin
Pavindeep
Pavinder
Pavit
Pavitarpal
Paviter
Pavithiran
Pavithran
Pavitpal
Pavkarn
Pavlo
Pavlos
Pavlos-Ioannis
Pavneet
Pavninder
Pawan
Pawandeep
Pawanpreet
Pawat
Pawee
Pawel *(0.01)*
Pawet
Paxian
Paxson
Paxton *(0.03)*
Payam
Paycen
Payden *(0.01)*
Paydon
Payge
Paymon
Payne *(0.01)*
Paynn
Payson
Payton *(0.16)*
Pazblo

Peair
Peairr E
Peanut
Pearce *(0.01)*
Pearl
Pearse
Pearson *(0.01)*
Peaton
Peder
Pedram
Pedraum
Pedrito
Pedro *(0.72)*
Pedro III
Pedro Luis
Pedrum
Peék
Peed
Peejay
Peer
Pei
Peighton
Peirce
Peirson
Pekelo
Pekto
Pelaa
Pele
Pelham
Pelmo
Pelton
Pembroke
Pemching
Peng
Peniel
Peniro
Penisimani
Penn
Peoro
Pepe
Pepper
Peraveen
Peraveenan
Perca
Percell
Percinta
Percio
Percival
Percy *(0.02)*
Peregrin
Peregrine
Perekina
Perez
Perfecto
Peris

Perius
Periyanth
Perkins
Permeet
Pern
Pernall
Pernell *(0.01)*
Perren
Perrence
Perria
Perrin *(0.01)*
Perrion
Perry *(0.16)*
Perry Danie
Perry'
Perrya
Perrye
Perryn
Pertie
Peruis
Pervez
Pervis
Peryis
Peshraw
Petar *(0.01)*
Pete *(0.05)*
Peter *(1.94)*
Peter Duy
Peter Hoan
Peter Jose
Peter Vinh
Peter-Anthony
Peter-Chakib
Peterech
Peterlee
Petersen
Peterson *(0.01)*
Peteru
Petllex
Petr
Petra
Petre
Petrioni
Petro
Petrocha-Roumi
Petronilo
Petros *(0.01)*
Petrus
Petter
Petteri
Petty
Peut
Peyam
Peydin
Peyson

Peyten
Peython
Peyton *(0.14)*
Peyton Michael
Peytonn
Pfnandrea
Phabian
Phadarius
Phadrian
Phaivanh
Phalen
Pham
Phaniel
Phanushan
Pharaoh
Pharell
Pharen
Phares
Pharez
Pharilien
Pharlen
Pharles
Pharoh
Pharon
Pharris
Pharryn
Phashod
Phat
Phatarios
Phaylyn
Phayon
Phebe
Phelan
Phelix *(0.01)*
Phelps
Pheng *(0.01)*
Phenian
Phenix
Phenxue
Pheonix
Pheonté
Phetanutphone
Pheth
Phethsarat
Phetpaseuth
Phetsalod
Pheybian
Pheylan
Phflanico
Phi *(0.01)*
Phi Long
Phi-Viet
Phiarune
Phibin
Phil *(0.01)*

Philander
Philandis
Philani
Philbert
Philémon
Phileman
Philemon
Phili Meric
Philip *(0.86)*
Philip Aaron
Philip Benjamin
Philip-Michael
Philip-Myles
Philipe *(0.02)*
Philipp *(0.01)*
Philippe *(0.51)*
Philippe Anto
Philippe Oliv
   (0.01)
Philippli
Philips
Phillip *(1.14)*
Phillip Charles
Phillip J.
Phillip James
Phillip Jordan
Phillip-Bernard
Phillip-Jo'allen
Phillip-Michael
Phillip-Tyler
Phillipe *(0.01)*
Phillipp
Phillippe *(0.01)*
Phillippee
Phillips
Phillon
Philmon
Philmore
Philonzo
Philundrick
Phineas
Phinehas
Phipsavart
Phishon
Phoenix *(0.05)*
Phonchit
Phong *(0.01)*
Phongseeyu
Phoojywg
Phosion
Photis
Phoumano
Phouthakhoune
Phoutthasone
Phu

Phuc
Phula
Phung
Phuong
Phuqui
Phylip
Phyllip
Phyllipe
Phyllmore La'roy
Phylon
Phynix
Piakai
Piarre
Picard
Pichest
Piérre
Piearre
Piedad
Pier
Pier Alexandr
   (0.01)
Pier Luc *(0.02)*
Pier Olivier *(0.02)*
Pierce *(0.10)*
Pierce Ryan
Piercen
Piere
Piero
Pierpont
Pierra
Pierre *(0.13)*
Pierre Alexan
   (0.03)
Pierre Andre
   (0.01)
Pierre Antoin
   (0.01)
Pierre Etienn
   (0.01)
Pierre Luc *(0.11)*
Pierre Marc *(0.01)*
Pierre Olivier
   (0.07)
Pierre Yves *(0.01)*
Pierre-Alexandre
Pierre-Alexis
Pierre-Andre
Pierre-Jean
Pierre-Luc *(0.01)*
Pierre-Mendes
Pierrick *(0.01)*
Pierrot
Pierrson
Piers *(0.01)*
Piersen

Piershawn
Pierson *(0.01)*
Piersun
Piet
Pieter *(0.01)*
Pieter Nicolaas
Pietro *(0.02)*
Piett
Pilar
Pileana
Piman
Pimis
Pinchos
Pinkerton
Pinsky
Pinytek
Pio
Piorence
Piotr *(0.02)*
Piper
Pir
Piragaash
Piranavan
Pirannavan
Pirasaanth
Pirassanna
Piraveen
Piraveenan
Piravien
Piravin
Piriyanth
Pirtham
Piruz
Pishoi
Pishoy
Pisinga
Pisith
Piston
Pita
Pitchaya
Pj
Placide
Placido
Plaskett
Plato
Platon
Platt
Platte
Play
Pleasant
Pleasure
Plennie
Ples
Plezour
Plinio

Plousha	Prahash	Prenston	Pritesh	Q'vontae	Qortez
Plug	Praise	Prentavious	Prithvi	Q'vontes	Qourtnei
Po-Yi	Prajedix	Prentice	Pritpal	Q'vontrae	Qra-Sawn
Po-Yu	Prakash	Prentis	Pritpaul	Qa	Qu'darius
Poetry	Prakatheesh	Prentiss	Priyan	Qa Vione	Qu'juan
Pok	Prana	Prerak	Priyank	Qa'shawn	Qu'nard
Polarius	Pranav (0.01)	Pres'had	Proctor	Qa'shon	Qu'ran
Pole	Pranavan	Prescott (0.01)	Prodromos	Qa'zim	Qu'ron
Polite	Pranay	President	Proeep	Qaadir	Qu'ton
Pollock	Praneel	Presley (0.01)	Promaé	Qadan	Qu'wan
Polly	Praneil	Presly	Promise	Qadeer	Qua Darrius
Polo	Pranit	Prestan	Prophet	Qadir	Qua'darius
Poly	Prannavan	Presten	Prosper	Qadre	Qua'derrick
Polyhronis	Praphon	Prester	Prosper-Edward	Qadree	Qua'dre
Pomsiri	Prarak	Prestin	Prudencio	Qadry	Qua'duoffius
Poneet	Prasad	Preston (0.63)	Pruitt	Qahir	Qua'juan
Ponpasert	Prasanna	Preston Randall	Pryce	Qahlil	Qua'larrious
Pontius	Prasannaa	Prestyn	Pryor	Qaim	Qua'mel
Pontsdailyont	Prasanth	Pretice	Przemek	Qaiss	Qua'sean
Poole	Prashan	Prett	Przemyslaw	Qaivs	Qua'shun
Poovegan	Prashant	Prevan	Psalms	Qantraus	Qua'son
Porfirio (0.02)	Prashanth	Previn	Psyheim	Qaron	Qua'tariyus
Poria`	Prat	Prevost	Puckett	Qaseem	Qua'taveus
Porita	Pratapvir	Prevuan	Pujan	Qashelby	Qua'tellius
Porteal	Prateek	Preyan	Pukar	Qashon	Qua'tez
Porter (0.03)	Prater	Preyas	Pukhraj	Qasid	Qua'twain
Pot	Pratheepan	Priadeepk	Punardeo	Qasim (0.01)	Qua'von
Poul	Pratibodh	Prianavan	Puneet	Qauntez	Quaadir
Poulos	Pratik	Price (0.01)	Puneetinder	Qavi	Quaay
Pouria	Pravdeep	Priceton	Punit	Qawmaine	Quace
Pouv	Praveen	Priciliano	Punnarah	Qays	Quadara
Pouya	Praveenen	Pride	Pupunu	Qayveon	Quadarious
Pouyea	Praveenram	Priest	Purav	Qazell	Quadaris
Powell (0.01)	Praven	Priestly	Purcell	Qazi	Quadarius (0.01)
Poya	Pravenon	Priit	Purmveer	Qei Antai	Quadauirs
Prabdeep	Pravesh	Primitivo	Purnell	Qeivhon	Quadavius
Prabdip	Pravikesh	Primitivo James	Pursodman	Qelon	Quadayton
Prabhas	Pravin	Primo	Purushoth	Qemoi	Quaddiem
Prabhat	Pravinth	Primus	Purvis	Qendarius	Quaddus
Prabhdeep	Pravion	Prince (0.03)	Puvanai	Qenyatta	Quade (0.03)
Prabhjas	Prayag	Prince Saad	Puya	Qeontay	Quadell
Prabhjit	Prayer	Prince Zechariah	Pwter	Qevin	Quaden
Prabhjot (0.01)	Prayin	Prince-Ezra	Pyerre	Qevon	Quadere
Prabhnoor	Prédarious	Princedeep	Pyoung	Qhalif	Quadon
Prabhpal	Preather	Princefabian	Pyron	Qhorban	Quadre
Prabhsimran	Preben	Princess-Senter	Pyus	Qhyshawn	Quadree
Prabhvir	Pred	Princeston		Qijuan	Quadrell
Prabjeet	Preddy	Princeton (0.01)	**-Q-**	Qion	Quadrice
Prabjit	Predrag	Princton		Qiydar	Quadrie
Prabjot	Preet	Princy	Q	Qjuanté	Quadrine
Pradeep	Preetkaran	Prine	Q Uran	Qodi	Quadrion
Pradeesh	Prell	Priness	Q'ashaw	Qonain	Quadrum
Praghanth	Prem	Printes	Q'darius	Qontéa	Quadry
Pragith	Premveer	Prisco	Q'nealus	Qoraish	Quadtavious
Pragvinderay	Prenell	Prit	Q'shawn	Qoree	Quaeise

Quaemonn	Quaneto	Quantu	Quavanté	Quenci	Queshan
Quaeshawn	Quang *(0.01)*	Quanvonte	Quavaris	Quency	Queshon
Quaevonn	Quang-Kiet-Bryan	Quanzavion	Quave	Quendal	Quesi
Quahim	Quanillias	Quanzay	Quavean	Quendale	Quesley
Quaid	Quanjayis	Quanzé	Quaveiyon	Quendarious	Quess
Quaidti	Quannel	Quanzeak	Quavell	Quendarius	Quest *(0.01)*
Quainton	Quanshae	Quanzel	Quaventeze	Quendarrius	Questen
Quaisaan	Quanshea	Quanzell	Quaveon	Quenderious	Questus
Quaison	Quanta	Quaquon	Quaviaun	Quendrick	Quetin
Qualan	Quantae	Quaran	Quavious	Quener	Quevin
Qualeek	Quantaé	Quardee	Quavis	Quenesha	Quevonte
Qualen	Quantaise	Quardell	Quavius	Quenicy	Queyshaun
Qualer	Quantario	Quarderius	Quavon	Quennel	Quezan
Qualik	Quantarious	Quardez	Quavonne	Quennell	Qui
Qualin	Quantaris	Quardre	Quavonta	Quenshawn	Qui'ari
Quallan	Quantarius	Quardrez	Quavonte	Quent Ron	Quianard
Qualyn	Quantas	Quark	Quawi	Quenta	Quianté
Quamain	Quantavian	Quarma	Quay	Quentan	Quick
Quamaine *(0.01)*	Quantavin	Quarmaine	Quay'shoan	Quentario	Quientá
Quaman	Quantavion	Quarry	Quay-Mec	Quentarius	Quientaveous
Quamane	Quantavious	Quartavious	Quayd	Quentarrius	Quienten
Quamar	*(0.01)*	Quartell	Quayde	Quentavious	Quientin
Quamarque	Quantavis	Quarterius	Quaye	*(0.01)*	Quienton
Quamayne	Quantavius *(0.01)*	Quarterrio	Quaylen	Quentavis	Quieric
Quame	Quantavous	Quartez	Quaymar	Quentavius	Quigan
Quamel	Quantay	Quartizz	Quaymere	Quentavrus	Quill
Quamelius	Quantaz	Quartus	Quayron	Quentay	Quillan
Quamell	Quante	Quarvalenta	Quaysan	Quentel	Quillen
Quamina	Quanté	Quas'ian	Quayshaun	Quentell	Quillin
Quamir	Quantel	Quasean	Quayshawn	Quenten *(0.01)*	Quillis
Quamy	Quantelius	Quashaan	Quayshon	Quenterias	Quillon
Quan *(0.01)*	Quantell	Quashad	Quayson	Quenterion	Quilo'
Quan Son	Quantelle	Quashan	Quayvaun	Quenterious	Quimar
Quan'drekus	Quantellis	Quashaud	Quayvon	Quenterius	Quimars-Jesus
Quan'tavius	Quantereis	Quashaun	Quazaidrick	Quenterrious	Quin *(0.01)*
Quan'te	Quanterio	Quashaunn	Quazza	Quenterrius	Quin Tera
Quan'tez	Quanterious	Quashawn *(0.01)*	Qucavon	Quenteze	Quin'chelle
Quan-Derrious	Quanterist	Quashon	Qudarius	Quentin *(0.33)*	Quin'darious
Quan-Minh	Quanterius	Quashone	Qudaruis	Quentin-Antone	Quin'darius
Quanah	Quanterrious	Quashun	Quddus	Quentine	Quin'ten
Quanard	Quanterris	Quasim	Qudrain	Quentis	Quin'terrius
Quanche	Quanteryion	Quatalius	Qudree	Quenton *(0.03)*	Quinard
Quancy	Quantez *(0.01)*	Quatarius	Que	Quentorrius	Quinawl
Quandarious	Quantico	Quatasce	Que Londis	Quentre	Quince
Quandarius	Quanties	Quatavious	Quecis	Quentrell	Quincee
Quandarrius	Quantiz	Quatavis	Quedell	Quentyn	Quincey *(0.01)*
Quandell	Quantonio	Quatavius	Queentrellus	Quentynn	Quinci
Quandrae	Quantral	Quataz	Quegee	Quenyenta	Quincy *(0.20)*
Quandre *(0.01)*	Quantravius	Quatez	Quei'trell	Quenzale	Quindale
Quandré	Quantre	Quatin	Queilan	Quenzavious	Quindariean
Quandreek	Quantrel	Quaton	Queion	Queondric	Quindarien
Quandrell	Quantrell	Quatravious	Queiturious	Queonte	Quindarious
Quane-Daris	Quantrelle	Quatre Lyn	Quejuan	Queroy	Quindarius *(0.01)*
Quanell	Quantrez	Quatrich	Quen'naldas	Ques	Quindarrius
Quanerious	Quantry	Quavante	Quen'travius	Ques T	Quindel

Quindell	Quintavion	Qujuan	Quy	Ra Jhan	Raashen
Quinderious	Quintavious (0.02)	Quleon	Quy-Dong	Ra Jon Akil	Raashod
Quinderus	Quintavis (0.01)	Qumaine	Quyen	Ra Mon	Raason
Quindez	Quintavius (0.02)	Qunetin	Quymane	Ra Shaad	Raattv
Quindray	Quintavus	Quntavies	Quynh	Ra Shawn	Rabee
Quindrey	Quintayvious	Quntavious	Quyterrious	Ra Shon	Rabeeh
Quindrius	Quinte	Qunterrius	Quzae	Ra'aed	Rabib
Quinétarius	Quintel	Quoatious	Qvon	Ra'darius	Rabie
Quinell	Quintele	Quoc (0.02)	Qwa Darius	Ra'eed	Rabih
Quinest	Quintell	Quoc Dung	Qwade	Ra'gene	Rabin
Quinjuante	Quintellis	Quoc Khuong	Qwadrick	Ra'heem	Rabon
Quinlan (0.03)	Quinten (0.09)	Quoc-Thai	Qwamari	Ra'heid	Racan
Quinlin	Quinterious	Quoc-Trung	Qwamaryah	Ra'heim	Race (0.01)
Quinn (0.32)	Quinterius	Quodadis	Qwane	Ra'jae	Racey
Quinn James	Quinterrio	Quomon	Qwantavious	Ra'jah	Rachaad
Quinn Lilomai	Quinterrious	Quon	Qwantavis	Ra'keem	Rachard
Quinn-Elliot	Quinterrius (0.01)	Quondarius	Qwantez	Ra'kjuan	Rachaun
Quinn-Tario	Quintese	Quonderrius	Qwenell	Ra'kuan	Rachavious
Quinncy	Quintevious	Quonnetavis	Qwentá	Ra'kueem	Rachazman
Quinndale	Quintez (0.01)	Quonshe	Qwentin	Ra'male	Rached
Quinndarius	Quinteze	Quontavious	Qweon	Ra'mone	Racheed
Quinnell	Quintilianus	Quontavius	Qweshawn	Ra'morrion	Rachel (0.01)
Quinnen	Quintin (0.15)	Quontel	Qwevonne	Ra'quan	Racherie
Quinnie	Quintine	Quonterace	Qwia	Ra'quell	Rachi
Quinnlin	Quintion	Quonterius	Qwintrell	Ra'quon	Rachid
Quinntavious	Quinton (0.37)	Quontravion	Qwonnta	Ra'san	Rachiim
Quinnten	Quinton Zackieu	Quordal	Qwontaveous	Ra'shad	Rachon
Quinntin	Quintonio	Quordarius	Qwontayvious	Ra'shard	Raciel
Quinnton	Quintorrius	Quordorole	Qwoy	Ra'shaud	Rackeem
Quinnzel	Quintravious	Quorey	Qwuantez	Ra'shaun	Rackim
Quinnzelle	Quintravius	Quortez	Qwunterius	Ra'shawn (0.01)	Rackwon
Quinshaun	Quintrel	Quory	Qwunzavius	Ra'shayne	Racquan
Quinshawn	Quintrell	Quoshad	Qwymann	Ra'sheam	Rad
Quinshea	Quintrevius	Quoshawn	Qylan	Ra'sheed	Radale
Quinshon	Quintrione	Quotavious	Qymyrys	Ra'suan	Radames
Quinshun	Quintus	Quotavius	Qynnshon	Ra'von	Radarrien
Quinson	Quintwan	Quovadias	Qynton	Ra'vonn	Radarrius
Quinsonta	Quintyn	Quovaun	Qyshawn	Ra-Keem	Radavius
Quinston	Quinza	Qur'aan		Raad	Rade
Quint	Quinzavies	Quran	**-R-**	Raafat	Radee
Quinta	Quinzelle	Qurell		Raafiq	Raden
Quintae	Quinzy	Quresh	R (0.03)	Raaheel	Radesmond
Quintan	Quion	Quron	R J	Raaheid	Radfan
Quintana	Quiondre	Qurtaz	R J Edward	Raaheim	Radford
Quintarian	Quiondré	Qusai	R L	Raahulan	Radhey
Quintario	Quirinius	Qushard	R Trease	Raajan	Radi
Quintarious	Quirino	Qushawn	R.	Raajinth	Radimar
Quintarius	Quiron	Qutavious	R. James	Raam	Radin
Quintarrius	Quishawn	Qutoris	R. Nickalus	Raamel	Radith
Quintarus	Quishon	Quvanté	R.D.	Raamen	Radja
Quintarvis	Quiten	Quvarious	R.L.	Raami	Radley
Quintaveious	Quiterrius	Quvonte	Ra	Raamiah	Radney
Quintaven	Quitman	Quwandré	Ra Dre	Raanan	Radom
Quintavian	Quiyaham	Quwante	Ra Gene	Raaquan	Radon
Quintavias		Quwillien	Ra Heem	Raashawn	Radosav

Radoslaw	Rafeeq	Rahiim	Raifert	Rajé	Rakib
Radrey	Rafer	Rahil	Raiford	Rajée	Rakie
Radu	Raffaele (0.01)	Rahill	Raigan	Rajeem	Rakiel
Radwan	Raffaello	Rahim (0.01)	Raige	Rajeen	Rakiev
Rady	Raffe	Rahime	Raihaan	Rajeeth	Rakiim
Rae	Raffel	Rahimullah	Raijon	Rajeev	Rakil
Rae Xhard	Raffi (0.01)	Rahium	Raiko	Rajeevh	Rakim (0.02)
Raékwon	Raffiel	Rahja	Raikwan	Rajeh	Rakinul
Raéquan	Raffiq	Rahjae	Railey	Rajelio	Rakip
Raéquon	Raffy	Rahjé	Raimanda	Rajen	Rakkan
Raéqwon	Rafi	Rahkal	Raimeise	Rajesh	Rakulan
Raésean	Rafiel	Rahkeem	Raimon	Raji	Rakunun
Raéshaun	Rafiki	Rahkeesh	Raimond	Rajin	Rakwane
Raéshawn	Rafiq	Rahkim	Raimondo	Rajinder	Rakwon
Raézhon	Rafique	Rahkman	Raimundo	Rajindra	Ralamar
Rae-Kwon	Ragan	Rahm	Rain	Rajish	Raleigh (0.02)
Raechaune	Ragavan	Rahmad	Raine (0.01)	Rajiv (0.01)	Ralf
Raed	Rageed	Rahman	Raine-Skyler	Rajkamal	Rali
Raedan	Rageh	Rahmeal	Rainee	Rajkanwar	Ralik
Raedarius	Ragen	Rahmel	Rainer	Rajkunvar	Raljot
Raedo	Raghav	Rahmere	Raines	Rajmel	Ralkeem
Raeem Croshay	Ragheb	Rahmi	Rainey	Rajneel	Ralona
Raefel	Raghulan	Rahmlee	Raini	Rajneish	Ralph (0.17)
Raeffel	Raghuraman	Rahn	Rainier	Rajohnte	Ralph Eric
Raegan	Ragiauan	Rahnard	Rainney	Rajon	Ralphael
Raeilon	Ragivan	Rahnee Jeremiah	Rainol	Rajoo	Ralphael-Jibri
Raejon	Ragnar	Rahod	Rainon	Rajpal	Ralpheal
Raekon	Ragu	Rahquan	Rainor	Rajpaul	Ralphel
Raekwan	Raguil	Rahsaan (0.01)	Rainy	Rajpreet	Ralphel'
Raekwon (0.06)	Ragulan	Rahsean	Raiquan	Raju	Ralphell
Rael	Rah'keem	Rahshai	Raiquen	Rajuan	Ralphiel
Raeland	Rah-Mel	Rahshard	Raiquon	Rajul	Ralphy
Raelyn	Rahaeim	Rahshawn	Raishawn	Rajun	Ralston
Raemil	Rahaze	Rahsheem	Raishon	Rajveer	Ram (0.01)
Raemon	Rahbar	Rahsheen	Raishun	Rajvir	Ramaar
Raemonn	Rahdames	Rahshid	Raistlin	Rakai	Ramachandra
Raenique	Rahe	Rahshmeer	Raistlyn	Rakan	Ramadan
Raequan (0.01)	Raheam	Rahson	Raj (0.01)	Rakavan	Ramadhan
Raequon	Rahean	Rahsontanoshstha	Raja	Rakedrick	Ramah
Raeqwon	Raheel	Rahtavian	Rajaah	Rakeel	Ramal
Raesean	Raheem (0.13)	Rahtriveo	Rajaahn	Rakeem (0.05)	Ramale
Raeshaun	Raheema	Rahul (0.05)	Rajah	Rakeem Amad	Ramalius
Raeshawn	Raheen (0.01)	Rahulan	Rajahe	Rakeeme	Ramall
Raeshe	Raheim (0.01)	Rahvin	Rajahmeel	Rakeen	Raman
Raeshon	Rahein	Rahyme	Rajai	Rakeez	Raman-Deep
Raeshun	Rahem	Rahzine	Rajain	Rakeill	Ramanan
Raevon	Rahevin	Rai	Rajajee	Rakeim	Ramanbeer
Raewkon	Raheym	Rai'shon	Rajan (0.02)	Rakel	Ramanda
Rafael (0.69)	Rahgené	Raiatea	Rajandeep	Rakem	Ramandeep (0.01)
Rafaele	Rahgul	Raibrinder	Rajandip	Rakeon	Ramanik
Rafaey	Rahi	Raid	Rajat	Rakesh	Ramanjeet
Rafal (0.01)	Rahib	Raidan	Rajbinder	Rakevion	Ramanjit
Rafat	Rahid	Raidel	Rajbir	Rakevious	Ramanpaul
Rafe	Rahiem	Raiden	Rajdeep	Rakheem	Ramanpreet
Rafeal	Rahien	Raider	Raje	Raki	Ramar

Ramarcus	Ramm	Randall David	Ranger	Raqjuan	Rashaude
Ramario	Rammie	Randall Jeric	Rangsey	Raquaill	Rashaun *(0.03)*
Ramases	Ramnik	Randall Jr	Rani	Raquan *(0.02)*	Rashawd
Ramavelan	Ramoan	Randall	Raniel	Raquané	Rashawn *(0.08)*
Ramazan	Ramon *(0.43)*	Osbourne	Ranier	Raquarius	Rashay
Rambert	Ramon Charles	Randall Tres	Ranim	Raqueil	Rashead
Ramces	Ramon Cristian	Randallon	Ranique	Raquel	Rashean
Ramdeo	Ramon'	Randam	Ranjet	Raquez	Rashed
Ramdy	Ramond *(0.01)*	Randan	Ranji'	Raquib	Rashee
Rame	Ramondi	Randarious	Ranjit	Raquiem	Rasheed *(0.05)*
Ramean	Ramondre	Randarius	Ranjodh	Raquill	Rasheek
Ramee	Ramone *(0.01)*	Randary	Ranjot	Raquish	Rasheem *(0.01)*
Rameed	Ramonenrique	Randdy	Rankin	Raqulan	Rasheen *(0.01)*
Rameek	Ramonte	Randee	Rannal	Raquon	Rasheid
Rameen	Ramonté	Randeep *(0.01)*	Rannel	Raquwan	Rasheim
Rameer	Ramos	Randel	Rannen	Raquwn	Rasheme
Ramees	Ramos Andrew	Randell *(0.02)*	Rannier	Raquwon	Rashi
Rameez	Ramsay	Randen	Rannylo	Raqwan	Rashica
Rameiko	Ramsee	Randerious	Ranon	Raqwann	Rashid *(0.02)*
Rameil	Ramses *(0.01)*	Randez	Ranous	Rarico	Rashid Rhawnish
Rameir	Ramsey *(0.04)*	Randhir	Ranquavious	Raricus	Rashidi
Rameke	Ramshad	Randi	Ranquavius	Rarshed	Rashie
Ramel *(0.01)*	Ramsie	Randie	Ransen	Rartosz	Rashied
Ramelio	Ramsin	Randiel	Ransford	Ras	Rashiem
Ramell	Ramson	Randip	Ranshad	Ras'deshaun	Rashion
Ramello	Ramsy	Randl	Ransis	Rasa	Rashmel
Ramelo	Ramuldo	Randle	Ransom *(0.01)*	Rasaan	Rashod *(0.01)*
Ramen	Ramun	Randoff	Rant	Rasaun	Rashodd
Ramere	Ramy *(0.01)*	Randolf	Ranta	Rasawn	Rashon *(0.01)*
Ramero	Ramzan	Randolfo	Rantavian	Raschaud	Rashone
Rames	Ramzee	Randolph *(0.06)*	Ranteg	Rase	Rashonn
Rameses	Ramzey	Random	Rantel	Rasean	Rashoud
Ramesh	Ramzez	Randon *(0.01)*	Rantez	Rasean-Tyrell	Rashpal
Ramey	Ramzi *(0.01)*	Randono	Ranton	Raseen	Rashrod
Ramez	Ramzy	Randrell	Rantorrance	Rash	Rashuan
Ramhar	Ran'quavious	Randsom	Rantrell	Rasha'd	Rashun
Rami *(0.04)*	Ran-Dale	Randtavius	Rantz	Rasha'un	Rashunn
Ramiel	Rana	Randy *(0.67)*	Ranujan	Rashaa'd	Rashuwn
Ramih	Ranadeep	Randy Jr	Ranulfo	Rashaad *(0.04)*	Rasia
Ramil	Ranail	Randy-James	Ranveer	Rashaam	Rasjit
Ramilio	Ranako	Randyallen	Ranvir	Rashaan *(0.03)*	Rasmus
Ramin	Ranan	Randyll	Rany	Rashaard	Rasmy
Raminder	Ranapreet	Randyn	Ranyodh	Rashad *(0.19)*	Rassel
Raminjeet	Ranard	Rane	Ranz	Rashad Antonio	Rasul
Ramio	Ranbir	Ranehesi	Ranzer	Rashada	Rasvan
Ramires	Rance *(0.01)*	Raneil	Ranzy	Rashadd	Ratana
Ramirez	Ranceford	Raneldon	Raonel	Rashade	Ratanak
Ramiro *(0.19)*	Ranch	Ranell	Raoul	Rashai	Ratavious
Ramiro Alejandr	Rand	Ranelle Arman	Raphael *(0.39)*	Rashamad	Ratavius
Ramis	Randace	Ranerquant	Raphael-Kahlil	Rashan *(0.01)*	Rateb
Ramit	Randahl	Raney	Raphawn	Rashann	Ratha
Ramitha	Randal *(0.05)*	Ranferi	Raphe	Rashany	Ratham
Ramitpal	Randal-Joseph	Ranferl	Rapheal *(0.01)*	Rashard *(0.03)*	Rathana
Ramius	Randale	Rangeer	Raphel	Rasharrd	Rathasar
Ramiz	Randall *(0.40)*	Rangel	Raphiel	Rashaud *(0.01)*	Ratib

Ratissa	Rawad	Rayfield	Raynal	Razak	Rece
Ratiyondre	Rawaz	Rayford	Raynaldo	Razel	Recha
Ratrell	Rawel	Rayhaan	Raynall	Razell	Recharde
Ratwinder	Rawen	Rayhan	Raynard (0.01)	Razhede	Rechazz
Raudel (0.02)	Rawhiem	Rayhem	Raynarde	Razhee	Reche
Raudip	Rawim	Rayimundo	Raynathan	Razhon	Rechu
Rauheem	Rawkea	Rayje	Raynathon	Razi	Recky
Raul (0.66)	Rawle	Rayjon	Rayne (0.01)	Raziel (0.01)	Reco
Raul John	Rawley	Rayjone	Raynee	Raziq	Red
Rauldel	Rawling	Raykale	Raynel	Razu	Reda
Rauldelis	Rawlings	Raykeem	Raynel-Jan	Rc	Redd
Raumir	Rawlyn	Raykez	Raynell	Rcnard	Reddrick
Raunel	Rawn	Raykwon	Raynere	Rdjustice	Redeate
Raunell	Rawshard	Raylan	Raynier	Re	Redel
Raurie	Rawshon	Raylen	Rayno	Re Kory	Redell
Raushaan	Raxem	Raylin	Raynoor	Rémone	Rederick
Raushan	Raxon	Raylon	Rayon	Rénell	Redge
Raushaun	Ray (0.22)	Raylun	Rayondre	Réo	Redh
Raushaundre	Ray Axl	Rayman	Raypheal	Réquan	Redin
Raushod	Ray Delle	Raymand	Rayqu'on	Réquin	Redjo
Raustin	Ray El	Raymann	Rayquan (0.01)	Résean	Redmond
Ravan	Ray Field	Rayme	Rayquashawn	Réshad	Redvers
Ravanna	Ray Shaun	Raymeanus	Rayquel	Réshaun	Ree
Ravaughn	Ray Webb	Raymel	Raysean (0.01)	Réshawn	Reece (0.11)
Ravean	Ray'keem	Raymell	Rayshaan	Résheem	Reeche
Raveen	Ray'shaun	Raymen	Rayshad	Réshuan	Reecie
Raveil	Ray'shean	Raymer	Rayshard	Réthaniel	Reed (0.23)
Raven (0.04)	Ray'var	Raymi	Rayshaud	Rea Nel	Reef
Raven-River	Ray'vell	Raymil	Rayshaun (0.01)	Rea'von	Reegan
Raveon	Ray'von	Raymius	Rayshawn (0.03)	Reace	Reegor
Ravez	Ray'zian	Raymome	Raysheed	Reachi	Reem
Ravi (0.03)	Ray-Deandre	Raymon (0.02)	Rayshon (0.01)	Reacy	Rees (0.01)
Ravijot	Ray-Mond	Raymonce	Rayshone	Read	Reese (0.09)
Ravin	Ray-Von	Raymond (1.32)	Rayshonn	Readale	Reesen
Ravinda	Rayaaz	Raymond George	Rayshord	Reade	Reeshay
Ravinder	Rayad	Raymond III	Rayshun	Reagan (0.03)	Reetam
Ravinderpal	Rayan (0.01)	Raymond Matthew	Rayshundre	Reagen	Reeve (0.01)
Ravindra	Rayaun	Raymond Niko	Rayshunn	Reaghan	Reeves
Ravine	Rayaz	Raymond-Laurent	Rayson	Reakwon	Reeyon
Ravion	Raybert	Raymond-Shu	Raytao	Real (0.01)	Refaat
Ravirajsinh	Rayce (0.01)	Raymondo	Raytavius	Reality	Refael
Ravis	Raychad	Raymone	Rayten	Reamond	Refoel
Ravji	Raychon	Raymong	Raytrawn	Reamual	Refugio (0.02)
Ravjit	Raydarius	Raymont	Rayvan	Reamullu	Refujio
Ravkirat	Raydell	Raymord	Rayvanell	Reanaldo	Rega
Ravneel	Rayden (0.02)	Raymun	Rayvant	Reann	Regal
Ravneet	Rayder	Raymund	Rayvaun	Reardon	Regan (0.03)
Ravon (0.01)	Raydin	Raymund Jesus	Rayven	Rease	Regarl
Ravon-Richard	Raydun	Raymund Matthew	Rayvis	Reazen	Regdrick
Ravone	Raye	Raymundo (0.09)	Rayvon (0.01)	Reazon	Regelio
Ravonn	Rayeddrick	Rayn	Rayvone	Rebecca	Regen
Ravonne	Rayedon	Raynair	Rayvontez	Rebekah	Regenald
Ravonte	Rayeed		Rayzone	Rebel	Regev
Ravuth	Rayen		Raz	Rebel-Lee	Regg
Ravyn	Rayfael		Raza	Recardo	Reggep

Reggie *(0.04)*	Reindon	Renaid	Renyck	Rexter	Rhamel
Regginald	Reindorf	Renald	Renz	Rexton	Rhandy
Regi	Reine	Renaldin	Renzo	Rexx	Rhane
Regie	Reinel	Renaldo *(0.01)*	Renzy	Rexzelle	Rhanel
Reginal *(0.01)*	Reiner	Renaldre	Renzzo	Rey *(0.04)*	Rhasaan
Reginal-Mahkie	Reinhard	Renale	Reo *(0.01)*	Reyad	Rhashaan
Reginald *(0.38)*	Reinhold	Renan	Reon	Reyan	Rhashaud
Reginald Brandon	Reinhold	Renandoes	Reonard	Reyaz	Rhasheed
Reginald Jo	Matthew	Renanta	Reondea	Reyce	Rhaven
Reginald-Mar	Reiniel	Renard *(0.02)*	Reontay	Reyd	Rhea
Reginald-Rolin	Reinier	Renardo	Reoshard	Reydelsel	Rheagan
Reginaldo	Reiny	Renato *(0.01)*	Reoto	Reyer	Rheal
Reginard	Reiondai	Renato Jesse	Requan	Reyes *(0.04)*	Rheam
Reginauld	Reis	Renaud *(0.03)*	Rese	Reyhan	Rhean
Regineau	Reise	Renauld	Resean	Reyly	Rheed
Reginold	Reison	Renault	Resha	Reymon	Rhema
Reginuld	Reiss	Renay	Reshad	Reymond *(0.01)*	Rhen
Region	Rejean *(0.01)*	Renbarren	Reshae	Reymound	Rheo
Regis *(0.01)*	Rejeeth	Rendell *(0.01)*	Reshanth	Reymund	Rhet
Regneaus	Rejhi	Render	Reshard	Reymundo *(0.02)*	Rhetlee
Regor	Rejino	Rendontey	Resharde	Reynal	Rhett *(0.11)*
Rehan *(0.01)*	Rejjan	Rendy	Reshaud	Reynald	Rhett Lee
Rehaz	Rejkard	Rene *(0.33)*	Reshaun	Reynaldo *(0.09)*	Rheyce
Rehland	Rekwahn	René	Reshawd	Reynaldy	Rhian
Rehman	Rekwane	Rene-Antonio	Reshawn *(0.01)*	Reynard	Rhianon
Rehmat	Relijah	Renedo	Reshayne	Reynaud	Rhidley
Rei'chuan	Rellkwaun	Renee *(0.01)*	Reshea	Reynauldo	Rhiheem
Reice	Remaliah	Renegem	Reshead	Reynerio	Rhiley
Reichaun	Remarcus	Reneil	Reshod	Reynier	Rhine
Reichel	Remaro	Renel	Reshon	Reynol	Rhiron
Reichle	Remaz	Renell	Ressy	Reynold	Rhiston
Reid *(0.28)*	Remberto	Renen	Reston	Reynold Lowen	Rhiver
Reidar	Remello	Reneque	Resty	Reynolds	Rhobbie
Reif	Remeo	Renfort	Retha	Reyon	Rhodec
Reigan	Remey	Renick	Rethyl	Reyshaan	Rhoderick
Reighan	Remi *(0.06)*	Reniel	Reuban	Reysin	Rhodri
Reighn	Remi-Gabriel	Renier	Reuben *(0.10)*	Reyu	Rhonald
Reign	Remiah	Renison	Reuber	Reyven	Rhondda
Reiker	Remigio	Renjamin	Reubin	Reyvon	Rhonell
Reiki	Remijio	Renn	Reuel	Reza *(0.01)*	Rhotonda
Reiko	Remington *(0.06)*	Rennard	Reuven	Rezamond	Rhouri
Reiland	Reminton	Rennice	Revan	Rezaul	Rhoynald
Reiley	Remize	Rennick	Revard	Rezzin	Rhuben
Reilley	Remko	Rennie	Revaughn	Rha'san	Rhyan *(0.01)*
Reilly *(0.05)*	Remmington	Rennold	Revel	Rhad	Rhyce
Reily	Remmy	Renny	Revelation	Rhaed	Rhydon
Reimer	Remo	Reno *(0.05)*	Revell	Rhafiki	Rhygis
Reimon	Remon	Renol	Revelle	Rhaheim	Rhyheem
Reimon Niel	Remone	Renold	Reven	Rhahime	Rhyheim
Reimundo	Remy *(0.05)*	Renous	Revenel	Rhai	Rhyidh
Rein	Remyck	Renquez	Revon	Rhailyn	Rhylan
Reinald	Ren	Rens	Revonte	Rhajaan	Rhyland
Reinaldo *(0.02)*	Ren Drick	Rentavious	Rex *(0.06)*	Rhajee	Rhylee
Reinan	Ren-Chieh	Renton	Rexford	Rhakeem	Rhyley
Reinard	Renado	Renwick	Rexmay	Rhaman	Rhyme

Rhymeeke
Rhymerais
Rhyne
Rhyquon
Rhys *(0.04)*
Rhys Michael
Rhyse
Rhysheen
Rhyston
Ri'chard
Ri'onne
Riá
Riad
Rian *(0.01)*
Riaz
Ribahin
Ribelino
Ric
Ric'quan
Ric'queze
Ric-Teanny
Ricade
Ricardale
Ricardi
Ricardito
Ricardo *(1.39)*
Ricardo Jr
Ricardoe
Ricca
Riccardo *(0.01)*
Riccarrdo
Ricco *(0.01)*
Rice
Ricesell
Rich
Richad
Richand
Richard *(3.88)*
Richard Austin
Richard Christi
Richard David
Richard II
Richard Jr
Richard Lynn
Richard Minh
Richard William
Richard-Deniro
Richardo
Richardre
Richardson
Richaud
Richdell
Richelyn
Richeman
Richer

Richerd
Richers
Richey
Richi
Richial
Richie *(0.03)*
Richie Ricardo
Richird
Richky
Richlon
Richly
Richmon
Richmond *(0.01)*
Richmondreachi
Richmore
Richorias
Richrd
Richshod
Richwill
Richy
Rick *(0.11)*
Rickee
Rickeem
Rickeen
Rickell
Ricken
Rickey *(0.10)*
Ricki *(0.01)*
Rickia
Rickie *(0.03)*
Rickilee
Ricklyn
Rickman
Ricktez
Rickvir
Rickwinder
Ricky *(0.61)*
Ricky Jr
Ricky Kadar
Ricky-Ryan
Rickyeon
Rickyjoe
Rico *(0.07)*
Ricorey
Ricquais
Ricquell
Ricquone
Ricshay
Rictavious
Rida
Ridarius
Ridda
Riddick
Rider *(0.01)*
Ridge *(0.04)*

Ridgley
Ridhwaan
Ridley
Ridvan
Ridwaan
Ridwaanur
Ried
Riel
Rielen
Rieley
Rielly
Riely
Riese
Rifat
Riffinsky
Rigas
Rigby
Rigdon
Rigekaanth
Rigel *(0.01)*
Riggs
Rigit
Rigo *(0.02)*
Rigo-Verto
Rigobert
Rigoberto *(0.13)*
Rigsbee
Riguel
Riis
Rij
Rijad
Rik
Riker *(0.01)*
Rikesh
Rikhil
Riki
Rikker
Rikkey
Rikki *(0.01)*
Rikley
Rikondja
Rikoy
Rikuo
Rikwavis
Riky
Rilde
Rilee
Riley *(1.03)*
Riley Joseph
Rilley-Joseph
Rily
Rilyn
Rimas
Rimirez
Rimon

Rinaldi
Rindel
Rinesh
Riney
Ringo
Rini
Rinku
Rino
Rinz
Rio *(0.02)*
Rio Day
Rio De Jane
Riolando
Rion
Rione
Rionin
Riordan
Riot
Rip
Ripandeep
Ripken
Ripley
Riquel
Riqui
Risaban
Risanth
Rischard
Risha'ard
Rishaad
Rishab
Rishabh
Rishad
Rishal
Rishard
Rishav
Rishawn
Rishay
Rishi *(0.02)*
Rishikesh
Rishjaun
Rishon
Rishone
Risi
Risler
Rissell
Risto
Riston
Risun
Rit'chard
Ritan
Ritch
Ritchard
Ritchie *(0.02)*
Ritchy
Ritesh

Rithi
Ritho
Rithy
Ritish
Rittaporn
Ritvik
Ritwan
Rivan
Rivarius
River *(0.11)*
Rivera-Wilcox
Rivers
Riverton
Riviera
Rivor
Rixon
Riyaad
Riyad
Riyadh
Riyah
Riyan
Riyaz
Riyazh
Riyoberto
Riyod
Riza
Rizek
Rizgar
Rizwaan
Rizwan
Rizzano
Rj
Rjay
Rlonte
Ro Darius
Ro Shaun
Ro Velle
Ro'jahmene
Ro'melle
Ro-Derick
Roam
Roan
Roand
Roandy
Roarke
Rob *(0.01)*
Roba
Robah
Robal
Robar
Robb
Robben
Robbert
Robbey
Robbi

Robbie *(0.04)*
Robbin
Robby *(0.03)*
Robdriquz
Robe
Robel *(0.01)*
Roben
Robena
Robens
Robenson
Rober
Roberson
Robert *(8.67)*
Robert Alexander
Robert Alexis
Robert Austin
Robert Earl
Robert Hont
Robert III
Robert Jay
Robert Jr
Robert Ky'rion
Robert Michael
Robert Tres'
Robert William
Robert-Alexander
Robert-Anthony
Robert-Dillion
Robert-Eli
Robert-Harold
Robert-James
Robert-Lee
Robert-Michael
Robert.oscar
Roberta
Roberte
Robertino
Roberto *(0.91)*
Roberto Octavius
Roberto Vicente
Roberto-Alejandr
Robertoadaly
Roberts
Robertson
Robeson
Robeto
Robie
Robiel
Robilin
Robin *(0.17)*
Robin-Johannes
Robins
Robinson
Robinton
Robiu

Roble
Robleh
Robreon
Robrico
Robson
Roby
Robyn *(0.01)*
Robynne-Tyronne
Roccas
Rocci
Rocco *(0.03)*
Roccorosano
Roceam
Roch *(0.01)*
Rochaad
Rochane
Rochelle
Rochester
Rochield
Rochon
Rociel
Rocio
Rock *(0.01)*
Rockell
Rocket
Rockey
Rockford
Rockie
Rockim
Rocking
Rockland
Rocko
Rockquan
Rockwell
Rocky *(0.07)*
Rocque
Rocquell
Rocquez
Rocqui
Rocsoe
Rod *(0.01)*
Rod Darius
Rod Derius
Rod'darius
Rodalfo
Rodareo
Rodareun
Rodarion
Rodarius
Rodd
Roddean
Rodderial
Rodderick
Roddrick
Roddrigues

Roddy
Roddy Jr
Rodeam
Rodel
Rodelle
Roden
Rodeny
Roderic
Roderick *(0.19)*
Roderick Bry
Roderico
Roderik
Roderious
Roderius
Roderrick
Rodger *(0.01)*
Rodgerick
Rodgers
Rodgric
Rodi
Rodick
Rodiero
Rodiguz
Rodin
Rodlin
Rodmil
Rodnei
Rodneill
Rodnell
Rodnelle
Rodney *(0.46)*
Rodney Paul
Rodnick
Rodny
Rodolfo *(0.25)*
Rodquez
Rodrakus
Rodrecius
Rodreckis
Rodrecus
Rodreuta
Rodric
Rodricaus
Rodricco
Rodrick *(0.04)*
Rodricqous
Rodricus
Rodriekus
Rodrigo *(0.22)*
Rodrigquez
Rodriguez *(0.01)*
Rodrique
Rodriques
Rodriquez *(0.01)*
Rodriquiez

Rodrius
Rodrus
Rodsco
Rodshawn
Rodterius
Rodulfo
Rodzavien
Rodzell
Roe
Roe Mello
Roee
Roel *(0.02)*
Roelle
Roemell
Roemello *(0.01)*
Roemon
Roenick
Roey
Rofel
Roferson
Rog'dravious
Rogan
Rogdrick
Roge
Rogeem
Rogein
Rogelio *(0.22)*
Rogen
Roger *(0.44)*
Roger-Tankor
Roger-Wayne
Rogerick
Rogerio
Rogers
Rogiens
Roginald
Rognee
Rogrick
Rohail
Rohan *(0.05)*
Roheem
Rohelio
Rohin
Rohinesh
Rohit *(0.02)*
Rohith
Rohn
Rohnalzo
Rohshawn
Roi
Roi Bel-Amour
Roi-El
Roiess
Roitravious
Rojaza

Rojclio
Rojee
Rojée
Rojelio *(0.01)*
Rojshawn
Roke
Rokeem
Rokel
Rokheam
Roki
Roko
Roktim
Rolan
Roland *(0.12)*
Rolando *(0.18)*
Rolandon
Roldan
Rolde
Roleen
Rolf
Rolfe
Rolin
Rolland *(0.01)*
Rollans
Rollden
Rolle
Rollie
Rollin *(0.01)*
Rollins
Rollsky
Rolman
Rolondo
Rolono
Rolshawn
Rolston
Rom
Rom-And
Roma
Romahd
Romai
Romaiel
Romailo
Romain *(0.01)*
Romain Elliott
Romaine
Romal
Romales
Romalice
Romall
Romallis
Romallo
Roman *(0.27)*
Romance
Romando
Romandré

Romane
Romanel
Romani
Romann
Romanne
Romano
Romanon
Romante
Romanual
Romao
Romar
Romarcus
Romarico
Romario *(0.05)*
Romarius
Romaro
Romarrio
Romas
Romaus
Rome
Roméu'l
Romeal
Romecio
Romeike
Romeilo
Romeiro
Romel *(0.03)*
Romele
Romelin
Romelio
Romell *(0.01)*
Romello *(0.04)*
Romello-Carm
Romellow
Romelo *(0.01)*
Romelo-William
Romen
Romeo *(0.04)*
Romeollo
Romer
Romeral
Romeraux
Romere
Romerio
Romeris
Romero *(0.01)*
Romeryo
Rometrius
Romg
Romhanyi
Romi
Romiel
Romielo
Romil
Romillo

Romin
Romit
Rommel *(0.02)*
Rommello
Rommie
Rommy
Romneesh
Romnel
Romo
Romoad
Romon
Romonal
Romond
Romondo
Romontae
Romonte
Romontre
Romtin
Romuald
Romualdo
Romulo
Romulus
Romy
Romyko
Ron *(0.06)*
Ron Darius
Ron Derrick
Ron Zell
Ron'darius
Ron'shad
Ron'shay
Ronaele
Ronak *(0.01)*
Ronal
Ronald *(0.96)*
Ronald Alexande
Ronald James
Ronald Joseph
Ronald Jr
Ronald Robert
Ronald Spencer
Ronaldo *(0.02)*
Ronalds
Ronaldy
Ronan *(0.01)*
Ronard
Ronat
Ronate
Ronatiio
Ronaveer
Rond
Rondal
Rondale
Rondall
Rondarious

Rondarius	Ronny *(0.03)*	Roque *(0.01)*	Rossi	Royal *(0.01)*	Ruchell
Rondel	Ronquel	Rordon	Rossie	Royale	Ruchir
Rondell *(0.01)*	Ronquerris	Rori	Rossini	Royall	Ruchit
Ronderick	Ronquil	Roric	Rosslan	Royan	Rucker
Ronderious	Ronquis	Roriquez	Rosston	Royce *(0.08)*	Rudd
Ronderrick	Ronrico	Rorrie	Rossy	Roychester	Ruddene
Rondetrich	Ronshawn	Rorry	Rostam	Roydarius	Ruddy
Rondexter	Ronson	Rory *(0.11)*	Rosten	Roydavid	Ruderick
Rondicious	Ronsonie	Roryck	Rostislav	Royden	Rudgerry
Rondney	Rontae	Rosa	Roston	Roydreakus	Rudi
Rondo	Rontarius	Rosalino	Rostum	Roye	Rudie
Rondon	Rontarrius	Rosalio *(0.02)*	Rostyn	Royell	Rudiz
Rondre	Rontavian	Rosano	Rot'ciy	Royer	Rudnath
Rondrell	Rontavious	Rosario *(0.02)*	Rotanok	Roylis	Rudnel
Rondrequis	Rontavis	Rosbie	Rotel	Roymell	Rudo
Rondrevious	Rontavius	Rosby	Roth	Roymone	Rudolf
Rondrez	Rontay	Roscher	Rothanack	Roynell	Rudolfo
Rondric	Ronte	Rosco	Rotney	Royquel	Rudolph *(0.04)*
Rondrick	Rontel	Roscoe *(0.02)*	Rouacha	Royriecus	Rudolpho
Rondriques	Rontelyn	Roscole	Roubins	Royshon	Rudon
Rondy	Ronterio	Roselle	Roudy	Roytai	Rudra
Rone	Ronterious	Rosember	Roulston	Roytavious	Rudy *(0.25)*
Ronea	Ronterries	Rosemberg	Roumelle	Roytez	Rue
Roneal	Ronterrious	Rosemond	Rouney	Roytrell	Rueban
Roneek	Rontez	Rosendio	Rourke	Royundre	Rueben *(0.02)*
Roneil	Rontorius	Rosendo *(0.03)*	Rouse	Royvonta	Ruebin
Ronel *(0.01)*	Rontravis	Rosento	Rousevel	Royz	Ruel
Ronell *(0.01)*	Rontre	Rosevelt	Rousner	Royzell	Ruell
Ronelle	Rontrell	Roseyvel	Rovandel	Rozario	Rueshad
Ronen	Rontrevius	Roshad *(0.01)*	Rovel	Rozell	Ruevim
Roney	Rontrey	Roshain	Rovelle	Rozier	Rufaro
Ronez	Rontrez	Roshall	Rovert	Rozzey	Rufat
Rong	Rony *(0.01)*	Roshan *(0.02)*	Roverto	Rs	Rufeal
Roni	Ronyam	Roshane	Rovonta	Rsandy	Rufino *(0.01)*
Ronico	Ronyeah	Roshard	Rovontae	Rsei	Rufus *(0.02)*
Ronier	Ronyell	Roshaun	Rovonté	Ru'shaun	Rugen
Ronil	Ronzal	Roshawn	Rovortis	Ruaidhri	Ruger
Ronit	Ronzel	Roshawnski	Rovoyin	Ruairi	Ruggery
Ronjel	Ronzeld	Rosheem	Rowan *(0.03)*	Ruairi'	Rui
Ronkel	Ronzelle	Rosheim	Rowdie	Ruairidh	Ruisdael
Ronkeria	Ronzicus	Roshen	Rowdy *(0.01)*	Rual	Ruiz
Ronmarcus	Ronzo	Roshi	Rowe	Ruan	Rujuhn
Ronmel	Roodney	Roshida	Rowea	Ruandi	Rukshan
Ronnald	Roodson	Roshir	Rowell	Ruark	Rulberto
Ronndell	Roody	Roshoad	Rowen	Ruayen	Ruley
Ronnel	Roojerry	Roshon	Rowland	Ruban	Rully
Ronnell *(0.01)*	Rook	Roshord	Rowlando	Rubean	Rulon
Ronnelle	Rooldolph	Roshun	Rowley	Ruben *(0.76)*	Rulondo
Ronney	Roop	Rosier	Rowmontoe	Rubens	Rumae
Ronnie *(0.26)*	Roopinder	Rosny	Rowyn	Rubianny	Rumal
Ronnie Dévonte	Rooservelt	Ross *(0.38)*	Roy *(0.32)*	Rubicela	Rumaldo
Ronnie Lee	Roosevelt *(0.04)*	Rossana	Roy Derrick	Rubiel	Rumalus
Ronnie-Maurel	Roosvelt	Rossano	Roy Don	Rubin *(0.01)*	Ruman
Ronnijoe	Roper	Rosscol	Roy Edward Jr	Rubinson	Rumeal
Ronniy	Roperto	Rosser	Roy Mark	Ruby	Rumel

Rumesh	Ruthann	Rydder	Ryne Christopher	Saadallah	Sabir
Ruminder	Ruthran	Rydell	Ryne Joseph	Saadat	Sable
Rumman	Rutledge	Ryden	Rynell	Saadiah	Sablond
Rummeal	Rutvik	Ryder *(0.07)*	Ryneque	Saadiq	Sabo
Rumtin	Ruupan	Rydge	Ryner	Saadya	Sabona
Run	Ruvaid	Rydon	Rynn	Saafir	Saboor
Run-Hong	Ruvern	Rydreques	Ryo *(0.01)*	Saafir-Ahmid	Sabrean
Rune	Ruven	Rye	Ryohei	Saagar	Sabri
Runell	Ruvim	Ryechic	Ryoji	Saagarkumar	Sabrie
Rungrote	Ruvium	Ryein	Ryon *(0.01)*	Saaheb	Sabrina *(0.01)*
Runy	Ruvon	Ryeker	Ryosuke	Saahil	Sabryn
Rupchand	Ruvoun	Ryeland	Ryota	Saaid	Sabyn
Rupert *(0.01)*	Ruxter	Ryeleigh	Ryou	Saaif	Sacardus
Ruperto	Ruyer	Ryely	Ryrecus	Saaijan	Sacaremento
Ruperto Jr	Ruyssell	Ryen *(0.01)*	Rysan	Saajan	Sacario
Ruperto Santiago	Ruzo	Ryer	Ryse	Saajanpreet	Sacha *(0.02)*
Rupin	Ruzshanth	Ryerson	Ryshaun	Saajenjeet	Sachbir
Rupinder	Rvaraidh	Ryese	Rysheed	Saajid	Sachery
Rurel	Ry	Ryeshene	Rysheek	Saam	Sachiel
Rurik	Ry Drick	Ryez	Rysheem	Saamer	Sachin *(0.01)*
Rury	Ry Keem	Ryheem	Ryshie	Saar	Sachith
Rusdy	Ry'chon	Ryhem	Rytirius	Saarangan	Sachneet
Rusean	Ry'dealous	Ryian	Ryu	Saardar	Sack Sith
Rush	Ry'kel	Ryiann	Ryuhei	Saavan	Sacra
Rushabh	Ry'kell	Ryiemmle	Ryun	Saawan	Sacral
Rushan	Ry'mone	Ryien	Ryus	Saba	Sacramento
Rushane	Ryad	Ryikeem	Ryusei	Sabah	Sadabius
Rushaud	Ryaime	Ryk	Ryuta	Sabaian	Sadair
Rushawn	Ryair	Ryker *(0.05)*	Ryyan	Saban	Sadale
Rushi	Ryall	Rykess	Ryzarius	Sabastain	Sadarian
Rushil	Ryam	Rykken	Ryzen	Sabastian *(0.02)*	Sadaris
Rushine	Ryan *(11.24)*	Rykley		Sabastiano	Sadarius
Rushton	Ryan Calvin	Ryky	**-S-**	Sabastien *(0.01)*	Sadat
Ruslan	Ryan James	Rylan *(0.08)*		Sabastin	Saddarion
Russ	Ryan John	Ryland *(0.04)*	S *(0.03)*	Sabastion	Saddauius
Russel *(0.03)*	Ryan Jr	Ryle	S Sukhvir	Sabaston	Sade
Russel Thomas	Ryan Omar	Rylean	S Von	Sabata	Sadeek
Russell *(0.52)*	Ryan-Anthony	Rylec	S.	Sabatino	Sadek
Russell-Joseph	Ryan-Nathaniel	Ryledenn	Sa	Sabato	Saderous
Russelle	Ryan-Scott	Rylee *(0.02)*	Sa Ku	Sabazz	Saderrick
Russhane	Ryana	Ryleigh	Sa Mir	Sabba	Sadi
Russton	Ryandeep	Rylen	Sa Vaun	Sabbastiun	Sadig
Russuane	Ryane	Ryley *(0.10)*	Sa'ad	Sabbath	Sadik
Rust	Ryanell	Rylie *(0.01)*	Sa'd	Sabe	Sadiki
Rustam	Ryanjeet	Rylier	Sa'darius	Sabearien	Sadiq
Rustamjeet	Ryanley	Rylin	Sa'eed	Sabeel	Sadler
Ruste	Ryann *(0.01)*	Ryllie	Sa'mard	Saben	Sadman
Rusten	Ryano	Rylon	Sa'quan	Saber	Sadrach
Rustin *(0.01)*	Ryare	Rylyn	Sa'valis	Sabestian	Sadrian
Rustom	Ryashown	Rylynn	Sa'von	Sabian	Sadrick
Ruston	Ryce	Rynado	Sa'vonn	Sabien	Sady
Rusty *(0.05)*	Ryche	Rynalder	Sa'youn	Sabijan	Sae
Rustyn	Rycheelm	Rynard	Sa-Von	Sabin	Saévon
Rutavies	Rycher	Ryndon	Saabashton	Sabino *(0.01)*	Sae-Won
Rutger *(0.01)*	Ryckiel	Ryne *(0.04)*	Saad *(0.01)*	Sabio	Saed

Saeder	Sahir	Sajdeep	Salem *(0.01)*	Samauel	Samrat
Saeed	Sahirtaj	Saje	Salento	Samaundre	Samron
Saeeda	Sahne	Sajed	Salers	Sambathany	Samsiva
Saeem	Sahvon	Sajeed	Salesi	Sambit	Samson *(0.06)*
Saequan	Sai	Sajeel	Sali	Sambou	Samtavious
Saesheon	Sai'quan	Sajeesan	Salih	Samdarsh	Samuael
Saevon	Sai'von	Sajeev	Salik	Samdiel	Samuail
Saf'yuan	Sai-Srinivas	Sajeevan	Salil	Samdor	Samual *(0.03)*
Safari	Saic	Sajevan	Salim *(0.01)*	Samdri	Samuel *(6.66)*
Safarian	Saichy	Sajhmori	Saljoq	Sameeh	Samuel Christop
Safe	Said *(0.01)*	Sajid	Salko	Sameem	Samuel Elias
Safeer	Saidall	Sajill	Salle	Sameer *(0.03)*	Samuel Miguel
Safet	Saide	Sajin	Sally	Sameh	Samuel Steven
Saffa	Saideep	Sajind	Salmaan	Sameko	Samuel-Hunter
Safi	Saied	Sajir	Salman *(0.02)*	Samel	Samuel-Joseph
Safi-Ul-Lah	Saieed	Sajjad	Salmit	Samendra	Samuel-Lee
Safian	Saieesan	Sajjan	Salmon	Sameon	Samuel-Tre
Safraz	Saier	Sajo	Saloman	Samer *(0.03)*	Samuela
Safwaan	Saiesan	Sajoesph	Salome	Sameul	Samuele
Safwan	Saievon	Sakarai	Salomon *(0.02)*	Samhain	Samuell
Sagal	Saif *(0.02)*	Sakari	Salters	Sami *(0.05)*	Samuelle
Sagan	Saif Allah	Sakasteow	Salton	Samidh	Samuelu
Sagar *(0.03)*	Saif El Din	Sakeem	Salud	Samier	Samule
Sage *(0.10)*	Saif-Ullah	Sakentrey	Salum	Samih	Samuri
Sage Michael	Saifaldin	Sakhile	Salvador *(0.51)*	Samip	Samvecheth
Sageevan	Saifeldden	Sakia	Salvadore	Samir *(0.05)*	Samy *(0.02)*
Sagen	Saiffullah	Sakile	Salvator	Samirali	Samydra
Sager	Saige *(0.01)*	Sakilye	Salvatore *(0.09)*	Samiu	Samyuth
Sagiv	Saiharan	Sakima	Salvattore	Samiuddin	San
Sagor	Saihou	Sakishan	Salviano	Samiuela	San Vinnichi
Sagwinder	Saijuran	Sakohawitsere	Salvin	Samiul	San'joshua
Sahab	Saikirthi	Sakori	Salvintino	Samley	San'quan
Sahain	Sailesh	Sakthi	Sam *(0.25)*	Sammad	San'ton
Sahajpal	Sailor	Sakweontaris	Sam Alexander	Sammer	Sanad
Sahal	Saim	Sal *(0.01)*	Sam Shyunn	Sammi	Sanahan
Sahalet	Saime	Sala	Sam-Calin	Sammie *(0.01)*	Sanamanca
Sahamaa	Saimion	Sala'h Ad-Di'n	Sama	Sammier	Sanamjot
Sahan	Saimullah	Salaam	Samad	Sammnuel	Sanampreet
Sahand	Sainath	Salaar	Samadhi	Sammurelle	Sanan
Saharat	Saint	Salah *(0.01)*	Samaer	Sammy *(0.09)*	Sanath
Saharus	Saint-John	Salah'urdeen	Samal	Samnang	Sanayan
Sahat	Saintano	Salahadine	Saman	Samneet	Sanchaz
Sahdarian	Saion	Salahaldin	Samandeep	Samolu	Sanchez *(0.01)*
Sahed	Sairam	Salaheddene	Samanjera	Samon	Sancheze
Saheed	Sairse	Salahideen	Samante	Samon'te	Sandale
Saheel	Sais	Salahudeen	Samantha *(0.01)*	Samonte	Sandario
Saheenan	Saishan	Salam	Samar	Samonté	Sandeep *(0.02)*
Sahel	Saivon	Salama	Samarge	Samora K.	Sander
Sahem	Saivontre	Salar	Samari	Samori	Sanders
Sahen	Saiyed	Salas	Samariel	Samosir	Sanderson
Sahfar	Saiyeed	Salathiel	Samario Glenn	Sampeir	Sandford
Sahi	Saiyong	Salazar	Samartha	Samprati	Sandi
Sahib	Sajan	Salden	Samatar *(0.01)*	Sampson *(0.01)*	Sandino
Sahid	Sajankumar	Saleem *(0.01)*	Samater	Samr	Sandip
Sahil *(0.03)*	Sajanpreet	Saleh *(0.01)*	Samaudrick	Samraj	Sandler

Sandon	Santania	Sard	Satinder	Savkaran	Sayyid
Sandor	Santanna	Sardjeet	Satish	Savo	Sayzer
Sandravious	Santaonio	Sarek	Sativa	Savon (0.04)	Scandal
Sandre	Santario	Sargent	Satnam	Savonce	Scattiny
Sandré	Santarius	Sargon	Satnam Dillon	Savone	Scbaston
Sandro (0.02)	Santavia	Sari	Satorry	Savontae	Scenthuran
Sandrof	Santavious	Sariel	Satoru	Savonté	Schad
Sandstrom	Santavius	Sarif	Satoshi	Savorio	Schade
Sandun	Santavous	Sarim	Satrion	Savory	Schaefer
Sandwaine	Santeep	Sarithy	Satsuki	Savoy	Schafer
Sandy (0.01)	Santerius	Sarius	Sattbir	Savraj	Schaffer
Saned	Santerra	Sarjan	Sattya	Savreet	Schaller
Saneel	Santez	Sarjana	Saturn	Savvas	Schallum
Saneet	Santhuran	Sarkis (0.02)	Saturnino (0.01)	Sawal	Schammua-
Sanford	Santi	Sarmad	Satveer	Sawayz	Daniel
Sang	Santiago (0.17)	Sarmir	Satvir	Sawndale	Scharn
Sang Giovan	Santiago Alfonso	Sarn	Satwan	Sawson	Schauncey
Sangeesh	Santiel	Sarpreet	Satwinder	Sawyer (0.19)	Schawn
Sangeevan	Santino (0.03)	Sarris	Satya	Sawyer Chase	Schayne
Sanggam	Santion	Sartaaj	Satyam	Saxon (0.01)	Schenaider
Sangjoon	Santito	Sartaj	Satyen	Saxsin	Schevene
Sangpou	Santo (0.01)	Sartao	Sau	Saxton	Schiffer
Sangwan	Santoni	Sarthak	Sau L	Saxxon	Schirack
Sanibo	Santonio	Sarthe	Saud	Say	Schmell
Sanice	Santorrio (0.01)	Sartori	Saudéion	Say-Von	Schmydt
Sanjay (0.02)	Santos (0.08)	Sarun	Saul (0.28)	Saya	Schneider
Sanjaya	Santrél	Sarwan	Saul Ezequiel	Sayadeth	Schnellen
Sanje	Santrell	Sary	Saul-Daniel	Sayaf	Schneur
Sanjeen	Santwan	Sasan	Saulo	Sayan	Schoen
Sanjeet	Santwon	Sascha	Saumon	Saybeon	Schon
Sanjeev	Sanuel	Saseddrick	Saunders	Saye	Schubert
Sanjey	Sanvir	Sash	Saurabh	Sayed	Schue
Sanjit	Sanyog	Sasha (0.03)	Saurav	Sayeddal	Schuylar
Sanjo	Saodara	Sashank	Saurubh	Sayeed	Schuyler (0.05)
Sanjor	Saomouny	Sasquel	Sav'veon	Sayem	Schylar
Sankalp	Sapario	Sastavion	Sava	Sayer	Schyler (0.01)
Sankeeth	Saphelle	Sastun	Savaje	Sayers	Schylre
Sanket	Sappreet	Sata	Savalas	Sayf	Schylur
Sanmartise	Saqeeb	Satao	Savalias	Sayil	Sciguard
Sanmeet	Saqib (0.01)	Satasin	Savan	Sayjon	Scionti
Sanned	Saqron	Satch	Savannah	Saylor	Scipio
Sannid	Saquan (0.01)	Satchel (0.01)	Savarra	Sayma	Scogtt
Sannie	Saquandric	Satchithanandan	Savaughn	Sayorn	Scoitt
Sanny	Saquané	Satchytan	Saveion	Sayorous	Scorpio
Sanode	Saquin	Satemo	Saveion Mck	Sayquoine	Scot (0.01)
Sanpras	Saquon	Satesh	Savelle	Sayr	Scotch
Sanqua	Saquoya	Sathasivam	Saveon	Sayre	Scotland
Sanquan	Saqwan	Satheesan	Saverio	Saysavanh	Scott (2.27)
Sanquavius	Saqwone	Sathes	Savhon	Sayton	Scott Aleks
Sanquentin	Sara	Sathira	Saviahn	Sayvaun	Scott Douglas
Sanquez	Sarah (0.01)	Sathursan	Savian	Sayvon	Scott-Jearld
Sanraj	Saran	Sathusan	Savieus	Sayvone	Scottalan
Sant	Saranyan	Sathvik	Savino	Sayvonté	Scottey
Santana (0.03)	Sarav	Sathya	Savio	Sayyad	Scotti
Santana Joshua	Saravanan	Sathyah	Savion (0.01)	Sayyaf	Scottie (0.04)

Scottinder	Seantrei	Seeraj-Addeen	Selo	Senussi	Serreyratha
Scottland	Seantrel	Seevola	Selso	Seon	Sersie
Scotty *(0.05)*	Seantrell	Sefer	Selvacoumar	Seondre	Servan
Scout	Seantri	Sefita	Selvan	Seong	Servando *(0.02)*
Scsott	Sears	Sefjuan	Selvin	Seongjun	Servellas
Scully	Sease	Sefkan	Selwyn	Sepand	Servio
Scyllir	Season	Sefton	Sem	Sepano	Sesar
Se Derek	Seaton *(0.01)*	Segal	Sema'd	Sepehr	Sessions
Se Drick	Seaver	Segrick	Sema'j	Sepncer	Set
Séan	Seb	Segun	Semaj *(0.03)*	Sepuloni	Setanta
Séderrick	Sebaron	Segundo	Semaj'	Sequan	Setelo
Séquin	Sebashtian	Sehajpaul	Semajay	Sequnne	Seth *(1.49)*
Séron	Sebastain	Seham	Semaje	Sequoia	Seth Mark
Sévaughn	Sebastian *(0.67)*	Sehm	Semard	Sequorey	Seth'mikel
Sévé	Sebastian-Alexa	Sehtaj	Semartea	Sequoya	Seti
Séviaun	Sebastian-Kane	Seibeon	Semcongwon	Sequoyah	Seton
Sévon	Sebastiane	Seibin	Semere	Seqwill	Setorius
Se-Hoon	Sebastiano *(0.01)*	Seichi	Semia	Seqwon	Seumas
Seabastian	Sebastiasn	Seid	Semian	Serafim	Seumus
Seaborn	Sebastien *(0.40)*	Seiervon	Semier	Serafin *(0.01)*	Seung
Seabrin	Sebastin	Seif	Semih	Serahtullaa	Seung-Tai
Sead	Sebastine	Seif-Allah	Semion	Serai	Seungho
Seadric	Sebastine Micha	Seifullah	Semir	Seran	Sevag
Seager	Sebastion *(0.01)*	Seigal	Semisi	Serastian	Sevak
Sealand	Sebastyen	Seigan	Semko	Serayne	Sevan
Sealtiel	Sebatian	Seiger	Semmes	Serbando	Sevarias
Seamas	Sebien	Seiji	Semo	Serdric	Sevastian
Seamus *(0.06)*	Sebron	Seile	Sen-Tonio	Serech	Sevastjan
Seamuson	Sebyan	Sein	Senabeh	Sereno	Seve
Sean *(3.97)*	Secdrick	Seiquon	Senad	Serez	Seveantae
Sean Anthony	Secondino	Seith	Senarchi	Serfaraz	Sevearn
Sean Astin	Secoy	Seiviohne	Senard	Serg	Seven
Sean Christopher	Secquoyah	Seivon	Sender	Serge *(0.01)*	Seveon
Sean Edward	Secundino	Seiya	Seneca	Sergei	Severian
Sean Ellis	Sedale	Seizi	Senen	Sergey *(0.01)*	Severiano
Sean Kaarlo	Sedarion	Sejeon	Senerl	Serghey	Severik
Sean Kevin	Sedarious	Sekedric	Sengathith	Sergi	Severin
Sean Michael	Sedarius	Sekondi	Sengphet	Sergia	Severo
Sean Thomas	Seddon	Sekou *(0.01)*	Seniasha	Sergii	Sevester
Sean'dre	Seddrick	Sekye	Senica	Sergio *(0.97)*	Seveyon
Sean-Dale	Sederian	Selah	Sennai	Sergio Jr	Seville
Sean-Keith	Sederick	Selassie	Sennay	Sergio-Andres	Sevin
Sean-Luc	Sederra	Selbey	Sennua	Serguei	Sevontae
Sean-Michael	Sedgwyck	Selby	Senoble	Serhat	Sevonte
Sean-Micheal	Sedhare	Selden	Senovain	Seric	Sevren
Sean-Patrick	Sedio Deonte	Seldon	Senquan	Serif	Sevrnn
Sean-Paul	Sedric *(0.01)*	Selemon	Senshi	Serigo	Sevryn
Sean-Thomas	Sedrick *(0.01)*	Selena	Sentaro	Serjio *(0.01)*	Sevy
Seanan	Sedrik	Selestino	Senthooran	Serjito	Sewanu
Seandale	Sedriq	Selestreon	Senthuoran	Sernaggio	Seward
Seandel	Sedriques	Selichiro	Senthuran	Sernard	Sexton
Seanjose	See	Selim	Sentrell	Serod	Seyanthan
Seanmichael	See-Hung	Sellaharan	Sentrelle	Seron	Seyar-Ahmad
Seann	Seena	Selleck	Sentron	Serpatrick	Seyed
Seanpatrick	Seenan	Sellers	Senturan	Serren	Seyh

Seyitgan	Shaan *(0.01)*	Shadonté	Shahiem	Shairlian	Shakwan
Seynen	Shaaz	Shadow *(0.01)*	Shahil	Shairric	Shakyle
Seyval	Shabach	Shadrach *(0.01)*	Shahin	Shairshah	Shalafi
Seyvon	Shabahat	Shadrack	Shahir	Shaitrustin	Shalan
Seyyed	Shaban	Shadre	Shahm	Shaiyan	Shalanda
Sezar	Shabarreon	Shadrick *(0.01)*	Shahmad	Shaiyannsanya	Shalaree
Sh Michael	Shabaz	Shadricus	Shahmeer	Shaiye	Shale
Sh'den	Shabazz *(0.01)*	Shadriq	Shahnawaz	Shaja	Shaleem
Sh'kel	Shabbar	Shadroc	Shahnaz	Shajen	Shalem
Sh-Donta	Shabbir	Shady *(0.01)*	Shahob	Shajevan	Shalen
Sha	Shabell	Shae *(0.02)*	Shahqeel	Shajgev	Shalico
Sha Corey	Shabir	Shaé	Shahram	Shaji	Shalik
Sha Kur	Shabiv A	Shaed	Shahroz	Shajuan	Shalin
Sha Quil	Shabonn	Shaedan	Shahrukh	Shajzad	Shaliq
Sha Ron	Shabree	Shaefer	Shahryar	Shaka	Shalique
Sha Vargo	Shacari	Shaek	Shahzab	Shakaem	Shallahn
Sha Vez	Shacayne	Shael	Shahzad	Shakana	Shalmar
Sha'brein	Shachar	Shaen	Shahzaib	Shakaray	Shalom *(0.01)*
Sha'bryant	Shacoby	Shaeson	Shahzain	Shakari	Shalon
Sha'bryonne	Shacorey	Shaeza	Shahzeb	Shakawis	Shalvin
Sha'cori	Shacorie	Shafeeq	Shai *(0.01)*	Shakayla	Shamaar
Sha'd	Shacoy	Shafeer	Shai'john	Shakeal	Shamal
Sha'darious	Shacquille	Shafeké	Shai'kavn	Shakeeb	Shamale
Sha'heim	Shad *(0.03)*	Shafer	Shai'ki	Shakeei	Shamall
Sha'keem	Shadab	Shaffer Christi	Shai-Li	Shakeel *(0.01)*	Shaman
Sha'keim	Shadai	Shafi	Shai-Quaine	Shakeem *(0.01)*	Shamar *(0.02)*
Sha'kim	Shadaine	Shafiaullah	Shai-Ron	Shakeen	Shamar Anton
Sha'mel	Shadarian	Shafick	Shaian	Shakeer	Shamarcus
Sha'ney	Shadarion	Shafinoll	Shaidren	Shakeil	Shamare
Sha'qown	Shadarius	Shafiq	Shaie	Shakeim	Shamaree
Sha'qua	Shadaryl	Shafique	Shaif	Shakeir	Shamarel
Sha'quan	Shaday	Shaft	Shaiharyar	Shakel	Shamari *(0.01)*
Sha'quann	Shadd	Shafwan	Shaihiem	Shakell	Shamarick
Sha'quayvis	Shadde	Shagan	Shaik	Shakem	Shamario
Sha'quean	Shaddi	Shaguan	Shaikeem	Shakeme	Shamarious
Sha'quel	Shaddoc	Shaguille	Shaikem	Shakenneth	Shamarjai
Sha'quil	Shaddrick	Shagun	Shaikh	Shaker	Shamarkis
Sha'quille	Shaddy	Shah	Shaikiem	Shakerian	Shamarko
Sha'ron	Shade *(0.01)*	Shah Zaib	Shaikwon	Shakib	Shamarrie
Sha'tone	Shadee	Shah'kier	Shail	Shakiel	Shamas
Sha'von	Shadeem	Shah-Baz	Shailabh	Shakil	Shamatiyah
Sha'vone	Shadell	Shahaun	Shaileik	Shakille	Shamaun
Sha'vos	Shaden	Shahbaz	Shailen	Shakim	Shamaury
Sha'voski	Shadi *(0.01)*	Shahe	Shailendra	Shakina	Shame
Sha-Ke	Shadie	Shaheabras	Shaimea	Shaking	Shameek
Sha-Keim	Shadiff	Shahed	Shaimiguel	Shakir *(0.01)*	Shameer
Sha-Lynn	Shadley	Shaheed *(0.01)*	Shain *(0.01)*	Shakis	Shameik
Sha-Quille	Shadliek	Shaheem *(0.01)*	Shaina	Shakoi	Shameiré
Sha-Ron	Shadman	Shaheen	Shaine *(0.01)*	Shakori	Shamel
Shaahid	Shadod	Shaheer	Shaine Rhea	Shakorrie	Shames
Shaaiuille	Shadoe	Shaheim	Shaineel	Shakoy	Shamiah
Shaakilo	Shadon	Shaheriyar	Shainor	Shakti	Shamicheal
Shaakir	Shadonis	Shaheryar	Shaiquan	Shakuel	Shamiek
Shaam	Shadonn	Shahezad	Shaiquann	Shakur *(0.02)*	Shamik
Shaamal	Shadonta	Shahid *(0.01)*	Shaiqui	Shakuur	Shamil

Shamin	Shanen	Shaqiel	Shaqul	Sharodrick	Shaunish
Shaminder	Shangaa	Shaqille	Shaqullie	Sharom	Shaunmichael
Shamir	Shangara	Shaqkill	Shaquoin	Sharome	Shaunn
Shammah	Shangeeth	Shaqkim	Shaquon *(0.01)*	Sharon	Shaunne
Shammai	Shangi	Shaqkn	Shaquoné	Sharone	Shaunqae
Shammarco	Shangobunni	Shaqon	Shaquore	Sharonne	Shaunquell
Shammon	Shaniko	Shaqquail	Shaquory	Sharonni	Shaunquille
Shamon	Shanil	Shaqquille	Shaqur	Sharqil	Shaunt
Shamond	Shanjievan	Shaquael	Shaquric	Sharquay	Shauntavious
Shamone	Shankar	Shaquail	Shaquris	Sharquis	Shaunte
Shamont	Shanket	Shaquale	Shaquwane	Sharr-Ard	Shaunté
Shamonte	Shanklin	Shaquam	Shaqville	Sharrell	Shauntez
Shamontierre	Shankuan	Shaquan *(0.06)*	Shaqwan	Sharri	Shauntrel
Shamoon	Shann	Shaquan Antonio	Shar	Sharrif	Shauntrell
Shamor	Shannan	Shaquand	Shar'qun	Sharrkar	Shauquel
Shamori	Shannard	Shaquane	Sharad	Sharrod	Shaurya
Shamos	Shanne	Shaquané	Sharaeel	Sharrold	Shauvan
Shams	Shannelle	Shaquann	Sharaf	Sharron	Shauvez
Shamsher	Shannen	Shaquaries	Sharan	Sharujan	Shauvon
Shamus *(0.02)*	Shannin	Shaquarn	Sharanjit	Sharukh	Shavan
Shan *(0.02)*	Shannon *(0.16)*	Shaquaunn	Sharard	Sharva	Shavanta
Shan Shree	Shannone	Shaquavis	Sharaz	Sharvar	Shavantae
Shan'darrius	Shano	Shaquawn	Shardbeer	Sharvay	Shavante
Shan'quinn	Shanol	Shaquay	Sharde	Sharvell	Shavar
Shanado	Shanon	Shaquayvion	Shardel	Sharvez	Shavarea
Shanae	Shanoojan	Shaquaz	Shardul	Sharyer	Shavaris
Shanahan	Shanoy	Shaqué	Shareef *(0.01)*	Shashank	Shavaughn
Shanard	Shanquel	Shaqueal	Shareem	Shashi	Shavauni
Shanas	Shanquelle	Shaqueil	Shareif	Shashoney	Shavaunté
Shance	Shanquille	Shaquel	Shareik	Shatarvis	Shavawnte
Shanchez	Shanroy	Shaquell	Sharem	Shateil	Shavayé
Shand	Shant *(0.01)*	Shaquelle	Sharence	Shatique	Shaveez
Shandarian	Shanta	Shaquem	Sharez	Shatoine	Shaveiles
Shandarius	Shantae	Shaquen	Sharhan	Shaton	Shavel
Shandarrell	Shantai	Shaquez	Shariah	Shatzie	Shavell
Shandeep	Shantanu	Shaqui'awan	Sharice	Shau	Shavelle
Shandel	Shantavious	Shaquian	Sharief	Shaughn	Shaven
Shanderius	Shante	Shaquiel	Sharif *(0.01)*	Shaughnessy	Shavez
Shanderus	Shantell	Shaquiell	Sharife	Shaugn	Shavez'e
Shandoff	Shantez	Shaquielle	Shariff	Shaukendrick	Shavia
Shandon	Shantia	Shaquier	Shariq	Shaul	Shavil
Shandor	Shantonio	Shaquil	Sharis	Shaumbe	Shavin
Shandrewick	Shantwan	Shaquile *(0.01)*	Sharjeel	Shaumont	Shavios
Shane *(1.76)*	Shantwon	Shaquill *(0.01)*	Sharkeem	Shaun *(0.34)*	Shavoie
Shane Degroat	Shanuel	Shaquilla	Sharkerian	Shaun'	Shavon *(0.01)*
Shane-Robert	Shanvir	Shaquille *(0.36)*	Sharkie	Shaun-Michael	Shavone
Shaneal	Shao-Yan	Shaquille	Sharkiem	Shaun-Stephone	Shavonta
Shanederian	Shapeck-Ahmad	Raheem	Sharley	Shaunak	Shavonte
Shaneef	Shaphan	Shaquillé	Sharlimon	Shaundel	Shavonté
Shaneel	Shapir	Shaquille-Aziz	Sharman	Shaundell	Shavontez
Shaneil	Shapour	Shaquillie	Sharmarke	Shaundra	Shavoski
Shaneion	Shapri	Shaquin	Sharmdisae	Shaundre	Shavoskie
Shanejoel	Shaq-Keil	Shaquinton	Sharmic	Shaune	Shavoy
Shanel	Shaqaun	Shaquire	Sharn	Shaunecey	Shaw
Shaneley	Shaqhari	Shaquize	Sharod *(0.02)*	Shaunessy	Shawan

Shawden	Shawntravius	Shazon	Sheldo	Sherik	Shi'zare
Shawki	Shawntre	Shéliek	Sheldom	Sherjeel	Shi-Quan
Shawma	Shawntrez	Shea (0.07)	Sheldon (0.28)	Sherl	Shi-Trell
Shawmar	Shawnyuate	Shea'lund	Sheldyn	Sherlby	Shi-Yu
Shawmelle	Shawon	Sheaden	Shelford	Sherlton	Shia
Shawn (1.73)	Shawondell	Sheadrah	Shellby	Shermain	Shibbir
Shawn Angelo	Shawtaz	Sheamus	Shelley	Shermaine	Shibreek
Shawn J.R.	Shawun	Shean	Shelly	Sherman (0.06)	Shie
Shawn Jr	Shay (0.06)	Sheanthan	Shelrich	Shermar	Shiely
Shawn Michael	Shay'qun	Sheardon	Shelson	Shermarke	Shien
Shawn Mikael	Shay'qwan	Shebby	Sheltarus	Shermiahh	Shieran
Shawn'tez	Shay-Quan	Shedaine	Shelten	Shermir	Shihab
Shawn-Douglas	Shaya	Shedane	Shelton (0.05)	Shermon	Shihaisha
Shawn-Dutton	Shayaa	Sheddrach	Shelvin	Sherneir	Shiheem
Shawn-E	Shayaan	Sheddryn	Shelvy	Shernerd	Shihei
Shawn-Johnathon	Shayan (0.03)	Shederick	Shem (0.01)	Sherod	Shiheim
Shawn-Michael	Shayanan	Shedly	Shema	Sheron	Shihiem
Shawn-Micheal	Shayann	Shedran	Shemar (0.01)	Sheroyd	Shijuan
Shawn-Stuart	Shaybren	Shedrekyus	Shemayah	Sherrarr	Shikean
Shawnaessy	Shayd	Shedric	Shemik	Sherrick	Shikeb
Shawnathan	Shayde	Shedrick (0.01)	Shemoria	Sherridan	Shikeem
Shawndale	Shayden (0.01)	Shedrique	Shemroy	Sherridell	Shikell
Shawndalema	Shaydin	Sheehan	Shemuel	Sherriff	Shikib
Shawndarias	Shaye (0.01)	Sheel	Shemus	Sherrod (0.01)	Shil
Shawndarious	Shayfer	Sheen	Shena	Sherrodric	Shileik
Shawndarrius	Shayheim	Sheeraz	Shenar	Sherrome	Shilo (0.01)
Shawnde	Shayian	Shefflan	Shenard	Sherron	Shiloe
Shawndell	Shaykwan	Sheh	Shenazar	Sherrone	Shiloh (0.02)
Shawndouglas	Shaylan	Shehab	Shendan	Sherry	Shilpen
Shawndre	Shayland	Shehalian	Sheneka	Sherun	Shimaq
Shawndreus	Shayler	Shehan	Shenell	Sherveen	Shimon (0.01)
Shawndric	Shaylon	Shehbaz	Shenequa	Sherveer	Shimron
Shawnee	Shaylor	Sheheryar	Sheng	Shervin	Shin
Shawnelious	Shaymas	Shehmeer	Sheng-Haw	Sherwan	Shine
Shawnell	Shaymus	Shehroz	Shenthan	Sherwin (0.01)	Shinean
Shawnesse	Shayn (0.01)	Shehroze	Shentory	Sherwin Bryan	Shing
Shawnkee	Shayne (0.17)	Shehryar	Sheon	Sherwood	Shing-Him
Shawnken	Shaynge	Shehu	Shepard	Sherwyn	Shing-Wai
Shawnly	Shaynne	Shehzad	Shepherd	Sheryar	Shingi
Shawnmichael	Shayon	Sheik	Shequan	Sheryas	Shini
Shawnovan	Shaypher	Sheikh	Shequel	Sheser	Shinji
Shawnquell	Shayse	Sheilfer	Shequill	Shester	Shinn
Shawnquevious	Shayson	Sheimar	Shequille	Sheung	Shinobi
Shawnquez	Shayton	Shekeal	Sher	Sheve	Shinpei
Shawnquise	Shayvai	Shekel	Sher'rod	Sheven	Shintaro
Shawntavious	Shayvon	Shekelton	Sherard	Shevin	Shion
Shawntavis	Shaz	Shekhar	Sheraz	Shevon	Shiquan
Shawntavy	Shazaad	Shekinah	Sherdell	Shevonte	Shiquane
Shawntee	Shazad	Sheku	Shereef	Shewond	Shiquann
Shawntell	Shazam	Shel	Shereen	Shey	Shiquarri
Shawnterian	Shazard	Shelbe	Sherer	Sheyenne	Shiquawn
Shawntesse	Shazeb	Shelby (0.14)	Sheridan (0.02)	Shi	Shiqueal
Shawntez	Shazia	Sheldan	Sheriden	Shi'heem	Shiquise
Shawnteze	Shazil	Shelden	Sherif	Shi'keize	Shiquoin
	Shazim	Sheldin	Sheriffe	Shi'quan	Shiqwade

Shiqwan	Shobradrick	Shota	Shunderick	Shyler	Sidny
Shiran	Shoen	Shotaro	Shunica	Shylio	Sidor
Shiraz	Shoghi	Shoua	Shunravion	Shylique	Siebe
Shire	Shogo	Shougo	Shunsuke	Shylo	Sieef
Shireff	Shoham	Shoumik	Shuntae	Shyloh	Siegfried
Shiriff	Shohei	Shoun	Shuntaro	Shylon	Sienda
Shirkeem	Shohn	Shoundeep	Shunterrius	Shylow	Sierra
Shirlin	Shoichi	Shovon	Shuntrease	Shymeak	Sierre
Shirlon	Shokelle	Shovonta	Shuntrell	Shymeek	Siesmon
Shiron	Shokoni	Shovonte	Shuquan	Shymeik	Sigelfredo
Shirrod	Sholan	Showin	Shuquann	Shymel	Sigfrido
Shirune	Sholom	Shown	Shuqwan	Shymer	Sigfried
Shirvon	Sholten	Shownney	Shurash	Shymere	Sigifredo *(0.01)*
Shirwa	Shoma	Shownny	Shurod	Shymiere	Sigismund
Shirwin	Shomara	Shownoo	Shuron	Shymon	Sigmond
Shishir	Shomari *(0.01)*	Shran	Shushep	Shynell	Signmund
Shiv *(0.01)*	Shomarii	Shrandon	Shusuke	Shypriece	Sigomond
Shiva	Shomas	Shravan	Shutharshan	Shyquan	Sigord
Shiva Teja	Shombie	Shrederick	Shuto	Shyron	Sihaan
Shivaaz	Shomen	Shredrick	Shuuma	Shyrone	Siholonder
Shivadas	Shomiron	Shreif	Shuvon	Shysheem	Siiuta Chuka
Shivalik	Shon *(0.03)*	Shrenik	Shuwyane	Shytawn	Sikandar
Shivam *(0.01)*	Shon' Drea	Shreyan	Shvan	Shyun	Sikander
Shivamohinder	Shonari	Shreyas	Shvertondd	Shyvez	Sil
Shivan	Shondale	Shri	Shveze	Shyvon	Silaf
Shivanandha	Shondarion	Shshuke	Shy'heim	Si	Silas *(0.07)*
Shivanshu	Shondaris	Shu	Shy'keem	Siah	Silbano
Shiveley	Shonderek	Shuabrin	Shy'kwan	Siale	Silbert
Shiven	Shondor	Shuaib	Shya	Siaosi	Siler
Shivesh	Shondrick	Shuan	Shyaam	Sias	Silila
Shivjot	Shone	Shubdip	Shyah	Siavash	Silvano *(0.01)*
Shivkaran	Shoneric	Shubhajyoti	Shyam *(0.01)*	Siaygnoun	Silver
Shivon	Shongo	Shubham	Shyan	Sibi	Silverio
Shivraj	Shonn	Shubhum	Shyand	Sibusiso	Silvestre *(0.03)*
Shiyam	Shonquél	Shucorey	Shybri	Sicha	Silvino *(0.01)*
Shiyel	Shonquell	Shucree	Shydamion	Sicinio	Silvio *(0.01)*
Shizuo	Shonquez	Shudarious	Shydarius	Sid'dale	Silviu
Shjonbrandon	Shont'z	Shudarius	Shyhed	Sidante	Sim
Shkwan	Shonta	Shudi	Shyheed	Sidanth	Sima
Shlomo	Shontarious	Shue	Shyheem *(0.01)*	Sidarius	Simandeep
Shmar	Shontazz	Shueb	Shyheid	Siddarath	Simao
Shmayl	Shonte	Shufon	Shyheim *(0.05)*	Siddartha	Simarbir
Shmu	Shontel	Shuhei	Shyhelm	Siddhaarth	Simarjit
Shmuel	Shonterrius	Shujaat	Shyhem	Siddhart	Simarpartap
Shneur	Shontez	Shukahreeous	Shyhiem	Siddharth	Simarre
Shneyor	Shontiz	Shukore	Shyhmé	Siddhartha	Simba
Shnyden	Shontori	Shukri	Shyige	Siddhi	Simcha
Shnyder	Shontrail	Shukur	Shyihem	Siddiq	Simenpal
Sho	Shontravius	Shumar	Shykeem	Sidhant	Simeon *(0.04)*
Shoaeb	Shontre	Shumarae	Shykeen	Sidharth	Simerjot
Shoaib	Shontrell	Shumate	Shykem	Sidi-Mohamed	Simernam
Shoaibur	Shontreyvious	Shumba	Shykeri	Sidiamond	Simey'on
Shoan	Shonynn	Shumon	Shyla	Sidley	Simione
Shobhit	Shorleh	Shun	Shylan	Sidney *(0.16)*	Simisola
Shobi	Shoshonee	Shundarius	Shylatron	Sidney-Cheick	Simitro

Simmie	Siomon	Siu	Skylarr	Sobih	Sonam
Simmy	Sione *(0.01)*	Siu-Hung	Skylayr	Socheat	Sonate
Simon *(0.86)*	Siopesoakai	Siumafua Heako	Skylen	Socorro	Sonatra
Simon Christian	Siosaia	Sivagaran	Skyler *(0.62)*	Socrate	Sondai Yao Ali
Simon Pierre	Sipenisa	Sivakumar	Skyler James	Socrates	Sondel
(0.02)	Sir *(0.01)*	Sivan	Skylier	Soctt	Sonedeep
Simon-Joshua	Sir Charles	Sivanathan	Skylin	Sodaba	Soneesh
Simondre	Sir Darion	Sivandeep	Skyller	Sodiq	Soner
Simone	Sir Donald	Sivano	Skyloer	Sofen	Song
Simpson	Sir Eric	Sivert	Skylon	Sofia	Soni
Simrait	Sir Jeffery	Sivisan	Skylor *(0.01)*	Sohaan	Sonit
Simraj	Sir Kalton	Sivitri	Skylor-Vince	Sohaib	Sonnie
Simran *(0.01)*	Sir Preston	Sixto	Skylore	Sohail *(0.01)*	Sonny *(0.07)*
Simrandeep	Sir Ron	Sixx	Skylour	Sohan	Sonny-Gene
Simranjeet	Sir Victor	Siya	Skylur	Soheil	Sonome
Simranjit *(0.01)*	Sir Vontintent	Siyad	Skylxr	Sohib	Sontavious
Simranpal	Sir'lawrence	Siyamson	Skylyr	Sohil	Sonthonyo
Simrat	Sir'ravious	Siyia	Skywise Conor	Sohiub	Sony
Simren	Sir'ron	Sjael	Skywren	Sohrab	Sonya
Simrit	Sir-Lawrence	Sjolanté	Slade *(0.03)*	Sohran	Soolim
Simritpaul	Sir. John	Sjon	Slader	Sohum	Soon
Simrum	Siraa'j	Skai	Slaimon	Sokchandavy	Soopawatt
Sims	Sirajuddin	Skie	Slanaker	Sokhountea	Soorya
Simson	Sirallen	Skieler	Slash	Sokun	Sooyoung
Sin	Sirandon	Skii'e	Slate	Sol	Sophath
Sina *(0.02)*	Sirbashgin	Skilar	Slater *(0.02)*	Solan	Sopheak
Sinan	Sircharles	Skiler	Slavko	Solar	Sopheaktra
Sinan-Saleh	Sircon	Skilur	Slayde	Solaris	Sophia
Sinanian	Sirenio	Skip	Slayman	Soliman	Sophie
Sinatra	Sirfame	Skkylar	Slayter	Solo-Man	Sophoeun
Sinbad	Sirfrusha	Sklar	Slayton	Solodeen	Sophonn
Sincere	Sirgio	Sklenni	Sleiman	Solom'een	Sopira
Sinclair	Siriaco	Sklyer	Sloan *(0.02)*	Soloman	Sopual
Sindeny	Sirjat	Skoda	Sloane	Solomon *(0.12)*	Sorabh
Sinder	Sirkeron	Skooter	Slone	Solomona	Soreeysa
Sindujan	Sirmarcus	Skotlan	Sly	Solon	Sorell
Sinesio	Siron	Skott	Slyder	Soloway	Soren *(0.02)*
Sineway	Sirott	Skulynkee	Slyman	Solumn	Soressa
Sing	Sirquittin	Skuylar	Smile	Solyman	Sorie
Singh *(0.01)*	Sirr Aheem	Sky *(0.04)*	Smir	Soma	Sorin
Sinian	Sirra	Sky'e	Smit	Somaje	Soriya
Sinisha	Sirrendrick	Sky'kir	Smith *(0.01)*	Somak	Sorkeiss
Sinjin *(0.01)*	Sirret	Skye *(0.02)*	Smokey	Somar	Soroush
Sinjun	Sirronta	Skyeler	Smoky	Somate	Sorqan
Sinnamon	Sirus	Skyelor	Snayder	Somdara	Sorren
Sinoe	Sisley	Skyer	Sndrew	Somerled	Sortorius
Sinom	Sisouvong	Skyhawk	Sneh	Someshar	Sosala
Sinquay	Sisto	Skykhanh	Snehal	Somjeet	Sosefa
Sinterio	Sitaleki	Skyla	Snorri	Sommy	Sosefo
Sinthujan	Siteichy	Skylaar	Snowden	Somondre	Soshane
Sintiller	Sitesh	Skylar *(0.24)*	Snyder	Somphorn	Soshiant
Siobhan	Sitini	Skylar Matthew	So	Somuth	Sosimo
Sioeli	Sitlali	Skylar Ray	So Happy	Somvang	Sotaro
Siole	Sitonius	Skylare	Sobanthany	Son *(0.01)*	Soterios
Siolui	Sitta	Skylarlee	Sobhi	Son-Steven	Soteris

Sotero	Squires	Stanley *(0.24)*	Stedmen	Stepane	Stevan *(0.02)*
Sotero Jr.	Sr. Michael	Stanley Mel	Stedson	Stepanie	Stevano
Sothea	Sratton	Stanly	Steel	Stepfan	Stevanoe
Sothyro	Sree	Stanquiz	Steele *(0.02)*	Stepfon	Stevaughn
Sou *(0.01)*	Sreejith	Stanshon	Steelion	Stepfone	Steve *(0.41)*
Soua	Sreekar	Stantavin	Steen	Steph'an	Stevean
Souber	Sri	Stantavious	Steenn	Steph'fon	Stevem
Soubhan	Sridhaman	Stanten	Steeve *(0.01)*	Stephain	Steven *(5.26)*
Soufian	Srijoy	Stanton *(0.01)*	Steeven *(0.02)*	Stephan *(0.20)*	Steven Buford
Souheil	Srikajan	Stanz	Steevn	Stephan-Jamar	Steven Ray
Soujanan	Srikar	Staphon	Stef	Stephanas	Steven-Alan
Soukichi	Sriman	Staphone	Stef'fon	Stephane *(0.08)*	Steven-Anthony
Soulivan	Srinath	Stapp	Stefa'n	Stephanie *(0.01)*	Steven-Bryant
Soumil	Sriram	Staquavous	Stefaan	Stephanne	Steven-David
Sounak	Srivatsan	Star	Stefah	Stephano	Steven-Myers
Soung	Srun	Stark	Stefan *(0.32)*	Stephanos	Steven-Patrick
Souphien	Ssebastien	Starke	Stefanao	Stephans	Steven-Richard
Souriya	St	Starlin	Stefane	Stephany	Stevens *(0.01)*
South	St Taurus	Starling	Stefano *(0.05)*	Stephaun *(0.01)*	Stevenson
Southern	St.	Starnes	Stefanos	Stephawn	Steveon
Souvick	St.jon	Starsky	Stefans	Stephayn	Stevie *(0.03)*
Sovannarith	Sta'cee	Startavius	Stefaun	Stephen *(2.89)*	Stevie-Ray
Sovannaroun	Sta-Von	Stary	Stefen *(0.01)*	Stephen Jr	Stevieon
Sovanny	Stac	Stas	Steffan *(0.03)*	Stephen Vincent	Stevin *(0.01)*
Sowah	Staccato	Stashawn	Steffano	Stepheno	Stevinson
Spanky	Stacee	Stashu	Steffen *(0.02)*	Stepheny	Stevion
Sparsh	Stacey *(0.04)*	Stassie	Steffens	Stephfen	Stevon *(0.01)*
Spartacus	Stacy *(0.05)*	Staten	Steffin	Stephfon	Stevontarious
Spearin	Stacy-Kane	Stathis	Steffon *(0.01)*	Stephin	Stevonte
Special	Stafan	Statler	Steffon Deshan	Stephion	Stevonté
Speed	Staffon	Staton	Steffond	Stephon *(0.13)*	Stevtavious
Spence	Staffony	Statravious	Steffone	Stephon'	Stevyn
Spencer *(2.02)*	Stafford *(0.01)*	Staurt	Stefhan	Stephon'e	Steward
Spencer Han	Stafhan	Staven	Stefhon	Stephone *(0.01)*	Stewart *(0.10)*
Spencer Kyle	Stafone	Stavinski	Stefon *(0.02)*	Stephonne	Steyson
Spencer Patrick	Stag	Stavion	Stefon'	Stephonta	Sthevennson
Spencer-Lynn	Staheli	Stavon	Stefone	Stephron	Stian
Spencer-Thomas	Stakesh	Stavros	Stefonne	Stephun	Stice
Spencer-Xavier	Staley	Stayton	Stefven	Stepnen	Stif
Spener	Stallin	Ste	Steidman	Stepten	Stifanos
Spenser *(0.06)*	Stallone	Ste Fon	Steilph	Sterett	Stile
Spike	Stamati	Stéfan	Stein	Stergios	Stiler
Spiliotopoulos	Stamford	Stéfon	Steiner	Sterlen	Stillborn
Spiridon	Stan	Stéfvonn	Stelfone	Sterlin *(0.01)*	Stillman
Spirit	Stanas	Stéphan	Stelianos	Sterling *(0.23)*	Stillmon
Spiro	Stance	Stévaughn	Stelios	Sterling Antoni	Stinnett
Spiros	Standley	Ste-Fon	Stella	Stern	Stipan
Springer Th	Standly	Steafan	Stelzon	Sterrett	Stirling *(0.01)*
Sprott	Stands	Stean	Sten	Steryling	Stiven
Spur	Stanely	Stearne	Stenford	Steston	Stjepan
Spyder	Stanford *(0.01)*	Steaven	Stennett	Steth	Stocken
Spyridon	Stanislav	Steavin	Stenor	Steton	Stockton *(0.01)*
Spyros	Stanislaw	Steavon	Stensen	Stetsen	Stockton-Cordt
Sqauille	Stanjik	Stecker	Stenson	Stetson *(0.06)*	Stoen
Squire	Stanleigh	Stedman *(0.01)*	Stepan	Stetzon	Stone *(0.04)*

Stoner
Stoney *(0.01)*
Stonie
Stoniy
Stony
Storey
Stori
Storm *(0.06)*
Storme
Stormey
Stormi
Stormin
Stormmie
Stormy *(0.01)*
Story
Stosh
Stowe
Stowen
Strachan
Strader
Stradford
Strahd
Strat
Straten
Straton
Stratton
Straven
Strawn
Streeter
String-Fellow
Strodney
Stroker
Stroud
Struan
Stryder
Stryker
Stuart *(0.28)*
Stuart-James
Stuary
Studreck
Stuward
Style
Styles
Stylianos
Stylon
Stylz
Stymie
Styver
Sua'heed
Suad
Suade
Suavae
Subarna
Suber
Subhan

Subishan
Suboor
Subothan
Subramaniam
Subret
Success
Sucre
Sudan
Sudarshan
Suddiq
Sudeep
Sudesh
Sudhan
Sudharsan
Sudharshen
Sudip
Sudrsan
Sueade
Suede *(0.01)*
Suedewolf
Sueng-Hyuk
Sufiyan
Sufwan
Sufyaan
Sufyan
Sugene
Sugirthan
Suhaas
Suhael
Suhaib
Suhail
Suhas
Suhayb
Suheb
Sui
Suihn
Sujan
Sujay
Sujean
Sujeen
Sujeethan
Sujeevan
Sujipan
Sujit
Sujith
Suk-Jun
Sukadeva
Sukharsh
Sukhbir
Sukhdeep
Sukhdip
Sukhip
Sukhjeet
Sukhjeevan
Sukhjinder

Sukhjit
Sukhjivan
Sukhjodh
Sukhjot
Sukhkamal
Sukhkaran
Sukhman
Sukhmandeep
Sukhmander
Sukhmanjit
Sukhmeet
Sukhpal
Sukhpiar
Sukhpneet
Sukhpreet *(0.01)*
Sukhraaj
Sukhraj
Sukhrajan
Sukhrajdeep
Sukhresh
Sukhshane
Sukhveer
Sukhvir *(0.01)*
Sukhwindar
Sukrani
Sulaiman
Sulakshan
Sulaymaan
Sulayman
Suleiman
Suleman
Sulfredo
Sulieman
Sulli
Sullivan *(0.02)*
Sully
Sulman
Sulomon
Sultan *(0.01)*
Sultan-Ismail
Sulviyon
Sulvontaye
Sulyman
Sum
Sumair
Sumanyu
Sumeer
Sumeet *(0.01)*
Sumer
Sumerinder
Sumit *(0.01)*
Summer
Summit
Sumner *(0.02)*
Sumontae

Sun
Sunam
Sundance
Sundar
Sundara
Sunday
Sundeep *(0.01)*
Sunden
Sunderland
Suneel
Suneet
Suneil
Sung
Sung Gi
Sung Jun
Sung-Ho
Sungho
Sungkook
Sungmeen
Sunil
Sunjay
Sunjeev
Sunjeevan
Sunjit
Sunjot
Sunni
Sunny *(0.04)*
Sunnynam
Sunpreet
Sunra
Sunshine
Sunveer
Sunvir
Supavannan
Supper
Supreet
Suprotik
Surachet
Surain
Suraj *(0.01)*
Surakhun
Sural
Surazdeep
Surell
Suresh
Surgi
Surgio
Surhman
Surinder
Surinderpal
Suriya
Surjit
Surking
Surmeet
Surya

Susan
Susana
Sushanth
Sushixit
Suta
Suthan
Sutharshan
Sutter
Suttle
Sutton *(0.01)*
Suveathan
Suverthan
Suvith
Suvon
Suvrat
Suyan
Suyog
Suzanne
Sved
Sven *(0.01)*
Svenn
Sverker
Swade
Swahili Jamel
Swain
Swaine
Swandrick
Swane
Swarain
Swaroop
Swasean
Swataveus
Swayde
Swayne
Swayze
Sweden
Sweetson
Swilling
Sy
Sy'kevious
Syad
Syam
Sychá
Syclayton
Syd
Syd Kevin
Syderious
Sydian
Sydne
Sydnee
Sydner
Sydney *(0.04)*
Syed *(0.08)*
Syed Abid
Syed Adam Azree

Syed Mehdi
Syed-Kashan
Syeed
Syheed
Syheem
Syid
Sykarno
Syl
Sylas *(0.01)*
Syles
Sylquell
Sylus
Sylvain *(0.03)*
Sylvan *(0.01)*
Sylvan-Stone
Sylvanious
Sylver-River
Sylverne
Sylvester *(0.05)*
Sylvestre
Sylvian
Sylvonta
Sym
Syman
Symeon
Symion
Symon
Syndarius
Syndey
Syngen
Synjen
Synjon
Syntorious
Syota
Syphone
Sypmith
Syrell
Syrick
Syril
Syris
Syrshawn
Syrus
Sytse
Syuhei
Syun
Sze
Szu-Raj
Szymon

-T-

T *(0.04)*
T Ashib
T J
T Keenan

T Michael	Ta'jon	Taboski	Taéori	Tahja	Taion
T Nicholas	Ta'jun	Taboure	Tae-Woong	Tahjab	Taiqee
T Rae	Ta'kari	Tabrez	Taechun	Tahjai	Taiquan
T Ranito	Ta'kein	Tabrian	Taed	Tahje	Taira
T'aaron	Ta'lib	Tabris	Taedron	Tahjé	Tairay
T'ai	Ta'lil	Tabrium	Taejel	Tahjee	Tairi
T'anthony	Ta'lonti	Tabriz	Taekwoun	Tahji	Tairo
T'ardre	Ta'marcus	Tabur	Taelon	Tahlan	Taisahn
T'astae	Ta'mel	Tabyus	Taelor	Tahlik	Taisei
T'jaun	Ta'phari	Tacante	Taelur	Tahlil	Taisen
T'jay	Ta'quan	Tacarey	Taelyn	Tahmid	Taish-On
T'jerron	Ta'qwan	Tacarious	Taeminn	Tahmoor	Taishaun
T'karryel	Ta'ray	Tacarldre	Taeon	Tahmos	Taishawn
T'marcus	Ta'rel	Tacarré	Taeqwon	Tahmyas	Taishon
T'mari	Ta'riq	Tacarry	Taeron	Tahnner	Taishyo
T'michael	Ta'ron	Tace	Taesahun	Tahran	Taison
T'mone	Ta'ronn	Tachon	Taeshawe	Tahray	Taissir
T'niko	Ta'shawn	Tacobi	Taeshawn	Tahree	Taistevion
T'nomal	Ta'shon	Tacoma	Taevaun	Tahrell	Taisto
T'ontray	Ta'shun	Tacorey	Taevéon	Tahrik	Tait (0.01)
T'quan	Ta'vante	Tacorion	Taeveon	Tahshawn	Taite
T'qwan	Ta'varis	Tacquille	Taevion	Tahsin	Taitmon
T'sean	Ta'varus	Tad (0.03)	Taevon	Tahvel	Taitusi
T'shane	Ta'vaughn	Tadam	Taevyon	Tahvon	Taivion
T'shun	Ta'vione	Tadan	Taewon	Tahwan	Taivon
T'vadis	Ta'von	Tadanrrian	Tafadzwa	Tahyr	Taiwain
T'varis	Ta'vone	Tadar	Tafari (0.01)	Tahza	Taiwan
T'veaciyea	Ta'vyon	Tadarious	Tafarie	Tai (0.02)	Taiwo
T'vonta	Ta-Jai	Tadaris	Tafario	Tai Wan	Taiye
T'voris	Ta-Shun	Tadarius (0.01)	Taft	Tai'asian	Taiyon
T'wan	Taa	Tadarrel	Tag	Tai'eric	Taiyou
T-Jae	Taahir	Tadarrius	Tagan	Tai'quan	Taj (0.03)
T-P	Taajaé	Tadaryn	Tagarious	Tai'ron	Taj Malik
T-Shawn	Taareq	Tadas	Tagart	Tai-Jahn	Tajae
T. (0.01)	Taariq	Tadashi	Tage	Tai-Tjing	Tajaé
T. Michael	Taarique	Tadavious	Taggart	Taibe	Tajaey
T.C.	Taaron	Tadayo	Taggert	Taiga	Tajah
T.J.	Taau	Tadd	Tago	Taigan	Tajahs
Ta	Tab	Taddeous	Tah	Taige	Tajai
Ta Jhay	Tabahri	Taddeus	Tah'jee	Taigen	Tajammal
Ta Marcus	Tabann	Tadele	Tah-Quan	Taijai	Tajan
Ta Quane	Tabares	Taden	Taha (0.01)	Taijalon	Tajarius
Ta Rik	Tabari	Tadeo	Tahajie	Taije	Tajarvis
Ta Ron	Tabarious	Tadeusz	Tahann	Taijh	Taje
Ta Seanby	Tabarius	Tadis	Taharqa	Taijier	Tajé
Ta Shaun	Tabarus	Tadorian	Tahdjai	Taijon	Tajee
Ta Shawn	Tabatha	Tadow	Tahdryan	Taijuan	Tajeh
Ta Varus	Tabb	Tadrick	Taheah	Taijun	Tajh
Ta'corey	Taber	Tadriel	Taheed	Taijuon	Tajh'bahatileik
Ta'corrious	Tabias	Tadrien	Taheer	Taike	Tajha
Ta'daviyon	Tabious	Tadrill	Taheim	Taiki	Tajhari
Ta'harge	Tabish	Tadros	Taher	Tailer	Tajhea
Ta'jacquis	Tabius	Tae	Taheran	Tailong	Taji
Ta'jean	Tabor	Tae Hyung	Tahir	Tailor	Tajia
Ta'ji	Taboris	Taé-Dashawne	Tahj (0.01)	Taimoor	Tajid

Tajik	Takyrim	Talor	Tamoreia	Tanner *(1.92)*	Taquon
Tajil	Tal *(0.01)*	Talton	Tamorus	Tanner William	Taqurius
Tajinder	Tal-Lim	Talvin	Tamos	Tannes	Taqwan
Tajmalik	Talah	Talvir	Tamour	Tannin	Tara
Tajohn	Talaha	Talvon	Tamoy	Tannir	Taradio
Tajon	Talaihaapepe	Talwinder	Tamres	Tannis	Tarae
Tajoris	Talajuwon	Talya	Tamrick	Tannon	Tarain
Tajpal	Talakai	Talyn	Tamrin	Tannor	Taraino
Tajprett	Talal	Tam *(0.01)*	Tamrrisk	Tano	Tarak
Tajuan	Talan	Tamadrick	Tamryn	Tanoh	Taralah
Tajveer	Talanzo	Tamaijá	Tamyon	Tanongsith	Taramis
Tajzahn	Talavou	Tamaine	Tamz	Tanor	Taran *(0.04)*
Tak-Wah	Talbot	Tamairis	Tan *(0.01)*	Tanques	Taranado
Takaaki	Taleb	Tamaiya	Tan-Moang	Tanrence	Tarance
Takaharu	Talecko	Tamal	Tana	Tanthalis	Tarandeep
Takahiro	Taleek	Tamar *(0.01)*	Tanahl	Tanual	Taranjit
Takanta	Taleem	Tamar'k	Tanaphol	Tanuel	Taranjot
Takari	Taleesun	Tamarack	Tanar	Tanveer *(0.01)*	Taranpreet
Takarius	Talem	Tamarcus	Tanara	Tanvi	Taranvir
Takashi	Talen *(0.01)*	Tamariae	Tanare	Tanvior	Tararey
Takayuki	Taler	Tamaric	Tanarut	Tanvir *(0.01)*	Tararez
Takeem	Talesh	Tamarick	Tanase	Tanweer	Tararius
Takeen	Talha	Tamarie	Tanay	Tanwinder	Taras
Takeo	Talhat	Tamarik	Tanbir	Tanwir	Taraus
Takeru	Tali	Tamario	Tandat	Tany	Taravarious
Takeshi	Taliat	Tamarion	Tandeep	Tanyen	Taray
Takevin	Talib	Tamaris	Tandin	Tanyon	Tard
Takevious	Talibay	Tamarius	Tandon	Tanyr	Tarderius
Takhori	Taliesin	Tamarkus	Tandy	Tanzel	Tare-Davni
Taki	Talijel	Tamarrick	Taneak	Tanzelle	Tareall
Taki'	Talik	Tamarus	Taneil	Tanzim	Tarean
Takia	Talin	Tamas	Tanell	Tanzimur	Tared
Takiah	Talio	Tamatra	Taner *(0.01)*	Tao	Tareecio
Takias	Talion	Tamaul	Tanes	Taofic	Tarek *(0.02)*
Takim	Taliq	Tamaz	Tanesha	Taonté	Tareke
Takima	Talis	Tamaza	Tanez	Tapan	Tarell *(0.01)*
Takin	Talisman	Tamba	Tango	Taprée	Taren *(0.01)*
Takker	Talison	Tameem	Tangy	Taqdeer	Tarence
Takoda *(0.01)*	Taljit	Tameer	Tania	Taqee-	Tareq
Takoma	Taljon	Tamell	Tanian	Mohammad	Tarevis
Takori	Tallal	Tamer	Taniela	Taqie	Tarey
Takory	Tallano	Tamerick	Tanieve	Taqu'el	Tarez
Takota	Tallen	Tameron	Tanim	Taquai	Tareze
Takquilla	Talley	Tamesh	Tanin	Taquan *(0.02)*	Targee
Takudzwa	Tallin	Tamidre	Taniqua	Taquann	Targie
Takuma	Tallis	Tamik	Tanis *(0.01)*	Taquarious	Taria
Takumi *(0.01)*	Tallon *(0.01)*	Tamim	Tanish	Taquarius	Tariano
Takunda	Talmadge	Tamin	Tanissan	Taquash	Taric
Takuro	Talmage	Tamir *(0.01)*	Tanjeet	Taquavious	Taricio
Takuto	Talmas	Tamity	Tanler	Taquawn	Tarick
Takuya	Talmon	Tammer	Tanmay	Taquell	Tariek
Takwan	Talon *(0.08)*	Tammy	Tanna	Taquerria	Tarif
Takwavis	Talon Alexander	Tamon	Tannar	Taquevious	Tarig
Takwon	Talonte	Tamone	Tannee	Taquille	Tarik *(0.05)*
Takyayukwiluti	Talonzale	Tamonte	Tannen	Taquinte	Tarikh

Tarin	Tarsheen	Tasren	Tavarin	Tavorian	Taylour
Tario	Tarson	Tassane	Tavario	Tavorious	Taylr
Tariq (0.05)	Tartorius	Tassium	Tavarious	Tavoris	Taymarcus
Tariq-Ur	Tartrend	Tasso	Tavaris (0.04)	Tavorise	Taymond
Tarique	Taruarus	Tatan	Tavarius (0.01)	Tavorres	Taymour
Taris	Taruis	Tatau	Tavarous	Tavorris	Tayne
Tarish	Taruka	Tataunati	Tavarres	Tavosia	Tayo
Tariu	Tarun	Tate (0.10)	Tavarrie	Tavoz	Tayon
Tarium	Tarus	Tate-Junior	Tavarus (0.01)	Tavrris	Tayona
Tarius	Tarvais	Taten	Tavarz	Tavunte	Tayrod
Tarkeith	Tarvarif	Tatenda	Tavas	Taw	Tayron
Tarlochan	Tarvaris	Tathan	Tavaughan	Tawaab	Tayrone
Tarlyn	Tarvers	Tathem	Tavaune	Tawain	Taysean
Tarman	Tarvez	Tathony	Tavein	Tawan	Tayshan
Tarmanpreet	Tarvie	Taton	Tavek	Tawanh	Tayshawn
Tarmar	Tarvis	Tatsuaki	Tavell	Tawann	Tayshiem
Tarmarcus	Tarvonte	Tatsuro	Tavelle	Tawaskea	Tayshun
Tarmarqus	Tarvorris	Tatsuya	Taven (0.01)	Tawaun	Taysir
Tarmo	Tarwinder	Tattinger	Tavender	Tawfeeq	Tayson
Tarnardus	Taryk	Tatum (0.01)	Taveon	Tawfige	Tayt
Tarndeep	Taryll	Tauafanga-'o-Lo	Taverae	Tawfik	Tayte
Tarnpreet	Taryn (0.01)	Tauai	Taveris	Tawfiq	Tayten
Tarnvir	Taryon	Taug	Taverris	Tawhe	Tayton
Taro	Tasa	Tauheed	Taverus	Tawion	Tayvan
Tarod	Tasbir	Tauhjai	Tavez	Tawon	Tayvaughn
Tarold	Tasca	Taunuuga	Tavhari	Taxiarhis	Tayven
Taron (0.02)	Tasdiq	Taurance	Tavian (0.01)	Tay'roy	Tayveon
Tarone	Tasha	Tauraun	Taviann	Tay'veion	Tayvin
Taronza	Tashaan	Taurean (0.01)	Tavias	Tay'veun	Tayvohn
Tarou	Tashan	Taurein	Tavielle	Tay'von	Tayvon (0.01)
Tarqi'	Tashar	Taurence	Tavien	Taya	Taywan
Tarquin	Tashard	Tauri	Tavieon	Tayab	Taywon
Tarquine	Tashaun	Taurice	Tavin (0.01)	Tayana	Tayyeb
Tarquinn	Tashawn (0.01)	Taurin	Tavinder	Tayber	Taz (0.01)
Tarquinnious	Tasheik	Taurino	Tavio	Taybor	Tazanleus
Tarral	Tashel	Taurion	Tavion (0.01)	Taycen	Tazarious
Tarran	Tasher	Tauris	Tavionne	Tayden	Tazavier
Tarrance (0.01)	Tashi	Taurone	Tavious	Tayey	Tazjon
Tarrandon	Tashiem	Taurrek	Tavirus	Taygan	Tazle
Tarrant	Tashod	Taurrence	Tavis (0.04)	Taygen	Tazmen
Tarrel	Tashoin	Taurus (0.01)	Tavish (0.01)	Tayidr	Tazmine
Tarrell (0.01)	Tashon	Taushi	Tavist	Taykerrian	Tazmir
Tarren (0.01)	Tashowntae	Tausif	Tavita	Taykia	Tazmond
Tarrence	Tashun	Tautahi	Tavius	Taykwan	Tazon
Tarrez	Tasi	Tauveli	Tavon (0.03)	Taylan	Tazshrée
Tarrick	Tasian	Tavairy	Tavonn	Taylar	Tazwell
Tarrik	Tasin	Tavan	Tavonne	Taylen	Tazz
Tarriké	Tasio	Tavante	Tavonni	Tayler (0.08)	Tazzeo
Tarrin	Tasjaa	Tavarae	Tavonta	Taylin	Tc
Tarrion	Tasker	Tavaras	Tavontae	Tayller	Tckur
Tarris	Tasmania	Tavaree	Tavontai	Tayllor	Te
Tarrius	Tasmin	Tavarence	Tavonte	Taylon (0.01)	Te Artis
Tarron	Tasmond	Tavares (0.02)	Tavonté	Taylor (2.92)	Te Kenyan
Tarry	Tasneef	Tavari	Tavorace	Taylor-Douglas	Te Rell
Tarryn	Tasneem	Tavaria	Tavoreo	Taylor-Ray	Te Various

Téandre	Tecorey	Tejas *(0.01)*	Temidayo	Terance *(0.02)*	Terr Yon
Téangelo	Tecumseh	Tejbir	Temitayo	Terando	Terra
Téchan	Ted *(0.06)*	Tejean	Temitayo Oluwas	Terane	Terrace
Tédarrel	Ted Uba	Tejinder	Temitope	Teravollis	Terrad
Tédarrius	Ted-James	Tejon	Temoni	Tercel	Terragan
Téjesse	Tedarius	Tejpal	Temoor	Terdarel	Terral
Téjonn	Tedaryl	Tejparpat	Temperance	Terdon	Terrall
Téjoun	Tedashi	Tejpaul	Tempest	Tereall	Terran *(0.02)*
Tékel	Tedd	Tejus	Templar	Terefe	Terrance *(0.39)*
Téman	Teddie	Tejveer	Temple	Terek	Terrance Dayqua
Témarco	Teddius	Tejvir	Temuchin	Terel *(0.01)*	Terrane
Téonta	Teddrick	Tek	Ten	Terell *(0.03)*	Terranton
Téquan	Teddy *(0.05)*	Tekais	Tenadore	Terelle *(0.01)*	Terraontre
Téray	Teddybear	Tekary	Tenario	Terelous	Terraries
Téron	Tededrain	Teke	Teneil	Teremi	Terrawn
Téshawn	Tedell	Tekeim	Tenerro	Teren	Terray
Téshon	Tederick	Tekenvila	Teng *(0.01)*	Terence *(0.14)*	Terreco
Tévion	Tedgrick	Tekesé	Tenin	Tereno	Terrel *(0.02)*
Tévon	Tedmund	Tekeyan	Tennessee	Terenz	Terrell *(0.26)*
Tévonn	Tedric	Tekoa	Tennie	Tereon	Terrelle *(0.01)*
Tévréountre	Tedrick	Tekoda	Tennison	Tereso	Terren *(0.01)*
Te-Corey	Tedrin	Tekorey	Tennyson	Teress	Terrence *(0.31)*
Te-Quan	Tedros	Tekorien	Teno	Terez *(0.01)*	Terrenyce
Tea	Tedvin	Tekwan	Tenry	Tereze	Terreon
Teacher	Tedvis	Tel	Tenson	Terezz	Terres
Teadric	Tedy	Telaine	Teny	Terfee	Terrese
Teadros	Tee	Telamegra	Tenzal	Teri	Terrez
Teag	Teeandre	Telarin	Tenzin	Terian	Terri
Teagan *(0.02)*	Teegan	Telayne	Tenzing	Teric	Terrial
Teage	Teejona	Teldon	Teo	Terick	Terriance
Teagen	Teemu-Thomas	Telito	Teodore	Terico	Terriaun
Teague *(0.01)*	Teenois	Tell	Teodorico	Teriel Antonio	Terriaus
Teaico	Teeroy	Tella	Teodoro *(0.01)*	Terik	Terribien
Teaj	Teetree-O	Teller	Teofilo	Terin	Terric
Teajay	Tefik	Telleran	Teon *(0.01)*	Terinco	Terrick *(0.01)*
Teak	Tefra	Tellis	Teonce	Terion	Terrico
Teakin	Tefrem	Tellvin	Teondre	Terione	Terricus
Teal	Teg	Telly *(0.01)*	Teontae	Teriq	Terriel
Teancum	Tegan *(0.01)*	Telmus	Teoprepio	Terique	Terriell
Teandre	Teghan	Telos	Teoun	Terius	Terrien
Tearance	Tegrea	Telson	Tephor	Teriyon	Terrik
Tearence	Teh'ron	Telus	Tequaious	Terizz	Terril
Tearin	Tehran	Telvan	Tequan *(0.01)*	Terjuan	Terrill *(0.02)*
Tearnce	Tehron	Telvin *(0.02)*	Tequavis	Terkelgin	Terrin *(0.01)*
Tearon	Tehvyn	Telvis	Tequerious	Terlet	Terrin-Micheal
Tearrance	Teigan	Temaj	Tequinn	Termaine *(0.01)*	Terrio
Teautla	Teige	Temall	Tequis	Termarkus	Terrion *(0.01)*
Teavin	Teighler	Temani	Tequon	Ternard	Terrione
Teayris	Teilhard	Temar	Ter-Zahn	Terome	Terriontez
Teb	Tein	Temarcus	Terack	Teron *(0.01)*	Terriquis
Tebelle	Teion	Temarlos	Terad	Terontae	Terris *(0.01)*
Tebray	Teiran	Temarr	Terah	Teroy	Terrish
Teco	Teistan	Temer	Terain	Terquan	Terrius
Tecobie	Teivon	Temerius	Terald	Terquez	Terriveo
Teconsa	Tej	Temesgen	Teran *(0.01)*	Terquise	Terrivio

Terriyon	Tevario	Tezera	Thanh-Hoang	Theilson	Therone
Terrod	Tevaris	Tezhawn	Thaniel	Thein	Therrel
Terrol	Tevarius	Tg	Thanish	Theland	Therrell
Terron (0.02)	Tevarkis	Thabo	Thanish-Afdal	Thelauxzan	Therrin
Terronavar	Tevarus	Thacarion	Thannujan	Thelbert	Therron
Terrone	Tevaughan	Thackary	Thanoosan	Thelbrick	Thershan
Terronn	Tevaughn	Thacker	Thanoozan	Theley	Theryn
Terrus	Tevell	Thackery	Thanos	Thelitus	Theryon
Terry (0.50)	Tevelle	Thad (0.01)	Thanual	Thell	Theryshian
Terry Ger'shon	Teven	Thadarius	Thanujan	Thelmon	Theshawn
Terry Jr	Teveon	Thadd	Thanujhan	Thelonious	Thesley
Terryain	Teveris	Thaddaeub	Thanuojan	Thelton	Thesolonica
Terryan	Tevianc	Thaddaeus	Thanushan	Themios	Thetheus
Terryl	Tevien	Thaddeaus	Thao	Themis	Thetis
Terrylee	Teviest	Thadden	Thape	Thenglee	Thiago
Terryll	Tevin (0.46)	Thaddeous	Tharakan	Thenigan	Thian
Terryn	Tevin Untrel	Thaddeus (0.08)	Tharan	Thenuson	Thiarie
Terryoine	Tevinn	Thaddis	Tharen	Theo (0.02)	Thiem
Terryon	Tevion	Thaddius	Tharin	Theoden	Thien (0.02)
Terryonte	Tevis (0.01)	Thade	Tharjan	Theodis	Thierry (0.06)
Tervarious	Tevish	Thadeaus	Tharon	Theodor	Thijmen
Tervaseus	Tevita (0.02)	Thadeous	Tharsan	Theodore (0.39)	Thilakxshan
Tervel	Tevitamaile	Thadeus (0.01)	Tharshan	Theodoros	Thilan
Tervon	Tevohn	Thadious	Tharshann	Theodric	Thilukshan
Tervontis	Tevon (0.02)	Thadius	Tharsmanth	Theodur	Thimmestry
Tery	Tevon'	Thai (0.01)	Thashunn	Theoharis	Thimothy
Teryian	Tevone	Thai-Binh	That	Theola	Thinderpal
Teryl	Tevonne	Thai-Minh	Thatavious	Theolonius	Thinesch
Teryn	Tevonte	Thaier	Thatcher	Theon	Thinh
Teryst	Tevor	Thaihoa	Thavia	Theonaldo	Thinojan
Tesean	Tevoris	Thailan	Thavinh	Theonta	Thiogest
Tesfaye	Tevorri	Thailar	Thavisit	Theophanis	Thiry
Teshaun	Tevoun	Thailyr	Thawan	Theophilus	Thishan
Teshawn (0.01)	Tevryn	Thain	Thawarnius	Theophlous	Thivaakaran
Teshay	Tevvan	Thaine	Thaxter	Theopolis	Thivagar
Teshon	Tevvin	Thair	Thaxton	Theorayn	Thivagaran
Tesmond	Tevyn (0.01)	Thairan	Thayden	Theoren (0.01)	Thivahar
Tesonski	Tewane	Thairee	Thayer	Theorin	Thivakar
Tess	Tewayne	Thairus	Thayne	Theoron	Thivethan
Tessa	Tewodros	Thajj	Thayvez	Theotis	Thivisan
Tessie	Tex	Thalamus	The	Theotrice	Thiviyan
Tessman	Texas	Thale	Thérontai	Thepvanon	Thivyaaxan
Teth	Teya	Thales	The-Chuong	Thequante	Thivyan
Teton	Teyan	Thalion	Theadore	Therald	Thiwasan
Tetsuaki	Teyante	Thalmus	Theandre	Theran	Thoams
Tetsuro	Teycavious	Thamas	Thearavuth	Theraz	Thoarne
Tetteh	Teyjaun	Thamell	Theard	Therell	Thoas
Teunis	Teyjon	Thamer	Thearn	Therence	Thob
Teuvo	Teylan	Than	Theartis	Thereon	Thoedore
Tev'eon	Teyland	Thane (0.02)	Theathus	Theresa	Thofiq
Teva	Teyler	Thaneshan	Thebe	Therin	Thom
Tevan (0.01)	Teylor	Thaney	Thedore	Therion	Thomarqis
Tevar	Teyrell	Thang	Thedrow	Therlow	Thomars
Tevaras	Teyrold	Thang-Phuoc	Theéanthony	Therman	Thomas (6.13)
Tevari	Teyvon	Thanh (0.02)	Theeron	Theron (0.04)	Thomas Jahliel

Thomas Jay	Thriston	Tiano	Tiger	Timijyn	Tino *(0.01)*
Thomas Jeremiah	Thuan	Tiant	Tigger	Timithay	Tinson
Thomas Keoni	Thubarakan	Tiante	Tighe *(0.01)*	Timithy	Tiny
Thomas Oladeji	Thuc	Tiaquille	Tighler	Timitris	Tinyu
Thomas Patrick	Thulasiram	Tiarell	Tigran	Timmarious	Tion
Thomas-Carlos	Thulasiyananth	Tiarnan	Tigranne	Timmesha	Tione
Thomas-James	Thuluxan	Tiarra	Tihami	Timmie *(0.01)*	Tiontay
Thomas-Jay	Thuluxjan	Tiaun	Tihares	Timmithy	Tionté
Thomas-John	Thunder *(0.01)*	Tiaunté	Tihryn	Timmorie	Tionzell
Thomas-	Thunku	Tiavelle	Tij	Timmothy *(0.01)*	Tioreon
Massalangolu	Thuong	Tiaviaus	Tijani	Timmy *(0.04)*	Tiphasan
Thomason	Thurgood	Tiawan	Tijash	Timo	Tipton
Thomaz	Thurlo	Tiberias	Tijlim	Timodei	Tiqeece
Thomchelik	Thurlow	Tiberio	Tijuan	Timofei-Thoma	Tiquan
Thomis	Thurman	Tiberious	Tikal	Timofey	Tiquawn
Thomley	Thurmond	Tiberiu	Tikeri	Timohty	Tiquay
Thommas	Thursten	Tiberius	Tiki	Timoll	Tiquhan
Thommy	Thurston *(0.01)*	Tibeson	Tikomir	Timon *(0.01)*	Tiquine
Thompson *(0.01)*	Thusan	Tibet	Tikwuan	Timond	Tiquon
Thomquai	Thusanth	Tibor	Til	Timone	Tiquoy
Thoms	Thushan	Tibril	Tilan	Timontai	Tiquwan
Thomsen	Thushanth	Tiburcio	Tilar	Timonte	Tiqwan
Thomson	Thusyanthan	Tical	Tilden	Timonté	Tirael
Thong	Thuvaarahan	Ticen	Tildon	Timonthy	Tiran
Thongsa	Thuvaataotan	Tico	Tiler	Timontrell	Tiras
Thony	Thuy	Ticorey	Tileur	Timophey	Tiray
Thor *(0.02)*	Thyagarajan	Ticortier	Tilford	Timoshon	Tirea
Thoran	Thyane	Tidal	Tilik	Timotei	Tireah
Thorbjorn	Thylan	Tidas	Tilkotmes	Timoteo *(0.01)*	Tiree
Thorburn	Thyron	Tidianne	Tilliman	Timothe *(0.01)*	Tirée
Thoren	Thys	Tidray	Tillman	Timothee *(0.01)*	Tirek
Thorgeon	Thyus	Tie	Tillman De	Timotheus	Tirell
Thorhallur	Ti	Tiegan	Tillo	Timothey	Tiren
Thorian	Ti Jhyrean	Tiegh	Tilmon	Timothie	Tirese
Thorin	Ti Juan	Tieken	Tilon	Timothy *(4.35)*	Tirik
Thorn	Ti'andré	Tielar	Tilonnie	Timothy Jake	Tirique
Thornara	Ti'cheveus	Tieler *(0.01)*	Tilston	Timothy Jr	Tiron
Thorndike	Ti'lhon	Tielor	Tilton	Timothy Michael	Tirrance
Thorne	Ti'lon	Tielque	Tilur	Timothy-Dalton	Tirrell *(0.01)*
Thornell	Ti'quan	Tielyr	Tilynn	Timothy-Lee	Tirry
Thornton	Ti-Jean	Tien	Tilyr	Timothy-Pierre	Tirtha
Thorriddh	Tia'quan	Tienhuy	Tim *(0.03)*	Timothy-Rien	Tirus
Thorson	Tia'wan	Tieran	Timaan	Timquezous	Tiryan
Thorstein	Tiago *(0.02)*	Tierdon	Timaj	Timucin	Tisaiah
Thorsten	Tiaheem	Tiere	Timar	Timur	Tisen
Thorvall	Tiajaun	Tieree	Timar'eus	Timurlane	Tishaan
Thoryn	Tiajé	Tierell	Timathy	Timyrus	Tishami
Thrace	Tiajuan	Tierice	Timauris	Tin *(0.01)*	Tishaun
Thrayland	Tiajuwan	Tiernan	Timber	Tina	Tishawn
Three	Tiamarie	Tierrance	Timburr	Tinas	Tishean
Three Feathers	Tian	Tierre	Timeaus	Tineil	Tishlum
Threeney	Tian Chuan	Tieshawn	Timeil	Ting	Tishon
Threston	Tiandre	Tiffany	Timel	Tinh	Tishun
Thrisstan	Tianna	Tifton	Timer	Tini	Tison
Thristan	Tianno	Tige	Timetric	Tinielle	Tita

Titan	Tobiah	Tolunte	Tomorik	Torauss	Torreek
Titarious	Tobiajah	Toluwani	Tomorrier	Torben	Torrell
Titerian	Tobian	Tom *(0.08)*	Tomos	Tore	Torren *(0.01)*
Tithus	Tobias *(0.09)*	Tom Paulus	Tomotsugu	Toréon	Torrenc
Tito *(0.01)*	Tobiath	Tom-Vu	Tomoya	Tore-Mozz	Torrence *(0.02)*
Titoriano	Tobie	Toma	Tomoyuki	Torean	Torres *(0.01)*
Titorrian	Tobijah	Toma'z	Tomson	Toreaun	Torrey *(0.04)*
Titouan	Tobin *(0.01)*	Tomah	Tomtom	Toree	Torrez
Titus *(0.05)*	Tobin Jacob	Tomahz	Tomus	Torehn	Torri
Tityus	Tobin Joseph	Tomarco	Tomy *(0.02)*	Torei	Torri'k
Tiuant	Tobore	Tomarié	Ton-Jai	Torel	Torrian *(0.01)*
Tiueti	Toby *(0.12)*	Tomarius	Tonas	Torell	Torriante
Tius	Tobyas	Tomarkist	Tonatiuh	Toren *(0.01)*	Torrie *(0.01)*
Tiviear	Tobyn	Tomarkus	Toncy	Torence	Torriel
Tivis	Tochi	Tomas *(0.22)*	Tonda	Toreno	Torrien
Tivon	Tocqueze	Tomas III	Tondell	Torenze	Torries
Tivonta	Tod *(0.01)*	Tomas-Jay	Tonder E	Toreus	Torrin *(0.01)*
Tivonte	Todario	Tomasi	Tondrez	Torey *(0.03)*	Torrion
Tiwan	Todarus	Tomasz *(0.02)*	Tondric	Toreyain	Torris
Tiwaun	Todd *(0.45)*	Tomaz	Tone	Torez	Torron
Tiwian	Todderick	Tome	Toné	Torgen	Torry *(0.01)*
Tiyell	Toddreckius	Tomek	Tonée	Tori *(0.01)*	Torryan
Tiynaan	Toddric	Tomeko	Tonee	Torian *(0.01)*	Tors
Tiyon	Toddrick	Tomell	Tonej	Toriano	Torson
Tiyren	Todryk	Tomer	Tonell	Toriaun	Torsten
Tiziano	Todven	Tomerrick	Toney *(0.01)*	Toribio	Toru
Tizoc	Toef	Tometrius	Tong *(0.01)*	Toric	Torvald
Tj *(0.01)*	Toei	Tomez'	Toni *(0.01)*	Torico	Torvorius
Tjad	Toeray	Tomi	Tonia	Torie	Tory *(0.07)*
Tjaden	Tohazie	Tomie	Tonie	Torien	Toryn
Tjark	Toheeb	Tomier	Tonino	Torieuanno	Torynce
Tjohn	Toheed	Tomika	Tonio	Torii	Tosh
Tk	Tohermain	Tomikazu	Tonisha	Torin *(0.05)*	Toshi
Tkhari	Tohi	Tomiko	Tonishaye	Torin Elie	Toshiki
Tkye	Tohlei	Tomislav *(0.01)*	Tonka	Torino	Toshio
Tlaloc	Tohn	Tomislav-Andrija	Tonko	Torion	Toshiya
Tlarence	Tohyup	Tomislay	Tonmaine	Torique	Toshiyuki
Tmel	Toi	Tomiya	Tonny *(0.01)*	Toris	Toshj
To'maz	Toie	Tomlinson	Tonshawn	Torishawme	Toshmari
To-Raan	Toimie	Tommas	Tontravius	Torison	Toshua
Toa	Toiriste	Tommaso	Tony *(0.75)*	Torius	Tosin
Toadriek	Tojyea	Tommel	Tony-Reid	Torivio	Tou *(0.02)*
Toan *(0.01)*	Tokensky	Tommer	Tonyo	Torke	Tou're
Toan Steven	Tokowski	Tommie *(0.03)*	Toochukwu	Torlando	Touche
Toare	Tolanda	Tommlie	Toon	Tornez	Toufic
Tobbie	Tolbert	Tommy *(0.57)*	Toosaa	Toron	Touhmong
Tobby	Tolby	Tommy Lee	Topaz	Toronto	Toui
Tobe	Tolentino	Tommy Truon	Tope	Toros	Toulmin
Tobechukwu	Tolia	Tommy-Lee	Tor	Torques	Toumani
Tobee	Tolice	Tomo	Tor'yanni	Torrance *(0.02)*	Toumy
Toben	Tolkien	Tomohiko	Tora	Torrawn	Touraine
Tober	Tollae	Tomohiro	Toran	Torre	Toure
Tobey	Tolly	Tomoki	Torance	Torré	Tourean-Tyrice
Tobi	Tolman	Tomone	Toras	Torrean	Tourvousier
Tobia	Toluafe	Tomonori	Torase	Torreas	Tousner

Toussant	Tradell	Tramarcus	Traskx	Travion *(0.03)*	Trayl
Tovano	Traden	Trameil	Trason	Travione	Traylan
Tovaris	Trae *(0.05)*	Tramel	Travaes	Traviontay	Traylee
Tovia	Traé	Tramell *(0.01)*	Travail	Travionté	Traylin
Tovon	Traéshawn	Tramelle	Travain	Traviontte	Trayllius
Townes	Traévon	Tramellé	Travaireon	Travioun	Traylon
Townley	Traedarious	Tramere	Travale	Travious	Traymain
Townsen	Traeden	Tramerius	Travante	Travirus	Traymon
Townsend	Traedon	Tramir	Travanté	Travis *(2.81)*	Traynard
Toy	Traegan	Trammell	Travanti Saquan	Travis Jr	Traynearious
Toyan	Traeger	Tramon	Travares	Travis Theodore	Traynor
Toyin	Traeon	Tramond	Travarious	Travis Weyburn	Trayon
Toyous	Traequan	Tramone	Travaris *(0.01)*	Travis-Roy	Trayone
Toyren	Traer	Tramoneya	Travarius	Traviss	Trayonté
Tr'amon	Traeten	Tramont	Travarous	Travist	Trayquan
Tr'e	Traevon *(0.01)*	Tramontae	Travarus	Travius *(0.01)*	Trayquane
Tr'rek	Traevond	Tramonte	Travarvs	Travlon	Trayquel
Tra *(0.01)*	Trafford	Trampas	Travaughen	Travolis	Trayqwon
Tra Von	Trafton John	Trampis	Travaughn	Travon *(0.13)*	Traysen
Trá	Tragejo	Trampus	Travauan	Travon'ta	Trayshaun
Tra'mon	Trager	Tran *(0.01)*	Travauris	Travond	Trayshawn
Tra'on	Trahan	Tranandez	Travay	Travondis	Trayson
Tra'quan	Trahmad	Tranard	Trave	Travone	Traytavious
Tra'quane	Trai *(0.01)*	Tranayle	Travees	Travonn	Trayten
Tra'quis	Traiden	Trandon	Travei	Travonne	Trayton *(0.01)*
Tra'shawn	Traie	Trane	Traveine	Travonntay	Trayvarous
Tra'shownco	Traige	Tranealius	Traveion	Travonta	Trayvaun
Tra'shun	Traijon	Tranell	Traveir	Travontae	Trayvéon
Tra'vacious	Trail	Trang	Traveiz	Travontaz	Trayven
Tra'vanté	Traile	Traniel	Travel	Travonte *(0.01)*	Trayveon
Tra'vaughn	Trainer	Tranquille	Travell *(0.02)*	Travonté	Trayveoun
Tra'vinsky	Traiquan	Tranroop	Travelle	Travonti	Trayvin
Tra'von *(0.01)*	Traise	Trantavious	Travelt	Travor	Trayvion *(0.01)*
Tra'vonta	Traisean	Tranya	Travelyan	Travoris	Trayvious
Tra'vonté	Traishoun	Traon	Traven *(0.01)*	Travorus	Trayvis
Tra-Deon	Traius	Traonte	Traveon *(0.02)*	Travosier	Trayvon *(0.07)*
Tra-Kwon	Traiveon	Trapper	Traveoun	Travous	Trayvond *(0.02)*
Tra-Van	Traivon	Traqon	Traver	Travus	Trayvone
Tra-Von	Trajan	Traquan *(0.01)*	Traveress	Travys	Trayvonne
Traa	Trajon	Traquell	Travers	Travyuan	Trayvontae
Trabeon	Trakece	Traquon	Traverus	Trawick	Trayvyon
Trabian	Trakeivance	Traqvas	Traves	Trax	Trazel
Trabias	Trakeno	Traqwan	Travette	Traxonte	Trazelle
Trace *(0.07)*	Trakevin	Traqwaun	Traveus	Traxton	Tre *(0.11)*
Tracen	Trakkor	Traron	Traveyon	Tray *(0.02)*	Tre Allen
Tracer	Traland	Trase	Travian	Tray Vius	Tre C
Tracey *(0.02)*	Tralen	Trasen	Travie	Tray Vond	Tre Cheise
Trachawn	Tralend	Trashaun	Traviea	Tray'von	Tre Jon
Traci	Tramacus	Trashawn *(0.01)*	Travien	Trayantay	Tre Kell
Tracii	Tramail	Trashean	Travieon	Traybeon	Tre Lee
Tracobie	Tramain	Trashon	Travier	Trayce	Tre Lunn
Tracy *(0.10)*	Tramaine *(0.01)*	Trashone	Traville	Traycen	Tre Mar
Trad	Traman	Trashun	Travin	Traycorieus	Tre Marquie
Tradarion	Tramane	Trasjohn	Travine	Traye	Tre Michael
Tradarious	Tramar	Trask	Travino	Trayion	Tre Mon

Tre Quan	Tréveon	Trebiel	Tremaine *(0.04)*	Trenttton	Trevant
Tre Shaun	Tréveonce	Trebor *(0.01)*	Tremane	Trentyn	Trevante *(0.01)*
Tre Vail	Tréveoone	Trebore	Tremar	Treon	Trevanté
Tre Varis	Tréveyun	Trebyn	Tremay	Treone	Trevantis
Tre Vaughn	Trévian	Trece	Tremay'ne	Treonte	Trevar *(0.01)*
Tre Vell	Trévijon	Trecoy	Tremayme	Trequan *(0.01)*	Trevares
Tre Veon	Trévion *(0.01)*	Tred	Tremayne *(0.02)*	Trequanne	Trevarié
Tre Vhonne	Trévionne	Tredacian	Tremeec	Trequaun	Trevarious
Tre Vion	Trévious	Tredarius	Tremek	Trequavious	Trevaris
Tre Vionne	Trévis	Tredavious	Tremel	Trequavius	Trevarius
Tre Von *(0.01)*	Trévius	Tredell	Tremel'es	Trequés	Trevaros
Tre Vonce	Trévon *(0.05)*	Treden	Tremele	Trequel	Trevarri
Tre Vone	Trévonce	Tredeon	Tremell	Trequian	Trevarus
Tre William	Trévond	Trederialo	Tremelle	Trequis	Trevathan
Tre Y	Trévone	Trederick	Tremelvion	Trequon	Trevaughan
Tre Zaul	Trévonious	Tredge	Tremiar	Treqwon	Trevaughh
Tré *(0.05)*	Trévonn	Tredreon	Tremico	Trerrell	Trevaughn *(0.02)*
Tré Chance	Trévonne	Tredrick	Tremon	Trerrion	Trevaugn
Tré Deandre	Trévonnte	Tredrion	Tremond	Tres	Trevaun
Tré-Jon	Trévonta	Treére	Tremone	Tresden	Trevaune
Tré-Vaughn	Trévontae	Trefor	Tremont	Tresean	Trevaunn
Tréa	Trévontay	Trefron	Tremonté	Tresen	Trevaus
Trébien	Trévonte	Treg	Tremonti	Treshaq	Treve
Tréchon	Trévonté	Tregan	Tremor	Tresharn	Trevélle
Trédon	Tréwil	Tregg	Tremorris	Treshaun *(0.01)*	Trevein
Tréjarvis	Tréy	Trei	Tren	Treshaun Shaqui	Treveion
Tréjaune	Tréyvous	Trei'von	Trenard	Treshawn *(0.01)*	Trevel
Tréjon	Tre-Andrew	Treigh	Trenay	Treshez	Trevell *(0.01)*
Tréjuan	Tre-Lonnie	Treighton	Trenayne	Treshon	Trevelle
Trékwan	Tre-Mon	Treion	Trence	Treshun	Treven *(0.01)*
Trékwane	Tre-Montaé	Treisha'ad	Trendan	Tresmon	Treveon *(0.01)*
Trélan	Tre-Quise	Trejan	Trendarious	Tresmond	Trever *(0.10)*
Trélante	Tre-Von	Trejavious	Trendell	Tresnaiis	Treves
Trémaine	Trea *(0.01)*	Trejohn	Trendon	Treson	Trevett
Trémayne	Trea'vie	Trejon	Trendowski	Tresor	Treveus
Tréon	Treadrick	Trejorn	Trenecy	Trestan	Treveyon
Tréquan	Treail	Trek	Trenell	Trestessa	Trevez
Tréquarious	Treamel	Trekael	Trenelyus	Trestin	Treveze
Trérell	Treamon	Trekar	Trenice	Treston *(0.01)*	Trevian
Tréron	Treandis	Trekele	Trenious	Trestton	Treviante
Trésean	Treante	Trekeno	Treniqua	Trestyn	Treviar
Tréshaun	Treanté	Trekker	Trenity	Treszante	Trevien
Tréshaune	Treaque	Trekuan	Trenjae	Treton	Trevijo
Tréshawn	Treashon	Trekus	Trennal	Treundous	Trevik
Tréshon	Treaun	Trelandon	Trennier	Trev	Trevin *(0.04)*
Tréshun	Treavan	Trelane	Trennin	Treva	Trevine
Trésione	Treavant	Trelanne	Trent *(0.46)*	Treva'nte	Trevinne
Trétez	Treaver	Trelante	Trentaurious	Trevahn	Trevino
Trévahn	Treavero	Trelis	Trentavious	Treval	Trevion *(0.03)*
Trévar	Treavin	Trell	Trentazia	Trevale	Trevione
Trévarus	Treavion	Trellas	Trenten *(0.02)*	Trevalian	Trevioné
Trévaughan	Treavon	Trellis	Trentez	Trevalle	Trevionne
Trévaughn	Treavor *(0.01)*	Trelon	Trentin	Trevan *(0.01)*	Trevious
Trévaun	Treaz	Trelyn	Trenton *(0.58)*	Trevance	Trevir
Trévell	Treber	Tremain	Trenton-Michael	Trevanion	Trevis *(0.02)*

Trevius	Treycen	Trezel	Tristram	Troyrell	Trystyn
Trevlin	Treydan	Trezelle	Tristyn (0.01)	Troyshaw	Tryton
Trevlyn	Treydarias	Trezjaun	Tristynne	Troyshawn	Tryvarious
Trevo'n	Treydarrius	Trezvon	Trit	Troyvonne	Tryvonne
Trevohn	Treydon	Tri (0.01)	Tritavious	Troyvonte	Tryzell
Trevoine	Treye	Tri'marcus	Tritin	Trozá	Tsani
Trevon (0.26)	Treyeon	Tri'shawn	Triton	Tru	Tsegai
Trevond (0.01)	Treyjen	Tri-Minh	Tritt	Truan	Tselote
Trevondisio	Treyjohn	Triakyce Taquan	Trittin	Truc	Tsenoh
Trevondrick	Treylan	Triandus	Tritton	Truce	Tsens
Trevone	Treylis	Triantifillos	Triumph	Trucker	Tshawn
Trevoné	Treylon	Tribec	Trivan	Trudell	Tshombe
Trevonn	Treymaine	Trico	Trivanté	True	Tshombé
Trevonne (0.01)	Treymane	Tricton	Trivaris	Trueman	Tshumbi
Trevonné	Treymar	Trie	Trivas	Truett	Tsim
Trevont	Treymarcus	Triet	Trivelle	Truitt	Tsimour
Trevonta	Treymel	Trieu	Triveon	Trumain	Tsubasa
Trevontae	Treymon	Trifily	Trivette	Trumaine	Tsun
Trevontaé	Treymont	Trifon	Trivolis	Trumale	Tsutomu
Trevontay	Treyon (0.01)	Trigg	Trivon	Truman (0.04)	Tsuyoshi
Trevonte (0.01)	Treyondian	Trijeet	Triwan	Trung (0.01)	Tsz
Trevonté	Treyonte	Trillian	Triyan	Trunghau	Tt'shard
Trevontes	Treyquane	Trimain	Triymeceus	Truong	Tu (0.01)
Trevonti	Treysan	Trimarcus	Trizden	Truson	Tu'shouney
Trevor (2.97)	Treyse	Trina	Trizhon	Trussie	Tua
Trevor Gordon	Treysean	Trindale	Tro	Trusten	Tuafafo
Trevor Lee	Treyshawn	Trinder	Troi	Trustin	Tuafono
Trevor-Anthony	Treyshon	Trinian	Troijuan	Trustis	Tuan (0.02)
Trevore	Treyson	Trinidad (0.01)	Tron	Truston	Tuan-Dat
Trevores	Treyton (0.01)	Trinidy	Tronard	Truth	Tubbie
Trevoris	Treytyn	Trinier	Trone	Truvette	Tuburis
Trevorlea-James	Treyvan	Trinity (0.02)	Tronell	Truvon	Tuck
Trevoughn	Treyvance	Trino	Trong (0.01)	Truvoseia	Tucker (0.29)
Trevour	Treyvard	Trinston	Tronsayne	Truxton	Tuckett
Trevoy	Treyvaughn	Trinten	Trontatvis	Truxtun	Tuckyr
Trevun	Treyven	Trintin	Tronte	Trvoné	Tucson
Trevus	Treyvenn	Trinton	Tropez	Trvor	Tudarries
Trevyn	Treyveon	Triphon	Troshawn	Try	Tudor
Trevyon	Treyveon Kindel	Tririce	Troskie	Tryan	Tueni
Trevyr	Treyvin	Tris	Troupe	Tryce	Tuff
Trewayne	Treyvion	Trisdan	Trovarie	Tryceton	Tuftin
Trewston	Treyvius	Trisden	Trovaughn	Trydell	Tufue
Trey (0.50)	Treyvoloski	Trishtan	Trovoy	Trygve	Tugg
Trey Shun	Treyvon (0.06)	Trishton	Trovoy	Trynce	Tuifga
Trey'von	Treyvond	Trison	Troy (1.11)	Trynton	Tujoshua
Trey'vond	Treyvone	Trissten	Troy'vale	Tryon	Tujuan
Trey-Alexander	Treyvonn	Trista	Troy-Austin	Tryountay	Tuker
Trey-C	Treyvonne	Tristain	Troy-Johnson	Tryquanta	Tukuafu
Trey-Robert	Treyvontae	Tristan (0.95)	Troy-Lamont	Tryson	Tuler
Trey-Von	Treyvonté	Tristan-Charles	Troyce	Trystan (0.02)	Tullio
Treyanté	Treyvun	Tristen (0.18)	Troydelle	Trysten (0.01)	Tully
Treyar	Trezail	Tristian (0.04)	Troydrick	Trystian	Tulu
Treybian	Trezdan	Tristin (0.08)	Troye	Trystin	Tulumbuyia
Treyce	Trezden	Tristinn	Troyer	Trystn	Tumaivin
Treycee	Trezdon	Triston (0.10)	Troylee	Tryston (0.01)	Tumelo

Tun
Tunnishwar
Tuo Yee Leng
Tuomas
Tuon
Tuong
Turak
Turan
Turandus
Ture
Turell
Turelle
Turhran
Turion
Turistian
Turki
Turkise
Turlo
Turner *(0.06)*
Turon
Turory
Turrel
Turrell
Turshard
Tusan
Tuscun
Tushar
Tushawn
Tushay
Tushon
Tuson
Tuuaiaigalelei
Tuuji
Tuvia
Tuvon
Tuwuan
Tuyler
Tvonnté
Twain
Twalyte
Twan
Twane
Twanzell
Twarn
Twavion
Twayne
Twfeg
Twincy
Twodros
Txawj
Ty *(0.39)*
Ty Ayre
Ty Francis
Ty Juan
Ty Kell

Ty Lon
Ty Quan
Ty Ran
Ty Relle
Ty Ren
Ty Rese
Ty Rin
Ty Ron
Ty Shon
Ty Von
Ty Water
Ty'arrance
Ty'berius
Ty'darrien
Ty'evian
Ty'juan
Ty'kece
Ty'kee
Ty'keem
Ty'keiss
Ty'kevis
Ty'kieceseon
Ty'lane
Ty'metrious
Ty'mont
Ty'qareus
Ty'quail
Ty'qual
Ty'quan
Ty'quane
Ty'quaveon
Ty'quavious
Ty'quawn
Ty'quentin
Ty'quez
Ty'quinn
Ty'qune
Ty'qwan
Ty'ree
Ty'reece
Ty'reese
Ty'rekk
Ty'rell
Ty'ri
Ty'rick
Ty'rik
Ty'ron
Ty'ronn
Ty'rus
Ty'sean
Ty'shae
Ty'shaun
Ty'shawn
Ty'sheam
Ty'shon

Ty'shuan
Ty'wuan
Ty-Austin
Ty-Edwin
Ty-Garrett
Ty-Jai
Ty-Jameer
Ty-Juan
Ty-Keontrai'
Ty-Lier
Ty-Shaun
Ty-Shawn
Ty-Trevon
Tyabre
Tyagnet
Tyair
Tyaire
Tyairr
Tyal
Tyale
Tyamo
Tyan
Tyanthony
Tyaquaná
Tyaquwon
Tyare
Tyas
Tybell
Tyberious
Tyberius
Tyberrius
Tybious
Tycardo
Tyce *(0.01)*
Tyceer
Tycen
Tycenen
Tychicus
Tyci
Tycon
Tycorey
Tycorick
Tycorius
Tycran
Tydarius
Tydarrius
Tyde
Tydell
Tyderian
Tyderious
Tydre
Tydrick
Tydron
Tydus
Tye *(0.05)*

Tye Wayne
Tyease
Tyeberius
Tyecell
Tyee
Tyekia
Tyekias
Tyelar
Tyelen
Tyeler
Tyelin
Tyelor
Tyer
Tyere
Tyerell
Tyeshawn
Tyevihenne
Tyevin
Tyewan
Tyewaune
Tyewon
Tyg
Tyga
Tyge
Tygée
Tyger
Tygh
Tyghe
Tygue
Tyhe
Tyheem
Tyhei
Tyheim
Tyhler
Tyhri
Tyhrone
Tyi
Tyi Virunte
Tyidous
Tyier
Tyion
Tyiquan
Tyiree
Tyirese
Tyishon
Tyjae
Tyjaé
Tyjavius
Tyjay
Tyjeik
Tyji
Tyjia
Tyjohn
Tyjon
Tyjuan *(0.01)*

Tyjuane
Tyjuaun
Tykaree
Tykareus
Tyke
Tykeam
Tykean
Tykearon
Tykee
Tykeim
Tykel
Tykell
Tykelli
Tyker
Tykese
Tyketis
Tykevious
Tykevius
Tykez
Tykine
Tykori
Tykwan
Tykwane
Tykwon
Tyla
Tylah
Tylan *(0.01)*
Tylance
Tyland
Tylandius
Tylane
Tylar *(0.03)*
Tylar-Jamai
Tylarr
Tyle
Tylea
Tyleak
Tylee
Tyleel
Tyleik
Tylen *(0.01)*
Tyleon
Tyler *(13.89)*
Tyler III
Tyler Ray
Tyler William
Tyler-David
Tyler-Davis
Tyler-James
Tyler-Jamison
Tyler-Janz
Tyler-Johnston
Tyler-Michael
Tyler-Ray
Tyler-Raymond

Tyler-Wallace
Tyler.james
Tylere
Tylerlee
Tyles
Tyley
Tylier
Tylik
Tylin
Tyllarr
Tyller
Tylo
Tyloer
Tylon *(0.01)*
Tylondus
Tylone
Tylonzo
Tylor *(0.23)*
Tylor-Cooper
Tylour
Tylr
Tylre
Tylyn
Tylyr
Tymain
Tymaine
Tymane
Tymar
Tymario
Tymarlis
Tymarlous
Tymashian
Tymberlin
Tymel
Tymele
Tymen
Tymere
Tymetheuz
Tymetris
Tymetrius
Tymir
Tymmar
Tymon *(0.01)*
Tymoteusz
Tymothy
Tymurius
Tynan *(0.01)*
Tynathan
Tyndale
Tyndall
Tyne
Tyneil
Tynell
Tyner
Tynevis

Tynnel	Tyrandon	Tyrie	Tysen *(0.01)*	Tywaine	Uligen
Tynor	Tyrane	Tyriece	Tysha	Tywan *(0.01)*	Uliscs
Tynquan	Tyrannus	Tyrieck	Tyshan	Tywane	Ulises *(0.14)*
Tynr	Tyranny	Tyriek	Tyshana	Tywann	Ulisse
Tyonne	Tyray	Tyriek Lamont	Tyshaun *(0.02)*	Tywaun	Ulisses *(0.01)*
Tyontae	Tyrce	Tyriel	Tyshauwn	Tywen	Ulric *(0.01)*
Typharaoh	Tyre *(0.03)*	Tyrielle	Tyshawn *(0.03)*	Tywon *(0.01)*	Ulrick
Typhonus	Tyré	Tyriese	Tyshe	Tywone	Ulrik
Typree	Tyrék	Tyrik *(0.01)*	Tysheem	Tywonne	Ulu
Typriest	Tyrea	Tyriko	Tysheik	Tywuane	Uluaki
Tyqaun	Tyrease	Tyrill	Tyshel	Tyz'ohn	Ulumasui
Tyqavious	Tyrece *(0.01)*	Tyrin *(0.06)*	Tyshian	Tyzhe	Uly
Tyqeon	Tyrecé	Tyrinn	Tyshiem	Tyzhé	Ulyl
Tyqhaum	Tyrecee	Tyrio	Tyshion	Tzaddi	Ulysee
Tyquaan	Tyreck	Tyrion	Tyshoan	Tze	Ulysees
Tyqual	Tyreco	Tyriq *(0.01)*	Tyshon *(0.01)*	Tzee	Ulyses *(0.01)*
Tyquan *(0.04)*	Tyree *(0.14)*	Tyriqu	Tyshone	Tzemach	Ulyssees
Tyquandre	Tyrée *(0.01)*	Tyrique	Tyshonne	Tzvi	Ulysses *(0.06)*
Tyquane	Tyreece	Tyris	Tyshun	Tzzi	Ulyssess
Tyquann	Tyreek *(0.01)*	Tyriss	Tyshunn		Ulyssius
Tyquantae	Tyreequéntavis	Tyrius	Tyshyn	**-U-**	Umair
Tyquarius	Tyreese *(0.01)*	Tyrmaine	Tysin		Umajan
Tyquavious	Tyrei	Tyro	Tysinger	U'laun	Umang
Tyquavius	Tyreice	Tyroby	Tysjai	Uaea	Umanga
Tyquayle	Tyreie	Tyrod	Tyson *(0.43)*	Uary	Umar *(0.01)*
Tyquel	Tyreik	Tyrohn	Tysond	Ubaid	Umar-Syed
Tyquell	Tyreil	Tyrome	Tystin	Ubaidullah	Umashankar
Tyquerrios	Tyreis	Tyron *(0.06)*	Tyswon	Ubaldo *(0.03)*	Umberto
Tyquese	Tyrek *(0.01)*	Tyrondrick	Tytanuel	Ube	Umer
Tyquez	Tyreke	Tyrone *(0.32)*	Tytavius	Ubiadurrahm	Umesh
Tyquil	Tyrekus	Tyrone Jr	Tython	Uchechukwu	Umit
Tyquine	Tyrel *(0.05)*	Tyronn	Tytrell	Uchenna	Umran
Tyquinn	Tyrel-Jacob	Tyronne	Tytrilocus	Udarian	Umut
Tyquise	Tyrell *(0.20)*	Tyroy	Tytron	Uday	Un Gu
Tyquon	Tyrell-Evan	Tyrquan	Tytua	Udenze	Una
Tyquone	Tyrelle *(0.01)*	Tyrrance	Tytus	Udhay	Unamed
Tyqurrius	Tyren *(0.02)*	Tyrre	Tyuan	Udlien	Uncas
Tyquwon	Tyreon	Tyrreck	Tyundre	Udonavon	Undra
Tyquyne	Tyreq	Tyrrel	Tyus *(0.02)*	Ugene	Undray
Tyqwain	Tyreque	Tyrrell	Tyvan	Ugochukwu	Undré
Tyqwan	Tyres	Tyrrin	Tyvanius	Ugonna	Undrea
Tyqwonzae	Tyrese *(0.01)*	Tyrronce	Tyvante	Ugur	Uneek
Tyr	Tyreses	Tyrrus	Tyvares	Uhola	Unek
Tyr'ee	Tyresius	Tyrue	Tyvas	Uilliam	Ungku
Tyra	Tyresse	Tyruence	Tyvel	Ujamaa	Unikque
Tyra'n	Tyrez *(0.01)*	Tyrun	Tyvic	Ujaree	Unique
Tyrae	Tyreze	Tyrus *(0.03)*	Tyvin	Ujjaval	Unique James
Tyraé	Tyrheal	Tyrvon	Tyvinn	Ujwal	Uniqué
Tyrael	Tyrhone	Tyryn	Tyvis	Ukaia	Unnal
Tyrail	Tyri	Tyryss	Tyvon *(0.02)*	Ukarya	Unnar
Tyraine	Tyrian	Tyrzell	Tyvone	Ukejeh	Unrico
Tyrak	Tyric	Tysahn	Tyvonne	Ukeme	Unsh
Tyral	Tyrice *(0.01)*	Tysan	Tyvonshae	Ukkuansm	Untereance
Tyran *(0.02)*	Tyrick	Tyse	Tyvonteis	Ulesius	Unteria
Tyrand	Tyricus	Tysean	Tywain	Ulices *(0.01)*	Unterria

Untorrey
Unwerdeep
Unyque
Upash
Upesh
Ur'kese
Ural
Uranwa
Urban
Urbano *(0.01)*
Urcell
Urel
Urelles
Uresi
Urgessa
Uri
Uria
Uriabram
Uriah *(0.04)*
Urian
Urias
Uric
Urice
Urick
Uricuas
Urie
Uriel *(0.17)*
Urihaan
Urijah
Urix
Urmit
Ursus
Urvinder
Usaia
Usaid
Usama *(0.01)*
Usamah
Usef
Ushan
Usher
Usiel
Usman *(0.01)*
Usoalii
Utah
Uthish
Uthmaan
Uttej
Utuq
Uvaldo
Uwachomadu
Uwadia
Uwen
Uyimwen
Uyioghosa
Uzair *(0.01)*

Uzayr
Uziel *(0.02)*
Uzochukwu
Uzoma
Uzzia
Uzziel

-V-

V
V'dre
Va
Va Darion
Va Shun
Va'dayle
Vaakesan
Vaamanan
Vachee
Vachon
Vachroan
Vadal
Vadale
Vadall
Vadaul
Vadaule
Vadel
Vaden
Vader
Vadil
Vadim *(0.01)*
Vadol
Vadoll
Vadrey
Vadual
Vaeamuni
Vahdim
Vahe *(0.01)*
Vahik
Vahio
Vahn
Vaibhav
Vaiden
Vail
Vaise
Vaisnavan
Vaiyshnavan
Vajon
Vajunius
Vaka
Vakale
Vakulan
Val
Val Jason
Val Ryan
Val'chez

Valante
Valanté
Valantis
Valantyn
Valarian
Valdemar *(0.01)*
Valdez
Valdibia
Valdrin
Valecia
Valee
Valen
Valente *(0.01)*
Valentin *(0.06)*
Valentine
Valentino *(0.04)*
Valentito
Valenton
Valeriano
Valerie
Valerina
Valerio
Valeriy
Valero
Valery
Valfre
Valier
Valis
Valissa
Valmik
Valmore
Valshone
Valton
Vamon
Vamsi
Van *(0.05)*
Van Buren
Van Dariul
Van Jeffrson
Van Pierre
Van Seyla
Van'ness
Van'quavyis
Van-Adam
Van-Oung
Vance *(0.07)*
Vance Matthew
Vancleto
Vandal
Vandan
Vandaz
Vandell
Vandervoort
Vandon
Vandrek

Vandrick
Vandrik
Vandy
Vandye
Vanessa
Vanetrius
Vang
Vanhdy
Vaninder
Vanja
Vanjarius
Vanlier
Vann *(0.01)*
Vanness
Vannhor
Vannin
Vannois
Vanquailus
Vanquez
Vanscooter
Vanshawn
Vantanez
Vantavious
Vanté
Vantee
Vantez
Vantha
Vantonio
Vantorious
Vantrail
Vantrelle
Vantrez
Vantrezman
Vanuman
Vanya
Vanyel
Vanzell
Vaquan
Varak
Varcy
Vardaan
Varek
Varga
Varian
Varick
Varinder
Varius
Varmanaa
Varnan
Varnell
Varnez
Varnzell
Varon
Varquis
Varrien

Varro
Varrol
Varron
Varry
Varshini
Vartan
Vartrel
Varun *(0.02)*
Vasanth
Vasco
Vascoe
Vasekan
Vasgar
Vashá
Vashad
Vashaun
Vashawn
Vashawnn
Vashon *(0.01)*
Vashonte
Vashun
Vasileos
Vasili
Vasilios *(0.01)*
Vasilios-Claude
Vasilis
Vasiliy
Vasily
Vasisth
Vasken
Vasper
Vasquan
Vasshaun
Vassilios
Vasso
Vasti
Vasu
Vaswar
Vatche
Vathana
Vatious
Vatr
Vatthana Matthew
Vauchon
Vaughan *(0.01)*
Vaughn *(0.08)*
Vaughn-Dele
Vaughnte
Vaughntre
Vaune
Vaux
Vavian
Vealor
Veasna
Vebushan

Vecente
Vecheslav
Vechet
Vedad
Vedang
Vedant
Vedat
Vedric
Vedyam
Veer
Vegas
Veidarshon
Velcin
Velmando
Velmir
Velton
Ven'tavius
Venancio
Vencent
Vendell
Veniamin
Venito'
Venitto
Venkat
Venkata
Venkateswar
Venkatsai
Vennie
Vennon
Venodan
Venom
Venshon
Venson
Ventavious
Ventavius
Venterries
Venton
Ventorro
Ventravious
Ventress
Ventroy
Ventson
Ventura
Venturi
Venugopal
Venujan
Venush
Venyamin
Venzel
Venzon
Veon
Veondre
Veonta
Veontae
Vequain

Vera	Vetaliy	Victron	Vinayak	Vinquan	Vitalino
Verachmiel	Veton	Victus	Vinayuk	Vinroy	Vitaliy
Verak	Vetone	Vida	Vincant	Vinsent	Vitaly
Vercell	Veylachez	Vidal (0.04)	Vincant Come	Vinsint	Vitalyk
Verdell	Veyni	Vidale	Vince (0.06)	Vinsion	Vitas
Verdi	Vianney	Vidall	Vinceint	Vinson (0.01)	Vithawatt
Verdiz	Vibaldo	Vidaryus	Vincenji	Vintavious	Vithursun
Verdrick	Vibert	Videll	Vincent (2.01)	Vinthushan	Vithusan
Vere	Vibhav	Videsh	Vincent Jr	Vinton	Vithushan
Verek	Vibhushan	Vidhu	Vincent-Michael	Vintrez	Vithushran
Vergil	Vibol	Vidieu	Vincente (0.02)	Vinu	Vithushsan
Verl	Vibulan	Vidur	Vincenté	Vinuu	Vito (0.02)
Verlan	Vibusaran	Viduran	Vincento	Vinze	Vittorio (0.01)
Verland	Vic	Vien	Vincenza	Vinzeal	Vitus
Verle	Vic'torrie	Vienthong	Vincenzio	Vinzell	Viukan
Verlen	Viccardo	Viet (0.02)	Vincenzo (0.05)	Vinzenz	Vivak
Verlenzo	Viccaro	Vignash	Vincenzo Manuel	Vipeisan	Vivek (0.03)
Verlin	Vicelio	Vihar	Vincenzo-	Vipin	Viven
Verlon	Vicent	Vihujan	Vincenzo-	Vipul	Vivesh
Verlyn	Vicente (0.18)	Vijal	Salvatore	Viradejd	Vivian
Vermaine	Vichai	Vijay (0.01)	Vinceson	Viraj	Viviano
Vermon	Vichea	Vijeyakrishnan	Vinchenzo	Viral	Vixay
Vern	Vichil	Vika	Vinci	Viraphet	Viyashar
Vernal	Vichon	Vikas (0.01)	Vincint	Virat	Vlad
Vernard	Vickash	Vikash	Vincinty	Virdevinder	Vladan
Vernardo	Vickey	Vikaskumar	Vincnet	Virean	Vlade
Vernarre	Vickie	Vikesh	Vincson	Viren	Vladimer
Verne	Vicklin	Viki	Vinctavious	Virgil (0.03)	Vladimere
Verneal	Vickram	Vikram (0.01)	Vindaris	Virgil Jr	Vladimir (0.04)
Vernel	Vickramjit	Vikramdeep	Vindeep	Virgilio (0.01)	Vladimyr
Vernell (0.01)	Vickrant	Vikramjit	Vineet	Virginio	Vladislav
Vernelle	Vickson	Vikran	Vineeth	Virjilio	Vladmir
Verner	Vicktor	Vikrant	Vinesh	Virkrant	Vlady
Vernial	Vicky	Vikrum	Vinh (0.02)	Virlan	Vlasis
Vernjit	Vicorio	Vikshar	Vinh-Son	Viron	Vo
Vernon (0.10)	Victavian	Viktor (0.01)	Vinicia	Virosh	Vois'el
Vernord	Victor (1.91)	Vilathap	Vinicio	Virquan	Vojislav
Vernoris	Victor Daniel	Vilayut	Vinicios	Virrell	Volarey
Vernzell	Victor Quen	Vili	Vinicius	Visaacan	Volkens
Veron	Victor Rashad	Viliami	Vinnee	Visael	Vollie
Verond	Victor-Laurent-	Viliamu	Vinney	Visente	Volney
Veronne	Victoralfonso	Villain	Vinni	Viseth	Volodimir
Veronte	Victorhugo	Villas	Vinnie	Vishaa	Voltaire
Verricchia	Victoria	Villis	Vinnie Marchell	Vishaal	Von (0.01)
Verron	Victoriano (0.01)	Villy	Vinny	Vishag	Von Ronstead
Vershaud	Victorien	Vilontario	Vinod	Vishal (0.04)	Von'dre
Vershawn	Victorino	Vilson	Vinodh	Vishek	Vonce
Vertis	Victorio	Vimal	Vinoj	Vishesh	Vonche
Verzell	Victorio Blas	Vimalan	Vinojan	Vishnu (0.01)	Vonchey
Vesal	Victorious	Vin	Vinojen	Vishnuwarthan	Vonda
Vesean	Victorjo	Vinaayak	Vinon	Vishok	Vondarius
Veshone	Victormanuel	Vinal	Vinood	Visizios	Vondariuse
Vessle	(0.01)	Vinashan	Vinoth	Vismark	Vondavious
Vestée	Victory	Vinay (0.01)	Vinothan	Visshan	Vondel
Vet	Victour	Vinayagar	Vinozshan	Vitaliano	Vondell

Vonderius	Vuk	Wafic	Walker-James	Warren *(0.24)*	Waynne
Vondeze	Vulfranito	Wagd	Walkind	Warren III	Wayquin
Vondray	Vulnet	Wagner	Wallace *(0.04)*	Warren-G	Wayson
Vondre	Vuong	Wagyns	Walleed	Warrez	Wayte
Vondrecus	Vutha	Wah	Waller	Warrin	Wazeen
Vong	Vuyou	Wahab	Wallesstein	Warrock	Wc
Vongsawan	Vy	Wahay	Walliam	Warsame	We-Laka
Vonisaam	Vyacheslav	Waheed	Wallie	Warsamn	Wean Naun
Vonlexis	Vybav	Waheedullah	Wallstein	Warthone	Webber
Vonnell	Vyerbraunn	Wahid	Wally *(0.01)*	Wasam	Weber
Vonnie	Vyon	Wahijadeen	Walner	Waseem *(0.01)*	Webster
Vonquail	Vyphot	Wahl	Walnick	Waseembeg	Wecley
Vonquez	Vyrin	Wai *(0.01)*	Walsh	Wasef	Wedge
Vonta	Vyron	Wai'quan	Walstine	Washad	Wedlin
Vontall	Vyschard	Wai-Dun	Walt	Washawn	Wedner
Vontarius	Vyshakh	Waid	Walt'ere	Washington	Weedmire
Vontate	Vyshnav	Wail	Walta	Wasi	Wei *(0.01)*
Vontavious	Vytal	Waino	Waltayvis	Wasif	Wei-Yin
Vontavius	Vytas	Wais	Walter *(0.45)*	Wasim	Weiland
Vonte	Vytautas	Waisses	Walter Emmett	Wasiq	Weison
Vonté		Waitus	Walther	Wasis	Welbon
Vontel	**-W-**	Wajahat	Walton *(0.01)*	Wasseem	Weldan
Vontell		Wajdy	Waltrell	Wassim	Welder
Vonterious	W *(0.02)*	Waji	Wamalwa	Wassua	Weldon *(0.01)*
Vonterius	W.	Wajih	Wamar	Wataru	Welford
Vontess	W.D.	Wakaar	Wambadi	Wathaniel	Welfredo
Vontez	Wa'el	Wakee	Waming	Watnel	Welles
Vontrae	Wa'il	Wakeim	Wamiq	Watrell	Wellesley
Vontre	Wa'keem	Wakeland	Wandell	Watron	Wellington
Vontrel	Wa'mere	Wakelo	Wandy	Watson	Wells
Vontrell *(0.01)*	Waail	Wakembie	Wang	Wattie	Welson
Vontrez	Waais	Wakien	Wanly	Waukeen	Welton
Vontrial	Waband	Wakim	Wanya *(0.02)*	Waun	Wen
Vontriel	Wabari	Wakiza	Wanyai	Waunneal	Wenceslao
Vontriele	Wacey	Wala	Wanyé	Waunyé	Wenci
Vonzele	Wachira	Walby	Waqaas	Wautese	Wendale
Vonzelle	Waco	Waldale	Waqar	Waverly	Wendall
Vonzeth	Wacothee	Waldemar	Waqas	Way	Wendavious
Vordie	Wacy	Walden	Waqem	Wayan	Wendel *(0.01)*
Vorris	Wad	Waldlie	Ward *(0.01)*	Wayde *(0.01)*	Wendell *(0.05)*
Vorshon	Wadada	Waldo *(0.01)*	Wardain	Waydus	Wenden
Vosean	Wadby	Waldrop	Wardan	Wayee	Wenny
Voshon	Waddah	Waldy	Wardell	Waylan	Wensen
Vou	Waddell	Waled	Warder	Wayland *(0.01)*	Wenseslado
Voyce	Wade *(0.25)*	Waleed *(0.02)*	Wardrer	Waylen	Wenthia
Voyd	Wadell	Waleem	Ware	Waylin	Wenzell
Voyez	Wadi	Waleen	Waren	Waylon *(0.05)*	Wequon
Voyo	Wadih	Wales	Wares	Wayman	Werenton
Vrujesh	Wadley	Walfed	Waring	Waymell	Werner
Vrushin	Wadon	Walfredo	Waris	Waymon	Wes *(0.01)*
Vryston	Wadson	Walfried	Warith	Waymond	Wesal
Vshon	Waeal	Wali	Warnel	Wayna	Wesam
Vthushan	Waed	Walid *(0.01)*	Warner *(0.01)*	Wayne *(0.30)*	Wesdell
Vu *(0.01)*	Wael *(0.01)*	Waliou	Warney	Wayne Joseph	Weseley
Vu Hung	Waell	Walker *(0.17)*	Warnton	Wayne-George	Wesle

Weslee
Wesley *(1.24)*
Weslie
Weslin
Wesly *(0.01)*
Weslyn
Wesner
Wess
Wessam
Wessel
Wessley
Wessman
West
Westan
Westcott
Westen
Western-Li
Westin *(0.02)*
Westland
Westlee
Westleigh
Westley *(0.04)*
Westly
Westlyn
Westmore
Weston *(0.26)*
Wetchley
Wevens
Weyekin-Ilp-Ilp
Weylan
Weyland
Weylin *(0.01)*
Weylyn
Weyman
Wezley
Whaid
Whaley
Whalion
Whatson
Whayne
Wheeler
Whesam
Whiley
Whitaker
Whitan
Whitcomb
White
Whitfield
Whitley
Whitman
Whitney *(0.01)*
Whittington
Whyette
Wiatt
Wiatte

Wicky
Widens
Widler
Widlyn
Wieber
Wigberto
Wikeez
Wiktor
Wil *(0.01)*
Wil-Gregory
Wilard
Wilbari
Wilber *(0.02)*
Wilbert *(0.04)*
Wilberto
Wilberton
Wilbertson
Wilbur *(0.02)*
Wilburn
Wilcarrius
Wilce
Wilchard
Wilcome
Wildarius
Wilder *(0.01)*
Wildo
Wildy
Wiley *(0.02)*
Wilferd
Wilfido
Wilford
Wilfred *(0.02)*
Wilfredo *(0.04)*
Wilfrido *(0.01)*
Wilgans
Wilganson
Wilguns
Wilhelm *(0.01)*
Wiliam
Wiliams
Wilian
Wilke
Wilkens
Wilkenson
Wilkins
Wilko
Wilks
Will *(0.11)*
Will-Franklin
Willa
Willagun B
Willaim
Willaims
Willam
Willan

Willard *(0.02)*
Willcanson
Wille
Willé
Willem *(0.01)*
Willetson
Willett
Willette
Willey
William *(9.67)*
William Chr
William D'mel
William III
William Joh
William John
William Jr
William Lan
William Peter
William Renner A
William-Adams
William-
  Alexandre
William-Dylan
William-Hinn
William-Lee
Williams *(0.02)*
Williamson
Willian
Willian Connor
Williard
Willie *(0.35)*
Willie Christop
Willie Henry
Williiam
Willim
Willimderri
Willio
Willis *(0.04)*
Willium
Willliam
Willmont
Willnard
Willon
Willonte
Willoughby
Willson
Willum
Willuster
Willy *(0.03)*
Willy John
Willyam
Wilmar
Wilmarth
Wilmer *(0.02)*
Wilmer-Jacory

Wilmorius
Wilmoth
Wilner
Wilno
Wilon
Wilquan
Wilsen
Wilshaun
Wilson *(0.18)*
Wilson Felix
Wiltavis
Wilton
Wilver
Wilvon
Wimanté
Win
Wincent
Winceslaw
Winchester
Windale
Windell
Windsor
Windy
Winfield
Winford
Winfred *(0.01)*
Winfrey
Winfu
Wing
Wing-Kwai
Wing-Yue
Winichy
Winifred
Winner
Winsen
Winsle
Winsley
Winslow
Winson
Winsten
Winstin
Winston *(0.11)*
Winston Cuyler
Winter *(0.01)*
Winthrop
Winton
Winzoir
Wirya
Wisaal
Wisam
Wisdom
Wise
Wisley
Wislyn
Wissam

Witimbert
Witmar
Witold
Witty
Wm Joshua
Wojciech
Wojcieh
Woles
Wolf
Wolfe
Wolfegang
Wolfgang *(0.03)*
Wolfgang Cody
Wolfgang Joseph
Wolfie
Wolfrid
Wolgens
Wolodymyr
Wolson
Womdee
Won
Won-June
Wonder
Wonjamiko
Woo
Woo-Jin
Wooby
Wood
Woodard
Woodfin
Woodie
Woodley
Woodroe
Woodrow *(0.01)*
Woodruff
Woods
Woodsen
Woodson
Woodward
Woody *(0.01)*
Worden
Worlderlin
Worlee
Worth
Wossen
Wouls
Wray *(0.01)*
Wreh
Wren
Wrennie
Wrex
Wright
Wrigley
Wriston
Wryke

Wualberto
Wualter
Wuilber
Wuilibaldo
Wuliams
Wuptichai
Wuttikrai
Wyan
Wyant
Wyat
Wyatt *(1.06)*
Wyatte
Wyckliffe
Wydreicus
Wyees
Wyeth
Wyett
Wyitt
Wykeem
Wykeen
Wykevious
Wykye
Wylan
Wylden
Wylder
Wyler
Wyley
Wylie *(0.01)*
Wyllie
Wyllis
Wyly
Wyman
Wymoth
Wyn
Wyndell
Wyndham
Wyndon
Wyne
Wynn
Wynston
Wynter
Wynton *(0.01)*
Wyron
Wysdom
Wysley
Wytt
Wyyontée

-X-

X
X Avier
X'aviare
X'avier
X'javion

X'xavier	Xenio	Y Samuel	Yaman	Yaser	Yediydeyah
X'zavair	Xenophon	Y'aaron	Yamarai	Yash *(0.01)*	Yee
X'zavier	Xenos	Y-Ian	Yamen	Yasha	Yee-Sean
X'zavius	Xeo-Fu	Y-Venny	Yames	Yashar	Yeehin
X-Zaviar	Xerez	Ya	Yamil *(0.01)*	Yashawn	Yehoshua
X.	Xerxes	Yaadram	Yamill	Yasheen	Yehosua Malachi
Xa'leon	Xeryous	Yaakov	Yamin	Yasika	Yehuda *(0.01)*
Xabian	Xeryus	Yaasiin	Yamir	Yasin *(0.01)*	Yehudah *(0.01)*
Xabryon	Xever	Yacario	Yamni	Yasine	Yehya
Xachary	Xhaner	Yacek	Yan *(0.06)*	Yasinjon	Yeimi
Xadrian	Xhemial	Yacine *(0.01)*	Yanal	Yasir *(0.01)*	Yeis
Xaevan	Xiadani	Yacir	Yanar	Yasmani	Yeison
Xahil	Xiaotian	Yacoub	Yanatan	Yasmany	Yekusiel
Xaire	Xin	Yacov	Yancey *(0.01)*	Yasper	Yelani
Xaiver *(0.01)*	Xinjie	Yacqub	Yancy *(0.01)*	Yassaky	Yelsing
Xajavier	Xiomar	Yadav	Yandy-Paul	Yasseen	Yency
Xakaryeh	Xiong	Yadean	Yang	Yasser	Yeng *(0.01)*
Xamil	Xiong-Fei	Yadhav	Yanick *(0.04)*	Yasshin	Yenifer
Xander *(0.01)*	Xisto	Yadin	Yanick-Herman	Yassin	Yenki
Xane	Xolotl	Yadira	Yanik *(0.01)*	Yassine	Yeon
Xanthus	Xonas	Yadnar	Yanis	Yasuhira	Yeong
Xaquarius	Xristopher	Yadriel	Yaniv	Yasuo	Yer
Xarian	Xsavier	Yadveer	Yankacton	Yasyf	Yerachmiel
Xaryus	Xuan	Yael	Yankee	Yat	Yered
Xashawn	Xuan-Long	Yafi	Yankees	Yateson	Yeremy
Xathan	Xuan-Tinh	Yagna	Yann *(0.03)*	Yathaven	Yerikk
Xavaeir	Xue Hong	Yahamoni	Yanni *(0.01)*	Yather	Yerman
Xavian	Xun	Yaharrie	Yanni Jay	Yathursan	Yernyl
Xaviar	Xvarien	Yahdiel	Yannic	Yatill	Yero
Xavias	Xvetrias	Yahdriel	Yannick *(0.14)*	Yatziel	Yerovy
Xavien	Xwistulaxw	Yaheem	Yannik	Yauncey	Yery
Xavier *(1.09)*	Xxavier	Yahern	Yannis	Yauncy	Yesean
Xavier Alexander	Xxzavien	Yahia	Yanny	Yaunqwave	Yesero
Xavier Char	Xyabrai	Yahir	Yanquier	Yavick	Yeshey
Xavier Diam	Xyja	Yahmarey	Yansey	Yavontaé	Yeshi
Xaviess	Xylon	Yahmin Christop	Yansy	Yavore	Yeshua
Xavion	Xzander	Yahnib	Yanté	Yaw	Yeshuah
Xavior	Xzavaier	Yahshua	Yantrell	Yaw-Wen	Yesid
Xavious	Xzaveion	Yahvalee	Yao	Yawer	Yetsebaot
Xavius	Xzaver	Yahya *(0.01)*	Yaoler	Yaxye	Yettra
Xavyer	Xzavia	Yahye *(0.01)*	Yaphet	Yazan	Yeung-Sum
Xaxier	Xzavian	Yahzeel	Yaqur	Yazdon	Yevgeniy
Xaysana	Xzavier *(0.02)*	Yair *(0.01)*	Yar	Yazeed	Yevin
Xazaviar	Xzavier-Christo	Yajeel	Yarden	Yazen	Yew
Xazavies	Xzavion	Yakaphar	Yardley	Yazide	Yewhnes
Xazier	Xzavior	Yakeem	Yared	Yazmahn	Yexson
Xcylur	Xzayvyayrr	Yakevis	Yariel	Ydeler	Yezen
Xdraveous	Xzoyloysius	Yaki	Yarko	Ye	Yezun
Xeduardo-Nicola	Xzvaier	Yakov	Yarlisan	Yéhudi	Yggdrassl
Xeemyeej	Xzyon	Yaku	Yarmani	Yea	Yhance
Xeilias		Yalda	Yarmon	Yeager	Yhaquille
Xeivier	**-Y-**	Yalexsy	Yarnell	Yechezkal	Yhaun
Xel-Ha		Yalwaiker	Yaseen	Yechezkel	Yhoang
Xemgin	Y	Yama	Yaseer	Yedaiel	Yhonnie
Xen	Y Sam	Yamaira	Yasen	Yedidya	Yhosvany

Yi	Yohannes	Yosif	Yueh Lin	Yvanson	Zaccharie
Yianni	Yohans	Yosmani	Yuepheng	Yvenert	Zacchary
Yiannis	Yohei	Yosmany	Yugo	Yvens	Zaccheaus
Yifei	Yom	Yosnier	Yuhei	Yvenson	Zacchery
Yihun	Ycmi	Yossaporn	Yuho	Yvensone	Zaccheus
Yik	Yon	Yossarian	Yuichi	Yvensonne	Zacchious
Yilin	Yona	Yosuf	Yuichiro	Yves *(0.01)*	Zacery
Yimmy Israel	Yonael	Yosuke	Yuji	Yves Langst	Zach *(0.01)*
Yimothy	Yonah	Yosvani	Yuk	Yves-Bernard	Zach Timothy
Yin	Yonas	Yota	Yukai	Yvon	Zachaciah
Ying	Yonase	Yotindra	Yukho	Yvonne	Zachaeriah
Ying-Jie	Yonason	You	Yuki	Yyves	Zachaery
Yinka	Yonata	You Guang	Yul		Zachaeus
Yiorgos	Yonatan *(0.02)*	Youki	Yulier	**-Z-**	Zacharai
Yirrah	Yonathan *(0.01)*	Youmans	Yulio		Zacharais
Yisehack	Yonaton	Youn	Yulo	Z *(0.01)*	Zacharay
Yiskoel	Yonattan	Youness	Yumail	Z'kevis	Zachare
Yisroel *(0.01)*	Yondon	Young *(0.02)*	Yumer	Z'kl	Zacharee
Yitshhaq	Yonel	Youngeun	Yumin	Z'ky	Zacharey *(0.01)*
Yitzchak	Yonelio	Youngjun	Yumito	Z'quan	Zacharha
Yitzchok	Yong	Youngsuk	Yumontre	Z'ykeisus	Zachari *(0.02)*
Yitzhak	Yonge	Younis	Yun	Z.	Zacharia *(0.05)*
Yiu	Yoni *(0.01)*	Youri *(0.01)*	Yung	Za Kavyon	Zachariah *(0.30)*
Yiu Shun	Yonic	Yousef *(0.03)*	Yunior	Za'aron	Zachariaha
Yiu-Yung	Yonis *(0.01)*	Yousef Khalil	Yunus	Za'darrien	Zacharian
Yiyuan	Yonkee	Youseph	Yuri *(0.01)*	Za'kerrious	Zacharias *(0.01)*
Yjuan	Yonnas	Yousif	Yuriah-Bronson	Za'qual	Zachariaus
Yliece	Yonny	Youssef *(0.03)*	Yuric	Za'quari	Zacharie *(0.04)*
Yll	Yonry	Yousseff	Yuriel	Za-Quan	Zacharie-Lyle
Yneil	Yony	Youston	Yuriell	Zaachary	Zachariha
Yo	Yoo	Yousuf	Yurinder	Zaahir Khaleefa	Zacharius
Yo-Hinace	Yoonninh	Youta	Yury	Zaal	Zacharry
Yoan *(0.02)*	Yoosuf	Yovam	Yusan	Zabair	Zachart
Yoandri	Yorai	Yovan	Yusef *(0.01)*	Zabbion	Zacharu
Yoandy	Yordan	Yovani *(0.03)*	Yusefra'sheed	Zabdiel	Zachary *(10.82)*
Yoann *(0.01)*	Yordi	Yovanni	Yuseph	Zabian	Zachary Christi
Yoban	Yordiandere	Yovanny	Yusera	Zabih	Zachary Nichola
Yobani *(0.01)*	Yordis	Yovany	Yusha	Zabion	Zachary Ta'shi
Yobel	Yorel	Yovni	Yushi	Zabriel	Zachary William
Yoceph	Yorell	Yowanes	Yusif	Zabrin	Zachary-Alex
Yodanis	Yorgo	Yowceph	Yusof	Zac	Zachary-
Yoe	Yorick	Ypaul	Yussuf	Zac'tavious	Alexander
Yoel *(0.01)*	York	Ysidro *(0.01)*	Yusuf *(0.04)*	Zacakary	Zachary-Eric
Yogarajah	Yorkis	Yu *(0.01)*	Yusufali	Zacari	Zachary-George
Yogaswara	Yosef *(0.01)*	Yu'shaun	Yusuke	Zacaria	Zachary-John
Yogeesaendooran	Yoselin	Yu'vaughn	Yuta	Zacariah	Zachary-Lucas-
Yogesh	Yoseph	Yu-Ning	Yutaro	Zacarias	Winfield
Yogi	Yoshihiko	Yu-Wing	Yuto	Zacarie	Zachary-Scott
Yogin	Yoshihiro	Yuchi	Yuuki *(0.01)*	Zacary *(0.01)*	Zachary-Ty
Yohan *(0.02)*	Yoshiki	Yudai	Yuval	Zaccari	Zacharya
Yohanan	Yoshimasa	Yudany	Yuvon	Zaccariah	Zacharyah
Yohance	Yoshiya	Yue	Yuvraj	Zaccarrius	Zacheem
Yohandi	Yoshua	Yue-Wen	Yuvrn	Zaccary	Zacheray
Yohanes	Yosiah	Yuebo	Yuya	Zacchaéus	Zacherey
Yohanne	Yosief	Yuechang	Yvan	Zacchaeus *(0.01)*	Zacheri

Zacheriah (0.01)
Zacherie
Zachery (0.60)
Zachery.mitchell
Zachhary
Zachiah
Zachiary
Zachius
Zachory (0.01)
Zachray
Zachrey (0.01)
Zachry (0.01)
Zachuery
Zachurie
Zachury
Zack (0.05)
Zackare
Zackaree
Zackari
Zackaria
Zackariah (0.01)
Zackarias
Zackarie
Zackary (0.54)
Zackary Dalton
Zackary-Tyler
Zackere
Zackeree
Zackerey
Zackeri
Zackeria
Zackeriah
Zackerie
Zackerry
Zackery (0.40)
Zackery Scott
Zackery-James
Zackery-Ty
Zackeus
Zackhary
Zackheaus
Zacki
Zackie
Zackiery
Zackiory
Zackone
Zackoriah
Zackory (0.01)
Zackrey
Zackry
Zackuriah
Zacorey
Zacori
Zacorious
Zacory

Zacry
Zad
Zadarian
Zade
Zaden
Zaderian
Zadian
Zadius
Zaed
Zaelin
Zaequan
Zafeer
Zafer
Zafir
Zafran
Zaghaun
Zahair
Zahar
Zahara
Zaharie
Zahary
Zahawadee
Zaheed
Zaheer
Zahid (0.01)
Zahin
Zahir
Zahrain
Zahrif
Zahron
Zahul
Zaia
Zaid (0.03)
Zaied
Zaiid
Zaikeese
Zaim
Zain (0.03)
Zaine
Zainul
Zainulabiddin
Zaion
Zaiquian
Zair
Zaire (0.01)
Zairee
Zak (0.01)
Zaka
Zakaraiya
Zakare
Zakaree
Zakareeya
Zakari (0.01)
Zakaria (0.02)
Zakariah

Zakarie
Zakarij
Zakarious
Zakarius
Zakariya (0.01)
Zakariye
Zakariyya
Zakary (0.10)
Zakee
Zakeel
Zakel
Zakelo
Zakendrick
Zaker
Zakeri
Zakeria
Zakeriah
Zakerie
Zakery (0.02)
Zakery-Mykel
Zakey
Zakeyion
Zakhariah
Zakhary
Zaki
Zakiayah
Zakie
Zakiem
Zakiry
Zakiy
Zakiya
Zakiyy
Zakk
Zakkari
Zakkary (0.02)
Zakkery
Zakki
Zakkyre
Zaknafein
Zakori
Zakree
Zakria
Zakriya
Zakry
Zakt
Zale
Zalen
Zaleon
Zalin
Zalon
Zamaan
Zamam
Zaman
Zamane
Zamar

Zamari
Zamarie
Zamariell
Zamarquus
Zameer
Zamemian
Zamion
Zamir
Zamon
Zamondie
Zamounte
Zamuel
Zan
Zana
Zanali
Zanavian
Zander
Zandore
Zandra
Zane (0.30)
Zanein
Zanevio
Zaniah
Zaniar
Zaniel
Zankevius
Zann
Zannie
Zanny
Zantana
Zantavius
Zanteze
Zanthanee
Zantias
Zantonio
Zantrez
Zantwoin
Zanyrius
Zaphniah
Zappa
Zaqaunze
Zaqckery
Zaqi
Zaquain
Zaquan
Zaquarius
Zaquary
Zaquiel
Zaquoine
Zaquon
Zaqurie
Zaqwan
Zara
Zaraphon
Zaravion

Zarayvion
Zarbree
Zarchary
Zared
Zareen
Zarek (0.01)
Zaren
Zarethus
Zariah
Zarian
Zarias
Zarif
Zariff
Zarik
Zarin
Zarion
Zarius
Zarko
Zarlo
Zaron
Zarqentice
Zarquez
Zarquis
Zarran
Zarren
Zarrick
Zarron
Zaryd
Zaryn
Zashius
Zatorris
Zatryl
Zaughn
Zavair
Zaveis
Zavell
Zaven
Zaverie
Zaverious
Zavery
Zaveyane
Zavian
Zavier (0.03)
Zavierre
Zavion
Zavionne
Zavior
Zavius
Zavon
Zavondric
Zavorea-Wilbert
Zavyon
Zavyr
Zaw
Zawad

Zawane
Zawnté
Zayahon
Zayan
Zaybrian
Zayd
Zaydrian
Zayin
Zaylin
Zayn
Zaynab
Zayne (0.02)
Zayniel
Zayquawn
Zayren
Zayrne
Zayroux
Zayrrick
Zayvone
Zazhariah
Zbigniew
Zchavonti
Zdravko
Zédarius
Zeadrick
Zeal
Zean
Zearl
Zearon
Zeavakerius
Zeb (0.01)
Zebadiah (0.01)
Zebariah
Zebb
Zebby
Zebedee
Zebediah
Zeberiah
Zebidiah
Zeboriah
Zebrik
Zebulan
Zebulee
Zebulin
Zebulon (0.02)
Zebulun
Zecharia (0.01)
Zechariach
Zechariah (0.09)
Zecharian
Zecharias
Zecharie
Zechary
Zechaviah
Zecheriah

Zechery	Zeno	Zeya	Zicieus	Zoheb	Zubeen
Zechia	Zenon	Zeyad	Zico	Zohn	Zuberi
Zechuriah	Zenquavion	Zeyid	Zide	Zokariah	Zubin
Zed	Zenquavious	Zh'tavius	Zied	Zol	Zuhab
Zedekiah	Zentavion	Zh'travius	Zieke	Zolan	Zuhaib
Zedikiah	Zenwa	Zha'von	Zievan	Zollan	Zuhair
Zedric	Zeon	Zhacqur	Ziggy	Zollie	Zuhayr
Zedrick	Zeonry	Zhaejuan	Zigwanis	Zoltan	Zuheer
Zeeshan	Zeontaye	Zhaire	Zijawaii	Zon	Zulkifly
Zeeyerack	Zepatrick	Zhaku	Zikomo	Zondaris	Zunair
Zef	Zeph	Zhamaal	Zilton	Zong	Zuntavious
Zefan	Zephan	Zhamar	Zimarian	Zonnie	Zuntriaus
Zeferino	Zephaniah *(0.01)*	Zhamartae	Zimir	Zonta	Zurah
Zeff	Zephery	Zhames	Zimon	Zontae	Zuri
Zeffan	Zephire	Zhamir	Zimorry	Zontonio	Zuriel
Zeffrey	Zephlynn	Zhan	Zimra	Zontray	Zvi
Zehulun	Zephnath	Zhane	Zinal	Zontrey	Zvonimir
Zeiad	Zephon	Zhané	Zinjin	Zoran	Zy'trell
Zeic	Zephrin	Zhante	Zinn	Zoravar	Zyaire
Zeid	Zeplin	Zhaokai	Zion *(0.01)*	Zoraver	Zyalan
Zeinthée	Zeppelin	Zhaquayle	Ziphion-Zadok	Zorawar	Zyarius
Zejuan	Zequan	Zhaqwaun	Ziquine	Zoren	Zychary
Zekariah	Zera	Zhari	Ziran	Zork	Zydraous
Zeke *(0.01)*	Zerach	Zharome	Zirece	Zorn	Zyi
Zekendrick	Zerdine	Zharvis	Zireese	Zoron	Zykee
Zekeriah	Zerek	Zhaven	Zishaan	Zorrine	Zykeem
Zekerya	Zerell	Zhebulen	Zishan	Zorrion	Zykeis
Zekiah	Zeren	Zhen	Ziyaad	Zorro	Zykiah
Zekiel	Zerick	Zheng	Ziyaan	Zory	Zyler
Zekis	Zernard	Zheray	Ziyad *(0.01)*	Zoser	Zylii
Zeky	Zeronne	Zhi	Zjackary	Zosim	Zylithe
Zelig	Zerquario	Zhicheng	Zjaquient	Zosima	Zymari
Zelik	Zerriaunh	Zhiming	Zjohdell	Zouber	Zyn
Zelma	Zerric	Zhiquae	Zmarak	Zouheir	Zyon
Zelner	Zerrick	Zhivá	Zo Earl	Zowl	Zyphlen
Zelos	Zerrod	Zhivago	Zo Lan	Zréshawn	Zyquis
Zemal	Zerry	Zhon	Zoaib	Zronsha	Zyre
Zemas	Zeshan *(0.01)*	Zhoushu	Zobain	Zsakhari	Zyrell
Zemenay	Zeshawn	Zi	Zodi	Zsakual	Zyren
Zemil	Zeterrian	Zia	Zodie	Zsavaris	Zyril
Zen	Zeth *(0.01)*	Zia'korey	Zoe *(0.01)*	Zshawn	Zyron
Zena	Zethan	Zia'u'llah	Zoee	Zsikia	Zyronjay
Zenaido	Zetrick	Ziab	Zoey	Zsolt	Zyrus
Zenan	Zetwon	Ziad	Zohaib	Zsombor	Zyved
Zenas	Zev *(0.01)*	Ziah	Zohair	Zu'cord	
Zenes	Zevahn	Zian	Zohair-Jahangir	Zubair	
Zenin	Zevar	Ziare	Zohak	Zubairul	
Zenith	Zevon	Ziaudoin	Zohar	Zubear	

Acknowledgments

I sincerely appreciate the cooperation of the 35 states and provinces of the United States and Canada (including the U.S. protectorate of Guam) who generously provided statistics for inclusion in this book. Thanks to the following:

Alabama Center for Health Statistics, for 1995 top 15 names.

Alaska Department of Health and Social Services, for 1995 complete data.

Arkansas Department of Health, for 1995 complete data.

California Vital Statistics Section, for 1994 names with a frequency greater than five.

Colorado Vital Records Section, for 1994 names with a frequency greater than two.

Delaware Health Statistics Center, for 1994 complete data.

Florida Department of Health and Rehabilitative Services, for 1995 complete data.

Georgia Division of Public Health, for 1995 complete data.

Guam Office of Vital Statistics, for 1995 complete data.

Hawaii Office of Health Status Monitoring, for 1995 data with a minimum frequency of 20.

Idaho Center for Vital Statistics and Health Policy, for 1995 complete data.

Illinois Division of Vital Records, for complete 1994 data.

Kansas Office of Health Care Information, for 1995 top 70 names.

Kentucky Office of Vital Statistics, for 1995 complete data.

Louisiana Vital Records Registry, for 1995 complete data.

Maine Office of Data, Research and Vital Statistics, for 1995 complete data.

Massachusetts Executive Office of Health and Human Services, for 1995 data with a minimum frequency of 5.

Michigan Office of the State Registrar and Center for Health Statistics, for complete 1994 data.

Minnesota Department of Health, for 1994 top 20 names.

Missouri Department of Health, for complete 1995 data.

Nebraska Bureau of Vital Statistics, for complete 1995 data.

North Carolina Vital Records, for complete 1994 data.

North Dakota Division of Vital Records, for complete 1995 data.

Oregon Health Division, for complete 1995 data.

Utah Bureau of Vital Records, for complete 1995 data.

Vermont Department of Health, for complete 1995 data.

Virginia Center for Health Statistics, for complete 1995 data.

Washington Department of Health, for complete 1994 data.

Alberta Vital Statistics, for complete 1995 data.

British Columbia Vital Statistics Agency, for complete 1995 data.

Manitoba Vital Statistics Agency, for 1995 data with a minimum frequency of 25.

Ontario Office of the Registrar General, for complete 1995 data.

Québec Direction des statistiques socio-demographiques, for complete 1995 data.

Saskatchewan Division of Vital Statistics, for complete 1995 data.

Yukon Registrar of Vital Statistics, for a short list of baby names used between 1978 and 1992.

Data for the most popular names in the years 2000, 1999, and 1998, and for the twentieth century were provided by the United States Social Security Administration.

Janet Schwegel, January 2001

⬛ Bibliography ⬛

Ames, Winthrop. What shall we name the baby? New York: Pocket Books, 1963.

Arthur, William, M.A. An etymological dictionary of family and Christian names. New York: Sheldon, Blakeman & Co., 1857.

Bains, Mohinder Singh. Punjabi Language School, Edmonton, Alberta, Canada. Personal correspondence, 1989.

Brar, Sandeep S. Sikh names and meanings. From the world wide web site www.sikhs.org/names.htm.

Browder, Sue. The new age baby name book. New York: Workman, 1974.

Chuks-orji, Ogonna. Names from Africa: their origin, meaning, and pronunciation. Chicago: Johnson, 1972.

Dinwiddie-Boyd, Elza. Proud heritage: 11,001 names for your African-American baby. New York: Avon, 1994.

Dunkling, Leslie Alan. The Guinness book of names. Guinness, 1986.

Dunkling, Leslie and William Gosling. The facts on file dictionary of first names. New York: Facts on file, 1983.

Ellefson, Connie Lockhart. The melting pot book of baby names, 3rd edition. Cincinnatti, Ohio: Betterway Books, 1995.

Fields, Maxine. Baby names from around the world. New York: Pocket Books, 1985.

Hanks, Patrick and Flavia Hodges. A dictionary of first names. Oxford: Oxford University Press, 1990.

Kolatch, Alfred J. The complete dictionary of English and Hebrew first names. New York: Jonathan David, 1984.

Kolatch, Alfred J. The Jonathan David dictionary of first names. New York: Penguin Books, 1980.

Kolatch, Alfred J. Today's best baby names. New York: Putnam, 1986.

Lansky, Bruce. The best baby name book in the whole wide world. Deephaven, Minnesota: Meadowbrook, 1984.

Lawson, Dr. Edwin D. Professor of Psychology, College at Fredonia, State University of New York. Board of Editors, NAMES. Personal correspondence, 1989.

Le, Rev. Thanh Trung. President, Nguon Sang Heritage Language School Association, Edmonton, Alberta, Canada. Personal correspondence, 1989.

McCue, Marion J. How to pick the right name for your baby. New York: Grosset & Dunlap, 1977.

Sanduga, Dean. Arab Link, Edmonton, Alberta, Canada. Personal correspondence, 1989.

Stewart, George R. American given names. New York: Oxford, 1979.

Woods, Richard D. Hispanic first names: a comprehensive dictionary of 250 years of Mexican-American usage. Connecticut: Greenwood Press, 1984.